Environmental Statutes

2004 Edition • Volume I

- Clean Air Act
- Clean Water Act
  - Estuary Restoration Act of 2000
- Oil Pollution Act
- Safe Drinking Water Act
- Resource Conservation and Recovery Act
- Comprehensive Environmental Response, Compensation, and Liability Act / Superfund Amendments and Reauthorization Act
  - Environmental Restoration
- Emergency Planning and Community Right-to-Know Act
- Toxic Substances Control Act
- Federal Insecticide, Fungicide, and Rodenticide Act
  - Food Quality Protection Act of 1994
- National Environmental Policy Act
- Pollution Prevention Act of 1990
- Occupational Safety and Health Act
- Transportation of Hazardous Materials Act

Government Institutes
An imprint of
The Scarecrow Press, Inc.
Lanham, Maryland • Toronto • Oxford
2004

G Government Institutes

Published in the United States of America
by Government Institutes, an imprint of The Scarecrow Press, Inc.
A wholly owned subsidiary of
The Rowman & Littlefield Publishing Group, Inc.
4501 Forbes Boulevard, Suite 200
Lanham, Maryland 20706
http://govinst.scarecrowpress.com

PO Box 317
Oxford
OX2 9RU, UK

Copyright © 2004 by Government Institutes

All rights reserved. No part of this publication may be reproduced, stored in a retrieval system, or transmitted in any form or by any means, electronic, mechanical, photocopying, recording, or otherwise, without the prior permission of the publisher.

The reader should not rely on this publication to address specific questions that apply to a particular set of facts. The author and the publisher make no representation or warranty, express or implied, as to the completeness, correctness, or utility of the information in this publication. In addition, the author and the publisher assume no liability of any kind whatsoever resulting from the use of or reliance upon the contents of this book.

ISBN 0-86587-977-X

Manufactured in the United States of America.

♾ The paper used in this publication meets the minimum requirements of American National Standard for Information Sciences—Permanence of Paper for Printed Library Materials, ANSI/NISO Z39.48-1992.

SUMMARY OF CONTENTS

VOLUME I

Clean Air Act	1
Clean Water Act	411
Estuary Restoration Act of 2000	675
Oil Pollution Act	685
Safe Drinking Water Act	783

VOLUME II

Resource Conservation and Recovery Act	897
Comprehensive Environmental Response, Compensation, and Liability Act/Superfund Amendments and Reauthorization Act	1065
Environmental Restoration	1217
Emergency Planning and Community-Right-to-Know Act	1267
Toxic Substances Control Act	1301
Federal Insecticide, Fungicide, and Rodenticide Act	1393
Food Quality Protection Act of 1994	1499
National Environmental Policy Act	1523
Pollution Prevention Act	1593
Occupational Safety and Health Act	1601
Transportation of Hazardous Materials Act	1639
Index	1683

CONTENTS
VOLUME I

AIR POLLUTION PREVENTION AND CONTROL [CLEAN AIR ACT]

SUBCHAPTER I—PROGRAMS AND ACTIVITIES

Part A—Air Quality and Emission Limitations

42 USC 7401	Congressional findings and declaration of purpose	1
42 USC 7402	Cooperative activities	8
42 USC 7403	Research, investigation, training, and other activities	9
42 USC 7404	Research relating to fuels and vehicles	17
42 USC 7405	Grants for support of air pollution planning and control programs	20
42 USC 7406	Interstate air quality agencies; program cost limitations	24
42 USC 7407	Air quality control regions	24
42 USC 7408	Air quality criteria and control techniques	32
42 USC 7409	National primary and secondary ambient air quality standards	35
42 USC 7410	State implementation plans for national primary and secondary ambient air quality standards	37
42 USC 741	Standards of performance for new stationary sources	49
42 USC 7412	Hazardous air pollutants	57
42 USC 7413	Federal enforcement	99
42 USC 7414	Recordkeeping, inspections, monitoring, and entry	107
42 USC 7415	International air pollution	110
42 USC 7416	Retention of State authority	112
42 USC 7417	Advisory committees	114
42 USC 7418	Control of pollution from Federal facilities	116
42 USC 7419	Primary nonferrous smelter orders	118
42 USC 7420	Noncompliance penalty	121
42 USC 7421	Consultation	126
42 USC 7422	Listing of certain unregulated pollutants	127
42 USC 7423	Stack heights	128
42 USC 7424	Assurance of adequacy of State plans	128
42 USC 7425	Measures to prevent economic disruption or unemployment	129
42 USC 7426	Interstate pollution abatement	131
42 USC 7427	Public notification	132
42 USC 7428	State boards	132
42 USC 7429	Solid waste combustion	133
42 USC 7430	Emission factors	138
42 USC 7431	Land use authority	138

Part B—Ozone Protection
Part C—Prevention of Significant Deterioration of Air Quality

Subpart i—Clean Air

42 USC 7470	Congressional declaration of purpose	139
42 USC 7471	Plan requirements	140

vi / Environmental Statutes

42 USC 7472	Initial classifications	140
42 USC 7473	Increments and ceilings	140
42 USC 7474	Area redesignation	142
42 USC 7475	Preconstruction requirements	144
42 USC 7476	Other pollutants	148
42 USC 7477	Enforcement	149
42 USC 7478	Period before plan approval	149
42 USC 7479	Definitions	150

Subpart ii—Visibility Protection

| 42 USC 7491 | Visibility protection for Federal class I areas | 151 |
| 42 USC 7492 | Visibility | 153 |

Part D—Plan Requirements for Nonattainment Areas

Subpart 1—Nonattainment Areas in General

42 USC 7501	Definitions	156
42 USC 7502	Nonattainment plan provisions in general	157
42 USC 7503	Permit requirements	160
42 USC 7504	Planning procedures	163
42 USC 7505	Environmental Protection Agency grants	164
42 USC 7505a	Maintenance plans	164
42 USC 7506	Limitations on certain Federal assistance	165
42 USC 7506a	Interstate transport commissions	168
42 USC 7507	New motor vehicle emission standards in nonattainment areas	169
42 USC 7508	Guidance documents	170
42 USC 7509	Sanctions and consequences of failure to attain	170
42 USC 7509a	International border areas	172

Subpart 2—Additional Provisions for Ozone Nonattainment Areas

42 USC 7511	Classifications and attainment dates	173
42 USC 7511a	Plan submissions and requirements	176
42 USC 7511b	Federal ozone measures	190
42 USC 7511c	Control of interstate ozone air pollution	195
42 USC 7511d	Enforcement for Severe and Extreme ozone nonattainment areas for failure to attain	196
42 USC 7511e	Transitional areas	197
42 USC 7511f	NO_x and VOC study	198

Subpart 3—Additional Provisions for Carbon Monoxide Nonattainment Areas

| 42 USC 7512 | Classification and attainment dates | 198 |
| 42 USC 7512a | Plan submissions and requirements | 200 |

Subpart 4—Additional Provisions for Particulate Matter Nonattainment Areas

42 USC 7513	Classifications and attainment dates	203
42 USC 7513a	Plan provisions and schedules for plan submissions	205
42 USC 7513b	Issuance of RACM and BACM guidance	207

Subpart 5—Additional Provisions for Areas Designated Nonattainment
for Sulfur Oxides, Nitrogen Dioxide, or Lead

42 USC 7514	Plan submission deadlines	207
42 USC 7514a	Attainment dates	207

Subpart 6—Savings Provisions

42 USC 7515	General savings clause	208

SUBCHAPTER II—EMISSION STANDARDS FOR MOVING SOURCES

Part A—Motor Vehicle Emission and Fuel Standards

42 USC 7521	Emission standards for new motor vehicles or new motor vehicle engines	209
42 USC 7522	Prohibited acts	226
42 USC 7523	Actions to restrain violations	230
42 USC 7524	Civil penalties	231
42 USC 7525	Motor vehicle and motor vehicle engine compliance testing and certification	233
42 USC 7541	Compliance by vehicles and engines in actual use	237
42 USC 7542	Information collection	244
42 USC 7543	State standards	245
42 USC 7544	State grants	247
42 USC 7545	Regulation of fuels	248
42 USC 7546	[repealed]	262
42 USC 7547	Nonroad engines and vehicles	262
42 USC 7548	Study of particulate emissions from motor vehicles	264
42 USC 7549	High altitude performance adjustments	264
42 USC 7550	Definitions	266
42 USC 7551	Study and report on fuel consumption	267
42 USC 7552	Motor vehicle compliance program fees	268
42 USC 7553	Prohibition on production of engines requiring leaded gasoline	268
42 USC 7554	Urban bus standards	269

Part B—Aircraft Emission Standards

42 USC 7571	Establishment of standards	270
42 USC 7572	Enforcement of standards	272
42 USC 7573	State standards and controls	273
42 USC 7574	Definitions	273

Part C—Clean Fuel Vehicles

42 USC 7581	Definitions	274
42 USC 7582	Requirements applicable to clean-fuel vehicles	275
42 USC 7583	Standards for light-duty clean-fuel vehicles	276
42 USC 7584	Administration and enforcement as per California standards	280
42 USC 7585	Standards for heavy-duty clean-fuel vehicles (GVWR above 8,500 up to 26,000 lbs.)	281
42 USC 7586	Centrally fueled fleets	281
42 USC 7587	Vehicle conversions	284

42 USC 7588	Federal agency fleets	285
42 USC 7589	California pilot test program	286
42 USC 7590	General provisions	288

SUBCHAPTER III—GENERAL PROVISIONS

42 USC 7601	Administration	290
42 USC 7602	Definitions	292
42 USC 7603	Emergency powers	295
42 USC 7604	Citizen suits	297
42 USC 7605	Representation in litigation	300
42 USC 7606	Federal procurement	301
42 USC 7607	Administrative proceedings and judicial review	304
42 USC 7608	Mandatory licensing	311
42 USC 7609	Policy review	312
42 USC 7610	Other authority	313
42 USC 7611	Records and audit	313
42 USC 7612	Economic impact analyses	314
42 USC 7613	[repealed]	316
42 USC 7614	Labor standards	317
42 USC 7615	Separability	317
42 USC 7616	Sewage treatment grants	317
42 USC 7617	Economic impact assessment	318
42 USC 7618	[repealed]	320
42 USC 7619	Air quality monitoring	320
42 USC 7620	Standardized air quality modeling	321
42 USC 7621	Employment effects	321
42 USC 7622	Employee protection	323
42 USC 7623	[repealed]	324
42 USC 7624	Cost of vapor recovery equipment	325
42 USC 7625	Vapor recovery for small business marketers of petroleum products	325
42 USC 7625–1	Exemptions for certain territories	326
42 USC 7625a	Statutory construction	327
42 USC 7626	Authorization of appropriations	328
42 USC 7627	Air pollution from Outer Continental Shelf activities	328

SUBCHAPTER IV—NOISE POLLUTION

42 USC 7641	Noise abatement	331
42 USC 7642	Authorization of appropriations	331

SUBCHAPTER IV-A—ACID DEPOSITION CONTROL

42 USC 7651	Findings and purposes	332
42 USC 7651a	Definitions	333
42 USC 7651b	Sulfur dioxide allowance program for existing and new units	336
42 USC 7651c	Phase I sulfur dioxide requirements	340
42 USC 7651d	Phase II sulfur dioxide requirements	351
42 USC 7651e	Allowances for States with emissions rates at or below 0.80 lbs/mmBtu	358
42 USC 7651f	Nitrogen oxides emission reduction program	358

42 USC 7651g	Permits and compliance plans	360
42 USC 7651h	Repowered sources	363
42 USC 7651i	Election for additional sources	365
42 USC 7651j	Excess emissions penalty	366
42 USC 7651k	Monitoring, reporting, and recordkeeping requirements	367
42 USC 7651l	General compliance with other provisions	369
42 USC 7651m	Enforcement	369
42 USC 7651n	Clean coal technology regulatory incentives	369
42 USC 7651o	Contingency guarantee, auctions, reserve	370

SUBCHAPTER V—PERMITS

42 USC 7661	Definitions	375
42 USC 7661a	Permit programs	375
42 USC 7661b	Permit applications	379
42 USC 7661c	Permit requirements and conditions	380
42 USC 7661d	Notification to Administrator and contiguous States	381
42 USC 7661e	Other authorities	383
42 USC 7661f	Small business stationary source technical and environmental compliance assistance program	383

SUBCHAPTER VI—STRATOSPHERIC OZONE PROTECTION

42 USC 7671	Definitions	387
42 USC 7671a	Listing of class I and class II substances	388
42 USC 7671b	Monitoring and reporting requirements	391
42 USC 7671c	Phase-out of production and consumption of class I substances	394
42 USC 7671d	Phase-out of production and consumption of class II substances	397
42 USC 7671e	Accelerated schedule	398
42 USC 7671f	Exchange authority	399
42 USC 7671g	National recycling and emission reduction program	400
42 USC 7671h	Servicing of motor vehicle air conditioners	401
42 USC 7671i	Nonessential products containing chlorofluorocarbons	402
42 USC 7671j	Labeling	403
42 USC 7671k	Safe alternatives policy	404
42 USC 7671l	Federal procurement	405
42 USC 7671m	Relationship to other laws	408
42 USC 7671n	Authority of Administrator	408
42 USC 7671o	Transfers among Parties to Montreal Protocol	408
42 USC 7671p	International cooperation	409
42 USC 7671q	Miscellaneous provisions	410

WATER POLLUTION PREVENTION AND CONTROL [CLEAN WATER ACT]

SUBCHAPTER I—RESEARCH AND RELATED PROGRAMS

33 USC 1251	Congressional declaration of goals and policy	411
33 USC 1252	Comprehensive programs for water pollution control	419
33 USC 1252a	Reservoir projects, water storage; modification; storage for other than for water quality, opinion of Federal agency,	

x / Environmental Statutes

	committee resolutions of approval; provisions inapplicable to projects with certain prescribed water quality benefits in relation to total project benefits	420
33 USC 1253	Interstate cooperation and uniform laws	421
33 USC 1254	Research, investigations, training, and information	421
33 USC 1254a	Research on effects of pollutants	429
33 USC 1255	Grants for research and development	429
33 USC 1256	Grants for pollution control programs	431
33 USC 1257	Mine water pollution control demonstrations	433
33 USC 1257a	State demonstration programs for cleanup of abandoned mines for use as waste disposal sites; authorization of appropriations	434
33 USC 1258	Pollution control in the Great Lakes	434
33 USC 1259	Training grants and contracts	435
33 USC 1260	Applications; allocation	436
33 USC 1261	Scholarships	437
33 USC 1262	Definitions and authorizations	438
33 USC 1263	Alaska village demonstration projects	439
33 USC 1263a	Grants to Alaska to improve sanitation in rural and Native villages	440
33 USC 1264	[Omitted]	441
33 USC 1265	In-place toxic pollutants	441
33 USC 1266	Hudson River reclamation demonstration project	441
33 USC 1267	Chesapeake Bay	442
33 USC 1268	Great Lakes	446
42 USC 1269	Long Island Sound	454
33 USC 1270	Lake Champlain Management Conference	456
33 USC 1271	Sediment survey and monitoring	459
33 USC 1271a	Research and development program	462
33 USC 1272	Environmental dredging	462
33 USC 1273	Lake Pontchartrain Basin	464
33 USC 1274	Wet weather watershed pilot projects	465

SUBCHAPTER II—GRANTS FOR CONSTRUCTION OF TREATMENT WORKS

33 USC 1281	Congressional declaration of purpose	466
33 USC 1281a	Total treatment system funding	475
33 USC 1281b	Availability of Farmers Home Administration funds for non-Federal share	475
33 USC 1282	Federal share	475
33 USC 1283	Plans, specifications, estimates, and payments	478
33 USC 1284	Limitations and conditions	481
33 USC 1285	Allotment of grant funds	486
33 USC 1286	Reimbursement and advanced construction	494
33 USC 1287	Authorization of appropriations	497
33 USC 1288	Areawide waste treatment management	498
33 USC 1289	Basin planning	505
33 USC 1290	Annual survey	505
33 USC 1291	Sewage collection systems	506
33 USC 1292	Definitions	506
33 USC 1293	Loan guarantees	507
33 USC 1293a	Contained spoil disposal facilities	508

Contents / xi

33 USC 1294	Public information and education on recycling and reuse of wastewater, use of land treatment, and reduction of wastewater volume	511
33 USC 1295	Requirements for American materials	511
33 USC 1296	Determination of priority of projects	511
33 USC 1297	Guidelines for cost-effectiveness analysis	512
33 USC 1298	Cost effectiveness	512
33 USC 1299	State certification of projects	513
33 USC 1300	Pilot program for alternative water source projects	513
33 USC 1301	Sewer overflow control grants	515

SUBCHAPTER III—STANDARDS AND ENFORCEMENT

33 USC 1311	Effluent limitations	517
33 USC 1312	Water quality related effluent limitations	530
33 USC 1313	Water quality standards and implementation plans	531
33 USC 1313a	Revised water quality standards	536
33 USC 1314	Information and guidelines	536
33 USC 1315	State reports on water quality; transmittal to Congress	543
33 USC 1316	National standards of performance	544
33 USC 1317	Toxic and pretreatment effluent standards	546
33 USC 1318	Records and reports; inspections	549
33 USC 1319	Enforcement	551
33 USC 1320	International pollution abatement	559
33 USC 1321	Oil and hazardous substance liability	560
33 USC 1322	Marine sanitation devices	590
33 USC 1323	Federal facilities pollution control	601
33 USC 1324	Clean lakes	603
33 USC 1325	National Study Commission	606
33 USC 1326	Thermal discharges	608
33 USC 1327	[Omitted]	609
33 USC 1328	Aquaculture	609
33 USC 1329	Nonpoint source management programs	609
33 USC 1330	National estuary program	615

SUBCHAPTER IV—PERMITS AND LICENSES

33 USC 1341	Certification	621
33 USC 1342	National pollutant discharge elimination system	623
33 USC 1343	Ocean discharge criteria	632
33 USC 1344	Permits for dredged or fill material	633
33 USC 1345	Disposal or use of sewage sludge	641
33 USC 1346	Coastal recreation water quality monitoring and notification	644

SUBCHAPTER V—GENERAL PROVISIONS

33 USC 1361	Administration	648
33 USC 1362	Definitions	649
33 USC 1363	Water Pollution Control Advisory Board	651
33 USC 1364	Emergency powers	653
33 USC 1365	Citizen suits	653
33 USC 1366	Appearance	655
33 USC 1367	Employee protection	655

33 USC 1368	Federal procurement	656
33 USC 1369	Administrative procedure and judicial review	657
33 USC 1370	State authority	659
33 USC 1371	Authority under other laws and regulations	659
33 USC 1372	Labor standards	660
33 USC 1373	Public health agency coordination	661
33 USC 1374	Effluent Standards and Water Quality Information Advisory Committee	661
33 USC 1375	Reports to Congress; detailed estimates and comprehensive study on costs; State estimates	662
33 USC 1375a	Report on coastal recreation waters	664
33 USC 1376	Authorization of appropriations	665
33 USC 1377	Indian tribes	665

SUBCHAPTER VI—STATE WATER POLLUTION CONTROL REVOLVING FUNDS

33 USC 1381	Grants to States for establishment of revolving funds	669
33 USC 1382	Capitalization grant agreements	669
33 USC 1383	Water pollution control revolving loan funds	670
33 USC 1384	Allotment of funds	671
33 USC 1385	Corrective action	672
33 USC 1386	Audits, reports, and fiscal controls; intended use plan	672
33 USC 1387	Authorization of appropriations	673

ESTUARY RESTORATION
[ESTUARY RESTORATION ACT OF 2000]

33 USC 2901	Purposes	675
33 USC 2902	Definitions	676
33 USC 2903	Estuary habitat restoration program	677
33 USC 2904	Establishment of Estuary Habitat Restoration Council	679
33 USC 2905	Estuary habitat restoration strategy	680
33 USC 2906	Monitoring of estuary habitat restoration projects	681
33 USC 2907	Reporting	682
33 USC 2908	Funding	682
33 USC 2909	General provisions	683

OIL POLLUTION
[OIL POLLUTION ACT OF 1990]
SUBCHAPTER I—OIL POLLUTION LIABILITY AND COMPENSATION

33 USC 2701	Definitions	685
33 USC 2702	Elements of liability	688
33 USC 2703	Defenses to liability	690
33 USC 2704	Limits on liability	691
33 USC 2705	Interest; partial payment of claims	693
33 USC 2706	Natural resources	694
33 USC 2707	Recovery by foreign claimants	697
33 USC 2708	Recovery by responsible party	698
33 USC 2709	Contribution	698

33 USC 2710	Indemnification agreements	699
33 USC 2711	Consultation on removal actions	699
33 USC 2712	Uses of Fund	699
33 USC 2713	Claims procedure	702
33 USC 2714	Designation of source and advertisement	703
33 USC 2715	Subrogation	704
33 USC 2716	Financial responsibility	705
33 USC 2716a	Financial responsibility civil penalties	708
33 USC 2717	Litigation, jurisdiction, and venue	709
33 USC 2718	Relationship to other law	710
33 USC 2719	State financial responsibility	711
33 USC 2720	Differentiation among fats, oils, and greases	711

Title II
Conforming Amendments

33 USC 1486	Oil Spill Liability Trust Fund	714
Sec. USC2002	Federal water pollution control act	714
Sec. USC2003	Deepwater port act	714
26 USC 9509	Oil Spill Liability Trust Fund	715

Title III
International Oil Pollution Prevention and Removal

Sec. USC3001	Sense of Congress regarding participation in international regime	720
Sec. USC3002	United States–Canada Great Lakes oil spill cooperation	720
Sec. USC3003	United States–Canada Lake Champlain oil spill cooperation	720
Sec. USC3004	Internation inventory of removal equipment and personnel	720
Sec. USC3005	Negotiations with Canada concerning tug escorts in Puget Sound	721

Title IV
Prevention and Removal

Subtitle A—Prevention

Sec. USC4101	Review of alcohol and drug abuse and other matters in issuing licenses, certificates of registry, and merchant mariners' documents	722
Sec. USC4102	Term of licenses, certificates of registry, and merchant mariners' documents; criminal record reviews in renewals	722
Sec. USC4103	Suspension and revocation of licences, certificates of registry, and merchant mariners' documents for alcohol and drug abuse	723
Sec. USC4104	Removal of master or individual in charge	724
Sec. USC4105	Access to national driver register	724
Sec. USC4106	Manning standards for foreign tank vessels	725
Sec. USC4107	Vessel traffic service systems	726
Sec. USC4108	Great Lakes pilotage	727
46 USC 3703	Regulations	727
Sec. USC4111	Study on tanker navigation safety standards	731
Sec. USC4112	Dredge modification study	731

xiv / Environmental Statutes

Sec. USC4113	Use of liners	732
Sec. USC4114	Tank vessel manning	732
46 USC 3703a	Tank vessel construction standards	732
Sec. USC4115	Establishment of double hull requirement for tank vessels	737
Sec. USC4116	Pilotage	739
Sec. USC4117	Maritime pollution prevention training program study	739
Sec. USC4118	Vessel communication equipment regulations	739

Subtitle B—Removal

Sec. USC4201	Federal removal authority	740
Sec. USC4202	National contingency planning and response system	740
14 USC 92 note	Coast Guard Vessel Design	741
Sec. USC4204	Determination of harmful quantities of oil and hazardous substances	741
Sec. USC4205	Coastwise oil spill response cooperatives	741

Subtitle C—Penalties and Miscellaneous

Sec. USC4301	Federal water pollution control act penalties	742
Sec. USC4302	Other penalties	742
Sec. USC4303	Financial responsibility civil penalties	743
Sec. USC4304	[Untitled]	744
Sec. USC4305	Inspection and entry	744
Sec. USC4306	Inspection and entry	744

SUBCHAPTER II—PRINCE WILLIAM SOUND PROVISIONS

33 USC 2731	Oil Spill Recovery Institute	745
33 USC 2732	Terminal and tanker oversight and monitoring	748
33 USC 2733	Bligh Reef light	755
33 USC 2734	Vessel traffic service system	755
33 USC 2735	Equipment and personnel requirements under tank vessel and facility response plans	756
33 USC 2736	Funding	757
33 USC 2737	Limitation	758
33 USC 2738	North Pacific Marine Research Institute	758

SUBCHAPTER III—MISCELLANEOUS

33 USC 2751	Savings provision	760
33 USC 2752	Annual appropriations	760
33 USC 2753	[Repealed]	761
43 USC 1334	Administration of leasing	761

SUBCHAPTER IV—OIL POLLUTION RESEARCH AND DEVELOPMENT PROGRAM

| 33 USC 2761 | Oil pollution research and development program | 766 |

TRANS-ALASKA PIPELINE
[as amended by Title VIII of Oil Pollution Act of 1990]

| 43 USC 1651 | Congressional findings and declaration | 771 |
| 43 USC 1652 | Authorizations for construction | 773 |

43 USC 1653	Liability for damages	774
43 USC 1654	Antitrust laws	779
43 USC 1655	Roads and airports	779
43 USC 1656	Civil penalties	779
43 USC 1642	Land conveyances	780
16 USC 3145	Wildlife resources portion of study and impact of potential oil spills in Arctic Ocean	781

SAFETY OF PUBLIC WATER SYSTEMS
[Safe Drinking Water Act]

Part A—Definitions

42 USC 300f	Definitions	783

Part B—Public Water Systems

42 USC 300g	Coverage	788
42 USC 300g-1	National drinking water regulations	788
42 USC 300g-2	State primary enforcement responsibility	802
42 USC 300g-3	Enforcement of drinking water regulations	803
42 USC 300g-4	Variances	810
42 USC 300g-5	Exemptions	816
42 USC 300g-6	Prohibition on use of lead pipes, solder, and flux	820
42 USC 300g-7	Monitoring of contaminants	823
42 USC 300g-8	Operator certification	824
42 USC 300g-9	Capacity development	826

Part C—Protection of Underground Sources of Drinking Water

42 USC 300h	Regulations for State programs	829
42 USC 300h-1	State primary enforcement responsibility	831
42 USC 300h-2	Enforcement of program	832
42 USC 300h-3	Interim regulation of underground injections	835
42 USC 300h-4	Optional demonstration by States relating to oil or natural gas	836
42 USC 300h-5	Regulation of State programs	837
42 USC 300h-6	Sole source aquifer demonstration program	838
42 USC 300h-7	State programs to establish wellhead protection areas	841
42 USC 300h-8	State ground water protection grants	845

Part D—Emergency Powers

42 USC 300i	Emergency powers	846
42 USC 300i-1	Tampering with public water systems	846

Part E—General Provisions

42 USC 300j	Assurances of availability of adequate supplies of chemicals necessary for treatment of water	847
42 USC 300j-1	Research, technical assistance, information, training of personnel	849
42 USC 300j-2	Grants for State programs	854
42 USC 300j-3	Special project grants and guaranteed loans	857

xvi / Environmental Statutes

42 USC 300j-3a	Grants to public sector agencies	858
42 USC 300j-3b	Contaminant standards or treatment technique guidelines	859
42 USC 300j-3c	National assistance program for water infrastructure and watersheds	860
42 USC 300j-4	Records and inspections	861
42 USC 300j-5	National Drinking Water Advisory Council	865
42 USC 300j-6	Federal agencies	867
42 USC 300j-7	Judicial review	869
42 USC 300j-8	Citizen's civil action	870
42 USC 300j-9	General provisions	872
42 USC 300j-10	Appointment of scientific, etc., personnel by Administrator of Environmental Protection Agency for implementation of responsibilities; compensation	875
42 USC 300j-11	Indian Tribes	875
42 USC 300j-12	State revolving loan funds	876
42 USC 300j-13	Source water quality assessment	884
42 USC 300j-14	Source water petition program	886
42 USC 300j-15	Water conservation plan	889
42 USC 300j-16	Assistance to colonias	889
42 USC 300j-17	Estrogenic substances screening program	890
42 USC 300j-18	Drinking water studies	890

Part F—Additional Requirements to Regulate Safety of Drinking Water

42 USC 300j-21	Definitions	893
42 USC 300j-22	Recall of drinking water coolers with lead-lined tanks	894
42 USC 300j-23	Drinking water coolers containing lead	894
42 USC 300j-24	Lead contamination in school drinking water	895
42 USC 300j-25	Federal assistance for State programs regarding lead contamination in school drinking water	896
42 USC 300j-26	Certification of testing laboratories	896

AIR POLLUTION PREVENTION AND CONTROL
[CLEAN AIR ACT]

as amended[1]
42 U.S.C. § 7401 et seq.

SUBCHAPTER I—PROGRAMS AND ACTIVITIES

Part A—Air Quality and Emission Limitations

CONGRESSIONAL FINDINGS AND DECLARATION OF PURPOSE

42 USC 7401

(a) Findings
   The Congress finds—
   (1) that the predominant part of the Nation's population is located in its rapidly expanding metropolitan and other urban areas, which generally cross the boundary lines of local jurisdictions and often extend into two or more States;
   (2) that the growth in the amount and complexity of air pollution brought about by urbanization, industrial development, and the increasing use of motor vehicles, has resulted in mounting dangers to the public health and welfare, including injury to agricultural crops and livestock, damage to and the deterioration of property, and hazards to air and ground transportation;
   (3) that air pollution prevention (that is, the reduction or elimination, through any measures, of the amount of pollutants produced or created at the source) and air pollution control at its source is the primary responsibility of States and local governments; and
   (4) that Federal financial assistance and leadership is essential for the development of cooperative Federal, State, regional, and local programs to prevent and control air pollution.
(b) Declaration
   The purposes of this subchapter are—
   (1) to protect and enhance the quality of the Nation's air resources so as to promote the public health and welfare and the productive capacity of its population;
   (2) to initiate and accelerate a national research and development program to achieve the prevention and control of air pollution;
   (3) to provide technical and financial assistance to State and local governments in connection with the development and execution of their air pollution prevention and control programs; and
   (4) to encourage and assist the development and operation of regional air pollution prevention and control programs.
(c) Pollution prevention
   A primary goal of this chapter is to encourage or otherwise promote reasonable Federal, State, and local governmental actions, consistent with the provisions of this chapter, for pollution prevention.

(July 14, 1955, ch. 360, title I, Sec. 101, formerly Sec. 1, as added Pub. L. 88-206, Sec. 1, Dec. 17, 1963, 77 Stat. 392; renumbered Sec. 101 and amended Pub. L. 89-272, title I, Sec. 101(2), (3), Oct. 20, 1965, 79 Stat. 992; Pub. L. 90-148, Sec. 2, Nov. 21, 1967, 81 Stat. 485; Pub. L. 101-549, title I, Sec. 108(k), Nov. 15, 1990, 104 Stat. 2468.)

---

[1] Editor's note: Text from Title 42, Chapter 85 of U.S. Code, as amended by Pub. L. 108-199, January 23, 2004; Pub. L 106-377, October 27, 2000; and Pub L. 106-246, July 13, 2000.

Codification

Section was formerly classified to section 1857 of this title.

Prior Provisions

Provisions similar to those in this section were contained in a prior section 1857 of this title, act of July 14, 1955, ch. 360, Sec. 1, 69 Stat. 322, prior to the general amendment of this chapter by Pub. L. 88-206.

Amendments

1990—Subsec. (a)(3). Pub. L. 101-549, Sec. 108(k)(1), amended par. (3) generally. Prior to amendment, par. (3) read as follows: "that the prevention and control of air pollution at its source is the primary responsibility of States and local governments; and".

Subsec. (b)(4). Pub. L. 101-549, Sec. 108(k)(2), inserted "prevention and" after "pollution".

Subsec. (c). Pub. L. 101-549, Sec. 108(k)(3), added subsec. (c).

1967—Subsec. (b)(1). Pub. L. 90-148 inserted "and enhance the quality of" after "to protect".

1965—Subsec. (b). Pub. L. 89-272 substituted "this title" for "this Act", which for purposes of codification has been changed to "this subchapter".

Effective Date of 1990 Amendment

Section 711(b) of Pub. L. 101-549 provided that:

"(1) Except as otherwise expressly provided, the amendments made by this Act [see Tables for classification] shall be effective on the date of enactment of this Act [Nov. 15, 1990].

(2) The Administrator's authority to assess civil penalties under section 205(c) of the Clean Air Act [42 U.S.C. 7524(c)], as amended by this Act, shall apply to violations that occur or continue on or after the date of enactment of this Act. Civil penalties for violations that occur prior to such date and do not continue after such date shall be assessed in accordance with the provisions of the Clean Air Act [42 U.S.C. 7401 et seq.] in effect immediately prior to the date of enactment of this Act.

(3) The civil penalties prescribed under sections 205(a) and 211(d)(1) of the Clean Air Act [42 U.S.C. 7524(a), 7545(d)(1)], as amended by this Act, shall apply to violations that occur on or after the date of enactment of this Act. Violations that occur prior to such date shall be subject to the civil penalty provisions prescribed in sections 205(a) and 211(d) of the Clean Air Act in effect immediately prior to the enactment of this Act. The injunctive authority prescribed under section 211(d)(2) of the Clean Air Act, as amended by this Act, shall apply to violations that occur or continue on or after the date of enactment of this Act.

(4) For purposes of paragraphs (2) and (3), where the date of a violation cannot be determined it will be assumed to be the date on which the violation is discovered."

Effective Date of 1977 Amendment; Pending Actions; Continuation of Rules, Contracts, Authorizations, Etc.; Implementation Plans

Section 406 of Pub. L. 95-95, as amended by Pub. L. 95-190, Sec. 14(b)(6), Nov. 16, 1977, 91 Stat. 1405, provided that:

"(a) No suit, action, or other proceeding lawfully commenced by or against the Administrator or any other officer or employee of the United States in his official capacity or in relation to the discharge of his official duties under the Clean Air Act [this chapter], as in effect immediately prior to the date of enactment of this Act [Aug. 7, 1977] shall abate by reason of the taking effect of the amendments made by this Act [see Short Title of 1977 Amendment note below]. The court may, on its own motion or that of any party made at any time within twelve months after such taking effect, allow the same to be maintained by or against the Administrator or such officer or employee.

(b) All rules, regulations, orders, determinations, contracts, certifications, authorizations, delegations, or other actions duly issued, made, or taken by or pursuant to the Clean Air Act [this chapter], as in effect immediately prior to the date of enactment of this Act [Aug. 7, 1977], and pertaining to any functions, powers, requirements, and duties under the Clean Air Act, as in effect immediately prior to the date of enactment of this Act, and not suspended by the Administrator or the courts, shall continue in full force and effect after the date of enactment of this Act until modified or rescinded in accordance with the Clean Air Act as amended by this Act [see Short Title of 1977 Amendment note below].

(c) Nothing in this Act [see Short Title of 1977 Amendment note below] nor any action taken pursuant to this Act shall in any way affect any requirement of an approved implementation plan in effect under section 110 of the Clean Air Act [section 7410 of this title] or any other provision of the Act in effect under the Clean Air Act before the date of enactment of this section [Aug. 7, 1977] until modified or rescinded in accordance with the Clean Air Act [this chapter] as amended by this Act [see Short Title of 1977 Amendment note below].

(d) (1) Except as otherwise expressly provided, the amendments made by this Act [see Short Title of 1977 Amendment note below] shall be effective on date of enactment [Aug. 7, 1977].

(2) Except as otherwise expressly provided, each State required to revise its applicable implementation plan by reason of any amendment made by this Act [see Short Title of 1977 Amendment note below] shall adopt and submit to the Administrator of the Environmental Protection Administration such plan revision before the later of the date—

(A) one year after the date of enactment of this Act [Aug. 7, 1977], or

(B) nine months after the date of promulgation by the Administrator of the Environmental Protection Administration of any regulations under an amendment made by this Act which are necessary for the approval of such plan revision."

Short Title of 1999 Amendment

Pub. L. 106-40, Sec. 1, Aug. 5, 1999, 113 Stat. 207, provided that: "This Act [amending section 7412 of this title and enacting provisions set out as notes under section 7412 of this title] may be cited as the 'Chemical Safety Information, Site Security and Fuels Regulatory Relief Act'."

Short Title of 1998 Amendment

Pub. L. 105-286, Sec. 1, Oct. 27, 1998, 112 Stat. 2773, provided that: "This Act [amending section 7511b of this title and enacting provisions set out as a note under section 7511b of this title] may be cited as the 'Border Smog Reduction Act of 1998'."

Short Title of 1990 Amendment

Pub. L. 101-549, Nov. 15, 1990, 104 Stat. 2399, is popularly known as the "Clean Air Act Amendments of 1990". See Tables for classification.

Short Title of 1981 Amendment

Pub. L. 97-23, Sec. 1, July 17, 1981, 95 Stat. 139, provided: "That this Act [amending sections 7410 and 7413 of this title] may be cited as the 'Steel Industry Compliance Extension Act of 1981'."

Short Title of 1977 Amendment

Pub. L. 95-95, Sec. 1, Aug. 7, 1977, 91 Stat. 685, provided that: "This Act [enacting sections 4362, 7419 to 7428, 7450 to 7459, 7470 to 7479, 7491, 7501 to 7508, 7548, 7549, 7551, 7617 to 7625, and 7626 of this title, amending sections 7403, 7405, 7407 to 7415, 7417, 7418, 7521 to 7525, 7541, 7543, 7544, 7545, 7550, 7571, 7601 to 7605, 7607, 7612, 7613, and 7616 of this title, repealing section 1857c-10 of this title, and enacting provisions set out as notes under this section, sections 7403, 7422, 7470, 7479, 7502, 7521, 7548, and 7621 of this title, and section 792 of Title 15, Commerce and Trade] may be cited as the 'Clean Air Act Amendments of 1977'."

Short Title of 1970 Amendment

Pub. L. 91-604, Sec. 1, Dec. 31, 1970, 84 Stat. 1676, provided: "That this Act [amending this chapter generally] may be cited as the 'Clean Air Amendments of 1970'."

Short Title of 1967 Amendment

Section 1 of Pub. L. 90-148 provided: "That this Act [amending this chapter generally] may be cited as the 'Air Quality Act of 1967'."

Short Title of 1966 Amendment

Pub. L. 89-675, Sec. 1, Oct. 15, 1966, 80 Stat. 954, provided: "That this Act [amending sections 7405 and 7616 of this title and repealing section 1857f-8 of this title] may be cited as the 'Clean Air Act Amendments of 1966'."

Short Title

Section 317, formerly section 14, of act July 14, 1955, as added by section 1 of Pub. L. 88-206, renumbered section 307 by section 101(4) of Pub. L. 89-272, renumbered section 310 by section 2 of Pub. L. 90-148, and renumbered section 317 by Pub. L. 91-604, Sec. 12(a), Dec. 31, 1970, 84 Stat. 1705, provided that: "This Act [enacting this chapter] may be cited as the 'Clean Air Act'."

Section 201 of title II of act July 14, 1955, as added by Pub. L. 89-272, title I, Sec. 101(8), Oct. 20, 1965, 79 Stat. 992, and amended by Pub. L. 90-148, Sec. 2, Nov. 2, 1967, 81 Stat. 499, provided that: "This title [enacting subchapter II of this chapter] may be cited as the 'National Emission Standards Act'." Prior to its amendment by Pub. L. 90-148, title II of act June 14, 1955, was known as the "Motor Vehicle Air Pollution Control Act".

Section 401 of title IV of act July 14, 1955, as added Dec. 31, 1970, Pub. L. 91-604, Sec. 14, 84 Stat. 1709, provided that: "This title [enacting subchapter IV of this chapter] may be cited as the 'Noise Pollution and Abatement Act of 1970'."

Savings Provision

Section 711(a) of Pub. L. 101-549 provided that: "Except as otherwise expressly provided in this Act [see Tables for classification], no suit, action, or other proceeding lawfully commenced by the Administrator or any other officer or employee of the United States in his official capacity or in relation to the discharge of his official duties under the Clean Air Act [42 U.S.C. 7401 et seq.], as in effect immediately prior to the date of enactment of this Act [Nov. 15, 1990], shall abate by reason of the taking effect of the amendments made by this Act."

Transfer of Functions

Reorg. Plan No. 3 of 1970, Sec. 2(a)(3), eff. Dec. 2, 1970, 35 F.R. 15623, 84 Stat. 2086, transferred to Administrator of Environmental Protection Agency functions vested by law in Secretary of Health, Education, and Welfare or in Department of Health, Education, and Welfare which are administered through Environmental Health Service, including functions exercised by National Air Pollution Control Administration, and Environmental Control Administration's Bureau of Solid Waste Management, Bureau of Water Hygiene, and Bureau of Radiological Health, except insofar as functions carried out by Bureau of Radiological Health pertain to regulation of radiation from consumer products, including electronic product radiation, radiation as used in healing arts, occupational exposure to radiation, and research, technical assistance, and training related to radiation from consumer products, radiation as used in healing arts, and occupational exposure to radiation.

Impact on Small Communities

Section 810 of Pub. L. 101-549 provided that: "Before implementing a provision of this Act [see Tables for classification], the Administrator of the Environmental Protection Agency shall consult with the Small Communities Coordinator of the Environmental Protection Agency to determine the impact of such provision on small communities, including the estimated cost of compliance with such provision."

Radon Assessment and Mitigation

Pub. L. 99-499, title I, Sec. 118(k), Oct. 17, 1986, 100 Stat. 1659, as amended by Pub. L. 105-362, title V, Sec. 501(i), Nov. 10, 1998, 112 Stat. 3284, provided that:

"(1) National assessment of radon gas.—No later than one year after the enactment of this Act [Oct. 17, 1986], the Administrator shall submit to the Congress a report which shall, to the extent possible—
  (A) identify the locations in the United States where radon is found in structures where people normally live or work, including educational institutions;
  (B) assess the levels of radon gas that are present in such structures;
  (C) determine the level of radon gas and radon daughters which poses a threat to human health and assess for each location identified under subparagraph (A) the extent of the threat to human health;
  (D) determine methods of reducing or eliminating the threat to human health of radon gas and radon daughters; and
  (E) include guidance and public information materials based on the findings or research of mitigating radon.
(2) Radon mitigation demonstration program.—
  (A) Demonstration program.—The Administrator shall conduct a demonstration program to test methods and technologies of reducing or eliminating radon gas and radon daughters where it poses a threat to human health. The Administrator shall take into consideration

any demonstration program underway in the Reading Prong of Pennsylvania, New Jersey, and New York and at other sites prior to enactment. The demonstration program under this section shall be conducted in the Reading Prong, and at such other sites as the Administrator considers appropriate.
  (B) Liability.—Liability, if any, for persons undertaking activities pursuant to the radon mitigation demonstration program authorized under this subsection shall be determined under principles of existing law.
(3) Construction of section.—Nothing in this subsection shall be construed to authorize the Administrator to carry out any regulatory program or any activity other than research, development, and related reporting, information dissemination, and coordination activities specified in this subsection. Nothing in paragraph (1) or (2) shall be construed to limit the authority of the Administrator or of any other agency or instrumentality of the United States under any other authority of law."

Spill Control Technology

Pub. L. 99-499, title I, Sec. 118(n), Oct. 17, 1986, 100 Stat. 1660, provided that:
"(1) Establishment of program.—Within 180 days of enactment of this subsection [Oct. 17, 1986], the Secretary of the United States Department of Energy is directed to carry out a program of testing and evaluation of technologies which may be utilized in responding to liquefied gaseous and other hazardous substance spills at the Liquefied Gaseous Fuels Spill Test Facility that threaten public health or the environment.
(2) Technology transfer.—In carrying out the program established under this subsection, the Secretary shall conduct a technology transfer program that, at a minimum—
  (A) documents and archives spill control technology;
  (B) investigates and analyzes significant hazardous spill incidents;
  (C) develops and provides generic emergency action plans;
  (D) documents and archives spill test results;
  (E) develops emergency action plans to respond to spills;
  (F) conducts training of spill response personnel; and
  (G) establishes safety standards for personnel engaged in spill response activities.
(3) Contracts and grants.—The Secretary is directed to enter into contracts and grants with a nonprofit organization in Albany County, Wyoming, that is capable of providing the necessary technical support and which is involved in environmental activities related to such hazardous substance related emergencies.
(4) Use of site.—The Secretary shall arrange for the use of the Liquefied Gaseous Fuels Spill Test Facility to carry out the provisions of this subsection."

Radon Gas and Indoor Air Quality Research

Pub. L. 99-499, title IV, Oct. 17, 1986, 100 Stat. 1758, provided that:
"SEC. 401. SHORT TITLE.

This title may be cited as the 'Radon Gas and Indoor Air Quality Research Act of 1986'.
SEC. 402. FINDINGS.

The Congress finds that:
(1) High levels of radon gas pose a serious health threat in structures in certain areas of the country.
(2) Various scientific studies have suggested that exposure to radon, including exposure to naturally occurring radon and indoor air pollutants, poses a public health risk.
(3) Existing Federal radon and indoor air pollutant research programs are fragmented and underfunded.
(4) An adequate information base concerning exposure to radon and indoor air pollutants should be developed by the appropriate Federal agencies.

SEC. 403. RADON GAS AND INDOOR AIR QUALITY RESEARCH PROGRAM.
(a) Design of Program.—The Administrator of the Environmental Protection Agency shall establish a research program with respect to radon gas and indoor air quality. Such program shall be designed to—
  (1) gather data and information on all aspects of indoor air quality in order to contribute to the understanding of health problems associated with the existence of air pollutants in the indoor environment;

(2) coordinate Federal, State, local, and private research and development efforts relating to the improvement of indoor air quality; and
(3) assess appropriate Federal Government actions to mitigate the environmental and health risks associated with indoor air quality problems.
(b) Program Requirements.—The research program required under this section shall include—
  (1) research and development concerning the identification, characterization, and monitoring of the sources and levels of indoor air pollution, including radon, which includes research and development relating to—
    (A) the measurement of various pollutant concentrations and their strengths and sources,
    (B) high-risk building types, and
    (C) instruments for indoor air quality data collection;
  (2) research relating to the effects of indoor air pollution and radon on human health;
  (3) research and development relating to control technologies or other mitigation measures to prevent or abate indoor air pollution (including the development, evaluation, and testing of individual and generic control devices and systems);
  (4) demonstration of methods for reducing or eliminating indoor air pollution and radon, including sealing, venting, and other methods that the Administrator determines may be effective;
  (5) research, to be carried out in conjunction with the Secretary of Housing and Urban Development, for the purpose of developing—
    (A) methods for assessing the potential for radon contamination of new construction, including (but not limited to) consideration of the moisture content of soil, porosity of soil, and radon content of soil; and
    (B) design measures to avoid indoor air pollution; and
  (6) the dissemination of information to assure the public availability of the findings of the activities under this section.
(c) Advisory Committees.—The Administrator shall establish a committee comprised of individuals representing Federal agencies concerned with various aspects of indoor air quality and an advisory group comprised of individuals representing the States, the scientific community, industry, and public interest organizations to assist him in carrying out the research program for radon gas and indoor air quality.
(d) Implementation Plan.—Not later than 90 days after the enactment of this Act [Oct. 17, 1986], the Administrator shall submit to the Congress a plan for implementation of the research program under this section. Such plan shall also be submitted to the EPA Science Advisory Board, which shall, within a reasonable period of time, submit its comments on such plan to Congress.
(e) Report.—Not later than 2 years after the enactment of this Act [Oct. 17, 1986], the Administrator shall submit to Congress a report respecting his activities under this section and making such recommendations as appropriate.

SEC. 404. CONSTRUCTION OF TITLE.

Nothing in this title shall be construed to authorize the Administrator to carry out any regulatory program or any activity other than research, development, and related reporting, information dissemination, and coordination activities specified in this title. Nothing in this title shall be construed to limit the authority of the Administrator or of any other agency or instrumentality of the United States under any other authority of law.

SEC. 405. AUTHORIZATIONS.

There are authorized to be appropriated to carry out the activities under this title and under section 118(k) of the Superfund Amendments and Reauthorization Act of 1986 (relating to radon gas assessment and demonstration program) [section 118(k) of Pub. L. 99-499, set out as a note above] not to exceed $5,000,000 for each of the fiscal years 1987, 1988, and 1989. Of such sums appropriated in fiscal years 1987 and 1988, two-fifths shall be reserved for the implementation of section 118(k)(2)."

Study of Odors and Odorous Emissions

Pub. L. 95-95, title IV, Sec. 403(b), Aug. 7, 1977, 91 Stat. 792, directed Administrator of Environmental Protection Agency to conduct a study and report to Congress not later than Jan. 1, 1979, on effects on public health and welfare of odors and odorous emissions, source of such emissions, technology or other measures available for control of such emissions and costs of such technology or measures, and costs and benefits of alternative measures or strategies to abate such emissions.

List of Chemical Contaminants From Environmental Pollution Found in Human Tissue

Pub. L. 95-95, title IV, Sec. 403(c), Aug. 7, 1977, 91 Stat. 792, directed Administrator of EPA, not later than twelve months after Aug. 7, 1977, to publish throughout the United States a list of all known chemical contaminants resulting from environmental pollution which have been found in human tissue including blood, urine, breast milk, and all other human tissue, such list to be prepared for the United States and to indicate approximate number of cases, range of levels found, and mean levels found, directed Administrator, not later than eighteen months after Aug. 7, 1977, to publish in same manner an explanation of what is known about the manner in which chemicals entered the environment and thereafter human tissue, and directed Administrator, in consultation with National Institutes of Health, the National Center for Health Statistics, and the National Center for Health Services Research and Development, to, if feasible, conduct an epidemiological study to demonstrate the relationship between levels of chemicals in the environment and in human tissue, such study to be made in appropriate regions or areas of the United States in order to determine any different results in such regions or areas, and the results of such study to be reported, as soon as practicable, to appropriate committee of Congress.

Study on Regional Air Quality

Pub. L. 95-95, title IV, Sec. 403(d), Aug. 7, 1977, 91 Stat. 793, directed Administrator of EPA to conduct a study of air quality in various areas throughout the country including the gulf coast region, such study to include analysis of liquid and solid aerosols and other fine particulate matter and contribution of such substances to visibility and public health problems in such areas, with Administrator to use environmental health experts from the National Institutes of Health and other outside agencies and organizations.

Railroad Emission Study

Pub. L. 95-95, title IV, Sec. 404, Aug. 7, 1977, 91 Stat. 793, as amended by H. Res. 549, Mar. 25, 1980, directed Administrator of EPA to conduct a study and investigation of emissions of air pollutants from railroad locomotives, locomotive engines, and secondary power sources on railroad rolling stock, in order to determine extent to which such emissions affect air quality in air quality control regions throughout the United States, technological feasibility and current state of technology for controlling such emissions, and status and effect of current and proposed State and local regulations affecting such emissions, and within one hundred and eighty days after commencing such study and investigation, Administrator to submit a report of such study and investigation, together with recommendations for appropriate legislation, to Senate Committee on Environment and Public Works and House Committee on Energy and Commerce.

Study and Report Concerning Economic Approaches to Controlling Air Pollution

Pub. L. 95-95, title IV, Sec. 405, Aug. 7, 1977, 91 Stat. 794, directed Administrator, in conjunction with Council of Economic Advisors, to undertake a study and assessment of economic measures for control of air pollution which could strengthen effectiveness of existing methods of controlling air pollution, provide incentives to abate air pollution greater than that required by Clean Air Act, and serve as primary incentive for controlling air pollution problems not addressed by Clean Air Act, and directed that not later than 2 years after Aug. 7, 1977, Administrator and Council conclude study and submit a report to President and Congress.

National Industrial Pollution Control Council

For provisions relating to establishment of National Industrial Pollution Control Council, see Ex. Ord. No. 11523, Apr. 9, 1970, 35 F.R. 5993, set out as a note under section 4321 of this title.

Federal Compliance With Pollution Control Standards

For provisions relating to responsibility of head of each Executive agency for compliance with applicable pollution control standards, see Ex. Ord. No. 12088, Oct. 13, 1978, 43 F.R. 47707, set out as a note under section 4321 of this title.

Executive Order No. 10779

Ex. Ord. No. 10779, Aug. 21, 1958, 23 F.R. 6487, which related to cooperation of Federal agencies with State and local authorities, was superseded by Ex. Ord. No. 11282, May 26, 1966, 31 F.R. 7663, formerly set out under section 7418 of this title.

Executive Order No. 11507

Ex. Ord. No. 11507, Feb. 4, 1970, 35 F.R. 2573, which provided for prevention, control, and abatement of air pollution at Federal facilities, was superseded by Ex. Ord. No. 11752, Dec. 17, 1973, 38 F.R. 34793, formerly set out as a note under section 4331 of this title.

Section Referred to in Other Sections

This section is referred to in sections 7471, 7476 of this title.

COOPERATIVE ACTIVITIES

42 USC 7402

(a) Interstate cooperation; uniform State laws; State compacts

The Administrator shall encourage cooperative activities by the States and local governments for the prevention and control of air pollution; encourage the enactment of improved and, so far as practicable in the light of varying conditions and needs, uniform State and local laws relating to the prevention and control of air pollution; and encourage the making of agreements and compacts between States for the prevention and control of air pollution.

(b) Federal cooperation

The Administrator shall cooperate with and encourage cooperative activities by all Federal departments and agencies having functions relating to the prevention and control of air pollution, so as to assure the utilization in the Federal air pollution control program of all appropriate and available facilities and resources within the Federal Government.

(c) Consent of Congress to compacts

The consent of the Congress is hereby given to two or more States to negotiate and enter into agreements or compacts, not in conflict with any law or treaty of the United States, for (1) cooperative effort and mutual assistance for the prevention and control of air pollution and the enforcement of their respective laws relating thereto, and (2) the establishment of such agencies, joint or otherwise, as they may deem desirable for making effective such agreements or compacts. No such agreement or compact shall be binding or obligatory upon any State a party thereto unless and until it has been approved by Congress. It is the intent of Congress that no agreement or compact entered into between States after November 21, 1967, which relates to the control and abatement of air pollution in an air quality control region, shall provide for participation by a State which is not included (in whole or in part) in such air quality control region.

(July 14, 1955, ch. 360, title I, Sec. 102, formerly Sec. 2, as added Pub. L. 88-206, Sec. 1, Dec. 17, 1963, 77 Stat. 393; renumbered Sec. 102, Pub. L. 89-272, title I, Sec. 101(3), Oct. 20, 1965, 79 Stat. 992; amended Pub. L. 90-148, Sec. 2, Nov. 21, 1967, 81 Stat. 485; Pub. L. 91-604, Sec. 15(c)(2), Dec. 31, 1970, 84 Stat. 1713.)

Codification

Section was formerly classified to section 1857a of this title.

Prior Provisions

Provisions similar to those in the first clause of subsec. (a) of this section were contained in subsec. (b)(1) of a prior section 1857a, of this title, act July 14, 1955, ch. 360, Sec. 2, 69 Stat. 322, prior to the general amendment of this chapter by Pub. L. 88-206.

Amendments

1970—Subsecs. (a), (b). Pub. L. 91-604 substituted "Administrator" for "Secretary" wherever appearing.

1967—Subsec. (c). Pub. L. 90-148 inserted declaration that it is the intent of Congress that no agreement or compact entered into between States after the date of enactment of the Air

Quality Act of 1967, which for purposes of codification was changed to November 21, 1967, the date of approval of such Act, relating to the control and abatement of air pollution in an air quality control region, shall provide for participation by a State which is not included (in whole or in part) in such air quality control region.

RESEARCH, INVESTIGATION, TRAINING, AND OTHER ACTIVITIES

42 USC 7403

(a) Research and development program for prevention and control of air pollution
The Administrator shall establish a national research and development program for the prevention and control of air pollution and as part of such program shall—
   (1) conduct, and promote the coordination and acceleration of, research, investigations, experiments, demonstrations, surveys, and studies relating to the causes, effects (including health and welfare effects), extent, prevention, and control of air pollution;
   (2) encourage, cooperate with, and render technical services and provide financial assistance to air pollution control agencies and other appropriate public or private agencies, institutions, and organizations, and individuals in the conduct of such activities;
   (3) conduct investigations and research and make surveys concerning any specific problem of air pollution in cooperation with any air pollution control agency with a view to recommending a solution of such problem, if he is requested to do so by such agency or if, in his judgment, such problem may affect any community or communities in a State other than that in which the source of the matter causing or contributing to the pollution is located;
   (4) establish technical advisory committees composed of recognized experts in various aspects of air pollution to assist in the examination and evaluation of research progress and proposals and to avoid duplication of research, and
   (5) conduct and promote coordination and acceleration of training for individuals relating to the causes, effects, extent, prevention, and control of air pollution.
(b) Authorized activities of Administrator in establishing research and development program
In carrying out the provisions of the preceding subsection the Administrator is authorized to—
   (1) collect and make available, through publications and other appropriate means, the results of and other information, including appropriate recommendations by him in connection therewith, pertaining to such research and other activities;
   (2) cooperate with other Federal departments and agencies, with air pollution control agencies, with other public and private agencies, institutions, and organizations, and with any industries involved, in the preparation and conduct of such research and other activities;
   (3) make grants to air pollution control agencies, to other public or nonprofit private agencies, institutions, and organizations, and to individuals, for purposes stated in subsection (a)(1) of this section;
   (4) contract with public or private agencies, institutions, and organizations, and with individuals, without regard to section 3324(a) and (b) of title 31 and section 5 of title 41;
   (5) establish and maintain research fellowships, in the Environmental Protection Agency and at public or nonprofit private educational institutions or research organizations;
   (6) collect and disseminate, in cooperation with other Federal departments and agencies, and with other public or private agencies, institutions, and organizations having related responsibilities, basic data on chemical, physical, and biological effects of varying air quality and other information pertaining to air pollution and the prevention and control thereof;
   (7) develop effective and practical processes, methods, and prototype devices for the prevention or control of air pollution; and
   (8) construct facilities, provide equipment, and employ staff as necessary to carry out this chapter.
In carrying out the provisions of subsection (a) of this section, the Administrator shall provide training for, and make training grants to, personnel of air pollution control agencies and other persons with suitable qualifications and make grants to such agencies, to other public or nonprofit private agencies, institutions, and organizations for the purposes stated in subsection (a)(5) of this section. Reasonable fees may be charged for such training provided to persons other than personnel of air pollution control agencies but such training shall be provided to such personnel of air pollution control agencies without charge.

(c) Air pollutant monitoring, analysis, modeling, and inventory research

In carrying out subsection (a) of this section, the Administrator shall conduct a program of research, testing, and development of methods for sampling, measurement, monitoring, analysis, and modeling of air pollutants. Such program shall include the following elements:

(1) Consideration of individual, as well as complex mixtures of, air pollutants and their chemical transformations in the atmosphere.

(2) Establishment of a national network to monitor, collect, and compile data with quantification of certainty in the status and trends of air emissions, deposition, air quality, surface water quality, forest condition, and visibility impairment, and to ensure the comparability of air quality data collected in different States and obtained from different nations.

(3) Development of improved methods and technologies for sampling, measurement, monitoring, analysis, and modeling to increase understanding of the sources of ozone percursors,[1] ozone formation, ozone transport, regional influences on urban ozone, regional ozone trends, and interactions of ozone with other pollutants. Emphasis shall be placed on those techniques which—

(A) improve the ability to inventory emissions of volatile organic compounds and nitrogen oxides that contribute to urban air pollution, including anthropogenic and natural sources;

(B) improve the understanding of the mechanism through which anthropogenic and biogenic volatile organic compounds react to form ozone and other oxidants; and

(C) improve the ability to identify and evaluate region- specific prevention and control options for ozone pollution.

(4) Submission of periodic reports to the Congress, not less than once every 5 years, which evaluate and assess the effectiveness of air pollution control regulations and programs using monitoring and modeling data obtained pursuant to this subsection.

(d) Environmental health effects research

(1) The Administrator, in consultation with the Secretary of Health and Human Services, shall conduct a research program on the short-term and long-term effects of air pollutants, including wood smoke, on human health. In conducting such research program the Administrator—

(A) shall conduct studies, including epidemiological, clinical, and laboratory and field studies, as necessary to identify and evaluate exposure to and effects of air pollutants on human health;

(B) may utilize, on a reimbursable basis, the facilities of existing Federal scientific laboratories and research centers; and

(C) shall consult with other Federal agencies to ensure that similar research being conducted in other agencies is coordinated to avoid duplication.

(2) In conducting the research program under this subsection, the Administrator shall develop methods and techniques necessary to identify and assess the risks to human health from both routine and accidental exposures to individual air pollutants and combinations thereof. Such research program shall include the following elements:

(A) The creation of an Interagency Task Force to coordinate such program. The Task Force shall include representatives of the National Institute for Environmental Health Sciences, the Environmental Protection Agency, the Agency for Toxic Substances and Disease Registry, the National Toxicology Program, the National Institute of Standards and Technology, the National Science Foundation, the Surgeon General, and the Department of Energy. This Interagency Task Force shall be chaired by a representative of the Environmental Protection Agency and shall convene its first meeting within 60 days after November 15, 1990.

(B) An evaluation, within 12 months after November 15, 1990, of each of the hazardous air pollutants listed under section 7412(b) of this title, to decide, on the basis of available information, their relative priority for preparation of environmental health assessments pursuant to subparagraph (C). The evaluation shall be based on reasonably anticipated toxicity to humans and exposure factors such as frequency of occurrence as an air pollutant and volume of emissions in populated areas. Such evaluation shall be reviewed by the Interagency Task Force established pursuant to subparagraph (A).

---

[1]So in original. Probably should be "precursors,".

(C) Preparation of environmental health assessments for each of the hazardous air pollutants referred to in subparagraph (B), beginning 6 months after the first meeting of the Interagency Task Force and to be completed within 96 months thereafter. No fewer than 24 assessments shall be completed and published annually. The assessments shall be prepared in accordance with guidelines developed by the Administrator in consultation with the Interagency Task Force and the Science Advisory Board of the Environmental Protection Agency. Each such assessment shall include—
  (i) an examination, summary, and evaluation of available toxicological and epidemiological information for the pollutant to ascertain the levels of human exposure which pose a significant threat to human health and the associated acute, subacute, and chronic adverse health effects;
  (ii) a determination of gaps in available information related to human health effects and exposure levels; and
  (iii) where appropriate, an identification of additional activities, including toxicological and inhalation testing, needed to identify the types or levels of exposure which may present significant risk of adverse health effects in humans.

(e) Ecosystem research

In carrying out subsection (a) of this section, the Administrator, in cooperation, where appropriate, with the Under Secretary of Commerce for Oceans and Atmosphere, the Director of the Fish and Wildlife Service, and the Secretary of Agriculture, shall conduct a research program to improve understanding of the short-term and long-term causes, effects, and trends of ecosystems damage from air pollutants on ecosystems. Such program shall include the following elements:

(1) Identification of regionally representative and critical ecosystems for research.
(2) Evaluation of risks to ecosystems exposed to air pollutants, including characterization of the causes and effects of chronic and episodic exposures to air pollutants and determination of the reversibility of those effects.
(3) Development of improved atmospheric dispersion models and monitoring systems and networks for evaluating and quantifying exposure to and effects of multiple environmental stresses associated with air pollution.
(4) Evaluation of the effects of air pollution on water quality, including assessments of the short-term and long-term ecological effects of acid deposition and other atmospherically derived pollutants on surface water (including wetlands and estuaries) and groundwater.
(5) Evaluation of the effects of air pollution on forests, materials, crops, biological diversity, soils, and other terrestrial and aquatic systems exposed to air pollutants.
(6) Estimation of the associated economic costs of ecological damage which have occurred as a result of exposure to air pollutants.

Consistent with the purpose of this program, the Administrator may use the estuarine research reserves established pursuant to section 1461 of title 16 to carry out this research.

(f) Liquefied Gaseous Fuels Spill Test Facility
  (1) The Administrator, in consultation with the Secretary of Energy and the Federal Coordinating Council for Science, Engineering, and Technology, shall oversee an experimental and analytical research effort, with the experimental research to be carried out at the Liquefied Gaseous Fuels Spill Test Facility. In consultation with the Secretary of Energy, the Administrator shall develop a list of chemicals and a schedule for field testing at the Facility. Analysis of a minimum of 10 chemicals per year shall be carried out, with the selection of a minimum of 2 chemicals for field testing each year. Highest priority shall be given to those chemicals that would present the greatest potential risk to human health as a result of an accidental release—
    (A) from a fixed site; or
    (B) related to the transport of such chemicals.
  (2) The purpose of such research shall be to—
    (A) develop improved predictive models for atmospheric dispersion which at a minimum—
      (i) describe dense gas releases in complex terrain including man-made structures or obstacles with variable winds;
      (ii) improve understanding of the effects of turbulence on dispersion patterns; and
      (iii) consider realistic behavior of aerosols by including physicochemical reactions with water vapor, ground deposition, and removal by water spray;

(B) evaluate existing and future atmospheric dispersion models by—
  (i) the development of a rigorous, standardized methodology for dense gas models; and
  (ii) the application of such methodology to current dense gas dispersion models using data generated from field experiments; and
(C) evaluate the effectiveness of hazard mitigation and emergency response technology for fixed site and transportation related accidental releases of toxic chemicals.

Models pertaining to accidental release shall be evaluated and improved periodically for their utility in planning and implementing evacuation procedures and other mitigative strategies designed to minimize human exposure to hazardous air pollutants released accidentally.

(3) The Secretary of Energy shall make available to interested persons (including other Federal agencies and businesses) the use of the Liquefied Gaseous Fuels Spill Test Facility to conduct research and other activities in connection with the activities described in this subsection.

(g) Pollution prevention and emissions control

In carrying out subsection (a) of this section, the Administrator shall conduct a basic engineering research and technology program to develop, evaluate, and demonstrate nonregulatory strategies and technologies for air pollution prevention. Such strategies and technologies shall be developed with priority on those pollutants which pose a significant risk to human health and the environment, and with opportunities for participation by industry, public interest groups, scientists, and other interested persons in the development of such strategies and technologies. Such program shall include the following elements:

(1) Improvements in nonregulatory strategies and technologies for preventing or reducing multiple air pollutants, including sulfur oxides, nitrogen oxides, heavy metals, PM-10 (particulate matter), carbon monoxide, and carbon dioxide, from stationary sources, including fossil fuel power plants. Such strategies and technologies shall include improvements in the relative cost effectiveness and long-range implications of various air pollutant reduction and nonregulatory control strategies such as energy conservation, including end-use efficiency, and fuel-switching to cleaner fuels. Such strategies and technologies shall be considered for existing and new facilities.

(2) Improvements in nonregulatory strategies and technologies for reducing air emissions from area sources.

(3) Improvements in nonregulatory strategies and technologies for preventing, detecting, and correcting accidental releases of hazardous air pollutants.

(4) Improvements in nonregulatory strategies and technologies that dispose of tires in ways that avoid adverse air quality impacts.

Nothing in this subsection shall be construed to authorize the imposition on any person of air pollution control requirements. The Administrator shall consult with other appropriate Federal agencies to ensure coordination and to avoid duplication of activities authorized under this subsection.

(h) NIEHS studies

(1) The Director of the National Institute of Environmental Health Sciences may conduct a program of basic research to identify, characterize, and quantify risks to human health from air pollutants. Such research shall be conducted primarily through a combination of university and medical school-based grants, as well as through intramural studies and contracts.

(2) The Director of the National Institute of Environmental Health Sciences shall conduct a program for the education and training of physicians in environmental health.

(3) The Director shall assure that such programs shall not conflict with research undertaken by the Administrator.

(4) There are authorized to be appropriated to the National Institute of Environmental Health Sciences such sums as may be necessary to carry out the purposes of this subsection.

(i) Coordination of research

The Administrator shall develop and implement a plan for identifying areas in which activities authorized under this section can be carried out in conjunction with other Federal ecological and air pollution research efforts. The plan, which shall be submitted to Congress within 6 months after November 15, 1990, shall include—

(1) an assessment of ambient monitoring stations and networks to determine cost effective ways to expand monitoring capabilities in both urban and rural environments;
(2) a consideration of the extent of the feasibility and scientific value of conducting the research program under subsection (e) of this section to include consideration of the effects of atmospheric processes and air pollution effects; and
(3) a methodology for evaluating and ranking pollution prevention technologies, such as those developed under subsection (g) of this section, in terms of their ability to reduce cost effectively the emissions of air pollutants and other airborne chemicals of concern.

Not later than 2 years after November 15, 1990, and every 4 years thereafter, the Administrator shall report to Congress on the progress made in implementing the plan developed under this subsection, and shall include in such report any revisions of the plan.

(j) Continuation of national acid precipitation assessment program
  (1) The acid precipitation research program set forth in the Acid Precipitation Act of 1980 [42 U.S.C. 8901 et seq.] shall be continued with modifications pursuant to this subsection.
  (2) The Acid Precipitation Task Force shall consist of the Administrator of the Environmental Protection Agency, the Secretary of Energy, the Secretary of the Interior, the Secretary of Agriculture, the Administrator of the National Oceanic and Atmospheric Administration, the Administrator of the National Aeronautics and Space Administration, and such additional members as the President may select. The President shall appoint a chairman for the Task Force from among its members within 30 days after November 15, 1990.
  (3) The responsibilities of the Task Force shall include the following:
    (A) Review of the status of research activities conducted to date under the comprehensive research plan developed pursuant to the Acid Precipitation Act of 1980 [42 U.S.C. 8901 et seq.], and development of a revised plan that identifies significant research gaps and establishes a coordinated program to address current and future research priorities. A draft of the revised plan shall be submitted by the Task Force to Congress within 6 months after November 15, 1990. The plan shall be available for public comment during the 60 day period after its submission, and a final plan shall be submitted by the President to the Congress within 45 days after the close of the comment period.
    (B) Coordination with participating Federal agencies, augmenting the agencies' research and monitoring efforts and sponsoring additional research in the scientific community as necessary to ensure the availability and quality of data and methodologies needed to evaluate the status and effectiveness of the acid deposition control program. Such research and monitoring efforts shall include, but not be limited to—
      (i) continuous monitoring of emissions of precursors of acid deposition;
      (ii) maintenance, upgrading, and application of models, such as the Regional Acid Deposition Model, that describe the interactions of emissions with the atmosphere, and models that describe the response of ecosystems to acid deposition; and
      (iii) analysis of the costs, benefits, and effectiveness of the acid deposition control program.
    (C) Publication and maintenance of a National Acid Lakes Registry that tracks the condition and change over time of a statistically representative sample of lakes in regions that are known to be sensitive to surface water acidification.
    (D) Submission every two years of a unified budget recommendation to the President for activities of the Federal Government in connection with the research program described in this subsection.
    (E) Beginning in 1992 and biennially thereafter, submission of a report to Congress describing the results of its investigations and analyses. The reporting of technical information about acid deposition shall be provided in a format that facilitates communication with policymakers and the public. The report shall include—
      (i) actual and projected emissions and acid deposition trends;
      (ii) average ambient concentrations of acid deposition percursors[2] and their transformation products;
      (iii) the status of ecosystems (including forests and surface waters), materials, and visibility affected by acid deposition;

---
[2] So in original. Probably should be "precursors".

(iv) the causes and effects of such deposition, including changes in surface water quality and forest and soil conditions;
(v) the occurrence and effects of episodic acidification, particularly with respect to high elevation watersheds; and
(vi) the confidence level associated with each conclusion to aid policymakers in use of the information.
(F) Beginning in 1996, and every 4 years thereafter, the report under subparagraph (E) shall include—
(i) the reduction in deposition rates that must be achieved in order to prevent adverse ecological effects; and
(ii) the costs and benefits of the acid deposition control program created by subchapter IV-A of this chapter.

(k) Air pollution conferences

If, in the judgment of the Administrator, an air pollution problem of substantial significance may result from discharge or discharges into the atmosphere, the Administrator may call a conference concerning this potential air pollution problem to be held in or near one or more of the places where such discharge or discharges are occurring or will occur. All interested persons shall be given an opportunity to be heard at such conference, either orally or in writing, and shall be permitted to appear in person or by representative in accordance with procedures prescribed by the Administrator. If the Administrator finds, on the basis of the evidence presented at such conference, that the discharge or discharges if permitted to take place or continue are likely to cause or contribute to air pollution subject to abatement under this part, the Administrator shall send such findings, together with recommendations concerning the measures which the Administrator finds reasonable and suitable to prevent such pollution, to the person or persons whose actions will result in the discharge or discharges involved; to air pollution agencies of the State or States and of the municipality or municipalities where such discharge or discharges will originate; and to the interstate air pollution control agency, if any, in the jurisdictional area of which any such municipality is located. Such findings and recommendations shall be advisory only, but shall be admitted together with the record of the conference, as part of the proceedings under subsections (b), (c), (d), (e), and (f) of section 7408 of this title.

(July 14, 1955, ch. 360, title I, Sec. 103, formerly Sec. 3, as added Pub. L. 88-206, Sec. 1, Dec. 17, 1963, 77 Stat. 394; renumbered Sec. 103 and amended Pub. L. 89-272, title I, Secs. 101(3), 103, Oct. 20, 1965, 79 Stat. 992, 996; Pub. L. 90-148, Sec. 2, Nov. 21, 1967, 81 Stat. 486; Pub. L. 91-604, Secs. 2(a), 4(2), 15(a)(2), (c)(2), Dec. 31, 1970, 84 Stat. 1676, 1689, 1710, 1713; Pub. L. 95-95, title I, Sec. 101(a), (b), Aug. 7, 1977, 91 Stat. 686, 687; Pub. L. 101-549, title IX, Sec. 901(a)-(c), Nov. 15, 1990, 104 Stat. 2700-2703.)

References in Text

The Acid Precipitation Act of 1980, referred to in subsec. (j)(1), (3)(A), is title VII of Pub. L. 96-294, June 30, 1980, 94 Stat. 770, which is classified generally to chapter 97 (Sec. 8901 et seq.) of this title. For complete classification of this Act to the Code, see Short Title note set out under section 8901 of this title and Tables.

Codification

In subsec. (b)(4), "section 3324(a) and (b) of title 31" substituted for reference to section 3648 of the Revised Statutes (31 U.S.C. 529) on authority of Pub. L. 97-258, Sec. 4(b), Sept. 13, 1982, 96 Stat. 1067, the first section of which enacted Title 31, Money and Finance.

Section was formerly classified to section 1857b of this title.

Prior Provisions

Provisions similar to those in subsec. (a)(3) of this section were contained in subsec. (a) of a prior section 1857b of this title, act July 14, 1955, ch. 360, Sec. 3, 69 Stat. 322, as amended Oct. 9, 1962, Pub. L. 87-761, Sec. 2, 76 Stat. 760, prior to the general amendment of this chapter by Pub. L. 88-206.

Provisions similar to those in this section were contained in prior sections 1857a to 1857d of this title, act July 14, 1955, ch. 360, Secs. 2 to 5, 69 Stat. 322 (section 1857b as amended Oct. 9, 1962, Pub. L. 87-761, Sec. 2, 76 Stat. 760; section 1857d as amended Sept. 22, 1959, Pub. L. 86-365, Sec.

1, 73 Stat. 646 and Oct. 9, 1962, Pub. L. 87-761, Sec. 1, 76 Stat. 760), prior to the general amendment of this chapter by Pub. L. 88-206.

Amendments

1990—Subsec. (a)(1). Pub. L. 101-549, Sec. 901(a)(1), inserted "(including health and welfare effects)" after "effects".

Subsec. (b)(8). Pub. L. 101-549, Sec. 901(a)(2), which directed amendment of subsec. (b) by adding par. (8) at end, was executed by adding par. (8) after par. (7) to reflect the probable intent of Congress.

Subsecs. (c) to (f). Pub. L. 101-549, Sec. 901(b), amended subsecs. (c) to (f) generally, substituting present provisions for provisions which related to: in subsec. (c), results of other scientific studies; in subsec. (d), construction of facilities; in subsec. (e), potential air pollution problems, conferences, and findings and recommendations of the Administrator; and, in subsec. (f), accelerated research programs.

Subsecs. (g) to (k). Pub. L. 101-549, Sec. 901(c), added subsecs. (g) to (k).

1977—Subsec. (a). Pub. L. 95-95, Sec. 101(b), struck out reference to "training" in par. (1) and added par. (5).

Subsec. (b). Pub. L. 95-95, Sec. 101(a), struck out par. (5) which provided for training and training grants to personnel of air pollution control agencies and other persons with suitable qualifications, redesignated pars. (6), (7), and (8) as (5), (6), and (7), respectively, and, following par. (7) as so redesignated, inserted provisions directing the Administrator, in carrying out subsec. (a), to provide training for, and make training grants to, personnel of air pollution control agencies and other persons with suitable qualifications and to make grants to such agencies, to other public or nonprofit private agencies, institutions, and organizations for the purposes stated in subsec. (a)(5) and allowing reasonable fees to be charged for such training provided to persons other than personnel of air pollution control agencies but requiring that such training be provided to such personnel of air pollution control agencies without charge.

1970—Subsec. (a). Pub. L. 91-604, Sec. 15(c)(2), substituted "Administrator" for "Secretary".

Subsec. (b). Pub. L. 91-604, Sec. 15(c)(2), substituted "Administrator" for "Secretary" and "Environmental Protection Agency" for "Department of Health, Education, and Welfare".

Subsec. (c). Pub. L. 91-604, Sec. 15(a)(2), (c)(2), substituted "Administrator" for "Secretary" and "air pollutants" for "air pollution agents (or combinations of agents)".

Subsec. (d). Pub. L. 91-604, Sec. 15(c)(2), substituted "Administrator" for "Secretary".

Subsec. (e). Pub. L. 91-604, Sec. 15(c)(2), substituted "Administrator" for "Secretary" wherever appearing, substituted "7415" for "7415(a)", and inserted references to subsecs. (b) and (c) of section 7415 of this title.

Subsec. (f). Pub. L. 91-604, Sec. 2(a), added subsec. (f).

1967—Subsec. (a). Pub. L. 90-148 substituted "establish technical advisory committees composed of recognized experts in various aspects of air pollution to assist in the examination and evaluation of research progress and proposals and to avoid duplication of research" for "initiate and conduct a program of research directed toward the development of improved, low-cost techniques for extracting sulfur from fuels" as cl. (4) and struck out cl. (5) which related to research programs relating to the control of hydrocarbon emissions from evaporation of gasoline and nitrogen and aldehyde oxide emission from gasoline and diesel powered vehicles and relating to the development of improved low-cost techniques to reduce emissions of oxides of sulfur produced by the combustion of sulfur-containing fuels.

Subsec. (c). Pub. L. 90-148 struck out provision for promulgation of criteria in the case of particular air pollution agents present in the air in certain quantities reflecting the latest scientific knowledge and allowing for availability and revision and provided for recommendation by Secretary of air quality criteria.

Subsec. (e). Pub. L. 90-148 substituted references to subsections (d), (e), and (f) of section 7415 of this title for references to subsections (c), (d), and (e) of section 7415 of this title in provision for admission of advisory findings and recommendations together with the record of the conference and made such findings and recommendations part of the proceedings of the conference, not merely part of the record of proceedings.

1965—Subsec. (a)(5). Pub. L. 89-272, Sec. 103(3), added par. (5).

Subsecs. (d), (e). Pub. L. 89-272, Sec. 103(4), added subsecs. (d) and (e).

Effective Date of 1977 Amendment

Amendment by Pub. L. 95-95 effective Aug. 7, 1977, except as otherwise expressly provided, see section 406(d) of Pub. L. 95-95, set out as a note under section 7401 of this title.

Modification or Rescission of Rules, Regulations, Orders, Determinations, Contracts, Certifications, Authorizations, Delegations, and Other Actions

All rules, regulations, orders, determinations, contracts, certifications, authorizations, delegations, or other actions duly issued, made, or taken by or pursuant to act July 14, 1955, the Clean Air Act, as in effect immediately prior to the date of enactment of Pub. L. 95-95 [Aug. 7, 1977] to continue in full force and effect until modified or rescinded in accordance with act July 14, 1955, as amended by Pub. L. 95-95 [this chapter], see section 406(b) of Pub. L. 95-95, set out as an Effective Date of 1977 Amendment note under section 7401 of this title.

Termination of Advisory Committees

Advisory committees in existence on Jan. 5, 1973, to terminate not later than the expiration of the 2-year period following Jan. 5, 1973, unless, in the case of a committee established by the President or an officer of the Federal Government, such committee is renewed by appropriate action prior to the expiration of such 2-year period, or in the case of a committee established by the Congress, its duration is otherwise provided by law. See section 14 of Pub. L. 92-463, Oct. 6, 1972, 86 Stat. 776, set out in the Appendix to Title 5, Government Organization and Employees.

Grants

Sec. 2603 of Pub. L. 106-246 provided that:

"(a) The Administrator of the Environmental Protection Agency shall make a grant for the purpose of carrying out the first year of a 2-year program to implement in five metropolitan areas pilot design programs developed under section 365(a)(2) of the Department of Transportation and Related Agencies Appropriations Act, 2000 (113 Stat. 1028-1029).

(b) The Administrator shall ensure that each pilot design program is implemented in accordance with recommendations developed by the National Telecommuting and Air Quality Steering Committee, in consultation with the local design teams.

(c) Grants received under subsection (a) may be used for–
  (1) protocol development in the five metropolitan areas;
  (2) marketing of the telecommute, emissions reduction, pollution credits strategy and recruitment of participating employers; and
  (3) data gathering on emissions reductions.

(d) In addition to the grant under subsection (a), for the purpose of carrying out the second year of the 2-year program referred to in subsection (a), the Administrator shall–
  (1) make a grant of $750,000 to the National Environmental Policy Institute (a nonprofit private entity incorporated under the laws of and located in the District of Columbia); and
  (2) make grants totaling $1,250,000 to local agencies within the five metropolitan areas referred to in subsection (a).

(e) Not later than 360 days from first day of the second year of the 2-year program referred to in subsection (a), the Administrator shall transmit to Congress a report on the results of the program."

National Acid Lakes Registry

Section 405 of Pub. L. 101-549 provided that: "The Administrator of the Environmental Protection Agency shall create a National Acid Lakes Registry that shall list, to the extent practical, all lakes that are known to be acidified due to acid deposition, and shall publish such list within one year of the enactment of this Act [Nov. 15, 1990]. Lakes shall be added to the registry as they become acidic or as data becomes available to show they are acidic. Lakes shall be deleted from the registry as they become nonacidic."

Assessment of International Air Pollution Control Technologies

Section 901(e) of Pub. L. 101-549 directed Administrator of Environmental Protection Agency to conduct a study that compares international air pollution control technologies of selected industrialized countries to determine if there exist air pollution control technologies in countries outside the United States that may have beneficial applications to this Nation's air pollution control efforts, including, with respect to each country studied, the topics of urban air quality, motor vehicle emissions, toxic air emissions, and acid deposition, and within 2 years after Nov. 15, 1990, submit to Congress a report detailing the results of such study.

Western States Acid Deposition Research

Section 901(g) of Pub. L. 101-549 provided that:
"(1) The Administrator of the Environmental Protection Agency shall sponsor monitoring and research and submit to Congress annual and periodic assessment reports on—
- (A) the occurrence and effects of acid deposition on surface waters located in that part of the United States west of the Mississippi River;
- (B) the occurrence and effects of acid deposition on high elevation ecosystems (including forests, and surface waters); and
- (C) the occurrence and effects of episodic acidification, particularly with respect to high elevation watersheds.
(2) The Administrator of the Environmental Protection Agency shall analyze data generated from the studies conducted under paragraph (1), data from the Western Lakes Survey, and other appropriate research and utilize predictive modeling techniques that take into account the unique geographic, climatological, and atmospheric conditions which exist in the western United States to determine the potential occurrence and effects of acid deposition due to any projected increases in the emission of sulfur dioxide and nitrogen oxides in that part of the United States located west of the Mississippi River. The Administrator shall include the results of the project conducted under this paragraph in the reports issued to Congress under paragraph (1)."

Consultation With Committee on Science of House of Representatives

Section 101(c) of Pub. L. 95-95 provided that: "The Administrator of the Environmental Protection Agency shall consult with the House Committee on Science and Technology [now Committee on Science] on the environmental and atmospheric research, development, and demonstration aspects of this Act [see Short Title of 1977 Amendment note set out under section 7401 of this title]. In addition, the reports and studies required by this Act that relate to research, development, and demonstration issues shall be transmitted to the Committee on Science and Technology [now Committee on Science] at the same time they are made available to other committees of the Congress."

Study of Substances Discharged From Exhausts of Motor Vehicles

Pub. L. 86-493, June 8, 1960, 74 Stat. 162, directed Surgeon General of Public Health Service to conduct a thorough study for purposes of determining, with respect to the various substances discharged from exhausts of motor vehicles, the amounts and kinds of such substances which, from the standpoint of human health, it is safe for motor vehicles to discharge into the atmosphere under the various conditions under which such vehicles may operate, and, not later than two years after June 8, 1960, submit to Congress a report on results of the study, together with such recommendations, if any, based upon the findings made in such study, as he deemed necessary for the protection of the public health.

Section Referred to in Other Sections

This section is referred to in section 7412 of this title.

RESEARCH RELATING TO FUELS AND VEHICLES

42 USC 7404

(a) Research programs; grants; contracts; pilot and demonstration plants; byproducts research
The Administrator shall give special emphasis to research and development into new and improved methods, having industry-wide application, for the prevention and control of air pollution resulting from the combustion of fuels. In furtherance of such research and development he shall—
  (1) conduct and accelerate research programs directed toward development of improved, cost-effective techniques for—

(A) control of combustion byproducts of fuels,
(B) removal of potential air pollutants from fuels prior to combustion,
(C) control of emissions from the evaporation of fuels,
(D) improving the efficiency of fuels combustion so as to decrease atmospheric emissions, and
(E) producing synthetic or new fuels which, when used, result in decreased atmospheric emissions.
  (2) provide for Federal grants to public or nonprofit agencies, institutions, and organizations and to individuals, and contracts with public or private agencies, institutions, or persons, for payment of (A) part of the cost of acquiring, constructing, or otherwise securing for research and development purposes, new or improved devices or methods having industrywide application of preventing or controlling discharges into the air of various types of pollutants; (B) part of the cost of programs to develop low emission alternatives to the present internal combustion engine; (C) the cost to purchase vehicles and vehicle engines, or portions thereof, for research, development, and testing purposes; and (D) carrying out the other provisions of this section, without regard to section 3324(a) and (b) of title 31 and section 5 of title 41: Provided, That research or demonstration contracts awarded pursuant to this subsection (including contracts for construction) may be made in accordance with, and subject to the limitations provided with respect to research contracts of the military departments in, section 2353 of title 10, except that the determination, approval, and certification required thereby shall be made by the Administrator; Provided further, That no grant may be made under this paragraph in excess of $1,500,000;
  (3) determine, by laboratory and pilot plant testing, the results of air pollution research and studies in order to develop new or improved processes and plant designs to the point where they can be demonstrated on a large and practical scale;
  (4) construct, operate, and maintain, or assist in meeting the cost of the construction, operation, and maintenance of new or improved demonstration plants or processes which have promise of accomplishing the purposes of this chapter;
  (5) study new or improved methods for the recovery and marketing of commercially valuable byproducts resulting from the removal of pollutants.
(b) Powers of Administrator in establishing research and development programs
  In carrying out the provisions of this section, the Administrator may—
  (1) conduct and accelerate research and development of cost-effective instrumentation techniques to facilitate determination of quantity and quality of air pollutant emissions, including, but not limited to, automotive emissions;
  (2) utilize, on a reimbursable basis, the facilities of existing Federal scientific laboratories;
  (3) establish and operate necessary facilities and test sites at which to carry on the research, testing, development, and programming necessary to effectuate the purposes of this section;
  (4) acquire secret processes, technical data, inventions, patent applications, patents, licenses, and an interest in lands, plants, and facilities, and other property or rights by purchase, license, lease, or donation; and
  (5) cause on-site inspections to be made of promising domestic and foreign projects, and cooperate and participate in their development in instances in which the purposes of the chapter will be served thereby.
(c) Clean alternative fuels
  The Administrator shall conduct a research program to identify, characterize, and predict air emissions related to the production, distribution, storage, and use of clean alternative fuels to determine the risks and benefits to human health and the environment relative to those from using conventional gasoline and diesel fuels. The Administrator shall consult with other Federal agencies to ensure coordination and to avoid duplication of activities authorized under this subsection.

(July 14, 1955, ch. 360, title I, Sec. 104, as added Pub. L. 90-148, Sec. 2, Nov. 21, 1967, 81 Stat. 487; amended Pub. L. 91-137, Dec. 5, 1969, 83 Stat. 283; Pub. L. 91-604, Secs. 2(b), (c), 13(a), 15(c)(2), Dec. 31, 1970, 84 Stat. 1676, 1677, 1709, 1713; Pub. L. 93-15, Sec. 1(a), Apr. 9, 1973, 87 Stat. 11; Pub. L. 93-319, Sec. 13(a), June 22, 1974, 88 Stat. 265; Pub. L. 101-549, title IX, Sec. 901(d), Nov. 15, 1990, 104 Stat. 2706.)

Codification

In subsec. (a)(2), "section 3324(a) and (b) of title 31" substituted for reference to section 3648 of the Revised Statutes (31 U.S.C. 529) on authority of Pub. L. 97-258, Sec. 4(b), Sept. 13, 1982, 96 Stat. 1067, the first section of which enacted Title 31, Money and Finance.

Section was formerly classified to section 1857b-1 of this title.

Prior Provisions

A prior section 104 of act July 14, 1955, was renumbered section 105 by Pub. L. 90-148 and is classified to section 7405 of this title.

Amendments

1990—Subsecs. (a)(1), (b)(1). Pub. L. 101-549, Sec. 901(d)(1), substituted "cost-effective" for "low-cost".

Subsec. (c). Pub. L. 101-549, Sec. 901(d)(2), amended subsec. (c) generally. Prior to amendment, subsec. (c) read as follows: "For the purposes of this section there are authorized to be appropriated $75,000,000 for the fiscal year ending June 30, 1971, $125,000,000 for the fiscal year ending June 30, 1972, $150,000,000 for the fiscal year ending June 30, 1973, and $150,000,000 for the fiscal year ending June 30, 1974, and $150,000,000 for the fiscal year ending June 30, 1975. Amounts appropriated pursuant to this subsection shall remain available until expended."

1974—Subsec. (c). Pub. L. 93-319 authorized appropriation of $150,000,000 for fiscal year ending June 30, 1975.

1973—Subsec. (c). Pub. L. 93-15 authorized appropriation of $150,000,000 for fiscal year ending June 30, 1974.

1970—Subsec. (a). Pub. L. 91-604, Sec. 15(c)(2), substituted "Administrator" for "Secretary".

Subsec. (a)(1). Pub. L. 91-604, Sec. 2(b), inserted provisions authorizing research programs directed toward development of techniques for improving the efficiency of fuels combustion so as to decrease atmospheric emissions, and producing synthetic or new fuels which result in decreased atmospheric emissions.

Subsec. (a)(2). Pub. L. 91-604, Sec. 2(c), added cls. (B) and (C) and redesignated former cl. (B) as (D).

Subsec. (b). Pub. L. 91-604, Sec. 15(c)(2), substituted "Administrator" for "Secretary".

Subsec. (c). Pub. L. 91-604, Sec. 13(a), substituted provisions authorizing appropriations for fiscal years ending June 30, 1971, 1972, and 1973, for provisions authorizing appropriations for fiscal years ending June 30, 1968 and 1969.

1969—Subsec. (c). Pub. L. 91-137 authorized appropriation of $45,000,000 for fiscal year ending June 30, 1970.

Hydrogen Fuel Cell Vehicle Study and Test Program

Section 807 of Pub. L. 101-549 provided that: "The Administrator of the Environmental Protection Agency, in conjunction with the National Aeronautics and Space Administration and the Department of Energy, shall conduct a study and test program on the development of a hydrogen fuel cell electric vehicle. The study and test program shall determine how best to transfer existing NASA hydrogen fuel cell technology into the form of a mass-producible, cost effective hydrogen fuel cell vehicle. Such study and test program shall include at a minimum a feasibility-design study, the construction of a prototype, and a demonstration. This study and test program should be completed and a report submitted to Congress within 3 years after the enactment of the Clean Air Act Amendments of 1990 [Nov. 15, 1990]. This study and test program should be performed in the university or universities which are best exhibiting the facilities and expertise to develop such a fuel cell vehicle."

Combustion of Contaminated Used Oil in Ships

Section 813 of Pub. L. 101-549 provided that: "Within 2 years after the enactment of the Clean Air Act Amendments of 1990 [Nov. 15, 1990], the Administrator of the Environmental Protection Agency shall complete a study and submit a report to Congress evaluating the health and environmental impacts of the combustion of contaminated used oil in ships, the reasons for using such oil for such purposes, the alternatives to such use, the costs of such alternatives, and other relevant factors and impacts. In preparing such study, the Administrator shall obtain the view and comments of all interested persons and shall consult with the Secretary of Transportation and the Secretary of the department in which the Coast Guard is operating."

Extension to Aug. 31, 1970 of Authorization Period for Fiscal Year 1970

Pub. L. 91-316, July 10, 1970, 84 Stat. 416, provided in part that the authorization contained in section 104(c) of the Clean Air Act [subsec. (c) of this section] for the fiscal year ending June 30, 1970, should remain available through Aug. 31, 1970, notwithstanding any provisions of this section.

GRANTS FOR SUPPORT OF AIR POLLUTION PLANNING AND CONTROL PROGRAMS

42 USC 7405

(a) Amounts; limitations; assurances of plan development capability
 (1) (A) The Administrator may make grants to air pollution control agencies, within the meaning of paragraph (1), (2), (3), (4), or (5) of section 7602 of this title, in an amount up to three-fifths of the cost of implementing programs for the prevention and control of air pollution or implementation of national primary and secondary ambient air quality standards. For the purpose of this section, "implementing" means any activity related to the planning, developing, establishing, carrying-out, improving, or maintaining of such programs.
  (B) Subject to subsections (b) and (c) of this section, an air pollution control agency which receives a grant under subparagraph (A) and which contributes less than the required two-fifths minimum shall have 3 years following November 15, 1990, in which to contribute such amount. If such an agency fails to meet and maintain this required level, the Administrator shall reduce the amount of the Federal contribution accordingly.
  (C) With respect to any air quality control region or portion thereof for which there is an applicable implementation plan under section 7410 of this title, grants under subparagraph (A) may be made only to air pollution control agencies which have substantial responsibilities for carrying out such applicable implementation plan.
 (2) Before approving any grant under this subsection to any air pollution control agency within the meaning of sections 7602(b)(2) and 7602(b)(4) of this title, the Administrator shall receive assurances that such agency provides for adequate representation of appropriate State, interstate, local, and (when appropriate) international, interests in the air quality control region.
 (3) Before approving any planning grant under this subsection to any air pollution control agency within the meaning of sections 7602(b)(2) and 7602(b)(4) of this title, the Administrator shall receive assurances that such agency has the capability of developing a comprehensive air quality plan for the air quality control region, which plan shall include (when appropriate) a recommended system of alerts to avert and reduce the risk of situations in which there may be imminent and serious danger to the public health or welfare from air pollutants and the various aspects relevant to the establishment of air quality standards for such air quality control region, including the concentration of industries, other commercial establishments, population and naturally occurring factors which shall affect such standards.
(b) Terms and conditions; regulations; factors for consideration; State expenditure limitations
 (1) From the sums available for the purposes of subsection (a) of this section for any fiscal year, the Administrator shall from time to time make grants to air pollution control agencies upon such terms and conditions as the Administrator may find necessary to carry out the purpose of this section. In establishing regulations for the granting of such funds the Administrator shall, so far as practicable, give due consideration to (A) the population, (B) the extent of the actual or potential air pollution problem, and (C) the financial need of the respective agencies.
 (2) Not more than 10 per centum of the total of funds appropriated or allocated for the purposes of subsection (a) of this section shall be granted for air pollution control programs in any one State. In the case of a grant for a program in an area crossing State boundaries,

the Administrator shall determine the portion of such grant that is chargeable to the percentage limitation under this subsection for each State into which such area extends. Subject to the provisions of paragraph (1) of this subsection, no State shall have made available to it for application less than one-half of 1 per centum of the annual appropriation for grants under this section for grants to agencies within such State.

(c) Maintenance of effort
   (1) No agency shall receive any grant under this section during any fiscal year when its expenditures of non-Federal funds for recurrent expenditures for air pollution control programs will be less than its expenditures were for such programs during the preceding fiscal year. In order for the Administrator to award grants under this section in a timely manner each fiscal year, the Administrator shall compare an agency's prospective expenditure level to that of its second preceding fiscal year. The Administrator shall revise the current regulations which define applicable nonrecurrent and recurrent expenditures, and in so doing, give due consideration to exempting an agency from the limitations of this paragraph and subsection (a) of this section due to periodic increases experienced by that agency from time to time in its annual expenditures for purposes acceptable to the Administrator for that fiscal year.
   (2) The Administrator may still award a grant to an agency not meeting the requirements of paragraph (l)[1] of this subsection if the Administrator, after notice and opportunity for public hearing, determines that a reduction in expenditures is attributable to a non-selective reduction in the expenditures in the programs of all Executive branch agencies of the applicable unit of Government. No agency shall receive any grant under this section with respect to the maintenance of a program for the prevention and control of air pollution unless the Administrator is satisfied that such a grant will be so used to supplement and, to the extent practicable, increase the level of State, local, or other non-Federal funds. No grants shall be made under this section until the Administrator has consulted with the appropriate official as designated by the Governor or Governors of the State or States affected.

(d) Reduction of payments; availability of reduced amounts; reduced amount as deemed paid to agency for purpose of determining amount of grant
The Administrator, with the concurrence of any recipient of a grant under this section, may reduce the payments to such recipient by the amount of the pay, allowances, traveling expenses, and any other costs in connection with the detail of any officer or employee to the recipient under section 7601 of this title, when such detail is for the convenience of, and at the request of, such recipient and for the purpose of carrying out the provisions of this chapter. The amount by which such payments have been reduced shall be available for payment of such costs by the Administrator, but shall, for the purpose of determining the amount of any grant to a recipient under subsection (a) of this section, be deemed to have been paid to such agency.

(e) Notice and opportunity for hearing when affected by adverse action
No application by a State for a grant under this section may be disapproved by the Administrator without prior notice and opportunity for a public hearing in the affected State, and no commitment or obligation of any funds under any such grant may be revoked or reduced without prior notice and opportunity for a public hearing in the affected State (or in one of the affected States if more than one State is affected).

(July 14, 1955, ch. 360, title I, Sec. 105, formerly Sec. 4, as added Pub. L. 88-206, Sec. 1, Dec. 17, 1963, 77 Stat. 395; renumbered Sec. 104 and amended Pub. L. 89-272, title I, Sec. 101(2)-(4), Oct. 20, 1965, 79 Stat. 992; Pub. L. 89-675, Sec. 3, Oct. 15, 1966, 80 Stat. 954; renumbered Sec. 105 and amended Pub. L. 90-148, Sec. 2, Nov. 21, 1967, 81 Stat. 489; Pub. L. 91-604, Secs. 3(a), (b)(1), 15(c)(2), Dec. 31, 1970, 84 Stat. 1677, 1713; Pub. L. 95-95, title I, Sec. 102, title III, Sec. 305(b), Aug. 7, 1977, 91 Stat. 687, 776; Pub. L. 101-549, title VIII, Sec. 802(a)-(e), Nov. 15, 1990, 104 Stat. 2687, 2688.)

Codification
Section was formerly classified to section 1857c of this title.

Prior Provisions
A prior section 105 of act July 14, 1955, was renumbered section 108 by Pub. L. 90-148 and is classified to section 7415 of this title.

Provisions similar to those in subsecs. (a) and (b) of this section were contained in a prior section 1857d of this title, act July 14, 1955, ch. 360, Sec. 5, 69 Stat. 322, as amended Sept. 22, 1959, Pub. L. 86-365, Sec. 1, 73 Stat. 646; Oct. 9, 1962, Pub. L. 87-761, Sec. 1, 76 Stat. 760, prior to the general amendment by Pub. L. 88-206.

Amendments

1990—Subsec. (a)(1)(A), (B). Pub. L. 101-549, Sec. 802(a), amended subpars. (A) and (B) generally. Prior to amendment, subpars. (A) and (B) read as follows:

"(A)The Administrator may make grants to air pollution control agencies in an amount up to two-thirds of the cost of planning, developing, establishing, or improving, and up to one-half of the cost of maintaining, programs for the prevention and control of air pollution or implementation of national primary and secondry [sic] ambient air quality standards.

(B) Subject to subparagraph (C), the Administrator may make grants to air pollution control agencies within the meaning of paragraph (1), (2), or (4) of section 7602(b) of this title in an amount up to three-fourths of the cost of planning, developing, establishing, or improving, and up to three-fifths of the cost of maintaining, any program for the prevention and control of air pollution or implementation of national primary and secondary ambient air quality standards in an area that includes two or more municipalities, whether in the same or different States."

Subsec. (a)(1)(C). Pub. L. 101-549, Sec. 802(b), substituted "subparagraph (A)" for "subparagraph (B)".

Subsec. (b)(1). Pub. L. 101-549, Sec. 802(c), designated existing provisions of subsec. (b) as par. (1), redesignated former cls. (1) to (3) as cls. (A) to (C), respectively, and struck out at end "No agency shall receive any grant under this section during any fiscal year when its expenditures of non-Federal funds for other than nonrecurrent expenditures for air pollution control programs will be less than its expenditures were for such programs during the preceding fiscal year, unless the Administrator, after notice and opportunity for public hearing, determines that a reduction in expenditures is attributable to a nonselective reduction in expenditures in the programs of all executive branch agencies of the applicable unit of Government; and no agency shall receive any grant under this section with respect to the maintenance of a program for the prevention and control of air pollution unless the Administrator is satisfied that such grant will be so used to supplement and, to the extent practicable, increase the level of State, local, or other non-Federal funds that would in the absence of such grant be made available for the maintenance of such program, and will in no event supplant such State, local, or other non-Federal funds. No grant shall be made under this section until the Administrator has consulted with the appropriate official as designated by the Governor or Governors of the State or States affected."

Subsec. (b)(2). Pub. L. 101-549, Sec. 802(d), redesignated subsec. (c) as subsec. (b)(2) and substituted "Subject to the provisions of paragraph (1) of this subsection, no State shall have made available to it for application less than one-half of 1 per centum of the annual appropriation for grants under this section for grants to agencies within such State." for "In fiscal year 1978 and subsequent fiscal years, subject to the provisions of subsection (b) of this section, no State shall receive less than one-half of 1 per centum of the annual appropriation for grants under this section for grants to agencies within such State."

Subsec. (c). Pub. L. 101-549, Sec. 802(e), added subsec. (c). Former subsec. (c) redesignated (b)(2).

1977—Subsec. (b). Pub. L. 95-95, Sec. 102(a), inserted ", unless the Administrator, after notice and opportunity for hearing, determines that a reduction in expenditures is attributable to a nonselective reduction in expenditures in the programs of all executive branch agencies of the applicable unit of Government" after "will be less than its expenditures were for such programs during the preceding fiscal year".

Subsec. (c). Pub. L. 95-95, Sec. 102(b), provided that in fiscal year 1978 and subsequent fiscal years, subject to provisions of subsec. (b) of this section, no State shall receive less than one-half of 1 per centum of the annual appropriation for grants under this section for grants to agencies within such State.

Subsec. (e). Pub. L. 95-95, Sec. 305(b), added subsec. (e).

1970—Subsec. (a)(1). Pub. L. 91-604, Sec. 3(a), substituted provisions authorizing the Administrator to make grants, for provisions authorizing the Secretary to make grants, and provisions authorizing grants for programs implementing national primary and secondary ambient air quality standards, for provisions authorizing grants for programs implementing air quality standards authorized by this subchapter, and inserted the provision requiring grants to air pollution control agencies be made to agencies having substantial responsibilities for carrying out the applicable implementation plan with respect to the air quality control region or portion thereof.

Subsecs. (a)(2), (3), (b), (c). Pub. L. 91-604, Sec. 15(c)(2), substituted "Administrator" for "Secretary" wherever appearing.

Subsec. (d). Pub. L. 91-604, Sec. 3(b)(1), added subsec. (d).

1967—Subsec. (a). Pub. L. 90-148 designated existing provisions as par. (1), substituted "regional air quality control program" for "regional air pollution control program," added planning to list of authorized activities, and added programs for implementation of air quality standards authorized by this chapter to list of authorized programs, and added pars. (2) and (3).

Subsec. (b). Pub. L. 90-148 made minor changes in the order of provisions.

Subsec. (c). Pub. L. 90-148 reduced percentage limitation on portion of total funds which might be granted for air pollution control programs in any one State from 12\1/2\ per centum to 10 per centum.

1966—Subsec. (a). Pub. L. 89-675, Sec. 3(a)(1), struck out provisions limiting available funds to 20 per centum of sums appropriated annually for purpose of this subchapter, inserted provisions allowing grants to air pollution control agencies up to one-half of cost of maintaining programs for prevention and control of air pollution, and authorized Secretary to make grants of up to three-fifths of cost of maintaining regional air pollution control programs.

Subsec. (b). Pub. L. 89-675, Sec. 3(a)(2), substituted "for the purpose of" for "under", permitted grantees to reduce annual expenditures to the extent that nonrecurrent costs are involved for purposes of application of the provision that no agency may receive grants during any fiscal year when its expenditures of non-Federal funds for air pollution control programs are less than its expenditures for such programs during the preceding year, and inserted provisions insuring that Federal funds will in no event be used to supplant State or local government funds in maintaining air pollution control programs.

Subsec. (c). Pub. L. 89-675, Sec. 3(b), substituted "total of funds appropriated or allocated for the purposes of subsection (a) of this section shall be granted for air pollution control programs" for "grant funds available under subsection (a) of this section shall be expended" and authorized the Secretary to determine the portion of grants to interstate agencies to be charged against the twelve and one-half percent limitation of grant funds to any one State.

1965—Subsec. (a). Pub. L. 89-272 substituted "this title" for "this Act", which for purposes of codification has been changed to "this subchapter", and "section 302(b)(2) and (4)" for "section 9(b)(2) and (4)", which for purposes of codification has been changed to "section 7602(b)(2) and (4) of this title".

Effective Date of 1977 Amendment

Amendment by Pub. L. 95-95 effective Aug. 7, 1977, except as otherwise expressly provided, see section 406(d) of Pub. L. 95-95, set out as a note under section 7401 of this title.

Modification or Rescission of Rules, Regulations, Orders, Determinations, Contracts, Certifications, Authorizations, Delegations, and Other Actions

All rules, regulations, orders, determinations, contracts, certifications, authorizations, delegations, or other actions duly issued, made, or taken by or pursuant to act July 14, 1955, the Clean Air Act, as in effect immediately prior to the date of enactment of Pub. L. 95-95 [Aug. 7, 1977] to continue in full force and effect until modified or rescinded in accordance with act July 14, 1955, as amended by Pub. L. 95-95 [this chapter], see section 406(b) of Pub. L. 95-95, set out as an Effective Date of 1977 Amendment note under section 7401 of this title.

Section Referred to in Other Sections

This section is referred to in sections 7509, 7601 of this title.

INTERSTATE AIR QUALITY AGENCIES; PROGRAM COST LIMITATIONS

42 USC 7406

For the purpose of developing implementation plans for any interstate air quality control region designated pursuant to section 7407 of this title or of implementing section 7506a of this title (relating to control of interstate air pollution) or section 7511c of this title (relating to control of interstate ozone pollution), the Administrator is authorized to pay, for two years, up to 100 per centum of the air quality planning program costs of any commission established under section 7506a of this title (relating to control of interstate air pollution) or section 7511c of this title (relating to control of interstate ozone pollution) or any agency designated by the Governors of the affected States, which agency shall be capable of recommending to the Governors plans for implementation of national primary and secondary ambient air quality standards and shall include representation from the States and appropriate political subdivisions within the air quality control region. After the initial two-year period the Administrator is authorized to make grants to such agency or such commission in an amount up to three-fifths of the air quality implementation program costs of such agency or commission.

(July 14, 1955, ch. 360, title I, Sec. 106, as added Pub. L. 90-148, Sec. 2, Nov. 21, 1967, 81 Stat. 490; amended Pub. L. 91-604, Sec. 3(c), Dec. 31, 1970, 84 Stat. 1677; Pub. L. 101-549, title I, Sec. 102(f)(2), title VIII, Sec. 802(f), Nov. 15, 1990, 104 Stat. 2420, 2688.)

Codification

Section was formerly classified to section 1857c-1 of this title.

Prior Provisions

A prior section 106 of act July 14, 1955, was renumbered section 117 by Pub. L. 91-604 and is classified to section 7417 of this title.

Amendments

1990—Pub. L. 101-549, Sec. 102(f)(2)(A), inserted "or of implementing section 7506a of this title (relating to control of interstate air pollution) or section 7511c of this title (relating to control of interstate ozone pollution)" after "section 7407 of this title".

Pub. L. 101-549, Sec. 102(f)(2)(B), which directed insertion of "any commission established under section 7506a of this title (relating to control of interstate air pollution) or section 7511c of this title (relating to control of interstate ozone pollution) or" after "program costs of", was executed by making the insertion after that phrase the first place it appeared to reflect the probable intent of Congress.

Pub. L. 101-549, Sec. 102(f)(2)(C), which directed insertion of "or such commission" after "such agency" in last sentence, was executed by making insertion after "such agency" the first place it appeared in the last sentence to reflect the probable intent of Congress.

Pub. L. 101-549, Secs. 102(f)(2)(D), 802(f), substituted "three-fifths of the air quality implementation program costs of such agency or commission" for "three-fourths of the air quality planning program costs of such agency".

1970—Pub. L. 91-604 struck out designation "(a)", substituted provisions authorizing Federal grants for the purpose of developing implementation plans and provisions requiring the designated State agency to be capable of recommending plans for implementation of national primary and secondary ambient air quality standards, for provisions authorizing Federal grants for the purpose of expediting the establishment of air quality standards and provisions requiring the designated State agency to be capable of recommending standards of air quality and plans for implementation thereof, respectively, and struck out subsec. (b) which authorized establishment of air quality planning commissions.

AIR QUALITY CONTROL REGIONS

42 USC 7407

(a) Responsibility of each State for air quality; submission of implementation plan

Each State shall have the primary responsibility for assuring air quality within the entire geographic area comprising such State by submitting an implementation plan for such State which will specify the manner in which national primary and secondary ambient air quality standards will be achieved and maintained within each air quality control region in such State.

(b) Designated regions

For purposes of developing and carrying out implementation plans under section 7410 of this title—
   (1) an air quality control region designated under this section before December 31, 1970, or a region designated after such date under subsection (c) of this section, shall be an air quality control region; and
   (2) the portion of such State which is not part of any such designated region shall be an air quality control region, but such portion may be subdivided by the State into two or more air quality control regions with the approval of the Administrator.

(c) Authority of Administrator to designate regions; notification of Governors of affected States

The Administrator shall, within 90 days after December 31, 1970, after consultation with appropriate State and local authorities, designate as an air quality control region any interstate area or major intrastate area which he deems necessary or appropriate for the attainment and maintenance of ambient air quality standards. The Administrator shall immediately notify the Governors of the affected States of any designation made under this subsection.

(d) Designations
   (1) Designations generally
      (A) Submission by Governors of initial designations following promulgation of new or revised standards

         By such date as the Administrator may reasonably require, but not later than 1 year after promulgation of a new or revised national ambient air quality standard for any pollutant under section 7409 of this title, the Governor of each State shall (and at any other time the Governor of a State deems appropriate the Governor may) submit to the Administrator a list of all areas (or portions thereof) in the State, designating as—
            (i) nonattainment, any area that does not meet (or that contributes to ambient air quality in a nearby area that does not meet) the national primary or secondary ambient air quality standard for the pollutant,
            (ii) attainment, any area (other than an area identified in clause (i)) that meets the national primary or secondary ambient air quality standard for the pollutant, or
            (iii) unclassifiable, any area that cannot be classified on the basis of available information as meeting or not meeting the national primary or secondary ambient air quality standard for the pollutant.

         The Administrator may not require the Governor to submit the required list sooner than 120 days after promulgating a new or revised national ambient air quality standard.

      (B) Promulgation by EPA of designations
         (i) Upon promulgation or revision of a national ambient air quality standard, the Administrator shall promulgate the designations of all areas (or portions thereof) submitted under subparagraph (A) as expeditiously as practicable, but in no case later than 2 years from the date of promulgation of the new or revised national ambient air quality standard. Such period may be extended for up to one year in the event the Administrator has insufficient information to promulgate the designations.
         (ii) In making the promulgations required under clause (i), the Administrator may make such modifications as the Administrator deems necessary to the designations of the areas (or portions thereof) submitted under subparagraph (A) (including to the boundaries of such areas or portions thereof). Whenever the Administrator intends to make a modification, the Administrator shall notify the State and provide such State with an opportunity to demonstrate why any proposed modification is inappropriate. The Administrator shall give such notification no later than 120 days before the date the Administrator promulgates the designation, including any modification thereto. If the Governor fails to submit the list in whole or in part, as required under subparagraph (A), the Administrator shall

promulgate the designation that the Administrator deems appropriate for any area (or portion thereof) not designated by the State.
   (iii) If the Governor of any State, on the Governor's own motion, under subparagraph (A), submits a list of areas (or portions thereof) in the State designated as nonattainment, attainment, or unclassifiable, the Administrator shall act on such designations in accordance with the procedures under paragraph (3) (relating to redesignation).
   (iv) A designation for an area (or portion thereof) made pursuant to this subsection shall remain in effect until the area (or portion thereof) is redesignated pursuant to paragraph (3) or (4).
  (C) Designations by operation of law
   (i) Any area designated with respect to any air pollutant under the provisions of paragraph (1)(A), (B), or (C) of this subsection (as in effect immediately before November 15, 1990) is designated, by operation of law, as a nonattainment area for such pollutant within the meaning of subparagraph (A)(i).
   (ii) Any area designated with respect to any air pollutant under the provisions of paragraph (1)(E) (as in effect immediately before November 15, 1990) is designated by operation of law, as an attainment area for such pollutant within the meaning of subparagraph (A)(ii).
   (iii) Any area designated with respect to any air pollutant under the provisions of paragraph (1)(D) (as in effect immediately before November 15, 1990) is designated, by operation of law, as an unclassifiable area for such pollutant within the meaning of subparagraph (A)(iii).
 (2) Publication of designations and redesignations
  (A) The Administrator shall publish a notice in the Federal Register promulgating any designation under paragraph (1) or (5), or announcing any designation under paragraph (4), or promulgating any redesignation under paragraph (3).
  (B) Promulgation or announcement of a designation under paragraph (1), (4) or (5) shall not be subject to the provisions of sections 553 through 557 of title 5 (relating to notice and comment), except nothing herein shall be construed as precluding such public notice and comment whenever possible.
 (3) Redesignation
  (A) Subject to the requirements of subparagraph (E), and on the basis of air quality data, planning and control considerations, or any other air quality-related considerations the Administrator deems appropriate, the Administrator may at any time notify the Governor of any State that available information indicates that the designation of any area or portion of an area within the State or interstate area should be revised. In issuing such notification, which shall be public, to the Governor, the Administrator shall provide such information as the Administrator may have available explaining the basis for the notice.
  (B) No later than 120 days after receiving a notification under subparagraph (A), the Governor shall submit to the Administrator such redesignation, if any, of the appropriate area (or areas) or portion thereof within the State or interstate area, as the Governor considers appropriate.
  (C) No later than 120 days after the date described in subparagraph (B) (or paragraph (1)(B)(iii)), the Administrator shall promulgate the redesignation, if any, of the area or portion thereof, submitted by the Governor in accordance with subparagraph (B), making such modifications as the Administrator may deem necessary, in the same manner and under the same procedure as is applicable under clause (ii) of paragraph (1)(B), except that the phrase "60 days" shall be substituted for the phrase "120 days" in that clause. If the Governor does not submit, in accordance with subparagraph (B), a redesignation for an area (or portion thereof) identified by the Administrator under subparagraph (A), the Administrator shall promulgate such redesignation, if any, that the Administrator deems appropriate.
  (D) The Governor of any State may, on the Governor's own motion, submit to the Administrator a revised designation of any area or portion thereof within the State. Within 18 months of receipt of a complete State redesignation submittal, the Administrator shall approve or deny such redesignation. The submission of a redesignation by a

Governor shall not affect the effectiveness or enforceability of the applicable implementation plan for the State.
- (E) The Administrator may not promulgate a redesignation of a nonattainment area (or portion thereof) to attainment unless—
    - (i) the Administrator determines that the area has attained the national ambient air quality standard;
    - (ii) the Administrator has fully approved the applicable implementation plan for the area under section 7410(k) of this title;
    - (iii) the Administrator determines that the improvement in air quality is due to permanent and enforceable reductions in emissions resulting from implementation of the applicable implementation plan and applicable Federal air pollutant control regulations and other permanent and enforceable reductions;
    - (iv) the Administrator has fully approved a maintenance plan for the area as meeting the requirements of section 7505a of this title; and
    - (v) the State containing such area has met all requirements applicable to the area under section 7410 of this title and part D of this subchapter.
- (F) The Administrator shall not promulgate any redesignation of any area (or portion thereof) from nonattainment to unclassifiable.
- (4) Nonattainment designations for ozone, carbon monoxide and particulate matter (PM-10)
    - (A) Ozone and carbon monoxide
        - (i) Within 120 days after November 15, 1990, each Governor of each State shall submit to the Administrator a list that designates, affirms or reaffirms the designation of, or redesignates (as the case may be), all areas (or portions thereof) of the Governor's State as attainment, nonattainment, or unclassifiable with respect to the national ambient air quality standards for ozone and carbon monoxide.
        - (ii) No later than 120 days after the date the Governor is required to submit the list of areas (or portions thereof) required under clause (i) of this subparagraph, the Administrator shall promulgate such designations, making such modifications as the Administrator may deem necessary, in the same manner, and under the same procedure, as is applicable under clause (ii) of paragraph (1)(B), except that the phrase "60 days" shall be substituted for the phrase "120 days" in that clause. If the Governor does not submit, in accordance with clause (i) of this subparagraph, a designation for an area (or portion thereof), the Administrator shall promulgate the designation that the Administrator deems appropriate.
        - (iii) No nonattainment area may be redesignated as an attainment area under this subparagraph.
        - (iv) Notwithstanding paragraph (1)(C)(ii) of this subsection, if an ozone or carbon monoxide nonattainment area located within a metropolitan statistical area or consolidated metropolitan statistical area (as established by the Bureau of the Census) is classified under part D of this subchapter as a Serious, Severe, or Extreme Area, the boundaries of such area are hereby revised (on the date 45 days after such classification) by operation of law to include the entire metropolitan statistical area or consolidated metropolitan statistical area, as the case may be, unless within such 45-day period the Governor (in consultation with State and local air pollution control agencies) notifies the Administrator that additional time is necessary to evaluate the application of clause (v). Whenever a Governor has submitted such a notice to the Administrator, such boundary revision shall occur on the later of the date 8 months after such classification or 14 months after November 15, 1990, unless the Governor makes the finding referred to in clause (v), and the Administrator concurs in such finding, within such period. Except as otherwise provided in this paragraph, a boundary revision under this clause or clause (v) shall apply for purposes of any State implementation plan revision required to be submitted after November 15, 1990.
        - (v) Whenever the Governor of a State has submitted a notice under clause (iv), the Governor, in consultation with State and local air pollution control agencies, shall undertake a study to evaluate whether the entire metropolitan statistical area or consolidated metropolitan statistical area should be included within the nonattainment area. Whenever a Governor finds and demonstrates to the satis-

faction of the Administrator, and the Administrator concurs in such finding, that with respect to a portion of a metropolitan statistical area or consolidated metropolitan statistical area, sources in the portion do not contribute significantly to violation of the national ambient air quality standard, the Administrator shall approve the Governor's request to exclude such portion from the nonattainment area. In making such finding, the Governor and the Administrator shall consider factors such as population density, traffic congestion, commercial development, industrial development, meteorological conditions, and pollution transport.

(B) PM-10 designations

By operation of law, until redesignation by the Administrator pursuant to paragraph (3)–

(i) each area identified in 52 Federal Register 29383 (Aug. 7, 1987) as a Group I area (except to the extent that such identification was modified by the Administrator before November 15, 1990) is designated nonattainment for PM-10;

(ii) any area containing a site for which air quality monitoring data show a violation of the national ambient air quality standard for PM-10 before January 1, 1989 (as determined under part 50, appendix K of title 40 of the Code of Federal Regulations) is hereby designated nonattainment for PM-10; and

(iii) each area not described in clause (i) or (ii) is hereby designated unclassifiable for PM-10.

Any designation for particulate matter (measured in terms of total suspended particulates) that the Administrator promulgated pursuant to this subsection (as in effect immediately before November 15, 1990) shall remain in effect for purposes of implementing the maximum allowable increases in concentrations of particulate matter (measured in terms of total suspended particulates) pursuant to section 7473(b) of this title, until the Administrator determines that such designation is no longer necessary for that purpose.

(5) Designations for lead

The Administrator may, in the Administrator's discretion at any time the Administrator deems appropriate, require a State to designate areas (or portions thereof) with respect to the national ambient air quality standard for lead in effect as of November 15, 1990, in accordance with the procedures under subparagraphs (A) and (B) of paragraph (1), except that in applying subparagraph (B)(i) of paragraph (1) the phrase "2 years from the date of promulgation of the new or revised national ambient air quality standard" shall be replaced by the phrase "1 year from the date the Administrator notifies the State of the requirement to designate areas with respect to the standard for lead".

(6) Designations-

(A) Submission- Notwithstanding any other provision of law, not later than February 15, 2004, the Governor of each State shall submit designations referred to in paragraph (1) for the July 1997 PM2.5 national ambient air quality standards for each area within the State, based on air quality monitoring data collected in accordance with any applicable Federal reference methods for the relevant areas.

(B) Promulgation- Notwithstanding any other provision of law, not later than December 31, 2004, the Administrator shall, consistent with paragraph (1), promulgate the designations referred to in subparagraph (A) for each area of each State for the July 1997 PM-2.5 national ambient air quality standards.

(7) Implementation Plan for Regional Haze-

(A) In General- Notwithstanding any other provision of law, not later than 3 years after the date on which the Administrator promulgates the designations referred to in paragraph (6)(B) for a State, the State shall submit, for the entire State, the State implementation plan revisions to meet the requirements promulgated by the Administrator under section 169B(e)(1) (referred to in this paragraph as 'regional haze requirements').

(B) No Preclusion of Other Provisions- Nothing in this paragraph precludes the implementation of the agreements and recommendations stemming from the Grand Canyon Visibility Transport Commission Report dated June 1996, including the submission of State implementation plan revisions by the States of Arizona, California, Colorado, Idaho, Nevada, New Mexico, Oregon, Utah, or Wyoming by December 31, 2003, for implementation of regional haze requirements applicable to those States.

(e) Redesignation of air quality control regions
  (1) Except as otherwise provided in paragraph (2), the Governor of each State is authorized, with the approval of the Administrator, to redesignate from time to time the air quality control regions within such State for purposes of efficient and effective air quality management. Upon such redesignation, the list under subsection (d) of this section shall be modified accordingly.
  (2) In the case of an air quality control region in a State, or part of such region, which the Administrator finds may significantly affect air pollution concentrations in another State, the Governor of the State in which such region, or part of a region, is located may redesignate from time to time the boundaries of so much of such air quality control region as is located within such State only with the approval of the Administrator and with the consent of all Governors of all States which the Administrator determines may be significantly affected.
  (3) No compliance date extension granted under section 7413(d)(5)[1] of this title (relating to coal conversion) shall cease to be effective by reason of the regional limitation provided in section 7413(d)(5)[1] of this title if the violation of such limitation is due solely to a redesignation of a region under this subsection.

(July 14, 1955, ch. 360, title I, Sec. 107, as added Pub. L. 91-604, Sec. 4(a), Dec. 31, 1970, 84 Stat. 1678; amended Pub. L. 95-95, title I, Sec. 103, Aug. 7, 1977, 91 Stat. 687; Pub. L. 101-549, title I, Sec. 101(a), Nov. 15, 1990, 104 Stat. 2399.)

References in Text

Section 7413 of this title, referred to in subsec. (e)(3), was amended generally by Pub. L. 101-549, title VII, Sec. 701, Nov. 15, 1990, 104 Stat. 2672, and, as so amended, subsec. (d) of section 7413 no longer relates to final compliance orders.

Codification

Section was formerly classified to section 1857c-2 of this title.

Prior Provisions

A prior section 107 of act July 14, 1955, as added Nov. 21, 1967, Pub. L. 90-148, Sec. 2, 81 Stat. 490, related to air quality control regions and was classified to section 1857c-2 of this title, prior to repeal by Pub. L. 91-604.

Another prior section 107 of act July 14, 1955, as added Dec. 17, 1963, Pub. L. 88-206, Sec. 1, 77 Stat. 399, was renumbered section 111 by Pub. L. 90-148 and is classified to section 7411 of this title.

Amendments

2004–Sec. 425(a) Pub. L. 108-199 added subsecs. (d)(6) and (d)(7).

1990–Subsec. (d). Pub. L. 101-549 amended subsec. (d) generally, substituting present provisions for provisions which required States to submit lists of regions not in compliance on Aug. 7, 1977, with certain air quality standards to be submitted to the Administrator, and which authorized States to revise and resubmit such lists from time to time.

1977–Subsecs. (d), (e). Pub. L. 95-95 added subsecs. (d) and (e).

Effective Date of 1977 Amendment

Amendment by Pub. L. 95-95 effective Aug. 7, 1977, except as otherwise expressly provided, see section 406(d) of Pub. L. 95-95, set out as a note under section 7401 of this title.

Relationship to Transportation Equity Act for the 21st Century

Except as provided in paragraphs (6) and (7) of section 107(d) of the Clean Air Act (as added by subsection (a)), section 6101, subsections (a) and (b) of section 6102, and section 6103 of the Transportation Equity Act for the 21st Century (42 U.S.C. 7407 note; 112 Stat. 463), as in effect on the day before the date of enactment of this Act, shall remain in effect.

---

[1] See References in Text note below.

Ozone and Particulate Matter Standards

Pub. L. 105-178, title VI, June 9, 1998, 112 Stat. 463, provided that:

"SEC. 6101. FINDINGS AND PURPOSE.

(a) The Congress finds that—
   (1) there is a lack of air quality monitoring data for fine particle levels, measured as PM-2.5, in the United States and the States should receive full funding for the monitoring efforts;
   (2) such data would provide a basis for designating areas as attainment or nonattainment for any PM-2.5 national ambient air quality standards pursuant to the standards promulgated in July 1997;
   (3) the President of the United States directed the Administrator of the Environmental Protection Agency (referred to in this title as the 'Administrator') in a memorandum dated July 16, 1997, to complete the next periodic review of the particulate matter national ambient air quality standards by July 2002 in order to determine 'whether to revise or maintain the standards';
   (4) the Administrator has stated that 3 years of air quality monitoring data for fine particle levels, measured as PM-2.5 and performed in accordance with any applicable Federal reference methods, is appropriate for designating areas as attainment or nonattainment pursuant to the July 1997 promulgated standards; and
   (5) the Administrator has acknowledged that in drawing boundaries for attainment and nonattainment areas for the July 1997 ozone national air quality standards, Governors would benefit from considering implementation guidance from EPA on drawing area boundaries.

(b) The purposes of this title are—
   (1) to ensure that 3 years of air quality monitoring data regarding fine particle levels are gathered for use in the determination of area attainment or nonattainment designations respecting any PM-2.5 national ambient air quality standards;
   (2) to ensure that the Governors have adequate time to consider implementation guidance from EPA on drawing area boundaries prior to submitting area designations respecting the July 1997 ozone national ambient air quality standards;
   (3) to ensure that the schedule for implementation of the July 1997 revisions of the ambient air quality standards for particulate matter and the schedule for the Environmental Protection Agency's visibility regulations related to regional haze are consistent with the timetable for implementation of such particulate matter standards as set forth in the President's Implementation Memorandum dated July 16, 1997.

SEC. 6102. PARTICULATE MATTER MONITORING PROGRAM.

(a) Through grants under section 103 of the Clean Air Act [42 U.S.C. 7403] the Administrator of the Environmental Protection Agency shall use appropriated funds no later than fiscal year 2000 to fund 100 percent of the cost of the establishment, purchase, operation and maintenance of a PM-2.5 monitoring network necessary to implement the national ambient air quality standards for PM-2.5 under section 109 of the Clean Air Act [42 U.S.C. 7409]. This implementation shall not result in a diversion or reprogramming of funds from other Federal, State or local Clean Air Act activities. Any funds previously diverted or reprogrammed from section 105 Clean Air Act [42 U.S.C. 7405] grants for PM-2.5 monitors must be restored to State or local air programs in fiscal year 1999.

(b) EPA and the States, consistent with their respective authorities under the Clean Air Act [42 U.S.C. 7401 et seq.], shall ensure that the national network (designated in subsection (a)) which consists of the PM-2.5 monitors necessary to implement the national ambient air quality standards is established by December 31, 1999.

(c) (1) The Governors shall be required to submit designations referred to in section 107(d)(1) of the Clean Air Act [42 U.S.C. 7407(d)(1)] for each area following promulgation of the July 1997 PM-2.5 national ambient air quality standard within 1 year after receipt of 3 years of air quality monitoring data performed in accordance with any applicable Federal reference methods for the relevant areas. Only data from the monitoring network designated in subsection (a) and other Federal reference method PM-2.5 monitors shall be considered for such designations. Nothing in the previous sentence shall be construed as affecting the

Governor's authority to designate an area initially as nonattainment, and the Administrator's authority to promulgate the designation of an area as nonattainment, under section 107(d)(1) of the Clean Air Act, based on its contribution to ambient air quality in a nearby nonattainment area.

(2) For any area designated as nonattainment for the July 1997 PM-2.5 national ambient air quality standard in accordance with the schedule set forth in this section, notwithstanding the time limit prescribed in paragraph (2) of section 169B(e) of the Clean Air Act [42 U.S.C. 7492(e)(2)], the Administrator shall require State implementation plan revisions referred to in such paragraph (2) to be submitted at the same time as State implementation plan revisions referred to in section 172 of the Clean Air Act [42 U.S.C. 7502] implementing the revised national ambient air quality standard for fine particulate matter are required to be submitted. For any area designated as attainment or unclassifiable for such standard, the Administrator shall require the State implementation plan revisions referred to in such paragraph (2) to be submitted 1 year after the area has been so designated. The preceding provisions of this paragraph shall not preclude the implementation of the agreements and recommendations set forth in the Grand Canyon Visibility Transport Commission Report dated June 1996.

(d) The Administrator shall promulgate the designations referred to in section 107(d)(1) of the Clean Air Act [42 U.S.C. 7407(d)(1)] for each area following promulgation of the July 1997 PM-2.5 national ambient air quality standard by the earlier of 1 year after the initial designations required under subsection (c)(1) are required to be submitted or December 31, 2005.

(e) The Administrator shall conduct a field study of the ability of the PM-2.5 Federal Reference Method to differentiate those particles that are larger than 2.5 micrograms in diameter. This study shall be completed and provided to the Committee on Commerce of the House of Representatives and the Committee on Environment and Public Works of the United States Senate no later than 2 years from the date of enactment of this Act [June 9, 1998].

SEC. 6103. OZONE DESIGNATION REQUIREMENTS.

(a) The Governors shall be required to submit the designations referred to in section 107(d)(1) of the Clean Air Act [42 U.S.C. 7407(d)(1)] within 2 years following the promulgation of the July 1997 ozone national ambient air quality standards.

(b) The Administrator shall promulgate final designations no later than 1 year after the designations required under subsection (a) are required to be submitted.

SEC. 6104. ADDITIONAL PROVISIONS.

Nothing in sections 6101 through 6103 shall be construed by the Administrator of Environmental Protection Agency or any court, State, or person to affect any pending litigation or to be a ratification of the ozone or PM-2.5 standards."

Pending Actions and Proceedings

Suits, actions, and other proceedings lawfully commenced by or against the Administrator or any other officer or employee of the United States in his official capacity or in relation to the discharge of his official duties under act July 14, 1955, the Clean Air Act, as in effect immediately prior to the enactment of Pub. L. 95-95 [Aug. 7, 1977], not to abate by reason of the taking effect of Pub. L. 95-95, see section 406(a) of Pub. L. 95-95, set out as an Effective Date of 1977 Amendment note under section 7401 of this title.

Modification or Rescission of Rules, Regulations, Orders, Determinations, Contracts, Certifications, Authorizations, Delegations, and Other Actions

All rules, regulations, orders, determinations, contracts, certifications, authorizations, delegations, or other actions duly issued, made, or taken by or pursuant to act July 14, 1955, the Clean Air Act, as in effect immediately prior to the date of enactment of Pub. L. 95-95 [Aug. 7, 1977] to continue in full force and effect until modified or rescinded in accordance with act July 14, 1955, as amended by Pub. L. 95-95 [this chapter], see section 406(b) of Pub. L. 95-95, set out as an Effective Date of 1977 Amendment note under section 7401 of this title.

Section Referred to in Other Sections

This section is referred to in sections 7406, 7429, 7471, 7472, 7477, 7501, 7502, 7505a, 7509, 7511, 7511e, 7512, 7513, 7513a, 7514, 7545, 7607, 7651d of this title; title 23 sections 101, 109, 149.

AIR QUALITY CRITERIA AND CONTROL TECHNIQUES
42 USC 7408

(a) Air pollutant list; publication and revision by Administrator; issuance of air quality criteria for air pollutants
   (1) For the purpose of establishing national primary and secondary ambient air quality standards, the Administrator shall within 30 days after December 31, 1970, publish, and shall from time to time thereafter revise, a list which includes each air pollutant—
      (A) emissions of which, in his judgment, cause or contribute to air pollution which may reasonably be anticipated to endanger public health or welfare;
      (B) the presence of which in the ambient air results from numerous or diverse mobile or stationary sources; and
      (C) for which air quality criteria had not been issued before December 31, 1970 but for which he plans to issue air quality criteria under this section.
   (2) The Administrator shall issue air quality criteria for an air pollutant within 12 months after he has included such pollutant in a list under paragraph (1). Air quality criteria for an air pollutant shall accurately reflect the latest scientific knowledge useful in indicating the kind and extent of all identifiable effects on public health or welfare which may be expected from the presence of such pollutant in the ambient air, in varying quantities. The criteria for an air pollutant, to the extent practicable, shall include information on—
      (A) those variable factors (including atmospheric conditions) which of themselves or in combination with other factors may alter the effects on public health or welfare of such air pollutant;
      (B) the types of air pollutants which, when present in the atmosphere, may interact with such pollutant to produce an adverse effect on public health or welfare; and
      (C) any known or anticipated adverse effects on welfare.
(b) Issuance by Administrator of information on air pollution control techniques; standing consulting committees for air pollutants; establishment; membership
   (1) Simultaneously with the issuance of criteria under subsection (a) of this section, the Administrator shall, after consultation with appropriate advisory committees and Federal departments and agencies, issue to the States and appropriate air pollution control agencies information on air pollution control techniques, which information shall include data relating to the cost of installation and operation, energy requirements, emission reduction benefits, and environmental impact of the emission control technology. Such information shall include such data as are available on available technology and alternative methods of prevention and control of air pollution. Such information shall also include data on alternative fuels, processes, and operating methods which will result in elimination or significant reduction of emissions.
   (2) In order to assist in the development of information on pollution control techniques, the Administrator may establish a standing consulting committee for each air pollutant included in a list published pursuant to subsection (a)(1) of this section, which shall be comprised of technically qualified individuals representative of State and local governments, industry, and the academic community. Each such committee shall submit, as appropriate, to the Administrator information related to that required by paragraph (1).
(c) Review, modification, and reissuance of criteria or information
   The Administrator shall from time to time review, and, as appropriate, modify, and reissue any criteria or information on control techniques issued pursuant to this section. Not later than six months after August 7, 1977, the Administrator shall revise and reissue criteria relating to concentrations of NO_2 over such period (not more than three hours) as he deems appropriate. Such criteria shall include a discussion of nitric and nitrous acids, nitrites, nitrates, nitrosamines, and other carcinogenic and potentially carcinogenic derivatives of oxides of nitrogen.
(d) Publication in Federal Register; availability of copies for general public
   The issuance of air quality criteria and information on air pollution control techniques shall be announced in the Federal Register and copies shall be made available to the general public.

(e) Transportation planning and guidelines

The Administrator shall, after consultation with the Secretary of Transportation, and after providing public notice and opportunity for comment, and with State and local officials, within nine months after November 15, 1990,[1] and periodically thereafter as necessary to maintain a continuous transportation-air quality planning process, update the June 1978 Transportation-Air Quality Planning Guidelines and publish guidance on the development and implementation of transportation and other measures necessary to demonstrate and maintain attainment of national ambient air quality standards. Such guidelines shall include information on—
  (1) methods to identify and evaluate alternative planning and control activities;
  (2) methods of reviewing plans on a regular basis as conditions change or new information is presented;
  (3) identification of funds and other resources necessary to implement the plan, including interagency agreements on providing such funds and resources;
  (4) methods to assure participation by the public in all phases of the planning process; and
  (5) such other methods as the Administrator determines necessary to carry out a continuous planning process.

(f) Information regarding processes, procedures, and methods to reduce or control pollutants in transportation; reduction of mobile source related pollutants; reduction of impact on public health
  (1) The Administrator shall publish and make available to appropriate Federal, State, and local environmental and transportation agencies not later than one year after November 15, 1990, and from time to time thereafter—
    (A) information prepared, as appropriate, in consultation with the Secretary of Transportation, and after providing public notice and opportunity for comment, regarding the formulation and emission reduction potential of transportation control measures related to criteria pollutants and their precursors, including, but not limited to—
      (i) programs for improved public transit;
      (ii) restriction of certain roads or lanes to, or construction of such roads or lanes for use by, passenger buses or high occupancy vehicles;
      (iii) employer-based transportation management plans, including incentives;
      (iv) trip-reduction ordinances;
      (v) traffic flow improvement programs that achieve emission reductions;
      (vi) fringe and transportation corridor parking facilities serving multiple occupancy vehicle programs or transit service;
      (vii) programs to limit or restrict vehicle use in downtown areas or other areas of emission concentration particularly during periods of peak use;
      (viii) programs for the provision of all forms of high-occupancy, shared-ride services;
      (ix) programs to limit portions of road surfaces or certain sections of the metropolitan area to the use of non-motorized vehicles or pedestrian use, both as to time and place;
      (x) programs for secure bicycle storage facilities and other facilities, including bicycle lanes, for the convenience and protection of bicyclists, in both public and private areas;
      (xi) programs to control extended idling of vehicles;
      (xii) programs to reduce motor vehicle emissions, consistent with subchapter II of this chapter, which are caused by extreme cold start conditions;
      (xiii) employer-sponsored programs to permit flexible work schedules;
      (xiv) programs and ordinances to facilitate non-automobile travel, provision and utilization of mass transit, and to generally reduce the need for single-occupant vehicle travel, as part of transportation planning and development efforts of a locality, including programs and ordinances applicable to new shopping centers, special events, and other centers of vehicle activity;
      (xv) programs for new construction and major reconstructions of paths, tracks or areas solely for the use by pedestrian or other non-motorized means of transportation when economically feasible and in the public interest. For purposes of this clause, the Administrator shall also consult with the Secretary of the Interior; and

---

[1] See Codification note below.

(xvi) program to encourage the voluntary removal from use and the marketplace of pre-1980 model year light duty vehicles and pre-1980 model light duty trucks.

(B) information on additional methods or strategies that will contribute to the reduction of mobile source related pollutants during periods in which any primary ambient air quality standard will be exceeded and during episodes for which an air pollution alert, warning, or emergency has been declared;

(C) information on other measures which may be employed to reduce the impact on public health or protect the health of sensitive or susceptible individuals or groups; and

(D) information on the extent to which any process, procedure, or method to reduce or control such air pollutant may cause an increase in the emissions or formation of any other pollutant.

(2) In publishing such information the Administrator shall also include an assessment of—

(A) the relative effectiveness of such processes, procedures, and methods;

(B) the potential effect of such processes, procedures, and methods on transportation systems and the provision of transportation services; and

(C) the environmental, energy, and economic impact of such processes, procedures, and methods.

(g) Assessment of risks to ecosystems

The Administrator may assess the risks to ecosystems from exposure to criteria air pollutants (as identified by the Administrator in the Administrator's sole discretion).

(h) RACT/BACT/LAER clearinghouse

The Administrator shall make information regarding emission control technology available to the States and to the general public through a central database. Such information shall include all control technology information received pursuant to State plan provisions requiring permits for sources, including operating permits for existing sources.

(July 14, 1955, ch. 360, title I, Sec. 108, as added Pub. L. 91-604, Sec. 4(a), Dec. 31, 1970, 84 Stat. 1678; amended Pub. L. 95-95, title I, Secs. 104, 105, title IV, Sec. 401(a), Aug. 7, 1977, 91 Stat. 689, 790; Pub. L. 101-549, title I, Secs. 108(a)-(c), (o), 111, Nov. 15, 1990, 104 Stat. 2465, 2466, 2469, 2470; Pub. L. 105-362, title XV, Sec. 1501(b), Nov. 10, 1998, 112 Stat. 3294.)

Codification

November 15, 1990, referred to in subsec. (e), was in the original "enactment of the Clean Air Act Amendments of 1989", and was translated as meaning the date of the enactment of Pub. L. 101-549, popularly known as the Clean Air Act Amendments of 1990, to reflect the probable intent of Congress.

Section was formerly classified to section 1857c-3 of this title.

Prior Provisions

A prior section 108 of act July 14, 1955, was renumbered section 115 by Pub. L. 91-604 and is classified to section 7415 of this title.

Amendments

1998–Subsec. (f)(3), (4). Pub. L. 105-362 struck out par. (3), which required reports by the Secretary of Transportation and the Administrator to be submitted to Congress by Jan. 1, 1993, and every 3 years thereafter, reviewing and analyzing existing State and local air quality related transportation programs, evaluating achievement of goals, and recommending changes to existing programs, and par. (4), which required that in each report after the first report the Secretary of Transportation include a description of the actions taken to implement the changes recommended in the preceding report.

1990–Subsec. (e). Pub. L. 101-549, Sec. 108(a), inserted first sentence and struck out former first sentence which read as follows: "The Administrator shall, after consultation with the Secretary of Transportation and the Secretary of Housing and Urban Development and State and local officials and within 180 days after August 7, 1977, and from time to time thereafter, publish guidelines on the basic program elements for the planning process assisted under section 7505 of this title."

Subsec. (f)(1). Pub. L. 101-549, Sec. 108(b), in introductory provisions, substituted present provisions for provisions relating to Federal agencies, States, and air pollution control agencies within either 6 months or one year after Aug. 7, 1977.

Subsec. (f)(1)(A). Pub. L. 101-549, Sec. 108(b), substituted present provisions for provisions relating to information prepared in cooperation with Secretary of Transportation, regarding processes, procedures, and methods to reduce certain pollutants.
Subsec. (f)(3), (4). Pub. L. 101-549, Sec. 111, added pars. (3) and (4).
Subsec. (g). Pub. L. 101-549, Sec. 108(o), added subsec. (g).
Subsec. (h). Pub. L. 101-549, Sec. 108(c), added subsec. (h).

1977—Subsec. (a)(1)(A). Pub. L. 95-95, Sec. 401(a), substituted "emissions of which, in his judgment, cause or contribute to air pollution which may reasonably be anticipated to endanger public health or welfare" for "which in his judgment has an adverse effect on public health or welfare".

Subsec. (b)(1). Pub. L. 95-95, Sec. 104(a), substituted "cost of installation and operation, energy requirements, emission reduction benefits, and environmental impact of the emission control technology" for "technology and costs of emission control".

Subsec. (c). Pub. L. 95-95, Sec. 104(b), inserted provision directing the Administrator, not later than six months after Aug. 7, 1977, to revise and reissue criteria relating to concentrations of NO_2 over such period (not more than three hours) as he deems appropriate, with the criteria to include a discussion of nitric and nitrous acids, nitrites, nitrates, nitrosamines, and other carcinogenic and potentially carcinogenic derivatives of oxides of nitrogen.

Subsecs. (e), (f). Pub. L. 95-95, Sec. 105, added subsecs. (e) and (f).

Effective Date of 1977 Amendment

Amendment by Pub. L. 95-95 effective Aug. 7, 1977, except as otherwise expressly provided, see section 406(d) of Pub. L. 95-95, set out as a note under section 7401 of this title.

Modification or Rescission of Rules, Regulations, Orders, Determinations, Contracts, Certifications, Authorizations, Delegations, and Other Actions

All rules, regulations, orders, determinations, contracts, certifications, authorizations, delegations, or other actions duly issued, made, or taken by or pursuant to act July 14, 1955, the Clean Air Act, as in effect immediately prior to the date of enactment of Pub. L. 95-95 [Aug. 7, 1977] to continue in full force and effect until modified or rescinded in accordance with act July 14, 1955, as amended by Pub. L. 95-95 [this chapter], see section 406(b) of Pub. L. 95-95, set out as an Effective Date of 1977 Amendment note under section 7401 of this title.

Section Referred to in Other Sections

This section is referred to in sections 7403, 7409, 7411, 7412, 7417, 7422, 7504, 7508, 7511a, 7511b, 7513b, 7602 of this title; title 23 sections 133, 149.

NATIONAL PRIMARY AND SECONDARY AMBIENT AIR QUALITY STANDARDS

42 USC 7409

(a) Promulgation
   (1) The Administrator—
      (A) within 30 days after December 31, 1970, shall publish proposed regulations prescribing a national primary ambient air quality standard and a national secondary ambient air quality standard for each air pollutant for which air quality criteria have been issued prior to such date; and
      (B) after a reasonable time for interested persons to submit written comments thereon (but no later than 90 days after the initial publication of such proposed standards) shall by regulation promulgate such proposed national primary and secondary ambient air quality standards with such modifications as he deems appropriate.
   (2) With respect to any air pollutant for which air quality criteria are issued after December 31, 1970, the Administrator shall publish, simultaneously with the issuance of such criteria and information, proposed national primary and secondary ambient air quality standards for any such pollutant. The procedure provided for in paragraph (1)(B) of this subsection shall apply to the promulgation of such standards.
(b) Protection of public health and welfare
   (1) National primary ambient air quality standards, prescribed under subsection (a) of this section shall be ambient air quality standards the attainment and maintenance of which

in the judgment of the Administrator, based on such criteria and allowing an adequate margin of safety, are requisite to protect the public health. Such primary standards may be revised in the same manner as promulgated.

(2) Any national secondary ambient air quality standard prescribed under subsection (a) of this section shall specify a level of air quality the attainment and maintenance of which in the judgment of the Administrator, based on such criteria, is requisite to protect the public welfare from any known or anticipated adverse effects associated with the presence of such air pollutant in the ambient air. Such secondary standards may be revised in the same manner as promulgated.

(c) National primary ambient air quality standard for nitrogen dioxide

The Administrator shall, not later than one year after August 7, 1977, promulgate a national primary ambient air quality standard for NO_2 concentrations over a period of not more than 3 hours unless, based on the criteria issued under section 7408(c) of this title, he finds that there is no significant evidence that such a standard for such a period is requisite to protect public health.

(d) Review and revision of criteria and standards; independent scientific review committee; appointment; advisory functions

(1) Not later than December 31, 1980, and at five-year intervals thereafter, the Administrator shall complete a thorough review of the criteria published under section 7408 of this title and the national ambient air quality standards promulgated under this section and shall make such revisions in such criteria and standards and promulgate such new standards as may be appropriate in accordance with section 7408 of this title and subsection (b) of this section. The Administrator may review and revise criteria or promulgate new standards earlier or more frequently than required under this paragraph.

(2) (A) The Administrator shall appoint an independent scientific review committee composed of seven members including at least one member of the National Academy of Sciences, one physician, and one person representing State air pollution control agencies.

(B) Not later than January 1, 1980, and at five-year intervals thereafter, the committee referred to in subparagraph (A) shall complete a review of the criteria published under section 7408 of this title and the national primary and secondary ambient air quality standards promulgated under this section and shall recommend to the Administrator any new national ambient air quality standards and revisions of existing criteria and standards as may be appropriate under section 7408 of this title and subsection (b) of this section.

(C) Such committee shall also (i) advise the Administrator of areas in which additional knowledge is required to appraise the adequacy and basis of existing, new, or revised national ambient air quality standards, (ii) describe the research efforts necessary to provide the required information, (iii) advise the Administrator on the relative contribution to air pollution concentrations of natural as well as anthropogenic activity, and (iv) advise the Administrator of any adverse public health, welfare, social, economic, or energy effects which may result from various strategies for attainment and maintenance of such national ambient air quality standards.

(July 14, 1955, ch. 360, title I, Sec. 109, as added Pub. L. 91-604, Sec. 4(a), Dec. 31, 1970, 84 Stat. 1679; amended Pub. L. 95-95, title I, Sec. 106, Aug. 7, 1977, 91 Stat. 691.)

Codification

Section was formerly classified to section 1857c-4 of this title.

Prior Provisions

A prior section 109 of act July 14, 1955, was renumbered section 116 by Pub. L. 91-604 and is classified to section 7416 of this title.

Amendments

1977—Subsec. (c). Pub. L. 95-95, Sec. 106(b), added subsec. (c).

Subsec. (d). Pub. L. 95-95, Sec. 106(a), added subsec. (d).

Effective Date of 1977 Amendment

Amendment by Pub. L. 95-95 effective Aug. 7, 1977, except as otherwise expressly provided, see section 406(d) of Pub. L. 95-95, set out as a note under section 7401 of this title.

Modification or Rescission of Rules, Regulations, Orders, Determinations, Contracts, Certifications, Authorizations, Delegations, and Other Actions

All rules, regulations, orders, determinations, contracts, certifications, authorizations, delegations, or other actions duly issued, made, or taken by or pursuant to act July 14, 1955, the Clean Air Act, as in effect immediately prior to the date of enactment of Pub. L. 95-95 [Aug. 7, 1977] to continue in full force and effect until modified or rescinded in accordance with act July 14, 1955, as amended by Pub. L. 95-95 [this chapter], see section 406(b) of Pub. L. 95-95, set out as an Effective Date of 1977 Amendment note under section 7401 of this title.

Termination of Advisory Committees

Advisory committees established after Jan. 5, 1973, to terminate not later than the expiration of the 2-year period beginning on the date of their establishment, unless, in the case of a committee established by the President or an officer of the Federal Government, such committee is renewed by appropriate action prior to the expiration of such 2-year period, or in the case of a committee established by the Congress, its duration is otherwise provided for by law. See section 14 of Pub. L. 92-463, Oct. 6, 1972, 86 Stat. 776, set out in the Appendix to Title 5, Government Organization and Employees.

Role of Secondary Standards

Pub. L. 101-549, title VIII, Sec. 817, Nov. 15, 1990, 104 Stat. 2697, provided that:

"(a) Report.—The Administrator shall request the National Academy of Sciences to prepare a report to the Congress on the role of national secondary ambient air quality standards in protecting welfare and the environment. The report shall:
  (1) include information on the effects on welfare and the environment which are caused by ambient concentrations of pollutants listed pursuant to section 108 [42 U.S.C. 7408] and other pollutants which may be listed;
  (2) estimate welfare and environmental costs incurred as a result of such effects;
  (3) examine the role of secondary standards and the State implementation planning process in preventing such effects;
  (4) determine ambient concentrations of each such pollutant which would be adequate to protect welfare and the environment from such effects;
  (5) estimate the costs and other impacts of meeting secondary standards; and
  (6) consider other means consistent with the goals and objectives of the Clean Air Act [42 U.S.C. 7401 et seq.] which may be more effective than secondary standards in preventing or mitigating such effects.
(b) Submission to Congress; Comments; Authorization.—(1) The report shall be transmitted to the Congress not later than 3 years after the date of enactment of the Clean Air Act Amendments of 1990 [Nov. 15, 1990].
  (2) At least 90 days before issuing a report the Administrator shall provide an opportunity for public comment on the proposed report. The Administrator shall include in the final report a summary of the comments received on the proposed report.
  (3) There are authorized to be appropriated such sums as are necessary to carry out this section."

Section Referred to in Other Sections

This section is referred to in sections 7407, 7410, 7415, 7607, 7612, 7651d of this title.

STATE IMPLEMENTATION PLANS FOR NATIONAL PRIMARY AND SECONDARY AMBIENT AIR QUALITY STANDARDS

42 USC 7410

(a) Adoption of plan by State; submission to Administrator; content of plan; revision; new sources; indirect source review program; supplemental or intermittent control systems

(1) Each State shall, after reasonable notice and public hearings, adopt and submit to the Administrator, within 3 years (or such shorter period as the Administrator may prescribe) after the promulgation of a national primary ambient air quality standard (or any revision thereof) under section 7409 of this title for any air pollutant, a plan which provides for implementation, maintenance, and enforcement of such primary standard in each air quality control region (or portion thereof) within such State. In addition, such State shall adopt and submit to the Administrator (either as a part of a plan submitted under the preceding sentence or separately) within 3 years (or such shorter period as the Administrator may prescribe) after the promulgation of a national ambient air quality secondary standard (or revision thereof), a plan which provides for implementation, maintenance, and enforcement of such secondary standard in each air quality control region (or portion thereof) within such State. Unless a separate public hearing is provided, each State shall consider its plan implementing such secondary standard at the hearing required by the first sentence of this paragraph.
(2) Each implementation plan submitted by a State under this chapter shall be adopted by the State after reasonable notice and public hearing. Each such plan shall—
   (A) include enforceable emission limitations and other control measures, means, or techniques (including economic incentives such as fees, marketable permits, and auctions of emissions rights), as well as schedules and timetables for compliance, as may be necessary or appropriate to meet the applicable requirements of this chapter;
   (B) provide for establishment and operation of appropriate devices, methods, systems, and procedures necessary to—
      (i) monitor, compile, and analyze data on ambient air quality, and
      (ii) upon request, make such data available to the Administrator;
   (C) include a program to provide for the enforcement of the measures described in subparagraph (A), and regulation of the modification and construction of any stationary source within the areas covered by the plan as necessary to assure that national ambient air quality standards are achieved, including a permit program as required in parts C and D of this subchapter;
   (D) contain adequate provisions—
      (i) prohibiting, consistent with the provisions of this subchapter, any source or other type of emissions activity within the State from emitting any air pollutant in amounts which will—(I) contribute significantly to nonattainment in, or interfere with maintenance by, any other State with respect to any such national primary or secondary ambient air quality standard, or (II) interfere with measures required to be included in the applicable implementation plan for any other State under part C of this subchapter to prevent significant deterioration of air quality or to protect visibility,
      (ii) insuring compliance with the applicable requirements of sections 7426 and 7415 of this title (relating to interstate and international pollution abatement);
   (E) provide (i) necessary assurances that the State (or, except where the Administrator deems inappropriate, the general purpose local government or governments, or a regional agency designated by the State or general purpose local governments for such purpose) will have adequate personnel, funding, and authority under State (and, as appropriate, local) law to carry out such implementation plan (and is not prohibited by any provision of Federal or State law from carrying out such implementation plan or portion thereof), (ii) requirements that the State comply with the requirements respecting State boards under section 7428 of this title, and (iii) necessary assurances that, where the State has relied on a local or regional government, agency, or instrumentality for the implementation of any plan provision, the State has responsibility for ensuring adequate implementation of such plan provision;
   (F) require, as may be prescribed by the Administrator—
      (i) the installation, maintenance, and replacement of equipment, and the implementation of other necessary steps, by owners or operators of stationary sources to monitor emissions from such sources,
      (ii) periodic reports on the nature and amounts of emissions and emissions-related data from such sources, and

(iii) correlation of such reports by the State agency with any emission limitations or standards established pursuant to this chapter, which reports shall be available at reasonable times for public inspection;
(G) provide for authority comparable to that in section 7603 of this title and adequate contingency plans to implement such authority;
(H) provide for revision of such plan—
  (i) from time to time as may be necessary to take account of revisions of such national primary or secondary ambient air quality standard or the availability of improved or more expeditious methods of attaining such standard, and
  (ii) except as provided in paragraph (3)(C), whenever the Administrator finds on the basis of information available to the Administrator that the plan is substantially inadequate to attain the national ambient air quality standard which it implements or to otherwise comply with any additional requirements established under this chapter;
(I) in the case of a plan or plan revision for an area designated as a nonattainment area, meet the applicable requirements of part D of this subchapter (relating to nonattainment areas);
(J) meet the applicable requirements of section 7421 of this title (relating to consultation), section 7427 of this title (relating to public notification), and part C of this subchapter (relating to prevention of significant deterioration of air quality and visibility protection);
(K) provide for—
  (i) the performance of such air quality modeling as the Administrator may prescribe for the purpose of predicting the effect on ambient air quality of any emissions of any air pollutant for which the Administrator has established a national ambient air quality standard, and
  (ii) the submission, upon request, of data related to such air quality modeling to the Administrator;
(L) require the owner or operator of each major stationary source to pay to the permitting authority, as a condition of any permit required under this chapter, a fee sufficient to cover—
  (i) the reasonable costs of reviewing and acting upon any application for such a permit, and
  (ii) if the owner or operator receives a permit for such source, the reasonable costs of implementing and enforcing the terms and conditions of any such permit (not including any court costs or other costs associated with any enforcement action), until such fee requirement is superseded with respect to such sources by the Administrator's approval of a fee program under subchapter V of this chapter; and
(M) provide for consultation and participation by local political subdivisions affected by the plan.
(3) (A) Repealed. Pub. L. 101-549, title I, Sec. 101(d)(1), Nov. 15, 1990, 104 Stat. 2409.
  (B) As soon as practicable, the Administrator shall, consistent with the purposes of this chapter and the Energy Supply and Environmental Coordination Act of 1974 [15 U.S.C. 791 et seq.], review each State's applicable implementation plans and report to the State on whether such plans can be revised in relation to fuel burning stationary sources (or persons supplying fuel to such sources) without interfering with the attainment and maintenance of any national ambient air quality standard within the period permitted in this section. If the Administrator determines that any such plan can be revised, he shall notify the State that a plan revision may be submitted by the State. Any plan revision which is submitted by the State shall, after public notice and opportunity for public hearing, be approved by the Administrator if the revision relates only to fuel burning stationary sources (or persons supplying fuel to such sources), and the plan as revised complies with paragraph (2) of this subsection. The Administrator shall approve or disapprove any revision no later than three months after its submission.
  (C) Neither the State, in the case of a plan (or portion thereof) approved under this subsection, nor the Administrator, in the case of a plan (or portion thereof) promulgated

under subsection (c) of this section, shall be required to revise an applicable implementation plan because one or more exemptions under section 7418 of this title (relating to Federal facilities), enforcement orders under section 7413(d)[1] of this title, suspensions under subsection (f) or (g) of this section (relating to temporary energy or economic authority), orders under section 7419 of this title (relating to primary nonferrous smelters), or extensions of compliance in decrees entered under section 7413(e)[1] of this title (relating to iron- and steel-producing operations) have been granted, if such plan would have met the requirements of this section if no such exemptions, orders, or extensions had been granted.

(4) Repealed. Pub. L. 101-549, title I, Sec. 101(d)(2), Nov. 15, 1990, 104 Stat. 2409.

(5) (A) (i) Any State may include in a State implementation plan, but the Administrator may not require as a condition of approval of such plan under this section, any indirect source review program. The Administrator may approve and enforce, as part of an applicable implementation plan, an indirect source review program which the State chooses to adopt and submit as part of its plan.

   (ii) Except as provided in subparagraph (B), no plan promulgated by the Administrator shall include any indirect source review program for any air quality control region, or portion thereof.

   (iii) Any State may revise an applicable implementation plan approved under this subsection to suspend or revoke any such program included in such plan, provided that such plan meets the requirements of this section.

   (B) The Administrator shall have the authority to promulgate, implement and enforce regulations under subsection (c) of this section respecting indirect source review programs which apply only to federally assisted highways, airports, and other major federally assisted indirect sources and federally owned or operated indirect sources.

   (C) For purposes of this paragraph, the term "indirect source means a facility, building, structure, installation, real property, road, or highway which attracts, or may attract, mobile sources of pollution. Such term includes parking lots, parking garages, and other facilities subject to any measure for management of parking supply (within the meaning of subsection (c)(2)(D)(ii) of this section), including regulation of existing off-street parking but such term does not include new or existing on-street parking. Direct emissions sources or facilities at, within, or associated with, any indirect source shall not be deemed indirect sources for the purpose of this paragraph.

   (D) For purposes of this paragraph the term "indirect source review program" means the facility-by-facility review of indirect sources of air pollution, including such measures as are necessary to assure, or assist in assuring, that a new or modified indirect source will not attract mobile sources of air pollution, the emissions from which would cause or contribute to air pollution concentrations—

      (i) exceeding any national primary ambient air quality standard for a mobile source-related air pollutant after the primary standard attainment date, or

      (ii) preventing maintenance of any such standard after such date.

   (E) For purposes of this paragraph and paragraph (2)(B), the term "transportation control measure" does not include any measure which is an "indirect source review program".

(6) No State plan shall be treated as meeting the requirements of this section unless such plan provides that in the case of any source which uses a supplemental, or intermittent control system for purposes of meeting the requirements of an order under section 7413(d)[1] of this title or section 7419 of this title (relating to primary nonferrous smelter orders), the owner or operator of such source may not temporarily reduce the pay of any employee by reason of the use of such supplemental or intermittent or other dispersion dependent control system.

(b) Extension of period for submission of plans

The Administrator may, wherever he determines necessary, extend the period for submission of any plan or portion thereof which implements a national secondary ambient air quality standard for a period not to exceed 18 months from the date otherwise required for submission of such plan.

---

[1] See References in Text note below.

(c) Preparation and publication by Administrator of proposed regulations setting forth implementation plan; transportation regulations study and report; parking surcharge; suspension authority; plan implementation
   (1) The Administrator shall promulgate a Federal implementation plan at any time within 2 years after the Administrator—
      (A) finds that a State has failed to make a required submission or finds that the plan or plan revision submitted by the State does not satisfy the minimum criteria established under subsection (k)(1)(A) of this section, or
      (B) disapproves a State implementation plan submission in whole or in part, unless the State corrects the deficiency, and the Administrator approves the plan or plan revision, before the Administrator promulgates such Federal implementation plan.
   (2) (A) Repealed. Pub. L. 101-549, title I, Sec. 101(d)(3)(A), Nov. 15, 1990, 104 Stat. 2409.
      (B) No parking surcharge regulation may be required by the Administrator under paragraph (1) of this subsection as a part of an applicable implementation plan. All parking surcharge regulations previously required by the Administrator shall be void upon June 22, 1974. This subparagraph shall not prevent the Administrator from approving parking surcharges if they are adopted and submitted by a State as part of an applicable implementation plan. The Administrator may not condition approval of any implementation plan submitted by a State on such plan's including a parking surcharge regulation.
      (C) Repealed. Pub. L. 101-549, title I, Sec. 101(d)(3)(B), Nov. 15, 1990, 104 Stat. 2409.
      (D) For purposes of this paragraph—
         (i) The term "parking surcharge regulation" means a regulation imposing or requiring the imposition of any tax, surcharge, fee, or other charge on parking spaces, or any other area used for the temporary storage of motor vehicles.
         (ii) The term "management of parking supply" shall include any requirement providing that any new facility containing a given number of parking spaces shall receive a permit or other prior approval, issuance of which is to be conditioned on air quality considerations.
         (iii) The term "preferential bus/carpool lane" shall include any requirement for the setting aside of one or more lanes of a street or highway on a permanent or temporary basis for the exclusive use of buses or carpools, or both.
      (E) No standard, plan, or requirement, relating to management of parking supply or preferential bus/carpool lanes shall be promulgated after June 22, 1974, by the Administrator pursuant to this section, unless such promulgation has been subjected to at least one public hearing which has been held in the area affected and for which reasonable notice has been given in such area. If substantial changes are made following public hearings, one or more additional hearings shall be held in such area after such notice.
   (3) Upon application of the chief executive officer of any general purpose unit of local government, if the Administrator determines that such unit has adequate authority under State or local law, the Administrator may delegate to such unit the authority to implement and enforce within the jurisdiction of such unit any part of a plan promulgated under this subsection. Nothing in this paragraph shall prevent the Administrator from implementing or enforcing any applicable provision of a plan promulgated under this subsection.
   (4) Repealed. Pub. L. 101-549, title I, Sec. 101(d)(3)(C), Nov. 15, 1990, 104 Stat. 2409.
   (5) (A) Any measure in an applicable implementation plan which requires a toll or other charge for the use of a bridge located entirely within one city shall be eliminated from such plan by the Administrator upon application by the Governor of the State, which application shall include a certification by the Governor that he will revise such plan in accordance with subparagraph (B).
      (B) In the case of any applicable implementation plan with respect to which a measure has been eliminated under subparagraph (A), such plan shall, not later than one year after August 7, 1977, be revised to include comprehensive measures to:
         (i) establish, expand, or improve public transportation measures to meet basic transportation needs, as expeditiously as is practicable; and
         (ii) implement transportation control measures necessary to attain and maintain national ambient air quality standards, and such revised plan shall, for the purpose

of implementing such comprehensive public transportation measures, include requirements to use (insofar as is necessary) Federal grants, State or local funds, or any combination of such grants and funds as may be consistent with the terms of the legislation providing such grants and funds. Such measures shall, as a substitute for the tolls or charges eliminated under subparagraph (A), provide for emissions reductions equivalent to the reductions which may reasonably be expected to be achieved through the use of the tolls or charges eliminated.

(C) Any revision of an implementation plan for purposes of meeting the requirements of subparagraph (B) shall be submitted in coordination with any plan revision required under part D of this subchapter.

(d), (e) Repealed. Pub. L. 101-549, title I, Sec. 101(d)(4), (5), Nov. 15, 1990, 104 Stat. 2409

(f) National or regional energy emergencies; determination by President
  (1) Upon application by the owner or operator of a fuel burning stationary source, and after notice and opportunity for public hearing, the Governor of the State in which such source is located may petition the President to determine that a national or regional energy emergency exists of such severity that—
    (A) a temporary suspension of any part of the applicable implementation plan or of any requirement under section 7651j of this title (concerning excess emissions penalties or offsets) may be necessary, and
    (B) other means of responding to the energy emergency may be inadequate. Such determination shall not be delegable by the President to any other person. If the President determines that a national or regional energy emergency of such severity exists, a temporary emergency suspension of any part of an applicable implementation plan or of any requirement under section 7651j of this title (concerning excess emissions penalties or offsets) adopted by the State may be issued by the Governor of any State covered by the President's determination under the condition specified in paragraph (2) and may take effect immediately.
  (2) A temporary emergency suspension under this subsection shall be issued to a source only if the Governor of such State finds that—
    (A) there exists in the vicinity of such source a temporary energy emergency involving high levels of unemployment or loss of necessary energy supplies for residential dwellings; and
    (B) such unemployment or loss can be totally or partially alleviated by such emergency suspension. Not more than one such suspension may be issued for any source on the basis of the same set of circumstances or on the basis of the same emergency.
  (3) A temporary emergency suspension issued by a Governor under this subsection shall remain in effect for a maximum of four months or such lesser period as may be specified in a disapproval order of the Administrator, if any. The Administrator may disapprove such suspension if he determines that it does not meet the requirements of paragraph (2).
  (4) This subsection shall not apply in the case of a plan provision or requirement promulgated by the Administrator under subsection (c) of this section, but in any such case the President may grant a temporary emergency suspension for a four month period of any such provision or requirement if he makes the determinations and findings specified in paragraphs (1) and (2).
  (5) The Governor may include in any temporary emergency suspension issued under this subsection a provision delaying for a period identical to the period of such suspension any compliance schedule (or increment of progress) to which such source is subject under section 1857c-10[2] of this title, as in effect before August 7, 1977, or section 7413(d)[2] of this title, upon a finding that such source is unable to comply with such schedule (or increment) solely because of the conditions on the basis of which a suspension was issued under this subsection.

(g) Governor's authority to issue temporary emergency suspensions
  (1) In the case of any State which has adopted and submitted to the Administrator a proposed plan revision which the State determines—
    (A) meets the requirements of this section, and
    (B) is necessary (i) to prevent the closing for one year or more of any source of air pollution, and (ii) to prevent substantial increases in unemployment which would result

---

[2]See References in Text note below.

from such closing, and which the Administrator has not approved or disapproved under this section within 12 months of submission of the proposed plan revision, the Governor may issue a temporary emergency suspension of the part of the applicable implementation plan for such State which is proposed to be revised with respect to such source. The determination under subparagraph (B) may not be made with respect to a source which would close without regard to whether or not the proposed plan revision is approved.
- (2) A temporary emergency suspension issued by a Governor under this subsection shall remain in effect for a maximum of four months or such lesser period as may be specified in a disapproval order of the Administrator. The Administrator may disapprove such suspension if he determines that it does not meet the requirements of this subsection.
- (3) The Governor may include in any temporary emergency suspension issued under this subsection a provision delaying for a period identical to the period of such suspension any compliance schedule (or increment of progress) to which such source is subject under section 1857c-10[2] of this title as in effect before August 7, 1977, or under section 7413(d)[2] of this title upon a finding that such source is unable to comply with such schedule (or increment) solely because of the conditions on the basis of which a suspension was issued under this subsection.

(h) Publication of comprehensive document for each State setting forth requirements of applicable implementation plan
- (1) Not later than 5 years after November 15, 1990, and every 3 years thereafter, the Administrator shall assemble and publish a comprehensive document for each State setting forth all requirements of the applicable implementation plan for such State and shall publish notice in the Federal Register of the availability of such documents.
- (2) The Administrator may promulgate such regulations as may be reasonably necessary to carry out the purpose of this subsection.

(i) Modification of requirements prohibited

Except for a primary nonferrous smelter order under section 7419 of this title, a suspension under subsection (f) or (g) of this section (relating to emergency suspensions), an exemption under section 7418 of this title (relating to certain Federal facilities), an order under section 7413(d)[2] of this title (relating to compliance orders), a plan promulgation under subsection (c) of this section, or a plan revision under subsection (a)(3) of this section; no order, suspension, plan revision, or other action modifying any requirement of an applicable implementation plan may be taken with respect to any stationary source by the State or by the Administrator.

(j) Technological systems of continuous emission reduction on new or modified stationary sources; compliance with performance standards

As a condition for issuance of any permit required under this subchapter, the owner or operator of each new or modified stationary source which is required to obtain such a permit must show to the satisfaction of the permitting authority that the technological system of continuous emission reduction which is to be used at such source will enable it to comply with the standards of performance which are to apply to such source and that the construction or modification and operation of such source will be in compliance with all other requirements of this chapter.

(k) Environmental Protection Agency action on plan submissions
- (1) Completeness of plan submissions
  - (A) Completeness criteria

    Within 9 months after November 15, 1990, the Administrator shall promulgate minimum criteria that any plan submission must meet before the Administrator is required to act on such submission under this subsection. The criteria shall be limited to the information necessary to enable the Administrator to determine whether the plan submission complies with the provisions of this chapter.
  - (B) Completeness finding

    Within 60 days of the Administrator's receipt of a plan or plan revision, but no later than 6 months after the date, if any, by which a State is required to submit the plan or revision, the Administrator shall determine whether the minimum criteria established

---

[2]See References in Text note below.

pursuant to subparagraph (A) have been met. Any plan or plan revision that a State submits to the Administrator, and that has not been determined by the Administrator (by the date 6 months after receipt of the submission) to have failed to meet the minimum criteria established pursuant to subparagraph (A), shall on that date be deemed by operation of law to meet such minimum criteria.

(C) Effect of finding of incompleteness

Where the Administrator determines that a plan submission (or part thereof) does not meet the minimum criteria established pursuant to subparagraph (A), the State shall be treated as not having made the submission (or, in the Administrator's discretion, part thereof).

(2) Deadline for action

Within 12 months of a determination by the Administrator (or a determination deemed by operation of law) under paragraph (1) that a State has submitted a plan or plan revision (or, in the Administrator's discretion, part thereof) that meets the minimum criteria established pursuant to paragraph (1), if applicable (or, if those criteria are not applicable, within 12 months of submission of the plan or revision), the Administrator shall act on the submission in accordance with paragraph (3).

(3) Full and partial approval and disapproval

In the case of any submittal on which the Administrator is required to act under paragraph (2), the Administrator shall approve such submittal as a whole if it meets all of the applicable requirements of this chapter. If a portion of the plan revision meets all the applicable requirements of this chapter, the Administrator may approve the plan revision in part and disapprove the plan revision in part. The plan revision shall not be treated as meeting the requirements of this chapter until the Administrator approves the entire plan revision as complying with the applicable requirements of this chapter.

(4) Conditional approval

The Administrator may approve a plan revision based on a commitment of the State to adopt specific enforceable measures by a date certain, but not later than 1 year after the date of approval of the plan revision. Any such conditional approval shall be treated as a disapproval if the State fails to comply with such commitment.

(5) Calls for plan revisions

Whenever the Administrator finds that the applicable implementation plan for any area is substantially inadequate to attain or maintain the relevant national ambient air quality standard, to mitigate adequately the interstate pollutant transport described in section 7506a of this title or section 7511c of this title, or to otherwise comply with any requirement of this chapter, the Administrator shall require the State to revise the plan as necessary to correct such inadequacies. The Administrator shall notify the State of the inadequacies, and may establish reasonable deadlines (not to exceed 18 months after the date of such notice) for the submission of such plan revisions. Such findings and notice shall be public. Any finding under this paragraph shall, to the extent the Administrator deems appropriate, subject the State to the requirements of this chapter to which the State was subject when it developed and submitted the plan for which such finding was made, except that the Administrator may adjust any dates applicable under such requirements as appropriate (except that the Administrator may not adjust any attainment date prescribed under part D of this subchapter, unless such date has elapsed).

(6) Corrections

Whenever the Administrator determines that the Administrator's action approving, disapproving, or promulgating any plan or plan revision (or part thereof), area designation, redesignation, classification, or reclassification was in error, the Administrator may in the same manner as the approval, disapproval, or promulgation revise such action as appropriate without requiring any further submission from the State. Such determination and the basis thereof shall be provided to the State and public.

(l) Plan revisions

Each revision to an implementation plan submitted by a State under this chapter shall be adopted by such State after reasonable notice and public hearing. The Administrator shall not approve a revision of a plan if the revision would interfere with any applicable requirement concerning attainment and reasonable further progress (as defined in section 7501 of this title), or any other applicable requirement of this chapter.

(m) Sanctions

The Administrator may apply any of the sanctions listed in section 7509(b) of this title at any time (or at any time after) the Administrator makes a finding, disapproval, or determination under paragraphs (1) through (4), respectively, of section 7509(a) of this title in relation to any plan or plan item (as that term is defined by the Administrator) required under this chapter, with respect to any portion of the State the Administrator determines reasonable and appropriate, for the purpose of ensuring that the requirements of this chapter relating to such plan or plan item are met. The Administrator shall, by rule, establish criteria for exercising his authority under the previous sentence with respect to any deficiency referred to in section 7509(a) of this title to ensure that, during the 24-month period following the finding, disapproval, or determination referred to in section 7509(a) of this title, such sanctions are not applied on a statewide basis where one or more political subdivisions covered by the applicable implementation plan are principally responsible for such deficiency.

(n) Savings clauses
  (1) Existing plan provisions
      Any provision of any applicable implementation plan that was approved or promulgated by the Administrator pursuant to this section as in effect before November 15, 1990, shall remain in effect as part of such applicable implementation plan, except to the extent that a revision to such provision is approved or promulgated by the Administrator pursuant to this chapter.
  (2) Attainment dates
      For any area not designated nonattainment, any plan or plan revision submitted or required to be submitted by a State—
      (A) in response to the promulgation or revision of a national primary ambient air quality standard in effect on November 15, 1990, or
      (B) in response to a finding of substantial inadequacy under subsection (a)(2) of this section (as in effect immediately before November 15, 1990), shall provide for attainment of the national primary ambient air quality standards within 3 years of November 15, 1990, or within 5 years of issuance of such finding of substantial inadequacy, whichever is later.
  (3) Retention of construction moratorium in certain areas
      In the case of an area to which, immediately before November 15, 1990, the prohibition on construction or modification of major stationary sources prescribed in subsection (a)(2)(I) of this section (as in effect immediately before November 15, 1990) applied by virtue of a finding of the Administrator that the State containing such area had not submitted an implementation plan meeting the requirements of section 7502(b)(6) of this title (relating to establishment of a permit program) (as in effect immediately before November 15, 1990) or 7502(a)(1) of this title (to the extent such requirements relate to provision for attainment of the primary national ambient air quality standard for sulfur oxides by December 31, 1982) as in effect immediately before November 15, 1990, no major stationary source of the relevant air pollutant or pollutants shall be constructed or modified in such area until the Administrator finds that the plan for such area meets the applicable requirements of section 7502(c)(5) of this title (relating to permit programs) or subpart 5 of part D of this subchapter (relating to attainment of the primary national ambient air quality standard for sulfur dioxide), respectively.

(o) Indian tribes
    If an Indian tribe submits an implementation plan to the Administrator pursuant to section 7601(d) of this title, the plan shall be reviewed in accordance with the provisions for review set forth in this section for State plans, except as otherwise provided by regulation promulgated pursuant to section 7601(d)(2) of this title. When such plan becomes effective in accordance with the regulations promulgated under section 7601(d) of this title, the plan shall become applicable to all areas (except as expressly provided otherwise in the plan) located within the exterior boundaries of the reservation, notwithstanding the issuance of any patent and including rights-of-way running through the reservation.

(p) Reports
    Any State shall submit, according to such schedule as the Administrator may prescribe, such reports as the Administrator may require relating to emission reductions, vehicle miles trav-

46 / Environmental Statutes

eled, congestion levels, and any other information the Administrator may deem necessary to assess the development effectiveness, need for revision, or implementation of any plan or plan revision required under this chapter.

(July 14, 1955, ch. 360, title I, Sec. 110, as added Pub. L. 91-604, Sec. 4(a), Dec. 31, 1970, 84 Stat. 1680; amended Pub. L. 93-319, Sec. 4, June 22, 1974, 88 Stat. 256; Pub. L. 95-95, title I, Secs. 107, 108, Aug. 7, 1977, 91 Stat. 691, 693; Pub. L. 95-190, Sec. 14(a)(1)-(6), Nov. 16, 1977, 91 Stat. 1399; Pub. L. 97-23, Sec. 3, July 17, 1981, 95 Stat. 142; Pub. L. 101-549, title I, Secs. 101(b)-(d), 102(h), 107(c), 108(d), title IV, Sec. 412, Nov. 15, 1990, 104 Stat. 2404-2408, 2422, 2464, 2466, 2634.)

References in Text

The Energy Supply and Environmental Coordination Act of 1974, referred to in subsec. (a)(3)(B), is Pub. L. 93-319, June 22, 1974, 88 Stat. 246, as amended, which is classified principally to chapter 16C (Sec. 791 et seq.) of Title 15, Commerce and Trade. For complete classification of this Act to the Code, see Short Title note set out under section 791 of Title 15 and Tables.

Section 7413 of this title, referred to in subsecs. (a)(3)(C), (6), (f)(5), (g)(3), and (i), was amended generally by Pub. L. 101-549, title VII, Sec. 701, Nov. 15, 1990, 104 Stat. 2672, and, as so amended, subsecs. (d) and (e) of section 7413 no longer relates to final compliance orders and steel industry compliance extension, respectively.

Section 1857c-10 of this title, as in effect before August 7, 1977, referred to in subsecs. (f)(5) and (g)(3), was in the original "section 119, as in effect before the date of the enactment of this paragraph", meaning section 119 of act July 14, 1955, ch. 360, title I, as added June 22, 1974, Pub. L. 93-319, Sec. 3, 88 Stat. 248, (which was classified to section 1857c-10 of this title) as in effect prior to the enactment of subsecs. (f)(5) and (g)(3) of this section by Pub. L. 95-95, Sec. 107, Aug. 7, 1977, 91 Stat. 691, effective Aug. 7, 1977. Section 112(b)(1) of Pub. L. 95-95 repealed section 119 of act July 14, 1955, ch. 360, title I, as added by Pub. L. 93-319, and provided that all references to such section 119 in any subsequent enactment which supersedes Pub. L. 93-319 shall be construed to refer to section 113(d) of the Clean Air Act and to paragraph (5) thereof in particular which is classified to section 7413(d)(5) of this title. Section 7413 of this title was subsequently amended generally by Pub. L. 101-549, title VII, Sec. 701, Nov. 15, 1990, 104 Stat. 2672, see note above. Section 117(b) of Pub. L. 95-95 added a new section 119 of act July 14, 1955, which is classified to section 7419 of this title.

Codification

Section was formerly classified to section 1857c-5 of this title.

Prior Provisions

A prior section 110 of act July 14, 1955, was renumbered section 117 by Pub. L. 91-604 and is classified to section 7417 of this title.

Amendments

1990—Subsec. (a)(1). Pub. L. 101-549, Sec. 101(d)(8), substituted "3 years (or such shorter period as the Administrator may prescribe)" for "nine months" in two places.

Subsec. (a)(2). Pub. L. 101-549, Sec. 101(b), amended par. (2) generally, substituting present provisions for provisions setting the time within which the Administrator was to approve or disapprove a plan or portion thereof and listing the conditions under which the plan or portion thereof was to be approved after reasonable notice and hearing.

Subsec. (a)(3)(A). Pub. L. 101-549, Sec. 101(d)(1), struck out subpar. (A) which directed Administrator to approve any revision of an implementation plan if it met certain requirements and had been adopted by the State after reasonable notice and public hearings.

Subsec. (a)(3)(D). Pub. L. 101-549, Sec. 101(d)(1), struck out subpar. (D) which directed that certain implementation plans be revised to include comprehensive measures and requirements.

Subsec. (a)(4). Pub. L. 101-549, Sec. 101(d)(2), struck out par. (4) which set forth requirements for review procedure.

Subsec. (c)(1). Pub. L. 101-549, Sec. 102(h), amended par. (1) generally, substituting present provisions for provisions relating to preparation and publication of regulations setting forth an implementation plan, after opportunity for a hearing, upon failure of a State to make required submission or revision.

Subsec. (c)(2)(A). Pub. L. 101-549, Sec. 101(d)(3)(A), struck out subpar. (A) which required a study and report on necessity of parking surcharge, management of parking supply, and preferential bus/carpool lane regulations to achieve and maintain national primary ambient air quality standards.

Subsec. (c)(2)(C). Pub. L. 101-549, Sec. 101(d)(3)(B), struck out subpar. (C) which authorized suspension of certain regulations and requirements relating to management of parking supply.

Subsec. (c)(4). Pub. L. 101-549, Sec. 101(d)(3)(C), struck out par. (4) which permitted Governors to temporarily suspend measures in implementation plans relating to retrofits, gas rationing, and reduction of on-street parking.

Subsec. (c)(5)(B). Pub. L. 101-549, Sec. 101(d)(3)(D), struck out "(including the written evidence required by part D)," after "include comprehensive measures".

Subsec. (d). Pub. L. 101-549, Sec. 101(d)(4), struck out subsec. (d) which defined an applicable implementation plan for purposes of this chapter.

Subsec. (e). Pub. L. 101-549, Sec. 101(d)(5), struck out subsec. (e) which permitted an extension of time for attainment of a national primary ambient air quality standard.

Subsec. (f)(1). Pub. L. 101-549, Sec. 412, inserted "or of any requirement under section 7651j of this title (concerning excess emissions penalties or offsets)" in subpar. (A) and in last sentence.

Subsec. (g)(1). Pub. L. 101-549, Sec. 101(d)(6), substituted "12 months of submission of the proposed plan revision" for "the required four month period" in closing provisions.

Subsec. (h)(1). Pub. L. 101-549, Sec. 101(d)(7), substituted "5 years after November 15, 1990, and every three years thereafter" for "one year after August 7, 1977, and annually thereafter" and struck out at end "Each such document shall be revised as frequently as practicable but not less often than annually."

Subsecs. (k) to (n). Pub. L. 101-549, Sec. 101(c), added subsecs. (k) to (n).

Subsec. (o). Pub. L. 101-549, Sec. 107(c), added subsec. (o).

Subsec. (p). Pub. L. 101-549, Sec. 108(d), added subsec. (p).

1981—Subsec. (a)(3)(C). Pub. L. 97-23 inserted reference to extensions of compliance in decrees entered under section 7413(e) of this title (relating to iron- and steel-producing operations).

1977—Subsec. (a)(2)(A). Pub. L. 95-95, Sec. 108(a)(1), substituted "(A) except as may be provided in subparagraph (I)(i) in the case of a plan" for "(A)(i) in the case of a plan".

Subsec. (a)(2)(B). Pub. L. 95-95, Sec. 108(a)(2), substituted "transportation controls, air quality maintenance plans, and preconstruction review of direct sources of air pollution as provided in subparagraph (D)" for "land use and transportation controls".

Subsec. (a)(2)(D). Pub. L. 95-95, Sec. 108(a)(3), substituted "it includes a program to provide for the enforcement of emission limitations and regulation of the modification, construction, and operation of any stationary source, including a permit program as required in parts C and D and a permit or equivalent program for any major emitting facility, within such region as necessary to assure (i) that national ambient air quality standards are achieved and maintained, and (ii) a procedure" for "it includes a procedure".

Subsec. (a)(2)(E). Pub. L. 95-95, Sec. 108(a)(4), substituted "it contains adequate provisions (i) prohibiting any stationary source within the State from emitting any air pollutant in amounts which will (I) prevent attainment or maintenance by any other State of any such national primary or secondary ambient air quality standard, or (II) interfere with measures required to be included in the applicable implementation plan for any other State under part C to prevent significant deterioration of air quality or to protect visibility, and (ii) insuring compliance with the requirements of section 7426 of this title, relating to interstate pollution abatement" for "it contains adequate provisions for intergovernmental cooperation, including measures necessary to insure that emissions of air pollutants from sources located in any air quality control region will not interfere with the attainment or maintenance of such primary or secondary standard in any portion of such region outside of such State or in any other air quality control region".

Subsec. (a)(2)(F). Pub. L. 95-95, Sec. 108(a)(5), added cl. (vi).

Subsec. (a)(2)(H). Pub. L. 95-190, Sec. 14(a)(1), substituted "1977;" for "1977".

Pub. L. 95-95, Sec. 108(a)(6), inserted "except as provided in paragraph (3)(C)," after "or (ii)" and "or to otherwise comply with any additional requirements established under the Clean Air Act Amendments of 1977" after "to achieve the national ambient air quality primary or secondary standard which it implements".

Subsec. (a)(2)(I). Pub. L. 95-95, Sec. 108(b), added subpar. (I).

Subsec. (a)(2)(J). Pub. L. 95-190, Sec. 14(a)(2), substituted "; and" for ", and".

Pub. L. 95-95, Sec. 108(b), added subpar. (J).
Subsec. (a)(2)(K). Pub. L. 95-95, Sec. 108(b) added subpar. (K).
Subsec. (a)(3)(C). Pub. L. 95-95, Sec. 108(c), added subpar. (C).
Subsec. (a)(3)(D). Pub. L. 95-190, Sec. 14(a)(4), added subpar. (D).
Subsec. (a)(5). Pub. L. 95-95, Sec. 108(3), added par. (5).
Subsec. (a)(5)(D). Pub. L. 95-190, Sec. 14(a)(3), struck out "preconstruction or premodification" before "review".
Subsec. (a)(6). Pub. L. 95-95, Sec. 108(3), added par. (6).
Subsec. (c)(1). Pub. L. 95-95, Sec. 108(d)(1), (2), substituted "plan which meets the requirements of this section" for "plan for any national ambient air quality primary or secondary standard within the time prescribed" in subpar. (A) and, in provisions following subpar. (C), directed that any portion of a plan relating to any measure described in first sentence of 7421 of this title (relating to consultation) or the consultation process required under such section 7421 of this title not be required to be promulgated before the date eight months after such date required for submission.
Subsec. (c)(3) to (5). Pub. L. 95-95, Sec. 108(d)(3), added pars. (3) to (5).
Subsec. (d). Pub. L. 95-95, Sec. 108(f), substituted "and which implements the requirements of this section" for "and which implements a national primary or secondary ambient air quality standard in a State".
Subsec. (f). Pub. L. 95-95, Sec. 107(a), substituted provisions relating to the handling of national or regional energy emergencies for provisions relating to the postponement of compliance by stationary sources or classes of moving sources with any requirement of applicable implementation plans.
Subsec. (g). Pub. L. 95-95, Sec. 108(g), added subsec. (g) relating to publication of comprehensive document.
Pub. L. 95-95, Sec. 107(b), added subsec. (g) relating to Governor's authority to issue temporary emergency suspensions.
Subsec. (h). Pub. L. 95-190, Sec. 14(a)(5), redesignated subsec. (g), added by Pub. L. 95-95, Sec. 108(g), as (h). Former subsec. (h) redesignated (i).
Subsec. (i). Pub. L. 95-190, Sec. 14(a)(5), redesignated subsec. (h), added by Pub. L. 95-95, Sec. 108(g), as (i). Former subsec. (i) redesignated (j) and amended.
Subsec. (j). Pub. L. 95-190 Sec. 14(a)(5), (6), redesignated subsec. (i), added by Pub. L. 95-95, Sec. 108(g), as (j) and in subsec. (j) as so redesignated, substituted "will enable such source" for "at such source will enable it".
1974—Subsec. (a)(3). Pub. L. 93-319, Sec. 4(a), designated existing provisions as subpar. (A) and added subpar. (B).
Subsec. (c). Pub. L. 93-319, Sec. 4(b), designated existing provisions as par. (1) and existing pars. (1), (2), and (3) as subpars. (A), (B), and (C), respectively, of such redesignated par. (1), and added par. (2).

Effective Date of 1977 Amendment

Amendment by Pub. L. 95-95 effective Aug. 7, 1977, except as otherwise expressly provided, see section 406(d) of Pub. L. 95-95, set out as a note under section 7401 of this title.

Pending Actions and Proceedings

Suits, actions, and other proceedings lawfully commenced by or against the Administrator or any other officer or employee of the United States in his official capacity or in relation to the discharge of his official duties under act July 14, 1955, the Clean Air Act, as in effect immediately prior to the enactment of Pub. L. 95-95 [Aug. 7, 1977], not to abate by reason of the taking effect of Pub. L. 95-95, see section 406(a) of Pub. L. 95-95, set out as an Effective Date of 1977 Amendment note under section 7401 of this title.

Modification or Rescission of Rules, Regulations, Orders, Determinations, Contracts, Certifications, Authorizations, Delegations, and Other Actions

All rules, regulations, orders, determinations, contracts, certifications, authorizations, delegations, or other actions duly issued, made, or taken by or pursuant to act July 14, 1955, the Clean Air Act, as in effect immediately prior to the date of enactment of Pub. L. 95-95 [Aug. 7, 1977] to continue in full force and effect until modified or rescinded in accordance with act July 14, 1955, as amended by Pub. L. 95-95 [this chapter], see section 406(b) of Pub. L. 95-95, set out as an Effective Date of 1977 Amendment note under section 7401 of this title.

Modification or Rescission of Implementation Plans Approved and In Effect Prior to Aug. 7, 1977

Nothing in the Clean Air Act Amendments of 1977 [Pub. L. 95-95] to affect any requirement of an approved implementation plan under this section or any other provision in effect under this chapter before Aug. 7, 1977, until modified or rescinded in accordance with this chapter as amended by the Clean Air Act Amendments of 1977, see section 406(c) of Pub. L. 95-95, set out as an Effective Date of 1977 Amendment note under section 7401 of this title.

Savings Provision

Section 16 of Pub. L. 91-604 provided that:
(a) (1) Any implementation plan adopted by any State and submitted to the Secretary of Health, Education, and Welfare, or to the Administrator pursuant to the Clean Air Act [this chapter] prior to enactment of this Act [Dec. 31, 1970] may be approved under section 110 of the Clean Air Act [this section] (as amended by this Act) [Pub. L. 91-604] and shall remain in effect, unless the Administrator determines that such implementation plan, or any portion thereof, is not consistent with applicable requirements of the Clean Air Act [this chapter] (as amended by this Act) and will not provide for the attainment of national primary ambient air quality standards in the time required by such Act. If the Administrator so determines, he shall, within 90 days after promulgation of any national ambient air quality standards pursuant to section 109(a) of the Clean Air Act [section 7409(a) of this title], notify the State and specify in what respects changes are needed to meet the additional requirements of such Act, including requirements to implement national secondary ambient air quality standards. If such changes are not adopted by the State after public hearings and within six months after such notification, the Administrator shall promulgate such changes pursuant to section 110(c) of such Act [subsec. (c) of this section].
(2) The amendments made by section 4(b) [amending sections 7403 and 7415 of this title] shall not be construed as repealing or modifying the powers of the Administrator with respect to any conference convened under section 108(d) of the Clean Air Act [section 7415 of this title] before the date of enactment of this Act [Dec. 31, 1970].
(b) Regulations or standards issued under this title II of the Clean Air Act [subchapter II of this chapter] prior to the enactment of this Act [Dec. 31, 1970] shall continue in effect until revised by the Administrator consistent with the purposes of such Act [this chapter]."

Federal Energy Administrator

"Federal Energy Administrator", for purposes of this chapter, to mean Administrator of Federal Energy Administration established by Pub. L. 93-275, May 7, 1974, 88 Stat. 97, which is classified to section 761 et seq. of Title 15, Commerce and Trade, but with the term to mean any officer of the United States designated as such by the President until Federal Energy Administrator takes office and after Federal Energy Administration ceases to exist, see section 798 of Title 15, Commerce and Trade.

Federal Energy Administration terminated and functions vested by law in Administrator thereof transferred to Secretary of Energy (unless otherwise specifically provided) by sections 7151(a) and 7293 of this title.

Section Referred to in Other Sections

This section is referred to in sections 6211, 6215, 7405, 7407, 7411, 7414, 7415, 7419, 7420, 7425, 7426, 7475, 7476, 7491, 7492, 7502, 7503, 7506, 7506a, 7509, 7511, 7511a, 7511c, 7512, 7545, 7586, 7589, 7590, 7602, 7607, 7619, 7625-1, 7651g, 7651j, 7661f, 8374, 9601 of this title.

STANDARDS OF PERFORMANCE FOR NEW STATIONARY SOURCES

42 USC 7411

(a) Definitions
    For purposes of this section:

(1) The term "standard of performance" means a standard for emissions of air pollutants which reflects the degree of emission limitation achievable through the application of the best system of emission reduction which (taking into account the cost of achieving such reduction and any nonair quality health and environmental impact and energy requirements) the Administrator determines has been adequately demonstrated.

(2) The term "new source" means any stationary source, the construction or modification of which is commenced after the publication of regulations (or, if earlier, proposed regulations) prescribing a standard of performance under this section which will be applicable to such source.

(3) The term "stationary source" means any building, structure, facility, or installation which emits or may emit any air pollutant. Nothing in subchapter II of this chapter relating to nonroad engines shall be construed to apply to stationary internal combustion engines.

(4) The term "modification" means any physical change in, or change in the method of operation of, a stationary source which increases the amount of any air pollutant emitted by such source or which results in the emission of any air pollutant not previously emitted.

(5) The term "owner or operator" means any person who owns, leases, operates, controls, or supervises a stationary source.

(6) The term "existing source" means any stationary source other than a new source.

(7) The term "technological system of continuous emission reduction" means—
   (A) a technological process for production or operation by any source which is inherently low-polluting or nonpolluting, or
   (B) a technological system for continuous reduction of the pollution generated by a source before such pollution is emitted into the ambient air, including precombustion cleaning or treatment of fuels.

(8) A conversion to coal (A) by reason of an order under section 2(a) of the Energy Supply and Environmental Coordination Act of 1974 [15 U.S.C. 792(a)] or any amendment thereto, or any subsequent enactment which supersedes such Act [15 U.S.C. 791 et seq.], or (B) which qualifies under section 7413(d)(5)(A)(ii)[1] of this title, shall not be deemed to be a modification for purposes of paragraphs (2) and (4) of this subsection.

(b) List of categories of stationary sources; standards of performance; information on pollution control techniques; sources owned or operated by United States; particular systems; revised standards

(1) (A) The Administrator shall, within 90 days after December 31, 1970, publish (and from time to time thereafter shall revise) a list of categories of stationary sources. He shall include a category of sources in such list if in his judgment it causes, or contributes significantly to, air pollution which may reasonably be anticipated to endanger public health or welfare.

(B) Within one year after the inclusion of a category of stationary sources in a list under subparagraph (A), the Administrator shall publish proposed regulations, establishing Federal standards of performance for new sources within such category. The Administrator shall afford interested persons an opportunity for written comment on such proposed regulations. After considering such comments, he shall promulgate, within one year after such publication, such standards with such modifications as he deems appropriate. The Administrator shall, at least every 8 years, review and, if appropriate, revise such standards following the procedure required by this subsection for promulgation of such standards. Notwithstanding the requirements of the previous sentence, the Administrator need not review any such standard if the Administrator determines that such review is not appropriate in light of readily available information on the efficacy of such standard. Standards of performance or revisions thereof shall become effective upon promulgation. When implementation and enforcement of any requirement of this chapter indicate that emission limitations and percent reductions beyond those required by the standards promulgated under this section are achieved in practice, the Administrator shall, when revising standards promulgated under this section, consider the emission limitations and percent reductions achieved in practice.

(2) The Administrator may distinguish among classes, types, and sizes within categories of new sources for the purpose of establishing such standards.

---

[1] See References in Text note below.

(3) The Administrator shall, from time to time, issue information on pollution control techniques for categories of new sources and air pollutants subject to the provisions of this section.
(4) The provisions of this section shall apply to any new source owned or operated by the United States.
(5) Except as otherwise authorized under subsection (h) of this section, nothing in this section shall be construed to require, or to authorize the Administrator to require, any new or modified source to install and operate any particular technological system of continuous emission reduction to comply with any new source standard of performance.
(6) The revised standards of performance required by enactment of subsection (a)(1)(A)(i) and (ii)[1] of this section shall be promulgated not later than one year after August 7, 1977. Any new or modified fossil fuel fired stationary source which commences construction prior to the date of publication of the proposed revised standards shall not be required to comply with such revised standards.

(c) State implementation and enforcement of standards of performance
(1) Each State may develop and submit to the Administrator a procedure for implementing and enforcing standards of performance for new sources located in such State. If the Administrator finds the State procedure is adequate, he shall delegate to such State any authority he has under this chapter to implement and enforce such standards.
(2) Nothing in this subsection shall prohibit the Administrator from enforcing any applicable standard of performance under this section.

(d) Standards of performance for existing sources; remaining useful life of source
(1) The Administrator shall prescribe regulations which shall establish a procedure similar to that provided by section 7410 of this title under which each State shall submit to the Administrator a plan which (A) establishes standards of performance for any existing source for any air pollutant (i) for which air quality criteria have not been issued or which is not included on a list published under section 7408(a) of this title or emitted from a source category which is regulated under section 7412 of this title but (ii) to which a standard of performance under this section would apply if such existing source were a new source, and (B) provides for the implementation and enforcement of such standards of performance. Regulations of the Administrator under this paragraph shall permit the State in applying a standard of performance to any particular source under a plan submitted under this paragraph to take into consideration, among other factors, the remaining useful life of the existing source to which such standard applies.
(2) The Administrator shall have the same authority—
(A) to prescribe a plan for a State in cases where the State fails to submit a satisfactory plan as he would have under section 7410(c) of this title in the case of failure to submit an implementation plan, and
(B) to enforce the provisions of such plan in cases where the State fails to enforce them as he would have under sections 7413 and 7414 of this title with respect to an implementation plan. In promulgating a standard of performance under a plan prescribed under this paragraph, the Administrator shall take into consideration, among other factors, remaining useful lives of the sources in the category of sources to which such standard applies.

(e) Prohibited acts
After the effective date of standards of performance promulgated under this section, it shall be unlawful for any owner or operator of any new source to operate such source in violation of any standard of performance applicable to such source.

(f) New source standards of performance
(1) For those categories of major stationary sources that the Administrator listed under subsection (b)(1)(A) of this section before November 15, 1990, and for which regulations had not been proposed by the Administrator by November 15, 1990, the Administrator shall—
(A) propose regulations establishing standards of performance for at least 25 percent of such categories of sources within 2 years after November 15, 1990;
(B) propose regulations establishing standards of performance for at least 50 percent of such categories of sources within 4 years after November 15, 1990; and

---
[1] See References in Text note below.

(C) propose regulations for the remaining categories of sources within 6 years after November 15, 1990.
(2) In determining priorities for promulgating standards for categories of major stationary sources for the purpose of paragraph (1), the Administrator shall consider—
   (A) the quantity of air pollutant emissions which each such category will emit, or will be designed to emit;
   (B) the extent to which each such pollutant may reasonably be anticipated to endanger public health or welfare; and
   (C) the mobility and competitive nature of each such category of sources and the consequent need for nationally applicable new source standards of performance.
(3) Before promulgating any regulations under this subsection or listing any category of major stationary sources as required under this subsection, the Administrator shall consult with appropriate representatives of the Governors and of State air pollution control agencies.

(g) Revision of regulations
   (1) Upon application by the Governor of a State showing that the Administrator has failed to specify in regulations under subsection (f)(1) of this section any category of major stationary sources required to be specified under such regulations, the Administrator shall revise such regulations to specify any such category.
   (2) Upon application of the Governor of a State, showing that any category of stationary sources which is not included in the list under subsection (b)(1)(A) of this section contributes significantly to air pollution which may reasonably be anticipated to endanger public health or welfare (notwithstanding that such category is not a category of major stationary sources), the Administrator shall revise such regulations to specify such category of stationary sources.
   (3) Upon application of the Governor of a State showing that the Administrator has failed to apply properly the criteria required to be considered under subsection (f)(2) of this section, the Administrator shall revise the list under subsection (b)(1)(A) of this section to apply properly such criteria.
   (4) Upon application of the Governor of a State showing that—
      (A) a new, innovative, or improved technology or process which achieves greater continuous emission reduction has been adequately demonstrated for any category of stationary sources, and
      (B) as a result of such technology or process, the new source standard of performance in effect under this section for such category no longer reflects the greatest degree of emission limitation achievable through application of the best technological system of continuous emission reduction which (taking into consideration the cost of achieving such emission reduction, and any non-air quality health and environmental impact and energy requirements) has been adequately demonstrated,
   the Administrator shall revise such standard of performance for such category accordingly.
   (5) Unless later deadlines for action of the Administrator are otherwise prescribed under this section, the Administrator shall, not later than three months following the date of receipt of any application by a Governor of a State, either—
      (A) find that such application does not contain the requisite showing and deny such application, or
      (B) grant such application and take the action required under this subsection.
   (6) Before taking any action required by subsection (f) of this section or by this subsection, the Administrator shall provide notice and opportunity for public hearing.

(h) Design, equipment, work practice, or operational standard; alternative emission limitation
   (1) For purposes of this section, if in the judgment of the Administrator, it is not feasible to prescribe or enforce a standard of performance, he may instead promulgate a design, equipment, work practice, or operational standard, or combination thereof, which reflects the best technological system of continuous emission reduction which (taking into consideration the cost of achieving such emission reduction, and any non-air quality health and environmental impact and energy requirements) the Administrator determines has been adequately demonstrated. In the event the Administrator promulgates a design or equipment standard under this subsection, he shall include as part of such standard such requirements as will assure the proper operation and maintenance of any such element of design or equipment.

(2) For the purpose of this subsection, the phrase "not feasible to prescribe or enforce a standard of performance" means any situation in which the Administrator determines that (A) a pollutant or pollutants cannot be emitted through a conveyance designed and constructed to emit or capture such pollutant, or that any requirement for, or use of, such a conveyance would be inconsistent with any Federal, State, or local law, or (B) the application of measurement methodology to a particular class of sources is not practicable due to technological or economic limitations.

(3) If after notice and opportunity for public hearing, any person establishes to the satisfaction of the Administrator that an alternative means of emission limitation will achieve a reduction in emissions of any air pollutant at least equivalent to the reduction in emissions of such air pollutant achieved under the requirements of paragraph (1), the Administrator shall permit the use of such alternative by the source for purposes of compliance with this section with respect to such pollutant.

(4) Any standard promulgated under paragraph (1) shall be promulgated in terms of standard of performance whenever it becomes feasible to promulgate and enforce such standard in such terms.

(5) Any design, equipment, work practice, or operational standard, or any combination thereof, described in this subsection shall be treated as a standard of performance for purposes of the provisions of this chapter (other than the provisions of subsection (a) of this section and this subsection).

(i) Country elevators

Any regulations promulgated by the Administrator under this section applicable to grain elevators shall not apply to country elevators (as defined by the Administrator) which have a storage capacity of less than two million five hundred thousand bushels.

(j) Innovative technological systems of continuous emission reduction

(1) (A) Any person proposing to own or operate a new source may request the Administrator for one or more waivers from the requirements of this section for such source or any portion thereof with respect to any air pollutant to encourage the use of an innovative technological system or systems of continuous emission reduction. The Administrator may, with the consent of the Governor of the State in which the source is to be located, grant a waiver under this paragraph, if the Administrator determines after notice and opportunity for public hearing, that—

   (i) the proposed system or systems have not been adequately demonstrated,

   (ii) the proposed system or systems will operate effectively and there is a substantial likelihood that such system or systems will achieve greater continuous emission reduction than that required to be achieved under the standards of performance which would otherwise apply, or achieve at least an equivalent reduction at lower cost in terms of energy, economic, or nonair quality environmental impact,

   (iii) the owner or operator of the proposed source has demonstrated to the satisfaction of the Administrator that the proposed system will not cause or contribute to an unreasonable risk to public health, welfare, or safety in its operation, function, or malfunction, and

   (iv) the granting of such waiver is consistent with the requirements of subparagraph (C). In making any determination under clause (ii), the Administrator shall take into account any previous failure of such system or systems to operate effectively or to meet any requirement of the new source performance standards. In determining whether an unreasonable risk exists under clause (iii), the Administrator shall consider, among other factors, whether and to what extent the use of the proposed technological system will cause, increase, reduce, or eliminate emissions of any unregulated pollutants; available methods for reducing or eliminating any risk to public health, welfare, or safety which may be associated with the use of such system; and the availability of other technological systems which may be used to conform to standards under this section without causing or contributing to such unreasonable risk. The Administrator may conduct such tests and may require the owner or operator of the proposed source to conduct such tests and provide such information as is necessary to carry out clause (iii) of this subparagraph. Such requirements shall include a requirement for prompt reporting of the emission of any unregulated pollutant from a system if such pollutant was not emitted, or was emitted in significantly lesser amounts without use of such system.

(B) A waiver under this paragraph shall be granted on such terms and conditions as the Administrator determines to be necessary to assure—
  (i) emissions from the source will not prevent attainment and maintenance of any national ambient air quality standards, and
  (ii) proper functioning of the technological system or systems authorized.

Any such term or condition shall be treated as a standard of performance for the purposes of subsection (e) of this section and section 7413 of this title.

(C) The number of waivers granted under this paragraph with respect to a proposed technological system of continuous emission reduction shall not exceed such number as the Administrator finds necessary to ascertain whether or not such system will achieve the conditions specified in clauses (ii) and (iii) of subparagraph (A).

(D) A waiver under this paragraph shall extend to the sooner of—
  (i) the date determined by the Administrator, after consultation with the owner or operator of the source, taking into consideration the design, installation, and capital cost of the technological system or systems being used, or
  (ii) the date on which the Administrator determines that such system has failed to—
    (I) achieve at least an equivalent continuous emission reduction to that required to be achieved under the standards of performance which would otherwise apply, or
    (II) comply with the condition specified in paragraph (1)(A)(iii),
  and that such failure cannot be corrected.

(E) In carrying out subparagraph (D)(i), the Administrator shall not permit any waiver for a source or portion thereof to extend beyond the date—
  (i) seven years after the date on which any waiver is granted to such source or portion thereof, or
  (ii) four years after the date on which such source or portion thereof commences operation,
  whichever is earlier.

(F) No waiver under this subsection shall apply to any portion of a source other than the portion on which the innovative technological system or systems of continuous emission reduction is used.

(2) (A) If a waiver under paragraph (1) is terminated under clause (ii) of paragraph (1)(D), the Administrator shall grant an extension of the requirements of this section for such source for such minimum period as may be necessary to comply with the applicable standard of performance under this section. Such period shall not extend beyond the date three years from the time such waiver is terminated.

(B) An extension granted under this paragraph shall set forth emission limits and a compliance schedule containing increments of progress which require compliance with the applicable standards of performance as expeditiously as practicable and include such measures as are necessary and practicable in the interim to minimize emissions. Such schedule shall be treated as a standard of performance for purposes of subsection (e) of this section and section 7413 of this title.

(July 14, 1955, ch. 360, title I, Sec. 111, as added Pub. L. 91-604, Sec. 4(a), Dec. 31, 1970, 84 Stat. 1683; amended Pub. L. 92-157, title III, Sec. 302(f), Nov. 18, 1971, 85 Stat. 464; Pub. L. 95-95, title I, Sec. 109(a)-(d)(1), (e), (f), title IV, Sec. 401(b), Aug. 7, 1977, 91 Stat. 697-703, 791; Pub. L. 95-190, Sec. 14(a)(7)-(9), Nov. 16, 1977, 91 Stat. 1399; Pub. L. 95-623, Sec. 13(a), Nov. 9, 1978, 92 Stat. 3457; Pub. L. 101-549, title I, Sec. 108(e)-(g), title III, Sec. 302(a), (b), title IV, Sec. 403(a), Nov. 15, 1990, 104 Stat. 2467, 2574, 2631.)

References in Text

Such Act, referred to in subsec. (a)(8), means Pub. L. 93-319, June 22, 1974, 88 Stat. 246, as amended, known as the Energy Supply and Environmental Coordination Act of 1974, which is classified principally to chapter 16C (Sec. 791 et seq.) of Title 15, Commerce and Trade. For complete classification of this Act to the Code, see Short Title note set out under section 791 of Title 15 and Tables.

Section 7413 of this title, referred to in subsec. (a)(8), was amended generally by Pub. L. 101-549, title VII, Sec. 701, Nov. 15, 1990, 104 Stat. 2672, and, as so amended, subsec. (d) of section 7413 no longer relates to final compliance orders.

Subsection (a)(1) of this section, referred to in subsec. (b)(6), was amended generally by Pub. L. 101-549, title VII, Sec. 403(a), Nov. 15, 1990, 104 Stat. 2631, and, as so amended, no longer contains subpars.

Codification

Section was formerly classified to section 1857c-6 of this title.

Prior Provisions

A prior section 111 of act July 14, 1955, was renumbered section 118 by Pub. L. 91-604 and is classified to section 7418 of this title.

Amendments

1990—Subsec. (a)(1). Pub. L. 101-549, Sec. 403(a), amended par. (1) generally, substituting provisions defining "standard of performance" with respect to any air pollutant for provisions defining such term with respect to subsec. (b) fossil fuel fired and other stationary sources and subsec. (d) particular sources.

Subsec. (a)(3). Pub. L. 101-549, Sec. 108(f), inserted at end "Nothing in subchapter II of this chapter relating to nonroad engines shall be construed to apply to stationary internal combustion engines."

Subsec. (b)(1)(B). Pub. L. 101-549, Sec. 108(e)(1), substituted "Within one year" for "Within 120 days", "within one year" for "within 90 days", and "every 8 years" for "every four years", inserted before last sentence "Notwithstanding the requirements of the previous sentence, the Administrator need not review any such standard if the Administrator determines that such review is not appropriate in light of readily available information on the efficacy of such standard.", and inserted at end "When implementation and enforcement of any requirement of this chapter indicate that emission limitations and percent reductions beyond those required by the standards promulgated under this section are achieved in practice, the Administrator shall, when revising standards promulgated under this section, consider the emission limitations and percent reductions achieved in practice."

Subsec. (d)(1)(A)(i). Pub. L. 101-549, Sec. 302(a), which directed the substitution of "7412(b)" for "7412(b)(1)(A)", could not be executed, because of the prior amendment by Pub. L. 101-549, Sec. 108(g), see below.

Pub. L. 101-549, Sec. 108(g), substituted "or emitted from a source category which is regulated under section 7412 of this title" for "or 7412(b)(1)(A)".

Subsec. (f)(1). Pub. L. 101-549, Sec. 108(e)(2), amended par. (1) generally, substituting present provisions for provisions requiring the Administrator to promulgate regulations listing the categories of major stationary sources not on the required list by Aug. 7, 1977, and regulations establishing standards of performance for such categories.

Subsec. (g)(5) to (8). Pub. L. 101-549, Sec. 302(b), redesignated par. (7) as (5) and struck out "or section 7412 of this title" after "this section", redesignated par. (8) as (6), and struck out former pars. (5) and (6) which read as follows:

"(5) Upon application by the Governor of a State showing that the Administrator has failed to list any air pollutant which causes, or contributes to, air pollution which may reasonably be anticipated to result in an increase in mortality or an increase in serious irreversible, or incapacitating reversible, illness as a hazardous air pollutant under section 7412 of this title the Administrator shall revise the list of hazardous air pollutants under such section to include such pollutant.

(6) Upon application by the Governor of a State showing that any category of stationary sources of a hazardous air pollutant listed under section 7412 of this title is not subject to emission standards under such section, the Administrator shall propose and promulgate such emission standards applicable to such category of sources."

1978—Subsecs. (d)(1)(A)(ii), (g)(4)(B). Pub. L. 95-623, Sec. 13(a)(2), substituted "under this section" for "under subsection (b) of this section".

Subsec. (h)(5). Pub. L. 95-623, Sec. 13(a)(1), added par. (5).

Subsec. (j). Pub. L. 95-623, Sec. 13(a)(3), substituted in pars. (1)(A) and (2)(A) "standards under this section" and "under this section" for "standards under subsection (b) of this section" and "under subsection (b) of this section", respectively.

1977—Subsec. (a)(1). Pub. L. 95-95, Sec. 109(c)(1)(A), added subpars. (A), (B), and (C), substituted "For the purpose of subparagraphs (A)(i) and (ii) and (B), a standard of performance shall reflect" for "a standard for emissions of air pollutants which reflects", "and the percentage reduction achievable" for "achievable", and "technological system of continuous emission reduction which (taking into consideration the cost of achieving such emission reduction, and any nonair quality health and environment impact and energy requirements)" for "system of emission reduction which (taking into account the cost of achieving such reduction)" in existing provisions, and inserted provision that, for the purpose of subparagraph (1)(A)(ii), any cleaning of the fuel or reduction in the pollution characteristics of the fuel after extraction and prior to combustion may be credited, as determined under regulations promulgated by the Administrator, to a source which burns such fuel.

Subsec. (a)(7). Pub. L. 95-95, Sec. 109(c)(1)(B), added par. (7) defining "technological system of continuous emission reduction".

Pub. L. 95-95, Sec. 109(f), added par. (7) directing that under certain circumstances a conversion to coal not be deemed a modification for purposes of pars. (2) and (4).

Subsec. (a)(7), (8). Pub. L. 95-190, Sec. 14(a)(7), redesignated second par. (7) as (8).

Subsec. (b)(1)(A). Pub. L. 95-95, Sec. 401(b), substituted "such list if in his judgment it causes, or contributes significantly to, air pollution which may reasonably be anticipated to endanger" for "such list if he determines it may contribute significantly to air pollution which causes or contributes to the endangerment of".

Subsec. (b)(1)(B). Pub. L. 95-95, Sec. 109(c)(2), substituted "shall, at least every four years, review and, if appropriate," for "may, from time to time,".

Subsec. (b)(5), (6). Pub. L. 95-95, Sec. 109(c)(3), added pars. (5) and (6).

Subsec. (c)(1). Pub. L. 95-95, Sec. 109(d)(1), struck out "(except with respect to new sources owned or operated by the United States)" after "implement and enforce such standards".

Subsec. (d)(1). Pub. L. 95-95, Sec. 109(b)(1), substituted "standards of performance" for "emission standards" and inserted provisions directing that regulations of the Administrator permit the State, in applying a standard of performance to any particular source under a submitted plan, to take into consideration, among other factors, the remaining useful life of the existing source to which the standard applies.

Subsec. (d)(2). Pub. L. 95-95, Sec. 109(b)(2), provided that, in promulgating a standard of performance under a plan, the Administrator take into consideration, among other factors, the remaining useful lives of the sources in the category of sources to which the standard applies.

Subsecs. (f) to (i). Pub. L. 95-95, Sec. 109(a), added subsecs. (f) to (i).

Subsecs. (j), (k). Pub. L. 95-190, Sec. 14(a)(8), (9), redesignated subsec. (k) as (j) and, as so redesignated, substituted "(B)" for "(8)" as designation for second subpar. in par. (2). Former subsec. (j), added by Pub. L. 95-95, Sec. 109(e), which related to compliance with applicable standards of performance, was struck out.

Pub. L. 95-95, Sec. 109(e), added subsec. (k).

1971—Subsec. (b)(1)(B). Pub. L. 92-157 substituted in first sentence "publish proposed" for "propose".

Effective Date of 1977 Amendment

Amendment by Pub. L. 95-95 effective Aug. 7, 1977, except as otherwise expressly provided, see section 406(d) of Pub. L. 95-95, set out as a note under section 7401 of this title.

Regulations

Section 403(b), (c) of Pub. L. 101-549 provided that:

"(b) Revised Regulations.—Not later than three years after the date of enactment of the Clean Air Act Amendments of 1990 [Nov. 15, 1990], the Administrator shall promulgate revised regulations for standards of performance for new fossil fuel fired electric utility units commencing construction after the date on which such regulations are proposed that, at a minimum, require any source subject to such revised standards to emit sulfur dioxide at a rate not greater than would have resulted from compliance by such source with the applicable standards of performance under this section [amending sections 7411 and 7479 of this title] prior to such revision.

(c) Applicability.—The provisions of subsections (a) [amending this section] and (b) apply only so long as the provisions of section 403(e) of the Clean Air Act [42 U.S.C. 7651b(e)] remain in effect."

Transfer of Functions

Enforcement functions of Administrator or other official in Environmental Protection Agency related to compliance with new source performance standards under this section with respect to pre-construction, construction, and initial operation of transportation system for Canadian and Alaskan natural gas transferred to Federal Inspector, Office of Federal Inspector for the Alaska Natural Gas Transportation System, until first anniversary of date of initial operation of Alaska Natural Gas Transportation System, see Reorg. Plan No. 1 of 1979, eff. July 1, 1979, Secs. 102(a), 203(a), 44 F.R. 33663, 33666, 93 Stat. 1373, 1376, set out in the Appendix to Title 5, Government Organization and Employees. Office of Federal Inspector for the Alaska Natural Gas Transportation System abolished and functions and authority vested in Inspector transferred to Secretary of Energy by section 3012(b) of Pub. L. 102-486, set out as an Abolition of Office of Federal Inspector note under section 719e of Title 15, Commerce and Trade.

Pending Actions and Proceedings

Suits, actions, and other proceedings lawfully commenced by or against the Administrator or any other officer or employee of the United States in his official capacity or in relation to the discharge of his official duties under act July 14, 1955, the Clean Air Act, as in effect immediately prior to the enactment of Pub. L. 95-95 [Aug. 7, 1977], not to abate by reason of the taking effect of Pub. L. 95-95, see section 406(a) of Pub. L. 95-95, set out as an Effective Date of 1977 Amendment note under section 7401 of this title.

Modification or Rescission of Rules, Regulations, Orders, Determinations, Contracts, Certifications, Authorizations, Delegations, and Other Actions

All rules, regulations, orders, determinations, contracts, certifications, authorizations, delegations, or other actions duly issued, made, or taken by or pursuant to act July 14, 1955, the Clean Air Act, as in effect immediately prior to the date of enactment of Pub. L. 95-95 [Aug. 7, 1977] to continue in full force and effect until modified or rescinded in accordance with act July 14, 1955, as amended by Pub. L. 95-95 [this chapter], see section 406(b) of Pub. L. 95-95, set out as an Effective Date of 1977 Amendment note under section 7401 of this title.

Section Referred to in Other Sections

This section is referred to in sections 7412, 7413, 7414, 7416, 7417, 7418, 7420, 7422, 7425, 7429, 7475, 7479, 7501, 7511a, 7511b, 7550, 7604, 7607, 7608, 7616, 7617, 7625-1, 7627, 7651a, 7651d, 7651f, 7651h, 7651n, 7661a, 9601 of this title.

HAZARDOUS AIR POLLUTANTS

42 USC 7412

(a) Definitions
   For purposes of this section, except subsection (r) of this section—
   (1) Major source
      The term "major source" means any stationary source or group of stationary sources located within a contiguous area and under common control that emits or has the potential to emit considering controls, in the aggregate, 10 tons per year or more of any hazardous air pollutant or 25 tons per year or more of any combination of hazardous air pollutants. The Administrator may establish a lesser quantity, or in the case of radionuclides different criteria, for a major source than that specified in the previous sentence, on the basis of the potency of the air pollutant, persistence, potential for bioaccumulation, other characteristics of the air pollutant, or other relevant factors.

(2) Area source
The term "area source" means any stationary source of hazardous air pollutants that is not a major source. For purposes of this section, the term "area source" shall not include motor vehicles or nonroad vehicles subject to regulation under subchapter II of this chapter.
(3) Stationary source
The term "stationary source" shall have the same meaning as such term has under section 7411(a) of this title.
(4) New source
The term "new source" means a stationary source the construction or reconstruction of which is commenced after the Administrator first proposes regulations under this section establishing an emission standard applicable to such source.
(5) Modification
The term "modification" means any physical change in, or change in the method of operation of, a major source which increases the actual emissions of any hazardous air pollutant emitted by such source by more than a de minimis amount or which results in the emission of any hazardous air pollutant not previously emitted by more than a de minimis amount.
(6) Hazardous air pollutant
The term "hazardous air pollutant" means any air pollutant listed pursuant to subsection (b) of this section.
(7) Adverse environmental effect
The term "adverse environmental effect" means any significant and widespread adverse effect, which may reasonably be anticipated, to wildlife, aquatic life, or other natural resources, including adverse impacts on populations of endangered or threatened species or significant degradation of environmental quality over broad areas.
(8) Electric utility steam generating unit
The term "electric utility steam generating unit" means any fossil fuel fired combustion unit of more than 25 megawatts that serves a generator that produces electricity for sale. A unit that cogenerates steam and electricity and supplies more than one-third of its potential electric output capacity and more than 25 megawatts electrical output to any utility power distribution system for sale shall be considered an electric utility steam generating unit.
(9) Owner or operator
The term "owner or operator" means any person who owns, leases, operates, controls, or supervises a stationary source.
(10) Existing source
The term "existing source" means any stationary source other than a new source.
(11) Carcinogenic effect
Unless revised, the term "carcinogenic effect" shall have the meaning provided by the Administrator under Guidelines for Carcinogenic Risk Assessment as of the date of enactment.[1] Any revisions in the existing Guidelines shall be subject to notice and opportunity for comment.

(b) List of pollutants
(1) Initial list
The Congress establishes for purposes of this section a list of hazardous air pollutants as follows:

CAS number	Chemical name
75070	Acetaldehyde
60355	Acetamide
75058	Acetonitrile
98862	Acetophenone
53963	2-Acetylaminofluorene
107028	Acrolein
79061	Acrylamide

[1] See References in Text note below.

CAS number	Chemical name
79107	Acrylic acid
107131	Acrylonitrile
107051	Allyl chloride
92671	4-Aminobiphenyl
62533	Aniline
90040	o-Anisidine
1332214	Asbestos
71432	Benzene (including benzene from gasoline)
92875	Benzidine
98077	Benzotrichloride
100447	Benzyl chloride
92524	Biphenyl
117817	Bis(2-ethylhexyl)phthalate (DEHP)
542881	Bis(chloromethyl)ether
75252	Bromoform
106990	1,3-Butadiene
156627	Calcium cyanamide
105602	Caprolactam
133062	Captan
63252	Carbaryl
75150	Carbon disulfide
56235	Carbon tetrachloride
463581	Carbonyl sulfide
120809	Catechol
133904	Chloramben
57749	Chlordane
7782505	Chlorine
79118	Chloroacetic acid
532274	2-Chloroacetophenone
108907	Chlorobenzene
510156	Chlorobenzilate
67663	Chloroform
107302	Chloromethyl methyl ether
126998	Chloroprene
1319773	Cresols/Cresylic acid (isomers and mixture)
95487	o-Cresol
108394	m-Cresol
106445	p-Cresol
98828	Cumene
94757	2,4-D, salts and esters
3547044	DDE
334883	Diazomethane
132649	Dibenzofurans
96128	1,2-Dibromo-3-chloropropane
84742	Dibutylphthalate
106467	1,4-Dichlorobenzene(p)
91941	3,3-Dichlorobenzidene
111444	Dichloroethyl ether (Bis(2-chloroethyl)ether)
542756	1,3-Dichloropropene
62737	Dichlorvos
111422	Diethanolamine
121697	N,N-Diethyl aniline (N,N-Dimethylaniline)
64675	Diethyl sulfate
119904	3,3-Dimethoxybenzidine
60117	Dimethyl aminoazobenzene
119937	3,3'-Dimethyl benzidine

CAS number	Chemical name
79447	Dimethyl carbamoyl chloride
68122	Dimethyl formamide
57147	1,1-Dimethyl hydrazine
131113	Dimethyl phthalate
77781	Dimethyl sulfate
534521	4,6-Dinitro-o-cresol, and salts
51285	2,4-Dinitrophenol
121142	2,4-Dinitrotoluene
123911	1,4-Dioxane (1,4-Diethyleneoxide)
122667	1,2-Diphenylhydrazine
106898	Epichlorohydrin (l-Chloro-2,3-epoxypropane)
106887	1,2-Epoxybutane
140885	Ethyl acrylate
100414	Ethyl benzene
51796	Ethyl carbamate (Urethane)
75003	Ethyl chloride (Chloroethane)
106934	Ethylene dibromide (Dibromoethane)
107062	Ethylene dichloride (1,2-Dichloroethane)
107211	Ethylene glycol
151564	Ethylene imine (Aziridine)
75218	Ethylene oxide
96457	Ethylene thiourea
75343	Ethylidene dichloride (1,1-Dichloroethane)
50000	Formaldehyde
76448	Heptachlor
118741	Hexachlorobenzene
87683	Hexachlorobutadiene
77474	Hexachlorocyclopentadiene
67721	Hexachloroethane
822060	Hexamethylene-1,6-diisocyanate
680319	Hexamethylphosphoramide
110543	Hexane
302012	Hydrazine
7647010	Hydrochloric acid
7664393	Hydrogen fluoride (Hydrofluoric acid)
123319	Hydroquinone
78591	Isophorone
58899	Lindane (all isomers)
108316	Maleic anhydride
67561	Methanol
72435	Methoxychlor
74839	Methyl bromide (Bromomethane)
74873	Methyl chloride (Chloromethane)
71556	Methyl chloroform (1,1,1-Trichloroethane)
78933	Methyl ethyl ketone (2-Butanone)
60344	Methyl hydrazine
74884	Methyl iodide (Iodomethane)
108101	Methyl isobutyl ketone (Hexone)
624839	Methyl isocyanate
80626	Methyl methacrylate
1634044	Methyl tert butyl ether
101144	4,4-Methylene bis(2-chloroaniline)
75092	Methylene chloride (Dichloromethane)
101688	Methylene diphenyl diisocyanate (MDI)
101779	4,4'-Methylenedianiline
91203	Naphthalene

CAS number	Chemical name
98953	Nitrobenzene
92933	4-Nitrobiphenyl
100027	4-Nitrophenol
79469	2-Nitropropane
684935	N-Nitroso-N-methylurea
62759	N-Nitrosodimethylamine
59892	N-Nitrosomorpholine
56382	Parathion
82688	Pentachloronitrobenzene (Quintobenzene)
87865	Pentachlorophenol
108952	Phenol
106503	p-Phenylenediamine
75445	Phosgene
7803512	Phosphine
7723140	Phosphorus
85449	Phthalic anhydride
1336363	Polychlorinated biphenyls (Aroclors)
1120714	1,3-Propane sultone
57578	beta-Propiolactone
123386	Propionaldehyde
114261	Propoxur (Baygon)
78875	Propylene dichloride (1,2-Dichloropropane)
75569	Propylene oxide
75558	1,2-Propylenimine (2-Methyl aziridine)
91225	Quinoline
106514	Quinone
100425	Styrene
96093	Styrene oxide
1746016	2,3,7,8-Tetrachlorodibenzo-p-dioxin
79345	1,1,2,2-Tetrachloroethane
127184	Tetrachloroethylene (Perchloroethylene)
7550450	Titanium tetrachloride
108883	Toluene
95807	2,4-Toluene diamine
584849	2,4-Toluene diisocyanate
95534	o-Toluidine
8001352	Toxaphene (chlorinated camphene)
120821	1,2,4-Trichlorobenzene
79005	1,1,2-Trichloroethane
79016	Trichloroethylene
95954	2,4,5-Trichlorophenol
88062	2,4,6-Trichlorophenol
121448	Triethylamine
1582098	Trifluralin
540841	2,2,4-Trimethylpentane
108054	Vinyl acetate
593602	Vinyl bromide
75014	Vinyl chloride
75354	Vinylidene chloride (1,1-Dichloroethylene)
1330207	Xylenes (isomers and mixture)
95476	o-Xylenes
108383	m-Xylenes
106423	p-Xylenes
0	Antimony Compounds
0	Arsenic Compounds (inorganic including arsine)
0	Beryllium Compounds

CAS number	Chemical name
0	Cadmium Compounds
0	Chromium Compounds
0	Cobalt Compounds
0	Coke Oven Emissions
0	Cyanide Compounds[1]
0	Glycol ethers[2]
0	Lead Compounds
0	Manganese Compounds
0	Mercury Compounds
0	Fine mineral fibers[3]
0	Nickel Compounds
0	Polycylic Organic Matter[4]
0	Radionuclides (including radon)[5]
0	Selenium Compounds

NOTE: For all listings above which contain the word "compounds" and for glycol ethers, the following applies: Unless otherwise specified, these listings are defined as including any unique chemical substance that contains the named chemical (i.e., antimony, arsenic, etc.) as part of that chemical's infrastructure.

(2) Revision of the list

The Administrator shall periodically review the list established by this subsection and publish the results thereof and, where appropriate, revise such list by rule, adding pollutants which present, or may present, through inhalation or other routes of exposure, a threat of adverse human health effects (including, but not limited to, substances which are known to be, or may reasonably be anticipated to be, carcinogenic, mutagenic, teratogenic, neurotoxic, which cause reproductive dysfunction, or which are acutely or chronically toxic) or adverse environmental effects whether through ambient concentrations, bioaccumulation, deposition, or otherwise, but not including releases subject to regulation under subsection (r) of this section as a result of emissions to the air. No air pollutant which is listed under section 7408(a) of this title may be added to the list under this section, except that the prohibition of this sentence shall not apply to any pollutant which independently meets the listing criteria of this paragraph and is a precursor to a pollutant which is listed under section 7408(a) of this title or to any pollutant which is in a class of pollutants listed under such section. No substance, practice, process or activity regulated under subchapter VI of this chapter shall be subject to regulation under this section solely due to its adverse effects on the environment.

(3) Petitions to modify the list

(A) Beginning at any time after 6 months after November 15, 1990, any person may petition the Administrator to modify the list of hazardous air pollutants under this subsection by adding or deleting a substance or, in case of listed pollutants without CAS numbers (other than coke oven emissions, mineral fibers, or polycyclic organic matter) removing certain unique substances. Within 18 months after receipt of a petition, the Administrator shall either grant or deny the petition by publishing a written ex-

---

[1]X'CN where X = H' or any other group where a formal dissociation may occur. For example KCN or Ca(CN)$_2$.

[2]Includes mono- and di- ethers of ethylene glycol, diethylene glycol, and triethylene glycol R-(OCH2CH2)$_n$-OR' where

n = 1, 2, or 3

R = alkyl or aryl groups

R' = R, H, or groups which, when removed, yield glycol ethers with the structure: R-(OCH2CH)$_n$-OH. Polymers are excluded from the glycol category.

[3]Includes mineral fiber emissions from facilities manufacturing or processing glass, rock, or slag fibers (or other mineral derived fibers) of average diameter 1 micrometer or less.

[4]Includes organic compounds with more than one benzene ring, and which have a boiling point greater than or equal to 100C.

[5]A type of atom which spontaneously undergoes radioactive decay.

planation of the reasons for the Administrator's decision. Any such petition shall include a showing by the petitioner that there is adequate data on the health or environmental defects[6] of the pollutant or other evidence adequate to support the petition. The Administrator may not deny a petition solely on the basis of inadequate resources or time for review.

(B) The Administrator shall add a substance to the list upon a showing by the petitioner or on the Administrator's own determination that the substance is an air pollutant and that emissions, ambient concentrations, bioaccumulation or deposition of the substance are known to cause or may reasonably be anticipated to cause adverse effects to human health or adverse environmental effects.

(C) The Administrator shall delete a substance from the list upon a showing by the petitioner or on the Administrator's own determination that there is adequate data on the health and environmental effects of the substance to determine that emissions, ambient concentrations, bioaccumulation or deposition of the substance may not reasonably be anticipated to cause any adverse effects to the human health or adverse environmental effects.

(D) The Administrator shall delete one or more unique chemical substances that contain a listed hazardous air pollutant not having a CAS number (other than coke oven emissions, mineral fibers, or polycyclic organic matter) upon a showing by the petitioner or on the Administrator's own determination that such unique chemical substances that contain the named chemical of such listed hazardous air pollutant meet the deletion requirements of subparagraph (C). The Administrator must grant or deny a deletion petition prior to promulgating any emission standards pursuant to subsection (d) of this section applicable to any source category or subcategory of a listed hazardous air pollutant without a CAS number listed under subsection (b) of this section for which a deletion petition has been filed within 12 months of November 15, 1990.

(4) Further information

If the Administrator determines that information on the health or environmental effects of a substance is not sufficient to make a determination required by this subsection, the Administrator may use any authority available to the Administrator to acquire such information.

(5) Test methods

The Administrator may establish, by rule, test measures and other analytic procedures for monitoring and measuring emissions, ambient concentrations, deposition, and bioaccumulation of hazardous air pollutants.

(6) Prevention of significant deterioration

The provisions of part C of this subchapter (prevention of significant deterioration) shall not apply to pollutants listed under this section.

(7) Lead

The Administrator may not list elemental lead as a hazardous air pollutant under this subsection.

(c) List of source categories

(1) In general

Not later than 12 months after November 15, 1990, the Administrator shall publish, and shall from time to time, but no less often than every 8 years, revise, if appropriate, in response to public comment or new information, a list of all categories and subcategories of major sources and area sources (listed under paragraph (3)) of the air pollutants listed pursuant to subsection (b) of this section. To the extent practicable, the categories and subcategories listed under this subsection shall be consistent with the list of source categories established pursuant to section 7411 of this title and part C of this subchapter. Nothing in the preceding sentence limits the Administrator's authority to establish subcategories under this section, as appropriate.

(2) Requirement for emissions standards

For the categories and subcategories the Administrator lists, the Administrator shall establish emissions standards under subsection (d) of this section, according to the schedule in this subsection and subsection (e) of this section.

---

[6] So in original. Probably should be "effects".

(3) Area sources
The Administrator shall list under this subsection each category or subcategory of area sources which the Administrator finds presents a threat of adverse effects to human health or the environment (by such sources individually or in the aggregate) warranting regulation under this section. The Administrator shall, not later than 5 years after November 15, 1990, and pursuant to subsection (k)(3)(B) of this section, list, based on actual or estimated aggregate emissions of a listed pollutant or pollutants, sufficient categories or subcategories of area sources to ensure that area sources representing 90 percent of the area source emissions of the 30 hazardous air pollutants that present the greatest threat to public health in the largest number of urban areas are subject to regulation under this section. Such regulations shall be promulgated not later than 10 years after November 15, 1990.

(4) Previously regulated categories
The Administrator may, in the Administrator's discretion, list any category or subcategory of sources previously regulated under this section as in effect before November 15, 1990.

(5) Additional categories
In addition to those categories and subcategories of sources listed for regulation pursuant to paragraphs (1) and (3), the Administrator may at any time list additional categories and subcategories of sources of hazardous air pollutants according to the same criteria for listing applicable under such paragraphs. In the case of source categories and subcategories listed after publication of the initial list required under paragraph (1) or (3), emission standards under subsection (d) of this section for the category or subcategory shall be promulgated within 10 years after November 15, 1990, or within 2 years after the date on which such category or subcategory is listed, whichever is later.

(6) Specific pollutants
With respect to alkylated lead compounds, polycyclic organic matter, hexachlorobenzene, mercury, polychlorinated biphenyls, 2,3,7,8-tetrachlorodibenzofurans and 2,3,7,8-tetrachlorodibenzo-p-dioxin, the Administrator shall, not later than 5 years after November 15, 1990, list categories and subcategories of sources assuring that sources accounting for not less than 90 per centum of the aggregate emissions of each such pollutant are subject to standards under subsection (d)(2) or (d)(4) of this section. Such standards shall be promulgated not later than 10 years after November 15, 1990. This paragraph shall not be construed to require the Administrator to promulgate standards for such pollutants emitted by electric utility steam generating units.

(7) Research facilities
The Administrator shall establish a separate category covering research or laboratory facilities, as necessary to assure the equitable treatment of such facilities. For purposes of this section, "research or laboratory facility" means any stationary source whose primary purpose is to conduct research and development into new processes and products, where such source is operated under the close supervision of technically trained personnel and is not engaged in the manufacture of products for commercial sale in commerce, except in a de minimis manner.

(8) Boat manufacturing
When establishing emissions standards for styrene, the Administrator shall list boat manufacturing as a separate subcategory unless the Administrator finds that such listing would be inconsistent with the goals and requirements of this chapter.

(9) Deletions from the list
   (A) Where the sole reason for the inclusion of a source category on the list required under this subsection is the emission of a unique chemical substance, the Administrator shall delete the source category from the list if it is appropriate because of action taken under either subparagraphs (C) or (D) of subsection (b)(3) of this section.
   (B) The Administrator may delete any source category from the list under this subsection, on petition of any person or on the Administrator's own motion, whenever the Administrator makes the following determination or determinations, as applicable:
      (i) In the case of hazardous air pollutants emitted by sources in the category that may result in cancer in humans, a determination that no source in the category (or group of sources in the case of area sources) emits such hazardous air pollutants in quantities which may cause a lifetime risk of cancer greater than one in one million to the individual in the population who is most exposed to emissions of such pollutants from the source (or group of sources in the case of area sources).

(ii) In the case of hazardous air pollutants that may result in adverse health effects in humans other than cancer or adverse environmental effects, a determination that emissions from no source in the category or subcategory concerned (or group of sources in the case of area sources) exceed a level which is adequate to protect public health with an ample margin of safety and no adverse environmental effect will result from emissions from any source (or from a group of sources in the case of area sources).

The Administrator shall grant or deny a petition under this paragraph within 1 year after the petition is filed.

(d) Emission standards
  (1) In general
    The Administrator shall promulgate regulations establishing emission standards for each category or subcategory of major sources and area sources of hazardous air pollutants listed for regulation pursuant to subsection (c) of this section in accordance with the schedules provided in subsections (c) and (e) of this section. The Administrator may distinguish among classes, types, and sizes of sources within a category or subcategory in establishing such standards except that, there shall be no delay in the compliance date for any standard applicable to any source under subsection (i) of this section as the result of the authority provided by this sentence.
  (2) Standards and methods
    Emissions standards promulgated under this subsection and applicable to new or existing sources of hazardous air pollutants shall require the maximum degree of reduction in emissions of the hazardous air pollutants subject to this section (including a prohibition on such emissions, where achievable) that the Administrator, taking into consideration the cost of achieving such emission reduction, and any non-air quality health and environmental impacts and energy requirements, determines is achievable for new or existing sources in the category or subcategory to which such emission standard applies, through application of measures, processes, methods, systems or techniques including, but not limited to, measures which—
    (A) reduce the volume of, or eliminate emissions of, such pollutants through process changes, substitution of materials or other modifications,
    (B) enclose systems or processes to eliminate emissions,
    (C) collect, capture or treat such pollutants when released from a process, stack, storage or fugitive emissions point,
    (D) are design, equipment, work practice, or operational standards (including requirements for operator training or certification) as provided in subsection (h) of this section, or
    (E) are a combination of the above.
    None of the measures described in subparagraphs (A) through (D) shall, consistent with the provisions of section 7414(c) of this title, in any way compromise any United States patent or United States trademark right, or any confidential business information, or any trade secret or any other intellectual property right.
  (3) New and existing sources
    The maximum degree of reduction in emissions that is deemed achievable for new sources in a category or subcategory shall not be less stringent than the emission control that is achieved in practice by the best controlled similar source, as determined by the Administrator. Emission standards promulgated under this subsection for existing sources in a category or subcategory may be less stringent than standards for new sources in the same category or subcategory but shall not be less stringent, and may be more stringent than—
    (A) the average emission limitation achieved by the best performing 12 percent of the existing sources (for which the Administrator has emissions information), excluding those sources that have, within 18 months before the emission standard is proposed or within 30 months before such standard is promulgated, whichever is later, first achieved a level of emission rate or emission reduction which complies, or would comply if the source is not subject to such standard, with the lowest achievable emission rate (as defined by section 7501 of this title) applicable to the source category and prevailing at the time, in the category or subcategory for categories and subcategories with 30 or more sources, or

66 / Environmental Statutes

    (B) the average emission limitation achieved by the best performing 5 sources (for which the Administrator has or could reasonably obtain emissions information) in the category or subcategory for categories or subcategories with fewer than 30 sources.

(4) Health threshold

With respect to pollutants for which a health threshold has been established, the Administrator may consider such threshold level, with an ample margin of safety, when establishing emission standards under this subsection.

(5) Alternative standard for area sources

With respect only to categories and subcategories of area sources listed pursuant to subsection (c) of this section, the Administrator may, in lieu of the authorities provided in paragraph (2) and subsection (f) of this section, elect to promulgate standards or requirements applicable to sources in such categories or subcategories which provide for the use of generally available control technologies or management practices by such sources to reduce emissions of hazardous air pollutants.

(6) Review and revision

The Administrator shall review, and revise as necessary (taking into account developments in practices, processes, and control technologies), emission standards promulgated under this section no less often than every 8 years.

(7) Other requirements preserved

No emission standard or other requirement promulgated under this section shall be interpreted, construed or applied to diminish or replace the requirements of a more stringent emission limitation or other applicable requirement established pursuant to section 7411 of this title, part C or D of this subchapter, or other authority of this chapter or a standard issued under State authority.

(8) Coke ovens

    (A) Not later than December 31, 1992, the Administrator shall promulgate regulations establishing emission standards under paragraphs (2) and (3) of this subsection for coke oven batteries. In establishing such standards, the Administrator shall evaluate—

        (i) the use of sodium silicate (or equivalent) luting compounds to prevent door leaks, and other operating practices and technologies for their effectiveness in reducing coke oven emissions, and their suitability for use on new and existing coke oven batteries, taking into account costs and reasonable commercial door warranties; and

        (ii) as a basis for emission standards under this subsection for new coke oven batteries that begin construction after the date of proposal of such standards, the Jewell design Thompson non-recovery coke oven batteries and other non-recovery coke oven technologies, and other appropriate emission control and coke production technologies, as to their effectiveness in reducing coke oven emissions and their capability for production of steel quality coke.

Such regulations shall require at a minimum that coke oven batteries will not exceed 8 per centum leaking doors, 1 per centum leaking lids, 5 per centum leaking offtakes, and 16 seconds visible emissions per charge, with no exclusion for emissions during the period after the closing of self-sealing oven doors. Notwithstanding subsection (i) of this section, the compliance date for such emission standards for existing coke oven batteries shall be December 31, 1995.

    (B) The Administrator shall promulgate work practice regulations under this subsection for coke oven batteries requiring, as appropriate—

        (i) the use of sodium silicate (or equivalent) luting compounds, if the Administrator determines that use of sodium silicate is an effective means of emissions control and is achievable, taking into account costs and reasonable commercial warranties for doors and related equipment; and

        (ii) door and jam cleaning practices.

Notwithstanding subsection (i) of this section, the compliance date for such work practice regulations for coke oven batteries shall be not later than the date 3 years after November 15, 1990.

    (C) For coke oven batteries electing to qualify for an extension of the compliance date for standards promulgated under subsection (f) of this section in accordance with subsection (i)(8) of this section, the emission standards under this subsection for coke oven batteries shall require that coke oven batteries not exceed 8 per centum leaking doors, 1 per centum leaking lids, 5 per centum leaking offtakes, and 16 seconds visible emissions per charge, with no exclusion for emissions during the period after the closing of self-sealing doors. Notwithstanding subsection (i) of this section, the compliance date for such emission standards for existing coke oven batteries seeking an extension shall be not later than the date 3 years after November 15, 1990.

(9) Sources licensed by the Nuclear Regulatory Commission

No standard for radionuclide emissions from any category or subcategory of facilities licensed by the Nuclear Regulatory Commission (or an Agreement State) is required to be promulgated under this section if the Administrator determines, by rule, and after consultation with the Nuclear Regulatory Commission, that the regulatory program established by the Nuclear Regulatory Commission pursuant to the Atomic Energy Act [42 U.S.C. 2011 et seq.] for such category or subcategory provides an ample margin of safety to protect the public health. Nothing in this subsection shall preclude or deny the right of any State or political subdivision thereof to adopt or enforce any standard or limitation respecting emissions of radionuclides which is more stringent than the standard or limitation in effect under section 7411 of this title or this section.

(10) Effective date

Emission standards or other regulations promulgated under this subsection shall be effective upon promulgation.

(e) Schedule for standards and review

(1) In general

The Administrator shall promulgate regulations establishing emission standards for categories and subcategories of sources initially listed for regulation pursuant to subsection (c)(1) of this section as expeditiously as practicable, assuring that—

(A) emission standards for not less than 40 categories and subcategories (not counting coke oven batteries) shall be promulgated not later than 2 years after November 15, 1990;

(B) emission standards for coke oven batteries shall be promulgated not later than December 31, 1992;

(C) emission standards for 25 per centum of the listed categories and subcategories shall be promulgated not later than 4 years after November 15, 1990;

(D) emission standards for an additional 25 per centum of the listed categories and subcategories shall be promulgated not later than 7 years after November 15, 1990; and

(E) emission standards for all categories and subcategories shall be promulgated not later than 10 years after November 15, 1990.

(2) Priorities

In determining priorities for promulgating standards under subsection (d) of this section, the Administrator shall consider—

(A) the known or anticipated adverse effects of such pollutants on public health and the environment;

(B) the quantity and location of emissions or reasonably anticipated emissions of hazardous air pollutants that each category or subcategory will emit; and

(C) the efficiency of grouping categories or subcategories according to the pollutants emitted, or the processes or technologies used.

(3) Published schedule

Not later than 24 months after November 15, 1990, and after opportunity for comment, the Administrator shall publish a schedule establishing a date for the promulgation of emission standards for each category and subcategory of sources listed pursuant to subsection (c)(1) and (3) of this section which shall be consistent with the requirements of paragraphs (1) and (2). The determination of priorities for the promulgation of standards pursuant to this paragraph is not a rulemaking and shall not be subject to judicial review, except that, failure to promulgate any standard pursuant to the schedule established by this paragraph shall be subject to review under section 7604 of this title.

(4) Judicial review

Notwithstanding section 7607 of this title, no action of the Administrator adding a pollutant to the list under subsection (b) of this section or listing a source category or subcategory under subsection (c) of this section shall be a final agency action subject to judicial review, except that any such action may be reviewed under such section 7607 of this title when the Administrator issues emission standards for such pollutant or category.

(5) Publicly owned treatment works

The Administrator shall promulgate standards pursuant to subsection (d) of this section applicable to publicly owned treatment works (as defined in title II of the Federal Water Pollution Control Act [33 U.S.C. 1281 et seq.]) not later than 5 years after November 15, 1990.

(f) Standard to protect health and environment

(1) Report

Not later than 6 years after November 15, 1990, the Administrator shall investigate and report, after consultation with the Surgeon General and after opportunity for public comment, to Congress on—

(A) methods of calculating the risk to public health remaining, or likely to remain, from sources subject to regulation under this section after the application of standards under subsection (d) of this section;

(B) the public health significance of such estimated remaining risk and the technologically and commercially available methods and costs of reducing such risks;

(C) the actual health effects with respect to persons living in the vicinity of sources, any available epidemiological or other health studies, risks presented by background concentrations of hazardous air pollutants, any uncertainties in risk assessment methodology or other health assessment technique, and any negative health or environmental consequences to the community of efforts to reduce such risks; and

(D) recommendations as to legislation regarding such remaining risk.

(2) Emission standards

(A) If Congress does not act on any recommendation submitted under paragraph (1), the Administrator shall, within 8 years after promulgation of standards for each category or subcategory of sources pursuant to subsection (d) of this section, promulgate standards for such category or subcategory if promulgation of such standards is required in order to provide an ample margin of safety to protect public health in accordance with this section (as in effect before November 15, 1990) or to prevent, taking into consideration costs, energy, safety, and other relevant factors, an adverse environmental effect. Emission standards promulgated under this subsection shall provide an ample margin of safety to protect public health in accordance with this section (as in effect before November 15, 1990), unless the Administrator determines that a more stringent standard is necessary to prevent, taking into consideration costs, energy, safety, and other relevant factors, an adverse environmental effect. If standards promulgated pursuant to subsection (d) of this section and applicable to a category or subcategory of sources emitting a pollutant (or pollutants) classified as a known, probable or possible human carcinogen do not reduce lifetime excess cancer risks to the individual most exposed to emissions from a source in the category or subcategory to less than one in one million, the Administrator shall promulgate standards under this subsection for such source category.

(B) Nothing in subparagraph (A) or in any other provision of this section shall be construed as affecting, or applying to the Administrator's interpretation of this section, as in effect before November 15, 1990, and set forth in the Federal Register of September 14, 1989 (54 Federal Register 38044).

(C) The Administrator shall determine whether or not to promulgate such standards and, if the Administrator decides to promulgate such standards, shall promulgate the standards 8 years after promulgation of the standards under subsection (d) of this section for each source category or subcategory concerned. In the case of categories or subcategories for which standards under subsection (d) of this section are required to be promulgated within 2 years after November 15, 1990, the Administrator shall have 9 years after promulgation of the standards under subsection (d) of this section to make the determination under the preceding sentence and, if required, to promulgate the standards under this paragraph.

(3) Effective date

Any emission standard established pursuant to this subsection shall become effective upon promulgation.

(4) Prohibition

No air pollutant to which a standard under this subsection applies may be emitted from any stationary source in violation of such standard, except that in the case of an existing source—

(A) such standard shall not apply until 90 days after its effective date, and

(B) the Administrator may grant a waiver permitting such source a period of up to 2 years after the effective date of a standard to comply with the standard if the Administrator finds that such period is necessary for the installation of controls and that steps will be taken during the period of the waiver to assure that the health of persons will be protected from imminent endangerment.

(5) Area sources

The Administrator shall not be required to conduct any review under this subsection or promulgate emission limitations under this subsection for any category or subcategory of area sources that is listed pursuant to subsection (c)(3) of this section and for which an emission standard is promulgated pursuant to subsection (d)(5) of this section.

(6) Unique chemical substances

In establishing standards for the control of unique chemical substances of listed pollutants without CAS numbers under this subsection, the Administrator shall establish such standards with respect to the health and environmental effects of the substances actually emitted by sources and direct transformation byproducts of such emissions in the categories and subcategories.

(g) Modifications

(1) Offsets

(A) A physical change in, or change in the method of operation of, a major source which results in a greater than de minimis increase in actual emissions of a hazardous air pollutant shall not be considered a modification, if such increase in the quantity of actual emissions of any hazardous air pollutant from such source will be offset by an equal or greater decrease in the quantity of emissions of another hazardous air pollutant (or pollutants) from such source which is deemed more hazardous, pursuant to guidance issued by the Administrator under subparagraph (B). The owner or operator of such source shall submit a showing to the Administrator (or the State) that such increase has been offset under the preceding sentence.

(B) The Administrator shall, after notice and opportunity for comment and not later than 18 months after November 15, 1990, publish guidance with respect to implementation of this subsection. Such guidance shall include an identification, to the extent practicable, of the relative hazard to human health resulting from emissions to the ambient air of each of the pollutants listed under subsection (b) of this section sufficient to facilitate the offset showing authorized by subparagraph (A). Such guidance shall not authorize offsets between pollutants where the increased pollutant (or more than one pollutant in a stream of pollutants) causes adverse effects to human health for which no safety threshold for exposure can be determined unless there are corresponding decreases in such types of pollutant(s).

(2) Construction, reconstruction and modifications

(A) After the effective date of a permit program under subchapter V of this chapter in any State, no person may modify a major source of hazardous air pollutants in such State, unless the Administrator (or the State) determines that the maximum achievable control technology emission limitation under this section for existing sources will be met. Such determination shall be made on a case-by-case basis where no applicable emissions limitations have been established by the Administrator.

(B) After the effective date of a permit program under subchapter V of this chapter in any State, no person may construct or reconstruct any major source of hazardous air pollutants, unless the Administrator (or the State) determines that the maximum achievable control technology emission limitation under this section for new sources will be met. Such determination shall be made on a case-by-case basis where no applicable emission limitations have been established by the Administrator.

(3) Procedures for modifications

The Administrator (or the State) shall establish reasonable procedures for assuring that the requirements applying to modifications under this section are reflected in the permit.

(h) Work practice standards and other requirements
  (1) In general
    For purposes of this section, if it is not feasible in the judgment of the Administrator to prescribe or enforce an emission standard for control of a hazardous air pollutant or pollutants, the Administrator may, in lieu thereof, promulgate a design, equipment, work practice, or operational standard, or combination thereof, which in the Administrator's judgment is consistent with the provisions of subsection (d) or (f) of this section. In the event the Administrator promulgates a design or equipment standard under this subsection, the Administrator shall include as part of such standard such requirements as will assure the proper operation and maintenance of any such element of design or equipment.
  (2) Definition
    For the purpose of this subsection, the phrase "not feasible to prescribe or enforce an emission standard" means any situation in which the Administrator determines that—
    (A) a hazardous air pollutant or pollutants cannot be emitted through a conveyance designed and constructed to emit or capture such pollutant, or that any requirement for, or use of, such a conveyance would be inconsistent with any Federal, State or local law, or
    (B) the application of measurement methodology to a particular class of sources is not practicable due to technological and economic limitations.
  (3) Alternative standard
    If after notice and opportunity for comment, the owner or operator of any source establishes to the satisfaction of the Administrator that an alternative means of emission limitation will achieve a reduction in emissions of any air pollutant at least equivalent to the reduction in emissions of such pollutant achieved under the requirements of paragraph (1), the Administrator shall permit the use of such alternative by the source for purposes of compliance with this section with respect to such pollutant.
  (4) Numerical standard required
    Any standard promulgated under paragraph (1) shall be promulgated in terms of an emission standard whenever it is feasible to promulgate and enforce a standard in such terms.
(i) Schedule for compliance
  (1) Preconstruction and operating requirements
    After the effective date of any emission standard, limitation, or regulation under subsection (d), (f) or (h) of this section, no person may construct any new major source or reconstruct any existing major source subject to such emission standard, regulation or limitation unless the Administrator (or a State with a permit program approved under subchapter V of this chapter) determines that such source, if properly constructed, reconstructed and operated, will comply with the standard, regulation or limitation.
  (2) Special rule
    Notwithstanding the requirements of paragraph (1), a new source which commences construction or reconstruction after a standard, limitation or regulation applicable to such source is proposed and before such standard, limitation or regulation is promulgated shall not be required to comply with such promulgated standard until the date 3 years after the date of promulgation if—
    (A) the promulgated standard, limitation or regulation is more stringent than the standard, limitation or regulation proposed; and
    (B) the source complies with the standard, limitation, or regulation as proposed during the 3-year period immediately after promulgation.
  (3) Compliance schedule for existing sources
    (A) After the effective date of any emissions standard, limitation or regulation promulgated under this section and applicable to a source, no person may operate such source in violation of such standard, limitation or regulation except, in the case of an existing source, the Administrator shall establish a compliance date or dates for each category or subcategory of existing sources, which shall provide for compliance as expeditiously as practicable, but in no event later than 3 years after the effective date of such standard, except as provided in subparagraph (B) and paragraphs (4) through (8).
    (B) The Administrator (or a State with a program approved under subchapter V of this chapter) may issue a permit that grants an extension permitting an existing source up

to 1 additional year to comply with standards under subsection (d) of this section if such additional period is necessary for the installation of controls. An additional extension of up to 3 years may be added for mining waste operations, if the 4-year compliance time is insufficient to dry and cover mining waste in order to reduce emissions of any pollutant listed under subsection (b) of this section.

(4) Presidential exemption

The President may exempt any stationary source from compliance with any standard or limitation under this section for a period of not more than 2 years if the President determines that the technology to implement such standard is not available and that it is in the national security interests of the United States to do so.

An exemption under this paragraph may be extended for 1 or more additional periods, each period not to exceed 2 years. The President shall report to Congress with respect to each exemption (or extension thereof) made under this paragraph.

(5) Early reduction

(A) The Administrator (or a State acting pursuant to a permit program approved under subchapter V of this chapter) shall issue a permit allowing an existing source, for which the owner or operator demonstrates that the source has achieved a reduction of 90 per centum or more in emissions of hazardous air pollutants (95 per centum in the case of hazardous air pollutants which are particulates) from the source, to meet an alternative emission limitation reflecting such reduction in lieu of an emission limitation promulgated under subsection (d) of this section for a period of 6 years from the compliance date for the otherwise applicable standard, provided that such reduction is achieved before the otherwise applicable standard under subsection (d) of this section is first proposed. Nothing in this paragraph shall preclude a State from requiring reductions in excess of those specified in this subparagraph as a condition of granting the extension authorized by the previous sentence.

(B) An existing source which achieves the reduction referred to in subparagraph (A) after the proposal of an applicable standard but before January 1, 1994, may qualify under subparagraph (A), if the source makes an enforceable commitment to achieve such reduction before the proposal of the standard. Such commitment shall be enforceable to the same extent as a regulation under this section.

(C) The reduction shall be determined with respect to verifiable and actual emissions in a base year not earlier than calendar year 1987, provided that, there is no evidence that emissions in the base year are artificially or substantially greater than emissions in other years prior to implementation of emissions reduction measures. The Administrator may allow a source to use a baseline year of 1985 or 1986 provided that the source can demonstrate to the satisfaction of the Administrator that emissions data for the source reflects verifiable data based on information for such source, received by the Administrator prior to November 15, 1990, pursuant to an information request issued under section 7414 of this title.

(D) For each source granted an alternative emission limitation under this paragraph there shall be established by a permit issued pursuant to subchapter V of this chapter an enforceable emission limitation for hazardous air pollutants reflecting the reduction which qualifies the source for an alternative emission limitation under this paragraph. An alternative emission limitation under this paragraph shall not be available with respect to standards or requirements promulgated pursuant to subsection (f) of this section and the Administrator shall, for the purpose of determining whether a standard under subsection (f) of this section is necessary, review emissions from sources granted an alternative emission limitation under this paragraph at the same time that other sources in the category or subcategory are reviewed.

(E) With respect to pollutants for which high risks of adverse public health effects may be associated with exposure to small quantities including, but not limited to, chlorinated dioxins and furans, the Administrator shall by regulation limit the use of offsetting reductions in emissions of other hazardous air pollutants from the source as counting toward the 90 per centum reduction in such high-risk pollutants qualifying for an alternative emissions limitation under this paragraph.

(6) Other reductions

Notwithstanding the requirements of this section, no existing source that has installed—

(A) best available control technology (as defined in section 7479(3) of this title), or
(B) technology required to meet a lowest achievable emission rate (as defined in section 7501 of this title), prior to the promulgation of a standard under this section applicable to such source and the same pollutant (or stream of pollutants) controlled pursuant to an action described in subparagraph (A) or (B) shall be required to comply with such standard under this section until the date 5 years after the date on which such installation or reduction has been achieved, as determined by the Administrator. The Administrator may issue such rules and guidance as are necessary to implement this paragraph.

(7) Extension for new sources

A source for which construction or reconstruction is commenced after the date an emission standard applicable to such source is proposed pursuant to subsection (d) of this section but before the date an emission standard applicable to such source is proposed pursuant to subsection (f) of this section shall not be required to comply with the emission standard under subsection (f) of this section until the date 10 years after the date construction or reconstruction is commenced.

(8) Coke ovens

(A) Any coke oven battery that complies with the emission limitations established under subsection (d)(8)(C) of this section, subparagraph (B), and subparagraph (C), and complies with the provisions of subparagraph (E), shall not be required to achieve emission limitations promulgated under subsection (f) of this section until January 1, 2020.

(B) (i) Not later than December 31, 1992, the Administrator shall promulgate emission limitations for coke oven emissions from coke oven batteries. Notwithstanding paragraph (3) of this subsection, the compliance date for such emission limitations for existing coke oven batteries shall be January 1, 1998. Such emission limitations shall reflect the lowest achievable emission rate as defined in section 7501 of this title for a coke oven battery that is rebuilt or a replacement at a coke oven plant for an existing battery. Such emission limitations shall be no less stringent than—

(I) 3 per centum leaking doors (5 per centum leaking doors for six meter batteries);
(II) 1 per centum leaking lids;
(III) 4 per centum leaking offtakes; and
(IV) 16 seconds visible emissions per charge,

with an exclusion for emissions during the period after the closing of self-sealing oven doors (or the total mass emissions equivalent). The rulemaking in which such emission limitations are promulgated shall also establish an appropriate measurement methodology for determining compliance with such emission limitations, and shall establish such emission limitations in terms of an equivalent level of mass emissions reduction from a coke oven battery, unless the Administrator finds that such a mass emissions standard would not be practicable or enforceable. Such measurement methodology, to the extent it measures leaking doors, shall take into consideration alternative test methods that reflect the best technology and practices actually applied in the affected industries, and shall assure that the final test methods are consistent with the performance of such best technology and practices.

(ii) If the Administrator fails to promulgate such emission limitations under this subparagraph prior to the effective date of such emission limitations, the emission limitations applicable to coke oven batteries under this subparagraph shall be—

(I) 3 per centum leaking doors (5 per centum leaking doors for six meter batteries);
(II) 1 per centum leaking lids;
(III) 4 per centum leaking offtakes; and
(IV) 16 seconds visible emissions per charge,

or the total mass emissions equivalent (if the total mass emissions equivalent is determined to be practicable and enforceable), with no exclusion for emissions during the period after the closing of self-sealing oven doors.

(C) Not later than January 1, 2007, the Administrator shall review the emission limitations promulgated under subparagraph (B) and revise, as necessary, such emission limitations to reflect the lowest achievable emission rate as defined in section 7501 of this title at the time for a coke oven battery that is rebuilt or a replacement at a coke oven plant for an existing battery. Such emission limitations shall be no less stringent than the emission limitation promulgated under subparagraph (B). Notwithstanding paragraph (2) of this subsection, the compliance date for such emission limitations for existing coke oven batteries shall be January 1, 2010.

(D) At any time prior to January 1, 1998, the owner or operator of any coke oven battery may elect to comply with emission limitations promulgated under subsection (f) of this section by the date such emission limitations would otherwise apply to such coke oven battery, in lieu of the emission limitations and the compliance dates provided under subparagraphs (B) and (C) of this paragraph. Any such owner or operator shall be legally bound to comply with such emission limitations promulgated under subsection (f) of this section with respect to such coke oven battery as of January 1, 2003. If no such emission limitations have been promulgated for such coke oven battery, the Administrator shall promulgate such emission limitations in accordance with subsection (f) of this section for such coke oven battery.

(E) Coke oven batteries qualifying for an extension under subparagraph (A) shall make available not later than January 1, 2000, to the surrounding communities the results of any risk assessment performed by the Administrator to determine the appropriate level of any emission standard established by the Administrator pursuant to subsection (f) of this section.

(F) Notwithstanding the provisions of this section, reconstruction of any source of coke oven emissions qualifying for an extension under this paragraph shall not subject such source to emission limitations under subsection (f) of this section more stringent than those established under subparagraphs (B) and (C) until January 1, 2020. For the purposes of this subparagraph, the term "reconstruction" includes the replacement of existing coke oven battery capacity with new coke oven batteries of comparable or lower capacity and lower potential emissions.

(j) Equivalent emission limitation by permit

(1) Effective date

The requirements of this subsection shall apply in each State beginning on the effective date of a permit program established pursuant to subchapter V of this chapter in such State, but not prior to the date 42 months after November 15, 1990.

(2) Failure to promulgate a standard

In the event that the Administrator fails to promulgate a standard for a category or subcategory of major sources by the date established pursuant to subsection (e)(1) and (3) of this section, and beginning 18 months after such date (but not prior to the effective date of a permit program under subchapter V of this chapter), the owner or operator of any major source in such category or subcategory shall submit a permit application under paragraph (3) and such owner or operator shall also comply with paragraphs (5) and (6).

(3) Applications

By the date established by paragraph (2), the owner or operator of a major source subject to this subsection shall file an application for a permit. If the owner or operator of a source has submitted a timely and complete application for a permit required by this subsection, any failure to have a permit shall not be a violation of paragraph (2), unless the delay in final action is due to the failure of the applicant to timely submit information required or requested to process the application. The Administrator shall not later than 18 months after November 15, 1990, and after notice and opportunity for comment, establish requirements for applications under this subsection including a standard application form and criteria for determining in a timely manner the completeness of applications.

(4) Review and approval

Permit applications submitted under this subsection shall be reviewed and approved or disapproved according to the provisions of section 7661d of this title. In the event that the Administrator (or the State) disapproves a permit application submitted under this subsection or determines that the application is incomplete, the applicant shall have up to 6 months to revise the application to meet the objections of the Administrator (or the State).

(5) Emission limitation
   The permit shall be issued pursuant to subchapter V of this chapter and shall contain emission limitations for the hazardous air pollutants subject to regulation under this section and emitted by the source that the Administrator (or the State) determines, on a case-by-case basis, to be equivalent to the limitation that would apply to such source if an emission standard had been promulgated in a timely manner under subsection (d) of this section. In the alternative, if the applicable criteria are met, the permit may contain an emissions limitation established according to the provisions of subsection (i)(5) of this section. For purposes of the preceding sentence, the reduction required by subsection (i)(5)(A) of this section shall be achieved by the date on which the relevant standard should have been promulgated under subsection (d) of this section. No such pollutant may be emitted in amounts exceeding an emission limitation contained in a permit immediately for new sources and, as expeditiously as practicable, but not later than the date 3 years after the permit is issued for existing sources or such other compliance date as would apply under subsection (i) of this section.
(6) Applicability of subsequent standards
   If the Administrator promulgates an emission standard that is applicable to the major source prior to the date on which a permit application is approved, the emission limitation in the permit shall reflect the promulgated standard rather than the emission limitation determined pursuant to paragraph (5), provided that the source shall have the compliance period provided under subsection (i) of this section. If the Administrator promulgates a standard under subsection (d) of this section that would be applicable to the source in lieu of the emission limitation established by permit under this subsection after the date on which the permit has been issued, the Administrator (or the State) shall revise such permit upon the next renewal to reflect the standard promulgated by the Administrator providing such source a reasonable time to comply, but no longer than 8 years after such standard is promulgated or 8 years after the date on which the source is first required to comply with the emissions limitation established by paragraph (5), whichever is earlier.

(k) Area source program
   (1) Findings and purpose
      The Congress finds that emissions of hazardous air pollutants from area sources may individually, or in the aggregate, present significant risks to public health in urban areas. Considering the large number of persons exposed and the risks of carcinogenic and other adverse health effects from hazardous air pollutants, ambient concentrations characteristic of large urban areas should be reduced to levels substantially below those currently experienced. It is the purpose of this subsection to achieve a substantial reduction in emissions of hazardous air pollutants from area sources and an equivalent reduction in the public health risks associated with such sources including a reduction of not less than 75 per centum in the incidence of cancer attributable to emissions from such sources.
   (2) Research program
      The Administrator shall, after consultation with State and local air pollution control officials, conduct a program of research with respect to sources of hazardous air pollutants in urban areas and shall include within such program—
      (A) ambient monitoring for a broad range of hazardous air pollutants (including, but not limited to, volatile organic compounds, metals, pesticides and products of incomplete combustion) in a representative number of urban locations;
      (B) analysis to characterize the sources of such pollution with a focus on area sources and the contribution that such sources make to public health risks from hazardous air pollutants; and
      (C) consideration of atmospheric transformation and other factors which can elevate public health risks from such pollutants.
      Health effects considered under this program shall include, but not be limited to, carcinogenicity, mutagenicity, teratogenicity, neurotoxicity, reproductive dysfunction and other acute and chronic effects including the role of such pollutants as precursors of ozone or acid aerosol formation. The Administrator shall report the preliminary results of such research not later than 3 years after November 15, 1990.

(3) National strategy
   (A) Considering information collected pursuant to the monitoring program authorized by paragraph (2), the Administrator shall, not later than 5 years after November 15, 1990, and after notice and opportunity for public comment, prepare and transmit to the Congress a comprehensive strategy to control emissions of hazardous air pollutants from area sources in urban areas.
   (B) The strategy shall—
      (i) identify not less than 30 hazardous air pollutants which, as the result of emissions from area sources, present the greatest threat to public health in the largest number of urban areas and that are or will be listed pursuant to subsection (b) of this section, and
      (ii) identify the source categories or subcategories emitting such pollutants that are or will be listed pursuant to subsection (c) of this section. When identifying categories and subcategories of sources under this subparagraph, the Administrator shall assure that sources accounting for 90 per centum or more of the aggregate emissions of each of the 30 identified hazardous air pollutants are subject to standards pursuant to subsection (d) of this section.
   (C) The strategy shall include a schedule of specific actions to substantially reduce the public health risks posed by the release of hazardous air pollutants from area sources that will be implemented by the Administrator under the authority of this or other laws (including, but not limited to, the Toxic Substances Control Act [15 U.S.C. 2601 et seq.], the Federal Insecticide, Fungicide and Rodenticide Act [7 U.S.C. 136 et seq.] and the Resource Conservation and Recovery Act [42 U.S.C. 6901 et seq.]) or by the States. The strategy shall achieve a reduction in the incidence of cancer attributable to exposure to hazardous air pollutants emitted by stationary sources of not less than 75 per centum, considering control of emissions of hazardous air pollutants from all stationary sources and resulting from measures implemented by the Administrator or by the States under this or other laws.
   (D) The strategy may also identify research needs in monitoring, analytical methodology, modeling or pollution control techniques and recommendations for changes in law that would further the goals and objectives of this subsection.
   (E) Nothing in this subsection shall be interpreted to preclude or delay implementation of actions with respect to area sources of hazardous air pollutants under consideration pursuant to this or any other law and that may be promulgated before the strategy is prepared.
   (F) The Administrator shall implement the strategy as expeditiously as practicable assuring that all sources are in compliance with all requirements not later than 9 years after November 15, 1990.
   (G) As part of such strategy the Administrator shall provide for ambient monitoring and emissions modeling in urban areas as appropriate to demonstrate that the goals and objectives of the strategy are being met.
(4) Areawide activities
   In addition to the national urban air toxics strategy authorized by paragraph (3), the Administrator shall also encourage and support areawide strategies developed by State or local air pollution control agencies that are intended to reduce risks from emissions by area sources within a particular urban area. From the funds available for grants under this section, the Administrator shall set aside not less than 10 per centum to support areawide strategies addressing hazardous air pollutants emitted by area sources and shall award such funds on a demonstration basis to those States with innovative and effective strategies. At the request of State or local air pollution control officials, the Administrator shall prepare guidelines for control technologies or management practices which may be applicable to various categories or subcategories of area sources.
(5) Report
   The Administrator shall report to the Congress at intervals not later than 8 and 12 years after November 15, 1990, on actions taken under this subsection and other parts of this chapter to reduce the risk to public health posed by the release of hazardous air pollutants from area sources. The reports shall also identify specific metropolitan areas that continue to experience high risks to public health as the result of emissions from area sources.

(l) State programs
   (1) In general
       Each State may develop and submit to the Administrator for approval a program for the implementation and enforcement (including a review of enforcement delegations previously granted) of emission standards and other requirements for air pollutants subject to this section or requirements for the prevention and mitigation of accidental releases pursuant to subsection (r) of this section. A program submitted by a State under this subsection may provide for partial or complete delegation of the Administrator's authorities and responsibilities to implement and enforce emissions standards and prevention requirements but shall not include authority to set standards less stringent than those promulgated by the Administrator under this chapter.
   (2) Guidance
       Not later than 12 months after November 15, 1990, the Administrator shall publish guidance that would be useful to the States in developing programs for submittal under this subsection. The guidance shall also provide for the registration of all facilities producing, processing, handling or storing any substance listed pursuant to subsection (r) of this section in amounts greater than the threshold quantity. The Administrator shall include as an element in such guidance an optional program begun in 1986 for the review of high-risk point sources of air pollutants including, but not limited to, hazardous air pollutants listed pursuant to subsection (b) of this section.
   (3) Technical assistance
       The Administrator shall establish and maintain an air toxics clearinghouse and center to provide technical information and assistance to State and local agencies and, on a cost recovery basis, to others on control technology, health and ecological risk assessment, risk analysis, ambient monitoring and modeling, and emissions measurement and monitoring. The Administrator shall use the authority of section 7403 of this title to examine methods for preventing, measuring, and controlling emissions and evaluating associated health and ecological risks. Where appropriate, such activity shall be conducted with not-for-profit organizations. The Administrator may conduct research on methods for preventing, measuring and controlling emissions and evaluating associated health and environment risks. All information collected under this paragraph shall be available to the public.
   (4) Grants
       Upon application of a State, the Administrator may make grants, subject to such terms and conditions as the Administrator deems appropriate, to such State for the purpose of assisting the State in developing and implementing a program for submittal and approval under this subsection. Programs assisted under this paragraph may include program elements addressing air pollutants or extremely hazardous substances other than those specifically subject to this section. Grants under this paragraph may include support for high-risk point source review as provided in paragraph (2) and support for the development and implementation of areawide area source programs pursuant to subsection (k) of this section.
   (5) Approval or disapproval
       Not later than 180 days after receiving a program submitted by a State, and after notice and opportunity for public comment, the Administrator shall either approve or disapprove such program. The Administrator shall disapprove any program submitted by a State, if the Administrator determines that—
       (A) the authorities contained in the program are not adequate to assure compliance by all sources within the State with each applicable standard, regulation or requirement established by the Administrator under this section;
       (B) adequate authority does not exist, or adequate resources are not available, to implement the program;
       (C) the schedule for implementing the program and assuring compliance by affected sources is not sufficiently expeditious; or
       (D) the program is otherwise not in compliance with the guidance issued by the Administrator under paragraph (2) or is not likely to satisfy, in whole or in part, the objectives of this chapter.
       If the Administrator disapproves a State program, the Administrator shall notify the State of any revisions or modifications necessary to obtain approval. The State may revise and

resubmit the proposed program for review and approval pursuant to the provisions of this subsection.
    (6) Withdrawal
    Whenever the Administrator determines, after public hearing, that a State is not administering and enforcing a program approved pursuant to this subsection in accordance with the guidance published pursuant to paragraph (2) or the requirements of paragraph (5), the Administrator shall so notify the State and, if action which will assure prompt compliance is not taken within 90 days, the Administrator shall withdraw approval of the program. The Administrator shall not withdraw approval of any program unless the State shall have been notified and the reasons for withdrawal shall have been stated in writing and made public.
    (7) Authority to enforce
    Nothing in this subsection shall prohibit the Administrator from enforcing any applicable emission standard or requirement under this section.
    (8) Local program
    The Administrator may, after notice and opportunity for public comment, approve a program developed and submitted by a local air pollution control agency (after consultation with the State) pursuant to this subsection and any such agency implementing an approved program may take any action authorized to be taken by a State under this section.
    (9) Permit authority
    Nothing in this subsection shall affect the authorities and obligations of the Administrator or the State under subchapter V of this chapter.
(m) Atmospheric deposition to Great Lakes and coastal waters
    (1) Deposition assessment
    The Administrator, in cooperation with the Under Secretary of Commerce for Oceans and Atmosphere, shall conduct a program to identify and assess the extent of atmospheric deposition of hazardous air pollutants (and in the discretion of the Administrator, other air pollutants) to the Great Lakes, the Chesapeake Bay, Lake Champlain and coastal waters. As part of such program, the Administrator shall—
        (A) monitor the Great Lakes, the Chesapeake Bay, Lake Champlain and coastal waters, including monitoring of the Great Lakes through the monitoring network established pursuant to paragraph (2) of this subsection and designing and deploying an atmospheric monitoring network for coastal waters pursuant to paragraph (4);
        (B) investigate the sources and deposition rates of atmospheric deposition of air pollutants (and their atmospheric transformation precursors);
        (C) conduct research to develop and improve monitoring methods and to determine the relative contribution of atmospheric pollutants to total pollution loadings to the Great Lakes, the Chesapeake Bay, Lake Champlain, and coastal waters;
        (D) evaluate any adverse effects to public health or the environment caused by such deposition (including effects resulting from indirect exposure pathways) and assess the contribution of such deposition to violations of water quality standards established pursuant to the Federal Water Pollution Control Act [33 U.S.C. 1251 et seq.] and drinking water standards established pursuant to the Safe Drinking Water Act [42 U.S.C. 300f et seq.]; and
        (E) sample for such pollutants in biota, fish, and wildlife of the Great Lakes, the Chesapeake Bay, Lake Champlain and coastal waters and characterize the sources of such pollutants.
    (2) Great Lakes monitoring network
    The Administrator shall oversee, in accordance with Annex 15 of the Great Lakes Water Quality Agreement, the establishment and operation of a Great Lakes atmospheric deposition network to monitor atmospheric deposition of hazardous air pollutants (and in the Administrator's discretion, other air pollutants) to the Great Lakes.
        (A) As part of the network provided for in this paragraph, and not later than December 31, 1991, the Administrator shall establish in each of the 5 Great Lakes at least 1 facility capable of monitoring the atmospheric deposition of hazardous air pollutants in both dry and wet conditions.
        (B) The Administrator shall use the data provided by the network to identify and track the movement of hazardous air pollutants through the Great Lakes, to determine the

portion of water pollution loadings attributable to atmospheric deposition of such pollutants, and to support development of remedial action plans and other management plans as required by the Great Lakes Water Quality Agreement.
(C) The Administrator shall assure that the data collected by the Great Lakes atmospheric deposition monitoring network is in a format compatible with databases sponsored by the International Joint Commission, Canada, and the several States of the Great Lakes region.
(3) Monitoring for the Chesapeake Bay and Lake Champlain
The Administrator shall establish at the Chesapeake Bay and Lake Champlain atmospheric deposition stations to monitor deposition of hazardous air pollutants (and in the Administrator's discretion, other air pollutants) within the Chesapeake Bay and Lake Champlain watersheds. The Administrator shall determine the role of air deposition in the pollutant loadings of the Chesapeake Bay and Lake Champlain, investigate the sources of air pollutants deposited in the watersheds, evaluate the health and environmental effects of such pollutant loadings, and shall sample such pollutants in biota, fish and wildlife within the watersheds, as necessary to characterize such effects.
(4) Monitoring for coastal waters
The Administrator shall design and deploy atmospheric deposition monitoring networks for coastal waters and their watersheds and shall make any information collected through such networks available to the public. As part of this effort, the Administrator shall conduct research to develop and improve deposition monitoring methods, and to determine the relative contribution of atmospheric pollutants to pollutant loadings. For purposes of this subsection, "coastal waters" shall mean estuaries selected pursuant to section 320(a)(2)(A) of the Federal Water Pollution Control Act [33 U.S.C. 1330(a)(2)(A)] or listed pursuant to section 320(a)(2)(B) of such Act [33 U.S.C. 1330(a)(2)(B)] or estuarine research reserves designated pursuant to section 1461 of title 16.
(5) Report
Within 3 years of November 15, 1990, and biennially thereafter, the Administrator, in cooperation with the Under Secretary of Commerce for Oceans and Atmosphere, shall submit to the Congress a report on the results of any monitoring, studies, and investigations conducted pursuant to this subsection. Such report shall include, at a minimum, an assessment of—
(A) the contribution of atmospheric deposition to pollution loadings in the Great Lakes, the Chesapeake Bay, Lake Champlain and coastal waters;
(B) the environmental and public health effects of any pollution which is attributable to atmospheric deposition to the Great Lakes, the Chesapeake Bay, Lake Champlain and coastal waters;
(C) the source or sources of any pollution to the Great Lakes, the Chesapeake Bay, Lake Champlain and coastal waters which is attributable to atmospheric deposition;
(D) whether pollution loadings in the Great Lakes, the Chesapeake Bay, Lake Champlain or coastal waters cause or contribute to exceedances of drinking water standards pursuant to the Safe Drinking Water Act [42 U.S.C. 300f et seq.] or water quality standards pursuant to the Federal Water Pollution Control Act [33 U.S.C. 1251 et seq.] or, with respect to the Great Lakes, exceedances of the specific objectives of the Great Lakes Water Quality Agreement; and
(E) a description of any revisions of the requirements, standards, and limitations pursuant to this chapter and other applicable Federal laws as are necessary to assure protection of human health and the environment.
(6) Additional regulation
As part of the report to Congress, the Administrator shall determine whether the other provisions of this section are adequate to prevent serious adverse effects to public health and serious or widespread environmental effects, including such effects resulting from indirect exposure pathways, associated with atmospheric deposition to the Great Lakes, the Chesapeake Bay, Lake Champlain and coastal waters of hazardous air pollutants (and their atmospheric transformation products). The Administrator shall take into consideration the tendency of such pollutants to bioaccumulate. Within 5 years after November 15, 1990, the Administrator shall, based on such report and determination, promulgate, in accordance with this section, such further emission standards or control measures as

may be necessary and appropriate to prevent such effects, including effects due to bioaccumulation and indirect exposure pathways. Any requirements promulgated pursuant to this paragraph with respect to coastal waters shall only apply to the coastal waters of the States which are subject to section 7627(a) of this title.

(n) Other provisions
  (1) Electric utility steam generating units
    (A) The Administrator shall perform a study of the hazards to public health reasonably anticipated to occur as a result of emissions by electric utility steam generating units of pollutants listed under subsection (b) of this section after imposition of the requirements of this chapter. The Administrator shall report the results of this study to the Congress within 3 years after November 15, 1990. The Administrator shall develop and describe in the Administrator's report to Congress alternative control strategies for emissions which may warrant regulation under this section. The Administrator shall regulate electric utility steam generating units under this section, if the Administrator finds such regulation is appropriate and necessary after considering the results of the study required by this subparagraph.
    (B) The Administrator shall conduct, and transmit to the Congress not later than 4 years after November 15, 1990, a study of mercury emissions from electric utility steam generating units, municipal waste combustion units, and other sources, including area sources. Such study shall consider the rate and mass of such emissions, the health and environmental effects of such emissions, technologies which are available to control such emissions, and the costs of such technologies.
    (C) The National Institute of Environmental Health Sciences shall conduct, and transmit to the Congress not later than 3 years after November 15, 1990, a study to determine the threshold level of mercury exposure below which adverse human health effects are not expected to occur. Such study shall include a threshold for mercury concentrations in the tissue of fish which may be consumed (including consumption by sensitive populations) without adverse effects to public health.
  (2) Coke oven production technology study
    (A) The Secretary of the Department of Energy and the Administrator shall jointly undertake a 6-year study to assess coke oven production emission control technologies and to assist in the development and commercialization of technically practicable and economically viable control technologies which have the potential to significantly reduce emissions of hazardous air pollutants from coke oven production facilities. In identifying control technologies, the Secretary and the Administrator shall consider the range of existing coke oven operations and battery design and the availability of sources of materials for such coke ovens as well as alternatives to existing coke oven production design.
    (B) The Secretary and the Administrator are authorized to enter into agreements with persons who propose to develop, install and operate coke production emission control technologies which have the potential for significant emissions reductions of hazardous air pollutants provided that Federal funds shall not exceed 50 per centum of the cost of any project assisted pursuant to this paragraph.
    (C) On completion of the study, the Secretary shall submit to Congress a report on the results of the study and shall make recommendations to the Administrator identifying practicable and economically viable control technologies for coke oven production facilities to reduce residual risks remaining after implementation of the standard under subsection (d) of this section.
    (D) There are authorized to be appropriated $5,000,000 for each of the fiscal years 1992 through 1997 to carry out the program authorized by this paragraph.
  (3) Publicly owned treatment works
    The Administrator may conduct, in cooperation with the owners and operators of publicly owned treatment works, studies to characterize emissions of hazardous air pollutants emitted by such facilities, to identify industrial, commercial and residential discharges that contribute to such emissions and to demonstrate control measures for such emissions. When promulgating any standard under this section applicable to publicly owned treatment works, the Administrator may provide for control measures that include pretreatment of discharges causing emissions of hazardous air pollutants and process or prod-

uct substitutions or limitations that may be effective in reducing such emissions. The Administrator may prescribe uniform sampling, modeling and risk assessment methods for use in implementing this subsection.

(4) Oil and gas wells; pipeline facilities

(A) Notwithstanding the provisions of subsection (a) of this section, emissions from any oil or gas exploration or production well (with its associated equipment) and emissions from any pipeline compressor or pump station shall not be aggregated with emissions from other similar units, whether or not such units are in a contiguous area or under common control, to determine whether such units or stations are major sources, and in the case of any oil or gas exploration or production well (with its associated equipment), such emissions shall not be aggregated for any purpose under this section.

(B) The Administrator shall not list oil and gas production wells (with its associated equipment) as an area source category under subsection (c) of this section, except that the Administrator may establish an area source category for oil and gas production wells located in any metropolitan statistical area or consolidated metropolitan statistical area with a population in excess of 1 million, if the Administrator determines that emissions of hazardous air pollutants from such wells present more than a negligible risk of adverse effects to public health.

(5) Hydrogen sulfide

The Administrator is directed to assess the hazards to public health and the environment resulting from the emission of hydrogen sulfide associated with the extraction of oil and natural gas resources. To the extent practicable, the assessment shall build upon and not duplicate work conducted for an assessment pursuant to section 8002(m) of the Solid Waste Disposal Act [42 U.S.C. 6982(m)] and shall reflect consultation with the States. The assessment shall include a review of existing State and industry control standards, techniques and enforcement. The Administrator shall report to the Congress within 24 months after November 15, 1990, with the findings of such assessment, together with any recommendations, and shall, as appropriate, develop and implement a control strategy for emissions of hydrogen sulfide to protect human health and the environment, based on the findings of such assessment, using authorities under this chapter including sections[7] 7411 of this title and this section.

(6) Hydrofluoric acid

Not later than 2 years after November 15, 1990, the Administrator shall, for those regions of the country which do not have comprehensive health and safety regulations with respect to hydrofluoric acid, complete a study of the potential hazards of hydrofluoric acid and the uses of hydrofluoric acid in industrial and commercial applications to public health and the environment considering a range of events including worst-case accidental releases and shall make recommendations to the Congress for the reduction of such hazards, if appropriate.

(7) RCRA facilities

In the case of any category or subcategory of sources the air emissions of which are regulated under subtitle C of the Solid Waste Disposal Act [42 U.S.C. 6921 et seq.], the Administrator shall take into account any regulations of such emissions which are promulgated under such subtitle and shall, to the maximum extent practicable and consistent with the provisions of this section, ensure that the requirements of such subtitle and this section are consistent.

(o) National Academy of Sciences study

(1) Request of the Academy

Within 3 months of November 15, 1990, the Administrator shall enter into appropriate arrangements with the National Academy of Sciences to conduct a review of—

(A) risk assessment methodology used by the Environmental Protection Agency to determine the carcinogenic risk associated with exposure to hazardous air pollutants from source categories and subcategories subject to the requirements of this section; and

(B) improvements in such methodology.

---

[7] So in original. Probably should be "section".

(2) Elements to be studied
In conducting such review, the National Academy of Sciences should consider, but not be limited to, the following—
    (A) the techniques used for estimating and describing the carcinogenic potency to humans of hazardous air pollutants; and
    (B) the techniques used for estimating exposure to hazardous air pollutants (for hypothetical and actual maximally exposed individuals as well as other exposed individuals).
(3) Other health effects of concern
To the extent practicable, the Academy shall evaluate and report on the methodology for assessing the risk of adverse human health effects other than cancer for which safe thresholds of exposure may not exist, including, but not limited to, inheritable genetic mutations, birth defects, and reproductive dysfunctions.
(4) Report
A report on the results of such review shall be submitted to the Senate Committee on Environment and Public Works, the House Committee on Energy and Commerce, the Risk Assessment and Management Commission established by section 303 of the Clean Air Act Amendments of 1990 and the Administrator not later than 30 months after November 15, 1990.
(5) Assistance
The Administrator shall assist the Academy in gathering any information the Academy deems necessary to carry out this subsection. The Administrator may use any authority under this chapter to obtain information from any person, and to require any person to conduct tests, keep and produce records, and make reports respecting research or other activities conducted by such person as necessary to carry out this subsection.
(6) Authorization
Of the funds authorized to be appropriated to the Administrator by this chapter, such amounts as are required shall be available to carry out this subsection.
(7) Guidelines for carcinogenic risk assessment
The Administrator shall consider, but need not adopt, the recommendations contained in the report of the National Academy of Sciences prepared pursuant to this subsection and the views of the Science Advisory Board, with respect to such report. Prior to the promulgation of any standard under subsection (f) of this section, and after notice and opportunity for comment, the Administrator shall publish revised Guidelines for Carcinogenic Risk Assessment or a detailed explanation of the reasons that any recommendations contained in the report of the National Academy of Sciences will not be implemented. The publication of such revised Guidelines shall be a final Agency action for purposes of section 7607 of this title.

(p) Mickey Leland National Urban Air Toxics Research Center
(1) Establishment
The Administrator shall oversee the establishment of a National Urban Air Toxics Research Center, to be located at a university, a hospital, or other facility capable of undertaking and maintaining similar research capabilities in the areas of epidemiology, oncology, toxicology, pulmonary medicine, pathology, and biostatistics. The center shall be known as the Mickey Leland National Urban Air Toxics Research Center. The geographic site of the National Urban Air Toxics Research Center should be further directed to Harris County, Texas, in order to take full advantage of the well developed scientific community presence on-site at the Texas Medical Center as well as the extensive data previously compiled for the comprehensive monitoring system currently in place.
(2) Board of Directors
The National Urban Air Toxics Research Center shall be governed by a Board of Directors to be comprised of 9 members, the appointment of which shall be allocated pro rata among the Speaker of the House, the Majority Leader of the Senate and the President. The members of the Board of Directors shall be selected based on their respective academic and professional backgrounds and expertise in matters relating to public health, environmental pollution and industrial hygiene. The duties of the Board of Directors shall be to determine policy and research guidelines, submit views from center sponsors and the public and issue periodic reports of center findings and activities.

(3) Scientific Advisory Panel

The Board of Directors shall be advised by a Scientific Advisory Panel, the 13 members of which shall be appointed by the Board, and to include eminent members of the scientific and medical communities. The Panel membership may include scientists with relevant experience from the National Institute of Environmental Health Sciences, the Center for Disease Control, the Environmental Protection Agency, the National Cancer Institute, and others, and the Panel shall conduct peer review and evaluate research results. The Panel shall assist the Board in developing the research agenda, reviewing proposals and applications, and advise on the awarding of research grants.

(4) Funding

The center shall be established and funded with both Federal and private source funds.

(q) Savings provision

(1) Standards previously promulgated

Any standard under this section in effect before the date of enactment of the Clean Air Act Amendments of 1990 [November 15, 1990] shall remain in force and effect after such date unless modified as provided in this section before the date of enactment of such Amendments or under such Amendments. Except as provided in paragraph (4), any standard under this section which has been promulgated, but has not taken effect, before such date shall not be affected by such Amendments unless modified as provided in this section before such date or under such Amendments. Each such standard shall be reviewed and, if appropriate, revised, to comply with the requirements of subsection (d) of this section within 10 years after the date of enactment of the Clean Air Act Amendments of 1990. If a timely petition for review of any such standard under section 7607 of this title is pending on such date of enactment, the standard shall be upheld if it complies with this section as in effect before that date. If any such standard is remanded to the Administrator, the Administrator may in the Administrator's discretion apply either the requirements of this section, or those of this section as in effect before the date of enactment of the Clean Air Act Amendments of 1990.

(2) Special rule

Notwithstanding paragraph (1), no standard shall be established under this section, as amended by the Clean Air Act Amendments of 1990, for radionuclide emissions from (A) elemental phosphorous plants, (B) grate calcination elemental phosphorous plants, (C) phosphogypsum stacks, or (D) any subcategory of the foregoing. This section, as in effect prior to the date of enactment of the Clean Air Act Amendments of 1990 [November 15, 1990], shall remain in effect for radionuclide emissions from such plants and stacks.

(3) Other categories

Notwithstanding paragraph (1), this section, as in effect prior to the date of enactment of the Clean Air Act Amendments of 1990 [November 15, 1990], shall remain in effect for radionuclide emissions from non-Department of Energy Federal facilities that are not licensed by the Nuclear Regulatory Commission, coal-fired utility and industrial boilers, underground uranium mines, surface uranium mines, and disposal of uranium mill tailings piles, unless the Administrator, in the Administrator's discretion, applies the requirements of this section as modified by the Clean Air Act Amendments of 1990 to such sources of radionuclides.

(4) Medical facilities

Notwithstanding paragraph (1), no standard promulgated under this section prior to November 15, 1990, with respect to medical research or treatment facilities shall take effect for two years following November 15, 1990, unless the Administrator makes a determination pursuant to a rulemaking under subsection (d)(9) of this section. If the Administrator determines that the regulatory program established by the Nuclear Regulatory Commission for such facilities does not provide an ample margin of safety to protect public health, the requirements of this section shall fully apply to such facilities. If the Administrator determines that such regulatory program does provide an ample margin of safety to protect the public health, the Administrator is not required to promulgate a standard under this section for such facilities, as provided in subsection (d)(9) of this section.

(r) Prevention of accidental releases

(1) Purpose and general duty

It shall be the objective of the regulations and programs authorized under this subsection to prevent the accidental release and to minimize the consequences of any such release of any substance listed pursuant to paragraph (3) or any other extremely hazardous substance. The owners and operators of stationary sources producing, processing, handling or storing such substances have a general duty in the same manner and to the same extent as section 654 of title 29 to identify hazards which may result from such releases using appropriate hazard assessment techniques, to design and maintain a safe facility taking such steps as are necessary to prevent releases, and to minimize the consequences of accidental releases which do occur. For purposes of this paragraph, the provisions of section 7604 of this title shall not be available to any person or otherwise be construed to be applicable to this paragraph. Nothing in this section shall be interpreted, construed, implied or applied to create any liability or basis for suit for compensation for bodily injury or any other injury or property damages to any person which may result from accidental releases of such substances.

(2) Definitions
   (A) The term "accidental release" means an unanticipated emission of a regulated substance or other extremely hazardous substance into the ambient air from a stationary source.
   (B) The term "regulated substance" means a substance listed under paragraph (3).
   (C) The term "stationary source" means any buildings, structures, equipment, installations or substance emitting stationary activities (i) which belong to the same industrial group, (ii) which are located on one or more contiguous properties, (iii) which are under the control of the same person (or persons under common control), and (iv) from which an accidental release may occur.
   (D) The term "retail facility" means a stationary source at which more than one-half of the income is obtained from direct sales to end users or at which more than one-half of the fuel sold, by volume, is sold through a cylinder exchange program.

(3) List of substances
The Administrator shall promulgate not later than 24 months after November 15, 1990, an initial list of 100 substances which, in the case of an accidental release, are known to cause or may reasonably be anticipated to cause death, injury, or serious adverse effects to human health or the environment. For purposes of promulgating such list, the Administrator shall use, but is not limited to, the list of extremely hazardous substances published under the Emergency Planning and Community Right-to-Know Act of 1986 [42 U.S.C. 11001 et seq.], with such modifications as the Administrator deems appropriate. The initial list shall include chlorine, anhydrous ammonia, methyl chloride, ethylene oxide, vinyl chloride, methyl isocyanate, hydrogen cyanide, ammonia, hydrogen sulfide, toluene diisocyanate, phosgene, bromine, anhydrous hydrogen chloride, hydrogen fluoride, anhydrous sulfur dioxide, and sulfur trioxide. The initial list shall include at least 100 substances which pose the greatest risk of causing death, injury, or serious adverse effects to human health or the environment from accidental releases. Regulations establishing the list shall include an explanation of the basis for establishing the list. The list may be revised from time to time by the Administrator on the Administrator's own motion or by petition and shall be reviewed at least every 5 years. No air pollutant for which a national primary ambient air quality standard has been established shall be included on any such list. No substance, practice, process, or activity regulated under subchapter VI of this chapter shall be subject to regulations under this subsection. The Administrator shall establish procedures for the addition and deletion of substances from the list established under this paragraph consistent with those applicable to the list in subsection (b) of this section.

(4) Factors to be considered
In listing substances under paragraph (3), the Administrator—
   (A) shall consider—
      (i) the severity of any acute adverse health effects associated with accidental releases of the substance;
      (ii) the likelihood of accidental releases of the substance; and
      (iii) the potential magnitude of human exposure to accidental releases of the substance; and
   (B) shall not list a flammable substance when used as a fuel or held for sale as a fuel at a retail facility under this subsection solely because of the explosive or flammable prop-

erties of the substance, unless a fire or explosion caused by the substance will result in acute adverse health effects from human exposure to the substance, including the unburned fuel or its combustion byproducts, other than those caused by the heat of the fire or impact of the explosion.

(5) Threshold quantity

At the time any substance is listed pursuant to paragraph (3), the Administrator shall establish by rule, a threshold quantity for the substance, taking into account the toxicity, reactivity, volatility, dispersibility, combustibility, or flammability of the substance and the amount of the substance which, as a result of an accidental release, is known to cause or may reasonably be anticipated to cause death, injury or serious adverse effects to human health for which the substance was listed. The Administrator is authorized to establish a greater threshold quantity for, or to exempt entirely, any substance that is a nutrient used in agriculture when held by a farmer.

(6) Chemical Safety Board

(A) There is hereby established an independent safety board to be known as the Chemical Safety and Hazard Investigation Board.

(B) The Board shall consist of 5 members, including a Chairperson, who shall be appointed by the President, by and with the advice and consent of the Senate. Members of the Board shall be appointed on the basis of technical qualification, professional standing, and demonstrated knowledge in the fields of accident reconstruction, safety engineering, human factors, toxicology, or air pollution regulation. The terms of office of members of the Board shall be 5 years. Any member of the Board, including the Chairperson, may be removed for inefficiency, neglect of duty, or malfeasance in office. The Chairperson shall be the Chief Executive Officer of the Board and shall exercise the executive and administrative functions of the Board.

(C) The Board shall—

(i) investigate (or cause to be investigated), determine and report to the public in writing the facts, conditions, and circumstances and the cause or probable cause of any accidental release resulting in a fatality, serious injury or substantial property damages;

(ii) issue periodic reports to the Congress, Federal, State and local agencies, including the Environmental Protection Agency and the Occupational Safety and Health Administration, concerned with the safety of chemical production, processing, handling and storage, and other interested persons recommending measures to reduce the likelihood or the consequences of accidental releases and proposing corrective steps to make chemical production, processing, handling and storage as safe and free from risk of injury as is possible and may include in such reports proposed rules or orders which should be issued by the Administrator under the authority of this section or the Secretary of Labor under the Occupational Safety and Health Act [29 U.S.C. 651 et seq.] to prevent or minimize the consequences of any release of substances that may cause death, injury or other serious adverse effects on human health or substantial property damage as the result of an accidental release; and

(iii) establish by regulation requirements binding on persons for reporting accidental releases into the ambient air subject to the Board's investigatory jurisdiction. Reporting releases to the National Response Center, in lieu of the Board directly, shall satisfy such regulations. The National Response Center shall promptly notify the Board of any releases which are within the Board's jurisdiction.

(D) The Board may utilize the expertise and experience of other agencies.

(E) The Board shall coordinate its activities with investigations and studies conducted by other agencies of the United States having a responsibility to protect public health and safety. The Board shall enter into a memorandum of understanding with the National Transportation Safety Board to assure coordination of functions and to limit duplication of activities which shall designate the National Transportation Safety Board as the lead agency for the investigation of releases which are transportation related. The Board shall not be authorized to investigate marine oil spills, which the National Transportation Safety Board is authorized to investigate. The Board shall enter into a memorandum of understanding with the Occupational Safety and Health Administration

so as to limit duplication of activities. In no event shall the Board forego an investigation where an accidental release causes a fatality or serious injury among the general public, or had the potential to cause substantial property damage or a number of deaths or injuries among the general public.
(F) The Board is authorized to conduct research and studies with respect to the potential for accidental releases, whether or not an accidental release has occurred, where there is evidence which indicates the presence of a potential hazard or hazards. To the extent practicable, the Board shall conduct such studies in cooperation with other Federal agencies having emergency response authorities, State and local governmental agencies and associations and organizations from the industrial, commercial, and nonprofit sectors.
(G) No part of the conclusions, findings, or recommendations of the Board relating to any accidental release or the investigation thereof shall be admitted as evidence or used in any action or suit for damages arising out of any matter mentioned in such report.
(H) Not later than 18 months after November 15, 1990, the Board shall publish a report accompanied by recommendations to the Administrator on the use of hazard assessments in preventing the occurrence and minimizing the consequences of accidental releases of extremely hazardous substances. The recommendations shall include a list of extremely hazardous substances which are not regulated substances (including threshold quantities for such substances) and categories of stationary sources for which hazard assessments would be an appropriate measure to aid in the prevention of accidental releases and to minimize the consequences of those releases that do occur. The recommendations shall also include a description of the information and analysis which would be appropriate to include in any hazard assessment. The Board shall also make recommendations with respect to the role of risk management plans as required by paragraph (8)(B)[8] in preventing accidental releases. The Board may from time to time review and revise its recommendations under this subparagraph.
(I) Whenever the Board submits a recommendation with respect to accidental releases to the Administrator, the Administrator shall respond to such recommendation formally and in writing not later than 180 days after receipt thereof. The response to the Board's recommendation by the Administrator shall indicate whether the Administrator will—
  (i) initiate a rulemaking or issue such orders as are necessary to implement the recommendation in full or in part, pursuant to any timetable contained in the recommendation;
  (ii) decline to initiate a rulemaking or issue orders as recommended.
Any determination by the Administrator not to implement a recommendation of the Board or to implement a recommendation only in part, including any variation from the schedule contained in the recommendation, shall be accompanied by a statement from the Administrator setting forth the reasons for such determination.
(J) The Board may make recommendations with respect to accidental releases to the Secretary of Labor. Whenever the Board submits such recommendation, the Secretary shall respond to such recommendation formally and in writing not later than 180 days after receipt thereof. The response to the Board's recommendation by the Administrator shall indicate whether the Secretary will—
  (i) initiate a rulemaking or issue such orders as are necessary to implement the recommendation in full or in part, pursuant to any timetable contained in the recommendation;
  (ii) decline to initiate a rulemaking or issue orders as recommended.
Any determination by the Secretary not to implement a recommendation or to implement a recommendation only in part, including any variation from the schedule contained in the recommendation, shall be accompanied by a statement from the Secretary setting forth the reasons for such determination.
(K) Within 2 years after November 15, 1990, the Board shall issue a report to the Administrator of the Environmental Protection Agency and to the Administrator of the Occupational Safety and Health Administration recommending the adoption of regulations for the preparation of risk management plans and general requirements for the

---

[8] So in original. Probably should be paragraph "(7)(B)".

prevention of accidental releases of regulated substances into the ambient air (including recommendations for listing substances under paragraph (3)) and for the mitigation of the potential adverse effect on human health or the environment as a result of accidental releases which should be applicable to any stationary source handling any regulated substance in more than threshold amounts. The Board may include proposed rules or orders which should be issued by the Administrator under authority of this subsection or by the Secretary of Labor under the Occupational Safety and Health Act [29 U.S.C. 651 et seq.]. Any such recommendations shall be specific and shall identify the regulated substance or class of regulated substances (or other substances) to which the recommendations apply. The Administrator shall consider such recommendations before promulgating regulations required by paragraph (7)(B).
(L) The Board, or upon authority of the Board, any member thereof, any administrative law judge employed by or assigned to the Board, or any officer or employee duly designated by the Board, may for the purpose of carrying out duties authorized by subparagraph (C)–
  (i) hold such hearings, sit and act at such times and places, administer such oaths, and require by subpoena or otherwise attendance and testimony of such witnesses and the production of evidence and may require by order that any person engaged in the production, processing, handling, or storage of extremely hazardous substances submit written reports and responses to requests and questions within such time and in such form as the Board may require; and
  (ii) upon presenting appropriate credentials and a written notice of inspection authority, enter any property where an accidental release causing a fatality, serious injury or substantial property damage has occurred and do all things therein necessary for a proper investigation pursuant to subparagraph (C) and inspect at reasonable times records, files, papers, processes, controls, and facilities and take such samples as are relevant to such investigation.
Whenever the Administrator or the Board conducts an inspection of a facility pursuant to this subsection, employees and their representatives shall have the same rights to participate in such inspections as provided in the Occupational Safety and Health Act [29 U.S.C. 651 et seq.].
(M) In addition to that described in subparagraph (L), the Board may use any information gathering authority of the Administrator under this chapter, including the subpoena power provided in section 7607(a)(1) of this title.
(N) The Board is authorized to establish such procedural and administrative rules as are necessary to the exercise of its functions and duties. The Board is authorized without regard to section 5 of title 41 to enter into contracts, leases, cooperative agreements or other transactions as may be necessary in the conduct of the duties and functions of the Board with any other agency, institution, or person.
(O) After the effective date of any reporting requirement promulgated pursuant to subparagraph (C)(iii) it shall be unlawful for any person to fail to report any release of any extremely hazardous substance as required by such subparagraph. The Administrator is authorized to enforce any regulation or requirements established by the Board pursuant to subparagraph (C)(iii) using the authorities of sections 7413 and 7414 of this title. Any request for information from the owner or operator of a stationary source made by the Board or by the Administrator under this section shall be treated, for purposes of sections 7413, 7414, 7416, 7420, 7603, 7604 and 7607 of this title and any other enforcement provisions of this chapter, as a request made by the Administrator under section 7414 of this title and may be enforced by the Chairperson of the Board or by the Administrator as provided in such section.
(P) The Administrator shall provide to the Board such support and facilities as may be necessary for operation of the Board.
(Q) Consistent with subsection[9] (G) and section 7414(c) of this title any records, reports or information obtained by the Board shall be available to the Administrator, the Secretary of Labor, the Congress and the public, except that upon a showing satisfactory to the Board by any person that records, reports, or information, or particular part thereof

---

[9] So in original. Probably should be "subparagraph".

(other than release or emissions data) to which the Board has access, if made public, is likely to cause substantial harm to the person's competitive position, the Board shall consider such record, report, or information or particular portion thereof confidential in accordance with section 1905 of title 18, except that such record, report, or information may be disclosed to other officers, employees, and authorized representatives of the United States concerned with carrying out this chapter or when relevant under any proceeding under this chapter. This subparagraph does not constitute authority to withhold records, reports, or information from the Congress.
- (R) Whenever the Board submits or transmits any budget estimate, budget request, supplemental budget request, or other budget information, legislative recommendation, prepared testimony for congressional hearings, recommendation or study to the President, the Secretary of Labor, the Administrator, or the Director of the Office of Management and Budget, it shall concurrently transmit a copy thereof to the Congress. No report of the Board shall be subject to review by the Administrator or any Federal agency or to judicial review in any court. No officer or agency of the United States shall have authority to require the Board to submit its budget requests or estimates, legislative recommendations, prepared testimony, comments, recommendations or reports to any officer or agency of the United States for approval or review prior to the submission of such recommendations, testimony, comments or reports to the Congress. In the performance of their functions as established by this chapter, the members, officers and employees of the Board shall not be responsible to or subject to supervision or direction, in carrying out any duties under this subsection, of any officer or employee or agent of the Environmental Protection Agency, the Department of Labor or any other agency of the United States except that the President may remove any member, officer or employee of the Board for inefficiency, neglect of duty or malfeasance in office. Nothing in this section shall affect the application of title 5 to officers or employees of the Board.
- (S) The Board shall submit an annual report to the President and to the Congress which shall include, but not be limited to, information on accidental releases which have been investigated by or reported to the Board during the previous year, recommendations for legislative or administrative action which the Board has made, the actions which have been taken by the Administrator or the Secretary of Labor or the heads of other agencies to implement such recommendations, an identification of priorities for study and investigation in the succeeding year, progress in the development of risk-reduction technologies and the response to and implementation of significant research findings on chemical safety in the public and private sector.

(7) Accident prevention
- (A) In order to prevent accidental releases of regulated substances, the Administrator is authorized to promulgate release prevention, detection, and correction requirements which may include monitoring, record-keeping, reporting, training, vapor recovery, secondary containment, and other design, equipment, work practice, and operational requirements. Regulations promulgated under this paragraph may make distinctions between various types, classes, and kinds of facilities, devices and systems taking into consideration factors including, but not limited to, the size, location, process, process controls, quantity of substances handled, potency of substances, and response capabilities present at any stationary source. Regulations promulgated pursuant to this subparagraph shall have an effective date, as determined by the Administrator, assuring compliance as expeditiously as practicable.
- (B) (i) Within 3 years after November 15, 1990, the Administrator shall promulgate reasonable regulations and appropriate guidance to provide, to the greatest extent practicable, for the prevention and detection of accidental releases of regulated substances and for response to such releases by the owners or operators of the sources of such releases. The Administrator shall utilize the expertise of the Secretaries of Transportation and Labor in promulgating such regulations. As appropriate, such regulations shall cover the use, operation, repair, replacement, and maintenance of equipment to monitor, detect, inspect, and control such releases, including training of persons in the use and maintenance of such equipment and in the conduct of periodic inspections. The regulations shall include procedures

and measures for emergency response after an accidental release of a regulated substance in order to protect human health and the environment. The regulations shall cover storage, as well as operations. The regulations shall, as appropriate, recognize differences in size, operations, processes, class and categories of sources and the voluntary actions of such sources to prevent such releases and respond to such releases. The regulations shall be applicable to a stationary source 3 years after the date of promulgation, or 3 years after the date on which a regulated substance present at the source in more than threshold amounts is first listed under paragraph (3), whichever is later.

(ii) The regulations under this subparagraph shall require the owner or operator of stationary sources at which a regulated substance is present in more than a threshold quantity to prepare and implement a risk management plan to detect and prevent or minimize accidental releases of such substances from the stationary source, and to provide a prompt emergency response to any such releases in order to protect human health and the environment. Such plan shall provide for compliance with the requirements of this subsection and shall also include each of the following:

(I) a hazard assessment to assess the potential effects of an accidental release of any regulated substance. This assessment shall include an estimate of potential release quantities and a determination of downwind effects, including potential exposures to affected populations. Such assessment shall include a previous release history of the past 5 years, including the size, concentration, and duration of releases, and shall include an evaluation of worst case accidental releases;

(II) a program for preventing accidental releases of regulated substances, including safety precautions and maintenance, monitoring and employee training measures to be used at the source; and

(III) a response program providing for specific actions to be taken in response to an accidental release of a regulated substance so as to protect human health and the environment, including procedures for informing the public and local agencies responsible for responding to accidental releases, emergency health care, and employee training measures.

At the time regulations are promulgated under this subparagraph, the Administrator shall promulgate guidelines to assist stationary sources in the preparation of risk management plans. The guidelines shall, to the extent practicable, include model risk management plans.

(iii) The owner or operator of each stationary source covered by clause (ii) shall register a risk management plan prepared under this subparagraph with the Administrator before the effective date of regulations under clause (i) in such form and manner as the Administrator shall, by rule, require. Plans prepared pursuant to this subparagraph shall also be submitted to the Chemical Safety and Hazard Investigation Board, to the State in which the stationary source is located, and to any local agency or entity having responsibility for planning for or responding to accidental releases which may occur at such source, and shall be available to the public under section 7414(c) of this title. The Administrator shall establish, by rule, an auditing system to regularly review and, if necessary, require revision in risk management plans to assure that the plans comply with this subparagraph. Each such plan shall be updated periodically as required by the Administrator, by rule.

(C) Any regulations promulgated pursuant to this subsection shall to the maximum extent practicable, consistent with this subsection, be consistent with the recommendations and standards established by the American Society of Mechanical Engineers (ASME), the American National Standards Institute (ANSI) or the American Society of Testing Materials (ASTM). The Administrator shall take into consideration the concerns of small business in promulgating regulations under this subsection.

(D) In carrying out the authority of this paragraph, the Administrator shall consult with the Secretary of Labor and the Secretary of Transportation and shall coordinate any requirements under this paragraph with any requirements established for comparable purposes by the Occupational Safety and Health Administration or the Department of Transportation. Nothing in this subsection shall be interpreted, construed or applied to impose requirements affecting, or to grant the Administrator, the Chemical Safety and Hazard Investigation Board, or any other agency any authority to regulate (including requirements for hazard assessment), the accidental release of radionuclides arising from the construction and operation of facilities licensed by the Nuclear Regulatory Commission.

(E) After the effective date of any regulation or requirement imposed under this subsection, it shall be unlawful for any person to operate any stationary source subject to such regulation or requirement in violation of such regulation or requirement. Each regulation or requirement under this subsection shall for purposes of sections 7413, 7414, 7416, 7420, 7604, and 7607 of this title and other enforcement provisions of this chapter, be treated as a standard in effect under subsection (d) of this section.

(F) Notwithstanding the provisions of subchapter V of this chapter or this section, no stationary source shall be required to apply for, or operate pursuant to, a permit issued under such subchapter solely because such source is subject to regulations or requirements under this subsection.

(G) In exercising any authority under this subsection, the Administrator shall not, for purposes of section 653(b)(1) of title 29, be deemed to be exercising statutory authority to prescribe or enforce standards or regulations affecting occupational safety and health.

(H) Public access to off-site consequence analysis information.—
  (i) Definitions.—In this subparagraph:
    (I) Covered person.—The term "covered person" means—
      (aa) an officer or employee of the United States;
      (bb) an officer or employee of an agent or contractor of the Federal Government;
      (cc) an officer or employee of a State or local government;
      (dd) an officer or employee of an agent or contractor of a State or local government;
      (ee) an individual affiliated with an entity that has been given, by a State or local government, responsibility for preventing, planning for, or responding to accidental releases;
      (ff) an officer or employee or an agent or contractor of an entity described in item (ee); and
      (gg) a qualified researcher under clause (vii).
    (II) Official use.—The term "official use" means an action of a Federal, State, or local government agency or an entity referred to in subclause (I)(ee) intended to carry out a function relevant to preventing, planning for, or responding to accidental releases.
    (III) Off-site consequence analysis information.—The term "off-site consequence analysis information" means those portions of a risk management plan, excluding the executive summary of the plan, consisting of an evaluation of 1 or more worst-case release scenarios or alternative release scenarios, and any electronic data base created by the Administrator from those portions.
    (IV) Risk management plan.—The term "risk management plan" means a risk management plan submitted to the Administrator by an owner or operator of a stationary source under subparagraph (B)(iii).
  (ii) Regulations.—Not later than 1 year after August 5, 1999, the President shall—
    (I) assess—
      (aa) the increased risk of terrorist and other criminal activity associated with the posting of off-site consequence analysis information on the Internet; and
      (bb) the incentives created by public disclosure of off-site consequence analysis information for reduction in the risk of accidental releases; and
    (II) based on the assessment under subclause (I), promulgate regulations governing the distribution of off-site consequence analysis information in a manner that, in the opinion of the President, minimizes the likelihood of accidental

releases and the risk described in subclause (I)(aa) and the likelihood of harm to public health and welfare, and—
- (aa) allows access by any member of the public to paper copies of off-site consequence analysis information for a limited number of stationary sources located anywhere in the United States, without any geographical restriction;
- (bb) allows other public access to off-site consequence analysis information as appropriate;
- (cc) allows access for official use by a covered person described in any of items (cc) through (ff) of clause (i)(I) (referred to in this subclause as a "State or local covered person") to off-site consequence analysis information relating to stationary sources located in the person's State;
- (dd) allows a State or local covered person to provide, for official use, off-site consequence analysis information relating to stationary sources located in the person's State to a State or local covered person in a contiguous State; and
- (ee) allows a State or local covered person to obtain for official use, by request to the Administrator, off-site consequence analysis information that is not available to the person under item (cc).

(iii) Availability under freedom of information act.—
- (I) First year.—Off-site consequence analysis information, and any ranking of stationary sources derived from the information, shall not be made available under section 552 of title 5 during the 1-year period beginning on August 5, 1999.
- (II) After first year.—If the regulations under clause (ii) are promulgated on or before the end of the period described in subclause (I), off-site consequence analysis information covered by the regulations, and any ranking of stationary sources derived from the information, shall not be made available under section 552 of title 5 after the end of that period.
- (III) Applicability.—Subclauses (I) and (II) apply to off-site consequence analysis information submitted to the Administrator before, on, or after August 5, 1999.

(iv) Availability of information during transition period.—
The Administrator shall make off-site consequence analysis information available to covered persons for official use in a manner that meets the requirements of items (cc) through (ee) of clause (ii)(II), and to the public in a form that does not make available any information concerning the identity or location of stationary sources, during the period—
- (I) beginning on August 5, 1999; and
- (II) ending on the earlier of the date of promulgation of the regulations under clause (ii) or the date that is 1 year after August 5, 1999.

(v) Prohibition on unauthorized disclosure of information by covered persons.—
- (I) In general.—Beginning on August 5, 1999, a covered person shall not disclose to the public off-site consequence analysis information in any form, or any statewide or national ranking of identified stationary sources derived from such information, except as authorized by this subparagraph (including the regulations promulgated under clause (ii)). After the end of the 1-year period beginning on August 5, 1999, if regulations have not been promulgated under clause (ii), the preceding sentence shall not apply.
- (II) Criminal penalties.—Notwithstanding section 7413 of this title, a covered person that willfully violates a restriction or prohibition established by this subparagraph (including the regulations promulgated under clause (ii)) shall, upon conviction, be fined for an infraction under section 3571 of title 18 (but shall not be subject to imprisonment) for each unauthorized disclosure of off-site consequence analysis information, except that subsection (d) of such section 3571 shall not apply to a case in which the offense results in pecuniary loss unless the defendant knew that such loss would occur. The disclosure of off-site consequence analysis information for each specific stationary source shall be considered a separate offense. The total of all penalties that may be im-

posed on a single person or organization under this item shall not exceed $1,000,000 for violations committed during any 1 calendar year.
(III) Applicability.—If the owner or operator of a stationary source makes off-site consequence analysis information relating to that stationary source available to the public without restriction—
(aa) subclauses (I) and (II) shall not apply with respect to the information; and
(bb) the owner or operator shall notify the Administrator of the public availability of the information.
(IV) List.—The Administrator shall maintain and make publicly available a list of all stationary sources that have provided notification under subclause (III)(bb).
(vi) Notice.—The Administrator shall provide notice of the definition of official use as provided in clause (i)(III) and examples of actions that would and would not meet that definition, and notice of the restrictions on further dissemination and the penalties established by this chapter to each covered person who receives off-site consequence analysis information under clause (iv) and each covered person who receives off-site consequence analysis information for an official use under the regulations promulgated under clause (ii).
(vii) Qualified researchers.—
(I) In general.—Not later than 180 days after August 5, 1999, the Administrator, in consultation with the Attorney General, shall develop and implement a system for providing off-site consequence analysis information, including facility identification, to any qualified researcher, including a qualified researcher from industry or any public interest group.
(II) Limitation on dissemination.—The system shall not allow the researcher to disseminate, or make available on the Internet, the off-site consequence analysis information, or any portion of the off-site consequence analysis information, received under this clause.
(viii) Read-only information technology system.—In consultation with the Attorney General and the heads of other appropriate Federal agencies, the Administrator shall establish an information technology system that provides for the availability to the public of off-site consequence analysis information by means of a central data base under the control of the Federal Government that contains information that users may read, but that provides no means by which an electronic or mechanical copy of the information may be made.
(ix) Voluntary industry accident prevention standards.—The Environmental Protection Agency, the Department of Justice, and other appropriate agencies may provide technical assistance to owners and operators of stationary sources and participate in the development of voluntary industry standards that will help achieve the objectives set forth in paragraph (1).
(x) Effect on state or local law.—
(I) In general.—Subject to subclause (II), this subparagraph (including the regulations promulgated under this subparagraph) shall supersede any provision of State or local law that is inconsistent with this subparagraph (including the regulations).
(II) Availability of information under state law.—
Nothing in this subparagraph precludes a State from making available data on the off-site consequences of chemical releases collected in accordance with State law.
(xi) Report.—
(I) In general.—Not later than 3 years after August 5, 1999, the Attorney General, in consultation with appropriate State, local, and Federal Government agencies, affected industry, and the public, shall submit to Congress a report that describes the extent to which regulations promulgated under this paragraph have resulted in actions, including the design and maintenance of safe facilities, that are effective in detecting, preventing, and minimizing the consequences of releases of regulated substances that may be caused by criminal activity. As part of this report, the Attorney General, using available data to

the extent possible, and a sampling of covered stationary sources selected at the discretion of the Attorney General, and in consultation with appropriate State, local, and Federal governmental agencies, affected industry, and the public, shall review the vulnerability of covered stationary sources to criminal and terrorist activity, current industry practices regarding site security, and security of transportation of regulated substances. The Attorney General shall submit this report, containing the results of the review, together with recommendations, if any, for reducing vulnerability of covered stationary sources to criminal and terrorist activity, to the Committee on Commerce of the United States House of Representatives and the Committee on Environment and Public Works of the United States Senate and other relevant committees of Congress.

(II) Interim report.—Not later than 12 months after August 5, 1999, the Attorney General shall submit to the Committee on Commerce of the United States House of Representatives and the Committee on Environment and Public Works of the United States Senate, and other relevant committees of Congress, an interim report that includes, at a minimum—
  (aa) the preliminary findings under subclause (I);
  (bb) the methods used to develop the findings; and
  (cc) an explanation of the activities expected to occur that could cause the findings of the report under subclause (I) to be different than the preliminary findings.

(III) Availability of information.—Information that is developed by the Attorney General or requested by the Attorney General and received from a covered stationary source for the purpose of conducting the review under subclauses (I) and (II) shall be exempt from disclosure under section 552 of title 5 if such information would pose a threat to national security.

(xii) Scope.—This subparagraph—
  (I) applies only to covered persons; and
  (II) does not restrict the dissemination of off-site consequence analysis information by any covered person in any manner or form except in the form of a risk management plan or an electronic data base created by the Administrator from off-site consequence analysis information.

(xiii) Authorization of appropriations.—There are authorized to be appropriated to the Administrator and the Attorney General such sums as are necessary to carry out this subparagraph (including the regulations promulgated under clause (ii)), to remain available until expended.

(8) Research on hazard assessments

The Administrator may collect and publish information on accident scenarios and consequences covering a range of possible events for substances listed under paragraph (3). The Administrator shall establish a program of long-term research to develop and disseminate information on methods and techniques for hazard assessment which may be useful in improving and validating the procedures employed in the preparation of hazard assessments under this subsection.

(9) Order authority

(A) In addition to any other action taken, when the Administrator determines that there may be an imminent and substantial endangerment to the human health or welfare or the environment because of an actual or threatened accidental release of a regulated substance, the Administrator may secure such relief as may be necessary to abate such danger or threat, and the district court of the United States in the district in which the threat occurs shall have jurisdiction to grant such relief as the public interest and the equities of the case may require. The Administrator may also, after notice to the State in which the stationary source is located, take other action under this paragraph including, but not limited to, issuing such orders as may be necessary to protect human health. The Administrator shall take action under section 7603 of this title rather than this paragraph whenever the authority of such section is adequate to protect human health and the environment.

(B) Orders issued pursuant to this paragraph may be enforced in an action brought in the appropriate United States district court as if the order were issued under section 7603 of this title.
(C) Within 180 days after November 15, 1990, the Administrator shall publish guidance for using the order authorities established by this paragraph. Such guidance shall provide for the coordinated use of the authorities of this paragraph with other emergency powers authorized by section 9606 of this title, sections 311(c), 308, 309 and 504(a) of the Federal Water Pollution Control Act [33 U.S.C. 1321(c), 1318, 1319, 1364(a)], sections 3007, 3008, 3013, and 7003 of the Solid Waste Disposal Act [42 U.S.C. 6927, 6928, 6934, 6973], sections 1445 and 1431 of the Safe Drinking Water Act [42 U.S.C. 300j-4, 300i], sections 5 and 7 of the Toxic Substances Control Act [15 U.S.C. 2604, 2606], and sections 7413, 7414, and 7603 of this title.

(10) Presidential review

The President shall conduct a review of release prevention, mitigation and response authorities of the various Federal agencies and shall clarify and coordinate agency responsibilities to assure the most effective and efficient implementation of such authorities and to identify any deficiencies in authority or resources which may exist. The President may utilize the resources and solicit the recommendations of the Chemical Safety and Hazard Investigation Board in conducting such review. At the conclusion of such review, but not later than 24 months after November 15, 1990, the President shall transmit a message to the Congress on the release prevention, mitigation and response activities of the Federal Government making such recommendations for change in law as the President may deem appropriate. Nothing in this paragraph shall be interpreted, construed or applied to authorize the President to modify or reassign release prevention, mitigation or response authorities otherwise established by law.

(11) State authority

Nothing in this subsection shall preclude, deny or limit any right of a State or political subdivision thereof to adopt or enforce any regulation, requirement, limitation or standard (including any procedural requirement) that is more stringent than a regulation, requirement, limitation or standard in effect under this subsection or that applies to a substance not subject to this subsection.

(s) Periodic report

Not later than January 15, 1993 and every 3 years thereafter, the Administrator shall prepare and transmit to the Congress a comprehensive report on the measures taken by the Agency and by the States to implement the provisions of this section. The Administrator shall maintain a database on pollutants and sources subject to the provisions of this section and shall include aggregate information from the database in each annual report. The report shall include, but not be limited to—

(1) a status report on standard-setting under subsections (d) and (f) of this section;
(2) information with respect to compliance with such standards including the costs of compliance experienced by sources in various categories and subcategories;
(3) development and implementation of the national urban air toxics program; and
(4) recommendations of the Chemical Safety and Hazard Investigation Board with respect to the prevention and mitigation of accidental releases.

(July 14, 1955, ch. 360, title I, Sec. 112, as added Pub. L. 91-604, Sec. 4(a), Dec. 31, 1970, 84 Stat. 1685; amended Pub. L. 95-95, title I, Secs. 109(d)(2), 110, title IV, Sec. 401(c), Aug. 7, 1977, 91 Stat. 701, 703, 791; Pub. L. 95-623, Sec. 13(b), Nov. 9, 1978, 92 Stat. 3458; Pub. L. 101-549, title III, Sec. 301, Nov. 15, 1990, 104 Stat. 2531; Pub. L. 102-187, Dec. 4, 1991, 105 Stat. 1285; Pub. L. 105-362, title IV, Sec. 402(b), Nov. 10, 1998, 112 Stat. 3283; Pub. L. 106-40, Secs. 2, 3(a), Aug. 5, 1999, 113 Stat. 207, 208.)

References in Text

The date of enactment, referred to in subsec. (a)(11), probably means the date of enactment of Pub. L. 101-549, which amended this section generally and was approved Nov. 15, 1990.

The Atomic Energy Act, referred to in subsec. (d)(9), probably means the Atomic Energy Act of 1954, act Aug. 1, 1946, ch. 724, as added by act Aug. 30, 1954, ch. 1073, Sec. 1, 68 Stat. 921, and

94 / Environmental Statutes

amended, which is classified generally to chapter 23 (Sec. 2011 et seq.) of this title. For complete classification of this Act to the Code, see Short Title note set out under section 2011 of this title and Tables.

The Federal Water Pollution Control Act, referred to in subsecs. (e)(5) and (m)(1)(D), (5)(D), is act June 30, 1948, ch. 758, as amended generally by Pub. L. 92-500, Sec. 2, Oct. 18, 1972, 86 Stat. 816, which is classified generally to chapter 26 (Sec. 1251 et seq.) of Title 33, Navigation and Navigable Waters. Title II of the Act is classified generally to subchapter II (Sec. 1281 et seq.) of chapter 26 of Title 33. For complete classification of this Act to the Code, see Short Title note set out under section 1251 of Title 33 and Tables.

The Toxic Substances Control Act, referred to in subsec. (k)(3)(C), is Pub. L. 94-469, Oct. 11, 1976, 90 Stat. 2003, as amended, which is classified generally to chapter 53 (Sec. 2601 et seq.) of Title 15, Commerce and Trade. For complete classification of this Act to the Code, see Short Title note set out under section 2601 of Title 15 and Tables.

The Federal Insecticide, Fungicide and Rodenticide Act, referred to in subsec. (k)(3)(C), probably means the Federal Insecticide, Fungicide, and Rodenticide Act, act June 25, 1947, ch. 125, as amended generally by Pub. L. 92-516, Oct. 21, 1972, 86 Stat. 973, which is classified generally to subchapter II (Sec. 136 et seq.) of chapter 6 of Title 7, Agriculture. For complete classification of this Act to the Code, see Short Title note set out under section 136 of Title 7 and Tables.

The Resource Conservation and Recovery Act, referred to in subsec. (k)(3)(C), probably means the Resource Conservation and Recovery Act of 1976, Pub. L. 94-580, Oct. 21, 1976, 90 Stat. 2796, as amended, which is classified generally to chapter 82 (Sec. 6901 et seq.) of this title. For complete classification of this Act to the Code, see Short Title of 1976 Amendment note set out under section 6901 of this title and Tables.

The Safe Drinking Water Act, referred to in subsec. (m)(1)(D), (5)(D), is title XIV of act July 1, 1944, as added Dec. 16, 1974, Pub. L. 93-523, Sec. 2(a), 88 Stat. 1660, as amended, which is classified generally to subchapter XII (Sec. 300f et seq.) of chapter 6A of this title. For complete classification of this Act to the Code, see Short Title note set out under section 201 of this title and Tables.

The Solid Waste Disposal Act, referred to in subsec. (n)(7), is title II of Pub. L. 89-272, Oct. 20, 1965, 79 Stat. 997, as amended generally by Pub. L. 94-580, Sec. 2, Oct. 21, 1976, 90 Stat. 2795. Subtitle C of the Act is classified generally to subchapter III (Sec. 6921 et seq.) of chapter 82 of this title. For complete classification of this Act to the Code, see Short Title note set out under section 6901 of this title and Tables.

Section 303 of the Clean Air Act Amendments of 1990, referred to in subsec. (o)(4), probably means section 303 of Pub. L. 101-549, which is set out below.

The Clean Air Act Amendments of 1990, referred to in subsec. (q)(1)-(3), probably means Pub. L. 101-549, Nov. 15, 1990, 104 Stat. 2399. For complete classification of this Act to the Code, see Short Title note set out under section 7401 of this title and Tables.

The Emergency Planning and Community Right-to-Know Act of 1986, referred to in subsec. (r)(3), is title III of Pub. L. 99-499, Oct. 17, 1986, 100 Stat. 1728, which is classified generally to chapter 116 (Sec. 11001 et seq.) of this title. For complete classification of this Act to the Code, see Short Title note set out under section 11001 of this title and Tables.

The Occupational Safety and Health Act, referred to in subsec. (r)(6)(C)(ii), (K), (L), probably means the Occupational Safety and Health Act of 1970, Pub. L. 91-596, Dec. 29, 1970, 84 Stat. 1590, as amended, which is classified principally to chapter 15 (Sec. 651 et seq.) of Title 29, Labor. For complete classification of this Act to the Code, see Short Title note set out under section 651 of Title 29 and Tables.

Codification

Section was formerly classified to section 1857c-7 of this title.

Amendments

1999–Subsec. (r)(2)(D). Pub. L. 106-40, Sec. 2(5), added subpar. (D).

    Subsec. (r)(4). Pub. L. 106-40, Sec. 2, substituted "Administrator–
    (A)   shall consider–" for "Administrator shall consider each of the following criteria–" in

introductory provisions, redesignated subpars. (A) to (C) as cls. (i) to (iii), respectively, of subpar. (A) and added subpar. (B).

Subsec. (r)(7)(H). Pub. L. 106-40, Sec. 3(a), added subpar. (H).

1998—Subsec. (n)(2)(C). Pub. L. 105-362 substituted "On completion of the study, the Secretary shall submit to Congress a report on the results of the study and" for "The Secretary shall prepare annual reports to Congress on the status of the research program and at the completion of the study".

1991—Subsec. (b)(1). Pub. L. 102-187 struck out "7783064 Hydrogen sulfide" from list of pollutants.

1990—Pub. L. 101-549 amended section generally, substituting present provisions for provisions which related to: in subsec. (a), definitions; in subsec. (b), list of hazardous air pollutants, emission standards, and pollution control techniques; in subsec. (c), prohibited acts and exemption; in subsec. (d), State implementation and enforcement; and in subsec. (e), design, equipment, work practice, and operational standards.

1978—Subsec. (e)(5). Pub. L. 95-623 added par. (5).

1977—Subsec. (a)(1). Pub. L. 95-95, Sec. 401(c), substituted "causes, or contributes to, air pollution which may reasonably be anticipated to result in an increase in mortality or an increase in serious irreversible, or incapacitating reversible, illness" for "may cause, or contribute to, an increase in mortality or an increase in serious irreversible, or incapacitating reversible, illness".

Subsec. (d)(1). Pub. L. 95-95, Sec. 109(d)(2), struck out "(except with respect to stationary sources owned or operated by the United States)" after "implement and enforce such standards".

Subsec. (e). Pub. L. 95-95, Sec. 110, added subsec. (e).

Change of Name

Committee on Energy and Commerce of House of Representatives treated as referring to Committee on Commerce of House of Representatives by section 1(a) of Pub. L. 104-14, set out as a note preceding section 21 of Title 2, The Congress.

Effective Date of 1977 Amendment

Amendment by Pub. L. 95-95 effective Aug. 7, 1977, except as otherwise expressly provided, see section 406(d) of Pub. L. 95-95, set out as a note under section 7401 of this title.

Pending Actions and Proceedings

Suits, actions, and other proceedings lawfully commenced by or against the Administrator or any other officer or employee of the United States in his official capacity or in relation to the discharge of his official duties under act July 14, 1955, the Clean Air Act, as in effect immediately prior to the enactment of Pub. L. 95-95 [Aug. 7, 1977], not to abate by reason of the taking effect of Pub. L. 95-95, see section 406(a) of Pub. L. 95-95, set out as an Effective Date of 1977 Amendment note under section 7401 of this title.

Modification or Rescission of Rules, Regulations, Orders, Determinations, Contracts, Certifications, Authorizations, Delegations, and Other Actions

All rules, regulations, orders, determinations, contracts, certifications, authorizations, delegations, or other actions duly issued, made, or taken by or pursuant to act July 14, 1955, the Clean Air Act, as in effect immediately prior to the date of enactment of Pub. L. 95-95 [Aug. 7, 1977] to continue in full force and effect until modified or rescinded in accordance with act July 14, 1955, as amended by Pub. L. 95-95 [this chapter], see section 406(b) of Pub. L. 95-95, set out as an Effective Date of 1977 Amendment note under section 7401 of this title.

Delegation of Authority

Memorandum of President of the United States, Aug. 19, 1993, 58 F.R. 52397, provided:

Memorandum for the Administrator of the Environmental Protection Agency

WHEREAS, the Environmental Protection Agency, the agencies and departments that are members of the National Response Team (authorized under Executive Order No. 12580, 52 Fed. Reg. 2923 (1987) [42 U.S.C. 9615 note]), and other Federal agencies and departments undertake emergency release prevention, mitigation, and response activities pursuant to various authorities;

By the authority vested in me as President by the Constitution and the laws of the United States of America, including section 112(r)(10) of the Clean Air Act (the "Act") (section 7412(r)(10) of title 42 of the United States Code) and section 301 of title 3 of the United States Code, and in order to provide for the delegation of certain functions under the Act [42 U.S.C. 7401 et seq.], I hereby:

(1) Authorize you, in coordination with agencies and departments that are members of the National Response Team and other appropriate agencies and departments, to conduct a review of release prevention, mitigation, and response authorities of Federal agencies in order to assure the most effective and efficient implementation of such authorities and to identify any deficiencies in authority or resources that may exist, to the extent such review is required by section 112(r)(10) of the Act; and

(2) Authorize you, in coordination with agencies and departments that are members of the National Response Team and other appropriate agencies and departments, to prepare and transmit a message to the Congress concerning the release prevention, mitigation, and response activities of the Federal Government with such recommendations for change in law as you deem appropriate, to the extent such message is required by section 112(r)(10) of the Act.

The authority delegated by this memorandum may be further redelegated within the Environmental Protection Agency.

You are hereby authorized and directed to publish this memorandum in the Federal Register.

William J. Clinton.

Memorandum of President of the United States, Jan. 27, 2000, 65 F.R. 8631, provided:

Memorandum for the Attorney General[,] the Administrator of the Environmental Protection Agency[, and] the Director of the Office of Management and Budget

By the authority vested in me as President by the Constitution and laws of the United States of America, including section 112(r)(7)(H) of the Clean Air Act ("Act") (42 U.S.C. 7412(r)(7)(H)), as added by section 3 of the Chemical Safety Information, Site Security and Fuels Regulatory Relief Act (Public Law 106-40), and section 301 of title 3, United States Code, I hereby delegate to:

(1) the Attorney General the authority vested in the President under section 112(r)(7)(H)(ii)(I)(aa) of the Act to assess the increased risk of terrorist and other criminal activity associated with the posting of off-site consequence analysis information on the Internet;

(2) the Administrator of the Environmental Protection Agency (EPA) the authority vested in the President under section 112(r)(7)(H)(ii)(I)(bb) of the Act to assess the incentives created by public disclosure of off-site consequence analysis information for reduction in the risk of accidental releases; and

(3) the Attorney General and the Administrator of EPA, jointly, the authority vested in the President under section 112(r)(7)(H)(ii)(II) of the Act to promulgate regulations, based on these assessments, governing the distribution of off-site consequence analysis information. These regulations, in proposed and final form, shall be subject to review and approval by the Director of the Office of Management and Budget.

The Administrator of EPA is authorized and directed to publish this memorandum in the Federal Register.

William J. Clinton.

Reports

Pub. L. 106-40, Sec. 3(b), Aug. 5, 1999, 113 Stat. 213, provided that:

"(1) Definition of accidental release.—In this subsection, the term 'accidental release' has the meaning given the term in section 112(r)(2) of the Clean Air Act (42 U.S.C. 7412(r)(2)).

(2) Report on status of certain amendments.—Not later than 2 years after the date of enactment of this Act [Aug. 5, 1999], the Comptroller General of the United States shall submit to Congress a report on the status of the development of amendments to the National Fire Protection Association Code for Liquefied Petroleum Gas that will result in the provision of information to local emergency response personnel concerning the off-site effects of accidental releases of substances exempted from listing under section 112(r)(4)(B) of the Clean Air Act (as added by section 3).

(3) Report on compliance with certain information submission requirements.—Not later than 3 years after the date of enactment of this Act, the Comptroller General of the United States shall submit to Congress a report that—

(A) describes the level of compliance with Federal and State requirements relating to the submission to local emergency response personnel of information intended to help the local emergency response personnel respond to chemical accidents or related environmental or public health threats; and
(B) contains an analysis of the adequacy of the information required to be submitted and the efficacy of the methods for delivering the information to local emergency response personnel."

Reevaluation of Regulations

Pub. L. 106-40, Sec. 3(c), Aug. 5, 1999, 113 Stat. 213, provided that: "The President shall reevaluate the regulations promulgated under this section within 6 years after the enactment of this Act [Aug. 5, 1999]. If the President determines not to modify such regulations, the President shall publish a notice in the Federal Register stating that such reevaluation has been completed and that a determination has been made not to modify the regulations. Such notice shall include an explanation of the basis of such decision."

Public Meeting During Moratorium Period

Pub. L. 106-40, Sec. 4, Aug. 5, 1999, 113 Stat. 214, provided that:

"(a) In General.—Not later than 180 days after the date of enactment of this Act [Aug. 5, 1999], each owner or operator of a stationary source covered by section 112(r)(7)(B)(ii) of the Clean Air Act [42 U.S.C. 7412(r)(7)(B)(ii)] shall convene a public meeting, after reasonable public notice, in order to describe and discuss the local implications of the risk management plan submitted by the stationary source pursuant to section 112(r)(7)(B)(iii) of the Clean Air Act, including a summary of the off-site consequence analysis portion of the plan. Two or more stationary sources may conduct a joint meeting. In lieu of conducting such a meeting, small business stationary sources as defined in section 507(c)(1) of the Clean Air Act [42 U.S.C. 7661f(c)(1)] may comply with this section by publicly posting a summary of the off-site consequence analysis information for their facility not later than 180 days after the enactment of this Act. Not later than 10 months after the date of enactment of this Act, each such owner or operator shall send a certification to the director of the Federal Bureau of Investigation stating that such meeting has been held, or that such summary has been posted, within 1 year prior to, or within 6 months after, the date of the enactment of this Act. This section shall not apply to sources that employ only Program 1 processes within the meaning of regulations promulgated under section 112(r)(7)(B)(i) of the Clean Air Act.

(b) Enforcement.—The Administrator of the Environmental Protection Agency may bring an action in the appropriate United States district court against any person who fails or refuses to comply with the requirements of this section, and such court may issue such orders, and take such other actions, as may be necessary to require compliance with such requirements."

Risk Assessment and Management Commission

Section 303 of Pub. L. 101-549 provided that:

"(a) Establishment.—There is hereby established a Risk Assessment and Management Commission (hereafter referred to in this section as the 'Commission'), which shall commence proceedings not later than 18 months after the date of enactment of the Clean Air Act Amendments of 1990 [Nov. 15, 1990] and which shall make a full investigation of the policy implications and appropriate uses of risk assessment and risk management in regulatory programs under various Federal laws to prevent cancer and other chronic human health effects which may result from exposure to hazardous substances.

(b) Charge.—The Commission shall consider—
(1) the report of the National Academy of Sciences authorized by section 112(o) of the Clean Air Act [42 U.S.C. 7412(o)], the use and limitations of risk assessment in establishing emission or effluent standards, ambient standards, exposure standards, acceptable concentration levels, tolerances or other environmental criteria for hazardous substances that present a risk of carcinogenic effects or other chronic health effects and the suitability of risk assessment for such purposes;
(2) the most appropriate methods for measuring and describing cancer risks or risks of other chronic health effects from exposure to hazardous substances considering such alternative approaches as the lifetime risk of cancer or other effects to the individual or individu-

als most exposed to emissions from a source or sources on both an actual and worst case basis, the range of such risks, the total number of health effects avoided by exposure reductions, effluent standards, ambient standards, exposures standards, acceptable concentration levels, tolerances and other environmental criteria, reductions in the number of persons exposed at various levels of risk, the incidence of cancer, and other public health factors;
   (3) methods to reflect uncertainties in measurement and estimation techniques, the existence of synergistic or antagonistic effects among hazardous substances, the accuracy of extrapolating human health risks from animal exposure data, and the existence of unquantified direct or indirect effects on human health in risk assessment studies;
   (4) risk management policy issues including the use of lifetime cancer risks to individuals most exposed, incidence of cancer, the cost and technical feasibility of exposure reduction measures and the use of site-specific actual exposure information in setting emissions standards and other limitations applicable to sources of exposure to hazardous substances; and
   (5) and comment on the degree to which it is possible or desirable to develop a consistent risk assessment methodology, or a consistent standard of acceptable risk, among various Federal programs.
(c) Membership.—Such Commission shall be composed of ten members who shall have knowledge or experience in fields of risk assessment or risk management, including three members to be appointed by the President, two members to be appointed by the Speaker of the House of Representatives, one member to be appointed by the Minority Leader of the House of Representatives, two members to be appointed by the Majority Leader of the Senate, one member to be appointed by the Minority Leader of the Senate, and one member to be appointed by the President of the National Academy of Sciences. Appointments shall be made not later than 18 months after the date of enactment of the Clean Air Act Amendments of 1990 [Nov. 15, 1990].
(d) Assistance from Agencies.—The Administrator of the Environmental Protection Agency and the heads of all other departments, agencies, and instrumentalities of the executive branch of the Federal Government shall, to the maximum extent practicable, assist the Commission in gathering such information as the Commission deems necessary to carry out this section subject to other provisions of law.
(e) Staff and Contracts.—
   (1) In the conduct of the study required by this section, the Commission is authorized to contract (in accordance with Federal contract law) with nongovernmental entities that are competent to perform research or investigations within the Commission's mandate, and to hold public hearings, forums, and workshops to enable full public participation.
   (2) The Commission may appoint and fix the pay of such staff as it deems necessary in accordance with the provisions of title 5, United States Code. The Commission may request the temporary assignment of personnel from the Environmental Protection Agency or other Federal agencies.
   (3) The members of the Commission who are not officers or employees of the United States, while attending conferences or meetings of the Commission or while otherwise serving at the request of the Chair, shall be entitled to receive compensation at a rate not in excess of the maximum rate of pay for Grade GS-18, as provided in the General Schedule under section 5332 of title 5 of the United States Code, including travel time, and while away from their homes or regular places of business they may be allowed travel expenses, including per diem in lieu of subsistence as authorized by law for persons in the Government service employed intermittently.
(f) Report.—A report containing the results of all Commission studies and investigations under this section, together with any appropriate legislative recommendations or administrative recommendations, shall be made available to the public for comment not later than 42 months after the date of enactment of the Clean Air Act Amendments of 1990 [Nov. 15, 1990] and shall be submitted to the President and to the Congress not later than 48 months after such date of enactment. In the report, the Commission shall make recommendations with respect to the appropriate use of risk assessment and risk management in Federal regulatory programs to prevent cancer or other chronic health effects which may result from exposure to hazardous substances. The Commission shall cease to exist upon the date determined by the Commission, but not later than 9 months after the submission of such report.

(g) Authorization.—There are authorized to be appropriated such sums as are necessary to carry out the activities of the Commission established by this section."

[References in laws to the rates of pay for GS-16, 17, or 18, or to maximum rates of pay under the General Schedule, to be considered references to rates payable under specified sections of Title 5, Government Organization and Employees, see section 529 [title I, Sec. 101(c)(1)] of Pub. L. 101-509, set out in a note under section 5376 of Title 5.]

Section Referred to in Other Sections

This section is referred to in sections 7403, 7411, 7413, 7414, 7416, 7417, 7418, 7420, 7422, 7429, 7479, 7511b, 7604, 7607, 7608, 7612, 7616, 7625-1, 7627, 7661, 7661a, 7661f, 9601 of this title.

FEDERAL ENFORCEMENT

42 USC 7413

(a) In general
  (1) Order to comply with SIP
    Whenever, on the basis of any information available to the Administrator, the Administrator finds that any person has violated or is in violation of any requirement or prohibition of an applicable implementation plan or permit, the Administrator shall notify the person and the State in which the plan applies of such finding. At any time after the expiration of 30 days following the date on which such notice of a violation is issued, the Administrator may, without regard to the period of violation (subject to section 2462 of title 28)—
    (A) issue an order requiring such person to comply with the requirements or prohibitions of such plan or permit,
    (B) issue an administrative penalty order in accordance with subsection (d) of this section, or
    (C) bring a civil action in accordance with subsection (b) of this section.
  (2) State failure to enforce SIP or permit program
    Whenever, on the basis of information available to the Administrator, the Administrator finds that violations of an applicable implementation plan or an approved permit program under subchapter V of this chapter are so widespread that such violations appear to result from a failure of the State in which the plan or permit program applies to enforce the plan or permit program effectively, the Administrator shall so notify the State. In the case of a permit program, the notice shall be made in accordance with subchapter V of this chapter. If the Administrator finds such failure extends beyond the 30th day after such notice (90 days in the case of such permit program), the Administrator shall give public notice of such finding. During the period beginning with such public notice and ending when such State satisfies the Administrator that it will enforce such plan or permit program (hereafter referred to in this section as "period of federally assumed enforcement"), the Administrator may enforce any requirement or prohibition of such plan or permit program with respect to any person by—
    (A) issuing an order requiring such person to comply with such requirement or prohibition,
    (B) issuing an administrative penalty order in accordance with subsection (d) of this section, or
    (C) bringing a civil action in accordance with subsection (b) of this section.
  (3) EPA enforcement of other requirements
    Except for a requirement or prohibition enforceable under the preceding provisions of this subsection, whenever, on the basis of any information available to the Administrator, the Administrator finds that any person has violated, or is in violation of, any other requirement or prohibition of this subchapter, section 7603 of this title, subchapter IV-A, subchapter V, or subchapter VI of this chapter, including, but not limited to, a requirement or prohibition of any rule, plan, order, waiver, or permit promulgated, issued, or approved under those provisions or subchapters, or for the payment of any fee owed to the United States under this chapter (other than subchapter II of this chapter), the Administrator may—

(A) issue an administrative penalty order in accordance with subsection (d) of this section,
(B) issue an order requiring such person to comply with such requirement or prohibition,
(C) bring a civil action in accordance with subsection (b) of this section or section 7605 of this title, or
(D) request the Attorney General to commence a criminal action in accordance with subsection (c) of this section.
(4) Requirements for orders
An order issued under this subsection (other than an order relating to a violation of section 7412 of this title) shall not take effect until the person to whom it is issued has had an opportunity to confer with the Administrator concerning the alleged violation. A copy of any order issued under this subsection shall be sent to the State air pollution control agency of any State in which the violation occurs. Any order issued under this subsection shall state with reasonable specificity the nature of the violation and specify a time for compliance which the Administrator determines is reasonable, taking into account the seriousness of the violation and any good faith efforts to comply with applicable requirements. In any case in which an order under this subsection (or notice to a violator under paragraph (1)) is issued to a corporation, a copy of such order (or notice) shall be issued to appropriate corporate officers. An order issued under this subsection shall require the person to whom it was issued to comply with the requirement as expeditiously as practicable, but in no event longer than one year after the date the order was issued, and shall be nonrenewable. No order issued under this subsection shall prevent the State or the Administrator from assessing any penalties nor otherwise affect or limit the State's or the United States authority to enforce under other provisions of this chapter, nor affect any person's obligations to comply with any section of this chapter or with a term or condition of any permit or applicable implementation plan promulgated or approved under this chapter.
(5) Failure to comply with new source requirements
Whenever, on the basis of any available information, the Administrator finds that a State is not acting in compliance with any requirement or prohibition of the chapter relating to the construction of new sources or the modification of existing sources, the Administrator may—
(A) issue an order prohibiting the construction or modification of any major stationary source in any area to which such requirement applies;[1]
(B) issue an administrative penalty order in accordance with subsection (d) of this section, or
(C) bring a civil action under subsection (b) of this section.
Nothing in this subsection shall preclude the United States from commencing a criminal action under subsection (c) of this section at any time for any such violation.
(b) Civil judicial enforcement
The Administrator shall, as appropriate, in the case of any person that is the owner or operator of an affected source, a major emitting facility, or a major stationary source, and may, in the case of any other person, commence a civil action for a permanent or temporary injunction, or to assess and recover a civil penalty of not more than $25,000 per day for each violation, or both, in any of the following instances:
(1) Whenever such person has violated, or is in violation of, any requirement or prohibition of an applicable implementation plan or permit. Such an action shall be commenced (A) during any period of federally assumed enforcement, or (B) more than 30 days following the date of the Administrator's notification under subsection (a)(1) of this section that such person has violated, or is in violation of, such requirement or prohibition.
(2) Whenever such person has violated, or is in violation of, any other requirement or prohibition of this subchapter, section 7603 of this title, subchapter IV-A, subchapter V, or subchapter VI of this chapter, including, but not limited to, a requirement or prohibition of any rule, order, waiver or permit promulgated, issued, or approved under this chapter, or for the payment of any fee owed the United States under this chapter (other than subchapter II of this chapter).

---

[1]So in original. The semicolon probably should be a comma.

(3) Whenever such person attempts to construct or modify a major stationary source in any area with respect to which a finding under subsection (a)(5) of this section has been made.

Any action under this subsection may be brought in the district court of the United States for the district in which the violation is alleged to have occurred, or is occurring, or in which the defendant resides, or where the defendant's principal place of business is located, and such court shall have jurisdiction to restrain such violation, to require compliance, to assess such civil penalty, to collect any fees owed the United States under this chapter (other than subchapter II of this chapter) and any noncompliance assessment and nonpayment penalty owed under section 7420 of this title, and to award any other appropriate relief. Notice of the commencement of such action shall be given to the appropriate State air pollution control agency. In the case of any action brought by the Administrator under this subsection, the court may award costs of litigation (including reasonable attorney and expert witness fees) to the party or parties against whom such action was brought if the court finds that such action was unreasonable.

(c) Criminal penalties

(1) Any person who knowingly violates any requirement or prohibition of an applicable implementation plan (during any period of federally assumed enforcement or more than 30 days after having been notified under subsection (a)(1) of this section by the Administrator that such person is violating such requirement or prohibition), any order under subsection (a) of this section, requirement or prohibition of section 7411(e) of this title (relating to new source performance standards), section 7412 of this title, section 7414 of this title (relating to inspections, etc.), section 7429 of this title (relating to solid waste combustion), section 7475(a) of this title (relating to preconstruction requirements), an order under section 7477 of this title (relating to preconstruction requirements), an order under section 7603 of this title (relating to emergency orders), section 7661a(a) or 7661b(c) of this title (relating to permits), or any requirement or prohibition of subchapter IV-A of this chapter (relating to acid deposition control), or subchapter VI of this chapter (relating to stratospheric ozone control), including a requirement of any rule, order, waiver, or permit promulgated or approved under such sections or subchapters, and including any requirement for the payment of any fee owed the United States under this chapter (other than subchapter II of this chapter) shall, upon conviction, be punished by a fine pursuant to title 18 or by imprisonment for not to exceed 5 years, or both. If a conviction of any person under this paragraph is for a violation committed after a first conviction of such person under this paragraph, the maximum punishment shall be doubled with respect to both the fine and imprisonment.

(2) Any person who knowingly—

(A) makes any false material statement, representation, or certification in, or omits material information from, or knowingly alters, conceals, or fails to file or maintain any notice, application, record, report, plan, or other document required pursuant to this chapter to be either filed or maintained (whether with respect to the requirements imposed by the Administrator or by a State);

(B) fails to notify or report as required under this chapter; or

(C) falsifies, tampers with, renders inaccurate, or fails to install any monitoring device or method required to be maintained or followed under this chapter[2]

shall, upon conviction, be punished by a fine pursuant to title 18 or by imprisonment for not more than 2 years, or both. If a conviction of any person under this paragraph is for a violation committed after a first conviction of such person under this paragraph, the maximum punishment shall be doubled with respect to both the fine and imprisonment.

(3) Any person who knowingly fails to pay any fee owed the United States under this subchapter, subchapter III, IV-A, V, or VI of this chapter shall, upon conviction, be punished by a fine pursuant to title 18 or by imprisonment for not more than 1 year, or both. If a conviction of any person under this paragraph is for a violation committed after a first conviction of such person under this paragraph, the maximum punishment shall be doubled with respect to both the fine and imprisonment.

(4) Any person who negligently releases into the ambient air any hazardous air pollutant listed pursuant to section 7412 of this title or any extremely hazardous substance listed

---

[2]So in original. Probably should be followed by a comma.

pursuant to section 11002(a)(2) of this title that is not listed in section 7412 of this title, and who at the time negligently places another person in imminent danger of death or serious bodily injury shall, upon conviction, be punished by a fine under title 18 or by imprisonment for not more than 1 year, or both. If a conviction of any person under this paragraph is for a violation committed after a first conviction of such person under this paragraph, the maximum punishment shall be doubled with respect to both the fine and imprisonment.

(5) (A) Any person who knowingly releases into the ambient air any hazardous air pollutant listed pursuant to section 7412 of this title or any extremely hazardous substance listed pursuant to section 11002(a)(2) of this title that is not listed in section 7412 of this title, and who knows at the time that he thereby places another person in imminent danger of death or serious bodily injury shall, upon conviction, be punished by a fine under title 18 or by imprisonment of not more than 15 years, or both. Any person committing such violation which is an organization shall, upon conviction under this paragraph, be subject to a fine of not more than $1,000,000 for each violation. If a conviction of any person under this paragraph is for a violation committed after a first conviction of such person under this paragraph, the maximum punishment shall be doubled with respect to both the fine and imprisonment. For any air pollutant for which the Administrator has set an emissions standard or for any source for which a permit has been issued under subchapter V of this chapter, a release of such pollutant in accordance with that standard or permit shall not constitute a violation of this paragraph or paragraph (4).

(B) In determining whether a defendant who is an individual knew that the violation placed another person in imminent danger of death or serious bodily injury—
  (i) the defendant is responsible only for actual awareness or actual belief possessed; and
  (ii) knowledge possessed by a person other than the defendant, but not by the defendant, may not be attributed to the defendant; except that in proving a defendant's possession of actual knowledge, circumstantial evidence may be used, including evidence that the defendant took affirmative steps to be shielded from relevant information.

(C) It is an affirmative defense to a prosecution that the conduct charged was freely consented to by the person endangered and that the danger and conduct charged were reasonably foreseeable hazards of—
  (i) an occupation, a business, or a profession; or
  (ii) medical treatment or medical or scientific experimentation conducted by professionally approved methods and such other person had been made aware of the risks involved prior to giving consent.
The defendant may establish an affirmative defense under this subparagraph by a preponderance of the evidence.

(D) All general defenses, affirmative defenses, and bars to prosecution that may apply with respect to other Federal criminal offenses may apply under subparagraph (A) of this paragraph and shall be determined by the courts of the United States according to the principles of common law as they may be interpreted in the light of reason and experience. Concepts of justification and excuse applicable under this section may be developed in the light of reason and experience.

(E) The term "organization" means a legal entity, other than a government, established or organized for any purpose, and such term includes a corporation, company, association, firm, partnership, joint stock company, foundation, institution, trust, society, union, or any other association of persons.

(F) The term "serious bodily injury" means bodily injury which involves a substantial risk of death, unconsciousness, extreme physical pain, protracted and obvious disfigurement or protracted loss or impairment of the function of a bodily member, organ, or mental faculty.

(6) For the purpose of this subsection, the term "person" includes, in addition to the entities referred to in section 7602(e) of this title, any responsible corporate officer.

(d) Administrative assessment of civil penalties

(1) The Administrator may issue an administrative order against any person assessing a civil administrative penalty of up to $25,000, per day of violation, whenever, on the basis of any available information, the Administrator finds that such person—
   (A) has violated or is violating any requirement or prohibition of an applicable implementation plan (such order shall be issued (i) during any period of federally assumed enforcement, or (ii) more than thirty days following the date of the Administrator's notification under subsection (a)(1) of this section of a finding that such person has violated or is violating such requirement or prohibition); or
   (B) has violated or is violating any other requirement or prohibition of this subchapter or subchapter III, IV-A, V, or VI of this chapter, including, but not limited to, a requirement or prohibition of any rule, order, waiver, permit, or plan promulgated, issued, or approved under this chapter, or for the payment of any fee owed the United States under this chapter (other than subchapter II of this chapter); or
   (C) attempts to construct or modify a major stationary source in any area with respect to which a finding under subsection (a)(5) of this section has been made.
The Administrator's authority under this paragraph shall be limited to matters where the total penalty sought does not exceed $200,000 and the first alleged date of violation occurred no more than 12 months prior to the initiation of the administrative action, except where the Administrator and the Attorney General jointly determine that a matter involving a larger penalty amount or longer period of violation is appropriate for administrative penalty action. Any such determination by the Administrator and the Attorney General shall not be subject to judicial review.

(2) (A) An administrative penalty assessed under paragraph (1) shall be assessed by the Administrator by an order made after opportunity for a hearing on the record in accordance with sections 554 and 556 of title 5. The Administrator shall issue reasonable rules for discovery and other procedures for hearings under this paragraph. Before issuing such an order, the Administrator shall give written notice to the person to be assessed an administrative penalty of the Administrator's proposal to issue such order and provide such person an opportunity to request such a hearing on the order, within 30 days of the date the notice is received by such person.
   (B) The Administrator may compromise, modify, or remit, with or without conditions, any administrative penalty which may be imposed under this subsection.

(3) The Administrator may implement, after consultation with the Attorney General and the States, a field citation program through regulations establishing appropriate minor violations for which field citations assessing civil penalties not to exceed $5,000 per day of violation may be issued by officers or employees designated by the Administrator. Any person to whom a field citation is assessed may, within a reasonable time as prescribed by the Administrator through regulation, elect to pay the penalty assessment or to request a hearing on the field citation. If a request for a hearing is not made within the time specified in the regulation, the penalty assessment in the field citation shall be final. Such hearing shall not be subject to section 554 or 556 of title 5, but shall provide a reasonable opportunity to be heard and to present evidence. Payment of a civil penalty required by a field citation shall not be a defense to further enforcement by the United States or a State to correct a violation, or to assess the statutory maximum penalty pursuant to other authorities in the chapter, if the violation continues.

(4) Any person against whom a civil penalty is assessed under paragraph (3) of this subsection or to whom an administrative penalty order is issued under paragraph (1) of this subsection may seek review of such assessment in the United States District Court for the District of Columbia or for the district in which the violation is alleged to have occurred, in which such person resides, or where such person's principal place of business is located, by filing in such court within 30 days following the date the administrative penalty order becomes final under paragraph (2), the assessment becomes final under paragraph (3), or a final decision following a hearing under paragraph (3) is rendered, and by simultaneously sending a copy of the filing by certified mail to the Administrator and the Attorney General. Within 30 days thereafter, the Administrator shall file in such court a certified copy, or certified index, as appropriate, of the record on which the administrative penalty order or assessment was issued. Such court shall not set aside or remand such order or assessment unless there is not substantial evidence in the record, taken as a

whole, to support the finding of a violation or unless the order or penalty assessment constitutes an abuse of discretion. Such order or penalty assessment shall not be subject to review by any court except as provided in this paragraph. In any such proceedings, the United States may seek to recover civil penalties ordered or assessed under this section.
  (5) If any person fails to pay an assessment of a civil penalty or fails to comply with an administrative penalty order—
    (A) after the order or assessment has become final, or
    (B) after a court in an action brought under paragraph (4) has entered a final judgment in favor of the Administrator, the Administrator shall request the Attorney General to bring a civil action in an appropriate district court to enforce the order or to recover the amount ordered or assessed (plus interest at rates established pursuant to section 6621(a)(2) of title 26 from the date of the final order or decision or the date of the final judgment, as the case may be). In such an action, the validity, amount, and appropriateness of such order or assessment shall not be subject to review. Any person who fails to pay on a timely basis a civil penalty ordered or assessed under this section shall be required to pay, in addition to such penalty and interest, the United States enforcement expenses, including but not limited to attorneys fees and costs incurred by the United States for collection proceedings and a quarterly nonpayment penalty for each quarter during which such failure to pay persists. Such nonpayment penalty shall be 10 percent of the aggregate amount of such person's outstanding penalties and nonpayment penalties accrued as of the beginning of such quarter.
(e) Penalty assessment criteria
  (1) In determining the amount of any penalty to be assessed under this section or section 7604(a) of this title, the Administrator or the court, as appropriate, shall take into consideration (in addition to such other factors as justice may require) the size of the business, the economic impact of the penalty on the business, the violator's full compliance history and good faith efforts to comply, the duration of the violation as established by any credible evidence (including evidence other than the applicable test method), payment by the violator of penalties previously assessed for the same violation, the economic benefit of noncompliance, and the seriousness of the violation. The court shall not assess penalties for noncompliance with administrative subpoenas under section 7607(a) of this title, or actions under section 7414 of this title, where the violator had sufficient cause to violate or fail or refuse to comply with such subpoena or action.
  (2) A penalty may be assessed for each day of violation. For purposes of determining the number of days of violation for which a penalty may be assessed under subsection (b) or (d)(1) of this section, or section 7604(a) of this title, or an assessment may be made under section 7420 of this title, where the Administrator or an air pollution control agency has notified the source of the violation, and the plaintiff makes a prima facie showing that the conduct or events giving rise to the violation are likely to have continued or recurred past the date of notice, the days of violation shall be presumed to include the date of such notice and each and every day thereafter until the violator establishes that continuous compliance has been achieved, except to the extent that the violator can prove by a preponderance of the evidence that there were intervening days during which no violation occurred or that the violation was not continuing in nature.
(f) Awards
  The Administrator may pay an award, not to exceed $10,000, to any person who furnishes information or services which lead to a criminal conviction or a judicial or administrative civil penalty for any violation of this subchapter or subchapter III, IV-A, V, or VI of this chapter enforced under this section. Such payment is subject to available appropriations for such purposes as provided in annual appropriation Acts. Any officer, or employee of the United States or any State or local government who furnishes information or renders service in the performance of an official duty is ineligible for payment under this subsection. The Administrator may, by regulation, prescribe additional criteria for eligibility for such an award.
(g) Settlements; public participation
  At least 30 days before a consent order or settlement agreement of any kind under this chapter to which the United States is a party (other than enforcement actions under this section, section 7420 of this title, or subchapter II of this chapter, whether or not involving civil or crimi-

nal penalties, or judgments subject to Department of Justice policy on public participation) is final or filed with a court, the Administrator shall provide a reasonable opportunity by notice in the Federal Register to persons who are not named as parties or intervenors to the action or matter to comment in writing. The Administrator or the Attorney General, as appropriate, shall promptly consider any such written comments and may withdraw or withhold his consent to the proposed order or agreement if the comments disclose facts or considerations which indicate that such consent is inappropriate, improper, inadequate, or inconsistent with the requirements of this chapter. Nothing in this subsection shall apply to civil or criminal penalties under this chapter.

(h) Operator

For purposes of the provisions of this section and section 7420 of this title, the term "operator", as used in such provisions, shall include any person who is senior management personnel or a corporate officer. Except in the case of knowing and willful violations, such term shall not include any person who is a stationary engineer or technician responsible for the operation, maintenance, repair, or monitoring of equipment and facilities and who often has supervisory and training duties but who is not senior management personnel or a corporate officer. Except in the case of knowing and willful violations, for purposes of subsection (c)(4) of this section, the term "a person" shall not include an employee who is carrying out his normal activities and who is not a part of senior management personnel or a corporate officer. Except in the case of knowing and willful violations, for purposes of paragraphs (1), (2), (3), and (5) of subsection (c) of this section the term "a person" shall not include an employee who is carrying out his normal activities and who is acting under orders from the employer.

(July 14, 1955, ch. 360, title I, Sec. 113, as added Pub. L. 91-604, Sec. 4(a), Dec. 31, 1970, 84 Stat. 1686; amended Pub. L. 92-157, title III, Sec. 302(b), (c), Nov. 18, 1971, 85 Stat. 464; Pub. L. 93-319, Sec. 6(a)(1)-(3), June 22, 1974, 88 Stat. 259; Pub. L. 95-95, title I, Secs. 111, 112(a), Aug. 7, 1977, 91 Stat. 704, 705; Pub. L. 95-190, Sec. 14(a)(10)-(21), (b)(1), Nov. 16, 1977, 91 Stat. 1400, 1404; Pub. L. 97-23, Sec. 2, July 17, 1981, 95 Stat. 139; Pub. L. 101-549, title VII, Sec. 701, Nov. 15, 1990, 104 Stat. 2672.)

Codification

Section was formerly classified to section 1857c-8 of this title.

Amendments

1990—Pub. L. 101-549 amended section generally, substituting present provisions for provisions which related to: in subsec. (a), finding of violation, notice, compliance order, civil action, State failure to enforce plan, and construction or modification of major stationary sources; in subsec. (b), violations by owners or operators of major stationary sources; in subsec. (c), penalties; in subsec. (d), final compliance orders; and in subsec. (e), steel industry compliance extension.

1981—Subsec. (c). Pub. L. 97-23 added subsec. (e).

1977—Subsec. (a)(5). Pub. L. 95-95, Sec. 111(a), added par. (5).

Subsec. (b). Pub. L. 95-95, Sec. 111(b), (c), substituted "shall, in the case of any person which is the owner or operator of a major stationary source, and may, in the case of any other person, commence a civil action for a permanent or temporary injunction, or to assess and recover a civil penalty of not more than $25,000 per day of violation, or both, whenever such person" for "may commence a civil action for appropriate relief, including a permanent or temporary injunction, whenever any person" in provisions preceding par. (1), inserted references to subsec. (d)(5) of this section, sections 7419 and 7620 of this title, and regulations under part in par. (3), inserted reference to subsec. (d) of this section in par. (4), added par. (5), and, in provisions following par. (5), authorized the commencement of civil actions to recover noncompliance penalties and nonpayment penalties under section 7420 of this title, expanded jurisdictional provisions to authorize actions in districts in which the violation occurred and to authorize the district court to restrain violations, to require compliance, to assess civil penalties, and to collect penalties under section 7420 of this title, enumerated factors to be taken into consideration in determining the amount of civil penalties, and authorized awarding of costs to the party or parties against whom the action was brought in cases where the court finds that the action was unreasonable.

Subsec. (b)(3). Pub. L. 95-190, Sec. 14(a)(10), (11), inserted "or" after "ozone);", and substituted "7624" for "7620", "conversion), section" for "conversion) section", and "orders), or" for "orders) or".

Subsec. (c)(1). Pub. L. 95-95, Sec. 111(d)(1), (2), substituted "any order issued under section 7419 of this title or under subsection (a) or (d) of this section" for "any order issued by the Administrator under subsection (a) of this section" in subpar. (B), struck out reference to section 119(g) (as in effect before the date of the enactment of Pub. L. 95-95) in subpar. (C), and added subpar. (D).

Subsec. (c)(1)(B). Pub. L. 95-190, Sec. 14(a)(12), inserted "or" after "section,".

Subsec. (c)(1)(D). Pub. L. 95-190, Sec. 14(a)(13), substituted "1977 subsection" for "1977) subsection" and "penalties), or" for "penalties) or".

Subsec. (c)(3). Pub. L. 95-95, Sec. 111(d)(3), added par. (3).

Subsec. (d). Pub. L. 95-95, Sec. 112(a), added subsec. (d).

Subsec. (d)(1). Pub. L. 95-190, Sec. 14(a)(14), substituted "to any stationary source which is unable to comply with any requirement of an applicable implementation plan an order" for "an order for any stationary source" and "such requirement" for "any requirement of an applicable implementation plan".

Subsec. (d)(1)(E). Pub. L. 95-190, Sec. 14(a)(15), inserted provision relating to exemption under section 7420(a)(2)(B) or (C) of this title, provision relating to noncompliance penalties effective July 1, 1979, and reference to subsec. (b)(3) or (g) of section 7420 of this title.

Subsec. (d)(2). Pub. L. 95-190, Sec. 14(a)(16), inserted provisions relating to determinations by the Administrator of compliance with requirements of this chapter of State orders issued under this subsection.

Subsec. (d)(4)(A). Pub. L. 95-190, Sec. 14(a)(17), substituted "title) upon" for "title upon".

Subsec. (d)(5)(A). Pub. L. 95-190, Sec. 14(a)(18), substituted "an additional period for" for "an additional period of".

Subsec. (d)(8). Pub. L. 95-190, Sec. 14(a)(19), struck out reference to par. (3) of this subsection.

Subsec. (d)(10). Pub. L. 95-190, Sec. 14(a)(20), substituted "in effect" for "issued", "Federal" for "other", and "and no action under" for "or".

Subsec. (d)(11). Pub. L. 95-190, Sec. 14(a)(21), substituted "and in effect" for "(and approved by the Administrator)".

1974—Subsec. (a)(3). Pub. L. 93-319, Sec. 6(a)(1), inserted reference to section 1857c-10(g) of this title (relating to energy-related authorities).

Subsecs. (b)(3), (c)(1)(C). Pub. L. 93-319, Sec. 6(a)(2), (3), inserted reference to section 1857c-10(g) of this title.

1971—Subsec. (b)(2). Pub. L. 92-157, Sec. 302(b), inserted "(A)" before "during" and ", or (B)" after "assumed enforcement".

Subsec. (c)(1)(A). Pub. L. 92-157, Sec. 302(c), inserted "(i)" before "during" and ", or (ii)" after "assumed enforcement".

Effective Date of 1977 Amendment

Amendment by Pub. L. 95-95 effective Aug. 7, 1977, except as otherwise expressly provided, see section 406(d) of Pub. L. 95-95, set out as a note under section 7401 of this title.

Pending Actions and Proceedings

Suits, actions, and other proceedings lawfully commenced by or against the Administrator or any other officer or employee of the United States in his official capacity or in relation to the discharge of his official duties under act July 14, 1955, the Clean Air Act, as in effect immediately prior to the enactment of Pub. L. 95-95 [Aug. 7, 1977], not to abate by reason of the taking effect of Pub. L. 95-95, see section 406(a) of Pub. L. 95-95, set out as an Effective Date of 1977 Amendment note under section 7401 of this title.

Modification or Rescission of Rules, Regulations, Orders, Determinations, Contracts, Certifications, Authorizations, Delegations, and Other Actions

All rules, regulations, orders, determinations, contracts, certifications, authorizations, delegations, or other actions duly issued, made, or taken by or pursuant to act July 14, 1955, the Clean Air Act, as in effect immediately prior to the date of enactment of Pub. L. 95-95 [Aug. 7, 1977] to continue in full force and effect until modified or rescinded in accordance with act July 14, 1955, as amended by Pub. L. 95-95 [this chapter], see section 406(b) of Pub. L. 95-95, set out as an Effective Date of 1977 Amendment note under section 7401 of this title.

Transfer of Functions

Federal Power Commission terminated and its functions, personnel, property, funds, etc., transferred to Secretary of Energy (except for certain functions transferred to Federal Energy Regulatory Commission) by sections 7151(b), 7171(a), 7172(a), 7291, and 7293 of this title.

Section Referred to in Other Sections

This section is referred to in sections 7407, 7410, 7411, 7412, 7414, 7419, 7420, 7421, 7425, 7426, 7429, 7604, 7606, 7607, 7627, 7651g, 7651j, 9606 of this title; title 15 section 792.

RECORDKEEPING, INSPECTIONS, MONITORING, AND ENTRY

42 USC 7414

(a) Authority of Administrator or authorized representative

For the purpose (i) of developing or assisting in the development of any implementation plan under section 7410 or section 7411(d) of this title, any standard of performance under section 7411 of this title, any emission standard under section 7412 of this title,,[1] or any regulation of solid waste combustion under section 7429 of this title, or any regulation under section 7429 of this title (relating to solid waste combustion), (ii) of determining whether any person is in violation of any such standard or any requirement of such a plan, or (iii) carrying out any provision of this chapter (except a provision of subchapter II of this chapter with respect to a manufacturer of new motor vehicles or new motor vehicle engines)—

(1) the Administrator may require any person who owns or operates any emission source, who manufactures emission control equipment or process equipment, who the Administrator believes may have information necessary for the purposes set forth in this subsection, or who is subject to any requirement of this chapter (other than a manufacturer subject to the provisions of section 7525(c) or 7542 of this title with respect to a provision of subchapter II of this chapter) on a one-time, periodic or continuous basis to—

(A) establish and maintain such records;
(B) make such reports;
(C) install, use, and maintain such monitoring equipment, and use such audit procedures, or methods;
(D) sample such emissions (in accordance with such procedures or methods, at such locations, at such intervals, during such periods and in such manner as the Administrator shall prescribe);
(E) keep records on control equipment parameters, production variables or other indirect data when direct monitoring of emissions is impractical;
(F) submit compliance certifications in accordance with subsection (a)(3) of this section; and
(G) provide such other information as the Administrator may reasonably require; and

(2) the Administrator or his authorized representative, upon presentation of his credentials—

(A) shall have a right of entry to, upon, or through any premises of such person or in which any records required to be maintained under paragraph (1) of this section are located, and
(B) may at reasonable times have access to and copy any records, inspect any monitoring equipment or method required under paragraph (1), and sample any emissions which such person is required to sample under paragraph (1).[2]

(3) The[3] Administrator shall in the case of any person which is the owner or operator of a major stationary source, and may, in the case of any other person, require enhanced monitoring and submission of compliance certifications. Compliance certifications shall in-

---

[1]So in original.
[2]The period probably should be "; and".
[3]So in original. Probably should not be capitalized.

clude (A) identification of the applicable requirement that is the basis of the certification, (B) the method used for determining the compliance status of the source, (C) the compliance status, (D) whether compliance is continuous or intermittent, (E) such other facts as the Administrator may require. Compliance certifications and monitoring data shall be subject to subsection (c) of this section. Submission of a compliance certification shall in no way limit the Administrator's authorities to investigate or otherwise implement this chapter. The Administrator shall promulgate rules to provide guidance and to implement this paragraph within 2 years after November 15, 1990.

(b) State enforcement
  (1) Each State may develop and submit to the Administrator a procedure for carrying out this section in such State. If the Administrator finds the State procedure is adequate, he may delegate to such State any authority he has to carry out this section.
  (2) Nothing in this subsection shall prohibit the Administrator from carrying out this section in a State.

(c) Availability of records, reports, and information to public; disclosure of trade secrets
  Any records, reports or information obtained under subsection (a) of this section shall be available to the public, except that upon a showing satisfactory to the Administrator by any person that records, reports, or information, or particular part thereof, (other than emission data) to which the Administrator has access under this section if made public, would divulge methods or processes entitled to protection as trade secrets of such person, the Administrator shall consider such record, report, or information or particular portion thereof confidential in accordance with the purposes of section 1905 of title 18, except that such record, report, or information may be disclosed to other officers, employees, or authorized representatives of the United States concerned with carrying out this chapter or when relevant in any proceeding under this chapter.

(d) Notice of proposed entry, inspection, or monitoring
  (1) In the case of any emission standard or limitation or other requirement which is adopted by a State, as part of an applicable implementation plan or as part of an order under section 7413(d)[4] of this title, before carrying out an entry, inspection, or monitoring under paragraph (2) of subsection (a) of this section with respect to such standard, limitation, or other requirement, the Administrator (or his representatives) shall provide the State air pollution control agency with reasonable prior notice of such action, indicating the purpose of such action. No State agency which receives notice under this paragraph of an action proposed to be taken may use the information contained in the notice to inform the person whose property is proposed to be affected of the proposed action. If the Administrator has reasonable basis for believing that a State agency is so using or will so use such information, notice to the agency under this paragraph is not required until such time as the Administrator determines the agency will no longer so use information contained in a notice under this paragraph. Nothing in this section shall be construed to require notification to any State agency of any action taken by the Administrator with respect to any standard, limitation, or other requirement which is not part of an applicable implementation plan or which was promulgated by the Administrator under section 7410(c) of this title.
  (2) Nothing in paragraph (1) shall be construed to provide that any failure of the Administrator to comply with the requirements of such paragraph shall be a defense in any enforcement action brought by the Administrator or shall make inadmissible as evidence in any such action any information or material obtained notwithstanding such failure to comply with such requirements.

(July 14, 1955, ch. 360, title I, Sec. 114, as added Pub. L. 91-604, Sec. 4(a), Dec. 31, 1970, 84 Stat. 1687; amended Pub. L. 93-319, Sec. 6(a)(4), June 22, 1974, 88 Stat. 259; Pub. L. 95-95, title I, Secs. 109(d)(3), 113, title III, Sec. 305(d), Aug. 7, 1977, 91 Stat. 701, 709, 776; Pub. L. 95-190, Sec. 14(a)(22), (23), Nov. 16, 1977, 91 Stat. 1400; Pub. L. 101-549, title III, Sec. 302(c), title VII, Sec. 702(a), (b), Nov. 15, 1990, 104 Stat. 2574, 2680, 2681.)

---

[4]See References in Text note below.

References in Text

Section 7413(d) of this title, referred to in subsec. (d)(1), was amended generally by Pub. L. 101-549, title VII, Sec. 701, Nov. 15, 1990, 104 Stat. 2672, and, as so amended, no longer relates to final compliance orders.

Codification

Section was formerly classified to section 1857c-9 of this title.

Amendments

1990—Subsec. (a). Pub. L. 101-549, Sec. 702(a)(1), which directed that "or" be struck out in first sentence immediately before "any emission standard under section 7412 of this title," could not be executed because of the prior amendment by Pub. L. 101-549, Sec. 302(c), see below.

Pub. L. 101-549, Sec. 702(a)(2), inserted "or any regulation under section 7429 of this title (relating to solid waste combustion)," before "(ii) of determining".

Pub. L. 101-549, Sec. 302(c), struck out "or" after "performance under section 7411 of this title," and inserted ", or any regulation of solid waste combustion under section 7429 of this title," after "standard under section 7412 of this title".

Subsec. (a)(1). Pub. L. 101-549, Sec. 702(a)(3), amended par. (1) generally. Prior to amendment, par. (1) read as follows: "the Administrator may require any person who owns or operates any emission source or who is subject to any requirement of this chapter (other than a manufacturer subject to the provisions of section 7525(c) or 7542 of this title) with respect to a provision of subchapter II of this chapter to (A) establish and maintain such records, (B) make such reports, (C) install, use, and maintain such monitoring equipment or methods, (D) sample such emissions (in accordance with such methods, at such locations, at such intervals, and in such manner as the Administrator shall prescribe), and (E) provide such other information as he may reasonably require; and".

Subsec. (a)(3). Pub. L. 101-549, Sec. 702(b), added par. (3).

1977—Subsec. (a). Pub. L. 95-190, Sec. 14(a)(22), inserted reference to subchapter II of this chapter and "new" before "motor" in two places.

Pub. L. 95-95, Sec. 305(d), substituted "carrying out any provision of this chapter (except with respect to a manufacturer of motor vehicles or motor vehicle engines)" for "carrying out sections 119 or 303" in cl. (iii) preceding par. (1), substituted "any person subject to any requirement of this chapter (other than a manufacturer subject to the provisions of sections 7525(c) or 7542 of this title)" for "the owner or operator of any emission source" in par. (1), substituted "any premises of such person" for "any premises in which an emission source is located" in subpar. (A) of par. (2), and substituted "emissions which such person is required to sample" for "emissions which the owner or operator of such source is required to sample" in subpar. (B) of subpar. (2).

Subsec. (a)(1). Pub. L. 95-190, Sec. 14(a)(23), inserted reference to subchapter II of this chapter and "who owns or operates any emission source or who is" after "any person".

Subsec. (b)(1). Pub. L. 95-95, Sec. 109(d)(3), struck out "(except with respect to new sources owned or operated by the United States)" after "to carry out this section".

Subsec. (d). Pub. L. 95-95, Sec. 113, added subsec. (d).

1974—Subsec. (a). Pub. L. 93-319 inserted reference to section 119.

Effective Date of 1977 Amendment

Amendment by Pub. L. 95-95 effective Aug. 7, 1977, except as otherwise expressly provided, see section 406(d) of Pub. L. 95-95, set out as a note under section 7401 of this title.

Pending Actions and Proceedings

Suits, actions, and other proceedings lawfully commenced by or against the Administrator or any other officer or employee of the United States in his official capacity or in relation to the discharge of his official duties under act July 14, 1955, the Clean Air Act, as in effect immediately prior to the enactment of Pub. L. 95-95 [Aug. 7, 1977], not to abate by reason of the taking effect of Pub. L. 95-95, see section 406(a) of Pub. L. 95-95, set out as an Effective Date of 1977 Amendment note under section 7401 of this title.

Modification or Rescission of Rules, Regulations, Orders, Determinations, Contracts, Certifications, Authorizations, Delegations, and Other Actions

All rules, regulations, orders, determinations, contracts, certifications, authorizations, delegations, or other actions duly issued, made, or taken by or pursuant to act July 14, 1955, the Clean Air Act, as in effect immediately prior to the date of enactment of Pub. L. 95-95 [Aug. 7, 1977] to continue in full force and effect until modified or rescinded in accordance with act July 14, 1955, as amended by Pub. L. 95-95 [this chapter], see section 406(b) of Pub. L. 95-95, set out as an Effective Date of 1977 Amendment note under section 7401 of this title.

Section Referred to in Other Sections

This section is referred to in sections 7411, 7412, 7413, 7429, 7607, 7627, 7651j, 7661a, 7661b, 7671k, 9606 of this title.

INTERNATIONAL AIR POLLUTION

42 USC 7415

(a) Endangerment of public health or welfare in foreign countries from pollution emitted in United States

Whenever the Administrator, upon receipt of reports, surveys or studies from any duly constituted international agency has reason to believe that any air pollutant or pollutants emitted in the United States cause or contribute to air pollution which may reasonably be anticipated to endanger public health or welfare in a foreign country or whenever the Secretary of State requests him to do so with respect to such pollution which the Secretary of State alleges is of such a nature, the Administrator shall give formal notification thereof to the Governor of the State in which such emissions originate.

(b) Prevention or elimination of endangerment

The notice of the Administrator shall be deemed to be a finding under section 7410(a)(2)(H)(ii) of this title which requires a plan revision with respect to so much of the applicable implementation plan as is inadequate to prevent or eliminate the endangerment referred to in subsection (a) of this section. Any foreign country so affected by such emission of pollutant or pollutants shall be invited to appear at any public hearing associated with any revision of the appropriate portion of the applicable implementation plan.

(c) Reciprocity

This section shall apply only to a foreign country which the Administrator determines has given the United States essentially the same rights with respect to the prevention or control of air pollution occurring in that country as is given that country by this section.

(d) Recommendations

Recommendations issued following any abatement conference conducted prior to August 7, 1977, shall remain in effect with respect to any pollutant for which no national ambient air quality standard has been established under section 7409 of this title unless the Administrator, after consultation with all agencies which were party to the conference, rescinds any such recommendation on grounds of obsolescence.

(July 14, 1955, ch. 360, title I, Sec. 115, formerly Sec. 5, as added Pub. L. 88-206, Sec. 1, Dec. 17, 1963, 77 Stat. 396; renumbered Sec. 105 and amended Pub. L. 89-272, title I, Secs. 101(2), (3), 102, Oct. 20, 1965, 79 Stat. 992, 995, renumbered Sec. 108 and amended Pub. L. 90-148, Sec. 2, Nov. 21, 1967, 81 Stat. 491, renumbered Sec. 115 and amended Pub. L. 91-604, Secs. 4(a), (b)(2)-(10), 15(c)(2), Dec. 31, 1970, 84 Stat. 1678, 1688, 1689, 1713; Pub. L. 95-95, title I, Sec. 114, Aug. 7, 1977, 91 Stat. 710.)

Codification

Section was formerly classified to section 1857d of this title.

Amendments

1977—Pub. L. 95-95 completely revised section by substituting provisions establishing a mechanism for the Administrator to trigger a revision of a State implementation plan under section 7410(a)(2)(H) upon a petition of an international agency or the Secretary of State if he finds that emissions originating in a State endanger the health or welfare of persons in a foreign country for provisions calling for the abatement of air pollution by means of conference procedures.

1970—Subsec. (a). Pub. L. 91-604, Sec. 4(b)(2), inserted "and which is covered by subsection (b) or (c) of this section" after "persons".

Subsec. (b). Pub. L. 91-604, Secs. 4(b)(3), (4), (5), 15(c)(2), redesignated former subsec. (d)(1)(A), (B), and (C) as (b)(1), (2), and (3), substituted "Administrator" for "Secretary" wherever appearing, and added subsec. (b)(4). Former subsec. (b), which related to the encouragement of municipal, State, and interstate action to abate air pollution, was struck out.

Subsec. (c). Pub. L. 91-604, Secs. 4(b)(3), (6), 15(c)(2), redesignated former subsec. (d)(1)(D) as (c) and substituted "Administrator" for "Secretary" and "Secretary of Health, Education, and Welfare" wherever appearing and "subsection" for "subparagraph" wherever appearing. Former subsec. (c), which related to the procedure for the promulgation of State air quality standards, was struck out.

Subsec. (d). Pub. L. 91-604, Secs. 4(b)(4), (6), (7), (8), 15(c)(2), redesignated former subsec. (d)(2) and (3) as (d)(1) and (2), in (d)(1) substituted "Administrator" for "Secretary" wherever appearing and "any conference under this section" for "such conference", and in (d)(2) substituted "Administrator" for "Secretary". Former subsec. (d)(1)(A), (B), and (C) were redesignated as (b)(1), (2), and (3), respectively, and subsec. (d)(1)(D) was redesignated as (c).

Subsec. (e). Pub. L. 91-604, Sec. 15(c)(2), substituted "Administrator" for "Secretary" wherever appearing.

Subsec. (f). Pub. L. 91-604, Sec. 15(c)(2), substituted "Administrator" for "Secretary" wherever appearing and "Environmental Protection Agency" for "Department of Health, Education, and Welfare".

Subsec. (g). Pub. L. 91-604, Secs. 4(b)(9), 15(c)(2), substituted "Administrator" for "Secretary" and "subsection (c)" for "subparagraph (D) of subsection (d)".

Subsecs. (i), (j). Pub. L. 91-604, Sec. 15(c)(2), substituted "Administrator" for "Secretary" wherever appearing.

Subsec. (k). Pub. L. 91-604, Sec. 4(b)(3), (10), substituted provisions relating to compliance with any requirement of an applicable implementation plan or with any standard prescribed under section 7411 of this title or section 7412 of this title, for provisions relating to the enjoining of imminent and substantial endangerment from pollution sources.

1967—Subsec. (b). Pub. L. 90-148 substituted reference to subsec. (c), (h), or (k) of this section for reference to subsec. (g) of this section.

Subsecs. (c), (d). Pub. L. 90-148 added subsec. (c), redesignated former subsec. (c) as (d), inserted in par. (2) provisions for the delivery prior to the conference of a Federal report to agencies and interested parties covering matters before the conference, raised from three weeks to thirty days the required notice of the conference, and inserted provisions for notice by newspapers, presentation of views on the Federal report, and transcript of proceedings. Former subsec. (d) redesignated (e).

Subsec. (e). Pub. L. 90-148 redesignated former subsec. (d) as (e). Former subsec. (e) redesignated (f) and amended.

Subsec. (f). Pub. L. 90-148 redesignated former subsec. (e) as (f) and inserted in par. (1) requirement that all interested parties be given a reasonable opportunity to present evidence to the hearing board. Former subsec. (f) redesignated (g) and amended.

Subsec. (g). Pub. L. 90-148 redesignated former subsec. (f) as (g) and substituted reference to subsec. (d) of this section for reference to subsec. (c) of this section. Former subsec. (g) redesignated (h) and amended.

Subsec. (h). Pub. L. 90-148 redesignated former subsec. (g) as (h) and substituted reference to subsec. (g) of this section for reference to subsec. (f) of this section. Former subsec. (h) redesignated (i) and amended.

112 / Environmental Statutes

Subsec. (i). Pub. L. 90-148 redesignated former subsec. (h) as (i) and substituted reference to subsec. (f) of this section for reference to subsec. (e) of this section and raised the per diem maximum from $50 to $100. Former subsec. (i) redesignated (j).

Subsec. (j). Pub. L. 90-148 redesignated former subsec. (i) as (j).

Subsec. (k). Pub. L. 90-148 added subsec. (k).

1965—Subsec. (b). Pub. L. 89-272, Sec. 101(2), substituted "this title" for "this Act", which for purposes of codification has been changed to "this subchapter".

Subsec. (c)(1)(D). Pub. L. 89-272, Sec. 102(a), added subpar. (D).

Subsec. (d)(3). Pub. L. 89-272, Sec. 101(2), substituted "subchapter" for "chapter".

Subsec. (f)(1). Pub. L. 89-272, Sec. 102(b), designated existing provisions as cl. (A) and added cl. (B).

Effective Date of 1977 Amendment

Amendment by Pub. L. 95-95 effective Aug. 7, 1977, except as otherwise expressly provided, see section 406(d) of Pub. L. 95-95, set out as a note under section 7401 of this title.

Modification or Rescission of Rules, Regulations, Orders, Determinations, Contracts, Certifications, Authorizations, Delegations, and Other Actions

All rules, regulations, orders, determinations, contracts, certifications, authorizations, delegations, or other actions duly issued, made, or taken by or pursuant to act July 14, 1955, the Clean Air Act, as in effect immediately prior to the date of enactment of Pub. L. 95-95 [Aug. 7, 1977] to continue in full force and effect until modified or rescinded in accordance with act July 14, 1955, as amended by Pub. L. 95-95 [this chapter], see section 406(b) of Pub. L. 95-95, set out as an Effective Date of 1977 Amendment note under section 7401 of this title.

United States-Canadian Negotiations on Air Quality

Pub. L. 95-426, title VI, Sec. 612, Oct. 7, 1978, 92 Stat. 990, provided that:

"(a) The Congress finds that—
  (1) the United States and Canada share a common environment along a 5,500 mile border;
  (2) the United States and Canada are both becoming increasingly concerned about the effects of pollution, particularly that resulting from power generation facilities, since the facilities of each country affect the environment of the other;
  (3) the United States and Canada have subscribed to international conventions; have joined in the environmental work of the United Nations, the Organization for Economic Cooperation and Development, and other international environmental forums; and have entered into and implemented effectively the provisions of the historic Boundary Waters Treaty of 1909; and
  (4) the United States and Canada have a tradition of cooperative resolution of issues of mutual concern which is nowhere more evident than in the environmental area.
(b) It is the sense of the Congress that the President should make every effort to negotiate a cooperative agreement with the Government of Canada aimed at preserving the mutual airshed of the United States and Canada so as to protect and enhance air resources and insure the attainment and maintenance of air quality protective of public health and welfare.
(c) It is further the sense of the Congress that the President, through the Secretary of State working in concert with interested Federal agencies and the affected States, should take whatever diplomatic actions appear necessary to reduce or eliminate any undesirable impact upon the United States and Canada resulting from air pollution from any source."

Section Referred to in Other Sections

This section is referred to in section 7410 of this title.

RETENTION OF STATE AUTHORITY

42 USC 7416

Except as otherwise provided in sections 1857c-10(c), (e), and (f) (as in effect before August 7, 1977), 7543, 7545(c)(4), and 7573 of this title (preempting certain State regulation of moving sources) nothing in this chapter shall preclude or deny the right of any State or political subdivision thereof to adopt or enforce (1) any standard or limitation respecting emissions of air pollutants or (2) any requirement respecting control or abatement of air pollution; except that if an emission standard or limitation is in effect under an applicable implementation plan or under section 7411 or section 7412 of this title, such State or political subdivision may not adopt or enforce any emission standard or limitation which is less stringent than the standard or limitation under such plan or section.

(July 14, 1955, ch. 360, title I, Sec. 116, formerly Sec. 109, as added Pub. L. 90-148, Sec. 2, Nov. 21, 1967, 81 Stat. 497; renumbered Sec. 116 and amended Pub. L. 91-604, Sec. 4(a), (c), Dec. 31, 1970, 84 Stat. 1678, 1689; Pub. L. 93-319, Sec. 6(b), June 22, 1974, 88 Stat. 259; Pub. L. 95-190, Sec. 14(a)(24), Nov. 16, 1977, 91 Stat. 1400.)

References in Text

1857c-10(c), (e), and (f) (as in effect before August 7, 1977), referred to in text, was in the original "119(c), (e), and (f) (as in effect before the date of the enactment of the Clean Air Act Amendments of 1977)" meaning section 119 of act July 14, 1955, ch. 360, title I, as added June 22, 1974, Pub. L. 93-319, Sec. 3, 88 Stat. 248, (which was classified to section 1857c-10 of this title) as in effect prior to the enactment of Pub. L. 95-95, Aug. 7, 1977, 91 Stat. 691, effective Aug. 7, 1977. Section 112(b)(1) of Pub. L. 95-95 repealed section 119 of act July 14, 1955, ch. 360, title I, as added by Pub. L. 93-319, and provided that all references to such section 119 in any subsequent enactment which supersedes Pub. L. 93-319 shall be construed to refer to section 113(d) of the Clean Air Act and to paragraph (5) thereof in particular which is classified to subsec. (d)(5) of section 7413 of this title. Section 7413 of this title was subsequently amended generally by Pub. L. 101-549, title VII, Sec. 701, Nov. 15, 1990, 104 Stat. 2672, and, as so amended, no longer relates to final compliance orders. Section 117(b) of Pub. L. 95-95 added a new section 119 of act July 14, 1955, which is classified to section 7419 of this title.

Codification

Section was formerly classified to section 1857d-1 of this title.

Amendments

1977—Pub. L. 95-190 inserted reference to specified provisions in effect before Aug. 7, 1977.

1974—Pub. L. 93-319 inserted reference to section 1857c-10(c), (e), and (f).

1970—Pub. L. 91-604, Sec. 4(c), substituted provisions which authorized any State or political subdivision thereof to adopt or enforce, except as otherwise provided, emission standards or limitations under the specified conditions, or any requirement respecting control or abatement of air pollution, for provisions which authorized any State, political subdivision, or intermunicipal or interstate agency to adopt standards and plans to achieve a higher level of air quality than approved by the Secretary.

Modification or Rescission of Rules, Regulations, Orders, Determinations, Contracts, Certifications, Authorizations, Delegations, and Other Actions

All rules, regulations, orders, determinations, contracts, certifications, authorizations, delegations, or other actions duly issued, made, or taken by or pursuant to act July 14, 1955, the Clean Air Act, as in effect immediately prior to the date of enactment of Pub. L. 95-95 [Aug. 7, 1977] to continue in full force and effect until modified or rescinded in accordance with act July 14, 1955, as amended by Pub. L. 95-95 [this chapter], see section 406(b) of Pub. L. 95-95, set out as an Effective Date of 1977 Amendment note under section 7401 of this title.

Section Referred to in Other Sections

This section is referred to in sections 7412, 7429, 7627, 7671m, 7671q of this title.

ADVISORY COMMITTEES

42 USC 7417

(a) Establishment; membership

In order to obtain assistance in the development and implementation of the purposes of this chapter including air quality criteria, recommended control techniques, standards, research and development, and to encourage the continued efforts on the part of industry to improve air quality and to develop economically feasible methods for the control and abatement of air pollution, the Administrator shall from time to time establish advisory committees. Committee members shall include, but not be limited to, persons who are knowledgeable concerning air quality from the standpoint of health, welfare, economics or technology.

(b) Compensation

The members of any other advisory committees appointed pursuant to this chapter who are not officers or employees of the United States while attending conferences or meetings or while otherwise serving at the request of the Administrator, shall be entitled to receive compensation at a rate to be fixed by the Administrator, but not exceeding $100 per diem, including traveltime, and while away from their homes or regular places of business they may be allowed travel expenses, including per diem in lieu of subsistence, as authorized by section 5703 of title 5 for persons in the Government service employed intermittently.

(c) [1]Consultations by Administrator

Prior to—
(1) issuing criteria for an air pollutant under section 7408(a)(2) of this title,
(2) publishing any list under section 7411(b)(1)(A)[2] or section 7412(b)(1)(A) of this title,
(3) publishing any standard under section 7411 or section 7412 of this title, or
(4) publishing any regulation under section 7521(a) of this title,

the Administrator shall, to the maximum extent practicable within the time provided, consult with appropriate advisory committees, independence experts, and Federal departments and agencies.

(July 14, 1955, ch. 360, title I, Sec. 117 formerly Sec. 6, as added Pub. L. 88-206, Sec. 1, Dec. 17, 1963, 77 Stat. 399; renumbered Sec. 106, Pub. L. 89-272, title I, Sec. 101(3), Oct. 20, 1965, 79 Stat. 992; renumbered Sec. 110 and amended Pub. L. 90-148, Sec. 2, Nov. 21, 1967, 81 Stat. 498; renumbered Sec. 117 and amended Pub. L. 91-604, Secs. 4(a), (d), 15(c)(2), Dec. 31, 1970, 84 Stat. 1678, 1689, 1713; Pub. L. 95-95, title I, Sec. 115, Aug. 7, 1977, 91 Stat. 711; Pub. L. 95-623, Sec. 13(c), Nov. 9, 1978, 92 Stat. 3458.)

References in Text

Section 7412(b)(1), referred to in subsec. (c)(2), was amended generally by Pub. L. 101-549, title III, Sec. 301, Nov. 15, 1990, 104 Stat. 2531, and, as so amended, no longer contains a subpar. (A).

Codification

Subsec. (c) was originally enacted as subsec. (f) but has been redesignated (c) for purposes of codification in view of the failure of Pub. L. 95-95 to redesignate subsec. (f) as (c) after repealing former subsecs. (a) and (b) and redesignating former subsecs. (d) and (e) as (a) and (b).

Section was formerly classified to section 1857e of this title.

Amendments

1978—Subsec. (c)(3). Pub. L. 95-623 substituted "7411" for "7411(b)(1)(B)" and "7412" for "7412(b)(1)(B)".

1977—Subsec. (a). Pub. L. 95-95, Sec. 115(1), (2), redesignated subsec. (d) as (a). Former subsec. (a), establishing an Air Quality Advisory Board in the Environmental Protection Agency, was struck out.

Subsec. (b). Pub. L. 95-95, Sec. 115(1)-(3), redesignated subsec. (e) as (b) and substituted "The members of any other advisory committees" for "The members of the Board and other advi-

---
[1]See Codification note below.
[2]See References in Text note below.

sory committees" and "conferences or meetings or while otherwise serving" for "conferences or meetings of the Board or while otherwise serving". Former subsec. (b), setting out the duties of the Air Quality Advisory Board, was struck out.

Subsecs. (c) to (e). Pub. L. 95-95, Sec. 115(1), (2), struck out subsec. (c) which related to clerical and technical assistance for the Air Quality Advisory Board, and redesignated subsecs. (d) and (e) as (a) and (b), respectively.

1970—Subsec. (a). Pub. L. 91-604, Sec. 15(c)(2), substituted "Environmental Protection Agency" for "Department of Health, Education, and Welfare" and "Administrator" for "Secretary".

Subsec. (b). Pub. L. 91-604, Sec. 15(c)(2), substituted "Administrator" for "Secretary" wherever appearing.

Subsec. (c). Pub. L. 91-604, Sec. 15(c)(2), substituted "Environmental Protection Agency" for "Department of Health, Education, and Welfare".

Subsecs. (d), (e). Pub. L. 91-604, Sec. 15(c)(2), substituted "Administrator" for "Secretary" wherever appearing.

Subsec. (f). Pub. L. 91-604, Sec. 4(d), added subsec. (f).

1967—Subsec. (a). Pub. L. 90-148 substituted provisions establishing in the Department of Health, Education, and Welfare an Air Quality Advisory Board and providing for the appointment and term of its members for provisions directing the Secretary to maintain liaison with manufacturers looking toward development of devices and fuels to reduce pollutants in automotive exhaust and to appoint a technical committee and call it together from time to time to evaluate progress and develop and recommend research programs.

Subsec. (b). Pub. L. 90-148 substituted provision setting out the duties of the Air Quality Advisory Board for provisions requiring the Secretary to make semi-annual reports to Congress on measures being taken toward the resolution of vehicle exhaust pollution problems.

Subsecs. (c) to (e). Pub. L. 90-148 added subsecs. (c) to (e).

Effective Date of 1977 Amendment

Amendment by Pub. L. 95-95 effective Aug. 7, 1977, except as otherwise expressly provided, see section 406(d) of Pub. L. 95-95, set out as a note under section 7401 of this title.

Modification or Rescission of Rules, Regulations, Orders, Determinations, Contracts, Certifications, Authorizations, Delegations, and Other Actions

All rules, regulations, orders, determinations, contracts, certifications, authorizations, delegations, or other actions duly issued, made, or taken by or pursuant to act July 14, 1955, the Clean Air Act, as in effect immediately prior to the date of enactment of Pub. L. 95-95 [Aug. 7, 1977] to continue in full force and effect until modified or rescinded in accordance with act July 14, 1955, as amended by Pub. L. 95-95 [this chapter], see section 406(b) of Pub. L. 95-95, set out as an Effective Date of 1977 Amendment note under section 7401 of this title.

Termination of Advisory Committees

Advisory committees in existence on Jan. 5, 1973, to terminate not later than the expiration of the 2-year period following Jan. 5, 1973, unless, in the case of a committee established by the President or an officer of the Federal Government, such committee is renewed by appropriate action prior to the expiration of such 2-year period, or in the case of a committee established by the Congress, its duration is otherwise provided by law. Advisory committees established after Jan. 5, 1973, to terminate not later than the expiration of the 2-year period beginning on the date of their establishment, unless, in the case of a committee established by the President or an officer of the Federal Government, such committee is renewed by appropriate action prior to the expiration of such 2-year period, or in the case of a committee established by the Congress, its duration is otherwise provided by law. See section 14 of Pub. L. 92-463, Oct. 6, 1972, 86 Stat. 776, set out in the Appendix to Title 5, Government Organization and Employees.

CONTROL OF POLLUTION FROM FEDERAL FACILITIES

42 USC 7418

(a) General compliance

Each department, agency, and instrumentality of the executive, legislative, and judicial branches of the Federal Government (1) having jurisdiction over any property or facility, or (2) engaged in any activity resulting, or which may result, in the discharge of air pollutants, and each officer, agent, or employee thereof, shall be subject to, and comply with, all Federal, State, interstate, and local requirements, administrative authority, and process and sanctions respecting the control and abatement of air pollution in the same manner, and to the same extent as any nongovernmental entity. The preceding sentence shall apply (A) to any requirement whether substantive or procedural (including any recordkeeping or reporting requirement, any requirement respecting permits and any other requirement whatsoever), (B) to any requirement to pay a fee or charge imposed by any State or local agency to defray the costs of its air pollution regulatory program, (C) to the exercise of any Federal, State, or local administrative authority, and (D) to any process and sanction, whether enforced in Federal, State, or local courts, or in any other manner. This subsection shall apply notwithstanding any immunity of such agencies, officers, agents, or employees under any law or rule of law. No officer, agent, or employee of the United States shall be personally liable for any civil penalty for which he is not otherwise liable.

(b) Exemption

The President may exempt any emission source of any department, agency, or instrumentality in the executive branch from compliance with such a requirement if he determines it to be in the paramount interest of the United States to do so, except that no exemption may be granted from section 7411 of this title, and an exemption from section 7412 of this title may be granted only in accordance with section 7412(i)(4) of this title. No such exemption shall be granted due to lack of appropriation unless the President shall have specifically requested such appropriation as a part of the budgetary process and the Congress shall have failed to make available such requested appropriation. Any exemption shall be for a period not in excess of one year, but additional exemptions may be granted for periods of not to exceed one year upon the President's making a new determination. In addition to any such exemption of a particular emission source, the President may, if he determines it to be in the paramount interest of the United States to do so, issue regulations exempting from compliance with the requirements of this section any weaponry, equipment, aircraft, vehicles, or other classes or categories of property which are owned or operated by the Armed Forces of the United States (including the Coast Guard) or by the National Guard of any State and which are uniquely military in nature. The President shall reconsider the need for such regulations at three-year intervals. The President shall report each January to the Congress all exemptions from the requirements of this section granted during the preceding calendar year, together with his reason for granting each such exemption.

(c) Government vehicles

Each department, agency, and instrumentality of executive, legislative, and judicial branches of the Federal Government shall comply with all applicable provisions of a valid inspection and maintenance program established under the provisions of subpart 2 of part D of this subchapter or subpart 3 of part D of this subchapter except for such vehicles that are considered military tactical vehicles.

(d) Vehicles operated on Federal installations

Each department, agency, and instrumentality of executive, legislative, and judicial branches of the Federal Government having jurisdiction over any property or facility shall require all employees which operate motor vehicles on the property or facility to furnish proof of compliance with the applicable requirements of any vehicle inspection and maintenance program established under the provisions of subpart 2 of part D of this subchapter or subpart 3 of part D of this subchapter for the State in which such property or facility is located (without regard to whether such vehicles are registered in the State). The installation shall use one of the following methods to establish proof of compliance—

(1) presentation by the vehicle owner of a valid certificate of compliance from the vehicle inspection and maintenance program;

(2) presentation by the vehicle owner of proof of vehicle registration within the geographic area covered by the vehicle inspection and maintenance program (except for any program whose enforcement mechanism is not through the denial of vehicle registration);

(3) another method approved by the vehicle inspection and maintenance program administrator.

(July 14, 1955, ch. 360, title I, Sec. 118, formerly, Sec. 7, as added Pub. L. 88-206, Sec. 1, Dec. 17, 1963, 77 Stat. 399; renumbered Sec. 107, Pub. L. 89-272, title I, Sec. 101(3), Oct. 20, 1965, 79 Stat. 992; renumbered Sec. 111 and amended Pub. L. 90-148, Sec. 2, Nov. 21, 1967, 81 Stat. 499; renumbered Sec. 118 and amended Pub. L. 91-604, Secs. 4(a), 5, Dec. 31, 1970, 84 Stat. 1678, 1689; Pub. L. 95-95, title I, Sec. 116, Aug. 7, 1977, 91 Stat. 711; Pub. L. 101-549, title I, Sec. 101(e), title II, Sec. 235, title III, Sec. 302(d), Nov. 15, 1990, 104 Stat. 2409, 2530, 2574.)

Codification

Section was formerly classified to section 1857f of this title.

Amendments

1990—Subsec. (a). Pub. L. 101-549, Sec. 235, inserted heading.

Pub. L. 101-549, Sec. 101(e), amended second sentence generally. Prior to amendment, second sentence read as follows: "The preceding sentence shall apply (A) to any requirement whether substantive or procedural (including any recordkeeping or reporting requirement, any requirement respecting permits and any other requirement whatsoever), (B) to the exercise of any Federal, State, or local administrative authority, and (C) to any process and sanction, whether enforced in Federal, State, or local courts or in any other manner."

Subsec. (b). Pub. L. 101-549, Sec. 302(d), substituted "section 7412(i)(4) of this title" for "section 7412(c) of this title".

Subsecs. (c), (d). Pub. L. 101-549, Sec. 235, added subsecs. (c) and (d).

1977—Subsec. (a). Pub. L. 95-95, Sec. 116(a), designated existing first sentence as subsec. (a) and inserted provisions enumerating the legal and administrative areas to which the compliance requirements apply and directing that agencies, officers, agents, and employees not be immune and that officers, agents, or employees of the United States not be personally liable for civil penalties for which they are not otherwise liable.

Subsec. (b). Pub. L. 95-95, Sec. 116(b), designated second and following existing sentences as subsec. (b) and inserted provisions authorizing the President to exempt weaponry, equipment, aircraft, vehicles, and other classes and categories of property of the Armed Forces and the National Guard from compliance but to reconsider the need for such an exemption at three-year intervals.

1970—Pub. L. 91-604, Sec. 5, struck out lettered designations (a) and (b), and, as so redesignated, substituted provisions requiring Federal facilities to comply with Federal, State, local, and interstate air pollution control and abatement requirements and provisions authorizing the President to exempt, under the specified terms and conditions, any emission source of any department, etc., in the executive branch from compliance with control and abatement requirements, for provisions requiring, to the extent practicable and consistent with the interests of the United States and within any available appropriations, Federal facilities to cooperate with the Department of Health, Education, and Welfare and with any air pollution control agency to prevent and control air pollution and provisions authorizing the Secretary to establish classes of potential pollution sources for which any Federal department or agency having jurisdiction over any facility was required to obtain a permit, under the specified terms and conditions, for the discharge of any matter into the air of the United States.

1967—Pub. L. 90-148 reenacted section without change.

Effective Date of 1977 Amendment

Amendment by Pub. L. 95-95 effective Aug. 7, 1977, except as otherwise expressly provided, see section 406(d) of Pub. L. 95-95, set out as a note under section 7401 of this title.

Pending Actions and Proceedings

Suits, actions, and other proceedings lawfully commenced by or against the Administrator or any other officer or employee of the United States in his official capacity or in relation to the discharge of his official duties under act July 14, 1955, the Clean Air Act, as in effect immediately prior to the enactment of Pub. L. 95-95 [Aug. 7, 1977], not to abate by reason of the taking effect of Pub. L. 95-95, see section 406(a) of Pub. L. 95-95, set out as an Effective Date of 1977 Amendment note under section 7401 of this title.

Modification or Rescission of Rules, Regulations, Orders, Determinations, Contracts, Certifications, Authorizations, Delegations, and Other Actions

All rules, regulations, orders, determinations, contracts, certifications, authorizations, delegations, or other actions duly issued, made, or taken by or pursuant to act July 14, 1955, the Clean Air Act, as in effect immediately prior to the date of enactment of Pub. L. 95-95 [Aug. 7, 1977] to continue in full force and effect until modified or rescinded in accordance with act July 14, 1955, as amended by Pub. L. 95-95 [this chapter], see section 406(b) of Pub. L. 95-95, set out as an Effective Date of 1977 Amendment note under section 7401 of this title.

Executive Order No. 11282

Ex. Ord. No. 11282, May 26, 1966, 31 F.R. 7663, which provided for the prevention, control, and abatement of air pollution from Federal activities, was superseded by Ex. Ord. No. 11507, Feb. 4, 1970, 35 F.R. 2573.

Executive Order No. 11507

Ex. Ord. No. 11507, Feb. 4, 1970, 35 F.R. 2573, which provided for the prevention, control, and abatement of air pollution at Federal facilities, was superseded by Ex. Ord. No. 11752, Dec. 17, 1973, 38 F.R. 34793, formerly set out as a note under section 4331 of this title.

Section Referred to in Other Sections

This section is referred to in sections 7410, 7423, 7604, 7671q of this title.

PRIMARY NONFERROUS SMELTER ORDERS

42 USC 7419

(a) Issuance; hearing; enforcement orders; statement of grounds for application; findings
 (1) Upon application by the owner or operator of a primary nonferrous smelter, a primary nonferrous smelter order under subsection (b) of this section may be issued—
  (A) by the Administrator, after thirty days' notice to the State, or
  (B) by the State in which such source is located, but no such order issued by the State shall take effect until the Administrator determines that such order has been issued in accordance with the requirements of this chapter.
 Not later than ninety days after submission by the State to the Administrator of notice of the issuance of a primary nonferrous smelter order under this section, the Administrator shall determine whether or not such order has been issued by the State in accordance with the requirements of this chapter. If the Administrator determines that such order has not been issued in accordance with such requirements, he shall conduct a hearing respecting the reasonably available control technology for primary nonferrous smelters.
 (2) (A) An order issued under this section to a primary nonferrous smelter shall be referred to as a "primary nonferrous smelter order". No primary nonferrous smelter may receive both an enforcement order under section 7413(d)[1] of this title and a primary nonferrous smelter order under this section.
  (B) Before any hearing conducted under this section, in the case of an application made by the owner or operator of a primary nonferrous smelter for a second order under this section, the applicant shall furnish the Administrator (or the State as the case may be) with a statement of the grounds on which such application is based (including all supporting documents and information). The statement of the grounds for the proposed order shall be provided by the Administrator or the State in any case in which such State or Administrator is acting on its own initiative. Such statement (including such documents and information) shall be made available to the public for a thirty-day period before such hearing and shall be considered as part of such hearing. No primary nonferrous smelter order may be granted unless the applicant establishes

---
[1]See References in Text note below.

that he meets the conditions required for the issuance of such order (or the Administrator or State establishes the meeting of such conditions when acting on their own initiative).
- (C) Any decision with respect to the issuance of a primary nonferrous smelter order shall be accompanied by a concise statement of the findings and of the basis of such findings.
- (3) For the purposes of sections 7410, 7604, and 7607 of this title, any order issued by the State and in effect pursuant to this subsection shall become part of the applicable implementation plan.

(b) Prerequisites to issuance of orders

A primary nonferrous smelter order under this section may be issued to a primary nonferrous smelter if—
- (1) such smelter is in existence on August 7, 1977;
- (2) the requirement of the applicable implementation plan with respect to which the order is issued is an emission limitation or standard for sulfur oxides which is necessary and intended to be itself sufficient to enable attainment and maintenance of national primary and secondary ambient air quality standards for sulfur oxides; and
- (3) such smelter is unable to comply with such requirement by the applicable date for compliance because no means of emission limitation applicable to such smelter which will enable it to achieve compliance with such requirement has been adequately demonstrated to be reasonably available (as determined by the Administrator, taking into account the cost of compliance, non-air quality health and environmental impact, and energy consideration).

(c) Second orders
- (1) A second order issued to a smelter under this section shall set forth compliance schedules containing increments of progress which require compliance with the requirement postponed as expeditiously as practicable. The increments of progress shall be limited to requiring compliance with subsection (d) of this section and, in the case of a second order, to procuring, installing, and operating the necessary means of emission limitation as expeditiously as practicable after the Administrator determines such means have been adequately demonstrated to be reasonably available within the meaning of subsection (b)(3) of this section.
- (2) Not in excess of two primary nonferrous smelter orders may be issued under this section to any primary nonferrous smelter. The first such order issued to a smelter shall not result in the postponement of the requirement with respect to which such order is issued beyond January 1, 1983. The second such order shall not result in the postponement of such requirement beyond January 1, 1988.

(d) Interim measures; continuous emission reduction technology
- (1) (A) Each primary nonferrous smelter to which an order is issued under this section shall be required to use such interim measures for the period during which such order is in effect as may be necessary in the judgment of the Administrator to assure attainment and maintenance of the national primary and secondary ambient air quality standards during such period, taking into account the aggregate effect on air quality of such order together with all variances, extensions, waivers, enforcement orders, delayed compliance orders and primary nonferrous smelter orders previously issued under this chapter.
  - (B) Such interim requirements shall include—
    - (i) a requirement that the source to which the order applies comply with such reporting requirements and conduct such monitoring as the Administrator determines may be necessary, and
    - (ii) such measures as the Administrator determines are necessary to avoid an imminent and substantial endangerment to health of persons.
  - (C) Such interim measures shall also, except as provided in paragraph (2), include continuous emission reduction technology. The Administrator shall condition the use of any such interim measures upon the agreement of the owner or operator of the smelter—
    - (i) to comply with such conditions as the Administrator determines are necessary to maximize the reliability and enforceability of such interim measures, as applied

to the smelter, in attaining and maintaining the national ambient air quality standards to which the order relates, and
  (ii) to commit reasonable resources to research and development of appropriate emission control technology.
(2) The requirement of paragraph (1) for the use of continuous emission reduction technology may be waived with respect to a particular smelter by the State or the Administrator, after notice and a hearing on the record, and upon a showing by the owner or operator of the smelter that such requirement would be so costly as to necessitate permanent or prolonged temporary cessation of operations of the smelter. Upon application for such waiver, the Administrator shall be notified and shall, within ninety days, hold a hearing on the record in accordance with section 554 of title 5. At such hearing the Administrator shall require the smelter involved to present information relating to any alleged cessation of operations and the detailed reasons or justifications therefor. On the basis of such hearing the Administrator shall make findings of fact as to the effect of such requirement and on the alleged cessation of operations and shall make such recommendations as he deems appropriate. Such report, findings, and recommendations shall be available to the public, and shall be taken into account by the State or the Administrator in making the decision whether or not to grant such waiver.
(3) In order to obtain information for purposes of a waiver under paragraph (2), the Administrator may, on his own motion, conduct an investigation and use the authority of section 7621 of this title.
(4) In the case of any smelter which on August 7, 1977, uses continuous emission reduction technology and supplemental controls and which receives an initial primary nonferrous smelter order under this section, no additional continuous emission reduction technology shall be required as a condition of such order unless the Administrator determines, at any time, after notice and public hearing, that such additional continuous emission reduction technology is adequately demonstrated to be reasonably available for the primary nonferrous smelter industry.

(e) Termination of orders
At any time during which an order under this section applies, the Administrator may enter upon a public hearing respecting the availability of technology. Any order under this section shall be terminated if the Administrator determines on the record, after notice and public hearing, that the conditions upon which the order was based no longer exist. If the owner or operator of the smelter to which the order is issued demonstrates that prompt termination of such order would result in undue hardship, the termination shall become effective at the earliest practicable date on which such undue hardship would not result, but in no event later than the date required under subsection (c) of this section.

(f) Violation of requirements
If the Administrator determines that a smelter to which an order is issued under this section is in violation of any requirement of subsection (c) or (d) of this section, he shall—
  (1) enforce such requirement under section 7413 of this title,
  (2) (after notice and opportunity for public hearing) revoke such order and enforce compliance with the requirement with respect to which such order was granted,
  (3) give notice of noncompliance and commence action under section 7420 of this title, or
  (4) take any appropriate combination of such actions.

(July 14, 1955, ch. 360, title I, Sec. 119, as added Pub. L. 95-95, title I, Sec. 117(b), Aug. 7, 1977, 91 Stat. 712; amended Pub. L. 95-190, Sec. 14(a)(25)-(27), Nov. 16, 1977, 91 Stat. 1401.)

References in Text

Section 7413(d) of this title, referred to in subsec. (a)(2)(A), was amended generally by Pub. L. 101-549, title VII, Sec. 701, Nov. 15, 1990, 104 Stat. 2672, and, as so amended, no longer relates to final compliance orders.

Prior Provisions

A prior section 119 of act July 14, 1955, ch. 360, title I, as added June 22, 1974, Pub. L. 93-319, Sec. 3, 88 Stat. 248, was classified to section 1857c-10 of this title and provided for the authority to deal with energy shortages, prior to repeal by Pub. L. 95-95, title I, Sec. 112(b)(1), Aug. 7, 1977, 91 Stat. 709, which provided that all references to such section 119 in any subsequent enactment which

Clean Air Act / 121

supersedes Pub. L. 93-319 shall be construed to refer to section 113(d) of the Clean Air Act and to paragraph (5) thereof in particular which is classified to section 7413(d)(5) of this title.

Amendments

1977—Subsec. (a)(3). Pub. L. 95-190, Sec. 14(a)(25), added par. (3).

Subsec. (d)(3). Pub. L. 95-190, Sec. 14(a)(26), substituted "7621" for "7619".

Subsec. (e). Pub. L. 95-190, Sec. 14(a)(27), substituted "an order under this section" for "such order".

Effective Date

Section effective Aug. 7, 1977, except as otherwise expressly provided, see section 406(d) of Pub. L. 95-95, set out as an Effective Date of 1977 Amendment note under section 7401 of this title.

Modification or Rescission of Rules, Regulations, Orders, Determinations, Contracts, Certifications, Authorizations, Delegations, and Other Actions

All rules, regulations, orders, determinations, contracts, certifications, authorizations, delegations, or other actions duly issued, made, or taken by or pursuant to act July 14, 1955, the Clean Air Act, as in effect immediately prior to the date of enactment of Pub. L. 95-95 [Aug. 7, 1977] to continue in full force and effect until modified or rescinded in accordance with act July 14, 1955, as amended by Pub. L. 95-95 [this chapter], see section 406(b) of Pub. L. 95-95, set out as an Effective Date of 1977 Amendment note under section 7401 of this title.

Section Referred to in Other Sections

This section is referred to in sections 7410, 7420, 7604, 7607, 7621 of this title; title 15 sections 793, 798.

NONCOMPLIANCE PENALTY

42 USC 7420

(a) Assessment and collection
   (1) (A) Not later than 6 months after August 7, 1977, and after notice and opportunity for a public hearing, the Administrator shall promulgate regulations requiring the assessment and collection of a noncompliance penalty against persons referred to in paragraph (2)(A).
      (B) (i) Each State may develop and submit to the Administrator a plan for carrying out this section in such State. If the Administrator finds that the State plan meets the requirements of this section, he may delegate to such State any authority he has to carry out this section.
         (ii) Notwithstanding a delegation to a State under clause (i), the Administrator may carry out this section in such State under the circumstances described in subsection (b)(2)(B) of this section.
   (2) (A) Except as provided in subparagraph (B) or (C) of this paragraph, the State or the Administrator shall assess and collect a noncompliance penalty against every person who owns or operates—
         (i) a major stationary source (other than a primary nonferrous smelter which has received a primary nonferrous smelter order under section 7419 of this title), which is not in compliance with any emission limitation, emission standard or compliance schedule under any applicable implementation plan (whether or not such source is subject to a Federal or State consent decree), or
         (ii) a stationary source which is not in compliance with an emission limitation, emission standard, standard of performance, or other requirement established under section 7411, 7477, 7603, or 7412 of this title, or
         (iii) a stationary source which is not in compliance with any requirement of subchapter IV-A, V, or VI of this chapter, or
         (iv) any source referred to in clause (i), (ii), or (iii) (for which an extension, order, or suspension referred to in subparagraph (B), or Federal or State consent decree is in effect), or a primary nonferrous smelter which has received a primary nonferrous smelter order under section 7419 of this title which is not in compliance with

any interim emission control requirement or schedule of compliance under such extension, order, suspension, or consent decree.

For purposes of subsection (d)(2) of this section, in the case of a penalty assessed with respect to a source referred to in clause (iii) of this subparagraph, the costs referred to in such subsection (d)(2) shall be the economic value of noncompliance with the interim emission control requirement or the remaining steps in the schedule of compliance referred to in such clause.

(B) Notwithstanding the requirements of subparagraph (A)(i) and (ii), the owner or operator of any source shall be exempted from the duty to pay a noncompliance penalty under such requirements with respect to that source if, in accordance with the procedures in subsection (b)(5) of this section, the owner or operator demonstrates that the failure of such source to comply with any such requirement is due solely to—
  (i) a conversion by such source from the burning of petroleum products or natural gas, or both, as the permanent primary energy source to the burning of coal pursuant to an order under section 7413(d)(5)[1] of this title or section 1857c-10[1] of this title (as in effect before August 7, 1977);
  (ii) in the case of a coal-burning source granted an extension under the second sentence of section 1857c-10(c)(1)[1] of this title (as in effect before August 7, 1977), a prohibition from using petroleum products or natural gas or both, by reason of an order under the provisions of section 792(a) and (b) of title 15 or under any legislation which amends or supersedes such provisions;
  (iii) the use of innovative technology sanctioned by an enforcement order under section 7413(d)(4)[1] of this title;
  (iv) an inability to comply with any such requirement, for which inability the source has received an order under section 7413(d)[1] of this title (or an order under section 7413 of this title issued before August 7, 1977) which has the effect of permitting a delay or violation of any requirement of this chapter (including a requirement of an applicable implementation plan) which inability results from reasons entirely beyond the control of the owner or operator of such source or of any entity controlling, controlled by, or under common control with the owner or operator of such source; or
  (v) the conditions by reason of which a temporary emergency suspension is authorized under section 7410(f) or (g) of this title.

An exemption under this subparagraph shall cease to be effective if the source fails to comply with the interim emission control requirements or schedules of compliance (including increments of progress) under any such extension, order, or suspension.

(C) The Administrator may, after notice and opportunity for public hearing, exempt any source from the requirements of this section with respect to a particular instance of noncompliance if he finds that such instance of noncompliance is de minimis in nature and in duration.

(b) Regulations

Regulations under subsection (a) of this section shall—
(1) permit the assessment and collection of such penalty by the State if the State has a delegation of authority in effect under subsection (a)(1)(B)(i) of this section;
(2) provide for the assessment and collection of such penalty by the Administrator, if—
  (A) the State does not have a delegation of authority in effect under subsection (a)(1)(B)(i) of this section, or
  (B) the State has such a delegation in effect but fails with respect to any particular person or source to assess or collect the penalty in accordance with the requirements of this section;
(3) require the States, or in the event the States fail to do so, the Administrator, to give a brief but reasonably specific notice of noncompliance under this section to each person referred to in subsection (a)(2)(A) of this section with respect to each source owned or operated by such person which is not in compliance as provided in such subsection, not later than July 1, 1979, or thirty days after the discovery of such noncompliance, whichever is later;

---

[1] See References in Text note below.

(4) require each person to whom notice is given under paragraph (3) to—
  (A) calculate the amount of the penalty owed (determined in accordance with subsection (d)(2) of this section) and the schedule of payments (determined in accordance with subsection (d)(3) of this section) for each such source and, within forty-five days after the issuance of such notice or after the denial of a petition under subparagraph (B), to submit that calculation and proposed schedule, together with the information necessary for an independent verification thereof, to the State and to the Administrator, or
  (B) submit a petition, within forty-five days after the issuance of such notice, challenging such notice of noncompliance or alleging entitlement to an exemption under subsection (a)(2)(B) of this section with respect to a particular source;
(5) require the Administrator to provide a hearing on the record (within the meaning of subchapter II of chapter 5 of title 5) and to make a decision on such petition (including findings of fact and conclusions of law) not later than ninety days after the receipt of any petition under paragraph (4)(B), unless the State agrees to provide a hearing which is substantially similar to such a hearing on the record and to make a decision on such petition (including such findings and conclusions) within such ninety-day period;
(6) (A) authorize the Administrator on his own initiative to review the decision of the State under paragraph (5) and disapprove it if it is not in accordance with the requirements of this section, and (B) require the Administrator to do so not later than sixty days after receipt of a petition under this subparagraph, notice, and public hearing and a showing by such petitioner that the State decision under paragraph (5) is not in accordance with the requirements of this section;
(7) require payment, in accordance with subsection (d) of this section, of the penalty by each person to whom notice of noncompliance is given under paragraph (3) with respect to each noncomplying source for which such notice is given unless there has been a final determination granting a petition under paragraph (4)(B) with respect to such source;
(8) authorize the State or the Administrator to adjust (and from time to time to readjust) the amount of the penalty assessment calculated or the payment schedule proposed by such owner or operator under paragraph (4), if the Administrator finds after notice and opportunity for a hearing on the record that the penalty or schedule does not meet the requirements of this section; and
(9) require a final adjustment of the penalty within 180 days after such source comes into compliance in accordance with subsection (d)(4) of this section.

In any case in which the State establishes a noncompliance penalty under this section, the State shall provide notice thereof to the Administrator. A noncompliance penalty established by a State under this section shall apply unless the Administrator, within ninety days after the date of receipt of notice of the State penalty assessment under this section, objects in writing to the amount of the penalty as less than would be required to comply with guidelines established by the Administrator. If the Administrator objects, he shall immediately establish a substitute noncompliance penalty applicable to such source.

(c) Contract to assist in determining amount of penalty assessment or payment schedule

If the owner or operator of any stationary source to whom a notice is issued under subsection (b)(3) of this section—
  (1) does not submit a timely petition under subsection (b)(4)(B) of this section, or
  (2) submits a petition under subsection (b)(4)(B) of this section which is denied, and fails to submit a calculation of the penalty assessment, a schedule for payment, and the information necessary for independent verification thereof, the State (or the Administrator, as the case may be) may enter into a contract with any person who has no financial interest in the owner or operator of the source (or in any person controlling, controlled by or under common control with such source) to assist in determining the amount of the penalty assessment or payment schedule with respect to such source. The cost of carrying out such contract may be added to the penalty to be assessed against the owner or operator of such source.

(d) Payment
  (1) All penalties assessed by the Administrator under this section shall be paid to the United States Treasury. All penalties assessed by the State under this section shall be paid to such State.

(2) The amount of the penalty which shall be assessed and collected with respect to any source under this section shall be equal to—
  (A) the amount determined in accordance with regulations promulgated by the Administrator under subsection (a) of this section, which is no less than the economic value which a delay in compliance beyond July 1, 1979, may have for the owner of such source, including the quarterly equivalent of the capital costs of compliance and debt service over a normal amortization period, not to exceed ten years, operation and maintenance costs foregone as a result of noncompliance, and any additional economic value which such a delay may have for the owner or operator of such source, minus
  (B) the amount of any expenditure made by the owner or operator of that source during any such quarter for the purpose of bringing that source into, and maintaining compliance with, such requirement, to the extent that such expenditures have not been taken into account in the calculation of the penalty under subparagraph (A).
  To the extent that any expenditure under subparagraph (B) made during any quarter is not subtracted for such quarter from the costs under subparagraph (A), such expenditure may be subtracted for any subsequent quarter from such costs. In no event shall the amount paid be less than the quarterly payment minus the amount attributed to actual cost of construction.
(3) (A) The assessed penalty required under this section shall be paid in quarterly installments for the period of covered noncompliance. All quarterly payments (determined without regard to any adjustment or any subtraction under paragraph (2)(B)) after the first payment shall be equal.
  (B) The first payment shall be due on the date six months after the date of issuance of the notice of noncompliance under subsection (b)(3) of this section with respect to any source or on January 1, 1980, whichever is later. Such first payment shall be in the amount of the quarterly installment for the upcoming quarter, plus the amount owed for any preceding period within the period of covered noncompliance for such source.
  (C) For the purpose of this section, the term "period of covered noncompliance" means the period which begins—
    (i) two years after August 7, 1977, in the case of a source for which notice of noncompliance under subsection (b)(3) of this section is issued on or before the date two years after August 7, 1977, or
    (ii) on the date of issuance of the notice of noncompliance under subsection (b)(3) of this section, in the case of a source for which such notice is issued after July 1, 1979,
  and ending on the date on which such source comes into (or for the purpose of establishing the schedule of payments, is estimated to come into) compliance with such requirement.
(4) Upon making a determination that a source with respect to which a penalty has been paid under this section is in compliance and is maintaining compliance with the applicable requirement, the State (or the Administrator as the case may be) shall review the actual expenditures made by the owner or operator of such source for the purpose of attaining and maintaining compliance, and shall within 180 days after such source comes into compliance—
  (A) provide reimbursement with interest (to be paid by the State or Secretary of the Treasury, as the case may be) at appropriate prevailing rates (as determined by the Secretary of the Treasury) for any overpayment by such person, or
  (B) assess and collect an additional payment with interest at appropriate prevailing rates (as determined by the Secretary of the Treasury) for any underpayment by such person.
(5) Any person who fails to pay the amount of any penalty with respect to any source under this section on a timely basis shall be required to pay in addition a quarterly nonpayment penalty for each quarter during which such failure to pay persists. Such nonpayment penalty shall be in an amount equal to 20 percent of the aggregate amount of such person's penalties and nonpayment penalties with respect to such source which are unpaid as of the beginning of such quarter.

(e) Judicial review
   Any action pursuant to this section, including any objection of the Administrator under the last sentence of subsection (b) of this section, shall be considered a final action for purposes of judicial review of any penalty under section 7607 of this title.
(f) Other orders, payments, sanctions, or requirements
   Any orders, payments, sanctions, or other requirements under this section shall be in addition to any other permits, orders, payments, sanctions, or other requirements established under this chapter, and shall in no way affect any civil or criminal enforcement proceedings brought under any provision of this chapter or State or local law.
(g) More stringent emission limitations or other requirements
   In the case of any emission limitation or other requirement approved or promulgated by the Administrator under this chapter after August 7, 1977, which is more stringent than the emission limitation or requirement for the source in effect prior to such approval or promulgation, if any, or where there was no emission limitation or requirement approved or promulgated before August 7, 1977, the date for imposition of the non-compliance penalty under this section, shall be either July 1, 1979, or the date on which the source is required to be in full compliance with such emission limitation or requirement, whichever is later, but in no event later than three years after the approval or promulgation of such emission limitation or requirement.

(July 14, 1955, ch. 360, title I, Sec. 120, as added Pub. L. 95-95, title I, Sec. 118, Aug. 7, 1977, 91 Stat. 714; amended Pub. L. 95-190, Sec. 14(a)(28)-(38), Nov. 16, 1977, 91 Stat. 1401; Pub. L. 101-549, title VII, Sec. 710(a), Nov. 15, 1990, 104 Stat. 2684.)

References in Text

Section 7413(d) of this title, referred to in subsec. (a)(2)(B), was amended generally by Pub. L. 101-549, title VII, Sec. 701, Nov. 15, 1990, 104 Stat. 2672, and, as so amended, no longer relates to final compliance orders.

Section 1857c-10 of this title (as in effect before August 7, 1977), referred to in subsec. (a)(2)(B)(i), was in the original "section 119 (as in effect before the date of the enactment of the Clean Air Act Amendments of 1977)", meaning section 119 of act July 14, 1955, ch. 360, title I, as added June 22, 1974, Pub. L. 93-319, Sec. 3, 88 Stat. 248, (which was classified to section 1857c-10 of this title) as in effect prior to the enactment of Pub. L. 95-95, Aug. 7, 1977, 91 Stat. 691, effective Aug. 7, 1977. Section 112(b)(1) of Pub. L. 95-95 repealed section 119 of act July 14, 1955, ch. 360, title I, as added by Pub. L. 93-319, and provided that all references to such section 119 in any subsequent enactment which supersedes Pub. L. 93-319 shall be construed to refer to section 113(d) of the Clean Air Act and to paragraph (5) thereof in particular which is classified to subsec. (d)(5) of section 7413 of this title. Section 7413(d) of this title was subsequently amended generally by Pub. L. 101-549, title VII, Sec. 701, Nov. 15, 1990, 104 Stat. 2672, and, as so amended, no longer relates to final compliance orders. Section 117(b) of Pub. L. 95-95 added a new section 119 of act July 14, 1955, which is classified to section 7419 of this title.

Section 1857c-10(c)(1) of this title (as in effect before August 7, 1977), referred to in subsec. (a)(2)(B)(ii), was in the original "section 119(c)(1) (as in effect before the date of the enactment of the Clean Air Act Amendments of 1977)." See paragraph set out above for explanation of codification.

Amendments

1990—Subsec. (a)(2)(A). Pub. L. 101-549 inserted reference to sections 7477 and 7603 of this title in cl. (ii), added cl. (iii), and redesignated former cl. (iii) as (iv) and inserted reference to cl. (iii).

1977—Subsec. (a)(2)(A). Pub. L. 95-190, Sec. 14(a)(28), (29), in cls. (i) and (iii) inserted provisions relating to consent decrees wherever appearing.

Subsec. (a)(2)(B). Pub. L. 95-190, Sec. 14(a)(30), (31), in cl. (i) inserted reference to section 7413(d)(5) of this title, and in cls. (i) and (ii) inserted provision relating to orders in effect under section 1857c-10 of this title before Aug. 7, 1977, wherever appearing.

Subsec. (b). Pub. L. 95-190, Sec. 14(a)(34)-(36), in closing provisions inserted provisions relating to notice to the Administrator when a noncompliance penalty is established by a State, and substituted references to noncompliance for references to delayed compliance in two places, "source" for "facility", and "receipt of notice of the State penalty assessment" for "publication of the proposed penalty".

126 / Environmental Statutes

Subsec. (b)(2)(A). Pub. L. 95-190, Sec. 14(a)(33), substituted "(a)(1)(B)(i)" for "(e)".
Subsec. (b)(8). Pub. L. 95-190, Sec. 14(a)(32), substituted "(4)" for "(6)".
Subsec. (d)(2)(A). Pub. L. 95-190, Sec. 14(a)(37), inserted provisions relating to inclusion of the economic value of a delay in compliance, and substituted "such a delay" for "a delay in compliance beyond July 1, 1979,".
Subsec. (e). Pub. L. 95-190, Sec. 14(a)(38), substituted "subsection, shall" for "subsection shall".

Effective Date

Section effective Aug. 7, 1977, except as otherwise expressly provided, see section 406(d) of Pub. L. 95-95, set out as an Effective Date of 1977 Amendment note under section 7401 of this title.

Section Referred to in Other Sections

This section is referred to in sections 7412, 7413, 7419, 7425, 7429, 7607, 7627, 7651j of this title.

CONSULTATION

42 USC 7421

In carrying out the requirements of this chapter requiring applicable implementation plans to contain—
 (1) any transportation controls, air quality maintenance plan requirements or preconstruction review of direct sources of air pollution, or
 (2) any measure referred to—
  (A) in part D of this subchapter (pertaining to nonattainment requirements), or
  (B) in part C of this subchapter (pertaining to prevention of significant deterioration),
and in carrying out the requirements of section 7413(d)[1] of this title (relating to certain enforcement orders), the State shall provide a satisfactory process of consultation with general purpose local governments, designated organizations of elected officials of local governments and any Federal land manager having authority over Federal land to which the State plan applies, effective with respect to any such requirement which is adopted more than one year after August 7, 1977, as part of such plan. Such process shall be in accordance with regulations promulgated by the Administrator to assure adequate consultation. The Administrator shall update as necessary the original regulations required and promulgated under this section (as in effect immediately before November 15, 1990) to ensure adequate consultation. Only a general purpose unit of local government, regional agency, or council of governments adversely affected by action of the Administrator approving any portion of a plan referred to in this subsection may petition for judicial review of such action on the basis of a violation of the requirements of this section.
(July 14, 1955, ch. 360, title I, Sec. 121, as added Pub. L. 95-95, title I, Sec. 119, Aug. 7, 1977, 91 Stat. 719; amended Pub. L. 101-549, title I, Sec. 108(h), Nov. 15, 1990, 104 Stat. 2467.)

References in Text

Section 7413(d) of this title, referred to in text, was amended generally by Pub. L. 101-549, title VII, Sec. 701, Nov. 15, 1990, 104 Stat. 2672, and, as so amended, no longer relates to final compliance orders.

Amendments

1990—Pub. L. 101-549 amended penultimate sentence generally. Prior to amendment, penultimate sentence read as follows: "Such regulations shall be promulgated after notice and opportunity for public hearing and not later than 6 months after August 7, 1977."

Effective Date

Section effective Aug. 7, 1977, except as otherwise expressly provided, see section 406(d) of Pub. L. 95-95, set out as an Effective Date of 1977 Amendment note under section 7401 of this title.

Section Referred to in Other Sections

This section is referred to in section 7410 of this title; title 15 section 1410.

LISTING OF CERTAIN UNREGULATED POLLUTANTS

42 USC 7422

(a) Radioactive pollutants, cadmium, arsenic, and polycyclic organic matter
Not later than one year after August 7, 1977 (two years for radioactive pollutants) and after notice and opportunity for public hearing, the Administrator shall review all available relevant information and determine whether or not emissions of radioactive pollutants (including source material, special nuclear material, and byproduct material), cadmium, arsenic and polycyclic organic matter into the ambient air will cause, or contribute to, air pollution which may reasonably be anticipated to endanger public health. If the Administrator makes an affirmative determination with respect to any such substance, he shall simultaneously with such determination include such substance in the list published under section 7408(a)(1) or 7412(b)(1)(A)[1] of this title (in the case of a substance which, in the judgment of the Administrator, causes, or contributes to, air pollution which may reasonably be anticipated to result in an increase in mortality or an increase in serious irreversible, or incapacitating reversible, illness), or shall include each category of stationary sources emitting such substance in significant amounts in the list published under section 7411(b)(1)(A) of this title, or take any combination of such actions.

(b) Revision authority
Nothing in subsection (a) of this section shall be construed to affect the authority of the Administrator to revise any list referred to in subsection (a) of this section with respect to any substance (whether or not enumerated in subsection (a) of this section).

(c) Consultation with Nuclear Regulatory Commission; interagency agreement; notice and hearing
  (1) Before listing any source material, special nuclear, or byproduct material (or component or derivative thereof) as provided in subsection (a) of this section, the Administrator shall consult with the Nuclear Regulatory Commission.
  (2) Not later than six months after listing any such material (or component or derivative thereof) the Administrator and the Nuclear Regulatory Commission shall enter into an interagency agreement with respect to those sources or facilities which are under the jurisdiction of the Commission. This agreement shall, to the maximum extent practicable consistent with this chapter, minimize duplication of effort and conserve administrative resources in the establishment, implementation, and enforcement of emission limitations, standards of performance, and other requirements and authorities (substantive and procedural) under this chapter respecting the emission of such material (or component or derivative thereof) from such sources or facilities.
  (3) In case of any standard or emission limitation promulgated by the Administrator, under this chapter or by any State (or the Administrator) under any applicable implementation plan under this chapter, if the Nuclear Regulatory Commission determines, after notice and opportunity for public hearing that the application of such standard or limitation to a source or facility within the jurisdiction of the Commission would endanger public health or safety, such standard or limitation shall not apply to such facilities or sources unless the President determines otherwise within ninety days from the date of such finding.

(July 14, 1955, ch. 360, title I, Sec. 122, as added Pub. L. 95-95, title I, Sec. 120(a), Aug. 7, 1977, 91 Stat. 720.)

References in Text

Section 7412(b)(1), referred to in subsec. (a), was amended generally by Pub. L. 101-549, title III, Sec. 301, Nov. 15, 1990, 104 Stat. 2531, and, as so amended, no longer contains a subpar. (A).

Effective Date

Section effective Aug. 7, 1977, except as otherwise expressly provided, see section 406(d) of Pub. L. 95-95, set out as an Effective Date of 1977 Amendment note under section 7401 of this title.

---

[1] See References in Text note below.

Transfer of Functions

For transfer of certain functions from Nuclear Regulatory Commission to Chairman thereof, see Reorg. Plan No. 1 of 1980, 45 F.R. 40561, 94 Stat. 3585, set out as a note under section 5841 of this title.

Study by Administrator of Environmental Protection Agency

Section 120(b) of Pub. L. 95-95 directed Administrator of Environmental Protection Agency to conduct a study, in conjunction with other appropriate agencies, concerning effect on public health and welfare of sulfates, radioactive pollutants, cadmium, arsenic, and polycyclic organic matter which are present or may reasonably be anticipated to occur in the ambient air, such study to include a thorough investigation of how sulfates are formed and how to protect public health and welfare from the injurious effects, if any, of sulfates, cadmium, arsenic, and polycyclic organic matter.

STACK HEIGHTS

42 USC 7423

(a) Heights in excess of good engineering practice; other dispersion techniques
 The degree of emission limitation required for control of any air pollutant under an applicable implementation plan under this subchapter shall not be affected in any manner by—
 (1) so much of the stack height of any source as exceeds good engineering practice (as determined under regulations promulgated by the Administrator), or
 (2) any other dispersion technique.
 The preceding sentence shall not apply with respect to stack heights in existence before December 31, 1970, or dispersion techniques implemented before such date. In establishing an emission limitation for coal-fired steam electric generating units which are subject to the provisions of section 7418 of this title and which commenced operation before July 1, 1957, the effect of the entire stack height of stacks for which a construction contract was awarded before February 8, 1974, may be taken into account.

(b) Dispersion technique
 For the purpose of this section, the term "dispersion technique" includes any intermittent or supplemental control of air pollutants varying with atmospheric conditions.

(c) Regulations; good engineering practice
 Not later than six months after August 7, 1977, the Administrator, shall after notice and opportunity for public hearing, promulgate regulations to carry out this section. For purposes of this section, good engineering practice means, with respect to stack heights, the height necessary to insure that emissions from the stack do not result in excessive concentrations of any air pollutant in the immediate vicinity of the source as a result of atmospheric downwash, eddies and wakes which may be created by the source itself, nearby structures or nearby terrain obstacles (as determined by the Administrator). For purposes of this section such height shall not exceed two and a half times the height of such source unless the owner or operator of the source demonstrates, after notice and opportunity for public hearing, to the satisfaction of the Administrator, that a greater height is necessary as provided under the preceding sentence. In no event may the Administrator prohibit any increase in any stack height or restrict in any manner the stack height of any source.

(July 14, 1955, ch. 360, title I, Sec. 123, as added Pub. L. 95-95, title I, Sec. 121, Aug. 7, 1977, 91 Stat. 721.)

Effective Date

Section effective Aug. 7, 1977, except as otherwise expressly provided, see section 406(d) of Pub. L. 95-95, set out as an Effective Date of 1977 Amendment note under section 7401 of this title.

ASSURANCE OF ADEQUACY OF STATE PLANS

42 USC 7424

(a) State review of implementation plans which relate to major fuel burning sources
 As expeditiously as practicable but not later than one year after August 7, 1977, each State

shall review the provisions of its implementation plan which relate to major fuel burning sources and shall determine—
(1) the extent to which compliance with requirements of such plan is dependent upon the use by major fuel burning stationary sources of petroleum products or natural gas,
(2) the extent to which such plan may reasonably be anticipated to be inadequate to meet the requirements of this chapter in such State on a reliable and long-term basis by reason of its dependence upon the use of such fuels, and
(3) the extent to which compliance with the requirements of such plan is dependent upon use of coal or coal derivatives which is not locally or regionally available.

Each State shall submit the results of its review and its determination under this paragraph to the Administrator promptly upon completion thereof.

(b) Plan revision
(1) Not later than eighteen months after August 7, 1977, the Administrator shall review the submissions of the States under subsection (a) of this section and shall require each State to revise its plan if, in the judgment of the Administrator, such plan revision is necessary to assure that such plan will be adequate to assure compliance with the requirements of this chapter in such State on a reliable and long-term basis, taking into account the actual or potential prohibitions on use of petroleum products or natural gas, or both, under any other authority of law.
(2) Before requiring a plan revision under this subsection, with respect to any State the Administrator shall take into account the report of the review conducted by such State under paragraph (1) and shall consult with the Governor of the State respecting such required revision.

(July 14, 1955, ch. 360, title I, Sec. 124, as added Pub. L. 95-95, title I, Sec. 122, Aug. 7, 1977, 91 Stat. 722.)

Effective Date

Section effective Aug. 7, 1977, except as otherwise expressly provided, see section 406(d) of Pub. L. 95-95, set out as an Effective Date of 1977 Amendment note under section 7401 of this title.

MEASURES TO PREVENT ECONOMIC DISRUPTION OR UNEMPLOYMENT

42 USC 7425

(a) Determination that action is necessary
After notice and opportunity for a public hearing—
(1) the Governor of any State in which a major fuel burning stationary source referred to in this subsection (or class or category thereof) is located,
(2) the Administrator, or
(3) the President (or his designee),
may determine that action under subsection (b) of this section is necessary to prevent or minimize significant local or regional economic disruption or unemployment which would otherwise result from use by such source (or class or category) of—
(A) coal or coal derivatives other than locally or regionally available coal,
(B) petroleum products,
(C) natural gas, or
(D) any combination of fuels referred to in subparagraphs (A) through (C),
to comply with the requirements of a State implementation plan.
(b) Use of locally or regionally available coal or coal derivatives to comply with implementation plan requirements
Upon a determination under subsection (a) of this section—
(1) such Governor, with the written consent of the President or his designee,
(2) the President's designee with the written consent of such Governor, or
(3) the President
may by rule or order prohibit any such major fuel burning stationary source (or class or category thereof) from using fuels other than locally or regionally available coal or coal derivatives to comply with implementation plan requirements. In taking any action under this sub-

section, the Governor, the President, or the President's designee as the case may be, shall take into account, the final cost to the consumer of such an action.

(c) Contracts; schedules

The Governor, in the case of action under subsection (b)(1) of this section, or the Administrator, in the case of an action under subsection (b)(2) or (3) of this section shall, by rule or order, require each source to which such action applies to—
  (1) enter into long-term contracts of at least ten years in duration (except as the President or his designee may otherwise permit or require by rule or order for good cause) for supplies of regionally available coal or coal derivatives,
  (2) enter into contracts to acquire any additional means of emission limitation which the Administrator or the State determines may be necessary to comply with the requirements of this chapter while using such coal or coal derivatives as fuel, and
  (3) comply with such schedules (including increments of progress), timetables and other requirements as may be necessary to assure compliance with the requirements of this chapter.

Requirements under this subsection shall be established simultaneously with, and as a condition of, any action under subsection (b) of this section.

(d) Existing or new major fuel burning stationary sources

This section applies only to existing or new major fuel burning stationary sources—
  (1) which have the design capacity to produce 250,000,000 Btu's per hour (or its equivalent), as determined by the Administrator, and
  (2) which are not in compliance with the requirements of an applicable implementation plan or which are prohibited from burning oil or natural gas, or both, under any other authority of law.

(e) Actions not to be deemed modifications of major fuel burning stationary sources

Except as may otherwise be provided by rule by the State or the Administrator for good cause, any action required to be taken by a major fuel burning stationary source under this section shall not be deemed to constitute a modification for purposes of section 7411(a)(2) and (4) of this title.

(f) Treatment of prohibitions, rules, or orders as requirements or parts of plans under other provisions

For purposes of sections 7413 and 7420 of this title a prohibition under subsection (b) of this section, and a corresponding rule or order under subsection (c) of this section, shall be treated as a requirement of section 7413 of this title. For purposes of any plan (or portion thereof) promulgated under section 7410(c) of this title, any rule or order under subsection (c) of this section corresponding to a prohibition under subsection (b) of this section, shall be treated as a part of such plan. For purposes of section 7413 of this title, a prohibition under subsection (b) of this section, applicable to any source, and a corresponding rule or order under subsection (c) of this section, shall be treated as part of the applicable implementation plan for the State in which subject source is located.

(g) Delegation of Presidential authority

The President may delegate his authority under this section to an officer or employee of the United States designated by him on a case-by-case basis or in any other manner he deems suitable.

(h) "Locally or regionally available coal or coal derivatives" defined

For the purpose of this section the term "locally or regionally available coal or coal derivatives" means coal or coal derivatives which is, or can in the judgment of the State or the Administrator feasibly be, mined or produced in the local or regional area (as determined by the Administrator) in which the major fuel burning stationary source is located.

(July 14, 1955, ch. 360, title I, Sec. 125, as added Pub. L. 95-95, title I, Sec. 122, Aug. 7, 1977, 91 Stat. 722.)

Effective Date

Section effective Aug. 7, 1977, except as otherwise expressly provided, see section 406(d) of Pub. L. 95-95, set out as an Effective Date of 1977 Amendment note under section 7401 of this title.

Section Referred to in Other Sections

This section is referred to in section 6215 of this title.

INTERSTATE POLLUTION ABATEMENT

42 USC 7426

(a) Written notice to all nearby States
Each applicable implementation plan shall—
   (1) require each major proposed new (or modified) source—
      (A) subject to part C of this subchapter (relating to significant deterioration of air quality) or
      (B) which may significantly contribute to levels of air pollution in excess of the national ambient air quality standards in any air quality control region outside the State in which such source intends to locate (or make such modification),
   to provide written notice to all nearby States the air pollution levels of which may be affected by such source at least sixty days prior to the date on which commencement of construction is to be permitted by the State providing notice, and
   (2) identify all major existing stationary sources which may have the impact described in paragraph (1) with respect to new or modified sources and provide notice to all nearby States of the identity of such sources not later than three months after August 7, 1977.

(b) Petition for finding that major sources emit or would emit prohibited air pollutants
Any State or political subdivision may petition the Administrator for a finding that any major source or group of stationary sources emits or would emit any air pollutant in violation of the prohibition of section 7410(a)(2)(D)(ii) of this title or this section. Within 60 days after receipt of any petition under this subsection and after public hearing, the Administrator shall make such a finding or deny the petition.

(c) Violations; allowable continued operation
Notwithstanding any permit which may have been granted by the State in which the source is located (or intends to locate), it shall be a violation of this section and the applicable implementation plan in such State—
   (1) for any major proposed new (or modified) source with respect to which a finding has been made under subsection (b) of this section to be constructed or to operate in violation of the prohibition of section 7410(a)(2)(D)(ii) of this title or this section, or
   (2) for any major existing source to operate more than three months after such finding has been made with respect to it.
The Administrator may permit the continued operation of a source referred to in paragraph (2) beyond the expiration of such three-month period if such source complies with such emission limitations and compliance schedules (containing increments of progress) as may be provided by the Administrator to bring about compliance with the requirements contained in section 7410(a)(2)(D)(ii) of this title or this section as expeditiously as practicable, but in no case later than three years after the date of such finding. Nothing in the preceding sentence shall be construed to preclude any such source from being eligible for an enforcement order under section 7413(d)[1] of this title after the expiration of such period during which the Administrator has permitted continuous operation.

(July 14, 1955, ch. 360, title I, Sec. 126, as added Pub. L. 95-95, title I, Sec. 123, Aug. 7, 1977, 91 Stat. 724; amended Pub. L. 95-190, Sec. 14(a)(39), Nov. 16, 1977, 91 Stat. 1401; Pub. L. 101-549, title I, Sec. 109(a), Nov. 15, 1990, 104 Stat. 2469.)

References in Text

Section 7413(d) of this title, referred to in subsec. (c), was amended generally by Pub. L. 101-549, title VII, Sec. 701, Nov. 15, 1990, 104 Stat. 2672, and, as so amended, no longer relates to final compliance orders.

Amendments

1990—Subsec. (b). Pub. L. 101-549, Sec. 109(a)(1), inserted "or group of stationary sources" after "any major source" and substituted "section 7410(a)(2)(D)(ii) of this title or this section" for "section 7410(a)(2)(E)(i) of this title".

Subsec. (c). Pub. L. 101-549, Sec. 109(a)(2)(A), which directed the insertion of "this section and" after "violation of", was executed by making the insertion after first reference to "violation of" to reflect the probable intent of Congress.

---

[1]See References in Text note below.

132 / Environmental Statutes

Pub. L. 101-549, Sec. 109(a)(2)(B), substituted "section 7410(a)(2)(D)(ii) of this title or this section" for "section 7410(a)(2)(E)(i) of this title" in par. (1) and penultimate sentence.

1977—Subsec. (a)(1). Pub. L. 95-190 substituted "(relating to significant deterioration of air quality)" for ", relating to significant deterioration of air quality".

Effective Date

Section effective Aug. 7, 1977, except as otherwise expressly provided, see section 406(d) of Pub. L. 95-95, set out as an Effective Date of 1977 Amendment note under section 7401 of this title.

Section Referred to in Other Sections

This section is referred to in sections 7410, 7607 of this title.

PUBLIC NOTIFICATION

42 USC 7427

(a) Warning signs; television, radio, or press notices or information

Each State plan shall contain measures which will be effective to notify the public during any calendar[2] on a regular basis of instances or areas in which any national primary ambient air quality standard is exceeded or was exceeded during any portion of the preceding calendar year to advise the public of the health hazards associated with such pollution, and to enhance public awareness of the measures which can be taken to prevent such standards from being exceeded and the ways in which the public can participate in regulatory and other efforts to improve air quality. Such measures may include the posting of warning signs on interstate highway access points to metropolitan areas or television, radio, or press notices or information.

(b) Grants

The Administrator is authorized to make grants to States to assist in carrying out the requirements of subsection (a) of this section.

(July 14, 1955, ch. 360, title I, Sec. 127, as added Pub. L. 95-95, title I, Sec. 124, Aug. 7, 1977, 91 Stat. 725.)

Effective Date

Section effective Aug. 7, 1977, except as otherwise expressly provided, see section 406(d) of Pub. L. 95-95, set out as an Effective Date of 1977 Amendment note under section 7401 of this title.

Section Referred to in Other Sections

This section is referred to in section 7410 of this title.

STATE BOARDS

42 USC 7428

(a)[1] Not later than the date one year after August 7, 1977, each applicable implementation plan shall contain requirements that—
   (1) any board or body which approves permits or enforcement orders under this chapter shall have at least a majority of members who represent the public interest and do not derive any significant portion of their income from persons subject to permits or enforcement orders under this chapter, and
   (2) any potential conflicts of interest by members of such board or body or the head of an executive agency with similar powers be adequately disclosed.

A State may adopt any requirements respecting conflicts of interest for such boards or bodies or heads of executive agencies, or any other entities which are more stringent than the requirements of paragraph (1) and (2), and the Administrator shall approve any such more stringent requirements submitted as part of an implementation plan.

---

[2]So in original. Probably should be "calendar year".
[1]So in original. Section enacted without a subsec. (b).

(July 14, 1955, ch. 360, title I, Sec. 128, as added Pub. L. 95-95, title I, Sec. 125, Aug. 7, 1977, 91 Stat. 725.)

Effective Date

Section effective Aug. 7, 1977, except as otherwise expressly provided, see section 406(d) of Pub. L. 95-95, set out as an Effective Date of 1977 Amendment note under section 7401 of this title.

Section Referred to in Other Sections

This section is referred to in section 7410 of this title.

SOLID WASTE COMBUSTION

42 USC 7429

(a) New source performance standards
   (1) In general
      (A) The Administrator shall establish performance standards and other requirements pursuant to section 7411 of this title and this section for each category of solid waste incineration units. Such standards shall include emissions limitations and other requirements applicable to new units and guidelines (under section 7411(d) of this title and this section) and other requirements applicable to existing units.
      (B) Standards under section 7411 of this title and this section applicable to solid waste incineration units with capacity greater than 250 tons per day combusting municipal waste shall be promulgated not later than 12 months after November 15, 1990. Nothing in this subparagraph shall alter any schedule for the promulgation of standards applicable to such units under section 7411 of this title pursuant to any settlement and consent decree entered by the Administrator before November 15, 1990: Provided, That, such standards are subsequently modified pursuant to the schedule established in this subparagraph to include each of the requirements of this section.
      (C) Standards under section 7411 of this title and this section applicable to solid waste incineration units with capacity equal to or less than 250 tons per day combusting municipal waste and units combusting hospital waste, medical waste and infectious waste shall be promulgated not later than 24 months after November 15, 1990.
      (D) Standards under section 7411 of this title and this section applicable to solid waste incineration units combusting commercial or industrial waste shall be proposed not later than 36 months after November 15, 1990, and promulgated not later than 48 months after November 15, 1990.
      (E) Not later than 18 months after November 15, 1990, the Administrator shall publish a schedule for the promulgation of standards under section 7411 of this title and this section applicable to other categories of solid waste incineration units.
   (2) Emissions standard
      Standards applicable to solid waste incineration units promulgated under section 7411 of this title and this section shall reflect the maximum degree of reduction in emissions of air pollutants listed under section[1] (a)(4) that the Administrator, taking into consideration the cost of achieving such emission reduction, and any non-air quality health and environmental impacts and energy requirements, determines is achievable for new or existing units in each category. The Administrator may distinguish among classes, types (including mass-burn, refuse-derived fuel, modular and other types of units), and sizes of units within a category in establishing such standards. The degree of reduction in emissions that is deemed achievable for new units in a category shall not be less stringent than the emissions control that is achieved in practice by the best controlled similar unit, as determined by the Administrator. Emissions standards for existing units in a category may be less stringent than standards for new units in the same category but shall not be less stringent than the average emissions limitation achieved by the best performing 12 percent of units in the category (excluding units which first met lowest achievable emissions rates 18 months before the date such standards are proposed or 30 months before the date such standards are promulgated, whichever is later).

---

[1] So in original. Probably should be "subsection".

(3) Control methods and technologies
Standards under section 7411 of this title and this section applicable to solid waste incineration units shall be based on methods and technologies for removal or destruction of pollutants before, during, or after combustion, and shall incorporate for new units siting requirements that minimize, on a site specific basis, to the maximum extent practicable, potential risks to public health or the environment.

(4) Numerical emissions limitations
The performance standards promulgated under section 7411 of this title and this section and applicable to solid waste incineration units shall specify numerical emission limitations for the following substances or mixtures: particulate matter (total and fine), opacity (as appropriate), sulfur dioxide, hydrogen chloride, oxides of nitrogen, carbon monoxide, lead, cadmium, mercury, and dioxins and dibenzofurans. The Administrator may promulgate numerical emissions limitations or provide for the monitoring of postcombustion concentrations of surrogate substances, parameters or periods of residence time in excess of stated temperatures with respect to pollutants other than those listed in this paragraph.

(5) Review and revision
Not later than 5 years following the initial promulgation of any performance standards and other requirements under this section and section 7411 of this title applicable to a category of solid waste incineration units, and at 5 year intervals thereafter, the Administrator shall review, and in accordance with this section and section 7411 of this title, revise such standards and requirements.

(b) Existing units
(1) Guidelines
Performance standards under this section and section 7411 of this title for solid waste incineration units shall include guidelines promulgated pursuant to section 7411(d) of this title and this section applicable to existing units. Such guidelines shall include, as provided in this section, each of the elements required by subsection (a) of this section (emissions limitations, notwithstanding any restriction in section 7411(d) of this title regarding issuance of such limitations), subsection (c) of this section (monitoring), subsection (d) of this section (operator training), subsection (e) of this section (permits), and subsection (h)(4)[2] of this section (residual risk).

(2) State plans
Not later than 1 year after the Administrator promulgates guidelines for a category of solid waste incineration units, each State in which units in the category are operating shall submit to the Administrator a plan to implement and enforce the guidelines with respect to such units. The State plan shall be at least as protective as the guidelines promulgated by the Administrator and shall provide that each unit subject to the guidelines shall be in compliance with all requirements of this section not later than 3 years after the State plan is approved by the Administrator but not later than 5 years after the guidelines were promulgated. The Administrator shall approve or disapprove any State plan within 180 days of the submission, and if a plan is disapproved, the Administrator shall state the reasons for disapproval in writing. Any State may modify and resubmit a plan which has been disapproved by the Administrator.

(3) Federal plan
The Administrator shall develop, implement and enforce a plan for existing solid waste incineration units within any category located in any State which has not submitted an approvable plan under this subsection with respect to units in such category within 2 years after the date on which the Administrator promulgated the relevant guidelines. Such plan shall assure that each unit subject to the plan is in compliance with all provisions of the guidelines not later than 5 years after the date the relevant guidelines are promulgated.

(c) Monitoring
The Administrator shall, as part of each performance standard promulgated pursuant to subsection (a) of this section and section 7411 of this title, promulgate regulations requiring the owner or operator of each solid waste incineration unit—

---

[2]So in original. Probably should be subsection "(h)(3)".

(1) to monitor emissions from the unit at the point at which such emissions are emitted into the ambient air (or within the stack, combustion chamber or pollution control equipment, as appropriate) and at such other points as necessary to protect public health and the environment;

(2) to monitor such other parameters relating to the operation of the unit and its pollution control technology as the Administrator determines are appropriate; and

(3) to report the results of such monitoring.

Such regulations shall contain provisions regarding the frequency of monitoring, test methods and procedures validated on solid waste incineration units, and the form and frequency of reports containing the results of monitoring and shall require that any monitoring reports or test results indicating an exceedance of any standard under this section shall be reported separately and in a manner that facilitates review for purposes of enforcement actions. Such regulations shall require that copies of the results of such monitoring be maintained on file at the facility concerned and that copies shall be made available for inspection and copying by interested members of the public during business hours.

(d) Operator training

Not later than 24 months after November 15, 1990, the Administrator shall develop and promote a model State program for the training and certification of solid waste incineration unit operators and high-capacity fossil fuel fired plant operators. The Administrator may authorize any State to implement a model program for the training of solid waste incineration unit operators and high-capacity fossil fuel fired plant operators, if the State has adopted a program which is at least as effective as the model program developed by the Administrator. Beginning on the date 36 months after the date on which performance standards and guidelines are promulgated under subsection (a) of this section and section 7411 of this title for any category of solid waste incineration units it shall be unlawful to operate any unit in the category unless each person with control over processes affecting emissions from such unit has satisfactorily completed a training program meeting the requirements established by the Administrator under this subsection.

(e) Permits

Beginning (1) 36 months after the promulgation of a performance standard under subsection (a) of this section and section 7411 of this title applicable to a category of solid waste incineration units, or (2) the effective date of a permit program under subchapter V of this chapter in the State in which the unit is located, whichever is later, each unit in the category shall operate pursuant to a permit issued under this subsection and subchapter V of this chapter. Permits required by this subsection may be renewed according to the provisions of subchapter V of this chapter. Notwithstanding any other provision of this chapter, each permit for a solid waste incineration unit combusting municipal waste issued under this chapter shall be issued for a period of up to 12 years and shall be reviewed every 5 years after date of issuance or reissuance. Each permit shall continue in effect after the date of issuance until the date of termination, unless the Administrator or State determines that the unit is not in compliance with all standards and conditions contained in the permit. Such determination shall be made at regular intervals during the term of the permit, such intervals not to exceed 5 years, and only after public comment and public hearing. No permit for a solid waste incineration unit may be issued under this chapter by an agency, instrumentality or person that is also responsible, in whole or part, for the design and construction or operation of the unit. Notwithstanding any other provision of this subsection, the Administrator or the State shall require the owner or operator of any unit to comply with emissions limitations or implement any other measures, if the Administrator or the State determines that emissions in the absence of such limitations or measures may reasonably be anticipated to endanger public health or the environment. The Administrator's determination under the preceding sentence is a discretionary decision.

(f) Effective date and enforcement

(1) New units

Performance standards and other requirements promulgated pursuant to this section and section 7411 of this title and applicable to new solid waste incineration units shall be effective as of the date 6 months after the date of promulgation.

(2) Existing units

Performance standards and other requirements promulgated pursuant to this section and section 7411 of this title and applicable to existing solid waste incineration units shall be effective as expeditiously as practicable after approval of a State plan under subsection (b)(2) of this section (or promulgation of a plan by the Administrator under subsection (b)(3) of this section) but in no event later than 3 years after the State plan is approved or 5 years after the date such standards or requirements are promulgated, whichever is earlier.

(3) Prohibition

After the effective date of any performance standard, emission limitation or other requirement promulgated pursuant to this section and section 7411 of this title, it shall be unlawful for any owner or operator of any solid waste incineration unit to which such standard, limitation or requirement applies to operate such unit in violation of such limitation, standard or requirement or for any other person to violate an applicable requirement of this section.

(4) Coordination with other authorities

For purposes of sections 7411(e), 7413, 7414, 7416, 7420, 7603, 7604, 7607 of this title and other provisions for the enforcement of this chapter, each performance standard, emission limitation or other requirement established pursuant to this section by the Administrator or a State or local government, shall be treated in the same manner as a standard of performance under section 7411 of this title which is an emission limitation.

(g) Definitions

For purposes of section 306 of the Clean Air Act Amendments of 1990 and this section only—

(1) Solid waste incineration unit

The term "solid waste incineration unit" means a distinct operating unit of any facility which combusts any solid waste material from commercial or industrial establishments or the general public (including single and multiple residences, hotels, and motels). Such term does not include incinerators or other units required to have a permit under section 3005 of the Solid Waste Disposal Act [42 U.S.C. 6925]. The term "solid waste incineration unit" does not include (A) materials recovery facilities (including primary or secondary smelters) which combust waste for the primary purpose of recovering metals, (B) qualifying small power production facilities, as defined in section 796(17)(C) of title 16, or qualifying cogeneration facilities, as defined in section 796(18)(B) of title 16, which burn homogeneous waste (such as units which burn tires or used oil, but not including refuse-derived fuel) for the production of electric energy or in the case of qualifying cogeneration facilities which burn homogeneous waste for the production of electric energy and steam or forms of useful energy (such as heat) which are used for industrial, commercial, heating or cooling purposes, or (C) air curtain incinerators provided that such incinerators only burn wood wastes, yard wastes and clean lumber and that such air curtain incinerators comply with opacity limitations to be established by the Administrator by rule.

(2) New solid waste incineration unit

The term "new solid waste incineration unit" means a solid waste incineration unit the construction of which is commenced after the Administrator proposes requirements under this section establishing emissions standards or other requirements which would be applicable to such unit or a modified solid waste incineration unit.

(3) Modified solid waste incineration unit

The term "modified solid waste incineration unit" means a solid waste incineration unit at which modifications have occurred after the effective date of a standard under subsection (a) of this section if (A) the cumulative cost of the modifications, over the life of the unit, exceed 50 per centum of the original cost of construction and installation of the unit (not including the cost of any land purchased in connection with such construction or installation) updated to current costs, or (B) the modification is a physical change in or change in the method of operation of the unit which increases the amount of any air pollutant emitted by the unit for which standards have been established under this section or section 7411 of this title.

(4) Existing solid waste incineration unit

The term "existing solid waste incineration unit" means a solid waste unit which is not a new or modified solid waste incineration unit.

(5) Municipal waste

The term "municipal waste" means refuse (and refuse-derived fuel) collected from the general public and from residential, commercial, institutional, and industrial sources consisting of paper, wood, yard wastes, food wastes, plastics, leather, rubber, and other combustible materials and non-combustible materials such as metal, glass and rock, provided that: (A) the term does not include industrial process wastes or medical wastes that are segregated from such other wastes; and (B) an incineration unit shall not be considered to be combusting municipal waste for purposes of section 7411 of this title or this section if it combusts a fuel feed stream, 30 percent or less of the weight of which is comprised, in aggregate, of municipal waste.

(6) Other terms

The terms "solid waste" and "medical waste" shall have the meanings established by the Administrator pursuant to the Solid Waste Disposal Act [42 U.S.C. 6901 et seq.].

(h) Other authority

(1) State authority

Nothing in this section shall preclude or deny the right of any State or political subdivision thereof to adopt or enforce any regulation, requirement, limitation or standard relating to solid waste incineration units that is more stringent than a regulation, requirement, limitation or standard in effect under this section or under any other provision of this chapter.

(2) Other authority under this chapter

Nothing in this section shall diminish the authority of the Administrator or a State to establish any other requirements applicable to solid waste incineration units under any other authority of law, including the authority to establish for any air pollutant a national ambient air quality standard, except that no solid waste incineration unit subject to performance standards under this section and section 7411 of this title shall be subject to standards under section 7412(d) of this title.

(3) Residual risk

The Administrator shall promulgate standards under section 7412(f) of this title for a category of solid waste incineration units, if promulgation of such standards is required under section 7412(f) of this title. For purposes of this[3] preceding sentence only—

(A) the performance standards under subsection (a) of this section and section 7411 of this title applicable to a category of solid waste incineration units shall be deemed standards under section 7412(d)(2) of this title, and

(B) the Administrator shall consider and regulate, if required, the pollutants listed under subsection (a)(4) of this section and no others.

(4) Acid rain

A solid waste incineration unit shall not be a utility unit as defined in subchapter IV-A of this chapter: Provided, That, more than 80 per centum of its annual average fuel consumption measured on a Btu basis, during a period or periods to be determined by the Administrator, is from a fuel (including any waste burned as a fuel) other than a fossil fuel.

(5) Requirements of parts C and D

No requirement of an applicable implementation plan under section 7475 of this title (relating to construction of facilities in regions identified pursuant to section 7407(d)(1)(A)(ii) or (iii) of this title) or under section 7502(c)(5) of this title (relating to permits for construction and operation in nonattainment areas) may be used to weaken the standards in effect under this section.

(July 14, 1955, ch. 360, title I, Sec. 129, as added Pub. L. 101-549, title III, Sec. 305(a), Nov. 15, 1990, 104 Stat. 2577.)

References in Text

Section 306 of the Clean Air Act Amendments of 1990, referred to in subsec. (g), probably means section 306 of Pub. L. 101-549, which is set out as a note under section 6921 of this title.

The Solid Waste Disposal Act, referred to in subsec. (g)(6), is title II of Pub. L. 89-272, Oct. 20, 1965, 79 Stat. 997, as amended generally by Pub. L. 94-580, Sec. 2, Oct. 21, 1976, 90 Stat. 2795, which is classified generally to chapter 82 (Sec. 6901 et seq.) of this title. For complete classification of this Act to the Code, see Short Title note set out under section 6901 of this title and Tables.

Review of Acid Gas Scrubbing Requirements

Section 305(c) of Pub. L. 101-549 provided that: "Prior to the promulgation of any performance standard for solid waste incineration units combusting municipal waste under section 111 or sec-

---

[3] So in original. Probably should be "the".

tion 129 of the Clean Air Act [42 U.S.C. 7411, 7429], the Administrator shall review the availability of acid gas scrubbers as a pollution control technology for small new units and for existing units (as defined in 54 Federal Register 52190 (December 20, 1989)[)], taking into account the provisions of subsection (a)(2) of section 129 of the Clean Air Act."

Section Referred to in Other Sections

This section is referred to in sections 7413, 7414, 7607 of this title.

EMISSION FACTORS

42 USC 7430

Within 6 months after November 15, 1990, and at least every 3 years thereafter, the Administrator shall review and, if necessary, revise, the methods ("emission factors") used for purposes of this chapter to estimate the quantity of emissions of carbon monoxide, volatile organic compounds, and oxides of nitrogen from sources of such air pollutants (including area sources and mobile sources). In addition, the Administrator shall establish emission factors for sources for which no such methods have previously been established by the Administrator. The Administrator shall permit any person to demonstrate improved emissions estimating techniques, and following approval of such techniques, the Administrator shall authorize the use of such techniques. Any such technique may be approved only after appropriate public participation. Until the Administrator has completed the revision required by this section, nothing in this section shall be construed to affect the validity of emission factors established by the Administrator before November 15, 1990.

(July 14, 1955, ch. 360, title I, Sec. 130, as added Pub. L. 101-549, title VIII, Sec. 804, Nov. 15, 1990, 104 Stat. 2689.)

LAND USE AUTHORITY

42 USC 7431

Nothing in this chapter constitutes an infringement on the existing authority of counties and cities to plan or control land use, and nothing in this chapter provides or transfers authority over such land use.

(July 14, 1955, ch. 360, title I, Sec. 131, as added Pub. L. 101-549, title VIII, Sec. 805, Nov. 15, 1990, 104 Stat. 2689.)

Part B—Ozone Protection[1]

Part C—Prevention of Significant Deterioration of Air Quality

Subpart i—Clean Air

CONGRESSIONAL DECLARATION OF PURPOSE

42 USC 7470

The purposes of this part are as follows:
   (1) to protect public health and welfare from any actual or potential adverse effect which in the Administrator's judgment may reasonably be anticipate[2] to occur from air pollution or from exposures to pollutants in other media, which pollutants originate as emissions to the ambient air)[3], notwithstanding attainment and maintenance of all national ambient air quality standards;
   (2) to preserve, protect, and enhance the air quality in national parks, national wilderness areas, national monuments, national seashores, and other areas of special national or regional natural, recreational, scenic, or historic value;
   (3) to insure that economic growth will occur in a manner consistent with the preservation of existing clean air resources;
   (4) to assure that emissions from any source in any State will not interfere with any portion of the applicable implementation plan to prevent significant deterioration of air quality for any other State; and
   (5) to assure that any decision to permit increased air pollution in any area to which this section applies is made only after careful evaluation of all the consequences of such a decision and after adequate procedural opportunities for informed public participation in the decisionmaking process.

(July 14, 1955, ch. 360, title I, Sec. 160, as added Pub. L. 95-95, title I, Sec. 127(a), Aug. 7, 1977, 91 Stat. 731.)

Effective Date

Subpart effective Aug. 7, 1977, except as otherwise expressly provided, see section 406(d) of Pub. L. 95-95, set out as an Effective Date of 1977 Amendment note under section 7401 of this title.

Guidance Document

Section 127(c) of Pub. L. 95-95 required Administrator, not later than 1 year after Aug. 7, 1977, to publish a guidance document to assist States in carrying out their functions under part C of title I of the Clean Air Act (this part) with respect to pollutants for which national ambient air quality standards are promulgated.

Study and Report on Progress Made in Program Relating to Significant Deterioration of Air Quality

Section 127(d) of Pub. L. 95-95 directed Administrator, not later than 2 years after Aug. 7, 1977, to complete a study and report to Congress on progress made in carrying out part C of title I of the Clean Air Act (this part) and the problems associated in carrying out such section.

Section Referred to in Other Sections

This section is referred to in section 7476 of this title.

---

[1] Repealed by section 601 of P.L. 101-549 (104 Stat. 2648).
[2] So in original. Probably should be "anticipated".

PLAN REQUIREMENTS

42 USC 7471

In accordance with the policy of section 7401(b)(1) of this title, each applicable implementation plan shall contain emission limitations and such other measures as may be necessary, as determined under regulations promulgated under this part, to prevent significant deterioration of air quality in each region (or portion thereof) designated pursuant to section 7407 of this title as attainment or unclassifiable.

(July 14, 1955, ch. 360, title I, Sec. 161, as added Pub. L. 95-95, title I, Sec. 127(a), Aug. 7, 1977, 91 Stat. 731; amended Pub. L. 101-549, title I, Sec. 110(1), Nov. 15, 1990, 104 Stat. 2470.)

Amendments

1990—Pub. L. 101-549 substituted "designated pursuant to section 7407 of this title as attainment or unclassifiable" for "identified pursuant to section 7407(d)(1)(D) or (E) of this title".

INITIAL CLASSIFICATIONS

42 USC 7472

(a) Areas designated as class I
Upon the enactment of this part, all—
  (1) international parks,
  (2) national wilderness areas which exceed 5,000 acres in size,
  (3) national memorial parks which exceed 5,000 acres in size, and
  (4) national parks which exceed six thousand acres in size,
and which are in existence on August 7, 1977, shall be class I areas and may not be redesignated. All areas which were redesignated as class I under regulations promulgated before August 7, 1977, shall be class I areas which may be redesignated as provided in this part. The extent of the areas designated as Class I under this section shall conform to any changes in the boundaries of such areas which have occurred subsequent to August 7, 1977, or which may occur subsequent to November 15, 1990.

(b) Areas designated as class II
All areas in such State designated pursuant to section 7407(d) of this title as attainment or unclassifiable which are not established as class I under subsection (a) of this section shall be class II areas unless redesignated under section 7474 of this title.

(July 14, 1955, ch. 360, title I, Sec. 162, as added Pub. L. 95-95, title I, Sec. 127(a), Aug. 7, 1977, 91 Stat. 731; amended Pub. L. 95-190, Sec. 14(a)(40), Nov. 16, 1977, 91 Stat. 1401; Pub. L. 101-549, title I, Secs. 108(m), 110(2), Nov. 15, 1990, 104 Stat. 2469, 2470.)

Amendments

1990—Subsec. (a). Pub. L. 101-549, Sec. 108(m), inserted at end "The extent of the areas designated as Class I under this section shall conform to any changes in the boundaries of such areas which have occurred subsequent to August 7, 1977, or which may occur subsequent to November 15, 1990."

Subsec. (b). Pub. L. 101-549, Sec. 110(2), substituted "designated pursuant to section 7407(d) of this title as attainment or unclassifiable" for "identified pursuant to section 7407(d)(1)(D) or (E) of this title".

1977—Subsec. (a)(4). Pub. L. 95-190 inserted a comma after "size".

Section Referred to in Other Sections

This section is referred to in sections 7474, 7478 of this title.

INCREMENTS AND CEILINGS

42 USC 7473

(a) Sulfur oxide and particulate matter; requirement that maximum allowable increases and maximum allowable concentrations not be exceeded

In the case of sulfur oxide and particulate matter, each applicable implementation plan shall contain measures assuring that maximum allowable increases over baseline concentrations of, and maximum allowable concentrations of, such pollutant shall not be exceeded. In the case of any maximum allowable increase (except an allowable increase specified under section 7475(d)(2)(C)(iv) of this title) for a pollutant based on concentrations permitted under national ambient air quality standards for any period other than an annual period, such regulations shall permit such maximum allowable increase to be exceeded during one such period per year.

(b) Maximum allowable increases in concentrations over baseline concentrations

(1) For any class I area, the maximum allowable increase in concentrations of sulfur dioxide and particulate matter over the baseline concentration of such pollutants shall not exceed the following amounts:

Pollutant	Maximum allowable increase (in micrograms per cubic meter)
Particulate matter:	
Annual geometric mean	5
Twenty-four-hour maximum	10
Sulfur dioxide:	
Annual arithmetic mean	2
Twenty-four-hour maximum	5
Three-hour maximum	25

(2) For any class II area, the maximum allowable increase in concentrations of sulfur dioxide and particulate matter over the baseline concentration of such pollutants shall not exceed the following amounts:

Pollutant	Maximum allowable increase (in micrograms per cubic meter)
Particulate matter:	
Annual geometric mean	19
Twenty-four-hour maximum	37
Sulfur dioxide:	
Annual arithmetic mean	20
Twenty-four-hour maximum	91
Three-hour maximum	512

(3) For any class III area, the maximum allowable increase in concentrations of sulfur dioxide and particulate matter over the baseline concentration of such pollutants shall not exceed the following amounts:

Pollutant	Maximum allowable increase (in micrograms per cubic meter)
Particulate matter:	
Annual geometric mean	37
Twenty-four-hour maximum	75
Sulfur dioxide:	
Annual arithmetic mean	40
Twenty-four-hour maximum	182
Three-hour maximum	700

(4) The maximum allowable concentration of any air pollutant in any area to which this part applies shall not exceed a concentration for such pollutant for each period of exposure equal to—

(A) the concentration permitted under the national secondary ambient air quality standard, or

(B) the concentration permitted under the national primary ambient air quality standard, whichever concentration is lowest for such pollutant for such period of exposure.

(c) Orders or rules for determining compliance with maximum allowable increases in ambient concentrations of air pollutants

(1) In the case of any State which has a plan approved by the Administrator for purposes of carrying out this part, the Governor of such State may, after notice and opportunity for

142 / Environmental Statutes

public hearing, issue orders or promulgate rules providing that for purposes of determining compliance with the maximum allowable increases in ambient concentrations of an air pollutant, the following concentrations of such pollutant shall not be taken into account:
- (A) concentrations of such pollutant attributable to the increase in emissions from stationary sources which have converted from the use of petroleum products, or natural gas, or both, by reason of an order which is in effect under the provisions of sections 792(a) and (b) of title 15 (or any subsequent legislation which supersedes such provisions) over the emissions from such sources before the effective date of such order.[1]
- (B) the concentrations of such pollutant attributable to the increase in emissions from stationary sources which have converted from using natural gas by reason of a natural gas curtailment pursuant to a natural gas curtailment plan in effect pursuant to the Federal Power Act [16 U.S.C. 791a et seq.] over the emissions from such sources before the effective date of such plan,
- (C) concentrations of particulate matter attributable to the increase in emissions from construction or other temporary emission-related activities, and
- (D) the increase in concentrations attributable to new sources outside the United States over the concentrations attributable to existing sources which are included in the baseline concentration determined in accordance with section 7479(4) of this title.

(2) No action taken with respect to a source under paragraph (1)(A) or (1)(B) shall apply more than five years after the effective date of the order referred to in paragraph (1)(A) or the plan referred to in paragraph (1)(B), whichever is applicable. If both such order and plan are applicable, no such action shall apply more than five years after the later of such effective dates.

(3) No action under this subsection shall take effect unless the Governor submits the order or rule providing for such exclusion to the Administrator and the Administrator determines that such order or rule is in compliance with the provisions of this subsection.

(July 14, 1955, ch. 360, title I, Sec. 163, as added Pub. L. 95-95, title I, Sec. 127(a), Aug. 7, 1977, 91 Stat. 732; amended Pub. L. 95-190, Sec. 14(a)(41), Nov. 16, 1977, 91 Stat. 1401.)

References In Text

The Federal Power Act, referred to in subsec. (c)(1)(B), is act June 10, 1920, ch. 285, 41 Stat. 1063, as amended, which is classified generally to chapter 12 (Sec. 791a et seq.) of Title 16, Conservation. For complete classification of this Act to the Code, see section 791a of Title 16 and Tables.

Amendments

1977—Subsec. (a). Pub. L. 95-190 inserted "section" before "7475".

Section Referred to in Other Sections

This section is referred to in sections 7407, 7476, 7478 of this title.

AREA REDESIGNATION

42 USC 7474

(a) Authority of States to redesignate areas
Except as otherwise provided under subsection (c) of this section, a State may redesignate such areas as it deems appropriate as class I areas. The following areas may be redesignated only as class I or II:
(1) an area which exceeds ten thousand acres in size and is a national monument, a national primitive area, a national preserve, a national recreation area, a national wild and scenic river, a national wildlife refuge, a national lakeshore or seashore, and
(2) a national park or national wilderness area established after August 7, 1977, which exceeds ten thousand acres in size.

The extent of the areas referred to in paragraph[2] (1) and (2) shall conform to any changes in the boundaries of such areas which have occurred subsequent to August 7, 1977, or which may occur subsequent to November 15, 1990. Any area (other than an area referred to in paragraph

---

[1] So in original. The period probably should be a comma.

[2] So in original. Probably should be "paragraphs".

(1) or (2) or an area established as class I under the first sentence of section 7472(a) of this title) may be redesignated by the State as class III if—
  (A) such redesignation has been specifically approved by the Governor of the State, after consultation with the appropriate Committees of the legislature if it is in session or with the leadership of the legislature if it is not in session (unless State law provides that such redesignation must be specifically approved by State legislation) and if general purpose units of local government representing a majority of the residents of the area so redesignated enact legislation (including for such units of local government resolutions where appropriate) concurring in the State's redesignation;
  (B) such redesignation will not cause, or contribute to, concentrations of any air pollutant which exceed any maximum allowable increase or maximum allowable concentration permitted under the classification of any other area; and
  (C) such redesignation otherwise meets the requirements of this part.
  Subparagraph (A) of this paragraph shall not apply to area redesignations by Indian tribes.
(b) Notice and hearing; notice to Federal land manager; written comments and recommendations; regulations; disapproval of redesignation
  (1) (A) Prior to redesignation of any area under this part, notice shall be afforded and public hearings shall be conducted in areas proposed to be redesignated and in areas which may be affected by the proposed redesignation. Prior to any such public hearing a satisfactory description and analysis of the health, environmental, economic, social, and energy effects of the proposed redesignation shall be prepared and made available for public inspection and prior to any such redesignation, the description and analysis of such effects shall be reviewed and examined by the redesignating authorities.
  (B) Prior to the issuance of notice under subparagraph (A) respecting the redesignation of any area under this subsection, if such area includes any Federal lands, the State shall provide written notice to the appropriate Federal land manager and afford adequate opportunity (but not in excess of 60 days) to confer with the State respecting the intended notice of redesignation and to submit written comments and recommendations with respect to such intended notice of redesignation. In redesignating any area under this section with respect to which any Federal land manager has submitted written comments and recommendations, the State shall publish a list of any inconsistency between such redesignation and such recommendations and an explanation of such inconsistency (together with the reasons for making such redesignation against the recommendation of the Federal land manager).
  (C) The Administrator shall promulgate regulations not later than six months after August 7, 1977, to assure, insofar as practicable, that prior to any public hearing on redesignation of any area, there shall be available for public inspection any specific plans for any new or modified major emitting facility which may be permitted to be constructed and operated only if the area in question is designated or redesignated as class III.
  (2) The Administrator may disapprove the redesignation of any area only if he finds, after notice and opportunity for public hearing, that such redesignation does not meet the procedural requirements of this section or is inconsistent with the requirements of section 7472(a) of this title or of subsection (a) of this section. If any such disapproval occurs, the classification of the area shall be that which was in effect prior to the redesignation which was disapproved.
(c) Indian reservations
  Lands within the exterior boundaries of reservations of federally recognized Indian tribes may be redesignated only by the appropriate Indian governing body. Such Indian governing body shall be subject in all respect to the provisions of subsection (e) of this section.
(d) Review of national monuments, primitive areas, and national preserves
  The Federal Land Manager shall review all national monuments, primitive areas, and national preserves, and shall recommend any appropriate areas for redesignation as class I where air quality related values are important attributes of the area. The Federal Land Manager shall report such recommendations, within[3] supporting analysis, to the Congress and the af-

---

[3] So in original. Probably should be "with".

fected States within one year after August 7, 1977. The Federal Land Manager shall consult with the appropriate States before making such recommendations.

(e) Resolution of disputes between State and Indian tribes
If any State affected by the redesignation of an area by an Indian tribe or any Indian tribe affected by the redesignation of an area by a State disagrees with such redesignation of any area, or if a permit is proposed to be issued for any new major emitting facility proposed for construction in any State which the Governor of an affected State or governing body of an affected Indian tribe determines will cause or contribute to a cumulative change in air quality in excess of that allowed in this part within the affected State or tribal reservation, the Governor or Indian ruling body may request the Administrator to enter into negotiations with the parties involved to resolve such dispute. If requested by any State or Indian tribe involved, the Administrator shall make a recommendation to resolve the dispute and protect the air quality related values of the lands involved. If the parties involved do not reach agreement, the Administrator shall resolve the dispute and his determination, or the results of agreements reached through other means, shall become part of the applicable plan and shall be enforceable as part of such plan. In resolving such disputes relating to area redesignation, the Administrator shall consider the extent to which the lands involved are of sufficient size to allow effective air quality management or have air quality related values of such an area.

(July 14, 1955, ch. 360, title I, Sec. 164, as added Pub. L. 95-95, title I, Sec. 127(a), Aug. 7, 1977, 91 Stat. 733; amended Pub. L. 95-190, Sec. 14(a)(42), (43), Nov. 16, 1977, 91 Stat. 1402; Pub. L. 101-549, title I, Sec. 108(n), Nov. 15, 1990, 104 Stat. 469.)

Amendments

1990—Subsec. (a). Pub. L. 101-549, which directed the insertion of "The extent of the areas referred to in paragraph (1) and (2) shall conform to any changes in the boundaries of such areas which have occurred subsequent to August 7, 1977, or which may occur subsequent to November 15, 1990." before "Any area (other than an area referred to in paragraph (1) or (2))", was executed by making the insertion before "Any area (other than an area referred to in paragraph (1) or (2)", to reflect the probable intent of Congress.

1977—Subsec. (b)(2). Pub. L. 95-190, Sec. 14(a)(42), inserted "or is inconsistent with the requirements of section 7472(a) of this title or of subsection (a) of this section" after "this section".

Subsec. (e). Pub. L. 95-190, Sec. 14(a)(43), inserted "an" after "If any State affected by the redesignation of".

Section Referred to in Other Sections

This section is referred to in sections 7472, 7478 of this title.

PRECONSTRUCTION REQUIREMENTS

42 USC 7475

(a) Major emitting facilities on which construction is commenced
No major emitting facility on which construction is commenced after August 7, 1977, may be constructed in any area to which this part applies unless—
  (1) a permit has been issued for such proposed facility in accordance with this part setting forth emission limitations for such facility which conform to the requirements of this part;
  (2) the proposed permit has been subject to a review in accordance with this section, the required analysis has been conducted in accordance with regulations promulgated by the Administrator, and a public hearing has been held with opportunity for interested persons including representatives of the Administrator to appear and submit written or oral presentations on the air quality impact of such source, alternatives thereto, control technology requirements, and other appropriate considerations;
  (3) the owner or operator of such facility demonstrates, as required pursuant to section 7410(j) of this title, that emissions from construction or operation of such facility will not cause, or contribute to, air pollution in excess of any (A) maximum allowable increase or maximum allowable concentration for any pollutant in any area to which this part applies more than one time per year, (B) national ambient air quality standard in any air quality

control region, or (C) any other applicable emission standard or standard of performance under this chapter;
(4) the proposed facility is subject to the best available control technology for each pollutant subject to regulation under this chapter emitted from, or which results from, such facility;
(5) the provisions of subsection (d) of this section with respect to protection of class I areas have been complied with for such facility;
(6) there has been an analysis of any air quality impacts projected for the area as a result of growth associated with such facility;
(7) the person who owns or operates, or proposes to own or operate, a major emitting facility for which a permit is required under this part agrees to conduct such monitoring as may be necessary to determine the effect which emissions from any such facility may have, or is having, on air quality in any area which may be affected by emissions from such source; and
(8) in the case of a source which proposes to construct in a class III area, emissions from which would cause or contribute to exceeding the maximum allowable increments applicable in a class II area and where no standard under section 7411 of this title has been promulgated subsequent to August 7, 1977, for such source category, the Administrator has approved the determination of best available technology as set forth in the permit.

(b) Exception

The demonstration pertaining to maximum allowable increases required under subsection (a)(3) of this section shall not apply to maximum allowable increases for class II areas in the case of an expansion or modification of a major emitting facility which is in existence on August 7, 1977, whose allowable emissions of air pollutants, after compliance with subsection (a)(4) of this section, will be less than fifty tons per year and for which the owner or operator of such facility demonstrates that emissions of particulate matter and sulfur oxides will not cause or contribute to ambient air quality levels in excess of the national secondary ambient air quality standard for either of such pollutants.

(c) Permit applications

Any completed permit application under section 7410 of this title for a major emitting facility in any area to which this part applies shall be granted or denied not later than one year after the date of filing of such completed application.

(d) Action taken on permit applications; notice; adverse impact on air quality related values; variance; emission limitations
  (1) Each State shall transmit to the Administrator a copy of each permit application relating to a major emitting facility received by such State and provide notice to the Administrator of every action related to the consideration of such permit.
  (2) (A) The Administrator shall provide notice of the permit application to the Federal Land Manager and the Federal official charged with direct responsibility for management of any lands within a class I area which may be affected by emissions from the proposed facility.
      (B) The Federal Land Manager and the Federal official charged with direct responsibility for management of such lands shall have an affirmative responsibility to protect the air quality related values (including visibility) of any such lands within a class I area and to consider, in consultation with the Administrator, whether a proposed major emitting facility will have an adverse impact on such values.
      (C) (i) In any case where the Federal official charged with direct responsibility for management of any lands within a class I area or the Federal Land Manager of such lands, or the Administrator, or the Governor of an adjacent State containing such a class I area files a notice alleging that emissions from a proposed major emitting facility may cause or contribute to a change in the air quality in such area and identifying the potential adverse impact of such change, a permit shall not be issued unless the owner or operator of such facility demonstrates that emissions of particulate matter and sulfur dioxide will not cause or contribute to concentrations which exceed the maximum allowable increases for a class I area.
          (ii) In any case where the Federal Land Manager demonstrates to the satisfaction of the State that the emissions from such facility will have an adverse impact on the air quality-related values (including visibility) of such lands, notwithstanding the

fact that the change in air quality resulting from emissions from such facility will not cause or contribute to concentrations which exceed the maximum allowable increases for a class I area, a permit shall not be issued.

(iii) In any case where the owner or operator of such facility demonstrates to the satisfaction of the Federal Land Manager, and the Federal Land Manager so certifies, that the emissions from such facility will have no adverse impact on the air quality-related values of such lands (including visibility), notwithstanding the fact that the change in air quality resulting from emissions from such facility will cause or contribute to concentrations which exceed the maximum allowable increases for class I areas, the State may issue a permit.

(iv) In the case of a permit issued pursuant to clause (iii), such facility shall comply with such emission limitations under such permit as may be necessary to assure that emissions of sulfur oxides and particulates from such facility will not cause or contribute to concentrations of such pollutant which exceed the following maximum allowable increases over the baseline concentration for such pollutants:

Maximum allowable increase
(in micrograms per cubic meter)

Particulate matter:
  Annual geometric mean... 19
  Twenty-four-hour maximum................................... 37
Sulfur dioxide:
  Annual arithmetic mean.. 20
  Twenty-four-hour maximum................................... 91
  Three-hour maximum.. 325

(D) (i) In any case where the owner or operator of a proposed major emitting facility who has been denied a certification under subparagraph (C)(iii) demonstrates to the satisfaction of the Governor, after notice and public hearing, and the Governor finds, that the facility cannot be constructed by reason of any maximum allowable increase for sulfur dioxide for periods of twenty-four hours or less applicable to any class I area and, in the case of Federal mandatory class I areas, that a variance under this clause will not adversely affect the air quality related values of the area (including visibility), the Governor, after consideration of the Federal Land Manager's recommendation (if any) and subject to his concurrence, may grant a variance from such maximum allowable increase. If such variance is granted, a permit may be issued to such source pursuant to the requirements of this subparagraph.

(ii) In any case in which the Governor recommends a variance under this subparagraph in which the Federal Land Manager does not concur, the recommendations of the Governor and the Federal Land Manager shall be transmitted to the President. The President may approve the Governor's recommendation if he finds that such variance is in the national interest. No Presidential finding shall be reviewable in any court. The variance shall take effect if the President approves the Governor's recommendations. The President shall approve or disapprove such recommendation within ninety days after his receipt of the recommendations of the Governor and the Federal Land Manager.

(iii) In the case of a permit issued pursuant to this subparagraph, such facility shall comply with such emission limitations under such permit as may be necessary to assure that emissions of sulfur oxides from such facility will not (during any day on which the otherwise applicable maximum allowable increases are exceeded) cause or contribute to concentrations which exceed the following maximum allowable increases for such areas over the baseline concentration for such pollutant and to assure that such emissions will not cause or contribute to concentrations which exceed the otherwise applicable maximum allowable increases for periods of exposure of 24 hours or less on more than 18 days during any annual period:

MAXIMUM ALLOWABLE INCREASE
(In micrograms per cubic meter)

Period of exposure	Low terrain areas	High terrain areas
24-hr maximum	36	62
3-hr maximum	130	221

(iv) For purposes of clause (iii), the term "high terrain area" means with respect to any facility, any area having an elevation of 900 feet or more above the base of the stack of such facility, and the term "low terrain area" means any area other than a high terrain area.

(e) Analysis; continuous air quality monitoring data; regulations; model adjustments
  (1) The review provided for in subsection (a) of this section shall be preceded by an analysis in accordance with regulations of the Administrator, promulgated under this subsection, which may be conducted by the State (or any general purpose unit of local government) or by the major emitting facility applying for such permit, of the ambient air quality at the proposed site and in areas which may be affected by emissions from such facility for each pollutant subject to regulation under this chapter which will be emitted from such facility.
  (2) Effective one year after August 7, 1977, the analysis required by this subsection shall include continuous air quality monitoring data gathered for purposes of determining whether emissions from such facility will exceed the maximum allowable increases or the maximum allowable concentration permitted under this part. Such data shall be gathered over a period of one calendar year preceding the date of application for a permit under this part unless the State, in accordance with regulations promulgated by the Administrator, determines that a complete and adequate analysis for such purposes may be accomplished in a shorter period. The results of such analysis shall be available at the time of the public hearing on the application for such permit.
  (3) The Administrator shall within six months after August 7, 1977, promulgate regulations respecting the analysis required under this subsection which regulations—
    (A) shall not require the use of any automatic or uniform buffer zone or zones,
    (B) shall require an analysis of the ambient air quality, climate and meteorology, terrain, soils and vegetation, and visibility at the site of the proposed major emitting facility and in the area potentially affected by the emissions from such facility for each pollutant regulated under this chapter which will be emitted from, or which results from the construction or operation of, such facility, the size and nature of the proposed facility, the degree of continuous emission reduction which could be achieved by such facility, and such other factors as may be relevant in determining the effect of emissions from a proposed facility on any air quality control region,
    (C) shall require the results of such analysis shall be available at the time of the public hearing on the application for such permit, and
    (D) shall specify with reasonable particularity each air quality model or models to be used under specified sets of conditions for purposes of this part. Any model or models designated under such regulations may be adjusted upon a determination, after notice and opportunity for public hearing, by the Administrator that such adjustment is necessary to take into account unique terrain or meteorological characteristics of an area potentially affected by emissions from a source applying for a permit required under this part.

(July 14, 1955, ch. 360, title I, Sec. 165, as added Pub. L. 95-95, title I, Sec. 127(a), Aug. 7, 1977, 91 Stat. 735; amended Pub. L. 95-190, Sec. 14(a)(44)-(51), Nov. 16, 1977, 91 Stat. 1402.)

Amendments

1977—Subsec. (a)(1). Pub. L. 95-190, Sec. 14(a)(44), substituted "part;" for "part:".

Subsec. (a)(3). Pub. L. 95-190, Sec. 14(a)(45), inserted provision making applicable requirement of section 7410(j) of this title.

Subsec. (b). Pub. L. 95-190, Sec. 14(a)(46), inserted "cause or" before "contribute" and struck out "actual" before "allowable emissions".

Subsec. (d)(2)(C). Pub. L. 95-190, Sec. 14(a)(47)-(49), in cl. (ii) substituted "contribute" for "contrbute", in cl. (iii) substituted "quality-related" for "quality related" and "concentrations which" for "concentrations, which", and in cl. (iv) substituted "such facility" for "such sources" and "will not cause or contribute to concentrations of such pollutant which exceed" for "together with all other sources, will not exceed".

Subsec. (d)(2)(D). Pub. L. 95-190, Sec. 14(a)(50), (51), in cl. (iii) substituted provisions relating to determinations of amounts of emissions of sulfur oxides from facilities, for provisions relating to determinations of amounts of emissions of sulfur oxides from sources operating under permits issued pursuant to this subpar., together with all other sources, and added cl. (iv).

Section Referred to in Other Sections

This section is referred to in sections 7413, 7429, 7473, 7476 of this title.

OTHER POLLUTANTS

42 USC 7476

(a) Hydrocarbons, carbon monoxide, petrochemical oxidants, and nitrogen oxides
In the case of the pollutants hydrocarbons, carbon monoxide, photochemical oxidants, and nitrogen oxides, the Administrator shall conduct a study and not later than two years after August 7, 1977, promulgate regulations to prevent the significant deterioration of air quality which would result from the emissions of such pollutants. In the case of pollutants for which national ambient air quality standards are promulgated after August 7, 1977, he shall promulgate such regulations not more than 2 years after the date of promulgation of such standards.

(b) Effective date of regulations
Regulations referred to in subsection (a) of this section shall become effective one year after the date of promulgation. Within 21 months after such date of promulgation such plan revision shall be submitted to the Administrator who shall approve or disapprove the plan within 25 months after such date or promulgation in the same manner as required under section 7410 of this title.

(c) Contents of regulations
Such regulations shall provide specific numerical measures against which permit applications may be evaluated, a framework for stimulating improved control technology, protection of air quality values, and fulfill the goals and purposes set forth in section 7401 and section 7470 of this title.

(d) Specific measures to fulfill goals and purposes
The regulations of the Administrator under subsection (a) of this section shall provide specific measures at least as effective as the increments established in section 7473 of this title to fulfill such goals and purposes, and may contain air quality increments, emission density requirements, or other measures.

(e) Area classification plan not required
With respect to any air pollutant for which a national ambient air quality standard is established other than sulfur oxides or particulate matter, an area classification plan shall not be required under this section if the implementation plan adopted by the State and submitted for the Administrator's approval or promulgated by the Administrator under section 7410(c) of this title contains other provisions which when considered as a whole, the Administrator finds will carry out the purposes in section 7470 of this title at least as effectively as an area classification plan for such pollutant. Such other provisions referred to in the preceding sentence need not require the establishment of maximum allowable increases with respect to such pollutant for any area to which this section applies.

(f) PM-10 increments
The Administrator is authorized to substitute, for the maximum allowable increases in particulate matter specified in section 7473(b) of this title and section 7475(d)(2)(C)(iv) of this title, maximum allowable increases in particulate matter with an aerodynamic diameter smaller than or equal to 10 micrometers. Such substituted maximum allowable increases shall be of equal stringency in effect as those specified in the provisions for which they are substituted. Until the Administrator promulgates regulations under the authority of this subsection, the current maximum allowable increases in concentrations of particulate matter shall remain in effect.

(July 14, 1955, ch. 360, title I, Sec. 166, as added Pub. L. 95-95, title I, Sec. 127(a), Aug. 7, 1977, 91 Stat. 739; amended Pub. L. 101-549, title I, Sec. 105(b), Nov. 15, 1990, 104 Stat. 2462.)

Amendments

1990—Subsec. (f). Pub. L. 101-549 added subsec. (f).

ENFORCEMENT

42 USC 7477

The Administrator shall, and a State may, take such measures, including issuance of an order, or seeking injunctive relief, as necessary to prevent the construction or modification of a major emitting facility which does not conform to the requirements of this part, or which is proposed to be constructed in any area designated pursuant to section 7407(d) of this title as attainment or unclassifiable ad which is not subject to an implementation plan which meets the requirements of this part.

(July 14, 1955, ch. 360, title I, Sec. 167, as added Pub. L. 95-95, title I, Sec. 127(a), Aug. 7, 1977, 91 Stat. 740; amended Pub. L. 101-549, title I, Sec. 110(3), title VII, Sec. 708, Nov. 15, 1990, 104 Stat. 2470, 2684.)

Amendments

1990—Pub. L. 101-549, Sec. 708, substituted "construction or modification of a major emitting facility" for "construction of a major emitting facility".

Pub. L. 101-549, Sec. 110(3), substituted "designated pursuant to section 7407(d) as attainment or unclassifiable" for "included in the list promulgated pursuant to paragraph (1)(D) or (E) of subsection (d) of section 7407 of this title".

Section Referred to in Other Sections

This section is referred to in sections 7413, 7420, 7607 of this title.

PERIOD BEFORE PLAN APPROVAL

42 USC 7478

(a) Existing regulations to remain in effect
   Until such time as an applicable implementation plan is in effect for any area, which plan meets the requirements of this part to prevent significant deterioration of air quality with respect to any air pollutant, applicable regulations under this chapter prior to August 7, 1977, shall remain in effect to prevent significant deterioration of air quality in any such area for any such pollutant except as otherwise provided in subsection (b) of this section.

(b) Regulations deemed amended; construction commenced after June 1, 1975
   If any regulation in effect prior to August 7, 1977, to prevent significant deterioration of air quality would be inconsistent with the requirements of section 7472(a), section 7473(b) or section 7474(a) of this title, then such regulations shall be deemed amended so as to conform with such requirements. In the case of a facility on which construction was commenced (in accordance with the definition of "commenced" in section 7479(2) of this title) after June 1, 1975, and prior to August 7, 1977, the review and permitting of such facility shall be in accordance with the regulations for the prevention of significant deterioration in effect prior to August 7, 1977.

(July 14, 1955, ch. 360, title I, Sec. 168, as added Pub. L. 95-95, title I, Sec. 127(a), Aug. 7, 1977, 91 Stat. 740; amended Pub. L. 95-190, Sec. 14(a)(52), Nov. 16, 1977, 91 Stat. 1402.)

Amendments

1977—Subsec. (b). Pub. L. 95-190 substituted "(in accordance with the definition of 'commenced' in section 7479(2) of this title)" for "in accordance with this definition".

DEFINITIONS

42 USC 7479

For purposes of this part—
(1) The term "major emitting facility" means any of the following stationary sources of air pollutants which emit, or have the potential to emit, one hundred tons per year or more of any air pollutant from the following types of stationary sources: fossil-fuel fired steam electric plants of more than two hundred and fifty million British thermal units per hour heat input, coal cleaning plants (thermal dryers), kraft pulp mills, Portland Cement plants, primary zinc smelters, iron and steel mill plants, primary aluminum ore reduction plants, primary copper smelters, municipal incinerators capable of charging more than fifty tons of refuse per day, hydrofluoric, sulfuric, and nitric acid plants, petroleum refineries, lime plants, phosphate rock processing plants, coke oven batteries, sulfur recovery plants, carbon black plants (furnace process), primary lead smelters, fuel conversion plants, sintering plants, secondary metal production facilities, chemical process plants, fossil-fuel boilers of more than two hundred and fifty million British thermal units per hour heat input, petroleum storage and transfer facilities with a capacity exceeding three hundred thousand barrels, taconite ore processing facilities, glass fiber processing plants, charcoal production facilities. Such term also includes any other source with the potential to emit two hundred and fifty tons per year or more of any air pollutant. This term shall not include new or modified facilities which are nonprofit health or education institutions which have been exempted by the State.
(2) (A) The term "commenced" as applied to construction of a major emitting facility means that the owner or operator has obtained all necessary preconstruction approvals or permits required by Federal, State, or local air pollution emissions and air quality laws or regulations and either has (i) begun, or caused to begin, a continuous program of physical on-site construction of the facility or (ii) entered into binding agreements or contractual obligations, which cannot be canceled or modified without substantial loss to the owner or operator, to undertake a program of construction of the facility to be completed within a reasonable time.
(B) The term "necessary preconstruction approvals or permits" means those permits or approvals, required by the permitting authority as a precondition to undertaking any activity under clauses (i) or (ii) of subparagraph (A) of this paragraph.
(C) The term "construction" when used in connection with any source or facility, includes the modification (as defined in section 7411(a) of this title) of any source or facility.
(3) The term "best available control technology" means an emission limitation based on the maximum degree of reduction of each pollutant subject to regulation under this chapter emitted from or which results from any major emitting facility, which the permitting authority, on a case-by-case basis, taking into account energy, environmental, and economic impacts and other costs, determines is achievable for such facility through application of production processes and available methods, systems, and techniques, including fuel cleaning, clean fuels, or treatment or innovative fuel combustion techniques for control of each such pollutant. In no event shall application of "best available control technology" result in emissions of any pollutants which will exceed the emissions allowed by any applicable standard established pursuant to section 7411 or 7412 of this title. Emissions from any source utilizing clean fuels, or any other means, to comply with this paragraph shall not be allowed to increase above levels that would have been required under this paragraph as it existed prior to November 15, 1990.
(4) The term "baseline concentration" means, with respect to a pollutant, the ambient concentration levels which exist at the time of the first application for a permit in an area subject to this part, based on air quality data available in the Environmental Protection Agency or a State air pollution control agency and on such monitoring data as the permit applicant is required to submit. Such ambient concentration levels shall take into account all projected emissions in, or which may affect, such area from any major emitting facility on which construction commenced prior to January 6, 1975, but which has not begun operation by the date of the baseline air quality concentration determination. Emissions of sulfur oxides and particulate matter from any major emitting facility on which con-

struction commenced after January 6, 1975, shall not be included in the baseline and shall be counted against the maximum allowable increases in pollutant concentrations established under this part.

(July 14, 1955, ch. 360, title I, Sec. 169, as added Pub. L. 95-95, title I, Sec. 127(a), Aug. 7, 1977, 91 Stat. 740; amended Pub. L. 95-190, Sec. 14(a)(54), Nov. 16, 1977, 91 Stat. 1402; Pub. L. 101-549, title III, Sec. 305(b), title IV, Sec. 403(d), Nov. 15, 1990, 104 Stat. 2583, 2631.)

Amendments

1990—Par. (1). Pub. L. 101-549, Sec. 305(b), struck out "two hundred and" after "municipal incinerators capable of charging more than".

Par. (3). Pub. L. 101-549, Sec. 403(d), directed the insertion of ", clean fuels," after "including fuel cleaning,", which was executed by making the insertion after "including fuel cleaning" to reflect the probable intent of Congress, and inserted at end "Emissions from any source utilizing clean fuels, or any other means, to comply with this paragraph shall not be allowed to increase above levels that would have been required under this paragraph as it existed prior to November 15, 1990."

1977—Par. (2)(C). Pub. L. 95-190 added subpar. (C).

Study of Major Emitting Facilities With Potential of Emitting 250 Tons Per Year

Section 127(b) of Pub. L. 95-95 directed Administrator, within 1 year after Aug. 7, 1977, to report to Congress on consequences of that portion of definition of "major emitting facility" under this subpart which applies to facilities with potential to emit 250 tons per year or more.

Section Referred to in Other Sections

This section is referred to in sections 7412, 7473, 7478, 7511a of this title.

Subpart ii—Visibility Protection

VISIBILITY PROTECTION FOR FEDERAL CLASS I AREAS

42 USC 7491

(a) Impairment of visibility; list of areas; study and report
  (1) Congress hereby declares as a national goal the prevention of any future, and the remedying of any existing, impairment of visibility in mandatory class I Federal areas which impairment results from manmade air pollution.
  (2) Not later than six months after August 7, 1977, the Secretary of the Interior in consultation with other Federal land managers shall review all mandatory class I Federal areas and identify those where visibility is an important value of the area. From time to time the Secretary of the Interior may revise such identifications. Not later than one year after August 7, 1977, the Administrator shall, after consultation with the Secretary of the Interior, promulgate a list of mandatory class I Federal areas in which he determines visibility is an important value.
  (3) Not later than eighteen months after August 7, 1977, the Administrator shall complete a study and report to Congress on available methods for implementing the national goal set forth in paragraph (1). Such report shall include recommendations for—
    (A) methods for identifying, characterizing, determining, quantifying, and measuring visibility impairment in Federal areas referred to in paragraph (1), and
    (B) modeling techniques (or other methods) for determining the extent to which manmade air pollution may reasonably be anticipated to cause or contribute to such impairment, and
    (C) methods for preventing and remedying such manmade air pollution and resulting visibility impairment.
  Such report shall also identify the classes or categories of sources and the types of air pollutants which, alone or in conjunction with other sources or pollutants, may reasonably be anticipated to cause or contribute significantly to impairment of visibility.
  (4) Not later than twenty-four months after August 7, 1977, and after notice and public hearing, the Administrator shall promulgate regulations to assure (A) reasonable progress to-

ward meeting the national goal specified in paragraph (1), and (B) compliance with the requirements of this section.

(b) Regulations

Regulations under subsection (a)(4) of this section shall—

(1) provide guidelines to the States, taking into account the recommendations under subsection (a)(3) of this section on appropriate techniques and methods for implementing this section (as provided in subparagraphs (A) through (C) of such subsection (a)(3)), and

(2) require each applicable implementation plan for a State in which any area listed by the Administrator under subsection (a)(2) of this section is located (or for a State the emissions from which may reasonably be anticipated to cause or contribute to any impairment of visibility in any such area) to contain such emission limits, schedules of compliance and other measures as may be necessary to make reasonable progress toward meeting the national goal specified in subsection (a) of this section, including—

(A) except as otherwise provided pursuant to subsection (c) of this section, a requirement that each major stationary source which is in existence on August 7, 1977, but which has not been in operation for more than fifteen years as of such date, and which, as determined by the State (or the Administrator in the case of a plan promulgated under section 7410(c) of this title) emits any air pollutant which may reasonably be anticipated to cause or contribute to any impairment of visibility in any such area, shall procure, install, and operate, as expeditiously as practicable (and maintain thereafter) the best available retrofit technology, as determined by the State (or the Administrator in the case of a plan promulgated under section 7410(c) of this title) for controlling emissions from such source for the purpose of eliminating or reducing any such impairment, and

(B) a long-term (ten to fifteen years) strategy for making reasonable progress toward meeting the national goal specified in subsection (a) of this section.

In the case of a fossil-fuel fired generating powerplant having a total generating capacity in excess of 750 megawatts, the emission limitations required under this paragraph shall be determined pursuant to guidelines, promulgated by the Administrator under paragraph (1).

(c) Exemptions

(1) The Administrator may, by rule, after notice and opportunity for public hearing, exempt any major stationary source from the requirement of subsection (b)(2)(A) of this section, upon his determination that such source does not or will not, by itself or in combination with other sources, emit any air pollutant which may reasonably be anticipated to cause or contribute to a significant impairment of visibility in any mandatory class I Federal area.

(2) Paragraph (1) of this subsection shall not be applicable to any fossil-fuel fired powerplant with total design capacity of 750 megawatts or more, unless the owner or operator of any such plant demonstrates to the satisfaction of the Administrator that such powerplant is located at such distance from all areas listed by the Administrator under subsection (a)(2) of this section that such powerplant does not or will not, by itself or in combination with other sources, emit any air pollutant which may reasonably be anticipated to cause or contribute to significant impairment of visibility in any such area.

(3) An exemption under this subsection shall be effective only upon concurrence by the appropriate Federal land manager or managers with the Administrator's determination under this subsection.

(d) Consultations with appropriate Federal land managers

Before holding the public hearing on the proposed revision of an applicable implementation plan to meet the requirements of this section, the State (or the Administrator, in the case of a plan promulgated under section 7410(c) of this title) shall consult in person with the appropriate Federal land manager or managers and shall include a summary of the conclusions and recommendations of the Federal land managers in the notice to the public.

(e) Buffer zones

In promulgating regulations under this section, the Administrator shall not require the use of any automatic or uniform buffer zone or zones.

(f) Nondiscretionary duty

For purposes of section 7604(a)(2) of this title, the meeting of the national goal specified in subsection (a)(1) of this section by any specific date or dates shall not be considered a "nondiscretionary duty" of the Administrator.

(g) Definitions

For the purpose of this section—

(1) in determining reasonable progress there shall be taken into consideration the costs of compliance, the time necessary for compliance, and the energy and nonair quality environmental impacts of compliance, and the remaining useful life of any existing source subject to such requirements;

(2) in determining best available retrofit technology the State (or the Administrator in determining emission limitations which reflect such technology) shall take into consideration the costs of compliance, the energy and nonair quality environmental impacts of compliance, any existing pollution control technology in use at the source, the remaining useful life of the source, and the degree of improvement in visibility which may reasonably be anticipated to result from the use of such technology;

(3) the term "manmade air pollution" means air pollution which results directly or indirectly from human activities;

(4) the term "as expeditiously as practicable" means as expeditiously as practicable but in no event later than five years after the date of approval of a plan revision under this section (or the date of promulgation of such a plan revision in the case of action by the Administrator under section 7410(c) of this title for purposes of this section);

(5) the term "mandatory class I Federal areas" means Federal areas which may not be designated as other than class I under this part;

(6) the terms "visibility impairment" and "impairment of visibility" shall include reduction in visual range and atmospheric discoloration; and

(7) the term "major stationary source" means the following types of stationary sources with the potential to emit 250 tons or more of any pollutant: fossil-fuel fired steam electric plants of more than 250 million British thermal units per hour heat input, coal cleaning plants (thermal dryers), kraft pulp mills, Portland Cement plants, primary zinc smelters, iron and steel mill plants, primary aluminum ore reduction plants, primary copper smelters, municipal incinerators capable of charging more than 250 tons of refuse per day, hydrofluoric, sulfuric, and nitric acid plants, petroleum refineries, lime plants, phosphate rock processing plants, coke oven batteries, sulfur recovery plants, carbon black plants (furnace process), primary lead smelters, fuel conversion plants, sintering plants, secondary metal production facilities, chemical process plants, fossil-fuel boilers of more than 250 million British thermal units per hour heat input, petroleum storage and transfer facilities with a capacity exceeding 300,000 barrels, taconite ore processing facilities, glass fiber processing plants, charcoal production facilities.

(July 14, 1955, ch. 360, title I, Sec. 169A, as added Pub. L. 95-95, title I, Sec. 128, Aug. 7, 1977, 91 Stat. 742.)

Effective Date

Subpart effective Aug. 7, 1977, except as otherwise expressly provided, see section 406(d) of Pub. L. 95-95, set out as an Effective Date of 1977 Amendment note under section 7401 of this title.

Section Referred to in Other Sections

This section is referred to in sections 7492, 7604 of this title.

VISIBILITY

42 USC 7492

(a) Studies

(1) The Administrator, in conjunction with the National Park Service and other appropriate Federal agencies, shall conduct research to identify and evaluate sources and source regions of both visibility impairment and regions that provide predominantly clean air in class I areas. A total of $8,000,000 per year for 5 years is authorized to be appropriated for the Environmental Protection Agency and the other Federal agencies to conduct this research. The research shall include—

(A) expansion of current visibility related monitoring in class I areas;
(B) assessment of current sources of visibility impairing pollution and clean air corridors;
(C) adaptation of regional air quality models for the assessment of visibility;
(D) studies of atmospheric chemistry and physics of visibility.
(2) Based on the findings available from the research required in subsection (a)(1) of this section as well as other available scientific and technical data, studies, and other available information pertaining to visibility source-receptor relationships, the Administrator shall conduct an assessment and evaluation that identifies, to the extent possible, sources and source regions of visibility impairment including natural sources as well as source regions of clear air for class I areas. The Administrator shall produce interim findings from this study within 3 years after November 15, 1990.
(b) Impacts of other provisions
Within 24 months after November 15, 1990, the Administrator shall conduct an assessment of the progress and improvements in visibility in class I areas that are likely to result from the implementation of the provisions of the Clean Air Act Amendments of 1990 other than the provisions of this section. Every 5 years thereafter the Administrator shall conduct an assessment of actual progress and improvement in visibility in class I areas. The Administrator shall prepare a written report on each assessment and transmit copies of these reports to the appropriate committees of Congress.
(c) Establishment of visibility transport regions and commissions
(1) Authority to establish visibility transport regions
Whenever, upon the Administrator's motion or by petition from the Governors of at least two affected States, the Administrator has reason to believe that the current or projected interstate transport of air pollutants from one or more States contributes significantly to visibility impairment in class I areas located in the affected States, the Administrator may establish a transport region for such pollutants that includes such States. The Administrator, upon the Administrator's own motion or upon petition from the Governor of any affected State, or upon the recommendations of a transport commission established under subsection (b) of this section[1] may—
(A) add any State or portion of a State to a visibility transport region when the Administrator determines that the interstate transport of air pollutants from such State significantly contributes to visibility impairment in a class I area located within the transport region, or
(B) remove any State or portion of a State from the region whenever the Administrator has reason to believe that the control of emissions in that State or portion of the State pursuant to this section will not significantly contribute to the protection or enhancement of visibility in any class I area in the region.
(2) Visibility transport commissions
Whenever the Administrator establishes a transport region under subsection (c)(1) of this section, the Administrator shall establish a transport commission comprised of (as a minimum) each of the following members:
(A) the Governor of each State in the Visibility Transport Region, or the Governor's designee;
(B) The[2] Administrator or the Administrator's designee; and
(C) A[2] representative of each Federal agency charged with the direct management of each class I area or areas within the Visibility Transport Region.
(3) Ex officio members
All representatives of the Federal Government shall be ex officio members.
(4) Federal Advisory Committee Act
The visibility transport commissions shall be exempt from the requirements of the Federal Advisory Committee Act [5 U.S.C. App.].
(d) Duties of visibility transport commissions
A Visibility Transport Commission—
(1) shall assess the scientific and technical data, studies, and other currently available information, including studies conducted pursuant to subsection (a)(1) of this section, pertain-

---

[1] So in original. Words "subsection (b) of this section" probably should be "paragraph (2)".

ing to adverse impacts on visibility from potential or projected growth in emissions from sources located in the Visibility Transport Region; and
  (2) shall, within 4 years of establishment, issue a report to the Administrator recommending what measures, if any, should be taken under this chapter to remedy such adverse impacts. The report required by this subsection shall address at least the following measures:
      (A) the establishment of clean air corridors, in which additional restrictions on increases in emissions may be appropriate to protect visibility in affected class I areas;
      (B) the imposition of the requirements of part D of this subchapter affecting the construction of new major stationary sources or major modifications to existing sources in such clean air corridors specifically including the alternative siting analysis provisions of section 7503(a)(5) of this title; and
      (C) the promulgation of regulations under section 7491 of this title to address long range strategies for addressing regional haze which impairs visibility in affected class I areas.
(e) Duties of Administrator
  (1) The Administrator shall, taking into account the studies pursuant to subsection (a)(1) of this section and the reports pursuant to subsection (d)(2) of this section and any other relevant information, within eighteen months of receipt of the report referred to in subsection (d)(2) of this section, carry out the Administrator's regulatory responsibilities under section 7491 of this title, including criteria for measuring "reasonable progress" toward the national goal.
  (2) Any regulations promulgated under section 7491 of this title pursuant to this subsection shall require affected States to revise within 12 months their implementation plans under section 7410 of this title to contain such emission limits, schedules of compliance, and other measures as may be necessary to carry out regulations promulgated pursuant to this subsection.
(f) Grand Canyon visibility transport commission
  The Administrator pursuant to subsection (c)(1) of this section shall, within 12 months, establish a visibility transport commission for the region affecting the visibility of the Grand Canyon National Park.

(July 14, 1955, ch. 360, title I, Sec. 169B, as added Pub. L. 101-549, title VIII, Sec. 816, Nov. 15, 1990, 104 Stat. 2695.)

References in Text

The Clean Air Act Amendments of 1990, referred to in subsec. (b), probably means Pub. L. 101-549, Nov. 15, 1990, 104 Stat. 2399. For complete classification of this Act to the Code, see Short Title note set out under section 7401 of this title and Tables.

The Federal Advisory Committee Act, referred to in subsec. (c)(4), is Pub. L. 92-463, Oct. 6, 1972, 86 Stat. 770, as amended, which is set out in the Appendix to Title 5, Government Organization and Employees.

Part D—Plan Requirements for Nonattainment Areas

Subpart 1—Nonattainment Areas in General

DEFINITIONS

42 USC 7501

For the purpose of this part—
(1) Reasonable further progress.—The term "reasonable further progress" means such annual incremental reductions in emissions of the relevant air pollutant as are required by this part or may reasonably be required by the Administrator for the purpose of ensuring attainment of the applicable national ambient air quality standard by the applicable date.
(2) Nonattainment area.—The term "nonattainment area" means, for any air pollutant, an area which is designated "nonattainment" with respect to that pollutant within the meaning of section 7407(d) of this title.
(3) The term "lowest achievable emission rate" means for any source, that rate of emissions which reflects—
 (A) the most stringent emission limitation which is contained in the implementation plan of any State for such class or category of source, unless the owner or operator of the proposed source demonstrates that such limitations are not achievable, or
 (B) the most stringent emission limitation which is achieved in practice by such class or category of source, whichever is more stringent.
In no event shall the application of this term permit a proposed new or modified source to emit any pollutant in excess of the amount allowable under applicable new source standards of performance.
(4) The terms "modifications" and "modified" mean the same as the term "modification" as used in section 7411(a)(4) of this title.

(July 14, 1955, ch. 360, title I, Sec. 171, as added Pub. L. 95-95, title I, Sec. 129(b), Aug. 7, 1977, 91 Stat. 745; amended Pub. L. 101-549, title I, Sec. 102(a)(2), Nov. 15, 1990, 104 Stat. 2412.)

Amendments

1990–Pub. L. 101-549, Sec. 102(a)(2)(A), struck out "and section 7410(a)(2)(I) of this title" after "purpose of this part".

Pars. (1), (2). Pub. L. 101-549, Sec. 102(a)(2)(B), (C), amended pars. (1) and (2) generally. Prior to amendment, pars. (1) and (2) read as follows:

"(1) The term 'reasonable further progress' means annual incremental reductions in emissions of the applicable air pollutant (including substantial reductions in the early years following approval or promulgation of plan provisions under this part and section 7410(a)(2)(I) of this title and regular reductions thereafter) which are sufficient in the judgment of the Administrator, to provide for attainment of the applicable national ambient air quality standard by the date required in section 7502(a) of this title.

(2) The term 'nonattainment area' means, for any air pollutant an area which is shown by monitored data or which is calculated by air quality modeling (or other methods determined by the Administrator to be reliable) to exceed any national ambient air quality standard for such pollutant. Such term includes any area identified under subparagraphs (A) through (C) of section 7407(d)(1) of this title."

Effective Date

Part effective Aug. 7, 1977, except as otherwise expressly provided, see section 406(d) of Pub. L. 95-95, set out as an Effective Date of 1977 Amendment note under section 7401 of this title.

Section Referred to in Other Sections

This section is referred to in sections 7410, 7412, 7503, 7513a of this title.

NONATTAINMENT PLAN PROVISIONS IN GENERAL

42 USC 7502

(a) Classifications and attainment dates
  (1) Classifications
    (A) On or after the date the Administrator promulgates the designation of an area as a nonattainment area pursuant to section 7407(d) of this title with respect to any national ambient air quality standard (or any revised standard, including a revision of any standard in effect on November 15, 1990), the Administrator may classify the area for the purpose of applying an attainment date pursuant to paragraph (2), and for other purposes. In determining the appropriate classification, if any, for a nonattainment area, the Administrator may consider such factors as the severity of nonattainment in such area and the availability and feasibility of the pollution control measures that the Administrator believes may be necessary to provide for attainment of such standard in such area.
    (B) The Administrator shall publish a notice in the Federal Register announcing each classification under subparagraph (A), except the Administrator shall provide an opportunity for at least 30 days for written comment. Such classification shall not be subject to the provisions of sections 553 through 557 of title 5 (concerning notice and comment) and shall not be subject to judicial review until the Administrator takes final action under subsection (k) or (l) of section 7410 of this title (concerning action on plan submissions) or section 7509 of this title (concerning sanctions) with respect to any plan submissions required by virtue of such classification.
    (C) This paragraph shall not apply with respect to nonattainment areas for which classifications are specifically provided under other provisions of this part.
  (2) Attainment dates for nonattainment areas
    (A) The attainment date for an area designated nonattainment with respect to a national primary ambient air quality standard shall be the date by which attainment can be achieved as expeditiously as practicable, but no later than 5 years from the date such area was designated nonattainment under section 7407(d) of this title, except that the Administrator may extend the attainment date to the extent the Administrator determines appropriate, for a period no greater than 10 years from the date of designation as nonattainment, considering the severity of nonattainment and the availability and feasibility of pollution control measures.
    (B) The attainment date for an area designated nonattainment with respect to a secondary national ambient air quality standard shall be the date by which attainment can be achieved as expeditiously as practicable after the date such area was designated nonattainment under section 7407(d) of this title.
    (C) Upon application by any State, the Administrator may extend for 1 additional year (hereinafter referred to as the "Extension Year") the attainment date determined by the Administrator under subparagraph (A) or (B) if—
      (i) the State has complied with all requirements and commitments pertaining to the area in the applicable implementation plan, and
      (ii) in accordance with guidance published by the Administrator, no more than a minimal number of exceedances of the relevant national ambient air quality standard has occurred in the area in the year preceding the Extension Year.
    No more than 2 one-year extensions may be issued under this subparagraph for a single nonattainment area.
    (D) This paragraph shall not apply with respect to nonattainment areas for which attainment dates are specifically provided under other provisions of this part.
(b) Schedule for plan submissions
At the time the Administrator promulgates the designation of an area as nonattainment with respect to a national ambient air quality standard under section 7407(d) of this title, the Administrator shall establish a schedule according to which the State containing such area shall submit a plan or plan revision (including the plan items) meeting the applicable requirements of subsection (c) of this section and section 7410(a)(2) of this title. Such schedule shall at a minimum, include a date or dates, extending no later than 3 years from the date of the

nonattainment designation, for the submission of a plan or plan revision (including the plan items) meeting the applicable requirements of subsection (c) of this section and section 7410(a)(2) of this title.

(c) Nonattainment plan provisions
The plan provisions (including plan items) required to be submitted under this part shall comply with each of the following:

(1) In general
Such plan provisions shall provide for the implementation of all reasonably available control measures as expeditiously as practicable (including such reductions in emissions from existing sources in the area as may be obtained through the adoption, at a minimum, of reasonably available control technology) and shall provide for attainment of the national primary ambient air quality standards.

(2) RFP
Such plan provisions shall require reasonable further progress.

(3) Inventory
Such plan provisions shall include a comprehensive, accurate, current inventory of actual emissions from all sources of the relevant pollutant or pollutants in such area, including such periodic revisions as the Administrator may determine necessary to assure that the requirements of this part are met.

(4) Identification and quantification
Such plan provisions shall expressly identify and quantify the emissions, if any, of any such pollutant or pollutants which will be allowed, in accordance with section 7503(a)(1)(B) of this title, from the construction and operation of major new or modified stationary sources in each such area. The plan shall demonstrate to the satisfaction of the Administrator that the emissions quantified for this purpose will be consistent with the achievement of reasonable further progress and will not interfere with attainment of the applicable national ambient air quality standard by the applicable attainment date.

(5) Permits for new and modified major stationary sources
Such plan provisions shall require permits for the construction and operation of new or modified major stationary sources anywhere in the nonattainment area, in accordance with section 7503 of this title.

(6) Other measures
Such plan provisions shall include enforceable emission limitations, and such other control measures, means or techniques (including economic incentives such as fees, marketable permits, and auctions of emission rights), as well as schedules and timetables for compliance, as may be necessary or appropriate to provide for attainment of such standard in such area by the applicable attainment date specified in this part.

(7) Compliance with section 7410(a)(2)
Such plan provisions shall also meet the applicable provisions of section 7410(a)(2) of this title.

(8) Equivalent techniques
Upon application by any State, the Administrator may allow the use of equivalent modeling, emission inventory, and planning procedures, unless the Administrator determines that the proposed techniques are, in the aggregate, less effective than the methods specified by the Administrator.

(9) Contingency measures
Such plan shall provide for the implementation of specific measures to be undertaken if the area fails to make reasonable further progress, or to attain the national primary ambient air quality standard by the attainment date applicable under this part. Such measures shall be included in the plan revision as contingency measures to take effect in any such case without further action by the State or the Administrator.

(d) Plan revisions required in response to finding of plan inadequacy
Any plan revision for a nonattainment area which is required to be submitted in response to a finding by the Administrator pursuant to section 7410(k)(5) of this title (relating to calls for plan revisions) must correct the plan deficiency (or deficiencies) specified by the Administrator and meet all other applicable plan requirements of section 7410 of this title and this part. The Administrator may reasonably adjust the dates otherwise applicable under such require-

ments to such revision (except for attainment dates that have not yet elapsed), to the extent necessary to achieve a consistent application of such requirements. In order to facilitate submittal by the States of adequate and approvable plans consistent with the applicable requirements of this chapter, the Administrator shall, as appropriate and from time to time, issue written guidelines, interpretations, and information to the States which shall be available to the public, taking into consideration any such guidelines, interpretations, or information provided before November 15, 1990.

(e) Future modification of standard

If the Administrator relaxes a national primary ambient air quality standard after November 15, 1990, the Administrator shall, within 12 months after the relaxation, promulgate requirements applicable to all areas which have not attained that standard as of the date of such relaxation. Such requirements shall provide for controls which are not less stringent than the controls applicable to areas designated nonattainment before such relaxation.

(July 14, 1955, ch. 360, title I, Sec. 172, as added Pub. L. 95-95, title I, Sec. 129(b), Aug. 7, 1977, 91 Stat. 746; amended Pub. L. 95-190, Sec. 14(a)(55), (56), Nov. 16, 1977, 91 Stat. 1402; Pub. L. 101-549, title I, Sec. 102(b), Nov. 15, 1990, 104 Stat. 2412.)

Amendments

1990—Pub. L. 101-549 amended section generally, substituting present provisions for provisions which related to: in subsec. (a), expeditious attainment of national ambient air quality standards; in subsec. (b), requisite provisions of plan; and in subsec. (c), attainment of applicable standard not later than July 1, 1987.

1977—Subsec. (b)(4). Pub. L. 95-190, Sec. 14(a)(55), substituted "subsection (a) of this section" for "paragraph (1)".

Subsec. (c). Pub. L. 95-190, Sec. 14(a)(56), substituted "December 31" for "July 1".

Nonattainment Areas

Section 129(a) of Pub. L. 95-95, as amended by Pub. L. 95-190, Sec. 14(b)(2), (3), Nov. 16, 1977, 91 Stat. 1404, provided that:

"(1) Before July 1, 1979, the interpretative regulation of the Administrator of the Environmental Protection Agency published in 41 Federal Register 55524-30, December 21, 1976, as may be modified by rule of the Administrator, shall apply except that the baseline to be used for determination of appropriate emission offsets under such regulation shall be the applicable implementation plan of the State in effect at the time of application for a permit by a proposed major stationary source (within the meaning of section 302 of the Clean Air Act) [section 7602 of this title].

(2) Before July 1, 1979, the requirements of the regulation referred to in paragraph (1) shall be waived by the Administrator with respect to any pollutant if he determines that the State has—

(A) an inventory of emissions of the applicable pollutant for each nonattainment area (as defined in section 171 of the Clean Air Act [section 7501 of this title]) that identifies the type, quantity, and source of such pollutant so as to provide information sufficient to demonstrate that the requirements of subparagraph (C) are being met;

(B) an enforceable permit program which—

(i) requires new or modified major stationary sources to meet emission limitations at least as stringent as required under the permit requirements referred to in paragraphs (2) and (3) of section 173 of the Clean Air Act [section 7503 of this title] (relating to lowest achievable emission rate and compliance by other sources) and which assures compliance with the annual reduction requirements of subparagraph (C); and

(ii) requires existing sources to achieve such reduction in emissions in the area as may be obtained through the adoption, at a minimum, of reasonably available control technology, and

(C) a program which requires reductions in total allowable emissions in the area prior to July 1, 1979, so as to provide for the same level of emission reduction as would result from the application of the regulation referred to in paragraph (1).

The Administrator shall terminate such waiver if in his judgment the reduction in emissions actually being attained is less than the reduction on which the waiver was conditioned pursuant to subparagraph (C), or if the Administrator determines that the State is no longer in compliance with any requirement of this paragraph. Upon application by the State, the Administrator may reinstate a waiver terminated under the preceding sentence if he is satisfied that such State is in compliance with all requirements of this subsection.

(3) Operating permits may be issued to those applicants who were properly granted construction permits, in accordance with the law and applicable regulations in effect at the time granted, for construction of a new or modified source in areas exceeding national primary air quality standards on or before the date of the enactment of this Act [Aug. 7, 1977] if such construction permits were granted prior to the date of the enactment of this Act and the person issued any such permit is able to demonstrate that the emissions from the source will be within the limitations set forth in such construction permit."

State Implementation Plan Revision

Section 129(c) of Pub. L. 95-95, as amended by Pub. L. 95-190, Sec. 14(b)(4), Nov. 16, 1977, 91 Stat. 1405, provided that: "Notwithstanding the requirements of section 406(d)(2) [set out as an Effective Date of 1977 Amendment note under section 7401 of this title] (relating to date required for submission of certain implementation plan revisions), for purposes of section 110(a)(2) of the Clean Air Act [section 7410(a)(2) of this title] each State in which there is any nonattainment area (as defined in part D of title I of the Clean Air Act) [this part] shall adopt and submit an implementation plan revision which meets the requirements of section 110(a)(2)(I) [section 7410(a)(2)(I) of this title] and part D of title I of the Clean Air Act [this part] not later than January 1, 1979. In the case of any State for which a plan revision adopted and submitted before such date has made the demonstration required under section 172(a)(2) of the Clean Air Act [subsec. (a)(2) of this section] (respecting impossibility of attainment before 1983), such State shall adopt and submit to the Administrator a plan revision before July 1, 1982, which meets the requirements of section 172(b) and (c) of such Act [subsecs. (b) and (c) of this section]."

Section Referred to in Other Sections

This section is referred to in sections 7410, 7429, 7503, 7509, 7511, 7511a, 7512, 7512a, 7513, 7513a, 7607 of this title.

PERMIT REQUIREMENTS

42 USC 7503

(a) In general

The permit program required by section 7502(b)(6)[1] of this title shall provide that permits to construct and operate may be issued if—

(1) in accordance with regulations issued by the Administrator for the determination of baseline emissions in a manner consistent with the assumptions underlying the applicable implementation plan approved under section 7410 of this title and this part, the permitting agency determines that—

(A) by the time the source is to commence operation, sufficient offsetting emissions reductions have been obtained, such that total allowable emissions from existing sources in the region, from new or modified sources which are not major emitting facilities, and from the proposed source will be sufficiently less than total emissions from existing sources (as determined in accordance with the regulations under this paragraph) prior to the application for such permit to construct or modify so as to represent (when considered together with the plan provisions required under section 7502 of this title) reasonable further progress (as defined in section 7501 of this title); or

(B) in the case of a new or modified major stationary source which is located in a zone (within the nonattainment area) identified by the Administrator, in consultation with the Secretary of Housing and Urban Development, as a zone to which economic development should be targeted, that emissions of such pollutant resulting from the proposed new or modified major stationary source will not cause or contribute to emissions levels which exceed the allowance permitted for such pollutant for such area from new or modified major stationary sources under section 7502(c) of this title;

---

[1]See References in Text note below.

(2) the proposed source is required to comply with the lowest achievable emission rate;
(3) the owner or operator of the proposed new or modified source has demonstrated that all major stationary sources owned or operated by such person (or by any entity controlling, controlled by, or under common control with such person) in such State are subject to emission limitations and are in compliance, or on a schedule for compliance, with all applicable emission limitations and standards under this chapter; and[2]
(4) the Administrator has not determined that the applicable implementation plan is not being adequately implemented for the nonattainment area in which the proposed source is to be constructed or modified in accordance with the requirements of this part; and
(5) an analysis of alternative sites, sizes, production processes, and environmental control techniques for such proposed source demonstrates that benefits of the proposed source significantly outweigh the environmental and social costs imposed as a result of its location, construction, or modification.

Any emission reductions required as a precondition of the issuance of a permit under paragraph (1) shall be federally enforceable before such permit may be issued.

(b) Prohibition on use of old growth allowances
Any growth allowance included in an applicable implementation plan to meet the requirements of section 7502(b)(5) of this title (as in effect immediately before November 15, 1990) shall not be valid for use in any area that received or receives a notice under section 7410(a)(2)(H)(ii) of this title (as in effect immediately before November 15, 1990) or under section 7410(k)(1) of this title that its applicable implementation plan containing such allowance is substantially inadequate.

(c) Offsets
(1) The owner or operator of a new or modified major stationary source may comply with any offset requirement in effect under this part for increased emissions of any air pollutant only by obtaining emission reductions of such air pollutant from the same source or other sources in the same nonattainment area, except that the State may allow the owner or operator of a source to obtain such emission reductions in another nonattainment area if (A) the other area has an equal or higher nonattainment classification than the area in which the source is located and (B) emissions from such other area contribute to a violation of the national ambient air quality standard in the nonattainment area in which the source is located. Such emission reductions shall be, by the time a new or modified source commences operation, in effect and enforceable and shall assure that the total tonnage of increased emissions of the air pollutant from the new or modified source shall be offset by an equal or greater reduction, as applicable, in the actual emissions of such air pollutant from the same or other sources in the area.
(2) Emission reductions otherwise required by this chapter shall not be creditable as emissions reductions for purposes of any such offset requirement. Incidental emission reductions which are not otherwise required by this chapter shall be creditable as emission reductions for such purposes if such emission reductions meet the requirements of paragraph (1).

(d) Control technology information
The State shall provide that control technology information from permits issued under this section will be promptly submitted to the Administrator for purposes of making such information available through the RACT/BACT/LAER clearinghouse to other States and to the general public.

(e) Rocket engines or motors
The permitting authority of a State shall allow a source to offset by alternative or innovative means emission increases from rocket engine and motor firing, and cleaning related to such firing, at an existing or modified major source that tests rocket engines or motors under the following conditions:
(1) Any modification proposed is solely for the purpose of expanding the testing of rocket engines or motors at an existing source that is permitted to test such engines on November 15, 1990.

---

[2] So in original. The word "and" probably should not appear.

162 / Environmental Statutes

(2) The source demonstrates to the satisfaction of the permitting authority of the State that it has used all reasonable means to obtain and utilize offsets, as determined on an annual basis, for the emissions increases beyond allowable levels, that all available offsets are being used, and that sufficient offsets are not available to the source.

(3) The source has obtained a written finding from the Department of Defense, Department of Transportation, National Aeronautics and Space Administration or other appropriate Federal agency, that the testing of rocket motors or engines at the facility is required for a program essential to the national security.

(4) The source will comply with an alternative measure, imposed by the permitting authority, designed to offset any emission increases beyond permitted levels not directly offset by the source. In lieu of imposing any alternative offset measures, the permitting authority may impose an emissions fee to be paid to such authority of a State which shall be an amount no greater than 1.5 times the average cost of stationary source control measures adopted in that area during the previous 3 years. The permitting authority shall utilize the fees in a manner that maximizes the emissions reductions in that area.

(July 14, 1955, ch. 360, title I, Sec. 173, as added Pub. L. 95-95, title I, Sec. 129(b), Aug. 7, 1977, 91 Stat. 748; amended Pub. L. 95-190, Sec. 14(a)(57), (58), Nov. 16, 1977, 91 Stat. 1403; Pub. L. 101-549, title I, Sec. 102(c), Nov. 15, 1990, 104 Stat. 2415.)

References in Text

Section 7502(b) of this title, referred to in subsec. (a), was amended generally by Pub. L. 101-549, title I, Sec. 102(b), Nov. 15, 1990, 104 Stat. 2412, and, as so amended, does not contain a par. (6). See section 7502(c)(5) of this title.

Amendments

1990—Pub. L. 101-549, Sec. 102(c)(1), made technical amendment to section catchline.

Pub. L. 101-549, Sec. 102(c)(2), (8), designated existing provisions as subsec. (a), inserted heading, and substituted "(1) shall be federally enforceable" for "(1)(A) shall be legally binding" in last sentence.

Subsec. (a)(1). Pub. L. 101-549, Sec. 102(c)(3), inserted at beginning "in accordance with regulations issued by the Administrator for the determination of baseline emissions in a manner consistent with the assumptions underlying the applicable implementation plan approved under section 7410 of this title and this part,".

Subsec. (a)(1)(A). Pub. L. 101-549, Sec. 102(c)(4), inserted "sufficient offsetting emissions reductions have been obtained, such that" after "to commence operation," and substituted "(as determined in accordance with the regulations under this paragraph)" for "allowed under the applicable implementation plan".

Subsec. (a)(1)(B). Pub. L. 101-549, Sec. 102(c)(5), inserted at beginning "in the case of a new or modified major stationary source which is located in a zone (within the nonattainment area) identified by the Administrator, in consultation with the Secretary of Housing and Urban Development, as a zone to which economic development should be targeted," and substituted "7502(c)" for "7502(b)".

Subsec. (a)(4). Pub. L. 101-549, Sec. 102(c)(6), inserted at beginning "the Administrator has not determined that", substituted "not being adequately implemented" for "being carried out", and substituted "; and" for period at end.

Subsec. (a)(5). Pub. L. 101-549, Sec. 102(c)(7), added par. (5).

Subsec. (b). Pub. L. 101-549, Sec. 102(c)(9), added subsec. (b).

Subsecs. (c) to (e). Pub. L. 101-549, Sec. 102(c)(10), added subsecs. (c) to (e).

1977—Par. (1)(A). Pub. L. 95-190, Sec. 14(a)(57), inserted "or modified" after "from new" and "applicable" before "implementation plan", and substituted "source" for "facility" wherever appearing.

Par. (4). Pub. L. 95-190, Sec. 14(a)(58), added par. (4).

Failure To Attain National Primary Ambient Air Quality Standards Under Clean Air Act

Pub. L. 100-202, Sec. 101(f) [title II], Dec. 22, 1987, 101 Stat. 1329-187, 1329-199, provided that: "No restriction or prohibition on construction, permitting, or funding under sections 110(a)(2)(I), 173(4),

176(a), 176(b), or 316 of the Clean Air Act [sections 7410(a)(2)(I), 7503(4), 7506(a), (b), 7616 of this title] shall be imposed or take effect during the period prior to August 31, 1988, by reason of (1) the failure of any nonattainment area to attain the national primary ambient air quality standard under the Clean Air Act [this chapter] for photochemical oxidants (ozone) or carbon monoxide (or both) by December 31, 1987, (2) the failure of any State to adopt and submit to the Administrator of the Environmental Protection Agency an implementation plan that meets the requirements of part D of title I of such Act [this part] and provides for attainment of such standards by December 31, 1987, (3) the failure of any State or designated local government to implement the applicable implementation plan, or (4) any combination of the foregoing. During such period and consistent with the preceding sentence, the issuance of a permit (including required offsets) under section 173 of such Act [this section] for the construction or modification of a source in a nonattainment area shall not be denied solely or partially by reason of the reference contained in section 171(l) of such Act [section 7501(1) of this title] to the applicable date established in section 172(a) [section 7502(a) of this title]. This subsection [probably means the first 3 sentences of this note] shall not apply to any restriction or prohibition in effect under sections 110(a)(2)(I), 173(4), 176(a), 176(b), or 316 of such Act prior to the enactment of this section [Dec. 22, 1987]. Prior to August 31, 1988, the Administrator of the Environmental Protection Agency shall evaluate air quality data and make determinations with respect to which areas throughout the nation have attained, or failed to attain, either or both of the national primary ambient air quality standards referred to in subsection (a) [probably means the first 3 sentences of this note] and shall take appropriate steps to designate those areas failing to attain either or both of such standards as nonattainment areas within the meaning of part D of title I of the Clean Air Act."

Section Referred to in Other Sections

This section is referred to in sections 7492, 7502, 7509, 7511a, 7513a of this title.

PLANNING PROCEDURES

42 USC 7504

(a) In general

For any ozone, carbon monoxide, or PM-10 nonattainment area, the State containing such area and elected officials of affected local governments shall, before the date required for submittal of the inventory described under sections 7511a(a)(1) and 7512a(a)(1) of this title, jointly review and update as necessary the planning procedures adopted pursuant to this subsection as in effect immediately before November 15, 1990, or develop new planning procedures pursuant to this subsection, as appropriate. In preparing such procedures the State and local elected officials shall determine which elements of a revised implementation plan will be developed, adopted, and implemented (through means including enforcement) by the State and which by local governments or regional agencies, or any combination of local governments, regional agencies, or the State. The implementation plan required by this part shall be prepared by an organization certified by the State, in consultation with elected officials of local governments and in accordance with the determination under the second sentence of this subsection. Such organization shall include elected officials of local governments in the affected area, and representatives of the State air quality planning agency, the State transportation planning agency, the metropolitan planning organization designated to conduct the continuing, cooperative and comprehensive transportation planning process for the area under section 134 of title 23, the organization responsible for the air quality maintenance planning process under regulations implementing this chapter, and any other organization with responsibilities for developing, submitting, or implementing the plan required by this part. Such organization may be one that carried out these functions before November 15, 1990.

(b) Coordination

The preparation of implementation plan provisions and subsequent plan revisions under the continuing transportation-air quality planning process described in section 7408(e) of this title shall be coordinated with the continuing, cooperative and comprehensive transportation planning process required under section 134 of title 23, and such planning processes shall take into account the requirements of this part.

(c) Joint planning
In the case of a nonattainment area that is included within more than one State, the affected States may jointly, through interstate compact or otherwise, undertake and implement all or part of the planning procedures described in this section.

(July 14, 1955, ch. 360, title I, Sec. 174, as added Pub. L. 95-95, title I, Sec. 129(b), Aug. 7, 1977, 91 Stat. 748; amended Pub. L. 101-549, title I, Sec. 102(d), Nov. 15, 1990, 104 Stat. 2417.)

Amendments

1990—Pub. L. 101-549 amended section generally, substituting present provisions for provisions which related to: in subsec. (a), preparation of implementation plan by designated organization; and in subsec. (b), coordination of plan preparation.

Section Referred to in Other Sections

This section is referred to in sections 7505, 7511a of this title.

ENVIRONMENTAL PROTECTION AGENCY GRANTS

42 USC 7505

(a) Plan revision development costs
The Administrator shall make grants to any organization of local elected officials with transportation or air quality maintenance planning responsibilities recognized by the State under section 7504(a) of this title for payment of the reasonable costs of developing a plan revision under this part.

(b) Uses of grant funds
The amount granted to any organization under subsection (a) of this section shall be 100 percent of any additional costs of developing a plan revision under this part for the first two fiscal years following receipt of the grant under this paragraph, and shall supplement any funds available under Federal law to such organization for transportation or air quality maintenance planning. Grants under this section shall not be used for construction.

(July 14, 1955, ch. 360, title I, Sec. 175, as added Pub. L. 95-95, title I, Sec. 129(b), Aug. 7, 1977, 91 Stat. 749.)

Section Referred to in Other Sections

This section is referred to in section 7626 of this title.

MAINTENANCE PLANS

42 USC 7505a

(a) Plan revision
Each State which submits a request under section 7407(d) of this title for redesignation of a nonattainment area for any air pollutant as an area which has attained the national primary ambient air quality standard for that air pollutant shall also submit a revision of the applicable State implementation plan to provide for the maintenance of the national primary ambient air quality standard for such air pollutant in the area concerned for at least 10 years after the redesignation. The plan shall contain such additional measures, if any, as may be necessary to ensure such maintenance.

(b) Subsequent plan revisions
8 years after redesignation of any area as an attainment area under section 7407(d) of this title, the State shall submit to the Administrator an additional revision of the applicable State implementation plan for maintaining the national primary ambient air quality standard for 10 years after the expiration of the 10-year period referred to in subsection (a) of this section.

(c) Nonattainment requirements applicable pending plan approval
Until such plan revision is approved and an area is redesignated as attainment for any area designated as a nonattainment area, the requirements of this part shall continue in force and effect with respect to such area.

(d) Contingency provisions

Each plan revision submitted under this section shall contain such contingency provisions as the Administrator deems necessary to assure that the State will promptly correct any violation of the standard which occurs after the redesignation of the area as an attainment area. Such provisions shall include a requirement that the State will implement all measures with respect to the control of the air pollutant concerned which were contained in the State implementation plan for the area before redesignation of the area as an attainment area. The failure of any area redesignated as an attainment area to maintain the national ambient air quality standard concerned shall not result in a requirement that the State revise its State implementation plan unless the Administrator, in the Administrator's discretion, requires the State to submit a revised State implementation plan.

(July 14, 1955, ch. 360, title I, Sec. 175A, as added Pub. L. 101-549, title I, Sec. 102(e), Nov. 15, 1990, 104 Stat. 2418.)

Section Referred to in Other Sections

This section is referred to in sections 7407, 7506 of this title; title 23 section 109.

LIMITATIONS ON CERTAIN FEDERAL ASSISTANCE

42 USC 7506

(a), (b) Repealed. Pub. L. 101-549, title I, Sec. 110(4), Nov. 15, 1990, 104 Stat. 2470

(c) Activities not conforming to approved or promulgated plans

(1) No department, agency, or instrumentality of the Federal Government shall engage in, support in any way or provide financial assistance for, license or permit, or approve, any activity which does not conform to an implementation plan after it has been approved or promulgated under section 7410 of this title. No metropolitan planning organization designated under section 134 of title 23, shall give its approval to any project, program, or plan which does not conform to an implementation plan approved or promulgated under section 7410 of this title. The assurance of conformity to such an implementation plan shall be an affirmative responsibility of the head of such department, agency, or instrumentality. Conformity to an implementation plan means—

(A) conformity to an implementation plan's purpose of eliminating or reducing the severity and number of violations of the national ambient air quality standards and achieving expeditious attainment of such standards; and

(B) that such activities will not—
  (i) cause or contribute to any new violation of any standard in any area;
  (ii) increase the frequency or severity of any existing violation of any standard in any area; or
  (iii) delay timely attainment of any standard or any required interim emission reductions or other milestones in any area.

The determination of conformity shall be based on the most recent estimates of emissions, and such estimates shall be determined from the most recent population, employment, travel and congestion estimates as determined by the metropolitan planning organization or other agency authorized to make such estimates.

(2) Any transportation plan or program developed pursuant to title 23 or chapter 53 of title 49 shall implement the transportation provisions of any applicable implementation plan approved under this chapter applicable to all or part of the area covered by such transportation plan or program. No Federal agency may approve, accept or fund any transportation plan, program or project unless such plan, program or project has been found to conform to any applicable implementation plan in effect under this chapter. In particular—

(A) no transportation plan or transportation improvement program may be adopted by a metropolitan planning organization designated under title 23 or chapter 53 of title 49, or be found to be in conformity by a metropolitan planning organization until a final determination has been made that emissions expected from implementation of such plans and programs are consistent with estimates of emissions from motor vehicles and necessary emissions reductions contained in the applicable implementation plan, and that the plan or program will conform to the requirements of paragraph (1)(B);

(B) no metropolitan planning organization or other recipient of funds under title 23 or chapter 53 of title 49 shall adopt or approve a transportation improvement program of projects until it determines that such program provides for timely implementation of transportation control measures consistent with schedules included in the applicable implementation plan;

(C) a transportation project may be adopted or approved by a metropolitan planning organization or any recipient of funds designated under title 23 or chapter 53 of title 49, or found in conformity by a metropolitan planning organization or approved, accepted, or funded by the Department of Transportation only if it meets either the requirements of subparagraph (D) or the following requirements—
  (i) such a project comes from a conforming plan and program;
  (ii) the design concept and scope of such project have not changed significantly since the conformity finding regarding the plan and program from which the project derived; and
  (iii) the design concept and scope of such project at the time of the conformity determination for the program was adequate to determine emissions.

(D) Any project not referred to in subparagraph (C) shall be treated as conforming to the applicable implementation plan only if it is demonstrated that the projected emissions from such project, when considered together with emissions projected for the conforming transportation plans and programs within the nonattainment area, do not cause such plans and programs to exceed the emission reduction projections and schedules assigned to such plans and programs in the applicable implementation plan.

(3) Until such time as the implementation plan revision referred to in paragraph (4)(C) is approved, conformity of such plans, programs, and projects will be demonstrated if—
  (A) the transportation plans and programs—
    (i) are consistent with the most recent estimates of mobile source emissions;
    (ii) provide for the expeditious implementation of transportation control measures in the applicable implementation plan; and
    (iii) with respect to ozone and carbon monoxide nonattainment areas, contribute to annual emissions reductions consistent with sections 7511a(b)(1) and 7512a(a)(7) of this title; and
  (B) the transportation projects—
    (i) come from a conforming transportation plan and program as defined in subparagraph (A) or for 12 months after November 15, 1990, from a transportation program found to conform within 3 years prior to November 15, 1990; and
    (ii) in carbon monoxide nonattainment areas, eliminate or reduce the severity and number of violations of the carbon monoxide standards in the area substantially affected by the project.

With regard to subparagraph (B)(ii), such determination may be made as part of either the conformity determination for the transportation program or for the individual project taken as a whole during the environmental review phase of project development.

(4) (A) No later than one year after November 15, 1990, the Administrator shall promulgate criteria and procedures for determining conformity (except in the case of transportation plans, programs, and projects) of, and for keeping the Administrator informed about, the activities referred to in paragraph (1). No later than one year after November 15, 1990, the Administrator, with the concurrence of the Secretary of Transportation, shall promulgate criteria and procedures for demonstrating and assuring conformity in the case of transportation plans, programs, and projects. A suit may be brought against the Administrator and the Secretary of Transportation under section 7604 of this title to compel promulgation of such criteria and procedures and the Federal district court shall have jurisdiction to order such promulgation.

(B) The procedures and criteria shall, at a minimum—
  (i) address the consultation procedures to be undertaken by metropolitan planning organizations and the Secretary of Transportation with State and local air quality agencies and State departments of transportation before such organizations and the Secretary make conformity determinations;
  (ii) address the appropriate frequency for making conformity determinations, but in no case shall such determinations for transportation plans and programs be less frequent than every three years; and

(iii) address how conformity determinations will be made with respect to maintenance plans.
(C) Such procedures shall also include a requirement that each State shall submit to the Administrator and the Secretary of Transportation within 24 months of November 15, 1990, a revision to its implementation plan that includes criteria and procedures for assessing the conformity of any plan, program, or project subject to the conformity requirements of this subsection.
(D) Compliance with the rules of the Administrator for determining the conformity of transportation plans, programs, and projects funded or approved under title 23 or chapter 53 of title 49 to State or Federal implementation plans shall not be required for traffic signal synchronization projects prior to the funding, approval or implementation of such projects. The supporting regional emissions analysis for any conformity determination made with respect to a transportation plan, program, or project shall consider the effect on emissions of any such project funded, approved, or implemented prior to the conformity determination.
(5) Applicability.—This subsection shall apply only with respect to—
(A) a nonattainment area and each pollutant for which the area is designated as a nonattainment area; and
(B) an area that was designated as a nonattainment area but that was later redesignated by the Administrator as an attainment area and that is required to develop a maintenance plan under section 7505a of this title with respect to the specific pollutant for which the area was designated nonattainment.
(6) Notwithstanding paragraph 5, this subsection shall not apply with respect to an area designated nonattainment under section 107(d)(1) [42 USC 7407 (d)(1)] until 1 year after that area is first designated nonattainment for a specific national ambient air quality standard. This paragraph only applies with respect to the national ambient air quality standard for which an area is newly designated nonattainment and does not affect the area's requirements with respect to all other national ambient air quality standards for which the area is designated nonattainment or has been redesignated from nonattainment to attainment with a maintenance plan pursuant to section 175(A) [42 USC 7505a] (including any pre-existing national ambient air quality standard for a pollutant for which a new or revised standard has been issued).
(d) Priority of achieving and maintaining national primary ambient air quality standards
Each department, agency, or instrumentality of the Federal Government having authority to conduct or support any program with air-quality related transportation consequences shall give priority in the exercise of such authority, consistent with statutory requirements for allocation among States or other jurisdictions, to the implementation of those portions of plans prepared under this section to achieve and maintain the national primary ambient air-quality standard. This paragraph extends to, but is not limited to, authority exercised under chapter 53 of title 49, title 23, and the Housing and Urban Development Act.

(July 14, 1955, ch. 360, title I, Sec. 176, as added Pub. L. 95-95, title I, Sec. 129(b), Aug. 7, 1977, 91 Stat. 749; amended Pub. L. 95-190, Sec. 14(a)(59), Nov. 16, 1977, 91 Stat. 1403; Pub. L. 101-549, title I, Secs. 101(f), 110(4), Nov. 15, 1990, 104 Stat. 2409, 2470; Pub. L. 104-59, title III, Sec. 305(b), Nov. 28, 1995, 109 Stat. 580; Pub. L. 104-260, Sec. 1, Oct. 9, 1996, 110 Stat. 3175.)

References in Text

The Housing and Urban Development Act, referred to in subsec. (d), may be the name for a series of acts sharing the same name but enacted in different years by Pub. L. 89-117, Aug. 10, 1965, 79 Stat. 451; Pub. L. 90-448, Aug. 1, 1968, 82 Stat. 476; Pub. L. 91-152, Dec. 24, 1969, 83 Stat. 379; and Pub. L. 91-609, Dec. 31, 1970, 84 Stat. 1770, respectively. For complete classification of these Acts to the Code, see Short Title notes set out under section 1701 of Title 12, Banks and Banking, and Tables.

Codification

In subsecs. (c)(2) and (d), "chapter 53 of title 49" substituted for "the Urban Mass Transportation Act [49 App. U.S.C. 1601 et seq.]" and in subsec. (c)(4)(D) substituted for "Federal Transit Act" on authority of Pub. L. 103-272, Sec. 6(b), July 5, 1994, 108 Stat. 1378 (the first section of which enacted subtitles II, III, and V to X of Title 49, Transportation), and of Pub. L. 102-240, title III,

Sec. 3003(b), Dec. 18, 1991, 105 Stat. 2088, which provided that references in laws to the Urban Mass Transportation Act of 1964 be deemed to be references to the Federal Transit Act.

Amendments

2000—Subsec. (a)(6). Pub L. 106-377 added par. (6).

1996—Subsec. (c)(4)(D). Pub. L. 104-260 added subpar. (D).

1995—Subsec. (c)(5). Pub. L. 104-59 added par. (5).

1990—Subsecs. (a), (b). Pub. L. 101-549, Sec. 110(4), struck out subsec. (a) which related to approval of projects or award of grants, and subsec. (b) which related to implementation of approved or promulgated plans.

Subsec. (c). Pub. L. 101-549, Sec. 101(f), designated existing provisions as par. (1), struck out "(1)", "(2)", "(3)", and "(4)" before "engage in", "support in", "license or", and "approve, any", respectively, substituted "conform to an implementation plan after it" for "conform to a plan after it", "conform to an implementation plan approved" for "conform to a plan approved", and "conformity to such an implementation plan shall" for "conformity to such a plan shall", inserted "Conformity to an implementation plan means—" followed immediately by subpars. (A) and (B) and closing provisions relating to determination of conformity being based on recent estimates of emissions and the determination of such estimates, and added pars. (2) to (4).

1977—Subsec. (a)(1). Pub. L. 95-190 inserted "national" before "primary".

INTERSTATE TRANSPORT COMMISSIONS

42 USC 7506a

(a) Authority to establish interstate transport regions

Whenever, on the Administrator's own motion or by petition from the Governor of any State, the Administrator has reason to believe that the interstate transport of air pollutants from one or more States contributes significantly to a violation of a national ambient air quality standard in one or more other States, the Administrator may establish, by rule, a transport region for such pollutant that includes such States. The Administrator, on the Administrator's own motion or upon petition from the Governor of any State, or upon the recommendation of a transport commission established under subsection (b) of this section, may—

(1) add any State or portion of a State to any region established under this subsection whenever the Administrator has reason to believe that the interstate transport of air pollutants from such State significantly contributes to a violation of the standard in the transport region, or

(2) remove any State or portion of a State from the region whenever the Administrator has reason to believe that the control of emissions in that State or portion of the State pursuant to this section will not significantly contribute to the attainment of the standard in any area in the region.

The Administrator shall approve or disapprove any such petition or recommendation within 18 months of its receipt. The Administrator shall establish appropriate proceedings for public participation regarding such petitions and motions, including notice and comment.

(b) Transport commissions

(1) Establishment

Whenever the Administrator establishes a transport region under subsection (a) of this section, the Administrator shall establish a transport commission comprised of (at a minimum) each of the following members:

(A) The Governor of each State in the region or the designee of each such Governor.

(B) The Administrator or the Administrator's designee.

(C) The Regional Administrator (or the Administrator's designee) for each Regional Office for each Environmental Protection Agency Region affected by the transport region concerned.

(D) An air pollution control official representing each State in the region, appointed by the Governor.

Decisions of, and recommendations and requests to, the Administrator by each transport commission may be made only by a majority vote of all members other than the Administrator and the Regional Administrators (or designees thereof).
(2) Recommendations
The transport commission shall assess the degree of interstate transport of the pollutant or precursors to the pollutant throughout the transport region, assess strategies for mitigating the interstate pollution, and recommend to the Administrator such measures as the Commission determines to be necessary to ensure that the plans for the relevant States meet the requirements of section 7410(a)(2)(D) of this title. Such commission shall not be subject to the provisions of the Federal Advisory Committee Act (5 U.S.C. App.).
(c) Commission requests
A transport commission established under subsection (b) of this section may request the Administrator to issue a finding under section 7410(k)(5) of this title that the implementation plan for one or more of the States in the transport region is substantially inadequate to meet the requirements of section 7410(a)(2)(D) of this title. The Administrator shall approve, disapprove, or partially approve and partially disapprove such a request within 18 months of its receipt and, to the extent the Administrator approves such request, issue the finding under section 7410(k)(5) of this title at the time of such approval. In acting on such request, the Administrator shall provide an opportunity for public participation and shall address each specific recommendation made by the commission. Approval or disapproval of such a request shall constitute final agency action within the meaning of section 7607(b) of this title.

(July 14, 1955, ch. 360, title I, Sec. 176A, as added Pub. L. 101-549, title I, Sec. 102(f)(1), Nov. 15, 1990, 104 Stat. 2419.)

References in Text

The Federal Advisory Committee Act, referred to in subsec. (b)(2), is Pub. L. 92-463, Oct. 6, 1972, 86 Stat. 770, as amended, which is set out in the Appendix to Title 5, Government Organization and Employees.

Section Referred to in Other Sections

This section is referred to in sections 7406, 7410, 7511c of this title.

NEW MOTOR VEHICLE EMISSION STANDARDS IN NONATTAINMENT AREAS

42 USC 7507

Notwithstanding section 7543(a) of this title, any State which has plan provisions approved under this part may adopt and enforce for any model year standards relating to control of emissions from new motor vehicles or new motor vehicle engines and take such other actions as are referred to in section 7543(a) of this title respecting such vehicles if—
   (1) such standards are identical to the California standards for which a waiver has been granted for such model year, and
   (2) California and such State adopt such standards at least two years before commencement of such model year (as determined by regulations of the Administrator).

Nothing in this section or in subchapter II of this chapter shall be construed as authorizing any such State to prohibit or limit, directly or indirectly, the manufacture or sale of a new motor vehicle or motor vehicle engine that is certified in California as meeting California standards, or to take any action of any kind to create, or have the effect of creating, a motor vehicle or motor vehicle engine different than a motor vehicle or engine certified in California under California standards (a "third vehicle") or otherwise create such a "third vehicle".

(July 14, 1955, ch. 360, title I, Sec. 177, as added Pub. L. 95-95, title I, Sec. 129(b), Aug. 7, 1977, 91 Stat. 750; amended Pub. L. 101-549, title II, Sec. 232, Nov. 15, 1990, 104 Stat. 2529.)

Amendments

1990—Pub. L. 101-549 added sentence at end prohibiting States from limiting or prohibiting sale or manufacture of new vehicles or engines certified in California as having met California standards and from taking any actions where effect of those actions would be to create a "third vehicle".

Section Referred to in Other Sections

This section is referred to in section 7589 of this title.

GUIDANCE DOCUMENTS

42 USC 7508

The Administrator shall issue guidance documents under section 7408 of this title for purposes of assisting States in implementing requirements of this part respecting the lowest achievable emission rate. Such a document shall be published not later than nine months after August 7, 1977, and shall be revised at least every two years thereafter.

(July 14, 1955, ch. 360, title I, Sec. 178, as added Pub. L. 95-95, title I, Sec. 129(b), Aug. 7, 1977, 91 Stat. 750.)

SANCTIONS AND CONSEQUENCES OF FAILURE TO ATTAIN

42 USC 7509

(a) State failure
For any implementation plan or plan revision required under this part (or required in response to a finding of substantial inadequacy as described in section 7410(k)(5) of this title), if the Administrator—
   (1) finds that a State has failed, for an area designated nonattainment under section 7407(d) of this title, to submit a plan, or to submit 1 or more of the elements (as determined by the Administrator) required by the provisions of this chapter applicable to such an area, or has failed to make a submission for such an area that satisfies the minimum criteria established in relation to any such element under section 7410(k) of this title,
   (2) disapproves a submission under section 7410(k) of this title, for an area designated nonattainment under section 7407 of this title, based on the submission's failure to meet one or more of the elements required by the provisions of this chapter applicable to such an area,
   (3) (A) determines that a State has failed to make any submission as may be required under this chapter, other than one described under paragraph (1) or (2), including an adequate maintenance plan, or has failed to make any submission, as may be required under this chapter, other than one described under paragraph (1) or (2), that satisfies the minimum criteria established in relation to such submission under section 7410(k)(1)(A) of this title, or
   (B) disapproves in whole or in part a submission described under subparagraph (A), or
   (4) finds that any requirement of an approved plan (or approved part of a plan) is not being implemented, unless such deficiency has been corrected within 18 months after the finding, disapproval, or determination referred to in paragraphs (1), (2), (3), and (4), one of the sanctions referred to in subsection (b) of this section shall apply, as selected by the Administrator, until the Administrator determines that the State has come into compliance, except that if the Administrator finds a lack of good faith, sanctions under both paragraph (1) and paragraph (2) of subsection (b) of this section shall apply until the Administrator determines that the State has come into compliance. If the Administrator has selected one of such sanctions and the deficiency has not been corrected within 6 months thereafter, sanctions under both paragraph (1) and paragraph (2) of subsection (b) of this section shall apply until the Administrator determines that the State has come into compliance. In addition to any other sanction applicable as provided in this section, the Administrator may withhold all or part of the grants for support of air pollution planning and control programs that the Administrator may award under section 7405 of this title.

(b) Sanctions
The sanctions available to the Administrator as provided in subsection (a) of this section are as follows:
   (1) Highway sanctions
      (A) The Administrator may impose a prohibition, applicable to a nonattainment area, on the approval by the Secretary of Transportation of any projects or the awarding by the

Secretary of any grants, under title 23 other than projects or grants for safety where the Secretary determines, based on accident or other appropriate data submitted by the State, that the principal purpose of the project is an improvement in safety to resolve a demonstrated safety problem and likely will result in a significant reduction in, or avoidance of, accidents. Such prohibition shall become effective upon the selection by the Administrator of this sanction.

    (B) In addition to safety, projects or grants that may be approved by the Secretary, notwithstanding the prohibition in subparagraph (A), are the following—
        (i) capital programs for public transit;
        (ii) construction or restriction of certain roads or lanes solely for the use of passenger buses or high occupancy vehicles;
        (iii) planning for requirements for employers to reduce employee work-trip-related vehicle emissions;
        (iv) highway ramp metering, traffic signalization, and related programs that improve traffic flow and achieve a net emission reduction;
        (v) fringe and transportation corridor parking facilities serving multiple occupancy vehicle programs or transit operations;
        (vi) programs to limit or restrict vehicle use in downtown areas or other areas of emission concentration particularly during periods of peak use, through road use charges, tolls, parking surcharges, or other pricing mechanisms, vehicle restricted zones or periods, or vehicle registration programs;
        (vii) programs for breakdown and accident scene management, nonrecurring congestion, and vehicle information systems, to reduce congestion and emissions; and
        (viii) such other transportation-related programs as the Administrator, in consultation with the Secretary of Transportation, finds would improve air quality and would not encourage single occupancy vehicle capacity.

In considering such measures, the State should seek to ensure adequate access to downtown, other commercial, and residential areas, and avoid increasing or relocating emissions and congestion rather than reducing them.

(2) Offsets

In applying the emissions offset requirements of section 7503 of this title to new or modified sources or emissions units for which a permit is required under this part, the ratio of emission reductions to increased emissions shall be at least 2 to 1.

(c) Notice of failure to attain

    (1) As expeditiously as practicable after the applicable attainment date for any nonattainment area, but not later than 6 months after such date, the Administrator shall determine, based on the area's air quality as of the attainment date, whether the area attained the standard by that date.

    (2) Upon making the determination under paragraph (1), the Administrator shall publish a notice in the Federal Register containing such determination and identifying each area that the Administrator has determined to have failed to attain. The Administrator may revise or supplement such determination at any time based on more complete information or analysis concerning the area's air quality as of the attainment date.

(d) Consequences for failure to attain

    (1) Within 1 year after the Administrator publishes the notice under subsection (c)(2) of this section (relating to notice of failure to attain), each State containing a nonattainment area shall submit a revision to the applicable implementation plan meeting the requirements of paragraph (2) of this subsection.

    (2) The revision required under paragraph (1) shall meet the requirements of section 7410 of this title and section 7502 of this title. In addition, the revision shall include such additional measures as the Administrator may reasonably prescribe, including all measures that can be feasibly implemented in the area in light of technological achievability, costs, and any nonair quality and other air quality-related health and environmental impacts.

    (3) The attainment date applicable to the revision required under paragraph (1) shall be the same as provided in the provisions of section 7502(a)(2) of this title, except that in applying such provisions the phrase "from the date of the notice under section 7509(c)(2) of this

title" shall be substituted for the phrase "from the date such area was designated nonattainment under section 7407(d) of this title" and for the phrase "from the date of designation as nonattainment".

(July 14, 1955, ch. 360, title I, Sec. 179, as added Pub. L. 101-549, title I, Sec. 102(g), Nov. 15, 1990, 104 Stat. 2420.)

Section Referred to in Other Sections

This section is referred to in sections 7410, 7502, 7511a, 7511d, 7512a, 7661a of this title.

INTERNATIONAL BORDER AREAS

42 USC 7509a

(a) Implementation plans and revisions
Notwithstanding any other provision of law, an implementation plan or plan revision required under this chapter shall be approved by the Administrator if—
  (1) such plan or revision meets all the requirements applicable to it under the[1] chapter other than a requirement that such plan or revision demonstrate attainment and maintenance of the relevant national ambient air quality standards by the attainment date specified under the applicable provision of this chapter, or in a regulation promulgated under such provision, and
  (2) the submitting State establishes to the satisfaction of the Administrator that the implementation plan of such State would be adequate to attain and maintain the relevant national ambient air quality standards by the attainment date specified under the applicable provision of this chapter, or in a regulation promulgated under such provision, but for emissions emanating from outside of the United States.

(b) Attainment of ozone levels
Notwithstanding any other provision of law, any State that establishes to the satisfaction of the Administrator that, with respect to an ozone nonattainment area in such State, such State would have attained the national ambient air quality standard for ozone by the applicable attainment date, but for emissions emanating from outside of the United States, shall not be subject to the provisions of section 7511(a)(2) or (5) of this title or section 7511d of this title.

(c) Attainment of carbon monoxide levels
Notwithstanding any other provision of law, any State that establishes to the satisfaction of the Administrator, with respect to a carbon monoxide nonattainment area in such State, that such State has attained the national ambient air quality standard for carbon monoxide by the applicable attainment date, but for emissions emanating from outside of the United States, shall not be subject to the provisions of section 7512(b)(2) or (9)[2] of this title.

(d) Attainment of PM-10 levels
Notwithstanding any other provision of law, any State that establishes to the satisfaction of the Administrator that, with respect to a PM-10 nonattainment area in such State, such State would have attained the national ambient air quality standard for carbon monoxide by the applicable attainment date, but for emissions emanating from outside the United States, shall not be subject to the provisions of section 7513(b)(2) of this title.

(July 14, 1955, ch. 360, title I, Sec. 179B, as added Pub. L. 101-549, title VIII, Sec. 818, Nov. 15, 1990, 104 Stat. 2697.)

Establishment of Program To Monitor and Improve Air Quality in Regions Along Border Between United States and Mexico

Section 815 of Pub. L. 101-549 provided that:

"(a) In General.—The Administrator of the Environmental Protection Agency (hereinafter referred to as the 'Administrator') is authorized, in cooperation with the Department of State and the affected States, to negotiate with representatives of Mexico to authorize a program to monitor and improve air quality in regions along the border between the United States and Mexico. The program established under this section shall not extend beyond July 1, 1995.

---
[1]So in original. Probably should be "this".

(b) Monitoring and Remediation.—
  (1) Monitoring.—The monitoring component of the program conducted under this section shall identify and determine sources of pollutants for which national ambient air quality standards (hereinafter referred to as 'NAAQS') and other air quality goals have been established in regions along the border between the United States and Mexico. Any such monitoring component of the program shall include, but not be limited to, the collection of meteorological data, the measurement of air quality, the compilation of an emissions inventory, and shall be sufficient to the extent necessary to successfully support the use of a state-of-the-art mathematical air modeling analysis. Any such monitoring component of the program shall collect and produce data projecting the level of emission reductions necessary in both Mexico and the United States to bring about attainment of both primary and secondary NAAQS, and other air quality goals, in regions along the border in the United States. Any such monitoring component of the program shall include to the extent possible, data from monitoring programs undertaken by other parties.
  (2) Remediation.—The Administrator is authorized to negotiate with appropriate representatives of Mexico to develop joint remediation measures to reduce the level of airborne pollutants to achieve and maintain primary and secondary NAAQS, and other air quality goals, in regions along the border between the United States and Mexico. Such joint remediation measures may include, but not be limited to measures included in the Environmental Protection Agency's Control Techniques and Control Technology documents. Any such remediation program shall also identify those control measures implementation of which in Mexico would be expedited by the use of material and financial assistance of the United States.
(c) Annual Reports.—The Administrator shall, each year the program authorized in this section is in operation, report to Congress on the progress of the program in bringing nonattainment areas along the border of the United States into attainment with primary and secondary NAAQS. The report issued by the Administrator under this paragraph shall include recommendations on funding mechanisms to assist in implementation of monitoring and remediation efforts.
(d) Funding and Personnel.—The Administrator may, where appropriate, make available, subject to the appropriations, such funds, personnel, and equipment as may be necessary to implement the provisions of this section. In those cases where direct financial assistance of the United States is provided to implement monitoring and remediation programs in Mexico, the Administrator shall develop grant agreements with appropriate representatives of Mexico to assure the accuracy and completeness of monitoring data and the performance of remediation measures which are financed by the United States. With respect to any control measures within Mexico funded by the United States, the Administrator shall, to the maximum extent practicable, utilize resources of Mexico where such utilization would reduce costs to the United States. Such funding agreements shall include authorization for the Administrator to—
  (1) review and agree to plans for monitoring and remediation;
  (2) inspect premises, equipment and records to insure compliance with the agreements established under and the purposes set forth in this section; and
  (3) where necessary, develop grant agreements with affected States to carry out the provisions of this section."

Subpart 2—Additional Provisions for Ozone Nonattainment Areas

CLASSIFICATIONS AND ATTAINMENT DATES

42 USC 7511

(a) Classification and attainment dates for 1989 nonattainment areas
  (1) Each area designated nonattainment for ozone pursuant to section 7407(d) of this title shall be classified at the time of such designation, under table 1, by operation of law, as a Marginal Area, a Moderate Area, a Serious Area, a Severe Area, or an Extreme Area based on the design value for the area. The design value shall be calculated according to

the interpretation methodology issued by the Administrator most recently before November 15, 1990. For each area classified under this subsection, the primary standard attainment date for ozone shall be as expeditiously as practicable but not later than the date provided in table 1.

TABLE 1

Area class	Design value*	Primary standard attainment date**
Marginal...................	0.121 up to 0.138...................	3 years after November 15, 1990
Moderate................	0.138 up to 0.160..................	6 years after November 15, 1990
Serious...................	0.160 up to 0.180..................	9 years after November 15, 1990
Severe....................	0.180 up to 0.280..................	15 years after November 15, 1990
Extreme..................	0.280 and above..................	20 years after November 15, 1990

*The design value is measured in parts per million (ppm).
**The primary standard attainment date is measured from November 15, 1990.

  (2) Notwithstanding table 1, in the case of a severe area with a 1988 ozone design value between 0.190 and 0.280 ppm, the attainment date shall be 17 years (in lieu of 15 years) after November 15, 1990.

  (3) At the time of publication of the notice under section 7407(d)(4) of this title (relating to area designations) for each ozone nonattainment area, the Administrator shall publish a notice announcing the classification of such ozone nonattainment area. The provisions of section 7502(a)(1)(B) of this title (relating to lack of notice and comment and judicial review) shall apply to such classification.

  (4) If an area classified under paragraph (1) (Table 1) would have been classified in another category if the design value in the area were 5 percent greater or 5 percent less than the level on which such classification was based, the Administrator may, in the Administrator's discretion, within 90 days after the initial classification, by the procedure required under paragraph (3), adjust the classification to place the area in such other category. In making such adjustment, the Administrator may consider the number of exceedances of the national primary ambient air quality standard for ozone in the area, the level of pollution transport between the area and other affected areas, including both intrastate and interstate transport, and the mix of sources and air pollutants in the area.

  (5) Upon application by any State, the Administrator may extend for 1 additional year (hereinafter referred to as the "Extension Year") the date specified in table 1 of paragraph (1) of this subsection if—

    (A) the State has complied with all requirements and commitments pertaining to the area in the applicable implementation plan, and

    (B) no more than 1 exceedance of the national ambient air quality standard level for ozone has occurred in the area in the year preceding the Extension Year.

No more than 2 one-year extensions may be issued under this paragraph for a single nonattainment area.

(b) New designations and reclassifications

  (1) New designations to nonattainment

Any area that is designated attainment or unclassifiable for ozone under section 7407(d)(4) of this title, and that is subsequently redesignated to nonattainment for ozone under section 7407(d)(3) of this title, shall, at the time of the redesignation, be classified by operation of law in accordance with table 1 under subsection (a) of this section. Upon its classification, the area shall be subject to the same requirements under section 7410 of this title, subpart 1 of this part, and this subpart that would have applied had the area been so classified at the time of the notice under subsection (a)(3) of this section, except that any absolute, fixed date applicable in connection with any such requirement is extended by operation of law by a period equal to the length of time between November 15, 1990, and the date the area is classified under this paragraph.

  (2) Reclassification upon failure to attain

    (A) Within 6 months following the applicable attainment date (including any extension thereof) for an ozone nonattainment area, the Administrator shall determine, based on the area's design value (as of the attainment date), whether the area attained the standard by that date. Except for any Severe or Extreme area, any area that the Ad-

ministrator finds has not attained the standard by that date shall be reclassified by operation of law in accordance with table 1 of subsection (a) of this section to the higher of—
- (i) the next higher classification for the area, or
- (ii) the classification applicable to the area's design value as determined at the time of the notice required under subparagraph (B).

No area shall be reclassified as Extreme under clause (ii).
- (B) The Administrator shall publish a notice in the Federal Register, no later than 6 months following the attainment date, identifying each area that the Administrator has determined under subparagraph (A) as having failed to attain and identifying the reclassification, if any, described under subparagraph (A).
- (3) Voluntary reclassification

The Administrator shall grant the request of any State to reclassify a nonattainment area in that State in accordance with table 1 of subsection (a) of this section to a higher classification. The Administrator shall publish a notice in the Federal Register of any such request and of action by the Administrator granting the request.
- (4) Failure of Severe Areas to attain standard
  - (A) If any Severe Area fails to achieve the national primary ambient air quality standard for ozone by the applicable attainment date (including any extension thereof), the fee provisions under section 7511d of this title shall apply within the area, the percent reduction requirements of section 7511a(c)(2)(B) and (C) of this title (relating to reasonable further progress demonstration and NO_x control) shall continue to apply to the area, and the State shall demonstrate that such percent reduction has been achieved in each 3-year interval after such failure until the standard is attained. Any failure to make such a demonstration shall be subject to the sanctions provided under this part.
  - (B) In addition to the requirements of subparagraph (A), if the ozone design value for a Severe Area referred to in subparagraph (A) is above 0.140 ppm for the year of the applicable attainment date, or if the area has failed to achieve its most recent milestone under section 7511a(g) of this title, the new source review requirements applicable under this subpart in Extreme Areas shall apply in the area and the term[1] "major source" and "major stationary source" shall have the same meaning as in Extreme Areas.
  - (C) In addition to the requirements of subparagraph (A) for those areas referred to in subparagraph (A) and not covered by subparagraph (B), the provisions referred to in subparagraph (B) shall apply after 3 years from the applicable attainment date unless the area has attained the standard by the end of such 3-year period.
  - (D) If, after November 15, 1990, the Administrator modifies the method of determining compliance with the national primary ambient air quality standard, a design value or other indicator comparable to 0.140 in terms of its relationship to the standard shall be used in lieu of 0.140 for purposes of applying the provisions of subparagraphs (B) and (C).
- (c) References to terms
  - (1) Any reference in this subpart to a "Marginal Area", a "Moderate Area", a "Serious Area", a "Severe Area", or an "Extreme Area" shall be considered a reference to a Marginal Area, a Moderate Area, a Serious Area, a Severe Area, or an Extreme Area as respectively classified under this section.
  - (2) Any reference in this subpart to "next higher classification" or comparable terms shall be considered a reference to the classification related to the next higher set of design values in table 1.

(July 14, 1955, ch. 360, title I, Sec. 181, as added Pub. L. 101-549, title I, Sec. 103, Nov. 15, 1990, 104 Stat. 2423.)

Exemptions for Stripper Wells

Section 819 of Pub. L. 101-549 provided that: "Notwithstanding any other provision of law, the amendments to the Clean Air Act made by section 103 of the Clean Air Act Amendments of 1990 [enacting this section and sections 7511a to 7511f of this title] (relating to additional provisions for ozone nonattainment areas), by section 104 of such amendments [enacting sections 7512 and 7512a

---

[1] So in original. Probably should be "terms".

of this title] (relating to additional provisions for carbon monoxide nonattainment areas), by section 105 of such amendments [enacting sections 7513 to 7513b of this title and amending section 7476 of this title] (relating to additional provisions for PM-10 nonattainment areas), and by section 106 of such amendments [enacting sections 7514 and 7514a of this title] (relating to additional provisions for areas designated as nonattainment for sulfur oxides, nitrogen dioxide, and lead) shall not apply with respect to the production of and equipment used in the exploration, production, development, storage or processing of—

"(1) oil from a stripper well property, within the meaning of the June 1979 energy regulations (within the meaning of section 4996(b)(7) of the Internal Revenue Code of 1986 [26 U.S.C. 4996(b)(7)], as in effect before the repeal of such section); and

(2) stripper well natural gas, as defined in section 108(b) of the Natural Gas Policy Act of 1978 (15 U.S.C. 3318(b)).[,]

except to the extent that provisions of such amendments cover areas designated as Serious pursuant to part D of title I of the Clean Air Act [this part] and having a population of 350,000 or more, or areas designated as Severe or Extreme pursuant to such part D."

Section Referred to in Other Sections

This section is referred to in sections 7509a, 7511a, 7511b, 7511d, 7521, 7545, 7607 of this title; title 23 section 149.

PLAN SUBMISSIONS AND REQUIREMENTS

42 USC 7511a

(a) Marginal Areas

Each State in which all or part of a Marginal Area is located shall, with respect to the Marginal Area (or portion thereof, to the extent specified in this subsection), submit to the Administrator the State implementation plan revisions (including the plan items) described under this subsection except to the extent the State has made such submissions as of November 15, 1990.

(1) Inventory

Within 2 years after November 15, 1990, the State shall submit a comprehensive, accurate, current inventory of actual emissions from all sources, as described in section 7502(c)(3) of this title, in accordance with guidance provided by the Administrator.

(2) Corrections to the State implementation plan

Within the periods prescribed in this paragraph, the State shall submit a revision to the State implementation plan that meets the following requirements—

(A) Reasonably available control technology corrections

For any Marginal Area (or, within the Administrator's discretion, portion thereof) the State shall submit, within 6 months of the date of classification under section 7511(a) of this title, a revision that includes such provisions to correct requirements in (or add requirements to) the plan concerning reasonably available control technology as were required under section 7502(b) of this title (as in effect immediately before November 15, 1990), as interpreted in guidance issued by the Administrator under section 7408 of this title before November 15, 1990.

(B) Savings clause for vehicle inspection and maintenance

(i) For any Marginal Area (or, within the Administrator's discretion, portion thereof), the plan for which already includes, or was required by section 7502(b)(11)(B) of this title (as in effect immediately before November 15, 1990) to have included, a specific schedule for implementation of a vehicle emission control inspection and maintenance program, the State shall submit, immediately after November 15, 1990, a revision that includes any provisions necessary to provide for a vehicle inspection and maintenance program of no less stringency than that of either the program defined in House Report Numbered 95-294, 95th Congress, 1st Session, 281-291 (1977) as interpreted in guidance of the Administrator issued pursuant to section 7502(b)(11)(B) of this title (as in effect immediately before November 15, 1990) or the program already included in the plan, whichever is more stringent.

(ii) Within 12 months after November 15, 1990, the Administrator shall review, revise, update, and republish in the Federal Register the guidance for the States for motor vehicle inspection and maintenance programs required by this chapter, taking into consideration the Administrator's investigations and audits of such program. The guidance shall, at a minimum, cover the frequency of inspections, the types of vehicles to be inspected (which shall include leased vehicles that are registered in the nonattainment area), vehicle maintenance by owners and operators, audits by the State, the test method and measures, including whether centralized or decentralized, inspection methods and procedures, quality of inspection, components covered, assurance that a vehicle subject to a recall notice from a manufacturer has complied with that notice, and effective implementation and enforcement, including ensuring that any retesting of a vehicle after a failure shall include proof of corrective action and providing for denial of vehicle registration in the case of tampering or misfueling. The guidance which shall be incorporated in the applicable State implementation plans by the States shall provide the States with continued reasonable flexibility to fashion effective, reasonable, and fair programs for the affected consumer. No later than 2 years after the Administrator promulgates regulations under section 7521(m)(3) of this title (relating to emission control diagnostics), the State shall submit a revision to such program to meet any requirements that the Administrator may prescribe under that section.

(C) Permit programs

Within 2 years after November 15, 1990, the State shall submit a revision that includes each of the following:

  (i) Provisions to require permits, in accordance with sections 7502(c)(5) and 7503 of this title, for the construction and operation of each new or modified major stationary source (with respect to ozone) to be located in the area.

  (ii) Provisions to correct requirements in (or add requirements to) the plan concerning permit programs as were required under section 7502(b)(6) of this title (as in effect immediately before November 15, 1990), as interpreted in regulations of the Administrator promulgated as of November 15, 1990.

(3) Periodic inventory

  (A) General requirement

  No later than the end of each 3-year period after submission of the inventory under paragraph (1) until the area is redesignated to attainment, the State shall submit a revised inventory meeting the requirements of subsection (a)(1) of this section.

  (B) Emissions statements

    (i) Within 2 years after November 15, 1990, the State shall submit a revision to the State implementation plan to require that the owner or operator of each stationary source of oxides of nitrogen or volatile organic compounds provide the State with a statement, in such form as the Administrator may prescribe (or accept an equivalent alternative developed by the State), for classes or categories of sources, showing the actual emissions of oxides of nitrogen and volatile organic compounds from that source. The first such statement shall be submitted within 3 years after November 15, 1990. Subsequent statements shall be submitted at least every year thereafter. The statement shall contain a certification that the information contained in the statement is accurate to the best knowledge of the individual certifying the statement.

    (ii) The State may waive the application of clause (i) to any class or category of stationary sources which emit less than 25 tons per year of volatile organic compounds or oxides of nitrogen if the State, in its submissions under subparagraphs[1] (1) or (3)(A), provides an inventory of emissions from such class or category of sources, based on the use of the emission factors established by the Administrator or other methods acceptable to the Administrator.

(4) General offset requirement

For purposes of satisfying the emission offset requirements of this part, the ratio of total emission reductions of volatile organic compounds to total increased emissions of such air pollutant shall be at least 1.1 to 1.

The Administrator may, in the Administrator's discretion, require States to submit a schedule for submitting any of the revisions or other items required under this subsection. The require-

---

[1] So in original. Probably should be "subparagraph".

ments of this subsection shall apply in lieu of any requirement that the State submit a demonstration that the applicable implementation plan provides for attainment of the ozone standard by the applicable attainment date in any Marginal Area. Section 7502(c)(9) of this title (relating to contingency measures) shall not apply to Marginal Areas.

(b) Moderate Areas

Each State in which all or part of a Moderate Area is located shall, with respect to the Moderate Area, make the submissions described under subsection (a) of this section (relating to Marginal Areas), and shall also submit the revisions to the applicable implementation plan described under this subsection.

(1) Plan provisions for reasonable further progress

(A) General rule

(i) By no later than 3 years after November 15, 1990, the State shall submit a revision to the applicable implementation plan to provide for volatile organic compound emission reductions, within 6 years after November 15, 1990, of at least 15 percent from baseline emissions, accounting for any growth in emissions after 1990. Such plan shall provide for such specific annual reductions in emissions of volatile organic compounds and oxides of nitrogen as necessary to attain the national primary ambient air quality standard for ozone by the attainment date applicable under this chapter. This subparagraph shall not apply in the case of oxides of nitrogen for those areas for which the Administrator determines (when the Administrator approves the plan or plan revision) that additional reductions of oxides of nitrogen would not contribute to attainment.

(ii) A percentage less than 15 percent may be used for purposes of clause (i) in the case of any State which demonstrates to the satisfaction of the Administrator that—

(I) new source review provisions are applicable in the nonattainment areas in the same manner and to the same extent as required under subsection (e) of this section in the case of Extreme Areas (with the exception that, in applying such provisions, the terms "major source" and "major stationary source" shall include (in addition to the sources described in section 7602 of this title) any stationary source or group of sources located within a contiguous area and under common control that emits, or has the potential to emit, at least 5 tons per year of volatile organic compounds);

(II) reasonably available control technology is required for all existing major sources (as defined in subclause (I)); and

(III) the plan reflecting a lesser percentage than 15 percent includes all measures that can feasibly be implemented in the area, in light of technological achievability.

To qualify for a lesser percentage under this clause, a State must demonstrate to the satisfaction of the Administrator that the plan for the area includes the measures that are achieved in practice by sources in the same source category in nonattainment areas of the next higher category.

(B) Baseline emissions

For purposes of subparagraph (A), the term "baseline emissions" means the total amount of actual VOC or NO_x emissions from all anthropogenic sources in the area during the calendar year 1990, excluding emissions that would be eliminated under the regulations described in clauses (i) and (ii) of subparagraph (D).

(C) General rule for creditability of reductions

Except as provided under subparagraph (D), emissions reductions are creditable toward the 15 percent required under subparagraph (A) to the extent they have actually occurred, as of 6 years after November 15, 1990, from the implementation of measures required under the applicable implementation plan, rules promulgated by the Administrator, or a permit under subchapter V of this chapter.

(D) Limits on creditability of reductions

Emission reductions from the following measures are not creditable toward the 15 percent reductions required under subparagraph (A):

(i) Any measure relating to motor vehicle exhaust or evaporative emissions promulgated by the Administrator by January 1, 1990.

(ii) Regulations concerning Reid Vapor Pressure promulgated by the Administrator by November 15, 1990, or required to be promulgated under section 7545(h) of this title.
(iii) Measures required under subsection (a)(2)(A) of this section (concerning corrections to implementation plans prescribed under guidance by the Administrator).
(iv) Measures required under subsection (a)(2)(B) of this section to be submitted immediately after November 15, 1990 (concerning corrections to motor vehicle inspection and maintenance programs).

(2) Reasonably available control technology

The State shall submit a revision to the applicable implementation plan to include provisions to require the implementation of reasonably available control technology under section 7502(c)(1) of this title with respect to each of the following:

(A) Each category of VOC sources in the area covered by a CTG document issued by the Administrator between November 15, 1990, and the date of attainment.
(B) All VOC sources in the area covered by any CTG issued before November 15, 1990.
(C) All other major stationary sources of VOCs that are located in the area.

Each revision described in subparagraph (A) shall be submitted within the period set forth by the Administrator in issuing the relevant CTG document. The revisions with respect to sources described in subparagraphs (B) and (C) shall be submitted by 2 years after November 15, 1990, and shall provide for the implementation of the required measures as expeditiously as practicable but no later than May 31, 1995.

(3) Gasoline vapor recovery

(A) General rule

Not later than 2 years after November 15, 1990, the State shall submit a revision to the applicable implementation plan to require all owners or operators of gasoline dispensing systems to install and operate, by the date prescribed under subparagraph (B), a system for gasoline vapor recovery of emissions from the fueling of motor vehicles. The Administrator shall issue guidance as appropriate as to the effectiveness of such system. This subparagraph shall apply only to facilities which sell more than 10,000 gallons of gasoline per month (50,000 gallons per month in the case of an independent small business marketer of gasoline as defined in section 7625-1[2] of this title).

(B) Effective date

The date required under subparagraph (A) shall be—
(i) 6 months after the adoption date, in the case of gasoline dispensing facilities for which construction commenced after November 15, 1990;
(ii) one year after the adoption date, in the case of gasoline dispensing facilities which dispense at least 100,000 gallons of gasoline per month, based on average monthly sales for the 2-year period before the adoption date; or
(iii) 2 years after the adoption date, in the case of all other gasoline dispensing facilities.

Any gasoline dispensing facility described under both clause (i) and clause (ii) shall meet the requirements of clause (i).

(C) Reference to terms

For purposes of this paragraph, any reference to the term "adoption date" shall be considered a reference to the date of adoption by the State of requirements for the installation and operation of a system for gasoline vapor recovery of emissions from the fueling of motor vehicles.

(4) Motor vehicle inspection and maintenance

For all Moderate Areas, the State shall submit, immediately after November 15, 1990, a revision to the applicable implementation plan that includes provisions necessary to provide for a vehicle inspection and maintenance program as described in subsection (a)(2)(B) of this section (without regard to whether or not the area was required by section 7502(b)(11)(B) of this title (as in effect immediately before November 15, 1990) to have included a specific schedule for implementation of such a program).

(5) General offset requirement

For purposes of satisfying the emission offset requirements of this part, the ratio of total emission reductions of volatile organic compounds to total increase emissions of such air pollutant shall be at least 1.15 to 1.

---

[2]So in original. Probably should be section "7625".

(c) Serious Areas

Except as otherwise specified in paragraph (4), each State in which all or part of a Serious Area is located shall, with respect to the Serious Area (or portion thereof, to the extent specified in this subsection), make the submissions described under subsection (b) of this section (relating to Moderate Areas), and shall also submit the revisions to the applicable implementation plan (including the plan items) described under this subsection. For any Serious Area, the terms "major source" and "major stationary source" include (in addition to the sources described in section 7602 of this title) any stationary source or group of sources located within a contiguous area and under common control that emits, or has the potential to emit, at least 50 tons per year of volatile organic compounds.

(1) Enhanced monitoring

In order to obtain more comprehensive and representative data on ozone air pollution, not later than 18 months after November 15, 1990, the Administrator shall promulgate rules, after notice and public comment, for enhanced monitoring of ozone, oxides of nitrogen, and volatile organic compounds. The rules shall, among other things, cover the location and maintenance of monitors. Immediately following the promulgation of rules by the Administrator relating to enhanced monitoring, the State shall commence such actions as may be necessary to adopt and implement a program based on such rules, to improve monitoring for ambient concentrations of ozone, oxides of nitrogen and volatile organic compounds and to improve monitoring of emissions of oxides of nitrogen and volatile organic compounds. Each State implementation plan for the area shall contain measures to improve the ambient monitoring of such air pollutants.

(2) Attainment and reasonable further progress demonstrations

Within 4 years after November 15, 1990, the State shall submit a revision to the applicable implementation plan that includes each of the following:

(A) Attainment demonstration

A demonstration that the plan, as revised, will provide for attainment of the ozone national ambient air quality standard by the applicable attainment date. This attainment demonstration must be based on photochemical grid modeling or any other analytical method determined by the Administrator, in the Administrator's discretion, to be at least as effective.

(B) Reasonable further progress demonstration

A demonstration that the plan, as revised, will result in VOC emissions reductions from the baseline emissions described in subsection (b)(1)(B) of this section equal to the following amount averaged over each consecutive 3-year period beginning 6 years after November 15, 1990, until the attainment date:

(i) at least 3 percent of baseline emissions each year; or

(ii) an amount less than 3 percent of such baseline emissions each year, if the State demonstrates to the satisfaction of the Administrator that the plan reflecting such lesser amount includes all measures that can feasibly be implemented in the area, in light of technological achievability.

To lessen the 3 percent requirement under clause (ii), a State must demonstrate to the satisfaction of the Administrator that the plan for the area includes the measures that are achieved in practice by sources in the same source category in nonattainment areas of the next higher classification. Any determination to lessen the 3 percent requirement shall be reviewed at each milestone under subsection (g) of this section and revised to reflect such new measures (if any) achieved in practice by sources in the same category in any State, allowing a reasonable time to implement such measures. The emission reductions described in this subparagraph shall be calculated in accordance with subsection (b)(1)(C) and (D) of this section (concerning creditability of reductions). The reductions creditable for the period beginning 6 years after November 15, 1990, shall include reductions that occurred before such period, computed in accordance with subsection (b)(1) of this section, that exceed the 15-percent amount of reductions required under subsection (b)(1)(A) of this section.

(C) NO_x control

The revision may contain, in lieu of the demonstration required under subparagraph (B), a demonstration to the satisfaction of the Administrator that the applicable implementation plan, as revised, provides for reductions of emissions of VOC's and oxides of nitrogen (calculated according to the creditability provisions of subsection (b)(1)(C) and (D) of this section), that would result in a reduction in ozone concentrations at least equivalent to that which would result from the amount of VOC emission reductions required under subparagraph (B). Within 1 year after November 15, 1990, the Administrator shall issue guidance concerning the conditions under which NO_x control may be substituted for VOC control or may be combined with VOC control in order to maximize the reduction in ozone air pollution. In accord with such guidance, a lesser percentage of VOCs may be accepted as an adequate demonstration for purposes of this subsection.

(3) Enhanced vehicle inspection and maintenance program

(A) Requirement for submission

Within 2 years after November 15, 1990, the State shall submit a revision to the applicable implementation plan to provide for an enhanced program to reduce hydrocarbon emissions and NO_x emissions from in-use motor vehicles registered in each urbanized area (in the nonattainment area), as defined by the Bureau of the Census, with a 1980 population of 200,000 or more.

(B) Effective date of State programs; guidance

The State program required under subparagraph (A) shall take effect no later than 2 years from November 15, 1990, and shall comply in all respects with guidance published in the Federal Register (and from time to time revised) by the Administrator for enhanced vehicle inspection and maintenance programs. Such guidance shall include—

(i) a performance standard achievable by a program combining emission testing, including on-road emission testing, with inspection to detect tampering with emission control devices and misfueling for all light-duty vehicles and all light-duty trucks subject to standards under section 7521 of this title; and

(ii) program administration features necessary to reasonably assure that adequate management resources, tools, and practices are in place to attain and maintain the performance standard.

Compliance with the performance standard under clause (i) shall be determined using a method to be established by the Administrator.

(C) State program

The State program required under subparagraph (A) shall include, at a minimum, each of the following elements—

(i) Computerized emission analyzers, including on-road testing devices.

(ii) No waivers for vehicles and parts covered by the emission control performance warranty as provided for in section 7541(b) of this title unless a warranty remedy has been denied in writing, or for tampering-related repairs.

(iii) In view of the air quality purpose of the program, if, for any vehicle, waivers are permitted for emissions-related repairs not covered by warranty, an expenditure to qualify for the waiver of an amount of $450 or more for such repairs (adjusted annually as determined by the Administrator on the basis of the Consumer Price Index in the same manner as provided in subchapter V of this chapter).

(iv) Enforcement through denial of vehicle registration (except for any program in operation before November 15, 1990, whose enforcement mechanism is demonstrated to the Administrator to be more effective than the applicable vehicle registration program in assuring that noncomplying vehicles are not operated on public roads).

(v) Annual emission testing and necessary adjustment, repair, and maintenance, unless the State demonstrates to the satisfaction of the Administrator that a biennial inspection, in combination with other features of the program which exceed the requirements of this chapter, will result in emission reductions which equal or exceed the reductions which can be obtained through such annual inspections.

(vi) Operation of the program on a centralized basis, unless the State demonstrates to the satisfaction of the Administrator that a decentralized program will be equally effective. An electronically connected testing system, a licensing system, or other measures (or any combination thereof) may be considered, in accordance with criteria established by the Administrator, as equally effective for such purposes.

(vii) Inspection of emission control diagnostic systems and the maintenance or repair of malfunctions or system deterioration identified by or affecting such diagnostics systems.

Each State shall biennially prepare a report to the Administrator which assesses the emission reductions achieved by the program required under this paragraph based on data collected during inspection and repair of vehicles. The methods used to assess the emission reductions shall be those established by the Administrator.

(4) Clean-fuel vehicle programs

(A) Except to the extent that substitute provisions have been approved by the Administrator under subparagraph (B), the State shall submit to the Administrator, within 42 months of November 15, 1990, a revision to the applicable implementation plan for each area described under part C of subchapter II of this chapter to include such measures as may be necessary to ensure the effectiveness of the applicable provisions of the clean-fuel vehicle program prescribed under part C of subchapter II of this chapter, including all measures necessary to make the use of clean alternative fuels in clean-fuel vehicles (as defined in part C of subchapter II of this chapter) economic from the standpoint of vehicle owners. Such a revision shall also be submitted for each area that opts into the clean fuel-vehicle program as provided in part C of subchapter II of this chapter.

(B) The Administrator shall approve, as a substitute for all or a portion of the clean-fuel vehicle program prescribed under part C of subchapter II of this chapter, any revision to the relevant applicable implementation plan that in the Administrator's judgment will achieve long-term reductions in ozone-producing and toxic air emissions equal to those achieved under part C of subchapter II of this chapter, or the percentage thereof attributable to the portion of the clean-fuel vehicle program for which the revision is to substitute. The Administrator may approve such revision only if it consists exclusively of provisions other than those required under this chapter for the area. Any State seeking approval of such revision must submit the revision to the Administrator within 24 months of November 15, 1990. The Administrator shall approve or disapprove any such revision within 30 months of November 15, 1990. The Administrator shall publish the revision submitted by a State in the Federal Register upon receipt. Such notice shall constitute a notice of proposed rulemaking on whether or not to approve such revision and shall be deemed to comply with the requirements concerning notices of proposed rulemaking contained in sections 553 through 557 of title 5 (related to notice and comment). Where the Administrator approves such revision for any area, the State need not submit the revision required by subparagraph (A) for the area with respect to the portions of the Federal clean-fuel vehicle program for which the Administrator has approved the revision as a substitute.

(C) If the Administrator determines, under section 7509 of this title, that the State has failed to submit any portion of the program required under subparagraph (A), then, in addition to any sanctions available under section 7509 of this title, the State may not receive credit, in any demonstration of attainment or reasonable further progress for the area, for any emission reductions from implementation of the corresponding aspects of the Federal clean-fuel vehicle requirements established in part C of subchapter II of this chapter.

(5) Transportation control

(A)[3] Beginning 6 years after November 15, 1990, and each third year thereafter, the State shall submit a demonstration as to whether current aggregate vehicle mileage, aggregate vehicle emissions, congestion levels, and other relevant parameters are consistent with those used for the area's demonstration of attainment. Where such parameters and emissions levels exceed the levels projected for purposes of the area's attainment demonstration, the State shall within 18 months develop and submit a revision of the applicable implementation plan that includes a transportation control measures program consisting of measures from, but not limited to, section 7408(f) of this title that will reduce emissions to levels that are consistent with emission levels projected in such demonstration. In considering such measures, the State should ensure

---

[3] So in original. No subpar. (B) has been enacted.

adequate access to downtown, other commercial, and residential areas and should avoid measures that increase or relocate emissions and congestion rather than reduce them. Such revision shall be developed in accordance with guidance issued by the Administrator pursuant to section 7408(e) of this title and with the requirements of section 7504(b) of this title and shall include implementation and funding schedules that achieve expeditious emissions reductions in accordance with implementation plan projections.

(6) De minimis rule

The new source review provisions under this part shall ensure that increased emissions of volatile organic compounds resulting from any physical change in, or change in the method of operation of, a stationary source located in the area shall not be considered de minimis for purposes of determining the applicability of the permit requirements established by this chapter unless the increase in net emissions of such air pollutant from such source does not exceed 25 tons when aggregated with all other net increases in emissions from the source over any period of 5 consecutive calendar years which includes the calendar year in which such increase occurred.

(7) Special rule for modifications of sources emitting less than 100 tons

In the case of any major stationary source of volatile organic compounds located in the area (other than a source which emits or has the potential to emit 100 tons or more of volatile organic compounds per year), whenever any change (as described in section 7411(a)(4) of this title) at that source results in any increase (other than a de minimis increase) in emissions of volatile organic compounds from any discrete operation, unit, or other pollutant emitting activity at the source, such increase shall be considered a modification for purposes of section 7502(c)(5) of this title and section 7503(a) of this title, except that such increase shall not be considered a modification for such purposes if the owner or operator of the source elects to offset the increase by a greater reduction in emissions of volatile organic compounds concerned from other operations, units, or activities within the source at an internal offset ratio of at least 1.3 to 1. If the owner or operator does not make such election, such change shall be considered a modification for such purposes, but in applying section 7503(a)(2) of this title in the case of any such modification, the best available control technology (BACT), as defined in section 7479 of this title, shall be substituted for the lowest achievable emission rate (LAER). The Administrator shall establish and publish policies and procedures for implementing the provisions of this paragraph.

(8) Special rule for modifications of sources emitting 100 tons or more

In the case of any major stationary source of volatile organic compounds located in the area which emits or has the potential to emit 100 tons or more of volatile organic compounds per year, whenever any change (as described in section 7411(a)(4) of this title) at that source results in any increase (other than a de minimis increase) in emissions of volatile organic compounds from any discrete operation, unit, or other pollutant emitting activity at the source, such increase shall be considered a modification for purposes of section 7502(c)(5) of this title and section 7503(a) of this title, except that if the owner or operator of the source elects to offset the increase by a greater reduction in emissions of volatile organic compounds from other operations, units, or activities within the source at an internal offset ratio of at least 1.3 to 1, the requirements of section 7503(a)(2) of this title (concerning the lowest achievable emission rate (LAER)) shall not apply.

(9) Contingency provisions

In addition to the contingency provisions required under section 7502(c)(9) of this title, the plan revision shall provide for the implementation of specific measures to be undertaken if the area fails to meet any applicable milestone. Such measures shall be included in the plan revision as contingency measures to take effect without further action by the State or the Administrator upon a failure by the State to meet the applicable milestone.

(10) General offset requirement

For purposes of satisfying the emission offset requirements of this part, the ratio of total emission reductions of volatile organic compounds to total increase emissions of such air pollutant shall be at least 1.2 to 1.

Any reference to "attainment date" in subsection (b) of this section, which is incorporated by reference into this subsection, shall refer to the attainment date for serious areas.

(d) Severe Areas

Each State in which all or part of a Severe Area is located shall, with respect to the Severe Area, make the submissions described under subsection (c) of this section (relating to Serious Areas), and shall also submit the revisions to the applicable implementation plan (including the plan items) described under this subsection. For any Severe Area, the terms "major source" and "major stationary source" include (in addition to the sources described in section 7602 of this title) any stationary source or group of sources located within a contiguous area and under common control that emits, or has the potential to emit, at least 25 tons per year of volatile organic compounds.

(1) Vehicle miles traveled

(A) Within 2 years after November 15, 1990, the State shall submit a revision that identifies and adopts specific enforceable transportation control strategies and transportation control measures to offset any growth in emissions from growth in vehicle miles traveled or numbers of vehicle trips in such area and to attain reduction in motor vehicle emissions as necessary, in combination with other emission reduction requirements of this subpart, to comply with the requirements of subsection[4] (b)(2)(B) and (c)(2)(B) of this section (pertaining to periodic emissions reduction requirements). The State shall consider measures specified in section 7408(f) of this title, and choose from among and implement such measures as necessary to demonstrate attainment with the national ambient air quality standards; in considering such measures, the State should ensure adequate access to downtown, other commercial, and residential areas and should avoid measures that increase or relocate emissions and congestion rather than reduce them.

(B) The State may also, in its discretion, submit a revision at any time requiring employers in such area to implement programs to reduce work-related vehicle trips and miles travelled by employees. Such revision shall be developed in accordance with guidance issued by the Administrator pursuant to section 7408(f) of this title and may require that employers in such area increase average passenger occupancy per vehicle in commuting trips between home and the workplace during peak travel periods. The guidance of the Administrator may specify average vehicle occupancy rates which vary for locations within a nonattainment area (suburban, center city, business district) or among nonattainment areas reflecting existing occupancy rates and the availability of high occupancy modes. Any State required to submit a revision under this subparagraph (as in effect before December 23, 1995) containing provisions requiring employers to reduce work-related vehicle trips and miles travelled by employees may, in accordance with State law, remove such provisions from the implementation plan, or withdraw its submission, if the State notifies the Administrator, in writing, that the State has undertaken, or will undertake, one or more alternative methods that will achieve emission reductions equivalent to those to be achieved by the removed or withdrawn provisions.

(2) Offset requirement

For purposes of satisfying the offset requirements pursuant to this part, the ratio of total emission reductions of VOCs to total increased emissions of such air pollutant shall be at least 1.3 to 1, except that if the State plan requires all existing major sources in the nonattainment area to use best available control technology (as defined in section 7479(3) of this title) for the control of volatile organic compounds, the ratio shall be at least 1.2 to 1.

(3) Enforcement under section 7511d

By December 31, 2000, the State shall submit a plan revision which includes the provisions required under section 7511d of this title.

Any reference to the term "attainment date" in subsection (b) or (c) of this section, which is incorporated by reference into this subsection (d), shall refer to the attainment date for Severe Areas.

(e) Extreme Areas

Each State in which all or part of an Extreme Area is located shall, with respect to the Extreme Area, make the submissions described under subsection (d) of this section (relating to Severe Areas), and shall also submit the revisions to the applicable implementation plan (including

---

[4] So in original. Probably should be "subsections".

the plan items) described under this subsection. The provisions of clause (ii) of subsection (c)(2)(B) of this section (relating to reductions of less than 3 percent), the provisions of paragraphs[5] (6), (7) and (8) of subsection (c) of this section (relating to de minimus rule and modification of sources), and the provisions of clause (ii) of subsection (b)(1)(A) of this section (relating to reductions of less than 15 percent) shall not apply in the case of an Extreme Area. For any Extreme Area, the terms "major source" and "major stationary source" includes (in addition to the sources described in section 7602 of this title) any stationary source or group of sources located within a contiguous area and under common control that emits, or has the potential to emit, at least 10 tons per year of volatile organic compounds.

(1) Offset requirement

For purposes of satisfying the offset requirements pursuant to this part, the ratio of total emission reductions of VOCs to total increased emissions of such air pollutant shall be at least 1.5 to 1, except that if the State plan requires all existing major sources in the nonattainment area to use best available control technology (as defined in section 7479(3) of this title) for the control of volatile organic compounds, the ratio shall be at least 1.2 to 1.

(2) Modifications

Any change (as described in section 7411(a)(4) of this title) at a major stationary source which results in any increase in emissions from any discrete operation, unit, or other pollutant emitting activity at the source shall be considered a modification for purposes of section 7502(c)(5) of this title and section 7503(a) of this title, except that for purposes of complying with the offset requirement pursuant to section 7503(a)(1) of this title, any such increase shall not be considered a modification if the owner or operator of the source elects to offset the increase by a greater reduction in emissions of the air pollutant concerned from other discrete operations, units, or activities within the source at an internal offset ratio of at least 1.3 to 1. The offset requirements of this part shall not be applicable in Extreme Areas to a modification of an existing source if such modification consists of installation of equipment required to comply with the applicable implementation plan, permit, or this chapter.

(3) Use of clean fuels or advanced control technology

For Extreme Areas, a plan revision shall be submitted within 3 years after November 15, 1990, to require, effective 8 years after November 15, 1990, that each new, modified, and existing electric utility and industrial and commercial boiler which emits more than 25 tons per year of oxides of nitrogen—

(A) burn as its primary fuel natural gas, methanol, or ethanol (or a comparably low polluting fuel), or

(B) use advanced control technology (such as catalytic control technology or other comparably effective control methods) for reduction of emissions of oxides of nitrogen.

For purposes of this subsection, the term "primary fuel" means the fuel which is used 90 percent or more of the operating time. This paragraph shall not apply during any natural gas supply emergency (as defined in title III of the Natural Gas Policy Act of 1978 [15 U.S.C. 3361 et seq.]).

(4) Traffic control measures during heavy traffic hours

For Extreme Areas, each implementation plan revision under this subsection may contain provisions establishing traffic control measures applicable during heavy traffic hours to reduce the use of high polluting vehicles or heavy-duty vehicles, notwithstanding any other provision of law.

(5) New technologies

The Administrator may, in accordance with section 7410 of this title, approve provisions of an implementation plan for an Extreme Area which anticipate development of new control techniques or improvement of existing control technologies, and an attainment demonstration based on such provisions, if the State demonstrates to the satisfaction of the Administrator that—

(A) such provisions are not necessary to achieve the incremental emission reductions required during the first 10 years after November 15, 1990; and

(B) the State has submitted enforceable commitments to develop and adopt contingency measures to be implemented as set forth herein if the anticipated technologies do not achieve planned reductions. Such contingency measures shall be submitted to the Administrator no later than 3 years before proposed implementation of the plan provisions and approved or disapproved by the Administrator in accordance with section 7410 of this title. The contingency measures shall be adequate to produce emission reductions sufficient, in conjunction with other approved plan provisions, to achieve the periodic emission reductions required by subsection (b)(1) or (c)(2) of this section and attainment by the applicable dates. If the Administrator determines that an Extreme Area has failed to achieve an emission reduction requirement set forth in subsection (b)(1) or (c)(2) of this section, and that such failure is due in whole or part to an inability to fully implement provisions approved pursuant to this subsection, the Administrator shall require the State to implement the contingency measures to the extent necessary to assure compliance with subsections (b)(1) and (c)(2) of this section. Any reference to the term "attainment date" in subsection (b), (c), or (d) of this section which is incorporated by reference into this subsection, shall refer to the attainment date for Extreme Areas.

(f) NO_x requirements
  (1) The plan provisions required under this subpart for major stationary sources of volatile organic compounds shall also apply to major stationary sources (as defined in section 7602 of this title and subsections (c), (d), and (e) of this section) of oxides of nitrogen. This subsection shall not apply in the case of oxides of nitrogen for those sources for which the Administrator determines (when the Administrator approves a plan or plan revision) that net air quality benefits are greater in the absence of reductions of oxides of nitrogen from the sources concerned. This subsection shall also not apply in the case of oxides of nitrogen for—
    (A) nonattainment areas not within an ozone transport region under section 7511c of this title, if the Administrator determines (when the Administrator approves a plan or plan revision) that additional reductions of oxides of nitrogen would not contribute to attainment of the national ambient air quality standard for ozone in the area, or
    (B) nonattainment areas within such an ozone transport region if the Administrator determines (when the Administrator approves a plan or plan revision) that additional reductions of oxides of nitrogen would not produce net ozone air quality benefits in such region.
  The Administrator shall, in the Administrator's determinations, consider the study required under section 7511f of this title.
  (2) (A) If the Administrator determines that excess reductions in emissions of NO_x would be achieved under paragraph (1), the Administrator may limit the application of paragraph (1) to the extent necessary to avoid achieving such excess reductions.
    (B) For purposes of this paragraph, excess reductions in emissions of NO_x are emission reductions for which the Administrator determines that net air quality benefits are greater in the absence of such reductions. Alternatively, for purposes of this paragraph, excess reductions in emissions of NO_x are, for—
      (i) nonattainment areas not within an ozone transport region under section 7511c of this title, emission reductions that the Administrator determines would not contribute to attainment of the national ambient air quality standard for ozone in the area, or
      (ii) nonattainment areas within such ozone transport region, emission reductions that the Administrator determines would not produce net ozone air quality benefits in such region.
  (3) At any time after the final report under section 7511f of this title is submitted to Congress, a person may petition the Administrator for a determination under paragraph (1) or (2) with respect to any nonattainment area or any ozone transport region under section 7511c of this title. The Administrator shall grant or deny such petition within 6 months after its filing with the Administrator.

(g) Milestones
  (1) Reductions in emissions
    6 years after November 15, 1990, and at intervals of every 3 years thereafter, the State shall determine whether each nonattainment area (other than an area classified as Marginal or Moderate) has achieved a reduction in emissions during the preceding intervals equivalent to the total emission reductions required to be achieved by the end of such

interval pursuant to subsection (b)(1) of this section and the corresponding requirements of subsections (c)(2)(B) and (C), (d), and (e) of this section. Such reduction shall be referred to in this section as an applicable milestone.
(2) Compliance demonstration
For each nonattainment area referred to in paragraph (1), not later than 90 days after the date on which an applicable milestone occurs (not including an attainment date on which a milestone occurs in cases where the standard has been attained), each State in which all or part of such area is located shall submit to the Administrator a demonstration that the milestone has been met. A demonstration under this paragraph shall be submitted in such form and manner, and shall contain such information and analysis, as the Administrator shall require, by rule. The Administrator shall determine whether or not a State's demonstration is adequate within 90 days after the Administrator's receipt of a demonstration which contains the information and analysis required by the Administrator.
(3) Serious and Severe Areas; State election
If a State fails to submit a demonstration under paragraph (2) for any Serious or Severe Area within the required period or if the Administrator determines that the area has not met any applicable milestone, the State shall elect, within 90 days after such failure or determination—
  (A) to have the area reclassified to the next higher classification,
  (B) to implement specific additional measures adequate, as determined by the Administrator, to meet the next milestone as provided in the applicable contingency plan, or
  (C) to adopt an economic incentive program as described in paragraph (4).
If the State makes an election under subparagraph (B), the Administrator shall, within 90 days after the election, review such plan and shall, if the Administrator finds the contingency plan inadequate, require further measures necessary to meet such milestone. Once the State makes an election, it shall be deemed accepted by the Administrator as meeting the election requirement. If the State fails to make an election required under this paragraph within the required 90-day period or within 6 months thereafter, the area shall be reclassified to the next higher classification by operation of law at the expiration of such 6-month period. Within 12 months after the date required for the State to make an election, the State shall submit a revision of the applicable implementation plan for the area that meets the requirements of this paragraph. The Administrator shall review such plan revision and approve or disapprove the revision within 9 months after the date of its submission.
(4) Economic incentive program
  (A) An economic incentive program under this paragraph shall be consistent with rules published by the Administrator and sufficient, in combination with other elements of the State plan, to achieve the next milestone. The State program may include a nondiscriminatory system, consistent with applicable law regarding interstate commerce, of State established emissions fees or a system of marketable permits, or a system of State fees on sale or manufacture of products the use of which contributes to ozone formation, or any combination of the foregoing or other similar measures. The program may also include incentives and requirements to reduce vehicle emissions and vehicle miles traveled in the area, including any of the transportation control measures identified in section 7408(f) of this title.
  (B) Within 2 years after November 15, 1990, the Administrator shall publish rules for the programs to be adopted pursuant to subparagraph (A). Such rules shall include model plan provisions which may be adopted for reducing emissions from permitted stationary sources, area sources, and mobile sources. The guidelines shall require that any revenues generated by the plan provisions adopted pursuant to subparagraph (A) shall be used by the State for any of the following:
    (i) Providing incentives for achieving emission reductions.
    (ii) Providing assistance for the development of innovative technologies for the control of ozone air pollution and for the development of lower-polluting solvents and surface coatings. Such assistance shall not provide for the payment of more than 75 percent of either the costs of any project to develop such a technology or the costs of development of a lower-polluting solvent or surface coating.

(iii) Funding the administrative costs of State programs under this chapter. Not more than 50 percent of such revenues may be used for purposes of this clause.
(5) Extreme Areas
If a State fails to submit a demonstration under paragraph (2) for any Extreme Area within the required period, or if the Administrator determines that the area has not met any applicable milestone, the State shall, within 9 months after such failure or determination, submit a plan revision to implement an economic incentive program which meets the requirements of paragraph (4). The Administrator shall review such plan revision and approve or disapprove the revision within 9 months after the date of its submission.
(h) Rural transport areas
  (1) Notwithstanding any other provision of section 7511 of this title or this section, a State containing an ozone nonattainment area that does not include, and is not adjacent to, any part of a Metropolitan Statistical Area or, where one exists, a Consolidated Metropolitan Statistical Area (as defined by the United States Bureau of the Census), which area is treated by the Administrator, in the Administrator's discretion, as a rural transport area within the meaning of paragraph (2), shall be treated by operation of law as satisfying the requirements of this section if it makes the submissions required under subsection (a) of this section (relating to marginal areas).
  (2) The Administrator may treat an ozone nonattainment area as a rural transport area if the Administrator finds that sources of VOC (and, where the Administrator determines relevant, NO_x) emissions within the area do not make a significant contribution to the ozone concentrations measured in the area or in other areas.
(i) Reclassified areas
Each State containing an ozone nonattainment area reclassified under section 7511(b)(2) of this title shall meet such requirements of subsections (b) through (d) of this section as may be applicable to the area as reclassified, according to the schedules prescribed in connection with such requirements, except that the Administrator may adjust any applicable deadlines (other than attainment dates) to the extent such adjustment is necessary or appropriate to assure consistency among the required submissions.
(j) Multi-State ozone nonattainment areas
  (1) Coordination among States
  Each State in which there is located a portion of a single ozone nonattainment area which covers more than one State (hereinafter in this section referred to as a "multi-State ozone nonattainment area") shall—
    (A) take all reasonable steps to coordinate, substantively and procedurally, the revisions and implementation of State implementation plans applicable to the nonattainment area concerned; and
    (B) use photochemical grid modeling or any other analytical method determined by the Administrator, in his discretion, to be at least as effective.
  The Administrator may not approve any revision of a State implementation plan submitted under this part for a State in which part of a multi-State ozone nonattainment area is located if the plan revision for that State fails to comply with the requirements of this subsection.
  (2) Failure to demonstrate attainment
  If any State in which there is located a portion of a multi-State ozone nonattainment area fails to provide a demonstration of attainment of the national ambient air quality standard for ozone in that portion within the required period, the State may petition the Administrator to make a finding that the State would have been able to make such demonstration but for the failure of one or more other States in which other portions of the area are located to commit to the implementation of all measures required under this section (relating to plan submissions and requirements for ozone nonattainment areas). If the Administrator makes such finding, the provisions of section 7509 of this title (relating to sanctions) shall not apply, by reason of the failure to make such demonstration, in the portion of the multi-State ozone nonattainment area within the State submitting such petition.

(July 14, 1955, ch. 360, title I, Sec. 182, as added Pub. L. 101-549, title I, Sec. 103, Nov. 15, 1990, 104 Stat. 2426; amended Pub. L. 104-70, Sec. 1, Dec. 23, 1995, 109 Stat. 773.)

References in Text

The Natural Gas Policy Act of 1978, referred to in subsec. (e)(3), is Pub. L. 95-621, Nov. 9, 1978, 92 Stat. 3350, as amended. Title III of the Act is classified generally to subchapter III (Sec. 3361 et seq.) of chapter 60 of Title 15, Commerce and Trade. For complete classification of this Act to the Code, see Short Title note set out under section 3301 of Title 15 and Tables.

Amendments

1995—Subsec. (d)(1)(B). Pub. L. 104-70 amended subpar. (B) generally. Prior to amendment, subpar. (B) read as follows: "Within 2 years after November 15, 1990, the State shall submit a revision requiring employers in such area to implement programs to reduce work-related vehicle trips and miles traveled by employees. Such revision shall be developed in accordance with guidance issued by the Administrator pursuant to section 7408(f) of this title and shall, at a minimum, require that each employer of 100 or more persons in such area increase average passenger occupancy per vehicle in commuting trips between home and the workplace during peak travel periods by not less than 25 percent above the average vehicle occupancy for all such trips in the area at the time the revision is submitted. The guidance of the Administrator may specify average vehicle occupancy rates which vary for locations within a nonattainment area (suburban, center city, business district) or among nonattainment areas reflecting existing occupancy rates and the availability of high occupancy modes. The revision shall provide that each employer subject to a vehicle occupancy requirement shall submit a compliance plan within 2 years after the date the revision is submitted which shall convincingly demonstrate compliance with the requirements of this paragraph not later than 4 years after such date."

Moratorium on Certain Emissions Testing Requirements

Pub. L. 104-59, title III, Sec. 348, Nov. 28, 1995, 109 Stat. 617, provided that:

"(a) In General.—The Administrator of the Environmental Protection Agency (hereinafter in this section referred to as the 'Administrator') shall not require adoption or implementation by a State of a test-only I/M240 enhanced vehicle inspection and maintenance program as a means of compliance with section 182 or 187 of the Clean Air Act (42 U.S.C. 7511a; 7512a), but the Administrator may approve such a program if a State chooses to adopt the program as a means of compliance with such section.

(b) Limitation on Plan Disapproval.—The Administrator shall not disapprove or apply an automatic discount to a State implementation plan revision under section 182 or 187 of the Clean Air Act (42 U.S.C. 7511a; 7512a) on the basis of a policy, regulation, or guidance providing for a discount of emissions credits because the inspection and maintenance program in such plan revision is decentralized or a test-and-repair program.

(c) Emissions Reduction Credits.—
   (1) State plan revision; approval.—Within 120 days of the date of the enactment of this subsection [Nov. 28, 1995], a State may submit an implementation plan revision proposing an interim inspection and maintenance program under section 182 or 187 of the Clean Air Act (42 U.S.C. 7511a; 7512a). The Administrator shall approve the program based on the full amount of credits proposed by the State for each element of the program if the proposed credits reflect good faith estimates by the State and the revision is otherwise in compliance with such Act. If, within such 120-day period, the State submits to the Administrator proposed revisions to the implementation plan, has all of the statutory authority necessary to implement the revisions, and has proposed a regulation to make the revisions, the Administrator may approve the revisions without regard to whether or not such regulation has been issued as a final regulation by the State.
   (2) Expiration of interim approval.—The interim approval shall expire on the earlier of (A) the last day of the 18-month period beginning on the date of the interim approval, or (B) the date of final approval. The interim approval may not be extended.
   (3) Final approval.—The Administrator shall grant final approval of the revision based on the credits proposed by the State during or after the period of interim approval if data collected on the operation of the State program demonstrates that the credits are appropriate and the revision is otherwise in compliance with the Clean Air Act [42 U.S.C. 7401 et seq.].
   (4) Basis of approval; no automatic discount.—Any determination with respect to interim or full approval shall be based on the elements of the program and shall not apply any automatic discount because the program is decentralized or a test-and-repair program."

Section Referred to in Other Sections

This section is referred to in sections 7504, 7506, 7511, 7511c, 7511d, 7512a, 7521 of this title.

FEDERAL OZONE MEASURES

42 USC 7511b

(a) Control techniques guidelines for VOC sources
Within 3 years after November 15, 1990, the Administrator shall issue control techniques guidelines, in accordance with section 7408 of this title, for 11 categories of stationary sources of VOC emissions for which such guidelines have not been issued as of November 15, 1990, not including the categories referred to in paragraphs (3) and (4) of subsection (b) of this section. The Administrator may issue such additional control techniques guidelines as the Administrator deems necessary.

(b) Existing and new CTGS
  (1) Within 36 months after November 15, 1990, and periodically thereafter, the Administrator shall review and, if necessary, update control technique guidance issued under section 7408 of this title before November 15, 1990.
  (2) In issuing the guidelines the Administrator shall give priority to those categories which the Administrator considers to make the most significant contribution to the formation of ozone air pollution in ozone nonattainment areas, including hazardous waste treatment, storage, and disposal facilities which are permitted under subtitle C of the Solid Waste Disposal Act [42 U.S.C. 6921 et seq.]. Thereafter the Administrator shall periodically review and, if necessary, revise such guidelines.
  (3) Within 3 years after November 15, 1990, the Administrator shall issue control techniques guidelines in accordance with section 7408 of this title to reduce the aggregate emissions of volatile organic compounds into the ambient air from aerospace coatings and solvents. Such control techniques guidelines shall, at a minimum, be adequate to reduce aggregate emissions of volatile organic compounds into the ambient air from the application of such coatings and solvents to such level as the Administrator determines may be achieved through the adoption of best available control measures. Such control technology guidance shall provide for such reductions in such increments and on such schedules as the Administrator determines to be reasonable, but in no event later than 10 years after the final issuance of such control technology guidance. In developing control technology guidance under this subsection, the Administrator shall consult with the Secretary of Defense, the Secretary of Transportation, and the Administrator of the National Aeronautics and Space Administration with regard to the establishment of specifications for such coatings. In evaluating VOC reduction strategies, the guidance shall take into account the applicable requirements of section 7412 of this title and the need to protect stratospheric ozone.
  (4) Within 3 years after November 15, 1990, the Administrator shall issue control techniques guidelines in accordance with section 7408 of this title to reduce the aggregate emissions of volatile organic compounds and PM-10 into the ambient air from paints, coatings, and solvents used in shipbuilding operations and ship repair. Such control techniques guidelines shall, at a minimum, be adequate to reduce aggregate emissions of volatile organic compounds and PM-10 into the ambient air from the removal or application of such paints, coatings, and solvents to such level as the Administrator determines may be achieved through the adoption of the best available control measures. Such control techniques guidelines shall provide for such reductions in such increments and on such schedules as the Administrator determines to be reasonable, but in no event later than 10 years after the final issuance of such control technology guidance. In developing control techniques guidelines under this subsection, the Administrator shall consult with the appropriate Federal agencies.

(c) Alternative control techniques
Within 3 years after November 15, 1990, the Administrator shall issue technical documents which identify alternative controls for all categories of stationary sources of volatile organic compounds and oxides of nitrogen which emit, or have the potential to emit 25 tons per year or more of such air pollutant. The Administrator shall revise and update such documents as the Administrator determines necessary.

(d) Guidance for evaluating cost-effectiveness

Within 1 year after November 15, 1990, the Administrator shall provide guidance to the States to be used in evaluating the relative cost-effectiveness of various options for the control of emissions from existing stationary sources of air pollutants which contribute to nonattainment of the national ambient air quality standards for ozone.

(e) Control of emissions from certain sources
   (1) Definitions
      For purposes of this subsection—
      (A) Best available controls
         The term "best available controls" means the degree of emissions reduction that the Administrator determines, on the basis of technological and economic feasibility, health, environmental, and energy impacts, is achievable through the application of the most effective equipment, measures, processes, methods, systems or techniques, including chemical reformulation, product or feedstock substitution, repackaging, and directions for use, consumption, storage, or disposal.
      (B) Consumer or commercial product
         The term "consumer or commercial product" means any substance, product (including paints, coatings, and solvents), or article (including any container or packaging) held by any person, the use, consumption, storage, disposal, destruction, or decomposition of which may result in the release of volatile organic compounds. The term does not include fuels or fuel additives regulated under section 7545 of this title, or motor vehicles, non-road vehicles, and non-road engines as defined under section 7550 of this title.
      (C) Regulated entities
         The term "regulated entities" means—
         (i) manufacturers, processors, wholesale distributors, or importers of consumer or commercial products for sale or distribution in interstate commerce in the United States; or
         (ii) manufacturers, processors, wholesale distributors, or importers that supply the entities listed under clause (i) with such products for sale or distribution in interstate commerce in the United States.
   (2) Study and report
      (A) Study
         The Administrator shall conduct a study of the emissions of volatile organic compounds into the ambient air from consumer and commercial products (or any combination thereof) in order to—
         (i) determine their potential to contribute to ozone levels which violate the national ambient air quality standard for ozone; and
         (ii) establish criteria for regulating consumer and commercial products or classes or categories thereof which shall be subject to control under this subsection.
         The study shall be completed and a report submitted to Congress not later than 3 years after November 15, 1990.
      (B) Consideration of certain factors
         In establishing the criteria under subparagraph (A)(ii), the Administrator shall take into consideration each of the following:
         (i) The uses, benefits, and commercial demand of consumer and commercial products.
         (ii) The health or safety functions (if any) served by such consumer and commercial products.
         (iii) Those consumer and commercial products which emit highly reactive volatile organic compounds into the ambient air.
         (iv) Those consumer and commercial products which are subject to the most cost-effective controls.
         (v) The availability of alternatives (if any) to such consumer and commercial products which are of comparable costs, considering health, safety, and environmental impacts.
   (3) Regulations to require emission reductions
      (A) In general
         Upon submission of the final report under paragraph (2), the Administrator shall list those categories of consumer or commercial products that the Administrator deter-

mines, based on the study, account for at least 80 percent of the VOC emissions, on a reactivity-adjusted basis, from consumer or commercial products in areas that violate the NAAQS for ozone. Credit toward the 80 percent emissions calculation shall be given for emission reductions from consumer or commercial products made after November 15, 1990. At such time, the Administrator shall divide the list into 4 groups establishing priorities for regulation based on the criteria established in paragraph (2). Every 2 years after promulgating such list, the Administrator shall regulate one group of categories until all 4 groups are regulated. The regulations shall require best available controls as defined in this section. Such regulations may exempt health use products for which the Administrator determines there is no suitable substitute. In order to carry out this section, the Administrator may, by regulation, control or prohibit any activity, including the manufacture or introduction into commerce, offering for sale, or sale of any consumer or commercial product which results in emission of volatile organic compounds into the ambient air.

(B) Regulated entities

Regulations under this subsection may be imposed only with respect to regulated entities.

(C) Use of CTGS

For any consumer or commercial product the Administrator may issue control techniques guidelines under this chapter in lieu of regulations required under subparagraph (A) if the Administrator determines that such guidance will be substantially as effective as regulations in reducing emissions of volatile organic compounds which contribute to ozone levels in areas which violate the national ambient air quality standard for ozone.

(4) Systems of regulation

The regulations under this subsection may include any system or systems of regulation as the Administrator may deem appropriate, including requirements for registration and labeling, self-monitoring and reporting, prohibitions, limitations, or economic incentives (including marketable permits and auctions of emissions rights) concerning the manufacture, processing, distribution, use, consumption, or disposal of the product.

(5) Special fund

Any amounts collected by the Administrator under such regulations shall be deposited in a special fund in the United States Treasury for licensing and other services, which thereafter shall be available until expended, subject to annual appropriation Acts, solely to carry out the activities of the Administrator for which such fees, charges, or collections are established or made.

(6) Enforcement

Any regulation established under this subsection shall be treated, for purposes of enforcement of this chapter, as a standard under section 7411 of this title and any violation of such regulation shall be treated as a violation of a requirement of section 7411(e) of this title.

(7) State administration

Each State may develop and submit to the Administrator a procedure under State law for implementing and enforcing regulations promulgated under this subsection. If the Administrator finds the State procedure is adequate, the Administrator shall approve such procedure. Nothing in this paragraph shall prohibit the Administrator from enforcing any applicable regulations under this subsection.

(8) Size, etc.

No regulations regarding the size, shape, or labeling of a product may be promulgated, unless the Administrator determines such regulations to be useful in meeting any national ambient air quality standard.

(9) State consultation

Any State which proposes regulations other than those adopted under this subsection shall consult with the Administrator regarding whether any other State or local subdivision has promulgated or is promulgating regulations on any products covered under this part. The Administrator shall establish a clearinghouse of information, studies, and regulations proposed and promulgated regarding products covered under this subsection and disseminate such information collected as requested by State or local subdivisions.

(f) Tank vessel standards
  (1) Schedule for standards
    (A) Within 2 years after November 15, 1990, the Administrator, in consultation with the Secretary of the Department in which the Coast Guard is operating, shall promulgate standards applicable to the emission of VOCs and any other air pollutant from loading and unloading of tank vessels (as that term is defined in section 2101 of title 46) which the Administrator finds causes, or contributes to, air pollution that may be reasonably anticipated to endanger public health or welfare. Such standards shall require the application of reasonably available control technology, considering costs, any nonair-quality benefits, environmental impacts, energy requirements and safety factors associated with alternative control techniques. To the extent practicable such standards shall apply to loading and unloading facilities and not to tank vessels.
    (B) Any regulation prescribed under this subsection (and any revision thereof) shall take effect after such period as the Administrator finds (after consultation with the Secretary of the department[1] in which the Coast Guard is operating) necessary to permit the development and application of the requisite technology, giving appropriate consideration to the cost of compliance within such period, except that the effective date shall not be more than 2 years after promulgation of such regulations.
  (2) Regulations on equipment safety
  Within 6 months after November 15, 1990, the Secretary of the Department in which the Coast Guard is operating shall issue regulations to ensure the safety of the equipment and operations which are to control emissions from the loading and unloading of tank vessels, under section 3703 of title 46 and section 1225 of title 33. The standards promulgated by the Administrator under paragraph (1) and the regulations issued by a State or political subdivision regarding emissions from the loading and unloading of tank vessels shall be consistent with the regulations regarding safety of the Department in which the Coast Guard is operating.
  (3) Agency authority
    (A) The Administrator shall ensure compliance with the tank vessel emission standards prescribed under paragraph (1)(A). The Secretary of the Department in which the Coast Guard is operating shall also ensure compliance with the tank vessel standards prescribed under paragraph (1)(A).
    (B) The Secretary of the Department in which the Coast Guard is operating shall ensure compliance with the regulations issued under paragraph (2).
  (4) State or local standards
  After the Administrator promulgates standards under this section, no State or political subdivision thereof may adopt or attempt to enforce any standard respecting emissions from tank vessels subject to regulation under paragraph (1) unless such standard is no less stringent than the standards promulgated under paragraph (1).
  (5) Enforcement
  Any standard established under paragraph (1)(A) shall be treated, for purposes of enforcement of this chapter, as a standard under section 7411 of this title and any violation of such standard shall be treated as a violation of a requirement of section 7411(e) of this title.
(g) Ozone design value study
The Administrator shall conduct a study of whether the methodology in use by the Environmental Protection Agency as of November 15, 1990, for establishing a design value for ozone provides a reasonable indicator of the ozone air quality of ozone nonattainment areas. The Administrator shall obtain input from States, local subdivisions thereof, and others. The study shall be completed and a report submitted to Congress not later than 3 years after November 15, 1990. The results of the study shall be subject to peer and public review before submitting it to Congress.
(h) Vehicles entering ozone nonattainment areas
  (1) Authority regarding ozone inspection and maintenance testing
    (A) In general
      No noncommercial motor vehicle registered in a foreign country and operated by a United States citizen or by an alien who is a permanent resident of the United States,

---

[1] So in original. Probably should be capitalized.

or who holds a visa for the purposes of employment or educational study in the United States, may enter a covered ozone nonattainment area from a foreign country bordering the United States and contiguous to the nonattainment area more than twice in a single calendar-month period, if State law has requirements for the inspection and maintenance of such vehicles under the applicable implementation plan in the nonattainment area.
- (B) Applicability
Subparagraph (A) shall not apply if the operator presents documentation at the United States border entry point establishing that the vehicle has complied with such inspection and maintenance requirements as are in effect and are applicable to motor vehicles of the same type and model year.
- (2) Sanctions for violations
The President may impose and collect from the operator of any motor vehicle who violates, or attempts to violate, paragraph (1) a civil penalty of not more than $200 for the second violation or attempted violation and $400 for the third and each subsequent violation or attempted violation.
- (3) State election
The prohibition set forth in paragraph (1) shall not apply in any State that elects to be exempt from the prohibition. Such an election shall take effect upon the President's receipt of written notice from the Governor of the State notifying the President of such election.
- (4) Alternative approach
The prohibition set forth in paragraph (1) shall not apply in a State, and the President may implement an alternative approach, if—
  - (A) the Governor of the State submits to the President a written description of an alternative approach to facilitate the compliance, by some or all foreign-registered motor vehicles, with the motor vehicle inspection and maintenance requirements that are—
    - (i) related to emissions of air pollutants;
    - (ii) in effect under the applicable implementation plan in the covered ozone nonattainment area; and
    - (iii) applicable to motor vehicles of the same types and model years as the foreign-registered motor vehicles; and
  - (B) the President approves the alternative approach as facilitating compliance with the motor vehicle inspection and maintenance requirements referred to in subparagraph (A).
- (5) Definition of covered ozone nonattainment area
In this section, the term "covered ozone nonattainment area" means a Serious Area, as classified under section 7511 of this title as of October 27, 1998.

(July 14, 1955, ch. 360, title I, Sec. 183, as added Pub. L. 101-549, title I, Sec. 103, Nov. 15, 1990, 104 Stat. 2443; amended Pub. L. 105-286, Sec. 2, Oct. 27, 1998, 112 Stat. 2773.)

References in Text

The Solid Waste Disposal Act, referred to in subsec. (b)(2), is title II of Pub. L. 89-272, Oct. 20, 1965, 79 Stat. 997, as amended generally by Pub. L. 94-580, Sec. 2, Oct. 21, 1976, 90 Stat. 2795. Subtitle C of the Act is classified generally to subchapter III (Sec. 6921 et seq.) of chapter 82 of this title. For complete classification of this Act to the Code, see Short Title note set out under section 6901 of this title and Tables.

Amendments

1998—Subsec. (h). Pub. L. 105-286 added subsec. (h).

Effective Date of 1998 Amendment; Publication of Prohibition

Pub. L. 105-286, Sec. 3, Oct. 27, 1998, 112 Stat. 2774, provided that:

"(a) In General.—The amendment made by section 2 [amending this section] takes effect 180 days after the date of the enactment of this Act [Oct. 27, 1998]. Nothing in that amendment shall require action that is inconsistent with the obligations of the United States under any international agreement.

(b) Information.—As soon as practicable after the date of the enactment of this Act, the appropriate agency of the United States shall distribute information to publicize the prohibition set forth in the amendment made by section 2."

Section Referred to in Other Sections
This section is referred to in section 7607 of this title.

CONTROL OF INTERSTATE OZONE AIR POLLUTION

42 USC 7511c

(a) Ozone transport regions

A single transport region for ozone (within the meaning of section 7506a(a) of this title), comprised of the States of Connecticut, Delaware, Maine, Maryland, Massachusetts, New Hampshire, New Jersey, New York, Pennsylvania, Rhode Island, Vermont, and the Consolidated Metropolitan Statistical Area that includes the District of Columbia, is hereby established by operation of law. The provisions of section 7506a(a)(1) and (2) of this title shall apply with respect to the transport region established under this section and any other transport region established for ozone, except to the extent inconsistent with the provisions of this section. The Administrator shall convene the commission required (under section 7506a(b) of this title) as a result of the establishment of such region within 6 months of November 15, 1990.

(b) Plan provisions for States in ozone transport regions
  (1) In accordance with section 7410 of this title, not later than 2 years after November 15, 1990 (or 9 months after the subsequent inclusion of a State in a transport region established for ozone), each State included within a transport region established for ozone shall submit a State implementation plan or revision thereof to the Administrator which requires the following—
    (A) that each area in such State that is in an ozone transport region, and that is a metropolitan statistical area or part thereof with a population of 100,000 or more comply with the provisions of section 7511a(c)(2)(A) of this title (pertaining to enhanced vehicle inspection and maintenance programs); and
    (B) implementation of reasonably available control technology with respect to all sources of volatile organic compounds in the State covered by a control techniques guideline issued before or after November 15, 1990.
  (2) Within 3 years after November 15, 1990, the Administrator shall complete a study identifying control measures capable of achieving emission reductions comparable to those achievable through vehicle refueling controls contained in section 7511a(b)(3) of this title, and such measures or such vehicle refueling controls shall be implemented in accordance with the provisions of this section. Notwithstanding other deadlines in this section, the applicable implementation plan shall be revised to reflect such measures within 1 year of completion of the study. For purposes of this section any stationary source that emits or has the potential to emit at least 50 tons per year of volatile organic compounds shall be considered a major stationary source and subject to the requirements which would be applicable to major stationary sources if the area were classified as a Moderate nonattainment area.

(c) Additional control measures
  (1) Recommendations
    Upon petition of any State within a transport region established for ozone, and based on a majority vote of the Governors on the Commission[1] (or their designees), the Commission[1] may, after notice and opportunity for public comment, develop recommendations for additional control measures to be applied within all or a part of such transport region if the commission determines such measures are necessary to bring any area in such region into attainment by the dates provided by this subpart. The commission shall transmit such recommendations to the Administrator.
  (2) Notice and review
    Whenever the Administrator receives recommendations prepared by a commission pursuant to paragraph (1) (the date of receipt of which shall hereinafter in this section be referred to as the "receipt date"), the Administrator shall—
    (A) immediately publish in the Federal Register a notice stating that the recommendations are available and provide an opportunity for public hearing within 90 days beginning on the receipt date; and

---
[1] So in original. Probably should not be capitalized.

(B) commence a review of the recommendations to determine whether the control measures in the recommendations are necessary to bring any area in such region into attainment by the dates provided by this subpart and are otherwise consistent with this chapter.

(3) Consultation

In undertaking the review required under paragraph (2)(B), the Administrator shall consult with members of the commission of the affected States and shall take into account the data, views, and comments received pursuant to paragraph (2)(A).

(4) Approval and disapproval

Within 9 months after the receipt date, the Administrator shall (A) determine whether to approve, disapprove, or partially disapprove and partially approve the recommendations; (B) notify the commission in writing of such approval, disapproval, or partial disapproval; and (C) publish such determination in the Federal Register. If the Administrator disapproves or partially disapproves the recommendations, the Administrator shall specify—

   (i) why any disapproved additional control measures are not necessary to bring any area in such region into attainment by the dates provided by this subpart or are otherwise not consistent with the[2] chapter; and

   (ii) recommendations concerning equal or more effective actions that could be taken by the commission to conform the disapproved portion of the recommendations to the requirements of this section.

(5) Finding

Upon approval or partial approval of recommendations submitted by a commission, the Administrator shall issue to each State which is included in the transport region and to which a requirement of the approved plan applies, a finding under section 7410(k)(5) of this title that the implementation plan for such State is inadequate to meet the requirements of section 7410(a)(2)(D) of this title. Such finding shall require each such State to revise its implementation plan to include the approved additional control measures within one year after the finding is issued.

(d) Best available air quality monitoring and modeling

For purposes of this section, not later than 6 months after November 15, 1990, the Administrator shall promulgate criteria for purposes of determining the contribution of sources in one area to concentrations of ozone in another area which is a nonattainment area for ozone. Such criteria shall require that the best available air quality monitoring and modeling techniques be used for purposes of making such determinations.

(July 14, 1955, ch. 360, title I, Sec. 184, as added Pub. L. 101-549, title I, Sec. 103, Nov. 15, 1990, 104 Stat. 2448.)

Section Referred to in Other Sections

This section is referred to in sections 7406, 7410, 7511a of this title.

ENFORCEMENT FOR SEVERE AND EXTREME OZONE NONATTAINMENT AREAS FOR FAILURE TO ATTAIN

42 USC 7511d

(a) General rule

Each implementation plan revision required under section 7511a(d) and (e) of this title (relating to the attainment plan for Severe and Extreme ozone nonattainment areas) shall provide that, if the area to which such plan revision applies has failed to attain the national primary ambient air quality standard for ozone by the applicable attainment date, each major stationary source of VOCs located in the area shall, except as otherwise provided under subsection (c) of this section, pay a fee to the State as a penalty for such failure, computed in accordance with subsection (b) of this section, for each calendar year beginning after the attainment date, until the area is redesignated as an attainment area for ozone. Each such plan revision should include procedures for assessment and collection of such fees.

---

[2]So in original. Probably should be "this".

(b) Computation of fee
  (1) Fee amount
    The fee shall equal $5,000, adjusted in accordance with paragraph (3), per ton of VOC emitted by the source during the calendar year in excess of 80 percent of the baseline amount, computed under paragraph (2).
  (2) Baseline amount
    For purposes of this section, the baseline amount shall be computed, in accordance with such guidance as the Administrator may provide, as the lower of the amount of actual VOC emissions ("actuals") or VOC emissions allowed under the permit applicable to the source (or, if no such permit has been issued for the attainment year, the amount of VOC emissions allowed under the applicable implementation plan ("allowables")) during the attainment year. Notwithstanding the preceding sentence, the Administrator may issue guidance authorizing the baseline amount to be determined in accordance with the lower of average actuals or average allowables, determined over a period of more than one calendar year. Such guidance may provide that such average calculation for a specific source may be used if that source's emissions are irregular, cyclical, or otherwise vary significantly from year to year.
  (3) Annual adjustment
    The fee amount under paragraph (1) shall be adjusted annually, beginning in the year beginning after 1990, in accordance with section 7661a(b)(3)(B)(v) of this title (relating to inflation adjustment).
(c) Exception
  Notwithstanding any provision of this section, no source shall be required to pay any fee under subsection (a) of this section with respect to emissions during any year that is treated as an Extension Year under section 7511(a)(5) of this title.
(d) Fee collection by Administrator
  If the Administrator has found that the fee provisions of the implementation plan do not meet the requirements of this section, or if the Administrator makes a finding that the State is not administering and enforcing the fee required under this section, the Administrator shall, in addition to any other action authorized under this subchapter, collect, in accordance with procedures promulgated by the Administrator, the unpaid fees required under subsection (a) of this section. If the Administrator makes such a finding under section 7509(a)(4) of this title, the Administrator may collect fees for periods before the determination, plus interest computed in accordance with section 6621(a)(2) of title 26 (relating to computation of interest on underpayment of Federal taxes), to the extent the Administrator finds such fees have not been paid to the State. The provisions of clauses (ii) through (iii) of section 7661a(b)(3)(C) of this title (relating to penalties and use of the funds, respectively) shall apply with respect to fees collected under this subsection.
(e) Exemptions for certain small areas
  For areas with a total population under 200,000 which fail to attain the standard by the applicable attainment date, no sanction under this section or under any other provision of this chapter shall apply if the area can demonstrate, consistent with guidance issued by the Administrator, that attainment in the area is prevented because of ozone or ozone precursors transported from other areas. The prohibition applies only in cases in which the area has met all requirements and implemented all measures applicable to the area under this chapter.

(July 14, 1955, ch. 360, title I, Sec. 185, as added Pub. L. 101-549, title I, Sec. 103, Nov. 15, 1990, 104 Stat. 2450.)

Section Referred to in Other Sections

This section is referred to in sections 7509a, 7511, 7511a of this title.

TRANSITIONAL AREAS

42 USC 7511e

If an area designated as an ozone nonattainment area as of November 15, 1990, has not violated the national primary ambient air quality standard for ozone for the 36-month period commencing on January 1, 1987, and ending on December 31, 1989, the Administrator shall suspend the appli-

198 / Environmental Statutes

cation of the requirements of this subpart to such area until December 31, 1991. By June 30, 1992, the Administrator shall determine by order, based on the area's design value as of the attainment date, whether the area attained such standard by December 31, 1991. If the Administrator determines that the area attained the standard, the Administrator shall require, as part of the order, the State to submit a maintenance plan for the area within 12 months of such determination. If the Administrator determines that the area failed to attain the standard, the Administrator shall, by June 30, 1992, designate the area as nonattainment under section 7407(d)(4) of this title.

(July 14, 1955, ch. 360, title I, Sec. 185A, as added Pub. L. 101-549, title I, Sec. 103, Nov. 15, 1990, 104 Stat. 2451.)

NO_x AND VOC STUDY

42 USC 7511f

The Administrator, in conjunction with the National Academy of Sciences, shall conduct a study on the role of ozone precursors in tropospheric ozone formation and control. The study shall examine the roles of NO_x and VOC emission reductions, the extent to which NO_x reductions may contribute (or be counterproductive) to achievement of attainment in different nonattainment areas, the sensitivity of ozone to the control of NO_x, the availability and extent of controls for NO_x, the role of biogenic VOC emissions, and the basic information required for air quality models. The study shall be completed and a proposed report made public for 30 days comment within 1 year of November 15, 1990, and a final report shall be submitted to Congress within 15 months after November 15, 1990. The Administrator shall utilize all available information and studies, as well as develop additional information, in conducting the study required by this section.

(July 14, 1955, ch. 360, title I, Sec. 185B, as added Pub. L. 101-549, title I, Sec. 103, Nov. 15, 1990, 104 Stat. 2452.)

Section Referred to in Other Sections

This section is referred to in section 7511a of this title.

Subpart 3—Additional Provisions for Carbon Monoxide Nonattainment Areas

CLASSIFICATION AND ATTAINMENT DATES

42 USC 7512

(a) Classification by operation of law and attainment dates for nonattainment areas
  (1) Each area designated nonattainment for carbon monoxide pursuant to section 7407(d) of this title shall be classified at the time of such designation under table 1, by operation of law, as a Moderate Area or a Serious Area based on the design value for the area. The design value shall be calculated according to the interpretation methodology issued by the Administrator most recently before November 15, 1990. For each area classified under this subsection, the primary standard attainment date for carbon monoxide shall be as expeditiously as practicable but not later than the date provided in table 1:

TABLE 3[1]

Area classification	Design value	Primary standard attainment date
Moderate	9.1-16.4 ppm	December 31, 1995
Serious	16.5 and above	December 31, 2000

  (2) At the time of publication of the notice required under section 7407 of this title (designating carbon monoxide nonattainment areas), the Administrator shall publish a notice announcing the classification of each such carbon monoxide nonattainment area. The provisions of section 7502(a)(1)(B) of this title (relating to lack of notice-and-comment and judicial review) shall apply with respect to such classification.

[1] So in original. Probably should be "TABLE 1".

(3) If an area classified under paragraph (1), table 1, would have been classified in another category if the design value in the area were 5 percent greater or 5 percent less than the level on which such classification was based, the Administrator may, in the Administrator's discretion, within 90 days after November 15, 1990, by the procedure required under paragraph (2), adjust the classification of the area. In making such adjustment, the Administrator may consider the number of exceedances of the national primary ambient air quality standard for carbon monoxide in the area, the level of pollution transport between the area and the other affected areas, and the mix of sources and air pollutants in the area. The Administrator may make the same adjustment for purposes of paragraphs (2), (3), (6), and (7) of section 7512a(a) of this title.

(4) Upon application by any State, the Administrator may extend for 1 additional year (hereinafter in this subpart referred to as the "Extension Year") the date specified in table 1 of subsection (a) of this section if—
  (A) the State has complied with all requirements and commitments pertaining to the area in the applicable implementation plan, and
  (B) no more than one exceedance of the national ambient air quality standard level for carbon monoxide has occurred in the area in the year preceding the Extension Year.
  No more than 2 one-year extensions may be issued under this paragraph for a single nonattainment area.

(b) New designations and reclassifications
  (1) New designations to nonattainment
    Any area that is designated attainment or unclassifiable for carbon monoxide under section 7407(d)(4) of this title, and that is subsequently redesignated to nonattainment for carbon monoxide under section 7407(d)(3) of this title, shall, at the time of the redesignation, be classified by operation of law in accordance with table 1 under subsections (a)(1) and (a)(4) of this section. Upon its classification, the area shall be subject to the same requirements under section 7410 of this title, subpart 1 of this part, and this subpart that would have applied had the area been so classified at the time of the notice under subsection (a)(2) of this section, except that any absolute, fixed date applicable in connection with any such requirement is extended by operation of law by a period equal to the length of time between November 15, 1990, and the date the area is classified.
  (2) Reclassification of Moderate Areas upon failure to attain
    (A) General rule
      Within 6 months following the applicable attainment date for a carbon monoxide nonattainment area, the Administrator shall determine, based on the area's design value as of the attainment date, whether the area has attained the standard by that date. Any Moderate Area that the Administrator finds has not attained the standard by that date shall be reclassified by operation of law in accordance with table 1 of subsection (a)(1) of this section as a Serious Area.
    (B) Publication of notice
      The Administrator shall publish a notice in the Federal Register, no later than 6 months following the attainment date, identifying each area that the Administrator has determined, under subparagraph (A), as having failed to attain and identifying the reclassification, if any, described under subparagraph (A).

(c) References to terms
  Any reference in this subpart to a "Moderate Area" or a "Serious Area" shall be considered a reference to a Moderate Area or a Serious Area, respectively, as classified under this section.

(July 14, 1955, ch. 360, title I, Sec. 186, as added Pub. L. 101-549, title I, Sec. 104, Nov. 15, 1990, 104 Stat. 2452.)

Section Referred to in Other Sections

This section is referred to in sections 7509a, 7512a, 7545, 7607 of this title; title 23 section 149.

PLAN SUBMISSIONS AND REQUIREMENTS
42 USC 7512a

(a) Moderate Areas
Each State in which all or part of a Moderate Area is located shall, with respect to the Moderate Area (or portion thereof, to the extent specified in guidance of the Administrator issued before November 15, 1990), submit to the Administrator the State implementation plan revisions (including the plan items) described under this subsection, within such periods as are prescribed under this subsection, except to the extent the State has made such submissions as of November 15, 1990:
(1) Inventory
No later than 2 years from November 15, 1990, the State shall submit a comprehensive, accurate, current inventory of actual emissions from all sources, as described in section 7502(c)(3) of this title, in accordance with guidance provided by the Administrator.
(2) (A) Vehicle miles traveled
No later than 2 years after November 15, 1990, for areas with a design value above 12.7 ppm at the time of classification, the plan revision shall contain a forecast of vehicle miles traveled in the nonattainment area concerned for each year before the year in which the plan projects the national ambient air quality standard for carbon monoxide to be attained in the area. The forecast shall be based on guidance which shall be published by the Administrator, in consultation with the Secretary of Transportation, within 6 months after November 15, 1990. The plan revision shall provide for annual updates of the forecasts to be submitted to the Administrator together with annual reports regarding the extent to which such forecasts proved to be accurate. Such annual reports shall contain estimates of actual vehicle miles traveled in each year for which a forecast was required.
(B) Special rule for Denver
Within 2 years after November 15, 1990, in the case of Denver, the State shall submit a revision that includes the transportation control measures as required in section 7511a(d)(1)(A) of this title except that such revision shall be for the purpose of reducing CO emissions rather than volatile organic compound emissions. If the State fails to include any such measure, the implementation plan shall contain an explanation of why such measure was not adopted and what emissions reduction measure was adopted to provide a comparable reduction in emissions, or reasons why such reduction is not necessary to attain the national primary ambient air quality standard for carbon monoxide.
(3) Contingency provisions
No later than 2 years after November 15, 1990, for areas with a design value above 12.7 ppm at the time of classification, the plan revision shall provide for the implementation of specific measures to be undertaken if any estimate of vehicle miles traveled in the area which is submitted in an annual report under paragraph (2) exceeds the number predicted in the most recent prior forecast or if the area fails to attain the national primary ambient air quality standard for carbon monoxide by the primary standard attainment date. Such measures shall be included in the plan revision as contingency measures to take effect without further action by the State or the Administrator if the prior forecast has been exceeded by an updated forecast or if the national standard is not attained by such deadline.
(4) Savings clause for vehicle inspection and maintenance provisions of the State implementation plan
Immediately after November 15, 1990, for any Moderate Area (or, within the Administrator's discretion, portion thereof), the plan for which is of the type described in section 7511a(a)(2)(B) of this title any provisions necessary to ensure that the applicable implementation plan includes the vehicle inspection and maintenance program described in section 7511a(a)(2)(B) of this title.
(5) Periodic inventory
No later than September 30, 1995, and no later than the end of each 3 year period thereafter, until the area is redesignated to attainment, a revised inventory meeting the requirements of subsection (a)(1) of this section.

(6) Enhanced vehicle inspection and maintenance
No later than 2 years after November 15, 1990, in the case of Moderate Areas with a design value greater than 12.7 ppm at the time of classification, a revision that includes provisions for an enhanced vehicle inspection and maintenance program as required in section 7511a(c)(3) of this title (concerning serious ozone nonattainment areas), except that such program shall be for the purpose of reducing carbon monoxide rather than hydrocarbon emissions.

(7) Attainment demonstration and specific annual emission reductions
In the case of Moderate Areas with a design value greater than 12.7 ppm at the time of classification, no later than 2 years after November 15, 1990, a revision to provide, and a demonstration that the plan as revised will provide, for attainment of the carbon monoxide NAAQS by the applicable attainment date and provisions for such specific annual emission reductions as are necessary to attain the standard by that date.

The Administrator may, in the Administrator's discretion, require States to submit a schedule for submitting any of the revisions or other items required under this subsection. In the case of Moderate Areas with a design value of 12.7 ppm or lower at the time of classification, the requirements of this subsection shall apply in lieu of any requirement that the State submit a demonstration that the applicable implementation plan provides for attainment of the carbon monoxide standard by the applicable attainment date.

(b) Serious Areas
(1) In general
Each State in which all or part of a Serious Area is located shall, with respect to the Serious Area, make the submissions (other than those required under subsection (a)(1)(B)[1] of this section) applicable under subsection (a) of this section to Moderate Areas with a design value of 12.7 ppm or greater at the time of classification, and shall also submit the revision and other items described under this subsection.

(2) Vehicle miles traveled
Within 2 years after November 15, 1990, the State shall submit a revision that includes the transportation control measures as required in section 7511a(d)(1) of this title except that such revision shall be for the purpose of reducing CO emissions rather than volatile organic compound emissions. In the case of any such area (other than an area in New York State) which is a covered area (as defined in section 7586(a)(2)(B) of this title) for purposes of the Clean Fuel Fleet program under part C of subchapter II of this chapter, if the State fails to include any such measure, the implementation plan shall contain an explanation of why such measure was not adopted and what emissions reduction measure was adopted to provide a comparable reduction in emissions, or reasons why such reduction is not necessary to attain the national primary ambient air quality standard for carbon monoxide.

(3) Oxygenated gasoline
(A) Within 2 years after November 15, 1990, the State shall submit a revision to require that gasoline sold, supplied, offered for sale or supply, dispensed, transported or introduced into commerce in the larger of—
(i) the Consolidated Metropolitan Statistical Area (as defined by the United States Office of Management and Budget) (CMSA) in which the area is located, or
(ii) if the area is not located in a CMSA, the Metropolitan Statistical Area (as defined by the United States Office of Management and Budget) in which the area is located,

be blended, during the portion of the year in which the area is prone to high ambient concentrations of carbon monoxide (as determined by the Administrator), with fuels containing such level of oxygen as is necessary, in combination with other measures, to provide for attainment of the carbon monoxide national ambient air quality standard by the applicable attainment date and maintenance of the national ambient air quality standard thereafter in the area. The revision shall provide that such requirement shall take effect no later than October 1, 1993, and shall include a program for implementation and enforcement of the requirement consistent with guidance to be issued by the Administrator.

---

[1]So in original. Subsec. (a)(1) of this section does not contain a subpar. (B).

(B) Notwithstanding subparagraph (A), the revision described in this paragraph shall not be required for an area if the State demonstrates to the satisfaction of the Administrator that the revision is not necessary to provide for attainment of the carbon monoxide national ambient air quality standard by the applicable attainment date and maintenance of the national ambient air quality standard thereafter in the area.

(c) Areas with significant stationary source emissions of CO
  (1) Serious Areas
  In the case of Serious Areas in which stationary sources contribute significantly to carbon monoxide levels (as determined under rules issued by the Administrator), the State shall submit a plan revision within 2 years after November 15, 1990, which provides that the term "major stationary source" includes (in addition to the sources described in section 7602 of this title) any stationary source which emits, or has the potential to emit, 50 tons per year or more of carbon monoxide.
  (2) Waivers for certain areas
  The Administrator may, on a case-by-case basis, waive any requirements that pertain to transportation controls, inspection and maintenance, or oxygenated fuels where the Administrator determines by rule that mobile sources of carbon monoxide do not contribute significantly to carbon monoxide levels in the area.
  (3) Guidelines
  Within 6 months after November 15, 1990, the Administrator shall issue guidelines for and rules determining whether stationary sources contribute significantly to carbon monoxide levels in an area.

(d) CO milestone
  (1) Milestone demonstration
  By March 31, 1996, each State in which all or part of a Serious Area is located shall submit to the Administrator a demonstration that the area has achieved a reduction in emissions of CO equivalent to the total of the specific annual emission reductions required by December 31, 1995. Such reductions shall be referred to in this subsection as the milestone.
  (2) Adequacy of demonstration
  A demonstration under this paragraph shall be submitted in such form and manner, and shall contain such information and analysis, as the Administrator shall require. The Administrator shall determine whether or not a State's demonstration is adequate within 90 days after the Administrator's receipt of a demonstration which contains the information and analysis required by the Administrator.
  (3) Failure to meet emission reduction milestone
  If a State fails to submit a demonstration under paragraph (1) within the required period, or if the Administrator notifies the State that the State has not met the milestone, the State shall, within 9 months after such a failure or notification, submit a plan revision to implement an economic incentive and transportation control program as described in section 7511a(g)(4) of this title. Such revision shall be sufficient to achieve the specific annual reductions in carbon monoxide emissions set forth in the plan by the attainment date.

(e) Multi-State CO nonattainment areas
  (1) Coordination among States
  Each State in which there is located a portion of a single nonattainment area for carbon monoxide which covers more than one State ("multi-State nonattainment area") shall take all reasonable steps to coordinate, substantively and procedurally, the revisions and implementation of State implementation plans applicable to the nonattainment area concerned. The Administrator may not approve any revision of a State implementation plan submitted under this part for a State in which part of a multi-State nonattainment area is located if the plan revision for that State fails to comply with the requirements of this subsection.
  (2) Failure to demonstrate attainment
  If any State in which there is located a portion of a multi-State nonattainment area fails to provide a demonstration of attainment of the national ambient air quality standard for carbon monoxide in that portion within the period required under this part the State may petition the Administrator to make a finding that the State would have been able to make such demonstration but for the failure of one or more other States in which other portions of the area are located to commit to the implementation of all measures required under

this section (relating to plan submissions for carbon monoxide nonattainment areas). If the Administrator makes such finding, in the portion of the nonattainment area within the State submitting such petition, no sanction shall be imposed under section 7509 of this title or under any other provision of this chapter, by reason of the failure to make such demonstration.

(f) Reclassified areas
Each State containing a carbon monoxide nonattainment area reclassified under section 7512(b)(2) of this title shall meet the requirements of subsection (b) of this section, as may be applicable to the area as reclassified, according to the schedules prescribed in connection with such requirements, except that the Administrator may adjust any applicable deadlines (other than the attainment date) where such deadlines are shown to be infeasible.

(g) Failure of Serious Area to attain standard
If the Administrator determines under section 7512(b)(2) of this title that the national primary ambient air quality standard for carbon monoxide has not been attained in a Serious Area by the applicable attainment date, the State shall submit a plan revision for the area within 9 months after the date of such determination. The plan revision shall provide that a program of incentives and requirements as described in section 7511a(g)(4) of this title shall be applicable in the area, and such program, in combination with other elements of the revised plan, shall be adequate to reduce the total tonnage of emissions of carbon monoxide in the area by at least 5 percent per year in each year after approval of the plan revision and before attainment of the national primary ambient air quality standard for carbon monoxide.

(July 14, 1955, ch. 360, title I, Sec. 187, as added Pub. L. 101-549, title I, Sec. 104, Nov. 15, 1990, 104 Stat. 2454.)

Moratorium on Certain Emissions Testing Requirements

For provisions prohibiting Administrator of Environmental Protection Agency from requiring adoption or implementation by State of test-only I/M240 enhanced vehicle inspection and maintenance program as means of compliance with this section, with further provisions relating to plan disapproval and emissions reduction credits, see section 348 of Pub. L. 104-59, set out as a note under section 7511a of this title.

Section Referred to in Other Sections

This section is referred to in sections 7504, 7506, 7512 of this title.

Subpart 4—Additional Provisions for Particulate Matter Nonattainment Areas

CLASSIFICATIONS AND ATTAINMENT DATES

42 USC 7513

(a) Initial classifications
Every area designated nonattainment for PM-10 pursuant to section 7407(d) of this title shall be classified at the time of such designation, by operation of law, as a moderate PM-10 nonattainment area (also referred to in this subpart as a "Moderate Area") at the time of such designation. At the time of publication of the notice under section 7407(d)(4) of this title (relating to area designations) for each PM-10 nonattainment area, the Administrator shall publish a notice announcing the classification of such area. The provisions of section 7502(a)(1)(B) of this title (relating to lack of notice-and-comment and judicial review) shall apply with respect to such classification.

(b) Reclassification as Serious
  (1) Reclassification before attainment date
    The Administrator may reclassify as a Serious PM-10 nonattainment area (identified in this subpart also as a "Serious Area") any area that the Administrator determines cannot practicably attain the national ambient air quality standard for PM-10 by the attainment

date (as prescribed in subsection (c) of this section) for Moderate Areas. The Administrator shall reclassify appropriate areas as Serious by the following dates:
- (A) For areas designated nonattainment for PM-10 under section 7407(d)(4) of this title, the Administrator shall propose to reclassify appropriate areas by June 30, 1991, and take final action by December 31, 1991.
- (B) For areas subsequently designated nonattainment, the Administrator shall reclassify appropriate areas within 18 months after the required date for the State's submission of a SIP for the Moderate Area.

(2) Reclassification upon failure to attain

Within 6 months following the applicable attainment date for a PM-10 nonattainment area, the Administrator shall determine whether the area attained the standard by that date. If the Administrator finds that any Moderate Area is not in attainment after the applicable attainment date—
- (A) the area shall be reclassified by operation of law as a Serious Area; and
- (B) the Administrator shall publish a notice in the Federal Register no later than 6 months following the attainment date, identifying the area as having failed to attain and identifying the reclassification described under subparagraph (A).

(c) Attainment dates

Except as provided under subsection (d) of this section, the attainment dates for PM-10 nonattainment areas shall be as follows:

(1) Moderate Areas

For a Moderate Area, the attainment date shall be as expeditiously as practicable but no later than the end of the sixth calendar year after the area's designation as nonattainment, except that, for areas designated nonattainment for PM-10 under section 7407(d)(4) of this title, the attainment date shall not extend beyond December 31, 1994.

(2) Serious Areas

For a Serious Area, the attainment date shall be as expeditiously as practicable but no later than the end of the tenth calendar year beginning after the area's designation as nonattainment, except that, for areas designated nonattainment for PM-10 under section 7407(d)(4) of this title, the date shall not extend beyond December 31, 2001.

(d) Extension of attainment date for Moderate Areas

Upon application by any State, the Administrator may extend for 1 additional year (hereinafter referred to as the "Extension Year") the date specified in paragraph[1] (c)(1) if—
(1) the State has complied with all requirements and commitments pertaining to the area in the applicable implementation plan; and
(2) no more than one exceedance of the 24-hour national ambient air quality standard level for PM-10 has occurred in the area in the year preceding the Extension Year, and the annual mean concentration of PM-10 in the area for such year is less than or equal to the standard level.

No more than 2 one-year extensions may be issued under the subsection for a single nonattainment area.

(e) Extension of attainment date for Serious Areas

Upon application by any State, the Administrator may extend the attainment date for a Serious Area beyond the date specified under subsection (c) of this section, if attainment by the date established under subsection (c) of this section would be impracticable, the State has complied with all requirements and commitments pertaining to that area in the implementation plan, and the State demonstrates to the satisfaction of the Administrator that the plan for that area includes the most stringent measures that are included in the implementation plan of any State or are achieved in practice in any State, and can feasibly be implemented in the area. At the time of such application, the State must submit a revision to the implementation plan that includes a demonstration of attainment by the most expeditious alternative date practicable. In determining whether to grant an extension, and the appropriate length of time for any such extension, the Administrator may consider the nature and extent of nonattainment, the types and numbers of sources or other emitting activities in the area (including the influence of uncontrollable natural sources and transboundary emissions from foreign countries),

---

[1]So in original. Probably should be "subsection".

the population exposed to concentrations in excess of the standard, the presence and concentration of potentially toxic substances in the mix of particulate emissions in the area, and the technological and economic feasibility of various control measures. The Administrator may not approve an extension until the State submits an attainment demonstration for the area. The Administrator may grant at most one such extension for an area, of no more than 5 years.

(f) Waivers for certain areas

The Administrator may, on a case-by-case basis, waive any requirement applicable to any Serious Area under this subpart where the Administrator determines that anthropogenic sources of PM-10 do not contribute significantly to the violation of the PM-10 standard in the area. The Administrator may also waive a specific date for attainment of the standard where the Administrator determines that nonanthropogenic sources of PM-10 contribute significantly to the violation of the PM-10 standard in the area.

(July 14, 1955, ch. 360, title I, Sec. 188, as added Pub. L. 101-549, title I, Sec. 105(a), Nov. 15, 1990, 104 Stat. 2458.)

Section Referred to in Other Sections

This section is referred to in sections 7509a, 7513a of this title; title 23 section 149.

PLAN PROVISIONS AND SCHEDULES FOR PLAN SUBMISSIONS

42 USC 7513a

(a) Moderate Areas
  (1) Plan provisions
     Each State in which all or part of a Moderate Area is located shall submit, according to the applicable schedule under paragraph (2), an implementation plan that includes each of the following:
     (A) For the purpose of meeting the requirements of section 7502(c)(5) of this title, a permit program providing that permits meeting the requirements of section 7503 of this title are required for the construction and operation of new and modified major stationary sources of PM-10.
     (B) Either (i) a demonstration (including air quality modeling) that the plan will provide for attainment by the applicable attainment date; or (ii) a demonstration that attainment by such date is impracticable.
     (C) Provisions to assure that reasonably available control measures for the control of PM-10 shall be implemented no later than December 10, 1993, or 4 years after designation in the case of an area classified as moderate after November 15, 1990.
  (2) Schedule for plan submissions
     A State shall submit the plan required under subparagraph (1) no later than the following:
     (A) Within 1 year of November 15, 1990, for areas designated nonattainment under section 7407(d)(4) of this title, except that the provision required under subparagraph (1)(A) shall be submitted no later than June 30, 1992.
     (B) 18 months after the designation as nonattainment, for those areas designated nonattainment after the designations prescribed under section 7407(d)(4) of this title.
(b) Serious Areas
  (1) Plan provisions
     In addition to the provisions submitted to meet the requirements of paragraph[1] (a)(1) (relating to Moderate Areas), each State in which all or part of a Serious Area is located shall submit an implementation plan for such area that includes each of the following:
     (A) A demonstration (including air quality modeling)—
        (i) that the plan provides for attainment of the PM-10 national ambient air quality standard by the applicable attainment date, or
        (ii) for any area for which the State is seeking, pursuant to section 7513(e) of this title, an extension of the attainment date beyond the date set forth in section 7513(c) of this title, that attainment by that date would be impracticable, and that the plan provides for attainment by the most expeditious alternative date practicable.

(B) Provisions to assure that the best available control measures for the control of PM-10 shall be implemented no later than 4 years after the date the area is classified (or reclassified) as a Serious Area.

(2) Schedule for plan submissions
A State shall submit the demonstration required for an area under paragraph (1)(A) no later than 4 years after reclassification of the area to Serious, except that for areas reclassified under section 7513(b)(2) of this title, the State shall submit the attainment demonstration within 18 months after reclassification to Serious. A State shall submit the provisions described under paragraph (1)(B) no later than 18 months after reclassification of the area as a Serious Area.

(3) Major sources
For any Serious Area, the terms "major source" and "major stationary source" include any stationary source or group of stationary sources located within a contiguous area and under common control that emits, or has the potential to emit, at least 70 tons per year of PM-10.

(c) Milestones
(1) Plan revisions demonstrating attainment submitted to the Administrator for approval under this subpart shall contain quantitative milestones which are to be achieved every 3 years until the area is redesignated attainment and which demonstrate reasonable further progress, as defined in section 7501(1) of this title, toward attainment by the applicable date.

(2) Not later than 90 days after the date on which a milestone applicable to the area occurs, each State in which all or part of such area is located shall submit to the Administrator a demonstration that all measures in the plan approved under this section have been implemented and that the milestone has been met. A demonstration under this subsection shall be submitted in such form and manner, and shall contain such information and analysis, as the Administrator shall require. The Administrator shall determine whether or not a State's demonstration under this subsection is adequate within 90 days after the Administrator's receipt of a demonstration which contains the information and analysis required by the Administrator.

(3) If a State fails to submit a demonstration under paragraph (2) with respect to a milestone within the required period or if the Administrator determines that the area has not met any applicable milestone, the Administrator shall require the State, within 9 months after such failure or determination to submit a plan revision that assures that the State will achieve the next milestone (or attain the national ambient air quality standard for PM-10, if there is no next milestone) by the applicable date.

(d) Failure to attain
In the case of a Serious PM-10 nonattainment area in which the PM-10 standard is not attained by the applicable attainment date, the State in which such area is located shall, after notice and opportunity for public comment, submit within 12 months after the applicable attainment date, plan revisions which provide for attainment of the PM-10 air quality standard and, from the date of such submission until attainment, for an annual reduction in PM-10 or PM-10 precursor emissions within the area of not less than 5 percent of the amount of such emissions as reported in the most recent inventory prepared for such area.

(e) PM-10 precursors
The control requirements applicable under plans in effect under this part for major stationary sources of PM-10 shall also apply to major stationary sources of PM-10 precursors, except where the Administrator determines that such sources do not contribute significantly to PM-10 levels which exceed the standard in the area. The Administrator shall issue guidelines regarding the application of the preceding sentence.

(July 14, 1955, ch. 360, title I, Sec. 189, as added Pub. L. 101-549, title I, Sec. 105(a), Nov. 15, 1990, 104 Stat. 2460.)

---

[1] So in original. Probably should be "subsection".

ISSUANCE OF RACM AND BACM GUIDANCE

42 USC 7513b

The Administrator shall issue, in the same manner and according to the same procedure as guidance is issued under section 7408(c) of this title, technical guidance on reasonably available control measures and best available control measures for urban fugitive dust, and emissions from residential wood combustion (including curtailments and exemptions from such curtailments) and prescribed silvicultural and agricultural burning, no later than 18 months following November 15, 1990. The Administrator shall also examine other categories of sources contributing to nonattainment of the PM-10 standard, and determine whether additional guidance on reasonably available control measures and best available control measures is needed, and issue any such guidance no later than 3 years after November 15, 1990. In issuing guidelines and making determinations under this section, the Administrator (in consultation with the State) shall take into account emission reductions achieved, or expected to be achieved, under subchapter IV-A of this chapter and other provisions of this chapter.

(July 14, 1955, ch. 360, title I, Sec. 190, as added Pub. L. 101-549, title I, Sec. 105(a), Nov. 15, 1990, 104 Stat. 2462.)

Subpart 5—Additional Provisions for Areas Designated Nonattainment for Sulfur Oxides, Nitrogen Dioxide, or Lead

PLAN SUBMISSION DEADLINES

42 USC 7514

(a) Submission
Any State containing an area designated or redesignated under section 7407(d) of this title as nonattainment with respect to the national primary ambient air quality standards for sulfur oxides, nitrogen dioxide, or lead subsequent to November 15, 1990, shall submit to the Administrator, within 18 months of the designation, an applicable implementation plan meeting the requirements of this part.

(b) States lacking fully approved State implementation plans
Any State containing an area designated nonattainment with respect to national primary ambient air quality standards for sulfur oxides or nitrogen dioxide under section 7407(d)(1)(C)(i) of this title, but lacking a fully approved implementation plan complying with the requirements of this chapter (including this part) as in effect immediately before November 15, 1990, shall submit to the Administrator, within 18 months of November 15, 1990, an implementation plan meeting the requirements of subpart 1 (except as otherwise prescribed by section 7514a of this title).

(July 14, 1955, ch. 360, title I, Sec. 191, as added Pub. L. 101-549, title I, Sec. 106, Nov. 15, 1990, 104 Stat. 2463.)

Section Referred to in Other Sections

This section is referred to in section 7514a of this title.

ATTAINMENT DATES

42 USC 7514a

(a) Plans under section 7514(a)
Implementation plans required under section 7514(a) of this title shall provide for attainment of the relevant primary standard as expeditiously as practicable but no later than 5 years from the date of the nonattainment designation.

(b) Plans under section 7514(b)
Implementation plans required under section 7514(b) of this title shall provide for attainment

of the relevant primary national ambient air quality standard within 5 years after November 15, 1990.

(c) Inadequate plans
Implementation plans for nonattainment areas for sulfur oxides or nitrogen dioxide with plans that were approved by the Administrator before November 15, 1990, but, subsequent to such approval, were found by the Administrator to be substantially inadequate, shall provide for attainment of the relevant primary standard within 5 years from the date of such finding.

(July 14, 1955, ch. 360, title I, Sec. 192, as added Pub. L. 101-549, title I, Sec. 106, Nov. 15, 1990, 104 Stat. 2463.)

Section Referred to in Other Sections

This section is referred to in section 7514 of this title.

Subpart 6—Savings Provisions

GENERAL SAVINGS CLAUSE

42 USC 7515

Each regulation, standard, rule, notice, order and guidance promulgated or issued by the Administrator under this chapter, as in effect before November 15, 1990, shall remain in effect according to its terms, except to the extent otherwise provided under this chapter, inconsistent with any provision of this chapter, or revised by the Administrator. No control requirement in effect, or required to be adopted by an order, settlement agreement, or plan in effect before November 15, 1990, in any area which is a nonattainment area for any air pollutant may be modified after November 15, 1990, in any manner unless the modification insures equivalent or greater emission reductions of such air pollutant.

(July 14, 1955, ch. 360, title I, Sec. 193, as added Pub. L. 101-549, title I, Sec. 108(1), Nov. 15, 1990, 104 Stat. 2469.)

SUBCHAPTER II—EMISSION STANDARDS FOR MOVING SOURCES

Part A—Motor Vehicle Emission and Fuel Standards

EMISSION STANDARDS FOR NEW MOTOR VEHICLES OR NEW MOTOR VEHICLE ENGINES

42 USC 7521

(a) Authority of Administrator to prescribe by regulation
Except as otherwise provided in subsection (b) of this section—
  (1) The Administrator shall by regulation prescribe (and from time to time revise) in accordance with the provisions of this section, standards applicable to the emission of any air pollutant from any class or classes of new motor vehicles or new motor vehicle engines, which in his judgment cause, or contribute to, air pollution which may reasonably be anticipated to endanger public health or welfare. Such standards shall be applicable to such vehicles and engines for their useful life (as determined under subsection (d) of this section, relating to useful life of vehicles for purposes of certification), whether such vehicles and engines are designed as complete systems or incorporate devices to prevent or control such pollution.
  (2) Any regulation prescribed under paragraph (1) of this subsection (and any revision thereof) shall take effect after such period as the Administrator finds necessary to permit the development and application of the requisite technology, giving appropriate consideration to the cost of compliance within such period.
  (3) (A) In general.—(i) Unless the standard is changed as provided in subparagraph (B), regulations under paragraph (1) of this subsection applicable to emissions of hydrocarbons, carbon monoxide, oxides of nitrogen, and particulate matter from classes or categories of heavy-duty vehicles or engines manufactured during or after model year 1983 shall contain standards which reflect the greatest degree of emission reduction achievable through the application of technology which the Administrator determines will be available for the model year to which such standards apply, giving appropriate consideration to cost, energy, and safety factors associated with the application of such technology.
    (ii) In establishing classes or categories of vehicles or engines for purposes of regulations under this paragraph, the Administrator may base such classes or categories on gross vehicle weight, horsepower, type of fuel used, or other appropriate factors.
  (B) Revised standards for heavy duty trucks.—(i) On the basis of information available to the Administrator concerning the effects of air pollutants emitted from heavy-duty vehicles or engines and from other sources of mobile source related pollutants on the public health and welfare, and taking costs into account, the Administrator may promulgate regulations under paragraph (1) of this subsection revising any standard promulgated under, or before the date of, the enactment of the Clean Air Act Amendments of 1990 (or previously revised under this subparagraph) and applicable to classes or categories of heavy-duty vehicles or engines.
    (ii) Effective for the model year 1998 and thereafter, the regulations under paragraph (1) of this subsection applicable to emissions of oxides of nitrogen (NO_x) from gasoline and diesel-fueled heavy duty trucks shall contain standards which provide that such emissions may not exceed 4.0 grams per brake horsepower hour (gbh).
  (C) Lead time and stability.—Any standard promulgated or revised under this paragraph and applicable to classes or categories of heavy-duty vehicles or engines shall apply for a period of no less than 3 model years beginning no earlier than the model year commencing 4 years after such revised standard is promulgated.

(D) Rebuilding practices.—The Administrator shall study the practice of rebuilding heavy-duty engines and the impact rebuilding has on engine emissions. On the basis of that study and other information available to the Administrator, the Administrator may prescribe requirements to control rebuilding practices, including standards applicable to emissions from any rebuilt heavy-duty engines (whether or not the engine is past its statutory useful life), which in the Administrator's judgment cause, or contribute to, air pollution which may reasonably be anticipated to endanger public health or welfare taking costs into account. Any regulation shall take effect after a period the Administrator finds necessary to permit the development and application of the requisite control measures, giving appropriate consideration to the cost of compliance within the period and energy and safety factors.

(E) Motorcycles.—For purposes of this paragraph, motorcycles and motorcycle engines shall be treated in the same manner as heavy-duty vehicles and engines (except as otherwise permitted under section 7525(f)(1)[1] of this title) unless the Administrator promulgates a rule reclassifying motorcycles as light-duty vehicles within the meaning of this section or unless the Administrator promulgates regulations under subsection (a) of this section applying standards applicable to the emission of air pollutants from motorcycles as a separate class or category. In any case in which such standards are promulgated for such emissions from motorcycles as a separate class or category, the Administrator, in promulgating such standards, shall consider the need to achieve equivalency of emission reductions between motorcycles and other motor vehicles to the maximum extent practicable.

(4) (A) Effective with respect to vehicles and engines manufactured after model year 1978, no emission control device, system, or element of design shall be used in a new motor vehicle or new motor vehicle engine for purposes of complying with requirements prescribed under this subchapter if such device, system, or element of design will cause or contribute to an unreasonable risk to public health, welfare, or safety in its operation or function.

(B) In determining whether an unreasonable risk exists under subparagraph (A), the Administrator shall consider, among other factors, (i) whether and to what extent the use of any device, system, or element of design causes, increases, reduces, or eliminates emissions of any unregulated pollutants; (ii) available methods for reducing or eliminating any risk to public health, welfare, or safety which may be associated with the use of such device, system, or element of design, and (iii) the availability of other devices, systems, or elements of design which may be used to conform to requirements prescribed under this subchapter without causing or contributing to such unreasonable risk. The Administrator shall include in the consideration required by this paragraph all relevant information developed pursuant to section 7548 of this title.

(5) (A) If the Administrator promulgates final regulations which define the degree of control required and the test procedures by which compliance could be determined for gasoline vapor recovery of uncontrolled emissions from the fueling of motor vehicles, the Administrator shall, after consultation with the Secretary of Transportation with respect to motor vehicle safety, prescribe, by regulation, fill pipe standards for new motor vehicles in order to insure effective connection between such fill pipe and any vapor recovery system which the Administrator determines may be required to comply with such vapor recovery regulations. In promulgating such standards the Administrator shall take into consideration limits on fill pipe diameter, minimum design criteria for nozzle retainer lips, limits on the location of the unleaded fuel restrictors, a minimum access zone surrounding a fill pipe, a minimum pipe or nozzle insertion angle, and such other factors as he deems pertinent.

(B) Regulations prescribing standards under subparagraph (A) shall not become effective until the introduction of the model year for which it would be feasible to implement such standards, taking into consideration the restraints of an adequate leadtime for design and production.

(C) Nothing in subparagraph (A) shall (i) prevent the Administrator from specifying different nozzle and fill neck sizes for gasoline with additives and gasoline without additives or (ii) permit the Administrator to require a specific location, configuration,

---

[1] See References in Text note below.

modeling, or styling of the motor vehicle body with respect to the fuel tank fill neck or fill nozzle clearance envelope.

 (D) For the purpose of this paragraph, the term "fill pipe" shall include the fuel tank fill pipe, fill neck, fill inlet, and closure.

(6) Onboard vapor recovery.—Within 1 year after November 15, 1990, the Administrator shall, after consultation with the Secretary of Transportation regarding the safety of vehicle-based ("onboard") systems for the control of vehicle refueling emissions, promulgate standards under this section requiring that new light-duty vehicles manufactured beginning in the fourth model year after the model year in which the standards are promulgated and thereafter shall be equipped with such systems. The standards required under this paragraph shall apply to a percentage of each manufacturer's fleet of new light-duty vehicles beginning with the fourth model year after the model year in which the standards are promulgated. The percentage shall be as specified in the following table:

IMPLEMENTATION SCHEDULE
FOR ONBOARD VAPOR RECOVERY REQUIREMENTS

Model year commencing after standards promulgated	Percentage*
Fourth	40
Fifth	80
After Fifth	100

*Percentages in the table refer to a percentage of the manufacturer's sales volume.

The standards shall require that such systems provide a minimum evaporative emission capture efficiency of 95 percent. The requirements of section 7511a(b)(3) of this title (relating to stage II gasoline vapor recovery) for areas classified under section 7511 of this title as moderate for ozone shall not apply after promulgation of such standards and the Administrator may, by rule, revise or waive the application of the requirements of such section 7511a(b)(3) of this title for areas classified under section 7511 of this title as Serious, Severe, or Extreme for ozone, as appropriate, after such time as the Administrator determines that onboard emissions control systems required under this paragraph are in widespread use throughout the motor vehicle fleet.

(b) Emissions of carbon monoxide, hydrocarbons, and oxides of nitrogen; annual report to Congress; waiver of emission standards; research objectives

 (1) (A) The regulations under subsection (a) of this section applicable to emissions of carbon monoxide and hydrocarbons from light-duty vehicles and engines manufactured during model years 1977 through 1979 shall contain standards which provide that such emissions from such vehicles and engines may not exceed 1.5 grams per vehicle mile of hydrocarbons and 15.0 grams per vehicle mile of carbon monoxide. The regulations under subsection (a) of this section applicable to emissions of carbon monoxide from light-duty vehicles and engines manufactured during the model year 1980 shall contain standards which provide that such emissions may not exceed 7.0 grams per vehicle mile. The regulations under subsection (a) of this section applicable to emissions of hydrocarbons from light-duty vehicles and engines manufactured during or after model year 1980 shall contain standards which require a reduction of at least 90 percent from emissions of such pollutant allowable under the standards under this section applicable to light-duty vehicles and engines manufactured in model year 1970. Unless waived as provided in paragraph (5), regulations under subsection (a) of this section applicable to emissions of carbon monoxide from light-duty vehicles and engines manufactured during or after the model year 1981 shall contain standards which require a reduction of at least 90 percent from emissions of such pollutant allowable under the standards under this section applicable to light-duty vehicles and engines manufactured in model year 1970.

 (B) The regulations under subsection (a) of this section applicable to emissions of oxides of nitrogen from light-duty vehicles and engines manufactured during model years 1977 through 1980 shall contain standards which provide that such emissions from such vehicles and engines may not exceed 2.0 grams per vehicle mile. The regulations under subsection (a) of this section applicable to emissions of oxides of nitrogen from light-duty vehicles and engines manufactured during the model year 1981 and thereafter shall contain standards which provide that such emissions from such vehicles and engines may not exceed 1.0 gram per vehicle mile. The Administrator shall prescribe standards in lieu of those required by the preceding sentence, which provide that emissions of oxides of nitrogen may not exceed 2.0 grams per vehicle mile for any light-duty vehicle manufactured during model years 1981 and 1982 by any manufacturer whose production, by corporate identity, for calendar year 1976 was less than three hundred thousand light-duty motor vehicles worldwide if the Administrator determines that—

    (i) the ability of such manufacturer to meet emission standards in the 1975 and subsequent model years was, and is, primarily dependent upon technology developed by other manufacturers and purchased from such manufacturers; and

    (ii) such manufacturer lacks the financial resources and technological ability to develop such technology.

  (C) The Administrator may promulgate regulations under subsection (a)(1) of this section revising any standard prescribed or previously revised under this subsection, as needed to protect public health or welfare, taking costs, energy, and safety into account. Any revised standard shall require a reduction of emissions from the standard that was previously applicable. Any such revision under this subchapter may provide for a phase-in of the standard. It is the intent of Congress that the numerical emission standards specified in subsections (a)(3)(B)(ii), (g), (h), and (i) of this section shall not be modified by the Administrator after November 15, 1990, for any model year before the model year 2004.

(2) Emission standards under paragraph (1), and measurement techniques on which such standards are based (if not promulgated prior to November 15, 1990), shall be promulgated by regulation within 180 days after November 15, 1990.

(3) For purposes of this part—

  (A) (i) The term "model year" with reference to any specific calendar year means the manufacturer's annual production period (as determined by the Administrator) which includes January 1 of such calendar year. If the manufacturer has no annual production period, the term "model year" shall mean the calendar year.

    (ii) For the purpose of assuring that vehicles and engines manufactured before the beginning of a model year were not manufactured for purposes of circumventing the effective date of a standard required to be prescribed by subsection (b) of this section, the Administrator may prescribe regulations defining "model year" otherwise than as provided in clause (i).

  (B) Repealed. Pub. L. 101-549, title II, Sec. 230(1), Nov. 15, 1990, 104 Stat. 2529.

  (C) The term "heavy duty vehicle" means a truck, bus, or other vehicle manufactured primarily for use on the public streets, roads, and highways (not including any vehicle operated exclusively on a rail or rails) which has a gross vehicle weight (as determined under regulations promulgated by the Administrator) in excess of six thousand pounds. Such term includes any such vehicle which has special features enabling off-street or off-highway operation and use.

(3)[2] Upon the petition of any manufacturer, the Administrator, after notice and opportunity for public hearing, may waive the standard required under subparagraph (B) of paragraph (1) to not exceed 1.5 grams of oxides of nitrogen per vehicle mile for any class or category of light-duty vehicles or engines manufactured by such manufacturer during any period of up to four model years beginning after the model year 1980 if the manufacturer demonstrates that such waiver is necessary to permit the use of an innovative power train technology, or innovative emission control device or system, in such class or category of vehicles or engines and that such technology or system was not utilized by more than 1 percent of the light-duty vehicles sold in the United States in the 1975 model year. Such waiver may be granted only if the Administrator determines—

  (A) that such waiver would not endanger public health,

  (B) that there is a substantial likelihood that the vehicles or engines will be able to comply with the applicable standard under this section at the expiration of the waiver, and

---

[2]So in original. Probably should be "(4)".

(C) that the technology or system has a potential for long-term air quality benefit and has the potential to meet or exceed the average fuel economy standard applicable under the Energy Policy and Conservation Act [42 U.S.C. 6201 et seq.] upon the expiration of the waiver.

No waiver under this subparagraph[3] granted to any manufacturer shall apply to more than 5 percent of such manufacturer's production or more than fifty thousand vehicles or engines, whichever is greater.

(c) Feasibility study and investigation by National Academy of Sciences; reports to Administrator and Congress; availability of information
   (1) The Administrator shall undertake to enter into appropriate arrangements with the National Academy of Sciences to conduct a comprehensive study and investigation of the technological feasibility of meeting the emissions standards required to be prescribed by the Administrator by subsection (b) of this section.
   (2) Of the funds authorized to be appropriated to the Administrator by this chapter, such amounts as are required shall be available to carry out the study and investigation authorized by paragraph (1) of this subsection.
   (3) In entering into any arrangement with the National Academy of Sciences for conducting the study and investigation authorized by paragraph (1) of this subsection, the Administrator shall request the National Academy of Sciences to submit semiannual reports on the progress of its study and investigation to the Administrator and the Congress, beginning not later than July 1, 1971, and continuing until such study and investigation is completed.
   (4) The Administrator shall furnish to such Academy at its request any information which the Academy deems necessary for the purpose of conducting the investigation and study authorized by paragraph (1) of this subsection. For the purpose of furnishing such information, the Administrator may use any authority he has under this chapter (A) to obtain information from any person, and (B) to require such person to conduct such tests, keep such records, and make such reports respecting research or other activities conducted by such person as may be reasonably necessary to carry out this subsection.

(d) Useful life of vehicles
The Administrator shall prescribe regulations under which the useful life of vehicles and engines shall be determined for purposes of subsection (a)(1) of this section and section 7541 of this title. Such regulations shall provide that except where a different useful life period is specified in this subchapter useful life shall—
   (1) in the case of light duty vehicles and light duty vehicle engines and light-duty trucks up to 3,750 lbs. LVW and up to 6,000 lbs. GVWR, be a period of use of five years or fifty thousand miles (or the equivalent), whichever first occurs, except that in the case of any requirement of this section which first becomes applicable after November 15, 1990, where the useful life period is not otherwise specified for such vehicles and engines, the period shall be 10 years or 100,000 miles (or the equivalent), whichever first occurs, with testing for purposes of in-use compliance under section 7541 of this title up to (but not beyond) 7 years or 75,000 miles (or the equivalent), whichever first occurs;
   (2) in the case of any other motor vehicle or motor vehicle engine (other than motorcycles or motorcycle engines), be a period of use set forth in paragraph (1) unless the Administrator determines that a period of use of greater duration or mileage is appropriate; and
   (3) in the case of any motorcycle or motorcycle engine, be a period of use the Administrator shall determine.

(e) New power sources or propulsion systems
In the event of a new power source or propulsion system for new motor vehicles or new motor vehicle engines is submitted for certification pursuant to section 7525(a) of this title, the Administrator may postpone certification until he has prescribed standards for any air pollutants emitted by such vehicle or engine which in his judgment cause, or contribute to, air pollution which may reasonably be anticipated to endanger the public health or welfare but for which standards have not been prescribed under subsection (a) of this section.

---

[3]So in original. Probably should be "paragraph".

(f)[4] High altitude regulations
  (1) The high altitude regulation in effect with respect to model year 1977 motor vehicles shall not apply to the manufacture, distribution, or sale of 1978 and later model year motor vehicles. Any future regulation affecting the sale or distribution of motor vehicles or engines manufactured before the model year 1984 in high altitude areas of the country shall take effect no earlier than model year 1981.
  (2) Any such future regulation applicable to high altitude vehicles or engines shall not require a percentage of reduction in the emissions of such vehicles which is greater than the required percentage of reduction in emissions from motor vehicles as set forth in subsection (b) of this section. This percentage reduction shall be determined by comparing any proposed high altitude emission standards to high altitude emissions from vehicles manufactured during model year 1970. In no event shall regulations applicable to high altitude vehicles manufactured before the model year 1984 establish a numerical standard which is more stringent than that applicable to vehicles certified under non-high altitude conditions.
  (3) Section 7607(d) of this title shall apply to any high altitude regulation referred to in paragraph (2) and before promulgating any such regulation, the Administrator shall consider and make a finding with respect to—
    (A) the economic impact upon consumers, individual high altitude dealers, and the automobile industry of any such regulation, including the economic impact which was experienced as a result of the regulation imposed during model year 1977 with respect to high altitude certification requirements;
    (B) the present and future availability of emission control technology capable of meeting the applicable vehicle and engine emission requirements without reducing model availability; and
    (C) the likelihood that the adoption of such a high altitude regulation will result in any significant improvement in air quality in any area to which it shall apply.
(g) Light-duty trucks up to 6,000 lbs. GVWR and light-duty vehicles; standards for model years after 1993
  (1) NMHC, CO, and NO_x
  Effective with respect to the model year 1994 and thereafter, the regulations under subsection (a) of this section applicable to emissions of nonmethane hydrocarbons (NMHC), carbon monoxide (CO), and oxides of nitrogen (NO_x) from light-duty trucks (LDTs) of up to 6,000 lbs. gross vehicle weight rating (GVWR) and light-duty vehicles (LDVs) shall contain standards which provide that emissions from a percentage of each manufacturer's sales volume of such vehicles and trucks shall comply with the levels specified in table G. The percentage shall be as specified in the implementation schedule below:

TABLE G—EMISSION STANDARDS FOR NMHC, CO, AND NO_x FROM LIGHT-DUTY TRUCKS OF UP TO 6,000 LBS. GVWR AND LIGHT-DUTYVEHICLES

Vehicle type	Column A (5 yrs/50,000 mi) NMHC CO NO_x	Column B (10 yrs/100,000 mi) NMHC CO NO_x
LDTs (0-3,750 lbs. LVW) and light-duty vehicles...............	0.25 3.4 0.4*	0.31 4.2 0.6*
LDTs (3,751-5,750 lbs. LVW)...	0.32 4.4 0.7**	0.40 5.5 0.97

Standards are expressed in grams per mile (gpm).
*In the case of diesel-fueled LDTs (0-3,750 lvw) and light-duty vehicles, before the model year 2004, in lieu of the 0.4 and 0.6 standards for NO_x, the applicable standards for NO_x shall be 1.0 gpm for a useful life of 5 years or 50,000 miles (or the equivalent), whichever first occurs, and 1.25 gpm for a useful life of 10 years or 100,000 miles (or the equivalent) whichever first occurs.
**This standard does not apply to diesel-fueled LDTs (3,751-5,750 lbs. LVW).

---

[4]Another subsec. (f) is set out after subsec. (m).

For standards under column A, for purposes of certification under section 7525 of this title, the applicable useful life shall be 5 years or 50,000 miles (or the equivalent), whichever first occurs.

For standards under column B, for purposes of certification under section 7525 of this title, the applicable useful life shall be 10 years or 100,000 miles (or the equivalent), whichever first occurs.

IMPLEMENTATION SCHEDULE FOR TABLE G STANDARDS	
Model year	Percentage*
1994	40
1995	80
after 1995	100

*Percentages in the table refer to a percentage of each manufacturer's sales volume.

(2) PM Standard

Effective with respect to model year 1994 and thereafter in the case of light-duty vehicles, and effective with respect to the model year 1995 and thereafter in the case of light-duty trucks (LDTs) of up to 6,000 lbs. gross vehicle weight rating (GVWR), the regulations under subsection (a) of this section applicable to emissions of particulate matter (PM) from such vehicles and trucks shall contain standards which provide that such emissions from a percentage of each manufacturer's sales volume of such vehicles and trucks shall not exceed the levels specified in the table below. The percentage shall be as specified in the Implementation Schedule below.

PM STANDARD FOR LDTS OF UP TO 6,000 LBS. GVWR	
Useful life period	Standard
5/50,000	0.08 gpm
10/100,000	0.10 gpm

The applicable useful life, for purposes of certification under section 7525 of this title and for purposes of in-use compliance under section 7541 of this title, shall be 5 years or 50,000 miles (or the equivalent), whichever first occurs, in the case of the 5/50,000 standard.

The applicable useful life, for purposes of certification under section 7525 of this title and for purposes of in-use compliance under section 7541 of this title, shall be 10 years or 100,000 miles (or the equivalent), whichever first occurs in the case of the 10/100,000 standard.

IMPLEMENTATION SCHEDULE FOR PM STANDARDS		
Model year	Light-duty vehicles	LDTs
1994	40%*	....
1995	80%*	40%*
1996	100%*	80%*
after 1996	100%*	100%*

*Percentages in the table refer to a percentage of each manufacturer's sales volume.

(h) Light-duty trucks of more than 6,000 lbs. GVWR; standards for model years after 1995

Effective with respect to the model year 1996 and thereafter, the regulations under subsection (a) of this section applicable to emissions of nonmethane hydrocarbons (NMHC), carbon monoxide (CO), oxides of nitrogen (NO_x), and particulate matter (PM) from light-duty trucks (LDTs) of more than 6,000 lbs. gross vehicle weight rating (GVWR) shall contain standards which provide that emissions from a specified percentage of each manufacturer's sales volume of such trucks shall comply with the levels specified in table H. The specified percentage shall be 50 percent in model year 1996 and 100 percent thereafter.

TABLE H—EMISSION STANDARDS FOR NMHC AND CO FROM GASOLINE AND DIESEL FUELED LIGHT-DUTY TRUCKS OF MORE THAN 6,000 LBS. GVWR

	Column A	Column B			
LDT Test weight	(5 yrs/50,000 mi) NMHC CO NO$_x$	(11 yrs/120,000 mi) NMHC CO NO$_x$ PM
3,751-5,750 lbs. TW	0.32 4.4 0.7*	0.46 6.4 0.98 0.10
Over 5,750 lbs. TW	0.39 5.0 1.1*	0.56 7.3 1.53 0.12

*Not applicable to diesel-fueled LDTs.

Standards are expressed in grams per mile (GPM).

For standards under column A, for purposes of certification under section 7525 of this title, the applicable useful life shall be 5 years or 50,000 miles (or the equivalent) whichever first occurs.

For standards under column B, for purposes of certification under section 7525 of this title, the applicable useful life shall be 11 years or 120,000 miles (or the equivalent), whichever first occurs.

(i) Phase II study for certain light-duty vehicles and light-duty trucks
  (1) The Administrator, with the participation of the Office of Technology Assessment, shall study whether or not further reductions in emissions from light-duty vehicles and light-duty trucks should be required pursuant to this subchapter. The study shall consider whether to establish with respect to model years commencing after January 1, 2003, the standards and useful life period for gasoline and diesel-fueled light-duty vehicles and light-duty trucks with a loaded vehicle weight (LVW) of 3,750 lbs. or less specified in the following table:

TABLE 3—PENDING EMISSION STANDARDS FOR GASOLINE AND DIESEL FUELED LIGHT-DUTY VEHICLES AND LIGHT-DUTY TRUCKS 3,750 LBS. LVW OR LESS

Pollutant	Emission level*
NMHC	0.125 GPM
NO$_x$	0.2 GPM
CO	1.7 GPM

*Emission levels are expressed in grams per mile (GPM). For vehicles andengines subject to this subsection for purposes of subsection (d) of this section and any reference thereto, the useful life of suchvehicles and engines shall be a period of 10 years or 100,000 miles (or the equivalent), whichever first occurs.

Such study shall also consider other standards and useful life periods which are more stringent or less stringent than those set forth in table 3 (but more stringent than those referred to in subsections (g) and (h) of this section).

(2) (A) As part of the study under paragraph (1), the Administrator shall examine the need for further reductions in emissions in order to attain or maintain the national ambient air quality standards, taking into consideration the waiver provisions of section 7543(b) of this title. As part of such study, the Administrator shall also examine—
  (i) the availability of technology (including the costs thereof), in the case of light-duty vehicles and light-duty trucks with a loaded vehicle weight (LVW) of 3,750 lbs. or less, for meeting more stringent emission standards than those provided in subsections (g) and (h) of this section for model years commencing not earlier than after January 1, 2003, and not later than model year 2006, including the lead time and safety and energy impacts of meeting more stringent emission standards; and
  (ii) the need for, and cost effectiveness of, obtaining further reductions in emissions from such light-duty vehicles and light-duty trucks, taking into consideration alternative means of attaining or maintaining the national primary ambient air quality standards pursuant to State implementation plans and other requirements of this chapter, including their feasibility and cost effectiveness.
(B) The Administrator shall submit a report to Congress no later than June 1, 1997, containing the results of the study under this subsection, including the results of the

examination conducted under subparagraph (A). Before submittal of such report the Administrator shall provide a reasonable opportunity for public comment and shall include a summary of such comments in the report to Congress.

(3) (A) Based on the study under paragraph (1) the Administrator shall determine, by rule, within 3 calendar years after the report is submitted to Congress, but not later than December 31, 1999, whether—
   (i) there is a need for further reductions in emissions as provided in paragraph (2)(A);
   (ii) the technology for meeting more stringent emission standards will be available, as provided in paragraph (2)(A)(i), in the case of light-duty vehicles and light-duty trucks with a loaded vehicle weight (LVW) of 3,750 lbs. or less, for model years commencing not earlier than January 1, 2003, and not later than model year 2006, considering the factors listed in paragraph (2)(A)(i); and
   (iii) obtaining further reductions in emissions from such vehicles will be needed and cost effective, taking into consideration alternatives as provided in paragraph (2)(A)(ii).

   The rulemaking under this paragraph shall commence within 3 months after submission of the report to Congress under paragraph (2)(B).

(B) If the Administrator determines under subparagraph (A) that—
   (i) there is no need for further reductions in emissions as provided in paragraph (2)(A);
   (ii) the technology for meeting more stringent emission standards will not be available as provided in paragraph (2)(A)(i), in the case of light-duty vehicles and light-duty trucks with a loaded vehicle weight (LVW) of 3,750 lbs. or less, for model years commencing not earlier than January 1, 2003, and not later than model year 2006, considering the factors listed in paragraph (2)(A)(i); or
   (iii) obtaining further reductions in emissions from such vehicles will not be needed or cost effective, taking into consideration alternatives as provided in paragraph (2)(A)(ii),

   the Administrator shall not promulgate more stringent standards than those in effect pursuant to subsections (g) and (h) of this section. Nothing in this paragraph shall prohibit the Administrator from exercising the Administrator's authority under subsection (a) of this section to promulgate more stringent standards for light-duty vehicles and light-duty trucks with a loaded vehicle weight (LVW) of 3,750 lbs. or less at any other time thereafter in accordance with subsection (a) of this section.

(C) If the Administrator determines under subparagraph (A) that—
   (i) there is a need for further reductions in emissions as provided in paragraph (2)(A);
   (ii) the technology for meeting more stringent emission standards will be available, as provided in paragraph (2)(A)(i), in the case of light-duty vehicles and light-duty trucks with a loaded vehicle weight (LVW) of 3,750 lbs. or less, for model years commencing not earlier than January 1, 2003, and not later than model year 2006, considering the factors listed in paragraph (2)(A)(i); and
   (iii) obtaining further reductions in emissions from such vehicles will be needed and cost effective, taking into consideration alternatives as provided in paragraph (2)(A)(ii),

   the Administrator shall either promulgate the standards (and useful life periods) set forth in Table 3 in paragraph (1) or promulgate alternative standards (and useful life periods) which are more stringent than those referred to in subsections (g) and (h) of this section. Any such standards (or useful life periods) promulgated by the Administrator shall take effect with respect to any such vehicles or engines no earlier than the model year 2003 but not later than model year 2006, as determined by the Administrator in the rule.

(D) Nothing in this paragraph shall be construed by the Administrator or by a court as a presumption that any standards (or useful life period) set forth in Table 3 shall be promulgated in the rulemaking required under this paragraph. The action required of the Administrator in accordance with this paragraph shall be treated as a nondiscretionary duty for purposes of section 7604(a)(2) of this title (relating to citizen suits).

(E) Unless the Administrator determines not to promulgate more stringent standards as provided in subparagraph (B) or to postpone the effective date of standards referred to in Table 3 in paragraph (1) or to establish alternative standards as provided in subparagraph (C), effective with respect to model years commencing after January 1, 2003, the regulations under subsection (a) of this section applicable to emissions of nonmethane hydrocarbons (NMHC), oxides of nitrogen (NO_x), and carbon monoxide (CO) from motor vehicles and motor vehicle engines in the classes specified in Table 3 in paragraph (1) above shall contain standards which provide that emissions may not exceed the pending emission levels specified in Table 3 in paragraph (1).

(j) Cold CO standard

(1) Phase I

Not later than 12 months after November 15, 1990, the Administrator shall promulgate regulations under subsection (a) of this section applicable to emissions of carbon monoxide from 1994 and later model year light-duty vehicles and light-duty trucks when operated at 20 degrees Fahrenheit. The regulations shall contain standards which provide that emissions of carbon monoxide from a manufacturer's vehicles when operated at 20 degrees Fahrenheit may not exceed, in the case of light-duty vehicles, 10.0 grams per mile, and in the case of light-duty trucks, a level comparable in stringency to the standard applicable to light-duty vehicles. The standards shall take effect after model year 1993 according to a phase-in schedule which requires a percentage of each manufacturer's sales volume of light-duty vehicles and light-duty trucks to comply with applicable standards after model year 1993. The percentage shall be as specified in the following table:

PHASE-IN SCHEDULE FOR COLD START STANDARDS	
Model Year	Percentage
1994............................	40
1995............................	80
1996 and after...........	100

(2) Phase II

(A) Not later than June 1, 1997, the Administrator shall complete a study assessing the need for further reductions in emissions of carbon monoxide and the maximum reductions in such emissions achievable from model year 2001 and later model year light-duty vehicles and light-duty trucks when operated at 20 degrees Fahrenheit.

(B) (i) If as of June 1, 1997, 6 or more nonattainment areas have a carbon monoxide design value of 9.5 ppm or greater, the regulations under subsection (a)(1) of this section applicable to emissions of carbon monoxide from model year 2002 and later model year light-duty vehicles and light-duty trucks shall contain standards which provide that emissions of carbon monoxide from such vehicles and trucks when operated at 20 degrees Fahrenheit may not exceed 3.4 grams per mile (gpm) in the case of light-duty vehicles and 4.4 grams per mile (gpm) in the case of light-duty trucks up to 6,000 GVWR and a level comparable in stringency in the case of light-duty trucks 6,000 GVWR and above.

(ii) In determining for purposes of this subparagraph whether 6 or more nonattainment areas have a carbon monoxide design value of 9.5 ppm or greater, the Administrator shall exclude the areas of Steubenville, Ohio, and Oshkosh, Wisconsin.

(3) Useful-life for phase I and phase II standards

In the case of the standards referred to in paragraphs (1) and (2), for purposes of certification under section 7525 of this title and in-use compliance under section 7541 of this title, the applicable useful life period shall be 5 years or 50,000 miles, whichever first occurs, except that the Administrator may extend such useful life period (for purposes of section 7525 of this title, or section 7541 of this title, or both) if he determines that it is feasible for vehicles and engines subject to such standards to meet such standards for a longer useful life. If the Administrator extends such useful life period, the Administrator may make an appropriate adjustment of applicable standards for such extended useful life. No such extended useful life shall extend beyond the useful life period provided in regulations under subsection (d) of this section.

(4) Heavy-duty vehicles and engines

The Administrator may also promulgate regulations under subsection (a)(1) of this section applicable to emissions of carbon monoxide from heavy-duty vehicles and engines when operated at cold temperatures.

(k) Control of evaporative emissions

The Administrator shall promulgate (and from time to time revise) regulations applicable to evaporative emissions of hydrocarbons from all gasoline-fueled motor vehicles—

(1) during operation; and

(2) over 2 or more days of nonuse;

under ozone-prone summertime conditions (as determined by regulations of the Administrator). The regulations shall take effect as expeditiously as possible and shall require the greatest degree of emission reduction achievable by means reasonably expected to be available for production during any model year to which the regulations apply, giving appropriate consideration to fuel volatility, and to cost, energy, and safety factors associated with the application of the appropriate technology. The Administrator shall commence a rulemaking under this subsection within 12 months after November 15, 1990. If final regulations are not promulgated under this subsection within 18 months after November 15, 1990, the Administrator shall submit a statement to the Congress containing an explanation of the reasons for the delay and a date certain for promulgation of such final regulations in accordance with this chapter. Such date certain shall not be later than 15 months after the expiration of such 18 month deadline.

(l) Mobile source-related air toxics

(1) Study

Not later than 18 months after November 15, 1990, the Administrator shall complete a study of the need for, and feasibility of, controlling emissions of toxic air pollutants which are unregulated under this chapter and associated with motor vehicles and motor vehicle fuels, and the need for, and feasibility of, controlling such emissions and the means and measures for such controls. The study shall focus on those categories of emissions that pose the greatest risk to human health or about which significant uncertainties remain, including emissions of benzene, formaldehyde, and 1,3 butadiene. The proposed report shall be available for public review and comment and shall include a summary of all comments.

(2) Standards

Within 54 months after November 15, 1990, the Administrator shall, based on the study under paragraph (1), promulgate (and from time to time revise) regulations under subsection (a)(1) of this section or section 7545(c)(1) of this title containing reasonable requirements to control hazardous air pollutants from motor vehicles and motor vehicle fuels. The regulations shall contain standards for such fuels or vehicles, or both, which the Administrator determines reflect the greatest degree of emission reduction achievable through the application of technology which will be available, taking into consideration the standards established under subsection (a) of this section, the availability and costs of the technology, and noise, energy, and safety factors, and lead time. Such regulations shall not be inconsistent with standards under subsection (a) of this section. The regulations shall, at a minimum, apply to emissions of benzene and formaldehyde.

(m) Emissions control diagnostics

(1) Regulations

Within 18 months after November 15, 1990, the Administrator shall promulgate regulations under subsection (a) of this section requiring manufacturers to install on all new light duty vehicles and light duty trucks diagnostics systems capable of—

(A) accurately identifying for the vehicle's useful life as established under this section, emission-related systems deterioration or malfunction, including, at a minimum, the catalytic converter and oxygen sensor, which could cause or result in failure of the vehicles to comply with emission standards established under this section,

(B) alerting the vehicle's owner or operator to the likely need for emission-related components or systems maintenance or repair,

(C) storing and retrieving fault codes specified by the Administrator, and

(D) providing access to stored information in a manner specified by the Administrator. The Administrator may, in the Administrator's discretion, promulgate regulations requiring manufacturers to install such onboard diagnostic systems on heavy-duty vehicles and engines.

(2) Effective date

The regulations required under paragraph (1) of this subsection shall take effect in model year 1994, except that the Administrator may waive the application of such regulations for model year 1994 or 1995 (or both) with respect to any class or category of motor vehicles if the Administrator determines that it would be infeasible to apply the regulations to that class or category in such model year or years, consistent with corresponding regulations or policies adopted by the California Air Resources Board for such systems.

(3) State inspection

The Administrator shall by regulation require States that have implementation plans containing motor vehicle inspection and maintenance programs to amend their plans within 2 years after promulgation of such regulations to provide for inspection of onboard diagnostics systems (as prescribed by regulations under paragraph (1) of this subsection) and for the maintenance or repair of malfunctions or system deterioration identified by or affecting such diagnostics systems. Such regulations shall not be inconsistent with the provisions for warranties promulgated under section 7541(a) and (b) of this title.

(4) Specific requirements

In promulgating regulations under this subsection, the Administrator shall require—

(A) that any connectors through which the emission control diagnostics system is accessed for inspection, diagnosis, service, or repair shall be standard and uniform on all motor vehicles and motor vehicle engines;

(B) that access to the emission control diagnostics system through such connectors shall be unrestricted and shall not require any access code or any device which is only available from a vehicle manufacturer; and

(C) that the output of the data from the emission control diagnostics system through such connectors shall be usable without the need for any unique decoding information or device.

(5) Information availability

The Administrator, by regulation, shall require (subject to the provisions of section 7542(c) of this title regarding the protection of methods or processes entitled to protection as trade secrets) manufacturers to provide promptly to any person engaged in the repairing or servicing of motor vehicles or motor vehicle engines, and the Administrator for use by any such persons, with any and all information needed to make use of the emission control diagnostics system prescribed under this subsection and such other information including instructions for making emission related diagnosis and repairs. No such information may be withheld under section 7542(c) of this title if that information is provided (directly or indirectly) by the manufacturer to franchised dealers or other persons engaged in the repair, diagnosing, or servicing of motor vehicles or motor vehicle engines. Such information shall also be available to the Administrator, subject to section 7542(c) of this title, in carrying out the Administrator's responsibilities under this section.

(f)[5] Model years after 1990

For model years prior to model year 1994, the regulations under subsection (a) of this section applicable to buses other than those subject to standards under section 7554 of this title shall contain a standard which provides that emissions of particulate matter (PM) from such buses may not exceed the standards set forth in the following table:

PM STANDARD FOR BUSES	
Model year	Standard*
1991	0.25
1992	0.25
1993 and thereafter	0.10

*Standards are expressed in grams per brake horsepower hour (g/bhp/hr).

---

[5] So in original. Probably should be "(n)".

(July 14, 1955, ch. 360, title II, Sec. 202, as added Pub. L. 89-272, title I, Sec. 101(8), Oct. 20, 1965, 79 Stat. 992; amended Pub. L. 90-148, Sec. 2, Nov. 21, 1967, 81 Stat. 499; Pub. L. 91-604, Sec. 6(a), Dec. 31, 1970, 84 Stat. 1690; Pub. L. 93-319, Sec. 5, June 22, 1974, 88 Stat. 258; Pub. L. 95-95, title II, Secs. 201, 202(b), 213(b), 214(a), 215-217, 224(a), (b), (g), title IV, Sec. 401(d), Aug. 7, 1977, 91 Stat. 751-753, 758-761, 765, 767, 769, 791; Pub. L. 95-190, Sec. 14(a)(60)-(65), (b)(5), Nov. 16, 1977, 91 Stat. 1403, 1405; Pub. L. 101-549, title II, Secs. 201-207, 227(b), 230(1)-(5), Nov. 15, 1990, 104 Stat. 2472-2481, 2507, 2529.)

References in Text

The enactment of the Clean Air Act Amendments of 1990, referred to in subsec. (a)(3)(B), probably means the enactment of Pub. L. 101-549, Nov. 15, 1990, 104 Stat. 2399, which was approved Nov. 15, 1990. For complete classification of this Act to the Code, see Short Title note set out under section 7401 of this title and Tables.

Section 7525(f)(1) of this title, referred to in subsec. (a)(3)(E), was redesignated section 7525(f) of this title by Pub. L. 101-549, title II, Sec. 230(8), Nov. 15, 1990, 104 Stat. 2529.

The Energy Policy and Conservation Act, referred to in subsec. (b)(3)(C), is Pub. L. 94-163, Dec. 22, 1975, 89 Stat. 871, as amended, which is classified principally to chapter 77 (Sec. 6201 et seq.) of this title. For complete classification of this Act to the Code, see Short Title note set out under section 6201 of this title and Tables.

Codification

Section was formerly classified to section 1857f-1 of this title.

Amendments

1990—Subsec. (a)(3)(A). Pub. L. 101-549, Sec. 201(1), added subpar. (A) and struck out former subpar. (A) which related to promulgation of regulations applicable to reduction of emissions from heavy-duty vehicles or engines manufactured during and after model year 1979 in the case of carbon monoxide, hydrocarbons, and oxides of nitrogen, and from vehicles manufactured during and after model year 1981 in the case of particulate matter.

Subsec. (a)(3)(B). Pub. L. 101-549, Sec. 201(1), added subpar. (B) and struck out former subpar. (B) which read as follows: "During the period of June 1 through December 31, 1978, in the case of hydrocarbons and carbon monoxide, or during the period of June 1 through December 31, 1980, in the case of oxides of nitrogen, and during each period of June 1 through December 31 of each third year thereafter, the Administrator may, after notice and opportunity for a public hearing promulgate regulations revising any standard prescribed as provided in subparagraph (A)(ii) for any class or category of heavy-duty vehicles or engines. Such standard shall apply only for the period of three model years beginning four model years after the model year in which such revised standard is promulgated. In revising any standard under this subparagraph for any such three model year period, the Administrator shall determine the maximum degree of emission reduction which can be achieved by means reasonably expected to be available for production of such period and shall prescribe a revised emission standard in accordance with such determination. Such revised standard shall require a reduction of emissions from any standard which applies in the previous model year."

Subsec. (a)(3)(C). Pub. L. 101-549, Sec. 201(1), added subpar. (C) and struck out former subpar. (C) which read as follows: "Action revising any standard for any period may be taken by the Administrator under subparagraph (B) only if he finds—
- (i) that compliance with the emission standards otherwise applicable for such model year cannot be achieved by technology, processes, operating methods, or other alternatives reasonably expected to be available for production for such model year without increasing cost or decreasing fuel economy to an excessive and unreasonable degree; and
- (ii) the National Academy of Sciences has not, pursuant to its study and investigation under subsection (c) of this section, issued a report substantially contrary to the findings of the Administrator under clause (i)."

Subsec. (a)(3)(D). Pub. L. 101-549, Sec. 201(1), added subpar. (D) and struck out former subpar. (D) which read as follows: "A report shall be made to the Congress with respect to any standard revised under subparagraph (B) which shall contain—

(i) a summary of the health effects found, or believed to be associated with, the pollutant covered by such standard,

(ii) an analysis of the cost-effectiveness of other strategies for attaining and maintaining national ambient air quality standards and carrying out regulations under part C of subchapter I (relating to significant deterioration) in relation to the cost-effectiveness for such purposes of standards which, but for such revision, would apply.

(iii) a summary of the research and development efforts and progress being made by each manufacturer for purposes of meeting the standards promulgated as provided in subparagraph (A)(ii) or, if applicable, subparagraph (E), and

(iv) specific findings as to the relative costs of compliance, and relative fuel economy, which may be expected to result from the application for any model year of such revised standard and the application for such model year of the standard, which, but for such revision, would apply."

Subsec. (a)(3)(E), (F). Pub. L. 101-549, Sec. 201, redesignated subpar. (F) as (E), inserted heading, and struck out former subpar. (E) which read as follows:

(i) The Administrator shall conduct a continuing pollutant-specific study concerning the effects of each air pollutant emitted from heavy-duty vehicles or engines and from other sources of mobile source related pollutants on the public health and welfare. The results of such study shall be published in the Federal Register and reported to the Congress not later than June 1, 1978, in the case of hydrocarbons and carbon monoxide, and June 1, 1980, in the case of oxides of nitrogen, and before June 1 of each third year thereafter.

(ii) On the basis of such study and such other information as is available to him (including the studies under section 7548 of this title), the Administrator may, after notice and opportunity for a public hearing, promulgate regulations under paragraph (1) of this subsection changing any standard prescribed in subparagraph (A)(ii) (or revised under subparagraph (B) or previously changed under this subparagraph). No such changed standard shall apply for any model year before the model year four years after the model year during which regulations containing such changed standard are promulgated."

Subsec. (a)(4)(A), (B). Pub. L. 101-549, Sec. 227(b), substituted "requirements prescribed under this subchapter" for "standards prescribed under this subsection".

Subsec. (a)(6). Pub. L. 101-549, Sec. 202, amended par. (6) generally. Prior to amendment, par. (6) read as follows: "The Administrator shall determine the feasibility and desirability of requiring new motor vehicles to utilize onboard hydrocarbon control technology which would avoid the necessity of gasoline vapor recovery of uncontrolled emissions emanating from the fueling of motor vehicles. The Administrator shall compare the costs and effectiveness of such technology to that of implementing and maintaining vapor recovery systems (taking into consideration such factors as fuel economy, economic costs of such technology, administrative burdens, and equitable distribution of costs). If the Administrator finds that it is feasible and desirable to employ such technology, he shall, after consultation with the Secretary of Transportation with respect to motor vehicle safety, prescribe, by regulation, standards requiring the use of onboard hydrocarbon technology which shall not become effective until the introduction to the model year for which it would be feasible to implement such standards, taking into consideration compliance costs and the restraints of an adequate lead time for design and production."

Subsec. (b)(1)(C). Pub. L. 101-549, Sec. 203(c), amended subpar. (C) generally. Prior to amendment, subpar. (C) read as follows: "Effective with respect to vehicles and engines manufactured after model year 1978 (or in the case of heavy-duty vehicles or engines, such later model year as the Administrator determines is the earliest feasible model year), the test procedure promulgated under paragraph (2) for measurement of evaporative emissions of hydrocarbons shall require that such emissions be measured from the vehicle or engine as a whole. Regulations to carry out this subparagraph shall be promulgated not later than two hundred and seventy days after August 7, 1977."

Subsec. (b)(2). Pub. L. 101-549, Sec. 203(d), amended par. (2) generally. Prior to amendment, par. (2) read as follows: "Emission standards under paragraph (1), and measurement techniques on which such standards are based (if not promulgated prior to December 31, 1970), shall be prescribed by regulation within 180 days after such date."

Subsec. (b)(3). Pub. L. 101-549, Sec. 230(4), redesignated par. (6) relating to waiver of standards for oxides of nitrogen as par. (3), struck out subpar. (A) designation before "Upon the petition", redesignated former cls. (i) to (iii) as subpars. (A) to (C), respectively, and struck out former subpar. (B) which authorized the Administrator to waive the standard under subsec. (b)(1)(B) of this section for emissions of oxides of nitrogen from light-duty vehicles and engines beginning in model year 1981 after providing notice and opportunity for a public hearing, and set forth conditions under which a waiver could be granted.

Subsec. (b)(3)(B). Pub. L. 101-549, Sec. 230(1), in the par. (3) defining terms for purposes of this part struck out subpar. (B) which defined "light duty vehicles and engines".

Subsec. (b)(4). Pub. L. 101-549, Sec. 230(2), struck out par. (4) which read as follows: "On July 1 of 1971, and of each year thereafter, the Administrator shall report to the Congress with respect to the development of systems necessary to implement the emission standards established pursuant to this section. Such reports shall include information regarding the continuing effects of such air pollutants subject to standards under this section on the public health and welfare, the extent and progress of efforts being made to develop the necessary systems, the costs associated with development and application of such systems, and following such hearings as he may deem advisable, any recommendations for additional congressional action necessary to achieve the purposes of this chapter. In gathering information for the purposes of this paragraph and in connection with any hearing, the provisions of section 7607(a) of this title (relating to subpenas) shall apply."

Subsec. (b)(5). Pub. L. 101-549, Sec. 230(3), struck out par. (5) which related to waivers for model years 1981 and 1982 of the effective date of the emissions standard required under par. (1)(A) for carbon monoxide applicable to light-duty vehicles and engines manufactured in those model years.

Subsec. (b)(6). Pub. L. 101-549, Sec. 230(4), redesignated par. (6) as (3).

Subsec. (b)(7). Pub. L. 101-549, Sec. 230(5), struck out par. (7) which read as follows: "The Congress hereby declares and establishes as a research objective, the development of propulsion systems and emission control technology to achieve standards which represent a reduction of at least 90 per centum from the average emissions of oxides of nitrogen actually measured from light duty motor vehicles manufactured in model year 1971 not subject to any Federal or State emission standard for oxides of nitrogen. The Administrator shall, by regulations promulgated within one hundred and eighty days after August 7, 1977, require each manufacturer whose sales represent at least 0.5 per centum of light duty motor vehicle sales in the United States, to build and, on a regular basis, demonstrate the operation of light duty motor vehicles that meet this research objective, in addition to any other applicable standards or requirements for other pollutants under this chapter. Such demonstration vehicles shall be submitted to the Administrator no later than model year 1979 and in each model year thereafter. Such demonstration shall, in accordance with applicable regulations, to the greatest extent possible, (A) be designed to encourage the development of new powerplant and emission control technologies that are fuel efficient, (B) assure that the demonstration vehicles are or could reasonably be expected to be within the productive capability of the manufacturers, and (C) assure the utilization of optimum engine, fuel, and emission control systems."

Subsec. (d). Pub. L. 101-549, Sec. 203(b)(1), substituted "provide that except where a different useful life period is specified in this subchapter" for "provide that".

Subsec. (d)(1). Pub. L. 101-549, Sec. 203(b)(2), (3), inserted "and light-duty trucks up to 3,750 lbs. LVW and up to 6,000 lbs. GVWR" after "engines" and substituted for semicolon at end ", except that in the case of any requirement of this section which first becomes applicable after November 15, 1990, where the useful life period is not otherwise specified for such vehicles and engines, the period shall be 10 years or 100,000 miles (or the equivalent), whichever first occurs, with testing for purposes of in-use compliance under section 7541 of this title up to (but not beyond) 7 years or 75,000 miles (or the equivalent), whichever first occurs;".

Subsec. (f). Pub. L. 101-549, Sec. 207(b), added (after subsec. (m) at end) subsec. (f) relating to regulations applicable to buses for model years after 1990.

224 / Environmental Statutes

Subsecs. (g) to (i). Pub. L. 101-549, Sec. 203(a), added subsecs. (g) to (i).

Subsecs. (j) to (m). Pub. L. 101-549, Secs. 204-207(a), added subsecs. (j) to (m).

1977—Subsec. (a)(1). Pub. L. 95-190, Sec. 14(a)(60), restructured subsec. (a) by providing for designation of par. (1) to precede "The Administrator" in place of "Except as".

Pub. L. 95-95, Sec. 401(d)(1), substituted "Except as otherwise provided in subsection (b) of this section the Administrator" for "The Administrator", "cause, or contribute to, air pollution which may reasonably be anticipated to endanger public health or welfare" for "causes or contributes to, or is likely to cause or contribute to, air pollution which endangers the public health or welfare", and "useful life (as determined under subsection (d) of this section, relating to useful life of vehicles for purposes of certification), whether such vehicles and engines are designed as complete systems or incorporate devices" for "useful life (as determined under subsection (d) of this section) whether such vehicles and engines are designed as complete systems or incorporated devices".

Subsec. (a)(2). Pub. L. 95-95, Sec. 214(a), substituted "prescribed under paragraph (1) of this subsection" for "prescribed under this subsection".

Subsec. (a)(3). Pub. L. 95-95, Sec. 224(a), added par. (3).

Subsec. (a)(3)(B). Pub. L. 95-190, Sec. 14(a)(61), (62), substituted provisions setting forth applicable periods of from June 1 through Dec. 31, 1978, June 1 through Dec. 31, 1980, and during each period of June 1 through Dec. 31 of each third year thereafter, for provisions setting forth applicable periods of from June 1 through Dec. 31, 1979, and during each period of June 1 through Dec. 31 of each third year after 1979, and substituted "from any" for "of from any".

Subsec. (a)(3)(E). Pub. L. 95-190, Sec. 14(a)(63), substituted "1978, in the case of hydrocarbons and carbon monoxide, and June 1, 1980, in the case of oxides of nitrogen" for "1979,".

Subsec. (a)(4). Pub. L. 95-95, Sec. 214(a), added par. (4).

Subsec. (a)(5). Pub. L. 95-95, Sec. 215, added par. (5).

Subsec. (a)(6). Pub. L. 95-95, Sec. 216, added par. (6).

Subsec. (b)(1)(A). Pub. L. 95-95, Sec. 201(a), substituted provisions setting the standards for emissions from light-duty vehicles and engines manufactured during the model years 1977 through 1980 for provisions which had set the standards for emissions from light-duty vehicles and engines manufactured during the model years 1975 and 1976, substituted "model year 1980" for "model year 1977" in provisions requiring a reduction of at least 90 per centum from the emissions allowable under standards for model year 1970, and inserted provisions that, unless waived as provided in par. (5), the standards for vehicles and engines manufactured during or after the model year 1981 represent a reduction of at least 90 per centum from the emissions allowable under standards for model year 1970.

Subsec. (b)(1)(B). Pub. L. 95-190, Sec. 14(a)(64), (65), substituted "calendar year 1976" for "model year 1976" and in cl. (i) substituted "other" for "United States".

Pub. L. 95-95, Sec. 201(b), substituted provisions setting the standards for emissions from light-duty vehicles and engines manufactured during the model years 1977 through 1980 for provisions which had set the standards for emissions from light-duty vehicles and engines manufactured during the model years 1975 through 1977, substituted provisions that the standards for model years 1981 and after allow emissions of no more than 1.0 gram per vehicle mile for provisions that the standards for model year 1978 and after require a reduction of at least 90 per centum from the average of emissions actually measured from light-duty vehicles manufactured during model year 1971 which were not subject to any Federal or State emission standards for oxides of nitrogen, and inserted provisions directing the Administrator to prescribe separate standards for model years 1981 and 1982 for manufacturers whose production, by corporate identity, for model year 1976 was less than three hundred thousand light-duty motor vehicles worldwide if the manufacturer's capability to meet emission standards depends upon United States technology and if the manufacturer cannot develop one.

Subsec. (b)(1)(C). Pub. L. 95-95, Sec. 217, added subpar. (C).

Subsec. (b)(3)(C). Pub. L. 95-95, Sec. 224(b), added subpar. (C).

Subsec. (b)(5). Pub. L. 95-95, Sec. 201(c), substituted provisions setting up a procedure under which a manufacturer may apply for a waiver for model years 1981 and 1982 of the effective date of the emission standards for carbon monoxide required by par. (1)(A) for provisions which had set up a procedure under which a manufacturer, after Jan. 1, 1975, could apply for a one-year suspension of the effective date of any emission standard required by par. (1)(A) for model year 1977.

Subsec. (b)(6). Pub. L. 95-95, Sec. 201(c), added par. (6).

Subsec. (b)(7). Pub. L. 95-95, Sec. 202(b), added par. (7).

Subsec. (d)(2). Pub. L. 95-95, Sec. 224(g), as amended by Pub. L. 95-190, Sec. 14(b)(5), to correct typographical error in directory language, inserted "(other than motorcycles or motorcycle engines)" after "motor vehicle or motor vehicle engine".

Subsec. (d)(3). Pub. L. 95-95, Sec. 224(g), added par. (3).

Subsec. (e). Pub. L. 95-95, Sec. 401(d)(2), substituted "which in his judgment cause, or contribute to, air pollution which may reasonably be anticipated to endanger" for "which cause or contribute to, or are likely to cause or contribute to, air pollution which endangers".

Subsec. (f). Pub. L. 95-95, Sec. 213(b), added subsec. (f).

1974—Subsec. (b)(1)(A). Pub. L. 93-319, Sec. 5(a), substituted "model year 1977" for "model year 1975" in provisions requiring a reduction of at least 90 per centum from the emissions allowable under standards for model year 1970 and inserted provisions covering regulations for model years 1975 and 1976.

Subsec. (b)(1)(B). Pub. L. 93-319, Sec. 5(b), substituted "model year 1978" for "model year 1976" in provisions requiring a reduction of at least 90 per centum from the average of emissions actually measured from vehicles manufactured during model year 1971 and inserted provisions covering regulations for model years 1975, 1976, and 1977.

Subsec. (b)(5). Pub. L. 93-319, Sec. 5(c), (d), substituted in subpar. (A), "At any time after January 1, 1975" for "At any time after January 1, 1972", "with respect to such manufacturer for light-duty vehicles and engines manufactured in model year 1977" for "with respect to such manufacturer", "sixty days" for "60 days", "paragraph (1)(A) of this subsection" for "paragraph (1)(A)", and "vehicles and engines manufactured during model year 1977" for "vehicles and engines manufactured during model year 1975", redesignated subpars. (C) to (E) as (B) to (D), respectively, and struck out former subpar. (B) which had allowed manufacturers, at any time after Jan. 1, 1973, to file with the Administrator an application requesting a 1-year suspension of the effective date of any emission standard required by subsec. (b)(1)(B) with respect to such manufacturer.

1970—Subsec. (a). Pub. L. 91-604 redesignated existing provisions as par. (1), substituted Administrator for Secretary as the issuing authority for standards, inserted references to the useful life of engines, and substituted the emission of any air pollutant for the emission of any kind of substance as the subject to be regulated, and added par. (2).

Subsec. (b). Pub. L. 91-604 added subsec. (b). Former subsec. (b) redesignated as par. (2) of subsec. (a).

Subsecs. (c) to (e). Pub. L. 91-604 added subsecs. (c) to (e).

1967—Pub. L. 90-148 reenacted section without change.

Effective Date of 1977 Amendment

Amendment by Pub. L. 95-95 effective Aug. 7, 1977, except as otherwise expressly provided, see section 406(d) of Pub. L. 95-95, set out as a note under section 7401 of this title.

Modification or Rescission of Rules, Regulations, Orders, Determinations, Contracts, Certifications, Authorizations, Delegations, and Other Actions

All rules, regulations, orders, determinations, contracts, certifications, authorizations, delegations, or other actions duly issued, made, or taken by or pursuant to act July 14, 1955, the Clean Air Act, as in effect immediately prior to the date of enactment of Pub. L. 95-95 [Aug. 7, 1977] to continue in full force and effect until modified or rescinded in accordance with act July 14, 1955, as amended by Pub. L. 95-95 [this chapter], see section 406(b) of Pub. L. 95-95, set out as an Effective Date of 1977 Amendment note under section 7401 of this title.

Study on Oxides of Nitrogen From Light-Duty Vehicles

Section 202(a) of Pub. L. 95-95 provided that the Administrator of the Environmental Protection Agency conduct a study of the public health implications of attaining an emission standard on oxides of nitrogen from light-duty vehicles of 0.4 gram per vehicle mile, the cost and technological capability of attaining such standard, and the need for such a standard to protect public health or welfare and that the Administrator submit a report of such study to the Congress, together with recommendations not later than July 1, 1980.

Study of Carbon Monoxide Intrusion Into Sustained-Use Vehicles

Section 226 of Pub. L. 95-95 provided that the Administrator, in conjunction with the Secretary of Transportation, study the problem of carbon monoxide intrusion into the passenger area of sustained-use motor vehicles and that within one year the EPA report to the Congress respecting the results of such study.

Continuing Comprehensive Studies and Investigations by National Academy of Sciences

Section 403(f) of Pub. L. 95-95 provided that: "The Administrator of the Environmental Protection Agency shall undertake to enter into appropriate arrangements with the National Academy of Sciences to conduct continuing comprehensive studies and investigations of the effects on public health and welfare of emissions subject to section 202(a) of the Clean Air Act [subsec. (a) of this section] (including sulfur compounds) and the technological feasibility of meeting emission standards required to be prescribed by the Administrator by section 202(b) of such Act [subsec. (b) of this section]. The Administrator shall report to the Congress within six months of the date of enactment of this section [Aug. 7, 1977] and each year thereafter regarding the status of the contractual arrangements and conditions necessary to implement this paragraph."

Study on Emission of Sulfur-Bearing Compounds From Motor Vehicles and Motor Vehicle and Aircraft Engines

Section 403(g) of Pub. L. 95-95 provided that the Administrator of the Environmental Protection Agency conduct a study and report to the Congress by the date one year after Aug. 7, 1977, on the emission of sulfur-bearing compounds from motor vehicles and motor vehicle engines and aircraft engines.

Section Referred to in Other Sections

This section is referred to in sections 7417, 7511a, 7522, 7525, 7541, 7543, 7545, 7547, 7548, 7549, 7550, 7554, 7585, 7607, 7608, 7617 of this title; title 49 section 30113.

PROHIBITED ACTS

42 USC 7522

(a) Enumerated prohibitions
 The following acts and the causing thereof are prohibited—
 (1) in the case of a manufacturer of new motor vehicles or new motor vehicle engines for distribution in commerce, the sale, or the offering for sale, or the introduction, or delivery for introduction, into commerce, or (in the case of any person, except as provided by regulation of the Administrator), the importation into the United States, of any new motor vehicle or new motor vehicle engine, manufactured after the effective date of regulations under this part which are applicable to such vehicle or engine unless such vehicle or engine is covered by a certificate of conformity issued (and in effect) under regulations prescribed under this part or part C in the case of clean-fuel vehicles (except as provided in subsection (b) of this section);
 (2) (A) for any person to fail or refuse to permit access to or copying of records or to fail to make reports or provide information required under section 7542 of this title;
  (B) for any person to fail or refuse to permit entry, testing or inspection authorized under section 7525(c) of this title or section 7542 of this title;
  (C) for any person to fail or refuse to perform tests, or have tests performed as required under section 7542 of this title;
  (D) for any manufacturer to fail to make information available as provided by regulation under section 7521(m)(5) of this title;

(3) (A) for any person to remove or render inoperative any device or element of design installed on or in a motor vehicle or motor vehicle engine in compliance with regulations under this subchapter prior to its sale and delivery to the ultimate purchaser, or for any person knowingly to remove or render inoperative any such device or element of design after such sale and delivery to the ultimate purchaser; or

(B) for any person to manufacture or sell, or offer to sell, or install, any part or component intended for use with, or as part of, any motor vehicle or motor vehicle engine, where a principal effect of the part or component is to bypass, defeat, or render inoperative any device or element of design installed on or in a motor vehicle or motor vehicle engine in compliance with regulations under this subchapter, and where the person knows or should know that such part or component is being offered for sale or installed for such use or put to such use; or

(4) for any manufacturer of a new motor vehicle or new motor vehicle engine subject to standards prescribed under section 7521 of this title or part C of this subchapter—

(A) to sell or lease any such vehicle or engine unless such manufacturer has complied with (i) the requirements of section 7541(a) and (b) of this title with respect to such vehicle or engine, and unless a label or tag is affixed to such vehicle or engine in accordance with section 7541(c)(3) of this title, or (ii) the corresponding requirements of part C of this subchapter in the case of clean fuel vehicles unless the manufacturer has complied with the corresponding requirements of part C of this subchapter[1]

(B) to fail or refuse to comply with the requirements of section 7541(c) or (e) of this title, or the corresponding requirements of part C of this subchapter in the case of clean fuel vehicles[1]

(C) except as provided in subsection (c)(3) of section 7541 of this title and the corresponding requirements of part C of this subchapter in the case of clean fuel vehicles, to provide directly or indirectly in any communication to the ultimate purchaser or any subsequent purchaser that the coverage of any warranty under this chapter is conditioned upon use of any part, component, or system manufactured by such manufacturer or any person acting for such manufacturer or under his control, or conditioned upon service performed by any such person, or

(D) to fail or refuse to comply with the terms and conditions of the warranty under section 7541(a) or (b) of this title or the corresponding requirements of part C of this subchapter in the case of clean fuel vehicles with respect to any vehicle; or

(5) for any person to violate section 7553 of this title, 7554 of this title, or part C of this subchapter or any regulations under section 7553 of this title, 7554 of this title, or part C of this subchapter.

No action with respect to any element of design referred to in paragraph (3) (including any adjustment or alteration of such element) shall be treated as a prohibited act under such paragraph (3) if such action is in accordance with section 7549 of this title. Nothing in paragraph (3) shall be construed to require the use of manufacturer parts in maintaining or repairing any motor vehicle or motor vehicle engine. For the purposes of the preceding sentence, the term "manufacturer parts" means, with respect to a motor vehicle engine, parts produced or sold by the manufacturer of the motor vehicle or motor vehicle engine. No action with respect to any device or element of design referred to in paragraph (3) shall be treated as a prohibited act under that paragraph if (i) the action is for the purpose of repair or replacement of the device or element, or is a necessary and temporary procedure to repair or replace any other item and the device or element is replaced upon completion of the procedure, and (ii) such action thereafter results in the proper functioning of the device or element referred to in paragraph (3). No action with respect to any device or element of design referred to in paragraph (3) shall be treated as a prohibited act under that paragraph if the action is for the purpose of a conversion of a motor vehicle for use of a clean alternative fuel (as defined in this subchapter) and if such vehicle complies with the applicable standard under section 7521 of this title when operating on such fuel, and if in the case of a clean alternative fuel vehicle (as defined by rule by the Administrator), the device or element is replaced upon completion of the conversion procedure and such action results in proper functioning of the device or element when the motor vehicle operates on conventional fuel.

---

[1]So in original. Probably should be followed by a comma.

(b) Exemptions; refusal to admit vehicle or engine into United States; vehicles or engines intended for export
  (1) The Administrator may exempt any new motor vehicle or new motor vehicle engine, from subsection (a) of this section, upon such terms and conditions as he may find necessary for the purpose of research, investigations, studies, demonstrations, or training, or for reasons of national security.
  (2) A new motor vehicle or new motor vehicle engine offered for importation or imported by any person in violation of subsection (a) of this section shall be refused admission into the United States, but the Secretary of the Treasury and the Administrator may, by joint regulation, provide for deferring final determination as to admission and authorizing the delivery of such a motor vehicle or engine offered for import to the owner or consignee thereof upon such terms and conditions (including the furnishing of a bond) as may appear to them appropriate to insure that any such motor vehicle or engine will be brought into conformity with the standards, requirements, and limitations applicable to it under this part. The Secretary of the Treasury shall, if a motor vehicle or engine is finally refused admission under this paragraph, cause disposition thereof in accordance with the customs laws unless it is exported, under regulations prescribed by such Secretary, within ninety days of the date of notice of such refusal or such additional time as may be permitted pursuant to such regulations, except that disposition in accordance with the customs laws may not be made in such manner as may result, directly or indirectly, in the sale, to the ultimate consumer, of a new motor vehicle or new motor vehicle engine that fails to comply with applicable standards of the Administrator under this part.
  (3) A new motor vehicle or new motor vehicle engine intended solely for export, and so labeled or tagged on the outside of the container and on the vehicle or engine itself, shall be subject to the provisions of subsection (a) of this section, except that if the country which is to receive such vehicle or engine has emission standards which differ from the standards prescribed under section 7521 of this title, then such vehicle or engine shall comply with the standards of such country which is to receive such vehicle or engine.

(July 14, 1955, ch. 360, title II, Sec. 203, as added Pub. L. 89-272, title I, Sec. 101(8), Oct. 20, 1965, 79 Stat. 993; amended Pub. L. 90-148, Sec. 2, Nov. 21, 1967, 81 Stat. 499; Pub. L. 91-604, Secs. 7(a), 11(a)(2)(A), 15(c)(2), Dec. 31, 1970, 84 Stat. 1693, 1705, 1713; Pub. L. 95-95, title II, Secs. 206, 211(a), 218(a), (d), 219(a), (b), Aug. 7, 1977, 91 Stat. 755, 757, 761, 762; Pub. L. 95-190, Sec. 14(a)(66)-(68), Nov. 16, 1977, 91 Stat. 1403; Pub. L. 101-549, title II, Secs. 228(a), (b), (e), 230(6), Nov. 15, 1990, 104 Stat. 2507, 2511, 2529.)

Codification

Section was formerly classified to section 1857f-2 of this title.

Amendments

1990—Subsec. (a). Pub. L. 101-549, Sec. 228(b)(2), inserted two sentences at end which set forth conditions under which actions with respect to devices or elements of design, referred to in par. (3), would not be deemed prohibited acts.

Subsec. (a)(1). Pub. L. 101-549, Sec. 228(e)(1), inserted "or part C of this subchapter in the case of clean-fuel vehicles" before "(except".

Subsec. (a)(2). Pub. L. 101-549, Sec. 228(a), amended par. (2) generally. Prior to amendment, par. (2) read as follows: "for any person to fail or refuse to permit access to or copying of records or to fail to make reports or provide information, required under section 7542 of this title or for any person to fail or refuse to permit entry, testing, or inspection authorized under section 7525(c) of this title;".

Subsec. (a)(3). Pub. L. 101-549, Sec. 228(b)(1), amended par. (3) generally. Prior to amendment, par. (3) read as follows:
  "(A) for any person to remove or render inoperative any device or element of design installed on or in a motor vehicle or motor vehicle engine in compliance with regulations under this subchapter prior to its sale and delivery to the ultimate purchaser, or for any manufacturer or dealer knowingly to remove or render inoperative any such device or element of design after such sale and delivery to the ultimate purchaser; or
  (B) for any person engaged in the business of repairing, servicing, selling, leasing, or trading motor vehicles or motor vehicle engines, or who operates a fleet of motor

vehicles, knowingly to remove or render inoperative any device or element of design installed on or in a motor vehicle or motor vehicle engine in compliance with regulations under this subchapter following its sale and delivery to the ultimate purchaser; or".

Subsec. (a)(4). Pub. L. 101-549, Sec. 228(e)(2), inserted "part C of this subchapter" after "section 7521 of this title".

Subsec. (a)(4)(A). Pub. L. 101-549, Sec. 228(e)(3), inserted cl. (i) designation and added cl. (ii).

Subsec. (a)(4)(B). Pub. L. 101-549, Sec. 228(e)(4), inserted at end "or the corresponding requirements of part C of this subchapter in the case of clean fuel vehicles".

Subsec. (a)(4)(C). Pub. L. 101-549, Sec. 228(e)(5), inserted "and the corresponding requirements of part C of this subchapter in the case of clean fuel vehicles" after "section 7541 of this title".

Subsec. (a)(4)(D). Pub. L. 101-549, Sec. 228(e)(6), inserted "or the corresponding requirements of part C of this subchapter in the case of clean fuel vehicles" before "with respect to any vehicle".

Subsec. (a)(5). Pub. L. 101-549, Sec. 228(e)(7), added par. (5).

Subsec. (c). Pub. L. 101-549, Sec. 230(6), struck out subsec. (c) which related to exemptions to permit modifications of emission control devices or systems.

1977—Subsec. (a). Pub. L. 95-190, Sec. 14(a)(68), in closing text inserted a period after "section 7549 of this title".

Pub. L. 95-95, Secs. 206, 211(a), 218(a), 219(a), (b), inserted "or for any person to fail or refuse to permit entry, testing, or inspection authorized under section 7525(c) of this title" in par. (2), designated existing provisions of par. (3) as subpar. (A) and added subpar. (B), added subpars. (C) and (D) in par. (4), and, following par. (4), inserted provisions that no action with respect to any element of design referred to in par. (3) (including adjustment or alteration of such element) be treated as a prohibited act under par. (3) if the action is in accordance with section 7549 of this title and that nothing in par. (3) be construed to require the use of manufacturer parts in maintaining or repairing motor vehicles or motor vehicle engines.

Subsec. (a)(3)(B). Pub. L. 95-190, Sec. 14(a)(66), substituted "purchaser;" for "purchaser,".

Subsec. (a)(4)(C). Pub. L. 95-190, Sec. 14(a)(67), inserted "or" after "such person,".

Subsec. (b)(3). Pub. L. 95-95, Sec. 218(d), substituted "section 7521 of this title" for "subsection (a) of this section" and "country which is to receive such vehicle or engine" for "country of export".

1970—Subsec. (a)(1). Pub. L. 91-604, Sec. 7(a)(1), struck out reference to the manufacture of new motor vehicles or new motor vehicle engines for sale, inserted provision for issuance by the Administrator of regulations regarding exceptions in the case of importation of new motor vehicles or new motor vehicle engines, and substituted "importation" into the United States of such units for "importation for sale or resale" into the United States of such units.

Subsec. (a)(2). Pub. L. 91-604, Sec. 7(a)(2), substituted "section 208" for "section 207", both of which, for purposes of codification, are translated as "section 7542 of this title".

Subsec. (a)(3). Pub. L. 91-604, Secs. 7(a)(3), 11(a)(2)(A), substituted "part" for "subchapter" and inserted provisions prohibiting the knowing removal or inoperation by manufacturers or dealers of devices or elements of design after sale and delivery to the ultimate purchaser.

Subsec. (a)(4). Pub. L. 91-604, Sec. 7(a)(4), added par. (4).

Subsec. (b)(1). Pub. L. 91-604, Secs. 7(a)(5), 15(c)(2), struck out reference to the exemption of a class of new motor vehicles or new motor vehicle engines, struck out the protection of the public health and welfare from the enumeration of purposes for which exemptions may be made, and substituted "Administrator" for "Secretary".

Subsec. (b)(2). Pub. L. 91-604, Secs. 7(a)(6), 11(a)(2)(A), 15(c)(2), substituted "Administrator" for "Secretary of Health, Education, and Welfare", "importation or imported by any person" for "importation by a manufacturer", and "part" for "subchapter".

Subsec. (b)(3). Pub. L. 91-604, Sec. 7(a)(7)(A), inserted provision that, if the country of export has emission standards which differ from the standards prescribed under subsec. (a), such vehicle or engine must comply with the standards of such country of export.

Subsec. (c). Pub. L. 91-604, Sec. 7(a)(7)(B), added subsec. (c).

230 / Environmental Statutes

1967—Subsec. (a). Pub. L. 90-148 substituted "conformity with regulations prescribed under this subchapter" for "conformity with regulations prescribed under section 7521 of this title" in par. (1).

Effective Date of 1977 Amendment

Amendment by Pub. L. 95-95 effective Aug. 7, 1977, except as otherwise expressly provided, see section 406(d) of Pub. L. 95-95, set out as a note under section 7401 of this title.

Modification or Rescission of Rules, Regulations, Orders, Determinations, Contracts, Certifications, Authorizations, Delegations, and Other Actions

All rules, regulations, orders, determinations, contracts, certifications, authorizations, delegations, or other actions duly issued, made, or taken by or pursuant to act July 14, 1955, the Clean Air Act, as in effect immediately prior to the date of enactment of Pub. L. 95-95 [Aug. 7, 1977] to continue in full force and effect until modified or rescinded in accordance with act July 14, 1955, as amended by Pub. L. 95-95 [this chapter], see section 406(b) of Pub. L. 95-95, set out as an Effective Date of 1977 Amendment note under section 7401 of this title.

Section Referred to in Other Sections

This section is referred to in sections 7523, 7524, 7549, 7550, 7587 of this title.

ACTIONS TO RESTRAIN VIOLATIONS

42 USC 7523

(a) Jurisdiction
   The district courts of the United States shall have jurisdiction to restrain violations of section 7522(a) of this title.

(b) Actions brought by or in name of United States; subpenas
   Actions to restrain such violations shall be brought by and in the name of the United States. In any such action, subpenas for witnesses who are required to attend a district court in any district may run into any other district.

(July 14, 1955, ch. 360, title II, Sec. 204, as added Pub. L. 89-272, title I, Sec. 101(8), Oct. 20, 1965, 79 Stat. 994; amended Pub. L. 90-148, Sec. 2, Nov. 21, 1967, 81 Stat. 500; Pub. L. 91-604, Sec. 7(b), Dec. 31, 1970, 84 Stat. 1694; Pub. L. 95-95, title II, Sec. 218(b), Aug. 7, 1977, 91 Stat. 761.)

Codification

Section was formerly classified to section 1857f-3 of this title.

Amendments

1977—Subsec. (a). Pub. L. 95-95 struck out "paragraph (1), (2), (3), or (4)" after "restrain violations of".

1970—Subsec. (a). Pub. L. 91-604 inserted reference to par. (4) of section 7522(a) of this title.

1967—Pub. L. 90-148 reenacted section without change.

Effective Date of 1977 Amendment

Amendment by Pub. L. 95-95 effective Aug. 7, 1977, except as otherwise expressly provided, see section 406(d) of Pub. L. 95-95, set out as a note under section 7401 of this title.

Pending Actions and Proceedings

Suits, actions, and other proceedings lawfully commenced by or against the Administrator or any other officer or employee of the United States in his official capacity or in relation to the discharge of his official duties under act July 14, 1955, the Clean Air Act, as in effect immediately prior to the enactment of Pub. L. 95-95 [Aug. 7, 1977], not to abate by reason of the taking effect of Pub. L. 95-95, see section 406(a) of Pub. L. 95-95, set out as an Effective Date of 1977 amendment note under section 7401 of this title.

CIVIL PENALTIES

42 USC 7524

(a) Violations

Any person who violates sections[1] 7522(a)(1), 7522(a)(4), or 7522(a)(5) of this title or any manufacturer or dealer who violates section 7522(a)(3)(A) of this title shall be subject to a civil penalty of not more than $25,000. Any person other than a manufacturer or dealer who violates section 7522(a)(3)(A) of this title or any person who violates section 7522(a)(3)(B) of this title shall be subject to a civil penalty of not more than $2,500. Any such violation with respect to paragraph (1), (3)(A), or (4) of section 7522(a) of this title shall constitute a separate offense with respect to each motor vehicle or motor vehicle engine. Any such violation with respect to section 7522(a)(3)(B) of this title shall constitute a separate offense with respect to each part or component. Any person who violates section 7522(a)(2) of this title shall be subject to a civil penalty of not more than $25,000 per day of violation.

(b) Civil actions

The Administrator may commence a civil action to assess and recover any civil penalty under subsection (a) of this section, section 7545(d) of this title, or section 7547(d) of this title. Any action under this subsection may be brought in the district court of the United States for the district in which the violation is alleged to have occurred or in which the defendant resides or has the Administrator's principal place of business, and the court shall have jurisdiction to assess a civil penalty. In determining the amount of any civil penalty to be assessed under this subsection, the court shall take into account the gravity of the violation, the economic benefit or savings (if any) resulting from the violation, the size of the violator's business, the violator's history of compliance with this subchapter, action taken to remedy the violation, the effect of the penalty on the violator's ability to continue in business, and such other matters as justice may require. In any such action, subpoenas for witnesses who are required to attend a district court in any district may run into any other district.

(c) Administrative assessment of certain penalties

(1) Administrative penalty authority

In lieu of commencing a civil action under subsection (b) of this section, the Administrator may assess any civil penalty prescribed in subsection (a) of this section, section 7545(d) of this title, or section 7547(d) of this title, except that the maximum amount of penalty sought against each violator in a penalty assessment proceeding shall not exceed $200,000, unless the Administrator and the Attorney General jointly determine that a matter involving a larger penalty amount is appropriate for administrative penalty assessment. Any such determination by the Administrator and the Attorney General shall not be subject to judicial review. Assessment of a civil penalty under this subsection shall be by an order made on the record after opportunity for a hearing in accordance with sections 554 and 556 of title 5. The Administrator shall issue reasonable rules for discovery and other procedures for hearings under this paragraph. Before issuing such an order, the Administrator shall give written notice to the person to be assessed an administrative penalty of the Administrator's proposal to issue such order and provide such person an opportunity to request such a hearing on the order, within 30 days of the date the notice is received by such person. The Administrator may compromise, or remit, with or without conditions, any administrative penalty which may be imposed under this section.

(2) Determining amount

In determining the amount of any civil penalty assessed under this subsection, the Administrator shall take into account the gravity of the violation, the economic benefit or savings (if any) resulting from the violation, the size of the violator's business, the violator's history of compliance with this subchapter, action taken to remedy the violation, the effect of the penalty on the violator's ability to continue in business, and such other matters as justice may require.

(3) Effect of Administrator's action

(A) Action by the Administrator under this subsection shall not affect or limit the Administrator's authority to enforce any provision of this chapter; except that any violation,

---

[1] So in original. Probably should be "section".

(i) with respect to which the Administrator has commenced and is diligently prosecuting an action under this subsection, or

(ii) for which the Administrator has issued a final order not subject to further judicial review and the violator has paid a penalty assessment under this subsection,

shall not be the subject of civil penalty action under subsection (b) of this section.

(B) No action by the Administrator under this subsection shall affect any person's obligation to comply with any section of this chapter.

(4) Finality of order

An order issued under this subsection shall become final 30 days after its issuance unless a petition for judicial review is filed under paragraph (5).

(5) Judicial review

Any person against whom a civil penalty is assessed in accordance with this subsection may seek review of the assessment in the United States District Court for the District of Columbia, or for the district in which the violation is alleged to have occurred, in which such person resides, or where such person's principal place of business is located, within the 30-day period beginning on the date a civil penalty order is issued. Such person shall simultaneously send a copy of the filing by certified mail to the Administrator and the Attorney General. The Administrator shall file in the court a certified copy, or certified index, as appropriate, of the record on which the order was issued within 30 days. The court shall not set aside or remand any order issued in accordance with the requirements of this subsection unless there is not substantial evidence in the record, taken as a whole, to support the finding of a violation or unless the Administrator's assessment of the penalty constitutes an abuse of discretion, and the court shall not impose additional civil penalties unless the Administrator's assessment of the penalty constitutes an abuse of discretion. In any proceedings, the United States may seek to recover civil penalties assessed under this section.

(6) Collection

If any person fails to pay an assessment of a civil penalty imposed by the Administrator as provided in this subsection—

(A) after the order making the assessment has become final, or

(B) after a court in an action brought under paragraph (5) has entered a final judgment in favor of the Administrator,

the Administrator shall request the Attorney General to bring a civil action in an appropriate district court to recover the amount assessed (plus interest at rates established pursuant to section 6621(a)(2) of title 26 from the date of the final order or the date of the final judgment, as the case may be). In such an action, the validity, amount, and appropriateness of the penalty shall not be subject to review. Any person who fails to pay on a timely basis the amount of an assessment of a civil penalty as described in the first sentence of this paragraph shall be required to pay, in addition to that amount and interest, the United States' enforcement expenses, including attorneys fees and costs for collection proceedings, and a quarterly nonpayment penalty for each quarter during which such failure to pay persists. The nonpayment penalty shall be in an amount equal to 10 percent of the aggregate amount of that person's penalties and nonpayment penalties which are unpaid as of the beginning of such quarter.

(July 14, 1955, ch. 360, title I, Sec. 205, as added Pub. L. 89-272, title I, Sec. 101(8), Oct. 20, 1965, 79 Stat. 994; amended Pub. L. 90-148, Sec. 2, Nov. 21, 1967, 81 Stat. 500; Pub. L. 91-604, Sec. 7(c), Dec. 31, 1970, 84 Stat. 1694; Pub. L. 95-95, title II, Sec. 219(c), Aug. 7, 1977, 91 Stat. 762; Pub. L. 101-549, title II, Sec. 228(c), Nov. 15, 1990, 104 Stat. 2508.)

Codification

Section was formerly classified to section 1857f-4 of this title.

Amendments

1990—Pub. L. 101-549 amended section generally. Prior to amendment, section read as follows: "Any person who violates paragraph (1), (2), or (4) of section 7522(a) of this title or any manufacturer, dealer, or other person who violates paragraph (3)(A) of section 7522(a) of this title shall be subject to a civil penalty of not more than $10,000. Any person who violates paragraph (3)(B) of such section 7522(a) shall be subject to a civil penalty of not more than $2,500.

Any such violation with respect to paragraph (1), (3), or (4) of section 7522(a) of this title shall constitute a separate offense with respect to each motor vehicle or motor vehicle engine."

1977—Pub. L. 95-95 substituted "Any person who violates paragraph (1), (2), or (4) of section 7522(a) of this title, or any manufacturer, dealer, or other person who violates paragraph (3)(A) of section 7522(a) of this title" for "Any person who violates paragraph (1), (2), (3), or (4) of section 7522(a) of this title" in provisions covering the civil penalty of $10,000, and inserted provisions for a civil penalty of not more than $2,500 for violations of par. (3)(B) of section 7522(a) of this title.

1970—Pub. L. 91-604 increased the upper limit of the allowable fine from "$1,000" to "$10,000".

1967—Pub. L. 90-148 reenacted section without change.

Effective Date of 1977 Amendment

Amendment by Pub. L. 95-95 effective Aug. 7, 1977, except as otherwise expressly provided, see section 406(d) of Pub. L. 95-95, set out as a note under section 7401 of this title.

Section Referred to in Other Sections

This section is referred to in sections 7545, 7549, 7607 of this title.

MOTOR VEHICLE AND MOTOR VEHICLE ENGINE COMPLIANCE TESTING AND CERTIFICATION

42 USC 7525

(a) Testing and issuance of certificate of conformity
   (1) The Administrator shall test, or require to be tested in such manner as he deems appropriate, any new motor vehicle or new motor vehicle engine submitted by a manufacturer to determine whether such vehicle or engine conforms with the regulations prescribed under section 7521 of this title. If such vehicle or engine conforms to such regulations, the Administrator shall issue a certificate of conformity upon such terms, and for such period (not in excess of one year), as he may prescribe. In the case of any original equipment manufacturer (as defined by the Administrator in regulations promulgated before November 15, 1990) of vehicles or vehicle engines whose projected sales in the United States for any model year (as determined by the Administrator) will not exceed 300, the Administrator shall not require, for purposes of determining compliance with regulations under section 7521 of this title for the useful life of the vehicle or engine, operation of any vehicle or engine manufactured during such model year for more than 5,000 miles or 160 hours, respectively, unless the Administrator, by regulation, prescribes otherwise. The Administrator shall apply any adjustment factors that the Administrator deems appropriate to assure that each vehicle or engine will comply during its useful life (as determined under section 7521(d) of this title) with the regulations prescribed under section 7521 of this title.
   (2) The Administrator shall test any emission control system incorporated in a motor vehicle or motor vehicle engine submitted to him by any person, in order to determine whether such system enables such vehicle or engine to conform to the standards required to be prescribed under section 7521(b) of this title. If the Administrator finds on the basis of such tests that such vehicle or engine conforms to such standards, the Administrator shall issue a verification of compliance with emission standards for such system when incorporated in vehicles of a class of which the tested vehicle is representative. He shall inform manufacturers and the National Academy of Sciences, and make available to the public, the results of such tests. Tests under this paragraph shall be conducted under such terms and conditions (including requirements for preliminary testing by qualified independent laboratories) as the Administrator may prescribe by regulations.
   (3) (A) A certificate of conformity may be issued under this section only if the Administrator determines that the manufacturer (or in the case of a vehicle or engine for import, any person) has established to the satisfaction of the Administrator that any emission control device, system, or element of design installed on, or incorporated in, such vehicle or engine conforms to applicable requirements of section 7521(a)(4) of this title.
   (B) The Administrator may conduct such tests and may require the manufacturer (or any such person) to conduct such tests and provide such information as is necessary to

carry out subparagraph (A) of this paragraph. Such requirements shall include a requirement for prompt reporting of the emission of any unregulated pollutant from a system, device, or element of design if such pollutant was not emitted, or was emitted in significantly lesser amounts, from the vehicle or engine without use of the system, device, or element of design.

(4) (A) Not later than 12 months after November 15, 1990, the Administrator shall revise the regulations promulgated under this subsection to add test procedures capable of determining whether model year 1994 and later model year light-duty vehicles and light-duty trucks, when properly maintained and used, will pass the inspection methods and procedures established under section 7541(b) of this title for that model year, under conditions reasonably likely to be encountered in the conduct of inspection and maintenance programs, but which those programs cannot reasonably influence or control. The conditions shall include fuel characteristics, ambient temperature, and short (30 minutes or less) waiting periods before tests are conducted. The Administrator shall not grant a certificate of conformity under this subsection for any 1994 or later model year vehicle or engine that the Administrator concludes cannot pass the test procedures established under this paragraph.

(B) From time to time, the Administrator may revise the regulations promulgated under subparagraph (A), as the Administrator deems appropriate.

(b) Testing procedures; hearing; judicial review; additional evidence

(1) In order to determine whether new motor vehicles or new motor vehicle engines being manufactured by a manufacturer do in fact conform with the regulations with respect to which the certificate of conformity was issued, the Administrator is authorized to test such vehicles or engines. Such tests may be conducted by the Administrator directly or, in accordance with conditions specified by the Administrator, by the manufacturer.

(2) (A) (i) If, based on tests conducted under paragraph (1) on a sample of new vehicles or engines covered by a certificate of conformity, the Administrator determines that all or part of the vehicles or engines so covered do not conform with the regulations with respect to which the certificate of conformity was issued and with the requirements of section 7521(a)(4) of this title, he may suspend or revoke such certificate in whole or in part, and shall so notify the manufacturer. Such suspension or revocation shall apply in the case of any new motor vehicles or new motor vehicle engines manufactured after the date of such notification (or manufactured before such date if still in the hands of the manufacturer), and shall apply until such time as the Administrator finds that vehicles and engines manufactured by the manufacturer do conform to such regulations and requirements. If, during any period of suspension or revocation, the Administrator finds that a vehicle or engine actually conforms to such regulations and requirements, he shall issue a certificate of conformity applicable to such vehicle or engine.

(ii) If, based on tests conducted under paragraph (1) on any new vehicle or engine, the Administrator determines that such vehicle or engine does not conform with such regulations and requirements, he may suspend or revoke such certificate insofar as it applies to such vehicle or engine until such time as he finds such vehicle or engine actually so conforms with such regulations and requirements, and he shall so notify the manufacturer.

(B) (i) At the request of any manufacturer the Administrator shall grant such manufacturer a hearing as to whether the tests have been properly conducted or any sampling methods have been properly applied, and make a determination on the record with respect to any suspension or revocation under subparagraph (A); but suspension or revocation under subparagraph (A) shall not be stayed by reason of such hearing.

(ii) In any case of actual controversy as to the validity of any determination under clause (i), the manufacturer may at any time prior to the 60th day after such determination is made file a petition with the United States court of appeals for the circuit wherein such manufacturer resides or has his principal place of business for a judicial review of such determination. A copy of the petition shall be forthwith transmitted by the clerk of the court to the Administrator or other officer designated by him for that purpose. The Administrator thereupon shall file in the

court the record of the proceedings on which the Administrator based his determination, as provided in section 2112 of title 28.
(iii) If the petitioner applies to the court for leave to adduce additional evidence, and shows to the satisfaction of the court that such additional evidence is material and that there were reasonable grounds for the failure to adduce such evidence in the proceeding before the Administrator, the court may order such additional evidence (and evidence in rebuttal thereof) to be taken before the Administrator, in such manner and upon such terms and conditions as the court may deem proper. The Administrator may modify his findings as to the facts, or make new findings, by reason of the additional evidence so taken and he shall file such modified or new findings, and his recommendation, if any, for the modification or setting aside of his original determination, with the return of such additional evidence.
(iv) Upon the filing of the petition referred to in clause (ii), the court shall have jurisdiction to review the order in accordance with chapter 7 of title 5 and to grant appropriate relief as provided in such chapter.

(c) Inspection
For purposes of enforcement of this section, officers or employees duly designated by the Administrator, upon presenting appropriate credentials to the manufacturer or person in charge, are authorized (1) to enter, at reasonable times, any plant or other establishment of such manufacturer, for the purpose of conducting tests of vehicles or engines in the hands of the manufacturer, or (2) to inspect, at reasonable times, records, files, papers, processes, controls, and facilities used by such manufacturer in conducting tests under regulations of the Administrator. Each such inspection shall be commenced and completed with reasonable promptness.

(d) Rules and regulations
The Administrator shall by regulation establish methods and procedures for making tests under this section.

(e) Publication of test results
The Administrator shall make available to the public the results of his tests of any motor vehicle or motor vehicle engine submitted by a manufacturer under subsection (a) of this section as promptly as possible after December 31, 1970, and at the beginning of each model year which begins thereafter. Such results shall be described in such nontechnical manner as will reasonably disclose to prospective ultimate purchasers of new motor vehicles and new motor vehicle engines the comparative performance of the vehicles and engines tested in meeting the standards prescribed under section 7521 of this title.

(f) High altitude regulations
All light duty[1] vehicles and engines manufactured during or after model year 1984 and all light-duty trucks manufactured during or after model year 1995 shall comply with the requirements of section 7521 of this title regardless of the altitude at which they are sold.

(g) Nonconformance penalty
(1) In the case of any class or category of heavy-duty vehicles or engines to which a standard promulgated under section 7521(a) of this title applies, except as provided in paragraph (2), a certificate of conformity shall be issued under subsection (a) of this section and shall not be suspended or revoked under subsection (b) of this section for such vehicles or engines manufactured by a manufacturer notwithstanding the failure of such vehicles or engines to meet such standard if such manufacturer pays a nonconformance penalty as provided under regulations promulgated by the Administrator after notice and opportunity for public hearing. In the case of motorcycles to which such a standard applies, such a certificate may be issued notwithstanding such failure if the manufacturer pays such a penalty.
(2) No certificate of conformity may be issued under paragraph (1) with respect to any class or category of vehicle or engine if the degree by which the manufacturer fails to meet any standard promulgated under section 7521(a) of this title with respect to such class or category exceeds the percentage determined under regulations promulgated by the Administrator to be practicable. Such regulations shall require such testing of vehicles or engines being produced as may be necessary to determine the percentage of the classes or catego-

---

[1] So in original. Probably should be "light-duty".

ries of vehicles or engines which are not in compliance with the regulations with respect to which a certificate of conformity was issued and shall be promulgated not later than one year after August 7, 1977.
(3) The regulations promulgated under paragraph (1) shall, not later than one year after August 7, 1977, provide for nonconformance penalties in amounts determined under a formula established by the Administrator. Such penalties under such formula—
   (A) may vary from pollutant-to-pollutant;
   (B) may vary by class or category or vehicle or engine;
   (C) shall take into account the extent to which actual emissions of any air pollutant exceed allowable emissions under the standards promulgated under section 7521 of this title;
   (D) shall be increased periodically in order to create incentives for the development of production vehicles or engines which achieve the required degree of emission reduction; and
   (E) shall remove any competitive disadvantage to manufacturers whose engines or vehicles achieve the required degree of emission reduction (including any such disadvantage arising from the application of paragraph (4)).
(4) In any case in which a certificate of conformity has been issued under this subsection, any warranty required under section 7541(b)(2) of this title and any action under section 7541(c) of this title shall be required to be effective only for the emission levels which the Administrator determines that such certificate was issued and not for the emission levels required under the applicable standard.
(5) The authorities of section 7542(a) of this title shall apply, subject to the conditions of section 7542(b)[2] of this title, for purposes of this subsection.
(h) Review and revision of regulations
Within 18 months after November 15, 1990, the Administrator shall review and revise as necessary the regulations under subsection[3] (a) and (b) of this section regarding the testing of motor vehicles and motor vehicle engines to insure that vehicles are tested under circumstances which reflect the actual current driving conditions under which motor vehicles are used, including conditions relating to fuel, temperature, acceleration, and altitude.

(July 14, 1955, ch. 360, title II, Sec. 206, as added Pub. L. 91-604, Sec. 8(a), Dec. 31, 1970, 84 Stat. 1694; amended Pub. L. 95-95, title II, Secs. 213(a), 214(b), (c), 220, 224(e), Aug. 7, 1977, 91 Stat. 758-760, 762, 768; Pub. L. 95-190, Sec. 14(a)(69), Nov. 16, 1977, 91 Stat. 1403; Pub. L. 101-549, title II, Secs. 208, 230(7), (8), Nov. 15, 1990, 104 Stat. 2483, 2529.)

References in Text

Section 7542 of this title, referred to in subsec. (g)(5), was amended generally by Pub. L. 101-549, title II, Sec. 211, Nov. 15, 1990, 104 Stat. 2487, and provisions formerly contained in section 7542(b) of this title are contained in section 7542(c).

Codification

Section was formerly classified to section 1857f-5 of this title.

Prior Provisions

A prior section 206 of act July 14, 1955, related to testing of motor vehicles and motor vehicle engines and was classified to section 1857f-5 of this title, prior to repeal by Pub. L. 91-604.

Amendments

1990—Subsec. (a)(1). Pub. L. 101-549, Sec. 208(b), inserted new third sentence and struck out former third sentence which read as follows: "In the case of any manufacturer of vehicles or vehicle engines whose projected sales in the United States for any model year (as determined by the Administrator) will not exceed three hundred, the regulations prescribed by the Administrator concerning testing by the manufacturer for purposes of determining compliance with regulations under section 7521 of this title for the useful life of the vehicle or engine shall not require operation of any vehicle or engine manufactured during such model year for more than five thousand miles or one hundred and sixty hours, respectively, but the Administrator shall apply such adjustment factors as he deems appropriate to assure that each such vehicle

---

[2] See References in Text note below.
[3] So in original. Probably should be "subsections".

or engine will comply during its useful life (as determined under section 7521(d) of this title) with the regulations prescribed under section 7521 of this title."

Subsec. (a)(4). Pub. L. 101-549, Sec. 208(a), added par. (4).

Subsec. (e). Pub. L. 101-549, Sec. 230(7), struck out "announce in the Federal Register and" after "The Administrator shall".

Subsec. (f). Pub. L. 101-549, Sec. 230(8), struck out par. (1) designation before "All light duty vehicles", inserted reference to all light-duty trucks manufactured during or after model year 1995, and struck out par. (2) which required the Administrator to report to Congress by Oct. 1, 1978, on the economic impact and technological feasibility of the requirements of former par. (1).

Subsec. (h). Pub. L. 101-549, Sec. 208(c), added subsec. (h).

1977–Subsec. (a)(1). Pub. L. 95-95, Sec. 220, inserted provisions covering testing by small manufacturers.

Subsec. (a)(3). Pub. L. 95-95, Sec. 214(b), added par. (3).

Subsec. (b)(2)(A)(i). Pub. L. 95-95, Sec. 214(c)(1), (2), substituted "certificate of conformity was issued and with the requirements of section 7521(a)(4) of this title, he may suspend" for "certificate of conformity was issued, he may suspend" and "such regulations and requirements" for "such regulations".

Subsec. (b)(2)(A)(ii). Pub. L. 95-95, Sec. 214(c)(2), substituted "such regulations and requirements" for "such regulations".

Subsec. (f). Pub. L. 95-95, Sec. 213(a), added subsec. (f).

Subsec. (g). Pub. L. 95-95, Sec. 224(e), added subsec. (g).

Subsec. (g)(3)(D). Pub. L. 95-190 inserted "shall" before "be".

Effective Date of 1977 Amendment

Amendment by Pub. L. 95-95 effective Aug. 7, 1977, except as otherwise expressly provided, see section 406(d) of Pub. L. 95-95, set out as a note under section 7401 of this title.

Effective Date

Section 8(b) of Pub. L. 91-604 provided that: "The amendments made by this section [enacting this section and section 7541 of this title] shall not apply to vehicles or engines imported into the United States before the sixtieth day after the date of enactment of this Act [Dec. 31, 1970]."

Modification or Rescission of Rules, Regulations, Orders, Determinations, Contracts, Certifications, Authorizations, Delegations, and Other Actions

All rules, regulations, orders, determinations, contracts, certifications, authorizations, delegations, or other actions duly issued, made, or taken by or pursuant to act July 14, 1955, the Clean Air Act, as in effect immediately prior to the date of enactment of Pub. L. 95-95 [Aug. 7, 1977] to continue in full force and effect until modified or rescinded in accordance with act July 14, 1955, as amended by Pub. L. 95-95 [this chapter], see section 406(b) of Pub. L. 95-95, set out as an Effective Date of 1977 Amendment note under section 7401 of this title.

Section Referred to in Other Sections

This section is referred to in sections 7414, 7521, 7522, 7541, 7545, 7547, 7550, 7552, 7554, 7583, 7587, 7607 of this title; title 15 section 2702; title 26 section 4064; title 49 section 32904.

COMPLIANCE BY VEHICLES AND ENGINES IN ACTUAL USE

42 USC 7541

(a) Warranty; certification; payment of replacement costs of parts, devices, or components designed for emission control
  (1) Effective with respect to vehicles and engines manufactured in model years beginning more than 60 days after December 31, 1970, the manufacturer of each new motor vehicle and new motor vehicle engine shall warrant to the ultimate purchaser and each subsequent purchaser that such vehicle or engine is (A) designed, built, and equipped so as to conform at the time of sale with applicable regulations under section 7521 of this title, and (B) free from defects in materials and workmanship which cause such vehicle or engine to

fail to conform with applicable regulations for its useful life (as determined under section 7521(d) of this title). In the case of vehicles and engines manufactured in the model year 1995 and thereafter such warranty shall require that the vehicle or engine is free from any such defects for the warranty period provided under subsection (i) of this section.
(2) In the case of a motor vehicle part or motor vehicle engine part, the manufacturer or rebuilder of such part may certify that use of such part will not result in a failure of the vehicle or engine to comply with emission standards promulgated under section 7521 of this title. Such certification shall be made only under such regulations as may be promulgated by the Administrator to carry out the purposes of subsection (b) of this section. The Administrator shall promulgate such regulations no later than two years following August 7, 1977.
(3) The cost of any part, device, or component of any light-duty vehicle that is designed for emission control and which in the instructions issued pursuant to subsection (c)(3) of this section is scheduled for replacement during the useful life of the vehicle in order to maintain compliance with regulations under section 7521 of this title, the failure of which shall not interfere with the normal performance of the vehicle, and the expected retail price of which, including installation costs, is greater than 2 percent of the suggested retail price of such vehicle, shall be borne or reimbursed at the time of replacement by the vehicle manufacturer and such replacement shall be provided without cost to the ultimate purchaser, subsequent purchaser, or dealer. The term "designed for emission control" as used in the preceding sentence means a catalytic converter, thermal reactor, or other component installed on or in a vehicle for the sole or primary purpose of reducing vehicle emissions (not including those vehicle components which were in general use prior to model year 1968 and the primary function of which is not related to emission control).
(b) Testing methods and procedures
If the Administrator determines that (i) there are available testing methods and procedures to ascertain whether, when in actual use throughout its[1] the warranty period (as determined under subsection (i) of this section), each vehicle and engine to which regulations under section 7521 of this title apply complies with the emission standards of such regulations, (ii) such methods and procedures are in accordance with good engineering practices, and (iii) such methods and procedures are reasonably capable of being correlated with tests conducted under section 7525(a)(1) of this title, then—
(1) he shall establish such methods and procedures by regulation, and
(2) at such time as he determines that inspection facilities or equipment are available for purposes of carrying out testing methods and procedures established under paragraph (1), he shall prescribe regulations which shall require manufacturers to warrant the emission control device or system of each new motor vehicle or new motor vehicle engine to which a regulation under section 7521 of this title applies and which is manufactured in a model year beginning after the Administrator first prescribes warranty regulations under this paragraph (2). The warranty under such regulations shall run to the ultimate purchaser and each subsequent purchaser and shall provide that if—
  (A) the vehicle or engine is maintained and operated in accordance with instructions under subsection (c)(3) of this section,
  (B) it fails to conform at any time during its[1] the warranty period (as determined under subsection (i) of this section) to the regulations prescribed under section 7521 of this title, and
  (C) such nonconformity results in the ultimate purchaser (or any subsequent purchaser) of such vehicle or engine having to bear any penalty or other sanction (including the denial of the right to use such vehicle or engine) under State or Federal law,
then such manufacturer shall remedy such nonconformity under such warranty with the cost thereof to be borne by the manufacturer. No such warranty shall be invalid on the basis of any part used in the maintenance or repair of a vehicle or engine if such part was certified as provided under subsection (a)(2) of this section.
(c) Nonconforming vehicles; plan for remedying nonconformity; instructions for maintenance and use; label or tag
Effective with respect to vehicles and engines manufactured during model years beginning more than 60 days after December 31, 1970—

---

[1] So in original. The word "its" probably should not appear.

(1) If the Administrator determines that a substantial number of any class or category of vehicles or engines, although properly maintained and used, do not conform to the regulations prescribed under section 7521 of this title, when in actual use throughout their useful life (as determined under section 7521(d) of this title), he shall immediately notify the manufacturer thereof of such nonconformity, and he shall require the manufacturer to submit a plan for remedying the nonconformity of the vehicles or engines with respect to which such notification is given. The plan shall provide that the nonconformity of any such vehicles or engines which are properly used and maintained will be remedied at the expense of the manufacturer. If the manufacturer disagrees with such determination of nonconformity and so advises the Administrator, the Administrator shall afford the manufacturer and other interested persons an opportunity to present their views and evidence in support thereof at a public hearing. Unless, as a result of such hearing the Administrator withdraws such determination of nonconformity, he shall, within 60 days after the completion of such hearing, order the manufacturer to provide prompt notification of such nonconformity in accordance with paragraph (2).

(2) Any notification required by paragraph (1) with respect to any class or category of vehicles or engines shall be given to dealers, ultimate purchasers, and subsequent purchasers (if known) in such manner and containing such information as the Administrator may by regulations require.

(3) (A) The manufacturer shall furnish with each new motor vehicle or motor vehicle engine written instructions for the proper maintenance and use of the vehicle or engine by the ultimate purchaser and such instructions shall correspond to regulations which the Administrator shall promulgate. The manufacturer shall provide in boldface type on the first page of the written maintenance instructions notice that maintenance, replacement, or repair of the emission control devices and systems may be performed by any automotive repair establishment or individual using any automotive part which has been certified as provided in subsection (a)(2) of this section.

(B) The instruction under subparagraph (A) of this paragraph shall not include any condition on the ultimate purchaser's using, in connection with such vehicle or engine, any component or service (other than a component or service provided without charge under the terms of the purchase agreement) which is identified by brand, trade, or corporate name; or directly or indirectly distinguishing between service performed by the franchised dealers of such manufacturer or any other service establishments with which such manufacturer has a commercial relationship, and service performed by independent automotive repair facilities with which such manufacturer has no commercial relationship; except that the prohibition of this subsection may be waived by the Administrator if—
(i) the manufacturer satisfies the Administrator that the vehicle or engine will function properly only if the component or service so identified is used in connection with such vehicle or engine, and
(ii) the Administrator finds that such a waiver is in the public interest.

(C) In addition, the manufacturer shall indicate by means of a label or tag permanently affixed to such vehicle or engine that such vehicle or engine is covered by a certificate of conformity issued for the purpose of assuring achievement of emissions standards prescribed under section 7521 of this title. Such label or tag shall contain such other information relating to control of motor vehicle emissions as the Administrator shall prescribe by regulation.

(4) Intermediate in-use standards.—
(A) Model years 1994 and 1995.—For light-duty trucks of up to 6,000 lbs. gross vehicle weight rating (GVWR) and light-duty vehicles which are subject to standards under table G of section 7521(g)(1) of this title in model years 1994 and 1995 (40 percent of the manufacturer's sales volume in model year 1994 and 80 percent in model year 1995), the standards applicable to NMHC, CO, and NO_x for purposes of this subsection shall be those set forth in table A below in lieu of the standards for such air pollutants otherwise applicable under this subchapter.

TABLE A—INTERMEDIATE IN-USE STANDARDS
LDTS UP TO 6,000 LBS. GVWR AND LIGHT-DUTY VEHICLES

Vehicle type	NMHC	CO	NO$_x$
Light-duty vehicles..................	0.32	3.4	0.4*
LDT's (0-3,750 LVW)..............	0.32	5.2	0.4*
LDT's (3,751-5,750 LVW)........	0.41	6.7	0.7*

*Not applicable to diesel-fueled vehicles.

(B) Model years 1996 and thereafter.—(i) In the model years 1996 and 1997, light-duty trucks (LDTs) up to 6,000 lbs. gross vehicle weight rating (GVWR) and light-duty vehicles which are not subject to final in-use standards under paragraph (5) (60 percent of the manufacturer's sales volume in model year 1996 and 20 percent in model year 1997) shall be subject to the standards set forth in table A of subparagraph (A) for NMHC, CO, and NO$_x$ for purposes of this subsection in lieu of those set forth in paragraph (5).

(ii) For LDTs of more than 6,000 lbs. GVWR—
    (I)   in model year 1996 which are subject to the standards set forth in Table H of section 7521(h) of this title (50%);
    (II)   in model year 1997 (100%); and
    (III)   in model year 1998 which are not subject to final in-use standards under paragraph (5) (50%);
the standards for NMHC, CO, and NO$_x$ for purposes of this subsection shall be those set forth in Table B below in lieu of the standards for such air pollutants otherwise applicable under this subchapter.

TABLE B—INTERMEDIATE IN-USE STANDARDS
LDTS MORE THAN 6,000 LBS. GVWR

Vehicle type	NMHC	CO	NO$_x$
LDTs (3,751-5,750 lbs. TW).......	0.40	5.5	0.88*
LDTs (over 5,750 lbs. TW)........	0.49	6.2	1.38*

*Not applicable to diesel-fueled vehicles.

(C) Useful life.—In the case of the in-use standards applicable under this paragraph, for purposes of applying this subsection, the applicable useful life shall be 5 years or 50,000 miles or the equivalent (whichever first occurs).

(5) Final in-use standards.—
(A) After the model year 1995, for purposes of applying this subsection, in the case of the percentage specified in the implementation schedule below of each manufacturer's sales volume of light-duty trucks of up to 6,000 lbs. gross vehicle weight rating (GVWR) and light duty[2] vehicles, the standards for NMHC, CO, and NO$_x$ shall be as provided in Table G in section 7521(g) of this title, except that in applying the standards set forth in Table G for purposes of determining compliance with this subsection, the applicable useful life shall be (i) 5 years or 50,000 miles (or the equivalent) whichever first occurs in the case of standards applicable for purposes of certification at 50,000 miles; and (ii) 10 years or 100,000 miles (or the equivalent), whichever first occurs in the case of standards applicable for purposes of certification at 100,000 miles, except that no testing shall be done beyond 7 years or 75,000 miles, or the equivalent whichever first occurs.

LDTS UP TO 6,000 LBS. GVWR AND LIGHT-DUTY VEHICLE SCHEDULE
FOR IMPLEMENTATION OF FINAL IN-USE STANDARDS

Model year	Percent
1996............................	40
1997............................	80
1998............................	100

---

[2]So in original. Probably should be "light-duty".

(B) After the model year 1997, for purposes of applying this subsection, in the case of the percentage specified in the implementation schedule below of each manufacturer's sales volume of light-duty trucks of more than 6,000 lbs. gross vehicle weight rating (GVWR), the standards for NMHC, CO, and NO_x shall be as provided in Table H in section 7521(h) of this title, except that in applying the standards set forth in Table H for purposes of determining compliance with this subsection, the applicable useful life shall be (i) 5 years or 50,000 miles (or the equivalent) whichever first occurs in the case of standards applicable for purposes of certification at 50,000 miles; and (ii) 11 years or 120,000 miles (or the equivalent), whichever first occurs in the case of standards applicable for purposes of certification at 120,000 miles, except that no testing shall be done beyond 7 years or 90,000 miles (or the equivalent) whichever first occurs.

LDTS OF MORE THAN 6,000 LBS. GVWR IMPLEMENTATION SCHEDULE FOR IMPLEMENTATION OF FINAL IN-USE STANDARDS

Model year	Percent
1998	50
1999	100

(6) Diesel vehicles; in-use useful life and testing.—(A) In the case of diesel-fueled light-duty trucks up to 6,000 lbs. GVWR and light-duty vehicles, the useful life for purposes of determining in-use compliance with the standards under section 7521(g) of this title for NO_x shall be a period of 10 years or 100,000 miles (or the equivalent), whichever first occurs, in the case of standards applicable for purposes of certification at 100,000 miles, except that testing shall not be done for a period beyond 7 years or 75,000 miles (or the equivalent) whichever first occurs.

(B) In the case of diesel-fueled light-duty trucks of 6,000 lbs. GVWR or more, the useful life for purposes of determining in-use compliance with the standards under section 7521(h) of this title for NO_x shall be a period of 11 years or 120,000 miles (or the equivalent), whichever first occurs, in the case of standards applicable for purposes of certification at 120,000 miles, except that testing shall not be done for a period beyond 7 years or 90,000 miles (or the equivalent) whichever first occurs.

(d) Dealer costs borne by manufacturer

Any cost obligation of any dealer incurred as a result of any requirement imposed by subsection (a), (b), or (c) of this section shall be borne by the manufacturer. The transfer of any such cost obligation from a manufacturer to any dealer through franchise or other agreement is prohibited.

(e) Cost statement

If a manufacturer includes in any advertisement a statement respecting the cost or value of emission control devices or systems, such manufacturer shall set forth in such statement the cost or value attributed to such devices or systems by the Secretary of Labor (through the Bureau of Labor Statistics). The Secretary of Labor, and his representatives, shall have the same access for this purpose to the books, documents, papers, and records of a manufacturer as the Comptroller General has to those of a recipient of assistance for purposes of section 7611 of this title.

(f) Inspection after sale to ultimate purchaser

Any inspection of a motor vehicle or a motor vehicle engine for purposes of subsection (c)(1) of this section, after its sale to the ultimate purchaser, shall be made only if the owner of such vehicle or engine voluntarily permits such inspection to be made, except as may be provided by any State or local inspection program.

(g) Replacement and maintenance costs borne by owner

For the purposes of this section, the owner of any motor vehicle or motor vehicle engine warranted under this section is responsible in the proper maintenance of such vehicle or engine to replace and to maintain, at his expense at any service establishment or facility of his choosing, such items as spark plugs, points, condensers, and any other part, item, or device related to emission control (but not designed for emission control under the terms of the last sentence of subsection (a)(3) of this section)),[3] unless such part, item, or device is covered by any warranty not mandated by this chapter.

---

[3] So in original. The second closing parenthesis probably should not appear.

242 / Environmental Statutes

(h) Dealer certification
   (1) Upon the sale of each new light-duty motor vehicle by a dealer, the dealer shall furnish to the purchaser a certificate that such motor vehicle conforms to the applicable regulations under section 7521 of this title, including notice of the purchaser's rights under paragraph (2).
   (2) If at any time during the period for which the warranty applies under subsection (b) of this section, a motor vehicle fails to conform to the applicable regulations under section 7521 of this title as determined under subsection (b) of this section such nonconformity shall be remedied by the manufacturer at the cost of the manufacturer pursuant to such warranty as provided in subsection (b)(2) of this section (without regard to subparagraph (C) thereof).
   (3) Nothing in section 7543(a) of this title shall be construed to prohibit a State from testing, or requiring testing of, a motor vehicle after the date of sale of such vehicle to the ultimate purchaser (except that no new motor vehicle manufacturer or dealer may be required to conduct testing under this paragraph).
(i) Warranty period
   (1) In general
      For purposes of subsection (a)(1) of this section and subsection (b) of this section, the warranty period, effective with respect to new light-duty trucks and new light-duty vehicles and engines, manufactured in the model year 1995 and thereafter, shall be the first 2 years or 24,000 miles of use (whichever first occurs), except as provided in paragraph (2). For purposes of subsection (a)(1) of this section and subsection (b) of this section, for other vehicles and engines the warranty period shall be the period established by the Administrator by regulation (promulgated prior to November 15, 1990) for such purposes unless the Administrator subsequently modifies such regulation.
   (2) Specified major emission control components
      In the case of a specified major emission control component, the warranty period for new light-duty trucks and new light-duty vehicles and engines manufactured in the model year 1995 and thereafter for purposes of subsection (a)(1) of this section and subsection (b) of this section shall be 8 years or 80,000 miles of use (whichever first occurs). As used in this paragraph, the term "specified major emission control component" means only a catalytic converter, an electronic emissions control unit, and an onboard emissions diagnostic device, except that the Administrator may designate any other pollution control device or component as a specified major emission control component if—
      (A) the device or component was not in general use on vehicles and engines manufactured prior to the model year 1990; and
      (B) the Administrator determines that the retail cost (exclusive of installation costs) of such device or component exceeds $200 (in 1989 dollars), adjusted for inflation or deflation as calculated by the Administrator at the time of such determination.
      For purposes of this paragraph, the term "onboard emissions diagnostic device" means any device installed for the purpose of storing or processing emissions related diagnostic information, but not including any parts or other systems which it monitors except specified major emissions control components. Nothing in this chapter shall be construed to provide that any part (other than a part referred to in the preceding sentence) shall be required to be warranted under this chapter for the period of 8 years or 80,000 miles referred to in this paragraph.
   (3) Instructions
      Subparagraph (A) of subsection (b)(2) of this section shall apply only where the Administrator has made a determination that the instructions concerned conform to the requirements of subsection (c)(3) of this section.

(July 14, 1955, ch. 360, title II, Sec. 207, as added Pub. L. 91-604, Sec. 8(a), Dec. 31, 1970, 84 Stat. 1696; amended Pub. L. 95-95, title II, Secs. 205, 208-210, 212, Aug. 7, 1977, 91 Stat. 754-756, 758; Pub. L. 95-190, Sec. 14(a)(70)-(72), Nov. 16, 1977, 91 Stat. 1403; Pub. L. 101-549, title II, Secs. 209, 210, 230(9), Nov. 15, 1990, 104 Stat. 2484, 2485, 2529.)

Codification

Section was formerly classified to section 1857f-5a of this title.

Prior Provisions

A prior section 207 of act July 14, 1955, was renumbered section 208 by Pub. L. 91-604 and is classified to section 7542 of this title.

Amendments

1990—Subsec. (a)(1). Pub. L. 101-549, Sec. 209(4), inserted at end "In the case of vehicles and engines manufactured in the model year 1995 and thereafter such warranty shall require that the vehicle or engine is free from any such defects for the warranty period provided under subsection (i) of this section."

Subsec. (b). Pub. L. 101-549, Sec. 209(1), (2), substituted "the warranty period (as determined under subsection (i) of this section)" for "useful life (as determined under section 7521(d) of this title)" in introductory provisions and par. (2)(B), and struck out closing provisions which read as follows: "For purposes of the warranty under this subsection, for the period after twenty-four months or twenty-four thousand miles (whichever first occurs) the term 'emission control device or system' means a catalytic converter, thermal reactor, or other component installed on or in a vehicle for the sole or primary purpose of reducing vehicle emissions. Such term shall not include those vehicle components which were in general use prior to model year 1968."

Subsec. (c)(4) to (6). Pub. L. 101-549, Sec. 210, added pars. (4) to (6).

Subsec. (g). Pub. L. 101-549, Sec. 230(9), substituted "the last sentence of subsection (a)(3) of this section)" for "the last three sentences of subsection (a)(1) of this section".

Subsec. (i). Pub. L. 101-549, Sec. 209(3), added subsec. (i).

1977—Subsec. (a). Pub. L. 95-190, Sec. 14(a)(70), designated provisions contained in cl. (3) of subsec. (a), formerly set out as containing cls. (1), (2), and (3), to be par. (3) of subsec. (a) after the amendment by Pub. L. 95-95, Sec. 209(b), which designated provisions of former subsec. (a) as par. (1) and former cls. (1) and (2) as (A) and (B) of par. (1) and added a new par. (2).

Pub. L. 95-95, Sec. 205, added cl. (3).

Subsec. (b). Pub. L. 95-95, Sec. 209(a), (c), inserted provisions to par. (2) that no warranty be held invalid on the basis of any part used in the maintenance or repair of a vehicle or engine if the part was certified as provided in subsec. (a)(2) of this section, and, following par. (2), inserted provisions defining "emission control device or system".

Subsec. (c)(3). Pub. L. 95-95, Sec. 208, designated existing provisions as subpars. (A) and (C), added requirement for the bold face printing of a required notice on the first page of the written maintenance instructions in subpar. (A), and added subpar. (B).

Subsec. (f). Pub. L. 95-190, Sec. 14(a)(71), redesignated subsec. (f) as added by Pub. L. 95-95, Sec. 212, as (h).

Subsec. (g). Pub. L. 95-95, Sec. 210, added subsec. (g).

Subsec. (h). Pub. L. 95-190, Sec. 14(a)(71), redesignated subsec. (f) as added by Pub. L. 95-95, Sec. 212, as (h).

Subsec. (h)(2). Pub. L. 95-190, Sec. 14(a)(72), substituted "determined under" for "determined and".

Effective Date of 1990 Amendment

Section 209 of Pub. L. 101-549 provided that the amendments made by that section are effective with respect to new motor vehicles and engines manufactured in model year 1995 and thereafter.

Effective Date of 1977 Amendment

Amendment by Pub. L. 95-95 effective Aug. 7, 1977, except as otherwise expressly provided, see section 406(d) of Pub. L. 95-95, set out as a note under section 7401 of this title.

Effective Date

Section not applicable to vehicles or engines imported into United States before sixtieth day after Dec. 31, 1970, see section 8(b) of Pub. L. 91-604, set out as a note under section 7525 of this title.

Modification or Rescission of Rules, Regulations, Orders, Determinations, Contracts, Certifications, Authorizations, Delegations, and Other Actions

All rules, regulations, orders, determinations, contracts, certifications, authorizations, delegations, or other actions duly issued, made, or taken by or pursuant to act July 14, 1955, the Clean Air Act, as in effect immediately prior to the date of enactment of Pub. L. 95-95 [Aug. 7, 1977] to continue in full force and effect until modified or rescinded in accordance with act July 14, 1955, as amended by Pub. L. 95-95 [this chapter], see section 406(b) of Pub. L. 95-95, set out as an Effective Date of 1977 Amendment note under section 7401 of this title.

Section Referred to in Other Sections

This section is referred to in sections 7511a, 7521, 7522, 7525, 7543, 7547, 7550, 7552, 7587, 7607 of this title.

INFORMATION COLLECTION

42 USC 7542

(a) Manufacturer's responsibility
Every manufacturer of new motor vehicles or new motor vehicle engines, and every manufacturer of new motor vehicle or engine parts or components, and other persons subject to the requirements of this part or part C of this subchapter, shall establish and maintain records, perform tests where such testing is not otherwise reasonably available under this part and part C of this subchapter (including fees for testing), make reports and provide information the Administrator may reasonably require to determine whether the manufacturer or other person has acted or is acting in compliance with this part and part C of this subchapter and regulations thereunder, or to otherwise carry out the provision of this part and part C of this subchapter, and shall, upon request of an officer or employee duly designated by the Administrator, permit such officer or employee at reasonable times to have access to and copy such records.

(b) Enforcement authority
For the purposes of enforcement of this section, officers or employees duly designated by the Administrator upon presenting appropriate credentials are authorized—
   (1) to enter, at reasonable times, any establishment of the manufacturer, or of any person whom the manufacturer engages to perform any activity required by subsection (a) of this section, for the purposes of inspecting or observing any activity conducted pursuant to subsection (a) of this section, and
   (2) to inspect records, files, papers, processes, controls, and facilities used in performing any activity required by subsection (a) of this section, by such manufacturer or by any person whom the manufacturer engages to perform any such activity.

(c) Availability to public; trade secrets
Any records, reports, or information obtained under this part or part C of this subchapter shall be available to the public, except that upon a showing satisfactory to the Administrator by any person that records, reports, or information, or a particular portion thereof (other than emission data), to which the Administrator has access under this section, if made public, would divulge methods or processes entitled to protection as trade secrets of that person, the Administrator shall consider the record, report, or information or particular portion thereof confidential in accordance with the purposes of section 1905 of title 18. Any authorized representative of the Administrator shall be considered an employee of the United States for purposes of section 1905 of title 18. Nothing in this section shall prohibit the Administrator or authorized representative of the Administrator from disclosing records, reports or information to other officers, employees or authorized representatives of the United States concerned with carrying out this chapter or when relevant in any proceeding under this chapter. Nothing in this section shall authorize the withholding of information by the Administrator or any officer or employee under the Administrator's control from the duly authorized committees of the Congress.

(July 14, 1955, ch. 360, title II, Sec. 208, formerly Sec. 207, as added Pub. L. 89-272, title I, Sec. 101(8), Oct. 20, 1965, 79 Stat. 994; amended Pub. L. 90-148, Sec. 2, Nov. 21, 1967, 81 Stat. 501; renumbered and amended Pub. L. 91-604, Secs. 8(a), 10(a), 11(a)(2)(A), 15(c)(2), Dec. 31, 1970, 84 Stat. 1694, 1700, 1705, 1713; Pub. L. 101-549, title II, Sec. 211, Nov. 15, 1990, 104 Stat. 2487.)

Codification

Section was formerly classified to section 1857f-6 of this title.

Prior Provisions

A prior section 208 of act July 14, 1955, as added Nov. 21, 1967, Pub. L. 90-148, Sec. 2, 81 Stat. 501, was renumbered section 209 by Pub. L. 91-604 and is classified to section 7543 of this title.

Another prior section 208 of act July 14, 1955, as added Oct. 20, 1965, Pub. L. 89-272, title I, Sec. 101(8), 79 Stat. 994, was renumbered section 212 by Pub. L. 90-148, renumbered section 213 by Pub. L. 91-604, renumbered 214 by Pub. L. 93-319, and renumbered section 216 by Pub. L. 95-95, and is classified to section 7550 of this title.

Amendments

1990—Pub. L. 101-549 amended section generally, substituting present provisions for provisions which related to: in subsec. (a), manufacturer's responsibility; and in subsec. (b), availability to public except for trade secrets.

1970—Subsec. (a). Pub. L. 91-604, Secs. 11(a)(2)(A), 15(c)(2), substituted "Administrator" for "Secretary" wherever appearing and "part" for "subchapter".

Subsec. (b). Pub. L. 91-604, Secs. 10(a), 15(c)(2), substituted provisions authorizing the Administrator to make available to the public any records, reports, of information obtained under subsec. (a) of this section, except those shown to the Administrator to be entitled to protection as trade secrets, for provisions that all information reported or otherwise obtained by the Secretary or his representative pursuant to subsec. (a) of this section, which information contains or relates to a trade secret or other matter referred to in section 1905 of title 18, be considered confidential for the purpose of such section 1905, and substituted "Administrator" for "Secretary".

1967—Pub. L. 90-148 reenacted section without change.

Section Referred to in Other Sections

This section is referred to in sections 7414, 7521, 7522, 7525, 7547, 7550, 7607 of this title.

STATE STANDARDS

42 USC 7543

(a) Prohibition

No State or any political subdivision thereof shall adopt or attempt to enforce any standard relating to the control of emissions from new motor vehicles or new motor vehicle engines subject to this part. No State shall require certification, inspection, or any other approval relating to the control of emissions from any new motor vehicle or new motor vehicle engine as condition precedent to the initial retail sale, titling (if any), or registration of such motor vehicle, motor vehicle engine, or equipment.

(b) Waiver

(1) The Administrator shall, after notice and opportunity for public hearing, waive application of this section to any State which has adopted standards (other than crankcase emission standards) for the control of emissions from new motor vehicles or new motor vehicle engines prior to March 30, 1966, if the State determines that the State standards will be, in the aggregate, at least as protective of public health and welfare as applicable Federal standards. No such waiver shall be granted if the Administrator finds that—

(A) the determination of the State is arbitrary and capricious,

(B) such State does not need such State standards to meet compelling and extraordinary conditions, or

(C) such State standards and accompanying enforcement procedures are not consistent with section 7521(a) of this title.

(2) If each State standard is at least as stringent as the comparable applicable Federal standard, such State standard shall be deemed to be at least as protective of health and welfare as such Federal standards for purposes of paragraph (1).

(3) In the case of any new motor vehicle or new motor vehicle engine to which State standards apply pursuant to a waiver granted under paragraph (1), compliance with such State standards shall be treated as compliance with applicable Federal standards for purposes of this subchapter.

(c) Certification of vehicle parts or engine parts

Whenever a regulation with respect to any motor vehicle part or motor vehicle engine part is in effect under section 7541(a)(2) of this title, no State or political subdivision thereof shall adopt or attempt to enforce any standard or any requirement of certification, inspection, or approval which relates to motor vehicle emissions and is applicable to the same aspect of such part. The preceding sentence shall not apply in the case of a State with respect to which a waiver is in effect under subsection (b) of this section.

(d) Control, regulation, or restrictions on registered or licensed motor vehicles
Nothing in this part shall preclude or deny to any State or political subdivision thereof the right otherwise to control, regulate, or restrict the use, operation, or movement of registered or licensed motor vehicles.

(e) Nonroad engines or vehicles
  (1) Prohibition on certain State standards
  No State or any political subdivision thereof shall adopt or attempt to enforce any standard or other requirement relating to the control of emissions from either of the following new nonroad engines or nonroad vehicles subject to regulation under this chapter—
    (A) New engines which are used in construction equipment or vehicles or used in farm equipment or vehicles and which are smaller than 175 horsepower.
    (B) New locomotives or new engines used in locomotives.
  Subsection (b) of this section shall not apply for purposes of this paragraph.
  (2) Other nonroad engines or vehicles
    (A) In the case of any nonroad vehicles or engines other than those referred to in subparagraph (A) or (B) of paragraph (1), the Administrator shall, after notice and opportunity for public hearing, authorize California to adopt and enforce standards and other requirements relating to the control of emissions from such vehicles or engines if California determines that California standards will be, in the aggregate, at least as protective of public health and welfare as applicable Federal standards. No such authorization shall be granted if the Administrator finds that—
      (i) the determination of California is arbitrary and capricious,
      (ii) California does not need such California standards to meet compelling and extraordinary conditions, or
      (iii) California standards and accompanying enforcement procedures are not consistent with this section.
    (B) Any State other than California which has plan provisions approved under part D of subchapter I of this chapter may adopt and enforce, after notice to the Administrator, for any period, standards relating to control of emissions from nonroad vehicles or engines (other than those referred to in subparagraph (A) or (B) of paragraph (1)) and take such other actions as are referred to in subparagraph (A) of this paragraph respecting such vehicles or engines if—
      (i) such standards and implementation and enforcement are identical, for the period concerned, to the California standards authorized by the Administrator under subparagraph (A), and
      (ii) California and such State adopt such standards at least 2 years before commencement of the period for which the standards take effect.
    The Administrator shall issue regulations to implement this subsection.

(July 14, 1955, ch. 360, title II, Sec. 209, formerly Sec. 208, as added Pub. L. 90-148, Sec. 2, Nov. 21, 1967, 81 Stat. 501; renumbered and amended Pub. L. 91-604, Secs. 8(a), 11(a)(2)(A), 15(c)(2), Dec. 31, 1970, 84 Stat. 1694, 1705, 1713; Pub. L. 95-95, title II, Secs. 207, 221, Aug. 7, 1977, 91 Stat. 755, 762; Pub. L. 101-549, title II, Sec. 222(b), Nov. 15, 1990, 104 Stat. 2502.)

Codification

Section was formerly classified to section 1857f-6a of this title.

Prior Provisions

A prior section 209 of act July 14, 1955, as added Nov. 21, 1967, Pub. L. 90-148, Sec. 2, 81 Stat. 502, was renumbered section 210 by Pub. L. 91-604 and is classified to section 7544 of this title.

Another prior section 209 of act July 14, 1955, ch. 360, title II, as added Oct. 20, 1965, Pub. L. 89-272, title I, Sec. 101(8), 79 Stat. 995, related to appropriations for the fiscal years ending June 30, 1966, 1967, 1968, and 1969, and was classified to section 1857f-8 of this title, prior to repeal by Pub. L. 89-675, Sec. 2(b), Oct. 15, 1966, 80 Stat. 954.

Amendments

1990—Subsec. (e). Pub. L. 101-549 added subsec. (e).

1977—Subsec. (b). Pub. L. 95-95, Sec. 207, designated existing provisions as par. (1), substituted "March 30, 1966, if the State determines that the State standards will be, in the aggregate, at least as protective of public health and welfare as applicable Federal standards" for "March 30, 1966, unless he finds that such State does not require standards more stringent than applicable Federal standards to meet compelling the extraordinary conditions or that such State standards and accompanying enforcement procedures are not consistent with section 7521(a) of this title", added subpars. (A), (B), and (C), and added pars. (2) and (3).

Subsecs. (c), (d). Pub. L. 95-95, Sec. 221, added subsec. (c) and redesignated former subsec. (c) as (d).

1970—Subsec. (a). Pub. L. 91-604, Sec. 11(a)(2)(A), substituted "part" for "subchapter".

Subsec. (b). Pub. L. 91-604, Sec. 15(c)(2), substituted "Administrator" for "Secretary".

Subsec. (c). Pub. L. 91-604, Sec. 11(a)(2)(A), substituted "part" for "subchapter".

Effective Date of 1977 Amendment

Amendment by Pub. L. 95-95 effective Aug. 7, 1977, except as otherwise expressly provided, see section 406(d) of Pub. L. 95-95, set out as a note under section 7401 of this title.

Modification or Rescission of Rules, Regulations, Orders, Determinations, Contracts, Certifications, Authorizations, Delegations, and Other Actions

All rules, regulations, orders, determinations, contracts, certifications, authorizations, delegations, or other actions duly issued, made, or taken by or pursuant to act July 14, 1955, the Clean Air Act, as in effect immediately prior to the date of enactment of Pub. L. 95-95 [Aug. 7, 1977] to continue in full force and effect until modified or rescinded in accordance with act July 14, 1955, as amended by Pub. L. 95-95 [this chapter], see section 406(b) of Pub. L. 95-95, set out as an Effective Date of 1977 Amendment note under section 7401 of this title.

Section Referred to in Other Sections

This section is referred to in sections 7416, 7507, 7521, 7541, 7545, 7547, 7583, 7584 of this title.

STATE GRANTS

42 USC 7544

The Administrator is authorized to make grants to appropriate State agencies in an amount up to two-thirds of the cost of developing and maintaining effective vehicle emission devices and systems inspection and emission testing and control programs, except that—
  (1) no such grant shall be made for any part of any State vehicle inspection program which does not directly relate to the cost of the air pollution control aspects of such a program;
  (2) no such grant shall be made unless the Secretary of Transportation has certified to the Administrator that such program is consistent with any highway safety program developed pursuant to section 402 of title 23; and
  (3) no such grant shall be made unless the program includes provisions designed to insure that emission control devices and systems on vehicles in actual use have not been discontinued or rendered inoperative.

Grants may be made under this section by way of reimbursement in any case in which amounts have been expended by the State before the date on which any such grant was made.

(July 14, 1955, ch. 360, title II, Sec. 210, formerly Sec. 209, as added Pub. L. 90-148, Sec. 2, Nov. 21, 1967, 81 Stat. 502; renumbered and amended Pub. L. 91-604, Secs. 8(a), 10(b), Dec. 31, 1970, 84 Stat. 1694, 1700; Pub. L. 95-95, title II, Sec. 204, Aug. 7, 1977, 91 Stat. 754.)

Codification

Section was formerly classified to section 1857f-6b of this title.

Prior Provisions

A prior section 210 of act July 14, 1955, was renumbered section 211 by Pub. L. 91-604 and is classified to section 7545 of this title.

Amendments

1977—Pub. L. 95-95 inserted provision allowing grants to be made by way of reimbursement in any case in which amounts have been expended by States before the date on which the grants were made.

1970—Pub. L. 91-604, Sec. 10(b), substituted provisions authorizing the Administrator to make grants to appropriate State agencies for the development and maintenance of effective vehicle emission devices and systems inspection and emission testing and control programs, for provisions authorizing the Secretary to make grants to appropriate State air pollution control agencies for the development of meaningful uniform motor vehicle emission device inspection and emission testing programs.

Effective Date of 1977 Amendment

Amendment by Pub. L. 95-95 effective Aug. 7, 1977, except as otherwise expressly provided, see section 406(d) of Pub. L. 95-95, set out as a note under section 7401 of this title.

REGULATION OF FUELS

42 USC 7545

(a) Authority of Administrator to regulate
    The Administrator may by regulation designate any fuel or fuel additive (including any fuel or fuel additive used exclusively in nonroad engines or nonroad vehicles) and, after such date or dates as may be prescribed by him, no manufacturer or processor of any such fuel or additive may sell, offer for sale, or introduce into commerce such fuel or additive unless the Administrator has registered such fuel or additive in accordance with subsection (b) of this section.

(b) Registration requirement
    (1) For the purpose of registration of fuels and fuel additives, the Administrator shall require—
        (A) the manufacturer of any fuel to notify him as to the commercial identifying name and manufacturer of any additive contained in such fuel; the range of concentration of any additive in the fuel; and the purpose-in-use of any such additive; and
        (B) the manufacturer of any additive to notify him as to the chemical composition of such additive.
    (2) For the purpose of registration of fuels and fuel additives, the Administrator may also require the manufacturer of any fuel or fuel additive—
        (A) to conduct tests to determine potential public health effects of such fuel or additive (including, but not limited to, carcinogenic, teratogenic, or mutagenic effects), and
        (B) to furnish the description of any analytical technique that can be used to detect and measure any additive in such fuel, the recommended range of concentration of such additive, and the recommended purpose-in-use of such additive, and such other information as is reasonable and necessary to determine the emissions resulting from the use of the fuel or additive contained in such fuel, the effect of such fuel or additive on the emission control performance of any vehicle, vehicle engine, nonroad engine or nonroad vehicle, or the extent to which such emissions affect the public health or welfare.
    Tests under subparagraph (A) shall be conducted in conformity with test procedures and protocols established by the Administrator. The result of such tests shall not be considered confidential.
    (3) Upon compliance with the provision of this subsection, including assurances that the Administrator will receive changes in the information required, the Administrator shall register such fuel or fuel additive.

(c) Offending fuels and fuel additives; control; prohibition
    (1) The Administrator may, from time to time on the basis of information obtained under subsection (b) of this section or other information available to him, by regulation, control or prohibit the manufacture, introduction into commerce, offering for sale, or sale of any fuel or fuel additive for use in a motor vehicle, motor vehicle engine, or nonroad engine or nonroad vehicle (A) if in the judgment of the Administrator any emission product of such

fuel or fuel additive causes, or contributes, to air pollution which may reasonably be anticipated to endanger the public health or welfare, or (B) if emission products of such fuel or fuel additive will impair to a significant degree the performance of any emission control device or system which is in general use, or which the Administrator finds has been developed to a point where in a reasonable time it would be in general use were such regulation to be promulgated.

(2) (A) No fuel, class of fuels, or fuel additive may be controlled or prohibited by the Administrator pursuant to clause (A) of paragraph (1) except after consideration of all relevant medical and scientific evidence available to him, including consideration of other technologically or economically feasible means of achieving emission standards under section 7521 of this title.

(B) No fuel or fuel additive may be controlled or prohibited by the Administrator pursuant to clause (B) of paragraph (1) except after consideration of available scientific and economic data, including a cost benefit analysis comparing emission control devices or systems which are or will be in general use and require the proposed control or prohibition with emission control devices or systems which are or will be in general use and do not require the proposed control or prohibition. On request of a manufacturer of motor vehicles, motor vehicle engines, fuels, or fuel additives submitted within 10 days of notice of proposed rulemaking, the Administrator shall hold a public hearing and publish findings with respect to any matter he is required to consider under this subparagraph. Such findings shall be published at the time of promulgation of final regulations.

(C) No fuel or fuel additive may be prohibited by the Administrator under paragraph (1) unless he finds, and publishes such finding, that in his judgment such prohibition will not cause the use of any other fuel or fuel additive which will produce emissions which will endanger the public health or welfare to the same or greater degree than the use of the fuel or fuel additive proposed to be prohibited.

(3) (A) For the purpose of obtaining evidence and data to carry out paragraph (2), the Administrator may require the manufacturer of any motor vehicle or motor vehicle engine to furnish any information which has been developed concerning the emissions from motor vehicles resulting from the use of any fuel or fuel additive, or the effect of such use on the performance of any emission control device or system.

(B) In obtaining information under subparagraph (A), section 7607(a) of this title (relating to subpenas) shall be applicable.

(4) (A) Except as otherwise provided in subparagraph (B) or (C), no State (or political subdivision thereof) may prescribe or attempt to enforce, for purposes of motor vehicle emission control, any control or prohibition respecting any characteristic or component of a fuel or fuel additive in a motor vehicle or motor vehicle engine—
  (i) if the Administrator has found that no control or prohibition of the characteristic or component of a fuel or fuel additive under paragraph (1) is necessary and has published his finding in the Federal Register, or
  (ii) if the Administrator has prescribed under paragraph (1) a control or prohibition applicable to such characteristic or component of a fuel or fuel additive, unless State prohibition or control is identical to the prohibition or control prescribed by the Administrator.

(B) Any State for which application of section 7543(a) of this title has at any time been waived under section 7543(b) of this title may at any time prescribe and enforce, for the purpose of motor vehicle emission control, a control or prohibition respecting any fuel or fuel additive.

(C) A State may prescribe and enforce, for purposes of motor vehicle emission control, a control or prohibition respecting the use of a fuel or fuel additive in a motor vehicle or motor vehicle engine if an applicable implementation plan for such State under section 7410 of this title so provides. The Administrator may approve such provision in an implementation plan, or promulgate an implementation plan containing such a provision, only if he finds that the State control or prohibition is necessary to achieve the national primary or secondary ambient air quality standard which the plan implements. The Administrator may find that a State control or prohibition is necessary to achieve that standard if no other measures that would bring about timely attainment exist, or if other measures exist and are technically possible to implement, but are unreasonable or impracticable. The Administrator may make a finding of necessity under this subparagraph even if the plan for the area does not contain an approved demonstration of timely attainment.

(d) Penalties and injunctions
  (1) Civil penalties
    Any person who violates subsection (a), (f), (g), (k), (l), (m), or (n) of this section or the regulations prescribed under subsection (c), (h), (i), (k), (l), (m), or (n) of this section or who fails to furnish any information or conduct any tests required by the Administrator under subsection (b) of this section shall be liable to the United States for a civil penalty of not more than the sum of $25,000 for every day of such violation and the amount of economic benefit or savings resulting from the violation. Any violation with respect to a regulation prescribed under subsection (c), (k), (l), or (m) of this section which establishes a regulatory standard based upon a multiday averaging period shall constitute a separate day of violation for each and every day in the averaging period. Civil penalties shall be assessed in accordance with subsections (b) and (c) of section 7524 of this title.
  (2) Injunctive authority
    The district courts of the United States shall have jurisdiction to restrain violations of subsections (a), (f), (g), (k), (l), (m), and (n) of this section and of the regulations prescribed under subsections (c), (h), (i), (k), (l), (m), and (n) of this section, to award other appropriate relief, and to compel the furnishing of information and the conduct of tests required by the Administrator under subsection (b) of this section. Actions to restrain such violations and compel such actions shall be brought by and in the name of the United States. In any such action, subpoenas for witnesses who are required to attend a district court in any district may run into any other district.

(e) Testing of fuels and fuel additives
  (1) Not later than one year after August 7, 1977, and after notice and opportunity for a public hearing, the Administrator shall promulgate regulations which implement the authority under subsection (b)(2)(A) and (B) of this section with respect to each fuel or fuel additive which is registered on the date of promulgation of such regulations and with respect to each fuel or fuel additive for which an application for registration is filed thereafter.
  (2) Regulations under subsection (b) of this section to carry out this subsection shall require that the requisite information be provided to the Administrator by each such manufacturer—
    (A) prior to registration, in the case of any fuel or fuel additive which is not registered on the date of promulgation of such regulations; or
    (B) not later than three years after the date of promulgation of such regulations, in the case of any fuel or fuel additive which is registered on such date.
  (3) In promulgating such regulations, the Administrator may—
    (A) exempt any small business (as defined in such regulations) from or defer or modify the requirements of, such regulations with respect to any such small business;
    (B) provide for cost-sharing with respect to the testing of any fuel or fuel additive which is manufactured or processed by two or more persons or otherwise provide for shared responsibility to meet the requirements of this section without duplication; or
    (C) exempt any person from such regulations with respect to a particular fuel or fuel additive upon a finding that any additional testing of such fuel or fuel additive would be duplicative of adequate existing testing.

(f) New fuels and fuel additives
  (1) (A) Effective upon March 31, 1977, it shall be unlawful for any manufacturer of any fuel or fuel additive to first introduce into commerce, or to increase the concentration in use of, any fuel or fuel additive for general use in light duty motor vehicles manufactured after model year 1974 which is not substantially similar to any fuel or fuel additive utilized in the certification of any model year 1975, or subsequent model year, vehicle or engine under section 7525 of this title.
    (B) Effective upon November 15, 1990, it shall be unlawful for any manufacturer of any fuel or fuel additive to first introduce into commerce, or to increase the concentration in use of, any fuel or fuel additive for use by any person in motor vehicles manufac-

tured after model year 1974 which is not substantially similar to any fuel or fuel additive utilized in the certification of any model year 1975, or subsequent model year, vehicle or engine under section 7525 of this title.

(2) Effective November 30, 1977, it shall be unlawful for any manufacturer of any fuel to introduce into commerce any gasoline which contains a concentration of manganese in excess of .0625 grams per gallon of fuel, except as otherwise provided pursuant to a waiver under paragraph (4).

(3) Any manufacturer of any fuel or fuel additive which prior to March 31, 1977, and after January 1, 1974, first introduced into commerce or increased the concentration in use of a fuel or fuel additive that would otherwise have been prohibited under paragraph (1)(A) if introduced on or after March 31, 1977 shall, not later than September 15, 1978, cease to distribute such fuel or fuel additive in commerce. During the period beginning 180 days after August 7, 1977, and before September 15, 1978, the Administrator shall prohibit, or restrict the concentration of any fuel additive which he determines will cause or contribute to the failure of an emission control device or system (over the useful life of any vehicle in which such device or system is used) to achieve compliance by the vehicle with the emission standards with respect to which it has been certified under section 7525 of this title.

(4) The Administrator, upon application of any manufacturer of any fuel or fuel additive, may waive the prohibitions established under paragraph (1) or (3) of this subsection or the limitation specified in paragraph (2) of this subsection, if he determines that the applicant has established that such fuel or fuel additive or a specified concentration thereof, and the emission products of such fuel or additive or specified concentration thereof, will not cause or contribute to a failure of any emission control device or system (over the useful life of any vehicle in which such device or system is used) to achieve compliance by the vehicle with the emission standards with respect to which it has been certified pursuant to section 7525 of this title. If the Administrator has not acted to grant or deny an application under this paragraph within one hundred and eighty days of receipt of such application, the waiver authorized by this paragraph shall be treated as granted.

(5) No action of the Administrator under this section may be stayed by any court pending judicial review of such action.

(g) Misfueling

(1) No person shall introduce, or cause or allow the introduction of, leaded gasoline into any motor vehicle which is labeled "unleaded gasoline only," which is equipped with a gasoline tank filler inlet designed for the introduction of unleaded gasoline, which is a 1990 or later model year motor vehicle, or which such person knows or should know is a vehicle designed solely for the use of unleaded gasoline.

(2) Beginning October 1, 1993, no person shall introduce or cause or allow the introduction into any motor vehicle of diesel fuel which such person knows or should know contains a concentration of sulfur in excess of 0.05 percent (by weight) or which fails to meet a cetane index minimum of 40 or such equivalent alternative aromatic level as prescribed by the Administrator under subsection (i)(2) of this section.

(h) Reid Vapor Pressure requirements

(1) Prohibition

Not later than 6 months after November 15, 1990, the Administrator shall promulgate regulations making it unlawful for any person during the high ozone season (as defined by the Administrator) to sell, offer for sale, dispense, supply, offer for supply, transport, or introduce into commerce gasoline with a Reid Vapor Pressure in excess of 9.0 pounds per square inch (psi). Such regulations shall also establish more stringent Reid Vapor Pressure standards in a nonattainment area as the Administrator finds necessary to generally achieve comparable evaporative emissions (on a per-vehicle basis) in nonattainment areas, taking into consideration the enforceability of such standards, the need of an area for emission control, and economic factors.

(2) Attainment areas

The regulations under this subsection shall not make it unlawful for any person to sell, offer for supply, transport, or introduce into commerce gasoline with a Reid Vapor Pressure of 9.0 pounds per square inch (psi) or lower in any area designated under section 7407

of this title as an attainment area. Notwithstanding the preceding sentence, the Administrator may impose a Reid vapor pressure requirement lower than 9.0 pounds per square inch (psi) in any area, formerly an ozone nonattainment area, which has been redesignated as an attainment area.
   (3) Effective date; enforcement
   The regulations under this subsection shall provide that the requirements of this subsection shall take effect not later than the high ozone season for 1992, and shall include such provisions as the Administrator determines are necessary to implement and enforce the requirements of this subsection.
   (4) Ethanol waiver
   For fuel blends containing gasoline and 10 percent denatured anhydrous ethanol, the Reid vapor pressure limitation under this subsection shall be one pound per square inch (psi) greater than the applicable Reid vapor pressure limitations established under paragraph (1); Provided, however, That a distributor, blender, marketer, reseller, carrier, retailer, or wholesale purchaser-consumer shall be deemed to be in full compliance with the provisions of this subsection and the regulations promulgated thereunder if it can demonstrate (by showing receipt of a certification or other evidence acceptable to the Administrator) that—
      (A) the gasoline portion of the blend complies with the Reid vapor pressure limitations promulgated pursuant to this subsection;
      (B) the ethanol portion of the blend does not exceed its waiver condition under subsection (f)(4) of this section; and
      (C) no additional alcohol or other additive has been added to increase the Reid Vapor Pressure of the ethanol portion of the blend.
   (5) Areas covered
   The provisions of this subsection shall apply only to the 48 contiguous States and the District of Columbia.
(i) Sulfur content requirements for diesel fuel
   (1) Effective October 1, 1993, no person shall manufacture, sell, supply, offer for sale or supply, dispense, transport, or introduce into commerce motor vehicle diesel fuel which contains a concentration of sulfur in excess of 0.05 percent (by weight) or which fails to meet a cetane index minimum of 40.
   (2) Not later than 12 months after November 15, 1990, the Administrator shall promulgate regulations to implement and enforce the requirements of paragraph (1). The Administrator may require manufacturers and importers of diesel fuel not intended for use in motor vehicles to dye such fuel in a particular manner in order to segregate it from motor vehicle diesel fuel. The Administrator may establish an equivalent alternative aromatic level to the cetane index specification in paragraph (1).
   (3) The sulfur content of fuel required to be used in the certification of 1991 through 1993 model year heavy-duty diesel vehicles and engines shall be 0.10 percent (by weight). The sulfur content and cetane index minimum of fuel required to be used in the certification of 1994 and later model year heavy-duty diesel vehicles and engines shall comply with the regulations promulgated under paragraph (2).
   (4) The States of Alaska and Hawaii may be exempted from the requirements of this subsection in the same manner as provided in section 7625[1] of this title. The Administrator shall take final action on any petition filed under section 7625[1] of this title or this paragraph for an exemption from the requirements of this subsection, within 12 months from the date of the petition.
(j) Lead substitute gasoline additives
   (1) After November 15, 1990, any person proposing to register any gasoline additive under subsection (a) of this section or to use any previously registered additive as a lead substitute may also elect to register the additive as a lead substitute gasoline additive for reducing valve seat wear by providing the Administrator with such relevant information regarding product identity and composition as the Administrator deems necessary for carrying out the responsibilities of paragraph (2) of this subsection (in addition to other information which may be required under subsection (b) of this section).

---

[1]So in original. Probably should be section "7625-1".

(2) In addition to the other testing which may be required under subsection (b) of this section, in the case of the lead substitute gasoline additives referred to in paragraph (1), the Administrator shall develop and publish a test procedure to determine the additives' effectiveness in reducing valve seat wear and the additives' tendencies to produce engine deposits and other adverse side effects. The test procedures shall be developed in cooperation with the Secretary of Agriculture and with the input of additive manufacturers, engine and engine components manufacturers, and other interested persons. The Administrator shall enter into arrangements with an independent laboratory to conduct tests of each additive using the test procedures developed and published pursuant to this paragraph. The Administrator shall publish the results of the tests by company and additive name in the Federal Register along with, for comparison purposes, the results of applying the same test procedures to gasoline containing 0.1 gram of lead per gallon in lieu of the lead substitute gasoline additive. The Administrator shall not rank or otherwise rate the lead substitute additives. Test procedures shall be established within 1 year after November 15, 1990. Additives shall be tested within 18 months of November 15, 1990, or 6 months after the lead substitute additives are identified to the Administrator, whichever is later.

(3) The Administrator may impose a user fee to recover the costs of testing of any fuel additive referred to in this subsection. The fee shall be paid by the person proposing to register the fuel additive concerned. Such fee shall not exceed $20,000 for a single fuel additive.

(4) There are authorized to be appropriated to the Administrator not more than $1,000,000 for the second full fiscal year after November 15, 1990, to establish test procedures and conduct engine tests as provided in this subsection. Not more than $500,000 per year is authorized to be appropriated for each of the 5 subsequent fiscal years.

(5) Any fees collected under this subsection shall be deposited in a special fund in the United States Treasury for licensing and other services which thereafter shall be available for appropriation, to remain available until expended, to carry out the Agency's activities for which the fees were collected.

(k) Reformulated gasoline for conventional vehicles

(1) EPA regulations

Within 1 year after November 15, 1990, the Administrator shall promulgate regulations under this section establishing requirements for reformulated gasoline to be used in gasoline-fueled vehicles in specified nonattainment areas. Such regulations shall require the greatest reduction in emissions of ozone forming volatile organic compounds (during the high ozone season) and emissions of toxic air pollutants (during the entire year) achievable through the reformulation of conventional gasoline, taking into consideration the cost of achieving such emission reductions, any nonair-quality and other air-quality related health and environmental impacts and energy requirements.

(2) General requirements

The regulations referred to in paragraph (1) shall require that reformulated gasoline comply with paragraph (3) and with each of the following requirements (subject to paragraph (7)):

(A) NO_x emissions

The emissions of oxides of nitrogen (NO_x) from baseline vehicles when using the reformulated gasoline shall be no greater than the level of such emissions from such vehicles when using baseline gasoline. If the Administrator determines that compliance with the limitation on emissions of oxides of nitrogen under the preceding sentence is technically infeasible, considering the other requirements applicable under this subsection to such gasoline, the Administrator may, as appropriate to ensure compliance with this subparagraph, adjust (or waive entirely), any other requirements of this paragraph (including the oxygen content requirement contained in subparagraph (B)) or any requirements applicable under paragraph (3)(A).

(B) Oxygen content

The oxygen content of the gasoline shall equal or exceed 2.0 percent by weight (subject to a testing tolerance established by the Administrator) except as otherwise required by this chapter. The Administrator may waive, in whole or in part, the application of this subparagraph for any ozone nonattainment area upon a determination by the Administrator that compliance with such requirement would prevent or interfere with the attainment by the area of a national primary ambient air quality standard.

(C) Benzene content
   The benzene content of the gasoline shall not exceed 1.0 percent by volume.
(D) Heavy metals
   The gasoline shall have no heavy metals, including lead or manganese. The Administrator may waive the prohibition contained in this subparagraph for a heavy metal (other than lead) if the Administrator determines that addition of the heavy metal to the gasoline will not increase, on an aggregate mass or cancer-risk basis, toxic air pollutant emissions from motor vehicles.

(3) More stringent of formula or performance standards
   The regulations referred to in paragraph (1) shall require compliance with the more stringent of either the requirements set forth in subparagraph (A) or the requirements of subparagraph (B) of this paragraph. For purposes of determining the more stringent provision, clause (i) and clause (ii) of subparagraph (B) shall be considered independently.
   (A) Formula
      (i) Benzene
         The benzene content of the reformulated gasoline shall not exceed 1.0 percent by volume.
      (ii) Aromatics
         The aromatic hydrocarbon content of the reformulated gasoline shall not exceed 25 percent by volume.
      (iii) Lead
         The reformulated gasoline shall have no lead content.
      (iv) Detergents
         The reformulated gasoline shall contain additives to prevent the accumulation of deposits in engines or vehicle fuel supply systems.
      (v) Oxygen content
         The oxygen content of the reformulated gasoline shall equal or exceed 2.0 percent by weight (subject to a testing tolerance established by the Administrator) except as otherwise required by this chapter.
   (B) Performance standard
      (i) VOC emissions
         During the high ozone season (as defined by the Administrator), the aggregate emissions of ozone forming volatile organic compounds from baseline vehicles when using the reformulated gasoline shall be 15 percent below the aggregate emissions of ozone forming volatile organic compounds from such vehicles when using baseline gasoline. Effective in calendar year 2000 and thereafter, 25 percent shall be substituted for 15 percent in applying this clause, except that the Administrator may adjust such 25 percent requirement to provide for a lesser or greater reduction based on technological feasibility, considering the cost of achieving such reductions in VOC emissions. No such adjustment shall provide for less than a 20 percent reduction below the aggregate emissions of such air pollutants from such vehicles when using baseline gasoline. The reductions required under this clause shall be on a mass basis.
      (ii) Toxics
         During the entire year, the aggregate emissions of toxic air pollutants from baseline vehicles when using the reformulated gasoline shall be 15 percent below the aggregate emissions of toxic air pollutants from such vehicles when using baseline gasoline. Effective in calendar year 2000 and thereafter, 25 percent shall be substituted for 15 percent in applying this clause, except that the Administrator may adjust such 25 percent requirement to provide for a lesser or greater reduction based on technological feasibility, considering the cost of achieving such reductions in toxic air pollutants. No such adjustment shall provide for less than a 20 percent reduction below the aggregate emissions of such air pollutants from such vehicles when using baseline gasoline. The reductions required under this clause shall be on a mass basis.
   Any reduction greater than a specific percentage reduction required under this subparagraph shall be treated as satisfying such percentage reduction requirement.

(4) Certification procedures
   (A) Regulations
      The regulations under this subsection shall include procedures under which the Administrator shall certify reformulated gasoline as complying with the requirements established pursuant to this subsection. Under such regulations, the Administrator shall establish procedures for any person to petition the Administrator to certify a fuel formulation, or slate of fuel formulations. Such procedures shall further require that the Administrator shall approve or deny such petition within 180 days of receipt. If the Administrator fails to act within such 180-day period, the fuel shall be deemed certified until the Administrator completes action on the petition.
   (B) Certification; equivalency
      The Administrator shall certify a fuel formulation or slate of fuel formulations as complying with this subsection if such fuel or fuels—
      (i) comply with the requirements of paragraph (2), and
      (ii) achieve equivalent or greater reductions in emissions of ozone forming volatile organic compounds and emissions of toxic air pollutants than are achieved by a reformulated gasoline meeting the applicable requirements of paragraph (3).
   (C) EPA determination of emissions level
      Within 1 year after November 15, 1990, the Administrator shall determine the level of emissions of ozone forming volatile organic compounds and emissions of toxic air pollutants emitted by baseline vehicles when operating on baseline gasoline. For purposes of this subsection, within 1 year after November 15, 1990, the Administrator shall, by rule, determine appropriate measures of, and methodology for, ascertaining the emissions of air pollutants (including calculations, equipment, and testing tolerances).
(5) Prohibition
   Effective beginning January 1, 1995, each of the following shall be a violation of this subsection:
   (A) The sale or dispensing by any person of conventional gasoline to ultimate consumers in any covered area.
   (B) The sale or dispensing by any refiner, blender, importer, or marketer of conventional gasoline for resale in any covered area, without (i) segregating such gasoline from reformulated gasoline, and (ii) clearly marking such conventional gasoline as "conventional gasoline, not for sale to ultimate consumer in a covered area".
   Any refiner, blender, importer or marketer who purchases property segregated and marked conventional gasoline, and thereafter labels, represents, or wholesales such gasoline as reformulated gasoline shall also be in violation of this subsection. The Administrator may impose sampling, testing, and recordkeeping requirements upon any refiner, blender, importer, or marketer to prevent violations of this section.
(6) Opt-in areas
   (A) Upon the application of the Governor of a State, the Administrator shall apply the prohibition set forth in paragraph (5) in any area in the State classified under subpart 2 of part D of subchapter I of this chapter as a Marginal, Moderate, Serious, or Severe Area (without regard to whether or not the 1980 population of the area exceeds 250,000). In any such case, the Administrator shall establish an effective date for such prohibition as he deems appropriate, not later than January 1, 1995, or 1 year after such application is received, whichever is later. The Administrator shall publish such application in the Federal Register upon receipt.
   (B) If the Administrator determines, on the Administrator's own motion or on petition of any person, after consultation with the Secretary of Energy, that there is insufficient domestic capacity to produce gasoline certified under this subsection, the Administrator shall, by rule, extend the effective date of such prohibition in Marginal, Moderate, Serious, or Severe Areas referred to in subparagraph (A) for one additional year, and may, by rule, renew such extension for 2 additional one-year periods. The Administrator shall act on any petition submitted under this paragraph within 6 months after receipt of the petition. The Administrator shall issue such extensions for areas with a lower ozone classification before issuing any such extension for areas with a higher classification.

(7) Credits
  (A) The regulations promulgated under this subsection shall provide for the granting of an appropriate amount of credits to a person who refines, blends, or imports and certifies a gasoline or slate of gasoline that—
    (i) has an oxygen content (by weight) that exceeds the minimum oxygen content specified in paragraph (2);
    (ii) has an aromatic hydrocarbon content (by volume) that is less than the maximum aromatic hydrocarbon content required to comply with paragraph (3); or
    (iii) has a benzene content (by volume) that is less than the maximum benzene content specified in paragraph (2).
  (B) The regulations described in subparagraph (A) shall also provide that a person who is granted credits may use such credits, or transfer all or a portion of such credits to another person for use within the same nonattainment area, for the purpose of complying with this subsection.
  (C) The regulations promulgated under subparagraphs (A) and (B) shall ensure the enforcement of the requirements for the issuance, application, and transfer of the credits. Such regulations shall prohibit the granting or transfer of such credits for use with respect to any gasoline in a nonattainment area, to the extent the use of such credits would result in any of the following:
    (i) An average gasoline aromatic hydrocarbon content (by volume) for the nonattainment (taking into account all gasoline sold for use in conventional gasoline-fueled vehicles in the nonattainment area) higher than the average fuel aromatic hydrocarbon content (by volume) that would occur in the absence of using any such credits.
    (ii) An average gasoline oxygen content (by weight) for the nonattainment area (taking into account all gasoline sold for use in conventional gasoline-fueled vehicles in the nonattainment area) lower than the average gasoline oxygen content (by weight) that would occur in the absence of using any such credits.
    (iii) An average benzene content (by volume) for the nonattainment area (taking into account all gasoline sold for use in conventional gasoline-fueled vehicles in the nonattainment area) higher than the average benzene content (by volume) that would occur in the absence of using any such credits.
(8) Anti-dumping rules
  (A) In general
  Within 1 year after November 15, 1990, the Administrator shall promulgate regulations applicable to each refiner, blender, or importer of gasoline ensuring that gasoline sold or introduced into commerce by such refiner, blender, or importer (other than reformulated gasoline subject to the requirements of paragraph (1)) does not result in average per gallon emissions (measured on a mass basis) of (i) volatile organic compounds, (ii) oxides of nitrogen, (iii) carbon monoxide, and (iv) toxic air pollutants in excess of such emissions of such pollutants attributable to gasoline sold or introduced into commerce in calendar year 1990 by that refiner, blender, or importer. Such regulations shall take effect beginning January 1, 1995.
  (B) Adjustments
  In evaluating compliance with the requirements of subparagraph (A), the Administrator shall make appropriate adjustments to insure that no credit is provided for improvement in motor vehicle emissions control in motor vehicles sold after the calendar year 1990.
  (C) Compliance determined for each pollutant independently
  In determining whether there is an increase in emissions in violation of the prohibition contained in subparagraph (A) the Administrator shall consider an increase in each air pollutant referred to in clauses (i) through (iv) as a separate violation of such prohibition, except that the Administrator shall promulgate regulations to provide that any increase in emissions of oxides of nitrogen resulting from adding oxygenates to gasoline may be offset by an equivalent or greater reduction (on a mass basis) in emissions of volatile organic compounds, carbon monoxide, or toxic air pollutants, or any combination of the foregoing.

(D) Compliance period

The Administrator shall promulgate an appropriate compliance period or appropriate compliance periods to be used for assessing compliance with the prohibition contained in subparagraph (A).

(E) Baseline for determining compliance

If the Administrator determines that no adequate and reliable data exists regarding the composition of gasoline sold or introduced into commerce by a refiner, blender, or importer in calendar year 1990, for such refiner, blender, or importer, baseline gasoline shall be substituted for such 1990 gasoline in determining compliance with subparagraph (A).

(9) Emissions from entire vehicle

In applying the requirements of this subsection, the Administrator shall take into account emissions from the entire motor vehicle, including evaporative, running, refueling, and exhaust emissions.

(10) Definitions

For purposes of this subsection—

(A) Baseline vehicles

The term "baseline vehicles" mean representative model year 1990 vehicles.

(B) Baseline gasoline

(i) Summertime

The term "baseline gasoline" means in the case of gasoline sold during the high ozone period (as defined by the Administrator) a gasoline which meets the following specifications:

BASELINE GASOLINE FUEL PROPERTIES

API Gravity	57.4
Sulfur, ppm	339
Benzene, %	1.53
RVP, psi	8.7
Octane, R+M/2	87.3
IBP, F	91
10%, F	128
50%, F	218
90%, F	330
End Point, F	415
Aromatics, %	32.0
Olefins, %	9.2
Saturates, %	58.8

(ii) Wintertime

The Administrator shall establish the specifications of "baseline gasoline" for gasoline sold at times other than the high ozone period (as defined by the Administrator). Such specifications shall be the specifications of 1990 industry average gasoline sold during such period.

(C) Toxic air pollutants

The term "toxic air pollutants" means the aggregate emissions of the following:
Benzene
1,3 Butadiene
Polycyclic organic matter (POM)
Acetaldehyde
Formaldehyde.

(D) Covered area

The 9 ozone nonattainment areas having a 1980 population in excess of 250,000 and having the highest ozone design value during the period 1987 through 1989 shall be "covered areas" for purposes of this subsection. Effective one year after the reclassification of any ozone nonattainment area as a Severe ozone nonattainment area under section 7511(b) of this title, such Severe area shall also be a "covered area" for purposes of this subsection.

(E) Reformulated gasoline
The term "reformulated gasoline" means any gasoline which is certified by the Administrator under this section as complying with this subsection.
(F) Conventional gasoline
The term "conventional gasoline" means any gasoline which does not meet specifications set by a certification under this subsection.
(l) Detergents
Effective beginning January 1, 1995, no person may sell or dispense to an ultimate consumer in the United States, and no refiner or marketer may directly or indirectly sell or dispense to persons who sell or dispense to ultimate consumers in the United States any gasoline which does not contain additives to prevent the accumulation of deposits in engines or fuel supply systems. Not later than 2 years after November 15, 1990, the Administrator shall promulgate a rule establishing specifications for such additives.
(m) Oxygenated fuels
(1) Plan revisions for CO nonattainment areas
(A) Each State in which there is located all or part of an area which is designated under subchapter I of this chapter as a nonattainment area for carbon monoxide and which has a carbon monoxide design value of 9.5 parts per million (ppm) or above based on data for the 2-year period of 1988 and 1989 and calculated according to the most recent interpretation methodology issued by the Administrator prior to November 15, 1990, shall submit to the Administrator a State implementation plan revision under section 7410 of this title and part D of subchapter I of this chapter for such area which shall contain the provisions specified under this subsection regarding oxygenated gasoline.
(B) A plan revision which contains such provisions shall also be submitted by each State in which there is located any area which, for any 2-year period after 1989 has a carbon monoxide design value of 9.5 ppm or above. The revision shall be submitted within 18 months after such 2-year period.
(2) Oxygenated gasoline in CO nonattainment areas
Each plan revision under this subsection shall contain provisions to require that any gasoline sold, or dispensed, to the ultimate consumer in the carbon monoxide nonattainment area or sold or dispensed directly or indirectly by fuel refiners or marketers to persons who sell or dispense to ultimate consumers, in the larger of—
(A) the Consolidated Metropolitan Statistical Area (CMSA) in which the area is located, or
(B) if the area is not located in a CMSA, the Metropolitan Statistical Area in which the area is located,
be blended, during the portion of the year in which the area is prone to high ambient concentrations of carbon monoxide to contain not less than 2.7 percent oxygen by weight (subject to a testing tolerance established by the Administrator). The portion of the year in which the area is prone to high ambient concentrations of carbon monoxide shall be as determined by the Administrator, but shall not be less than 4 months. At the request of a State with respect to any area designated as nonattainment for carbon monoxide, the Administrator may reduce the period specified in the preceding sentence if the State can demonstrate that because of meteorological conditions, a reduced period will assure that there will be no exceedances of the carbon monoxide standard outside of such reduced period. For areas with a carbon monoxide design value of 9.5 ppm or more of[2] November 15, 1990, the revision shall provide that such requirement shall take effect no later than November 1, 1992 (or at such other date during 1992 as the Administrator establishes under the preceding provisions of this paragraph). For other areas, the revision shall provide that such requirement shall take effect no later than November 1 of the third year after the last year of the applicable 2-year period referred to in paragraph (1) (or at such other date during such third year as the Administrator establishes under the preceding provisions of this paragraph) and shall include a program for implementation and enforcement of the requirement consistent with guidance to be issued by the Administrator.

---

[2]So in original. Probably should be "as of".

(3) Waivers
   (A) The Administrator shall waive, in whole or in part, the requirements of paragraph (2) upon a demonstration by the State to the satisfaction of the Administrator that the use of oxygenated gasoline would prevent or interfere with the attainment by the area of a national primary ambient air quality standard (or a State or local ambient air quality standard) for any air pollutant other than carbon monoxide.
   (B) The Administrator shall, upon demonstration by the State satisfactory to the Administrator, waive the requirement of paragraph (2) where the Administrator determines that mobile sources of carbon monoxide do not contribute significantly to carbon monoxide levels in an area.
   (C) (i) Any person may petition the Administrator to make a finding that there is, or is likely to be, for any area, an inadequate domestic supply of, or distribution capacity for, oxygenated gasoline meeting the requirements of paragraph (2) or fuel additives (oxygenates) necessary to meet such requirements. The Administrator shall act on such petition within 6 months after receipt of the petition.
      (ii) If the Administrator determines, in response to a petition under clause (i), that there is an inadequate supply or capacity described in clause (i), the Administrator shall delay the effective date of paragraph (2) for 1 year. Upon petition, the Administrator may extend such effective date for one additional year. No partial delay or lesser waiver may be granted under this clause.
      (iii) In granting waivers under this subparagraph the Administrator shall consider distribution capacity separately from the adequacy of domestic supply and shall grant such waivers in such manner as will assure that, if supplies of oxygenated gasoline are limited, areas having the highest design value for carbon monoxide will have a priority in obtaining oxygenated gasoline which meets the requirements of paragraph (2).
      (iv) As used in this subparagraph, the term distribution capacity includes capacity for transportation, storage, and blending.
(4) Fuel dispensing systems
   Any person selling oxygenated gasoline at retail pursuant to this subsection shall be required under regulations promulgated by the Administrator to label the fuel dispensing system with a notice that the gasoline is oxygenated and will reduce the carbon monoxide emissions from the motor vehicle.
(5) Guidelines for credit
   The Administrator shall promulgate guidelines, within 9 months after November 15, 1990, allowing the use of marketable oxygen credits from gasolines during that portion of the year specified in paragraph (2) with higher oxygen content than required to offset the sale or use of gasoline with a lower oxygen content than required. No credits may be transferred between nonattainment areas.
(6) Attainment areas
   Nothing in this subsection shall be interpreted as requiring an oxygenated gasoline program in an area which is in attainment for carbon monoxide, except that in a carbon monoxide nonattainment area which is redesignated as attainment for carbon monoxide, the requirements of this subsection shall remain in effect to the extent such program is necessary to maintain such standard thereafter in the area.
(7) Failure to attain CO standard
   If the Administrator determines under section 7512(b)(2) of this title that the national primary ambient air quality standard for carbon monoxide has not been attained in a Serious Area by the applicable attainment date, the State shall submit a plan revision for the area within 9 months after the date of such determination. The plan revision shall provide that the minimum oxygen content of gasoline referred to in paragraph (2) shall be 3.1 percent by weight unless such requirement is waived in accordance with the provisions of this subsection.

(n) Prohibition on leaded gasoline for highway use
After December 31, 1995, it shall be unlawful for any person to sell, offer for sale, supply, offer for supply, dispense, transport, or introduce into commerce, for use as fuel in any motor vehicle (as defined in section 7554(2)[3] of this title) any gasoline which contains lead or lead additives.

---

[3] So in original. Probably should be section "7550(2)".

260 / Environmental Statutes

(o) Fuel and fuel additive importers and importation
For the purposes of this section, the term "manufacturer" includes an importer and the term "manufacture" includes importation.

(July 14, 1955, ch. 360, title II, Sec. 211, formerly Sec. 210, as added Pub. L. 90-148, Sec. 2, Nov. 21, 1967, 81 Stat. 502; renumbered and amended Pub. L. 91-604, Secs. 8(a), 9(a), Dec. 31, 1970, 84 Stat. 1694, 1698; Pub. L. 92-157, title III, Sec. 302(d), (e), Nov. 18, 1971, 85 Stat. 464; Pub. L. 95-95, title II, Secs. 222, 223, title IV, Sec. 401(e), Aug. 7, 1977, 91 Stat. 762, 764, 791; Pub. L. 95-190, Sec. 14(a)(73), (74), Nov. 16, 1977, 91 Stat. 1403, 1404; Pub. L. 101-549, title II, Secs. 212-221, 228(d), Nov. 15, 1990, 104 Stat. 2488-2500, 2510.)

Codification

Section was formerly classified to section 1857f-6c of this title.

Prior Provisions

A prior section 211 of act July 14, 1955, as added Nov. 21, 1967, Pub. L. 90-148, Sec. 2, 81 Stat. 503, provided for a national emissions standards study and was classified to section 1857f-6d of this title, prior to repeal by section 8(a) of Pub. L. 91-604.

Amendments

1990—Subsec. (a). Pub. L. 101-549, Sec. 212, inserted "(including any fuel or fuel additive used exclusively in nonroad engines or nonroad vehicles)" after "fuel or fuel additive".

Subsecs. (b)(2)(B), (c)(1). Pub. L. 101-549, Sec. 212(b), (c), inserted reference to nonroad engine or nonroad vehicle.

Subsec. (c)(4)(A). Pub. L. 101-549, Sec. 213(a), substituted "any characteristic or component of a" for "use of a", inserted "of the characteristic or component of a fuel or fuel additive" after "control or prohibition" in cl. (i), and inserted "characteristic or component of a" after "such" in cl. (ii).

Subsec. (c)(4)(C). Pub. L. 101-549, Sec. 213(b), inserted last two sentences, authorizing Administrator to make a finding that State control or prohibition is necessary to achieve the standard.

Subsec. (d). Pub. L. 101-549, Sec. 228(d), amended subsec. (d) generally. Prior to amendment, subsec. (d) read as follows: "Any person who violates subsection (a) or (f) of this section or the regulations prescribed under subsection (c) of this section or who fails to furnish any information required by the Administrator under subsection (b) of this section shall forfeit and pay to the United States a civil penalty of $10,000 for each and every day of the continuance of such violation, which shall accrue to the United States and be recovered in a civil suit in the name of the United States, brought in the district where such person has his principal office or in any district in which he does business. The Administrator may, upon application therefor, remit or mitigate any forfeiture provided for in this subsection and he shall have authority to determine the facts upon all such applications."

Subsec. (f)(1). Pub. L. 101-549, Sec. 214(a), designated existing provisions as subpar. (A) and added subpar. (B).

Subsec. (f)(3). Pub. L. 101-549, Sec. 214(b), substituted reference to paragraph (1)(A) for reference to paragraph (1).

Subsec. (g). Pub. L. 101-549, Sec. 215, amended subsec. (g) generally, substituting present provisions for provisions which defined "gasoline", "refinery", and "small refinery" and which limited Administrator's authority to require small refineries to reduce average lead content per gallon of gasoline.

Subsec. (h). Pub. L. 101-549, Sec. 216, added subsec. (h).

Subsec. (i). Pub. L. 101-549, Sec. 217, added subsec. (i).

Subsec. (j). Pub. L. 101-549, Sec. 218(a), added subsec. (j).

Subsecs. (k) to (m). Pub. L. 101-549, Sec. 219, added subsecs. (k) to (m).

Subsec. (n). Pub. L. 101-549, Sec. 220, added subsec. (n).

Subsec. (o). Pub. L. 101-549, Sec. 221, added subsec. (o).

1977—Subsec. (c)(1)(A). Pub. L. 95-95, Sec. 401(e), substituted "if in the judgment of the Administrator any emission product of such fuel or fuel additive causes, or contributes, to air pollution which may reasonably be anticipated to endanger" for "if any emission products of such fuel or fuel additive will endanger".

Subsec. (d). Pub. L. 95-95, Sec. 222(b), inserted "or (f)" after "Any person who violates subsection (a)".

Subsecs. (e), (f). Pub. L. 95-95, Sec. 222(a), added subsecs. (e) and (f).

Subsec. (f)(2). Pub. L. 95-190, Sec. 14(a)(73), inserted provision relating to waiver under par. (4) of this subsec., and struck out "first" before "introduce".

Subsec. (f)(4). Pub. L. 95-190, Sec. 14(a)(74), inserted provision relating to applicability of limitation specified under par. (2) of this subsection.

Subsec. (g). Pub. L. 95-95, Sec. 223, added subsec. (g).

1971—Subsec. (c)(3)(A). Pub. L. 92-157, Sec. 302(d), substituted "purpose of obtaining" for "purpose of".

Subsec. (d). Pub. L. 92-157, Sec. 302(e), substituted "subsection (b)" for "subsection (c)" where appearing the second time.

1970—Subsec. (a). Pub. L. 91-604, Sec. 9(a), substituted "Administrator" for "Secretary" as the registering authority, inserted references to fuel additives, and substituted the selling, offering for sale, and introduction into commerce of fuel or fuel additives, for the delivery for introduction into interstate commerce or delivery to another person who can reasonably be expected to deliver fuel into interstate commerce.

Subsec. (b). Pub. L. 91-604, Sec. 9(a), designated existing provisions as pars. (1) and (3), added par. (2), and substituted "Administrator" for "Secretary" wherever appearing.

Subsec. (c). Pub. L. 91-604, Sec. 9(a), substituted provisions covering the control or prohibition of offending fuels and fuel additives, for provisions covering trade secrets and substituted "Administrator" for "Secretary" wherever appearing.

Subsec. (d). Pub. L. 91-604, Sec. 9(a), inserted references to failure to obey regulations prescribed under subsec. (c) and failure to furnish information required by the Administrator under subsec. (c), increased the daily civil penalty from $1,000 to $10,000 and substituted "Administrator" for "Secretary".

Subsec. (e). Pub. L. 91-604, Sec. 9(a), struck out subsec. (e) which directed the various United States Attorneys to prosecute for the recovery of forfeitures.

Effective Date of 1977 Amendment

Amendment by Pub. L. 95-95 effective Aug. 7, 1977, except as otherwise expressly provided, see section 406(d) of Pub. L. 95-95, set out as a note under section 7401 of this title.

Findings and Sense of Congress on Ethanol Usage

Pub. L. 100-203, title I, Sec. 1508, Dec. 22, 1987, 101 Stat. 1330-29, provided that:

"(a) Findings.—Congress finds that—
   (1) the United States is dependent for a large and growing share of its energy needs on the Middle East at a time when world petroleum reserves are declining;
   (2) the burning of gasoline causes pollution;
   (3) ethanol can be blended with gasoline to produce a cleaner source of fuel;
   (4) ethanol can be produced from grain, a renewable resource that is in considerable surplus in the United States;
   (5) the conversion of grain into ethanol would reduce farm program costs and grain surpluses; and
   (6) increasing the quantity of motor fuels that contain at least 10 percent ethanol from current levels to 50 percent by 1992 would create thousands of new jobs in ethanol production facilities.
   (b) Sense of Congress.—It is the sense of Congress that the Administrator of the Environmental Protection Agency should use authority provided under the Clean Air Act (42 U.S.C. 7401 et seq.) to require greater use of ethanol as motor fuel."

Agricultural Machinery: Study of Unleaded Fuel

Pub. L. 99-198, title XVII, Sec. 1765, Dec. 23, 1985, 99 Stat. 1653, directed Administrator of EPA and Secretary of Agriculture jointly to conduct a study of use of fuel containing lead additives, and alternative lubricating additives, in gasoline engines that are used in agricultural machinery, and designed to combust fuel containing such additives, study to analyze potential for mechanical problems (including but not limited to valve recession) that may be associated with use of other fuels in such engines, and not later than Jan. 1, 1987, Administrator and Secretary to publish results of the study, with Administrator to publish in Federal Register notice of publication of such study and a summary thereof; direct line to be used on a farm for farming purposes, including a determination of whether a modification of regulations limiting lead content of gasoline would be appropriate in the case of gasoline used on a farm for farming purposes, and submit to President and Congress a report containing the study, a summary of comments received during public hearing (including comments of Secretary), and findings and recommendations of Administrator made in accordance with clause (1), such report to be transmitted named congressional committees; directed Administrator between Jan. 1, 1986, and Dec. 31, 1987, to monitor actual lead content of leaded gasoline sold in the United States, with Administrator to determine average lead content of such gasoline for each 3-month period between Jan. 1, 1986, and Dec. 31, 1987, and if actual lead content falls below an average of 0.2 of a gram of lead per gallon in any such 3-month period, to report to Congress, and publish a notice thereof in Federal Register; provided that until Jan. 1, 1988, no regulation of Administrator issued under this section 211 could require an average lead content per gallon that is less than 0.1 of a gram per gallon; and authorized an appropriation.

Modification or Rescission of Rules, Regulations, Orders, Determinations, Contracts, Certifications, Authorizations, Delegations, and Other Actions

All rules, regulations, orders, determinations, contracts, certifications, authorizations, delegations, or other actions duly issued, made, or taken by or pursuant to act July 14, 1955, the Clean Air Act, as in effect immediately prior to the date of enactment of Pub. L. 95-95 [Aug. 7, 1977] to continue in full force and effect until modified or rescinded in accordance with act July 14, 1955, as amended by Pub. L. 95-95 [this chapter], see section 406(b) of Pub. L. 95-95, set out as an Effective Date of 1977 Amendment note under section 7401 of this title.

Section Referred to in Other Sections

This section is referred to in sections 7416, 7511a, 7511b, 7521, 7524, 7604, 7607, 7617, 7651i, 13220 of this title; title 26 section 4082.

42 USC 7546

Repealed. Pub. L. 101-549, title II, Sec. 230(10), Nov. 15, 1990, 104 Stat. 2529

Section, act July 14, 1955, ch. 360, title II, Sec. 212, as added Dec. 31, 1970, Pub. L. 91-604, Sec. 10(c), 84 Stat. 1700; amended Dec. 31, 1970, Pub. L. 91-605, Sec. 202(a), 84 Stat. 1739; Apr. 9, 1973, Pub. L. 93-15, Sec. 1(b), 87 Stat. 11; June 22, 1974, Pub. L. 93-319, Sec. 13(b), 88 Stat. 265, related to low-emission vehicles.

A prior section 212 of act July 14, 1955, was renumbered section 213 by Pub. L. 91-604, renumbered section 214 by Pub. L. 93-319, and renumbered section 216 by Pub. L. 95-95, and is classified to section 7550 of this title.

NONROAD ENGINES AND VEHICLES

42 USC 7547

(a) Emissions standards
   (1) The Administrator shall conduct a study of emissions from nonroad engines and nonroad vehicles (other than locomotives or engines used in locomotives) to determine if such emissions cause, or significantly contribute to, air pollution which may reasonably be anticipated to endanger public health or welfare. Such study shall be completed within 12 months of November 15, 1990.
   (2) After notice and opportunity for public hearing, the Administrator shall determine within 12 months after completion of the study under paragraph (1), based upon the results of such study, whether emissions of carbon monoxide, oxides of nitrogen, and volatile organic compounds from new and existing nonroad engines or nonroad vehicles (other than locomotives or engines used in locomotives) are significant contributors to ozone or carbon monoxide concentrations in more than 1 area which has failed to attain the national ambient air quality standards for ozone or carbon monoxide. Such determination shall be included in the regulations under paragraph (3).

(3) If the Administrator makes an affirmative determination under paragraph (2) the Administrator shall, within 12 months after completion of the study under paragraph (1), promulgate (and from time to time revise) regulations containing standards applicable to emissions from those classes or categories of new nonroad engines and new nonroad vehicles (other than locomotives or engines used in locomotives) which in the Administrator's judgment cause, or contribute to, such air pollution. Such standards shall achieve the greatest degree of emission reduction achievable through the application of technology which the Administrator determines will be available for the engines or vehicles to which such standards apply, giving appropriate consideration to the cost of applying such technology within the period of time available to manufacturers and to noise, energy, and safety factors associated with the application of such technology. In determining what degree of reduction will be available, the Administrator shall first consider standards equivalent in stringency to standards for comparable motor vehicles or engines (if any) regulated under section 7521 of this title, taking into account the technological feasibility, costs, safety, noise, and energy factors associated with achieving, as appropriate, standards of such stringency and lead time. The regulations shall apply to the useful life of the engines or vehicles (as determined by the Administrator).

(4) If the Administrator determines that any emissions not referred to in paragraph (2) from new nonroad engines or vehicles significantly contribute to air pollution which may reasonably be anticipated to endanger public health or welfare, the Administrator may promulgate (and from time to time revise) such regulations as the Administrator deems appropriate containing standards applicable to emissions from those classes or categories of new nonroad engines and new nonroad vehicles (other than locomotives or engines used in locomotives) which in the Administrator's judgment cause, or contribute to, such air pollution, taking into account costs, noise, safety, and energy factors associated with the application of technology which the Administrator determines will be available for the engines and vehicles to which such standards apply. The regulations shall apply to the useful life of the engines or vehicles (as determined by the Administrator).

(5) Within 5 years after November 15, 1990, the Administrator shall promulgate regulations containing standards applicable to emissions from new locomotives and new engines used in locomotives. Such standards shall achieve the greatest degree of emission reduction achievable through the application of technology which the Administrator determines will be available for the locomotives or engines to which such standards apply, giving appropriate consideration to the cost of applying such technology within the period of time available to manufacturers and to noise, energy, and safety factors associated with the application of such technology.

(b) Effective date

Standards under this section shall take effect at the earliest possible date considering the lead time necessary to permit the development and application of the requisite technology, giving appropriate consideration to the cost of compliance within such period and energy and safety.

(c) Safe controls

Effective with respect to new engines or vehicles to which standards under this section apply, no emission control device, system, or element of design shall be used in such a new nonroad engine or new nonroad vehicle for purposes of complying with such standards if such device, system, or element of design will cause or contribute to an unreasonable risk to public health, welfare, or safety in its operation or function. In determining whether an unreasonable risk exists, the Administrator shall consider factors including those described in section 7521(a)(4)(B) of this title.

(d) Enforcement

The standards under this section shall be subject to sections 7525, 7541, 7542, and 7543 of this title, with such modifications of the applicable regulations implementing such sections as the Administrator deems appropriate, and shall be enforced in the same manner as standards prescribed under section 7521 of this title. The Administrator shall revise or promulgate regulations as may be necessary to determine compliance with, and enforce, standards in effect under this section.

(July 14, 1955, ch. 360, title II, Sec. 213, as added Pub. L. 93-319, Sec. 10, June 22, 1974, 88 Stat. 261; amended Pub. L. 101-549, title II, Sec. 222(a), Nov. 15, 1990, 104 Stat. 2500.)

264 / Environmental Statutes

Codification
Section was formerly classified to section 1857f-6f of this title.

Prior Provisions
A prior section 213 of act July 14, 1955, was renumbered section 214 by Pub. L. 93-319 and renumbered section 216 by Pub. L. 95-95, and is classified to section 7550 of this title.

Amendments
1990—Pub. L. 101-549 amended section generally, substituting present provisions for provisions requiring Administrator and Secretary of Transportation to conduct study on fuel economy improvement for new motor vehicles manufactured during and after model year 1980.

Section Referred to in Other Sections
This section is referred to in sections 7524, 7607 of this title.

STUDY OF PARTICULATE EMISSIONS FROM MOTOR VEHICLES

42 USC 7548

(a) Study and analysis
  (1) The Administrator shall conduct a study concerning the effects on health and welfare of particulate emissions from motor vehicles or motor vehicle engines to which section 7521 of this title applies. Such study shall characterize and quantify such emissions and analyze the relationship of such emissions to various fuels and fuel additives.
  (2) The study shall also include an analysis of particulate emissions from mobile sources which are not related to engine emissions (including, but not limited to tire debris, and asbestos from brake lining).
(b) Report to Congress
  The Administrator shall report to the Congress the findings and results of the study conducted under subsection (a) of this section not later than two years after August 7, 1977. Such report shall also include recommendations for standards or methods to regulate particulate emissions described in paragraph (2) of subsection (a) of this section.

(July 14, 1955, ch. 360, title II, Sec. 214, as added Pub. L. 95-95, title II, Sec. 224(d), Aug. 7, 1977, 91 Stat. 767.)

Prior Provisions
A prior section 214 of act July 14, 1955, was renumbered section 216 by Pub. L. 95-95 and is classified to section 7550 of this title.

Effective Date
Section effective Aug. 7, 1977, except as otherwise expressly provided, see section 406(d) of Pub. L. 95-95, set out as an Effective Date of 1977 Amendment note under section 7401 of this title.

Study on Suspended Particulate Matter
Section 403(a) of Pub. L. 95-95 directed Administrator of EPA, not later than 18 months after Aug. 7, 1977, in cooperation with National Academy of Sciences, to study and report to Congress on relationship between size, weight, and chemical composition of suspended particulate matter and nature and degree of endangerment to public health or welfare presented by such particulate matter and availability of technology for controlling such particulate matter.

HIGH ALTITUDE PERFORMANCE ADJUSTMENTS

42 USC 7549

(a) Instruction of the manufacturer
  (1) Any action taken with respect to any element of design installed on or in a motor vehicle or motor vehicle engine in compliance with regulations under this subchapter (including any alteration or adjustment of such element), shall be treated as not in violation of section 7522(a) of this title if such action is performed in accordance with high altitude ad-

justment instructions provided by the manufacturer under subsection (b) of this section and approved by the Administrator.
   (2) If the Administrator finds that adjustments or modifications made pursuant to instructions of the manufacturer under paragraph (1) will not insure emission control performance with respect to each standard under section 7521 of this title at least equivalent to that which would result if no such adjustments or modifications were made, he shall disapprove such instructions. Such finding shall be based upon minimum engineering evaluations consistent with good engineering practice.
(b) Regulations
   (1) Instructions respecting each class or category of vehicles or engines to which this title applies providing for such vehicle and engine adjustments and modifications as may be necessary to insure emission control performance at different altitudes shall be submitted by the manufacturer to the Administrator pursuant to regulations promulgated by the Administrator.
   (2) Any knowing violation by a manufacturer of requirements of the Administrator under paragraph (1) shall be treated as a violation by such manufacturer of section 7522(a)(3) of this title for purposes of the penalties contained in section 7524 of this title.
   (3) Such instructions shall provide, in addition to other adjustments, for adjustments for vehicles moving from high altitude areas to low altitude areas after the initial registration of such vehicles.
(c) Manufacturer parts
   No instructions under this section respecting adjustments or modifications may require the use of any manufacturer parts (as defined in section 7522(a) of this title) unless the manufacturer demonstrates to the satisfaction of the Administrator that the use of such manufacturer parts is necessary to insure emission control performance.
(d) State inspection and maintenance programs
   Before January 1, 1981 the authority provided by this section shall be available in any high altitude State (as determined under regulations of the Administrator under regulations promulgated before August 7, 1977) but after December 31, 1980, such authority shall be available only in any such State in which an inspection and maintenance program for the testing of motor vehicle emissions has been instituted for the portions of the State where any national ambient air quality standard for auto-related pollutants has not been attained.
(e) High altitude testing
   (1) The Administrator shall promptly establish at least one testing center (in addition to the testing centers existing on November 15, 1990) located at a site that represents high altitude conditions, to ascertain in a reasonable manner whether, when in actual use throughout their useful life (as determined under section 7521(d) of this title), each class or category of vehicle and engines to which regulations under section 7521 of this title apply conforms to the emissions standards established by such regulations. For purposes of this subsection, the term "high altitude conditions" refers to high altitude as defined in regulations of the Administrator in effect as of November 15, 1990.
   (2) The Administrator, in cooperation with the Secretary of Energy and the Administrator of the Federal Transit Administration, and such other agencies as the Administrator deems appropriate, shall establish a research and technology assessment center to provide for the development and evaluation of less-polluting heavy-duty engines and fuels for use in buses, heavy-duty trucks, and non-road engines and vehicles, which shall be located at a high-altitude site that represents high-altitude conditions. In establishing and funding such a center, the Administrator shall give preference to proposals which provide for local cost-sharing of facilities and recovery of costs of operation through utilization of such facility for the purposes of this section.
   (3) The Administrator shall designate at least one center at high-altitude conditions to provide research on after-market emission components, dual-fueled vehicles and conversion kits, the effects of tampering on emissions equipment, testing of alternate fuels and conversion kits, and the development of curricula, training courses, and materials to maximize the effectiveness of inspection and maintenance programs as they relate to promoting effective control of vehicle emissions at high-altitude elevations. Preference shall be given to existing vehicle emissions testing and research centers that have established repu-

tations for vehicle emissions research and development and training, and that possess in-house Federal Test Procedure capacity.

(July 14, 1955, ch. 360, title II, Sec. 215, as added Pub. L. 95-95, title II, Sec. 211(b), Aug. 7, 1977, 91 Stat. 757; amended Pub. L. 95-190, Sec. 14(a)(75), Nov. 16, 1977, 91 Stat. 1404; Pub. L. 101-549, title II, Sec. 224, Nov. 15, 1990, 104 Stat. 2503; Pub. L. 102-240, title III, Sec. 3004(b), Dec. 18, 1991, 105 Stat. 2088.)

Codification

In subsec. (d), "August 7, 1977" substituted for "the date of enactment of this Act" to reflect the probable intent of Congress that such date of enactment meant the date of enactment of Pub. L. 95-95.

Amendments

1990—Subsec. (e). Pub. L. 101-549 added subsec. (e).

1977—Subsec. (d). Pub. L. 95-190 substituted "December 31, 1980" for "December 31, 1981".

Change of Name

"Federal Transit Administration" substituted for "Urban Mass Transit Administration" in subsec. (e)(2) pursuant to section 3004(a) of Pub. L. 102-240, set out as a note under section 107 of Title 49, Transportation.

Effective Date

Section effective Aug. 7, 1977, except as otherwise expressly provided, see section 406(d) of Pub. L. 95-95, set out as an Effective Date of 1977 Amendment note under section 7401 of this title.

Section Referred to in Other Sections

This section is referred to in section 7522 of this title.

DEFINITIONS

42 USC 7550

As used in this part—
(1) The term "manufacturer" as used in sections 7521, 7522, 7525, 7541, and 7542 of this title means any person engaged in the manufacturing or assembling of new motor vehicles, new motor vehicle engines, new nonroad vehicles or new nonroad engines, or importing such vehicles or engines for resale, or who acts for and is under the control of any such person in connection with the distribution of new motor vehicles, new motor vehicle engines, new nonroad vehicles or new nonroad engines, but shall not include any dealer with respect to new motor vehicles, new motor vehicle engines, new nonroad vehicles or new nonroad engines received by him in commerce.
(2) The term "motor vehicle" means any self-propelled vehicle designed for transporting persons or property on a street or highway.
(3) Except with respect to vehicles or engines imported or offered for importation, the term "new motor vehicle" means a motor vehicle the equitable or legal title to which has never been transferred to an ultimate purchaser; and the term "new motor vehicle engine" means an engine in a new motor vehicle or a motor vehicle engine the equitable or legal title to which has never been transferred to the ultimate purchaser; and with respect to imported vehicles or engines, such terms mean a motor vehicle and engine, respectively, manufactured after the effective date of a regulation issued under section 7521 of this title which is applicable to such vehicle or engine (or which would be applicable to such vehicle or engine had it been manufactured for importation into the United States).
(4) The term "dealer" means any person who is engaged in the sale or the distribution of new motor vehicles or new motor vehicle engines to the ultimate purchaser.
(5) The term "ultimate purchaser" means, with respect to any new motor vehicle or new motor vehicle engine, the first person who in good faith purchases such new motor vehicle or new engine for purposes other than resale.
(6) The term "commerce" means (A) commerce between any place in any State and any place outside thereof; and (B) commerce wholly within the District of Columbia.

(7) Vehicle curb weight, gross vehicle weight rating, light-duty truck, light-duty vehicle, and loaded vehicle weight.—The terms "vehicle curb weight", "gross vehicle weight rating"(GVWR), "light-duty truck" (LDT), light-duty vehicle,[1] and "loaded vehicle weight" (LVW) have the meaning provided in regulations promulgated by the Administrator and in effect as of November 15, 1990. The abbreviations in parentheses corresponding to any term referred to in this paragraph shall have the same meaning as the corresponding term.

(8) Test weight.—The term "test weight" and the abbreviation "tw" mean the vehicle curb weight added to the gross vehicle weight rating (gvwr) and divided by 2.

(9) Motor vehicle or engine part manufacturer.—The term "motor vehicle or engine part manufacturer" as used in sections 7541 and 7542 of this title means any person engaged in the manufacturing, assembling or rebuilding of any device, system, part, component or element of design which is installed in or on motor vehicles or motor vehicle engines.

(10) Nonroad engine.—The term "nonroad engine" means an internal combustion engine (including the fuel system) that is not used in a motor vehicle or a vehicle used solely for competition, or that is not subject to standards promulgated under section 7411 of this title or section 7521 of this title.

(11) Nonroad vehicle.—The term "nonroad vehicle" means a vehicle that is powered by a nonroad engine and that is not a motor vehicle or a vehicle used solely for competition.

(July 14, 1955, ch. 360, title II, Sec. 216, formerly Sec. 208, as added Pub. L. 89-272, title I, Sec. 101(8), Oct. 20, 1965, 79 Stat. 994; renumbered Sec. 212, and amended Pub. L. 90-148, Sec. 2, Nov. 21, 1967, 81 Stat. 503; renumbered Sec. 213, and amended Pub. L. 91-604, Secs. 8(a), 10(d), 11(a)(2)(A), Dec. 31, 1970, 84 Stat. 1694, 1703, 1705; renumbered Sec. 214, Pub. L. 93-319, Sec. 10, June 22, 1974, 88 Stat. 261; renumbered Sec. 216, Pub. L. 95-95, title II, Sec. 224(d), Aug. 7, 1977, 91 Stat. 767; Pub. L. 101-549, title II, Sec. 223, Nov. 15, 1990, 104 Stat. 2503.)

Codification

Section was formerly classified to section 1857f-7 of this title.

Amendments

1990—Par. (1). Pub. L. 101-549, Sec. 223(b), inserted references to new nonroad vehicles or new nonroad engines.

Pars. (7) to (11). Pub. L. 101-549, Sec. 223(a), added pars. (7) to (11).

1970—Pub. L. 91-604, Sec. 11(a)(2)(A), substituted "part" for "subchapter".

Par. (1). Pub. L. 91-604, Sec. 10(d)(1), inserted reference to section 7521 of this title.

Par. (3). Pub. L. 91-604, Sec. 10(d)(2), inserted provisions which defined such terms with respect to imported vehicles or engines.

1967—Pub. L. 90-148 inserted "as used in sections 7522, 7525, 7541, and 7542 of this title" after "manufacturer" in par. (1).

Section Referred to in Other Sections

This section is referred to in sections 7511b, 7545, 7581, 7602, 13211, 13271 of this title.

STUDY AND REPORT ON FUEL CONSUMPTION

42 USC 7551

Following each motor vehicle model year, the Administrator of the Environmental Protection Agency shall report to the Congress respecting the motor vehicle fuel consumption associated with the standards applicable for the immediately preceding model year.

(Pub. L. 95-95, title II, Sec. 203, Aug. 7, 1977, 91 Stat. 754; Pub. L. 97-375, title I, Sec. 106(a), Dec. 21, 1982, 96 Stat. 1820.)

Codification

Section was enacted as part of the Clean Air Act Amendments of 1977, and not as part of the Clean Air Act which comprises this chapter.

---

[1]So in original. Probably should be set off by quotation marks.

Amendments

1982—Subsec. (a). Pub. L. 97-375, Sec. 106(a)(2), struck out subsec. (a) designation.

Subsec. (b). Pub. L. 97-375, Sec. 106(a)(1), struck out subsec. (b) which directed the Secretaries of Energy and Transportation each to submit to Congress separate reports on fuel consumption as promptly as practicable after the submission by the Administrator of the fuel consumption report referred to in former subsec. (a) of this section.

Effective Date

Section effective Aug. 7, 1977, except as otherwise expressly provided, see section 406(d) of Pub. L. 95-95, set out as an Effective Date of 1977 Amendment note under section 7401 of this title.

MOTOR VEHICLE COMPLIANCE PROGRAM FEES

42 USC 7552

(a) Fee collection
Consistent with section 9701 of title 31, the Administrator may promulgate (and from time to time revise) regulations establishing fees to recover all reasonable costs to the Administrator associated with—
   (1) new vehicle or engine certification under section 7525(a) of this title or part C of this subchapter,
   (2) new vehicle or engine compliance monitoring and testing under section 7525(b) of this title or part C of this subchapter, and
   (3) in-use vehicle or engine compliance monitoring and testing under section 7541(c) of this title or part C of this subchapter.

The Administrator may establish for all foreign and domestic manufacturers a fee schedule based on such factors as the Administrator finds appropriate and equitable and nondiscriminatory, including the number of vehicles or engines produced under a certificate of conformity. In the case of heavy-duty engine and vehicle manufacturers, such fees shall not exceed a reasonable amount to recover an appropriate portion of such reasonable costs.

(b) Special Treasury fund
Any fees collected under this section shall be deposited in a special fund in the United States Treasury for licensing and other services which thereafter shall be available for appropriation, to remain available until expended, to carry out the Agency's activities for which the fees were collected.

(c) Limitation on fund use
Moneys in the special fund referred to in subsection (b) of this section shall not be used until after the first fiscal year commencing after the first July 1 when fees are paid into the fund.

(d) Administrator's testing authority
Nothing in this subsection shall be construed to limit the Administrator's authority to require manufacturer or confirmatory testing as provided in this part.

(July 14, 1955, ch. 360, title II, Sec. 217, as added Pub. L. 101-549, title II, Sec. 225, Nov. 15, 1990, 104 Stat. 2504.)

Section Referred to in Other Sections

This section is referred to in section 7607 of this title.

PROHIBITION ON PRODUCTION OF ENGINES REQUIRING LEADED GASOLINE

42 USC 7553

The Administrator shall promulgate regulations applicable to motor vehicle engines and nonroad engines manufactured after model year 1992 that prohibit the manufacture, sale, or introduction into commerce of any engine that requires leaded gasoline.

(July 14, 1955, ch. 360, title II, Sec. 218, as added Pub. L. 101-549, title II, Sec. 226, Nov. 15, 1990, 104 Stat. 2505.)

Section Referred to in Other Sections

This section is referred to in section 7522 of this title.

URBAN BUS STANDARDS

42 USC 7554

(a) Standards for model years after 1993

Not later than January 1, 1992, the Administrator shall promulgate regulations under section 7521(a) of this title applicable to urban buses for the model year 1994 and thereafter. Such standards shall be based on the best technology that can reasonably be anticipated to be available at the time such measures are to be implemented, taking costs, safety, energy, lead time, and other relevant factors into account. Such regulations shall require that such urban buses comply with the provisions of subsection (b) of this section (and subsection (c) of this subsection,[1] if applicable) in addition to compliance with the standards applicable under section 7521(a) of this title for heavy-duty vehicles of the same type and model year.

(b) PM standard

   (1) 50 percent reduction

   The standards under section 7521(a) of this title applicable to urban buses shall require that, effective for the model year 1994 and thereafter, emissions of particulate matter (PM) from urban buses shall not exceed 50 percent of the emissions of particulate matter (PM) allowed under the emission standard applicable under section 7521(a) of this title as of November 15, 1990, for particulate matter (PM) in the case of heavy-duty diesel vehicles and engines manufactured in the model year 1994.

   (2) Revised reduction

   The Administrator shall increase the level of emissions of particulate matter allowed under the standard referred to in paragraph (1) if the Administrator determines that the 50 percent reduction referred to in paragraph (1) is not technologically achievable, taking into account durability, costs, lead time, safety, and other relevant factors. The Administrator may not increase such level of emissions above 70 percent of the emissions of particulate matter (PM) allowed under the emission standard applicable under section 7521(a) of this title as of November 15, 1990, for particulate matter (PM) in the case of heavy-duty diesel vehicles and engines manufactured in the model year 1994.

   (3) Determination as part of rule

   As part of the rulemaking under subsection (a) of this section, the Administrator shall make a determination as to whether the 50 percent reduction referred to in paragraph (1) is technologically achievable, taking into account durability, costs, lead time, safety, and other relevant factors.

(c) Low-polluting fuel requirement

   (1) Annual testing

   Beginning with model year 1994 buses, the Administrator shall conduct annual tests of a representative sample of operating urban buses subject to the particulate matter (PM) standard applicable pursuant to subsection (b) of this section to determine whether such buses comply with such standard in use over their full useful life.

   (2) Promulgation of additional low-polluting fuel requirement

      (A) If the Administrator determines, based on the testing under paragraph (1), that urban buses subject to the particulate matter (PM) standard applicable pursuant to subsection (b) of this section do not comply with such standard in use over their full useful life, he shall revise the standards applicable to such buses to require (in addition to compliance with the PM standard applicable pursuant to subsection (b) of this section) that all new urban buses purchased or placed into service by owners or operators of urban buses in all metropolitan statistical areas or consolidated metropolitan statistical areas with a 1980 population of 750,000 or more shall be capable of operating, and shall be exclusively operated, on low-polluting fuels. The Administrator shall establish the pass-fail rate for purposes of testing under this subparagraph.

      (B) The Administrator shall promulgate a schedule phasing in any low-polluting fuel requirement established pursuant to this paragraph to an increasing percentage of new urban buses purchased or placed into service in each of the first 5 model years commencing 3 years after the determination under subparagraph (A). Under such sched-

---

[1]So in original. Probably should be "section,".

ule 100 percent of new urban buses placed into service in the fifth model year commencing 3 years after the determination under subparagraph (A) shall comply with the low-polluting fuel requirement established pursuant to this paragraph.
  (C) The Administrator may extend the requirements of this paragraph to metropolitan statistical areas or consolidated metropolitan statistical areas with a 1980 population of less than 750,000, if the Administrator determines that a significant benefit to public health could be expected to result from such extension.
(d) Retrofit requirements
  Not later than 12 months after November 15, 1990, the Administrator shall promulgate regulations under section 7521(a) of this title requiring that urban buses which—
  (1) are operating in areas referred to in subparagraph (A) of subsection (c)(2) of this section (or subparagraph (C) of subsection (c)(2) of this section if the Administrator has taken action under that subparagraph);
  (2) were not subject to standards in effect under the regulations under subsection (a) of this section; and
  (3) have their engines replaced or rebuilt after January 1, 1995,
  shall comply with an emissions standard or emissions control technology requirement established by the Administrator in such regulations. Such emissions standard or emissions control technology requirement shall reflect the best retrofit technology and maintenance practices reasonably achievable.
(e) Procedures for administration and enforcement
  The Administrator shall establish, within 18 months after November 15, 1990, and in accordance with section 7525(h) of this title, procedures for the administration and enforcement of standards for buses subject to standards under this section, testing procedures, sampling protocols, in-use compliance requirements, and criteria governing evaluation of buses. Procedures for testing (including, but not limited to, certification testing) shall reflect actual operating conditions.
(f) Definitions
  For purposes of this section—
  (1) Urban bus
    The term "urban bus" has the meaning provided under regulations of the Administrator promulgated under section 7521(a) of this title.
  (2) Low-polluting fuel
    The term "low-polluting fuel" means methanol, ethanol, propane, or natural gas, or any comparably low-polluting fuel. In determining whether a fuel is comparably low-polluting, the Administrator shall consider both the level of emissions of air pollutants from vehicles using the fuel and the contribution of such emissions to ambient levels of air pollutants. For purposes of this paragraph, the term "methanol" includes any fuel which contains at least 85 percent methanol unless the Administrator increases such percentage as he deems appropriate to protect public health and welfare.
(July 14, 1955, ch. 360, title II, Sec. 219, as added Pub. L. 101-549, title II, Sec. 227[(a)], Nov. 15, 1990, 104 Stat. 2505.)

Section Referred to in Other Sections

This section is referred to in sections 7521, 7522, 7545 of this title.

Part B—Aircraft Emission Standards

ESTABLISHMENT OF STANDARDS

42 USC 7571

(a) Study; proposed standards; hearings; issuance of regulations
  (1) Within 90 days after December 31, 1970, the Administrator shall commence a study and investigation of emissions of air pollutants from aircraft in order to determine—

(A) the extent to which such emissions affect air quality in air quality control regions throughout the United States, and
(B) the technological feasibility of controlling such emissions.
(2) (A) The Administrator shall, from time to time, issue proposed emission standards applicable to the emission of any air pollutant from any class or classes of aircraft engines which in his judgment causes, or contributes to, air pollution which may reasonably be anticipated to endanger public health or welfare.
(B) (i) The Administrator shall consult with the Administrator of the Federal Aviation Administration on aircraft engine emission standards.
(ii) The Administrator shall not change the aircraft engine emission standards if such change would significantly increase noise and adversely affect safety.
(3) The Administrator shall hold public hearings with respect to such proposed standards. Such hearings shall, to the extent practicable, be held in air quality control regions which are most seriously affected by aircraft emissions. Within 90 days after the issuance of such proposed regulations, he shall issue such regulations with such modifications as he deems appropriate. Such regulations may be revised from time to time.
(b) Effective date of regulations

Any regulation prescribed under this section (and any revision thereof) shall take effect after such period as the Administrator finds necessary (after consultation with the Secretary of Transportation) to permit the development and application of the requisite technology, giving appropriate consideration to the cost of compliance within such period.
(c) Regulations which create hazards to aircraft safety

Any regulations in effect under this section on August 7, 1977, or proposed or promulgated thereafter, or amendments thereto, with respect to aircraft shall not apply if disapproved by the President, after notice and opportunity for public hearing, on the basis of a finding by the Secretary of Transportation that any such regulation would create a hazard to aircraft safety. Any such finding shall include a reasonably specific statement of the basis upon which the finding was made.

(July 14, 1955, ch. 360, title II, Sec. 231, as added Pub. L. 91-604, Sec. 11(a)(1), Dec. 31, 1970, 84 Stat. 1703; amended Pub. L. 95-95, title II, Sec. 225, title IV, Sec. 401(f), Aug. 7, 1977, 91 Stat. 769, 791; Pub. L. 104-264, title IV, Sec. 406(b), Oct. 9, 1996, 110 Stat. 3257.)

Codification

Section was formerly classified to section 1857f-9 of this title.

Amendments

1996—Subsec. (a)(2). Pub. L. 104-264 designated existing provisions as subpar. (A) and added subpar. (B).

1977—Subsec. (a)(2). Pub. L. 95-95, Sec. 401(f), substituted "The Administrator shall, from time to time, issue proposed emission standards applicable to the emission of any air pollutant from any class or classes of aircraft engines which in his judgment causes, or contributes to, air pollution which may reasonably be anticipated to endanger public health or welfare" for "Within 180 days after commencing such study and investigation, the Administrator shall publish a report of such study and investigation and shall issue proposed emission standards applicable to emissions of any air pollutant from any class or classes of aircraft or aircraft engines which in his judgment cause or contribute to or are likely to cause or contribute to air pollution which endangers the public health or welfare".

Subsec. (c). Pub. L. 95-95, Sec. 225, substituted "Any regulations in effect under this section on August 7, 1977, or proposed or promulgated thereafter, or amendments thereto, with respect to aircraft shall not apply if disapproved by the President, after notice and opportunity for public hearing, on the basis of a finding by the Secretary of Transportation that any such regulation would create a hazard to aircraft safety" for "Any regulations under this section, or amendments thereto, with respect to aircraft, shall be prescribed only after consultation with the Secretary of Transportation in order to assure appropriate consideration for aircraft safety" and inserted provision that findings include a reasonably specific statement of the basis upon which the finding was made.

Effective Date of 1996 Amendment

Except as otherwise specifically provided, amendment by Pub. L. 104-264 applicable only to fiscal years beginning after Sept. 30, 1996, and not to be construed as affecting funds made available for a fiscal year ending before Oct. 1, 1996, see section 3 of Pub. L. 104-264, set out as a note under section 106 of Title 49, Transportation.

Effective Date of 1977 Amendment

Amendment by Pub. L. 95-95 effective Aug. 7, 1977, except as otherwise expressly provided, see section 406(d) of Pub. L. 95-95, set out as a note under section 7401 of this title.

Modification or Rescission of Rules, Regulations, Orders, Determinations, Contracts, Certifications, Authorizations, Delegations, and Other Actions

All rules, regulations, orders, determinations, contracts, certifications, authorizations, delegations, or other actions duly issued, made, or taken by or pursuant to act July 14, 1955, the Clean Air Act, as in effect immediately prior to the date of enactment of Pub. L. 95-95 [Aug. 7, 1977] to continue in full force and effect until modified or rescinded in accordance with act July 14, 1955, as amended by Pub. L. 95-95 [this chapter], see section 406(b) of Pub. L. 95-95, set out as an Effective Date of 1977 Amendment note under section 7401 of this title.

Study and Investigation of Uninstalled Aircraft Engines

Pub. L. 101-549, title II, Sec. 233, Nov. 15, 1990, 104 Stat. 2529, provided that:

"(a) Study.–The Administrator of the Environmental Protection Agency and the Secretary of Transportation, in consultation with the Secretary of Defense, shall commence a study and investigation of the testing of uninstalled aircraft engines in enclosed test cells that shall address at a minimum the following issues and such other issues as they shall deem appropriate—

(1) whether technologies exist to control some or all emissions of oxides of nitrogen from test cells;
(2) the effectiveness of such technologies;
(3) the cost of implementing such technologies;
(4) whether such technologies affect the safety, design, structure, operation, or performance of aircraft engines;
(5) whether such technologies impair the effectiveness and accuracy of aircraft engine safety design, and performance tests conducted in test cells; and
(6) the impact of not controlling such oxides of nitrogen in the applicable nonattainment areas and on other sources, stationary and mobile, on oxides of nitrogen in such areas.

(b) Report, Authority To Regulate.–Not later than 24 months after enactment of the Clean Air Act Amendments of 1990 [Nov. 15, 1990], the Administrator of the Environmental Protection Agency and the Secretary of Transportation shall submit to Congress a report of the study conducted under this section. Following the completion of such study, any of the States may adopt or enforce any standard for emissions of oxides of nitrogen from test cells only after issuing a public notice stating whether such standards are in accordance with the findings of the study."

Section Referred to in Other Sections

This section is referred to in sections 7572, 7607, 7617 of this title; title 49 section 44714.

ENFORCEMENT OF STANDARDS

42 USC 7572

(a) Regulations to insure compliance with standards

The Secretary of Transportation, after consultation with the Administrator, shall prescribe regulations to insure compliance with all standards prescribed under section 7571 of this title by the Administrator. The regulations of the Secretary of Transportation shall include provisions making such standards applicable in the issuance, amendment, modification, suspension, or revocation of any certificate authorized by part A of subtitle VII of title 49 or the Department of Transportation Act. Such Secretary shall insure that all necessary inspections are accomplished, and,[1] may execute any power or duty vested in him by any other provision of law in the execution of all powers and duties vested in him under this section.

---

[1] So in original. The comma probably should not appear.

(b) Notice and appeal rights

In any action to amend, modify, suspend, or revoke a certificate in which violation of an emission standard prescribed under section 7571 of this title or of a regulation prescribed under subsection (a) of this section is at issue, the certificate holder shall have the same notice and appeal rights as are prescribed for such holders in part A of subtitle VII of title 49 or the Department of Transportation Act, except that in any appeal to the National Transportation Safety Board, the Board may amend, modify, or revoke the order of the Secretary of Transportation only if it finds no violation of such standard or regulation and that such amendment, modification, or revocation is consistent with safety in air transportation.

(July 14, 1955, ch. 360, title II, Sec. 232, as added Pub. L. 91-604, Sec. 11(a)(1), Dec. 31, 1970, 84 Stat. 1704.)

References in Text

The Department of Transportation Act, referred to in subsecs. (a) and (b), is Pub. L. 89-670, Oct. 15, 1966, 80 Stat. 931, as amended, which was classified principally to sections 1651 to 1660 of former Title 49, Transportation. The Act was repealed and the provisions thereof reenacted in Title 49, Transportation, by Pub. L. 97-449, Jan. 12, 1983, 96 Stat. 2413, and Pub. L. 103-272, July 5, 1994, 108 Stat. 745. The Act was also repealed by Pub. L. 104-287, Sec. 7(5), Oct. 11, 1996, 110 Stat. 3400. For disposition of sections of former Title 49, see Table at the beginning of Title 49.

Codification

In subsecs. (a) and (b), "part A of subtitle VII of title 49" substituted for "the Federal Aviation Act [49 App. U.S.C. 1301 et seq.]" and "the Federal Aviation Act of 1958 [49 App. U.S.C. 1301 et seq.]" on authority of Pub. L. 103-272, Sec. 6(b), July 5, 1994, 108 Stat. 1378, the first section of which enacted subtitles II, III, and V to X of Title 49, Transportation.

Section was formerly classified to section 1857f-10 of this title.

STATE STANDARDS AND CONTROLS

42 USC 7573

No State or political subdivision thereof may adopt or attempt to enforce any standard respecting emissions of any air pollutant from any aircraft or engine thereof unless such standard is identical to a standard applicable to such aircraft under this part.

(July 14, 1955, ch. 360, title II, Sec. 233, as added Pub. L. 91-604, Sec. 11(a)(1), Dec. 31, 1970, 84 Stat. 1704.)

Codification

Section was formerly classified to section 1857f-11 of this title.

Section Referred to in Other Sections

This section is referred to in section 7416 of this title.

DEFINITIONS

42 USC 7574

Terms used in this part (other than Administrator) shall have the same meaning as such terms have under section 40102(a) of title 49.

(July 14, 1955, ch. 360, title II, Sec. 234, as added Pub. L. 91-604, Sec. 11(a)(1), Dec. 31, 1970, 84 Stat. 1705.)

Codification

In text, "section 40102(a) of title 49" substituted for "section 101 of the Federal Aviation Act of 1958" on authority of Pub. L. 103-272, Sec. 6(b), July 5, 1994, 108 Stat. 1378, the first section of which enacted subtitles II, III, and V to X of Title 49, Transportation.

Section was formerly classified to section 1857f-12 of this title.

Part C—Clean Fuel Vehicles

DEFINITIONS

42 USC 7581

For purposes of this part—
(1) Terms defined in part A
The definitions applicable to part A under section 7550 of this title shall also apply for purposes of this part.
(2) Clean alternative fuel
The term "clean alternative fuel" means any fuel (including methanol, ethanol, or other alcohols (including any mixture thereof containing 85 percent or more by volume of such alcohol with gasoline or other fuels), reformulated gasoline, diesel, natural gas, liquefied petroleum gas, and hydrogen) or power source (including electricity) used in a clean-fuel vehicle that complies with the standards and requirements applicable to such vehicle under this subchapter when using such fuel or power source. In the case of any flexible fuel vehicle or dual fuel vehicle, the term "clean alternative fuel" means only a fuel with respect to which such vehicle was certified as a clean-fuel vehicle meeting the standards applicable to clean-fuel vehicles under section 7583(d)(2) of this title when operating on clean alternative fuel (or any CARB standards which replaces such standards pursuant to section 7583(e) of this title).
(3) NMOG
The term nonmethane organic gas ("NMOG") means the sum of nonoxygenated and oxygenated hydrocarbons contained in a gas sample, including, at a minimum, all oxygenated organic gases containing 5 or fewer carbon atoms (i.e., aldehydes, ketones, alcohols, ethers, etc.), and all known alkanes, alkenes, alkynes, and aromatics containing 12 or fewer carbon atoms. To demonstrate compliance with a NMOG standard, NMOG emissions shall be measured in accordance with the "California Non-Methane Organic Gas Test Procedures". In the case of vehicles using fuels other than base gasoline, the level of NMOG emissions shall be adjusted based on the reactivity of the emissions relative to vehicles using base gasoline.
(4) Base gasoline
The term "base gasoline" means gasoline which meets the following specifications:

SPECIFICATIONS OF BASE GASOLINE USED AS BASIS FOR REACTIVITY	
Readjustment:	
API gravity............	57.8
Sulfur, ppm...............	317
Color.......................	Purple
Benzene, vol. %.........	1.35
Reid vapor pressure.....	8.7
Drivability....................	1195
Antiknock index..........	87.3
Distillation, D-86 deg.F	
IBP.............	92
10%............................	126
50%............................	219
90%............................	327
EP..............................	414
Hydrocarbon Type, Vol. % FIA:	
Aromatics.................	30.9
Olefins......................	8.2
Saturates...................	60.9

The Administrator shall modify the definitions of NMOG, base gasoline, and the methods for making reactivity adjustments, to conform to the definitions and method used in California under the Low-Emission Vehicle and Clean Fuel Regulations of the California Air Resources Board, so long as the California definitions are, in the aggregate, at least as protective of public health and welfare as the definitions in this section.

(5) Covered fleet
The term "covered fleet" means 10 or more motor vehicles which are owned or operated by a single person. In determining the number of vehicles owned or operated by a single person for purposes of this paragraph, all motor vehicles owned or operated, leased or otherwise controlled by such person, by any person who controls such person, by any person controlled by such person, and by any person under common control with such person shall be treated as owned by such person. The term "covered fleet" shall not include motor vehicles held for lease or rental to the general public, motor vehicles held for sale by motor vehicle dealers (including demonstration vehicles), motor vehicles used for motor vehicle manufacturer product evaluations or tests, law enforcement and other emergency vehicles, or nonroad vehicles (including farm and construction vehicles).

(6) Covered fleet vehicle
The term "covered fleet vehicle" means only a motor vehicle which is—
   (i) in a vehicle class for which standards are applicable under this part; and
   (ii) in a covered fleet which is centrally fueled (or capable of being centrally fueled). No vehicle which under normal operations is garaged at a personal residence at night shall be considered to be a vehicle which is capable of being centrally fueled within the meaning of this paragraph.

(7) Clean-fuel vehicle
The term "clean-fuel vehicle" means a vehicle in a class or category of vehicles which has been certified to meet for any model year the clean-fuel vehicle standards applicable under this part for that model year to clean-fuel vehicles in that class or category.

(July 14, 1955, ch. 360, title II, Sec. 241, as added Pub. L. 101-549, title II, Sec. 229(a), Nov. 15, 1990, 104 Stat. 2511.)

REQUIREMENTS APPLICABLE TO CLEAN-FUEL VEHICLES

42 USC 7582

(a) Promulgation of standards
Not later than 24 months after November 15, 1990, the Administrator shall promulgate regulations under this part containing clean-fuel vehicle standards for the clean-fuel vehicles specified in this part.

(b) Other requirements
Clean-fuel vehicles of up to 8,500 gvwr subject to standards set forth in this part shall comply with all motor vehicle requirements of this subchapter (such as requirements relating to onboard diagnostics, evaporative emissions, etc.) which are applicable to conventional gasoline-fueled vehicles of the same category and model year, except as provided in section 7584 of this title with respect to administration and enforcement, and except to the extent that any such requirement is in conflict with the provisions of this part. Clean-fuel vehicles of 8,500 gvwr or greater subject to standards set forth in this part shall comply with all requirements of this subchapter which are applicable in the case of conventional gasoline-fueled or diesel fueled vehicles of the same category and model year, except as provided in section 7584 of this title with respect to administration and enforcement, and except to the extent that any such requirement is in conflict with the provisions of this part.

(c) In-use useful life and testing
(1) In the case of light-duty vehicles and light-duty trucks up to 6,000 lbs gvwr, the useful life for purposes of determining in-use compliance with the standards under section 7583 of this title shall be—
   (A) a period of 5 years or 50,000 miles (or the equivalent) whichever first occurs, in the case of standards applicable for purposes of certification at 50,000 miles; and
   (B) a period of 10 years or 100,000 miles (or the equivalent) whichever first occurs, in the case of standards applicable for purposes of certification at 100,000 miles, except that in-use testing shall not be done for a period beyond 7 years or 75,000 miles (or the equivalent) whichever first occurs.
(2) In the case of light-duty trucks of more than 6,000 lbs gvwr, the useful life for purposes of determining in-use compliance with the standards under section 7583 of this title shall be—

(A) a period of 5 years or 50,000 miles (or the equivalent) whichever first occurs in the case of standards applicable for purposes of certification at 50,000 miles; and
(B) a period of 11 years or 120,000 miles (or the equivalent) whichever first occurs in the case of standards applicable for purposes of certification at 120,000 miles, except that in-use testing shall not be done for a period beyond 7 years or 90,000 miles (or the equivalent) whichever first occurs.

(July 14, 1955, ch. 360, title II, Sec. 242, as added Pub. L. 101-549, title II, Sec. 229(a), Nov. 15, 1990, 104 Stat. 2513.)

Section Referred to in Other Sections

This section is referred to in sections 7583, 7587 of this title.

STANDARDS FOR LIGHT-DUTY CLEAN-FUEL VEHICLES

42 USC 7583

(a) Exhaust standards for light-duty vehicles and certain light-duty trucks
The standards set forth in this subsection shall apply in the case of clean-fuel vehicles which are light-duty trucks of up to 6,000 lbs. gross vehicle weight rating (gvwr) (but not including light-duty trucks of more than 3,750 lbs. loaded vehicle weight (lvw)) or light-duty vehicles:
(1) Phase I
Beginning with model year 1996, for the air pollutants specified in the following table, the clean-fuel vehicle standards under this section shall provide that vehicle exhaust emissions shall not exceed the levels specified in the following table:

PHASE I CLEAN FUEL VEHICLE EMISSION STANDARDS
FOR LIGHT-DUTY TRUCKS OF UP TO 3,750 LBS. LVW AND
UP TO 6,000 LBS. GVWR AND LIGHT-DUTY VEHICLES

Pollutant	NMOG	CO	NO_x	PM	HCHO (formaldehyde)
50,000 mile standard.........	0.125	3.4	0.4	......	0.015
100,000 mile standard........	0.156	4.2	0.6	0.08*	0.018

Standards are expressed in grams per mile (gpm).
*Standards for particulates (PM) shall apply only to diesel-fueled vehicles.

In the case of the 50,000 mile standards and the 100,000 mile standards, for purposes of certification, the applicable useful life shall be 50,000 miles or 100,000 miles, respectively.
(2) Phase II
Beginning with model year 2001, for air pollutants specified in the following table, the clean-fuel vehicle standards under this section shall provide that vehicle exhaust emissions shall not exceed the levels specified in the following table.

PHASE II CLEAN FUEL VEHICLE EMISSION STANDARDS
FOR LIGHT-DUTY TRUCKS OF UP TO 3,750 LBS. LVW AND
UP TO 6,000 LBS. GVWR AND LIGHT-DUTY VEHICLES

Pollutant	NMOG	CO	NO_x	PM*	HCHO (formaldehyde)
50,000 mile standard..........	0.075	3.4	0.2	.....	0.015
100,000 mile standard.........	0.090	4.2	0.3	0.08	0.018

Standards are expressed in grams per mile (gpm).
*Standards for particulates (PM) shall apply only to diesel-fueled vehicles.

In the case of the 50,000 mile standards and the 100,000 mile standards, for purposes of certification, the applicable useful life shall be 50,000 miles or 100,000 miles, respectively.
(b) Exhaust standards for light-duty trucks of more than 3,750 lbs. LVW and up to 5,750 lbs. LVW and up to 6,000 lbs. GVWR

The standards set forth in this paragraph shall apply in the case of clean-fuel vehicles which are light-duty trucks of more than 3,750 lbs. loaded vehicle weight (lvw) but not more than 5,750 lbs. lvw and not more than 6,000 lbs. gross weight rating (GVWR):

(1) Phase I

Beginning with model year 1996, for the air pollutants specified in the following table, the clean-fuel vehicle standards under this section shall provide that vehicle exhaust emissions shall not exceed the levels specified in the following table.

PHASE I CLEAN FUEL VEHICLE EMISSION STANDARDS FOR LIGHT-DUTY TRUCKS OF MORE THAN 3,750 LBS. AND UP TO 5,750 LBS. LVW AND UP TO 6,000 LBS. GVWR

Pollutant	NMOG	CO	NO_x	PM*	HCHO (formaldehyde)
50,000 mile standard..........	0.160	4.4	0.7	.....	0.018
100,000 mile standard.........	0.200	5.5	0.9	0.08	0.023

Standards are expressed in grams per mile (gpm).
*Standards for particulates (PM) shall apply only to diesel-fueled vehicles.

In the case of the 50,000 mile standards and the 100,000 mile standards, for purposes of certification, the applicable useful life shall be 50,000 miles or 100,000 miles, respectively.

(2) Phase II

Beginning with model year 2001, for the air pollutants specified in the following table, the clean-fuel vehicle standards under this section shall provide that vehicle exhaust emissions shall not exceed the levels specified in the following table.

PHASE II CLEAN FUEL VEHICLE EMISSION STANDARDS FOR LIGHT-DUTY TRUCKS OF MORE THAN 3,750 LBS. LVW AND UP TO 5,750 LBS. LVW AND UP TO 6,000 LBS. GVWR

Pollutant	NMOG	CO	NO_x	PM*	HCHO (formaldehyde)
50,000 mile standard..........	0.100	4.4	0.4	.....	0.018
100,000 mile standard.........	0.130	5.5	0.5	0.08	0.023

Standards are expressed in grams per mile (gpm).
*Standards for particulates (PM) shall apply only to diesel-fueled vehicles.

In the case of the 50,000 mile standards and the 100,000 mile standards, for purposes of certification, the applicable useful life shall be 50,000 miles or 100,000 miles, respectively.

(c) Exhaust standards for light-duty trucks greater than 6,000 lbs. GVWR

The standards set forth in this subsection shall apply in the case of clean-fuel vehicles which are light-duty trucks of more than 6,000 lbs. gross weight rating (GVWR) and less than or equal to 8,500 lbs. GVWR, beginning with model year 1998. For the air pollutants specified in the following table, the clean-fuel vehicle standards under this section shall provide that vehicle exhaust emissions of vehicles within the test weight categories specified in the following table shall not exceed the levels specified in such table.

CLEAN FUEL VEHICLE EMISSION STANDARDS FOR LIGHT DUTY TRUCKS GREATER THAN 6,000 LBS. GVWR
Test Weight Category: Up to 3,750 lbs. tw

Pollutant	NMOG	CO	NO_x	PM*	HCHO (formaldehyde)
50,000 mile standard........	0.125	3.4	0.4**	.....	0.015
120,000 mile standard.......	0.180	5.0	0.6	0.08	0.022

Test Weight Category: Above 3,750 but not above 5,750 lbs. tw

Pollutant	NMOG	CO	NO_x	PM*	HCHO (formaldehyde)
50,000 mile standard........	0.160	4.4	0.7**	.....	0.018
120,000 mile standard......	0.230	6.4	1.0	0.10	0.027

Test Weight Category: Above 5,750 tw but not above 8,500 lbs. gvwr

Pollutant	NMOG	CO	NO_x	PM*	HCHO (formaldehyde)
50,000 mile standard.......	0.195	5.0	1.1**	.....	0.022
120,000 mile standard......	0.280	7.3	1.5	0.12	0.032

Standards are expressed in grams per mile (gpm).
*Standards for particulates (PM) shall apply only to diesel-fueled vehicles.
**Standard not applicable to diesel-fueled vehicles.

> For the 50,000 mile standards and the 120,000 mile standards set forth in the table, the applicable useful life for purposes of certification shall be 50,000 miles or 120,000 miles, respectively.

(d) Flexible and dual-fuel vehicles
(1) In general
> The Administrator shall establish standards and requirements under this section for the model year 1996 and thereafter for vehicles weighing not more than 8,500 lbs. gvwr which are capable of operating on more than one fuel. Such standards shall require that such vehicles meet the exhaust standards applicable under subsection[1] (a), (b), and (c) of this section for CO, NO_x, and HCHO, and if appropriate, PM for single-fuel vehicles of the same vehicle category and model year.

(2) Exhaust NMOG standard for operation on clean alternative fuel
> In addition to standards for the pollutants referred to in paragraph (1), the standards established under paragraph (1) shall require that vehicle exhaust emissions of NMOG not exceed the levels (expressed in grams per mile) specified in the tables below when the vehicle is operated on the clean alternative fuel for which such vehicle is certified:

NMOG STANDARDS FOR FLEXIBLE- AND DUAL-FUELED VEHICLES WHEN OPERATING ON CLEAN ALTERNATIVE FUEL
LIGHT-DUTY TRUCKS UP TO 6,000 LBS. GVWR AND LIGHT-DUTY VEHICLES

Vehicle Type	Column A (50,000 mi.) Standard (gpm)	Column B (100,000 mi.) Standard (gpm)
Beginning MY 1996:		
LDT's (0-3,750 lbs. LVW) and light-duty vehicles.....	0.125	0.156
LDT's (3,751-5,750 lbs. LVW)....	0.160	0.20
Beginning MY 2001:		
LDT's (0-3,750 lbs. LVW) and light-duty vehicles.....	0.075	0.090
LDT's (3,751-5,750 lbs. LVW)....	0.100	0.130

> For standards under column A, for purposes of certification under section 7525 of this title, the applicable useful life shall be 50,000 miles.
> For standards under column B, for purposes of certification under section 7525 of this title, the applicable useful life shall be 100,000 miles.

---

[1] So in original. Probably should be "subsections".

Clean Air Act / 279

LIGHT-DUTY TRUCKS MORE THAN 6,000 LBS. GVWR

Vehicle Type	Column A (50,000 mi.) Standard	Column B (120,000 mi.) Standard
Beginning MY 1998:		
LDT's (0-3,750 lbs. TW)..........	0.125	0.180
LDT's (3,751-5,750 lbs. TW).....	0.160	0.230
LDT's (above 5,750 lbs. TW).....	0.195	0.280

For standards under column A, for purposes of certification under section 7525 of this title, the applicable useful life shall be 50,000 miles.

For standards under column B, for purposes of certification under section 7525 of this title, the applicable useful life shall be 120,000 miles.

(3) NMOG standard for operation on conventional fuel

In addition to the standards referred to in paragraph (1), the standards established under paragraph (1) shall require that vehicle exhaust emissions of NMOG not exceed the levels (expressed in grams per mile) specified in the tables below:

NMOG STANDARDS FOR FLEXIBLE- AND DUAL-FUELED VEHICLES WHEN OPERATING ON CONVENTIONAL FUEL
LIGHT-DUTY TRUCKS OF UP TO 6,000 LBS. GVWR AND LIGHT-DUTY VEHICLES

Vehicle Type	Column A (50,000 mi.) Standard (gpm)	Column B (100,000 mi.) Standard (gpm)
Beginning MY 1996:		
LDT's (0-3,750 lbs. LVW) and light-duty vehicles....	0.25	0.31
LDT's (3,751-5,750 lbs. LVW)....	0.32	0.40
Beginning MY 2001:		
LDT's (0-3,750 lbs. LVW) and light-duty vehicles....	0.125	0.156
LDT's (3,751-5,750 lbs. LVW)....	0.160	0.200

For standards under column A, for purposes of certification under section 7525 of this title, the applicable useful life shall be 50,000 miles.

For standards under column B, for purposes of certification under section 7525 of this title, the applicable useful life shall be 100,000 miles.

LIGHT-DUTY TRUCKS OF UP TO 6,000 LBS. GVWR

Vehicle Type	Column A (50,000 mi.) Standard	Column B (120,000 mi.) Standard
Beginning MY 1998:		
LDT's (0-3,750 lbs. TW).....	0.25	0.36
LDT's (3,751-5,750 lbs. TW).....	0.32	0.46
LDT's (above 5,750 lbs. TW).....	0.39	0.56

For standards under column A, for purposes of certification under section 7525 of this title, the applicable useful life shall be 50,000 miles.

For standards under column B, for purposes of certification under section 7525 of this title, the applicable useful life shall be 120,000 miles.

(e) Replacement by CARB standards

(1) Single set of CARB standards

If the State of California promulgates regulations establishing and implementing a single set of standards applicable in California pursuant to a waiver approved under section 7543 of this title to any category of vehicles referred to in subsection (a), (b), (c), or (d) of this section and such set of standards is, in the aggregate, at least as protective of public health and welfare as the otherwise applicable standards set forth in section 7582 of this title and subsection (a), (b), (c), or (d) of this section, such set of California standards shall apply to clean-fuel vehicles in such category in lieu of the standards otherwise applicable under section 7582 of this title and subsection (a), (b), (c), or (d) of this section, as the case may be.

(2) Multiple sets of CARB standards
If the State of California promulgates regulations establishing and implementing several different sets of standards applicable in California pursuant to a waiver approved under section 7543 of this title to any category of vehicles referred to in subsection (a), (b), (c), or (d) of this section and each of such sets of California standards is, in the aggregate, at least as protective of public health and welfare as the otherwise applicable standards set forth in section 7582 of this title and subsection (a), (b), (c), or (d) of this section, such standards shall be treated as "qualifying California standards" for purposes of this paragraph. Where more than one set of qualifying standards are established and administered by the State of California, the least stringent set of qualifying California standards shall apply to the clean-fuel vehicles concerned in lieu of the standards otherwise applicable to such vehicles under section 7582 of this title and this section.

(f) Less stringent CARB standards
If the Low-Emission Vehicle and Clean Fuels Regulations of the California Air Resources Board applicable to any category of vehicles referred to in subsection (a), (b), (c), or (d) of this section are modified after November 15, 1990, to provide an emissions standard which is less stringent than the otherwise applicable standard set forth in subsection (a), (b), (c), or (d) of this section, or if any effective date contained in such regulations is delayed, such modified standards or such delay (or both, as the case may be) shall apply, for an interim period, in lieu of the standard or effective date otherwise applicable under subsection (a), (b), (c), or (d) of this section to any vehicles covered by such modified standard or delayed effective date. The interim period shall be a period of not more than 2 model years from the effective date otherwise applicable under subsection (a), (b), (c), or (d) of this section. After such interim period, the otherwise applicable standard set forth in subsection (a), (b), (c), or (d) of this section shall take effect with respect to such vehicles (unless subsequently replaced under subsection (e) of this section).

(g) Not applicable to heavy-duty vehicles
Notwithstanding any provision of the Low-Emission Vehicle and Clean Fuels Regulations of the California Air Resources Board nothing in this section shall apply to heavy-duty engines in vehicles of more than 8,500 lbs. GVWR.

(July 14, 1955, ch. 360, title II, Sec. 243, as added Pub. L. 101-549, title II, Sec. 229(a), Nov. 15, 1990, 104 Stat. 2514.)

Section Referred to in Other Sections

This section is referred to in sections 7581, 7582, 7586, 7587 of this title.

ADMINISTRATION AND ENFORCEMENT AS PER CALIFORNIA STANDARDS

42 USC 7584

Where the numerical clean-fuel vehicle standards applicable under this part to vehicles of not more than 8,500 lbs. GVWR are the same as numerical emission standards applicable in California under the Low-Emission Vehicle and Clean Fuels Regulations of the California Air Resources Board ("CARB"), such standards shall be administered and enforced by the Administrator—
  (1) in the same manner and with the same flexibility as the State of California administers and enforces corresponding standards applicable under the Low-Emission Vehicle and Clean Fuels Regulations of the California Air Resources Board ("CARB"); and
  (2) subject to the same requirements, and utilizing the same interpretations and policy judgments, as are applicable in the case of such CARB standards, including, but not limited to, requirements regarding certification, production-line testing, and in-use compliance,

unless the Administrator determines (in promulgating the rules establishing the clean fuel vehicle program under this section) that any such administration and enforcement would not meet the criteria for a waiver under section 7543 of this title. Nothing in this section shall apply in the case of standards under section 7585 of this title for heavy-duty vehicles.

(July 14, 1955, ch. 360, title II, Sec. 244, as added Pub. L. 101-549, title II, Sec. 229(a), Nov. 15, 1990, 104 Stat. 2519.)

Section Referred to in Other Sections

This section is referred to in sections 7582, 7587 of this title.

STANDARDS FOR HEAVY-DUTY CLEAN-FUEL VEHICLES
(GVWR ABOVE 8,500 UP TO 26,000 LBS.)

42 USC 7585

(a) Model years after 1997; combined NO_x and NMHC standard
For classes or categories of heavy-duty vehicles or engines manufactured for the model year 1998 or thereafter and having a GVWR greater than 8,500 lbs. and up to 26,000 lbs. GVWR, the standards under this part for clean-fuel vehicles shall require that combined emissions of oxides of nitrogen (NO_x) and nonmethane hydrocarbons (NMHC) shall not exceed 3.15 grams per brake horsepower hour (equivalent to 50 percent of the combined emission standards applicable under section 7521 of this title for such air pollutants in the case of a conventional model year 1994 heavy-duty diesel-fueled vehicle or engine). No standard shall be promulgated as provided in this section for any heavy-duty vehicle of more than 26,000 lbs. GVWR.

(b) Revised standards that are less stringent
  (1) The Administrator may promulgate a revised less stringent standard for the vehicles or engines referred to in subsection (a) of this section if the Administrator determines that the 50 percent reduction required under subsection (a) of this section is not technologically feasible for clean diesel-fueled vehicles and engines, taking into account durability, costs, lead time, safety, and other relevant factors. To provide adequate lead time the Administrator shall make a determination with regard to the technological feasibility of such 50 percent reduction before December 31, 1993.
  (2) Any person may at any time petition the Administrator to make a determination under paragraph (1). The Administrator shall act on such a petition within 6 months after the petition is filed.
  (3) Any revised less stringent standards promulgated as provided in this subsection shall require at least a 30 percent reduction in lieu of the 50 percent reduction referred to in paragraph (1).

(July 14, 1955, ch. 360, title II, Sec. 245, as added Pub. L. 101-549, title II, Sec. 229(a), Nov. 15, 1990, 104 Stat. 2519.)

Section Referred to in Other Sections

This section is referred to in sections 7584, 7587, 7589 of this title.

CENTRALLY FUELED FLEETS

42 USC 7586

(a) Fleet program required for certain nonattainment areas
  (1) SIP revision
  Each State in which there is located all or part of a covered area (as defined in paragraph (2)) shall submit, within 42 months after November 15, 1990, a State implementation plan revision under section 7410 of this title and part D of subchapter I of this chapter to establish a clean-fuel vehicle program for fleets under this section.
  (2) Covered areas
  For purposes of this subsection, each of the following shall be a "covered area":
    (A) Ozone nonattainment areas
    Any ozone nonattainment area with a 1980 population of 250,000 or more classified under subpart 2 of part D of subchapter I of this chapter as Serious, Severe, or Extreme based on data for the calendar years 1987, 1988, and 1989. In determining the ozone nonattainment areas to be treated as covered areas pursuant to this subparagraph, the Administrator shall use the most recent interpretation methodology issued by the Administrator prior to November 15, 1990.

(B) Carbon monoxide nonattainment areas
Any carbon monoxide nonattainment area with a 1980 population of 250,000 or more and a carbon monoxide design value at or above 16.0 parts per million based on data for calendar years 1988 and 1989 (as calculated according to the most recent interpretation methodology issued prior to November 15, 1990, by the United States Environmental Protection Agency), excluding those carbon monoxide nonattainment areas in which mobile sources do not contribute significantly to carbon monoxide exceedances.

(3) Plan revisions for reclassified areas
In the case of ozone nonattainment areas reclassified as Serious, Severe, or Extreme under part D of subchapter I of this chapter with a 1980 population of 250,000 or more, the State shall submit a plan revision meeting the requirements of this subsection within 1 year after reclassification. Such plan revision shall implement the requirements applicable under this subsection at the time of reclassification and thereafter, except that the Administrator may adjust for a limited period the deadlines for compliance where compliance with such deadlines would be infeasible.

(4) Consultation; consideration of factors
Each State required to submit an implementation plan revision under this subsection shall develop such revision in consultation with fleet operators, vehicle manufacturers, fuel producers and distributors, motor vehicle fuel, and other interested parties, taking into consideration operational range, specialty uses, vehicle and fuel availability, costs, safety, resale values of vehicles and equipment and other relevant factors.

(b) Phase-in of requirements
The plan revision required under this section shall contain provisions requiring that at least a specified percentage of all new covered fleet vehicles in model year 1998 and thereafter purchased by each covered fleet operator in each covered area shall be clean-fuel vehicles and shall use clean alternative fuels when operating in the covered area. For the applicable model years (MY) specified in the following table and thereafter, the specified percentage shall be as provided in the table for the vehicle types set forth in the table:

CLEAN FUEL VEHICLE PHASE-IN REQUIREMENTS FOR FLEETS			
Vehicle Type	MY1998	MY1999	MY2000
Light-duty trucks up to 6,000 lbs. GVWR and light-duty vehicles...	30%	50%	70%
Heavy-duty trucks above 8,500 lbs. GVWR......	50%	50%	50%

The term MY refers to model year.

(c) Accelerated standard for light-duty trucks up to 6,000 lbs. GVWR and light-duty vehicles
Notwithstanding the model years for which clean-fuel vehicle standards are applicable as provided in section 7583 of this title, for purposes of this section, light duty[1] trucks of up to 6,000 lbs. GVWR and light-duty vehicles manufactured in model years 1998 through model year 2000 shall be treated as clean-fuel vehicles only if such vehicles comply with the standards applicable under section 7583 of this title for vehicles in the same class for the model year 2001. The requirements of subsection (b) of this section shall take effect on the earlier of the following:

(1) The first model year after model year 1997 in which new light-duty trucks up to 6,000 lbs. GVWR and light-duty vehicles which comply with the model year 2001 standards under section 7583 of this title are offered for sale in California.

(2) Model year 2001.
Whenever the effective date of subsection (b) of this section is delayed pursuant to paragraph (1) of this subsection, the phase-in schedule under subsection (b) of this section shall be modified to commence with the model year referred to in paragraph (1) in lieu of model year 1998.

---

[1] So in original. Probably should be "light-duty".

(d) Choice of vehicles and fuel

The plan revision under this subsection shall provide that the choice of clean-fuel vehicles and clean alternative fuels shall be made by the covered fleet operator subject to the requirements of this subsection.

(e) Availability of clean alternative fuel

The plan revision shall require fuel providers to make clean alternative fuel available to covered fleet operators at locations at which covered fleet vehicles are centrally fueled.

(f) Credits

(1) Issuance of credits

The State plan revision required under this section shall provide for the issuance by the State of appropriate credits to a fleet operator for any of the following (or any combination thereof):

(A) The purchase of more clean-fuel vehicles than required under this section.

(B) The purchase of clean fuel[2] vehicles which meet more stringent standards established by the Administrator pursuant to paragraph (4).

(C) The purchase of vehicles in categories which are not covered by this section but which meet standards established for such vehicles under paragraph (4).

(2) Use of credits; limitations based on weight classes

(A) Use of credits

Credits under this subsection may be used by the person holding such credits to demonstrate compliance with this section or may be traded or sold for use by any other person to demonstrate compliance with other requirements applicable under this section in the same nonattainment area. Credits obtained at any time may be held or banked for use at any later time, and when so used, such credits shall maintain the same value as if used at an earlier date.

(B) Limitations based on weight classes

Credits issued with respect to the purchase of vehicles of up to 8,500 lbs. GVWR may not be used to demonstrate compliance by any person with the requirements applicable under this subsection to vehicles of more than 8,500 lbs. GVWR. Credits issued with respect to the purchase of vehicles of more than 8,500 lbs. GVWR may not be used to demonstrate compliance by any person with the requirements applicable under this subsection to vehicles weighing up to 8,500 lbs. GVWR.

(C) Weighting

Credits issued for purchase of a clean fuel[2] vehicle under this subsection shall be adjusted with appropriate weighting to reflect the level of emission reduction achieved by the vehicle.

(3) Regulations and administration

Within 12 months after November 15, 1990, the Administrator shall promulgate regulations for such credit program. The State shall administer the credit program established under this subsection.

(4) Standards for issuing credits for cleaner vehicles

Solely for purposes of issuing credits under paragraph (1)(B), the Administrator shall establish under this paragraph standards for Ultra-Low Emission Vehicles ("ULEV"s) and Zero Emissions Vehicles ("ZEV"s) which shall be more stringent than those otherwise applicable to clean-fuel vehicles under this part. The Administrator shall certify clean fuel[1] vehicles as complying with such more stringent standards, and administer and enforce such more stringent standards, in the same manner as in the case of the otherwise applicable clean-fuel vehicle standards established under this section. The standards established by the Administrator under this paragraph for vehicles under 8,500 lbs. GVWR or greater shall conform as closely as possible to standards which are established by the State of California for ULEV and ZEV vehicles in the same class. For vehicles of 8,500 lbs. GVWR or more, the Administrator shall promulgate comparable standards for purposes of this subsection.

(5) Early fleet credits

The State plan revision shall provide credits under this subsection to fleet operators that purchase vehicles certified to meet clean-fuel vehicle standards under this part during any

---

[2] So in original. Probably should be "clean-fuel".

period after approval of the plan revision and prior to the effective date of the fleet program under this section.

(g) Availability to public

At any facility owned or operated by a department, agency, or instrumentality of the United States where vehicles subject to this subsection are supplied with clean alternative fuel, such fuel shall be offered for sale to the public for use in other vehicles during reasonable business times and subject to national security concerns, unless such fuel is commercially available for vehicles in the vicinity of such Federal facilities.

(h) Transportation control measures

The Administrator shall by rule, within 1 year after November 15, 1990, ensure that certain transportation control measures including time-of-day or day-of-week restrictions, and other similar measures that restrict vehicle usage, do not apply to any clean-fuel vehicle that meets the requirements of this section. This subsection shall apply notwithstanding subchapter I of this chapter.

(July 14, 1955, ch. 360, title II, Sec. 246, as added Pub. L. 101-549, title II, Sec. 229(a), Nov. 15, 1990, 104 Stat. 2520.)

Section Referred to in Other Sections

This section is referred to in sections 7512a, 7587, 7589 of this title.

VEHICLE CONVERSIONS

42 USC 7587

a) Conversion of existing and new conventional vehicles to clean-fuel vehicles

The requirements of section 7586 of this title may be met through the conversion of existing or new gasoline or diesel-powered vehicles to clean-fuel vehicles which comply with the applicable requirements of that section. For purposes of such provisions the conversion of a vehicle to clean fuel[1] vehicle shall be treated as the purchase of a clean fuel[1] vehicle. Nothing in this part shall be construed to provide that any covered fleet operator subject to fleet vehicle purchase requirements under section 7586 of this title shall be required to convert existing or new gasoline or diesel-powered vehicles to clean-fuel vehicles or to purchase converted vehicles.

(b) Regulations

The Administrator shall, within 24 months after November 15, 1990, consistent with the requirements of this subchapter applicable to new vehicles, promulgate regulations governing conversions of conventional vehicles to clean-fuel vehicles. Such regulations shall establish criteria for such conversions which will ensure that a converted vehicle will comply with the standards applicable under this part to clean-fuel vehicles. Such regulations shall provide for the application to such conversions of the same provisions of this subchapter (including provisions relating to administration enforcement) as are applicable to standards under section[2] 7582, 7583, 7584, and 7585 of this title, except that in the case of conversions the Administrator may modify the applicable regulations implementing such provisions as the Administrator deems necessary to implement this part.

(c) Enforcement

Any person who converts conventional vehicles to clean fuel[1] vehicles pursuant to subsection (b) of this section, shall be considered a manufacturer for purposes of sections 7525 and 7541 of this title and related enforcement provisions. Nothing in the preceding sentence shall require a person who performs such conversions to warrant any part or operation of a vehicle other than as required under this part. Nothing in this paragraph shall limit the applicability of any other warranty to unrelated parts or operations.

(d) Tampering

The conversion from a vehicle capable of operating on gasoline or diesel fuel only to a clean-fuel vehicle shall not be considered a violation of section 7522(a)(3) of this title if such conversion complies with the regulations promulgated under subsection (b) of this section.

---

[1]So in original. Probably should be "clean-fuel".
[2]So in original. Probably should be "sections".

(e) Safety
The Secretary of Transportation shall, if necessary, promulgate rules under applicable motor vehicle laws regarding the safety of vehicles converted from existing and new vehicles to clean-fuel vehicles.

(July 14, 1955, ch. 360, title II, Sec. 247, as added Pub. L. 101-549, title II, Sec. 229(a), Nov. 15, 1990, 104 Stat. 2523.)

Section Referred to in Other Sections

This section is referred to in sections 13236, 13257 of this title.

FEDERAL AGENCY FLEETS

42 USC 7588

(a) Additional provisions applicable
The provisions of this section shall apply, in addition to the other provisions of this part, in the case of covered fleet vehicles owned or operated by an agency, department, or instrumentality of the United States, except as otherwise provided in subsection (e) of this section.

(b) Cost of vehicles to Federal agency
Notwithstanding the provisions of section 491 of title 40, the Administrator of General Services shall not include the incremental costs of clean-fuel vehicles in the amount to be reimbursed by Federal agencies if the Administrator of General Services determines that appropriations provided pursuant to this paragraph are sufficient to provide for the incremental cost of such vehicles over the cost of comparable conventional vehicles.

(c) Limitations on appropriations
Funds appropriated pursuant to the authorization under this paragraph shall be applicable only—
   (1) to the portion of the cost of acquisition, maintenance and operation of vehicles acquired under this subparagraph which exceeds the cost of acquisition, maintenance and operation of comparable conventional vehicles;
   (2) to the portion of the costs of fuel storage and dispensing equipment attributable to such vehicles which exceeds the costs for such purposes required for conventional vehicles; and
   (3) to the portion of the costs of acquisition of clean-fuel vehicles which represents a reduction in revenue from the disposal of such vehicles as compared to revenue resulting from the disposal of comparable conventional vehicles.

(d) Vehicle costs
The incremental cost of vehicles acquired under this part over the cost of comparable conventional vehicles shall not be applied to any calculation with respect to a limitation under law on the maximum cost of individual vehicles which may be required by the United States.

(e) Exemptions
The requirements of this part shall not apply to vehicles with respect to which the Secretary of Defense has certified to the Administrator that an exemption is needed based on national security consideration.

(f) Acquisition requirement
Federal agencies, to the extent practicable, shall obtain clean-fuel vehicles from original equipment manufacturers.

(g) Authorization of appropriations
There are authorized to be appropriated such sums as may be required to carry out the provisions of this section: Provided, That such sums as are appropriated for the Administrator of General Services pursuant to the authorization under this section shall be added to the General Supply Fund established in section 756 of title 40.

(July 14, 1955, ch. 360, title II, Sec. 248, as added Pub. L. 101-549, title II, Sec. 229(a), Nov. 15, 1990, 104 Stat. 2524.)

CALIFORNIA PILOT TEST PROGRAM

42 USC 7589

(a) Establishment
The Administrator shall establish a pilot program in the State of California to demonstrate the effectiveness of clean-fuel vehicles in controlling air pollution in ozone nonattainment areas.

(b) Applicability
The provisions of this section shall only apply to light-duty trucks and light-duty vehicles, and such provisions shall apply only in the State of California, except as provided in subsection (f) of this section.

(c) Program requirements
Not later than 24 months after November 15, 1990, the Administrator shall promulgate regulations establishing requirements under this section applicable in the State of California. The regulations shall provide the following:
(1) Clean-fuel vehicles
Clean-fuel vehicles shall be produced, sold, and distributed (in accordance with normal business practices and applicable franchise agreements) to ultimate purchasers in California (including owners of covered fleets referred to in section 7586 of this title) in numbers that meet or exceed the following schedule:

Model Years	Number of Clean-Fuel Vehicles
1996, 1997, 1998....................	150,000 vehicles
1999 and thereafter................	300,000 vehicles

(2) Clean alternative fuels
(A) Within 2 years after November 15, 1990, the State of California shall submit a revision of the applicable implementation plan under part D of subchapter I of this chapter and section 7410 of this title containing a clean fuel plan that requires that clean alternative fuels on which the clean-fuel vehicles required under this paragraph can operate shall be produced and distributed by fuel suppliers and made available in California. At a minimum, sufficient clean alternative fuels shall be produced, distributed and made available to assure that all clean-fuel vehicles required under this section can operate, to the maximum extent practicable, exclusively on such fuels in California. The State shall require that clean alternative fuels be made available and offered for sale at an adequate number of locations with sufficient geographic distribution to ensure convenient refueling with clean alternative fuels, considering the number of, and type of, such vehicles sold and the geographic distribution of such vehicles within the State. The State shall determine the clean alternative fuels to be produced, distributed, and made available based on motor vehicle manufacturers' projections of future sales of such vehicles and consultations with the affected local governments and fuel suppliers.
(B) The State may by regulation grant persons subject to the requirements prescribed under this paragraph an appropriate amount of credits for exceeding such requirements, and any person granted credits may transfer some or all of the credits for use by one or more persons in demonstrating compliance with such requirements. The State may make the credits available for use after consideration of enforceability, environmental, and economic factors and upon such terms and conditions as the State finds appropriate.
(C) The State may also by regulation establish specifications for any clean alternative fuel produced and made available under this paragraph as the State finds necessary to reduce or eliminate an unreasonable risk to public health, welfare, or safety associated with its use or to ensure acceptable vehicle maintenance and performance characteristics.
(D) If a retail gasoline dispensing facility would have to remove or replace one or more motor vehicle fuel underground storage tanks and accompanying piping in order to comply with the provisions of this section, and it had removed and replaced such tank or tanks and accompanying piping in order to comply with subtitle I of the Solid Waste Disposal Act [42 U.S.C. 6991 et seq.] prior to November 15, 1990, it shall not be

required to comply with this subsection until a period of 7 years has passed from the date of the removal and replacement of such tank or tanks.
- (E) Nothing in this section authorizes any State other than California to adopt provisions regarding clean alternative fuels.
- (F) If the State of California fails to adopt a clean fuel program that meets the requirements of this paragraph, the Administrator shall, within 4 years after November 15, 1990, establish a clean fuel program for the State of California under this paragraph and section 7410(c) of this title that meets the requirements of this paragraph.

(d) Credits for motor vehicle manufacturers
   (1) The Administrator may (by regulation) grant a motor vehicle manufacturer an appropriate amount of credits toward fulfillment of such manufacturer's share of the requirements of subsection (c)(1) of this section for any of the following (or any combination thereof):
      (A) The sale of more clean-fuel vehicles than required under subsection (c)(1) of this section.
      (B) The sale of clean fuel[1] vehicles which meet standards established by the Administrator as provided in paragraph (3) which are more stringent than the clean-fuel vehicle standards otherwise applicable to such clean-fuel vehicle. A manufacturer granted credits under this paragraph may transfer some or all of the credits for use by one or more other manufacturers in demonstrating compliance with the requirements prescribed under this paragraph. The Administrator may make the credits available for use after consideration of enforceability, environmental, and economic factors and upon such terms and conditions as he finds appropriate. The Administrator shall grant credits in accordance with this paragraph, notwithstanding any requirements of State law or any credits granted with respect to the same vehicles under any State law, rule, or regulation.
   (2) Regulations and administration.—The Administrator shall administer the credit program established under this subsection. Within 12 months after November 15, 1990, the Administrator shall promulgate regulations for such credit program.
   (3) Standards for issuing credits for cleaner vehicles.—The more stringent standards and other requirements (including requirements relating to the weighting of credits) established by the Administrator for purposes of the credit program under 7585(e)[2] of this title (relating to credits for clean fuel[1] vehicles in the fleets program) shall also apply for purposes of the credit program under this paragraph.

(e) Program evaluation
   (1) Not later than June 30, 1994 and again in connection with the report under paragraph (2), the Administrator shall provide a report to the Congress on the status of the California Air Resources Board Low-Emissions Vehicles and Clean Fuels Program. Such report shall examine the capability, from a technological standpoint, of motor vehicle manufacturers and motor vehicle fuel suppliers to comply with the requirements of such program and with the requirements of the California Pilot Program under this section.
   (2) Not later than June 30, 1998, the Administrator shall complete and submit a report to Congress on the effectiveness of the California pilot program under this section. The report shall evaluate the level of emission reductions achieved under the program, the costs of the program, the advantages and disadvantages of extending the program to other nonattainment areas, and desirability of continuing or expanding the program in California.
   (3) The program under this section cannot be extended or terminated by the Administrator except by Act of Congress enacted after November 15, 1990. Section 7507 of this title does not apply to the program under this section.

(f) Voluntary opt-in for other States
   (1) EPA regulations
      Not later than 2 years after November 15, 1990, the Administrator shall promulgate regulations establishing a voluntary opt-in program under this subsection pursuant to which—
      (A) clean-fuel vehicles which are required to be produced, sold, and distributed in the State of California under this section, and

---

[1] So in original. Probably should be "clean-fuel".
[2] So in original. Probably should be "section 7586(f)".

288 / Environmental Statutes

(B) clean alternative fuels required to be produced and distributed under this section by may also be sold and used in other States which submit plan revisions under paragraph (2).

(2) Plan revisions

Any State in which there is located all or part of an ozone nonattainment area classified under subpart D of subchapter I of this chapter as Serious, Severe, or Extreme may submit a revision of the applicable implementation plan under part D of subchapter I of this chapter and section 7410 of this title to provide incentives for the sale or use in such an area or State of clean-fuel vehicles which are required to be produced, sold, and distributed in the State of California, and for the use in such an area or State of clean alternative fuels required to be produced and distributed by fuel suppliers and made available in California. Such plan provisions shall not take effect until 1 year after the State has provided notice of such provisions to motor vehicle manufacturers and to fuel suppliers.

(3) Incentives

The incentives referred to in paragraph (2) may include any or all of the following:

(A) A State registration fee on new motor vehicles registered in the State which are not clean-fuel vehicles in the amount of at least 1 percent of the cost of the vehicle. The proceeds of such fee shall be used to provide financial incentives to purchasers of clean-fuel vehicles and to vehicle dealers who sell high volumes or high percentages of clean-fuel vehicles and to defray the administrative costs of the incentive program.

(B) Provisions to exempt clean-fuel vehicles from high occupancy vehicle or trip reduction requirements.

(C) Provisions to provide preference in the use of existing parking spaces for clean-fuel vehicles.

The incentives under this paragraph shall not apply in the case of covered fleet vehicles.

(4) No sales or production mandate

The regulations and plan revisions under paragraphs (1) and (2) shall not include any production or sales mandate for clean-fuel vehicles or clean alternative fuels. Such regulations and plan revisions shall also provide that vehicle manufacturers and fuel suppliers may not be subject to penalties or sanctions for failing to produce or sell clean-fuel vehicles or clean alternative fuels.

(July 14, 1955, ch. 360, title II, Sec. 249, as added Pub. L. 101-549, title II, Sec. 229(a), Nov. 15, 1990, 104 Stat. 2525.)

References in Text

The Solid Waste Disposal Act, referred to in subsec. (c)(2)(D), is title II of Pub. L. 89-272, Oct. 20, 1965, 79 Stat. 997, as amended generally by Pub. L. 94-580, Sec. 2, Oct. 21, 1976, 90 Stat. 2795. Subtitle I of the Act is classified generally to subchapter IX (Sec. 6991 et seq.) of chapter 82 of this title. For complete classification of this Act to the Code, see Short Title note set out under section 6901 of this title and Tables.

November 15, 1990, referred to in subsec. (e)(3), was in the original "the date of the Clean Air Act Amendments of 1990", which was translated as meaning the date of enactment of Pub. L. 101-549, which enacted this section, to reflect the probable intent of Congress.

GENERAL PROVISIONS

42 USC 7590

(a) State refueling facilities

If any State adopts enforceable provisions in an implementation plan applicable to a nonattainment area which provides that existing State refueling facilities will be made available to the public for the purchase of clean alternative fuels or that State-operated refueling facilities for such fuels will be constructed and operated by the State and made available to the public at reasonable times, taking into consideration safety, costs, and other relevant factors, in approving such plan under section 7410 of this title and part D,[1] the Administrator may credit a State with the emission reductions for purposes of part D[1] attributable to such actions.

---

[1] So in original. Probably should be "part D of subchapter I of this chapter".

(b) No production mandate

The Administrator shall have no authority under this part to mandate the production of clean-fuel vehicles except as provided in the California pilot test program or to specify as applicable the models, lines, or types of, or marketing or price practices, policies, or strategies for, vehicles subject to this part. Nothing in this part shall be construed to give the Administrator authority to mandate marketing or pricing practices, policies, or strategies for fuels.

(c) Tank and fuel system safety

The Secretary of Transportation shall, in accordance with chapter 301 of title 49, promulgate applicable regulations regarding the safety and use of fuel storage cylinders and fuel systems, including appropriate testing and retesting, in conversions of motor vehicles.

(d) Consultation with Department of Energy and Department of Transportation

The Administrator shall coordinate with the Secretaries of the Department of Energy and the Department of Transportation in carrying out the Administrator's duties under this part.

(July 14, 1955, ch. 360, title II, Sec. 250, as added Pub. L. 101-549, title II, Sec. 229(a), Nov. 15, 1990, 104 Stat. 2528.)

Codification

In subsec. (c), "chapter 301 of title 49" substituted for "the National Motor Vehicle Traffic Safety Act of 1966 [15 U.S.C. 1381 et seq.]", meaning "the National Traffic and Motor Vehicle Safety Act of 1966 [15 U.S.C. 1381 et seq.]", on authority of Pub. L. 103-272, Sec. 6(b), July 5, 1994, 108 Stat. 1378, the first section of which enacted subtitles II, III, and V to X of Title 49, Transportation.

SUBCHAPTER III—GENERAL PROVISIONS

ADMINISTRATION

42 USC 7601

(a) Regulations; delegation of powers and duties; regional officers and employees
   (1) The Administrator is authorized to prescribe such regulations as are necessary to carry out his functions under this chapter. The Administrator may delegate to any officer or employee of the Environmental Protection Agency such of his powers and duties under this chapter, except the making of regulations subject to section 7607(d) of this title, as he may deem necessary or expedient.
   (2) Not later than one year after August 7, 1977, the Administrator shall promulgate regulations establishing general applicable procedures and policies for regional officers and employees (including the Regional Administrator) to follow in carrying out a delegation under paragraph (1), if any. Such regulations shall be designed—
       (A) to assure fairness and uniformity in the criteria, procedures, and policies applied by the various regions in implementing and enforcing the chapter;
       (B) to assure at least an adequate quality audit of each State's performance and adherence to the requirements of this chapter in implementing and enforcing the chapter, particularly in the review of new sources and in enforcement of the chapter; and
       (C) to provide a mechanism for identifying and standardizing inconsistent or varying criteria, procedures, and policies being employed by such officers and employees in implementing and enforcing the chapter.
(b) Detail of Environmental Protection Agency personnel to air pollution control agencies
   Upon the request of an air pollution control agency, personnel of the Environmental Protection Agency may be detailed to such agency for the purpose of carrying out the provisions of this chapter.
(c) Payments under grants; installments; advances or reimbursements
   Payments under grants made under this chapter may be made in installments, and in advance or by way of reimbursement, as may be determined by the Administrator.
(d) Tribal authority
   (1) Subject to the provisions of paragraph (2), the Administrator—
       (A) is authorized to treat Indian tribes as States under this chapter, except for purposes of the requirement that makes available for application by each State no less than one-half of 1 percent of annual appropriations under section 7405 of this title; and
       (B) may provide any such Indian tribe grant and contract assistance to carry out functions provided by this chapter.
   (2) The Administrator shall promulgate regulations within 18 months after November 15, 1990, specifying those provisions of this chapter for which it is appropriate to treat Indian tribes as States. Such treatment shall be authorized only if—
       (A) the Indian tribe has a governing body carrying out substantial governmental duties and powers;
       (B) the functions to be exercised by the Indian tribe pertain to the management and protection of air resources within the exterior boundaries of the reservation or other areas within the tribe's jurisdiction; and
       (C) the Indian tribe is reasonably expected to be capable, in the judgment of the Administrator, of carrying out the functions to be exercised in a manner consistent with the terms and purposes of this chapter and all applicable regulations.
   (3) The Administrator may promulgate regulations which establish the elements of tribal implementation plans and procedures for approval or disapproval of tribal implementation plans and portions thereof.
   (4) In any case in which the Administrator determines that the treatment of Indian tribes as identical to States is inappropriate or administratively infeasible, the Administrator may provide, by regulation, other means by which the Administrator will directly administer such provisions so as to achieve the appropriate purpose.

(5) Until such time as the Administrator promulgates regulations pursuant to this subsection, the Administrator may continue to provide financial assistance to eligible Indian tribes under section 7405 of this title.

(July 14, 1955, ch. 360, title III, Sec. 301, formerly Sec. 8, as added Pub. L. 88-206, Sec. 1, Dec. 17, 1963, 77 Stat. 400, renumbered Pub. L. 89-272, title I, Sec. 101(4), Oct. 20, 1965, 79 Stat. 992; amended Pub. L. 90-148, Sec. 2, Nov. 21, 1967, 81 Stat. 504; Pub. L. 91-604, Secs. 3(b)(2), 15(c)(2), Dec. 31, 1970, 84 Stat. 1677, 1713; Pub. L. 95-95, title III, Sec. 305(e), Aug. 7, 1977, 91 Stat. 776; Pub. L. 101-549, title I, Secs. 107(d), 108(i), Nov. 15, 1990, 104 Stat. 2464, 2467.)

Codification

Section was formerly classified to section 1857g of this title.

Amendments

1990—Subsec. (a)(1). Pub. L. 101-549, Sec. 108(i), inserted "subject to section 7607(d) of this title" after "regulations".

Subsec. (d). Pub. L. 101-549, Sec. 107(d), added subsec. (d).

1977—Subsec. (a). Pub. L. 95-95 designated existing provisions as par. (1) and added par. (2).

1970—Subsec. (a). Pub. L. 91-604, Sec. 15(c)(2), substituted "Administrator" for "Secretary" and "Environmental Protection Agency" for "Department of Health, Education, and Welfare".

Subsec. (b). Pub. L. 91-604, Sec. 3(b)(2), substituted "Environmental Protection Agency" for "Public Health Service" and struck out provisions covering the payment of salaries and allowances.

Subsec. (c). Pub. L. 91-604, Sec. 15(c)(2), substituted "Administrator" for "Secretary".

1967—Pub. L. 90-148 reenacted section without change.

Effective Date of 1977 Amendment

Amendment by Pub. L. 95-95 effective Aug. 7, 1977, except as otherwise expressly provided, see section 406(d) of Pub. L. 95-95, set out as a note under section 7401 of this title.

Modification or Rescission of Rules, Regulations, Orders, Determinations, Contracts, Certifications, Authorizations, Delegations, and Other Actions

All rules, regulations, orders, determinations, contracts, certifications, authorizations, delegations, or other actions duly issued, made, or taken by or pursuant to act July 14, 1955, the Clean Air Act, as in effect immediately prior to the date of enactment of Pub. L. 95-95 [Aug. 7, 1977] to continue in full force and effect until modified or rescinded in accordance with act July 14, 1955, as amended by Pub. L. 95-95 [this chapter], see section 406(b) of Pub. L. 95-95, set out as an Effective Date of 1977 Amendment note under section 7401 of this title.

Disadvantaged Business Concerns; Use of Quotas Prohibited

Title X of Pub. L. 101-549 provided that:

"SEC. 1001. DISADVANTAGED BUSINESS CONCERNS.

(a) In General.—In providing for any research relating to the requirements of the amendments made by the Clean Air Act Amendments of 1990 [Pub. L. 101-549, see Tables for classification] which uses funds of the Environmental Protection Agency, the Administrator of the Environmental Protection Agency shall, to the extent practicable, require that not less than 10 percent of total Federal funding for such research will be made available to disadvantaged business concerns.

(b) Definition.—
 (1) (A) For purposes of subsection (a), the term 'disadvantaged business concern' means a concern—
  (i) which is at least 51 percent owned by one or more socially and economically disadvantaged individuals or, in the case of a publicly traded company, at least 51 percent of the stock of which is owned by one or more socially and economically disadvantaged individuals; and
  (ii) the management and daily business operations of which are controlled by such individuals.
 (B) (i) A for-profit business concern is presumed to be a disadvantaged business concern for purposes of subsection (a) if it is at least 51 percent owned by, or in the case of

a concern which is a publicly traded company at least 51 percent of the stock of the company is owned by, one or more individuals who are members of the following groups:
- (I) Black Americans.
- (II) Hispanic Americans.
- (III) Native Americans.
- (IV) Asian Americans.
- (V) Women.
- (VI) Disabled Americans.

(ii) The presumption established by clause (i) may be rebutted with respect to a particular business concern if it is reasonably established that the individual or individuals referred to in that clause with respect to that business concern are not experiencing impediments to establishing or developing such concern as a result of the individual's identification as a member of a group specified in that clause.

(C) The following institutions are presumed to be disadvantaged business concerns for purposes of subsection (a):
- (i) Historically black colleges and universities, and colleges and universities having a student body in which 40 percent of the students are Hispanic.
- (ii) Minority institutions (as that term is defined by the Secretary of Education pursuant to the General Education Provision Act (20 U.S.C. 1221 et seq.)).
- (iii) Private and voluntary organizations controlled by individuals who are socially and economically disadvantaged.

(D) A joint venture may be considered to be a disadvantaged business concern under subsection (a), notwithstanding the size of such joint venture, if—
- (i) a party to the joint venture is a disadvantaged business concern; and
- (ii) that party owns at least 51 percent of the joint venture.

A person who is not an economically disadvantaged individual or a disadvantaged business concern, as a party to a joint venture, may not be a party to more than 2 awarded contracts in a fiscal year solely by reason of this subparagraph.

(E) Nothing in this paragraph shall prohibit any member of a racial or ethnic group that is not listed in subparagraph (B)(i) from establishing that they have been impeded in establishing or developing a business concern as a result of racial or ethnic discrimination.

SEC. 1002. USE OF QUOTAS PROHIBITED.—

Nothing in this title shall permit or require the use of quotas or a requirement that has the effect of a quota in determining eligibility under section 1001."

Section Referred to in Other Sections

This section is referred to in sections 7405, 7410, 7602 of this title.

DEFINITIONS

42 USC 7602

When used in this chapter—

(a) The term "Administrator" means the Administrator of the Environmental Protection Agency.

(b) The term "air pollution control agency" means any of the following:
- (1) A single State agency designated by the Governor of that State as the official State air pollution control agency for purposes of this chapter.
- (2) An agency established by two or more States and having substantial powers or duties pertaining to the prevention and control of air pollution.
- (3) A city, county, or other local government health authority, or, in the case of any city, county, or other local government in which there is an agency other than the health authority charged with responsibility for enforcing ordinances or laws relating to the prevention and control of air pollution, such other agency.
- (4) An agency of two or more municipalities located in the same State or in different States and having substantial powers or duties pertaining to the prevention and control of air pollution.

(5) An agency of an Indian tribe.
(c) The term "interstate air pollution control agency" means—
  (1) an air pollution control agency established by two or more States, or
  (2) an air pollution control agency of two or more municipalities located in different States.
(d) The term "State" means a State, the District of Columbia, the Commonwealth of Puerto Rico, the Virgin Islands, Guam, and American Samoa and includes the Commonwealth of the Northern Mariana Islands.
(e) The term "person" includes an individual, corporation, partnership, association, State, municipality, political subdivision of a State, and any agency, department, or instrumentality of the United States and any officer, agent, or employee thereof.
(f) The term "municipality" means a city, town, borough, county, parish, district, or other public body created by or pursuant to State law.
(g) The term "air pollutant" means any air pollution agent or combination of such agents, including any physical, chemical, biological, radioactive (including source material, special nuclear material, and byproduct material) substance or matter which is emitted into or otherwise enters the ambient air. Such term includes any precursors to the formation of any air pollutant, to the extent the Administrator has identified such precursor or precursors for the particular purpose for which the term "air pollutant" is used.
(h) All language referring to effects on welfare includes, but is not limited to, effects on soils, water, crops, vegetation, manmade materials, animals, wildlife, weather, visibility, and climate, damage to and deterioration of property, and hazards to transportation, as well as effects on economic values and on personal comfort and well-being, whether caused by transformation, conversion, or combination with other air pollutants.
(i) The term "Federal land manager" means, with respect to any lands in the United States, the Secretary of the department with authority over such lands.
(j) Except as otherwise expressly provided, the terms "major stationary source" and "major emitting facility" mean any stationary facility or source of air pollutants which directly emits, or has the potential to emit, one hundred tons per year or more of any air pollutant (including any major emitting facility or source of fugitive emissions of any such pollutant, as determined by rule by the Administrator).
(k) The terms "emission limitation" and "emission standard" mean a requirement established by the State or the Administrator which limits the quantity, rate, or concentration of emissions of air pollutants on a continuous basis, including any requirement relating to the operation or maintenance of a source to assure continuous emission reduction, and any design, equipment, work practice or operational standard promulgated under this chapter..[1]
(l) The term "standard of performance" means a requirement of continuous emission reduction, including any requirement relating to the operation or maintenance of a source to assure continuous emission reduction.
(m) The term "means of emission limitation" means a system of continuous emission reduction (including the use of specific technology or fuels with specified pollution characteristics).
(n) The term "primary standard attainment date" means the date specified in the applicable implementation plan for the attainment of a national primary ambient air quality standard for any air pollutant.
(o) The term "delayed compliance order" means an order issued by the State or by the Administrator to an existing stationary source, postponing the date required under an applicable implementation plan for compliance by such source with any requirement of such plan.
(p) The term "schedule and timetable of compliance" means a schedule of required measures including an enforceable sequence of actions or operations leading to compliance with an emission limitation, other limitation, prohibition, or standard.
(q) For purposes of this chapter, the term "applicable implementation plan" means the portion (or portions) of the implementation plan, or most recent revision thereof, which has been approved under section 7410 of this title, or promulgated under section 7410(c) of this title, or promulgated or approved pursuant to regulations promulgated under section 7601(d) of this title and which implements the relevant requirements of this chapter.

---

[1] So in original.

294 / Environmental Statutes

(r) Indian Tribe.–The term "Indian tribe" means any Indian tribe, band, nation, or other organized group or community, including any Alaska Native village, which is Federally recognized as eligible for the special programs and services provided by the United States to Indians because of their status as Indians.

(s) VOC.–The term "VOC" means volatile organic compound, as defined by the Administrator.

(t) PM-10.–The term "PM-10" means particulate matter with an aerodynamic diameter less than or equal to a nominal ten micrometers, as measured by such method as the Administrator may determine.

(u) NAAQS and CTG.–The term "NAAQS" means national ambient air quality standard. The term "CTG" means a Control Technique Guideline published by the Administrator under section 7408 of this title.

(v) NO_x.–The term "NO_x" means oxides of nitrogen.

(w) CO.–The term "CO" means carbon monoxide.

(x) Small Source.–The term "small source" means a source that emits less than 100 tons of regulated pollutants per year, or any class of persons that the Administrator determines, through regulation, generally lack technical ability or knowledge regarding control of air pollution.

(y) Federal Implementation Plan.–The term "Federal implementation plan" means a plan (or portion thereof) promulgated by the Administrator to fill all or a portion of a gap or otherwise correct all or a portion of an inadequacy in a State implementation plan, and which includes enforceable emission limitations or other control measures, means or techniques (including economic incentives, such as marketable permits or auctions of emissions allowances), and provides for attainment of the relevant national ambient air quality standard.

(z) Stationary Source.–The term "stationary source" means generally any source of an air pollutant except those emissions resulting directly from an internal combustion engine for transportation purposes or from a nonroad engine or nonroad vehicle as defined in section 7550 of this title.

(July 14, 1955, ch. 360, title III, Sec. 302, formerly Sec. 9, as added Pub. L. 88-206, Sec. 1, Dec. 17, 1963, 77 Stat. 400, renumbered Pub. L. 89-272, title I, Sec. 101(4), Oct. 20, 1965, 79 Stat. 992; amended Pub. L. 90-148, Sec. 2, Nov. 21, 1967, 81 Stat. 504; Pub. L. 91-604, Sec. 15(a)(1), (c)(1), Dec. 31, 1970, 84 Stat. 1710, 1713; Pub. L. 95-95, title II, Sec. 218(c), title III, Sec. 301, Aug. 7, 1977, 91 Stat. 761, 769; Pub. L. 95-190, Sec. 14(a)(76), Nov. 16, 1977, 91 Stat. 1404; Pub. L. 101-549, title I, Secs. 101(d)(4), 107(a), (b), 108(j), 109(b), title III, Sec. 302(e), title VII, Sec. 709, Nov. 15, 1990, 104 Stat. 2409, 2464, 2468, 2470, 2574, 2684.)

Codification

Section was formerly classified to section 1857h of this title.

Prior Provisions

Provisions similar to those in subsecs. (b) and (d) of this section were contained in a section 1857e of this title, act July 14, 1955, ch. 360, Sec. 6, 69 Stat. 323, prior to the general amendment of this chapter by Pub. L. 88-206.

Amendments

1990–Subsec. (b)(1) to (3). Pub. L. 101-549, Sec. 107(a)(1), (2), struck out "or" at end of par. (3) and substituted periods for semicolons at end of pars. (1) to (3).

Subsec. (b)(5). Pub. L. 101-549, Sec. 107(a)(3), added par. (5).

Subsec. (g). Pub. L. 101-549, Sec. 108(j)(2), inserted at end "Such term includes any precursors to the formation of any air pollutant, to the extent the Administrator has identified such precursor or precursors for the particular purpose for which the term 'air pollutant' is used."

Subsec. (h). Pub. L. 101-549, Sec. 109(b), inserted before period at end ", whether caused by transformation, conversion, or combination with other air pollutants".

Subsec. (k). Pub. L. 101-549, Sec. 303(e), inserted before period at end ", and any design, equipment, work practice or operational standard promulgated under this chapter."

Subsec. (q). Pub. L. 101-549, Sec. 101(d)(4), added subsec. (q).

Subsec. (r). Pub. L. 101-549, Sec. 107(b), added subsec. (r).

Subsecs. (s) to (y). Pub. L. 101-549, Sec. 108(j)(1), added subsecs. (s) to (y).

Subsec. (z). Pub. L. 101-549, Sec. 709, added subsec. (z).

1977—Subsec. (d). Pub. L. 95-95, Sec. 218(c), inserted "and includes the Commonwealth of the Northern Mariana Islands" after "American Samoa".

Subsec. (e). Pub. L. 95-190 substituted "individual, corporation" for "individual corporation".

Pub. L. 95-95, Sec. 301(b), expanded definition of "person" to include agencies, departments, and instrumentalities of the United States and officers, agents, and employees thereof.

Subsec. (g). Pub. L. 95-95, Sec. 301(c), expanded definition of "air pollutant" so as, expressly, to include physical, chemical, biological, and radioactive substances or matter emitted into or otherwise entering the ambient air.

Subsecs. (i) to (p). Pub. L. 95-95, Sec. 301(a), added subsecs. (i) to (p).

1970—Subsec. (a). Pub. L. 91-604, Sec. 15(c)(1), substituted definition of "Administrator" as meaning Administrator of the Environmental Protection Agency for definition of "Secretary" as meaning Secretary of Health, Education, and Welfare.

Subsecs. (g), (h). Pub. L. 91-604, Sec. 15(a)(1), added subsec. (g) defining "air pollutant", redesignated former subsec. (g) as (h) and substituted references to effects on soil, water, crops, vegetation, manmade materials, animals, wildlife, weather, visibility, and climate for references to injury to agricultural crops and livestock, and inserted references to effects on economic values and on personal comfort and well being.

1967—Pub. L. 90-148 reenacted section without change.

Effective Date of 1977 Amendment

Amendment by Pub. L. 95-95 effective Aug. 7, 1977, except as otherwise expressly provided, see section 406(d) of Pub. L. 95-95, set out as a note under section 7401 of this title.

Section Referred to in Other Sections

This section is referred to in sections 7405, 7413, 7511a, 7512a, 7661, 8302 of this title; title 26 section 169.

EMERGENCY POWERS

42 USC 7603

Notwithstanding any other provision of this chapter, the Administrator, upon receipt of evidence that a pollution source or combination of sources (including moving sources) is presenting an imminent and substantial endangerment to public health or welfare, or the environment, may bring suit on behalf of the United States in the appropriate United States district court to immediately restrain any person causing or contributing to the alleged pollution to stop the emission of air pollutants causing or contributing to such pollution or to take such other action as may be necessary. If it is not practicable to assure prompt protection of public health or welfare or the environment by commencement of such a civil action, the Administrator may issue such orders as may be necessary to protect public health or welfare or the environment. Prior to taking any action under this section, the Administrator shall consult with appropriate State and local authorities and attempt to confirm the accuracy of the information on which the action proposed to be taken is based. Any order issued by the Administrator under this section shall be effective upon issuance and shall remain in effect for a period of not more than 60 days, unless the Administrator brings an action pursuant to the first sentence of this section before the expiration of that period. Whenever the Administrator brings such an action within the 60-day period, such order shall remain in effect for an additional 14 days or for such longer period as may be authorized by the court in which such action is brought.

(July 14, 1955, ch. 360, title III, Sec. 303, as added Pub. L. 91-604, Sec. 12(a), Dec. 31, 1970, 84 Stat. 1705; amended Pub. L. 95-95, title III, Sec. 302(a), Aug. 7, 1977, 91 Stat. 770; Pub. L. 101-549, title VII, Sec. 704, Nov. 15, 1990, 104 Stat. 2681.)

Codification

Section was formerly classified to section 1857h-1 of this title.

Prior Provisions

A prior section 303 of act July 14, 1955, was renumbered section 310 by Pub. L. 91-604 and is classified to section 7610 of this title.

Amendments

1990—Pub. L. 101-549, Sec. 704(2)-(5), struck out subsec. (a) designation before "Notwithstanding any other", struck out subsec. (b) which related to violation of or failure or refusal to comply with subsec. (a) orders, and substituted new provisions for provisions following first sentence which read as follows: "If it is not practicable to assure prompt protection of the health of persons solely by commencement of such a civil action, the Administrator may issue such orders as may be necessary to protect the health of persons who are, or may be, affected by such pollution source (or sources). Prior to taking any action under this section, the Administrator shall consult with the State and local authorities in order to confirm the correctness of the information on which the action proposed to be taken is based and to ascertain the action which such authorities are, or will be, taking. Such order shall be effective for a period of not more than twenty-four hours unless the Administrator brings an action under the first sentence of this subsection before the expiration of such period. Whenever the Administrator brings such an action within such period, such order shall be effective for a period of forty-eight hours or such longer period as may be authorized by the court pending litigation or thereafter."

Pub. L. 101-549, Sec. 704(1), which directed that "public health or welfare, or the environment" be substituted for "the health of persons and that appropriate State or local authorities have not acted to abate such sources", was executed by making the substitution for "the health of persons, and that appropriate State or local authorities have not acted to abate such sources" to reflect the probable intent of Congress.

1977—Pub. L. 95-95 designated existing provisions as subsec. (a), inserted provisions that, if it is not practicable to assure prompt protection of the health of persons solely by commencement of a civil action, the Administrator may issue such orders as may be necessary to protect the health of persons who are, or may be, affected by such pollution source (or sources), that, prior to taking any action under this section, the Administrator consult with the State and local authorities in order to confirm the correctness of the information on which the action proposed to be taken is based and to ascertain the action which such authorities are, or will be, taking, that the order be effective for a period of not more than twenty-four hours unless the Administrator brings an action under the first sentence of this subsection before the expiration of such period, and that, whenever the Administrator brings such an action within such period, such order be effective for a period of forty-eight hours or such longer period as may be authorized by the court pending litigation or thereafter, and added subsec. (b).

Effective Date of 1977 Amendment

Amendment by Pub. L. 95-95 effective Aug. 7, 1977, except as otherwise expressly provided, see section 406(d) of Pub. L. 95-95, set out as a note under section 7401 of this title.

Pending Actions and Proceedings

Suits, actions, and other proceedings lawfully commenced by or against the Administrator or any other officer or employee of the United States in his official capacity or in relation to the discharge of his official duties under act July 14, 1955, the Clean Air Act, as in effect immediately prior to the enactment of Pub. L. 95-95 [Aug. 7, 1977], not to abate by reason of the taking effect of Pub. L. 95-95, see section 406(a) of Pub. L. 95-95, set out as an Effective Date of 1977 Amendment note under section 7401 of this title.

Modification or Rescission of Rules, Regulations, Orders, Determinations, Contracts, Certifications, Authorizations, Delegations, and Other Actions

All rules, regulations, orders, determinations, contracts, certifications, authorizations, delegations, or other actions duly issued, made, or taken by or pursuant to act July 14, 1955, the Clean Air Act, as in effect immediately prior to the date of enactment of Pub. L. 95-95 [Aug. 7, 1977] to continue in full force and effect until modified or rescinded in accordance with act July 14, 1955, as amended by Pub. L. 95-95 [this chapter], see section 406(b) of Pub. L. 95-95, set out as an Effective Date of 1977 Amendment note under section 7401 of this title.

Section Referred to in Other Sections

This section is referred to in sections 7410, 7412, 7413, 7420, 7429, 7607, 7661c, 9606 of this title; title 15 section 717z.

CITIZEN SUITS

42 USC 7604

(a) Authority to bring civil action; jurisdiction

Except as provided in subsection (b) of this section, any person may commence a civil action on his own behalf—
   (1) against any person (including (i) the United States, and (ii) any other governmental instrumentality or agency to the extent permitted by the Eleventh Amendment to the Constitution) who is alleged to have violated (if there is evidence that the alleged violation has been repeated) or to be in violation of (A) an emission standard or limitation under this chapter or (B) an order issued by the Administrator or a State with respect to such a standard or limitation,
   (2) against the Administrator where there is alleged a failure of the Administrator to perform any act or duty under this chapter which is not discretionary with the Administrator, or
   (3) against any person who proposes to construct or constructs any new or modified major emitting facility without a permit required under part C of subchapter I of this chapter (relating to significant deterioration of air quality) or part D of subchapter I of this chapter (relating to nonattainment) or who is alleged to have violated (if there is evidence that the alleged violation has been repeated) or to be in violation of any condition of such permit.

The district courts shall have jurisdiction, without regard to the amount in controversy or the citizenship of the parties, to enforce such an emission standard or limitation, or such an order, or to order the Administrator to perform such act or duty, as the case may be, and to apply any appropriate civil penalties (except for actions under paragraph (2)). The district courts of the United States shall have jurisdiction to compel (consistent with paragraph (2) of this subsection) agency action unreasonably delayed, except that an action to compel agency action referred to in section 7607(b) of this title which is unreasonably delayed may only be filed in a United States District Court within the circuit in which such action would be reviewable under section 7607(b) of this title. In any such action for unreasonable delay, notice to the entities referred to in subsection (b)(1)(A) of this section shall be provided 180 days before commencing such action.

(b) Notice

No action may be commenced—
   (1) under subsection (a)(1) of this section—
      (A) prior to 60 days after the plaintiff has given notice of the violation (i) to the Administrator, (ii) to the State in which the violation occurs, and (iii) to any alleged violator of the standard, limitation, or order, or
      (B) if the Administrator or State has commenced and is diligently prosecuting a civil action in a court of the United States or a State to require compliance with the standard, limitation, or order, but in any such action in a court of the United States any person may intervene as a matter of right.
   (2) under subsection (a)(2) of the section prior to 60 days after the plaintiff has given notice of such action to the Administrator,

except that such action may be brought immediately after such notification in the case of an action under this section respecting a violation of section 7412(i)(3)(A) or (f)(4) of this title or an order issued by the Administrator pursuant to section 7413(a) of this title. Notice under this subsection shall be given in such manner as the Administrator shall prescribe by regulation.

(c) Venue; intervention by Administrator; service of complaint; consent judgment
   (1) Any action respecting a violation by a stationary source of an emission standard or limitation or an order respecting such standard or limitation may be brought only in the judicial district in which such source is located.
   (2) In any action under this section, the Administrator, if not a party, may intervene as a matter of right at any time in the proceeding. A judgment in an action under this section to which the United States is not a party shall not, however, have any binding effect upon the United States.

298 / Environmental Statutes

    (3) Whenever any action is brought under this section the plaintiff shall serve a copy of the complaint on the Attorney General of the United States and on the Administrator. No consent judgment shall be entered in an action brought under this section in which the United States is not a party prior to 45 days following the receipt of a copy of the proposed consent judgment by the Attorney General and the Administrator during which time the Government may submit its comments on the proposed consent judgment to the court and parties or may intervene as a matter of right.

(d) Award of costs; security

The court, in issuing any final order in any action brought pursuant to subsection (a) of this section, may award costs of litigation (including reasonable attorney and expert witness fees) to any party, whenever the court determines such award is appropriate. The court may, if a temporary restraining order or preliminary injunction is sought, require the filing of a bond or equivalent security in accordance with the Federal Rules of Civil Procedure.

(e) Nonrestriction of other rights

Nothing in this section shall restrict any right which any person (or class of persons) may have under any statute or common law to seek enforcement of any emission standard or limitation or to seek any other relief (including relief against the Administrator or a State agency). Nothing in this section or in any other law of the United States shall be construed to prohibit, exclude, or restrict any State, local, or interstate authority from—

    (1) bringing any enforcement action or obtaining any judicial remedy or sanction in any State or local court, or

    (2) bringing any administrative enforcement action or obtaining any administrative remedy or sanction in any State or local administrative agency, department or instrumentality,

against the United States, any department, agency, or instrumentality thereof, or any officer, agent, or employee thereof under State or local law respecting control and abatement of air pollution. For provisions requiring compliance by the United States, departments, agencies, instrumentalities, officers, agents, and employees in the same manner as nongovernmental entities, see section 7418 of this title.

(f) "Emission standard or limitation under this chapter" defined

For purposes of this section, the term "emission standard or limitation under this chapter" means—

    (1) a schedule or timetable of compliance, emission limitation, standard of performance or emission standard,

    (2) a control or prohibition respecting a motor vehicle fuel or fuel additive, or[1]

    (3) any condition or requirement of a permit under part C of subchapter I of this chapter (relating to significant deterioration of air quality) or part D of subchapter I of this chapter (relating to nonattainment),,[2] section 7419 of this title (relating to primary nonferrous smelter orders), any condition or requirement under an applicable implementation plan relating to transportation control measures, air quality maintenance plans, vehicle inspection and maintenance programs or vapor recovery requirements, section 7545(e) and (f) of this title (relating to fuels and fuel additives), section 7491 of this title (relating to visibility protection), any condition or requirement under subchapter VI of this chapter (relating to ozone protection), or any requirement under section 7411 or 7412 of this title (without regard to whether such requirement is expressed as an emission standard or otherwise);[3] or

    (4) any other standard, limitation, or schedule established under any permit issued pursuant to subchapter V of this chapter or under any applicable State implementation plan approved by the Administrator, any permit term or condition, and any requirement to obtain a permit as a condition of operations.[4]

which is in effect under this chapter (including a requirement applicable by reason of section 7418 of this title) or under an applicable implementation plan.

(g) Penalty fund

    (1) Penalties received under subsection (a) of this section shall be deposited in a special fund in the United States Treasury for licensing and other services. Amounts in such fund are

---

[1] So in original. The word "or" probably should not appear.
[2] So in original.
[3] So in original. The semicolon probably should be a comma.
[4] So in original. The period probably should be a comma.

authorized to be appropriated and shall remain available until expended, for use by the Administrator to finance air compliance and enforcement activities. The Administrator shall annually report to the Congress about the sums deposited into the fund, the sources thereof, and the actual and proposed uses thereof.

(2) Notwithstanding paragraph (1) the court in any action under this subsection to apply civil penalties shall have discretion to order that such civil penalties, in lieu of being deposited in the fund referred to in paragraph (1), be used in beneficial mitigation projects which are consistent with this chapter and enhance the public health or the environment. The court shall obtain the view of the Administrator in exercising such discretion and selecting any such projects. The amount of any such payment in any such action shall not exceed $100,000.

(July 14, 1955, ch. 360, title III, Sec. 304, as added Pub. L. 91-604, Sec. 12(a), Dec. 31, 1970, 84 Stat. 1706; amended Pub. L. 95-95, title III, Sec. 303(a)-(c), Aug. 7, 1977, 91 Stat. 771, 772; Pub. L. 95-190, Sec. 14(a) (77), (78), Nov. 16, 1977, 91 Stat. 1404; Pub. L. 101-549, title III, Sec. 302(f), title VII, Sec. 707(a)-(g), Nov. 15, 1990, 104 Stat. 2574, 2682, 2683.)

References in Text

The Federal Rules of Civil Procedure, referred to in subsec. (d), are set out in the Appendix to Title 28, Judiciary and Judicial Procedure.

Codification

Section was formerly classified to section 1857h-2 of this title.

Prior Provisions

A prior section 304 of act July 14, 1955, was renumbered section 311 by Pub. L. 91-604 and is classified to section 7611 of this title.

Amendments

1990—Subsec. (a). Pub. L. 101-549, Sec. 707(a), (f), in closing provisions, inserted before period at end ", and to apply any appropriate civil penalties (except for actions under paragraph (2))" and inserted sentences at end giving courts jurisdiction to compel agency action unreasonably delayed and requiring 180 days notice prior to commencement of action.

Subsec. (a)(1), (3). Pub. L. 101-549, Sec. 707(g), inserted "to have violated (if there is evidence that the alleged violation has been repeated) or" before "to be in violation".

Subsec. (b). Pub. L. 101-549, Sec. 302(f), substituted "section 7412(i)(3)(A) or (f)(4)" for "section 7412(c)(1)(B)" in closing provisions.

Subsec. (c)(2). Pub. L. 101-549, Sec. 707(c), amended par. (2) generally. Prior to amendment, par. (2) read as follows: "In such action under this section, the Administrator, if not a party, may intervene as a matter of right."

Subsec. (c)(3). Pub. L. 101-549, Sec. 707(d), added subsec. (c)(3).

Subsec. (f)(3). Pub. L. 101-549, Sec. 707(e), struck out "any condition or requirement of section 7413(d) of this title (relating to certain enforcement orders)" before ", section 7419 of this title", substituted "subchapter VI of this chapter" for "part B of subchapter I of this chapter", and substituted "; or" for period at end.

Subsec. (f)(4). Pub. L. 101-549, Sec. 707(e), which directed that par. (4) be added at end of subsec. (f), was executed by adding par. (4) after par. (3), to reflect the probable intent of Congress.

Subsec. (g). Pub. L. 101-549, Sec. 707(b), added subsec. (g).

1977—Subsec. (a)(3). Pub. L. 95-190, Sec. 14(a)(77), inserted "or modified" after "new".

Pub. L. 95-95, Sec. 303(a), added subsec. (a)(3).

Subsec. (e). Pub. L. 95-95, Sec. 303(c), inserted provisions which prohibited any construction of this section or any other law of the United States which would prohibit, exclude, or restrict any State, local, or interstate authority from bringing any enforcement action or obtaining any judicial remedy or sanction in any State or local court against the United States or bringing any administrative enforcement action or obtaining any administrative remedy or sanction against the United States in any State or local administrative agency, department, or instrumentality under State or local law.

300 / Environmental Statutes

Subsec. (f)(3). Pub. L. 95-190, Sec. 14(a)(78), inserted ", or" after "(relating to ozone protection)", substituted "any condition or requirement under an" for "requirements under an", and struck out "or" before "section 7491".

Pub. L. 95-95, Sec. 303(b), added par. (3).

Effective Date of 1990 Amendment

Section 707(g) of Pub. L. 101-549 provided that: "The amendment made by this subsection [amending this section] shall take effect with respect to actions brought after the date 2 years after the enactment of the Clean Air Act Amendments of 1990 [Nov. 15, 1990]."

Effective Date of 1977 Amendment

Amendment by Pub. L. 95-95 effective Aug. 7, 1977, except as otherwise expressly provided, see section 406(d) of Pub. L. 95-95, set out as a note under section 7401 of this title.

Pending Actions and Proceedings

Suits, actions, and other proceedings lawfully commenced by or against the Administrator or any other officer or employee of the United States in his official capacity or in relation to the discharge of his official duties under act July 14, 1955, the Clean Air Act, as in effect immediately prior to the enactment of Pub. L. 95-95 [Aug. 7, 1977], not to abate by reason of the taking effect of Pub. L. 95-95, see section 406(a) of Pub. L. 95-95, set out as an Effective Date of 1977 Amendment note under section 7401 of this title.

Modification or Rescission of Rules, Regulations, Orders, Determinations, Contracts, Certifications, Authorizations, Delegations, and Other Actions

All rules, regulations, orders, determinations, contracts, certifications, authorizations, delegations, or other actions duly issued made, or taken by or pursuant to act July 14, 1955, the Clean Air Act, as in effect immediately prior to the date of enactment of Pub. L. 95-95 [Aug. 7, 1977] to continue in full force and effect until modified or rescinded in accordance with act July 14, 1955, as amended by Pub. L. 95-95 [this chapter], see section 406(b) of Pub. L. 95-95, set out as an Effective Date of 1977 Amendment note under section 7401 of this title.

Section Referred to in Other Sections

This section is referred to in sections 7412, 7413, 7419, 7429, 7491, 7506, 7521, 7617, 7627, 7651j of this title.

REPRESENTATION IN LITIGATION

42 USC 7605

(a) Attorney General; attorneys appointed by Administrator
The Administrator shall request the Attorney General to appear and represent him in any civil action instituted under this chapter to which the Administrator is a party. Unless the Attorney General notifies the Administrator that he will appear in such action, within a reasonable time, attorneys appointed by the Administrator shall appear and represent him.

(b) Memorandum of understanding regarding legal representation
In the event the Attorney General agrees to appear and represent the Administrator in any such action, such representation shall be conducted in accordance with, and shall include participation by, attorneys appointed by the Administrator to the extent authorized by, the memorandum of understanding between the Department of Justice and the Environmental Protection Agency, dated June 13, 1977, respecting representation of the agency by the department in civil litigation.

(July 14, 1955, ch. 360, title III, Sec. 305, as added Pub. L. 91-604, Sec. 12(a), Dec. 31, 1970, 84 Stat. 1707; amended Pub. L. 95-95, title III, Sec. 304(a), Aug. 7, 1977, 91 Stat. 772.)

Codification

Section was formerly classified to section 1857h-3 of this title.

Prior Provisions

A prior section 305 of act July 14, 1955, as added Nov. 21, 1967, Pub. L. 90-148, Sec. 2, 81 Stat. 505, was renumbered section 312 by Pub. L. 91-604 and is classified to section 7612 of this title.

Another prior section 305 of act July 14, 1955, ch. 360, title III, formerly Sec. 12, as added Dec. 17, 1963, Pub. L. 88-206, Sec. 1, 77 Stat. 401, was renumbered section 305 by Pub. L. 89-272, renumbered section 308 by Pub. L. 90-148, and renumbered section 315 by Pub. L. 91-604, and is classified to section 7615 of this title.

Amendments
1977—Pub. L. 95-95 designated existing provisions as subsec. (a) and added subsec. (b).

Effective Date of 1977 Amendment
Amendment by Pub. L. 95-95 effective Aug. 7, 1977, except as otherwise expressly provided, see section 406(d) of Pub. L. 95-95, set out as a note under section 7401 of this title.

Pending Actions and Proceedings
Suits, actions, and other proceedings lawfully commenced by or against the Administrator or any other officer or employee of the United States in his official capacity or in relation to the discharge of his official duties under act July 14, 1955, the Clean Air Act, as in effect immediately prior to the enactment of Pub. L. 95-95 [Aug. 7, 1977], not to abate by reason of the taking effect of Pub. L. 95-95, see section 406(a) of Pub. L. 95-95, set out as an Effective Date of 1977 Amendment note under section 7401 of this title.

Modification or Rescission of Rules, Regulations, Orders, Determinations, Contracts, Certifications, Authorizations, Delegations, and Other Actions
All rules, regulations, orders, determinations, contracts, certifications, authorizations, delegations, or other actions duly issued, made, or taken by or pursuant to act July 14, 1955, the Clean Air Act, as in effect immediately prior to the date of enactment of Pub. L. 95-95 [Aug. 7, 1977] to continue in full force and effect until modified or rescinded in accordance with act July 14, 1955, as amended by Pub. L. 95-95 [this chapter], see section 406(b) of Pub. L. 95-95, set out as an Effective Date of 1977 Amendment note under section 7401 of this title.

Section Referred to in Other Sections
This section is referred to in section 7413 of this title.

FEDERAL PROCUREMENT

42 USC 7606

(a) Contracts with violators prohibited
   No Federal agency may enter into any contract with any person who is convicted of any offense under section 7413(c) of this title for the procurement of goods, materials, and services to perform such contract at any facility at which the violation which gave rise to such conviction occurred if such facility is owned, leased, or supervised by such person. The prohibition in the preceding sentence shall continue until the Administrator certifies that the condition giving rise to such a conviction has been corrected. For convictions arising under section 7413(c)(2) of this title, the condition giving rise to the conviction also shall be considered to include any substantive violation of this chapter associated with the violation of 7413(c)(2) of this title. The Administrator may extend this prohibition to other facilities owned or operated by the convicted person.

(b) Notification procedures
   The Administrator shall establish procedures to provide all Federal agencies with the notification necessary for the purposes of subsection (a) of this section.

(c) Federal agency contracts
   In order to implement the purposes and policy of this chapter to protect and enhance the quality of the Nation's air, the President shall, not more than 180 days after December 31, 1970, cause to be issued an order (1) requiring each Federal agency authorized to enter into contracts and each Federal agency which is empowered to extend Federal assistance by way of grant, loan, or contract to effectuate the purpose and policy of this chapter in such contracting or assistance activities, and (2) setting forth procedures, sanctions, penalties, and such other provisions, as the President determines necessary to carry out such requirement.

302 / Environmental Statutes

(d) Exemptions; notification to Congress
The President may exempt any contract, loan, or grant from all or part of the provisions of this section where he determines such exemption is necessary in the paramount interest of the United States and he shall notify the Congress of such exemption.

(e) Annual report to Congress
The President shall annually report to the Congress on measures taken toward implementing the purpose and intent of this section, including but not limited to the progress and problems associated with implementation of this section.

(July 14, 1955, ch. 360, title III, Sec. 306, as added Pub. L. 91-604, Sec. 12(a), Dec. 31, 1970, 84 Stat. 1707; amended Pub. L. 101-549, title VII, Sec. 705, Nov. 15, 1990, 104 Stat. 2682.)

Codification

Section was formerly classified to section 1857h-4 of this title.

Prior Provisions

A prior section 306 of act July 14, 1955, ch. 360, title III, as added Nov. 21, 1967, Pub. L. 90-148, Sec. 2, 81 Stat. 506, was renumbered section 313 by Pub. L. 91-604 and is classified to section 7613 of this title.

Another prior section 306 of act July 14, 1955, ch. 360, title III, formerly Sec. 13, as added Dec. 17, 1963, Pub. L. 88-206, Sec. 1, 77 Stat. 401, renumbered Sec. 306, Oct. 20, 1965, Pub. L. 89-272, title I, Sec. 101(4), 79 Stat. 992, renumbered Sec. 309, Nov. 21, 1967, Pub. L. 90-148, Sec. 2, 81 Stat. 506, renumbered Sec. 316, Dec. 31, 1970, Pub. L. 91-604, Sec. 12(a), 84 Stat. 1705, related to appropriations and was classified to section 1857l of this title, prior to repeal by section 306 of Pub. L. 95-95. See section 7626 of this title.

Amendments

1990—Subsec. (a). Pub. L. 101-549 substituted "section 7413(c)" for "section 7413(c)(1)" and inserted sentences at end relating to convictions arising under section 7413(c)(2) of this title and extension of prohibition to other facilities owned by convicted persons.

Federal Acquisition Regulation: Contractor Certification or Contract Clause for Acquisition of Commercial Items

Pub. L. 103-355, title VIII, Sec. 8301(g), Oct. 13, 1994, 108 Stat. 3397, provided that: "The Federal Acquisition Regulation may not contain a requirement for a certification by a contractor under a contract for the acquisition of commercial items, or a requirement that such a contract include a contract clause, in order to implement a prohibition or requirement of section 306 of the Clean Air Act (42 U.S.C. 7606) or a prohibition or requirement issued in the implementation of that section, since there is nothing in such section 306 that requires such a certification or contract clause."

Executive Order No. 11602

Ex. Ord. No. 11602, June 29, 1971, 36 F.R. 12475, which related to the administration of the Clean Air Act with respect to Federal contracts, grants, or loans, was superseded by Ex. Ord. No. 11738, Sept. 10, 1973, 38 F.R. 25161, set out below.

Ex. Ord. No. 11738. Administration of the Clean Air Act and the Federal Water Pollution Control Act With Respect to Federal Contracts, Grants, or Loans

Ex. Ord. No. 11738, Sept. 10, 1973, 38 F.R. 25161, provided:

By virtue of the authority vested in me by the provisions of the Clean Air Act, as amended (42 U.S.C. 1857 et seq.) [42 U.S.C. 7401 et seq.], particularly section 306 of that Act as added by the Clean Air Amendments of 1970 (Public Law 91-604) [this section], and the Federal Water Pollution Control Act (33 U.S.C. 1251 et seq.), particularly section 508 of that Act as added by the Federal Water Pollution Control Act Amendments of 1972 (Public Law 92-500) [33 U.S.C. 1368], it is hereby ordered as follows:

Section 1. Policy. It is the policy of the Federal Government to improve and enhance environmental quality. In furtherance of that policy, the program prescribed in this Order is instituted to assure that each Federal agency empowered to enter into contracts for the procurement of goods, materials, or services and each Federal agency empowered to extend Federal assistance by way of grant, loan, or contract shall undertake such procurement and assistance activities in a manner that will result in effective enforcement of the Clean Air Act [this chapter] (hereinafter referred to as "the Air Act") and the Federal Water Pollution Control Act (hereinafter referred to as "the Water Act") [33 U.S.C. 1251 et seq.].

Sec. 2. Designation of Facilities. (a) The Administrator of the Environmental Protection Agency (hereinafter referred to as "the Administrator") shall be responsible for the attainment of the purposes and objectives of this Order.

(b) In carrying out his responsibilities under this Order, the Administrator shall, in conformity with all applicable requirements of law, designate facilities which have given rise to a conviction for an offense under section 113(c)(1) of the Air Act [42 U.S.C. 7413(c)(1)] or section 309(c) of the Water Act [33 U.S.C. 1319(c)]. The Administrator shall, from time to time, publish and circulate to all Federal agencies lists of those facilities, together with the names and addresses of the persons who have been convicted of such offenses. Whenever the Administrator determines that the condition which gave rise to a conviction has been corrected, he shall promptly remove the facility and the name and address of the person concerned from the list.

Sec. 3. Contracts, Grants, or Loans. (a) Except as provided in section 8 of this Order, no Federal agency shall enter into any contract for the procurement of goods, materials, or services which is to be performed in whole or in part in a facility then designated by the Administrator pursuant to section 2.

(b) Except as provided in section 8 of this Order, no Federal agency authorized to extend Federal assistance by way of grant, loan, or contract shall extend such assistance in any case in which it is to be used to support any activity or program involving the use of a facility then designated by the Administrator pursuant to section 2.

Sec. 4. Procurement, Grant, and Loan Regulations. The Federal Procurement Regulations, the Armed Services Procurement Regulations, and to the extent necessary, any supplemental or comparable regulations issued by any agency of the Executive Branch shall, following consultation with the Administrator, be amended to require, as a condition of entering into, renewing, or extending any contract for the procurement of goods, materials, or services or extending any assistance by way of grant, loan, or contract, inclusion of a provision requiring compliance with the Air Act, the Water Act, and standards issued pursuant thereto in the facilities in which the contract is to be performed, or which are involved in the activity or program to receive assistance.

Sec. 5. Rules and Regulations. The Administrator shall issue such rules, regulations, standards, and guidelines as he may deem necessary or appropriate to carry out the purposes of this Order.

Sec. 6. Cooperation and Assistance. The head of each Federal agency shall take such steps as may be necessary to insure that all officers and employees of this agency whose duties entail compliance or comparable functions with respect to contracts, grants, and loans are familiar with the provisions of this Order. In addition to any other appropriate action, such officers and employees shall report promptly any condition in a facility which may involve noncompliance with the Air Act or the Water Act or any rules, regulations, standards, or guidelines issued pursuant to this Order to the head of the agency, who shall transmit such reports to the Administrator.

Sec. 7. Enforcement. The Administrator may recommend to the Department of Justice or other appropriate agency that legal proceedings be brought or other appropriate action be taken whenever he becomes aware of a breach of any provision required, under the amendments issued pursuant to section 4 of this Order, to be included in a contract or other agreement.

Sec. 8. Exemptions—Reports to Congress. (a) Upon a determination that the paramount interest of the United States so requires—

(1) The head of a Federal agency may exempt any contract, grant, or loan, and, following consultation with the Administrator, any class of contracts, grants or loans from the provisions of this Order. In any such case, the head of the Federal agency granting such exemption shall (A) promptly notify the Administrator of such exemption and the justification therefor; (B) review the necessity for each such exemption annually; and (C) report to the Administrator annually all such exemptions in effect. Exemptions granted pursuant to this section shall be for a period not to exceed one year.

Additional exemptions may be granted for periods not to exceed one year upon the making of a new determination by the head of the Federal agency concerned.

(2) The Administrator may, by rule or regulation, exempt any or all Federal agencies from any or all of the provisions of this Order with respect to any class or classes of contracts, grants, or loans, which (A) involve less than specified dollar amounts, or (B) have a minimal potential impact upon the environment, or (C) involve persons who are not prime contractors or direct recipients of Federal assistance by way of contracts, grants, or loans.

(b) Federal agencies shall reconsider any exemption granted under subsection (a) whenever requested to do so by the Administrator.

(c) The Administrator shall annually notify the President and the Congress of all exemptions granted, or in effect, under this Order during the preceding year.

Sec. 9. Related Actions. The imposition of any sanction or penalty under or pursuant to this Order shall not relieve any person of any legal duty to comply with any provisions of the Air Act or the Water Act.

Sec. 10. Applicability. This Order shall not apply to contracts, grants, or loans involving the use of facilities located outside the United States.

Sec. 11. Uniformity. Rules, regulations, standards, and guidelines issued pursuant to this order and section 508 of the Water Act [33 U.S.C. 1368] shall, to the maximum extent feasible, be uniform with regulations issued pursuant to this order, Executive Order No. 11602 of June 29, 1971 [formerly set out above], and section 306 of the Air Act [this section].

Sec. 12. Order Superseded. Executive Order No. 11602 of June 29, 1971, is hereby superseded.

Richard Nixon.

Section Referred to in Other Sections

This section is referred to in section 7607 of this title.

ADMINISTRATIVE PROCEEDINGS AND JUDICIAL REVIEW

42 USC 7607

(a) Administrative subpenas; confidentiality; witnesses

In connection with any determination under section 7410(f) of this title, or for purposes of obtaining information under section 7521(b)(4)[1] or 7545(c)(3) of this title, any investigation, monitoring, reporting requirement, entry, compliance inspection, or administrative enforcement proceeding under the[2] chapter (including but not limited to section 7413, section 7414, section 7420, section 7429, section 7477, section 7524, section 7525, section 7542, section 7603, or section 7606 of this title),,[3] the Administrator may issue subpenas for the attendance and testimony of witnesses and the production of relevant papers, books, and documents, and he may administer oaths. Except for emission data, upon a showing satisfactory to the Administrator by such owner or operator that such papers, books, documents, or information or particular part thereof, if made public, would divulge trade secrets or secret processes of such owner or operator, the Administrator shall consider such record, report, or information or particular portion thereof confidential in accordance with the purposes of section 1905 of title 18, except that such paper, book, document, or information may be disclosed to other officers, employees, or authorized representatives of the United States concerned with carrying out this chapter, to persons carrying out the National Academy of Sciences' study and investigation provided for in section 7521(c) of this title, or when relevant in any proceeding under this chapter. Witnesses summoned shall be paid the same fees and mileage that are paid witnesses in the courts of the United States. In case of contumacy or refusal to obey a subpena served upon any person under this subparagraph, the district court of the United States for any district in which such person is found or resides or transacts business, upon application by the United States and after notice to such person, shall have jurisdiction to issue an order requiring such person to appear and give testimony before the Administrator to appear and produce

---

[1] See References in Text note below.
[2] So in original. Probably should be "this".
[3] So in original.

papers, books, and documents before the Administrator, or both, and any failure to obey such order of the court may be punished by such court as a contempt thereof.
(b) Judicial review
  (1) A petition for review of action of the Administrator in promulgating any national primary or secondary ambient air quality standard, any emission standard or requirement under section 7412 of this title, any standard of performance or requirement under section 7411 of this title, any standard under section 7521 of this title (other than a standard required to be prescribed under section 7521(b)(1) of this title), any determination under section 7521(b)(5)[1] of this title, any control or prohibition under section 7545 of this title, any standard under section 7571 of this title, any rule issued under section 7413, 7419, or under section 7420 of this title, or any other nationally applicable regulations promulgated, or final action taken, by the Administrator under this chapter may be filed only in the United States Court of Appeals for the District of Columbia. A petition for review of the Administrator's action in approving or promulgating any implementation plan under section 7410 of this title or section 7411(d) of this title, any order under section 7411(j) of this title, under section 7412 of this title,,[3] under section 7419 of this title, or under section 7420 of this title, or his action under section 1857c-10(c)(2)(A), (B), or (C) of this title (as in effect before August 7, 1977) or under regulations thereunder, or revising regulations for enhanced monitoring and compliance certification programs under section 7414(a)(3) of this title, or any other final action of the Administrator under this chapter (including any denial or disapproval by the Administrator under subchapter I of this chapter) which is locally or regionally applicable may be filed only in the United States Court of Appeals for the appropriate circuit. Notwithstanding the preceding sentence a petition for review of any action referred to in such sentence may be filed only in the United States Court of Appeals for the District of Columbia if such action is based on a determination of nationwide scope or effect and if in taking such action the Administrator finds and publishes that such action is based on such a determination. Any petition for review under this subsection shall be filed within sixty days from the date notice of such promulgation, approval, or action appears in the Federal Register, except that if such petition is based solely on grounds arising after such sixtieth day, then any petition for review under this subsection shall be filed within sixty days after such grounds arise. The filing of a petition for reconsideration by the Administrator of any otherwise final rule or action shall not affect the finality of such rule or action for purposes of judicial review nor extend the time within which a petition for judicial review of such rule or action under this section may be filed, and shall not postpone the effectiveness of such rule or action.
  (2) Action of the Administrator with respect to which review could have been obtained under paragraph (1) shall not be subject to judicial review in civil or criminal proceedings for enforcement. Where a final decision by the Administrator defers performance of any nondiscretionary statutory action to a later time, any person may challenge the deferral pursuant to paragraph (1).
(c) Additional evidence
  In any judicial proceeding in which review is sought of a determination under this chapter required to be made on the record after notice and opportunity for hearing, if any party applies to the court for leave to adduce additional evidence, and shows to the satisfaction of the court that such additional evidence is material and that there were reasonable grounds for the failure to adduce such evidence in the proceeding before the Administrator, the court may order such additional evidence (and evidence in rebuttal thereof) to be taken before the Administrator, in such manner and upon such terms and conditions as to[4] the court may deem proper. The Administrator may modify his findings as to the facts, or make new findings, by reason of the additional evidence so taken and he shall file such modified or new findings, and his recommendation, if any, for the modification or setting aside of his original determination, with the return of such additional evidence.
(d) Rulemaking
  (1) This subsection applies to—
    (A) the promulgation or revision of any national ambient air quality standard under section 7409 of this title,

---

[4] So in original. The word "to" probably should not appear.

(B) the promulgation or revision of an implementation plan by the Administrator under section 7410(c) of this title,
(C) the promulgation or revision of any standard of performance under section 7411 of this title, or emission standard or limitation under section 7412(d) of this title, any standard under section 7412(f) of this title, or any regulation under section 7412(g)(1)(D) and (F) of this title, or any regulation under section 7412(m) or (n) of this title,
(D) the promulgation of any requirement for solid waste combustion under section 7429 of this title,
(E) the promulgation or revision of any regulation pertaining to any fuel or fuel additive under section 7545 of this title,
(F) the promulgation or revision of any aircraft emission standard under section 7571 of this title,
(G) the promulgation or revision of any regulation under subchapter IV-A of this chapter (relating to control of acid deposition),
(H) promulgation or revision of regulations pertaining to primary nonferrous smelter orders under section 7419 of this title (but not including the granting or denying of any such order),
(I) promulgation or revision of regulations under subchapter VI of this chapter (relating to stratosphere and ozone protection),
(J) promulgation or revision of regulations under part C of subchapter I of this chapter (relating to prevention of significant deterioration of air quality and protection of visibility),
(K) promulgation or revision of regulations under section 7521 of this title and test procedures for new motor vehicles or engines under section 7525 of this title, and the revision of a standard under section 7521(a)(3) of this title,
(L) promulgation or revision of regulations for noncompliance penalties under section 7420 of this title,
(M) promulgation or revision of any regulations promulgated under section 7541 of this title (relating to warranties and compliance by vehicles in actual use),
(N) action of the Administrator under section 7426 of this title (relating to interstate pollution abatement),
(O) the promulgation or revision of any regulation pertaining to consumer and commercial products under section 7511b(e) of this title,
(P) the promulgation or revision of any regulation pertaining to field citations under section 7413(d)(3) of this title,
(Q) the promulgation or revision of any regulation pertaining to urban buses or the clean-fuel vehicle, clean-fuel fleet, and clean fuel programs under part C of subchapter II of this chapter,
(R) the promulgation or revision of any regulation pertaining to nonroad engines or nonroad vehicles under section 7547 of this title,
(S) the promulgation or revision of any regulation relating to motor vehicle compliance program fees under section 7552 of this title,
(T) the promulgation or revision of any regulation under subchapter IV-A of this chapter (relating to acid deposition),
(U) the promulgation or revision of any regulation under section 7511b(f) of this title pertaining to marine vessels, and
(V) such other actions as the Administrator may determine.
The provisions of section 553 through 557 and section 706 of title 5 shall not, except as expressly provided in this subsection, apply to actions to which this subsection applies. This subsection shall not apply in the case of any rule or circumstance referred to in subparagraphs (A) or (B) of subsection 553(b) of title 5.
(2) Not later than the date of proposal of any action to which this subsection applies, the Administrator shall establish a rulemaking docket for such action (hereinafter in this subsection referred to as a "rule"). Whenever a rule applies only within a particular State, a second (identical) docket shall be simultaneously established in the appropriate regional office of the Environmental Protection Agency.
(3) In the case of any rule to which this subsection applies, notice of proposed rulemaking shall be published in the Federal Register, as provided under section 553(b) of title 5, shall be accompanied by a statement of its basis and purpose and shall specify the period avail-

able for public comment (hereinafter referred to as the "comment period"). The notice of proposed rulemaking shall also state the docket number, the location or locations of the docket, and the times it will be open to public inspection. The statement of basis and purpose shall include a summary of—
(A) the factual data on which the proposed rule is based;
(B) the methodology used in obtaining the data and in analyzing the data; and
(C) the major legal interpretations and policy considerations underlying the proposed rule.

The statement shall also set forth or summarize and provide a reference to any pertinent findings, recommendations, and comments by the Scientific Review Committee established under section 7409(d) of this title and the National Academy of Sciences, and, if the proposal differs in any important respect from any of these recommendations, an explanation of the reasons for such differences. All data, information, and documents referred to in this paragraph on which the proposed rule relies shall be included in the docket on the date of publication of the proposed rule.

(4) (A) The rulemaking docket required under paragraph (2) shall be open for inspection by the public at reasonable times specified in the notice of proposed rulemaking. Any person may copy documents contained in the docket. The Administrator shall provide copying facilities which may be used at the expense of the person seeking copies, but the Administrator may waive or reduce such expenses in such instances as the public interest requires. Any person may request copies by mail if the person pays the expenses, including personnel costs to do the copying.

(B) (i) Promptly upon receipt by the agency, all written comments and documentary information on the proposed rule received from any person for inclusion in the docket during the comment period shall be placed in the docket. The transcript of public hearings, if any, on the proposed rule shall also be included in the docket promptly upon receipt from the person who transcribed such hearings. All documents which become available after the proposed rule has been published and which the Administrator determines are of central relevance to the rulemaking shall be placed in the docket as soon as possible after their availability.

(ii) The drafts of proposed rules submitted by the Administrator to the Office of Management and Budget for any interagency review process prior to proposal of any such rule, all documents accompanying such drafts, and all written comments thereon by other agencies and all written responses to such written comments by the Administrator shall be placed in the docket no later than the date of proposal of the rule. The drafts of the final rule submitted for such review process prior to promulgation and all such written comments thereon, all documents accompanying such drafts, and written responses thereto shall be placed in the docket no later than the date of promulgation.

(5) In promulgating a rule to which this subsection applies (i) the Administrator shall allow any person to submit written comments, data, or documentary information; (ii) the Administrator shall give interested persons an opportunity for the oral presentation of data, views, or arguments, in addition to an opportunity to make written submissions; (iii) a transcript shall be kept of any oral presentation; and (iv) the Administrator shall keep the record of such proceeding open for thirty days after completion of the proceeding to provide an opportunity for submission of rebuttal and supplementary information.

(6) (A) The promulgated rule shall be accompanied by (i) a statement of basis and purpose like that referred to in paragraph (3) with respect to a proposed rule and (ii) an explanation of the reasons for any major changes in the promulgated rule from the proposed rule.

(B) The promulgated rule shall also be accompanied by a response to each of the significant comments, criticisms, and new data submitted in written or oral presentations during the comment period.

(C) The promulgated rule may not be based (in part or whole) on any information or data which has not been placed in the docket as of the date of such promulgation.

(7) (A) The record for judicial review shall consist exclusively of the material referred to in paragraph (3), clause (i) of paragraph (4)(B), and subparagraphs (A) and (B) of paragraph (6).

(B) Only an objection to a rule or procedure which was raised with reasonable specificity during the period for public comment (including any public hearing) may be raised during judicial review. If the person raising an objection can demonstrate to the Administrator that it was impracticable to raise such objection within such time or if the grounds for such objection arose after the period for public comment (but within the time specified for judicial review) and if such objection is of central relevance to the outcome of the rule, the Administrator shall convene a proceeding for reconsideration of the rule and provide the same procedural rights as would have been afforded had the information been available at the time the rule was proposed. If the Administrator refuses to convene such a proceeding, such person may seek review of such refusal in the United States court of appeals for the appropriate circuit (as provided in subsection (b) of this section). Such reconsideration shall not postpone the effectiveness of the rule. The effectiveness of the rule may be stayed during such reconsideration, however, by the Administrator or the court for a period not to exceed three months.

(8) The sole forum for challenging procedural determinations made by the Administrator under this subsection shall be in the United States court of appeals for the appropriate circuit (as provided in subsection (b) of this section) at the time of the substantive review of the rule. No interlocutory appeals shall be permitted with respect to such procedural determinations. In reviewing alleged procedural errors, the court may invalidate the rule only if the errors were so serious and related to matters of such central relevance to the rule that there is a substantial likelihood that the rule would have been significantly changed if such errors had not been made.

(9) In the case of review of any action of the Administrator to which this subsection applies, the court may reverse any such action found to be—

(A) arbitrary, capricious, an abuse of discretion, or otherwise not in accordance with law;

(B) contrary to constitutional right, power, privilege, or immunity;

(C) in excess of statutory jurisdiction, authority, or limitations, or short of statutory right; or

(D) without observance of procedure required by law, if (i) such failure to observe such procedure is arbitrary or capricious, (ii) the requirement of paragraph (7)(B) has been met, and (iii) the condition of the last sentence of paragraph (8) is met.

(10) Each statutory deadline for promulgation of rules to which this subsection applies which requires promulgation less than six months after date of proposal may be extended to not more than six months after date of proposal by the Administrator upon a determination that such extension is necessary to afford the public, and the agency, adequate opportunity to carry out the purposes of this subsection.

(11) The requirements of this subsection shall take effect with respect to any rule the proposal of which occurs after ninety days after August 7, 1977.

(e) Other methods of judicial review not authorized

Nothing in this chapter shall be construed to authorize judicial review of regulations or orders of the Administrator under this chapter, except as provided in this section.

(f) Costs

In any judicial proceeding under this section, the court may award costs of litigation (including reasonable attorney and expert witness fees) whenever it determines that such award is appropriate.

(g) Stay, injunction, or similar relief in proceedings relating to noncompliance penalties

In any action respecting the promulgation of regulations under section 7420 of this title or the administration or enforcement of section 7420 of this title no court shall grant any stay, injunctive, or similar relief before final judgment by such court in such action.

(h) Public participation

It is the intent of Congress that, consistent with the policy of subchapter II of chapter 5 of title 5, the Administrator in promulgating any regulation under this chapter, including a regulation subject to a deadline, shall ensure a reasonable period for public participation of at least 30 days, except as otherwise expressly provided in section[5] 7407(d), 7502(a), 7511(a) and (b), and 7512(a) and (b) of this title.

---

[5]So in original. Probably should be "sections".

(July 14, 1955, ch. 360, title III, Sec. 307, as added Pub. L. 91-604, Sec. 12(a), Dec. 31, 1970, 84 Stat. 1707; amended Pub. L. 92-157, title III, Sec. 302(a), Nov. 18, 1971, 85 Stat. 464; Pub. L. 93-319, Sec. 6(c), June 22, 1974, 88 Stat. 259; Pub. L. 95-95, title III, Secs. 303(d), 305(a), (c), (f)-(h), Aug. 7, 1977, 91 Stat. 772, 776, 777; Pub. L. 95-190, Sec. 14(a)(79), (80), Nov. 16, 1977, 91 Stat. 1404; Pub. L. 101-549, title I, Secs. 108(p), 110(5), title III, Sec. 302(g), (h), title VII, Secs. 702(c), 703, 706, 707(h), 710(b), Nov. 15, 1990, 104 Stat. 2469, 2470, 2574, 2681-2684.)

References in Text

Section 7521(b)(4) of this title, referred to in subsec. (a), was repealed by Pub. L. 101-549, title II, Sec. 203(2), Nov. 15, 1990, 104 Stat. 2529.

Section 7521(b)(5) of this title, referred to in subsec. (b)(1), was repealed by Pub. L. 101-549, title II, Sec. 203(3), Nov. 15, 1990, 104 Stat. 2529.

Section 1857c-10(c)(2)(A), (B), or (C) of this title (as in effect before August 7, 1977), referred to in subsec. (b)(1), was in the original "section 119(c)(2)(A), (B), or (C) (as in effect before the date of enactment of the Clean Air Act Amendments of 1977)", meaning section 119 of act July 14, 1955, ch. 360, title I, as added June 22, 1974, Pub. L. 93-319, Sec. 3, 88 Stat. 248, (which was classified to section 1857c-10 of this title) as in effect prior to the enactment of Pub. L. 95-95, Aug. 7, 1977, 91 Stat. 691, effective Aug. 7, 1977. Section 112(b)(1) of Pub. L. 95-95 repealed section 119 of act July 14, 1955, ch. 360, title I, as added by Pub. L. 93-319, and provided that all references to such section 119 in any subsequent enactment which supersedes Pub. L. 93-319 shall be construed to refer to section 113(d) of the Clean Air Act and to paragraph (5) thereof in particular which is classified to subsec. (d)(5) of section 7413 of this title. Section 7413(d) of this title was subsequently amended generally by Pub. L. 101-549, title VII, Sec. 701, Nov. 15, 1990, 104 Stat. 2672, and, as so amended, no longer relates to final compliance orders. Section 117(b) of Pub. L. 95-95 added a new section 119 of act July 14, 1955, which is classified to section 7419 of this title.

Part C of subchapter I of this chapter, referred to in subsec. (d)(1)(J), was in the original "subtitle C of title I", and was translated as reading "part C of title I" to reflect the probable intent of Congress, because title I does not contain subtitles.

Codification

In subsec. (h), "subchapter II of chapter 5 of title 5" was substituted for "the Administrative Procedures Act" on authority of Pub. L. 89-554, Sec. 7(b), Sept. 6, 1966, 80 Stat. 631, the first section of which enacted Title 5, Government Organization and Employees.

Section was formerly classified to section 1857h-5 of this title.

Prior Provisions

A prior section 307 of act July 14, 1955, was renumbered section 314 by Pub. L. 91-604 and is classified to section 7614 of this title.

Another prior section 307 of act July 14, 1955, ch. 360, title III, formerly Sec. 14, as added Dec. 17, 1963, Pub. L. 88-206, Sec. 1, 77 Stat. 401, was renumbered section 307 by Pub. L. 89-272, renumbered section 310 by Pub. L. 90-148, and renumbered section 317 by Pub. L. 91-604, and is set out as a Short Title note under section 7401 of this title.

Amendments

1990—Subsec. (a). Pub. L. 101-549, Sec. 703, struck out par. (1) designation at beginning, inserted provisions authorizing issuance of subpoenas and administration of oaths for purposes of investigations, monitoring, reporting requirements, entries, compliance inspections, or administrative enforcement proceedings under this chapter, and struck out "or section 7521(b)(5)" after "section 7410(f)".

Subsec. (b)(1). Pub. L. 101-549, Sec. 706, struck out "under section 7413(d) of this title" before ", under section 7419 of this title" and inserted at end: "The filing of a petition for reconsideration by the Administrator of any otherwise final rule or action shall not affect the finality of such rule or action for purposes of judicial review nor extend the time within which a petition for judicial review of such rule or action under this section may be filed, and shall not postpone the effectiveness of such rule or action."

Pub. L. 101-549, Sec. 702(c), inserted "or revising regulations for enhanced monitoring and compliance certification programs under section 7414(a)(3) of this title," before "or any other final action of the Administrator".

Pub. L. 101-549, Sec. 302(g), substituted "section 7412" for "section 7412(c)".

Subsec. (b)(2). Pub. L. 101-549, Sec. 707(h), inserted sentence at end authorizing challenge to deferrals of performance of nondiscretionary statutory actions.

Subsec. (d)(1)(C). Pub. L. 101-549, Sec. 110(5)(A), amended subpar. (C) generally. Prior to amendment, subpar. (C) read as follows: "the promulgation or revision of any standard of performance under section 7411 of this title or emission standard under section 7412 of this title,".

Subsec. (d)(1)(D), (E). Pub. L. 101-549, Sec. 302(h), added subpar. (D) and redesignated former subpar. (D) as (E). Former subpar. (E) redesignated (F).

Subsec. (d)(1)(F). Pub. L. 101-549, Sec. 302(h), redesignated subpar. (E) as (F). Former subpar. (F) redesignated (G).

Pub. L. 101-549, Sec. 110(5)(B), amended subpar. (F) generally. Prior to amendment, subpar. (F) read as follows: "promulgation or revision of regulations pertaining to orders for coal conversion under section 7413(d)(5) of this title (but not including orders granting or denying any such orders),".

Subsec. (d)(1)(G), (H). Pub. L. 101-549, Sec. 302(h), redesignated subpars. (F) and (G) as (G) and (H), respectively. Former subpar. (H) redesignated (I).

Subsec. (d)(1)(I). Pub. L. 101-549, Sec. 710(b), which directed that subpar. (H) be amended by substituting "subchapter VI of this chapter" for "part B of subchapter I of this chapter", was executed by making the substitution in subpar. (I), to reflect the probable intent of Congress and the intervening redesignation of subpar. (H) as (I) by Pub. L. 101-549, Sec. 302(h), see below.

Pub. L. 101-549, Sec. 302(h), redesignated subpar. (H) as (I). Former subpar. (I) redesignated (J).

Subsec. (d)(1)(J) to (M). Pub. L. 101-549, Sec. 302(h), redesignated subpars. (I) to (L) as (J) to (M), respectively. Former subpar. (M) redesignated (N).

Subsec. (d)(1)(N). Pub. L. 101-549, Sec. 302(h), redesignated subpar. (M) as (N). Former subpar. (N) redesignated (O).

Pub. L. 101-549, Sec. 110(5)(C), added subpar. (N) and redesignated former subpar. (N) as (U).

Subsec. (d)(1)(O) to (T). Pub. L. 101-549, Sec. 302(h), redesignated subpars. (N) to (S) as (O) to (T), respectively. Former subpar. (T) redesignated (U).

Pub. L. 101-549, Sec. 110(5)(C), added subpars. (O) to (T).

Subsec. (d)(1)(U). Pub. L. 101-549, Sec. 302(h), redesignated subpar. (T) as (U). Former subpar. (U) redesignated (V).

Pub. L. 101-549, Sec. 110(5)(C), redesignated former subpar. (N) as (U).

Subsec. (d)(1)(V). Pub. L. 101-549, Sec. 302(h), redesignated subpar. (U) as (V).

Subsec. (h). Pub. L. 101-549, Sec. 108(p), added subsec. (h).

1977—Subsec. (b)(1). Pub. L. 95-190 in text relating to filing of petitions for review in the United States Court of Appeals for the District of Columbia inserted provision respecting requirements under sections 7411 and 7412 of this title, and substituted provisions authorizing review of any rule issued under section 7413, 7419, or 7420 of this title, for provisions authorizing review of any rule or order issued under section 7420 of this title, relating to noncompliance penalties, and in text relating to filing of petitions for review in the United States Court of Appeals for the appropriate circuit inserted provision respecting review under section 7411(j), 7412(c), 7413(d), or 7419 of this title, provision authorizing review under section 1857c-10(c)(2)(A), (B), or (C) to the period prior to Aug. 7, 1977, and provisions authorizing review of denials or disapprovals by the Administrator under subchapter I of this chapter.

Pub. L. 95-95, Sec. 305(c), (h), inserted rules or orders issued under section 7420 of this title (relating to noncompliance penalties) and any other nationally applicable regulations promulgated, or final action taken, by the Administrator under this chapter to the enumeration of actions of the Administrator for which a petition for review may be filed only in the United States Court of Appeals for the District of Columbia, added the approval or promulgation by the Administrator of orders under section 7420 of this title, or any other final action of the Administrator under this chapter which is locally or regionally applicable to the enumeration of actions by the Administrator for which a petition for review may be filed only in the United States Court of Appeals for the appropriate circuit, inserted provision that petitions otherwise

Clean Air Act / 311

capable of being filed in the Court of Appeals for the appropriate circuit may be filed only in the Court of Appeals for the District of Columbia if the action is based on a determination of nationwide scope, and increased from 30 days to 60 days the period during which the petition must be filed.

Subsec. (d). Pub. L. 95-95, Sec. 305(a), added subsec. (d).

Subsec. (e). Pub. L. 95-95, Sec. 303(d), added subsec. (e).

Subsec. (f). Pub. L. 95-95, Sec. 305(f), added subsec. (f).

Subsec. (g). Pub. L. 95-95, Sec. 305(g), added subsec. (g).

1974—Subsec. (b)(1). Pub. L. 93-319 inserted reference to the Administrator's action under section 1857c-10(c)(2)(A), (B), or (C) of this title or under regulations thereunder and substituted reference to the filing of a petition within 30 days from the date of promulgation, approval, or action for reference to the filing of a petition within 30 days from the date of promulgation or approval.

1971—Subsec. (a)(1). Pub. L. 92-157 substituted reference to section "7545(c)(3)" for "7545(c)(4)" of this title.

Effective Date of 1977 Amendment

Amendment by Pub. L. 95-95 effective Aug. 7, 1977, except as otherwise expressly provided, see section 406(d) of Pub. L. 95-95, set out as a note under section 7401 of this title.

Termination of Advisory Committees

Advisory committees established after Jan. 5, 1973, to terminate not later than the expiration of the 2-year period beginning on the date of their establishment, unless, in the case of a committee established by the President or an officer of the Federal Government, such committee is renewed by appropriate action prior to the expiration of such 2-year period, or in the case of a committee established by the Congress, its duration is otherwise provided for by law. See section 14 of Pub. L. 92-463, Oct. 6, 1972, 86 Stat. 776, set out in the Appendix to Title 5, Government Organization and Employees.

Pending Actions and Proceedings

Suits, actions, and other proceedings lawfully commenced by or against the Administrator or any other officer or employee of the United States in his official capacity or in relation to the discharge of his official duties under act July 14, 1955, the Clean Air Act, as in effect immediately prior to the enactment of Pub. L. 95-95 [Aug. 7, 1977], not to abate by reason of the taking effect of Pub. L. 95-95, see section 406(a) of Pub. L. 95-95, set out as an Effective Date of 1977 Amendment note under section 7401 of this title.

Modification or Rescission of Rules, Regulations, Orders, Determinations, Contracts, Certifications, Authorizations, Delegations, and Other Actions

All rules, regulations, orders, determinations, contracts, certifications, authorizations, delegations, or other actions duly issued, made, or taken by or pursuant to act July 14, 1955, the Clean Air Act, as in effect immediately prior to the date of enactment of Pub. L. 95-95 [Aug. 7, 1977] to continue in full force and effect until modified or rescinded in accordance with act July 14, 1955, as amended by Pub. L. 95-95 [this chapter], see section 406(b) of Pub. L. 95-95, set out as an Effective Date of 1977 Amendment note under section 7401 of this title.

Section Referred to in Other Sections

This section is referred to in sections 7412, 7413, 7419, 7420, 7429, 7506a, 7521, 7545, 7601, 7604, 7617, 7625-1, 7661d of this title.

MANDATORY LICENSING

42 USC 7608

Whenever the Attorney General determines, upon application of the Administrator—
 (1) that—
  (A) in the implementation of the requirements of section 7411, 7412, or 7521 of this title, a right under any United States letters patent, which is being used or intended for pub-

lic or commercial use and not otherwise reasonably available, is necessary to enable any person required to comply with such limitation to so comply, and

(B) there are no reasonable alternative methods to accomplish such purpose, and

(2) that the unavailability of such right may result in a substantial lessening of competition or tendency to create a monopoly in any line of commerce in any section of the country,

the Attorney General may so certify to a district court of the United States, which may issue an order requiring the person who owns such patent to license it on such reasonable terms and conditions as the court, after hearing, may determine. Such certification may be made to the district court for the district in which the person owning the patent resides, does business, or is found.

(July 14, 1955, ch. 360, title III, Sec. 308, as added Pub. L. 91-604, Sec. 12(a), Dec. 31, 1970, 84 Stat. 1708.)

Codification

Section was formerly classified to section 1857h-6 of this title.

Prior Provisions

A prior section 308 of act July 14, 1955, was renumbered section 315 by Pub. L. 91-604 and is classified to section 7615 of this title.

Modification or Rescission of Rules, Regulations, Orders, Determinations, Contracts, Certifications, Authorizations, Delegations, and Other Actions

All rules, regulations, orders, determinations, contracts, certifications, authorizations, delegations, or other actions duly issued, made, or taken by or pursuant to act July 14, 1955, the Clean Air Act, as in effect immediately prior to the date of enactment of Pub. L. 95-95 [Aug. 7, 1977] to continue in full force and effect until modified or rescinded in accordance with act July 14, 1955, as amended by Pub. L. 95-95 [this chapter], see section 406(b) of Pub. L. 95-95, set out as an Effective Date of 1977 Amendment note under section 7401 of this title.

POLICY REVIEW

42 USC 7609

(a) Environmental impact

The Administrator shall review and comment in writing on the environmental impact of any matter relating to duties and responsibilities granted pursuant to this chapter or other provisions of the authority of the Administrator, contained in any (1) legislation proposed by any Federal department or agency, (2) newly authorized Federal projects for construction and any major Federal agency action (other than a project for construction) to which section 4332(2)(C) of this title applies, and (3) proposed regulations published by any department or agency of the Federal Government. Such written comment shall be made public at the conclusion of any such review.

(b) Unsatisfactory legislation, action, or regulation

In the event the Administrator determines that any such legislation, action, or regulation is unsatisfactory from the standpoint of public health or welfare or environmental quality, he shall publish his determination and the matter shall be referred to the Council on Environmental Quality.

(July 14, 1955, ch. 360, title III, Sec. 309, as added Pub. L. 91-604, Sec. 12(a), Dec. 31, 1970, 84 Stat. 1709.)

Codification

Section was formerly classified to section 1857h-7 of this title.

Prior Provisions

A prior section 309 of act July 14, 1955, ch. 360, title III, formerly Sec. 13, as added Dec. 17, 1963, Pub. L. 88-206, Sec. 1, 77 Stat. 401; renumbered Sec. 306, Oct. 20, 1965, Pub. L. 89-272, title I, Sec. 101(4), 79 Stat. 992; renumbered Sec. 309, Nov. 21, 1967, Pub. L. 90-148, Sec. 2, 81 Stat. 506; renumbered Sec. 316, Dec. 31, 1970, Pub. L. 91-604, Sec. 12(a), 84 Stat. 1705, related to appropriations and was classified to section 1857l of this title, prior to repeal by section 306 of Pub. L. 95-95. See section 7626 of this title.

Modification or Rescission of Rules, Regulations, Orders, Determinations, Contracts, Certifications, Authorizations, Delegations, and Other Actions

All rules, regulations, orders, determinations, contracts, certifications, authorizations, delegations, or other actions duly issued, made, or taken by or pursuant to act July 14, 1955, the Clean Air Act, as in effect immediately prior to the date of enactment of Pub. L. 95-95 [Aug. 7, 1977] to continue in full force and effect until modified or rescinded in accordance with act July 14, 1955, as amended by Pub. L. 95-95 [this chapter], see section 406(b) of Pub. L. 95-95, set out as an Effective Date of 1977 Amendment note under section 7401 of this title.

OTHER AUTHORITY

42 USC 7610

(a) Authority and responsibilities under other laws not affected
Except as provided in subsection (b) of this section, this chapter shall not be construed as superseding or limiting the authorities and responsibilities, under any other provision of law, of the Administrator or any other Federal officer, department, or agency.

(b) Nonduplication of appropriations
No appropriation shall be authorized or made under section 241, 243, or 246 of this title for any fiscal year after the fiscal year ending June 30, 1964, for any purpose for which appropriations may be made under authority of this chapter.

(July 14, 1955, ch. 360, title III, Sec. 310, formerly Sec. 10, as added Pub. L. 88-206, Sec. 1, Dec. 17, 1963, 77 Stat. 401; renumbered Sec. 303, Pub. L. 89-272, title I, Sec. 101(4), Oct. 20, 1965, 79 Stat. 992; amended Pub. L. 90-148, Sec. 2, Nov. 21, 1967, 81 Stat. 505; renumbered Sec. 310 and amended Pub. L. 91-604, Secs. 12(a), 15(c)(2), Dec. 31, 1970, 84 Stat. 1705, 1713.)

Codification

Section was formerly classified to section 1857i of this title.

Prior Provisions

A prior section 310 of act July 14, 1955, was renumbered section 317 by Pub. L. 91-604 and is set out as a Short Title note under section 7401 of this title.

Provisions similar to those in subsec. (a) of this section were contained in section 1857f of this title, act July 14, 1955, ch. 360, Sec. 7, 69 Stat. 323, prior to the general amendment of this chapter by Pub. L. 88-206.

Amendments

1970—Subsec. (a). Pub. L. 91-604, Sec. 15(c)(2), substituted "Administrator" for "Secretary".

1967—Subsec. (b). Pub. L. 90-148 substituted reference to section 246 of this title for reference to section 246(c) of this title.

Modification or Rescission of Rules, Regulations, Orders, Determinations, Contracts, Certifications, Authorizations, Delegations, and Other Actions

All rules, regulations, orders, determinations, contracts, certifications, authorizations, delegations, or other actions duly issued, made, or taken by or pursuant to act July 14, 1955, the Clean Air Act, as in effect immediately prior to the date of enactment of Pub. L. 95-95 [Aug. 7, 1977] to continue in full force and effect until modified or rescinded in accordance with act July 14, 1955, as amended by Pub. L. 95-95 [this chapter], see section 406(b) of Pub. L. 95-95, set out as an Effective Date of 1977 Amendment note under section 7401 of this title.

RECORDS AND AUDIT

42 USC 7611

(a) Recipients of assistance to keep prescribed records
Each recipient of assistance under this chapter shall keep such records as the Administrator shall prescribe, including records which fully disclose the amount and disposition by such recipient of the proceeds of such assistance, the total cost of the project or undertaking in

connection with which such assistance is given or used, and the amount of that portion of the cost of the project or undertaking supplied by other sources, and such other records as will facilitate an effective audit.

(b) Audits
The Administrator and the Comptroller General of the United States, or any of their duly authorized representatives, shall have access for the purpose of audit and examinations to any books, documents, papers, and records of the recipients that are pertinent to the grants received under this chapter.

(July 14, 1955, ch. 360, title III, Sec. 311, formerly Sec. 11, as added Pub. L. 88-206, Sec. 1, Dec. 17, 1963, 77 Stat. 401; renumbered Sec. 304, Pub. L. 89-272, title I, Sec. 101(4), Oct. 20, 1965, 79 Stat. 992; amended Pub. L. 90-148, Sec. 2, Nov. 21, 1967, 81 Stat. 505; renumbered Sec. 311 and amended Pub. L. 91-604, Secs. 12(a), 15(c)(2), Dec. 31, 1970, 84 Stat. 1705, 1713.)

Codification

Section was formerly classified to section 1857j of this title.

Amendments

1970—Pub. L. 91-604, Sec. 15(c)(2), substituted "Administrator" for "Secretary" and "Secretary of Health, Education, and Welfare".

1967—Pub. L. 90-148 reenacted section without change.

Modification or Rescission of Rules, Regulations, Orders, Determinations, Contracts, Certifications, Authorizations, Delegations, and Other Actions

All rules, regulations, orders, determinations, contracts, certifications, authorizations, delegations, or other actions duly issued, made, or taken by or pursuant to act July 14, 1955, the Clean Air Act, as in effect immediately prior to the date of enactment of Pub. L. 95-95 [Aug. 7, 1977] to continue in full force and effect until modified or rescinded in accordance with act July 14, 1955, as amended by Pub. L. 95-95 [this chapter], see section 406(b) of Pub. L. 95-95, set out as an Effective Date of 1977 Amendment note under section 7401 of this title.

Section Referred to in Other Sections

This section is referred to in sections 4905, 7541 of this title.

ECONOMIC IMPACT ANALYSES

42 USC 7612

(a) Cost-benefit analysis
The Administrator, in consultation with the Secretary of Commerce, the Secretary of Labor, and the Council on Clean Air Compliance Analysis (as established under subsection (f) of this section), shall conduct a comprehensive analysis of the impact of this chapter on the public health, economy, and environment of the United States. In performing such analysis, the Administrator should consider the costs, benefits and other effects associated with compliance with each standard issued for—
  (1) a criteria air pollutant subject to a standard issued under section 7409 of this title;
  (2) a hazardous air pollutant listed under section 7412 of this title, including any technology-based standard and any risk-based standard for such pollutant;
  (3) emissions from mobile sources regulated under subchapter II of this chapter;
  (4) a limitation under this chapter for emissions of sulfur dioxide or nitrogen oxides;
  (5) a limitation under subchapter VI of this chapter on the production of any ozone-depleting substance; and
  (6) any other section of this chapter.

(b) Benefits
In describing the benefits of a standard described in subsection (a) of this section, the Administrator shall consider all of the economic, public health, and environmental benefits of efforts to comply with such standard. In any case where numerical values are assigned to such benefits, a default assumption of zero value shall not be assigned to such benefits unless supported by specific data. The Administrator shall assess how benefits are measured in order to

Clean Air Act / 315

assure that damage to human health and the environment is more accurately measured and taken into account.

(c) Costs

In describing the costs of a standard described in subsection (a) of this section, the Administrator shall consider the effects of such standard on employment, productivity, cost of living, economic growth, and the overall economy of the United States.

(d) Initial report

Not later than 12 months after November 15, 1990, the Administrator, in consultation with the Secretary of Commerce, the Secretary of Labor, and the Council on Clean Air Compliance Analysis, shall submit a report to the Congress that summarizes the results of the analysis described in subsection (a) of this section, which reports—

(1) all costs incurred previous to November 15, 1990, in the effort to comply with such standards; and

(2) all benefits that have accrued to the United States as a result of such costs.

(e) Biennial updates; future projections

Not later than 24 months after November 15, 1990, and every 24 months thereafter, the Administrator, in consultation with the Secretary of Commerce, the Secretary of Labor, and the Council on Clean Air Compliance Analysis, shall submit a report to the Congress that updates the report issued pursuant to subsection (d) of this section, and which, in addition, makes projections into the future regarding expected costs, benefits, and other effects of compliance with standards pursuant to this chapter as listed in subsection (a) of this section.

(f) Appointment of Advisory Council on Clean Air Compliance Analysis

Not later than 6 months after November 15, 1990, the Administrator, in consultation with the Secretary of Commerce and the Secretary of Labor, shall appoint an Advisory Council on Clean Air Compliance Analysis of not less than nine members (hereafter in this section referred to as the "Council"). In appointing such members, the Administrator shall appoint recognized experts in the fields of the health and environmental effects of air pollution, economic analysis, environmental sciences, and such other fields that the Administrator determines to be appropriate.

(g) Duties of Advisory Council

The Council shall—

(1) review the data to be used for any analysis required under this section and make recommendations to the Administrator on the use of such data;

(2) review the methodology used to analyze such data and make recommendations to the Administrator on the use of such methodology; and

(3) prior to the issuance of a report required under subsection (d) or (e) of this section, review the findings of such report, and make recommendations to the Administrator concerning the validity and utility of such findings.

(July 14, 1955, ch. 360, title III, Sec. 312, formerly Sec. 305, as added Pub. L. 90-148, Sec. 2, Nov. 21, 1967, 81 Stat. 505; renumbered Sec. 312 and amended Pub. L. 91-604, Secs. 12(a), 15(c)(2), Dec. 31, 1970, 84 Stat. 1705, 1713; Pub. L. 95-95, title II, Sec. 224(c), Aug. 7, 1977, 91 Stat. 767; Pub. L. 101-549, title VIII, Sec. 812(a), Nov. 15, 1990, 104 Stat. 2691.)

Codification

Section was formerly classified to section 1857j-1 of this title.

Amendments

1990—Pub. L. 101-549 amended section generally, substituting present provisions for provisions which related to: in subsec. (a), detailed cost estimate, comprehensive cost and economic impact studies, and annual reevaluation; in subsec. (b), personnel study and report to President and Congress; and in subsec. (c), cost-effectiveness analyses.

1977—Subsec. (c). Pub. L. 95-95 added subsec. (c).

1970—Pub. L. 91-604, Sec. 15(c)(2), substituted "Administrator" for "Secretary" wherever appearing.

Effective Date of 1977 Amendment

Amendment by Pub. L. 95-95 effective Aug. 7, 1977, except as otherwise expressly provided, see section 406(d) of Pub. L. 95-95, set out as a note under section 7401 of this title.

316 / Environmental Statutes

Termination of Advisory Councils

Advisory councils established after Jan. 5, 1973, to terminate not later than the expiration of the 2-year period beginning on the date of their establishment, unless, in the case of a council established by the President or an officer of the Federal Government, such council is renewed by appropriate action prior to the expiration of such 2-year period, or in the case of a council established by Congress, its duration is otherwise provided by law. See sections 3(2) and 14 of Pub. L. 92-463, Oct. 6, 1972, 86 Stat. 770, 776, set out in the Appendix to Title 5, Government Organization and Employees.

Equivalent Air Quality Controls Among Trading Nations

Section 811 of Pub. L. 101-549 provided that:

"(a) Findings.—The Congress finds that—
  (1) all nations have the responsibility to adopt and enforce effective air quality standards and requirements and the United States, in enacting this Act [see Tables for classification], is carrying out its responsibility in this regard;
  (2) as a result of complying with this Act, businesses in the United States will make significant capital investments and incur incremental costs in implementing control technology standards;
  (3) such compliance may impair the competitiveness of certain United States jobs, production, processes, and products if foreign goods are produced under less costly environmental standards and requirements than are United States goods; and
  (4) mechanisms should be sought through which the United States and its trading partners can agree to eliminate or reduce competitive disadvantages.
(b) Action by the President.—
  (1) In general.—Within 18 months after the date of the enactment of the Clean Air Act Amendments of 1990 [Nov. 15, 1990], the President shall submit to the Congress a report—
    (A) identifying and evaluating the economic effects of—
      (i) the significant air quality standards and controls required under this Act, and
      (ii) the differences between the significant standards and controls required under this Act and similar standards and controls adopted and enforced by the major trading partners of the United States,
    on the international competitiveness of United States manufacturers; and
    (B) containing a strategy for addressing such economic effects through trade consultations and negotiations.
  (2) Additional reporting requirements.—(A) The evaluation required under paragraph (1)(A) shall examine the extent to which the significant air quality standards and controls required under this Act are comparable to existing internationally-agreed norms.
    (B) The strategy required to be developed under paragraph (1)(B) shall include recommended options (such as the harmonization of standards and trade adjustment measures) for reducing or eliminating competitive disadvantages caused by differences in standards and controls between the United States and each of its major trading partners.
  (3) Public comment.—Interested parties shall be given an opportunity to submit comments regarding the evaluations and strategy required in the report under paragraph (1). The President shall take any such comment into account in preparing the report.
  (4) Interim report.—Within 9 months after the date of the enactment of the Clean Air Act Amendments of 1990 [Nov. 15, 1990], the President shall submit to the Congress an interim report on the progress being made in complying with paragraph (1)."

GAO Reports on Costs and Benefits

Section 812(b) of Pub. L. 101-549, which directed Comptroller General, commencing on second year after Nov. 15, 1990, and annually thereafter, in consultation with other agencies, to report to Congress on pollution control strategies and technologies required by Clean Air Act Amendments of 1990, was repealed by Pub. L. 104-316, title I, Sec. 122(r), Oct. 19, 1996, 110 Stat. 3838.

---

42 USC 7613

Repealed. Pub. L. 101-549, title VIII, Sec. 803, Nov. 15, 1990, 104 Stat. 2689

Section, act July 14, 1955, ch. 360, title III, Sec. 313, formerly Sec. 306, as added Nov. 21, 1967, Pub. L. 90-148, Sec. 2, 81 Stat. 506; renumbered Sec. 313 and amended Dec. 31, 1970, Pub. L. 91-604,

Secs. 12(a), 15(c)(2), 84 Stat. 1705, 1713; Aug. 7, 1977, Pub. L. 95-95, title III, Sec. 302(b), 91 Stat. 771, required annual report to Congress on progress of programs under this chapter.

LABOR STANDARDS

42 USC 7614

The Administrator shall take such action as may be necessary to insure that all laborers and mechanics employed by contractors or subcontractors on projects assisted under this chapter shall be paid wages at rates not less than those prevailing for the same type of work on similar construction in the locality as determined by the Secretary of Labor, in accordance with the Act of March 3, 1931, as amended, known as the Davis-Bacon Act (46 Stat. 1494; 40 U.S.C. 276a–276a-5). The Secretary of Labor shall have, with respect to the labor standards specified in this subsection, the authority and functions set forth in Reorganization Plan Numbered 14 of 1950 (15 F.R. 3176; 64 Stat. 1267) and section 276c of title 40.

(July 14, 1955, ch. 360, title III, Sec. 314, formerly Sec. 307, as added Pub. L. 90-148, Sec. 2, Nov. 21, 1967, 81 Stat. 506; renumbered Sec. 314 and amended Pub. L. 91-604, Secs. 12(a), 15(c)(2), Dec. 31, 1970, 84 Stat. 1705, 1713.)

References in Text

The Davis-Bacon Act, referred to in text, is act Mar. 3, 1931, ch. 411, 46 Stat. 1494, as amended, which is classified generally to sections 276a to 276a-5 of Title 40, Public Buildings, Property, and Works. For complete classification of this Act to the Code, see Short Title note set out under section 276a of Title 40 and Tables.

Reorganization Plan Numbered 14 of 1950, referred to in text, is set out in the Appendix to Title 5, Government Organization and Employees.

Codification

Section was formerly classified to section 1857j-3 of this title.

Amendments

1970–Pub. L. 91-604, Sec. 15(c)(2), substituted "Administrator" for "Secretary" meaning the Secretary of Health, Education, and Welfare.

SEPARABILITY

42 USC 7615

If any provision of this chapter, or the application of any provision of this chapter to any person or circumstance, is held invalid, the application of such provision to other persons or circumstances, and the remainder of this chapter shall not be affected thereby.

(July 14, 1955, ch. 360, title III, Sec. 315, formerly Sec. 12, as added Pub. L. 88-206, Sec. 1, Dec. 17, 1963, 77 Stat. 401; renumbered Sec. 305, Pub. L. 89-272, title I, Sec. 101(4), Oct. 20, 1965, 79 Stat. 992; renumbered Sec. 308 and amended, Pub. L. 90-148, Sec. 2, Nov. 21, 1967, 81 Stat. 506; renumbered Sec. 315, Pub. L. 91-604, Sec. 12(a), Dec. 31, 1970, 84 Stat. 1705.)

Codification

Section was formerly classified to section 1857k of this title.

Amendments

1967–Pub. L. 90-148 reenacted section without change.

SEWAGE TREATMENT GRANTS

42 USC 7616

(a) Construction
No grant which the Administrator is authorized to make to any applicant for construction of sewage treatment works in any area in any State may be withheld, conditioned, or restricted by the Administrator on the basis of any requirement of this chapter except as provided in subsection (b) of this section.

318 / Environmental Statutes

(b) Withholding, conditioning, or restriction of construction grants
The Administrator may withhold, condition, or restrict the making of any grant for construction referred to in subsection (a) of this section only if he determines that—
   (1) such treatment works will not comply with applicable standards under section 7411 or 7412 of this title,
   (2) the State does not have in effect, or is not carrying out, a State implementation plan approved by the Administrator which expressly quantifies and provides for the increase in emissions of each air pollutant (from stationary and mobile sources in any area to which either part C or part D of subchapter I of this chapter applies for such pollutant) which increase may reasonably be anticipated to result directly or indirectly from the new sewage treatment capacity which would be created by such construction.
   (3) the construction of such treatment works would create new sewage treatment capacity which—
      (A) may reasonably be anticipated to cause or contribute to, directly or indirectly, an increase in emissions of any air pollutant in excess of the increase provided for under the provisions referred to in paragraph (2) for any such area, or
      (B) would otherwise not be in conformity with the applicable implementation plan, or
   (4) such increase in emissions would interfere with, or be inconsistent with, the applicable implementation plan for any other State.
In the case of construction of a treatment works which would result, directly or indirectly, in an increase in emissions of any air pollutant from stationary and mobile sources in an area to which part D of subchapter I of this chapter applies, the quantification of emissions referred to in paragraph (2) shall include the emissions of any such pollutant resulting directly or indirectly from areawide and nonmajor stationary source growth (mobile and stationary) for each such area.
(c) National Environmental Policy Act
Nothing in this section shall be construed to amend or alter any provision of the National Environmental Policy Act [42 U.S.C. 4321 et seq.] or to affect any determination as to whether or not the requirements of such Act have been met in the case of the construction of any sewage treatment works.
(July 14, 1955, ch. 360, title III, Sec. 316, as added Pub. L. 95-95, title III, Sec. 306, Aug. 7, 1977, 91 Stat. 777.)

References in Text

The National Environmental Policy Act, referred to in subsec. (c), probably means the National Environmental Policy Act of 1969, Pub. L. 91-190, Jan. 1, 1970, 83 Stat. 852, as amended, which is classified generally to chapter 55 (Sec. 4321 et seq.) of this title. For complete classification of this Act to the Code, see Short Title note set out under section 4321 of this title and Tables.

Prior Provisions

A prior section 316 of act July 14, 1955, ch. 360, title III, formerly Sec. 13, as added Dec. 17, 1963, Pub. L. 88-206, Sec. 1, 77 Stat. 401; renumbered Sec. 306 and amended Oct. 20, 1965, Pub. L. 89-272, title I, Sec. 101(4), (6), (7), 79 Stat. 992; Oct. 15, 1966, Pub. L. 89-675, Sec. 2(a), 80 Stat. 954; renumbered Sec. 309 and amended Nov. 21, 1967, Pub. L. 90-148, Sec. 2, 81 Stat. 506; renumbered Sec. 316 and amended Dec. 31, 1970, Pub. L. 91-604, Secs. 12(a), 13(b), 84 Stat. 1705, 1709; Apr. 9, 1973, Pub. L. 93-15, Sec. 1(c), 87 Stat. 11; June 22, 1974, Pub. L. 93-319, Sec. 13(c), 88 Stat. 265, authorized appropriations for air pollution control, prior to repeal by section 306 of Pub. L. 95-95. See section 7626 of this title.

Effective Date

Section effective Aug. 7, 1977, except as otherwise expressly provided, see section 406(d) of Pub. L. 95-95, set out as an Effective Date of 1977 Amendment note under section 7401 of this title.

ECONOMIC IMPACT ASSESSMENT

42 USC 7617

(a) Notice of proposed rulemaking; substantial revisions
This section applies to action of the Administrator in promulgating or revising—
   (1) any new source standard of performance under section 7411 of this title,

(2) any regulation under section 7411(d) of this title,
(3) any regulation under part B[1] of subchapter I of this chapter (relating to ozone and stratosphere protection),
(4) any regulation under part C of subchapter I of this chapter (relating to prevention of significant deterioration of air quality),
(5) any regulation establishing emission standards under section 7521 of this title and any other regulation promulgated under that section,
(6) any regulation controlling or prohibiting any fuel or fuel additive under section 7545(c) of this title, and
(7) any aircraft emission standard under section 7571 of this title.

Nothing in this section shall apply to any standard or regulation described in paragraphs (1) through (7) of this subsection unless the notice of proposed rulemaking in connection with such standard or regulation is published in the Federal Register after the date ninety days after August 7, 1977. In the case of revisions of such standards or regulations, this section shall apply only to revisions which the Administrator determines to be substantial revisions.

(b) Preparation of assessment by Administrator

Before publication of notice of proposed rulemaking with respect to any standard or regulation to which this section applies, the Administrator shall prepare an economic impact assessment respecting such standard or regulation. Such assessment shall be included in the docket required under section 7607(d)(2) of this title and shall be available to the public as provided in section 7607(d)(4) of this title. Notice of proposed rulemaking shall include notice of such availability together with an explanation of the extent and manner in which the Administrator has considered the analysis contained in such economic impact assessment in proposing the action. The Administrator shall also provide such an explanation in his notice of promulgation of any regulation or standard referred to in subsection (a) of this section. Each such explanation shall be part of the statements of basis and purpose required under sections 7607(d)(3) and 7607(d)(6) of this title.

(c) Analysis

Subject to subsection (d) of this section, the assessment required under this section with respect to any standard or regulation shall contain an analysis of—
(1) the costs of compliance with any such standard or regulation, including extent to which the costs of compliance will vary depending on (A) the effective date of the standard or regulation, and (B) the development of less expensive, more efficient means or methods of compliance with the standard or regulation;
(2) the potential inflationary or recessionary effects of the standard or regulation;
(3) the effects on competition of the standard or regulation with respect to small business;
(4) the effects of the standard or regulation on consumer costs; and
(5) the effects of the standard or regulation on energy use.

Nothing in this section shall be construed to provide that the analysis of the factors specified in this subsection affects or alters the factors which the Administrator is required to consider in taking any action referred to in subsection (a) of this section.

(d) Extensiveness of assessment

The assessment required under this section shall be as extensive as practicable, in the judgment of the Administrator taking into account the time and resources available to the Environmental Protection Agency and other duties and authorities which the Administrator is required to carry out under this chapter.

(e) Limitations on construction of section

Nothing in this section shall be construed—
(1) to alter the basis on which a standard or regulation is promulgated under this chapter;
(2) to preclude the Administrator from carrying out his responsibility under this chapter to protect public health and welfare; or
(3) to authorize or require any judicial review of any such standard or regulation, or any stay or injunction of the proposal, promulgation, or effectiveness of such standard or regulation on the basis of failure to comply with this section.

(f) Citizen suits

The requirements imposed on the Administrator under this section shall be treated as

---

[1]See References in Text note below.

320 / Environmental Statutes

nondiscretionary duties for purposes of section 7604(a)(2) of this title, relating to citizen suits. The sole method for enforcement of the Administrator's duty under this section shall be by bringing a citizen suit under such section 7604(a)(2) for a court order to compel the Administrator to perform such duty. Violation of any such order shall subject the Administrator to penalties for contempt of court.

(g) Costs
In the case of any provision of this chapter in which costs are expressly required to be taken into account, the adequacy or inadequacy of any assessment required under this section may be taken into consideration, but shall not be treated for purposes of judicial review of any such provision as conclusive with respect to compliance or noncompliance with the requirement of such provision to take cost into account.

(July 14, 1955, ch. 360, title III, Sec. 317, as added Pub. L. 95-95, title III, Sec. 307, Aug. 7, 1977, 91 Stat. 778; amended Pub. L. 95-623, Sec. 13(d), Nov. 9, 1978, 92 Stat. 3458.)

References in Text

Part B of subchapter I of this chapter, referred to in subsec. (a)(3), was repealed by Pub. L. 101-549, title VI, Sec. 601, Nov. 15, 1990, 104 Stat. 2648. See subchapter VI (Sec. 7671 et seq.) of this chapter.

Codification

Another section 317 of act July 14, 1955, is set out as a Short Title note under section 7401 of this title.

Amendments

1978—Subsec. (a)(1). Pub. L. 95-623 substituted "section 7411" for "section 7411(b)".

Effective Date

Section effective Aug. 7, 1977, except as otherwise expressly provided, see section 406(d) of Pub. L. 95-95, set out as an Effective Date of 1977 Amendment note under section 7401 of this title.

42 USC 7618

Repealed. Pub. L. 101-549, title I, Sec. 108(q), Nov. 15, 1990, 104 Stat. 2469

Section, act July 14, 1955, ch. 360, title III, Sec. 318, as added Aug. 7, 1977, Pub. L. 95-95, title III, Sec. 308, 91 Stat. 780, related to financial disclosure and conflicts of interest.

AIR QUALITY MONITORING

42 USC 7619

Not later than one year after August 7, 1977, and after notice and opportunity for public hearing, the Administrator shall promulgate regulations establishing an air quality monitoring system throughout the United States which—
  (1) utilizes uniform air quality monitoring criteria and methodology and measures such air quality according to a uniform air quality index,
  (2) provides for air quality monitoring stations in major urban areas and other appropriate areas throughout the United States to provide monitoring such as will supplement (but not duplicate) air quality monitoring carried out by the States required under any applicable implementation plan,
  (3) provides for daily analysis and reporting of air quality based upon such uniform air quality index, and
  (4) provides for recordkeeping with respect to such monitoring data and for periodic analysis and reporting to the general public by the Administrator with respect to air quality based upon such data.

The operation of such air quality monitoring system may be carried out by the Administrator or by such other departments, agencies, or entities of the Federal Government (including the National Weather Service) as the President may deem appropriate. Any air quality monitoring system required under any applicable implementation plan under section 7410 of this title shall, as soon as practicable following promulgation of regulations under this section, utilize the standard criteria and methodology, and measure air quality according to the standard index, established under such regulations.

(July 14, 1955, ch. 360, title III, Sec. 319, as added Pub. L. 95-95, title III, Sec. 309, Aug. 7, 1977, 91 Stat. 781.)

Effective Date

Section effective Aug. 7, 1977, except as otherwise expressly provided, see section 406(d) of Pub. L. 95-95, set out as an Effective Date of 1977 Amendment note under section 7401 of this title.

STANDARDIZED AIR QUALITY MODELING

42 USC 7620

(a) Conferences
Not later than six months after August 7, 1977, and at least every three years thereafter, the Administrator shall conduct a conference on air quality modeling. In conducting such conference, special attention shall be given to appropriate modeling necessary for carrying out part C of subchapter I of this chapter (relating to prevention of significant deterioration of air quality).

(b) Conferees
The conference conducted under this section shall provide for participation by the National Academy of Sciences, representatives of State and local air pollution control agencies, and appropriate Federal agencies, including the National Science Foundation; the National Oceanic and Atmospheric Administration, and the National Institute of Standards and Technology.

(c) Comments; transcripts
Interested persons shall be permitted to submit written comments and a verbatim transcript of the conference proceedings shall be maintained.

(d) Promulgation and revision of regulations relating to air quality modeling
The comments submitted and the transcript maintained pursuant to subsection (c) of this section shall be included in the docket required to be established for purposes of promulgating or revising any regulation relating to air quality modeling under part C of subchapter I of this chapter.

(July 14, 1955, ch. 360, title III, Sec. 320, as added Pub. L. 95-95, title III, Sec. 310, Aug. 7, 1977, 91 Stat. 782; amended Pub. L. 100-418, title V, Sec. 5115(c), Aug. 23, 1988, 102 Stat. 1433.)

Amendments

1988—Subsec. (b). Pub. L. 100-418 substituted "National Institute of Standards and Technology" for "National Bureau of Standards".

Effective Date

Section effective Aug. 7, 1977, except as otherwise expressly provided, see section 406(d) of Pub. L. 95-95, set out as an Effective Date of 1977 Amendment note under section 7401 of this title.

EMPLOYMENT EFFECTS

42 USC 7621

(a) Continuous evaluation of potential loss or shifts of employment
The Administrator shall conduct continuing evaluations of potential loss or shifts of employment which may result from the administration or enforcement of the provision of this chapter and applicable implementation plans, including where appropriate, investigating threatened plant closures or reductions in employment allegedly resulting from such administration or enforcement.

(b) Request for investigation; hearings; record; report
Any employee, or any representative of such employee, who is discharged or laid off, threatened with discharge or layoff, or whose employment is otherwise adversely affected or threatened to be adversely affected because of the alleged results of any requirement imposed or proposed to be imposed under this chapter, including any requirement applicable to Federal

facilities and any requirement imposed by a State or political subdivision thereof, may request the Administrator to conduct a full investigation of the matter. Any such request shall be reduced to writing, shall set forth with reasonable particularity the grounds for the request, and shall be signed by the employee, or representative of such employee, making the request. The Administrator shall thereupon investigate the matter and, at the request of any party, shall hold public hearings on not less than five days' notice. At such hearings, the Administrator shall require the parties, including the employer involved, to present information relating to the actual or potential effect of such requirements on employment and the detailed reasons or justification therefor. If the Administrator determines that there are no reasonable grounds for conducting a public hearing he shall notify (in writing) the party requesting such hearing of such a determination and the reasons therefor. If the Administrator does convene such a hearing, the hearing shall be on the record. Upon receiving the report of such investigation, the Administrator shall make findings of fact as to the effect of such requirements on employment and on the alleged actual or potential discharge, layoff, or other adverse effect on employment, and shall make such recommendations as he deems appropriate. Such report, findings, and recommendations shall be available to the public.

(c) Subpenas; confidential information; witnesses; penalty
In connection with any investigation or public hearing conducted under subsection (b) of this section or as authorized in section 7419 of this title (relating to primary nonferrous smelter orders), the Administrator may issue subpenas for the attendance and testimony of witnesses and the production of relevant papers, books and documents, and he may administer oaths. Except for emission data, upon a showing satisfactory to the Administrator by such owner or operator that such papers, books, documents, or information or particular part thereof, if made public, would divulge trade secrets or secret processes of such owner, or operator, the Administrator shall consider such record, report, or information or particular portion thereof confidential in accordance with the purposes of section 1905 of title 18, except that such paper, book, document, or information may be disclosed to other officers, employees, or authorized representatives of the United States concerned with carrying out this chapter, or when relevant in any proceeding under this chapter. Witnesses summoned shall be paid the same fees and mileage that are paid witnesses in the courts of the United States. In cases of contumacy or refusal to obey a subpena served upon any person under this subparagraph, the district court of the United States for any district in which such person is found or resides or transacts business, upon application by the United States and after notice to such person, shall have jurisdiction to issue an order requiring such person to appear and give testimony before the Administrator, to appear and produce papers, books, and documents before the Administrator, or both, and any failure to obey such order of the court may be punished by such court as a contempt thereof.

(d) Limitations on construction of section
Nothing in this section shall be construed to require or authorize the Administrator, the States, or political subdivisions thereof, to modify or withdraw any requirement imposed or proposed to be imposed under this chapter.

(July 14, 1955, ch. 360, title III, Sec. 321, as added Pub. L. 95-95, title III, Sec. 311, Aug. 7, 1977, 91 Stat. 782.)

Effective Date

Section effective Aug. 7, 1977, except as otherwise expressly provided, see section 406(d) of Pub. L. 95-95, set out as an Effective Date of 1977 Amendment note under section 7401 of this title.

Study of Potential Dislocation of Employees

Section 403(e) of Pub. L. 95-95 provided that the Secretary of Labor, in consultation with the Administrator, conduct a study of potential dislocation of employees due to implementation of laws administered by the Administrator and that the Secretary submit to Congress the results of the study not more than one year after Aug. 7, 1977.

Section Referred to in Other Sections

This section is referred to in section 7419 of this title.

EMPLOYEE PROTECTION

42 USC 7622

(a) Discharge or discrimination prohibited

No employer may discharge any employee or otherwise discriminate against any employee with respect to his compensation, terms, conditions, or privileges of employment because the employee (or any person acting pursuant to a request of the employee)–
   (1) commenced, caused to be commenced, or is about to commence or cause to be commenced a proceeding under this chapter or a proceeding for the administration or enforcement of any requirement imposed under this chapter or under any applicable implementation plan,
   (2) testified or is about to testify in any such proceeding, or
   (3) assisted or participated or is about to assist or participate in any manner in such a proceeding or in any other action to carry out the purposes of this chapter.

(b) Complaint charging unlawful discharge or discrimination; investigation; order
   (1) Any employee who believes that he has been discharged or otherwise discriminated against by any person in violation of subsection (a) of this section may, within thirty days after such violation occurs, file (or have any person file on his behalf) a complaint with the Secretary of Labor (hereinafter in this subsection referred to as the "Secretary") alleging such discharge or discrimination. Upon receipt of such a complaint, the Secretary shall notify the person named in the complaint of the filing of the complaint.
   (2) (A) Upon receipt of a complaint filed under paragraph (1), the Secretary shall conduct an investigation of the violation alleged in the complaint. Within thirty days of the receipt of such complaint, the Secretary shall complete such investigation and shall notify in writing the complainant (and any person acting in his behalf) and the person alleged to have committed such violation of the results of the investigation conducted pursuant to this subparagraph. Within ninety days of the receipt of such complaint the Secretary shall, unless the proceeding on the complaint is terminated by the Secretary on the basis of a settlement entered into by the Secretary and the person alleged to have committed such violation, issue an order either providing the relief prescribed by subparagraph (B) or denying the complaint. An order of the Secretary shall be made on the record after notice and opportunity for public hearing. The Secretary may not enter into a settlement terminating a proceeding on a complaint without the participation and consent of the complainant.
      (B) If, in response to a complaint filed under paragraph (1), the Secretary determines that a violation of subsection (a) of this section has occurred, the Secretary shall order the person who committed such violation to (i) take affirmative action to abate the violation, and (ii) reinstate the complainant to his former position together with the compensation (including back pay), terms, conditions, and privileges of his employment, and the Secretary may order such person to provide compensatory damages to the complainant. If an order is issued under this paragraph, the Secretary, at the request of the complainant, shall assess against the person against whom the order is issued a sum equal to the aggregate amount of all costs and expenses (including attorneys' and expert witness fees) reasonably incurred, as determined by the Secretary, by the complainant for, or in connection with, the bringing of the complaint upon which the order was issued.

(c) Review
   (1) Any person adversely affected or aggrieved by an order issued under subsection (b) of this section may obtain review of the order in the United States court of appeals for the circuit in which the violation, with respect to which the order was issued, allegedly occurred. The petition for review must be filed within sixty days from the issuance of the Secretary's order. Review shall conform to chapter 7 of title 5. The commencement of proceedings under this subparagraph shall not, unless ordered by the court, operate as a stay of the Secretary's order.
   (2) An order of the Secretary with respect to which review could have been obtained under paragraph (1) shall not be subject to judicial review in any criminal or other civil proceeding.

(d) Enforcement of order by Secretary
Whenever a person has failed to comply with an order issued under subsection (b)(2) of this section, the Secretary may file a civil action in the United States district court for the district in which the violation was found to occur to enforce such order. In actions brought under this subsection, the district courts shall have jurisdiction to grant all appropriate relief including, but not limited to, injunctive relief, compensatory, and exemplary damages.

(e) Enforcement of order by person on whose behalf order was issued
(1) Any person on whose behalf an order was issued under paragraph (2) of subsection (b) of this section may commence a civil action against the person to whom such order was issued to require compliance with such order. The appropriate United States district court shall have jurisdiction, without regard to the amount in controversy or the citizenship of the parties, to enforce such order.
(2) The court, in issuing any final order under this subsection, may award costs of litigation (including reasonable attorney and expert witness fees) to any party whenever the court determines such award is appropriate.

(f) Mandamus
Any nondiscretionary duty imposed by this section shall be enforceable in a mandamus proceeding brought under section 1361 of title 28.

(g) Deliberate violation by employee
Subsection (a) of this section shall not apply with respect to any employee who, acting without direction from his employer (or the employer's agent), deliberately causes a violation of any requirement of this chapter.

(July 14, 1955, ch. 360, title III, Sec. 322, as added Pub. L. 95-95, title III, Sec. 312, Aug. 7, 1977, 91 Stat. 783.)

Effective Date

Section effective Aug. 7, 1977, except as otherwise expressly provided, see section 406(d) of Pub. L. 95-95, set out as an Effective Date of 1977 Amendment note under section 7401 of this title.

Federal Rules of Civil Procedure

Injunctions, see rule 65, Title 28, Appendix, Judiciary and Judicial Procedure.

Writ of mandamus abolished in United States district courts, but relief available by appropriate action or motion, see rule 81.

---

42 USC 7623

Repealed. Pub. L. 96-300, Sec. 1(c), July 2, 1980, 94 Stat. 831

Section, act July 14, 1955, ch. 360, title III, Sec. 323, as added Aug. 7, 1977, Pub. L. 95-95, title III, Sec. 313, 91 Stat. 785; amended Nov. 16, 1977, Pub. L. 95-190, Sec. 14(a)(81), 91 Stat. 1404; S. Res. 4, Feb. 4, 1977; H. Res. 549, Mar. 25, 1980; July 2, 1980, Pub. L. 96-300, Sec. 1(a), 94 Stat. 831, established a National Commission on Air Quality, prescribed numerous subjects for study and report to Congress, enumerated specific questions for study and investigation, required specific identification of loss or irretrievable commitment of resources, and provided for appointment and confirmation of its membership, cooperation of Federal executive agencies, submission of a National Academy of Sciences study to Congress, compensation and travel expenses, termination of Commission, appointment and compensation of staff, and public participation.

Effective Date of Repeal

Section 1(c) of Pub. L. 96-300 provided that this section is repealed on date on which National Commission on Air Quality ceases to exist pursuant to provisions of former subsec. (g) of this section, which provided that not later than Mar. 1, 1981, a report be submitted containing results of all Commission studies and investigations and that Commission cease to exist on Mar. 1, 1981, if report is not submitted on Mar. 1, 1981, or Commission would cease to exist on such date, but not later than May 1, 1981, as determined and ordered by Commission if report is submitted on Mar. 1, 1981.

National Commission on Air Quality; Extension Prohibition

Section 1(d) of Pub. L. 96-300 provided that nothing in any other authority of law shall be construed to authorize or permit the extension of the National Commission on Air Quality pursuant to any Executive order or other Executive or agency action.

COST OF VAPOR RECOVERY EQUIPMENT

42 USC 7624

(a) Costs to be borne by owner of retail outlet
The regulations under this chapter applicable to vapor recovery with respect to mobile source fuels at retail outlets of such fuels shall provide that the cost of procurement and installation of such vapor recovery shall be borne by the owner of such outlet (as determined under such regulations). Except as provided in subsection (b) of this section, such regulations shall provide that no lease of a retail outlet by the owner thereof which is entered into or renewed after August 7, 1977, may provide for a payment by the lessee of the cost of procurement and installation of vapor recovery equipment. Such regulations shall also provide that the cost of procurement and installation of vapor recovery equipment may be recovered by the owner of such outlet by means of price increases in the cost of any product sold by such owner, notwithstanding any provision of law.

(b) Payment by lessee
The regulations of the Administrator referred to in subsection (a) of this section shall permit a lease of a retail outlet to provide for payment by the lessee of the cost of procurement and installation of vapor recovery equipment over a reasonable period (as determined in accordance with such regulations), if the owner of such outlet does not sell, trade in, or otherwise dispense any product at wholesale or retail at such outlet.

(July 14, 1955, ch. 360, title III, Sec. 323, formerly Sec. 324, as added Pub. L. 95-95, title III, Sec. 314(a), Aug. 7, 1977, 91 Stat. 788; amended Pub. L. 95-190, Sec. 14(a)(82), Nov. 16, 1977, 91 Stat. 1404; renumbered Sec. 323 and amended Pub. L. 96-300, Sec. 1(b), (c), July 2, 1980, 94 Stat. 831.)

Prior Provisions

A prior section 323 of act July 14, 1955, was classified to section 7623 of this title prior to repeal by Pub. L. 96-300, Sec. 1(c), July 2, 1980, 94 Stat. 831.

Amendments

1980—Pub. L. 96-300, Sec. 1(b), which directed that last sentence of this section be struck out was probably intended to strike sentence purportedly added by Pub. L. 95-190. See 1977 Amendment note below and section 7623(i) of this title.

1977—Pub. L. 95-190 which purported to amend subsec. (j) of this section by inserting "The Commission may appoint and fix the pay of such staff as it deems necessary." after "(j)" was not executed to this section because it did not contain a subsec. (j). See 1980 Amendment note above.

Effective Date

Section effective Aug. 7, 1977, except as otherwise expressly provided, see section 406(d) of Pub. L. 95-95, set out as an Effective Date of 1977 Amendment note under section 7401 of this title.

Section Referred to in Other Sections

This section is referred to in sections 7413, 7625a of this title.

VAPOR RECOVERY FOR SMALL BUSINESS MARKETERS OF PETROLEUM PRODUCTS

42 USC 7625

(a) Marketers of gasoline
The regulations under this chapter applicable to vapor recovery from fueling of motor vehicles at retail outlets of gasoline shall not apply to any outlet owned by an independent small business marketer of gasoline having monthly sales of less than 50,000 gallons. In the case of

any other outlet owned by an independent small business marketer, such regulations shall provide, with respect to independent small business marketers of gasoline, for a three-year phase-in period for the installation of such vapor recovery equipment at such outlets under which such marketers shall have—
  (1) 33 percent of such outlets in compliance at the end of the first year during which such regulations apply to such marketers,
  (2) 66 percent at the end of such second year, and
  (3) 100 percent at the end of the third year.
(b) State requirements
  Nothing in subsection (a) of this section shall be construed to prohibit any State from adopting or enforcing, with respect to independent small business marketers of gasoline having monthly sales of less than 50,000 gallons, any vapor recovery requirements for mobile source fuels at retail outlets. Any vapor recovery requirement which is adopted by a State and submitted to the Administrator as part of its implementation plan may be approved and enforced by the Administrator as part of the applicable implementation plan for that State.
(c) Refiners
  For purposes of this section, an independent small business marketer of gasoline is a person engaged in the marketing of gasoline who would be required to pay for procurement and installation of vapor recovery equipment under section 7624 of this title or under regulations of the Administrator, unless such person—
  (1) (A) is a refiner, or
    (B) controls, is controlled by, or is under common control with, a refiner,
    (C) is otherwise directly or indirectly affiliated (as determined under the regulations of the Administrator) with a refiner or with a person who controls, is controlled by, or is under a common control with a refiner (unless the sole affiliation referred to herein is by means of a supply contract or an agreement
  or contract to use a trademark, trade name, service mark, or other identifying symbol or name owned by such refiner or any such person), or
  (2) receives less than 50 percent of his annual income from refining or marketing of gasoline.
  For the purpose of this section, the term "refiner" shall not include any refiner whose total refinery capacity (including the refinery capacity of any person who controls, is controlled by, or is under common control with, such refiner) does not exceed 65,000 barrels per day. For purposes of this section, "control" of a corporation means ownership of more than 50 percent of its stock.

(July 14, 1955, ch. 360, title III, Sec. 324, formerly Sec. 325, as added Pub. L. 95-95, title III, Sec. 314(b), Aug. 7, 1977, 91 Stat. 789; renumbered Sec. 324, Pub. L. 96-300, Sec. 1(c), July 2, 1980, 94 Stat. 831.)

Prior Provisions

A prior section 324 of act July 14, 1955, was renumbered section 323 by Pub. L. 96-300 and is classified to section 7624 of this title.

Effective Date

Section effective Aug. 7, 1977, except as otherwise expressly provided, see section 406(d) of Pub. L. 95-95, set out as an Effective Date of 1977 Amendment note under section 7401 of this title.

Section Referred to in Other Sections

This section is referred to in section 7511a of this title.

EXEMPTIONS FOR CERTAIN TERRITORIES

42 USC 7625-1

(a) (1) Upon petition by the governor[1] of Guam, American Samoa, the Virgin Islands, or the Commonwealth of the Northern Mariana Islands, the Administrator is authorized to exempt any person or source or class of persons or sources in such territory from any requirement under this chapter other than section 7412 of this title or any requirement un-

---

[1]So in original. Probably should be capitalized.

der section 7410 of this title or part D of subchapter I of this chapter necessary to attain or maintain a national primary ambient air quality standard. Such exemption may be granted if the Administrator finds that compliance with such requirement is not feasible or is unreasonable due to unique geographical, meteorological, or economic factors of such territory, or such other local factors as the Administrator deems significant. Any such petition shall be considered in accordance with section 7607(d) of this title and any exemption under this subsection shall be considered final action by the Administrator for the purposes of section 7607(b) of this title.
- (2) The Administrator shall promptly notify the Committees on Energy and Commerce and on Natural Resources of the House of Representatives and the Committees on Environment and Public Works and on Energy and Natural Resources of the Senate upon receipt of any petition under this subsection and of the approval or rejection of such petition and the basis for such action.

(b) Notwithstanding any other provision of this chapter, any fossil fuel fired steam electric power plant operating within Guam as of December 8, 1983, is hereby exempted from:
- (1) any requirement of the new source performance standards relating to sulfur dioxide promulgated under section 7411 of this title as of December 8, 1983; and
- (2) any regulation relating to sulfur dioxide standards or limitations contained in a State implementation plan approved under section 7410 of this title as of December 8, 1983: Provided, That such exemption shall expire eighteen months after December 8, 1983, unless the Administrator determines that such plant is making all emissions reductions practicable to prevent exceedances of the national ambient air quality standards for sulfur dioxide.

(July 14, 1955, ch. 360, title III, Sec. 325, as added Pub. L. 98-213, Sec. 11, Dec. 8, 1983, 97 Stat. 1461; amended Pub. L. 101-549, title VIII, Sec. 806, Nov. 15, 1990, 104 Stat. 2689; Pub. L. 103-437, Sec. 15(s), Nov. 2, 1994, 108 Stat. 4594.)

Prior Provisions

A prior section 325 of act July 14, 1955, was renumbered section 326 by Pub. L. 98-213 and is classified to section 7625a of this title.

Another prior section 325 of act July 14, 1955, was renumbered section 324 by Pub. L. 96-300 and is classified to section 7625 of this title.

Amendments

1994—Subsec. (a)(2). Pub. L. 103-437 substituted "Natural Resources" for "Interior and Insular Affairs" before "of the House".

1990—Subsec. (a)(1). Pub. L. 101-549, which directed the insertion of "the Virgin Islands," after "American Samoa," in "[s]ection 324(a)(1) of the Clean Air Act (42 U.S.C. 7625-1(a)(1))", was executed by making the insertion in subsec. (a)(1) of this section to reflect the probable intent of Congress.

Change of Name

Committee on Energy and Commerce of House of Representatives treated as referring to Committee on Commerce of House of Representatives and Committee on Natural Resources of House of Representatives treated as referring to Committee on Resources of House of Representatives by section 1(a) of Pub. L. 104-14, set out as a note preceding section 21 of Title 2, The Congress.

Section Referred to in Other Sections

This section is referred to in section 7545 of this title.

STATUTORY CONSTRUCTION

42 USC 7625a

The parenthetical cross references in any provision of this chapter to other provisions of the chapter, or other provisions of law, where the words "relating to" or "pertaining to" are used, are made only for convenience, and shall be given no legal effect.

(July 14, 1955, ch. 360, title III, Sec. 326, as added Pub. L. 95-190, Sec. 14(a)(84), Nov. 16, 1977, 91 Stat. 1404; renumbered Sec. 325, Pub. L. 96-300, Sec. 1(c), July 2, 1980, 94 Stat. 831; renumbered Sec. 326, Pub. L. 98-213, Sec. 11, Dec. 8, 1983, 97 Stat. 1461.)

Prior Provisions

A prior section 326 of act July 14, 1955, was renumbered section 327 by Pub. L. 98-213 and is classified to section 7626 of this title.

AUTHORIZATION OF APPROPRIATIONS

42 USC 7626

(a) In general
There are authorized to be appropriated to carry out this chapter such sums as may be necessary for the 7 fiscal years commencing after November 15, 1990.

(b) Grants for planning
There are authorized to be appropriated (1) not more than $50,000,000 to carry out section 7505 of this title beginning in fiscal year 1991, to be available until expended, to develop plan revisions required by subpart 2, 3, or 4 of part D of subchapter I of this chapter, and (2) not more than $15,000,000 for each of the 7 fiscal years commencing after November 15, 1990, to make grants to the States to prepare implementation plans as required by subpart 2, 3, or 4 of part D of subchapter I of this chapter.

(July 14, 1955, ch. 360, title III, Sec. 327, formerly Sec. 325, as added Pub. L. 95-95, title III, Sec. 315, Aug. 7, 1977, 91 Stat. 790; renumbered Sec. 327 and amended Pub. L. 95-190, Sec. 14(a)(83), Nov. 16, 1977, 91 Stat. 1404; renumbered Sec. 326, Pub. L. 96-300, Sec. 1(c), July 2, 1980, 94 Stat. 831; renumbered Sec. 327, Pub. L. 98-213, Sec. 11, Dec. 8, 1983, 97 Stat. 1461; Pub. L. 101-549, title VIII, Sec. 822, Nov. 15, 1990, 104 Stat. 2699.)

Prior Provisions

Provisions similar to those in this section were contained in section 1857l of this title, act July 14, 1955, ch. 360, title III, Sec. 316, formerly Sec. 13, as added Dec. 17, 1963, Pub. L. 88-206, Sec. 1, 77 Stat. 401; renumbered Sec. 306 and amended Oct. 20, 1965, Pub. L. 89-272, title I, Sec. 101(4), (6), (7), 79 Stat. 992; Oct. 15, 1966, Pub. L. 89-675, Sec. 2(a), 80 Stat. 954; renumbered Sec. 309 and amended Nov. 21, 1967, Pub. L. 90-148, Sec. 2, 81 Stat. 506; renumbered Sec. 316 and amended Dec. 31, 1970, Pub. L. 91-604, Secs. 12(a), 13(b), 84 Stat. 1705, 1709; Apr. 9, 1973, Pub. L. 93-15, Sec. 1(c), 87 Stat. 11; June 22, 1974, Pub. L. 93-319, Sec. 13(c), 88 Stat. 265, prior to repeal by section 306 of Pub. L. 95-95.

Amendments

1990—Pub. L. 101-549 amended section generally, substituting present provisions for provisions authorizing specific appropriations for certain programs and periods and appropriations of $200,000,000 for fiscal years 1978 through 1981 to carry out the other programs under this chapter.

1977—Subsec. (b)(4). Pub. L. 95-190 substituted "section 7403(a)(5)" for "section 7403(b)(5)".

Effective Date

Section effective Aug. 7, 1977, except as otherwise expressly provided, see section 406(d) of Pub. L. 95-95, set out as an Effective Date of 1977 Amendment note under section 7401 of this title.

AIR POLLUTION FROM OUTER CONTINENTAL SHELF ACTIVITIES

42 USC 7627

(a) Applicable requirements for certain areas
  (1) In general
    Not later than 12 months after November 15, 1990, following consultation with the Secretary of the Interior and the Commandant of the United States Coast Guard, the Administrator, by rule, shall establish requirements to control air pollution from Outer Continen-

tal Shelf sources located offshore of the States along the Pacific, Arctic and Atlantic Coasts, and along the United States Gulf Coast off the State of Florida eastward of longitude 87 degrees and 30 minutes ("OCS sources") to attain and maintain Federal and State ambient air quality standards and to comply with the provisions of part C of subchapter I of this chapter. For such sources located within 25 miles of the seaward boundary of such States, such requirements shall be the same as would be applicable if the source were located in the corresponding onshore area, and shall include, but not be limited to, State and local requirements for emission controls, emission limitations, offsets, permitting, monitoring, testing, and reporting. New OCS sources shall comply with such requirements on the date of promulgation and existing OCS sources shall comply on the date 24 months thereafter. The Administrator shall update such requirements as necessary to maintain consistency with onshore regulations. The authority of this subsection shall supersede section 5(a)(8) of the Outer Continental Shelf Lands Act [43 U.S.C. 1334(a)(8)] but shall not repeal or modify any other Federal, State, or local authorities with respect to air quality. Each requirement established under this section shall be treated, for purposes of sections 7413, 7414, 7416, 7420, and 7604 of this title, as a standard under section 7411 of this title and a violation of any such requirement shall be considered a violation of section 7411(e) of this title.

(2) Exemptions

The Administrator may exempt an OCS source from a specific requirement in effect under regulations under this subsection if the Administrator finds that compliance with a pollution control technology requirement is technically infeasible or will cause an unreasonable threat to health and safety. The Administrator shall make written findings explaining the basis of any exemption issued pursuant to this subsection and shall impose another requirement equal to or as close in stringency to the original requirement as possible. The Administrator shall ensure that any increase in emissions due to the granting of an exemption is offset by reductions in actual emissions, not otherwise required by this chapter, from the same source or other sources in the area or in the corresponding onshore area. The Administrator shall establish procedures to provide for public notice and comment on exemptions proposed pursuant to this subsection.

(3) State procedures

Each State adjacent to an OCS source included under this subsection may promulgate and submit to the Administrator regulations for implementing and enforcing the requirements of this subsection. If the Administrator finds that the State regulations are adequate, the Administrator shall delegate to that State any authority the Administrator has under this chapter to implement and enforce such requirements. Nothing in this subsection shall prohibit the Administrator from enforcing any requirement of this section.

(4) Definitions

For purposes of subsections (a) and (b) of this section—

(A) Outer Continental Shelf

The term "Outer Continental Shelf" has the meaning provided by section 2 of the Outer Continental Shelf Lands Act (43 U.S.C. 1331).

(B) Corresponding onshore area

The term "corresponding onshore area" means, with respect to any OCS source, the onshore attainment or nonattainment area that is closest to the source, unless the Administrator determines that another area with more stringent requirements with respect to the control and abatement of air pollution may reasonably be expected to be affected by such emissions. Such determination shall be based on the potential for air pollutants from the OCS source to reach the other onshore area and the potential of such air pollutants to affect the efforts of the other onshore area to attain or maintain any Federal or State ambient air quality standard or to comply with the provisions of part C of subchapter I of this chapter.

(C) Outer Continental Shelf source

The terms "Outer Continental Shelf source" and "OCS source" include any equipment, activity, or facility which—

(i) emits or has the potential to emit any air pollutant,

(ii) is regulated or authorized under the Outer Continental Shelf Lands Act [43 U.S.C. 1331 et seq.], and

330 / Environmental Statutes

   (iii) is located on the Outer Continental Shelf or in or on waters above the Outer Continental Shelf.

  Such activities include, but are not limited to, platform and drill ship exploration, construction, development, production, processing, and transportation. For purposes of this subsection, emissions from any vessel servicing or associated with an OCS source, including emissions while at the OCS source or en route to or from the OCS source within 25 miles of the OCS source, shall be considered direct emissions from the OCS source.

  (D) New and existing OCS sources

  The term "new OCS source" means an OCS source which is a new source within the meaning of section 7411(a) of this title. The term "existing OCS source" means any OCS source other than a new OCS source.

(b) Requirements for other offshore areas

For portions of the United States Gulf Coast Outer Continental Shelf that are adjacent to the States not covered by subsection (a) of this section which are Texas, Louisiana, Mississippi, and Alabama, the Secretary shall consult with the Administrator to assure coordination of air pollution control regulation for Outer Continental Shelf emissions and emissions in adjacent onshore areas. Concurrently with this obligation, the Secretary shall complete within 3 years of November 15, 1990, a research study examining the impacts of emissions from Outer Continental Shelf activities in such areas that fail to meet the national ambient air quality standards for either ozone or nitrogen dioxide. Based on the results of this study, the Secretary shall consult with the Administrator and determine if any additional actions are necessary. There are authorized to be appropriated such sums as may be necessary to provide funding for the study required under this section.

(c) Coastal waters

 (1) The study report of section 7412(n)[1] of this title shall apply to the coastal waters of the United States to the same extent and in the same manner as such requirements apply to the Great Lakes, the Chesapeake Bay, and their tributary waters.

 (2) The regulatory requirements of section 7412(n)[1] of this title shall apply to the coastal waters of the States which are subject to subsection (a) of this section, to the same extent and in the same manner as such requirements apply to the Great Lakes, the Chesapeake Bay, and their tributary waters.

(July 14, 1955, ch. 360, title III, Sec. 328, as added Pub. L. 101-549, title VIII, Sec. 801, Nov. 15, 1990, 104 Stat. 2685.)

References in Text

The Outer Continental Shelf Lands Act, referred to in subsec. (a)(4)(C)(ii), is act Aug. 7, 1953, ch. 345, 67 Stat. 462, as amended, which is classified generally to subchapter III (Sec. 1331 et seq.) of chapter 29 of Title 43, Public Lands. For complete classification of this Act to the Code, see Short Title note set out under section 1331 of Title 43 and Tables.

Section Referred to in Other Sections

This section is referred to in section 7412 of this title.

---

[1] So in original. Probably should be section "7412(m)".

SUBCHAPTER IV—NOISE POLLUTION

NOISE ABATEMENT

42 USC 7641

(a) Office of Noise Abatement and Control
The Administrator shall establish within the Environmental Protection Agency an Office of Noise Abatement and Control, and shall carry out through such Office a full and complete investigation and study of noise and its effect on the public health and welfare in order to (1) identify and classify causes and sources of noise, and (2) determine—
- (A) effects at various levels;
- (B) projected growth of noise levels in urban areas through the year 2000;
- (C) the psychological and physiological effect on humans;
- (D) effects of sporadic extreme noise (such as jet noise near airports) as compared with constant noise;
- (E) effect on wildlife and property (including values);
- (F) effect of sonic booms on property (including values); and
- (G) such other matters as may be of interest in the public welfare.

(b) Investigation techniques; report and recommendations
In conducting such investigation, the Administrator shall hold public hearings, conduct research, experiments, demonstrations, and studies. The Administrator shall report the results of such investigation and study, together with his recommendations for legislation or other action, to the President and the Congress not later than one year after December 31, 1970.

(c) Abatement of noise from Federal activities
In any case where any Federal department or agency is carrying out or sponsoring any activity resulting in noise which the Administrator determines amounts to a public nuisance or is otherwise objectionable, such department or agency shall consult with the Administrator to determine possible means of abating such noise.

(July 14, 1955, ch. 360, title IV, Sec. 402, as added Pub. L. 91-604, Sec. 14, Dec. 31, 1970, 84 Stat. 1709.)

Codification

Another section 402 of act July 14, 1955, as added by Pub. L. 101-549, title IV, Sec. 401, Nov. 15, 1990, 104 Stat. 2585, is classified to section 7651a of this title.

Section was formerly classified to section 1858 of this title.

AUTHORIZATION OF APPROPRIATIONS

42 USC 7642

There is authorized to be appropriated such amount, not to exceed $30,000,000, as may be necessary for the purposes of this subchapter.

(July 14, 1955, ch. 360, title IV, Sec. 403, as added Pub. L. 91-604, Sec. 14, Dec. 31, 1970, 84 Stat. 1710.)

Codification

Another section 403 of act July 14, 1955, as added by Pub. L. 101-549, title IV, Sec. 401, Nov. 15, 1990, 104 Stat. 2589, is classified to section 7651b of this title.

Section was formerly classified to section 1858a of this title.

SUBCHAPTER IV-A—ACID DEPOSITION CONTROL

FINDINGS AND PURPOSES

42 USC 7651

(a) Findings
The Congress finds that—
(1) the presence of acidic compounds and their precursors in the atmosphere and in deposition from the atmosphere represents a threat to natural resources, ecosystems, materials, visibility, and public health;
(2) the principal sources of the acidic compounds and their precursors in the atmosphere are emissions of sulfur and nitrogen oxides from the combustion of fossil fuels;
(3) the problem of acid deposition is of national and international significance;
(4) strategies and technologies for the control of precursors to acid deposition exist now that are economically feasible, and improved methods are expected to become increasingly available over the next decade;
(5) current and future generations of Americans will be adversely affected by delaying measures to remedy the problem;
(6) reduction of total atmospheric loading of sulfur dioxide and nitrogen oxides will enhance protection of the public health and welfare and the environment; and
(7) control measures to reduce precursor emissions from steam-electric generating units should be initiated without delay.

(b) Purposes
The purpose of this subchapter is to reduce the adverse effects of acid deposition through reductions in annual emissions of sulfur dioxide of ten million tons from 1980 emission levels, and, in combination with other provisions of this chapter, of nitrogen oxides emissions of approximately two million tons from 1980 emission levels, in the forty-eight contiguous States and the District of Columbia. It is the intent of this subchapter to effectuate such reductions by requiring compliance by affected sources with prescribed emission limitations by specified deadlines, which limitations may be met through alternative methods of compliance provided by an emission allocation and transfer system. It is also the purpose of this subchapter to encourage energy conservation, use of renewable and clean alternative technologies, and pollution prevention as a long-range strategy, consistent with the provisions of this subchapter, for reducing air pollution and other adverse impacts of energy production and use.

(July 14, 1955, ch. 360, title IV, Sec. 401, as added Pub. L. 101-549, title IV, Sec. 401, Nov. 15, 1990, 104 Stat. 2584.)

Codification

Another section 401 of act July 14, 1955, as added by Pub. L. 91-604, Sec. 14, Dec. 31, 1970, 84 Stat. 1709, is set out as a Short Title note under section 7401 of this title.

Acid Deposition Standards

Section 404 of Pub. L. 101-549 directed Administrator of Environmental Protection Agency, not later than 36 months after Nov. 15, 1990, to transmit to Congress a report on the feasibility and effectiveness of an acid deposition standard or standards to protect sensitive and critically sensitive aquatic and terrestrial resources.

Industrial SO_2 Emissions

Section 406 of Pub. L. 101-549 provided that:
"(a) Report.—Not later than January 1, 1995 and every 5 years thereafter, the Administrator of the Environmental Protection Agency shall transmit to the Congress a report containing an inventory of national annual sulfur dioxide emissions from industrial sources (as defined in title IV of the Act [42 U.S.C. 7651 et seq.]), including units subject to section 405(g)(6) of the Clean Air Act [42 U.S.C. 7651d(g)(6)], for all years for which data are available, as well as the likely trend in such emissions over the following twenty-year period. The reports shall also contain estimates of the actual emission reduction in each year resulting from promulgation of the diesel fuel desulfurization regulations under section 214 [42 U.S.C. 7548].

(b) 5.60 Million Ton Cap.—Whenever the inventory required by this section indicates that sulfur dioxide emissions from industrial sources, including units subject to section 405(g)(5) of the Clean Air Act [42 U.S.C. 7651d(g)(5)], may reasonably be expected to reach levels greater than 5.60 million tons per year, the Administrator of the Environmental Protection Agency shall take such actions under the Clean Air Act [42 U.S.C. 7401 et seq.] as may be appropriate to ensure that such emissions do not exceed 5.60 million tons per year. Such actions may include the promulgation of new and revised standards of performance for new sources, including units subject to section 405(g)(5) of the Clean Air Act, under section 111(b) of the Clean Air Act [42 U.S.C. 7411(b)], as well as promulgation of standards of performance for existing sources, including units subject to section 405(g)(5) of the Clean Air Act, under authority of this section. For an existing source regulated under this section, 'standard of performance' means a standard which the Administrator determines is applicable to that source and which reflects the degree of emission reduction achievable through the application of the best system of continuous emission reduction which (taking into consideration the cost of achieving such emission reduction, and any nonair quality health and environmental impact and energy requirements) the Administrator determines has been adequately demonstrated for that category of sources.

(c) Election.—Regulations promulgated under section 405(b) of the Clean Air Act [42 U.S.C. 7651d(b)] shall not prohibit a source from electing to become an affected unit under section 410 of the Clean Air Act [42 U.S.C. 7651i]."

Sense of Congress on Emission Reductions Costs

Section 407 of Pub. L. 101-549 provided that: "It is the sense of the Congress that the Clean Air Act Amendments of 1990 [Pub. L. 101-549, see Tables for classification], through the allowance program, allocates the costs of achieving the required reductions in emissions of sulfur dioxide and oxides of nitrogen among sources in the United States. Broad based taxes and emissions fees that would provide for payment of the costs of achieving required emissions reductions by any party or parties other than the sources required to achieve the reductions are undesirable."

Monitoring of Acid Rain Program in Canada

Section 408 of Pub. L. 101-549 provided that:

"(a) Reports to Congress.—The Administrator of the Environmental Protection Agency, in consultation with the Secretary of State, the Secretary of Energy, and other persons the Administrator deems appropriate, shall prepare and submit a report to Congress on January 1, 1994, January 1, 1999, and January 1, 2005.

(b) Contents.—The report to Congress shall analyze the current emission levels of sulfur dioxide and nitrogen oxides in each of the provinces participating in Canada's acid rain control program, the amount of emission reductions of sulfur dioxide and oxides of nitrogen achieved by each province, the methods utilized by each province in making those reductions, the costs to each province and the employment impacts in each province of making and maintaining those reductions.

(c) Compliance.—Beginning on January 1, 1999, the reports shall also assess the degree to which each province is complying with its stated emissions cap."

DEFINITIONS

42 USC 7651a

As used in this subchapter:
(1) The term "affected source" means a source that includes one or more affected units.
(2) The term "affected unit" means a unit that is subject to emission reduction requirements or limitations under this subchapter.
(3) The term "allowance" means an authorization, allocated to an affected unit by the Administrator under this subchapter, to emit, during or after a specified calendar year, one ton of sulfur dioxide.
(4) The term "baseline" means the annual quantity of fossil fuel consumed by an affected unit, measured in millions of British Thermal Units ("mmBtu's"), calculated as follows:
   (A) For each utility unit that was in commercial operation prior to January 1, 1985, the baseline shall be the annual average quantity of mmBtu's consumed in fuel during

calendar years 1985, 1986, and 1987, as recorded by the Department of Energy pursuant to Form 767. For any utility unit for which such form was not filed, the baseline shall be the level specified for such unit in the 1985 National Acid Precipitation Assessment Program (NAPAP) Emissions Inventory, Version 2, National Utility Reference File (NURF) or in a corrected data base as established by the Administrator pursuant to paragraph (3). For nonutility units, the baseline is the NAPAP Emissions Inventory, Version 2. The Administrator, in the Administrator's sole discretion, may exclude periods during which a unit is shutdown for a continuous period of four calendar months or longer, and make appropriate adjustments under this paragraph. Upon petition of the owner or operator of any unit, the Administrator may make appropriate baseline adjustments for accidents that caused prolonged outages.
- (B) For any other nonutility unit that is not included in the NAPAP Emissions Inventory, Version 2, or a corrected data base as established by the Administrator pursuant to paragraph (3), the baseline shall be the annual average quantity, in mmBtu consumed in fuel by that unit, as calculated pursuant to a method which the administrator shall prescribe by regulation to be promulgated not later than eighteen months after November 15, 1990.
- (C) The Administrator shall, upon application or on his own motion, by December 31, 1991, supplement data needed in support of this subchapter and correct any factual errors in data from which affected Phase II units' baselines or actual 1985 emission rates have been calculated. Corrected data shall be used for purposes of issuing allowances under the[1] subchapter. Such corrections shall not be subject to judicial review, nor shall the failure of the Administrator to correct an alleged factual error in such reports be subject to judicial review.
- (5) The term "capacity factor" means the ratio between the actual electric output from a unit and the potential electric output from that unit.
- (6) The term "compliance plan" means, for purposes of the requirements of this subchapter, either—
  - (A) a statement that the source will comply with all applicable requirements under this subchapter, or
  - (B) where applicable, a schedule and description of the method or methods for compliance and certification by the owner or operator that the source is in compliance with the requirements of this subchapter.
- (7) The term "continuous emission monitoring system" (CEMS) means the equipment as required by section 7651k of this title, used to sample, analyze, measure, and provide on a continuous basis a permanent record of emissions and flow (expressed in pounds per million British thermal units (lbs/mmBtu), pounds per hour (lbs/hr) or such other form as the Administrator may prescribe by regulations under section 7651k of this title).
- (8) The term "existing unit" means a unit (including units subject to section 7411 of this title) that commenced commercial operation before November 15, 1990. Any unit that commenced commercial operation before November 15, 1990, which is modified, reconstructed, or repowered after November 15, 1990, shall continue to be an existing unit for the purposes of this subchapter. For the purposes of this subchapter, existing units shall not include simple combustion turbines, or units which serve a generator with a nameplate capacity of 25MWe or less.
- (9) The term "generator" means a device that produces electricity and which is reported as a generating unit pursuant to Department of Energy Form 860.
- (10) The term "new unit" means a unit that commences commercial operation on or after November 15, 1990.
- (11) The term "permitting authority" means the Administrator, or the State or local air pollution control agency, with an approved permitting program under part B[2] of title III of the Act.
- (12) The term "repowering" means replacement of an existing coal-fired boiler with one of the following clean coal technologies: atmospheric or pressurized fluidized bed combustion, integrated gasification combined cycle, magnetohydrodynamics, direct and indirect coal-fired turbines, integrated gasification fuel cells, or as determined by the Administrator, in consultation with the Secretary of Energy, a derivative of one or more of these technolo-

---

[1] So in original. Probably should be "this".
[2] See References in Text note below.

gies, and any other technology capable of controlling multiple combustion emissions simultaneously with improved boiler or generation efficiency and with significantly greater waste reduction relative to the performance of technology in widespread commercial use as of November 15, 1990. Notwithstanding the provisions of section 7651h(a) of this title, for the purpose of this subchapter, the term "repowering" shall also include any oil and/or gas-fired unit which has been awarded clean coal technology demonstration funding as of January 1, 1991, by the Department of Energy.

(13) The term "reserve" means any bank of allowances established by the Administrator under this subchapter.

(14) The term "State" means one of the 48 contiguous States and the District of Columbia.

(15) The term "unit" means a fossil fuel-fired combustion device.

(16) The term "actual 1985 emission rate", for electric utility units means the annual sulfur dioxide or nitrogen oxides emission rate in pounds per million Btu as reported in the NAPAP Emissions Inventory, Version 2, National Utility Reference File. For nonutility units, the term "actual 1985 emission rate" means the annual sulfur dioxide or nitrogen oxides emission rate in pounds per million Btu as reported in the NAPAP Emission Inventory, Version 2.

(17)(A) The term "utility unit" means—
  (i) a unit that serves a generator in any State that produces electricity for sale, or
  (ii) a unit that, during 1985, served a generator in any State that produced electricity for sale.
(B) Notwithstanding subparagraph (A), a unit described in subparagraph (A) that—
  (i) was in commercial operation during 1985, but
  (ii) did not, during 1985, serve a generator in any State that produced electricity for sale shall not be a utility unit for purposes of this subchapter.
(C) A unit that cogenerates steam and electricity is not a "utility unit" for purposes of this subchapter unless the unit is constructed for the purpose of supplying, or commences construction after November 15, 1990, and supplies, more than one-third of its potential electric output capacity and more than 25 megawatts electrical output to any utility power distribution system for sale.

(18) The term "allowable 1985 emissions rate" means a federally enforceable emissions limitation for sulfur dioxide or oxides of nitrogen, applicable to the unit in 1985 or the limitation applicable in such other subsequent year as determined by the Administrator if such a limitation for 1985 does not exist. Where the emissions limitation for a unit is not expressed in pounds of emissions per million Btu, or the averaging period of that emissions limitation is not expressed on an annual basis, the Administrator shall calculate the annual equivalent of that emissions limitation in pounds per million Btu to establish the allowable 1985 emissions rate.

(19) The term "qualifying phase I technology" means a technological system of continuous emission reduction which achieves a 90 percent reduction in emissions of sulfur dioxide from the emissions that would have resulted from the use of fuels which were not subject to treatment prior to combustion.

(20) The term "alternative method of compliance" means a method of compliance in accordance with one or more of the following authorities:
  (A) a substitution plan submitted and approved in accordance with subsections[3] 7651c(b) and (c) of this title;
  (B) a Phase I extension plan approved by the Administrator under section 7651c(d) of this title, using qualifying phase I technology as determined by the Administrator in accordance with that section; or
  (C) repowering with a qualifying clean coal technology under section 7651h of this title.

(21) The term "commenced" as applied to construction of any new electric utility unit means that an owner or operator has undertaken a continuous program of construction or that an owner or operator has entered into a contractual obligation to undertake and complete, within a reasonable time, a continuous program of construction.

(22) The term "commenced commercial operation" means to have begun to generate electricity for sale.

(23) The term "construction" means fabrication, erection, or installation of an affected unit.

---

[3] So in original. Probably should be "section".

336 / Environmental Statutes

(24) The term "industrial source" means a unit that does not serve a generator that produces electricity, a "nonutility unit" as defined in this section, or a process source as defined in section 7651i(e)[4] of this title.
(25) The term "nonutility unit" means a unit other than a utility unit.
(26) The term "designated representative" means a responsible person or official authorized by the owner or operator of a unit to represent the owner or operator in matters pertaining to the holding, transfer, or disposition of allowances allocated to a unit, and the submission of and compliance with permits, permit applications, and compliance plans for the unit.
(27) The term "life-of-the-unit, firm power contractual arrangement" means a unit participation power sales agreement under which a utility or industrial customer reserves, or is entitled to receive, a specified amount or percentage of capacity and associated energy generated by a specified generating unit (or units) and pays its proportional amount of such unit's total costs, pursuant to a contract either—
  (A) for the life of the unit;
  (B) for a cumulative term of no less than 30 years, including contracts that permit an election for early termination; or
  (C) for a period equal to or greater than 25 years or 70 percent of the economic useful life of the unit determined as of the time the unit was built, with option rights to purchase or re-lease some portion of the capacity and associated energy generated by the unit (or units) at the end of the period.
(28) The term "basic Phase II allowance allocations" means:
  (A) For calendar years 2000 through 2009 inclusive, allocations of allowances made by the Administrator pursuant to section 7651b of this title and subsections (b)(1), (3), and (4); (c)(1), (2), (3), and (5); (d)(1), (2), (4), and (5); (e); (f); (g)(1), (2), (3), (4), and (5); (h)(1); (i) and (j) of section 7651d of this title.
  (B) For each calendar year beginning in 2010, allocations of allowances made by the Administrator pursuant to section 7651b of this title and subsections (b)(1), (3), and (4); (c)(1), (2), (3), and (5); (d)(1), (2), (4) and (5); (e); (f); (g)(1), (2), (3), (4), and (5); (h)(1) and (3); (i) and (j) of section 7651d of this title.
(29) The term "Phase II bonus allowance allocations" means, for calendar year 2000 through 2009, inclusive, and only for such years, allocations made by the Administrator pursuant to section 7651b of this title, subsections (a)(2), (b)(2), (c)(4), (d)(3) (except as otherwise provided therein), and (h)(2) of section 7651d of this title, and section 7651e of this title.

(July 14, 1955, ch. 360, title IV, Sec. 402, as added Pub. L. 101-549, title IV, Sec. 401, Nov. 15, 1990, 104 Stat. 2585.)

References in Text

Part B of title III of the Act, referred to in par. (11), means title III of the Clean Air Act, act July 14, 1955, ch. 360, as added, which is classified to subchapter III of this chapter, but title III does not contain parts. For provisions of the Clean Air Act relating to permits, see subchapter V (Sec. 7661 et seq.) of this chapter.

Codification

Another section 402 of act July 14, 1955, as added by Pub. L. 91-604, Sec. 14, Dec. 31, 1970, 84 Stat. 1709, is classified to section 7641 of this title.

Section Referred to in Other Sections

This section is referred to in sections 7651c, 7651g, 7651h of this title.

SULFUR DIOXIDE ALLOWANCE PROGRAM FOR EXISTING AND NEW UNITS

42 USC 7651b

(a) Allocations of annual allowances for existing and new units
  (1)[1] For the emission limitation programs under this subchapter, the Administrator shall allocate annual allowances for the unit, to be held or distributed by the designated representa-

---
[4] So in original. Probably should be section "7651i(d)".
[1] So in original. No pars. (2) and (3) have been enacted.

tive of the owner or operator of each affected unit at an affected source in accordance with this subchapter, in an amount equal to the annual tonnage emission limitation calculated under section 7651c, 7651d, 7651e, 7651h, or 7651i of this title except as otherwise specifically provided elsewhere in this subchapter. Except as provided in sections 7651d(a)(2), 7651d(a)(3), 7651h and 7651i of this title, beginning January 1, 2000, the Administrator shall not allocate annual allowances to emit sulfur dioxide pursuant to section 7651d of this title in such an amount as would result in total annual emissions of sulfur dioxide from utility units in excess of 8.90 million tons except that the Administrator shall not take into account unused allowances carried forward by owners and operators of affected units or by other persons holding such allowances, following the year for which they were allocated. If necessary to meeting the restrictions imposed in the preceding sentence, the Administrator shall reduce, pro rata, the basic Phase II allowance allocations for each unit subject to the requirements of section 7651d of this title. Subject to the provisions of section 7651o of this title, the Administrator shall allocate allowances for each affected unit at an affected source annually, as provided in paragraphs (2) and (3) \1\ and section 7651g of this title. Except as provided in sections 7651h and 7651i of this title, the removal of an existing affected unit or source from commercial operation at any time after November 15, 1990 (whether before or after January 1, 1995, or January 1, 2000) shall not terminate or otherwise affect the allocation of allowances pursuant to section 7651c or 7651d of this title to which the unit is entitled. Allowances shall be allocated by the Administrator without cost to the recipient, except for allowances sold by the Administrator pursuant to section 7651o of this title. Not later than December 31, 1991, the Administrator shall publish a proposed list of the basic Phase II allowance allocations, the Phase II bonus allowance allocations and, if applicable, allocations pursuant to section 7651d(a)(3) of this title for each unit subject to the emissions limitation requirements of section 7651d of this title for the year 2000 and the year 2010. After notice and opportunity for public comment, but not later than December 31, 1992, the Administrator shall publish a final list of such allocations, subject to the provisions of section 7651d(a)(2) of this title. Any owner or operator of an existing unit subject to the requirements of section 7651d(b) or (c) of this title who is considering applying for an extension of the emission limitation requirement compliance deadline for that unit from January 1, 2000, until not later than December 31, 2000, pursuant to section 7651h of this title, shall notify the Administrator no later than March 31, 1991. Such notification shall be used as the basis for estimating the basic Phase II allowances under this subsection. Prior to June 1, 1998, the Administrator shall publish a revised final statement of allowance allocations, subject to the provisions of section 7651d(a)(2) of this title and taking into account the effect of any compliance date extensions granted pursuant to section 7651h of this title on such allocations. Any person who may make an election concerning the amount of allowances to be allocated to a unit or units shall make such election and so inform the Administrator not later than March 31, 1991, in the case of an election under section 7651d of this title (or June 30, 1991, in the case of an election under section 7651e of this title). If such person fails to make such election, the Administrator shall set forth for each unit owned or operated by such person, the amount of allowances reflecting the election that would, in the judgment of the Administrator, provide the greatest benefit for the owner or operator of the unit. If such person is a Governor who may make an election under section 7651e of this title and the Governor fails to make an election, the Administrator shall set forth for each unit in the State the amount of allowances reflecting the election that would, in the judgment of the Administrator, provide the greatest benefit for units in the State.

(b) Allowance transfer system

Allowances allocated under this subchapter may be transferred among designated representatives of the owners or operators of affected sources under this subchapter and any other person who holds such allowances, as provided by the allowance system regulations to be promulgated by the Administrator not later than eighteen months after November 15, 1990. Such regulations shall establish the allowance system prescribed under this section, including, but not limited to, requirements for the allocation, transfer, and use of allowances under this subchapter. Such regulations shall prohibit the use of any allowance prior to the calendar year for which the allowance was allocated, and shall provide, consistent with the purposes of this subchapter, for the identification of unused allowances, and for such unused allowances to be carried forward and added to allowances allocated in subsequent years, including allowances allocated to units subject to Phase I requirements (as described in section 7651c of this title) which are applied to emissions limitations requirements in Phase II (as described in section 7651d of this title). Transfers of allowances shall not be effective until written certification of the transfer, signed by a responsible official of each party to the transfer, is received and recorded by the Administrator. Such regulations shall permit the transfer of allowances prior to the issuance of such allowances. Recorded pre-allocation transfers shall be deducted by the Administrator from the number of allowances which would otherwise be allocated to the transferor, and added to those allowances allocated to the transferee. Pre-allocation transfers shall not affect the prohibition contained in this subsection against the use of allowances prior to the year for which they are allocated.

(c) Interpollutant trading

Not later than January 1, 1994, the Administrator shall furnish to the Congress a study evaluating the environmental and economic consequences of amending this subchapter to permit trading sulfur dioxide allowances for nitrogen oxides allowances.

(d) Allowance tracking system

(1) The Administrator shall promulgate, not later than 18 months after November 15, 1990, a system for issuing, recording, and tracking allowances, which shall specify all necessary procedures and requirements for an orderly and competitive functioning of the allowance system. All allowance allocations and transfers shall, upon recordation by the Administrator, be deemed a part of each unit's permit requirements pursuant to section 7651g of this title, without any further permit review and revision.

(2) In order to insure electric reliability, such regulations shall not prohibit or affect temporary increases and decreases in emissions within utility systems, power pools, or utilities entering into allowance pool agreements, that result from their operations, including emergencies and central dispatch, and such temporary emissions increases and decreases shall not require transfer of allowances among units nor shall it require recordation. The owners or operators of such units shall act through a designated representative. Notwithstanding the preceding sentence, the total tonnage of emissions in any calendar year (calculated at the end thereof) from all units in such a utility system, power pool, or allowance pool agreements shall not exceed the total allowances for such units for the calendar year concerned.

(e) New utility units

After January 1, 2000, it shall be unlawful for a new utility unit to emit an annual tonnage of sulfur dioxide in excess of the number of allowances to emit held for the unit by the unit's owner or operator. Such new utility units shall not be eligible for an allocation of sulfur dioxide allowances under subsection (a)(1) of this section, unless the unit is subject to the provisions of subsection (g)(2) or (3) of section 7651d of this title. New utility units may obtain allowances from any person, in accordance with this subchapter. The owner or operator of any new utility unit in violation of this subsection shall be liable for fulfilling the obligations specified in section 7651j of this title.

(f) Nature of allowances

An allowance allocated under this subchapter is a limited authorization to emit sulfur dioxide in accordance with the provisions of this subchapter. Such allowance does not constitute a property right. Nothing in this subchapter or in any other provision of law shall be construed to limit the authority of the United States to terminate or limit such authorization. Nothing in this section relating to allowances shall be construed as affecting the application of, or compliance with, any other provision of this chapter to an affected unit or source, including the provisions related to applicable National Ambient Air Quality Standards and State implementation plans. Nothing in this section shall be construed as requiring a change of any kind in any State law regulating electric utility rates and charges or affecting any State law regarding such State regulation or as limiting State regulation (including any prudency review) under such a State law. Nothing in this section shall be construed as modifying the Federal Power Act [16 U.S.C. 791a et seq.] or as affecting the authority of the Federal Energy Regulatory Commission under that Act. Nothing in this subchapter shall be construed to interfere with or impair any program for competitive bidding for power supply in a State in which such program is established. Allowances, once allocated to a person by the Administrator, may be received, held, and temporarily or permanently transferred in accordance with this subchapter and the regulations of the Administrator without regard to whether or not a permit is in effect under subchapter V of this chapter or section 7651g of this title with respect to the unit for which such allowance was originally allocated and recorded. Each permit under this subchapter and each permit issued under subchapter V of this chapter for any affected unit shall provide that the affected unit may not emit an annual tonnage of sulfur dioxide in excess of the allowances held for that unit.

(g) Prohibition

It shall be unlawful for any person to hold, use, or transfer any allowance allocated under this subchapter, except in accordance with regulations promulgated by the Administrator. It shall be unlawful for any affected unit to emit sulfur dioxide in excess of the number of allowances held for that unit for that year by the owner or operator of the unit. Upon the allocation of allowances under this subchapter, the prohibition contained in the preceding sentence shall supersede any other emission limitation applicable under this subchapter to the units for which such allowances are allocated. Allowances may not be used prior to the calendar year for which they are allocated. Nothing in this section or in the allowance system regulations shall relieve the Administrator of the Administrator's permitting, monitoring and enforcement obligations under this chapter, nor relieve affected sources of their requirements and liabilities under this chapter.

(h) Competitive bidding for power supply

Nothing in this subchapter shall be construed to interfere with or impair any program for competitive bidding for power supply in a State in which such program is established.

(i) Applicability of antitrust laws

(1) Nothing in this section affects—
  (A) the applicability of the antitrust laws to the transfer, use, or sale of allowances, or
  (B) the authority of the Federal Energy Regulatory Commission under any provision of law respecting unfair methods of competition or anticompetitive acts or practices.

(2) As used in this section, "antitrust laws" means those Acts set forth in section 12 of title 15.

(j) Public Utility Holding Company Act

The acquisition or disposition of allowances pursuant to this subchapter including the issuance of securities or the undertaking of any other financing transaction in connection with such allowances shall not be subject to the provisions of the Public Utility Holding Company Act of 1935 [15 U.S.C. 79 et seq.].

(July 14, 1955, ch. 360, title IV, Sec. 403, as added Pub. L. 101-549, title IV, Sec. 401, Nov. 15, 1990, 104 Stat. 2589.)

References in Text

The Federal Power Act, referred to in subsec. (f), is act June 10, 1920, ch. 285, 41 Stat. 1063, as amended, which is classified generally to chapter 12 (Sec. 791a et seq.) of Title 16, Conservation. For complete classification of this Act to the Code, see section 791a of Title 16 and Tables.

The Public Utility Holding Company Act of 1935, referred to in subsec. (j), is act Aug. 26, 1935, ch. 687, title I, 49 Stat. 838, as amended, which is classified generally to chapter 2C (Sec. 79 et seq.) of Title 15, Commerce and Trade. For complete classification of this Act to the Code, see section 79 of Title 15 and Tables.

Codification

Another section 403 of act July 14, 1955, as added by Pub. L. 91-604, Sec. 14, Dec. 31, 1970, 84 Stat. 1710, is classified to section 7642 of this title.

Fossil Fuel Use

Section 402 of title IV of Pub. L. 101-549 provided that:

"(a) Contracts for Hydroelectric Energy.—Any person who, after the date of the enactment of the Clean Air Act Amendments of 1990 [Nov. 15, 1990], enters into a contract under which such person receives hydroelectric energy in return for the provision of electric energy by such person shall use allowances held by such person as necessary to satisfy such person's obligations under such contract.

(b) Federal Power Marketing Administration.—A Federal Power Marketing Administration shall not be subject to the provisions and requirements of this title [enacting this subchapter, amending sections 7410, 7411, and 7479 of this title, and enacting provisions set out as notes under sections 7403, 7411, and 7651 of this title] with respect to electric energy generated by hydroelectric facilities and marketed by such Power Marketing Administration. Any person who sells or provides electric energy to a Federal Power Marketing Administration shall comply with the provisions and requirements of this title."

Section Referred to in Other Sections

This section is referred to in sections 7651a, 7651c, 7651d, 7651e, 7651g, 7651h, 7651i, 7651j of this title.

PHASE I SULFUR DIOXIDE REQUIREMENTS

42 USC 7651c

(a) Emission limitations
  (1) After January 1, 1995, each source that includes one or more affected units listed in table A is an affected source under this section. After January 1, 1995, it shall be unlawful for any affected unit (other than an eligible phase I unit under subsection (d)(2) of this section) to emit sulfur dioxide in excess of the tonnage limitation stated as a total number of allowances in table A for phase I, unless (A) the emissions reduction requirements applicable to such unit have been achieved pursuant to subsection (b) or (d) of this section, or (B) the owner or operator of such unit holds allowances to emit not less than the unit's total annual emissions, except that, after January 1, 2000, the emissions limitations established in this section shall be superseded by those established in section 7651d of this title. The owner or operator of any unit in violation of this section shall be fully liable for such violation including, but not limited to, liability for fulfilling the obligations specified in section 7651j of this title.
  (2) Not later than December 31, 1991, the Administrator shall determine the total tonnage of reductions in the emissions of sulfur dioxide from all utility units in calendar year 1995 that will occur as a result of compliance with the emissions limitation requirements of this section, and shall establish a reserve of allowances equal in amount to the number of tons determined thereby not to exceed a total of 3.50 million tons. In making such a determination, the Administrator shall compute for each unit subject to the emissions limitation requirements of this section the difference between:
   (A) the product of its baseline multiplied by the lesser of each unit's allowable 1985 emissions rate and its actual 1985 emissions rate, divided by 2,000, and
   (B) the product of each unit's baseline multiplied by 2.50 lbs/mmBtu divided by 2,000, and sum the computations. The Administrator shall adjust the foregoing calculation to reflect projected calendar year 1995 utilization of the units subject to the emissions limitations of this subchapter that the Administrator finds would have occurred in the absence of the imposition of such requirements. Pursuant to subsection (d) of this section, the Administrator shall allocate allowances from the reserve established hereinunder until the earlier of such time as all such allowances in the reserve are allocated or December 31, 1999.
  (3) In addition to allowances allocated pursuant to paragraph (1), in each calendar year beginning in 1995 and ending in 1999, inclusive, the Administrator shall allocate for each unit on Table A that is located in the States of Illinois, Indiana, or Ohio (other than units at Kyger Creek, Clifty Creek and Joppa Steam), allowances in an amount equal to 200,000 multiplied by the unit's pro rata share of the total number of allowances allocated for all units on Table A in the 3 States (other than units at Kyger Creek, Clifty Creek, and Joppa Steam) pursuant to paragraph (1). Such allowances shall be excluded from the calculation of the reserve under paragraph (2).
(b) Substitutions
  The owner or operator of an affected unit under subsection (a) of this section may include in its section 7651g of this title permit application and proposed compliance plan a proposal to reassign, in whole or in part, the affected unit's sulfur dioxide reduction requirements to any other unit(s) under the control of such owner or operator. Such proposal shall specify—

(1) the designation of the substitute unit or units to which any part of the reduction obligations of subsection (a) of this section shall be required, in addition to, or in lieu of, any original affected units designated under such subsection;

(2) the original affected unit's baseline, the actual and allowable 1985 emissions rate for sulfur dioxide, and the authorized annual allowance allocation stated in table A;

(3) calculation of the annual average tonnage for calendar years 1985, 1986, and 1987, emitted by the substitute unit or units, based on the baseline for each unit, as defined in section 7651a(d)[1] of this title, multiplied by the lesser of the unit's actual or allowable 1985 emissions rate;

(4) the emissions rates and tonnage limitations that would be applicable to the original and substitute affected units under the substitution proposal;

(5) documentation, to the satisfaction of the Administrator, that the reassigned tonnage limits will, in total, achieve the same or greater emissions reduction than would have been achieved by the original affected unit and the substitute unit or units without such substitution; and

(6) such other information as the Administrator may require.

(c) Administrator's action on substitution proposals

(1) The Administrator shall take final action on such substitution proposal in accordance with section 7651g(c) of this title if the substitution proposal fulfills the requirements of this subsection. The Administrator may approve a substitution proposal in whole or in part and with such modifications or conditions as may be consistent with the orderly functioning of the allowance system and which will ensure the emissions reductions contemplated by this subchapter. If a proposal does not meet the requirements of subsection (b) of this section, the Administrator shall disapprove it. The owner or operator of a unit listed in table A shall not substitute another unit or units without the prior approval of the Administrator.

(2) Upon approval of a substitution proposal, each substitute unit, and each source with such unit, shall be deemed affected under this subchapter, and the Administrator shall issue a permit to the original and substitute affected source and unit in accordance with the approved substitution plan and section 7651g of this title. The Administrator shall allocate allowances for the original and substitute affected units in accordance with the approved substitution proposal pursuant to section 7651b of this title. It shall be unlawful for any source or unit that is allocated allowances pursuant to this section to emit sulfur dioxide in excess of the emissions limitation provided for in the approved substitution permit and plan unless the owner or operator of each unit governed by the permit and approved substitution plan holds allowances to emit not less than the units total annual emissions. The owner or operator of any original or substitute affected unit operated in violation of this subsection shall be fully liable for such violation, including liability for fulfilling the obligations specified in section 7651j of this title. If a substitution proposal is disapproved, the Administrator shall allocate allowances to the original affected unit or units in accordance with subsection (a) of this section.

(d) Eligible phase I extension units

(1) The owner or operator of any affected unit subject to an emissions limitation requirement under this section may petition the Administrator in its permit application under section 7651g of this title for an extension of 2 years of the deadline for meeting such requirement, provided that the owner or operator of any such unit holds allowances to emit not less than the unit's total annual emissions for each of the 2 years of the period of extension. To qualify for such an extension, the affected unit must either employ a qualifying phase I technology, or transfer its phase I emissions reduction obligation to a unit employing a qualifying phase I technology. Such transfer shall be accomplished in accordance with a compliance plan, submitted and approved under section 7651g of this title, that shall govern operations at all units included in the transfer, and that specifies the emissions reduction requirements imposed pursuant to this subchapter.

(2) Such extension proposal shall—

(A) specify the unit or units proposed for designation as an eligible phase I extension unit;

(B) provide a copy of an executed contract, which may be contingent upon the Administrator approving the proposal, for the design engineering, and construction of the

---

[1] So in original. Probably should be section "7651a(4)".

qualifying phase I technology for the extension unit, or for the unit or units to which the extension unit's emission reduction obligation is to be transferred;
- (C) specify the unit's or units' baseline, actual 1985 emissions rate, allowable 1985 emissions rate, and projected utilization for calendar years 1995 through 1999;
- (D) require CEMS on both the eligible phase I extension unit or units and the transfer unit or units beginning no later than January 1, 1995; and
- (E) specify the emission limitation and number of allowances expected to be necessary for annual operation after the qualifying phase I technology has been installed.

(3) The Administrator shall review and take final action on each extension proposal in order of receipt, consistent with section 7651g of this title, and for an approved proposal shall designate the unit or units as an eligible phase I extension unit. The Administrator may approve an extension proposal in whole or in part, and with such modifications or conditions as may be necessary, consistent with the orderly functioning of the allowance system, and to ensure the emissions reductions contemplated by the[2] subchapter.

(4) In order to determine the number of proposals eligible for allocations from the reserve under subsection (a)(2) of this section and the number of allowances remaining available after each proposal is acted upon, the Administrator shall reduce the total number of allowances remaining available in the reserve by the number of allowances calculated according to subparagraphs (A), (B) and (C) until either no allowances remain available in the reserve for further allocation or all approved proposals have been acted upon. If no allowances remain available in the reserve for further allocation before all proposals have been acted upon by the Administrator, any pending proposals shall be disapproved. The Administrator shall calculate allowances equal to—
- (A) the difference between the lesser of the average annual emissions in calendar years 1988 and 1989 or the projected emissions tonnage for calendar year 1995 of each eligible phase I extension unit, as designated under paragraph (3), and the product of the unit's baseline multiplied by an emission rate of 2.50 lbs/mmBtu, divided by 2,000;
- (B) the difference between the lesser of the average annual emissions in calendar years 1988 and 1989 or the projected emissions tonnage for calendar year 1996 of each eligible phase I extension unit, as designated under paragraph (3), and the product of the unit's baseline multiplied by an emission rate of 2.50 lbs/mmBtu, divided by 2,000; and
- (C) the amount by which (i) the product of each unit's baseline multiplied by an emission rate of 1.20 lbs/mmBtu, divided by 2,000, exceeds (ii) the tonnage level specified under subparagraph (E) of paragraph (2) of this subsection multiplied by a factor of 3.

(5) Each eligible Phase I extension unit shall receive allowances determined under subsection (a)(1) or (c) of this section. In addition, for calendar year 1995, the Administrator shall allocate to each eligible Phase I extension unit, from the allowance reserve created pursuant to subsection (a)(2) of this section, allowances equal to the difference between the lesser of the average annual emissions in calendar years 1988 and 1989 or its projected emissions tonnage for calendar year 1995 and the product of the unit's baseline multiplied by an emission rate of 2.50 lbs/mmBtu, divided by 2,000. In calendar year 1996, the Administrator shall allocate for each eligible unit, from the allowance reserve created pursuant to subsection (a)(2) of this section, allowances equal to the difference between the lesser of the average annual emissions in calendar years 1988 and 1989 or its projected emissions tonnage for calendar year 1996 and the product of the unit's baseline multiplied by an emission rate of 2.50 lbs/mmBtu, divided by 2,000. It shall be unlawful for any source or unit subject to an approved extension plan under this subsection to emit sulfur dioxide in excess of the emissions limitations provided for in the permit and approved extension plan, unless the owner or operator of each unit governed by the permit and approved plan holds allowances to emit not less than the unit's total annual emissions.

(6) In addition to allowances specified in paragraph (5), the Administrator shall allocate for each eligible Phase I extension unit employing qualifying Phase I technology, for calendar years 1997, 1998, and 1999, additional allowances, from any remaining allowances in the reserve created pursuant to subsection (a)(2) of this section, following the reduction in the reserve provided for in paragraph (4), not to exceed the amount by which (A) the product of each eligible unit's baseline times an emission rate of 1.20 lbs/mmBtu, divided by 2,000, exceeds (B) the tonnage level specified under subparagraph (E) of paragraph (2) of this subsection.

---

[2] So in original. Probably should be "this".

(7) After January 1, 1997, in addition to any liability under this chapter, including under section 7651j of this title, if any eligible phase I extension unit employing qualifying phase I technology or any transfer unit under this subsection emits sulfur dioxide in excess of the annual tonnage limitation specified in the extension plan, as approved in paragraph (3) of this subsection, the Administrator shall, in the calendar year following such excess, deduct allowances equal to the amount of such excess from such unit's annual allowance allocation.

(e) Allocation of allowances

(1) In the case of a unit that receives authorization from the Governor of the State in which such unit is located to make reductions in the emissions of sulfur dioxide prior to calendar year 1995 and that is part of a utility system that meets the following requirements: (A) the total coal-fired generation within the utility system as a percentage of total system generation decreased by more than 20 percent between January 1, 1980, and December 31, 1985; and (B) the weighted capacity factor of all coal-fired units within the utility system averaged over the period from January 1, 1985, through December 31, 1987, was below 50 percent, the Administrator shall allocate allowances under this paragraph for the unit pursuant to this subsection. The Administrator shall allocate allowances for a unit that is an affected unit pursuant to section 7651d of this title (but is not also an affected unit under this section) and part of a utility system that includes 1 or more affected units under section 7651d of this title for reductions in the emissions of sulfur dioxide made during the period 1995-1999 if the unit meets the requirements of this subsection and the requirements of the preceding sentence, except that for the purposes of applying this subsection to any such unit, the prior year concerned as specified below, shall be any year after January 1, 1995 but prior to January 1, 2000.

(2) In the case of an affected unit under this section described in subparagraph (A), the allowances allocated under this subsection for early reductions in any prior year may not exceed the amount which (A) the product of the unit's baseline multiplied by the unit's 1985 actual sulfur dioxide emission rate (in lbs. per mmBtu), divided by 2,000, exceeds (B) the allowances specified for such unit in Table A. In the case of an affected unit under section 7651d of this title described in subparagraph (A), the allowances awarded under this subsection for early reductions in any prior year may not exceed the amount by which (i) the product of the quantity of fossil fuel consumed by the unit (in mmBtu) in the prior year multiplied by the lesser of 2.50 or the most stringent emission rate (in lbs. per mmBtu) applicable to the unit under the applicable implementation plan, divided by 2,000, exceeds (ii) the unit's actual tonnage of sulfur dioxide emission for the prior year concerned. Allowances allocated under this subsection for units referred to in subparagraph (A) may be allocated only for emission reductions achieved as a result of physical changes or changes in the method of operation made after November 15, 1990, including changes in the type or quality of fossil fuel consumed.

(3) In no event shall the provisions of this paragraph be interpreted as an event of force majeur or a commercial impracticability[3] or in any other way as a basis for excused nonperformance by a utility system under a coal sales contract in effect before November 15, 1990.

TABLE A.—AFFECTED SOURCES AND UNITS IN PHASE I AND THEIR SULFUR DIOXIDE ALLOWANCES (TONS)

State	Plant Name	Generator	Phase I Allowances
Alabama................	Colbert.............	1	13,570
		2	15,310
		3	15,400
		4	15,410
		5	37,180
	E.C. Gaston..........	1	18,100
		2	18,540
		3	18,310
		4	19,280
		5	59,840

---

[3] So in original. Probably should be "impracticability".

State	Plant Name	Generator	Phase I Allowances
Florida	Big Bend	1	28,410
		2	27,100
		3	26,740
	Crist	6	19,200
		7	31,680
Georgia	Bowen	1	56,320
		2	54,770
		3	71,750
		4	71,740
	Hammond	1	8,780
		2	9,220
		3	8,910
		4	37,640
	J. McDonough	1	19,910
		2	20,600
	Wansley	1	70,770
		2	65,430
	Yates	1	7,210
		2	7,040
		3	6,950
		4	8,910
		5	9,410
		6	24,760
		7	21,480
Illinois	Baldwin	1	42,010
		2	44,420
		3	42,550
	Coffeen	1	11,790
		2	35,670
	Grand Tower	4	5,910
	Hennepin	2	18,410
	Joppa Steam	1	12,590
		2	10,770
		3	12,270
		4	11,360
		5	11,420
		6	10,620
	Kincaid	1	31,530
		2	33,810
	Meredosia	3	13,890
	Vermilion	2	8,880
Indiana	Bailly	7	11,180
		8	15,630
	Breed	1	18,500
	Cayuga	1	33,370
		2	34,130
	Clifty Creek	1	20,150
		2	19,810
		3	20,410
		4	20,080
		5	19,360
		6	20,380

State	Plant Name	Generator	Phase I Allowances
	E. W. Stout	5	3,880
		6	4,770
		7	23,610
	F. B. Culley	2	4,290
		3	16,970
	F. E. Ratts	1	8,330
		2	8,480
	Gibson	1	40,400
		2	41,010
		3	41,080
		4	40,320
	H. T. Pritchard	6	5,770
	Michigan City	12	23,310
	Petersburg	1	16,430
		2	32,380
	R. Gallagher	1	6,490
		2	7,280
		3	6,530
		4	7,650
	Tanners Creek	4	24,820
	Wabash River	1	4,000
		2	2,860
		3	3,750
		5	3,670
		6	12,280
	Warrick	4	26,980
Iowa	Burlington	1	10,710
	Des Moines	7	2,320
	George Neal	1	1,290
	M.L. Kapp	2	13,800
	Prairie Creek	4	8,180
	Riverside	5	3,990
Kansas	Quindaro	2	4,220
Kentucky	Coleman	1	11,250
		2	12,840
		3	12,340
	Cooper	1	7,450
		2	15,320
	E.W. Brown	1	7,110
		2	10,910
		3	26,100
	Elmer Smith	1	6,520
		2	14,410
	Ghent	1	28,410
	Green River	4	7,820
	H.L. Spurlock	1	22,780
	Henderson II	1	13,340
		2	12,310
	Paradise	3	59,170
	Shawnee	10	10,170

346 / Environmental Statutes

State	Plant Name	Generator	Phase I Allowances
Maryland................	Chalk Point..........	1	21,910
		2	24,330
	C. P. Crane..........	1	10,330
		2	9,230
	Morgantown..........	1	35,260
		2	38,480
Michigan................	J. H. Campbell.......	1	19,280
		2	23,060
Minnesota................	High Bridge..........	6	4,270
Mississippi...............	Jack Watson..........	4	17,910
		5	36,700
Missouri.................	Asbury...............	1	16,190
	James River..........	5	4,850
	Labadie..............	1	40,110
		2	37,710
		3	40,310
		4	35,940
	Montrose............	1	7,390
		2	8,200
		3	10,090
	New Madrid..........	1	28,240
		2	32,480
	Sibley...............	3	15,580
	Sioux................	1	22,570
		2	23,690
	Thomas Hill..........	1	10,250
		2	19,390
New Hampshire.............	Merrimack............	1	10,190
		2	22,000
New Jersey................	B.L. England.........	1	9,060
		2	11,720
New York..................	Dunkirk..............	3	12,600
		4	14,060
	Greenidge............	4	7,540
	Milliken.............	1	11,170
		2	12,410
	Northport............	1	19,810
		2	24,110
		3	26,480
	Port Jefferson.......	3	10,470
		4	12,330
Ohio.....................	Ashtabula............	5	16,740
	Avon Lake............	8	11,650
		9	30,480
	Cardinal.............	1	34,270
		2	38,320
	Conesville...........	1	4,210
		2	4,890
		3	5,500
		4	48,770

State	Plant Name	Generator	Phase I Allowances
	Eastlake............	1	7,800
		2	8,640
		3	10,020
		4	14,510
		5	34,070
	Edgewater............	4	5,050
	Gen. J.M. Gavin......	1	79,080
		2	80,560
	Kyger Creek..........	1	19,280
		2	18,560
		3	17,910
		4	18,710
		5	18,740
	Miami Fort...........	5	760
		6	11,380
		7	38,510
	Muskingum River......	1	14,880
		2	14,170
		3	13,950
		4	11,780
		5	40,470
	Niles................	1	6,940
		2	9,100
	Picway...............	5	4,930
	R.E. Burger..........	3	6,150
		4	10,780
		5	12,430
	W.H. Sammis..........	5	24,170
		6	39,930
		7	43,220
	W.C. Beckjord........	5	8,950
		6	23,020
Pennsylvania...............	Armstrong............	1	14,410
		2	15,430
	Brunner Island.......	1	27,760
		2	31,100
		3	53,820
	Cheswick.............	1	39,170
	Conemaugh............	1	59,790
		2	66,450
	Hatfield's Ferry.....	1	37,830
		2	37,320
		3	40,270
	Martins Creek........	1	12,660
		2	12,820
	Portland.............	1	5,940
		2	10,230
	Shawville............	1	10,320
		2	10,320
		3	14,220
		4	14,070
	Sunbury..............	3	8,760
		4	11,450

State	Plant Name	Generator	Phase I Allowances
Tennessee..................	Allen................	1	15,320
		2	16,770
		3	15,670
	Cumberland...........	1	86,700
		2	94,840
	Gallatin.............	1	17,870
		2	17,310
		3	20,020
		4	21,260
	Johnsonville.........	1	7,790
		2	8,040
		3	8,410
		4	7,990
		5	8,240
		6	7,890
		7	8,980
		8	8,700
		9	7,080
		10	7,550
West Virginia.............	Albright.............	3	12,000
	Fort Martin..........	1	41,590
		2	41,200
	Harrison.............	1	48,620
		2	46,150
		3	41,500
	Kammer...............	1	18,740
		2	19,460
		3	17,390
	Mitchell.............	1	43,980
		2	45,510
	Mount Storm..........	1	43,720
		2	35,580
		3	42,430
Wisconsin.................	Edgewater............	4	24,750
	La Crosse/Genoa......	3	22,700
	Nelson Dewey.........	1	6,010
		2	6,680
	N. Oak Creek.........	1	5,220
		2	5,140
		3	5,370
		4	6,320
	Pulliam..............	8	7,510
	S. Oak Creek.........	5	9,670
		6	12,040
		7	16,180
		8	15,790

(f) Energy conservation and renewable energy
  (1) Definitions
    As used in this subsection:
      (A) Qualified energy conservation measure
        The term "qualified energy conservation measure" means a cost effective measure, as identified by the Administrator in consultation with the Secretary of Energy, that increases

the efficiency of the use of electricity provided by an electric utility to its customers.
- (B) Qualified renewable energy

    The term "qualified renewable energy" means energy derived from biomass, solar, geothermal, or wind as identified by the Administrator in consultation with the Secretary of Energy.
- (C) Electric utility

    The term "electric utility" means any person, State agency, or Federal agency, which sells electric energy.

(2) Allowances for emissions avoided through energy conservation and renewable energy
- (A) In general

    The regulations under paragraph (4) of this subsection shall provide that for each ton of sulfur dioxide emissions avoided by an electric utility, during the applicable period, through the use of qualified energy conservation measures or qualified renewable energy, the Administrator shall allocate a single allowance to such electric utility, on a first-come-first-served basis from the Conservation and Renewable Energy Reserve established under subsection (g) of this section, up to a total of 300,000 allowances for allocation from such Reserve.
- (B) Requirements for issuance

    The Administrator shall allocate allowances to an electric utility under this subsection only if all of the following requirements are met:
    - (i) Such electric utility is paying for the qualified energy conservation measures or qualified renewable energy directly or through purchase from another person.
    - (ii) The emissions of sulfur dioxide avoided through the use of qualified energy conservation measures or qualified renewable energy are quantified in accordance with regulations promulgated by the Administrator under this subsection.
    - (iii) (I) Such electric utility has adopted and is implementing a least cost energy conservation and electric power plan which evaluates a range of resources, including new power supplies, energy conservation, and renewable energy resources, in order to meet expected future demand at the lowest system cost.

        (II) The qualified energy conservation measures or qualified renewable energy, or both, are consistent with that plan.

        (III) Electric utilities subject to the jurisdiction of a State regulatory authority must have such plan approved by such authority. For electric utilities not subject to the jurisdiction of a State regulatory authority such plan shall be approved by the entity with rate-making authority for such utility.
    - (iv) In the case of qualified energy conservation measures undertaken by a State regulated electric utility, the Secretary of Energy certifies that the State regulatory authority with jurisdiction over the electric rates of such electric utility has established rates and charges which ensure that the net income of such electric utility after implementation of specific cost effective energy conservation measures is at least as high as such net income would have been if the energy conservation measures had not been implemented. Upon the date of any such certification by the Secretary of Energy, all allowances which, but for this paragraph, would have been allocated under subparagraph (A) before such date, shall be allocated to the electric utility. This clause is not a requirement for qualified renewable energy.
    - (v) Such utility or any subsidiary of the utility's holding company owns or operates at least one affected unit.
- (C) Period of applicability

    Allowances under this subsection shall be allocated only with respect to kilowatt hours of electric energy saved by qualified energy conservation measures or generated by qualified renewable energy after January 1, 1992 and before the earlier of (i) December 31, 2000, or (ii) the date on which any electric utility steam generating unit owned or operated by the electric utility to which the allowances are allocated becomes subject to this subchapter (including those sources that elect to become affected by this subchapter, pursuant to section 7651i of this title).
- (D) Determination of avoided emissions
    - (i) Application

        In order to receive allowances under this subsection, an electric utility shall make an application which—

350 / Environmental Statutes

      (I) designates the qualified energy conservation measures implemented and the qualified renewable energy sources used for purposes of avoiding emissions,[4]
      (II) calculates, in accordance with subparagraphs (F) and (G), the number of tons of emissions avoided by reason of the implementation of such measures or the use of such renewable energy sources; and
      (III) demonstrates that the requirements of subparagraph (B) have been met.
    Such application for allowances by a State-regulated electric utility shall require approval by the State regulatory authority with jurisdiction over such electric utility. The authority shall review the application for accuracy and compliance with this subsection and the rules under this subsection. Electric utilities whose retail rates are not subject to the jurisdiction of a State regulatory authority shall apply directly to the Administrator for such approval.
  (E) Avoided emissions from qualified energy conservation measures
    For the purposes of this subsection, the emission tonnage deemed avoided by reason of the implementation of qualified energy conservation measures for any calendar year shall be a tonnage equal to the product of multiplying—
    (i) the kilowatt hours that would otherwise have been supplied by the utility during such year in the absence of such qualified energy conservation measures, by
    (ii) 0.004,
    and dividing by 2,000.
  (F) Avoided emissions from the use of qualified renewable energy
    The emissions tonnage deemed avoided by reason of the use of qualified renewable energy by an electric utility for any calendar year shall be a tonnage equal to the product of multiplying—
    (i) the actual kilowatt hours generated by, or purchased from, qualified renewable energy, by
    (ii) 0.004,
    and dividing by 2,000.
  (G) Prohibitions
    (i) No allowances shall be allocated under this subsection for the implementation of programs that are exclusively informational or educational in nature.
    (ii) No allowances shall be allocated for energy conservation measures or renewable energy that were operational before January 1, 1992.
(3) Savings provision
  Nothing in this subsection precludes a State or State regulatory authority from providing additional incentives to utilities to encourage investment in demand-side resources.
(4) Regulations
  Not later than 18 months after November 15, 1990, and in conjunction with the regulations required to be promulgated under subsections (b) and (c) of this section, the Administrator shall, in consultation with the Secretary of Energy, promulgate regulations under this subsection. Such regulations shall list energy conservation measures and renewable energy sources which may be treated as qualified energy conservation measures and qualified renewable energy for purposes of this subsection. Allowances shall only be allocated if all requirements of this subsection and the rules promulgated to implement this subsection are complied with. The Administrator shall review the determinations of each State regulatory authority under this subsection to encourage consistency from electric utility to electric utility and from State to State in accordance with the Administrator's rules. The Administrator shall publish the findings of this review no less than annually.
(g) Conservation and Renewable Energy Reserve
  The Administrator shall establish a Conservation and Renewable Energy Reserve under this subsection. Beginning on January 1, 1995, the Administrator may allocate from the Conservation and Renewable Energy Reserve an amount equal to a total of 300,000 allowances for emissions of sulfur dioxide pursuant to section 7651b of this title. In order to provide 300,000 allowances for such reserve, in each year beginning in calendar year 2000 and until calendar year 2009, inclusive, the Administrator shall reduce each unit's basic Phase II allowance allocation on the basis of its pro rata share of 30,000 allowances. If allowances remain in the reserve after January 2, 2010, the Administrator shall allocate such allowances for affected

---
[4] So in original. The comma probably should be a semicolon.

units under section 7651d of this title on a pro rata basis. For purposes of this subsection, for any unit subject to the emissions limitation requirements of section 7651d of this title, the term "pro rata basis" refers to the ratio which the reductions made in such unit's allowances in order to establish the reserve under this subsection bears to the total of such reductions for all such units.

(h) Alternative allowance allocation for units in certain utility systems with optional baseline
  (1) Optional baseline for units in certain systems
    In the case of a unit subject to the emissions limitation requirements of this section which (as of November 15, 1990)—
    (A) has an emission rate below 1.0 lbs/mmBtu,
    (B) has decreased its sulfur dioxide emissions rate by 60 percent or greater since 1980, and
    (C) is part of a utility system which has a weighted average sulfur dioxide emissions rate for all fossil fueled-fired units below 1.0 lbs/mmBtu,
    at the election of the owner or operator of such unit, the unit's baseline may be calculated (i) as provided under section 7651a(d)[5] of this title, or (ii) by utilizing the unit's average annual fuel consumption at a 60 percent capacity factor. Such election shall be made no later than March 1, 1991.
  (2) Allowance allocation
    Whenever a unit referred to in paragraph (1) elects to calculate its baseline as provided in clause (ii) of paragraph (1), the Administrator shall allocate allowances for the unit pursuant to section 7651b(a)(1) of this title, this section, and section 7651d of this title (as basic Phase II allowance allocations) in an amount equal to the baseline selected multiplied by the lower of the average annual emission rate for such unit in 1989, or 1.0 lbs./mmBtu. Such allowance allocation shall be in lieu of any allocation of allowances under this section and section 7651d of this title.

(July 14, 1955, ch. 360, title IV, Sec. 404, as added Pub. L. 101-549, title IV, Sec. 401, Nov. 15, 1990, 104 Stat. 2592.)

Section Referred to in Other Sections

This section is referred to in sections 7651a, 7651b, 7651d, 7651f, 7651g, 7651i, 7651j, 7651k, 7651o of this title.

PHASE II SULFUR DIOXIDE REQUIREMENTS

42 USC 7651d

(a) Applicability
  (1) After January 1, 2000, each existing utility unit as provided below is subject to the limitations or requirements of this section. Each utility unit subject to an annual sulfur dioxide tonnage emission limitation under this section is an affected unit under this subchapter. Each source that includes one or more affected units is an affected source. In the case of an existing unit that was not in operation during calendar year 1985, the emission rate for a calendar year after 1985, as determined by the Administrator, shall be used in lieu of the 1985 rate. The owner or operator of any unit operated in violation of this section shall be fully liable under this chapter for fulfilling the obligations specified in section 7651j of this title.
  (2) In addition to basic Phase II allowance allocations, in each year beginning in calendar year 2000 and ending in calendar year 2009, inclusive, the Administrator shall allocate up to 530,000 Phase II bonus allowances pursuant to subsections (b)(2), (c)(4), (d)(3)(A) and (B), and (h)(2) of this section and section 7651e of this title. Not later than June 1, 1998, the Administrator shall calculate, for each unit granted an extension pursuant to section 7651h of this title the difference between (A) the number of allowances allocated for the unit in calendar year 2000, and (B) the product of the unit's baseline multiplied by 1.20 lbs/mmBtu, divided by 2000, and sum the computations. In each year, beginning in calendar year 2000 and ending in calendar year 2009, inclusive, the Administrator shall deduct from each unit's basic Phase II allowance allocation its pro rata share of 10 percent of the sum calculated pursuant to the preceding sentence.

---

[5]So in original. Probably should be section "7651a(4)".

(3) In addition to basic Phase II allowance allocations and Phase II bonus allowance allocations, beginning January 1, 2000, the Administrator shall allocate for each unit listed on Table A in section 7651c of this title (other than units at Kyger Creek, Clifty Creek, and Joppa Steam) and located in the States of Illinois, Indiana, Ohio, Georgia, Alabama, Missouri, Pennsylvania, West Virginia, Kentucky, or Tennessee allowances in an amount equal to 50,000 multiplied by the unit's pro rata share of the total number of basic allowances allocated for all units listed on Table A (other than units at Kyger Creek, Clifty Creek, and Joppa Steam). Allowances allocated pursuant to this paragraph shall not be subject to the 8,900,000 ton limitation in section 7651b(a) of this title.

(b) Units equal to, or above, 75 MWe and 1.20 lbs/mmBtu
  (1) Except as otherwise provided in paragraph (3), after January 1, 2000, it shall be unlawful for any existing utility unit that serves a generator with nameplate capacity equal to, or greater, than 75 MWe and an actual 1985 emission rate equal to or greater than 1.20 lbs/mmBtu to exceed an annual sulfur dioxide tonnage emission limitation equal to the product of the unit's baseline multiplied by an emission rate equal to 1.20 lbs/mmBtu, divided by 2,000, unless the owner or operator of such unit holds allowances to emit not less than the unit's total annual emissions.
  (2) In addition to allowances allocated pursuant to paragraph (1) and section 7651b(a)(1) of this title as basic Phase II allowance allocations, beginning January 1, 2000, and for each calendar year thereafter until and including 2009, the Administrator shall allocate annually for each unit subject to the emissions limitation requirements of paragraph (1) with an actual 1985 emissions rate greater than 1.20 lbs/mmBtu and less than 2.50 lbs/mmBtu and a baseline capacity factor of less than 60 percent, allowances from the reserve created pursuant to subsection (a)(2) of this section in an amount equal to 1.20 lbs/mmBtu multiplied by 50 percent of the difference, on a Btu basis, between the unit's baseline and the unit's fuel consumption at a 60 percent capacity factor.
  (3) After January 1, 2000, it shall be unlawful for any existing utility unit with an actual 1985 emissions rate equal to or greater than 1.20 lbs/mmBtu whose annual average fuel consumption during 1985, 1986, and 1987 on a Btu basis exceeded 90 percent in the form of lignite coal which is located in a State in which, as of July 1, 1989, no county or portion of a county was designated nonattainment under section 7407 of this title for any pollutant subject to the requirements of section 7409 of this title to exceed an annual sulfur dioxide tonnage limitation equal to the product of the unit's baseline multiplied by the lesser of the unit's actual 1985 emissions rate or its allowable 1985 emissions rate, divided by 2,000, unless the owner or operator of such unit holds allowances to emit not less than the unit's total annual emissions.
  (4) After January 1, 2000, the Administrator shall allocate annually for each unit, subject to the emissions limitation requirements of paragraph (1), which is located in a State with an installed electrical generating capacity of more than 30,000,000 kw in 1988 and for which was issued a prohibition order or a proposed prohibition order (from burning oil), which unit subsequently converted to coal between January 1, 1980 and December 31, 1985, allowances equal to the difference between (A) the product of the unit's annual fuel consumption, on a Btu basis, at a 65 percent capacity factor multiplied by the lesser of its actual or allowable emissions rate during the first full calendar year after conversion, divided by 2,000, and (B) the number of allowances allocated for the unit pursuant to paragraph (1): Provided, That the number of allowances allocated pursuant to this paragraph shall not exceed an annual total of five thousand. If necessary to meeting the restriction imposed in the preceding sentence the Administrator shall reduce, pro rata, the annual allowances allocated for each unit under this paragraph.

(c) Coal or oil-fired units below 75 MWe and above 1.20 lbs/mmBtu
  (1) Except as otherwise provided in paragraph (3), after January 1, 2000, it shall be unlawful for a coal or oil-fired existing utility unit that serves a generator with nameplate capacity of less than 75 MWe and an actual 1985 emission rate equal to, or greater than, 1.20 lbs/mmBtu and which is a unit owned by a utility operating company whose aggregate nameplate fossil fuel steam-electric capacity is, as of December 31, 1989, equal to, or greater than, 250 MWe to exceed an annual sulfur dioxide emissions limitation equal to the product of the unit's baseline multiplied by an emission rate equal to 1.20 lbs/mmBtu, divided

by 2,000, unless the owner or operator of such unit holds allowances to emit not less than the unit's total annual emissions.

(2) After January 1, 2000, it shall be unlawful for a coal or oil-fired existing utility unit that serves a generator with nameplate capacity of less than 75 MWe and an actual 1985 emission rate equal to, or greater than, 1.20 lbs/mmBtu (excluding units subject to section 7411 of this title or to a federally enforceable emissions limitation for sulfur dioxide equivalent to an annual rate of less than 1.20 lbs/mmBtu) and which is a unit owned by a utility operating company whose aggregate nameplate fossil fuel steam-electric capacity is, as of December 31, 1989, less than 250 MWe, to exceed an annual sulfur dioxide tonnage emissions limitation equal to the product of the unit's baseline multiplied by the lesser of its actual 1985 emissions rate or its allowable 1985 emissions rate, divided by 2,000, unless the owner or operator of such unit holds allowances to emit not less than the unit's total annual emissions.

(3) After January 1, 2000, it shall be unlawful for any existing utility unit with a nameplate capacity below 75 MWe and an actual 1985 emissions rate equal to, or greater than, 1.20 lbs/mmBtu which became operational on or before December 31, 1965, which is owned by a utility operating company with, as of December 31, 1989, a total fossil fuel steam-electric generating capacity greater than 250 MWe, and less than 450 MWe which serves fewer than 78,000 electrical customers as of November 15, 1990, to exceed an annual sulfur dioxide emissions tonnage limitation equal to the product of its baseline multiplied by the lesser of its actual or allowable 1985 emission rate, divided by 2,000, unless the owner or operator holds allowances to emit not less than the units[1] total annual emissions. After January 1, 2010, it shall be unlawful for each unit subject to the emissions limitation requirements of this paragraph to exceed an annual emissions tonnage limitation equal to the product of its baseline multiplied by an emissions rate of 1.20 lbs/mmBtu, divided by 2,000, unless the owner or operator holds allowances to emit not less than the unit's total annual emissions.

(4) In addition to allowances allocated pursuant to paragraph (1) and section 7651b(a)(1) of this title as basic Phase II allowance allocations, beginning January 1, 2000, and for each calendar year thereafter until and including 2009, inclusive, the Administrator shall allocate annually for each unit subject to the emissions limitation requirements of paragraph (1) with an actual 1985 emissions rate equal to, or greater than, 1.20 lbs/mmBtu and less than 2.50 lbs/mmBtu and a baseline capacity factor of less than 60 percent, allowances from the reserve created pursuant to subsection (a)(2) of this section in an amount equal to 1.20 lbs/mmBtu multiplied by 50 percent of the difference, on a Btu basis, between the unit's baseline and the unit's fuel consumption at a 60 percent capacity factor.

(5) After January 1, 2000, it shall be unlawful for any existing utility unit with a nameplate capacity below 75 MWe and an actual 1985 emissions rate equal to, or greater than, 1.20 lbs/mmBtu which is part of an electric utility system which, as of November 15, 1990, (A) has at least 20 percent of its fossil-fuel capacity controlled by flue gas desulfurization devices, (B) has more than 10 percent of its fossil-fuel capacity consisting of coal-fired units of less than 75 MWe, and (C) has large units (greater than 400 MWe) all of which have difficult or very difficult FGD Retrofit Cost Factors (according to the Emissions and the FGD Retrofit Feasibility at the 200 Top Emitting Generating Stations, prepared for the United States Environmental Protection Agency on January 10, 1986) to exceed an annual sulfur dioxide emissions tonnage limitation equal to the product of its baseline multiplied by an emissions rate of 2.5 lbs/mmBtu, divided by 2,000, unless the owner or operator holds allowances to emit not less than the unit's total annual emissions. After January 1, 2010, it shall be unlawful for each unit subject to the emissions limitation requirements of this paragraph to exceed an annual emissions tonnage limitation equal to the product of its baseline multiplied by an emissions rate of 1.20 lbs/mmBtu, divided by 2,000, unless the owner or operator holds for use allowances to emit not less than the unit's total annual emissions.

(d) Coal-fired units below 1.20 lbs/mmBtu

(1) After January 1, 2000, it shall be unlawful for any existing coal-fired utility unit the lesser of whose actual or allowable 1985 sulfur dioxide emissions rate is less than 0.60 lbs/mmBtu to exceed an annual sulfur dioxide tonnage emission limitation equal to the product of the

---

[1] So in original. Probably should be "unit's".

354 / Environmental Statutes

unit's baseline multiplied by (A) the lesser of 0.60 lbs/mmBtu or the unit's allowable 1985 emissions rate, and (B) a numerical factor of 120 percent, divided by 2,000, unless the owner or operator of such unit holds allowances to emit not less than the unit's total annual emissions.

(2) After January 1, 2000, it shall be unlawful for any existing coal-fired utility unit the lesser of whose actual or allowable 1985 sulfur dioxide emissions rate is equal to, or greater than, 0.60 lbs/mmBtu and less than 1.20 lbs/mmBtu to exceed an annual sulfur dioxide tonnage emissions limitation equal to the product of the unit's baseline multiplied by (A) the lesser of its actual 1985 emissions rate or its allowable 1985 emissions rate, and (B) a numerical factor of 120 percent, divided by 2,000, unless the owner or operator of such unit holds allowances to emit not less than the unit's total annual emissions.

(3) (A) In addition to allowances allocated pursuant to paragraph (1) and section 7651b(a)(1) of this title as basic Phase II allowance allocations, at the election of the designated representative of the operating company, beginning January 1, 2000, and for each calendar year thereafter until and including 2009, the Administrator shall allocate annually for each unit subject to the emissions limitation requirements of paragraph (1) allowances from the reserve created pursuant to subsection (a)(2) of this section in an amount equal to the amount by which (i) the product of the lesser of 0.60 lbs/mmBtu or the unit's allowable 1985 emissions rate multiplied by the unit's baseline adjusted to reflect operation at a 60 percent capacity factor, divided by 2,000, exceeds (ii) the number of allowances allocated for the unit pursuant to paragraph (1) and section 7651b(a)(1) of this title as basic Phase II allowance allocations.

(B) In addition to allowances allocated pursuant to paragraph (2) and section 7651b(a)(1) of this title as basic Phase II allowance allocations, at the election of the designated representative of the operating company, beginning January 1, 2000, and for each calendar year thereafter until and including 2009, the Administrator shall allocate annually for each unit subject to the emissions limitation requirements of paragraph (2) allowances from the reserve created pursuant to subsection (a)(2) of this section in an amount equal to the amount by which (i) the product of the lesser of the unit's actual 1985 emissions rate or its allowable 1985 emissions rate multiplied by the unit's baseline adjusted to reflect operation at a 60 percent capacity factor, divided by 2,000, exceeds (ii) the number of allowances allocated for the unit pursuant to paragraph (2) and section 7651b(a)(1) of this title as basic Phase II allowance allocations.

(C) An operating company with units subject to the emissions limitation requirements of this subsection may elect the allocation of allowances as provided under subparagraphs (A) and (B). Such election shall apply to the annual allowance allocation for each and every unit in the operating company subject to the emissions limitation requirements of this subsection. The Administrator shall allocate allowances pursuant to subparagraphs (A) and (B) only in accordance with this subparagraph.

(4) Notwithstanding any other provision of this section, at the election of the owner or operator, after January 1, 2000, the Administrator shall allocate in lieu of allocation, pursuant to paragraph (1), (2), (3), (5), or (6), allowances for a unit subject to the emissions limitation requirements of this subsection which commenced commercial operation on or after January 1, 1981 and before December 31, 1985, which was subject to, and in compliance with, section 7411 of this title in an amount equal to the unit's annual fuel consumption, on a Btu basis, at a 65 percent capacity factor multiplied by the unit's allowable 1985 emissions rate, divided by 2,000.

(5) For the purposes of this section, in the case of an oil- and gas-fired unit which has been awarded a clean coal technology demonstration grant as of January 1, 1991, by the United States Department of Energy, beginning January 1, 2000, the Administrator shall allocate for the unit allowances in an amount equal to the unit's baseline multiplied by 1.20 lbs/mmBtu, divided by 2,000.

(e) Oil and gas-fired units equal to or greater than 0.60 lbs/mmBtu and less than 1.20 lbs/mmBtu

After January 1, 2000, it shall be unlawful for any existing oil and gas-fired utility unit the lesser of whose actual or allowable 1985 sulfur dioxide emission rate is equal to, or greater than, 0.60 lbs/mmBtu, but less than 1.20 lbs/mmBtu to exceed an annual sulfur dioxide tonnage limitation equal to the product of the unit's baseline multiplied by (A) the lesser of the unit's allowable 1985 emissions rate or its actual 1985 emissions rate and (B) a numerical

factor of 120 percent divided by 2,000, unless the owner or operator of such unit holds allowances to emit not less than the unit's total annual emissions.
(f) Oil and gas-fired units less than 0.60 lbs/mmBtu
 (1) After January 1, 2000, it shall be unlawful for any oil and gas-fired existing utility unit the lesser of whose actual or allowable 1985 emission rate is less than 0.60 lbs/mmBtu and whose average annual fuel consumption during the period 1980 through 1989 on a Btu basis was 90 percent or less in the form of natural gas to exceed an annual sulfur dioxide tonnage emissions limitation equal to the product of the unit's baseline multiplied by (A) the lesser of 0.60 lbs/mmBtu or the unit's allowable 1985 emissions, and (B) a numerical factor of 120 percent, divided by 2,000, unless the owner or operator of such unit holds allowances to emit not less than the unit's total annual emissions.
 (2) In addition to allowances allocated pursuant to paragraph (1) as basic Phase II allowance allocations and section 7651b(a)(1) of this title, beginning January 1, 2000, the Administrator shall, in the case of any unit operated by a utility that furnishes electricity, electric energy, steam, and natural gas within an area consisting of a city and 1 contiguous county, and in the case of any unit owned by a State authority, the output of which unit is furnished within that same area consisting of a city and 1 contiguous county, the Administrator shall allocate for each unit in the utility its pro rata share of 7,000 allowances and for each unit in the State authority its pro rata share of 2,000 allowances.
(g) Units that commence operation between 1986 and December 31, 1995
 (1) After January 1, 2000, it shall be unlawful for any utility unit that has commenced commercial operation on or after January 1, 1986, but not later than September 30, 1990 to exceed an annual tonnage emission limitation equal to the product of the unit's annual fuel consumption, on a Btu basis, at a 65 percent capacity factor multiplied by the unit's allowable 1985 sulfur dioxide emission rate (converted, if necessary, to pounds per mmBtu), divided by 2,000 unless the owner or operator of such unit holds allowances to emit not less than the unit's total annual emissions.
 (2) After January 1, 2000, the Administrator shall allocate allowances pursuant to section 7651b of this title to each unit which is listed in table B of this paragraph in an annual amount equal to the amount specified in table B.

TABLE B	
Unit	Allowances
Brandon Shores..................	8,907
Miller 4..............................	9,197
TNP One 2........................	4,000
Zimmer 1..........................	18,458
Spruce 1............................	7,647
Clover 1.............................	2,796
Clover 2.............................	2,796
Twin Oak 2.......................	1,760
Twin Oak 1.......................	9,158
Cross 1..............................	6,401
Malakoff 1.........................	1,759

Notwithstanding any other paragraph of this subsection, for units subject to this paragraph, the Administrator shall not allocate allowances pursuant to any other paragraph of this subsection, Provided[2] that the owner or operator of a unit listed on Table B may elect an allocation of allowances under another paragraph of this subsection in lieu of an allocation under this paragraph.
 (3) Beginning January 1, 2000, the Administrator shall allocate to the owner or operator of any utility unit that commences commercial operation, or has commenced commercial operation, on or after October 1, 1990, but not later than December 31, 1992 allowances in an amount equal to the product of the unit's annual fuel consumption, on a Btu basis, at a 65 percent capacity factor multiplied by the lesser of 0.30 lbs/mmBtu or the unit's allowable sulfur dioxide emission rate (converted, if necessary, to pounds per mmBtu), divided by 2,000.

---

[2]So in original. Probably should not be capitalized.

356 / Environmental Statutes

(4) Beginning January 1, 2000, the Administrator shall allocate to the owner or operator of any utility unit that has commenced construction before December 31, 1990 and that commences commercial operation between January 1, 1993 and December 31, 1995, allowances in an amount equal to the product of the unit's annual fuel consumption, on a Btu basis, at a 65 percent capacity factor multiplied by the lesser of 0.30 lbs/mmBtu or the unit's allowable sulfur dioxide emission rate (converted, if necessary, to pounds per mmBtu), divided by 2,000.

(5) After January 1, 2000, it shall be unlawful for any existing utility unit that has completed conversion from predominantly gas fired existing operation to coal fired operation between January 1, 1985 and December 31, 1987, for which there has been allocated a proposed or final prohibition order pursuant to section 301(b)[3] of the Powerplant and Industrial Fuel Use Act of 1978 (42 U.S.C. 8301 et seq, repealed 1987) to exceed an annual sulfur dioxide tonnage emissions limitation equal to the product of the unit's annual fuel consumption, on a Btu basis, at a 65 percent capacity factor multiplied by the lesser of 1.20 lbs/mmBtu or the unit's allowable 1987 sulfur dioxide emissions rate, divided by 2,000, unless the owner or operator of such unit has obtained allowances equal to its actual emissions.

(6) (A)[4]Unless the Administrator has approved a designation of such facility under section 7651i of this title, the provisions of this subchapter shall not apply to a "qualifying small power production facility" or "qualifying cogeneration facility" (within the meaning of section 796(17)(C) or 796(18)(B) of title 16) or to a "new independent power production facility" as defined in section 7651o of this title except that clause (iii)[5] of such definition in section 7651o of this title shall not apply for purposes of this paragraph if, as of November 15, 1990,
 (i) an applicable power sales agreement has been executed;
 (ii) the facility is the subject of a State regulatory authority order requiring an electric utility to enter into a power sales agreement with, purchase capacity from, or (for purposes of establishing terms and conditions of the electric utility's purchase of power) enter into arbitration concerning, the facility;
 (iii) an electric utility has issued a letter of intent or similar instrument committing to purchase power from the facility at a previously offered or lower price and a power sales agreement is executed within a reasonable period of time; or
 (iv) the facility has been selected as a winning bidder in a utility competitive bid solicitation.

(h) Oil and gas-fired units less than 10 percent oil consumed
 (1) After January 1, 2000, it shall be unlawful for any oil- and gas-fired utility unit whose average annual fuel consumption during the period 1980 through 1989 on a Btu basis exceeded 90 percent in the form of natural gas to exceed an annual sulfur dioxide tonnage limitation equal to the product of the unit's baseline multiplied by the unit's actual 1985 emissions rate divided by 2,000 unless the owner or operator of such unit holds allowances to emit not less than the unit's total annual emissions.
 (2) In addition to allowances allocated pursuant to paragraph (1) and section 7651b(a)(1) of this title as basic Phase II allowance allocations, beginning January 1, 2000, and for each calendar year thereafter until and including 2009, the Administrator shall allocate annually for each unit subject to the emissions limitation requirements of paragraph (1) allowances from the reserve created pursuant to subsection (a)(2) of this section in an amount equal to the unit's baseline multiplied by 0.050 lbs/mmBtu, divided by 2,000.
 (3) In addition to allowances allocated pursuant to paragraph (1) and section 7651b(a)(1) of this title, beginning January 1, 2010, the Administrator shall allocate annually for each unit subject to the emissions limitation requirements of paragraph (1) allowances in an amount equal to the unit's baseline multiplied by 0.050 lbs/mmBtu, divided by 2,000.

(i) Units in high growth States
 (1) In addition to allowances allocated pursuant to this section and section 7651b(a)(1) of this title as basic Phase II allowance allocations, beginning January 1, 2000, the Administrator shall allocate annually allowances for each unit, subject to an emissions limitation requirement under this section, and located in a State that—

---
[3]See References in Text note below.
[4]So in original. No subpar. (B) has been enacted.
[5]So in original. Probably means clause "(C)".

(A) has experienced a growth in population in excess of 25 percent between 1980 and 1988 according to State Population and Household Estimates, With Age, Sex, and Components of Change: 1981-1988 allocated by the United States Department of Commerce, and

(B) had an installed electrical generating capacity of more than 30,000,000 kw in 1988, in an amount equal to the difference between (A) the number of allowances that would be allocated for the unit pursuant to the emissions limitation requirements of this section applicable to the unit adjusted to reflect the unit's annual average fuel consumption on a Btu basis of any three consecutive calendar years between 1980 and 1989 (inclusive) as elected by the owner or operator and (B) the number of allowances allocated for the unit pursuant to the emissions limitation requirements of this section: Provided, That the number of allowances allocated pursuant to this subsection shall not exceed an annual total of 40,000. If necessary to meeting the 40,000 allowance restriction imposed under this subsection the Administrator shall reduce, pro rata, the additional annual allowances allocated to each unit under this subsection.

(2) Beginning January 1, 2000, in addition to allowances allocated pursuant to this section and section 7651b(a)(1) of this title as basic Phase II allowance allocations, the Administrator shall allocate annually for each unit subject to the emissions limitation requirements of subsection (b)(1) of this section, (A) the lesser of whose actual or allowable 1980 emissions rate has declined by 50 percent or more as of November 15, 1990, (B) whose actual emissions rate is less than 1.2 lbs/mmBtu as of January 1, 2000, (C) which commenced operation after January 1, 1970, (D) which is owned by a utility company whose combined commercial and industrial kilowatt-hour sales have increased by more than 20 percent between calendar year 1980 and November 15, 1990, and (E) whose company-wide fossil-fuel sulfur dioxide emissions rate has declined 40 per centum or more from 1980 to 1988, allowances in an amount equal to the difference between (i) the number of allowances that would be allocated for the unit pursuant to the emissions limitation requirements of subsection (b)(1) of this section adjusted to reflect the unit's annual average fuel consumption on a Btu basis for any three consecutive years between 1980 and 1989 (inclusive) as elected by the owner or operator and (ii) the number of allowances allocated for the unit pursuant to the emissions limitation requirements of subsection (b)(1) of this section: Provided, That the number of allowances allocated pursuant to this paragraph shall not exceed an annual total of 5,000. If necessary to meeting the 5,000-allowance restriction imposed in the last clause of the preceding sentence the Administrator shall reduce, pro rata, the additional allowances allocated to each unit pursuant to this paragraph.

(j) Certain municipally owned power plants

Beginning January 1, 2000, in addition to allowances allocated pursuant to this section and section 7651b(a)(1) of this title as basic Phase II allowance allocations, the Administrator shall allocate annually for each existing municipally owned oil and gas-fired utility unit with nameplate capacity equal to, or less than, 40 MWe, the lesser of whose actual or allowable 1985 sulfur dioxide emission rate is less than 1.20 lbs/mmBtu, allowances in an amount equal to the product of the unit's annual fuel consumption on a Btu basis at a 60 percent capacity factor multiplied by the lesser of its allowable 1985 emission rate or its actual 1985 emission rate, divided by 2,000.

(July 14, 1955, ch. 360, title IV, Sec. 405, as added Pub. L. 101-549, title IV, Sec. 401, Nov. 15, 1990, 104 Stat. 2605.)

References in Text

Section 301(b) of the Powerplant and Industrial Fuel Use Act of 1978, referred to in subsec. (g)(5), is section 301(b) of Pub. L. 95-620, which is classified to section 8341(b) of this title. A prior section 301(b) of Pub. L. 95-620, title III, Nov. 9, 1978, 92 Stat. 3305, which was formerly classified to section 8341(b) of this title, was repealed by Pub. L. 97-35, title X, Sec. 1021(a), Aug. 13, 1981, 95 Stat. 614.

Section Referred to in Other Sections

This section is referred to in sections 7651a, 7651b, 7651c, 7651e, 7651f, 7651g, 7651h, 7651i, 7651j of this title.

ALLOWANCES FOR STATES WITH EMISSIONS RATES AT OR BELOW 0.80 LBS/MMBTU

42 USC 7651e

(a) Election of Governor
In addition to basic Phase II allowance allocations, upon the election of the Governor of any State, with a 1985 state-wide annual sulfur dioxide emissions rate equal to or less than, 0.80 lbs/mmBtu, averaged over all fossil fuel-fired utility steam generating units, beginning January 1, 2000, and for each calendar year thereafter until and including 2009, the Administrator shall allocate, in lieu of other Phase II bonus allowance allocations, allowances from the reserve created pursuant to section 7651d(a)(2) of this title to all such units in the State in an amount equal to 125,000 multiplied by the unit's pro rata share of electricity generated in calendar year 1985 at fossil fuel-fired utility steam units in all States eligible for the election.

(b) Notification of Administrator
Pursuant to section 7651b(a)(1) of this title, each Governor of a State eligible to make an election under paragraph[1] (a) shall notify the Administrator of such election. In the event that the Governor of any such State fails to notify the Administrator of the Governor's elections, the Administrator shall allocate allowances pursuant to section 7651d of this title.

(c) Allowances after January 1, 2010
After January 1, 2010, the Administrator shall allocate allowances to units subject to the provisions of this section pursuant to section 7651d of this title.

(July 14, 1955, ch. 360, title IV, Sec. 406, as added Pub. L. 101-549, title IV, Sec. 401, Nov. 15, 1990, 104 Stat. 2613.)

Section Referred to in Other Sections

This section is referred to in sections 7651a, 7651b, 7651d, 7651j of this title.

NITROGEN OXIDES EMISSION REDUCTION PROGRAM

42 USC 7651f

(a) Applicability
On the date that a coal-fired utility unit becomes an affected unit pursuant to sections 7651c, 7651d,[2] 7651h of this title, or on the date a unit subject to the provisions of section 7651c(d) or 7651h(b) of this title, must meet the SO_2 reduction requirements, each such unit shall become an affected unit for purposes of this section and shall be subject to the emission limitations for nitrogen oxides set forth herein.

(b) Emission limitations
  (1) Not later than eighteen months after November 15, 1990, the Administrator shall by regulation establish annual allowable emission limitations for nitrogen oxides for the types of utility boilers listed below, which limitations shall not exceed the rates listed below: Provided, That the Administrator may set a rate higher than that listed for any type of utility boiler if the Administrator finds that the maximum listed rate for that boiler type cannot be achieved using low NO_x burner technology. The maximum allowable emission rates are as follows:
  (A) for tangentially fired boilers, 0.45 lb/mmBtu;
  (B) for dry bottom wall-fired boilers (other than units applying cell burner technology), 0.50 lb/mmBtu.
  After January 1, 1995, it shall be unlawful for any unit that is an affected unit on that date and is of the type listed in this paragraph to emit nitrogen oxides in excess of the emission rates set by the Administrator pursuant to this paragraph.
  (2) Not later than January 1, 1997, the Administrator shall, by regulation, establish allowable emission limitations on a lb/mmBtu, annual average basis, for nitrogen oxides for the following types of utility boilers:
  (A) wet bottom wall-fired boilers;

---
[1] So in original. Probably should be "subsection".
[2] So in original. Probably should be followed by "or".

(B) cyclones;
(C) units applying cell burner technology;
(D) all other types of utility boilers.

The Administrator shall base such rates on the degree of reduction achievable through the retrofit application of the best system of continuous emission reduction, taking into account available technology, costs and energy and environmental impacts; and which is comparable to the costs of nitrogen oxides controls set pursuant to subsection (b)(1) of this section. Not later than January 1, 1997, the Administrator may revise the applicable emission limitations for tangentially fired and dry bottom, wall-fired boilers (other than cell burners) to be more stringent if the Administrator determines that more effective low NO_x burner technology is available: Provided, That, no unit that is an affected unit pursuant to section 7651c of this title and that is subject to the requirements of subsection (b)(1) of this section, shall be subject to the revised emission limitations, if any.

(c) Revised performance standards
   (1) Not later than January 1, 1993, the Administrator shall propose revised standards of performance to section 7411 of this title for nitrogen oxides emissions from fossil-fuel fired steam generating units, including both electric utility and nonutility units. Not later than January 1, 1994, the Administrator shall promulgate such revised standards of performance. Such revised standards of performance shall reflect improvements in methods for the reduction of emissions of oxides of nitrogen.

(d) Alternative emission limitations
   The permitting authority shall, upon request of an owner or operator of a unit subject to this section, authorize an emission limitation less stringent than the applicable limitation established under subsection (b)(1) or (b)(2) of this section upon a determination that—
   (1) a unit subject to subsection (b)(1) of this section cannot meet the applicable limitation using low NO_x burner technology; or
   (2) a unit subject to subsection (b)(2) of this section cannot meet the applicable rate using the technology on which the Administrator based the applicable emission limitation.

The permitting authority shall base such determination upon a showing satisfactory to the permitting authority, in accordance with regulations established by the Administrator not later than eighteen months after November 15, 1990, that the owner or operator—
   (1) has properly installed appropriate control equipment designed to meet the applicable emission rate;
   (2) has properly operated such equipment for a period of fifteen months (or such other period of time as the Administrator determines through the regulations), and provides operating and monitoring data for such period demonstrating that the unit cannot meet the applicable emission rate; and
   (3) has specified an emission rate that such unit can meet on an annual average basis.

The permitting authority shall issue an operating permit for the unit in question, in accordance with section 7651g of this title and part B[3] of title III—
   (i) that permits the unit during the demonstration period referred to in subparagraph (2) above, to emit at a rate in excess of the applicable emission rate;
   (ii) at the conclusion of the demonstration period to revise the operating permit to reflect the alternative emission rate demonstrated in paragraphs (2) and (3) above.

Units subject to subsection (b)(1) of this section for which an alternative emission limitation is established shall not be required to install any additional control technology beyond low NO_x burners. Nothing in this section shall preclude an owner or operator from installing and operating an alternative NO_x control technology capable of achieving the applicable emission limitation. If the owner or operator of a unit subject to the emissions limitation requirements of subsection (b)(1) of this section demonstrates to the satisfaction of the Administrator that the technology necessary to meet such requirements is not in adequate supply to enable its installation and operation at the unit, consistent with system reliability, by January 1, 1995, then the Administrator shall extend the deadline for compliance for the unit by a period of 15 months. Any owner or operator may petition the Administrator to make a determination under the previous sentence. The Administrator shall grant or deny such petition within 3 months of submittal.

---

[3] See References in Text note below.

(e) Emissions averaging

In lieu of complying with the applicable emission limitations under subsection (b)(1), (2), or (d) of this section, the owner or operator of two or more units subject to one or more of the applicable emission limitations set pursuant to these sections, may petition the permitting authority for alternative contemporaneous annual emission limitations for such units that ensure that (1) the actual annual emission rate in pounds of nitrogen oxides per million Btu averaged over the units in question is a rate that is less than or equal to (2) the Btu-weighted average annual emission rate for the same units if they had been operated, during the same period of time, in compliance with limitations set in accordance with the applicable emission rates set pursuant to subsections (b)(1) and (2) of this section.

If the permitting authority determines, in accordance with regulations issued by the Administrator not later than eighteen months after November 15, 1990;[4] that the conditions in the paragraph above can be met, the permitting authority shall issue operating permits for such units, in accordance with section 7651g of this title and part B [3] of title III, that allow alternative contemporaneous annual emission limitations. Such emission limitations shall only remain in effect while both units continue operation under the conditions specified in their respective operating permits.

(July 14, 1955, ch. 360, title IV, Sec. 407, as added Pub. L. 101-549, title IV, Sec. 401, Nov. 15, 1990, 104 Stat. 2613.)

References in Text

Part B of title III, referred to in subsecs. (d) and (e), means title III of the Clean Air Act, act July 14, 1955, ch. 360, as added, which is classified to subchapter III of this chapter, but title III does not contain parts. For provisions of the Clean Air Act relating to permits, see subchapter V (Sec. 7661 et seq.) of this chapter.

Section Referred to in Other Sections

This section is referred to in sections 7651g, 7651j of this title.

PERMITS AND COMPLIANCE PLANS

42 USC 7651g

(a) Permit program

The provisions of this subchapter shall be implemented, subject to section 7651b of this title, by permits issued to units subject to this subchapter (and enforced) in accordance with the provisions of subchapter V of this chapter, as modified by this subchapter. Any such permit issued by the Administrator, or by a State with an approved permit program, shall prohibit—
  (1) annual emissions of sulfur dioxide in excess of the number of allowances to emit sulfur dioxide the owner or operator, or the designated representative of the owners or operators, of the unit hold for the unit,
  (2) exceedances of applicable emissions rates,
  (3) the use of any allowance prior to the year for which it was allocated, and
  (4) contravention of any other provision of the permit.

Permits issued to implement this subchapter shall be issued for a period of 5 years, notwithstanding subchapter V of this chapter. No permit shall be issued that is inconsistent with the requirements of this subchapter, and subchapter V of this chapter as applicable.

(b) Compliance plan

Each initial permit application shall be accompanied by a compliance plan for the source to comply with its requirements under this subchapter. Where an affected source consists of more than one affected unit, such plan shall cover all such units, and for purposes of section 7661a(c) of this title, such source shall be considered a "facility". Nothing in this section regarding compliance plans or in subchapter V of this chapter shall be construed as affecting allowances. Except as provided under subsection (c)(1)(B) of this section, submission of a statement by the owner or operator, or the designated representative of the owners and operators, of a unit subject to the emissions limitation requirements of sections 7651c, 7651d, and 7651f of this title, that the unit will meet the applicable emissions limitation requirements of such

---

[4]So in original. The semicolon probably should be a comma.

sections in a timely manner or that, in the case of the emissions limitation requirements of sections 7651c and 7651d of this title, the owners and operators will hold allowances to emit not less than the total annual emissions of the unit, shall be deemed to meet the proposed and approved compliance planning requirements of this section and subchapter V of this chapter, except that, for any unit that will meet the requirements of this subchapter by means of an alternative method of compliance authorized under section 7651c(b), (c), (d), or (f) of this title[1] section 7651f(d) or (e) of this title, section 7651h of this title and section 7651i of this title, the proposed and approved compliance plan, permit application and permit shall include, pursuant to regulations promulgated by the Administrator, for each alternative method of compliance a comprehensive description of the schedule and means by which the unit will rely on one or more alternative methods of compliance in the manner and time authorized under this subchapter. Recordation by the Administrator of transfers of allowances shall amend automatically all applicable proposed or approved permit applications, compliance plans and permits. The Administrator may also require—

(1) for a source, a demonstration of attainment of national ambient air quality standards, and
(2) from the owner or operator of two or more affected sources, an integrated compliance plan providing an overall plan for achieving compliance at the affected sources.

(c) First phase permits

The Administrator shall issue permits to affected sources under sections 7651c and 7651f of this title.

(1) Permit application and compliance plan

(A) Not later than 27 months after November 15, 1990, the designated representative of the owners or operators, or the owner and operator, of each affected source under sections 7651c and 7651f of this title shall submit a permit application and compliance plan for that source in accordance with regulations issued by the Administrator under paragraph (3). The permit application and the compliance plan shall be binding on the owner or operator or the designated representative of owners and operators for purposes of this subchapter and section 7651a(a)[2] of this title, and shall be enforceable in lieu of a permit until a permit is issued by the Administrator for the source.

(B) In the case of a compliance plan for an affected source under sections 7651c and 7651f of this title for which the owner or operator proposes to meet the requirements of that section by reducing utilization of the unit as compared with its baseline or by shutting down the unit, the owner or operator shall include in the proposed compliance plan a specification of the unit or units that will provide electrical generation to compensate for the reduced output at the affected source, or a demonstration that such reduced utilization will be accomplished through energy conservation or improved unit efficiency. The unit to be used for such compensating generation, which is not otherwise an affected unit under sections 7651c and 7651f of this title, shall be deemed an affected unit under section 7651c of this title, subject to all of the requirements for such units under this subchapter, except that allowances shall be allocated to such compensating unit in the amount of an annual limitation equal to the product of the unit's baseline multiplied by the lesser of the unit's actual 1985 emissions rate or its allowable 1985 emissions rate, divided by 2,000.

(2) EPA action on compliance plans

The Administrator shall review each proposed compliance plan to determine whether it satisfies the requirements of this subchapter, and shall approve or disapprove such plan within 6 months after receipt of a complete submission. If a plan is disapproved, it may be resubmitted for approval with such changes as the Administrator shall require consistent with the requirements of this subchapter and within such period as the Administrator prescribes as part of such disapproval.

(3) Regulations; issuance of permits

Not later than 18 months after November 15, 1990, the Administrator shall promulgate regulations, in accordance with subchapter V of this chapter, to implement a Federal permit program to issue permits for affected sources under this subchapter. Following promulgation, the Administrator shall issue a permit to implement the requirements of section 7651c of this title and the allowances provided under section 7651b of this title to the

---

[1] So in original. Probably should be followed by a comma.
[2] So in original. Section 7651a of this title does not contain subsections.

owner or operator of each affected source under section 7651c of this title. Such a permit shall supersede any permit application and compliance plan submitted under paragraph (1).

(4) Fees

During the years 1995 through 1999 inclusive, no fee shall be required to be paid under section 7661a(b)(3) of this title or under section 7410(a)(2)(L) of this title with respect to emissions from any unit which is an affected unit under section 7651c of this title.

(d) Second phase permits

(1) To provide for permits for (A) new electric utility steam generating units required under section 7651b(e) of this title to have allowances, (B) affected units or sources under section 7651d of this title, and (C) existing units subject to nitrogen oxide emission reductions under section 7651f of this title, each State in which one or more such units or sources are located shall submit in accordance with subchapter V of this chapter, a permit program for approval as provided by that subchapter. Upon approval of such program, for the units or sources subject to such approved program the Administrator shall suspend the issuance of permits as provided in subchapter V of this chapter.

(2) The owner or operator or the designated representative of each affected source under section 7651d of this title shall submit a permit application and compliance plan for that source to the permitting authority, not later than January 1, 1996.

(3) Not later than December 31, 1997, each State with an approved permit program shall issue permits to the owner or operator, or the designated representative of the owners and operators, of affected sources under section 7651d of this title that satisfy the requirements of subchapter V of this chapter and this subchapter and that submitted to such State a permit application and compliance plan pursuant to paragraph (2). In the case of a State without an approved permit program by July 1, 1996, the Administrator shall, not later than January 1, 1998, issue a permit to the owner or operator or the designated representative of each such affected source. In the case of affected sources for which applications and plans are timely received under paragraph (2), the permit application and the compliance plan, including amendments thereto, shall be binding on the owner or operator or the designated representative of the owners or operators and shall be enforceable as a permit for purposes of this subchapter and subchapter V of this chapter until a permit is issued by the permitting authority for the affected source. The provisions of section 558(c) of title 5 (relating to renewals) shall apply to permits issued by a permitting authority under this subchapter and subchapter V of this chapter.

(4) The permit issued in accordance with this subsection for an affected source shall provide that the affected units at the affected source may not emit an annual tonnage of sulfur dioxide in excess of the number of allowances to emit sulfur dioxide the owner or operator or designated representative hold for the unit.

(e) New units

The owner or operator of each source that includes a new electric utility steam generating unit shall submit a permit application and compliance plan to the permitting authority not later than 24 months before the later of (1) January 1, 2000, or (2) the date on which the unit commences operation. The permitting authority shall issue a permit to the owner or operator, or the designated representative thereof, of the unit that satisfies the requirements of subchapter V of this chapter and this subchapter.

(f) Units subject to certain other limits

The owner or operator, or designated representative thereof, of any unit subject to an emission rate requirement under section 7651f of this title shall submit a permit application and compliance plan for such unit to the permitting authority, not later than January 1, 1998. The permitting authority shall issue a permit to the owner or operator that satisfies the requirements of subchapter V of this chapter and this subchapter, including any appropriate monitoring and reporting requirements.

(g) Amendment of application and compliance plan

At any time after the submission of an application and compliance plan under this section, the applicant may submit a revised application and compliance plan, in accordance with the requirements of this section. In considering any permit application and compliance plan under this subchapter, the permitting authority shall ensure coordination with the applicable electric ratemaking authority, in the case of regulated utilities, and with unregulated public utilities.

(h) Prohibition
   (1) It shall be unlawful for an owner or operator, or designated representative, required to submit a permit application or compliance plan under this subchapter to fail to submit such application or plan in accordance with the deadlines specified in this section or to otherwise fail to comply with regulations implementing this section.
   (2) It shall be unlawful for any person to operate any source subject to this subchapter except in compliance with the terms and requirements of a permit application and compliance plan (including amendments thereto) or permit issued by the Administrator or a State with an approved permit program. For purposes of this subsection, compliance, as provided in section 7661c(f) of this title, with a permit issued under subchapter V of this chapter which complies with this subchapter for sources subject to this subchapter shall be deemed compliance with this subsection as well as section 7661a(a) of this title.
   (3) In order to ensure reliability of electric power, nothing in this subchapter or subchapter V of this chapter shall be construed as requiring termination of operations of an electric utility steam generating unit for failure to have an approved permit or compliance plan, except that any such unit may be subject to the applicable enforcement provisions of section 7413 of this title.
(i) Multiple owners
   No permit shall be issued under this section to an affected unit until the designated representative of the owners or operators has filed a certificate of representation with regard to matters under this subchapter, including the holding and distribution of allowances and the proceeds of transactions involving allowances. Where there are multiple holders of a legal or equitable title to, or a leasehold interest in, such a unit, or where a utility or industrial customer purchases power from an affected unit (or units) under life-of-the-unit, firm power contractual arrangements, the certificate shall state (1) that allowances and the proceeds of transactions involving allowances will be deemed to be held or distributed in proportion to each holder's legal, equitable, leasehold, or contractual reservation or entitlement, or (2) if such multiple holders have expressly provided for a different distribution of allowances by contract, that allowances and the proceeds of transactions involving allowances will be deemed to be held or distributed in accordance with the contract. A passive lessor, or a person who has an equitable interest through such lessor, whose rental payments are not based, either directly or indirectly, upon the revenues or income from the affected unit shall not be deemed to be a holder of a legal, equitable, leasehold, or contractual interest for the purpose of holding or distributing allowances as provided in this subsection, during either the term of such leasehold or thereafter, unless expressly provided for in the leasehold agreement. Except as otherwise provided in this subsection, where all legal or equitable title to or interest in an affected unit is held by a single person, the certification shall state that all allowances received by the unit are deemed to be held for that person.

(July 14, 1955, ch. 360, title IV, Sec. 408, as added Pub. L. 101-549, title IV, Sec. 401, Nov. 15, 1990, 104 Stat. 2616.)

Section Referred to in Other Sections

This section is referred to in sections 7651b, 7651c, 7651f, 7651h, 7651i of this title.

REPOWERED SOURCES

42 USC 7651h

(a) Availability
   Not later than December 31, 1997, the owner or operator of an existing unit subject to the emissions limitation requirements of section 7651d(b) and (c) of this title may demonstrate to the permitting authority that one or more units will be repowered with a qualifying clean coal technology to comply with the requirements under section 7651d of this title. The owner or operator shall, as part of any such demonstration, provide, not later than January 1, 2000, satisfactory documentation of a preliminary design and engineering effort for such repowering and an executed and binding contract for the majority of the equipment to repower such unit and such other information as the Administrator may require by regulation. The replacement of an existing utility unit with a new utility unit using a repowering technology referred

to in section 7651a(2)[1] of this title which is located at a different site, shall be treated as repowering of the existing unit for purposes of this subchapter, if—
(1) the replacement unit is designated by the owner or operator to replace such existing unit, and
(2) the existing unit is retired from service on or before the date on which the designated replacement unit enters commercial operation.

(b) Extension
   (1) An owner or operator satisfying the requirements of subsection (a) of this section shall be granted an extension of the emission limitation requirement compliance date for that unit from January 1, 2000, to December 31, 2003. The extension shall be specified in the permit issued to the source under section 7651g of this title, together with any compliance schedule and other requirements necessary to meet second phase requirements by the extended date. Any unit that is granted an extension under this section shall not be eligible for a waiver under section 7411(j) of this title, and shall continue to be subject to requirements under this subchapter as if it were a unit subject to section 7651d of this title.
   (2) If (A) the owner or operator of an existing unit has been granted an extension under paragraph (1) in order to repower such unit with a clean coal unit, and (B) such owner or operator demonstrates to the satisfaction of the Administrator that the repowering technology to be utilized by such unit has been properly constructed and tested on such unit, but nevertheless has been unable to achieve the emission reduction limitations and is economically or technologically infeasible, such existing unit may be retrofitted or repowered with equipment or facilities utilizing another clean coal technology or other available control technology.

(c) Allowances
   (1) For the period of the extension under this section, the Administrator shall allocate to the owner or operator of the affected unit, annual allowances for sulfur dioxide equal to the affected unit's baseline multiplied by the lesser of the unit's federally approved State Implementation Plan emissions limitation or its actual emission rate for 1995 in lieu of any other allocation. Such allowances may not be transferred or used by any other source to meet emission requirements under this subchapter. The source owner or operator shall notify the Administrator sixty days in advance of the date on which the affected unit for which the extension has been granted is to be removed from operation to install the repowering technology.
   (2) Effective on that date, the unit shall be subject to the requirements of section 7651d of this title. Allowances for the year in which the unit is removed from operation to install the repowering technology shall be calculated as the product of the unit's baseline multiplied by 1.20 lbs/mmBtu, divided by 2,000, and prorated accordingly, and are transferable.
   (3) Allowances for such existing utility units for calendar years after the year the repowering is complete shall be calculated as the product of the existing unit's baseline multiplied by 1.20 lbs/mmBtu, divided by 2,000.
   (4) Notwithstanding the provisions of section 7651b(a) and (e) of this title, allowances shall be allocated under this section for a designated replacement unit which replaces an existing unit (as provided in the last sentence of subsection (a) of this section) in lieu of any further allocations of allowances for the existing unit.
   (5) For the purpose of meeting the aggregate emissions limitation requirement set forth in section 7651b(a)(1) of this title, the units with an extension under this subsection shall be treated in each calendar year during the extension period as holding allowances allocated under paragraph (3).

(d) Control requirements
   Any unit qualifying for an extension under this section that does not increase actual hourly emissions for any pollutant regulated under the[2] chapter shall not be subject to any standard of performance under section 7411 of this title. Notwithstanding the provisions of this subsection, no new unit (1) designated as a replacement for an existing unit, (2) qualifying for the extension under subsection (b) of this section, and (3) located at a different site than the existing unit shall receive an exemption from the requirements imposed under section 7411 of this title.

---

[1] So in original. Probably should be section "7651a(12)".
[2] So in original. Probably should be "this".

(e) Expedited permitting

State permitting authorities and, where applicable, the Administrator, are encouraged to give expedited consideration to permit applications under parts C and D of subchapter I of this chapter for any source qualifying for an extension under this section.

(f) Prohibition

It shall be unlawful for the owner or operator of a repowered source to fail to comply with the requirement of this section, or any regulations of permit requirements to implement this section, including the prohibition against emitting sulfur dioxide in excess of allowances held.

(July 14, 1955, ch. 360, title IV, Sec. 409, as added Pub. L. 101-549, title IV, Sec. 401, Nov. 15, 1990, 104 Stat. 2619.)

Section Referred to in Other Sections

This section is referred to in sections 7651a, 7651b, 7651d, 7651f, 7651g, 7651j of this title.

ELECTION FOR ADDITIONAL SOURCES

42 USC 7651i

(a) Applicability

The owner or operator of any unit that is not, nor will become, an affected unit under section 7651b(e), 7651c, or 7651d of this title, or that is a process source under subsection (d) of this section, that emits sulfur dioxide, may elect to designate that unit or source to become an affected unit and to receive allowances under this subchapter. An election shall be submitted to the Administrator for approval, along with a permit application and proposed compliance plan in accordance with section 7651g of this title. The Administrator shall approve a designation that meets the requirements of this section, and such designated unit, or source, shall be allocated allowances, and be an affected unit for purposes of this subchapter.

(b) Establishment of baseline

The baseline for a unit designated under this section shall be established by the Administrator by regulation, based on fuel consumption and operating data for the unit for calendar years 1985, 1986, and 1987, or if such data is not available, the Administrator may prescribe a baseline based on alternative representative data.

(c) Emission limitations

Annual emissions limitations for sulfur dioxide shall be equal to the product of the baseline multiplied by the lesser of the unit's 1985 actual or allowable emission rate in lbs/mmBtu, or, if the unit did not operate in 1985, by the lesser of the unit's actual or allowable emission rate for a calendar year after 1985 (as determined by the Administrator), divided by 2,000.

(d) Process sources

Not later than 18 months after November 15, 1990, the Administrator shall establish a program under which the owner or operator of a process source that emits sulfur dioxide may elect to designate that source as an affected unit for the purpose of receiving allowances under this subchapter. The Administrator shall, by regulation, define the sources that may be designated; specify the emissions limitation; specify the operating, emission baseline, and other data requirements; prescribe CEMS or other monitoring requirements; and promulgate permit, reporting, and any other requirements necessary to implement such a program.

(e) Allowances and permits

The Administrator shall issue allowances to an affected unit under this section in an amount equal to the emissions limitation calculated under subsection (c) or (d) of this section, in accordance with section 7651b of this title. Such allowance may be used in accordance with, and shall be subject to, the provisions of section 7651b of this title. Affected sources under this section shall be subject to the requirements of sections 7651b, 7651g, 7651j, 7651k, 7651l, and 7651m of this title.

(f) Limitation

Any unit designated under this section shall not transfer or bank allowances produced as a result of reduced utilization or shutdown, except that, such allowances may be transferred or carried forward for use in subsequent years to the extent that the reduced utilization or shutdown results from the replacement of thermal energy from the unit designated under this section, with thermal energy generated by any other unit or units subject to the requirements of this subchapter, and the designated unit's allowances are transferred or carried forward for use at such other replacement unit or units. In no case may the Administrator allocate to a source designated under this section allowances in an amount greater than the emissions resulting from operation of the source in full compliance with the requirements of this chapter. No such allowances shall authorize operation of a unit in violation of any other requirements of this chapter.

(g) Implementation

The Administrator shall issue regulations to implement this section not later than eighteen months after November 15, 1990.

(h) Small diesel refineries

The Administrator shall issue allowances to owners or operators of small diesel refineries who produce diesel fuel after October 1, 1993, meeting the requirements of subsection[1] 7545(i) of this title.

  (1) Allowance period

  Allowances may be allocated under this subsection only for the period from October 1, 1993, through December 31, 1999.

  (2) Allowance determination

  The number of allowances allocated pursuant to this paragraph shall equal the annual number of pounds of sulfur dioxide reduction attributable to desulfurization by a small refinery divided by 2,000. For the purposes of this calculation, the concentration of sulfur removed from diesel fuel shall be the difference between 0.274 percent (by weight) and 0.050 percent (by weight).

  (3) Refinery eligibility

  As used in this subsection, the term "small refinery" shall mean a refinery or portion of a refinery—

    (A) which, as of November 15, 1990, has bona fide crude oil throughput of less than 18,250,000 barrels per year, as reported to the Department of Energy, and

    (B) which, as of November 15, 1990, is owned or controlled by a refiner with a total combined bona fide crude oil throughput of less than 50,187,500 barrels per year, as reported to the Department of Energy.

  (4) Limitation per refinery

  The maximum number of allowances that can be annually allocated to a small refinery pursuant to this subsection is one thousand and five hundred.

  (5) Limitation on total

  In any given year, the total number of allowances allocated pursuant to this subsection shall not exceed thirty-five thousand.

  (6) Required certification

  The Administrator shall not allocate any allowances pursuant to this subsection unless the owner or operator of a small diesel refinery shall have certified, at a time and in a manner prescribed by the Administrator, that all motor diesel fuel produced by the refinery for which allowances are claimed, including motor diesel fuel for off-highway use, shall have met the requirements of subsection[1] 1545(i) of this title.

(July 14, 1955, ch. 360, title IV, Sec. 410, as added Pub. L. 101-549, title IV, Sec. 401, Nov. 15, 1990, 104 Stat. 2621.)

Section Referred to in Other Sections

This section is referred to in sections 7651a, 7651b, 7651c, 7651d, 7651g, 7651j, 7651o of this title.

EXCESS EMISSIONS PENALTY

42 USC 7651j

(a) Excess emissions penalty

The owner or operator of any unit or process source subject to the requirements of sections[1] 7651b, 7651c, 7651d, 7651e, 7651f or 7651h of this title, or designated under section 7651i of this title, that emits sulfur dioxide or nitrogen oxides for any calendar year in excess of the

---

[1] So in original. Probably should be "section".

unit's emissions limitation requirement or, in the case of sulfur dioxide, of the allowances the owner or operator holds for use for the unit for that calendar year shall be liable for the payment of an excess emissions penalty, except where such emissions were authorized pursuant to section 7410(f) of this title. That penalty shall be calculated on the basis of the number of tons emitted in excess of the unit's emissions limitation requirement or, in the case of sulfur dioxide, of the allowances the operator holds for use for the unit for that year, multiplied by $2,000. Any such penalty shall be due and payable without demand to the Administrator as provided in regulations to be issued by the Administrator by no later than eighteen months after November 15, 1990. Any such payment shall be deposited in the United States Treasury pursuant to the Miscellaneous Receipts Act.[2] Any penalty due and payable under this section shall not diminish the liability of the unit's owner or operator for any fine, penalty or assessment against the unit for the same violation under any other section of this chapter.

(b) Excess emissions offset
The owner or operator of any affected source that emits sulfur dioxide during any calendar year in excess of the unit's emissions limitation requirement or of the allowances held for the unit for the calendar year, shall be liable to offset the excess emissions by an equal tonnage amount in the following calendar year, or such longer period as the Administrator may prescribe. The owner or operator of the source shall, within sixty days after the end of the year in which the excess emissions occured,[3] submit to the Administrator, and to the State in which the source is located, a proposed plan to achieve the required offsets. Upon approval of the proposed plan by the Administrator, as submitted, modified or conditioned, the plan shall be deemed at a condition of the operating permit for the unit without further review or revision of the permit. The Administrator shall also deduct allowances equal to the excess tonnage from those allocated for the source for the calendar year, or succeeding years during which offsets are required, following the year in which the excess emissions occurred.

(c) Penalty adjustment
The Administrator shall, by regulation, adjust the penalty specified in subsection (a) of this section for inflation, based on the Consumer Price Index, on November 15, 1990, and annually thereafter.

(d) Prohibition
It shall be unlawful for the owner or operator of any source liable for a penalty and offset under this section to fail (1) to pay the penalty under subsection (a) of this section, (2) to provide, and thereafter comply with, a compliance plan as required by subsection (b) of this section, or (3) to offset excess emissions as required by subsection (b) of this section.

(e) Savings provision
Nothing in this subchapter shall limit or otherwise affect the application of section 7413, 7414, 7420, or 7604 of this title except as otherwise explicitly provided in this subchapter.

(July 14, 1955, ch. 360, title IV, Sec. 411, as added Pub. L. 101-549, title IV, Sec. 401, Nov. 15, 1990, 104 Stat. 2623.)

References in Text

The Miscellaneous Receipts Act, referred to in subsec. (a), is not a recognized popular name for an act. For provisions relating to deposit of monies, see section 3302 of Title 31, Money and Finance.

Section Referred to in Other Sections

This section is referred to in sections 7410, 7651b, 7651c, 7651d, 7651i, 7651k of this title.

MONITORING, REPORTING, AND RECORDKEEPING REQUIREMENTS

42 USC 7651k

(a) Applicability
The owner and operator of any source subject to this subchapter shall be required to install and operate CEMS on each affected unit at the source, and to quality assure the data for sulfur dioxide, nitrogen oxides, opacity and volumetric flow at each such unit. The Adminis-

---

[2] See References in Text note below.
[3] So in original. Probably should be "occurred,".

trator shall, by regulations issued not later than eighteen months after November 15, 1990, specify the requirements for CEMS, for any alternative monitoring system that is demonstrated as providing information with the same precision, reliability, accessibility, and timeliness as that provided by CEMS, and for recordkeeping and reporting of information from such systems. Such regulations may include limitations or the use of alternative compliance methods by units equipped with an alternative monitoring system as may be necessary to preserve the orderly functioning of the allowance system, and which will ensure the emissions reductions contemplated by this subchapter. Where 2 or more units utilize a single stack, a separate CEMS shall not be required for each unit, and for such units the regulations shall require that the owner or operator collect sufficient information to permit reliable compliance determinations for each such unit.

(b) First phase requirements
Not later than thirty-six months after November 15, 1990, the owner or operator of each affected unit under section 7651c of this title, including, but not limited to, units that become affected units pursuant to subsections (b) and (c) of this section and eligible units under subsection (d) of this section, shall install and operate CEMS, quality assure the data, and keep records and reports in accordance with the regulations issued under subsection (a) of this section.

(c) Second phase requirements
Not later than January 1, 1995, the owner or operator of each affected unit that has not previously met the requirements of subsections (a) and (b) of this section shall install and operate CEMS, quality assure the data, and keep records and reports in accordance with the regulations issued under subsection (a) of this section. Upon commencement of commercial operation of each new utility unit, the unit shall comply with the requirements of subsection (a) of this section.

(d) Unavailability of emissions data
If CEMS data or data from an alternative monitoring system approved by the Administrator under subsection (a) of this section is not available for any affected unit during any period of a calendar year in which such data is required under this subchapter, and the owner or operator cannot provide information, satisfactory to the Administrator, on emissions during that period, the Administrator shall deem the unit to be operating in an uncontrolled manner during the entire period for which the data was not available and shall, by regulation which shall be issued not later than eighteen months after November 15, 1990, prescribe means to calculate emissions for that period. The owner or operator shall be liable for excess emissions fees and offsets under section 7651j of this title in accordance with such regulations. Any fee due and payable under this subsection shall not diminish the liability of the unit's owner or operator for any fine, penalty, fee or assessment against the unit for the same violation under any other section of this chapter.

(e) Prohibition
It shall be unlawful for the owner or operator of any source subject to this subchapter to operate a source without complying with the requirements of this section, and any regulations implementing this section.

(July 14, 1955, ch. 360, title IV, Sec. 412, as added Pub. L. 101-549, title IV, Sec. 401, Nov. 15, 1990, 104 Stat. 2624.)

Information Gathering on Greenhouse Gases Contributing to Global Climate Change

Section 821 of Pub. L. 101-549 provided that:

"(a) Monitoring.—The Administrator of the Environmental Protection Agency shall promulgate regulations within 18 months after the enactment of the Clean Air Act Amendments of 1990 [Nov. 15, 1990] to require that all affected sources subject to title V of the Clean Air Act [probably means title IV of the Clean Air Act as added by Pub. L. 101-549, which is classified to section 7651 et seq. of this title] shall also monitor carbon dioxide emissions according to the same timetable as in section 511(b) and (c) [probably means section 412(b) and (c) of the Clean Air Act, which is classified to section 7651k(b) and (c) of this title]. The regulations shall require that such data be reported to the Administrator. The provisions of section 511(e) of title V of the Clean Air Act [probably means section 412(e) of title IV of the Clean Air Act,

which is classified to section 7651k(e) of this title] shall apply for purposes of this section in the same manner and to the same extent as such provision applies to the monitoring and data referred to in section 511 [probably means section 412 of the Clean Air Act, which is classified to section 7651k of this title].
(b) Public Availability of Carbon Dioxide Information.—For each unit required to monitor and provide carbon dioxide data under subsection (a), the Administrator shall compute the unit's aggregate annual total carbon dioxide emissions, incorporate such data into a computer data base, and make such aggregate annual data available to the public."

Section Referred to in Other Sections
This section is referred to in sections 7651a, 7651i of this title.

GENERAL COMPLIANCE WITH OTHER PROVISIONS
42 USC 7651l

Except as expressly provided, compliance with the requirements of this subchapter shall not exempt or exclude the owner or operator of any source subject to this subchapter from compliance with any other applicable requirements of this chapter.

(July 14, 1955, ch. 360, title IV, Sec. 413, as added Pub. L. 101-549, title IV, Sec. 401, Nov. 15, 1990, 104 Stat. 2625.)

Section Referred to in Other Sections
This section is referred to in section 7651i of this title.

ENFORCEMENT
42 USC 7651m

It shall be unlawful for any person subject to this subchapter to violate any prohibition of, requirement of, or regulation promulgated pursuant to this subchapter shall be a violation of this chapter. In addition to the other requirements and prohibitions provided for in this subchapter, the operation of any affected unit to emit sulfur dioxide in excess of allowances held for such unit shall be deemed a violation, with each ton emitted in excess of allowances held constituting a separate violation.

(July 14, 1955, ch. 360, title IV, Sec. 414, as added Pub. L. 101-549, title IV, Sec. 401, Nov. 15, 1990, 104 Stat. 2625.)

Section Referred to in Other Sections
This section is referred to in section 7651i of this title.

CLEAN COAL TECHNOLOGY REGULATORY INCENTIVES
42 USC 7651n

(a) "Clean coal technology" defined
   For purposes of this section, "clean coal technology" means any technology, including technologies applied at the precombustion, combustion, or post combustion stage, at a new or existing facility which will achieve significant reductions in air emissions of sulfur dioxide or oxides of nitrogen associated with the utilization of coal in the generation of electricity, process steam, or industrial products, which is not in widespread use as of November 15, 1990.
(b) Revised regulations for clean coal technology demonstrations
   (1) Applicability
      This subsection applies to physical or operational changes to existing facilities for the sole purpose of installation, operation, cessation, or removal of a temporary or permanent clean coal technology demonstration project. For the purposes of this section, a clean coal technology demonstration project shall mean a project using funds appropriated under the heading "Department of Energy–Clean Coal Technology", up to a total amount of

$2,500,000,000 for commercial demonstration of clean coal technology, or similar projects funded through appropriations for the Environmental Protection Agency. The Federal contribution for a qualifying project shall be at least 20 percent of the total cost of the demonstration project.

(2) Temporary projects
Installation, operation, cessation, or removal of a temporary clean coal technology demonstration project that is operated for a period of five years or less, and which complies with the State implementation plans for the State in which the project is located and other requirements necessary to attain and maintain the national ambient air quality standards during and after the project is terminated, shall not subject such facility to the requirements of section 7411 of this title or part C or D of subchapter I of this chapter.

(3) Permanent projects
For permanent clean coal technology demonstration projects that constitute repowering as defined in section 7651a(l)[1] of this title, any qualifying project shall not be subject to standards of performance under section 7411 of this title or to the review and permitting requirements of part C[2] for any pollutant the potential emissions of which will not increase as a result of the demonstration project.

(4) EPA regulations
Not later than 12 months after November 15, 1990, the Administrator shall promulgate regulations or interpretive rulings to revise requirements under section 7411 of this title and parts C and D,[2] as appropriate, to facilitate projects consistent in[3] this subsection. With respect to parts C and D,[2] such regulations or rulings shall apply to all areas in which EPA is the permitting authority. In those instances in which the State is the permitting authority under part C or D,[2] any State may adopt and submit to the Administrator for approval revisions to its implementation plan to apply the regulations or rulings promulgated under this subsection.

(c) Exemption for reactivation of very clean units
Physical changes or changes in the method of operation associated with the commencement of commercial operations by a coal-fired utility unit after a period of discontinued operation shall not subject the unit to the requirements of section 7411 of this title or part C of the Act[2] where the unit (1) has not been in operation for the two-year period prior to the enactment of the Clean Air Act Amendments of 1990 [November 15, 1990], and the emissions from such unit continue to be carried in the permitting authority's emissions inventory at the time of enactment, (2) was equipped prior to shut-down with a continuous system of emissions control that achieves a removal efficiency for sulfur dioxide of no less than 85 percent and a removal efficiency for particulates of no less than 98 percent, (3) is equipped with low-NO_x burners prior to the time of commencement, and (4) is otherwise in compliance with the requirements of this chapter.

(July 14, 1955, ch. 360, title IV, Sec. 415, as added Pub. L. 101-549, title IV, Sec. 401, Nov. 15, 1990, 104 Stat. 2625.)

References in Text

Parts C and D and part C of the Act, referred to in subsecs. (b)(3), (4) and (c), probably mean parts C and D of subchapter I of this chapter.

CONTINGENCY GUARANTEE, AUCTIONS, RESERVE

42 USC 7651o

(a) Definitions
For purposes of this section—
(1) The term "independent power producer" means any person who owns or operates, in whole or in part, one or more new independent power production facilities.
(2) The term "new independent power production facility" means a facility that—

---

[1] So in original. Probably should be section "7651a(12)".
[2] See References in Text note below.
[3] So in original. Probably should be "with".

(A) is used for the generation of electric energy, 80 percent or more of which is sold at wholesale;
(B) is nonrecourse project-financed (as such term is defined by the Secretary of Energy within 3 months of November 15, 1990);
(C) does not generate electric energy sold to any affiliate (as defined in section 79b(a)(11) of title 15) of the facility's owner or operator unless the owner or operator of the facility demonstrates that it cannot obtain allowances from the affiliate; and
(D) is a new unit required to hold allowances under this subchapter.
(3) The term "required allowances" means the allowances required to operate such unit for so much of the unit's useful life as occurs after January 1, 2000.
(b) Special reserve of allowances
Within 36 months after November 15, 1990, the Administrator shall promulgate regulations establishing a Special Allowance Reserve containing allowances to be sold under this section. For purposes of establishing the Special Allowance Reserve, the Administrator shall withhold—
(1) 2.8 percent of the allocation of allowances for each year from 1995 through 1999 inclusive; and
(2) 2.8 percent of the basic Phase II allowance allocation of allowances for each year beginning in the year 2000
which would (but for this subsection) be issued for each affected unit at an affected source. The Administrator shall record such withholding for purposes of transferring the proceeds of the allowance sales under this subsection. The allowances so withheld shall be deposited in the Reserve under this section.
(c) Direct sale at $1,500 per ton
(1) Subaccount for direct sales
In accordance with regulations under this section, the Administrator shall establish a Direct Sale Subaccount in the Special Allowance Reserve established under this section. The Direct Sale Subaccount shall contain allowances in the amount of 50,000 tons per year for each year beginning in the year 2000.
(2) Sales
Allowances in the subaccount shall be offered for direct sale to any person at the times and in the amounts specified in table 1 at a price of $1,500 per allowance, adjusted by the Consumer Price Index in the same manner as provided in paragraph (3). Requests to purchase allowances from the Direct Sale Subaccount established under paragraph (1) shall be approved in the order of receipt until no allowances remain in such subaccount, except that an opportunity to purchase such allowances shall be provided to the independent power producers referred to in this subsection before such allowances are offered to any other person. Each applicant shall be required to pay 50 percent of the total purchase price of the allowances within 6 months after the approval of the request to purchase. The remainder shall be paid on or before the transfer of the allowances.

TABLE 1—NUMBER OF ALLOWANCES AVAILABLE FOR SALE AT $1,500 PER TON

Year of Sale	Spot Sale (same year)	Advance Sale
1993-1999		25,000
2000 and after	25,000	25,000

Allowances sold in the spot sale in any year are allowances which may only be used in that year (unless banked for use in a later year).
Allowances sold in the advance sale in any year are allowances which may only be used in the 7th year after the year in which they are first offered for sale (unless banked for use in a later year).
(3) Entitlement to written guarantee
Any independent power producer that submits an application to the Administrator establishing that such independent power producer—
(A) proposes to construct a new independent power production facility for which allowances are required under this subchapter;
(B) will apply for financing to construct such facility after January 1, 1990, and before the date of the first auction under this section;

(C) has submitted to each owner or operator of an affected unit listed in table A (in section 7651c of this title) a written offer to purchase the required allowances for $750 per ton; and
(D) has not received (within 180 days after submitting offers to purchase under subparagraph (C)) an acceptance of the offer to purchase the required allowances,

shall, within 30 days after submission of such application, be entitled to receive the Administrator's written guarantee (subject to the eligibility requirements set forth in paragraph (4)) that such required allowances will be made available for purchase from the Direct Sale Subaccount established under this subsection and at a guaranteed price. The guaranteed price at which such allowances shall be made available for purchase shall be $1,500 per ton, adjusted by the percentage, if any, by which the Consumer Price Index (as determined under section 7661a(b)(3)(B)(v) of this title) for the year in which the allowance is purchased exceeds the Consumer Price Index for the calendar year 1990.

(4) Eligibility requirements

The guarantee issued by the Administrator under paragraph (3) shall be subject to a demonstration by the independent power producer, satisfactory to the Administrator, that—
(A) the independent power producer has—
  (i) made good faith efforts to purchase the required allowances from the owners or operators of affected units to which allowances will be allocated, including efforts to purchase at annual auctions under this section, and from industrial sources that have elected to become affected units pursuant to section 7651i of this title; and
  (ii) such bids and efforts were unsuccessful in obtaining the required allowances; and
(B) the independent power producer will continue to make good faith efforts to purchase the required allowances from the owners or operators of affected units and from industrial sources.

(5) Issuance of guaranteed allowances from Direct Sale Subaccount under this section

From the allowances available in the Direct Sale Subaccount established under this subsection, upon payment of the guaranteed price, the Administrator shall issue to any person exercising the right to purchase allowances pursuant to a guarantee under this subsection the allowances covered by such guarantee. Persons to which guarantees under this subsection have been issued shall have the opportunity to purchase allowances pursuant to such guarantee from such subaccount before the allowances in such reserve are offered for sale to any other person.

(6) Proceeds

Notwithstanding section 3302 of title 31 or any other provision of law, the Administrator shall require that the proceeds of any sale under this subsection be transferred, within 90 days after the sale, without charge, on a pro rata basis to the owners or operators of the affected units from whom the allowances were withheld under subsection (b) of this section and that any unsold allowances be transferred to the Subaccount for Auction Sales established under subsection (d) of this section. No proceeds of any sale under this subsection shall be held by any officer or employee of the United States or treated for any purpose as revenue to the United States or to the Administrator.

(7) Termination of subaccount

If the Administrator determines that, during any period of 2 consecutive calendar years, less than 20 percent of the allowances available in the subaccount for direct sales established under this subsection have been purchased under this paragraph, the Administrator shall terminate the subaccount and transfer such allowances to the Auction Subaccount under subsection (d) of this section.

(d) Auction sales

(1) Subaccount for auctions

The Administrator shall establish an Auction Subaccount in the Special Reserve established under this section. The Auction Subaccount shall contain allowances to be sold at auction under this section in the amount of 150,000 tons per year for each year from 1995 through 1999, inclusive and 250,000 tons per year for each year beginning in the calendar year 2000.

(2) Annual auctions

Commencing in 1993 and in each year thereafter, the Administrator shall conduct auctions at which the allowances referred to in paragraph (1) shall be offered for sale in accordance with regulations promulgated by the Administrator, in consultation with the Secretary of the Treasury, within 12 months of November 15, 1990. The allowances referred to in paragraph (1) shall be offered for sale at auction in the amounts specified in table 2. The auction shall be open to any person. A person wishing to bid for such allowances shall submit (by a date set by the Administrator) to the Administrator (on a sealed bid schedule provided by the Administrator) offers to purchase specified numbers of allowances at specified prices. Such regulations shall specify that the auctioned allowances shall be allocated and sold on the basis of bid price, starting with the highest-priced bid and continuing until all allowances for sale at such auction have been allocated. The regulations shall not permit that a minimum price be set for the purchase of withheld allowances. Allowances purchased at the auction may be used for any purpose and at any time after the auction, subject to the provisions of this subchapter.

TABLE 2–NUMBER OF ALLOWANCES AVAILABLE FOR AUCTION

Year of Sale	Spot Auction (same year)	Advance Auction
1993	50,000*	100,000
1994	50,000*	100,000
1995	50,000*	100,000
1996	150,000	100,000
1997	150,000	100,000
1998	150,000	100,000
1999	150,000	100,000
2000 and after	100,000	100,000

Allowances sold in the spot sale in any year are allowances which may only be used in that year (unless banked for use in a later year), except as otherwise noted. Allowances sold in the advance auction in any year are allowances which may only be used in the 7th year after the year in which they are first offered for sale (unless banked for use in a later year).
*Available for use only in 1995 (unless banked for use in a later year).

(3) Proceeds
   (A) Notwithstanding section 3302 of title 31 or any other provision of law, within 90 days of receipt, the Administrator shall transfer the proceeds from the auction under this section, on a pro rata basis, to the owners or operators of the affected units at an affected source from whom allowances were withheld under subsection (b) of this section. No funds transferred from a purchaser to a seller of allowances under this paragraph shall be held by any officer or employee of the United States or treated for any purpose as revenue to the United States or the Administrator.
   (B) At the end of each year, any allowances offered for sale but not sold at the auction shall be returned without charge, on a pro rata basis, to the owner or operator of the affected units from whose allocation the allowances were withheld.

(4) Additional auction participants
   Any person holding allowances or to whom allowances are allocated by the Administrator may submit those allowances to the Administrator to be offered for sale at auction under this subsection. The proceeds of any such sale shall be transferred at the time of sale by the purchaser to the person submitting such allowances for sale. The holder of allowances offered for sale under this paragraph may specify a minimum sale price. Any person may purchase allowances offered for auction under this paragraph. Such allowances shall be allocated and sold to purchasers on the basis of bid price after the auction under paragraph (2) is complete. No funds transferred from a purchaser to a seller of allowances under this paragraph shall be held by any officer or employee of the United States or treated for any purpose as revenue to the United States or the Administrator.

(5) Recording by EPA
   The Administrator shall record and publicly report the nature, prices and results of each auction under this subsection, including the prices of successful bids, and shall record the transfers of allowances as a result of each auction in accordance with the requirements of this section. The transfer of allowances at such auction shall be recorded in accordance with the regulations promulgated by the Administrator under this subchapter.

(e) Changes in sales, auctions, and withholding
Pursuant to rulemaking after public notice and comment the Administrator may at any time after the year 1998 (in the case of advance sales or advance auctions) and 2005 (in the case of spot sales or spot auctions) decrease the number of allowances withheld and sold under this section.

(f) Termination of auctions
The Administrator may terminate the withholding of allowances and the auction sales under this section if the Administrator determines that, during any period of 3 consecutive calendar years after 2002, less than 20 percent of the allowances available in the auction subaccount have been purchased. Pursuant to regulations under this section, the Administrator may by delegation or contract provide for the conduct of sales or auctions under the Administrator's supervision by other departments or agencies of the United States Government or by nongovernmental agencies, groups, or organizations.

(July 14, 1955, ch. 360, title IV, Sec. 416, as added Pub. L. 101-549, title IV, Sec. 401, Nov. 15, 1990, 104 Stat. 2626.)

Section Referred to in Other Sections

This section is referred to in sections 7651b, 7651d of this title.

SUBCHAPTER V—PERMITS

DEFINITIONS

42 USC 7661

As used in this subchapter—
- (1) Affected source
  The term "affected source" shall have the meaning given such term in subchapter IV-A of this chapter.
- (2) Major source
  The term "major source" means any stationary source (or any group of stationary sources located within a contiguous area and under common control) that is either of the following:
  - (A) A major source as defined in section 7412 of this title.
  - (B) A major stationary source as defined in section 7602 of this title or part D of subchapter I of this chapter.
- (3) Schedule of compliance
  The term "schedule of compliance" means a schedule of remedial measures, including an enforceable sequence of actions or operations, leading to compliance with an applicable implementation plan, emission standard, emission limitation, or emission prohibition.
- (4) Permitting authority
  The term "permitting authority" means the Administrator or the air pollution control agency authorized by the Administrator to carry out a permit program under this subchapter.

(July 14, 1955, ch. 360, title V, Sec. 501, as added Pub. L. 101-549, title V, Sec. 501, Nov. 15, 1990, 104 Stat. 2635.)

PERMIT PROGRAMS

42 USC 7661a

(a) Violations

After the effective date of any permit program approved or promulgated under this subchapter, it shall be unlawful for any person to violate any requirement of a permit issued under this subchapter, or to operate an affected source (as provided in subchapter IV-A of this chapter), a major source, any other source (including an area source) subject to standards or regulations under section 7411 or 7412 of this title, any other source required to have a permit under parts[1] C or D of subchapter I of this chapter, or any other stationary source in a category designated (in whole or in part) by regulations promulgated by the Administrator (after notice and public comment) which shall include a finding setting forth the basis for such designation, except in compliance with a permit issued by a permitting authority under this subchapter. (Nothing in this subsection shall be construed to alter the applicable requirements of this chapter that a permit be obtained before construction or modification.) The Administrator may, in the Administrator's discretion and consistent with the applicable provisions of this chapter, promulgate regulations to exempt one or more source categories (in whole or in part) from the requirements of this subsection if the Administrator finds that compliance with such requirements is impracticable, infeasible, or unnecessarily burdensome on such categories, except that the Administrator may not exempt any major source from such requirements.

(b) Regulations

The Administrator shall promulgate within 12 months after November 15, 1990, regulations establishing the minimum elements of a permit program to be administered by any air pollution control agency. These elements shall include each of the following:
- (1) Requirements for permit applications, including a standard application form and criteria for determining in a timely fashion the completeness of applications.
- (2) Monitoring and reporting requirements.
- (3) (A) A requirement under State or local law or interstate compact that the owner or operator of all sources subject to the requirement to obtain a permit under this subchapter

---

[1]So in original. Probably should be "part".

pay an annual fee, or the equivalent over some other period, sufficient to cover all reasonable (direct and indirect) costs required to develop and administer the permit program requirements of this subchapter, including section 7661f of this title, including the reasonable costs of—
   (i) reviewing and acting upon any application for such a permit,
   (ii) if the owner or operator receives a permit for such source, whether before or after November 15, 1990, implementing and enforcing the terms and conditions of any such permit (not including any court costs or other costs associated with any enforcement action),
   (iii) emissions and ambient monitoring,
   (iv) preparing generally applicable regulations, or guidance,
   (v) modeling, analyses, and demonstrations, and
   (vi) preparing inventories and tracking emissions.
(B) The total amount of fees collected by the permitting authority shall conform to the following requirements:
   (i) The Administrator shall not approve a program as meeting the requirements of this paragraph unless the State demonstrates that, except as otherwise provided in subparagraphs (ii) through (v) of this subparagraph, the program will result in the collection, in the aggregate, from all sources subject to subparagraph (A), of an amount not less than $25 per ton of each regulated pollutant, or such other amount as the Administrator may determine adequately reflects the reasonable costs of the permit program.
   (ii) As used in this subparagraph, the term "regulated pollutant" shall mean (I) a volatile organic compound; (II) each pollutant regulated under section 7411 or 7412 of this title; and (III) each pollutant for which a national primary ambient air quality standard has been promulgated (except that carbon monoxide shall be excluded from this reference).
   (iii) In determining the amount under clause (i), the permitting authority is not required to include any amount of regulated pollutant emitted by any source in excess of 4,000 tons per year of that regulated pollutant.
   (iv) The requirements of clause (i) shall not apply if the permitting authority demonstrates that collecting an amount less than the amount specified under clause (i) will meet the requirements of subparagraph (A).
   (v) The fee calculated under clause (i) shall be increased (consistent with the need to cover the reasonable costs authorized by subparagraph (A)) in each year beginning after 1990, by the percentage, if any, by which the Consumer Price Index for the most recent calendar year ending before the beginning of such year exceeds the Consumer Price Index for the calendar year 1989. For purposes of this clause—
      (I) the Consumer Price Index for any calendar year is the average of the Consumer Price Index for all-urban consumers published by the Department of Labor, as of the close of the 12-month period ending on August 31 of each calendar year, and
      (II) the revision of the Consumer Price Index which is most consistent with the Consumer Price Index for calendar year 1989 shall be used.
(C) (i) If the Administrator determines, under subsection (d) of this section, that the fee provisions of the operating permit program do not meet the requirements of this paragraph, or if the Administrator makes a determination, under subsection (i) of this section, that the permitting authority is not adequately administering or enforcing an approved fee program, the Administrator may, in addition to taking any other action authorized under this subchapter, collect reasonable fees from the sources identified under subparagraph (A). Such fees shall be designed solely to cover the Administrator's costs of administering the provisions of the permit program promulgated by the Administrator.
   (ii) Any source that fails to pay fees lawfully imposed by the Administrator under this subparagraph shall pay a penalty of 50 percent of the fee amount, plus interest on the fee amount computed in accordance with section 6621(a)(2) of title 26 (relating to computation of interest on underpayment of Federal taxes).

(iii) Any fees, penalties, and interest collected under this subparagraph shall be deposited in a special fund in the United States Treasury for licensing and other services, which thereafter shall be available for appropriation, to remain available until expended, subject to appropriation, to carry out the Agency's activities for which the fees were collected. Any fee required to be collected by a State, local, or interstate agency under this subsection shall be utilized solely to cover all reasonable (direct and indirect) costs required to support the permit program as set forth in subparagraph (A).
(4) Requirements for adequate personnel and funding to administer the program.
(5) A requirement that the permitting authority have adequate authority to:
   (A) issue permits and assure compliance by all sources required to have a permit under this subchapter with each applicable standard, regulation or requirement under this chapter;
   (B) issue permits for a fixed term, not to exceed 5 years;
   (C) assure that upon issuance or renewal permits incorporate emission limitations and other requirements in an applicable implementation plan;
   (D) terminate, modify, or revoke and reissue permits for cause;
   (E) enforce permits, permit fee requirements, and the requirement to obtain a permit, including authority to recover civil penalties in a maximum amount of not less than $10,000 per day for each violation, and provide appropriate criminal penalties; and
   (F) assure that no permit will be issued if the Administrator objects to its issuance in a timely manner under this subchapter.
(6) Adequate, streamlined, and reasonable procedures for expeditiously determining when applications are complete, for processing such applications, for public notice, including offering an opportunity for public comment and a hearing, and for expeditious review of permit actions, including applications, renewals, or revisions, and including an opportunity for judicial review in State court of the final permit action by the applicant, any person who participated in the public comment process, and any other person who could obtain judicial review of that action under applicable law.
(7) To ensure against unreasonable delay by the permitting authority, adequate authority and procedures to provide that a failure of such permitting authority to act on a permit application or permit renewal application (in accordance with the time periods specified in section 7661b of this title or, as appropriate, subchapter IV-A of this chapter) shall be treated as a final permit action solely for purposes of obtaining judicial review in State court of an action brought by any person referred to in paragraph (6) to require that action be taken by the permitting authority on such application without additional delay.
(8) Authority, and reasonable procedures consistent with the need for expeditious action by the permitting authority on permit applications and related matters, to make available to the public any permit application, compliance plan, permit, and monitoring or compliance report under section 7661b(e) of this title, subject to the provisions of section 7414(c) of this title.
(9) A requirement that the permitting authority, in the case of permits with a term of 3 or more years for major sources, shall require revisions to the permit to incorporate applicable standards and regulations promulgated under this chapter after the issuance of such permit. Such revisions shall occur as expeditiously as practicable and consistent with the procedures established under paragraph (6) but not later than 18 months after the promulgation of such standards and regulations. No such revision shall be required if the effective date of the standards or regulations is a date after the expiration of the permit term. Such permit revision shall be treated as a permit renewal if it complies with the requirements of this subchapter regarding renewals.
(10) Provisions to allow changes within a permitted facility (or one operating pursuant to section 7661b(d) of this title) without requiring a permit revision, if the changes are not modifications under any provision of subchapter I of this chapter and the changes do not exceed the emissions allowable under the permit (whether expressed therein as a rate of emissions or in terms of total emissions:[2] Provided, That the facility provides the Administrator and the permitting authority with written notification in advance of the proposed changes which shall be a minimum of 7 days, unless the permitting authority provides in its regulations a different timeframe for emergencies.

---

[2] So in original. A closing parenthesis probably should precede the colon.

(c) Single permit
A single permit may be issued for a facility with multiple sources.
(d) Submission and approval
(1) Not later than 3 years after November 15, 1990, the Governor of each State shall develop and submit to the Administrator a permit program under State or local law or under an interstate compact meeting the requirements of this subchapter. In addition, the Governor shall submit a legal opinion from the attorney general (or the attorney for those State air pollution control agencies that have independent legal counsel), or from the chief legal officer of an interstate agency, that the laws of the State, locality, or the interstate compact provide adequate authority to carry out the program. Not later than 1 year after receiving a program, and after notice and opportunity for public comment, the Administrator shall approve or disapprove such program, in whole or in part. The Administrator may approve a program to the extent that the program meets the requirements of this chapter, including the regulations issued under subsection (b) of this section. If the program is disapproved, in whole or in part, the Administrator shall notify the Governor of any revisions or modifications necessary to obtain approval. The Governor shall revise and resubmit the program for review under this section within 180 days after receiving notification.
(2) (A) If the Governor does not submit a program as required under paragraph (1) or if the Administrator disapproves a program submitted by the Governor under paragraph (1), in whole or in part, the Administrator may, prior to the expiration of the 18-month period referred to in subparagraph (B), in the Administrator's discretion, apply any of the sanctions specified in section 7509(b) of this title.
(B) If the Governor does not submit a program as required under paragraph (1), or if the Administrator disapproves any such program submitted by the Governor under paragraph (1), in whole or in part, 18 months after the date required for such submittal or the date of such disapproval, as the case may be, the Administrator shall apply sanctions under section 7509(b) of this title in the same manner and subject to the same deadlines and other conditions as are applicable in the case of a determination, disapproval, or finding under section 7509(a) of this title.
(C) The sanctions under section 7509(b)(2) of this title shall not apply pursuant to this paragraph in any area unless the failure to submit or the disapproval referred to in subparagraph (A) or (B) relates to an air pollutant for which such area has been designated a nonattainment area (as defined in part D of subchapter I of this chapter).
(3) If a program meeting the requirements of this subchapter has not been approved in whole for any State, the Administrator shall, 2 years after the date required for submission of such a program under paragraph (1), promulgate, administer, and enforce a program under this subchapter for that State.
(e) Suspension
The Administrator shall suspend the issuance of permits promptly upon publication of notice of approval of a permit program under this section, but may, in such notice, retain jurisdiction over permits that have been federally issued, but for which the administrative or judicial review process is not complete. The Administrator shall continue to administer and enforce federally issued permits under this subchapter until they are replaced by a permit issued by a permitting program. Nothing in this subsection should be construed to limit the Administrator's ability to enforce permits issued by a State.
(f) Prohibition
No partial permit program shall be approved unless, at a minimum, it applies, and ensures compliance with, this subchapter and each of the following:
(1) All requirements established under subchapter IV-A of this chapter applicable to "affected sources".
(2) All requirements established under section 7412 of this title applicable to "major sources", "area sources," and "new sources".
(3) All requirements of subchapter I of this chapter (other than section 7412 of this title) applicable to sources required to have a permit under this subchapter.
Approval of a partial program shall not relieve the State of its obligation to submit a complete program, nor from the application of any sanctions under this chapter for failure to submit an approvable permit program.

(g) Interim approval
If a program (including a partial permit program) submitted under this subchapter substantially meets the requirements of this subchapter, but is not fully approvable, the Administrator may by rule grant the program interim approval. In the notice of final rulemaking, the Administrator shall specify the changes that must be made before the program can receive full approval. An interim approval under this subsection shall expire on a date set by the Administrator not later than 2 years after such approval, and may not be renewed. For the period of any such interim approval, the provisions of subsection (d)(2) of this section, and the obligation of the Administrator to promulgate a program under this subchapter for the State pursuant to subsection (d)(3) of this section, shall be suspended. Such provisions and such obligation of the Administrator shall apply after the expiration of such interim approval.

(h) Effective date
The effective date of a permit program, or partial or interim program, approved under this subchapter, shall be the effective date of approval by the Administrator. The effective date of a permit program, or partial permit program, promulgated by the Administrator shall be the date of promulgation.

(i) Administration and enforcement
  (1) Whenever the Administrator makes a determination that a permitting authority is not adequately administering and enforcing a program, or portion thereof, in accordance with the requirements of this subchapter, the Administrator shall provide notice to the State and may, prior to the expiration of the 18-month period referred to in paragraph (2), in the Administrator's discretion, apply any of the sanctions specified in section 7509(b) of this title.
  (2) Whenever the Administrator makes a determination that a permitting authority is not adequately administering and enforcing a program, or portion thereof, in accordance with the requirements of this subchapter, 18 months after the date of the notice under paragraph (1), the Administrator shall apply the sanctions under section 7509(b) of this title in the same manner and subject to the same deadlines and other conditions as are applicable in the case of a determination, disapproval, or finding under section 7509(a) of this title.
  (3) The sanctions under section 7509(b)(2) of this title shall not apply pursuant to this subsection in any area unless the failure to adequately enforce and administer the program relates to an air pollutant for which such area has been designated a nonattainment area.
  (4) Whenever the Administrator has made a finding under paragraph (1) with respect to any State, unless the State has corrected such deficiency within 18 months after the date of such finding, the Administrator shall, 2 years after the date of such finding, promulgate, administer, and enforce a program under this subchapter for that State. Nothing in this paragraph shall be construed to affect the validity of a program which has been approved under this subchapter or the authority of any permitting authority acting under such program until such time as such program is promulgated by the Administrator under this paragraph.

(July 14, 1955, ch. 360, title V, Sec. 502, as added Pub. L. 101-549, title V, Sec. 501, Nov. 15, 1990, 104 Stat. 2635.)

Section Referred to in Other Sections

This section is referred to in sections 7413, 7511d, 7651g, 7651o, 7661b, 7661c of this title.

PERMIT APPLICATIONS

42 USC 7661b

(a) Applicable date
Any source specified in section 7661a(a) of this title shall become subject to a permit program, and required to have a permit, on the later of the following dates—
  (1) the effective date of a permit program or partial or interim permit program applicable to the source; or
  (2) the date such source becomes subject to section 7661a(a) of this title.

(b) Compliance plan
  (1) The regulations required by section 7661a(b) of this title shall include a requirement that the applicant submit with the permit application a compliance plan describing how the source will comply with all applicable requirements under this chapter. The compliance plan shall include a schedule of compliance, and a schedule under which the permittee will submit progress reports to the permitting authority no less frequently than every 6 months.
  (2) The regulations shall further require the permittee to periodically (but no less frequently than annually) certify that the facility is in compliance with any applicable requirements of the permit, and to promptly report any deviations from permit requirements to the permitting authority.
(c) Deadline
  Any person required to have a permit shall, not later than 12 months after the date on which the source becomes subject to a permit program approved or promulgated under this subchapter, or such earlier date as the permitting authority may establish, submit to the permitting authority a compliance plan and an application for a permit signed by a responsible official, who shall certify the accuracy of the information submitted. The permitting authority shall approve or disapprove a completed application (consistent with the procedures established under this subchapter for consideration of such applications), and shall issue or deny the permit, within 18 months after the date of receipt thereof, except that the permitting authority shall establish a phased schedule for acting on permit applications submitted within the first full year after the effective date of a permit program (or a partial or interim program). Any such schedule shall assure that at least one-third of such permits will be acted on by such authority annually over a period of not to exceed 3 years after such effective date. Such authority shall establish reasonable procedures to prioritize such approval or disapproval actions in the case of applications for construction or modification under the applicable requirements of this chapter.
(d) Timely and complete applications
  Except for sources required to have a permit before construction or modification under the applicable requirements of this chapter, if an applicant has submitted a timely and complete application for a permit required by this subchapter (including renewals), but final action has not been taken on such application, the source's failure to have a permit shall not be a violation of this chapter, unless the delay in final action was due to the failure of the applicant timely to submit information required or requested to process the application. No source required to have a permit under this subchapter shall be in violation of section 7661a(a) of this title before the date on which the source is required to submit an application under subsection (c) of this section.
(e) Copies; availability
  A copy of each permit application, compliance plan (including the schedule of compliance), emissions or compliance monitoring report, certification, and each permit issued under this subchapter, shall be available to the public. If an applicant or permittee is required to submit information entitled to protection from disclosure under section 7414(c) of this title, the applicant or permittee may submit such information separately. The requirements of section 7414(c) of this title shall apply to such information. The contents of a permit shall not be entitled to protection under section 7414(c) of this title.

(July 14, 1955, ch. 360, title V, Sec. 503, as added Pub. L. 101-549, title V, Sec. 501, Nov. 15, 1990, 104 Stat. 2641.)

Section Referred to in Other Sections

This section is referred to in sections 7413, 7661a, 7661c of this title.

PERMIT REQUIREMENTS AND CONDITIONS

42 USC 7661c

(a) Conditions
  Each permit issued under this subchapter shall include enforceable emission limitations and standards, a schedule of compliance, a requirement that the permittee submit to the permitting authority, no less often than every 6 months, the results of any required monitoring, and

such other conditions as are necessary to assure compliance with applicable requirements of this chapter, including the requirements of the applicable implementation plan.

(b) Monitoring and analysis

The Administrator may by rule prescribe procedures and methods for determining compliance and for monitoring and analysis of pollutants regulated under this chapter, but continuous emissions monitoring need not be required if alternative methods are available that provide sufficiently reliable and timely information for determining compliance. Nothing in this subsection shall be construed to affect any continuous emissions monitoring requirement of subchapter IV-A of this chapter, or where required elsewhere in this chapter.

(c) Inspection, entry, monitoring, certification, and reporting

Each permit issued under this subchapter shall set forth inspection, entry, monitoring, compliance certification, and reporting requirements to assure compliance with the permit terms and conditions. Such monitoring and reporting requirements shall conform to any applicable regulation under subsection (b) of this section. Any report required to be submitted by a permit issued to a corporation under this subchapter shall be signed by a responsible corporate official, who shall certify its accuracy.

(d) General permits

The permitting authority may, after notice and opportunity for public hearing, issue a general permit covering numerous similar sources. Any general permit shall comply with all requirements applicable to permits under this subchapter. No source covered by a general permit shall thereby be relieved from the obligation to file an application under section 7661b of this title.

(e) Temporary sources

The permitting authority may issue a single permit authorizing emissions from similar operations at multiple temporary locations. No such permit shall be issued unless it includes conditions that will assure compliance with all the requirements of this chapter at all authorized locations, including, but not limited to, ambient standards and compliance with any applicable increment or visibility requirements under part C of subchapter I of this chapter. Any such permit shall in addition require the owner or operator to notify the permitting authority in advance of each change in location. The permitting authority may require a separate permit fee for operations at each location.

(f) Permit shield

Compliance with a permit issued in accordance with this subchapter shall be deemed compliance with section 7661a of this title. Except as otherwise provided by the Administrator by rule, the permit may also provide that compliance with the permit shall be deemed compliance with other applicable provisions of this chapter that relate to the permittee if—
(1) the permit includes the applicable requirements of such provisions, or
(2) the permitting authority in acting on the permit application makes a determination relating to the permittee that such other provisions (which shall be referred to in such determination) are not applicable and the permit includes the determination or a concise summary thereof.

Nothing in the preceding sentence shall alter or affect the provisions of section 7603 of this title, including the authority of the Administrator under that section.

(July 14, 1955, ch. 360, title V, Sec. 504, as added Pub. L. 101-549, title V, Sec. 501, Nov. 15, 1990, 104 Stat. 2642.)

Section Referred to in Other Sections

This section is referred to in section 7651g of this title.

NOTIFICATION TO ADMINISTRATOR AND CONTIGUOUS STATES

42 USC 7661d

(a) Transmission and notice
   (1) Each permitting authority—
      (A) shall transmit to the Administrator a copy of each permit application (and any application for a permit modification or renewal) or such portion thereof, including any

compliance plan, as the Administrator may require to effectively review the application and otherwise to carry out the Administrator's responsibilities under this chapter, and

    (B) shall provide to the Administrator a copy of each permit proposed to be issued and issued as a final permit.

  (2) The permitting authority shall notify all States—

    (A) whose air quality may be affected and that are contiguous to the State in which the emission originates, or

    (B) that are within 50 miles of the source,

of each permit application or proposed permit forwarded to the Administrator under this section, and shall provide an opportunity for such States to submit written recommendations respecting the issuance of the permit and its terms and conditions. If any part of those recommendations are not accepted by the permitting authority, such authority shall notify the State submitting the recommendations and the Administrator in writing of its failure to accept those recommendations and the reasons therefor.

(b) Objection by EPA

  (1) If any permit contains provisions that are determined by the Administrator as not in compliance with the applicable requirements of this chapter, including the requirements of an applicable implementation plan, the Administrator shall, in accordance with this subsection, object to its issuance. The permitting authority shall respond in writing if the Administrator (A) within 45 days after receiving a copy of the proposed permit under subsection (a)(1) of this section, or (B) within 45 days after receiving notification under subsection (a)(2) of this section, objects in writing to its issuance as not in compliance with such requirements. With the objection, the Administrator shall provide a statement of the reasons for the objection. A copy of the objection and statement shall be provided to the applicant.

  (2) If the Administrator does not object in writing to the issuance of a permit pursuant to paragraph (1), any person may petition the Administrator within 60 days after the expiration of the 45-day review period specified in paragraph (1) to take such action. A copy of such petition shall be provided to the permitting authority and the applicant by the petitioner. The petition shall be based only on objections to the permit that were raised with reasonable specificity during the public comment period provided by the permitting agency (unless the petitioner demonstrates in the petition to the Administrator that it was impracticable to raise such objections within such period or unless the grounds for such objection arose after such period). The petition shall identify all such objections. If the permit has been issued by the permitting agency, such petition shall not postpone the effectiveness of the permit. The Administrator shall grant or deny such petition within 60 days after the petition is filed. The Administrator shall issue an objection within such period if the petitioner demonstrates to the Administrator that the permit is not in compliance with the requirements of this chapter, including the requirements of the applicable implementation plan. Any denial of such petition shall be subject to judicial review under section 7607 of this title. The Administrator shall include in regulations under this subchapter provisions to implement this paragraph. The Administrator may not delegate the requirements of this paragraph.

  (3) Upon receipt of an objection by the Administrator under this subsection, the permitting authority may not issue the permit unless it is revised and issued in accordance with subsection (c) of this section. If the permitting authority has issued a permit prior to receipt of an objection by the Administrator under paragraph (2) of this subsection, the Administrator shall modify, terminate, or revoke such permit and the permitting authority may thereafter only issue a revised permit in accordance with subsection (c) of this section.

(c) Issuance or denial

If the permitting authority fails, within 90 days after the date of an objection under subsection (b) of this section, to submit a permit revised to meet the objection, the Administrator shall issue or deny the permit in accordance with the requirements of this subchapter. No objection shall be subject to judicial review until the Administrator takes final action to issue or deny a permit under this subsection.

(d) Waiver of notification requirements
   (1) The Administrator may waive the requirements of subsections (a) and (b) of this section at the time of approval of a permit program under this subchapter for any category (including any class, type, or size within such category) of sources covered by the program other than major sources.
   (2) The Administrator may, by regulation, establish categories of sources (including any class, type, or size within such category) to which the requirements of subsections (a) and (b) of this section shall not apply. The preceding sentence shall not apply to major sources.
   (3) The Administrator may exclude from any waiver under this subsection notification under subsection (a)(2) of this section. Any waiver granted under this subsection may be revoked or modified by the Administrator by rule.
(e) Refusal of permitting authority to terminate, modify, or revoke and reissue
   If the Administrator finds that cause exists to terminate, modify, or revoke and reissue a permit under this subchapter, the Administrator shall notify the permitting authority and the source of the Administrator's finding. The permitting authority shall, within 90 days after receipt of such notification, forward to the Administrator under this section a proposed determination of termination, modification, or revocation and reissuance, as appropriate. The Administrator may extend such 90 day period for an additional 90 days if the Administrator finds that a new or revised permit application is necessary, or that the permitting authority must require the permittee to submit additional information. The Administrator may review such proposed determination under the provisions of subsections (a) and (b) of this section. If the permitting authority fails to submit the required proposed determination, or if the Administrator objects and the permitting authority fails to resolve the objection within 90 days, the Administrator may, after notice and in accordance with fair and reasonable procedures, terminate, modify, or revoke and reissue the permit.

(July 14, 1955, ch. 360, title V, Sec. 505, as added Pub. L. 101-549, title V, Sec. 501, Nov. 15, 1990, 104 Stat. 2643.)

Section Referred to in Other Sections

This section is referred to in section 7412 of this title.

OTHER AUTHORITIES

42 USC 7661e

(a) In general
   Nothing in this subchapter shall prevent a State, or interstate permitting authority, from establishing additional permitting requirements not inconsistent with this chapter.
(b) Permits implementing acid rain provisions
   The provisions of this subchapter, including provisions regarding schedules for submission and approval or disapproval of permit applications, shall apply to permits implementing the requirements of subchapter IV-A of this chapter except as modified by that subchapter.

(July 14, 1955, ch. 360, title V, Sec. 506, as added Pub. L. 101-549, title V, Sec. 501, Nov. 15, 1990, 104 Stat. 2645.)

SMALL BUSINESS STATIONARY SOURCE TECHNICAL AND ENVIRONMENTAL COMPLIANCE ASSISTANCE PROGRAM

42 USC 7661f

(a) Plan revisions
   Consistent with sections 7410 and 7412 of this title, each State shall, after reasonable notice and public hearings, adopt and submit to the Administrator as part of the State implementation plan for such State or as a revision to such State implementation plan under section 7410 of this title, plans for establishing a small business stationary source technical and environmental compliance assistance program. Such submission shall be made within 24 months after November 15, 1990. The Administrator shall approve such program if it includes each of the following:

(1) Adequate mechanisms for developing, collecting, and coordinating information concerning compliance methods and technologies for small business stationary sources, and programs to encourage lawful cooperation among such sources and other persons to further compliance with this chapter.
(2) Adequate mechanisms for assisting small business stationary sources with pollution prevention and accidental release detection and prevention, including providing information concerning alternative technologies, process changes, products, and methods of operation that help reduce air pollution.
(3) A designated State office within the relevant State agency to serve as ombudsman for small business stationary sources in connection with the implementation of this chapter.
(4) A compliance assistance program for small business stationary sources which assists small business stationary sources in determining applicable requirements and in receiving permits under this chapter in a timely and efficient manner.
(5) Adequate mechanisms to assure that small business stationary sources receive notice of their rights under this chapter in such manner and form as to assure reasonably adequate time for such sources to evaluate compliance methods and any relevant or applicable proposed or final regulation or standard issued under this chapter.
(6) Adequate mechanisms for informing small business stationary sources of their obligations under this chapter, including mechanisms for referring such sources to qualified auditors or, at the option of the State, for providing audits of the operations of such sources to determine compliance with this chapter.
(7) Procedures for consideration of requests from a small business stationary source for modification of—
   (A) any work practice or technological method of compliance, or
   (B) the schedule of milestones for implementing such work practice or method of compliance preceding any applicable compliance date,
   based on the technological and financial capability of any such small business stationary source. No such modification may be granted unless it is in compliance with the applicable requirements of this chapter, including the requirements of the applicable implementation plan. Where such applicable requirements are set forth in Federal regulations, only modifications authorized in such regulations may be allowed.
(b) Program
   The Administrator shall establish within 9 months after November 15, 1990, a small business stationary source technical and environmental compliance assistance program. Such program shall—
   (1) assist the States in the development of the program required under subsection (a) of this section (relating to assistance for small business stationary sources);
   (2) issue guidance for the use of the States in the implementation of these programs that includes alternative control technologies and pollution prevention methods applicable to small business stationary sources; and
   (3) provide for implementation of the program provisions required under subsection (a)(4) of this section in any State that fails to submit such a program under that subsection.
(c) Eligibility
   (1) Except as provided in paragraphs (2) and (3), for purposes of this section, the term "small business stationary source" means a stationary source that—
      (A) is owned or operated by a person that employs 100 or fewer individuals,
      (B) is a small business concern as defined in the Small Business Act [15 U.S.C. 631 et seq.];
      (C) is not a major stationary source;
      (D) does not emit 50 tons or more per year of any regulated pollutant; and
      (E) emits less than 75 tons per year of all regulated pollutants.
   (2) Upon petition by a source, the State may, after notice and opportunity for public comment, include as a small business stationary source for purposes of this section any stationary source which does not meet the criteria of subparagraphs[1] (C), (D), or (E) of paragraph (1) but which does not emit more than 100 tons per year of all regulated pollutants.
   (3) (A) The Administrator, in consultation with the Administrator of the Small Business Administration and after providing notice and opportunity for public comment, may exclude from the small business stationary source definition under this section any

---

[1] So in original. Probably should be "subparagraph".

category or subcategory of sources that the Administrator determines to have sufficient technical and financial capabilities to meet the requirements of this chapter without the application of this subsection.
- (B) The State, in consultation with the Administrator and the Administrator of the Small Business Administration and after providing notice and opportunity for public hearing, may exclude from the small business stationary source definition under this section any category or subcategory of sources that the State determines to have sufficient technical and financial capabilities to meet the requirements of this chapter without the application of this subsection.

(d) Monitoring

The Administrator shall direct the Agency's Office of Small and Disadvantaged Business Utilization through the Small Business Ombudsman (hereinafter in this section referred to as the "Ombudsman") to monitor the small business stationary source technical and environmental compliance assistance program under this section. In carrying out such monitoring activities, the Ombudsman shall—
  (1) render advisory opinions on the overall effectiveness of the Small Business Stationary Source Technical and Environmental Compliance Assistance Program, difficulties encountered, and degree and severity of enforcement;
  (2) make periodic reports to the Congress on the compliance of the Small Business Stationary Source Technical and Environmental Compliance Assistance Program with the requirements of the Paperwork Reduction Act,[2] the Regulatory Flexibility Act [5 U.S.C. 601 et seq.], and the Equal Access to Justice Act;
  (3) review information to be issued by the Small Business Stationary Source Technical and Environmental Compliance Assistance Program for small business stationary sources to ensure that the information is understandable by the layperson; and
  (4) have the Small Business Stationary Source Technical and Environmental Compliance Assistance Program serve as the secretariat for the development and dissemination of such reports and advisory opinions.

(e) Compliance Advisory Panel
  (1) There shall be created a Compliance Advisory Panel (hereinafter referred to as the "Panel") on the State level of not less than 7 individuals. This Panel shall—
    (A) render advisory opinions concerning the effectiveness of the small business stationary source technical and environmental compliance assistance program, difficulties encountered, and degree and severity of enforcement;
    (B) make periodic reports to the Administrator concerning the compliance of the State Small Business Stationary Source Technical and Environmental Compliance Assistance Program with the requirements of the Paperwork Reduction Act,[2] the Regulatory Flexibility Act [5 U.S.C. 601 et seq.], and the Equal Access to Justice Act;
    (C) review information for small business stationary sources to assure such information is understandable by the layperson; and
    (D) have the Small Business Stationary Source Technical and Environmental Compliance Assistance Program serve as the secretariat for the development and dissemination of such reports and advisory opinions.
  (2) The Panel shall consist of—
    (A) 2 members, who are not owners, or representatives of owners, of small business stationary sources, selected by the Governor to represent the general public;
    (B) 2 members selected by the State legislature who are owners, or who represent owners, of small business stationary sources (1 member each by the majority and minority leadership of the lower house, or in the case of a unicameral State legislature, 2 members each shall be selected by the majority leadership and the minority leadership, respectively, of such legislature, and subparagraph (C) shall not apply);
    (C) 2 members selected by the State legislature who are owners, or who represent owners, of small business stationary sources (1 member each by the majority and minority leadership of the upper house, or the equivalent State entity); and
    (D) 1 member selected by the head of the department or agency of the State responsible for air pollution permit programs to represent that agency.

---

[2] See References in Text note below.

(f) Fees
   The State (or the Administrator) may reduce any fee required under this chapter to take into account the financial resources of small business stationary sources.

(g) Continuous emission monitors
   In developing regulations and CTGs under this chapter that contain continuous emission monitoring requirements, the Administrator, consistent with the requirements of this chapter, before applying such requirements to small business stationary sources, shall consider the necessity and appropriateness of such requirements for such sources. Nothing in this subsection shall affect the applicability of subchapter IV-A of this chapter provisions relating to continuous emissions monitoring.

(h) Control technique guidelines
   The Administrator shall consider, consistent with the requirements of this chapter, the size, type, and technical capabilities of small business stationary sources (and sources which are eligible under subsection (c)(2) of this section to be treated as small business stationary sources) in developing CTGs applicable to such sources under this chapter.

(July 14, 1955, ch. 360, title V, Sec. 507, as added Pub. L. 101-549, title V, Sec. 501, Nov. 15, 1990, 104 Stat. 2645.)

References in Text

The Small Business Act, referred to in subsec. (c)(1)(B), is Pub. L. 85-536, July 18, 1958, 72 Stat. 384, as amended, which is classified generally to chapter 14A (Sec. 631 et seq.) of Title 15, Commerce and Trade. For complete classification of this Act to the Code, see Short Title note set out under section 631 of Title 15 and Tables.

The Paperwork Reduction Act, referred to in subsecs. (d)(2) and (e)(1)(B), probably means the Paperwork Reduction Act of 1980, Pub. L. 96-511, Dec. 11, 1980, 94 Stat. 2812, as amended, which was classified principally to chapter 35 (Sec. 3501 et seq.) of Title 44, Public Printing and Documents, prior to the general amendment of that chapter by Pub. L. 104-13, Sec. 2, May 22, 1995, 109 Stat. 163. For complete classification of this Act to the Code, see Short Title of 1980 Amendment note set out under section 101 of Title 44 and Tables.

The Regulatory Flexibility Act, referred to in subsecs. (d)(2) and (e)(1)(B), is Pub. L. 96-354, Sept. 19, 1980, 94 Stat. 1164, which is classified generally to chapter 6 (Sec. 601 et seq.) of Title 5, Government Organization and Employees. For complete classification of this Act to the Code, see Short Title note set out under section 601 of Title 5 and Tables.

The Equal Access to Justice Act, referred to in subsecs. (d)(2) and (e)(1)(B), is title II of Pub. L. 96-481, Oct. 21, 1980, 94 Stat. 2325. For complete classification of this Act to the Code, see Short Title note set out under section 504 of Title 5.

Section Referred to in Other Sections

This section is referred to in section 7661a of this title.

SUBCHAPTER VI—STRATOSPHERIC OZONE PROTECTION

DEFINITIONS

42 USC 7671

As used in this subchapter—
  (1) Appliance
      The term "appliance" means any device which contains and uses a class I or class II substance as a refrigerant and which is used for household or commercial purposes, including any air conditioner, refrigerator, chiller, or freezer.
  (2) Baseline year
      The term "baseline year" means—
      (A) the calendar year 1986, in the case of any class I substance listed in Group I or II under section 7671a(a) of this title,
      (B) the calendar year 1989, in the case of any class I substance listed in Group III, IV, or V under section 7671a(a) of this title, and
      (C) a representative calendar year selected by the Administrator, in the case of—
          (i) any substance added to the list of class I substances after the publication of the initial list under section 7671a(a) of this title, and
          (ii) any class II substance.
  (3) Class I substance
      The term "class I substance" means each of the substances listed as provided in section 7671a(a) of this title.
  (4) Class II substance
      The term "class II substance" means each of the substances listed as provided in section 7671a(b) of this title.
  (5) Commissioner
      The term "Commissioner" means the Commissioner of the Food and Drug Administration.
  (6) Consumption
      The term "consumption" means, with respect to any substance, the amount of that substance produced in the United States, plus the amount imported, minus the amount exported to Parties to the Montreal Protocol. Such term shall be construed in a manner consistent with the Montreal Protocol.
  (7) Import
      The term "import" means to land on, bring into, or introduce into, or attempt to land on, bring into, or introduce into, any place subject to the jurisdiction of the United States, whether or not such landing, bringing, or introduction constitutes an importation within the meaning of the customs laws of the United States.
  (8) Medical device
      The term "medical device" means any device (as defined in the Federal Food, Drug, and Cosmetic Act (21 U.S.C. 321)), diagnostic product, drug (as defined in the Federal Food, Drug, and Cosmetic Act), and drug delivery system—
      (A) if such device, product, drug, or drug delivery system utilizes a class I or class II substance for which no safe and effective alternative has been developed, and where necessary, approved by the Commissioner; and
      (B) if such device, product, drug, or drug delivery system, has, after notice and opportunity for public comment, been approved and determined to be essential by the Commissioner in consultation with the Administrator.
  (9) Montreal Protocol
      The terms "Montreal Protocol" and "the Protocol" mean the Montreal Protocol on Substances that Deplete the Ozone Layer, a protocol to the Vienna Convention for the Protection of the Ozone Layer, including adjustments adopted by Parties thereto and amendments that have entered into force.
  (10) Ozone-depletion potential
      The term "ozone-depletion potential" means a factor established by the Administrator to reflect the ozone-depletion potential of a substance, on a mass per kilogram basis, as compared to chlorofluorocarbon-11 (CFC-11). Such factor shall be based upon the substance's

388 / Environmental Statutes

atmospheric lifetime, the molecular weight of bromine and chlorine, and the substance's ability to be photolytically disassociated, and upon other factors determined to be an accurate measure of relative ozone-depletion potential.

(11) Produce, produced, and production

The terms "produce", "produced", and "production", refer to the manufacture of a substance from any raw material or feedstock chemical, but such terms do not include—

(A) the manufacture of a substance that is used and entirely consumed (except for trace quantities) in the manufacture of other chemicals, or

(B) the reuse or recycling of a substance.

(July 14, 1955, ch. 360, title VI, Sec. 601, as added Pub. L. 101-549, title VI, Sec. 602(a), Nov. 15, 1990, 104 Stat. 2649.)

References in Text

The customs laws of the United States, referred to in par. (7), are classified generally to Title 19, Customs Duties.

The Federal Food, Drug, and Cosmetic Act, referred to in par. (8), is act June 25, 1938, ch. 675, 52 Stat. 1040, as amended, which is classified generally to chapter 9 (Sec. 301 et seq.) of Title 21, Food and Drugs. For complete classification of this Act to the Code, see section 301 of Title 21 and Tables.

Section Referred to in Other Sections

This section is referred to in sections 7671a, 7671i of this title.

LISTING OF CLASS I AND CLASS II SUBSTANCES

42 USC 7671a

(a) List of class I substances

Within 60 days after November 15, 1990, the Administrator shall publish an initial list of class I substances, which list shall contain the following substances:

Group I
- chlorofluorocarbon-11 (CFC-11)
- chlorofluorocarbon-12 (CFC-12)
- chlorofluorocarbon-113 (CFC-113)
- chlorofluorocarbon-114 (CFC-114)
- chlorofluorocarbon-115 (CFC-115)

Group II
- halon-1211
- halon-1301
- halon-2402

Group III
- chlorofluorocarbon-13 (CFC-13)
- chlorofluorocarbon-111 (CFC-111)
- chlorofluorocarbon-112 (CFC-112)
- chlorofluorocarbon-211 (CFC-211)
- chlorofluorocarbon-212 (CFC-212)
- chlorofluorocarbon-213 (CFC-213)
- chlorofluorocarbon-214 (CFC-214)
- chlorofluorocarbon-215 (CFC-215)
- chlorofluorocarbon-216 (CFC-216)
- chlorofluorocarbon-217 (CFC-217)

Group IV
- carbon tetrachloride

Group V
- methyl chloroform

The initial list under this subsection shall also include the isomers of the substances listed above, other than 1,1,2-trichloroethane (an isomer of methyl chloroform). Pursuant to subsection (c) of this section, the Administrator shall add to the list of class I substances any other

substance that the Administrator finds causes or contributes significantly to harmful effects on the stratospheric ozone layer. The Administrator shall, pursuant to subsection (c) of this section, add to such list all substances that the Administrator determines have an ozone depletion potential of 0.2 or greater.
(b) List of class II substances
Simultaneously with publication of the initial list of class I substances, the Administrator shall publish an initial list of class II substances, which shall contain the following substances:

  hydrochlorofluorocarbon-21 (HCFC-21)
  hydrochlorofluorocarbon-22 (HCFC-22)
  hydrochlorofluorocarbon-31 (HCFC-31)
  hydrochlorofluorocarbon-121 (HCFC-121)
  hydrochlorofluorocarbon-122 (HCFC-122)
  hydrochlorofluorocarbon-123 (HCFC-123)
  hydrochlorofluorocarbon-124 (HCFC-124)
  hydrochlorofluorocarbon-131 (HCFC-131)
  hydrochlorofluorocarbon-132 (HCFC-132)
  hydrochlorofluorocarbon-133 (HCFC-133)
  hydrochlorofluorocarbon-141 (HCFC-141)
  hydrochlorofluorocarbon-142 (HCFC-142)
  hydrochlorofluorocarbon-221 (HCFC-221)
  hydrochlorofluorocarbon-222 (HCFC-222)
  hydrochlorofluorocarbon-223 (HCFC-223)
  hydrochlorofluorocarbon-224 (HCFC-224)
  hydrochlorofluorocarbon-225 (HCFC-225)
  hydrochlorofluorocarbon-226 (HCFC-226)
  hydrochlorofluorocarbon-231 (HCFC-231)
  hydrochlorofluorocarbon-232 (HCFC-232)
  hydrochlorofluorocarbon-233 (HCFC-233)
  hydrochlorofluorocarbon-234 (HCFC-234)
  hydrochlorofluorocarbon-235 (HCFC-235)
  hydrochlorofluorocarbon-241 (HCFC-241)
  hydrochlorofluorocarbon-242 (HCFC-242)
  hydrochlorofluorocarbon-243 (HCFC-243)
  hydrochlorofluorocarbon-244 (HCFC-244)
  hydrochlorofluorocarbon-251 (HCFC-251)
  hydrochlorofluorocarbon-252 (HCFC-252)
  hydrochlorofluorocarbon-253 (HCFC-253)
  hydrochlorofluorocarbon-261 (HCFC-261)
  hydrochlorofluorocarbon-262 (HCFC-262)
  hydrochlorofluorocarbon-271 (HCFC-271)

The initial list under this subsection shall also include the isomers of the substances listed above. Pursuant to subsection (c) of this section, the Administrator shall add to the list of class II substances any other substance that the Administrator finds is known or may reasonably be anticipated to cause or contribute to harmful effects on the stratospheric ozone layer.
(c) Additions to the lists
 (1) The Administrator may add, by rule, in accordance with the criteria set forth in subsection (a) or (b) of this section, as the case may be, any substance to the list of class I or class II substances under subsection (a) or (b) of this section. For purposes of exchanges under section 7661f[1] of this title, whenever a substance is added to the list of class I substances the Administrator shall, to the extent consistent with the Montreal Protocol, assign such substance to existing Group I, II, III, IV, or V or place such substance in a new Group.
 (2) Periodically, but not less frequently than every 3 years after November 15, 1990, the Administrator shall list, by rule, as additional class I or class II substances those substances which the Administrator finds meet the criteria of subsection (a) or (b) of this section, as the case may be.
 (3) At any time, any person may petition the Administrator to add a substance to the list of class I or class II substances. Pursuant to the criteria set forth in subsection (a) or (b) of this

---

[1] So in original. Probably should be section "7671f".

section as the case may be, within 180 days after receiving such a petition, the Administrator shall either propose to add the substance to such list or publish an explanation of the petition denial. In any case where the Administrator proposes to add a substance to such list, the Administrator shall add, by rule, (or make a final determination not to add) such substance to such list within 1 year after receiving such petition. Any petition under this paragraph shall include a showing by the petitioner that there are data on the substance adequate to support the petition. If the Administrator determines that information on the substance is not sufficient to make a determination under this paragraph, the Administrator shall use any authority available to the Administrator, under any law administered by the Administrator, to acquire such information.
(4) Only a class II substance which is added to the list of class I substances may be removed from the list of class II substances. No substance referred to in subsection (a) of this section, including methyl chloroform, may be removed from the list of class I substances.

(d) New listed substances
In the case of any substance added to the list of class I or class II substances after publication of the initial list of such substances under this section, the Administrator may extend any schedule or compliance deadline contained in section 7671c or 7671d of this title to a later date than specified in such sections if such schedule or deadline is unattainable, considering when such substance is added to the list. No extension under this subsection may extend the date for termination of production of any class I substance to a date more than 7 years after January 1 of the year after the year in which the substance is added to the list of class I substances. No extension under this subsection may extend the date for termination of production of any class II substance to a date more than 10 years after January 1 of the year after the year in which the substance is added to the list of class II substances.

(e) Ozone-depletion and global warming potential
Simultaneously with publication of the lists under this section and simultaneously with any addition to either of such lists, the Administrator shall assign to each listed substance a numerical value representing the substance's ozone-depletion potential. In addition, the Administrator shall publish the chlorine and bromine loading potential and the atmospheric lifetime of each listed substance. One year after November 15, 1990 (one year after the addition of a substance to either of such lists in the case of a substance added after the publication of the initial lists of such substances), and after notice and opportunity for public comment, the Administrator shall publish the global warming potential of each listed substance. The preceding sentence shall not be construed to be the basis of any additional regulation under this chapter. In the case of the substances referred to in table 1, the ozone-depletion potential shall be as specified in table 1, unless the Administrator adjusts the substance's ozone-depletion potential based on criteria referred to in section 7671(10) of this title:

TABLE 1	
Substance	Ozone-depletion potential
chlorofluorocarbon-11 (CFC-11)	1.0
chlorofluorocarbon-12 (CFC-12)	1.0
chlorofluorocarbon-13 (CFC-13)	1.0
chlorofluorocarbon-111 (CFC-111)	1.0
chlorofluorocarbon-112 (CFC-112)	1.0
chlorofluorocarbon-113 (CFC-113)	0.8
chlorofluorocarbon-114 (CFC-114)	1.0
chlorofluorocarbon-115 (CFC-115)	0.6
chlorofluorocarbon-211 (CFC-211)	1.0
chlorofluorocarbon-212 (CFC-212)	1.0
chlorofluorocarbon-213 (CFC-213)	1.0
chlorofluorocarbon-214 (CFC-214)	1.0
chlorofluorocarbon-215 (CFC-215)	1.0
chlorofluorocarbon-216 (CFC-216)	1.0
chlorofluorocarbon-217 (CFC-217)	1.0
halon-1211	3.0
halon-1301	10.0
halon-2402	6.0

Substance	Ozone-depletion potential
carbon tetrachloride..	1.1
methyl chloroform..	0.1
hydrochlorofluorocarbon-22 (HCFC-22).........................	0.05
hydrochlorofluorocarbon-123 (HCFC-123).......................	0.02
hydrochlorofluorocarbon-124 (HCFC-124).......................	0.02
hydrochlorofluorocarbon-141(b) (HCFC-141(b)).................	0.1
hydrochlorofluorocarbon-142(b) (HCFC-142(b)).................	0.06

Where the ozone-depletion potential of a substance is specified in the Montreal Protocol, the ozone-depletion potential specified for that substance under this section shall be consistent with the Montreal Protocol.

(July 14, 1955, ch. 360, title VI, Sec. 602, as added Pub. L. 101-549, title VI, Sec. 602(a), Nov. 15, 1990, 104 Stat. 2650.)

Section Referred to in Other Sections

This section is referred to in sections 7671, 7671f of this title.

MONITORING AND REPORTING REQUIREMENTS

42 USC 7671b

(a) Regulations

Within 270 days after November 15, 1990, the Administrator shall amend the regulations of the Administrator in effect on such date regarding monitoring and reporting of class I and class II substances. Such amendments shall conform to the requirements of this section. The amended regulations shall include requirements with respect to the time and manner of monitoring and reporting as required under this section.

(b) Production, import, and export level reports

On a quarterly basis, or such other basis (not less than annually) as determined by the Administrator, each person who produced, imported, or exported a class I or class II substance shall file a report with the Administrator setting forth the amount of the substance that such person produced, imported, and exported during the preceding reporting period. Each such report shall be signed and attested by a responsible officer. No such report shall be required from a person after April 1 of the calendar year after such person permanently ceases production, importation, and exportation of the substance and so notifies the Administrator in writing.

(c) Baseline reports for class I substances

Unless such information has previously been reported to the Administrator, on the date on which the first report under subsection (b) of this section is required to be filed, each person who produced, imported, or exported a class I substance (other than a substance added to the list of class I substances after the publication of the initial list of such substances under this section) shall file a report with the Administrator setting forth the amount of such substance that such person produced, imported, and exported during the baseline year. In the case of a substance added to the list of class I substances after publication of the initial list of such substances under this section, the regulations shall require that each person who produced, imported, or exported such substance shall file a report with the Administrator within 180 days after the date on which such substance is added to the list, setting forth the amount of the substance that such person produced, imported, and exported in the baseline year.

(d) Monitoring and reports to Congress

(1) The Administrator shall monitor and, not less often than every 3 years following November 15, 1990, submit a report to Congress on the production, use and consumption of class I and class II substances. Such report shall include data on domestic production, use and consumption, and an estimate of worldwide production, use and consumption of such substances. Not less frequently than every 6 years the Administrator shall report to Congress on the environmental and economic effects of any stratospheric ozone depletion.

(2) The Administrators of the National Aeronautics and Space Administration and the National Oceanic and Atmospheric Administration shall monitor, and not less often than every 3 years following November 15, 1990, submit a report to Congress on the current

average tropospheric concentration of chlorine and bromine and on the level of stratospheric ozone depletion. Such reports shall include updated projections of—
 (A) peak chlorine loading;
 (B) the rate at which the atmospheric abundance of chlorine is projected to decrease after the year 2000; and
 (C) the date by which the atmospheric abundance of chlorine is projected to return to a level of two parts per billion.

Such updated projections shall be made on the basis of current international and domestic controls on substances covered by this subchapter as well as on the basis of such controls supplemented by a year 2000 global phase out of all halocarbon emissions (the base case). It is the purpose of the Congress through the provisions of this section to monitor closely the production and consumption of class II substances to assure that the production and consumption of such substances will not:
 (i) increase significantly the peak chlorine loading that is projected to occur under the base case established for purposes of this section;
 (ii) reduce significantly the rate at which the atmospheric abundance of chlorine is projected to decrease under the base case; or
 (iii) delay the date by which the average atmospheric concentration of chlorine is projected under the base case to return to a level of two parts per billion.

(e) Technology status report in 2015
The Administrator shall review, on a periodic basis, the progress being made in the development of alternative systems or products necessary to manufacture and operate appliances without class II substances. If the Administrator finds, after notice and opportunity for public comment, that as a result of technological development problems, the development of such alternative systems or products will not occur within the time necessary to provide for the manufacture of such equipment without such substances prior to the applicable deadlines under section 7671d of this title, the Administrator shall, not later than January 1, 2015, so inform the Congress.

(f) Emergency report
If, in consultation with the Administrators of the National Aeronautics and Space Administration and the National Oceanic and Atmospheric Administration, and after notice and opportunity for public comment, the Administrator determines that the global production, consumption, and use of class II substances are projected to contribute to an atmospheric chlorine loading in excess of the base case projections by more than \5/10\ths parts per billion, the Administrator shall so inform the Congress immediately. The determination referred to in the preceding sentence shall be based on the monitoring under subsection (d) of this section and updated not less often than every 3 years.

(July 14, 1955, ch. 360, title VI, Sec. 603, as added Pub. L. 101-549, title VI, Sec. 602(a), Nov. 15, 1990, 104 Stat. 2653.)

Methane Studies

Section 603 of Pub. L. 101-549 provided that:

"(a) Economically Justified Actions.—Not later than 2 years after enactment of this Act [Nov. 15, 1990], the Administrator shall prepare and submit a report to the Congress that identifies activities, substances, processes, or combinations thereof that could reduce methane emissions and that are economically and technologically justified with and without consideration of environmental benefit.

(b) Domestic Methane Source Inventory and Control.—Not later than 2 years after the enactment of this Act [Nov. 15, 1990], the Administrator, in consultation and coordination with the Secretary of Energy and the Secretary of Agriculture, shall prepare and submit to the Congress reports on each of the following:
 (1) Methane emissions associated with natural gas extraction, transportation, distribution, storage, and use. Such report shall include an inventory of methane emissions associated with such activities within the United States. Such emissions include, but are not limited to, accidental and intentional releases from natural gas and oil wells, pipelines, processing facilities, and gas burners. The report shall also include an inventory of methane generation with such activities.

(2) Methane emissions associated with coal extraction, transportation, distribution, storage, and use. Such report shall include an inventory of methane emissions associated with such activities within the United States. Such emissions include, but are not limited to, accidental and intentional releases from mining shafts, degasification wells, gas recovery wells and equipment, and from the processing and use of coal. The report shall also include an inventory of methane generation with such activities.

(3) Methane emissions associated with management of solid waste. Such report shall include an inventory of methane emissions associated with all forms of waste management in the United States, including storage, treatment, and disposal.

(4) Methane emissions associated with agriculture. Such report shall include an inventory of methane emissions associated with rice and livestock production in the United States.

(5) Methane emissions associated with biomass burning. Such report shall include an inventory of methane emissions associated with the intentional burning of agricultural wastes, wood, grasslands, and forests.

(6) Other methane emissions associated with human activities. Such report shall identify and inventory other domestic sources of methane emissions that are deemed by the Administrator and other such agencies to be significant.

(c) International Studies.—
  (1) Methane emissions.—Not later than 2 years after the enactment of this Act [Nov. 15, 1990], the Administrator shall prepare and submit to the Congress a report on methane emissions from countries other than the United States. Such report shall include inventories of methane emissions associated with the activities listed in subsection (b).
  (2) Preventing increases in methane concentrations.—Not later than 2 years after the enactment of this Act [Nov. 15, 1990], the Administrator shall prepare and submit to the Congress a report that analyzes the potential for preventing an increase in atmospheric concentrations of methane from activities and sources in other countries. Such report shall identify and evaluate the technical options for reducing methane emission from each of the activities listed in subsection (b), as well as other activities or sources that are deemed by the Administrator in consultation with other relevant Federal agencies and departments to be significant and shall include an evaluation of costs. The report shall identify the emissions reductions that would need to be achieved to prevent increasing atmospheric concentrations of methane. The report shall also identify technology transfer programs that could promote methane emissions reductions in lesser developed countries.

(d) Natural Sources.—Not later than 2 years after the enactment of this Act [Nov. 15, 1990], the Administrator shall prepare and submit to the Congress a report on—
  (1) methane emissions from biogenic sources such as (A) tropical, temperate, and subarctic forests, (B) tundra, and (C) freshwater and saltwater wetlands; and
  (2) the changes in methane emissions from biogenic sources that may occur as a result of potential increases in temperatures and atmospheric concentrations of carbon dioxide.

(e) Study of Measures To Limit Growth in Methane Concentrations.—
Not later than 2 years after the completion of the studies in subsections (b), (c), and (d), the Administrator shall prepare and submit to the Congress a report that presents options outlining measures that could be implemented to stop or reduce the growth in atmospheric concentrations of methane from sources within the United States referred to in paragraphs (1) through (6) of subsection (b). This study shall identify and evaluate the technical options for reducing methane emissions from each of the activities listed in subsection (b), as well as other activities or sources deemed by such agencies to be significant, and shall include an evaluation of costs, technology, safety, energy, and other factors. The study shall be based on the other studies under this section. The study shall also identify programs of the United States and international lending agencies that could be used to induce lesser developed countries to undertake measures that will reduce methane emissions and the resource needs of such programs.

(f) Information Gathering.—In carrying out the studies under this section, the provisions and requirements of section 114 of the Clean Air Act [42 U.S.C. 7414] shall be available for purposes of obtaining information to carry out such studies.

(g) Consultation and Coordination.—In preparing the studies under this section the Administrator shall consult and coordinate with the Secretary of Energy, the Administrators of the National Aeronautics and Space Administration and the National Oceanic and Atmospheric

Administration, and the heads of other relevant Federal agencies and departments. In the case of the studies under subsections (a), (b), and (e), such consultation and coordination shall include the Secretary of Agriculture."

PHASE-OUT OF PRODUCTION AND CONSUMPTION OF CLASS I SUBSTANCES
42 USC 7671c

(a) Production phase-out
Effective on January 1 of each year specified in Table 2, it shall be unlawful for any person to produce any class I substance in an annual quantity greater than the relevant percentage specified in Table 2. The percentages in Table 2 refer to a maximum allowable production as a percentage of the quantity of the substance produced by the person concerned in the baseline year.

TABLE 2

Date	Carbon Tetrachloride	Methyl Chloroform	Other Class I Substances
1991	100%	100%	85%
1992	90%	100%	80%
1993	80%	90%	75%
1994	70%	85%	65%
1995	15%	70%	50%
1996	15%	50%	40%
1997	15%	50%	15%
1998	15%	50%	15%
1999	15%	50%	15%
2000		20%	
2001		20%	

(b) Termination of production of class I substances
Effective January 1, 2000 (January 1, 2002 in the case of methyl chloroform), it shall be unlawful for any person to produce any amount of a class I substance.

(c) Regulations regarding production and consumption of class I substances
The Administrator shall promulgate regulations within 10 months after November 15, 1990, phasing out the production of class I substances in accordance with this section and other applicable provisions of this subchapter. The Administrator shall also promulgate regulations to insure that the consumption of class I substances in the United States is phased out and terminated in accordance with the same schedule (subject to the same exceptions and other provisions) as is applicable to the phase-out and termination of production of class I substances under this subchapter.

(d) Exceptions for essential uses of methyl chloroform, medical devices, and aviation safety
  (1) Essential uses of methyl chloroform
  Notwithstanding the termination of production required by subsection (b) of this section, during the period beginning on January 1, 2002, and ending on January 1, 2005, the Administrator, after notice and opportunity for public comment, may, to the extent such action is consistent with the Montreal Protocol, authorize the production of limited quantities of methyl chloroform solely for use in essential applications (such as nondestructive testing for metal fatigue and corrosion of existing airplane engines and airplane parts susceptible to metal fatigue) for which no safe and effective substitute is available. Notwithstanding this paragraph, the authority to produce methyl chloroform for use in medical devices shall be provided in accordance with paragraph (2).
  (2) Medical devices
  Notwithstanding the termination of production required by subsection (b) of this section, the Administrator, after notice and opportunity for public comment, shall, to the extent such action is consistent with the Montreal Protocol, authorize the production of limited quantities of class I substances solely for use in medical devices if such authorization is determined by the Commissioner, in consultation with the Administrator, to be necessary for use in medical devices.

(3) Aviation safety
  (A) Notwithstanding the termination of production required by subsection (b) of this section, the Administrator, after notice and opportunity for public comment, may, to the extent such action is consistent with the Montreal Protocol, authorize the production of limited quantities of halon-1211 (bromochlorodifluoromethane), halon-1301 (bromotrifluoromethane), and halon-2402 (dibromotetrafluoroethane) solely for purposes of aviation safety if the Administrator of the Federal Aviation Administration, in consultation with the Administrator, determines that no safe and effective substitute has been developed and that such authorization is necessary for aviation safety purposes.
  (B) The Administrator of the Federal Aviation Administration shall, in consultation with the Administrator, examine whether safe and effective substitutes for methyl chloroform or alternative techniques will be available for nondestructive testing for metal fatigue and corrosion of existing airplane engines and airplane parts susceptible to metal fatigue and whether an exception for such uses of methyl chloroform under this paragraph will be necessary for purposes of airline safety after January 1, 2005 and provide a report to Congress in 1998.
(4) Cap on certain exceptions
  Under no circumstances may the authority set forth in paragraphs (1), (2), and (3) of subsection (d) of this section be applied to authorize any person to produce a class I substance in annual quantities greater than 10 percent of that produced by such person during the baseline year.
(5) Sanitation and food protection
  To the extent consistent with the Montreal Protocol's quarantine and preshipment provisions, the Administrator shall exempt the production, importation, and consumption of methyl bromide to fumigate commodities entering or leaving the United States or any State (or political subdivision thereof) for purposes of compliance with Animal and Plant Health Inspection Service requirements or with any international, Federal, State, or local sanitation or food protection standard.
(6) Critical uses
  To the extent consistent with the Montreal Protocol, the Administrator, after notice and the opportunity for public comment, and after consultation with other departments or instrumentalities of the Federal Government having regulatory authority related to methyl bromide, including the Secretary of Agriculture, may exempt the production, importation, and consumption of methyl bromide for critical uses.

(e) Developing countries
  (1) Exception
    Notwithstanding the phase-out and termination of production required under subsections (a) and (b) of this section, the Administrator, after notice and opportunity for public comment, may, consistent with the Montreal Protocol, authorize the production of limited quantities of a class I substance in excess of the amounts otherwise allowable under subsection (a) or (b) of this section, or both, solely for export to, and use in, developing countries that are Parties to the Montreal Protocol and are operating under article 5 of such Protocol. Any production authorized under this paragraph shall be solely for purposes of satisfying the basic domestic needs of such countries.
  (2) Cap on exception
    (A) Under no circumstances may the authority set forth in paragraph (1) be applied to authorize any person to produce a class I substance in any year for which a production percentage is specified in Table 2 of subsection (a) of this section in an annual quantity greater than the specified percentage, plus an amount equal to 10 percent of the amount produced by such person in the baseline year.
    (B) Under no circumstances may the authority set forth in paragraph (1) be applied to authorize any person to produce a class I substance in the applicable termination year referred to in subsection (b) of this section, or in any year thereafter, in an annual quantity greater than 15 percent of the baseline quantity of such substance produced by such person.
    (C) An exception authorized under this subsection shall terminate no later than January 1, 2010 (2012 in the case of methyl chloroform).

(3) Methyl bromide
Notwithstanding the phaseout and termination of production of methyl bromide pursuant to subsection (h) of this section, the Administrator may, consistent with the Montreal Protocol, authorize the production of limited quantities of methyl bromide, solely for use in developing countries that are Parties to the Copenhagen Amendments to the Montreal Protocol.

(f) National security
The President may, to the extent such action is consistent with the Montreal Protocol, issue such orders regarding production and use of CFC-114 (chlorofluorocarbon-114), halon-1211, halon-1301, and halon-2402, at any specified site or facility or on any vessel as may be necessary to protect the national security interests of the United States if the President finds that adequate substitutes are not available and that the production and use of such substance are necessary to protect such national security interest. Such orders may include, where necessary to protect such interests, an exemption from any prohibition or requirement contained in this subchapter. The President shall notify the Congress within 30 days of the issuance of an order under this paragraph providing for any such exemption. Such notification shall include a statement of the reasons for the granting of the exemption. An exemption under this paragraph shall be for a specified period which may not exceed one year. Additional exemptions may be granted, each upon the President's issuance of a new order under this paragraph. Each such additional exemption shall be for a specified period which may not exceed one year. No exemption shall be granted under this paragraph due to lack of appropriation unless the President shall have specifically requested such appropriation as a part of the budgetary process and the Congress shall have failed to make available such requested appropriation.

(g) Fire suppression and explosion prevention
(1) Notwithstanding the production phase-out set forth in subsection (a) of this section, the Administrator, after notice and opportunity for public comment, may, to the extent such action is consistent with the Montreal Protocol, authorize the production of limited quantities of halon-1211, halon-1301, and halon-2402 in excess of the amount otherwise permitted pursuant to the schedule under subsection (a) of this section solely for purposes of fire suppression or explosion prevention if the Administrator, in consultation with the Administrator of the United States Fire Administration, determines that no safe and effective substitute has been developed and that such authorization is necessary for fire suppression or explosion prevention purposes. The Administrator shall not authorize production under this paragraph for purposes of fire safety or explosion prevention training or testing of fire suppression or explosion prevention equipment. In no event shall the Administrator grant an exception under this paragraph that permits production after December 31, 1999.
(2) The Administrator shall periodically monitor and assess the status of efforts to obtain substitutes for the substances referred to in paragraph (1) for purposes of fire suppression or explosion prevention and the probability of such substitutes being available by December 31, 1999. The Administrator, as part of such assessment, shall consider any relevant assessments under the Montreal Protocol and the actions of the Parties pursuant to Article 2B of the Montreal Protocol in identifying essential uses and in permitting a level of production or consumption that is necessary to satisfy such uses for which no adequate alternatives are available after December 31, 1999. The Administrator shall report to Congress the results of such assessment in 1994 and again in 1998.
(3) Notwithstanding the termination of production set forth in subsection (b) of this section, the Administrator, after notice and opportunity for public comment, may, to the extent consistent with the Montreal Protocol, authorize the production of limited quantities of halon-1211, halon-1301, and halon-2402 in the period after December 31, 1999, and before December 31, 2004, solely for purposes of fire suppression or explosion prevention in association with domestic production of crude oil and natural gas energy supplies on the North Slope of Alaska, if the Administrator, in consultation with the Administrator of the United States Fire Administration, determines that no safe and effective substitute has been developed and that such authorization is necessary for fire suppression and explosion prevention purposes. The Administrator shall not authorize production under the paragraph for purposes of fire safety or explosion prevention training or testing of fire suppression or explosion prevention equipment. In no event shall the Administrator au-

thorize under this paragraph any person to produce any such halon in an amount greater than 3 percent of that produced by such person during the baseline year.
(h) Methyl bromide
Notwithstanding subsections (b) and (d) of this section, the Administrator shall not terminate production of methyl bromide prior to January 1, 2005. The Administrator shall promulgate rules for reductions in, and terminate the production, importation, and consumption of, methyl bromide under a schedule that is in accordance with, but not more stringent than, the phaseout schedule of the Montreal Protocol Treaty as in effect on October 21, 1998.

(July 14, 1955, ch. 360, title VI, Sec. 604, as added Pub. L. 101-549, title VI, Sec. 602(a), Nov. 15, 1990, 104 Stat. 2655; amended Pub. L. 105-277, div. A, Sec. 101(a) [title VII, Sec. 764], Oct. 21, 1998, 112 Stat. 2681, 2681-36.)

Amendments

1998—Subsec. (d)(5), (6). Pub. L. 105-277, Sec. 101(a) [title VII, Sec. 764(b)], added pars. (5) and (6).

Subsec. (e)(3). Pub. L. 105-277, Sec. 101(a) [title VII, Sec. 764(c)], added par. (3).

Subsec. (h). Pub. L. 105-277, Sec. 101(a) [title VII, Sec. 764(a)], added subsec. (h).

Section Referred to in Other Sections

This section is referred to in sections 7671a, 7671e of this title.

PHASE-OUT OF PRODUCTION AND CONSUMPTION OF CLASS II SUBSTANCES

42 USC 7671d

(a) Restriction of use of class II substances
Effective January 1, 2015, it shall be unlawful for any person to introduce into interstate commerce or use any class II substance unless such substance—
   (1) has been used, recovered, and recycled;
   (2) is used and entirely consumed (except for trace quantities) in the production of other chemicals; or
   (3) is used as a refrigerant in appliances manufactured prior to January 1, 2020.
As used in this subsection, the term "refrigerant" means any class II substance used for heat transfer in a refrigerating system.
(b) Production phase-out
   (1) Effective January 1, 2015, it shall be unlawful for any person to produce any class II substance in an annual quantity greater than the quantity of such substance produced by such person during the baseline year.
   (2) Effective January 1, 2030, it shall be unlawful for any person to produce any class II substance.
(c) Regulations regarding production and consumption of class II substances
By December 31, 1999, the Administrator shall promulgate regulations phasing out the production, and restricting the use, of class II substances in accordance with this section, subject to any acceleration of the phase-out of production under section 7671e of this title. The Administrator shall also promulgate regulations to insure that the consumption of class II substances in the United States is phased out and terminated in accordance with the same schedule (subject to the same exceptions and other provisions) as is applicable to the phase-out and termination of production of class II substances under this subchapter.
(d) Exceptions
   (1) Medical devices
      (A) In general
         Notwithstanding the termination of production required under subsection (b)(2) of this section and the restriction on use referred to in subsection (a) of this section, the Administrator, after notice and opportunity for public comment, shall, to the extent such action is consistent with the Montreal Protocol, authorize the production and use of limited quantities of class II substances solely for purposes of use in medical devices if such authorization is determined by the Commissioner, in consultation with the Administrator, to be necessary for use in medical devices.

(B) Cap on exception
Under no circumstances may the authority set forth in subparagraph (A) be applied to authorize any person to produce a class II substance in annual quantities greater than 10 percent of that produced by such person during the baseline year.
(2) Developing countries
  (A) In general
  Notwithstanding the provisions of subsection (a) or (b) of this section, the Administrator, after notice and opportunity for public comment, may authorize the production of limited quantities of a class II substance in excess of the quantities otherwise permitted under such provisions solely for export to and use in developing countries that are Parties to the Montreal Protocol, as determined by the Administrator. Any production authorized under this subsection shall be solely for purposes of satisfying the basic domestic needs of such countries.
  (B) Cap on exception
    (i) Under no circumstances may the authority set forth in subparagraph (A) be applied to authorize any person to produce a class II substance in any year following the effective date of subsection (b)(1) of this section and before the year 2030 in annual quantities greater than 110 percent of the quantity of such substance produced by such person during the baseline year.
    (ii) Under no circumstances may the authority set forth in subparagraph (A) be applied to authorize any person to produce a class II substance in the year 2030, or any year thereafter, in an annual quantity greater than 15 percent of the quantity of such substance produced by such person during the baseline year.
    (iii) Each exception authorized under this paragraph shall terminate no later than January 1, 2040.

(July 14, 1955, ch. 360, title VI, Sec. 605, as added Pub. L. 101-549, title VI, Sec. 602(a), Nov. 15, 1990, 104 Stat. 2658.)

Section Referred to in Other Sections

This section is referred to in sections 7671a, 7671b, 7671e of this title.

ACCELERATED SCHEDULE

42 USC 7671e

(a) In general
The Administrator shall promulgate regulations, after notice and opportunity for public comment, which establish a schedule for phasing out the production and consumption of class I and class II substances (or use of class II substances) that is more stringent than set forth in section 7671c or 7671d of this title, or both, if—
  (1) based on an assessment of credible current scientific information (including any assessment under the Montreal Protocol) regarding harmful effects on the stratospheric ozone layer associated with a class I or class II substance, the Administrator determines that such more stringent schedule may be necessary to protect human health and the environment against such effects,
  (2) based on the availability of substitutes for listed substances, the Administrator determines that such more stringent schedule is practicable, taking into account technological achievability, safety, and other relevant factors, or
  (3) the Montreal Protocol is modified to include a schedule to control or reduce production, consumption, or use of any substance more rapidly than the applicable schedule under this subchapter.

In making any determination under paragraphs (1) and (2), the Administrator shall consider the status of the period remaining under the applicable schedule under this subchapter.

(b) Petition
Any person may petition the Administrator to promulgate regulations under this section. The Administrator shall grant or deny the petition within 180 days after receipt of any such petition. If the Administrator denies the petition, the Administrator shall publish an explanation of why the petition was denied. If the Administrator grants such petition, such final regula-

tions shall be promulgated within 1 year. Any petition under this subsection shall include a showing by the petitioner that there are data adequate to support the petition. If the Administrator determines that information is not sufficient to make a determination under this subsection, the Administrator shall use any authority available to the Administrator, under any law administered by the Administrator, to acquire such information.

(July 14, 1955, ch. 360, title VI, Sec. 606, as added Pub. L. 101-549, title VI, Sec. 602(a), Nov. 15, 1990, 104 Stat. 2660.)

Section Referred to in Other Sections

This section is referred to in section 7671d of this title.

EXCHANGE AUTHORITY

42 USC 7671f

(a) Transfers

The Administrator shall, within 10 months after November 15, 1990, promulgate rules under this subchapter providing for the issuance of allowances for the production of class I and II substances in accordance with the requirements of this subchapter and governing the transfer of such allowances. Such rules shall insure that the transactions under the authority of this section will result in greater total reductions in the production in each year of class I and class II substances than would occur in that year in the absence of such transactions.

(b) Interpollutant transfers

　(1) The rules under this section shall permit a production allowance for a substance for any year to be transferred for a production allowance for another substance for the same year on an ozone depletion weighted basis.

　(2) Allowances for substances in each group of class I substances (as listed pursuant to section 7671a of this title) may only be transferred for allowances for other substances in the same Group.

　(3) The Administrator shall, as appropriate, establish groups of class II substances for trading purposes and assign class II substances to such groups. In the case of class II substances, allowances may only be transferred for allowances for other class II substances that are in the same Group.

(c) Trades with other persons

The rules under this section shall permit 2 or more persons to transfer production allowances (including interpollutant transfers which meet the requirements of subsections (a) and (b) of this section) if the transferor of such allowances will be subject, under such rules, to an enforceable and quantifiable reduction in annual production which—

　(1) exceeds the reduction otherwise applicable to the transferor under this subchapter,

　(2) exceeds the production allowances transferred to the transferee, and

　(3) would not have occurred in the absence of such transaction.

(d) Consumption

The rules under this section shall also provide for the issuance of consumption allowances in accordance with the requirements of this subchapter and for the trading of such allowances in the same manner as is applicable under this section to the trading of production allowances under this section.

(July 14, 1955, ch. 360, title VI, Sec. 607, as added Pub. L. 101-549, title VI, Sec. 602(a), Nov. 15, 1990, 104 Stat. 2660.)

Section Referred to in Other Sections

This section is referred to in section 7671a of this title.

NATIONAL RECYCLING AND EMISSION REDUCTION PROGRAM
42 USC 7671g

(a) In general
  (1) The Administrator shall, by not later than January 1, 1992, promulgate regulations establishing standards and requirements regarding the use and disposal of class I substances during the service, repair, or disposal of appliances and industrial process refrigeration. Such standards and requirements shall become effective not later than July 1, 1992.
  (2) The Administrator shall, within 4 years after November 15, 1990, promulgate regulations establishing standards and requirements regarding use and disposal of class I and II substances not covered by paragraph (1), including the use and disposal of class II substances during service, repair, or disposal of appliances and industrial process refrigeration. Such standards and requirements shall become effective not later than 12 months after promulgation of the regulations.
  (3) The regulations under this subsection shall include requirements that—
    (A) reduce the use and emission of such substances to the lowest achievable level, and
    (B) maximize the recapture and recycling of such substances.
  Such regulations may include requirements to use alternative substances (including substances which are not class I or class II substances) or to minimize use of class I or class II substances, or to promote the use of safe alternatives pursuant to section 7671k of this title or any combination of the foregoing.

(b) Safe disposal
  The regulations under subsection (a) of this section shall establish standards and requirements for the safe disposal of class I and II substances. Such regulations shall include each of the following—
  (1) Requirements that class I or class II substances contained in bulk in appliances, machines or other goods shall be removed from each such appliance, machine or other good prior to the disposal of such items or their delivery for recycling.
  (2) Requirements that any appliance, machine or other good containing a class I or class II substance in bulk shall not be manufactured, sold, or distributed in interstate commerce or offered for sale or distribution in interstate commerce unless it is equipped with a servicing aperture or an equally effective design feature which will facilitate the recapture of such substance during service and repair or disposal of such item.
  (3) Requirements that any product in which a class I or class II substance is incorporated so as to constitute an inherent element of such product shall be disposed of in a manner that reduces, to the maximum extent practicable, the release of such substance into the environment. If the Administrator determines that the application of this paragraph to any product would result in producing only insignificant environmental benefits, the Administrator shall include in such regulations an exception for such product.

(c) Prohibitions
  (1) Effective July 1, 1992, it shall be unlawful for any person, in the course of maintaining, servicing, repairing, or disposing of an appliance or industrial process refrigeration, to knowingly vent or otherwise knowingly release or dispose of any class I or class II substance used as a refrigerant in such appliance (or industrial process refrigeration) in a manner which permits such substance to enter the environment. De minimis releases associated with good faith attempts to recapture and recycle or safely dispose of any such substance shall not be subject to the prohibition set forth in the preceding sentence.
  (2) Effective 5 years after November 15, 1990, paragraph (1) shall also apply to the venting, release, or disposal of any substitute substance for a class I or class II substance by any person maintaining, servicing, repairing, or disposing of an appliance or industrial process refrigeration which contains and uses as a refrigerant any such substance, unless the Administrator determines that venting, releasing, or disposing of such substance does not pose a threat to the environment. For purposes of this paragraph, the term "appliance" includes any device which contains and uses as a refrigerant a substitute substance and which is used for household or commercial purposes, including any air conditioner, refrigerator, chiller, or freezer.

(July 14, 1955, ch. 360, title VI, Sec. 608, as added Pub. L. 101-549, title VI, Sec. 602(a), Nov. 15, 1990, 104 Stat. 2661.)

SERVICING OF MOTOR VEHICLE AIR CONDITIONERS

42 USC 7671h

(a) Regulations
Within 1 year after November 15, 1990, the Administrator shall promulgate regulations in accordance with this section establishing standards and requirements regarding the servicing of motor vehicle air conditioners.

(b) Definitions
As used in this section—
  (1) The term "refrigerant" means any class I or class II substance used in a motor vehicle air conditioner. Effective 5 years after November 15, 1990, the term "refrigerant" shall also include any substitute substance.
  (2) (A) The term "approved refrigerant recycling equipment" means equipment certified by the Administrator (or an independent standards testing organization approved by the Administrator) to meet the standards established by the Administrator and applicable to equipment for the extraction and reclamation of refrigerant from motor vehicle air conditioners. Such standards shall, at a minimum, be at least as stringent as the standards of the Society of Automotive Engineers in effect as of November 15, 1990, and applicable to such equipment (SAE standard J-1990).
    (B) Equipment purchased before the proposal of regulations under this section shall be considered certified if it is substantially identical to equipment certified as provided in subparagraph (A).
  (3) The term "properly using" means, with respect to approved refrigerant recycling equipment, using such equipment in conformity with standards established by the Administrator and applicable to the use of such equipment. Such standards shall, at a minimum, be at least as stringent as the standards of the Society of Automotive Engineers in effect as of November 15, 1990, and applicable to the use of such equipment (SAE standard J-1989).
  (4) The term "properly trained and certified" means training and certification in the proper use of approved refrigerant recycling equipment for motor vehicle air conditioners in conformity with standards established by the Administrator and applicable to the performance of service on motor vehicle air conditioners. Such standards shall, at a minimum, be at least as stringent as specified, as of November 15, 1990, in SAE standard J-1989 under the certification program of the National Institute for Automotive Service Excellence (ASE) or under a similar program such as the training and certification program of the Mobile Air Conditioning Society (MACS).

(c) Servicing motor vehicle air conditioners
Effective January 1, 1992, no person repairing or servicing motor vehicles for consideration may perform any service on a motor vehicle air conditioner involving the refrigerant for such air conditioner without properly using approved refrigerant recycling equipment and no such person may perform such service unless such person has been properly trained and certified. The requirements of the previous sentence shall not apply until January 1, 1993 in the case of a person repairing or servicing motor vehicles for consideration at an entity which performed service on fewer than 100 motor vehicle air conditioners during calendar year 1990 and if such person so certifies, pursuant to subsection (d)(2) of this section, to the Administrator by January 1, 1992.

(d) Certification
  (1) Effective 2 years after November 15, 1990, each person performing service on motor vehicle air conditioners for consideration shall certify to the Administrator either—
    (A) that such person has acquired, and is properly using, approved refrigerant recycling equipment in service on motor vehicle air conditioners involving refrigerant and that each individual authorized by such person to perform such service is properly trained and certified; or
    (B) that such person is performing such service at an entity which serviced fewer than 100 motor vehicle air conditioners in 1991.
  (2) Effective January 1, 1993, each person who certified under paragraph (1)(B) shall submit a certification under paragraph (1)(A).

(3) Each certification under this subsection shall contain the name and address of the person certifying under this subsection and the serial number of each unit of approved recycling equipment acquired by such person and shall be signed and attested by the owner or another responsible officer. Certifications under paragraph (1)(A) may be made by submitting the required information to the Administrator on a standard form provided by the manufacturer of certified refrigerant recycling equipment.

(e) Small containers of class I or class II substances
Effective 2 years after November 15, 1990, it shall be unlawful for any person to sell or distribute, or offer for sale or distribution, in interstate commerce to any person (other than a person performing service for consideration on motor vehicle air-conditioning systems in compliance with this section) any class I or class II substance that is suitable for use as a refrigerant in a motor vehicle air-conditioning system and that is in a container which contains less than 20 pounds of such refrigerant.

(July 14, 1955, ch. 360, title VI, Sec. 609, as added Pub. L. 101-549, title VI, Sec. 602(a), Nov. 15, 1990, 104 Stat. 2662.)

NONESSENTIAL PRODUCTS CONTAINING CHLOROFLUOROCARBONS

42 USC 7671i

(a) Regulations
The Administrator shall promulgate regulations to carry out the requirements of this section within 1 year after November 15, 1990.

(b) Nonessential products
The regulations under this section shall identify nonessential products that release class I substances into the environment (including any release occurring during manufacture, use, storage, or disposal) and prohibit any person from selling or distributing any such product, or offering any such product for sale or distribution, in interstate commerce. At a minimum, such prohibition shall apply to—
(1) chlorofluorocarbon-propelled plastic party streamers and noise horns,
(2) chlorofluorocarbon-containing cleaning fluids for noncommercial electronic and photographic equipment, and
(3) other consumer products that are determined by the Administrator—
  (A) to release class I substances into the environment (including any release occurring during manufacture, use, storage, or disposal), and
  (B) to be nonessential.
  In determining whether a product is nonessential, the Administrator shall consider the purpose or intended use of the product, the technological availability of substitutes for such product and for such class I substance, safety, health, and other relevant factors.

(c) Effective date
Effective 24 months after November 15, 1990, it shall be unlawful for any person to sell or distribute, or offer for sale or distribution, in interstate commerce any nonessential product to which regulations under subsection (a) of this section implementing subsection (b) of this section are applicable.

(d) Other products
(1) Effective January 1, 1994, it shall be unlawful for any person to sell or distribute, or offer for sale or distribution, in interstate commerce—
  (A) any aerosol product or other pressurized dispenser which contains a class II substance; or
  (B) any plastic foam product which contains, or is manufactured with, a class II substance.
(2) The Administrator is authorized to grant exceptions from the prohibition under subparagraph (A) of paragraph (1) where—
  (A) the use of the aerosol product or pressurized dispenser is determined by the Administrator to be essential as a result of flammability or worker safety concerns, and
  (B) the only available alternative to use of a class II substance is use of a class I substance which legally could be substituted for such class II substance.

(3) Subparagraph (B) of paragraph (1) shall not apply to—
   (A) a foam insulation product, or
   (B) an integral skin, rigid, or semi-rigid foam utilized to provide for motor vehicle safety in accordance with Federal Motor Vehicle Safety Standards where no adequate substitute substance (other than a class I or class II substance) is practicable for effectively meeting such Standards.
(e) Medical devices
   Nothing in this section shall apply to any medical device as defined in section 7671(8) of this title.
(July 14, 1955, ch. 360, title VI, Sec. 610, as added Pub. L. 101-549, title VI, Sec. 602(a), Nov. 15, 1990, 104 Stat. 2664.)

LABELING

42 USC 7671j

(a) Regulations
   The Administrator shall promulgate regulations to implement the labeling requirements of this section within 18 months after November 15, 1990, after notice and opportunity for public comment.
(b) Containers containing class I or class II substances and products containing class I substances
   Effective 30 months after November 15, 1990, no container in which a class I or class II substance is stored or transported, and no product containing a class I substance, shall be introduced into interstate commerce unless it bears a clearly legible and conspicuous label stating: "Warning: Contains [insert name of substance], a substance which harms public health and environment by destroying ozone in the upper atmosphere".
(c) Products containing class II substances
   (1) After 30 months after November 15, 1990, and before January 1, 2015, no product containing a class II substance shall be introduced into interstate commerce unless it bears the label referred to in subsection (b) of this section if the Administrator determines, after notice and opportunity for public comment, that there are substitute products or manufacturing processes (A) that do not rely on the use of such class II substance, (B) that reduce the overall risk to human health and the environment, and (C) that are currently or potentially available.
   (2) Effective January 1, 2015, the requirements of subsection (b) of this section shall apply to all products containing a class II substance.
(d) Products manufactured with class I and class II substances
   (1) In the case of a class II substance, after 30 months after November 15, 1990, and before January 1, 2015, if the Administrator, after notice and opportunity for public comment, makes the determination referred to in subsection (c) of this section with respect to a product manufactured with a process that uses such class II substance, no such product shall be introduced into interstate commerce unless it bears a clearly legible and conspicuous label stating:
   "Warning: Manufactured with [insert name of substance], a substance which harms public health and environment by destroying ozone in the upper atmosphere"[1]
   (2) In the case of a class I substance, effective 30 months after November 15, 1990, and before January 1, 2015, the labeling requirements of this subsection shall apply to all products manufactured with a process that uses such class I substance unless the Administrator determines that there are no substitute products or manufacturing processes that (A) do not rely on the use of such class I substance, (B) reduce the overall risk to human health and the environment, and (C) are currently or potentially available.
(e) Petitions
   (1) Any person may, at any time after 18 months after November 15, 1990, petition the Administrator to apply the requirements of this section to a product containing a class II substance or a product manufactured with a class I or II substance which is not otherwise subject to such requirements. Within 180 days after receiving such petition, the Adminis-

---

[1] So in original. Probably should be followed by a period.

trator shall, pursuant to the criteria set forth in subsection (c) of this section, either propose to apply the requirements of this section to such product or publish an explanation of the petition denial. If the Administrator proposes to apply such requirements to such product, the Administrator shall, by rule, render a final determination pursuant to such criteria within 1 year after receiving such petition.
  (2) Any petition under this paragraph[2] shall include a showing by the petitioner that there are data on the product adequate to support the petition.
  (3) If the Administrator determines that information on the product is not sufficient to make the required determination the Administrator shall use any authority available to the Administrator under any law administered by the Administrator to acquire such information.
  (4) In the case of a product determined by the Administrator, upon petition or on the Administrator's own motion, to be subject to the requirements of this section, the Administrator shall establish an effective date for such requirements. The effective date shall be 1 year after such determination or 30 months after November 15, 1990, whichever is later.
  (5) Effective January 1, 2015, the labeling requirements of this subsection[3] shall apply to all products manufactured with a process that uses a class I or class II substance.
(f) Relationship to other law
  (1) The labeling requirements of this section shall not constitute, in whole or part, a defense to liability or a cause for reduction in damages in any suit, whether civil or criminal, brought under any law, whether Federal or State, other than a suit for failure to comply with the labeling requirements of this section.
  (2) No other approval of such label by the Administrator under any other law administered by the Administrator shall be required with respect to the labeling requirements of this section.

(July 14, 1955, ch. 360, title VI, Sec. 611, as added Pub. L. 101-549, title VI, Sec. 602(a), Nov. 15, 1990, 104 Stat. 2665.)

SAFE ALTERNATIVES POLICY

42 USC 7671k

(a) Policy
  To the maximum extent practicable, class I and class II substances shall be replaced by chemicals, product substitutes, or alternative manufacturing processes that reduce overall risks to human health and the environment.
(b) Reviews and reports
  The Administrator shall—
  (1) in consultation and coordination with interested members of the public and the heads of relevant Federal agencies and departments, recommend Federal research programs and other activities to assist in identifying alternatives to the use of class I and class II substances as refrigerants, solvents, fire retardants, foam blowing agents, and other commercial applications and in achieving a transition to such alternatives, and, where appropriate, seek to maximize the use of Federal research facilities and resources to assist users of class I and class II substances in identifying and developing alternatives to the use of such substances as refrigerants, solvents, fire retardants, foam blowing agents, and other commercial applications;
  (2) examine in consultation and coordination with the Secretary of Defense and the heads of other relevant Federal agencies and departments, including the General Services Administration, Federal procurement practices with respect to class I and class II substances and recommend measures to promote the transition by the Federal Government, as expeditiously as possible, to the use of safe substitutes;
  (3) specify initiatives, including appropriate intergovernmental, international, and commercial information and technology transfers, to promote the development and use of safe substitutes for class I and class II substances, including alternative chemicals, product substitutes, and alternative manufacturing processes; and

---

[2]So in original. Probably should be "paragraph".
[3]So in original. Probably should be "section".

(4) maintain a public clearinghouse of alternative chemicals, product substitutes, and alternative manufacturing processes that are available for products and manufacturing processes which use class I and class II substances.

(c) Alternatives for class I or II substances

Within 2 years after November 15, 1990, the Administrator shall promulgate rules under this section providing that it shall be unlawful to replace any class I or class II substance with any substitute substance which the Administrator determines may present adverse effects to human health or the environment, where the Administrator has identified an alternative to such replacement that—

(1) reduces the overall risk to human health and the environment; and
(2) is currently or potentially available.

The Administrator shall publish a list of (A) the substitutes prohibited under this subsection for specific uses and (B) the safe alternatives identified under this subsection for specific uses.

(d) Right to petition

Any person may petition the Administrator to add a substance to the lists under subsection (c) of this section or to remove a substance from either of such lists. The Administrator shall grant or deny the petition within 90 days after receipt of any such petition. If the Administrator denies the petition, the Administrator shall publish an explanation of why the petition was denied. If the Administrator grants such petition the Administrator shall publish such revised list within 6 months thereafter. Any petition under this subsection shall include a showing by the petitioner that there are data on the substance adequate to support the petition. If the Administrator determines that information on the substance is not sufficient to make a determination under this subsection, the Administrator shall use any authority available to the Administrator, under any law administered by the Administrator, to acquire such information.

(e) Studies and notification

The Administrator shall require any person who produces a chemical substitute for a class I substance to provide the Administrator with such person's unpublished health and safety studies on such substitute and require producers to notify the Administrator not less than 90 days before new or existing chemicals are introduced into interstate commerce for significant new uses as substitutes for a class I substance. This subsection shall be subject to section 7414(c) of this title.

(July 14, 1955, ch. 360, title VI, Sec. 612, as added Pub. L. 101-549, title VI, Sec. 602(a), Nov. 15, 1990, 104 Stat. 2667.)

Section Referred to in Other Sections

This section is referred to in sections 7671g, 7671l of this title.

FEDERAL PROCUREMENT

42 USC 7671l

Not later than 18 months after November 15, 1990, the Administrator, in consultation with the Administrator of the General Services Administration and the Secretary of Defense, shall promulgate regulations requiring each department, agency, and instrumentality of the United States to conform its procurement regulations to the policies and requirements of this subchapter and to maximize the substitution of safe alternatives identified under section 7671k of this title for class I and class II substances. Not later than 30 months after November 15, 1990, each department, agency, and instrumentality of the United States shall so conform its procurement regulations and certify to the President that its regulations have been modified in accordance with this section.

(July 14, 1955, ch. 360, title VI, Sec. 613, as added Pub. L. 101-549, title VI, Sec. 602(a), Nov. 15, 1990, 104 Stat. 2668.)

Ex. Ord. No. 12843. Procurement Requirements and Policies for Federal Agencies for Ozone-Depleting Substances

Ex. Ord. No. 12843, Apr. 21, 1993, 58 F.R. 21881, provided:

WHEREAS, the essential function of the stratospheric ozone layer is shielding the Earth from dangerous ultraviolet radiation; and

WHEREAS, the production and consumption of substances that cause the depletion of stratospheric ozone are being rapidly phased out on a worldwide basis with the support and encouragement of the United States; and

WHEREAS, the Montreal Protocol on Substances that Deplete the Ozone Layer, to which the United States is a signatory, calls for a phaseout of the production and consumption of these substances; and

WHEREAS, the Federal Government, as one of the principal users of these substances, is able through affirmative procurement practices to reduce significantly the use of these substances and to provide leadership in their phaseout; and

WHEREAS, the use of alternative substances and new technologies to replace these ozone-depleting substances may contribute positively to the economic competitiveness on the world market of U.S. manufacturers of these innovative safe alternatives;

NOW, THEREFORE, I, WILLIAM JEFFERSON CLINTON, by the authority vested in me as President by the Constitution and the laws of the United States of America, including the 1990 amendments to the Clean Air Act ("Clean Air Act Amendments"), Public Law 101-549 [see Tables for classification], and in order to reduce the Federal Government's procurement and use of substances that cause stratospheric ozone depletion, do hereby order as follows:

Section 1. Federal Agencies. Federal agencies shall, to the extent practicable:

(a) conform their procurement regulations and practices to the policies and requirements of Title VI of the Clean Air Act Amendments [enacting this subchapter and repealing part B (Sec. 7451 et seq.) of subchapter I of this chapter], which deal with stratospheric ozone protection;

(b) maximize the use of safe alternatives to ozone-depleting substances;

(c) evaluate the present and future uses of ozone-depleting substances, including making assessments of existing and future needs for such materials and evaluate their use of and plans for recycling;

(d) revise their procurement practices and implement cost-effective programs both to modify specifications and contracts that require the use of ozone-depleting substances and to substitute non-ozone-depleting substances to the extent economically practicable; and

(e) exercise leadership, develop exemplary practices, and disseminate information on successful efforts in phasing out ozone-depleting substances.

Sec. 2. Definitions. (a) "Federal agency" means any executive department, military department, or independent agency within the meaning of 5 U.S.C. 101, 102, or 104(1), respectively.

(b) "Procurement" and "acquisition" are used interchangeably to refer to the processes through which Federal agencies purchase products and services.

(c) "Procurement regulations, policies and procedures" encompasses the complete acquisition process, including the generation of product descriptions by individuals responsible for determining which substances must be acquired by the agency to meet its mission.

(d) "Ozone-depleting substances" means the substances controlled internationally under the Montreal Protocol and nationally under Title VI of the Clean Air Act Amendments. This includes both Class I and Class II substances as follows:

   (i) "Class I substance" means any substance designated as Class I in the Federal Register notice of July 30, 1992 (57 Fed. Reg. 33753), including chlorofluorocarbons, halons, carbon tetrachloride, and methyl chloroform and any other substance so designated by the Environmental Protection Agency ("EPA") by regulation at a later date; and

   (ii) "Class II substance" means any substance designated as Class II in the Federal Register notice of July 30, 1992 (57 Fed. Reg. 33753), including hydrochlorofluorocarbons and any other substances so designated by EPA by regulation at a later date.

(e) "Recycling" is used to encompass recovery and reclamation, as well as the reuse of controlled substances.

Sec. 3. Policy. It is the policy of the Federal Government that Federal agencies: (i) implement cost-effective programs to minimize the procurement of materials and substances that contribute to the depletion of stratospheric ozone; and (ii) give preference to the procurement of alternative chemicals, products, and manufacturing processes that reduce overall risks to human health and the environment by lessening the depletion of ozone in the upper atmosphere. In implementing this policy, prior to final promulgation of EPA regulations on Federal procurement, Federal agencies shall begin conforming their procurement policies to the general requirements of Title VI of the Clean Air Act Amendments by:

(a) minimizing, where economically practicable, the procurement of products containing or manufactured with Class I substances in anticipation of the phaseout schedule to be promulgated by EPA for Class I substances, and maximizing the use of safe alternatives. In developing their procurement policies, agencies should be aware of the phaseout schedule for Class II substances;

(b) amending existing contracts, to the extent permitted by law and where practicable, to be consistent with the phaseout schedules for Class I substances. In awarding contracts, agencies should be aware of the phaseout schedule for Class II substances in awarding contracts;

(c) implementing policies and practices that recognize the increasingly limited availability of Class I substances as production levels capped by the Montreal Protocol decline until final phaseout. Such practices shall include, but are not limited to:
   (i) reducing emissions and recycling ozone-depleting substances;
   (ii) ceasing the purchase of nonessential products containing or manufactured with ozone-depleting substances; and
   (iii) requiring that new contracts provide that any acquired products containing or manufactured with Class I or Class II substances be labeled in accordance with section 611 of the Clean Air Act Amendments [probably means section 611 of the Clean Air Act, 42 U.S.C. 7671j].

Sec. 4. Responsibilities. Not later than 6 months after the effective date of this Executive order, each Federal agency, where feasible, shall have in place practices that, where economically practicable, minimize the procurement of Class I substances. Agencies also shall be aware of the phaseout schedule for Class II substances. Agency practices may include, but are not limited to:

(a) altering existing equipment and/or procedures to make use of safe alternatives;

(b) specifying the use of safe alternatives and of goods and services, where available, that do not require the use of Class I substances in new procurements and that limit the use of Class II substances consistent with section 612 of the Clean Air Act Amendments [probably means section 612 of the Clean Air Act, 42 U.S.C. 7671k]; and

(c) amending existing contracts, to the extent permitted by law and where practicable, to require the use of safe alternatives.

Sec. 5. Reporting Requirements. Not later than 6 months after the effective date of this Executive order, each Federal agency shall submit to the Office of Management and Budget a report regarding the implementation of this order. The report shall include a certification by each agency that its regulations and procurement practices are being amended to comply with this order.

Sec. 6. Exceptions. Exceptions to compliance with this Executive order may be made in accordance with section 604 of the Clean Air Act Amendments [probably means section 604 of the Clean Air Act, 42 U.S.C. 7671c] and with the provisions of the Montreal Protocol.

Sec. 7. Effective Date. This Executive order is effective 30 days after the date of issuance. Although full implementation of this order must await revisions to the Federal Acquisition Regulations ("FAR"), it is expected that Federal agencies will take all appropriate actions in the interim to implement those aspects of the order that are not dependent upon regulatory revision.

Sec. 8. Federal Acquisition Regulatory Councils. Pursuant to section 6(a) of the Office of Federal Procurement Policy Act, as amended, 41 U.S.C. 405(a), the Defense Acquisition Regulatory Council and the Civilian Agency Acquisition Council shall ensure that the policies established herein are incorporated in the FAR within 180 days from the date this order is issued.

Sec. 9. Judicial Review. This order does not create any right or benefit, substantive or procedural, enforceable by a non-Federal party against the United States, its officers or employees, or any other person.

William J. Clinton.

RELATIONSHIP TO OTHER LAWS

42 USC 7671m

(a) State laws
Notwithstanding section 7416 of this title, during the 2-year period beginning on November 15, 1990, no State or local government may enforce any requirement concerning the design of any new or recalled appliance for the purpose of protecting the stratospheric ozone layer.

(b) Montreal Protocol
This subchapter as added by the Clean Air Act Amendments of 1990 shall be construed, interpreted, and applied as a supplement to the terms and conditions of the Montreal Protocol, as provided in Article 2, paragraph 11 thereof, and shall not be construed, interpreted, or applied to abrogate the responsibilities or obligations of the United States to implement fully the provisions of the Montreal Protocol. In the case of conflict between any provision of this subchapter and any provision of the Montreal Protocol, the more stringent provision shall govern. Nothing in this subchapter shall be construed, interpreted, or applied to affect the authority or responsibility of the Administrator to implement Article 4 of the Montreal Protocol with other appropriate agencies.

(c) Technology export and overseas investment
Upon November 15, 1990, the President shall—
(1) prohibit the export of technologies used to produce a class I substance;
(2) prohibit direct or indirect investments by any person in facilities designed to produce a class I or class II substance in nations that are not parties to the Montreal Protocol; and
(3) direct that no agency of the government provide bilateral or multilateral subsidies, aids, credits, guarantees, or insurance programs, for the purpose of producing any class I substance.

(July 14, 1955, ch. 360, title VI, Sec. 614, as added Pub. L. 101-549, title VI, Sec. 602(a), Nov. 15, 1990, 104 Stat. 2668.)

References in Text

The Clean Air Act Amendments of 1990, referred to in subsec. (b), probably means Pub. L. 101-549, Nov. 15, 1990, 104 Stat. 2399. For complete classification of this Act to the Code, see Short Title of 1990 Amendment note set out under section 7401 of this title and Tables.

AUTHORITY OF ADMINISTRATOR

42 USC 7671n

If, in the Administrator's judgment, any substance, practice, process, or activity may reasonably be anticipated to affect the stratosphere, especially ozone in the stratosphere, and such effect may reasonably be anticipated to endanger public health or welfare, the Administrator shall promptly promulgate regulations respecting the control of such substance, practice, process, or activity, and shall submit notice of the proposal and promulgation of such regulation to the Congress.

(July 14, 1955, ch. 360, title VI, Sec. 615, as added Pub. L. 101-549, title VI, Sec. 602(a), Nov. 15, 1990, 104 Stat. 2669.)

TRANSFERS AMONG PARTIES TO MONTREAL PROTOCOL

42 USC 7671o

(a) In general
Consistent with the Montreal Protocol, the United States may engage in transfers with other Parties to the Protocol under the following conditions:
(1) The United States may transfer production allowances to another Party if, at the time of such transfer, the Administrator establishes revised production limits for the United States such that the aggregate national United States production permitted under the revised production limits equals the lesser of (A) the maximum production level permitted for the substance or substances concerned in the transfer year under the Protocol minus the pro-

duction allowances transferred, (B) the maximum production level permitted for the substance or substances concerned in the transfer year under applicable domestic law minus the production allowances transferred, or (C) the average of the actual national production level of the substance or substances concerned for the 3 years prior to the transfer minus the production allowances transferred.

(2) The United States may acquire production allowances from another Party if, at the time of such transfer, the Administrator finds that the other Party has revised its domestic production limits in the same manner as provided with respect to transfers by the United States in this subsection.

(b) Effect of transfers on production limits
The Administrator is authorized to reduce the production limits established under this chapter as required as a prerequisite to transfers under paragraph (1) of subsection (a) of this section or to increase production limits established under this chapter to reflect production allowances acquired under a transfer under paragraph (2) of subsection (a) of this section.

(c) Regulations
The Administrator shall promulgate, within 2 years after November 15, 1990, regulations to implement this section.

(d) "Applicable domestic law" defined
In the case of the United States, the term "applicable domestic law" means this chapter.

(July 14, 1955, ch. 360, title VI, Sec. 616, as added Pub. L. 101-549, title VI, Sec. 602(a), Nov. 15, 1990, 104 Stat. 2669.)

INTERNATIONAL COOPERATION

42 USC 7671p

(a) In general
The President shall undertake to enter into international agreements to foster cooperative research which complements studies and research authorized by this subchapter, and to develop standards and regulations which protect the stratosphere consistent with regulations applicable within the United States. For these purposes the President through the Secretary of State and the Assistant Secretary of State for Oceans and International Environmental and Scientific Affairs, shall negotiate multilateral treaties, conventions, resolutions, or other agreements, and formulate, present, or support proposals at the United Nations and other appropriate international forums and shall report to the Congress periodically on efforts to arrive at such agreements.

(b) Assistance to developing countries
The Administrator, in consultation with the Secretary of State, shall support global participation in the Montreal Protocol by providing technical and financial assistance to developing countries that are Parties to the Montreal Protocol and operating under article 5 of the Protocol. There are authorized to be appropriated not more than $30,000,000 to carry out this section in fiscal years 1991, 1992 and 1993 and such sums as may be necessary in fiscal years 1994 and 1995. If China and India become Parties to the Montreal Protocol, there are authorized to be appropriated not more than an additional $30,000,000 to carry out this section in fiscal years 1991, 1992, and 1993.

(July 14, 1955, ch. 360, title VI, Sec. 617, as added Pub. L. 101-549, title VI, Sec. 602(a), Nov. 15, 1990, 104 Stat. 2669.)

Authority of Secretary of State

Except as otherwise provided, Secretary of State to have and exercise any authority vested by law in any official or office of Department of State and references to such officials or offices deemed to refer to Secretary of State or Department of State, as appropriate, see section 2651a of Title 22, Foreign Relations and Intercourse, and section 161(d) of Pub. L. 103-236, set out as a note under section 2651a of Title 22.

MISCELLANEOUS PROVISIONS

42 USC 7671q

For purposes of section 7416 of this title, requirements concerning the areas addressed by this subchapter for the protection of the stratosphere against ozone layer depletion shall be treated as requirements for the control and abatement of air pollution. For purposes of section 7418 of this title, the requirements of this subchapter and corresponding State, interstate, and local requirements, administrative authority, and process, and sanctions respecting the protection of the stratospheric ozone layer shall be treated as requirements for the control and abatement of air pollution within the meaning of section 7418 of this title.

(July 14, 1955, ch. 360, title VI, Sec. 618, as added Pub. L. 101-549, title VI, Sec. 602(a), Nov. 15, 1990, 104 Stat. 2670.)

WATER POLLUTION PREVENTION AND CONTROL
[CLEAN WATER ACT]

as amended[1]
33 U.S.C. § 1251 et seq.

SUBCHAPTER I—RESEARCH AND RELATED PROGRAMS

CONGRESSIONAL DECLARATION OF GOALS AND POLICY

33 USC 1251

(a) Restoration and maintenance of chemical, physical and biological integrity of Nation's waters; national goals for achievement of objective

The objective of this chapter is to restore and maintain the chemical, physical, and biological integrity of the Nation's waters. In order to achieve this objective it is hereby declared that, consistent with the provisions of this chapter—
 (1) it is the national goal that the discharge of pollutants into the navigable waters be eliminated by 1985;
 (2) it is the national goal that wherever attainable, an interim goal of water quality which provides for the protection and propagation of fish, shellfish, and wildlife and provides for recreation in and on the water be achieved by July 1, 1983;
 (3) it is the national policy that the discharge of toxic pollutants in toxic amounts be prohibited;
 (4) it is the national policy that Federal financial assistance be provided to construct publicly owned waste treatment works;
 (5) it is the national policy that areawide waste treatment management planning processes be developed and implemented to assure adequate control of sources of pollutants in each State;
 (6) it is the national policy that a major research and demonstration effort be made to develop technology necessary to eliminate the discharge of pollutants into the navigable waters, waters of the contiguous zone, and the oceans; and
 (7) it is the national policy that programs for the control of nonpoint sources of pollution be developed and implemented in an expeditious manner so as to enable the goals of this chapter to be met through the control of both point and nonpoint sources of pollution.

(b) Congressional recognition, preservation, and protection of primary responsibilities and rights of States

It is the policy of the Congress to recognize, preserve, and protect the primary responsibilities and rights of States to prevent, reduce, and eliminate pollution, to plan the development and use (including restoration, preservation, and enhancement) of land and water resources, and to consult with the Administrator in the exercise of his authority under this chapter. It is the policy of Congress that the States manage the construction grant program under this chapter and implement the permit programs under sections 1342 and 1344 of this title. It is further the policy of the Congress to support and aid research relating to the prevention, reduction, and elimination of pollution and to provide Federal technical services and financial aid to State and interstate agencies and municipalities in connection with the prevention, reduction, and elimination of pollution.

---

[1]Editor's note: Text from Title 33, Chapter 26 of U.S. Code, amended by Pub. L. 108-136, November 24, 2003; Pub. L. 107-295, Nov. 25, 2002 ; Pub. L. 107-303, Nov. 27, 2992; Pub. L. 107-73, July 25, 2001; Pub. L. 106-554, Dec. 21, 2000; Pub. L. 106-541, Dec. 11, 2000; Pub. L. 106-457, Nov. 7, 2000; Pub. L. 106-377, Oct. 27, 2000; and Pub. L. 106-284, Oct. 10, 2000.

412 / Environmental Statutes

(c) Congressional policy toward Presidential activities with foreign countries

It is further the policy of Congress that the President, acting through the Secretary of State and such national and international organizations as he determines appropriate, shall take such action as may be necessary to insure that to the fullest extent possible all foreign countries shall take meaningful action for the prevention, reduction, and elimination of pollution in their waters and in international waters and for the achievement of goals regarding the elimination of discharge of pollutants and the improvement of water quality to at least the same extent as the United States does under its laws.

(d) Administrator of Environmental Protection Agency to administer chapter

Except as otherwise expressly provided in this chapter, the Administrator of the Environmental Protection Agency (hereinafter in this chapter called "Administrator") shall administer this chapter.

(e) Public participation in development, revision, and enforcement of any regulation, etc.

Public participation in the development, revision, and enforcement of any regulation, standard, effluent limitation, plan, or program established by the Administrator or any State under this chapter shall be provided for, encouraged, and assisted by the Administrator and the States. The Administrator, in cooperation with the States, shall develop and publish regulations specifying minimum guidelines for public participation in such processes.

(f) Procedures utilized for implementing chapter

It is the national policy that to the maximum extent possible the procedures utilized for implementing this chapter shall encourage the drastic minimization of paperwork and interagency decision procedures, and the best use of available manpower and funds, so as to prevent needless duplication and unnecessary delays at all levels of government.

(g) Authority of States over water

It is the policy of Congress that the authority of each State to allocate quantities of water within its jurisdiction shall not be superseded, abrogated or otherwise impaired by this chapter. It is the further policy of Congress that nothing in this chapter shall be construed to supersede or abrogate rights to quantities of water which have been established by any State. Federal agencies shall co-operate with State and local agencies to develop comprehensive solutions to prevent, reduce and eliminate pollution in concert with programs for managing water resources.

(June 30, 1948, ch. 758, title I, Sec. 101, as added Pub. L. 92-500, Sec. 2, Oct. 18, 1972, 86 Stat. 816; amended Pub. L. 95-217, Secs. 5(a), 26(b), Dec. 27, 1977, 91 Stat. 1567, 1575; Pub. L. 100-4, title III, Sec. 316(b), Feb. 4, 1987, 101 Stat. 60.)

Codification

The Federal Water Pollution Control Act, comprising this chapter, was originally enacted by act June 30, 1948, ch. 758, 62 Stat. 1155, and amended by acts July 17, 1952, ch. 927, 66 Stat. 755; July 9, 1956, ch. 518, Secs. 1, 2, 70 Stat. 498-507; June 25, 1959, Pub. L. 86-70, 73 Stat. 141; July 12, 1960, Pub. L. 86-624, 74 Stat. 411; July 20, 1961, Pub. L. 87-88, 75 Stat. 204; Oct. 2, 1965, Pub. L. 89-234, 79 Stat. 903; Nov. 3, 1966, Pub. L. 89-753, 80 Stat. 1246; Apr. 3, 1970, Pub. L. 91-224, 84 Stat. 91; Dec. 31, 1970, Pub. L. 91-611, 84 Stat. 1818; July 9, 1971, Pub. L. 92-50, 85 Stat. 124; Oct. 13, 1971, Pub. L. 92-137, 85 Stat. 379; Mar. 1, 1972, Pub. L. 92-240, 86 Stat. 47, and was formerly classified first to section 466 et seq. of this title and later to section 1151 et seq. of this title. The act is shown herein, however, as having been added by Pub. L. 92-500 without reference to such intervening amendments because of the extensive amendment, reorganization, and expansion of the act's provisions by Pub. L. 92-500.

Amendments

1987—Subsec. (a)(7). Pub. L. 100-4 added par. (7).

1977—Subsec. (b). Pub. L. 95-217, Sec. 26(b), inserted provisions expressing Congressional policy that the States manage the construction grant program under this chapter and implement the permit program under sections 1342 and 1344 of this title.

Subsec. (g). Pub. L. 95-217, Sec. 5(a), added subsec. (g).

Short Title of 2002 Amendment

Pub. L. 107-303, table of contents, Sec. 1, Nov. 27, 2002, 116 Stat. 2355, provided that: "This Act may be cited as the ``Great Lakes and Lake Champlain Act of 2002".

Pub. L. 107-303, title I, Sec. 101, Nov. 27, 2002, 116 Stat. 2355 provided that: This title may be cited as the "Great Lakes Legacy Act of 2002".

Pub. L. 107-303, title II, Sec. 201, Nov. 27, 2002, 116 Stat. 2358, provided that: This title may be cited as the "Daniel Patrick Moynihan Lake Champlain Basin Program Act of 2002".

Short Title of 2000 Amendment

Pub. L. 106-457, title II, Sec. 201, Nov. 7, 2000, 114 Stat. 1967, provided that: "This title [amending section 1267 of this title and enacting provisions set out as a note under section 1267 of this title] may be cited as the 'Chesapeake Bay Restoration Act of 2000'."

Pub. L. 106-457, title IV, Sec. 401, Nov. 7, 2000, 114 Stat. 1973, provided that: "This title [amending section 1269 of this title] may be cited as the 'Long Island Sound Restoration Act'."

Pub. L. 106-457, title V, Sec. 501, Nov. 7, 2000, 114 Stat. 1973, provided that: "This title [enacting section 1273 of this title] may be cited as the 'Lake Pontchartrain Basin Restoration Act of 2000'."

Pub. L. 106-457, title VI, Sec. 601, Nov. 7, 2000, 114 Stat. 1975, provided that: "This title [enacting section 1300 of this title] may be cited as the 'Alternative Water Sources Act of 2000'."

Pub. L. 106-284, Sec. 1, Oct. 10, 2000, 114 Stat. 870, provided that: "This Act [enacting sections 1346 and 1375a of this title and amending sections 1254, 1313, 1314, 1362, and 1377 of this title] may be cited as the 'Beaches Environmental Assessment and Coastal Health Act of 2000'."

Short Title of 1994 Amendment

Pub. L. 103-431, Sec. 1, Oct. 31, 1994, 108 Stat. 4396, provided that: "This Act [amending section 1311 of this title] may be cited as the 'Ocean Pollution Reduction Act'."

Short Title of 1990 Amendment

Pub. L. 101-596, Sec. 1, Nov. 16, 1990, 104 Stat. 3000, provided that: "This Act [enacting sections 1269 and 1270 of this title, amending sections 1268, 1324, and 1416 of this title, and enacting provisions set out as notes under this section and section 1270 of this title] may be cited as the 'Great Lakes Critical Programs Act of 1990'."

Pub. L. 101-596, title II, Sec. 201, Nov. 16, 1990, 104 Stat. 3004, provided that: "This part [probably means title, enacting section 1269 of this title and amending section 1416 of this title] may be cited as the 'Long Island Sound Improvement Act of 1990'."

Pub. L. 101-596, title III, Sec. 301, Nov. 16, 1990, 104 Stat. 3006, provided that: "This title [enacting section 1270 of this title, amending section 1324 of this title, and enacting provisions set out as a note under section 1270 of this title] may be cited as the 'Lake Champlain Special Designation Act of 1990'."

Short Title of 1988 Amendment

Pub. L. 100-653, title X, Sec. 1001, Nov. 14, 1988, 102 Stat. 3835, provided that: "This title [amending section 1330 of this title and enacting provisions set out as notes under section 1330 of this title] may be cited as the 'Massachusetts Bay Protection Act of 1988'."

Short Title of 1987 Amendment

Section 1(a) of Pub. L. 100-4 provided that: "This Act [enacting sections 1254a, 1267, 1268, 1281b, 1329, 1330, 1377, 1381 to 1387, and 1414a of this title, amending this section and sections 1254, 1256, 1262, 1281, 1282 to 1285, 1287, 1288, 1291, 1311 to 1313, 1314, 1317 to 1322, 1324, 1342, 1344, 1345, 1361, 1362, 1365, 1369, 1375, and 1376 of this title, and enacting provisions set out as notes under this section, sections 1284, 1311, 1317, 1319, 1330, 1342, 1345, 1362, 1375, and 1414a of this title, and section 1962d-20 of Title 42, The Public Health and Welfare] may be cited as the 'Water Quality Act of 1987'."

Short Title of 1981 Amendment

Pub. L. 97-117, Sec. 1, Dec. 29, 1981, 95 Stat. 1623, provided that: "This Act [enacting sections 1298, 1299, and 1313a of this title, amending sections 1281 to 1285, 1287, 1291, 1292, 1296, 1311, and 1314 of this title, and enacting provisions set out as notes under sections 1311 and 1375 of this title] may be cited as the 'Municipal Wastewater Treatment Construction Grant Amendments of 1981'."

Short Title of 1977 Amendment

Section 1 of Pub. L. 95-217 provided: "That this Act [enacting sections 1281a, 1294 to 1296, and 1297 of this title, amending this section and sections 1252, 1254 to 1256, 1259, 1262, 1263, 1281, 1282 to 1288, 1291, 1292, 1311, 1314, 1315, 1317 to 1319, 1321 to 1324, 1328, 1341, 1342, 1344, 1345, 1362, 1364, 1375, and 1376 of this title, enacting provisions set out as notes under this section and sections 1284, 1286, 1314, 1321, 1342, 1344, and 1376 of this title, and amending provisions set out as a note under this section] may be cited as the 'Clean Water Act of 1977'."

Short Title

Section 1 of Pub. L. 92-500 provided that: "That this Act [enacting this chapter, amending section 24 of Title 12, Banks and Banking, sections 633 and 636 of Title 15, Commerce and Trade, and section 711 of former Title 31, Money and Finance, and enacting provisions set out as notes under this section and sections 1281 and 1361 of this title] may be cited as the 'Federal Water Pollution Control Act Amendments of 1972'."

Section 519, formerly section 518, of Act June 30, 1948, ch. 758, title V, as added Oct. 18, 1972, Pub. L. 92-500, Sec. 2, 86 Stat. 896, and amended Dec. 27, 1977, Pub. L. 95-217, Sec. 2, 91 Stat. 1566, and renumbered Sec. 519, Feb. 4, 1987, Pub. L. 100-4, title V, Sec. 506, 101 Stat. 76, provided that: "This Act [this chapter] may be cited as the 'Federal Water Pollution Control Act' (commonly referred to as the Clean Water Act)."

Savings Provision

Section 4 of Pub. L. 92-500 provided that:

"(a) No suit, action, or other proceeding lawfully commenced by or against the Administrator or any other officer or employee of the United States in his official capacity or in relation to the discharge of his official duties under the Federal Water Pollution Control Act as in effect immediately prior to the date of enactment of this Act [Oct. 18, 1972] shall abate by reason of the taking effect of the amendment made by section 2 of this Act [which enacted this chapter]. The court may, on its own motion or that of any party made at any time within twelve months after such taking effect, allow the same to be maintained by or against the Administrator or such officer or employee.

"(b) All rules, regulations, orders, determinations, contracts, certifications, authorizations, delegations, or other actions duly issued, made, or taken by or pursuant to the Federal Water Pollution Control Act as in effect immediately prior to the date of enactment of this Act [Oct. 18, 1972], and pertaining to any functions, powers, requirements, and duties under the Federal Water Pollution Control Act as in effect immediately prior to the date of enactment of this Act [Oct. 18, 1972] shall continue in full force and effect after the date of enactment of this Act [Oct. 18, 1972] until modified or rescinded in accordance with the Federal Water Pollution Control Act as amended by this Act [this chapter].

"(c) The Federal Water Pollution Control Act as in effect immediately prior to the date of enactment of this Act [Oct. 18, 1972] shall remain applicable to all grants made from funds authorized for the fiscal year ending June 30, 1972, and prior fiscal years, including any increases in the monetary amount of any such grant which may be paid from authorizations for fiscal years beginning after June 30, 1972, except as specifically otherwise provided in section 202 of the Federal Water Pollution Control Act as amended by this Act [section 1282 of this title] and in subsection (c) of section 3 of this Act."

Separability

Section 512 of act June 30, 1948, ch. 758, title V, as added Oct. 18, 1972, Pub. L. 92-500, Sec. 2, 86 Stat. 894, provided that: "If any provision of this Act [this chapter], or the application of any provision of this Act [this chapter] to any person or circumstance, is held invalid, the application of such provision to other persons or circumstances, and the remainder of this Act [this chapter], shall not be affected thereby."

National Shellfish Indicator Program

Pub. L. 102-567, title III, Sec. 308, Oct. 29, 1992, 106 Stat. 4286; as amended by Pub. L. 105-362, title II, Sec. 201(b), Nov. 10, 1998, 112 Stat. 3282, provided that:

"(a) Establishment of a Research Program.—The Secretary of Commerce, in cooperation with the Secretary of Health and Human Services and the Administrator of the Environmental Protection Agency, shall establish and administer a 5-year national shellfish research program (hereafter in this section referred to as the 'Program') for the purpose of improving existing classification systems for shellfish growing waters using the latest technological advancements in microbiology and epidemiological methods. Within 12 months after the date of enactment of this Act [Oct. 29, 1992], the Secretary of Commerce, in cooperation with the advisory committee established under subsection (b) and the Consortium, shall develop a comprehensive 5-year plan for the Program which shall at a minimum provide for—

  (1) an environmental assessment of commercial shellfish growing areas in the United States, including an evaluation of the relationships between indicators of fecal contamination and human enteric pathogens;
  (2) the evaluation of such relationships with respect to potential health hazards associated with human consumption of shellfish;
  (3) a comparison of the current microbiological methods used for evaluating indicator bacteria and human enteric pathogens in shellfish and shellfish growing waters with new technological methods designed for this purpose;
  (4) the evaluation of current and projected systems for human sewage treatment in eliminating viruses and other human enteric pathogens which accumulate in shellfish;
  (5) the design of epidemiological studies to relate microbiological data, sanitary survey data, and human shellfish consumption data to actual hazards to health associated with such consumption; and
  (6) recommendations for revising Federal shellfish standards and improving the capabilities of Federal and State agencies to effectively manage shellfish and ensure the safety of shellfish intended for human consumption.

(b) Advisory Committee.—(1) For the purpose of providing oversight of the Program on a continuing basis, an advisory committee (hereafter in this section referred to as the 'Committee') shall be established under a memorandum of understanding between the Interstate Shellfish Sanitation Conference and the National Marine Fisheries Service.

  (2) The Committee shall—
    (A) identify priorities for achieving the purpose of the Program;
    (B) review and recommend approval or disapproval of Program work plans and plans of operation;
    (C) review and comment on all subcontracts and grants to be awarded under the Program;
    (D) receive and review progress reports from the Consortium and program subcontractors and grantees; and
    (E) provide such other advice on the Program as is appropriate.
  (3) The Committee shall consist of at least ten members and shall include—
    (A) three members representing agencies having authority under State law to regulate the shellfish industry, of whom one shall represent each of the Atlantic, Pacific, and Gulf of Mexico shellfish growing regions;
    (B) three members representing persons engaged in the shellfish industry in the Atlantic, Pacific, and Gulf of Mexico shellfish growing regions (who shall be appointed from among at least six recommendations by the industry members of the Interstate Shellfish Sanitation Conference Executive Board), of whom one shall represent the shellfish industry in each region;
    (C) three members, of whom one shall represent each of the following Federal agencies: the National Oceanic and Atmospheric Administration, the Environmental Protection Agency, and the Food and Drug Administration; and
    (D) one member representing the Shellfish Institute of North America.
  (4) The Chairman of the Committee shall be selected from among the Committee members described in paragraph (3)(A).

(5) The Committee shall establish and maintain a subcommittee of scientific experts to provide advice, assistance, and information relevant to research funded under the Program, except that no individual who is awarded, or whose application is being considered for, a grant or subcontract under the Program may serve on such subcommittee. The membership of the subcommittee shall, to the extent practicable, be regionally balanced with experts who have scientific knowledge concerning each of the Atlantic, Pacific, and Gulf of Mexico shellfish growing regions. Scientists from the National Academy of Sciences and appropriate Federal agencies (including the National Oceanic and Atmospheric Administration, Food and Drug Administration, Centers for Disease Control, National Institutes of Health, Environmental Protection Agency, and National Science Foundation) shall be considered for membership on the subcommittee.

(6) Members of the Committee and its scientific subcommittee established under this subsection shall not be paid for serving on the Committee or subcommittee, but shall receive travel expenses as authorized by section 5703 of title 5, United States Code.

(c) Contract With Consortium.—Within 30 days after the date of enactment of this Act [Oct. 29, 1992], the Secretary of Commerce shall seek to enter into a cooperative agreement or contract with the Consortium under which the Consortium will—
  (1) be the academic administrative organization and fiscal agent for the Program;
  (2) award and administer such grants and subcontracts as are approved by the Committee under subsection (b);
  (3) develop and implement a scientific peer review process for evaluating grant and subcontractor applications prior to review by the Committee;
  (4) in cooperation with the Secretary of Commerce and the Committee, procure the services of a scientific project director;
  (5) develop and submit budgets, progress reports, work plans, and plans of operation for the Program to the Secretary of Commerce and the Committee; and
  (6) make available to the Committee such staff, information, and assistance as the Committee may reasonably require to carry out its activities.

(d) Authorization of Appropriations.—
  (1) Of the sums authorized under section 4(a) of the National Oceanic and Atmospheric Administration Marine Fisheries Program Authorization Act (Public Law 98-210; 97 Stat. 1409), there are authorized to be appropriated to the Secretary of Commerce $5,200,000 for each of the fiscal years 1993 through 1997 for carrying out the Program. Of the amounts appropriated pursuant to this authorization, not more than 5 percent of such appropriation may be used for administrative purposes by the National Oceanic and Atmospheric Administration. The remaining 95 percent of such appropriation shall be used to meet the administrative and scientific objectives of the Program.
  (2) The Interstate Shellfish Sanitation Conference shall not administer appropriations authorized under this section, but may be reimbursed from such appropriations for its expenses in arranging for travel, meetings, workshops, or conferences necessary to carry out the Program.

(e) Definitions.—As used in this section, the term—
  (1) 'Consortium' means the Louisiana Universities Marine Consortium; and
  (2) 'shellfish' means any species of oyster, clam, or mussel that is harvested for human consumption."

Limitation on Payments

Section 2 of Pub. L. 100-4 provided that: "No payments may be made under this Act [see Short Title of 1987 Amendment note above] except to the extent provided in advance in appropriation Acts."

Seafood Processing Study;
Submittal of Results to Congress not Later Than January 1, 1979

Pub. L. 95-217, Sec. 74, Dec. 27, 1977, 91 Stat. 1609, provided that the Administrator of the Environmental Protection Agency conduct a study to examine the geographical, hydrological, and biological characteristics of marine waters to determine the effects of seafood processes which dispose of untreated natural wastes into such waters and to include in this study an examination of technologies which may be used in such processes to facilitate the use of the nutrients in these wastes or to reduce the discharge of such wastes into the marine environment and to submit the result of this study to Congress not later than Jan. 1, 1979.

Standards

For provisions relating to the responsibility of the head of each Executive agency for compliance with applicable pollution control standards, see Ex. Ord. No. 12088, Oct. 13, 1978, 43 F.R. 47707, set out as a note under section 4321 of Title 42, The Public Health and Welfare.

Oversight Study

Section 5 of Pub. L. 92-500 authorized the Comptroller General of the United States to conduct a study and review of the research, pilot, and demonstration programs related to prevention and control of water pollution conducted, supported, or assisted by any Federal agency pursuant to any Federal law or regulation and assess conflicts between these programs and their coordination and efficacy, and to report to Congress thereon by Oct. 1, 1973.

International Trade Study

Section 6 of Pub. L. 92-500 provided that:

"(a) The Secretary of Commerce, in cooperation with other interested Federal agencies and with representatives of industry and the public, shall undertake immediately an investigation and study to determine—

"(1) the extent to which pollution abatement and control programs will be imposed on, or voluntarily undertaken by, United States manufacturers in the near future and the probable short- and long-range effects of the costs of such programs (computed to the greatest extent practicable on an industry-by-industry basis) on (A) the production costs of such domestic manufacturers, and (B) the market prices of the goods produced by them;

"(2) the probable extent to which pollution abatement and control programs will be implemented in foreign industrial nations in the near future and the extent to which the production costs (computed to the greatest extent practicable on an industry-by-industry basis) of foreign manufacturers will be affected by the costs of such programs;

"(3) the probable competitive advantage which any article manufactured in a foreign nation will likely have in relation to a comparable article made in the United States if that foreign nation—

"(A) does not require its manufacturers to implement pollution abatement and control programs.

"(B) requires a lesser degree of pollution abatement and control in its programs, or

"(C) in any way reimburses or otherwise subsidizes its manufacturers for the costs of such program;

"(4) alternative means by which any competitive advantage accruing to the products of any foreign nation as a result of any factor described in paragraph (3) may be (A) accurately and quickly determined, and (B) equalized, for example, by the imposition of a surcharge or duty, on a foreign product in an amount necessary to compensate for such advantage; and

"(5) the impact, if any, which the imposition of a compensating tariff of other equalizing measure may have in encouraging foreign nations to implement pollution and abatement control programs.

"(b) The Secretary shall make an initial report to the President and Congress within six months after the date of enactment of this section [Oct. 18, 1972] of the results of the study and investigation carried out pursuant to this section and shall make additional reports thereafter at such times as he deems appropriate taking into account the development of relevant data, but not less than once every twelve months."

International Agreements

Section 7 of Pub. L. 92-500 provided that: "The President shall undertake to enter into international agreement to apply uniform standards of performance for the control of the discharge and emission of pollutants from new sources, uniform controls over the discharge and emission of toxic pollutants, and uniform controls over the discharge of pollutants into the ocean. For this purpose the President shall negotiate multilateral treaties, conventions, resolutions, or other agreements, and formulate, present, or support proposals at the United Nations and other appropriate international forums."

National Policies and Goal Study

Section 10 of Pub. L. 92-500 directed President to make a full and complete investigation and study of all national policies and goals established by law to determine what the relationship should be between these policies and goals, taking into account the resources of the Nation, and to report results of his investigation and study together with his recommendations to Congress not later than two years after Oct. 18, 1972.

Efficiency Study

Section 11 of Pub. L. 92-500 directed President, by utilization of the General Accounting Office, to conduct a full and complete investigation and study of ways and means of most effectively using all of the various resources, facilities, and personnel of the Federal Government in order to most efficiently carry out the provisions of this chapter and to report results of his investigation and study together with his recommendations to Congress not later than two hundred and seventy days after Oct. 18, 1972.

Sex Discrimination

Section 13 of Pub. L. 92-500 provided that: "No person in the United States shall on the ground of sex be excluded from participation in, be denied the benefits of, or be subjected to discrimination under any program or activity receiving Federal assistance under this Act [see Short Title note above] the Federal Water Pollution Control Act [this chapter], or the Environmental Financing Act [set out as a note under section 1281 of this title]. This section shall be enforced through agency provisions and rules similar to those already established, with respect to racial and other discrimination, under title VI of the Civil Rights Act of 1964 [section 2000d et seq. of Title 42, The Public Health and Welfare]. However, this remedy is not exclusive and will not prejudice or cut off any other legal remedies available to a discriminatee."

Contiguous Zone of United States

For extension of contiguous zone of United States, see Proc. No. 7219, set out as a note under section 1331 of Title 43, Public Lands.

Prevention, Control, and Abatement of Environmental Pollution at Federal Facilities

Ex. Ord. No. 12088, Oct. 13, 1978, 43 F.R. 47707, set out as a note under section 4321 of Title 42, The Public Health and Welfare, provides for the prevention, control, and abatement of environmental pollution at federal facilities.

Executive Order No. 11548

Ex. Ord. No. 11548, July 20, 1970, 35 F.R. 11677, which related to the delegation of Presidential functions, was superseded by Ex. Ord. No. 11735, Aug. 3, 1973, 38 F.R. 21243, formerly set out as a note under section 1321 of this title.

Ex. Ord. No. 11742. Delegation of Functions to Secretary of State Respecting the Negotiation of International Agreements Relating to the Enhancement of the Environment

Ex. Ord. No. 11742, Oct. 23, 1973, 38 F.R. 29457, provided:

Under and by virtue of the authority vested in me by section 301 of title 3 of the United States Code and as President of the United States, I hereby authorize and empower the Secretary of State, in coordination with the Council on Environmental Quality, the Environmental Protection Agency, and other appropriate Federal agencies, to perform, without the approval, ratification, or other action of the President, the functions vested in the President by Section 7 of the Federal Water Pollution Control Act Amendments of 1972 (Public Law 92-500; 86 Stat. 898) with respect to international agreements relating to the enhancement of the environment.

Richard Nixon.

Definition of "Administrator"

Section 1(d) of Pub. L. 100-4 provided that: "For purposes of this Act [see Short Title of 1987 Amendment note above], the term 'Administrator' means the Administrator of the Environmental Protection Agency."

Section Referred to in Other Sections

This section is referred to in sections 1267, 1268, 1300, 1311, 1377 of this title.

COMPREHENSIVE PROGRAMS FOR WATER POLLUTION CONTROL

33 USC 1252

(a) Preparation and development

The Administrator shall, after careful investigation, and in cooperation with other Federal agencies, State water pollution control agencies, interstate agencies, and the municipalities and industries involved, prepare or develop comprehensive programs for preventing, reducing, or eliminating the pollution of the navigable waters and ground waters and improving the sanitary condition of surface and underground waters. In the development of such comprehensive programs due regard shall be given to the improvements which are necessary to conserve such waters for the protection and propagation of fish and aquatic life and wildlife, recreational purposes, and the withdrawal of such waters for public water supply, agricultural, industrial, and other purposes. For the purpose of this section, the Administrator is authorized to make joint investigations with any such agencies of the condition of any waters in any State or States, and of the discharges of any sewage, industrial wastes, or substance which may adversely affect such waters.

(b) Planning for reservoirs; storage for regulation of streamflow

(1) In the survey or planning of any reservoir by the Corps of Engineers, Bureau of Reclamation, or other Federal agency, consideration shall be given to inclusion of storage for regulation of streamflow, except that any such storage and water releases shall not be provided as a substitute for adequate treatment or other methods of controlling waste at the source.

(2) The need for and the value of storage for regulation of streamflow (other than for water quality) including but not limited to navigation, salt water intrusion, recreation, esthetics, and fish and wildlife, shall be determined by the Corps of Engineers, Bureau of Reclamation, or other Federal agencies.

(3) The need for, the value of, and the impact of, storage for water quality control shall be determined by the Administrator, and his views on these matters shall be set forth in any report or presentation to Congress proposing authorization or construction of any reservoir including such storage.

(4) The value of such storage shall be taken into account in determining the economic value of the entire project of which it is a part, and costs shall be allocated to the purpose of regulation of streamflow in a manner which will insure that all project purposes, share equitably in the benefit of multiple-purpose construction.

(5) Costs of regulation of streamflow features incorporated in any Federal reservoir or other impoundment under the provisions of this chapter shall be determined and the beneficiaries identified and if the benefits are widespread or national in scope, the costs of such features shall be nonreimbursable.

(6) No license granted by the Federal Energy Regulatory for a hydroelectric power project shall include storage for regulation of streamflow for the purpose of water quality control unless the Administrator shall recommend its inclusion and such reservoir storage capacity shall not exceed such proportion of the total storage required for the water quality control plan as the drainage area of such reservoir bears to the drainage area of the river basin or basins involved in such water quality control plan.

(c) Basins; grants to State agencies

(1) The Administrator shall, at the request of the Governor of a State, or a majority of the Governors when more than one State is involved, make a grant to pay not to exceed 50 per centum of the administrative expenses of a planning agency for a period not to exceed three years, which period shall begin after October 18, 1972, if such agency provides for adequate representation of appropriate State, interstate, local, or (when appropriate) international interests in the basin or portion thereof involved and is capable of developing an effective, comprehensive water quality control plan for a basin or portion thereof.

(2) Each planning agency receiving a grant under this subsection shall develop a comprehensive pollution control plan for the basin or portion thereof which—

420 / Environmental Statutes

(A) is consistent with any applicable water quality standards effluent and other limitations, and thermal discharge regulations established pursuant to current law within the basin;
(B) recommends such treatment works as will provide the most effective and economical means of collection, storage, treatment, and elimination of pollutants and recommends means to encourage both municipal and industrial use of such works;
(C) recommends maintenance and improvement of water quality within the basin or portion thereof and recommends methods of adequately financing those facilities as may be necessary to implement the plan; and
(D) as appropriate, is developed in cooperation with, and is consistent with any comprehensive plan prepared by the Water Resources Council, any areawide waste management plans developed pursuant to section 1288 of this title, and any State plan developed pursuant to section 1313(e) of this title.
(3) For the purposes of this subsection the term "basin" includes, but is not limited to, rivers and their tributaries, streams, coastal waters, sounds, estuaries, bays, lakes, and portions thereof as well as the lands drained thereby.

(June 30, 1948, ch. 758, title I, Sec. 102, as added Pub. L. 92-500, Sec. 2, Oct. 18, 1972, 86 Stat. 817; amended Pub. L. 95-91, title IV, Sec. 402(a)(1)(A), Aug. 4, 1977, 91 Stat. 583; Pub. L. 95-217, Sec. 5(b), Dec. 27, 1977, 91 Stat. 1567; Pub. L. 104-66, title II, Sec. 2021(a), Dec. 21, 1995, 109 Stat. 726.)

Amendments

1995—Subsec. (d). Pub. L. 104-66 struck out subsec. (d) which read as follows: "The Administrator, after consultation with the States, and River Basin Commissions established under the Water Resources Planning Act, shall submit a report to Congress on or before July 1, 1978, which analyzes the relationship between programs under this chapter, and the programs by which State and Federal agencies allocate quantities of water. Such report shall include recommendations concerning the policy in section 1251(g) of this title to improve coordination of efforts to reduce and eliminate pollution in concert with programs for managing water resources."
1977—Subsec. (d). Pub. L. 95-217 added subsec. (d).

Transfer of Functions

"Federal Energy Regulatory Commission" substituted for "Federal Power Commission" in subsec. (b)(6) on authority of Pub. L. 95-91, title IV, Sec. 402(a)(1)(A), Aug. 4, 1977, 91 Stat. 583, which is classified to section 7172(a)(1)(A) of Title 42, The Public Health and Welfare.

Executive Order No. 10014

Ex. Ord. No. 10014, Nov. 3, 1948, 13 F.R. 6601, which related to the cooperation of Federal and State agencies to prevent pollution of surface and underground waters, was superseded by Ex. Ord. No. 11258, Nov. 17, 1965, 30 F.R. 14483.

Section Referred to in Other Sections

This section is referred to in section 1252a of this title.

RESERVOIR PROJECTS, WATER STORAGE; MODIFICATION; STORAGE FOR OTHER THAN FOR WATER QUALITY, OPINION OF FEDERAL AGENCY, COMMITTEE RESOLUTIONS OF APPROVAL; PROVISIONS INAPPLICABLE TO PROJECTS WITH CERTAIN PRESCRIBED WATER QUALITY BENEFITS IN RELATION TO TOTAL PROJECT BENEFITS

33 USC 1252a

In the case of any reservoir project authorized for construction by the Corps of Engineers, Bureau of Reclamation, or other Federal agency when the Administrator of the Environmental Protection Agency determines pursuant to section 1252(b) of this title that any storage in such project for regulation of streamflow for water quality is not needed, or is needed in a different amount, such project may be modified accordingly by the head of the appropriate agency, and any storage no longer required for water quality may be utilized for other authorized purposes of the project when, in the opinion of the head of such agency, such use is justified. Any such modification of a project where the benefits attributable to water quality are 15 per centum or more but not greater than 25 per centum of the total project benefits shall take effect only upon the adoption of resolutions approving such modification by the appropriate committees of the Senate and House of Representatives. The provisions of the section shall not apply to any project where the benefits attributable to water quality exceed 25 per centum of the total project benefits.

(Pub. L. 93-251, title I, Sec. 65, Mar. 7, 1974, 88 Stat. 30.)

Codification

Section was not enacted as part of the Federal Water Pollution Control Act which comprises this chapter.

INTERSTATE COOPERATION AND UNIFORM LAWS

33 USC 1253

(a) The Administrator shall encourage cooperative activities by the States for the prevention, reduction, and elimination of pollution, encourage the enactment of improved and, so far as practicable, uniform State laws relating to the prevention, reduction, and elimination of pollution; and encourage compacts between States for the prevention and control of pollution.

(b) The consent of the Congress is hereby given to two or more States to negotiate and enter into agreements or compacts, not in conflict with any law or treaty of the United States, for (1) cooperative effort and mutual assistance for the prevention and control of pollution and the enforcement of their respective laws relating thereto, and (2) the establishment of such agencies, joint or otherwise, as they may deem desirable for making effective such agreements and compacts. No such agreement or compact shall be binding or obligatory upon any State a party thereto unless and until it has been approved by the Congress.

(June 30, 1948, ch. 758, title I, Sec. 103, as added Pub. L. 92-500, Sec. 2, Oct. 18, 1972, 86 Stat. 818.)

RESEARCH, INVESTIGATIONS, TRAINING, AND INFORMATION

33 USC 1254

(a) Establishment of national programs; cooperation; investigations; water quality surveillance system; reports

The Administrator shall establish national programs for the prevention, reduction, and elimination of pollution and as part of such programs shall—

(1) in cooperation with other Federal, State, and local agencies, conduct and promote the coordination and acceleration of, research, investigations, experiments, training, demonstrations, surveys, and studies relating to the causes, effects, extent, prevention, reduction, and elimination of pollution;

(2) encourage, cooperate with, and render technical services to pollution control agencies and other appropriate public or private agencies, institutions, and organizations, and individuals, including the general public, in the conduct of activities referred to in paragraph (1) of this subsection;

(3) conduct, in cooperation with State water pollution control agencies and other interested agencies, organizations and persons, public investigations concerning the pollution of any navigable waters, and report on the results of such investigations;

(4) establish advisory committees composed of recognized experts in various aspects of pollution and representatives of the public to assist in the examination and evaluation of research progress and proposals and to avoid duplication of research;

(5) in cooperation with the States, and their political subdivisions, and other Federal agencies establish, equip, and maintain a water quality surveillance system for the purpose of monitoring the quality of the navigable waters and ground waters and the contiguous zone and the oceans and the Administrator shall, to the extent practicable, conduct such surveillance by utilizing the resources of the National Aeronautics and Space Administration, the National Oceanic and Atmospheric Administration, the United States Geological Survey, and the Coast Guard, and shall report on such quality not later than 90 days after the date of convening of each session of Congress; and

(6) initiate and promote the coordination and acceleration of research designed to develop the most effective practicable tools and techniques for measuring the social and economic costs and benefits of activities which are subject to regulation under this chapter; and shall transmit a report on the results of such research to the Congress not later than January 1, 1974.

(b) Authorized activities of Administrator

In carrying out the provisions of subsection (a) of this section the Administrator is authorized to—

(1) collect and make available, through publications and other appropriate means, the results of and other information, including appropriate recommendations by him in connection therewith, pertaining to such research and other activities referred to in paragraph (1) of subsection (a) of this section;

(2) cooperate with other Federal departments and agencies, State water pollution control agencies, interstate agencies, other public and private agencies, institutions, organizations, industries involved, and individuals, in the preparation and conduct of such research and other activities referred to in paragraph (1) of subsection (a) of this section;

(3) make grants to State water pollution control agencies, interstate agencies, other public or nonprofit private agencies, institutions, organizations, and individuals, for purposes stated in paragraph (1) of subsection (a) of this section;

(4) contract with public or private agencies, institutions, organizations, and individuals, without regard to section 3324(a) and (b) of title 31 and section 5 of title 41, referred to in paragraph (1) of subsection (a) of this section;

(5) establish and maintain research fellowships at public or nonprofit private educational institutions or research organizations;

(6) collect and disseminate, in cooperation with other Federal departments and agencies, and with other public or private agencies, institutions, and organizations having related responsibilities, basic data on chemical, physical, and biological effects of varying water quality and other information pertaining to pollution and the prevention, reduction, and elimination thereof; and

(7) develop effective and practical processes, methods, and prototype devices for the prevention, reduction, and elimination of pollution.

(c) Research and studies on harmful effects of pollutants; cooperation with Secretary of Health and Human Services

In carrying out the provisions of subsection (a) of this section the Administrator shall conduct research on, and survey the results of other scientific studies on, the harmful effects on the health or welfare of persons caused by pollutants. In order to avoid duplication of effort, the Administrator shall, to the extent practicable, conduct such research in cooperation with and through the facilities of the Secretary of Health and Human Services.

(d) Sewage treatment; identification and measurement of effects of pollutants; augmented streamflow

In carrying out the provisions of this section the Administrator shall develop and demonstrate under varied conditions (including conducting such basic and applied research, studies, and experiments as may be necessary):

(1) Practicable means of treating municipal sewage, and other waterborne wastes to implement the requirements of section 1281 of this title;

(2) Improved methods and procedures to identify and measure the effects of pollutants, including those pollutants created by new technological developments; and

(3) Methods and procedures for evaluating the effects on water quality of augmented streamflows to control pollution not susceptible to other means of prevention, reduction, or elimination.

(e) Field laboratory and research facilities

The Administrator shall establish, equip, and maintain field laboratory and research facilities, including, but not limited to, one to be located in the northeastern area of the United States, one in the Middle Atlantic area, one in the southeastern area, one in the midwestern area, one in the southwestern area, one in the Pacific Northwest, and one in the State of Alaska, for the conduct of research, investigations, experiments, field demonstrations and studies, and training relating to the prevention, reduction and elimination of pollution. Insofar as practicable, each such facility shall be located near institutions of higher learning in which graduate training in such research might be carried out. In conjunction with the development of criteria under section 1343 of this title, the Administrator shall construct the facilities authorized for the National Marine Water Quality Laboratory established under this subsection.

(f) Great Lakes water quality research

The Administrator shall conduct research and technical development work, and make studies, with respect to the quality of the waters of the Great Lakes, including an analysis of the present and projected future water quality of the Great Lakes under varying conditions of waste treatment and disposal, an evaluation of the water quality needs of those to be served by such waters, an evaluation of municipal, industrial, and vessel waste treatment and disposal practices with respect to such waters, and a study of alternate means of solving pollution problems (including additional waste treatment measures) with respect to such waters.

(g) Treatment works pilot training programs; employment needs forecasting; training projects and grants; research fellowships; technical training; report to the President and transmittal to Congress

(1) For the purpose of providing an adequate supply of trained personnel to operate and maintain existing and future treatment works and related activities, and for the purpose of enhancing substantially the proficiency of those engaged in such activities, the Administrator shall finance pilot programs, in cooperation with State and interstate agencies, municipalities, educational institutions, and other organizations and individuals, of manpower development and training and retraining of persons in, on entering into, the field of operation and maintenance of treatment works and related activities. Such program and any funds expended for such a program shall supplement, not supplant, other manpower and training programs and funds available for the purposes of this paragraph. The Administrator is authorized, under such terms and conditions as he deems appropriate, to enter into agreements with one or more States, acting jointly or severally, or with other public or private agencies or institutions for the development and implementation of such a program.

(2) The Administrator is authorized to enter into agreements with public and private agencies and institutions, and individuals to develop and maintain an effective system for forecasting the supply of, and demand for, various professional and other occupational categories needed for the prevention, reduction, and elimination of pollution in each region, State, or area of the United States and, from time to time, to publish the results of such forecasts.

(3) In furtherance of the purposes of this chapter, the Administrator is authorized to—

(A) make grants to public or private agencies and institutions and to individuals for training projects, and provide for the conduct of training by contract with public or private agencies and institutions and with individuals without regard to section 3324(a) and (b) of title 31 and section 5 of title 41;

(B) establish and maintain research fellowships in the Environmental Protection Agency with such stipends and allowances, including traveling and subsistence expenses, as he may deem necessary to procure the assistance of the most promising research fellows; and

(C) provide, in addition to the program established under paragraph (1) of this subsection, training in technical matters relating to the causes, prevention, reduction, and elimination of pollution for personnel of public agencies and other persons with suitable qualifications.

(4) The Administrator shall submit, through the President, a report to the Congress not later than December 31, 1973, summarizing the actions taken under this subsection and the effectiveness of such actions, and setting forth the number of persons trained, the occupational categories for which training was provided, the effectiveness of other Federal, State, and local training programs in this field, together with estimates of future needs, recommendations on improving training programs, and such other information and recommendations, including legislative recommendations, as he deems appropriate.

(h) Lake pollution

The Administrator is authorized to enter into contracts with, or make grants to, public or private agencies and organizations and individuals for (A) the purpose of developing and demonstrating new or improved methods for the prevention, removal, reduction, and elimination of pollution in lakes, including the undesirable effects of nutrients and vegetation, and (B) the construction of publicly owned research facilities for such purpose.

(i) Oil pollution control studies

The Administrator, in cooperation with the Secretary of the Department in which the Coast Guard is operating, shall—

(1) engage in such research, studies, experiments, and demonstrations as he deems appropriate, relative to the removal of oil from any waters and to the prevention, control, and elimination of oil and hazardous substances pollution;

(2) publish from time to time the results of such activities; and

(3) from time to time, develop and publish in the Federal Register specifications and other technical information on the various chemical compounds used in the control of oil and hazardous substances spills.

In carrying out this subsection, the Administrator may enter into contracts with, or make grants to, public or private agencies and organizations and individuals.

(j) Solid waste disposal equipment for vessels

The Secretary of the department in which the Coast Guard is operating shall engage in such research, studies, experiments, and demonstrations as he deems appropriate relative to equipment which is to be installed on board a vessel and is designed to receive, retain, treat, or discharge human body wastes and the wastes from toilets and other receptacles intended to receive or retain body wastes with particular emphasis on equipment to be installed on small recreational vessels. The Secretary of the department in which the Coast Guard is operating shall report to Congress the results of such research, studies, experiments, and demonstrations prior to the effective date of any regulations established under section 1322 of this title. In carrying out this subsection the Secretary of the department in which the Coast Guard is operating may enter into contracts with, or make grants to, public or private organizations and individuals.

(k) Land acquisition

In carrying out the provisions of this section relating to the conduct by the Administrator of demonstration projects and the development of field laboratories and research facilities, the Administrator may acquire land and interests therein by purchase, with appropriated or donated funds, by donation, or by exchange for acquired or public lands under his jurisdiction which he classifies as suitable for disposition. The values of the properties so exchanged either shall be approximately equal, or if they are not approximately equal, the values shall be equalized by the payment of cash to the grantor or to the Administrator as the circumstances require.

(l) Collection and dissemination of scientific knowledge on effects and control of pesticides in water

(1) The Administrator shall, after consultation with appropriate local, State, and Federal agencies, public and private organizations, and interested individuals, as soon as practicable but not later than January 1, 1973, develop and issue to the States for the purpose of carrying out this chapter the latest scientific knowledge available in indicating the kind and extent of effects on health and welfare which may be expected from the presence of pesticides in the water in varying quantities. He shall revise and add to such information whenever necessary to reflect developing scientific knowledge.

(2) The President shall, in consultation with appropriate local, State, and Federal agencies, public and private organizations, and interested individuals, conduct studies and investigations of methods to control the release of pesticides into the environment which study shall include examination of the persistency of pesticides in the water environment and alternatives thereto. The President shall submit reports, from time to time, on such investigations to Congress together with his recommendations for any necessary legislation.

(m) Waste oil disposal study

(1) The Administrator shall, in an effort to prevent degradation of the environment from the disposal of waste oil, conduct a study of (A) the generation of used engine, machine, cooling, and similar waste oil, including quantities generated, the nature and quality of such oil, present collecting methods and disposal practices, and alternate uses of such oil; (B) the long-term, chronic biological effects of the disposal of such waste oil; and (C) the po-

tential market for such oils, including the economic and legal factors relating to the sale of products made from such oils, the level of subsidy, if any, needed to encourage the purchase by public and private nonprofit agencies of products from such oil, and the practicability of Federal procurement, on a priority basis, of products made from such oil. In conducting such study, the Administrator shall consult with affected industries and other persons.
- (2) The Administrator shall report the preliminary results of such study to Congress within six months after October 18, 1972, and shall submit a final report to Congress within 18 months after such date.

(n) Comprehensive studies of effects of pollution on estuaries and estuarine zones
- (1) The Administrator shall, in cooperation with the Secretary of the Army, the Secretary of Agriculture, the Water Resources Council, and with other appropriate Federal, State, interstate, or local public bodies and private organizations, institutions, and individuals, conduct and promote, and encourage contributions to, continuing comprehensive studies of the effects of pollution, including sedimentation, in the estuaries and estuarine zones of the United States on fish and wildlife, on sport and commercial fishing, on recreation, on water supply and water power, and on other beneficial purposes. Such studies shall also consider the effect of demographic trends, the exploitation of mineral resources and fossil fuels, land and industrial development, navigation, flood and erosion control, and other uses of estuaries and estuarine zones upon the pollution of the waters therein.
- (2) In conducting such studies, the Administrator shall assemble, coordinate, and organize all existing pertinent information on the Nation's estuaries and estuarine zones; carry out a program of investigations and surveys to supplement existing information in representative estuaries and estuarine zones; and identify the problems and areas where further research and study are required.
- (3) For the purpose of this subsection, the term "estuarine zones" means an environmental system consisting of an estuary and those transitional areas which are consistently influenced or affected by water from an estuary such as, but not limited to, salt marshes, coastal and intertidal areas, bays, harbors, lagoons, inshore waters, and channels, and the term "estuary" means all or part of the mouth of a river or stream or other body of water having unimpaired natural connection with open sea and within which the sea water is measurably diluted with fresh water derived from land drainage.

(o) Methods of reducing total flow of sewage and unnecessary water consumption; reports
- (1) The Administrator shall conduct research and investigations on devices, systems, incentives, pricing policy, and other methods of reducing the total flow of sewage, including, but not limited to, unnecessary water consumption in order to reduce the requirements for, and the costs of, sewage and waste treatment services. Such research and investigations shall be directed to develop devices, systems, policies, and methods capable of achieving the maximum reduction of unnecessary water consumption.
- (2) The Administrator shall report the preliminary results of such studies and investigations to the Congress within one year after October 18, 1972, and annually thereafter not later than 90 days after the date of convening of each session of Congress. Such report shall include recommendations for any legislation that may be required to provide for the adoption and use of devices, systems, policies, or other methods of reducing water consumption and reducing the total flow of sewage. Such report shall include an estimate of the benefits to be derived from adoption and use of such devices, systems, policies, or other methods and also shall reflect estimates of any increase in private, public, or other cost that would be occasioned thereby.

(p) Agricultural pollution
In carrying out the provisions of subsection (a) of this section the Administrator shall, in cooperation with the Secretary of Agriculture, other Federal agencies, and the States, carry out a comprehensive study and research program to determine new and improved methods and the better application of existing methods of preventing, reducing, and eliminating pollution from agriculture, including the legal, economic, and other implications of the use of such methods.

(q) Sewage in rural areas; national clearinghouse for alternative treatment information; clearinghouse on small flows

(1) The Administrator shall conduct a comprehensive program of research and investigation and pilot project implementation into new and improved methods of preventing, reducing, storing, collecting, treating, or otherwise eliminating pollution from sewage in rural and other areas where collection of sewage in conventional, communitywide sewage collection systems is impractical, uneconomical, or otherwise infeasible, or where soil conditions or other factors preclude the use of septic tank and drainage field systems.

(2) The Administrator shall conduct a comprehensive program of research and investigation and pilot project implementation into new and improved methods for the collection and treatment of sewage and other liquid wastes combined with the treatment and disposal of solid wastes.

(3) The Administrator shall establish, either within the Environmental Protection Agency, or through contract with an appropriate public or private non-profit organization, a national clearinghouse which shall (A) receive reports and information resulting from research, demonstrations, and other projects funded under this chapter related to paragraph (1) of this subsection and to subsection (e)(2) of section 1255 of this title; (B) coordinate and disseminate such reports and information for use by Federal and State agencies, municipalities, institutions, and persons in developing new and improved methods pursuant to this subsection; and (C) provide for the collection and dissemination of reports and information relevant to this subsection from other Federal and State agencies, institutions, universities, and persons.

(4) Small flows clearinghouse.—Notwithstanding section 1285(d) of this title, from amounts that are set aside for a fiscal year under section 1285(i) of this title and are not obligated by the end of the 24-month period of availability for such amounts under section 1285(d) of this title, the Administrator shall make available $1,000,000 or such unobligated amount, whichever is less, to support a national clearinghouse within the Environmental Protection Agency to collect and disseminate information on small flows of sewage and innovative or alternative wastewater treatment processes and techniques, consistent with paragraph (3). This paragraph shall apply with respect to amounts set aside under section 1285(i) of this title for which the 24-month period of availability referred to in the preceding sentence ends on or after September 30, 1986.

(r) Research grants to colleges and universities

The Administrator is authorized to make grants to colleges and universities to conduct basic research into the structure and function of freshwater aquatic ecosystems, and to improve understanding of the ecological characteristics necessary to the maintenance of the chemical, physical, and biological integrity of freshwater aquatic ecosystems.

(s) River Study Centers

The Administrator is authorized to make grants to one or more institutions of higher education (regionally located and to be designated as "River Study Centers") for the purpose of conducting and reporting on interdisciplinary studies on the nature of river systems, including hydrology, biology, ecology, economics, the relationship between river uses and land uses, and the effects of development within river basins on river systems and on the value of water resources and water related activities. No such grant in any fiscal year shall exceed $1,000,000.

(t) Thermal discharges

The Administrator shall, in cooperation with State and Federal agencies and public and private organizations, conduct continuing comprehensive studies of the effects and methods of control of thermal discharges. In evaluating alternative methods of control the studies shall consider (1) such data as are available on the latest available technology, economic feasibility including cost-effectiveness analysis, and (2) the total impact on the environment, considering not only water quality but also air quality, land use, and effective utilization and conservation of freshwater and other natural resources. Such studies shall consider methods of minimizing adverse effects and maximizing beneficial effects of thermal discharges. The results of these studies shall be reported by the Administrator as soon as practicable, but not later than 270 days after October 18, 1972, and shall be made available to the public and the States, and considered as they become available by the Administrator in carrying out section 1326 of this title and by the States in proposing thermal water quality standards.

(u) Authorization of appropriations

There is authorized to be appropriated (1) not to exceed $100,000,000 per fiscal year for the fiscal year ending June 30, 1973, the fiscal year ending June 30, 1974, and the fiscal year ending June 30, 1975, not to exceed $14,039,000 for the fiscal year ending September 30, 1980, not to exceed $20,697,000 for the fiscal year ending September 30, 1981, not to exceed $22,770,000 for the fiscal year ending September 30, 1982, such sums as may be necessary for fiscal years 1983 through 1985, and not to exceed $22,770,000 per fiscal year for each of the fiscal years 1986 through 1990, for carrying out the provisions of this section, other than subsections (g)(1) and (2), (p), (r), and (t) of this section, except that such authorizations are not for any research, development, or demonstration activity pursuant to such provisions; (2) not to exceed $7,500,000 for fiscal years 1973, 1974, and 1975, $2,000,000 for fiscal year 1977, $3,000,000 for fiscal year 1978, $3,000,000 for fiscal year 1979, $3,000,000 for fiscal year 1980, $3,000,000 for fiscal year 1981, $3,000,000 for fiscal year 1982, such sums as may be necessary for fiscal years 1983 through 1985, and $3,000,000 per fiscal year for each of the fiscal years 1986 through 1990, for carrying out the provisions of subsection (g)(1) of this section; (3) not to exceed $2,500,000 for fiscal years 1973, 1974, and 1975, $1,000,000 for fiscal year 1977, $1,500,000 for fiscal year 1978, $1,500,000 for fiscal year 1979, $1,500,000 for fiscal year 1980, $1,500,000 for fiscal year 1981, $1,500,000 for fiscal year 1982, such sums as may be necessary for fiscal years 1983 through 1985, and $1,500,000 per fiscal year for each of the fiscal years 1986 through 1990, for carrying out the provisions of subsection (g)(2) of this section; (4) not to exceed $10,000,000 for each of the fiscal years ending June 30, 1973, June 30, 1974, and June 30, 1975, for carrying out the provisions of subsection (p) of this section; (5) not to exceed $15,000,000 per fiscal year for the fiscal years ending June 30, 1973, June 30, 1974, and June 30, 1975, for carrying out the provisions of subsection (r) of this section; and (6) not to exceed $10,000,000 per fiscal year for the fiscal years ending June 30, 1973, June 30, 1974, and June 30, 1975, for carrying out the provisions of subsection (t) of this section.

(v) Studies Concerning Pathogen Indicators in Coastal Recreation Waters
Not later than 18 months after the date of the enactment of this subsection, after consultation and in cooperation with appropriate Federal, State, tribal, and local officials (including local health officials), the Administrator shall initiate, and, not later than 3 years after the date of the enactment of this subsection, shall complete, in cooperation with the heads of other Federal agencies, studies to provide additional information for use in developing—
  (1) an assessment of potential human health risks resulting from exposure to pathogens in coastal recreation waters, including nongastrointestinal effects;
  (2) appropriate and effective indicators for improving detection in a timely manner in coastal recreation waters of the presence of pathogens that are harmful to human health;
  (3) appropriate, accurate, expeditious, and cost-effective methods (including predictive models) for detecting in a timely manner in coastal recreation waters the presence of pathogens that are harmful to human health; and
  (4) guidance for State application of the criteria for pathogens and pathogen indicators to be published under section 304(a)(9) to account for the diversity of geographic and aquatic conditions.

(June 30, 1948, ch. 758, title I, Sec. 104, as added Pub. L. 92-500, Sec. 2, Oct. 18, 1972, 86 Stat. 819; amended Pub. L. 93-207, Sec. 1(1), Dec. 28, 1973, 87 Stat. 906; Pub. L. 93-592, Sec. 1, Jan. 2, 1975, 88 Stat. 1924; Pub. L. 95-217, Secs. 4(a), (b), 6, 7, Dec. 27, 1977, 91 Stat. 1566, 1567; Pub. L. 95-576, Sec. 1(a), Nov. 2, 1978, 92 Stat. 2467; Pub. L. 96-88, title V, Sec. 509(b), Oct. 17, 1979, 93 Stat. 695; Pub. L. 96-483, Sec. 1(a), Oct. 21, 1980, 94 Stat. 2360; Pub. L. 100-4, title I, Secs. 101(a), 102, Feb. 4, 1987, 101 Stat. 8, 9; Pub. L. 102-154, title I, Nov. 13, 1991, 105 Stat. 1000; Pub. L. 105-362, title V, Sec. 501(a)(1), (d)(2)(A), Nov. 10, 1998, 112 Stat. 3283.)

Codification

In subsecs. (b)(4) and (g)(3)(A), "section 3324(a) and (b) of title 31" substituted for reference to section 3648 of the Revised Statutes [31 U.S.C. 529] on authority of Pub. L. 97-258, Sec. 4(b), Sept. 13, 1982, 96 Stat. 1067, the first section of which enacted Title 31, Money and Finance.

Amendments

2000—Subsec. (v). Pub. L. 106-284, Sec. 3(a) added subsec. (v).

1998—Subsec. (a)(5). Pub. L. 105-362, Sec. 501(d)(2)(A)(i), substituted "not later than 90 days after the date of convening of each session of Congress" for "in the report required under subsection (a) of section 1375 of this title".

Subsec. (n)(3), (4). Pub. L. 105-362, Sec. 501(a)(1), redesignated par. (4) as (3) and struck out former par. (3) which read as follows: "The Administrator shall submit to Congress, from time to time, reports of the studies authorized by this subsection but at least one such report during any six-year period. Copies of each such report shall be made available to all interested parties, public and private."

Subsec. (o)(2). Pub. L. 105-362, Sec. 501(d)(2)(A)(ii), substituted "not later than 90 days after the date of convening of each session of Congress" for "in the report required under subsection (a) of section 1375 of this title".

1987—Subsec. (q)(4). Pub. L. 100-4, Sec. 102, added par. (4).

Subsec. (u). Pub. L. 100-4, Sec. 101(a), in cl. (1) struck out "and" after "1975,", "1980,", and "1981," and inserted "such sums as may be necessary for fiscal years 1983 through 1985, and not to exceed $22,770,000 per fiscal year for each of the fiscal years 1986 through 1990,", in cl. (2) struck out "and" after "1981," and inserted "such sums as may be necessary for fiscal years 1983 through 1985, and $3,000,000 per fiscal year for each of the fiscal years 1986 through 1990,", and in cl. (3) struck out "and" after "1981," and inserted "such sums as may be necessary for fiscal years 1983 through 1985, and $1,500,000 per fiscal year for each of the fiscal years 1986 through 1990,".

1980—Subsec. (u). Pub. L. 96-483 in par. (1) inserted authorization of not to exceed $20,697,000 and $22,770,000 for fiscal years ending Sept. 30, 1981, and 1982, respectively; in par. (2) inserted authorization of the sum of $3,000,000 for each of fiscal years 1981 and 1982; and in par. (3) inserted authorization of the sum of $1,500,000 for each of fiscal years 1981 and 1982.

1978—Subsec. (u)(1). Pub. L. 95-576 authorized appropriation of not to exceed $14,039,000 for fiscal year ending Sept. 30, 1980 and prohibited use of authorizations for any research, development, or demonstration activity pursuant to provisions of this section.

1977—Subsec. (n)(3). Pub. L. 95-217, Sec. 6, substituted "any six-year period" for "any three year period".

Subsec. (q)(3). Pub. L. 95-217, Sec. 7, added par. (3).

Subsec. (u)(2). Pub. L. 95-217, Sec. 4(a), substituted "1975, $2,000,000 for fiscal year 1977, $3,000,000 for fiscal year 1978, $3,000,000 for fiscal year 1979, and $3,000,000 for fiscal year 1980," for "1975".

Subsec. (u)(3). Pub. L. 95-217, Sec. 4(b), substituted "1975, $1,000,000 for fiscal year 1977, $1,500,000 for fiscal year 1978, $1,500,000 for fiscal year 1979, and $1,500,000 for fiscal year 1980," for "1975".

1975—Subsec. (u)(1). Pub. L. 93-592, Sec. 1(a), substituted "the fiscal year ending June 30, 1974, and the fiscal year ending June 30, 1975," for "and the fiscal year ending June 30, 1974,".

Subsec. (u)(2). Pub. L. 93-592, Sec. 1(b), substituted "fiscal years 1973, 1974, and 1975" for "fiscal years 1973 and 1974".

Subsec. (u)(3). Pub. L. 93-592, Sec. 1(c), substituted "fiscal years 1973, 1974, and 1975" for "fiscal year 1973".

Subsec. (u)(4), (5), (6). Pub. L. 93-592, Sec. 1(d)-(f), substituted "June 30, 1974, and June 30, 1975," for "and June 30, 1974,".

1973—Subsec. (u)(2). Pub. L. 93-207 substituted "fiscal years 1973 and 1974" for "fiscal year 1973".

Change of Name

"United States Geological Survey" substituted for "Geological Survey" in subsec. (a)(5) pursuant to provision of title I of Pub. L. 102-154, set out as a note under section 31 of Title 43, Public Lands.

"Secretary of Health and Human Services" substituted for "Secretary of Health, Education, and Welfare" in subsec. (c) pursuant to section 509(b) of Pub. L. 96-88 which is classified to section 3508(b) of Title 20, Education.

Transfer of Functions

Enforcement functions of Secretary or other official in Department of Agriculture, insofar as they involve lands and programs under jurisdiction of that Department, related to compliance with this chapter with respect to pre-construction, construction, and initial operation of transportation system for Canadian and Alaskan natural gas were transferred to the Federal Inspector, Office of Federal Inspector for the Alaska Natural Gas Transportation System, until the first anniversary of date of initial operation of the Alaska Natural Gas Transportation System, see Reorg. Plan No. 1 of 1979, Secs. 102(f), 203(a), 44 F.R. 33663, 33666, 93 Stat. 1373, 1376, effective July 1, 1979, set out in the Appendix to Title 5, Government Organization and Employees. Office of Federal Inspector for the Alaska Natural Gas Transportation System abolished and functions and authority vested in Inspector transferred to Secretary of Energy by section 3012(b) of Pub. L. 102-486, set out as an Abolition of Office of Federal Inspector note under section 719e of Title 15, Commerce and Trade.

Columbia River Basin System; Protection From Oil Spills and Discharges; Criteria for Evaluation and Report to Congress by Commandant of Coast Guard in Consultation With Federal, Etc., Agencies

Pub. L. 95-308, Sec. 8, June 30, 1978, 92 Stat. 359, set forth Congressional findings and declarations and evaluation criteria with respect to protection from oil spills and discharges and betterment of the Columbia River Basin system, with such evaluation by the Commandant of the Coast Guard to begin within 180 days after June 30, 1978, and immediate submission of the evaluation to appropriate Congressional committees.

Contiguous Zone of United States

For extension of contiguous zone of United States, see Proc. No. 7219, Sept. 2, 1999, 64 F.R. 48701, set out as a note under section 1331 of Title 43, Public Lands.

Section Referred to in Other Sections

This section is referred to in sections 1254a, 1255, 1263, 1322, 1330, 1376, 1377 of this title.

RESEARCH ON EFFECTS OF POLLUTANTS

33 USC 1254a

In carrying out the provisions of section 1254(a) of this title, the Administrator shall conduct research on the harmful effects on the health and welfare of persons caused by pollutants in water, in conjunction with the United States Fish and Wildlife Service, the National Oceanic and Atmospheric Administration, and other Federal, State, and interstate agencies carrying on such research. Such research shall include, and shall place special emphasis on, the effect that bioaccumulation of these pollutants in aquatic species has upon reducing the value of aquatic commercial and sport industries. Such research shall further study methods to reduce and remove these pollutants from the relevant affected aquatic species so as to restore and enhance these valuable resources.

(Pub. L. 100-4, title I, Sec. 105, Feb. 4, 1987, 101 Stat. 15.)

Codification

Section was enacted as part of the Water Quality Act of 1987, and not as part of the Federal Water Pollution Control Act which comprises this chapter.

Definition

Administrator means the Administrator of the Environmental Protection Agency, see section 1(d) of Pub. L. 100-4, set out as a note under section 1251 of this title.

GRANTS FOR RESEARCH AND DEVELOPMENT

33 USC 1255

(a) Demonstration projects covering storm waters, advanced waste treatment and water purification methods, and joint treatment systems for municipal and industrial wastes

The Administrator is authorized to conduct in the Environmental Protection Agency, and to make grants to any State, municipality, or intermunicipal or interstate agency for the purpose of assisting in the development of—

  (1) any project which will demonstrate a new or improved method of preventing, reducing, and eliminating the discharge into any waters of pollutants from sewers which carry storm water or both storm water and pollutants; or

(2) any project which will demonstrate advanced waste treatment and water purification methods (including the temporary use of new or improved chemical additives which provide substantial immediate improvements to existing treatment processes), or new or improved methods of joint treatment systems for municipal and industrial wastes;
and to include in such grants such amounts as are necessary for the purpose of reports, plans, and specifications in connection therewith.

(b) Demonstration projects for advanced treatment and environmental enhancement techniques to control pollution in river basins
The Administrator is authorized to make grants to any State or States or interstate agency to demonstrate, in river basins or portions thereof, advanced treatment and environmental enhancement techniques to control pollution from all sources, within such basins or portions thereof, including nonpoint sources, together with in stream[1] water quality improvement techniques.

(c) Research and demonstration projects for prevention of water pollution by industry
In order to carry out the purposes of section 1311 of this title, the Administrator is authorized to (1) conduct in the Environmental Protection Agency, (2) make grants to persons, and (3) enter into contracts with persons, for research and demonstration projects for prevention of pollution of any waters by industry including, but not limited to, the prevention, reduction, and elimination of the discharge of pollutants. No grant shall be made for any project under this subsection unless the Administrator determines that such project will develop or demonstrate a new or improved method of treating industrial wastes or otherwise prevent pollution by industry, which method shall have industrywide application.

(d) Accelerated and priority development of waste management and waste treatment methods and identification and measurement methods
In carrying out the provisions of this section, the Administrator shall conduct, on a priority basis, an accelerated effort to develop, refine, and achieve practical application of:
   (1) waste management methods applicable to point and nonpoint sources of pollutants to eliminate the discharge of pollutants, including, but not limited to, elimination of runoff of pollutants and the effects of pollutants from inplace or accumulated sources;
   (2) advanced waste treatment methods applicable to point and nonpoint sources, including inplace or accumulated sources of pollutants, and methods for reclaiming and recycling water and confining pollutants so they will not migrate to cause water or other environmental pollution; and
   (3) improved methods and procedures to identify and measure the effects of pollutants on the chemical, physical, and biological integrity of water, including those pollutants created by new technological developments.

(e) Research and demonstration projects covering agricultural pollution and pollution from sewage in rural areas; dissemination of information
   (1) The Administrator is authorized to (A) make, in consultation with the Secretary of Agriculture, grants to persons for research and demonstration projects with respect to new and improved methods of preventing, reducing, and eliminating pollution from agriculture, and (B) disseminate, in cooperation with the Secretary of Agriculture, such information obtained under this subsection, section 1254(p) of this title, and section 1314 of this title as will encourage and enable the adoption of such methods in the agricultural industry.
   (2) The Administrator is authorized, (A) in consultation with other interested Federal agencies, to make grants for demonstration projects with respect to new and improved methods of preventing, reducing, storing, collecting, treating, or otherwise eliminating pollution from sewage in rural and other areas where collection of sewage in conventional, community-wide sewage collection systems is impractical, uneconomical, or otherwise infeasible, or where soil conditions or other factors preclude the use of septic tank and drainage field systems, and (B) in cooperation with other interested Federal and State agencies, to disseminate such information obtained under this subsection as will encourage and enable the adoption of new and improved methods developed pursuant to this subsection.

(f) Limitations
Federal grants under subsection (a) of this section shall be subject to the following limitations:
   (1) No grant shall be made for any project unless such project shall have been approved by the appropriate State water pollution control agency or agencies and by the Administrator;

---
[1] So in original.

(2) No grant shall be made for any project in an amount exceeding 75 per centum of cost thereof as determined by the Administrator; and
(3) No grant shall be made for any project unless the Administrator determines that such project will serve as a useful demonstration for the purpose set forth in clause (1) or (2) of subsection (a) of this section.

(g) Maximum grants
Federal grants under subsections (c) and (d) of this section shall not exceed 75 per centum of the cost of the project.

(h) Authorization of appropriations
For the purpose of this section there is authorized to be appropriated $75,000,000 per fiscal year for the fiscal year ending June 30, 1973, the fiscal year ending June 30, 1974, and the fiscal year ending June 30, 1975, and from such appropriations at least 10 per centum of the funds actually appropriated in each fiscal year shall be available only for the purposes of subsection (e) of this section.

(i) Assistance for research and demonstration projects
The Administrator is authorized to make grants to a municipality to assist in the costs of operating and maintaining a project which received a grant under this section, section 1254 of this title, or section 1263 of this title prior to December 27, 1977, so as to reduce the operation and maintenance costs borne by the recipients of services from such project to costs comparable to those for projects assisted under subchapter II of this chapter.

(j) Assistance for recycle, reuse, and land treatment projects
The Administrator is authorized to make a grant to any grantee who received an increased grant pursuant to section 1282(a)(2) of this title. Such grant may pay up to 100 per centum of the costs of technical evaluation of the operation of the treatment works, costs of training of persons (other than employees of the grantee), and costs of disseminating technical information on the operation of the treatment works.

(June 30, 1948, ch. 758, title I, Sec. 105, as added Pub. L. 92-500, Sec. 2, Oct. 18, 1972, 86 Stat. 825; amended Pub. L. 93-592, Sec. 2, Jan. 2, 1975, 88 Stat. 1925; Pub. L. 95-217, Secs. 8, 9, Dec. 27, 1977, 91 Stat. 1568.)

Amendments

1977—Subsecs. (i), (j). Pub. L. 95-217 added subsecs. (i) and (j).
1975—Subsec. (h). Pub. L. 93-592 substituted "the fiscal year ending June 30, 1974, and the fiscal year ending June 30, 1975," for "and the fiscal year ending June 30, 1974,".

Transfer of Functions

Enforcement functions of Secretary or other official in Department of Agriculture, insofar as they involve lands and programs under jurisdiction of that Department, related to compliance with this chapter with respect to pre-construction, construction, and initial operation of transportation system for Canadian and Alaskan natural gas were transferred to the Federal Inspector, Office of Federal Inspector for the Alaska Natural Gas Transportation System, until the first anniversary of date of initial operation of the Alaska Natural Gas Transportation System, see Reorg. Plan No. 1 of 1979, Secs. 102(f), 203(a), 44 F.R. 33663, 33666, 93 Stat. 1373, 1376, effective July 1, 1979, set out in the Appendix to Title 5, Government Organization and Employees. Office of Federal Inspector for the Alaska Natural Gas Transportation System abolished and functions and authority vested in Inspector transferred to Secretary of Energy by section 3012(b) of Pub. L. 102-486, set out as an Abolition of Office of Federal Inspector note under section 719e of Title 15, Commerce and Trade.

Section Referred to in Other Sections

This section is referred to in sections 1254, 1263, 1376 of this title.

GRANTS FOR POLLUTION CONTROL PROGRAMS

33 USC 1256

(a) Authorization of appropriations for State and interstate programs
There are hereby authorized to be appropriated the following sums, to remain available until expended, to carry out the purpose of this section—

432 / Environmental Statutes

   (1) $60,000,000 for the fiscal year ending June 30, 1973; and
   (2) $75,000,000 for the fiscal year ending June 30, 1974, and the fiscal year ending June 30, 1975, $100,000,000 per fiscal year for the fiscal years 1977, 1978, 1979, and 1980, $75,000,000 per fiscal year for the fiscal years 1981 and 1982, such sums as may be necessary for fiscal years 1983 through 1985, and $75,000,000 per fiscal year for each of the fiscal years 1986 through 1990;
   for grants to States and to interstate agencies to assist them in administering programs for the prevention, reduction, and elimination of pollution, including enforcement directly or through appropriate State law enforcement officers or agencies.
(b) Allotments
   From the sums appropriated in any fiscal year, the Administrator shall make allotments to the several States and interstate agencies in accordance with regulations promulgated by him on the basis of the extent of the pollution problem in the respective States.
(c) Maximum annual payments
   The Administrator is authorized to pay to each State and interstate agency each fiscal year either—
   (1) the allotment of such State or agency for such fiscal year under subsection (b) of this section, or
   (2) the reasonable costs as determined by the Administrator of developing and carrying out a pollution program by such State or agency during such fiscal year,
   which ever amount is the lesser.
(d) Limitations
   No grant shall be made under this section to any State or interstate agency for any fiscal year when the expenditure of non-Federal funds by such State or interstate agency during such fiscal year for the recurrent expenses of carrying out its pollution control program are less than the expenditure by such State or interstate agency of non-Federal funds for such recurrent program expenses during the fiscal year ending June 30, 1971.
(e) Grants prohibited to States not establishing water quality monitoring procedures or adequate emergency and contingency plans
   Beginning in fiscal year 1974 the Administrator shall not make any grant under this section to any State which has not provided or is not carrying out as a part of its program—
   (1) the establishment and operation of appropriate devices, methods, systems, and procedures necessary to monitor, and to compile and analyze data on (including classification according to eutrophic condition), the quality of navigable waters and to the extent practicable, ground waters including biological monitoring; and provision for annually updating such data and including it in the report required under section 1315 of this title;
   (2) authority comparable to that in section 1364 of this title and adequate contingency plans to implement such authority.
(f) Conditions
   Grants shall be made under this section on condition that—
   (1) Such State (or interstate agency) files with the Administrator within one hundred and twenty days after October 18, 1972:
      (A) a summary report of the current status of the State pollution control program, including the criteria used by the State in determining priority of treatment works; and
      (B) such additional information, data, and reports as the Administrator may require.
   (2) No federally assumed enforcement as defined in section 1319(a)(2) of this title is in effect with respect to such State or interstate agency.
   (3) Such State (or interstate agency) submits within one hundred and twenty days after October 18, 1972, and before October 1 of each year thereafter for the Administrator's approval of its program for the prevention, reduction, and elimination of pollution in accordance with purposes and provisions of this chapter in such form and content as the Administrator may prescribe.
(g) Reallotment of unpaid allotments
   Any sums allotted under subsection (b) of this section in any fiscal year which are not paid shall be reallotted by the Administrator in accordance with regulations promulgated by him.
(June 30, 1948, ch. 758, title I, Sec. 106, as added Pub. L. 92-500, Sec. 2, Oct. 18, 1972, 86 Stat. 827; amended Pub. L. 93-592, Sec. 3, Jan. 2, 1975, 88 Stat. 1925; Pub. L. 94-273, Sec. 3(20), Apr. 21,

1976, 90 Stat. 377; Pub. L. 95-217, Sec. 4(c), Dec. 27, 1977, 91 Stat. 1566; Pub. L. 96-483, Sec. 1(b), Oct. 21, 1980, 94 Stat. 2360; Pub. L. 100-4, title I, Sec. 101(b), Feb. 4, 1987, 101 Stat. 9.)

Amendments

1987—Subsec. (a)(2). Pub. L. 100-4 inserted ", such sums as may be necessary for fiscal years 1983 through 1985, and $75,000,000 per fiscal year for each of the fiscal years 1986 through 1990" after "1982".

1980—Subsec. (a)(2). Pub. L. 96-483 inserted authorization of the sum of $75,000,000 per fiscal year for fiscal years 1981 and 1982.

1977—Subsec. (a)(2). Pub. L. 95-217 substituted "and the fiscal year ending June 30, 1975, $100,000,000 per fiscal year for the fiscal years 1977, 1978, 1979, and 1980" for "and the fiscal year ending June 30, 1975".

1976—Subsec. (f)(3). Pub. L. 94-273 substituted "October" for "July".

1975—Subsec. (a)(2). Pub. L. 93-592 substituted "June 30, 1974, and the fiscal year ending June 30, 1975;" for "June 30, 1974;".

Section Referred to in Other Sections

This section is referred to in sections 1376, 1377 of this title.

MINE WATER POLLUTION CONTROL DEMONSTRATIONS

33 USC 1257

(a) Comprehensive approaches to elimination or control of mine water pollution
The Administrator in cooperation with the Appalachian Regional Commission and other Federal agencies is authorized to conduct, to make grants for, or to contract for, projects to demonstrate comprehensive approaches to the elimination or control of acid or other mine water pollution resulting from active or abandoned mining operations and other environmental pollution affecting water quality within all or part of a watershed or river basin, including siltation from surface mining. Such projects shall demonstrate the engineering and economic feasibility and practicality of various abatement techniques which will contribute substantially to effective and practical methods of acid or other mine water pollution elimination or control, and other pollution affecting water quality, including techniques that demonstrate the engineering and economic feasibility and practicality of using sewage sludge materials and other municipal wastes to diminish or prevent pollution affecting water quality from acid, sedimentation, or other pollutants and in such projects to restore affected lands to usefulness for forestry, agriculture, recreation, or other beneficial purposes.

(b) Consistency of projects with objectives of Appalachian Regional Development Act of 1965
Prior to undertaking any demonstration project under this section in the Appalachian region (as defined in section 403 of the Appalachian Regional Development Act of 1965, as amended [40 App. U.S.C. 403]), the Appalachian Regional Commission shall determine that such demonstration project is consistent with the objectives of the Appalachian Regional Development Act of 1965, as amended [40 App. U.S.C. 1 et seq].

(c) Watershed selection
The Administrator, in selecting watersheds for the purposes of this section, shall be satisfied that the project area will not be affected adversely by the influx of acid or other mine water pollution from nearby sources.

(d) Conditions upon Federal participation
Federal participation in such projects shall be subject to the conditions—
  (1) that the State shall acquire any land or interests therein necessary for such project; and
  (2) that the State shall provide legal and practical protection to the project area to insure against any activities which will cause future acid or other mine water pollution.

(e) Authorization of appropriations
There is authorized to be appropriated $30,000,000 to carry out the provisions of this section, which sum shall be available until expended.

(June 30, 1948, ch. 758, title I, Sec. 107, as added Pub. L. 92-500, Sec. 2, Oct. 18, 1972, 86 Stat. 828.)

References in Text
The Appalachian Regional Development Act of 1965, as amended, referred to in subsec. (b), is Pub. L. 89-4, Mar. 9, 1965, 79 Stat. 5, as amended, which is classified generally to Sec. 1 et seq. of the Appendix to Title 40, Public Buildings, Property, and Works. For complete classification of this Act to the Code, see section 1 of the Appendix to Title 40 and Tables.

Section Referred to in Other Sections
This section is referred to in section 1376 of this title.

STATE DEMONSTRATION PROGRAMS FOR CLEANUP OF ABANDONED MINES FOR USE AS WASTE DISPOSAL SITES; AUTHORIZATION OF APPROPRIATIONS

33 USC 1257a

The Administrator of the Environmental Protection Agency is authorized to make grants to States to undertake a demonstration program for the cleanup of State-owned abandoned mines which can be used as hazardous waste disposal sites. The State shall pay 10 per centum of project costs. At a minimum, the Administrator shall undertake projects under such program in the States of Ohio, Illinois, and West Virginia. There are authorized to be appropriated $10,000,000 per fiscal year for each of the fiscal years ending September 30, 1982, September 30, 1983, and September 30, 1984, to carry out this section. Such projects shall be undertaken in accordance with all applicable laws and regulations.

(Pub. L. 96-483, Sec. 12, Oct. 21, 1980, 94 Stat. 2363.)

Codification
Section was not enacted as part of the Federal Water Pollution Control Act which comprises this chapter.

POLLUTION CONTROL IN THE GREAT LAKES

33 USC 1258

(a) Demonstration projects
   The Administrator, in cooperation with other Federal departments, agencies, and instrumentalities is authorized to enter into agreements with any State, political subdivision, interstate agency, or other public agency, or combination thereof, to carry out one or more projects to demonstrate new methods and techniques and to develop preliminary plans for the elimination or control of pollution, within all or any part of the watersheds of the Great Lakes. Such projects shall demonstrate the engineering and economic feasibility and practicality of removal of pollutants and prevention of any polluting matter from entering into the Great Lakes in the future and other reduction and remedial techniques which will contribute substantially to effective and practical methods of pollution prevention, reduction, or elimination.

(b) Conditions of Federal participation
   Federal participation in such projects shall be subject to the condition that the State, political subdivision, interstate agency, or other public agency, or combination thereof, shall pay not less than 25 per centum of the actual project costs, which payment may be in any form, including, but not limited to, land or interests therein that is needed for the project, and personal property or services the value of which shall be determined by the Administrator.

(c) Authorization of appropriations
   There is authorized to be appropriated $20,000,000 to carry out the provisions of subsections (a) and (b) of this section, which sum shall be available until expended.

(d) Lake Erie demonstration program
   (1) In recognition of the serious conditions which exist in Lake Erie, the Secretary of the Army, acting through the Chief of Engineers, is directed to design and develop a demonstration waste water management program for the rehabilitation and environmental repair of Lake Erie. Prior to the initiation of detailed engineering and design, the program, along with the specific recommendations of the Chief of Engineers, and recommenda-

tions for its financing, shall be submitted to the Congress for statutory approval. This authority is in addition to, and not in lieu of, other waste water studies aimed at eliminating pollution emanating from select sources around Lake Erie.
(2) This program is to be developed in cooperation with the Environmental Protection Agency, other interested departments, agencies, and instrumentalities of the Federal Government, and the States and their political subdivisions. This program shall set forth alternative systems for managing waste water on a regional basis and shall provide local and State governments with a range of choice as to the type of system to be used for the treatment of waste water. These alternative systems shall include both advanced waste treatment technology and land disposal systems including aerated treatment-spray irrigation technology and will also include provisions for the disposal of solid wastes, including sludge. Such program should include measures to control point sources of pollution, area sources of pollution, including acid-mine drainage, urban runoff and rural runoff, and in place sources of pollution, including bottom loads, sludge banks, and polluted harbor dredgings.
(e) Authorization of appropriations for Lake Erie demonstration program
There is authorized to be appropriated $5,000,000 to carry out the provisions of subsection (d) of this section, which sum shall be available until expended.

(June 30, 1948, ch. 758, title I, Sec. 108, as added Pub. L. 92-500, Sec. 2, Oct. 18, 1972, 86 Stat. 828.)

Section Referred to in Other Sections

This section is referred to in section 1376 of this title.

TRAINING GRANTS AND CONTRACTS

33 USC 1259

(a) The Administrator is authorized to make grants to or contracts with institutions of higher education, or combinations of such institutions, to assist them in planning, developing, strengthening, improving, or carrying out programs or projects for the preparation of undergraduate students to enter an occupation which involves the design, operation, and maintenance of treatment works, and other facilities whose purpose is water quality control. Such grants or contracts may include payment of all or part of the cost of programs or projects such as—
  (A) planning for the development or expansion of programs or projects for training persons in the operation and maintenance of treatment works;
  (B) training and retraining of faculty members;
  (C) conduct of short-term or regular session institutes for study by persons engaged in, or preparing to engage in, the preparation of students preparing to enter an occupation involving the operation and maintenance of treatment works;
  (D) carrying out innovative and experimental programs of cooperative education involving alternate periods of full-time or part-time academic study at the institution and periods of full-time or part-time employment involving the operation and maintenance of treatment works; and
  (E) research into, and development of, methods of training students or faculty, including the preparation of teaching materials and the planning of curriculum.
(b) (1) The Administrator may pay 100 per centum of any additional cost of construction of treatment works required for a facility to train and upgrade waste treatment works operation and maintenance personnel and for the costs of other State treatment works operator training programs, including mobile training units, classroom rental, specialized instructors, and instructional material.
  (2) The Administrator shall make no more than one grant for such additional construction in any State (to serve a group of States, where, in his judgment, efficient training programs require multi-State programs), and shall make such grant after consultation with and approval by the State or States on the basis of (A) the suitability of such facility for training operation and maintenance personnel for treatment works throughout such State or States; and (B) a commitment by the State agency or agencies to carry out at such facility a program of training approved by the Administrator. In any case where a grant is made to serve two or more States, the Administrator is authorized to make an additional grant for a supplemental facility in each such State.

436 / Environmental Statutes

(3) The Administrator may make such grant out of the sums allocated to a State under section 1285 of this title, except that in no event shall the Federal cost of any such training facilities exceed $500,000.
(4) The Administrator may exempt a grant under this section from any requirement under section 1284(a)(3) of this title. Any grantee who received a grant under this section prior to enactment of the Clean Water Act of 1977 shall be eligible to have its grant increased by funds made available under such Act.

(June 30, 1948, ch. 758, title I, Sec. 109, as added Pub. L. 92-500, Sec. 2, Oct. 18, 1972, 86 Stat. 829; amended Pub. L. 95-217, Sec. 10, Dec. 27, 1977, 91 Stat. 1568.)

References in Text

Prior to the date of enactment of the Clean Water Act of 1977, referred to in subsec. (b)(4), means prior to the enactment of Pub. L. 95-217, Dec. 27, 1977, 91 Stat. 1566, which was approved Dec. 27, 1977.

Such Act, referred to in subsec. (b)(4), means Pub. L. 95-217, Dec. 27, 1977, 91 Stat. 1566, as amended, known as the Clean Water Act of 1977. For complete classification of this Act to the Code, see Short Title of 1977 Amendment note set out under section 1251 of this title and Tables.

Amendments

1977—Subsec. (b)(1). Pub. L. 95-217, Sec. 10(c), (d), substituted "cost of construction of treatment works required for a facility to train and upgrade waste treatment works operation and maintenance personnel and for the costs of other State treatment works operator training programs, including mobile training units, classroom rental, specialized instructors, and instructional material" for "cost of construction of a treatment works required for a facility to train and upgrade waste treatment works operation and maintenance personnel".

Subsec. (b)(2). Pub. L. 95-217, Sec. 10(e), authorized Administrator to make an additional grant for a supplemental facility in each of the States in any case where a grant is made to serve two or more States.

Subsec. (b)(3). Pub. L. 95-217, Sec. 10(a), substituted "$500,000" for "$250,000".

Subsec. (b)(4). Pub. L. 95-217, Sec. 10(b), added par. (4).

Section Referred to in Other Sections

This section is referred to in sections 1260, 1262 of this title.

APPLICATIONS; ALLOCATION

33 USC 1260

(1) A grant or contract authorized by section 1259 of this title may be made only upon application to the Administrator at such time or times and containing such information as he may prescribe, except that no such application shall be approved unless it—
   (A) sets forth programs, activities, research, or development for which a grant is authorized under section 1259 of this title and describes the relation to any program set forth by the applicant in an application, if any, submitted pursuant to section 1261 of this title;
   (B) provides such fiscal control and fund accounting procedures as may be necessary to assure proper disbursement of and accounting for Federal funds paid to the applicant under this section; and
   (C) provides for making such reports, in such form and containing such information, as the Administrator may require to carry out his functions under this section, and for keeping such records and for affording such access thereto as the Administrator may find necessary to assure the correctness and verification of such reports.
(2) The Administrator shall allocate grants or contracts under section 1259 of this title in such manner as will most nearly provide an equitable distribution of the grants or contracts throughout the United States among institutions of higher education which show promise of being able to use funds effectively for the purpose of this section.
(3) (A) Payments under this section may be used in accordance with regulations of the Administrator, and subject to the terms and conditions set forth in an application ap-

proved under paragraph (1), to pay part of the compensation of students employed in connection with the operation and maintenance of treatment works, other than as an employee in connection with the operation and maintenance of treatment works or as an employee in any branch of the Government of the United States, as part of a program for which a grant has been approved pursuant to this section.
- (B) Departments and agencies of the United States are encouraged, to the extent consistent with efficient administration, to enter into arrangements with institutions of higher education for the full-time, part-time, or temporary employment, whether in the competitive or excepted service, of students enrolled in programs set forth in applications approved under paragraph (1).

(June 30, 1948, ch. 758, title I, Sec. 110, as added Pub. L. 92-500, Sec. 2, Oct. 18, 1972, 86 Stat. 830.)

Section Referred to in Other Sections

This section is referred to in sections 1261, 1262 of this title.

SCHOLARSHIPS

33 USC 1261

(1) The Administrator is authorized to award scholarships in accordance with the provisions of this section for undergraduate study by persons who plan to enter an occupation involving the operation and maintenance of treatment works. Such scholarships shall be awarded for such periods as the Administrator may determine but not to exceed four academic years.

(2) The Administrator shall allocate scholarships under this section among institutions of higher education with programs approved under the provisions of this section for the use of individuals accepted into such programs in such manner and according to such plan as will insofar as practicable—
- (A) provide an equitable distribution of such scholarships throughout the United States; and
- (B) attract recent graduates of secondary schools to enter an occupation involving the operation and maintenance of treatment works.

(3) The Administrator shall approve a program of any institution of higher education for the purposes of this section only upon application by the institution and only upon his finding—
- (A) that such program has a principal objective the education and training of persons in the operation and maintenance of treatment works;
- (B) that such program is in effect and of high quality, or can be readily put into effect and may reasonably be expected to be of high quality;
- (C) that the application describes the relation of such program to any program, activity, research, or development set forth by the applicant in an application, if any, submitted pursuant to section 1260 of this title; and
- (D) that the application contains satisfactory assurances that (i) the institution will recommend to the Administrator for the award of scholarships under this section, for study in such program, only persons who have demonstrated to the satisfaction of the institution a serious intent, upon completing the program, to enter an occupation involving the operation and maintenance of treatment works, and (ii) the institution will make reasonable continuing efforts to encourage recipients of scholarships under this section, enrolled in such program, to enter occupations involving the operation and maintenance of treatment works upon completing the program.

(4) (A) The Administrator shall pay to persons awarded scholarships under this section such stipends (including such allowances for subsistence and other expenses for such persons and their dependents) as he may determine to be consistent with prevailing practices under comparable supported programs.
- (B) The Administrator shall (in addition to the stipends paid to persons under paragraph (1)) pay to the institution of higher education at which such person is pursuing his course of study such amount as he may determine to be consistent with prevailing practices under comparable federally supported programs.

(5) A person awarded a scholarship under the provisions of this section shall continue to receive the payments provided in this section only during such periods as the Administrator finds that he is maintaining satisfactory proficiency and devoting full time to study or research in the field in which such scholarship was awarded in an institution of higher education, and is not engaging in gainful employment other than employment approved by the Administrator by or pursuant to regulation.

(6) The Administrator shall by regulation provide that any person awarded a scholarship under this section shall agree in writing to enter and remain in an occupation involving the design, operation, or maintenance of treatment works for such period after completion of his course of studies as the Administrator determines appropriate.

(June 30, 1948, ch. 758, title I, Sec. 111, as added Pub. L. 92-500, Sec. 2, Oct. 18, 1972, 86 Stat. 831.)

Section Referred to in Other Sections

This section is referred to in sections 1260, 1262 of this title.

DEFINITIONS AND AUTHORIZATIONS

33 USC 1262

(a) As used in sections 1259 through 1262 of this title—
   (1) The term "institution of higher education" means an educational institution described in the first sentence of section 1001 of title 20 (other than an institution of any agency of the United States) which is accredited by a nationally recognized accrediting agency or association approved by the Administrator for this purpose. For purposes of this subsection, the Administrator shall publish a list of nationally recognized accrediting agencies or associations which he determines to be reliable authority as to the quality of training offered.
   (2) The term "academic year" means an academic year or its equivalent, as determined by the Administrator.

(b) The Administrator shall annually report his activities under sections 1259 through 1262 of this title, including recommendations for needed revisions in the provisions thereof.

(c) There are authorized to be appropriated $25,000,000 per fiscal year for the fiscal years ending June 30, 1973, June 30, 1974, and June 30, 1975, $6,000,000 for the fiscal year ending September 30, 1977, $7,000,000 for the fiscal year ending September 30, 1978, $7,000,000 for the fiscal year ending September 30, 1979, $7,000,000 for the fiscal year ending September 30, 1980, $7,000,000 for the fiscal year ending September 30, 1981, $7,000,000 for the fiscal year ending September 30, 1982, such sums as may be necessary for fiscal years 1983 through 1985, and $7,000,000 per fiscal year for each of the fiscal years 1986 through 1990, to carry out sections 1259 through 1262 of this title.

(June 30, 1948, ch. 758, title I, Sec. 112, as added Pub. L. 92-500, Sec. 2, Oct. 18, 1972, 86 Stat. 832; amended Pub. L. 93-592, Sec. 4, Jan. 2, 1975, 88 Stat. 1925; Pub. L. 95-217, Sec. 4(d), Dec. 27, 1977, 91 Stat. 1566; Pub. L. 96-483, Sec. 1(c), Oct. 21, 1980, 94 Stat. 2360; Pub. L. 100-4, title I, Sec. 101(c), Feb. 4, 1987, 101 Stat. 9; Pub. L. 105-244, title I, Sec. 102(a)(11), Oct. 7, 1998, 112 Stat. 1620.)

Amendments

1998—Subsec. (a)(1). Pub. L. 105-244 substituted "section 1001" for "section 1141".

1987—Subsec. (c). Pub. L. 100-4 struck out "and" after "1981," and inserted "such sums as may be necessary for fiscal years 1983 through 1985, and $7,000,000 per fiscal year for each of the fiscal years 1986 through 1990," after "1982,".

1980—Subsec. (c). Pub. L. 96-483 inserted authorization of the sum of $7,000,000 for each of fiscal years ending Sept. 30, 1981 and 1982.

1977—Subsec. (c). Pub. L. 95-217 substituted "June 30, 1975, $6,000,000 for the fiscal year ending September 30, 1977, $7,000,000 for the fiscal year ending September 30, 1978, $7,000,000 for the fiscal year ending September 30, 1979, and $7,000,000 for the fiscal year ending September 30, 1980," for "June 30, 1975,".

1975—Subsec. (c). Pub. L. 93-592 substituted "June 30, 1974, and June 30, 1975," for "and June 30, 1974,".

Effective Date of 1998 Amendment

Amendment by Pub. L. 105-244 effective Oct. 1, 1998, except as otherwise provided in Pub. L. 105-244, see section 3 of Pub. L. 105-244, set out as a note under section 1001 of Title 20, Education.

Section Referred to in Other Sections

This section is referred to in section 1376 of this title.

ALASKA VILLAGE DEMONSTRATION PROJECTS

33 USC 1263

(a) Central community facilities for safe water; elimination or control of pollution

The Administrator is authorized to enter into agreements with the State of Alaska to carry out one or more projects to demonstrate methods to provide for central community facilities for safe water and eliminate or control of pollution in those native villages of Alaska without such facilities. Such project shall include provisions for community safe water supply systems, toilets, bathing and laundry facilities, sewage disposal facilities, and other similar facilities, and educational and informational facilities and programs relating to health and hygiene. Such demonstration projects shall be for the further purpose of developing preliminary plans for providing such safe water and such elimination or control of pollution for all native villages in such State.

(b) Utilization of personnel and facilities of Department of Health and Human Services

In carrying out this section the Administrator shall cooperate with the Secretary of Health and Human Services for the purpose of utilizing such of the personnel and facilities of that Department as may be appropriate.

(c) Omitted

(d) Authorization of appropriations

There is authorized to be appropriated not to exceed $2,000,000 to carry out this section. In addition, there is authorized to be appropriated to carry out this section not to exceed $200,000 for the fiscal year ending September 30, 1978, and $220,000 for the fiscal year ending September 30, 1979.

(e) Study to develop comprehensive program for achieving sanitation services; report to Congress

The Administrator is authorized to coordinate with the Secretary of the Department of Health and Human Services, the Secretary of the Department of Housing and Urban Development, the Secretary of the Department of the Interior, the Secretary of the Department of Agriculture, and the heads of any other departments or agencies he may deem appropriate to conduct a joint study with representatives of the State of Alaska and the appropriate Native organizations (as defined in Public Law 92-203) to develop a comprehensive program for achieving adequate sanitation services in Alaska villages. This study shall be coordinated with the programs and projects authorized by sections 1254(q) and 1255(e)(2) of this title. The Administrator shall submit a report of the results of the study, together with appropriate supporting data and such recommendations as he deems desirable, to the Committee on Environment and Public Works of the Senate and to the Committee on Public Works and Transportation of the House of Representatives not later than December 31, 1979. The Administrator shall also submit recommended administrative actions, procedures, and any proposed legislation necessary to implement the recommendations of the study no later than June 30, 1980.

(f) Technical, financial, and management assistance

The Administrator is authorized to provide technical, financial and management assistance for operation and maintenance of the demonstration projects constructed under this section, until such time as the recommendations of subsection (e) of this section are implemented.

(g) "Village" and "sanitation services" defined

For the purpose of this section, the term "village" shall mean an incorporated or unincorporated community with a population of ten to six hundred people living within a two-mile radius. The term "sanitation services" shall mean water supply, sewage disposal, solid waste disposal and other services necessary to maintain generally accepted standards of personal hygiene and public health.

(June 30, 1948, ch. 758, title I, Sec. 113, as added Pub. L. 92-500, Sec. 2, Oct. 18, 1972, 86 Stat. 832; amended Pub. L. 95-217, Sec. 11, Dec. 27, 1977, 91 Stat. 1568; Pub. L. 96-88, title V, Sec. 509(b), Oct. 17, 1979, 93 Stat. 695.)

References in Text

Public Law 92-203, referred to in subsec. (e), is Pub. L. 92-203, Dec. 18, 1971, 85 Stat. 688, as amended, known as the Alaska Native Claims Settlement Act, which is classified generally to chapter 33 (Sec. 1601 et seq.) of Title 43, Public Lands. For complete classification of this Act to the Code, see Short Title note set out under section 1601 of Title 43 and Tables.

Codification

Subsec. (c) authorized the Administrator to report to Congress the results of the demonstration project accompanied by his recommendations for the establishment of a statewide project not later than July 1, 1973.

Amendments

1977—Subsec. (d). Pub. L. 95-217, Sec. 11(b), authorized additional appropriations of not to exceed $200,000 for the fiscal year ending Sept. 30, 1978, and $220,000, for the fiscal year ending Sept. 30, 1979, to carry out this section.

Subsecs. (e) to (g). Pub. L. 95-217, Sec. 11(a), added subsecs. (e), (f), and (g).

Change of Name

"Secretary of Health and Human Services" substituted for "Secretary of Health, Education, and Welfare" in subsec. (b), and "Secretary of the Department of Health and Human Services" substituted for "Secretary of the Department of Health, Education, and Welfare" in subsec. (e), pursuant to section 509(b) of Pub. L. 96-88 which is classified to section 3508(b) of Title 20, Education.

Committee on Public Works and Transportation of House of Representatives treated as referring to Committee on Transportation and Infrastructure of House of Representatives by section 1(a) of Pub. L. 104-14, set out as a note preceding section 21 of Title 2, The Congress.

Corps Capability Study, Alaska

Pub. L. 104-303, title IV, Sec. 401, Oct. 12, 1996, 110 Stat. 3740, provided that: "Not later than 18 months after the date of the enactment of this Act [Oct. 12, 1996], the Secretary shall report to Congress on the advisability and capability in the Corps of Engineers to implement rural sanitation projects for rural and Native villages in Alaska."

Section Referred to in Other Sections

This section is referred to in sections 1255, 1376 of this title.

GRANTS TO ALASKA TO IMPROVE SANITATION IN RURAL AND NATIVE VILLAGES

33 USC 1263a

(a) In general

The Administrator of the Environmental Protection Agency may make grants to the State of Alaska for the benefit of rural and Native villages in Alaska to pay the Federal share of the cost of—
  (1) the development and construction of public water systems and wastewater systems to improve the health and sanitation conditions in the villages; and
  (2) training, technical assistance, and educational programs relating to the operation and management of sanitation services in rural and Native villages.

(b) Federal share

The Federal share of the cost of the activities described in subsection (a) of this section shall be 50 percent.

(c) Administrative expenses

The State of Alaska may use an amount not to exceed 4 percent of any grant made available under this subsection[1] for administrative expenses necessary to carry out the activities described in subsection (a) of this section.

---

[1] So in original. Probably should be "section".

(d) Consultation with State of Alaska

The Administrator shall consult with the State of Alaska on a method of prioritizing the allocation of grants under subsection (a) of this section according to the needs of, and relative health and sanitation conditions in, each eligible village.

(e) Authorization of appropriations

There are authorized to be appropriated to carry out this section $40,000,000 for each of fiscal years 2001 through 2005.

(Pub. L. 104-182, title III, Sec. 303, Aug. 6, 1996, 110 Stat. 1683; Pub. L. 106-457, title IX, Sec. 903, Nov. 7, 2000, 114 Stat. 1982.)

Codification

Section was enacted as part of the Safe Drinking Water Act Amendments of 1996, and not as part of the Federal Water Pollution Control Act which comprises this chapter.

Amendments

2000—Subsec. (e). Pub. L. 106-457 substituted "to carry out this section $40,000,000 for each of fiscal years 2001 through 2005" for "$15,000,000 for each of the fiscal years 1997 through 2000 to carry out this section".

33 USC 1264

Omitted

Codification

Section, act June 30, 1948, ch. 758, title I, Sec. 114, as added Oct. 18, 1972, Pub. L. 92-500, Sec. 2, 86 Stat. 833, authorized the Administrator, in consultation with the Tahoe Regional Planning Agency, the Secretary of Agriculture, other Federal agencies, representatives of State and local governments, and members of the public, to conduct a thorough and complete study on the need of extending Federal oversight and control in order to preserve the fragile ecology of Lake Tahoe and to report the results of this study to Congress not later than one year after Oct. 18, 1972.

IN-PLACE TOXIC POLLUTANTS

33 USC 1265

The Administrator is directed to identify the location of in-place pollutants with emphasis on toxic pollutants in harbors and navigable waterways and is authorized, acting through the Secretary of the Army, to make contracts for the removal and appropriate disposal of such materials from critical port and harbor areas. There is authorized to be appropriated $15,000,000 to carry out the provisions of this section, which sum shall be available until expended.

(June 30, 1948, ch. 758, title I, Sec. 115, as added Pub. L. 92-500, Sec. 2, Oct. 18, 1972, 86 Stat. 833.)

Section Referred to in Other Sections

This section is referred to in sections 1266, 1376 of this title.

HUDSON RIVER RECLAMATION DEMONSTRATION PROJECT

33 USC 1266

(a) The Administrator is authorized to enter into contracts and other agreements with the State of New York to carry out a project to demonstrate methods for the selective removal of polychlorinated biphenyls contaminating bottom sediments of the Hudson River, treating such sediments as required, burying such sediments in secure landfills, and installing monitoring systems for such landfills. Such demonstration project shall be for the purpose of determining the feasibility of indefinite storage in secure landfills of toxic substances and of ascertaining the improvement of the rate of recovery of a toxic contaminated national waterway. No pollutants removed pursuant to this paragraph shall be placed in any landfill unless the Administrator first determines that disposal of the pollutants in such landfill would provide a higher standard of protection of the public health, safety, and welfare than disposal of such pollutants by any other method including, but not limited to, incineration or a chemical destruction process.

(b) The Administrator is authorized to make grants to the State of New York to carry out this section from funds allotted to such State under section 1285(a) of this title, except that the amount of any such grant shall be equal to 75 per centum of the cost of the project and such grant shall be made on condition that non-Federal sources provide the remainder of the cost of such project. The authority of this section shall be available until September 30, 1983. Funds allotted to the State of New York under section 1285(a) of this title shall be available under this subsection only to the extent that funds are not available, as determined by the Administrator, to the State of New York for the work authorized by this section under section 1265 or 1321 of this title or a comprehensive hazardous substance response and clean up fund. Any funds used under the authority of this subsection shall be deducted from any estimate of the needs of the State of New York prepared under section 1375 of this title. The Administrator may not obligate or expend more than $20,000,000 to carry out this section.

(June 30, 1948, ch. 758, title I, Sec. 116, as added Pub. L. 96-483, Sec. 10, Oct. 21, 1980, 94 Stat. 2363; amended Pub. L. 105-362, title V, Sec. 501(d)(2)(B), Nov. 10, 1998, 112 Stat. 3284.)

Amendments

1998—Subsec. (b). Pub. L. 105-362 substituted "section 1375 of this title" for "section 1375(b) of this title" in penultimate sentence.

CHESAPEAKE BAY

33 USC 1267

(a) Definitions.—In this section, the following definitions apply:
   (1) Administrative cost.—The term "administrative cost" means the cost of salaries and fringe benefits incurred in administering a grant under this section.
   (2) Chesapeake Bay Agreement.—The term "Chesapeake Bay Agreement" means the formal, voluntary agreements executed to achieve the goal of restoring and protecting the Chesapeake Bay ecosystem and the living resources of the Chesapeake Bay ecosystem and signed by the Chesapeake Executive Council.
   (3) Chesapeake Bay ecosystem.—The term "Chesapeake Bay ecosystem" means the ecosystem of the Chesapeake Bay and its watershed.
   (4) Chesapeake Bay Program.—The term "Chesapeake Bay Program" means the program directed by the Chesapeake Executive Council in accordance with the Chesapeake Bay Agreement.
   (5) Chesapeake Executive Council.—The term "Chesapeake Executive Council" means the signatories to the Chesapeake Bay Agreement.
   (6) Signatory jurisdiction.—The term "signatory jurisdiction" means a jurisdiction of a signatory to the Chesapeake Bay Agreement.
(b) Continuation of Chesapeake Bay Program
   (1) In general.—In cooperation with the Chesapeake Executive Council (and as a member of the Council), the Administrator shall continue the Chesapeake Bay Program.
   (2) Program Office
      (A) In general.—The Administrator shall maintain in the Environmental Protection Agency a Chesapeake Bay Program Office.
      (B) Function.—The Chesapeake Bay Program Office shall provide support to the Chesapeake Executive Council by—
         (i) implementing and coordinating science, research, modeling, support services, monitoring, data collection, and other activities that support the Chesapeake Bay Program;
         (ii) developing and making available, through publications, technical assistance, and other appropriate means, information pertaining to the environmental quality and living resources of the Chesapeake Bay ecosystem;
         (iii) in cooperation with appropriate Federal, State, and local authorities, assisting the signatories to the Chesapeake Bay Agreement in developing and implementing

specific action plans to carry out the responsibilities of the signatories to the Chesapeake Bay Agreement;
  - (iv) coordinating the actions of the Environmental Protection Agency with the actions of the appropriate officials of other Federal agencies and State and local authorities in developing strategies to—
    - (I) improve the water quality and living resources in the Chesapeake Bay ecosystem; and
    - (II) obtain the support of the appropriate officials of the agencies and authorities in achieving the objectives of the Chesapeake Bay Agreement; and
  - (v) implementing outreach programs for public information, education, and participation to foster stewardship of the resources of the Chesapeake Bay.
- (c) Interagency agreements.—The Administrator may enter into an interagency agreement with a Federal agency to carry out this section.
- (d) Technical assistance and assistance grants
  - (1) In general.—In cooperation with the Chesapeake Executive Council, the Administrator may provide technical assistance, and assistance grants, to nonprofit organizations, State and local governments, colleges, universities, and interstate agencies to carry out this section, subject to such terms and conditions as the Administrator considers appropriate.
  - (2) Federal share
    - (A) In general.—Except as provided in subparagraph (B), the Federal share of an assistance grant provided under paragraph (1) shall be determined by the Administrator in accordance with guidance issued by the Administrator.
    - (B) Small watershed grants program.—The Federal share of an assistance grant provided under paragraph (1) to carry out an implementing activity under subsection (g)(2) of this section shall not exceed 75 percent of eligible project costs, as determined by the Administrator.
  - (3) Non-Federal share.—An assistance grant under paragraph (1) shall be provided on the condition that non-Federal sources provide the remainder of eligible project costs, as determined by the Administrator.
  - (4) Administrative costs.—Administrative costs shall not exceed 10 percent of the annual grant award.
- (e) Implementation and monitoring grants
  - (1) In general.—If a signatory jurisdiction has approved and committed to implement all or substantially all aspects of the Chesapeake Bay Agreement, on the request of the chief executive of the jurisdiction, the Administrator—
    - (A) shall make a grant to the jurisdiction for the purpose of implementing the management mechanisms established under the Chesapeake Bay Agreement, subject to such terms and conditions as the Administrator considers appropriate; and
    - (B) may make a grant to a signatory jurisdiction for the purpose of monitoring the Chesapeake Bay ecosystem.
  - (2) Proposals
    - (A) In general.—A signatory jurisdiction described in paragraph (1) may apply for a grant under this subsection for a fiscal year by submitting to the Administrator a comprehensive proposal to implement management mechanisms established under the Chesapeake Bay Agreement.
    - (B) Contents.—A proposal under subparagraph (A) shall include—
      - (i) a description of proposed management mechanisms that the jurisdiction commits to take within a specified time period, such as reducing or preventing pollution in the Chesapeake Bay and its watershed or meeting applicable water quality standards or established goals and objectives under the Chesapeake Bay Agreement; and
      - (ii) the estimated cost of the actions proposed to be taken during the fiscal year.
  - (3) Approval.—If the Administrator finds that the proposal is consistent with the Chesapeake Bay Agreement and the national goals established under section 1251(a) of this title, the Administrator may approve the proposal for an award.
  - (4) Federal share.—The Federal share of a grant under this subsection shall not exceed 50 percent of the cost of implementing the management mechanisms during the fiscal year.

(5) Non-Federal share.—A grant under this subsection shall be made on the condition that non-Federal sources provide the remainder of the costs of implementing the management mechanisms during the fiscal year.
(6) Administrative costs.—Administrative costs shall not exceed 10 percent of the annual grant award.
(7) Reporting.—On or before October 1 of each fiscal year, the Administrator shall make available to the public a document that lists and describes, in the greatest practicable degree of detail—
    (A) all projects and activities funded for the fiscal year;
    (B) the goals and objectives of projects funded for the previous fiscal year; and
    (C) the net benefits of projects funded for previous fiscal years.
(f) Federal facilities and budget coordination
    (1) Subwatershed planning and restoration.—A Federal agency that owns or operates a facility (as defined by the Administrator) within the Chesapeake Bay watershed shall participate in regional and subwatershed planning and restoration programs.
    (2) Compliance with agreement.—The head of each Federal agency that owns or occupies real property in the Chesapeake Bay watershed shall ensure that the property, and actions taken by the agency with respect to the property, comply with the Chesapeake Bay Agreement, the Federal Agencies Chesapeake Ecosystem Unified Plan, and any subsequent agreements and plans.
    (3) Budget coordination
        (A) In general.—As part of the annual budget submission of each Federal agency with projects or grants related to restoration, planning, monitoring, or scientific investigation of the Chesapeake Bay ecosystem, the head of the agency shall submit to the President a report that describes plans for the expenditure of the funds under this section.
        (B) Disclosure to the Council.—The head of each agency referred to in subparagraph (A) shall disclose the report under that subparagraph with the Chesapeake Executive Council as appropriate.
(g) Chesapeake Bay Program
    (1) Management strategies.—The Administrator, in coordination with other members of the Chesapeake Executive Council, shall ensure that management plans are developed and implementation is begun by signatories to the Chesapeake Bay Agreement to achieve and maintain—
        (A) the nutrient goals of the Chesapeake Bay Agreement for the quantity of nitrogen and phosphorus entering the Chesapeake Bay and its watershed;
        (B) the water quality requirements necessary to restore living resources in the Chesapeake Bay ecosystem;
        (C) the Chesapeake Bay Basinwide Toxins Reduction and Prevention Strategy goal of reducing or eliminating the input of chemical contaminants from all controllable sources to levels that result in no toxic or bioaccumulative impact on the living resources of the Chesapeake Bay ecosystem or on human health;
        (D) habitat restoration, protection, creation, and enhancement goals established by Chesapeake Bay Agreement signatories for wetlands, riparian forests, and other types of habitat associated with the Chesapeake Bay ecosystem; and
        (E) the restoration, protection, creation, and enhancement goals established by the Chesapeake Bay Agreement signatories for living resources associated with the Chesapeake Bay ecosystem.
    (2) Small watershed grants program.—The Administrator, in cooperation with the Chesapeake Executive Council, shall—
        (A) establish a small watershed grants program as part of the Chesapeake Bay Program; and
        (B) offer technical assistance and assistance grants under subsection (d) of this section to local governments and nonprofit organizations and individuals in the Chesapeake Bay region to implement—
            (i) cooperative tributary basin strategies that address the water quality and living resource needs in the Chesapeake Bay ecosystem; and

(ii) locally based protection and restoration programs or projects within a watershed that complement the tributary basin strategies, including the creation, restoration, protection, or enhancement of habitat associated with the Chesapeake Bay ecosystem.
(h) Study of Chesapeake Bay Program
  (1) In general.—Not later than April 22, 2003, and every 5 years thereafter, the Administrator, in coordination with the Chesapeake Executive Council, shall complete a study and submit to Congress a comprehensive report on the results of the study.
  (2) Requirements.—The study and report shall—
    (A) assess the state of the Chesapeake Bay ecosystem;
    (B) compare the current state of the Chesapeake Bay ecosystem with its state in 1975, 1985, and 1995;
    (C) assess the effectiveness of management strategies being implemented on November 7, 2000, and the extent to which the priority needs are being met;
    (D) make recommendations for the improved management of the Chesapeake Bay Program either by strengthening strategies being implemented on November 7, 2000, or by adopting new strategies; and
    (E) be presented in such a format as to be readily transferable to and usable by other watershed restoration programs.
(i) Special study of living resource response
  (1) In general.—Not later than 180 days after November 7, 2000, the Administrator shall commence a 5-year special study with full participation of the scientific community of the Chesapeake Bay to Establish and expand understanding of the response of the living resources of the Chesapeake Bay ecosystem to improvements in water quality that have resulted from investments made through the Chesapeake Bay Program.
  (2) Requirements.—The study shall—
    (A) determine the current status and trends of living resources, including grasses, benthos, phytoplankton, zooplankton, fish, and shellfish;
    (B) establish to the extent practicable the rates of recovery of the living resources in response to improved water quality condition;
    (C) evaluate and assess interactions of species, with particular attention to the impact of changes within and among Trophic levels; and
    (D) recommend management actions to optimize the return of a healthy and balanced ecosystem in response to improvements in the quality and character of the waters of the Chesapeake Bay.
(j) Authorization of appropriations.—There is authorized to be appropriated to carry out this section $40,000,000 for each of fiscal years 2001 through 2005. Such sums shall remain available until expended.
(June 30, 1948, ch. 758, title I, Sec. 117, as added Pub. L. 100-4, title I, Sec. 103, Feb. 4, 1987, 101 Stat. 10; amended Pub. L. 106-457, title II, Sec. 203, Nov. 7, 2000, 114 Stat. 1967.)

Codification

November 7, 2000, referred to in subsecs. (h)(2)(C), (D), and (i)(1), was in the original "the date of enactment of this section", which was translated as meaning the date of enactment of Pub. L. 106-457, which amended this Section generally, to reflect the probable intent of Congress.

Amendments

2000—Pub. L. 106-457 amended section generally, substituting subsecs. (a) to (j) for former subsecs. (a) to (d), which related to continuation of the Chesapeake Bay Program and establishment and maintenance in the Environmental Protection Agency of an office, division, or branch of Chesapeake Bay Programs, interstate development plan grants, progress reports from grant recipient States, and authorization of appropriations.

Findings and Purposes

Pub. L. 106-457, title II, Sec. 202, Nov. 7, 2000, 114 Stat. 1967, provided that:
"(a) Findings.—Congress finds that—
  (1) the Chesapeake Bay is a national treasure and a resource of worldwide significance;

(2) over many years, the productivity and water quality of the Chesapeake Bay and its watershed were diminished by pollution, excessive sedimentation, shoreline erosion, the impacts of population growth and development in the Chesapeake Bay watershed, and other factors;
(3) the Federal Government (acting through the Administrator of the Environmental Protection Agency), the Governor of the State of Maryland, the Governor of the Commonwealth of Virginia, the Governor of the Commonwealth of Pennsylvania, the Chairperson of the Chesapeake Bay Commission, and the mayor of the District of Columbia, as Chesapeake Bay Agreement signatories, have committed to a comprehensive cooperative program to achieve improved water quality and improvements in the productivity of living resources of the Bay;
(4) the cooperative program described in paragraph (3) serves as a national and international model for the management of estuaries; and
(5) there is a need to expand Federal support for monitoring, management, and restoration activities in the Chesapeake Bay and the tributaries of the Bay in order to meet and further the original and subsequent goals and commitments of the Chesapeake Bay Program.
(b) Purposes.—The purposes of this title [amending this section and enacting provisions set out as a note under section 1251 of this title] are—
(1) to expand and strengthen cooperative efforts to restore and protect the Chesapeake Bay; and
(2) to achieve the goals established in the Chesapeake Bay Agreement."

Nutrient Loading Resulting From Dredged Material Disposal

Pub. L. 106-53, title IV, Sec. 457, Aug. 17, 1999, 113 Stat. 332, provided that:

"(a) Study.—The Secretary shall conduct a study of nutrient loading that occurs as a result of discharges of dredged material into open-water sites in the Chesapeake Bay.

(b) Report.—Not later than 18 months after the date of enactment of this Act [Aug. 17, 1999], the secretary shall submit to Congress a report on the results of the study."

Section Referred to in Other Sections

This section is referred to in section 2902 of this title.

GREAT LAKES

33 USC 1268

(a) Findings, purpose, and definitions
  (1) Findings
    The Congress finds that—
    (A) the Great Lakes are a valuable national resource, continuously serving the people of the United States and other nations as an important source of food, fresh water, recreation, beauty, and enjoyment;
    (B) the United States should seek to attain the goals embodied in the Great Lakes Water Quality Agreement of 1978, as amended by the Water Quality Agreement of 1987 and any other agreements and amendments, with particular emphasis on goals related to toxic pollutants; and
    (C) the Environmental Protection Agency should take the lead in the effort to meet those goals, working with other Federal agencies and State and local authorities.
  (2) Purpose
    It is the purpose of this section to achieve the goals embodied in the Great Lakes Water Quality Agreement of 1978, as amended by the Water Quality Agreement of 1987 and any other agreements and amendments, through improved organization and definition of mission on the part of the Agency, funding of State grants for pollution control in the Great Lakes area, and improved accountability for implementation of such agreement.
  (3) Definitions
    For purposes of this section, the term—
    (A) "Agency" means the Environmental Protection Agency;

(B) "Great Lakes" means Lake Ontario, Lake Erie, Lake Huron (including Lake St. Clair), Lake Michigan, and Lake Superior, and the connecting channels (Saint Mary's River, Saint Clair River, Detroit River, Niagara River, and Saint Lawrence River to the Canadian Border);

(C) "Great Lakes System" means all the streams, rivers, lakes, and other bodies of water within the drainage basin of the Great Lakes;

(D) "Program Office" means the Great Lakes National Program Office established by this section;

(E) "Research Office" means the Great Lakes Research Office established by subsection (d) of this section;

(F) "area of concern" means a geographic area located within the Great Lakes, in which beneficial uses are impaired and which has been officially designated as such under Annex 2 of the Great Lakes Water Quality Agreement;

(G) "Great Lakes States" means the States of Illinois, Indiana, Michigan, Minnesota, New York, Ohio, Pennsylvania, and Wisconsin;

(H) "Great Lakes Water Quality Agreement" means the bilateral agreement, between the United States and Canada which was signed in 1978 and amended by the Protocol of 1987;

(I) "Lakewide Management Plan" means a written document which embodies a systematic and comprehensive ecosystem approach to restoring and protecting the beneficial uses of the open waters of each of the Great Lakes, in accordance with article VI and Annex 2 of the Great Lakes Water Quality Agreement; and

(J) "Remedial Action Plan" means a written document which embodies a systematic and comprehensive ecosystem approach to restoring and protecting the beneficial uses of areas of concern, in accordance with article VI and Annex 2 of the Great Lakes Water Quality Agreement.

(b) Great Lakes National Program Office

The Great Lakes National Program Office (previously established by the Administrator) is hereby established within the Agency. The Program Office shall be headed by a Director who, by reason of management experience and technical expertise relating to the Great Lakes, is highly qualified to direct the development of programs and plans on a variety of Great Lakes issues. The Great Lakes National Program Office shall be located in a Great Lakes State.

(c) Great Lakes management

(1) Functions

The Program Office shall—

(A) in cooperation with appropriate Federal, State, tribal, and international agencies, and in accordance with section 1251(e) of this title, develop and implement specific action plans to carry out the responsibilities of the United States under the Great Lakes Water Quality Agreement of 1978, as amended by the Water Quality Agreement of 1987 and any other agreements and amendments,;[1]

(B) establish a Great Lakes system-wide surveillance network to monitor the water quality of the Great Lakes, with specific emphasis on the monitoring of toxic pollutants;

(C) serve as the liaison with, and provide information to, the Canadian members of the International Joint Commission and the Canadian counterpart to the Agency;

(D) coordinate actions of the Agency (including actions by headquarters and regional offices thereof) aimed at improving Great Lakes water quality; and

(E) coordinate actions of the Agency with the actions of other Federal agencies and State and local authorities, so as to ensure the input of those agencies and authorities in developing water quality strategies and obtain the support of those agencies and authorities in achieving the objectives of such agreement.

(2) Great Lakes water quality guidance

(A) By June 30, 1991, the Administrator, after consultation with the Program Office, shall publish in the Federal Register for public notice and comment proposed water quality guidance for the Great Lakes System. Such guidance shall conform with the objectives and provisions of the Great Lakes Water Quality Agreement, shall be no less restrictive than the provisions of this chapter and national water quality criteria and

---

[1] So in original.

guidance, shall specify numerical limits on pollutants in ambient Great Lakes waters to protect human health, aquatic life, and wildlife, and shall provide guidance to the Great Lakes States on minimum water quality standards, antidegradation policies, and implementation procedures for the Great Lakes System.
- (B) By June 30, 1992, the Administrator, in consultation with the Program Office, shall publish in the Federal Register, pursuant to this section and the Administrator's authority under this chapter, final water quality guidance for the Great Lakes System.
- (C) Within two years after such Great Lakes guidance is published, the Great Lakes States shall adopt water quality standards, antidegradation policies, and implementation procedures for waters within the Great Lakes System which are consistent with such guidance. If a Great Lakes State fails to adopt such standards, policies, and procedures, the Administrator shall promulgate them not later than the end of such two-year period. When reviewing any Great Lakes State's water quality plan, the agency shall consider the extent to which the State has complied with the Great Lakes guidance issued pursuant to this section.
- (3) Remedial Action Plans
  - (A) For each area of concern for which the United States has agreed to draft a Remedial Action Plan, the Program Office shall ensure that the Great Lakes State in which such area of concern is located—
    - (i) submits a Remedial Action Plan to the Program Office by June 30, 1991;
    - (ii) submits such Remedial Action Plan to the International Joint Commission by January 1, 1992; and
    - (iii) includes such Remedial Action Plans within the State's water quality plan by January 1, 1993.
  - (B) For each area of concern for which Canada has agreed to draft a Remedial Action Plan, the Program Office shall, pursuant to subparagraph (c)(1)(C) of this section, work with Canada to assure the submission of such Remedial Action Plans to the International Joint Commission by June 30, 1991, and to finalize such Remedial Action Plans by January 1, 1993.
  - (C) For any area of concern designated as such subsequent to November 16, 1990, the Program Office shall (i) if the United States has agreed to draft the Remedial Action Plan, ensure that the Great Lakes State in which such area of concern is located submits such Plan to the Program Office within two years of the area's designation, submits it to the International Joint Commission no later than six months after submitting it to the Program Office, and includes such Plan in the State's water quality plan no later than one year after submitting it to the Commission; and (ii) if Canada has agreed to draft the Remedial Action Plan, work with Canada, pursuant to subparagraph (c)(1)(C) of this section, to ensure the submission of such Plan to the International Joint Commission within two years of the area's designation and the finalization of such Plan no later than eighteen months after submitting it to such Commission.
  - (D) The Program Office shall compile formal comments on individual Remedial Action Plans made by the International Joint Commission pursuant to section 4(d) of Annex 2 of the Great Lakes Water Quality Agreement and, upon request by a member of the public, shall make such comments available for inspection and copying. The Program Office shall also make available, upon request, formal comments made by the Environmental Protection Agency on individual Remedial Action Plans.
  - (E) Report.—Not later than 1 year after the date of enactment of this subparagraph, the Administrator shall submit to Congress a report on such actions, time periods, and resources as are necessary to fulfill the duties of the Agency relating to oversight of Remedial Action plans under—
    - (i) this paragraph; and
    - (ii) the Great Lakes Water Quality Agreement.
- (4) Lakewide Management Plans
  The Administrator, in consultation with the Program Office shall—
  - (A) by January 1, 1992, publish in the Federal Register a proposed Lakewide Management Plan for Lake Michigan and solicit public comments;

(B) by January 1, 1993, submit a proposed Lakewide Management Plan for Lake Michigan to the International Joint Commission for review; and

(C) by January 1, 1994, publish in the Federal Register a final Lakewide Management Plan for Lake Michigan and begin implementation.

Nothing in this subparagraph shall preclude the simultaneous development of Lakewide Management Plans for the other Great Lakes.

(5) Spills of oil and hazardous materials

The Program Office, in consultation with the Coast Guard, shall identify areas within the Great Lakes which are likely to experience numerous or voluminous spills of oil or other hazardous materials from land based facilities, vessels, or other sources and, in consultation with the Great Lakes States, shall identify weaknesses in Federal and State programs and systems to prevent and respond to such spills. This information shall be included on at least a biennial basis in the report required by this section.

(6) 5-year plan and program

The Program Office shall develop, in consultation with the States, a five-year plan and program for reducing the amount of nutrients introduced into the Great Lakes. Such program shall incorporate any management program for reducing nutrient runoff from nonpoint sources established under section 1329 of this title and shall include a program for monitoring nutrient runoff into, and ambient levels in, the Great Lakes.

(7) 5-year study and demonstration projects

(A) The Program Office shall carry out a five-year study and demonstration projects relating to the control and removal of toxic pollutants in the Great Lakes, with emphasis on the removal of toxic pollutants from bottom sediments. In selecting locations for conducting demonstration projects under this paragraph, priority consideration shall be given to projects at the following locations: Saginaw Bay, Michigan; Sheboygan Harbor, Wisconsin; Grand Calumet River, Indiana; Ashtabula River, Ohio; and Buffalo River, New York.

(B) The Program Office shall—

(i) by December 31, 1990, complete chemical, physical, and biological assessments of the contaminated sediments at the locations selected for the study and demonstration projects;

(ii) by December 31, 1990, announce the technologies that will be demonstrated at each location and the numerical standard of protection intended to be achieved at each location;

(iii) by December 31, 1992, complete full or pilot scale demonstration projects on site at each location of promising technologies to remedy contaminated sediments; and

(iv) by December 31, 1993, issue a final report to Congress on its findings.

(C) The Administrator, after providing for public review and comment, shall publish information concerning the public health and environmental consequences of contaminants in Great Lakes sediment. Information published pursuant to this subparagraph shall include specific numerical limits to protect health, aquatic life, and wildlife from the bioaccumulation of toxins. The Administrator shall, at a minimum, publish information pursuant to this subparagraph within 2 years of November 16, 1990.

(8) Administrator's responsibility

The Administrator shall ensure that the Program Office enters into agreements with the various organizational elements of the Agency involved in Great Lakes activities and the appropriate State agencies specifically delineating—

(A) the duties and responsibilities of each such element in the Agency with respect to the Great Lakes;

(B) the time periods for carrying out such duties and responsibilities; and

(C) the resources to be committed to such duties and responsibilities.

(9) Budget item

The Administrator shall, in the Agency's annual budget submission to Congress, include a funding request for the Program Office as a separate budget line item.

(10) Comprehensive report

Within 90 days after the end of each fiscal year, the Administrator shall submit to Congress a comprehensive report which—

(A) describes the achievements in the preceding fiscal year in implementing the Great Lakes Water Quality Agreement of 1978, as amended by the Water Quality Agreement of 1987 and any other agreements and amendments, and shows by categories (including judicial enforcement, research, State cooperative efforts, and general administration) the amounts expended on Great Lakes water quality initiatives in such preceding fiscal year;

(B) describes the progress made in such preceding fiscal year in implementing the system of surveillance of the water quality in the Great Lakes System, including the monitoring of groundwater and sediment, with particular reference to toxic pollutants;

(C) describes the long-term prospects for improving the condition of the Great Lakes; and

(D) provides a comprehensive assessment of the planned efforts to be pursued in the succeeding fiscal year for implementing the Great Lakes Water Quality Agreement of 1978, as amended by the Water Quality Agreement of 1987 and any other agreements and amendments,,[2] which assessment shall—

   (i) show by categories (including judicial enforcement, research, State cooperative efforts, and general administration) the amount anticipated to be expended on Great Lakes water quality initiatives in the fiscal year to which the assessment relates; and

   (ii) include a report of current programs administered by other Federal agencies which make available resources to the Great Lakes water quality management efforts.

(11) Confined disposal facilities

(A) The Administrator, in consultation with the Assistant Secretary of the Army for Civil Works, shall develop and implement, within one year of November 16, 1990, management plans for every Great Lakes confined disposal facility.

(B) The plan shall provide for monitoring of such facilities, including—

   (i) water quality at the site and in the area of the site;
   (ii) sediment quality at the site and in the area of the site;
   (iii) the diversity, productivity, and stability of aquatic organisms at the site and in the area of the site; and
   (iv) such other conditions as the Administrator deems appropriate.

(C) The plan shall identify the anticipated use and management of the site over the following twenty-year period including the expected termination of dumping at the site, the anticipated need for site management, including pollution control, following the termination of the use of the site.

(D) The plan shall identify a schedule for review and revision of the plan which shall not be less frequent than five years after adoption of the plan and every five years thereafter.

(12) Remediation of sediment contamination in areas of concern.—

(A) In general.—In accordance with this paragraph, the Administrator, acting through the Program Office, may carry out projects that meet the requirements of subparagraph (B).

(B) Eligible projects.—A project meets the requirements of this subparagraph if the projects to be carried out in an area of concern located wholly or partially in the United States and the project—

   (i) monitors or evaluates contaminated sediment;
   (ii) subject to subparagraph (D), implements a plan to remediate contaminated sediment; or
   (iii) prevents further or renewed contamination of sediment.

(C) Priority.—In selecting projects to carry out under this paragraph, the Administrator shall give priority to a project that—

   (i) constitutes remedial action for contaminated sediment;
   (ii) (I) has been identified in a Remedial Action Plan submitted under paragraph (3); and (II) is ready to be implemented;
   (iii) will use an innovative approach, technology, or technique that may provide greater environmental benefits, or equivalent environmental benefits at a reduced cost; or

---

[2] So in original.

(iv) includes remediation to be commenced not later than 1 year after the date of receipt of funds for the project.
(D) Limitation.—The Administrator may not carry out a project under this paragraph for remediation of contaminated sediments located in an area of concern—
  (i) if an evaluation of remedial alternatives for the area of concern has not been conducted, including a review of the short-term and long-term effects of the alternatives on human health and the environment; or
  (ii) if the Administrator determines that the area of concern is likely to suffer significant further or renewed contamination from existing sources of pollutants causing sediment contamination following completion of the project.
(E) Non-federal share.—
  (i) In general.—The non-Federal share of the cost of a project carried out under this paragraph shall be at least 35 percent.
  (ii) In-kind contributions.—The non-Federal share of the cost of a project carried out under this paragraph may include the value of in-kind services contributed by a non-Federal sponsor.
  (iii) Non-federal share.—The non-Federal share of the cost of a project carried out under this paragraph—
    (I) may include monies paid pursuant to, or the value of any in-kind service performed under, an administrative order on consent or judicial consent decree; but
    (II) may not include any funds paid pursuant to, or the value of any in-kind service performed under, a unilateral administrative order or court order.
  (iv) Operation and maintenance.—The non-Federal share of the cost of the operation and maintenance of a project carried out under this paragraph shall be 100 percent.
(F) Maintenance of effort.—The Administrator may not carry out a project under this paragraph unless the non-Federal sponsor enters into such agreements with the Administrator as the Administrator may require to ensure that the non-Federal sponsor will maintain its aggregate expenditures from all other sources for remediation programs in the area of concern in which the project is located at or above the average level of such expenditures in the 2 fiscal years preceding the date on which the project is initiated.
(G) Coordination.—In carrying out projects under this paragraph, the Administrator shall coordinate with the Secretary of the Army, and with the Governors of States in which the projects are located, to ensure that Federal and State assistance for remediation in areas of concern is used as efficiently as practicable.
(H) Authorization of appropriations.—
  (i) In general.—In addition to other amounts authorized under this section, there is authorized to be appropriated to carry out this paragraph $50,000,000 for each of fiscal years 2004 through 2008.
  (ii) Availability.—Funds made available under clause (i) shall remain available until expended.
(13) Public information program.—
(A) In general.—The Administrator, acting through the Program Office and in coordination with States, Indian tribes, local governments, and other entities, may carry out a public information program to provide information relating to the remediation of contaminated sediment to the public in areas of concern that are located wholly or partially in the United States.
(B) Authorization of appropriations.—There is authorized to be appropriated to carry out this paragraph $1,000,000 for each of fiscal years 2004 through 2008.
(d) Great Lakes research
  (1) Establishment of Research Office
  There is established within the National Oceanic and Atmospheric Administration the Great Lakes Research Office.
  (2) Identification of issues
  The Research Office shall identify issues relating to the Great Lakes resources on which research is needed. The Research Office shall submit a report to Congress on such issues

452 / Environmental Statutes

before the end of each fiscal year which shall identify any changes in the Great Lakes system[3] with respect to such issues.

(3) Inventory

The Research Office shall identify and inventory Federal, State, university, and tribal environmental research programs (and, to the extent feasible, those of private organizations and other nations) relating to the Great Lakes system,[3] and shall update that inventory every four years.

(4) Research exchange

The Research Office shall establish a Great Lakes research exchange for the purpose of facilitating the rapid identification, acquisition, retrieval, dissemination, and use of information concerning research projects which are ongoing or completed and which affect the Great Lakes System.

(5) Research program

The Research Office shall develop, in cooperation with the Coordination Office, a comprehensive environmental research program and data base for the Great Lakes system.[3] The data base shall include, but not be limited to, data relating to water quality, fisheries, and biota.

(6) Monitoring

The Research Office shall conduct, through the Great Lakes Environmental Research Laboratory, the National Sea Grant College program, other Federal laboratories, and the private sector, appropriate research and monitoring activities which address priority issues and current needs relating to the Great Lakes.

(7) Location

The Research Office shall be located in a Great Lakes State.

(e) Research and management coordination

(1) Joint plan

Before October 1 of each year, the Program Office and the Research Office shall prepare a joint research plan for the fiscal year which begins in the following calendar year.

(2) Contents of plan

Each plan prepared under paragraph (1) shall—

(A) identify all proposed research dedicated to activities conducted under the Great Lakes Water Quality Agreement of 1978, as amended by the Water Quality Agreement of 1987 and any other agreements and amendments,;[4]

(B) include the Agency's assessment of priorities for research needed to fulfill the terms of such Agreement; and

(C) identify all proposed research that may be used to develop a comprehensive environmental data base for the Great Lakes System and establish priorities for development of such data base.

(3) Health research report

(A) Not later than September 30, 1994, the Program Office, in consultation with the Research Office, the Agency for Toxic Substances and Disease Registry, and Great Lakes States shall submit to the Congress a report assessing the adverse effects of water pollutants in the Great Lakes System on the health of persons in Great Lakes States and the health of fish, shellfish, and wildlife in the Great Lakes System. In conducting research in support of this report, the Administrator may, where appropriate, provide for research to be conducted under cooperative agreements with Great Lakes States.

(B) There is authorized to be appropriated to the Administrator to carry out this section not to exceed $3,000,000 for each of fiscal years 1992, 1993, and 1994.

(f) Interagency cooperation

The head of each department, agency, or other instrumentality of the Federal Government which is engaged in, is concerned with, or has authority over programs relating to research, monitoring, and planning to maintain, enhance, preserve, or rehabilitate the environmental quality and natural resources of the Great Lakes, including the Chief of Engineers of the Army, the Chief of the Soil Conservation Service, the Commandant of the Coast Guard, the Director of the Fish and Wildlife Service, and the Administrator of the National Oceanic and Atmospheric Administration, shall submit an annual report to the Administrator with respect

---

[3]So in original. Probably should be capitalized.

[4]So in original.

to the activities of that agency or office affecting compliance with the Great Lakes Water Quality Agreement of 1978, as amended by the Water Quality Agreement of 1987 and any other agreements and amendments,.[4]

(g) Relationship to existing Federal and State laws and international treaties
Nothing in this section shall be construed
  (1) to affect the jurisdiction, powers, or prerogatives of any department, agency, or officer of the Federal Government or of any State government, or of any tribe, nor any powers, jurisdiction, or prerogatives of any international body created by treaty with authority relating to the Great Lakes; or
  (2) to affect any other Federal or State authority that is being used or may be used to facilitate the cleanup and protection of the Great Lakes.

(h) Authorizations of Great Lakes appropriations
There are authorized to be appropriated to the Administrator to carry out this section not to exceed—
  (1) $11,000,000;
  (2) such sums as are necessary for each of fiscal years 1992 through 2003; and
  (3) $25,000,000 for each of fiscal years 2004 through 2008.

(June 30, 1948, ch. 758, title I, Sec. 118, as added Pub. L. 100-4, title I, Sec. 104, Feb. 4, 1987, 101 Stat. 11; amended Pub. L. 100-688, title I, Sec. 1008, Nov. 18, 1988, 102 Stat. 4151; Pub. L. 101-596, title I, Secs. 101-106, Nov. 16, 1990, 104 Stat. 3000-3004.)

Codification

November 16, 1990, referred to in subsec. (c)(3)(C), (7)(C), was in the original "the enactment of this Act", and "the date of the enactment of this title" which were translated as meaning the date of enactment of Pub. L. 101-596, title I of which enacted subsec. (c)(3), (7)(C), to reflect the probable intent of Congress.

Amendments

2002—Subsec. (c)(3) added subpar. (E).
  Subsec. (c) added (12) and (13).
  Subsec. (g) and (h) amended.
1990—Subsec. (a)(3)(F) to (J). Pub. L. 101-596, Sec. 103, added subpars. (F) to (J).
  Subsec. (c)(2) to (11). Pub. L. 101-596, Secs. 101, 102, 104, added pars. (2) to (5) after par. (1) and renumbered existing paragraphs accordingly, which was executed by renumbering pars. (2) to (6) as (6) to (10), respectively, redesignated existing provisions of par. (7) as subpar. (A) and added subpars. (B) and (C), and added par. (11).
  Subsec. (e)(3). Pub. L. 101-596, Sec. 106, added par. (3).
  Subsec. (h). Pub. L. 101-596, Sec. 105, substituted "and 1990, and $25,000,000 for fiscal year 1991" for "1990, and 1991" in introductory provisions and inserted "or $3,300,000, whichever is the lesser," after "30 percent" in par. (3).
1988—Subsecs. (a)(1)(B), (2), (c)(1)(A), (6)(A), (D), (e)(2)(A), (f). Pub. L. 100-688 inserted ", as amended by the Water Quality Agreement of 1987 and any other agreements and amendments," after "the Great Lakes Water Quality Agreement of 1978".

Great Lakes Remedial Action Plans and Sediment Remediation

Pub. L. 101-640, title IV, Sec. 401, Nov. 28, 1990, 104 Stat. 4644, as amended by Pub. L. 104-303, title V, Sec. 515, Oct. 12, 1996, 110 Stat. 3763; Pub. L. 106-53, title V, Sec. 505, Aug. 17, 1999, 113 Stat. 338; Pub. L. 106-541, Sec. 344, Dec. 11, 2000, 114 Stat. 2613 provided that:

"(a) Great Lakes Remedial Action Plans.—
  (1) In general.—The Secretary may provide technical, planning, and engineering assistance to State and local governments and nongovernmental entities designated by a State or local government in the development and implementation of remedial action plans for Areas of Concern in the Great Lakes identified under the Great Lakes Water Quality Agreement of 1978.
  (2) Non-federal share.—

---

[4]So in original.

(A) In general.—Non-Federal interests shall contribute, in cash or by providing in-kind contributions, 35 percent of costs of activities for which assistance is provided under paragraph (1).

(B) Contributions by entities.—Nonprofit public or private entities may contribute all or a portion of the non-Federal share.

(b) Sediment Remediation Projects.—
  (1) In general.—The Secretary, in consultation with the Administrator of the Environmental Protection Agency (acting through the Great Lakes National Program Office), may conduct pilot- and full-scale projects of promising technologies to remediate contaminated sediments in freshwater coastal regions in the Great Lakes basin. The Secretary shall conduct not fewer than 3 full-scale projects under this subsection.
  (2) Site selection for projects.—In selecting the sites for the technology projects, the Secretary shall give priority consideration to Saginaw Bay, Michigan, Sheboygan Harbor, Wisconsin, Grand Calumet River, Indiana, Ashtabula River, Ohio, Buffalo River, New York, and Duluth-Superior Harbor, Minnesota and Wisconsin.
  (3) Non-federal share.—Non-Federal interests shall contribute 35 percent of costs of projects under this subsection. Such costs may be paid in cash or by providing in-kind contributions.

(c) Authorization of Appropriations.—There is authorized to be appropriated to the Secretary to carry out this section $10,000,000 for each of fiscal years 2001 through 2006."

Section Referred to in Other Sections

This section is referred to in title 16 section 1447b.

LONG ISLAND SOUND

42 USC 1269

(a) Office of Management Conference of the Long Island Sound Study
The Administrator shall continue the Management Conference of the Long Island Sound Study (hereinafter referred to as the "Conference") as established pursuant to section 1330 of this title, and shall establish an office (hereinafter referred to as the "Office") to be located on or near Long Island Sound.

(b) Administration and staffing of Office
The Office shall be headed by a Director, who shall be detailed by the Administrator, following consultation with the Administrators of EPA regions I and II, from among the employees of the Agency who are in civil service. The Administrator shall delegate to the Director such authority and detail such additional staff as may be necessary to carry out the duties of the Director under this section.

(c) Duties of Office
The Office shall assist the Management Conference of the Long Island Sound Study in carrying out its goals. Specifically, the Office shall—
  (1) assist and support the implementation of the Comprehensive Conservation and Management Plan for Long Island Sound developed pursuant to section 1330 of this title, including efforts to establish, within the process for granting watershed general permits, a system for promoting innovative methodologies and technologies that are cost-effective and consistent with the goals of the Plan;
  (2) conduct or commission studies deemed necessary for strengthened implementation of the Comprehensive Conservation and Management Plan including, but not limited to—
    (A) population growth and the adequacy of wastewater treatment facilities,
    (B) the use of biological methods for nutrient removal in sewage treatment plants,
    (C) contaminated sediments, and dredging activities,
    (D) nonpoint source pollution abatement and land use activities in the Long Island Sound watershed,
    (E) wetland protection and restoration,
    (F) atmospheric deposition of acidic and other pollutants into Long Island Sound,
    (G) water quality requirements to sustain fish, shellfish, and wildlife populations, and the use of indicator species to assess environmental quality,

(H) State water quality programs, for their adequacy pursuant to implementation of the Comprehensive Conservation and Management Plan, and
(I) options for long-term financing of wastewater treatment projects and water pollution control programs.
(3) coordinate the grant, research and planning programs authorized under this section;
(4) coordinate activities and implementation responsibilities with other Federal agencies which have jurisdiction over Long Island Sound and with national and regional marine monitoring and research programs established pursuant to the Marine Protection, Research, and Sanctuaries Act [16 U.S.C. 1431 et seq., 1447 et seq.; 33 U.S.C. 1401 et seq., 2801 et seq.];
(5) provide administrative and technical support to the conference;
(6) collect and make available to the public publications, and other forms of information the conference determines to be appropriate, relating to the environmental quality of Long Island Sound;
(7) not more than two years after the date of the issuance of the final Comprehensive Conservation and Management Plan for Long Island Sound under section 1330 of this title, and biennially thereafter, issue a report to the Congress which—
(A) summarizes the progress made by the States in implementing the Comprehensive Conservation and Management Plan;
(B) summarizes any modifications to the Comprehensive Conservation and Management Plan in the twelve-month period immediately preceding such report; and
(C) incorporates specific recommendations concerning the implementation of the Comprehensive Conservation and Management Plan; and
(8) convene conferences and meetings for legislators from State governments and political subdivisions thereof for the purpose of making recommendations for coordinating legislative efforts to facilitate the environmental restoration of Long Island Sound and the implementation of the Comprehensive Conservation and Management Plan.

(d) Grants
(1) The Administrator is authorized to make grants for projects and studies which will help implement the Long Island Sound Comprehensive Conservation and Management Plan. Special emphasis shall be given to implementation, research and planning, enforcement, and citizen involvement and education.
(2) State, interstate, and regional water pollution control agencies, and other public or nonprofit private agencies, institutions, and organizations held to be eligible for grants pursuant to this subsection.
(3) Citizen involvement and citizen education grants under this subsection shall not exceed 95 per centum of the costs of such work. All other grants under this subsection shall not exceed 50 per centum of the research, studies, or work. All grants shall be made on the condition that the non-Federal share of such costs are provided from non-Federal sources.

(c) Assistance to Distressed Communities.—
(1) Eligible communities.—For the purposes of this subsection, a distressed community is any community that meets affordability criteria established by the State in which the community is located, if such criteria are developed after public review and comment.
(2) Priority.—In making assistance available under this section for the upgrading of wastewater treatment facilities, the Administrator may give priority to a distressed community.

(f) Authorizations
(1) There is authorized to be appropriated to the Administrator for the implementation of this section, other than subsection (d) of this section, such sums as may be necessary for each of the fiscal years 2001 through 2005.
(2) There is authorized to be appropriated to the Administrator for the implementation of subsection (d) of this section not to exceed $3,000,000 for each of the fiscal years 1991 through 2001.

(June 30, 1948, ch. 758, title I, Sec. 119, as added Pub. L. 101-596, title II, Sec. 202, Nov. 16, 1990, 104 Stat. 3004; amended Pub. L. 104-303, title V, Sec. 583, Oct. 12, 1996, 110 Stat. 3791; Pub. L. 106-457, Title IV, Sec. 402-404, 114 Stat. 1973.)

References in Text

The Marine Protection, Research, and Sanctuaries Act, referred to in subsec. (c)(4), probably means the Marine Protection, Research, and Sanctuaries Act of 1972, Pub. L. 92-532, Oct. 23,

1972, 86 Stat. 1052, as amended, which is classified generally to chapters 32 (Sec. 1431 et seq.) and 32A (Sec. 1447 et seq.) of Title 16, Conservation, and chapters 27 (Sec. 1401 et seq.) and 41 (Sec. 2801 et seq.) of this title. For complete classification of this Act to the Code, see Short Title note set out under section 1401 of this title and Tables.

Amendments

2000—Subsec. (c)(1). Pub. L. 106-457, Sec. 402 inserted inserted text after "watershed general permits" until semicolon.

Subsec. (e). Pub. L. 106-457, Sec. 403 added subsec. (e) and redesignated old subsec. (e) as subsec. (f).

Subsec. (f). Pub. L. 106-457, Sec. 404 substituted "2001 through 2005." for "1991 through 2001" in par. (1) and "not to exceed $40,000,000 for each of fiscal years 2001 through 2005" for "not to exceed $3,000,000 for each of the fiscal years 1991 through 2001." in par. (2).

1996—Subsec. (e). Pub. L. 104-303 substituted "2001" for "1996" in pars. (1) and (2).

LAKE CHAMPLAIN MANAGEMENT CONFERENCE

33 USC 1270

(a) Establishment.—
  (1) In general.—There is established a Lake Champlain Management Conference to develop a comprehensive pollution prevention, control, and restoration plan for Lake Champlain. The Administrator shall convene the management conference within ninety days of November 16, 1990.
  (2) Implementation.— The Administrator—
    (A) may provide support to the State of Vermont, the State of New York, and the New England Interstate Water Pollution Control Commission for the implementation of the Lake Champlain Basin Program; and
    (B) shall coordinate actions of the Environmental Protection Agency under subparagraph (A) with the actions of other appropriate Federal agencies.
(b) Membership
  The Members of the Management Conference shall be comprised of—
  (1) the Governors of the States of Vermont and New York;
  (2) each interested Federal agency, not to exceed a total of five members;
  (3) the Vermont and New York Chairpersons of the Vermont, New York, Quebec Citizens Advisory Committee for the Environmental Management of Lake Champlain;
  (4) four representatives of the State legislature of Vermont;
  (5) four representatives of the State legislature of New York;
  (6) six persons representing local governments having jurisdiction over any land or water within the Lake Champlain basin, as determined appropriate by the Governors; and
  (7) eight persons representing affected industries, nongovernmental organizations, public and private educational institutions, and the general public, as determined appropriate by the trigovernmental Citizens Advisory Committee for the Environmental Management of Lake Champlain, but not to be current members of the Citizens Advisory Committee.
(c) Technical Advisory Committee
  (1) The Management Conference shall, not later than one hundred and twenty days after November 16, 1990, appoint a Technical Advisory Committee.
  (2) Such Technical Advisory Committee shall consist of officials of: appropriate departments and agencies of the Federal Government; the State governments of New York and Vermont; and governments of political subdivisions of such States; and public and private research institutions.
(d) Research program[1]
  The Management Conference shall establish a multi-disciplinary environmental research program for Lake Champlain. Such research program shall be planned and conducted jointly with the Lake Champlain Research Consortium.

(e) Pollution prevention, control, and restoration plan
   (1) Not later than three years after November 16, 1990, the Management Conference shall publish a pollution prevention, control, and restoration plan for Lake Champlain.
   (2) The Plan developed pursuant to this section shall—
      (A) identify corrective actions and compliance schedules addressing point and nonpoint sources of pollution necessary to restore and maintain the chemical, physical, and biological integrity of water quality, a balanced, indigenous population of shellfish, fish and wildlife, recreational, and economic activities in and on the lake;
      (B) incorporate environmental management concepts and programs established in State and Federal plans and programs in effect at the time of the development of such plan;
      (C) clarify the duties of Federal and State agencies in pollution prevention and control activities, and to the extent allowable by law, suggest a timetable for adoption by the appropriate Federal and State agencies to accomplish such duties within a reasonable period of time;
      (D) describe the methods and schedules for funding of programs, activities, and projects identified in the Plan, including the use of Federal funds and other sources of funds;
      (E) include a strategy for pollution prevention and control that includes the promotion of pollution prevention and management practices to reduce the amount of pollution generated in the Lake Champlain basin; and
      (F) be reviewed and revised, as necessary, at least once every 5 years, in consultation with the Adminstrator and other appropriate Federal agencies.
   (3) The Administrator, in cooperation with the Management Conference, shall provide for public review and comment on the draft Plan. At a minimum, the Management Conference shall conduct one public meeting to hear comments on the draft plan in the State of New York and one such meeting in the State of Vermont.
   (4) Not less than one hundred and twenty days after the publication of the Plan required pursuant to this section, the Administrator shall approve such plan if the plan meets the requirements of this section and the Governors of the States of New York and Vermont concur.
   (5) Upon approval of the plan, such plan shall be deemed to be an approved management program for the purposes of section 1329(h) of this title and such plan shall be deemed to be an approved comprehensive conservation and management plan pursuant to section 1330 of this title.
(f) Grant assistance
   (1) The Administrator may, in consultation with participants in the Lake Champlain Basin Program, make grants to State, interstate, and regional water pollution control agencies, and public or nonprofit agencies, institutions, and organizations.
   (2) Grants under this subsection shall be made for assisting research, surveys, studies, and modeling and technical and supporting work necessary for the development and implementation of the Plan.
   (3) The amount of grants to any person under this subsection for a fiscal year shall not exceed 75 per centum of the costs of such research, survey, study and work and shall be made available on the condition that non-Federal share of such costs are provided from non-Federal sources.
   (4) The Administrator may establish such requirements for the administration of grants as he determines to be appropriate.
(g) Definitions.—In this section:
   (1) Lake champlain basin program.—The term 'Lake Champlain Basin Program' means the coordinated efforts among the Federal Government, State governments, and local governments to implement the Plan.
   (2) Lake champlain drainage basin.—The term "Lake Champlain drainage basin" means all or part of Clinton, Franklin, Warren, Essex, and Washington counties in the State of New York and all or part of Franklin, Hamilton, Grand Isle, Chittenden, Addison, Rutland, Bennington, Lamoille, Orange, Washington, Orleans, and Caledonia counties in Vermont, that contain all of the streams, rivers, lakes, and other bodies of water, including wetlands, that drain into Lake Champlain.
   (3) Plan.—The term 'Plan' means the plan developed under subsection (e).

(h) No Effect on Certain Authority.—Nothing in this section—
  (1) affects the jurisdiction or powers of—
    (A) any department or agency of the Federal Government or any State government; or
    (B) any international organization or entity related to Lake Champlain created by treaty or memorandum to which the United States is a signatory;
  (2) provides new regulatory authority for the Environmental Protection Agency; or
  (3) affects section 304 of the Great Lakes Critical Programs Act of 1990 (Public Law 101-596; 33 U.S.C. 1270 note.)
(i) Authorization
  There are authorized to be appropriated to the Environmental Protection Agency to carry out this section—
  (1) $2,000,000;
  (2) such sums as are necessary for each of fiscal years 1996 through 2003; and
  (3) $11,000,000 for each of fiscal years 2004 through 2008.

(June 30, 1948, ch. 758, title I, Sec. 120, as added Pub. L. 101-596, title III, Sec. 303, Nov. 16, 1990, 104 Stat. 3006.)

Federal Program Coordination

Section 304 of Pub. L. 101-596, as amended by Pub. L. 104-127, title III, Sec. 336(a)(2)(F), Apr. 4, 1996, 110 Stat. 1005, provided that:

"(a) Designation of Lake Champlain as a Priority Area Under the Environmental Quality Incentives Program.—
  (1) In general.—Notwithstanding any other provision of law, the Lake Champlain basin, as defined under section 120(h) of the Federal Water Pollution Control Act [33 U.S.C. 1270(h)], shall be designated by the Secretary of Agriculture as a priority area under the environmental quality incentives program established under chapter 4 of subtitle D of title XII of the Food Security Act of 1985 [16 U.S.C. 3839aa et seq.].
  (2) Technical assistance reimbursement.—To carry out the purposes of this subsection, the technical assistance reimbursement from the Agricultural Stabilization and Conservation Service authorized under the Soil Conservation and Domestic Allotment Act [16 U.S.C. 590a et seq.], shall be increased from 5 per centum to 10 per centum.
  (3) Comprehensive agricultural monitoring.—The Secretary, in consultation with the Management Conference and appropriate State and Federal agencies, shall develop a comprehensive agricultural monitoring and evaluation network for all major drainages within the Lake Champlain basin.
  (4) Allocation of funds.—In allocating funds under this subsection, the Secretary of Agriculture shall consult with the Management Conference established under section 120 of the Federal Water Pollution Control Act and to the extent allowable by law, allocate funds to those agricultural enterprises located at sites that the Management Conference determines to be priority sites, on the basis of a concern for ensuring implementation of nonpoint source pollution controls throughout the Lake Champlain basin.
(b) Cooperation of the United States Geological Survey of the Department of the Interior.—For the purpose of enhancing and expanding basic data collection and monitoring in operation in the Lake Champlain basin, as defined under section 120 of the Federal Water Pollution Control Act [33 U.S.C. 1270], the Secretary of the Interior, acting through the heads of water resources divisions of the New York and New England districts of the United States Geological Survey, shall—
  (1) in cooperation with appropriate universities and private research institutions, and the appropriate officials of the appropriate departments and agencies of the States of New York and Vermont, develop an integrated geographic information system of the Lake Champlain basin;
  (2) convert all partial recording sites in the Lake Champlain basin to continuous monitoring stations with full gauging capabilities and status; and
  (3) establish such additional continuous monitoring station sites in the Lake Champlain basin as are necessary to carry out basic data collection and monitoring, as defined by the Secretary of the Interior, including groundwater mapping, and water quality and sediment data collection.

Clean Water Act / 459

(c) Cooperation of the United States Fish and Wildlife Service of the Department of the Interior.—
  (1) Resource conservation program.—The Secretary of the Interior, acting through the United States Fish and Wildlife Service, in cooperation with the Lake Champlain Fish and Wildlife Management Cooperative and the Management Conference established pursuant to this subsection shall—
    (A) establish and implement a fisheries resources restoration, development and conservation program, including dedicating a level of hatchery production within the Lake Champlain basin at or above the level that existed immediately preceding the date of enactment of this Act [Nov. 16, 1990]; and
    (B) conduct a wildlife species and habitat assessment survey in the Lake Champlain basin, including—
      (i) a survey of Federal threatened and endangered species, listed or proposed for listing under the Endangered Species Act of 1973 (16 U.S.C. 1531 et seq.), New York State and State of Vermont threatened and endangered species and other species of special concern, migratory nongame species of management concern, and national resources plan species;
      (ii) a survey of wildlife habitats such as islands, wetlands, and riparian areas; and
      (iii) a survey of migratory bird populations breeding, migrating and wintering within the Lake Champlain basin.
  (2) To accomplish the purposes of paragraph (1), the Director of the United States Fish and Wildlife Service is authorized to carry out activities related to—
    (A) controlling sea lampreys and other nonindigenous aquatic animal nuisances;
    (B) improving the health of fishery resources;
    (C) conducting investigations about and assessing the status of fishery resources, and disseminating that information to all interested parties; and
    (D) conducting and periodically updating a survey of the fishery resources and their habitats and food chains in the Lake Champlain basin.
(d) Authorizations.—(1) There is authorized to be appropriated to the Department of Agriculture $2,000,000 for each of fiscal years 1991, 1992, 1993, 1994, and 1995 to carry out subsection (a) of this section.
  (2) There is authorized to be appropriated to the Department of [the] Interior $1,000,000 for each of fiscal years 1991, 1992, 1993, 1994, and 1995 to carry out subsections (b) and (c) of this section."

Amendments

2002–Subsec. (a). Pub. L. 107-303 added par (2); Subsec. (e). Pub. L. 107-303 added par. (F); Subsec. (f)(1). Pub. L. 107-303 changed "the Management Conference" to "participants in the Lake Champlain Basin Program; Subsec. (f)(2). Pub. L. 107-303 deleted "development of the Plan" and all that follows and inserted "development and implementation of the Plan."; Subsec. (g). Pub. L. 107-303 changed the section to include pars (1), (2), and (3); Subsec. (h). Pub. L. 107-303 struck par. (h) and new material was inserted; Subsec. (i). Pub. L. 107-303 added pars. (2) and (3).

SEDIMENT SURVEY AND MONITORING

33 USC 1271

(a) Survey
  (1) In general
    The Administrator, in consultation with the Administrator of the National Oceanic and Atmospheric Administration and the Secretary, shall conduct a comprehensive national survey of data regarding aquatic sediment quality in the United States. The Administrator shall compile all existing information on the quantity, chemical and physical composition, and geographic location of pollutants in aquatic sediment, including the probable source of such pollutants and identification of those sediments which are contaminated pursuant to section 501(b)(4).[1]

---

[1] See References in Text note below.

(2) Report

Not later than 24 months after October 31, 1992, the Administrator shall report to the Congress the findings, conclusions, and recommendations of such survey, including recommendations for actions necessary to prevent contamination of aquatic sediments and to control sources of contamination.

(b) Monitoring

(1) In general

The Administrator, in consultation with the Administrator of the National Oceanic and Atmospheric Administration and the Secretary, shall conduct a comprehensive and continuing program to assess aquatic sediment quality. The program conducted pursuant to this subsection shall, at a minimum—

(A) identify the location of pollutants in aquatic sediment;

(B) identify the extent of pollutants in sediment and those sediments which are contaminated pursuant to section 501(b)(4);[1]

(C) establish methods and protocols for monitoring the physical, chemical, and biological effects of pollutants in aquatic sediment and of contaminated sediment;

(D) develop a system for the management, storage, and dissemination of data concerning aquatic sediment quality;

(E) provide an assessment of aquatic sediment quality trends over time;

(F) identify locations where pollutants in sediment may pose a threat to the quality of drinking water supplies, fisheries resources, and marine habitats; and

(G) establish a clearing house for information on technology, methods, and practices available for the remediation, decontamination, and control of sediment contamination.

(2) Report

The Administrator shall submit to Congress a report on the findings of the monitoring under paragraph (1) on the date that is 2 years after the date specified in subsection (a)(2) of this section and biennially thereafter.

(Pub. L. 102-580, title V, Sec. 503, Oct. 31, 1992, 106 Stat. 4865.)

References in Text

Section 501(b)(4), referred to in subsecs. (a)(1) and (b)(1)(B), means section 501(b)(4) of Pub. L. 102-580, which is set out below.

Codification

Section was enacted as part of the Water Resources Development Act of 1992 and also as part of the National Contaminated Sediment Assessment and Management Act, and not as part of the Federal Water Pollution Control Act which comprises this chapter.

Availability of Contaminated Sediments Information

Section 327 of Pub. L. 102-580 directed Secretary to conduct national study on information that was currently available on contaminated sediments of surface waters of United States and compile information obtained for the purpose of identifying location and nature of contaminated sediments and, not later than 1 year after Oct. 31, 1992, to transmit to Congress a report on the results of the study.

National Contaminated Sediment Assessment and Management; Short Title; Definitions; Task Force

Sections 501 and 502 of title V of Pub. L. 102-580 provided that:

"SEC. 501. SHORT TITLE AND DEFINITIONS.

(a) Short Title.—This title [enacting this section, amending sections 1412 to 1416, 1420, and 1421 of this title, and enacting provisions set out below] may be cited as the 'National Contaminated Sediment Assessment and Management Act'.

(b) Definitions.—For the purposes of sections 502 and 503 of this title [enacting this section and provisions set out below]—

(1) the term 'aquatic sediment' means sediment underlying the navigable waters of the United States;

---

[1] See References in Text note below.

(2) the term 'navigable waters' has the same meaning as in section 502(7) of the Federal Water Pollution Control Act (33 U.S.C. 1362(7));
(3) the term 'pollutant' has the same meaning as in section 502(6) of the Federal Water Pollution Control Act (33 U.S.C. 1362(6)); except that such term does not include dredge spoil, rock, sand, or cellar dirt;
(4) the term 'contaminated sediment' means aquatic sediment which—
    (A) contains chemical substances in excess of appropriate geochemical, toxicological or sediment quality criteria or measures; or
    (B) is otherwise considered by the Administrator to pose a threat to human health or the environment; and
(5) the term 'Administrator' means the Administrator of the Environmental Protection Agency.

SEC. 502. NATIONAL CONTAMINATED SEDIMENT TASK FORCE.

(a) Establishment.—There is established a National Contaminated Sediment Task Force (hereinafter referred to in this section as the 'Task Force'). The Task Force shall—
   (1) advise the Administrator and the Secretary in the implementation of this title;
   (2) review and comment on reports concerning aquatic sediment quality and the extent and seriousness of aquatic sediment contamination throughout the Nation;
   (3) review and comment on programs for the research and development of aquatic sediment restoration methods, practices, and technologies;
   (4) review and comment on the selection of pollutants for development of aquatic sediment criteria and the schedule for the development of such criteria;
   (5) advise appropriate officials in the development of guidelines for restoration of contaminated sediment;
   (6) make recommendations to appropriate officials concerning practices and measures—
       (A) to prevent the contamination of aquatic sediments; and
       (B) to control sources of sediment contamination; and
   (7) review and assess the means and methods for locating and constructing permanent, cost-effective long-term disposal sites for the disposal of dredged material that is not suitable for ocean dumping (as determined under the Marine Protection, Research, and Sanctuaries Act of 1972 (33 U.S.C. 1401 et seq.) [also 16 U.S.C. 1431 et seq., 1447 et seq.; 33 U.S.C. 2801 et seq.]).

(b) Membership.—
   (1) In general.—The membership of the Task Force shall include 1 representative of each of the following:
       (A) The Administrator.
       (B) The Secretary.
       (C) The National Oceanic and Atmospheric Administration.
       (D) The United States Fish and Wildlife Service.
       (E) The Geological Survey [now United States Geological Survey].
       (F) The Department of Agriculture.
   (2) Additional members.—Additional members of the Task Force shall be jointly selected by the Administrator and the Secretary, and shall include—
       (A) not more than 3 representatives of States;
       (B) not more than 3 representatives of ports, agriculture, and manufacturing; and
       (C) not more than 3 representatives of public interest organizations with a demonstrated interest in aquatic sediment contamination.
   (3) Cochairmen.—The Administrator and the Secretary shall serve as cochairmen of the Task Force.
   (4) Clerical and technical assistance.—Such clerical and technical assistance as may be necessary to discharge the duties of the Task Force shall be provided by the personnel of the Environmental Protection Agency and the Army Corps of Engineers.
   (5) Compensation for additional members.—The additional members of the Task Force selected under paragraph (2) shall, while attending meetings or conferences of the Task Force, be compensated at a rate to be fixed by the cochairmen, but not to exceed the daily equivalent of the base rate of pay in effect for grade GS-15 of the General Schedule under section 5332 of title 5, United States Code, for each day (including travel time) during which they are engaged in the actual performance of duties vested in the Task Force.

While away from their homes or regular places of business in the performance of services for the Task Force, such members shall be allowed travel expenses, including per diem in lieu of subsistence, in the same manner as persons employed intermittently in the Government service are allowed expenses under section 5703(b) of title 5, United States Code.

(c) Report.–Within 2 years after the date of the enactment of this Act [Oct. 31, 1992], the Task Force shall submit to Congress a report stating the findings and recommendations of the Task Force."

Authorization of Appropriations

Section 509(b) of Pub. L. 102-580 provided that: "There is authorized to be appropriated to the Administrator to carry out sections 502 and 503 [enacting this section and provisions set out above] such sums as may be necessary."

"Secretary" Defined

Secretary means the Secretary of the Army, see section 3 of Pub. L. 102-580, set out as a note under section 2201 of this title.

RESEARCH AND DEVELOPMENT PROGRAM

33 USC 1271a

(a) In General.–In coordination with other Federal, State, and local officials, the Administrator of the Environmental Protection Agency may conduct research on the development and use of innovative approaches, technologies, and techniques for the remediation of sediment contamination in areas of concern that are located wholly or partially in the United States.

(b) Authorization of Appropriations.–
  (1) In general.–In addition to amounts authorized under other laws, there is authorized to be appropriated to carry out this section $3,000,000 for each of fiscal years 2004 through 2008.
  (2) Availability.–Funds appropriated under paragraph (1) shall remain available until expended.

ENVIRONMENTAL DREDGING

33 USC 1272

(a) Operation and maintenance of navigation projects

  Whenever necessary to meet the requirements of the Federal Water Pollution Control Act [33 U.S.C. 1251 et seq.], the Secretary, in consultation with the Administrator of the Environmental Protection Agency, may remove and remediate, as part of operation and maintenance of a navigation project, contaminated sediments outside the boundaries of and adjacent to the navigation channel.

(b) Nonproject specific
  (1) In general.–The Secretary may remove and remediate contaminated sediments from the navigable waters of the United States for the purpose of environmental enhancement and water quality improvement if such removal and remediation is requested by a non-Federal sponsor and the sponsor agrees to pay 35 percent of the cost of such removal and remediation.
  (2) Maximum amount.–The Secretary may not expend more than $50,000,000 in a fiscal year to carry out this subsection.

(c) Joint plan requirement

  The Secretary may only remove and remediate contaminated sediments under subsection (b) of this section in accordance with a joint plan developed by the Secretary and interested Federal, State, and local government officials. Such plan must include an opportunity for public comment, a description of the work to be undertaken, the method to be used for dredged material disposal, the roles and responsibilities of the Secretary and non-Federal sponsors, and identification of sources of funding.

Clean Water Act / 463

(d) Disposal costs

Costs of disposal of contaminated sediments removed under this section shall be a[1] shared as a cost of construction.

(e) Limitation on statutory construction

Nothing in this section shall be construed to affect the rights and responsibilities of any person under the Comprehensive Environmental Response, Compensation, and Liability Act of 1980 [42 U.S.C. 9601 et seq.].

(f) Priority work

In carrying out this section, the Secretary shall give priority to work in the following areas:
(1) Brooklyn Waterfront, New York.
(2) Buffalo Harbor and River, New York.
(3) Ashtabula River, Ohio.
(4) Mahoning River, Ohio.
(5) Lower Fox River, Wisconsin.
(6) Passaic River and Newark Bay, New Jersey.
(7) Snake Creek, Bixby, Oklahoma.
(8) Willamette River, Oregon.

(g) Nonprofit entities

Notwithstanding section 1962d-5b of title 42, for any project carried out under this section, a non-Federal sponsor may include a nonprofit entity, with the consent of the affected local government.

(Pub. L. 101-640, title III, Sec. 312, Nov. 28, 1990, 104 Stat. 4639; Pub. L. 104-303, title II, Sec. 205, Oct. 12, 1996, 110 Stat. 3679; Pub. L. 106-53, title II, Sec. 224, Aug. 17, 1999, 113 Stat. 297; Pub. L. 106-541, title II, Sec. 210(a), Dec. 11, 2000, 114 Stat. 2592.)

References in Text

The Federal Water Pollution Control Act, referred to in subsec. (a), is act June 30, 1948, ch. 758, as amended generally by Pub. L. 92-500, Sec. 2, Oct. 18, 1972, 86 Stat. 816, which is classified generally to this chapter (Sec. 1251 et seq.). For complete classification of this Act to the Code, see Short Title note set out under section 1251 of this title and Tables.

The Comprehensive Environmental Response, Compensation, and Liability Act of 1980, referred to in subsec. (e), is Pub. L. 96-510, Dec. 11, 1980, 94 Stat. 2767, as amended, which is classified principally to chapter 103 (Sec. 9601 et seq.) of Title 42, The Public Health and Welfare. For complete classification of this Act to the Code, see Short Title note set out under section 9601 of Title 42 and Tables.

Codification

Section was formerly set out as a note under section 1252 of this title.

Section was enacted as part of the Water Resources Development Act of 1990, and not as part of the Federal Water Pollution Control Act which comprises this chapter.

Amendments

2000—Subsec. (g). Pub. L. 106-541 added subsec. (g).

1999—Subsec. (b)(1). Pub. L. 106-53, Sec. 224(1)(A), substituted "35 percent" for "50 percent". Subsec. (b)(2). Pub. L. 106-53, Sec. 224(1)(B), substituted "$50,000,000" for "$20,000,000". Subsec. (d). Pub. L. 106-53, Sec. 224(2), substituted "shared as a cost of construction" for "non-Federal responsibility". Subsec. (f)(6) to (8). Pub. L. 106-53, Sec. 224(3), added pars. (6) to (8).

1996—Subsec. (a). Pub. L. 104-303, Sec. 205(1), inserted "and remediate" after "remove". Subsec. (b)(1). Pub. L. 104-303, Sec. 205(1), (2)(A), inserted "and remediate" after "remove" and inserted "and remediation" after "removal" in two places. Subsec. (b)(2). Pub. L. 104-303, Sec. 205(2)(B), substituted "$20,000,000" for "$10,000,000". Subsec. (c). Pub. L. 104-303, Sec. 205(1), inserted "and remediate" after "remove". Subsec. (f). Pub. L. 104-303, Sec. 205(3), added subsec. (f) and struck out heading and text of former subsec. (f). Text read as follows: "This section shall not be

---

[1] So in original. The word "a" probably should not appear.

effective after the last day of the 5-year period beginning on November 28, 1990; except that the Secretary may complete any project commenced under this section on or before such last day."

LAKE PONTCHARTRAIN BASIN

33 USC 1273

(a) Establishment of restoration program
   The Administrator shall establish within the Environmental Protection Agency the Lake Pontchartrain Basin Restoration Program.
(b) Purpose
   The purpose of the program shall be to restore the ecological health of the Basin by developing and funding restoration projects and related scientific and public education projects.
(c) Duties
   In carrying out the program, the Administrator shall—
   (1) provide administrative and technical assistance to a management conference convened for the Basin under section 1330 of this title;
   (2) assist and support the activities of the management conference, including the implementation of recommendations of the management conference;
   (3) support environmental monitoring of the Basin and research to provide necessary technical and scientific information;
   (4) develop a comprehensive research plan to address the technical needs of the program;
   (5) coordinate the grant, research, and planning programs authorized under this section; and
   (6) collect and make available to the public publications, and other forms of information the management conference determines to be appropriate, relating to the environmental quality of the Basin.
(d) Grants
   The Administrator may make grants—
   (1) for restoration projects and studies recommended by a management conference convened for the Basin under section 1330 of this title; and
   (2) for public education projects recommended by the management conference.
(e) Definitions
   In this section, the following definitions apply:
   (1) Basin
      The term "Basin" means the Lake Pontchartrain Basin, a 5,000 square mile watershed encompassing 16 parishes in the State of Louisiana and 4 counties in the State of Mississippi.
   (2) Program
      The term "program" means the Lake Pontchartrain Basin Restoration Program established under subsection (a) of this section.
(f) Authorization of appropriations
   (1) In general
      There is authorized to be appropriated to carry out this section $20,000,000 for each of fiscal years 2001 through 2005. Such sums shall remain available until expended.
   (2) Public education projects
      Not more than 15 percent of the amount appropriated pursuant to paragraph (1) in a fiscal year may be expended on grants for public education projects under subsection (d)(2) of this section.

(June 30, 1948, ch. 758, title I, Sec. 121, as added Pub. L. 106-457, title V, Sec. 502, Nov. 7, 2000, 114 Stat. 1973.)

Codification

Another section 121 of act June 30, 1948, ch. 758, is classified to section 1274 of this title.

WET WEATHER WATERSHED PILOT PROJECTS

33 USC 1274

(a) In general

The Administrator, in coordination with the States, may provide technical assistance and grants for treatment works to carry out pilot projects relating to the following areas of wet weather discharge control:

(1) Watershed management of wet weather discharges

The management of municipal combined sewer overflows, sanitary sewer overflows, and stormwater discharges, on an integrated watershed or subwatershed basis for the purpose of demonstrating the effectiveness of a unified wet weather approach.

(2) Stormwater best management practices

The control of pollutants from municipal separate storm sewer systems for the purpose of demonstrating and determining controls that are cost-effective and that use innovative technologies in reducing such pollutants from stormwater discharges.

(b) Administration

The Administrator, in coordination with the States, shall provide municipalities participating in a pilot project under this section the ability to engage in innovative practices, including the ability to unify separate wet weather control efforts under a single permit.

(c) Funding

(1) In general

There is authorized to be appropriated to carry out this section $10,000,000 for fiscal year 2002, $15,000,000 for fiscal year 2003, and $20,000,000 for fiscal year 2004. Such funds shall remain available until expended.

(2) Stormwater

The Administrator shall make available not less than 20 percent of amounts appropriated for a fiscal year pursuant to this subsection to carry out the purposes of subsection (a)(2) of this section.

(3) Administrative expenses

The Administrator may retain not to exceed 4 percent of any amounts appropriated for a fiscal year pursuant to this subsection for the reasonable and necessary costs of administering this section.

(d) Report to Congress

Not later than 5 years after December 21, 2000, the Administrator shall transmit to Congress a report on the results of the pilot projects conducted under this section and their possible application nationwide.

(June 30, 1948, ch. 758, title I, Sec. 121, as added Pub. L. 106-554, Sec. 1(a)(4) [div. B, title I, Sec. 112(b)], Dec. 21, 2000, 114 Stat. 2763, 2763A-225.)

Codification

Another section 121 of act June 30, 1948, ch. 758, is classified to section 1273 of this title.

SUBCHAPTER II—GRANTS FOR CONSTRUCTION OF TREATMENT WORKS

CONGRESSIONAL DECLARATION OF PURPOSE

33 USC 1281

(a) Development and implementation of waste treatment management plans and practices

It is the purpose of this subchapter to require and to assist the development and implementation of waste treatment management plans and practices which will achieve the goals of this chapter.

(b) Application of technology: confined disposal of pollutants; consideration of advanced techniques

Waste treatment management plans and practices shall provide for the application of the best practicable waste treatment technology before any discharge into receiving waters, including reclaiming and recycling of water, and confined disposal of pollutants so they will not migrate to cause water or other environmental pollution and shall provide for consideration of advanced waste treatment techniques.

(c) Waste treatment management area and scope

To the extent practicable, waste treatment management shall be on an areawide basis and provide control or treatment of all point and nonpoint sources of pollution, including in place or accumulated pollution sources.

(d) Waste treatment management construction of revenue producing facilities

The Administrator shall encourage waste treatment management which results in the construction of revenue producing facilities providing for—

(1) the recycling of potential sewage pollutants through the production of agriculture, silviculture, or aquaculture products, or any combination thereof;

(2) the confined and contained disposal of pollutants not recycled;

(3) the reclamation of wastewater; and

(4) the ultimate disposal of sludge in a manner that will not result in environmental hazards.

(e) Waste treatment management integration of facilities

The Administrator shall encourage waste treatment management which results in integrating facilities for sewage treatment and recycling with facilities to treat, dispose of, or utilize other industrial and municipal wastes, including but not limited to solid waste and waste heat and thermal discharges. Such integrated facilities shall be designed and operated to produce revenues in excess of capital and operation and maintenance costs and such revenues shall be used by the designated regional management agency to aid in financing other environmental improvement programs.

(f) Waste treatment management "open space" and recreational considerations

The Administrator shall encourage waste treatment management which combines "open space" and recreational considerations with such management.

(g) Grants to construct publicly owned treatment works

(1) The Administrator is authorized to make grants to any State, municipality, or intermunicipal or interstate agency for the construction of publicly owned treatment works. On and after October 1, 1984, grants under this subchapter shall be made only for projects for secondary treatment or more stringent treatment, or any cost effective alternative thereto, new interceptors and appurtenances, and infiltration-in-flow correction. Notwithstanding the preceding sentences, the Administrator may make grants on and after October 1, 1984, for (A) any project within the definition set forth in section 1292(2) of this title, other than for a project referred to in the preceding sentence, and (B) any purpose for which a grant may be made under sections[1] 1329(h) and (i) of this title (including any innovative and alternative approaches for the control of nonpoint sources of pollution), except that not more than 20 per centum (as determined by the Governor of the State) of

---

[1] So in original. Probably should be "section".

the amount allotted to a State under section 1285 of this title for any fiscal year shall be obligated in such State under authority of this sentence.
(2) The Administrator shall not make grants from funds authorized for any fiscal year beginning after June 30, 1974, to any State, municipality, or intermunicipal or interstate agency for the erection, building, acquisition, alteration, remodeling, improvement, or extension of treatment works unless the grant applicant has satisfactorily demonstrated to the Administrator that—
   (A) alternative waste management techniques have been studied and evaluated and the works proposed for grant assistance will provide for the application of the best practicable waste treatment technology over the life of the works consistent with the purposes of this subchapter; and
   (B) as appropriate, the works proposed for grant assistance will take into account and allow to the extent practicable the application of technology at a later date which will provide for the reclaiming or recycling of water or otherwise eliminate the discharge of pollutants.
(3) The Administrator shall not approve any grant after July 1, 1973, for treatment works under this section unless the applicant shows to the satisfaction of the Administrator that each sewer collection system discharging into such treatment works is not subject to excessive infiltration.
(4) The Administrator is authorized to make grants to applicants for treatment works grants under this section for such sewer system evaluation studies as may be necessary to carry out the requirements of paragraph (3) of this subsection. Such grants shall be made in accordance with rules and regulations promulgated by the Administrator. Initial rules and regulations shall be promulgated under this paragraph not later than 120 days after October 18, 1972.
(5) The Administrator shall not make grants from funds authorized for any fiscal year beginning after September 30, 1978, to any State, municipality, or intermunicipal or interstate agency for the erection, building, acquisition, alteration, remodeling, improvement, or extension of treatment works unless the grant applicant has satisfactorily demonstrated to the Administrator that innovative and alternative wastewater treatment processes and techniques which provide for the reclaiming and reuse of water, otherwise eliminate the discharge of pollutants, and utilize recycling techniques, land treatment, new or improved methods of waste treatment management for municipal and industrial waste (discharged into municipal systems) and the confined disposal of pollutants, so that pollutants will not migrate to cause water or other environmental pollution, have been fully studied and evaluated by the applicant taking into account subsection (d) of this section and taking into account and allowing to the extent practicable the more efficient use of energy and resources.
(6) The Administrator shall not make grants from funds authorized for any fiscal year beginning after September 30, 1978, to any State, municipality, or intermunicipal or interstate agency for the erection, building, acquisition, alteration, remodeling, improvement, or extension of treatment works unless the grant applicant has satisfactorily demonstrated to the Administrator that the applicant has analyzed the potential recreation and open space opportunities in the planning of the proposed treatment works.

(h) Grants to construct privately owned treatment works

A grant may be made under this section to construct a privately owned treatment works serving one or more principal residences or small commercial establishments constructed prior to, and inhabited on, December 27, 1977, where the Administrator finds that—
(1) a public body otherwise eligible for a grant under subsection (g) of this section has applied on behalf of a number of such units and certified that public ownership of such works is not feasible;
(2) such public body has entered into an agreement with the Administrator which guarantees that such treatment works will be properly operated and maintained and will comply with all other requirements of section 1284 of this title and includes a system of charges to assure that each recipient of waste treatment services under such a grant will pay its proportionate share of the cost of operation and maintenance (including replacement); and

(3) the total cost and environmental impact of providing waste treatment services to such residences or commercial establishments will be less than the cost of providing a system of collection and central treatment of such wastes.

(i) Waste treatment management methods, processes, and techniques to reduce energy requirements

The Administrator shall encourage waste treatment management methods, processes, and techniques which will reduce total energy requirements.

(j) Grants for treatment works utilizing processes and techniques of guidelines under section 1314(d)(3) of this title

The Administrator is authorized to make a grant for any treatment works utilizing processes and techniques meeting the guidelines promulgated under section 1314(d)(3) of this title, if the Administrator determines it is in the public interest and if in the cost effectiveness study made of the construction grant application for the purpose of evaluating alternative treatment works, the life cycle cost of the treatment works for which the grant is to be made does not exceed the life cycle cost of the most cost effective alternative by more than 15 per centum.

(k) Limitation on use of grants for publicly owned treatment works

No grant made after November 15, 1981, for a publicly owned treatment works, other than for facility planning and the preparation of construction plans and specifications, shall be used to treat, store, or convey the flow of any industrial user into such treatment works in excess of a flow per day equivalent to fifty thousand gallons per day of sanitary waste. This subsection shall not apply to any project proposed by a grantee which is carrying out an approved project to prepare construction plans and specifications for a facility to treat wastewater, which received its grant approval before May 15, 1980. This subsection shall not be in effect after November 15, 1981.

(l) Grants for facility plans, or plans, specifications, and estimates for proposed project for construction of treatment works; limitations, allotments, advances, etc.

(1) After December 29, 1981, Federal grants shall not be made for the purpose of providing assistance solely for facility plans, or plans, specifications, and estimates for any proposed project for the construction of treatment works. In the event that the proposed project receives a grant under this section for construction, the Administrator shall make an allowance in such grant for non-Federal funds expended during the facility planning and advanced engineering and design phase at the prevailing Federal share under section 1282(a) of this title, based on the percentage of total project costs which the Administrator determines is the general experience for such projects.

(2) (A) Each State shall use a portion of the funds allotted to such State each fiscal year, but not to exceed 10 per centum of such funds, to advance to potential grant applicants under this subchapter the costs of facility planning or the preparation of plans, specifications, and estimates.

(B) Such an advance shall be limited to the allowance for such costs which the Administrator establishes under paragraph (1) of this subsection, and shall be provided only to a potential grant applicant which is a small community and which in the judgment of the State would otherwise be unable to prepare a request for a grant for construction costs under this section.

(C) In the event a grant for construction costs is made under this section for a project for which an advance has been made under this paragraph, the Administrator shall reduce the amount of such grant by the allowance established under paragraph (1) of this subsection. In the event no such grant is made, the State is authorized to seek repayment of such advance on such terms and conditions as it may determine.

(m) Grants for State of California projects

(1) Notwithstanding any other provisions of this subchapter, the Administrator is authorized to make a grant from any funds otherwise allotted to the State of California under section 1285 of this title to the project (and in the amount) specified in Order WQG 81-1 of the California State Water Resources Control Board.

(2) Notwithstanding any other provision of this chapter, the Administrator shall make a grant from any funds otherwise allotted to the State of California to the city of Eureka, California, in connection with project numbered C-06-2772, for the purchase of one hundred and

thirty-nine acres of property as environmental mitigation for siting of the proposed treatment plant.
  (3) Notwithstanding any other provision of this chapter, the Administrator shall make a grant from any funds otherwise allotted to the State of California to the city of San Diego, California, in connection with that city's aquaculture sewage process (total resources recovery system) as an innovative and alternative waste treatment process.
(n) Water quality problems; funds, scope, etc.
  (1) On and after October 1, 1984, upon the request of the Governor of an affected State, the Administrator is authorized to use funds available to such State under section 1285 of this title to address water quality problems due to the impacts of discharges from combined storm water and sanitary sewer overflows, which are not otherwise eligible under this subsection, where correction of such discharges is a major priority for such State.
  (2) Beginning fiscal year 1983, the Administrator shall have available $200,000,000 per fiscal year in addition to those funds authorized in section 1287 of this title to be utilized to address water quality problems of marine bays and estuaries subject to lower levels of water quality due to the impacts of discharges from combined storm water and sanitary sewer overflows from adjacent urban complexes, not otherwise eligible under this subsection. Such sums may be used as deemed appropriate by the Administrator as provided in paragraphs (1) and (2) of this subsection, upon the request of and demonstration of water quality benefits by the Governor of an affected State.
(o) Capital financing plan
  The Administrator shall encourage and assist applicants for grant assistance under this subchapter to develop and file with the Administrator a capital financing plan which, at a minimum—
  (1) projects the future requirements for waste treatment services within the applicant's jurisdiction for a period of no less than ten years;
  (2) projects the nature, extent, timing, and costs of future expansion and reconstruction of treatment works which will be necessary to satisfy the applicant's projected future requirements for waste treatment services; and
  (3) sets forth with specificity the manner in which the applicant intends to finance such future expansion and reconstruction.
(p) Time limit on resolving certain disputes
  In any case in which a dispute arises with respect to the awarding of a contract for construction of treatment works by a grantee of funds under this subchapter and a party to such dispute files an appeal with the Administrator under this subchapter for resolution of such dispute, the Administrator shall make a final decision on such appeal within 90 days of the filing of such appeal.

(June 30, 1948, ch. 758, title II, Sec. 201, as added Pub. L. 92-500, Sec. 2, Oct. 18, 1972, 86 Stat. 833; amended Pub. L. 95-217, Secs. 12-16, Dec. 27, 1977, 91 Stat. 1569, 1570; Pub. L. 96-483, Secs. 2(d), 3, Oct. 21, 1980, 94 Stat. 2361; Pub. L. 97-117, Secs. 2(a), 3(a), 4-6, 10(c), Dec. 29, 1981, 95 Stat. 1623-1626; Pub. L. 100-4, title II, Sec. 201, title III, Sec. 316(c), Feb. 4, 1987, 101 Stat. 15, 60.)

Amendments

1987—Subsec. (g)(1). Pub. L. 100-4, Sec. 316(c), substituted "sentences, the Administrator" for "sentence, the Administrator" and inserted "(A)" after "October 1, 1984, for" and "and (B) any purpose for which a grant may be made under sections 1329(h) and (i) of this title (including any innovative and alternative approaches for the control of nonpoint sources of pollution)," before "except that".

Subsec. (p). Pub. L. 100-4, Sec. 201, added subsec. (p).

1981—Subsec. (g)(1). Pub. L. 97-117, Sec. 2(a), inserted provisions restricting, on or after Oct. 1, 1984, the categories of projects eligible for grants under this subchapter and providing an exception to the restriction for projects, other than specified projects, within the definition set forth in section 1292(2) of this title, but limiting such exception to not more than 20 per centum, as determined by the Governor of the State, of the amount allotted to a State under section 1285 of this title for any fiscal year.

Subsec. (k). Pub. L. 97-117, Sec. 10(c), inserted provision that subsection not be in effect after Nov. 15, 1981.

Subsec. (l). Pub. L. 97-117, Sec. 3(a), added subsec. (l).
Subsec. (m). Pub. L. 97-117, Sec. 4, added subsec. (m).
Subsec. (n). Pub. L. 97-117, Sec. 5, added subsec. (n).
Subsec. (o). Pub. L. 97-117, Sec. 6, added subsec. (o).
1980—Subsec. (h). Pub. L. 96-483, Sec. 2(d), struck out text following par. (3), relating to payment to the United States by commercial users of that portion of the cost of construction applicable to treatment of commercial wastes to the extent attributable to the Federal share of the cost of construction.
Subsec. (k). Pub. L. 96-483, Sec. 3, added subsec. (k).
1977—Subsec. (g)(5). Pub. L. 95-217, Sec. 12, added par. (5).
Subsec. (g)(6). Pub. L. 95-217, Sec. 13, added par. (6).
Subsec. (h). Pub. L. 95-217, Sec. 14, added subsec. (h).
Subsec. (i). Pub. L. 95-217, Sec. 15, added subsec. (i).
Subsec. (j). Pub. L. 95-217, Sec. 16, added subsec. (j).

Effective Date of 1980 Amendment

Section 2(g) of Pub. L. 96-483 provided that: "The amendments made by this section [amending sections 1281, 1284, and 1293 of this title, enacting provisions set out as notes under section 1284 of this title, and amending provisions set out as a note under section 1284 of this title] shall take effect on December 27, 1977."

Environmental Protection Agency State and Tribal Assistance Grants

Pub. L. 105-174, title III, May 1, 1998, 112 Stat. 92, provided that: "Notwithstanding any other provision of law, eligible recipients of the funds appropriated to the Environmental Protection Agency in the State and Tribal Assistance Grants account since fiscal year 1997 and hereafter for multi-media or single media grants, other than Performance Partnership Grants authorized pursuant to Public Law 104-134 and Public Law 105-65 [see Grants to Indian Tribes for Pollution Prevention, Control, and Abatement notes set out below], for pollution prevention, control, and abatement and related activities have been and shall be those entities eligible for grants under the Agency's organic statutes."

Privatization of Infrastructure Assets

Pub. L. 104-303, title V, Sec. 586, Oct. 12, 1996, 110 Stat. 3791, provided that:

"(a) In General.—Notwithstanding the provisions of title II of the Federal Water Pollution Control Act (33 U.S.C. 1281 et seq.), Executive Order 12803 [5 U.S.C. 601 note], or any other law or authority, an entity that received Federal grant assistance for an infrastructure asset under the Federal Water Pollution Control Act [33 U.S.C. 1251 et seq.] shall not be required to repay any portion of the grant upon the lease or concession of the asset only if—
   (1) ownership of the asset remains with the entity that received the grant; and
   (2) the Administrator of the Environmental Protection Agency determines that the lease or concession furthers the purposes of such Act and approves the lease or concession.
(b) Limitation.—The Administrator shall not approve a total of more than 5 leases and concessions under this section."

Grants to States To Administer Completion and Closeout of Construction Grants Program

Pub. L. 104-204, title III, Sept. 26, 1996, 110 Stat. 2912, provided in part: "That notwithstanding any other provision of law, beginning in fiscal year 1997 the Administrator may make grants to States, from funds available for obligation in the State under title II of the Federal Water Pollution Control Act [33 U.S.C. 1281 et seq.], as amended, for administering the completion and closeout of the State's construction grants program, based on a budget annually negotiated with the State".

Wastewater Assistance to Colonias

Pub. L. 104-182, title III, Sec. 307, Aug. 6, 1996, 110 Stat. 1688, provided that:

"(a) Definitions.—As used in this section:
   (1) Border state.—The term 'border State' means Arizona, California, New Mexico, and Texas.
   (2) Eligible community.—The term 'eligible community' means a low-income community with economic hardship that—

(A) is commonly referred to as a colonia;
(B) is located along the United States-Mexico border (generally in an unincorporated area); and
(C) lacks basic sanitation facilities such as household plumbing or a proper sewage disposal system.
(3) Treatment works.—The term 'treatment works' has the meaning provided in section 212(2) of the Federal Water Pollution Control Act (33 U.S.C. 1292(2)).

(b) Grants for Wastewater Assistance.—The Administrator of the Environmental Protection Agency and the heads of other appropriate Federal agencies are authorized to award grants to a border State to provide assistance to eligible communities for the planning, design, and construction or improvement of sewers, treatment works, and appropriate connections for wastewater treatment.

(c) Use of Funds.—Each grant awarded pursuant to subsection (b) shall be used to provide assistance to one or more eligible communities with respect to which the residents are subject to a significant health risk (as determined by the Administrator or the head of the Federal agency making the grant) attributable to the lack of access to an adequate and affordable treatment works for wastewater.

(d) Cost Sharing.—The amount of a grant awarded pursuant to this section shall not exceed 50 percent of the costs of carrying out the project that is the subject of the grant.

(e) Authorization of Appropriations.—There are authorized to be appropriated to carry out this section $25,000,000 for each of the fiscal years 1997 through 1999."

Grants to Indian Tribes for Pollution Prevention, Control and Abatement

Pub. L. 105-65, title III, Oct. 27, 1997, 111 Stat. 1373, provided in part that: "$745,000,000 for grants to States, federally recognized tribes, and air pollution control agencies for multi-media or single media pollution prevention, control and abatement and related activities pursuant to the provisions set forth under this heading in Public Law 104-134 [see below], provided that eligible recipients of these funds and the funds made available for this purpose since fiscal year 1996 and hereafter include States, federally recognized tribes, interstate agencies, tribal consortia, and air pollution control agencies, as provided in authorizing statutes, subject to such terms and conditions as the Administrator shall establish, and for making grants under section 103 of the Clean Air Act [42 U.S.C. 7403] for particulate matter monitoring and data collection activities".

Pub. L. 105-65, title III, Oct. 27, 1997, 111 Stat. 1374, provided in part: "That, hereafter from funds appropriated under this heading ["Environmental Protection Agency" and "state and tribal assistance grants"], the Administrator is authorized to make grants to federally recognized Indian governments for the development of multi-media environmental programs: Provided further, That, hereafter, the funds available under this heading for grants to States, federally recognized tribes, and air pollution control agencies for multi-media or single media pollution prevention, control and abatement and related activities may also be used for the direct implementation by the Federal Government of a program required by law in the absence of an acceptable State or tribal program".

Similar provisions were contained in the following prior appropriation acts:

Pub. L. 104-204, title III, Sept. 26, 1996, 110 Stat. 2912.

Pub. L. 104-134, title I, Sec. 101(e) [title III], Apr. 26, 1996, 110 Stat. 1321-257, 1321-299, renumbered title I, Pub. L. 104-140, Sec. 1(a), May 2, 1996, 110 Stat. 1327.

Pub. L. 103-327, title III, Sept. 28, 1994, 108 Stat. 2320.

Pub. L. 103-124, title III, Oct. 28, 1993, 107 Stat. 1293.

Pub. L. 102-389, title III, Oct. 6, 1992, 106 Stat. 1597.

Pub. L. 102-139, title III, Oct. 28, 1991, 105 Stat. 762.

Pub. L. 101-507, title III, Nov. 5, 1990, 104 Stat. 1372.

Pub. L. 104-134, title I, Sec. 101(e) [title III], Apr. 26, 1996, 110 Stat. 1321-257, 1321-299; renumbered title I, Pub. L. 104-140, Sec. 1(a), May 2, 1996, 110 Stat. 1327, provided in part: "That beginning in fiscal year 1996 and each fiscal year thereafter, and notwithstanding any other provision of law, the Administrator is authorized to make grants annually from funds appropriated under this heading ["Environmental Protection Agency" and "state and tribal assistance grants"], subject to such terms and conditions as the Administrator shall establish, to any State or federally recognized Indian tribe for multimedia or single media pollution prevention, control and abatement and related environmental activities at the request of the Governor or other appropriate State official or the tribe".

State Management of Construction Grant Activities

Pub. L. 104-134, title I, Sec. 101(e) [title III], Apr. 26, 1996, 110 Stat. 1321-257, 1321-299; renumbered title I, Pub. L. 104-140, Sec. 1(a), May 2, 1996, 110 Stat. 1327, provided in part: "That of the funds appropriated in the Construction Grants and Water Infrastructure/State Revolving Funds accounts since the appropriation for the fiscal year ending September 30, 1992, and hereafter, for making grants for wastewater treatment works construction projects, portions may be provided by the recipients to States for managing construction grant activities, on condition that the States agree to reimburse the recipients from State funding sources".

Grants to Trust Territory of the Pacific Islands, American Samoa, Guam, Northern Mariana Islands, and Virgin Islands; Waiver of Collector Sewers Limitation

Pub. L. 99-396, Sec. 12(b), Aug. 27, 1986, 100 Stat. 841, provided that: "In awarding grants to the Trust Territory of the Pacific Islands, American Samoa, Guam, the Northern Mariana Islands and the Virgin Islands under section 201(g)(1) of the Clean Water Act (33 U.S.C. 1251 et seq.) [subsec. (g)(1) of this section], the Administrator of the Environmental Protection Agency may waive limitations regarding grant eligibility for sewerage facilities and related appurtenances, insofar as such limitations relate to collector sewers, based upon a determination that applying such limitations could hinder the alleviation of threats to public health and water quality. In making such a determination, the Administrator shall take into consideration the public health and water quality benefits to be derived and the availability of alternate funding sources. The Administrator shall not award grants under this section for the operation and maintenance of sewerage facilities, for construction of facilities which are not an essential component of the sewerage facilities, or any other activities or facilities which are not concerned with the management of wastewater to alleviate threats to public health and water quality." [For termination of Trust Territory of the Pacific Islands, see note set out preceding section 1681 of Title 48, Territories and Insular Possessions.]

Environmental Financing Authority

Section 12 of Pub. L. 92-500, as amended by Pub. L. 97-258, Sec. 4(b), Sept. 13, 1982, 96 Stat. 1067, provided that:

"(a) [Short Title] This section may be cited as the Environmental Financing Act of 1972.

(b) [Establishment] There is hereby created a body corporate to be known as the Environmental Financing Authority, which shall have succession until dissolved by Act of Congress. The Authority shall be subject to the general supervision and direction of the Secretary of the Treasury. The Authority shall be an instrumentality of the United States Government and shall maintain such offices as may be necessary or appropriate in the conduct of its business.

(c) [Congressional Declaration of Purpose] The purpose of this section is to assure that inability to borrow necessary funds on reasonable terms does not prevent any State or local public body from carrying out any project for construction of waste treatment works determined eligible for assistance pursuant to subsection (e) of this section.

(d) [Board of Directors] (1) The Authority shall have a Board of Directors consisting of five persons, one of whom shall be the Secretary of the Treasury or his designee as Chairman of the Board, and four of whom shall be appointed by the President from among the officers or employees of the Authority or of any department or agency of the United States Government.

(2) The Board of Directors shall meet at the call of its Chairman. The Board shall determine the general policies which shall govern the operations of the Authority. The Chairman of the Board shall select and effect the appointment of qualified persons to fill the offices as may be provided for in the bylaws, with such executive functions, powers, and duties as may be prescribed by the bylaws or by the Board of Directors, and such persons shall be the executive officers of the Authority and shall discharge all such executive functions,

powers, and duties. The members of the Board, as such, shall not receive compensation for their services.

(e) [Purchase of State and Local Obligations] (1) Until July 1, 1975, the Authority is authorized to make commitments to purchase, and to purchase on terms and conditions determined by the Authority, any obligation or participation therein which is issued by a State or local public body to finance the non-Federal share of the cost of any project for the construction of waste treatment works which the Administrator of the Environmental Protection Agency has determined to be eligible for Federal financial assistance under the Federal Water Pollution Control Act [this chapter].

(2) No commitment shall be entered into, and no purchase shall be made, unless the Administrator of the Environmental Protection Agency (A) has certified that the public body is unable to obtain on reasonable terms sufficient credit to finance its actual needs; (B) has approved the project as eligible under the Federal Water Pollution Control Act [this chapter], and (C) has agreed to guarantee timely payment of principal and interest on the obligation. The Administrator is authorized to guarantee such timely payments and to issue regulations as he deems necessary and proper to protect such guarantees. Appropriations are hereby authorized to be made to the Administrator in such sums as are necessary to make payments under such guarantees, and such payments are authorized to be made from such appropriations.

(3) No purchase shall be made of obligations issued to finance projects, the permanent financing of which occurred prior to the enactment of this section [Oct. 18, 1972].

(4) Any purchase by the Authority shall be upon such terms and conditions as to yield a return at a rate determined by the Secretary of the Treasury taking into consideration (A) the current average yield on outstanding marketable obligations of the United States of comparable maturity or in its stead whenever the Authority has sufficient of its own long-term obligations outstanding, the current average yield on outstanding obligations of the Authority of comparable maturity; and (B) the market yields on municipal bonds.

(5) The Authority is authorized to charge fees for its commitments and other services adequate to cover all expenses and to provide for the accumulation of reasonable contingency reserves and such fees shall be included in the aggregate project costs.

(f) [Initial Capital] To provide initial capital to the Authority the Secretary of the Treasury is authorized to advance the funds necessary for this purpose. Each such advance shall be upon such terms and conditions as to yield a return at a rate not less than a rate determined by the Secretary of the Treasury taking into consideration the current average yield on outstanding marketable obligations of the United States of comparable maturities. Interest payments on such advances may be deferred, at the discretion of the Secretary, but any such deferred payments shall themselves bear interest at the rate specified in this section. There is authorized to be appropriated not to exceed $100,000,000, which shall be available for the purposes of this subsection.

(g) [Issuance of Obligations] (1) The Authority is authorized, with the approval of the Secretary of the Treasury, to issue and have outstanding obligations having such maturities and bearing such rate or rates of interest as may be determined by the Authority. Such obligations may be redeemable at the option of the Authority before maturity in such manner as may be stipulated therein.

(2) As authorized in appropriation Acts, and such authorizations may be without fiscal year limitations, the Secretary of the Treasury may in his discretion purchase or agree to purchase any obligations issued pursuant to paragraph (1) of this subsection, and for such purpose the Secretary of the Treasury is authorized to use as a public debt transaction the proceeds of the sale of any securities hereafter issued under chapter 31 of title 31, as now or hereafter in force, and the purposes for which securities may be issued under chapter 31 of title 31, as now or hereafter in force, are extended to include such purchases. Each purchase of obligations by the Secretary of the Treasury under this subsection shall be upon such terms and conditions as to yield a return at a rate not less than a rate determined by the Secretary of the Treasury, taking into consideration the current average yield on outstanding marketable obligations of the United States of comparable maturities. The Secretary of the Treasury may sell, upon such terms and conditions and at such price or prices as he shall determine, any of the obligations acquired by him under this paragraph. All purchases and sales by the Secretary of the Treasury of such obligations

under this paragraph shall be treated as public debt transactions of the United States. (As amended Pub. L. 97-258, Sec. 4(b), Sept. 13, 1982, 96 Stat. 1067.)

(h) [Interest Differential] The Secretary of the Treasury is authorized and directed to make annual payments to the Authority in such amounts as are necessary to equal the amount by which the dollar amount of interest expense accrued by the Authority on account of its obligations exceeds the dollar amount of interest income accrued by the Authority on account of obligations purchased by it pursuant to subsection (e) of this section.

(i) [Powers] The Authority shall have power—
   (1) to sue and be sued, complain and defend, in its corporate name;
   (2) to adopt, alter, and use a corporate seal, which shall be judicially noticed;
   (3) to adopt, amend, and repeal bylaws, rules, and regulations as may be necessary for the conduct of its business;
   (4) to conduct its business, carry on its operations, and have offices and exercise the powers granted by this section in any State without regard to any qualification or similar statute in any State;
   (5) to lease, purchase, or otherwise acquire, own, hold, improve, use, or otherwise deal in and with any property, real, personal, or mixed, or any interest therein, wherever situated;
   (6) to accept gifts or donations of services, or of property, real, personal, or mixed, tangible or intangible, in aid of any of the purposes of the Authority;
   (7) to sell, convey, mortgage, pledge, lease, exchange, and otherwise dispose of its property and assets;
   (8) to appoint such officers, attorneys, employees, and agents as may be required, to define their duties, to fix and to pay such compensation for their services as may be determined, subject to the civil service and classification laws, to require bonds for them and pay the premium thereof; and
   (9) to enter into contracts, to execute instruments, to incur liabilities, and to do all things as are necessary or incidental to the proper management of its affairs and the proper conduct of its business.

(j) [Tax Exemption, Exemptions] The Authority, its property, its franchise, capital, reserves, surplus, security holdings, and other funds, and its income shall be exempt from all taxation now or hereafter imposed by the United States or by any State or local taxing authority; except that (A) any real property and any tangible personal property of the Authority shall be subject to Federal, State, and local taxation to the same extent according to its value as other such property is taxed, and (B) any and all obligations issued by the Authority shall be subject both as to principal and interest to Federal, State, and local taxation to the same extent as the obligations of private corporations are taxed.

(k) [Nature of Obligations] All obligations issued by the Authority shall be lawful investments, and may be accepted as security for all fiduciary, trust, and public funds, the investment or deposit of which shall be under authority or control of the United States or of any officer or officers thereof. All obligations issued by the Authority pursuant to this section shall be deemed to be exempt securities within the meaning of laws administered by the Securities and Exchange Commission, to the same extent as securities which are issued by the United States.

(l) [Preparation of Obligations by Secretary of the Treasury] In order to furnish obligations for delivery by the Authority, the Secretary of the Treasury is authorized to prepare such obligations in such form as the Authority may approve, such obligations when prepared to be held in the Treasury subject to delivery upon order by the Authority. The engraved plates, dies, bed pieces, and so forth, executed in connection therewith, shall remain in the custody of the Secretary of the Treasury. The Authority shall reimburse the Secretary of the Treasury for any expenditures made in the preparation, custody, and delivery of such obligations.

(m) [Annual Report to Congress] The Authority shall, as soon as practicable after the end of each fiscal year, transmit to the President and the Congress an annual report of its operations and activities.

(n) [Subsec. (n) amended section 24 of Title 12, Banks and Banking, and is not set out herein.]

(o) [Financial Controls] The budget and audit provisions of chapter 91 of title 31 shall be applicable to the Environmental Financing Authority in the same manner as they are applied to the wholly owned Government corporations. (As amended Pub. L. 97-258, Sec. 4(b), Sept. 13, 1982, 96 Stat. 1067.)

(p) [Subsec. (p) amended section 711 of former Title 31, Money and Finance, and is not set out herein.]"

Section Referred to in Other Sections

This section is referred to in sections 1254, 1281a, 1281b, 1282, 1283, 1284, 1285, 1286, 1288, 1291, 1292, 1297, 1298, 1311, 1314, 1371, 1382, 1383 of this title.

TOTAL TREATMENT SYSTEM FUNDING

33 USC 1281a

Notwithstanding any other provision of law, in any case where the Administrator of the Environmental Protection Agency finds that the total of all grants made under section 1281 of this title for the same treatment works exceeds the actual construction costs for such treatment works (as defined in this chapter) such excess amount shall be a grant of the Federal share (as defined in this chapter) of the cost of construction of a sewage collection system if—
  (1) such sewage collection system was constructed as part of the same total treatment system as the treatment works for which such grants under section 1281 of this title were approved, and
  (2) an application for assistance for the construction of such sewage collection system was filed in accordance with section 3102 of title 42 before all such grants under section 1281 of this title were made and such grant under section 3102 of title 42 could not be approved due to lack of funding under such section 3102 of title 42.

The total of all grants for sewage collection systems made under this section shall not exceed $2,800,000.

(Pub. L. 95-217, Sec. 78, Dec. 27, 1977, 91 Stat. 1611.)

References in Text

Section 3102 of title 42, referred to in par. (2), was omitted from the Code pursuant to section 5316 of Title 42, The Public Health and Welfare, which terminated the authority to make grants or loans under that section after Jan. 1, 1975.

Codification

Section was enacted as part of the Clean Water Act of 1977, Pub. L. 95-217, and not as part of the Federal Water Pollution Control Act which comprises this chapter.

AVAILABILITY OF FARMERS HOME ADMINISTRATION FUNDS FOR NON-FEDERAL SHARE

33 USC 1281b

Notwithstanding any other provision of law, Federal assistance made available by the Farmers Home Administration to any political subdivision of a State may be used to provide the non-Federal share of the cost of any construction project carried out under section 1281 of this title.

(Pub. L. 100-4, title II, Sec. 202(f), Feb. 4, 1987, 101 Stat. 16.)

Codification

Section was enacted as part of the Water Quality Act of 1987, and not as part of the Federal Water Pollution Control Act which comprises this chapter.

FEDERAL SHARE

33 USC 1282

(a) Amount of grants for treatment works
  (1) The amount of any grant for treatment works made under this chapter from funds authorized for any fiscal year beginning after June 30, 1971, and ending before October 1, 1984, shall be 75 per centum of the cost of construction thereof (as approved by the Administra-

tor), and for any fiscal year beginning on or after October 1, 1984, shall be 55 per centum of the cost of construction thereof (as approved by the Administrator), unless modified to a lower percentage rate uniform throughout a State by the Governor of that State with the concurrence of the Administrator. Within ninety days after October 21, 1980, the Administrator shall issue guidelines for concurrence in any such modification, which shall provide for the consideration of the unobligated balance of sums allocated to the State under section 1285 of this title, the need for assistance under this subchapter in such State, and the availability of State grant assistance to replace the Federal share reduced by such modification. The payment of any such reduced Federal share shall not constitute an obligation on the part of the United States or a claim on the part of any State or grantee to reimbursement for the portion of the Federal share reduced in any such State. Any grant (other than for reimbursement) made prior to October 18, 1972, from any funds authorized for any fiscal year beginning after June 30, 1971, shall, upon the request of the applicant, be increased to the applicable percentage under this section. Notwithstanding the first sentence of this paragraph, in any case where a primary, secondary, or advanced waste treatment facility or its related interceptors or a project for infiltration-in-flow correction has received a grant for erection, building, acquisition, alteration, remodeling, improvement, extension, or correction before October 1, 1984, all segments and phases of such facility, interceptors, and project for infiltration-in-flow correction shall be eligible for grants at 75 per centum of the cost of construction thereof for any grant made pursuant to a State obligation which obligation occurred before October 1, 1990. Notwithstanding the first sentence of this paragraph, in the case of a project for which an application for a grant under this subchapter has been made to the Administrator before October 1, 1984, and which project is under judicial injunction on such date prohibiting its construction, such project shall be eligible for grants at 75 percent of the cost of construction thereof. Notwithstanding the first sentence of this paragraph, in the case of the Wyoming Valley Sanitary Authority project mandated by judicial order under a proceeding begun prior to October 1, 1984, and a project for wastewater treatment for Altoona, Pennsylvania, such projects shall be eligible for grants at 75 percent of the cost of construction thereof.

(2) The amount of any grant made after September 30, 1978, and before October 1, 1981, for any eligible treatment works or significant portion thereof utilizing innovative or alternative wastewater treatment processes and techniques referred to in section 1281(g)(5) of this title shall be 85 per centum of the cost of construction thereof, unless modified by the Governor of the State with the concurrence of the Administrator to a percentage rate no less than 15 per centum greater than the modified uniform percentage rate in which the Administrator has concurred pursuant to paragraph (1) of this subsection. The amount of any grant made after September 30, 1981, for any eligible treatment works or unit processes and techniques thereof utilizing innovative or alternative wastewater treatment processes and techniques referred to in section 1281(g)(5) of this title shall be a percentage of the cost of construction thereof equal to 20 per centum greater than the percentage in effect under paragraph (1) of this subsection for such works or unit processes and techniques, but in no event greater than 85 per centum of the cost of construction thereof. No grant shall be made under this paragraph for construction of a treatment works in any State unless the proportion of the State contribution to the non-Federal share of construction costs for all treatment works in such State receiving a grant under this paragraph is the same as or greater than the proportion of the State contribution (if any) to the non-Federal share of construction costs for all treatment works receiving grants in such State under paragraph (1) of this subsection.

(3) In addition to any grant made pursuant to paragraph (2) of this subsection, the Administrator is authorized to make a grant to fund all of the costs of the modification or replacement of any facilities constructed with a grant made pursuant to paragraph (2) if the Administrator finds that such facilities have not met design performance specifications unless such failure is attributable to negligence on the part of any person and if such failure has significantly increased capital or operating and maintenance expenditures. In addition, the Administrator is authorized to make a grant to fund all of the costs of the modification or replacement of biodisc equipment (rotating biological contactors) in any publicly owned treatment works if the Administrator finds that such equipment has failed to meet design performance specifications, unless such failure is attributable to negli-

gence on the part of any person, and if such failure has significantly increased capital or operating and maintenance expenditures.
  (4) For the purposes of this section, the term "eligible treatment works" means those treatment works in each State which meet the requirements of section 1281(g)(5) of this title and which can be fully funded from funds available for such purpose in such State.
(b) Amount of grants for construction of treatment works not commenced prior to July 1, 1971
  The amount of the grant for any project approved by the Administrator after January 1, 1971, and before July 1, 1971, for the construction of treatment works, the actual erection, building or acquisition of which was not commenced prior to July 1, 1971, shall, upon the request of the applicant, be increased to the applicable percentage under subsection (a) of this section for grants for treatment works from funds for fiscal years beginning after June 30, 1971, with respect to the cost of such actual erection, building, or acquisition. Such increased amount shall be paid from any funds allocated to the State in which the treatment works is located without regard to the fiscal year for which such funds were authorized. Such increased amount shall be paid for such project only if—
  (1) a sewage collection system that is a part of the same total waste treatment system as the treatment works for which such grant was approved is under construction or is to be constructed for use in conjunction with such treatment works, and if the cost of such sewage collection system exceeds the cost of such treatment works, and
  (2) the State water pollution control agency or other appropriate State authority certifies that the quantity of available ground water will be insufficient, inadequate, or unsuitable for public use, including the ecological preservation and recreational use of surface water bodies, unless effluents from publicly-owned treatment works after adequate treatment are returned to the ground water consistent with acceptable technological standards.
(c) Availability of sums allotted to Puerto Rico
  Notwithstanding any other provision of law, sums allotted to the Commonwealth of Puerto Rico under section 1285 of this title for fiscal year 1981 shall remain available for obligation for the fiscal year for which authorized and for the period of the next succeeding twenty-four months. Such sums and any unobligated funds available to Puerto Rico from allotments for fiscal years ending prior to October 1, 1981, shall be available for obligation by the Administrator of the Environmental Protection Agency only to fund the following systems: Aguadilla, Arecibo, Mayaguez, Carolina, and Camuy Hatillo. These funds may be used by the commonwealth of Puerto Rico to fund the non-Federal share of the costs of such projects. To the extent that these funds are used to pay the non-Federal share, the Commonwealth of Puerto Rico shall repay to the Environmental Protection Agency such amounts on terms and conditions developed and approved by the Administrator in consultation with the Governor of the Commonwealth of Puerto Rico. Agreement on such terms and conditions, including the payment of interest to be determined by the Secretary of the Treasury, shall be reached prior to the use of these funds for the Commonwealth's non-Federal share. No Federal funds awarded under this provision shall be used to replace local governments funds previously expended on these projects.

(June 30, 1948, ch. 758, title II, Sec. 202, as added Pub. L. 92-500, Sec. 2, Oct. 18, 1972, 86 Stat. 834; amended Pub. L. 95-217, Sec. 17, Dec. 27, 1977, 91 Stat. 1571; Pub. L. 96-483, Sec. 9, Oct. 21, 1980, 94 Stat. 2362; Pub. L. 97-117, Secs. 7, 8(a), (b), Dec. 29, 1981, 95 Stat. 1625; Pub. L. 97-357, title V, Sec. 501, Oct. 19, 1982, 96 Stat. 1712; Pub. L. 100-4, title II, Sec. 202(a)-(d), Feb. 4, 1987, 101 Stat. 15, 16.)

Amendments

1987—Subsec. (a)(1). Pub. L. 100-4, Sec. 202(a), inserted "for any grant made pursuant to a State obligation which obligation occurred before October 1, 1990" before period at end of last sentence.

Pub. L. 100-4, Sec. 202(b), inserted at end "Notwithstanding the first sentence of this paragraph, in the case of a project for which an application for a grant under this subchapter has been made to the Administrator before October 1, 1984, and which project is under judicial injunction on such date prohibiting its construction, such project shall be eligible for grants at 75 percent of the cost of construction thereof."

Pub. L. 100-4, Sec. 202(c), inserted at end "Notwithstanding the first sentence of this paragraph, in the case of the Wyoming Valley Sanitary Authority project mandated by judicial order under a proceeding begun prior to October 1, 1984, and a project for wastewater treatment for Altoona, Pennsylvania, such projects shall be eligible for grants at 75 percent of the cost of construction thereof."

Subsec. (a)(3). Pub. L. 100-4, Sec. 202(d), inserted at end "In addition, the Administrator is authorized to make a grant to fund all of the costs of the modification or replacement of biodisc equipment (rotating biological contactors) in any publicly owned treatment works if the Administrator finds that such equipment has failed to meet design performance specifications, unless such failure is attributable to negligence on the part of any person, and if such failure has significantly increased capital or operating and maintenance expenditures."

1982—Subsec. (c). Pub. L. 97-357 added subsec. (c).

1981—Subsec. (a)(1). Pub. L. 97-117, Sec. 7, inserted "and ending before October 30, 1984," after "June 30, 1971," and "and for any fiscal year beginning on or after October 1, 1984, shall be 55 per centum of the cost of construction thereof (as approved by the Administrator)," after "(as approved by the Administrator)," and provision that notwithstanding first sentence of this paragraph, in any case where primary, secondary, or advanced waste treatment facility or its related interceptors or a project for infiltration-in-flow correction has received a grant for building, acquisition, etc., before Oct. 1, 1984, all segments and phases be eligible for grants at 75 per centum of the cost of construction.

Subsec. (a)(2). Pub. L. 97-117, Sec. 8(a), inserted provision that the amount of any grant made after Sept. 30, 1981, for any eligible treatment works or unit processes or techniques, utilizing innovative or alternative wastewater treatment processes or techniques referred to in section 1281(g)(5) of this title be a percentage of the cost of construction equal to 20 per centum greater than the percentage in effect under par. (1) of this subsection, but in no event greater than 85 per centum of the cost of construction.

Subsec. (a)(4). Pub. L. 97-117, Sec. 8(b), struck out "in the fiscal years ending September 30, 1979, September 30, 1980, and September 30, 1981" after "purpose in such State" and provision that excluded from term "eligible treatment works" collector sewers, interceptors, storm or sanitary sewers or the separation thereof, or major sewer rehabilitation.

1980—Subsec. (a)(1). Pub. L. 96-483, Sec. 9(a), inserted provisions relating to modification to a lower percentage rate by the Governor of the State and issuance of guidelines by the Administrator for the concurrence in any such modification.

Subsec. (a)(2). Pub. L. 96-483, Sec. 9(b), inserted provision relating to the modification by the Governor of the State to a percentage rate no less than 15 per centum greater than the modified uniform rate in which the Administrator has concurred.

1977—Subsec. (a). Pub. L. 95-217 designated existing provisions as par. (1) and added pars. (2) to (4).

Promulgation of Federal Shares

Act July 9, 1956, ch. 518, Sec. 4, 70 Stat. 507, authorized the Surgeon General to promulgate Federal shares under the Federal Water Pollution Control Grant Program as soon as possible after July 9, 1956, in the manner specified in the Water Pollution Control Act, act June 30, 1948, ch. 758, 62 Stat. 1155, and provided that such shares were to be conclusive for the purposes of section 5 of act June 30, 1948.

Section Referred to in Other Sections

This section is referred to in sections 1255, 1281, 1283, 1285 of this title.

PLANS, SPECIFICATIONS, ESTIMATES, AND PAYMENTS

33 USC 1283

(a) Submission; contractual nature of approval by Administrator; agreement on eligible costs; single grant
  (1) Each applicant for a grant shall submit to the Administrator for his approval, plans, specifications, and estimates for each proposed project for the construction of treatment works for which a grant is applied for under section 1281(g)(1) of this title from funds allotted to

the State under section 1285 of this title and which otherwise meets the requirements of this chapter. The Administrator shall act upon such plans, specifications, and estimates as soon as practicable after the same have been submitted, and his approval of any such plans, specifications, and estimates shall be deemed a contractual obligation of the United States for the payment of its proportional contribution to such project.
  (2) Agreement on eligible costs.—
    (A) Limitation on modifications.—Before taking final action on any plans, specifications, and estimates submitted under this subsection after the 60th day following February 4, 1987, the Administrator shall enter into a written agreement with the applicant which establishes and specifies which items of the proposed project are eligible for Federal payments under this section. The Administrator may not later modify such eligibility determinations unless they are found to have been made in violation of applicable Federal statutes and regulations.
    (B) Limitation on effect.—Eligibility determinations under this paragraph shall not preclude the Administrator from auditing a project pursuant to section 1361 of this title, or other authority, or from withholding or recovering Federal funds for costs which are found to be unreasonable, unsupported by adequate documentation, or otherwise unallowable under applicable Federal cost principles, or which are incurred on a project which fails to meet the design specifications or effluent limitations contained in the grant agreement and permit pursuant to section 1342 of this title for such project.
  (3) In the case of a treatment works that has an estimated total cost of $8,000,000 or less (as determined by the Administrator), and the population of the applicant municipality is twenty-five thousand or less (according to the most recent United States census), upon completion of an approved facility plan, a single grant may be awarded for the combined Federal share of the cost of preparing construction plans and specifications, and the building and erection of the treatment works.
(b) Periodic payments
  The Administrator shall, from time to time as the work progresses, make payments to the recipient of a grant for costs of construction incurred on a project. These payments shall at no time exceed the Federal share of the cost of construction incurred to the date of the voucher covering such payment plus the Federal share of the value of the materials which have been stockpiled in the vicinity of such construction in conformity to plans and specifications for the project.
(c) Final payments
  After completion of a project and approval of the final voucher by the Administrator, he shall pay out of the appropriate sums the unpaid balance of the Federal share payable on account of such project.
(d) Projects eligible
  Nothing in this chapter shall be construed to require, or to authorize the Administrator to require, that grants under this chapter for construction of treatment works be made only for projects which are operable units usable for sewage collection, transportation, storage, waste treatment, or for similar purposes without additional construction.
(e) Technical and legal assistance in administration and enforcement of contracts; intervention in civil actions
  At the request of a grantee under this subchapter, the Administrator is authorized to provide technical and legal assistance in the administration and enforcement of any contract in connection with treatment works assisted under this subchapter, and to intervene in any civil action involving the enforcement of such a contract.
(f) Design/build projects
  (1) Agreement
    Consistent with State law, an applicant who proposes to construct waste water treatment works may enter into an agreement with the Administrator under this subsection providing for the preparation of construction plans and specifications and the erection of such treatment works, in lieu of proceeding under the other provisions of this section.
  (2) Limitation on projects
    Agreements under this subsection shall be limited to projects under an approved facility plan which projects are—

(A) treatment works that have an estimated total cost of $8,000,000 or less; and
(B) any of the following types of waste water treatment systems: aerated lagoons, trickling filters, stabilization ponds, land application systems, sand filters, and subsurface disposal systems.
(3) Required terms
An agreement entered into under this subsection shall—
(A) set forth an amount agreed to as the maximum Federal contribution to the project, based upon a competitively bid document of basic design data and applicable standard construction specifications and a determination of the federally eligible costs of the project at the applicable Federal share under section 1282 of this title;
(B) set forth dates for the start and completion of construction of the treatment works by the applicant and a schedule of payments of the Federal contribution to the project;
(C) contain assurances by the applicant that (i) engineering and management assistance will be provided to manage the project; (ii) the proposed treatment works will be an operable unit and will meet all the requirements of this subchapter; and (iii) not later than 1 year after the date specified as the date of completion of construction of the treatment works, the treatment works will be operating so as to meet the requirements of any applicable permit for such treatment works under section 1342 of this title;
(D) require the applicant to obtain a bond from the contractor in an amount determined necessary by the Administrator to protect the Federal interest in the project; and
(E) contain such other terms and conditions as are necessary to assure compliance with this subchapter (except as provided in paragraph (4) of this subsection).
(4) Limitation on application
Subsections (a), (b), and (c) of this section shall not apply to grants made pursuant to this subsection.
(5) Reservation to assure compliance
The Administrator shall reserve a portion of the grant to assure contract compliance until final project approval as defined by the Administrator. If the amount agreed to under paragraph (3)(A) exceeds the cost of designing and constructing the treatment works, the Administrator shall reallot the amount of the excess to the State in which such treatment works are located for the fiscal year in which such audit is completed.
(6) Limitation on obligations
The Administrator shall not obligate more than 20 percent of the amount allotted to a State for a fiscal year under section 1285 of this title for grants pursuant to this subsection.
(7) Allowance
The Administrator shall determine an allowance for facilities planning for projects constructed under this subsection in accordance with section 1281(l) of this title.
(8) Limitation on Federal contributions
In no event shall the Federal contribution for the cost of preparing construction plans and specifications and the building and erection of treatment works pursuant to this subsection exceed the amount agreed upon under paragraph (3).
(9) Recovery action
In any case in which the recipient of a grant made pursuant to this subsection does not comply with the terms of the agreement entered into under paragraph (3), the Administrator is authorized to take such action as may be necessary to recover the amount of the Federal contribution to the project.
(10) Prevention of double benefits
A recipient of a grant made pursuant to this subsection shall not be eligible for any other grants under this subchapter for the same project.

(June 30, 1948, ch. 758, title II, Sec. 203, as added Pub. L. 92-500, Sec. 2, Oct. 18, 1972, 86 Stat. 835; amended Pub. L. 93-243, Sec. 2, Jan. 2, 1974, 87 Stat. 1069; Pub. L. 95-217, Secs. 18, 19, Dec. 27, 1977, 91 Stat. 1571, 1572; Pub. L. 96-483, Sec. 6, Oct. 21, 1980, 94 Stat. 2362; Pub. L. 97-117, Sec. 9, Dec. 29, 1981, 95 Stat. 1626; Pub. L. 100-4, title II, Secs. 203, 204, Feb. 4, 1987, 101 Stat. 16, 17.)

Amendments

1987—Subsec. (a). Pub. L. 100-4, Sec. 203, designated provision relating to submission of plans, specifications, and estimates, and provision relating to contractual nature of approval by Administrator as par. (1), designated provision relating to requirements for awarding single grant for combined Federal share of cost of preparing plans and specifications, and building and erection of treatment works as par. (3), and added par. (2).

Subsec. (f). Pub. L. 100-4, Sec. 204, added subsec. (f).

1981—Subsec. (a). Pub. L. 97-117 substituted "$8,000,000" for "$4,000,000" and struck out provision that, if any State is found by the Administrator to have unusually high costs of construction, the Administrator may authorize a single grant where the estimated total cost of the treatment works does not exceed $5,000,000.

1980—Subsec. (a). Pub. L. 96-483 substituted "$4,000,000" and "$5,000,000" for "$2,000,000" and "$3,000,000", respectively.

1977—Subsec. (a). Pub. L. 95-217, Sec. 18, provided that, in the case of a treatment works that has an estimated total cost of $2,000,000 or less (as determined by the Administrator), and the population of the applicant municipality is twenty-five thousand or less (according to the most recent United States census), upon completion of an approved facility plan, a single grant may be awarded for the combined Federal share of the cost of preparing construction plans and specifications, and the building and erection of the treatment works, and that, if any State is found by the Administrator to have unusually high costs of construction, the Administrator may authorize a single grant where the estimated total cost of the treatment works does not exceed $3,000,000.

Subsec. (e). Pub. L. 95-217, Sec. 19, added subsec. (e).

1974—Subsec. (d). Pub. L. 93-243 added subsec. (d).

Section Referred to in Other Sections

This section is referred to in sections 1284, 1285, 1311 of this title.

LIMITATIONS AND CONDITIONS

33 USC 1284

(a) Determinations by Administrator

Before approving grants for any project for any treatment works under section 1281(g)(1) of this title the Administrator shall determine—

(1) that any required areawide waste treatment management plan under section 1288 of this title (A) is being implemented for such area and the proposed treatment works are included in such plan, or (B) is being developed for such area and reasonable progress is being made toward its implementation and the proposed treatment works will be included in such plan;

(2) that (A) the State in which the project is to be located (i) is implementing any required plan under section 1313(e) of this title and the proposed treatment works are in conformity with such plan, or (ii) is developing such a plan and the proposed treatment works will be in conformity with such plan, and (B) such State is in compliance with section 1315(b) of this title;

(3) that such works have been certified by the appropriate State water pollution control agency as entitled to priority over such other works in the State in accordance with any applicable State plan under section 1313(e) of this title, except that any priority list developed pursuant to section 1313(e)(3)(H) of this title may be modified by such State in accordance with regulations promulgated by the Administrator to give higher priority for grants for the Federal share of the cost of preparing construction drawings and specifications for any treatment works utilizing processes and techniques meeting the guidelines promulgated under section 1314(d)(3) of this title and for grants for the combined Federal share of the cost of preparing construction drawings and specifications and the building and erection of any treatment works meeting the requirements of the next to the last sentence of section 1283(a) of this title which utilizes processes and techniques meeting the guidelines promulgated under section 1314(d)(3) of this title.[1]

(4) that the applicant proposing to construct such works agrees to pay the non-Federal costs of such works and has made adequate provisions satisfactory to the Administrator for assur-

---

[1] So in original. The period probably should be a semicolon.

ing proper and efficient operation, including the employment of trained management and operations personnel, and the maintenance of such works in accordance with a plan of operation approved by the State water pollution control agency or, as appropriate, the interstate agency, after construction thereof;

(5) that the size and capacity of such works relate directly to the needs to be served by such works, including sufficient reserve capacity. The amount of reserve capacity provided shall be approved by the Administrator on the basis of a comparison of the cost of constructing such reserves as a part of the works to be funded and the anticipated cost of providing expanded capacity at a date when such capacity will be required, after taking into account, in accordance with regulations promulgated by the Administrator, efforts to reduce total flow of sewage and unnecessary water consumption. The amount of reserve capacity eligible for a grant under this subchapter shall be determined by the Administrator taking into account the projected population and associated commercial and industrial establishments within the jurisdiction of the applicant to be served by such treatment works as identified in an approved facilities plan, an areawide plan under section 1288 of this title, or an applicable municipal master plan of development. For the purpose of this paragraph, section 1288 of this title, and any such plan, projected population shall be determined on the basis of the latest information available from the United States Department of Commerce or from the States as the Administrator, by regulation, determines appropriate. Beginning October 1, 1984, no grant shall be made under this subchapter to construct that portion of any treatment works providing reserve capacity in excess of existing needs (including existing needs of residential, commercial, industrial, and other users) on the date of approval of a grant for the erection, building, acquisition, alteration, remodeling, improvement, or extension of a project for secondary treatment or more stringent treatment or new interceptors and appurtenances, except that in no event shall reserve capacity of a facility and its related interceptors to which this subsection applies be in excess of existing needs on October 1, 1990. In any case in which an applicant proposes to provide reserve capacity greater than that eligible for Federal financial assistance under this subchapter, the incremental costs of the additional reserve capacity shall be paid by the applicant;

(6) that no specification for bids in connection with such works shall be written in such a manner as to contain proprietary, exclusionary, or discriminatory requirements other than those based upon performance, unless such requirements are necessary to test or demonstrate a specific thing or to provide for necessary interchangeability of parts and equipment. When in the judgment of the grantee, it is impractical or uneconomical to make a clear and accurate description of the technical requirements, a "brand name or equal" description may be used as a means to define the performance or other salient requirements of a procurement, and in doing so the grantee need not establish the existence of any source other than the brand or source so named.

(b) Additional determinations; issuance of guidelines; approval by Administrator; system of charges

(1) Notwithstanding any other provision of this subchapter, the Administrator shall not approve any grant for any treatment works under section 1281(g)(1) of this title after March 1, 1973, unless he shall first have determined that the applicant (A) has adopted or will adopt a system of charges to assure that each recipient of waste treatment services within the applicant's jurisdiction, as determined by the Administrator, will pay its proportionate share (except as otherwise provided in this paragraph) of the costs of operation and maintenance (including replacement) of any waste treatment services provided by the applicant; and (B) has legal, institutional, managerial, and financial capability to insure adequate construction, operation, and maintenance of treatment works throughout the applicant's jurisdiction, as determined by the Administrator. In any case where an applicant which, as of December 27, 1977, uses a system of dedicated ad valorem taxes and the Administrator determines that the applicant has a system of charges which results in the distribution of operation and maintenance costs for treatment works within the applicant's jurisdiction, to each user class, in proportion to the contribution to the total cost of operation and maintenance of such works by each user class (taking into account total waste water loading of such works, the constituent elements of the wastes, and other appropriate factors), and such applicant is otherwise in compliance with clause (A) of this paragraph

with respect to each industrial user, then such dedicated ad valorem tax system shall be deemed to be the user charge system meeting the requirements of clause (A) of this paragraph for the residential user class and such small non-residential user classes as defined by the Administrator. In defining small non-residential users, the Administrator shall consider the volume of wastes discharged into the treatment works by such users and the constituent elements of such wastes as well as such other factors as he deems appropriate. A system of user charges which imposes a lower charge for low-income residential users (as defined by the Administrator) shall be deemed to be a user charge system meeting the requirements of clause (A) of this paragraph if the Administrator determines that such system was adopted after public notice and hearing.
  (2) The Administrator shall, within one hundred and eighty days after October 18, 1972, and after consultation with appropriate State, interstate, municipal, and intermunicipal agencies, issue guidelines applicable to payment of waste treatment costs by industrial and nonindustrial recipients of waste treatment services which shall establish (A) classes of users of such services, including categories of industrial users; (B) criteria against which to determine the adequacy of charges imposed on classes and categories of users reflecting all factors that influence the cost of waste treatment, including strength, volume, and delivery flow rate characteristics of waste; and (C) model systems and rates of user charges typical of various treatment works serving municipal-industrial communities.
  (3) Approval by the Administrator of a grant to an interstate agency established by interstate compact for any treatment works shall satisfy any other requirement that such works be authorized by Act of Congress.
  (4) A system of charges which meets the requirement of clause (A) of paragraph (1) of this subsection may be based on something other than metering the sewage or water supply flow of residential recipients of waste treatment services, including ad valorem taxes. If the system of charges is based on something other than metering the Administrator shall require (A) the applicant to establish a system by which the necessary funds will be available for the proper operation and maintenance of the treatment works; and (B) the applicant to establish a procedure under which the residential user will be notified as to that portion of his total payment which will be allocated to the cost of the waste treatment services.
(c) Applicability of reserve capacity restrictions to primary, secondary, or advanced waste treatment facilities or related interceptors
  The next to the last sentence of paragraph (5) of subsection (a) of this section shall not apply in any case where a primary, secondary, or advanced waste treatment facility or its related interceptors has received a grant for erection, building, acquisition, alteration, remodeling, improvement, or extension before October 1, 1984, and all segments and phases of such facility and interceptors shall be funded based on a 20-year reserve capacity in the case of such facility and a 20-year reserve capacity in the case of such interceptors, except that, if a grant for such interceptors has been approved prior to December 29, 1981, such interceptors shall be funded based on the approved reserve capacity not to exceed 40 years.
(d) Engineering requirements; certification by owner and operator; contractual assurances, etc.
  (1) A grant for the construction of treatment works under this subchapter shall provide that the engineer or engineering firm supervising construction or providing architect engineering services during construction shall continue its relationship to the grant applicant for a period of one year after the completion of construction and initial operation of such treatment works. During such period such engineer or engineering firm shall supervise operation of the treatment works, train operating personnel, and prepare curricula and training material for operating personnel. Costs associated with the implementation of this paragraph shall be eligible for Federal assistance in accordance with this subchapter.
  (2) On the date one year after the completion of construction and initial operation of such treatment works, the owner and operator of such treatment works shall certify to the Administrator whether or not such treatment works meet the design specifications and effluent limitations contained in the grant agreement and permit pursuant to section 1342 of this title for such works. If the owner and operator of such treatment works cannot certify that such treatment works meet such design specifications and effluent limitations, any failure to meet such design specifications and effluent limitations shall be corrected in a timely manner, to allow such affirmative certification, at other than Federal expense.

(3) Nothing in this section shall be construed to prohibit a grantee under this subchapter from requiring more assurances, guarantees, or indemnity or other contractual requirements from any party to a contract pertaining to a project assisted under this subchapter, than those provided under this subsection.

(June 30, 1948, ch. 758, title II, Sec. 204, as added Pub. L. 92-500, Sec. 2, Oct. 18, 1972, 86 Stat. 835; amended Pub. L. 95-217, Secs. 20-24, Dec. 27, 1977, 91 Stat. 1572, 1573; Pub. L. 96-483, Sec. 2(a), (b), Oct. 21, 1980, 94 Stat. 2360, 2361; Pub. L. 97-117, Secs. 10(a), (b), 11, 12, Dec. 29, 1981, 95 Stat. 1626, 1627; Pub. L. 100-4, title II, Sec. 205(a)-(c), Feb. 4, 1987, 101 Stat. 18.)

Amendments

1987—Subsec. (a)(1). Pub. L. 100-4, Sec. 205(a), amended par. (1) generally. Prior to amendment, par. (1) read as follows: "that such works are included in any applicable areawide waste treatment management plan developed under section 1288 of this title;".

Subsec. (a)(2). Pub. L. 100-4, Sec. 205(b), amended par. (2) generally. Prior to amendment, par. (2) read as follows: "that such works are in conformity with any applicable State plan under section 1313(e) of this title;".

Subsec. (b)(1). Pub. L. 100-4, Sec. 205(c), inserted at end "A system of user charges which imposes a lower charge for low-income residential users (as defined by the Administrator) shall be deemed to be a user charge system meeting the requirements of clause (A) of this paragraph if the Administrator determines that such system was adopted after public notice and hearing."

1981—Subsec. (a)(5). Pub. L. 97-117, Sec. 10(a), inserted provision that beginning Oct. 1, 1984, no grant be made under this subchapter to construct that portion of any treatment works providing reserve capacity in excess of existing needs on the date of approval of a grant for the erection, building, etc., of a project for secondary treatment or more stringent treatment or new interceptors and appurtenances, except that in no event shall reserve capacity of a facility and its related interceptors to which this subsection applies be in excess of existing needs on Oct. 1, 1990, and that in any case in which an applicant proposes to provide reserve capacity greater than that eligible for Federal financial assistance under this subchapter, the incremental costs of the additional reserve capacity be paid by the applicant.

Subsec. (a)(6). Pub. L. 97-117, Sec. 11, struck out ", or at least two brand names or trade names of comparable quality or utility are listed and are followed by the words 'or equal' " after "parts and equipment" and inserted provision that when in the judgment of the grantee, it is impractical or uneconomical to make a clear and accurate description of the technical requirements, a "brand name or equal" description be used as a means to define performance or other salient requirements of a procurement, and in doing so the grantee need not establish the existence of any source other than the brand or source so named.

Subsec. (c). Pub. L. 97-117, Sec. 10(b), added subsec. (c).

Subsec. (d). Pub. L. 97-117, Sec. 12, added subsec. (d).

1980—Subsec. (b)(1). Pub. L. 96-483, Sec. 2(a), redesignated cl. (C) as (B). Former cl. (B) relating to payment, as a condition of approval of a grant, to an applicant by industrial users of that portion of cost of construction allocable to the treatment of such industrial waste to the extent attributable to the Federal share of the cost of construction, was struck out.

Subsec. (b)(3) to (6). Pub. L. 96-483, Sec. 2(b), redesignated pars. (4) and (5) as (3) and (4), respectively. Former par. (3) relating to a formula determining the amount the grantee shall retain of the revenues derived from the payment of costs by industrial users of waste treatment services, to the extent costs are attributable to the Federal share of eligible project costs, and former par. (6) relating to the exemption from the requirements of par. (1)(B) of industrial users with a flow of twenty-five thousand gallons or less per day, were struck out.

1977—Subsec. (a)(3). Pub. L. 95-217, Sec. 20, provided that any priority list developed pursuant to section 1313(e)(3)(H) of this title may be modified by such State in accordance with regulations promulgated by the Administrator to give higher priority for grants for the Federal share of the cost of preparing construction drawings and specifications for any treatment works utilizing processes and techniques meeting the guidelines promulgated under section 1314(d)(3) of this title and for grants for the combined Federal share of the cost of preparing construction drawings and specifications and the building and erection of any treatment works meeting the requirements of the next to the last sentence of section 1283(a) of this title which utilizes processes and techniques meeting the guidelines promulgated under section 1314(d)(3) of this title.

Subsec. (a)(5). Pub. L. 95-217, Sec. 21, provided that efforts to reduce total flow of sewage and unnecessary water consumption be taken into account, in accordance with regulations promulgated by the Administrator, that the amount of reserve capacity eligible for a grant under this subchapter be determined by the Administrator taking into account the projected population and associated commercial and industrial establishments within the jurisdiction of the applicant to be served by such treatment works as identified in an approved facilities plan, an areawide plan under section 1288 of this title, or an applicable municipal master plan of development, and that, for the purpose of this paragraph, section 1288 of this title, and any such plan, projected population be determined on the basis of the latest information available from the United States Department of Commerce or from the States as the Administrator, by regulation, determines appropriate.

Subsec. (b)(1). Pub. L. 95-217, Secs. 22(a)(1), (2), 24(c), inserted "(except as otherwise provided in this paragraph)" after "proportionate share" in cl. (A) and "(which such portion, in the discretion of the applicant, may be recovered from industrial users of the total waste treatment system as distinguished from the treatment works for which the grant is made)" in cl. (B) and, at end of existing provisions, inserted sentences under which a dedicated ad valorem tax system is to be deemed the user charge system meeting the requirements of cl. (A) for the residential user class and such small non-residential user classes as defined by the Administrator in cases where an applicant, as of Dec. 27, 1977, uses a system of dedicated ad valorem taxes and the Administrator determines that the applicant has a system of charges which results in the distribution of operation and maintenance costs for treatment works within the applicant's jurisdiction, to each user class, in proportion to the contribution to the total cost of operation and maintenance of such works by each user class (taking into account total waste water loading of such works, the constituent elements of the wastes, and other appropriate factors), and such applicant is otherwise in compliance with cl. (A) of this paragraph with respect to each industrial user.

Subsec. (b)(3). Pub. L. 95-217, Secs. 23, 24(a), substituted "necessary for the administrative costs associated with the requirement of paragraph (1)(B) of this subsection and future expansion" for "necessary for future expansion" in cl. (B) and, at end of existing provisions, inserted sentence under which, subject to the approval of the Administrator, the following: "Not a grantee that received a grant prior to Dec. 27, 1977, may reduce the amounts required to be paid to such grantee by any industrial user of waste treatment services under such paragraph, if such grantee requires such industrial user to adopt other means of reducing the demand for waste treatment services through reduction in the total flow of sewage or unnecessary water consumption, in proportion to such reduction as determined in accordance with regulations promulgated by the Administrator".

Subsec. (b)(5), (6). Pub. L. 95-217, Secs. 22(b), 24(b), added pars. (5) and (6).

Effective Date of 1987 Amendment

Section 205(d) of Pub. L. 100-4 provided that: "This section [amending this section] shall take effect on the date of the enactment of this Act [Feb. 4, 1987], except that the amendments made by subsections (a) and (b) [amending this section] shall take effect on the last day of the two-year period beginning on such date of enactment."

Effective Date of 1980 Amendment

Amendment by Pub. L. 96-483 effective Dec. 27, 1977, see section 2(g) of Pub. L. 96-483, set out as a note under section 1281 of this title.

Elimination of Inapplicable Conditions or Requirements From Certain Grants

Section 2(c) of Pub. L. 96-483 provided that: "The Administrator of the Environmental Protection Agency shall take such action as may be necessary to remove from any grant made under section 201(g)(1) of the Federal Water Pollution Control Act [section 1281(g)(1) of this title] after March 1, 1973, and prior to the date of enactment of this Act [Oct. 21, 1980], any condition or requirement no longer applicable as a result of the repeals made by subsections (a) and (b) of this section [amending subsec. (b) of this section] or release any grant recipient of the obligations established by such conditions or other requirement."

Section 2(c) of Pub. L. 96-483, set out above, effective Dec. 27, 1977, see section 2(g) of Pub. L. 96-483, set out as an Effective Date of 1980 Amendment note under section 1281 of this title.

Cost Recovery;
Suspension of Grant Requirements That Industrial Users Make Payments

Section 75 of Pub. L. 95-217, as amended by Pub. L. 96-148, Sec. 1, Dec. 16, 1979, 93 Stat. 1088; Pub. L. 96-483, Sec. 2(f), Oct. 21, 1980, 94 Stat. 2361, directed Administrator of Environmental Protection Agency to study and report to Congress not later than last day of twelfth month which begins after Dec. 27, 1977, cost recovery procedures from industrial users of treatment works to the extent construction costs are attributable to the Federal share of the cost of construction.

Section Referred to in Other Sections

This section is referred to in sections 1259, 1281, 1285, 1311, 1342, 1382 of this title.

ALLOTMENT OF GRANT FUNDS

33 USC 1285

(a) Funds for fiscal years during period June 30, 1972, and September 30, 1977; determination of amount

Sums authorized to be appropriated pursuant to section 1287 of this title for each fiscal year beginning after June 30, 1972, and before September 30, 1977, shall be allotted by the Administrator not later than the January 1st immediately preceding the beginning of the fiscal year for which authorized, except that the allotment for fiscal year 1973 shall be made not later than 30 days after October 18, 1972. Such sums shall be allotted among the States by the Administrator in accordance with regulations promulgated by him, in the ratio that the estimated cost of constructing all needed publicly owned treatment works in each State bears to the estimated cost of construction of all needed publicly owned treatment works in all of the States. For the fiscal years ending June 30, 1973, and June 30, 1974, such ratio shall be determined on the basis of table III of House Public Works Committee Print No. 92-50. For the fiscal year ending June 30, 1975, such ratio shall be determined one-half on the basis of table I of House Public Works Committee Print Numbered 93-28 and one-half on the basis of table II of such print, except that no State shall receive an allotment less than that which it received for the fiscal year ending June 30, 1972, as set forth in table III of such print. Allotments for fiscal years which begin after the fiscal year ending June 30, 1975, shall be made only in accordance with a revised cost estimate made and submitted to Congress in accordance with section 1375 of this title and only after such revised cost estimate shall have been approved by law specifically enacted after October 18, 1972.

(b) Availability and use of funds allotted for fiscal years during period June 30, 1972, and September 30, 1977; reallotment

(1) Any sums allotted to a State under subsection (a) of this section shall be available for obligation under section 1283 of this title on and after the date of such allotment. Such sums shall continue available for obligation in such State for a period of one year after the close of the fiscal year for which such sums are authorized. Any amounts so allotted which are not obligated by the end of such one-year period shall be immediately reallotted by the Administrator, in accordance with regulations promulgated by him, generally on the basis of the ratio used in making the last allotment of sums under this section. Such reallotted sums shall be added to the last allotments made to the States. Any sum made available to a State by reallotment under this subsection shall be in addition to any funds otherwise allotted to such State for grants under this subchapter during any fiscal year.

(2) Any sums which have been obligated under section 1283 of this title and which are released by the payment of the final voucher for the project shall be immediately credited to the State to which such sums were last allotted. Such released sums shall be added to the amounts last allotted to such State and shall be immediately available for obligation in the same manner and to the same extent as such last allotment.

(c) Funds for fiscal years during period October 1, 1977, and September 30, 1981; funds for fiscal years 1982 to 1990; determination of amount

(1) Sums authorized to be appropriated pursuant to section 1287 of this title for the fiscal years during the period beginning October 1, 1977, and ending September 30, 1981, shall be allotted for each such year by the Administrator not later than the tenth day which begins after December 27, 1977. Notwithstanding any other provision of law, sums authorized for the fiscal years ending September 30, 1978, September 30, 1979, September 30, 1980, and September 30, 1981, shall be allotted in accordance with table 3 of Committee Print Numbered 95-30 of the Committee on Public Works and Transportation of the House of Representatives.

(2) Sums authorized to be appropriated pursuant to section 1287 of this title for the fiscal years 1982, 1983, 1984, and 1985 shall be allotted for each such year by the Administrator not later than the tenth day which begins after December 29, 1981. Notwithstanding any other provision of law, sums authorized for the fiscal year ending September 30, 1982, shall be allotted in accordance with table 3 of Committee Print Numbered 95-30 of the Committee on Public Works and Transportation of the House of Representatives. Sums authorized for the fiscal years ending September 30, 1983, September 30, 1984, September 30, 1985, and September 30, 1986, shall be allotted in accordance with the following table:

States:	Fiscal Years 1983 through 1985[1]
Alabama	.011398
Alaska	.006101
Arizona	.006885
Arkansas	.006668
California	.072901
Colorado	.008154
Connecticut	.012487
Delaware	.004965
District of Columbia	.004965
Florida	.034407
Georgia	.017234
Hawaii	.007895
Idaho	.004965
Illinois	.046101
Indiana	.024566
Iowa	.013796
Kansas	.009201
Kentucky	.012973
Louisiana	.011205
Maine	.007788
Maryland	.024653
Massachusetts	.034608
Michigan	.043829
Minnesota	.018735
Mississippi	.009184
Missouri	.028257
Montana	.004965
Nebraska	.005214
Nevada	.004965
New Hampshire	.010186
New Jersey	.041654
New Mexico	.004965
New York	.113097
North Carolina	.018396
North Dakota	.004965
Ohio	.057383
Oklahoma	.008235

[1] So in original. Probably should be "1986".

488 / Environmental Statutes

Oregon	.011515
Pennsylvania	.040377
Rhode Island	.006750
South Carolina	.010442
South Dakota	.004965
Tennessee	.014807
Texas	.038726
Utah	.005371
Vermont	.004965
Virginia	.020861
Washington	.017726
West Virginia	.015890
Wisconsin	.027557
Wyoming	.004965
Samoa	.000915
Guam	.000662
Northern Marianas	.000425
Puerto Rico	.013295
Pacific Trust Territories	.001305
Virgin Islands	.000531
United States totals	.999996

(3) Fiscal years 1987-1990.—Sums authorized to be appropriated pursuant to section 1287 of this title for the fiscal years 1987, 1988, 1989, and 1990 shall be allotted for each such year by the Administrator not later than the 10th day which begins after February 4, 1987. Sums authorized for such fiscal years shall be allotted in accordance with the following table:

States:

Alabama	.011309
Alaska	.006053
Arizona	.006831
Arkansas	.006616
California	.072333
Colorado	.008090
Connecticut	.012390
Delaware	.004965
District of Columbia	.004965
Florida	.034139
Georgia	.017100
Hawaii	.007833
Idaho	.004965
Illinois	.045741
Indiana	.024374
Iowa	.013688
Kansas	.009129
Kentucky	.012872
Louisiana	.011118
Maine	.007829
Maryland	.024461
Massachusetts	.034338
Michigan	.043487
Minnesota	.018589
Mississippi	.009112
Missouri	.028037
Montana	.004965
Nebraska	.005173
Nevada	.004965

New Hampshire	.010107
New Jersey	.041329
New Mexico	.004965
New York	.111632
North Carolina	.018253
North Dakota	.004965
Ohio	.056936
Oklahoma	.008171
Oregon	.011425
Pennsylvania	.040062
Rhode Island	.006791
South Carolina	.010361
South Dakota	.004965
Tennessee	.014692
Texas	.046226
Utah	.005329
Vermont	.004965
Virginia	.020698
Washington	.017588
West Virginia	.015766
Wisconsin	.027342
Wyoming	.004965
American Samoa	.000908
Guam	.000657
Northern Marianas	.000422
Puerto Rico	.013191
Pacific Trust Territories	.001295
Virgin Islands	.000527

(d) Availability and use of funds; reallotment

Sums allotted to the States for a fiscal year shall remain available for obligation for the fiscal year for which authorized and for the period of the next succeeding twelve months. The amount of any allotment not obligated by the end of such twenty-four-month period shall be immediately reallotted by the Administrator on the basis of the same ratio as applicable to sums allotted for the then current fiscal year, except that none of the funds reallotted by the Administrator for fiscal year 1978 and for fiscal years thereafter shall be allotted to any State which failed to obligate any of the funds being reallotted. Any sum made available to a State by reallotment under this subsection shall be in addition to any funds otherwise allotted to such State for grants under this subchapter during any fiscal year.

(e) Minimum allotment; additional appropriations; ratio of amount available

For the fiscal years 1978, 1979, 1980, 1981, 1982, 1983, 1984, 1985, 1986, 1987, 1988, 1989, and 1990, no State shall receive less than one-half of 1 per centum of the total allotment under subsection (c) of this section, except that in the case of Guam, Virgin Islands, American Samoa, and the Trust Territories not more than thirty-three one-hundredths of 1 per centum in the aggregate shall be allotted to all four of these jurisdictions. For the purpose of carrying out this subsection there are authorized to be appropriated, subject to such amounts as are provided in appropriation Acts, not to exceed $75,000,000 for each of fiscal years 1978, 1979, 1980, 1981, 1982, 1983, 1984, 1985, 1986, 1987, 1988, 1989, and 1990. If for any fiscal year the amount appropriated under authority of this subsection is less than the amount necessary to carry out this subsection, the amount each State receives under this subsection for such year shall bear the same ratio to the amount such State would have received under this subsection in such year if the amount necessary to carry it out had been appropriated as the amount appropriated for such year bears to the amount necessary to carry out this subsection for such year.

(f) Omitted

(g) Reservation of funds; State management assistance

   (1) The Administrator is authorized to reserve each fiscal year not to exceed 2 per centum of the amount authorized under section 1287 of this title for purposes of the allotment made

to each State under this section on or after October 1, 1977, except in the case of any fiscal year beginning on or after October 1, 1981, and ending before October 1, 1994, in which case the percentage authorized to be reserved shall not exceed 4 per centum.[2] or $400,000 whichever amount is the greater. Sums so reserved shall be available for making grants to such State under paragraph (2) of this subsection for the same period as sums are available from such allotment under subsection (d) of this section, and any such grant shall be available for obligation only during such period. Any grant made from sums reserved under this subsection which has not been obligated by the end of the period for which available shall be added to the amount last allotted to such State under this section and shall be immediately available for obligation in the same manner and to the same extent as such last allotment. Sums authorized to be reserved by this paragraph shall be in addition to and not in lieu of any other funds which may be authorized to carry out this subsection.

(2) The Administrator is authorized to grant to any State from amounts reserved to such State under this subsection, the reasonable costs of administering any aspects of sections 1281, 1283, 1284, and 1292 of this title the responsibility for administration of which the Administrator has delegated to such State. The Administrator may increase such grant to take into account the reasonable costs of administering an approved program under section 1342 or 1344 of this title, administering a state-wide waste treatment management planning program under section 1288(b)(4) of this title, and managing waste treatment construction grants for small communities.

(h) Alternate systems for small communities

The Administrator shall set aside from funds authorized for each fiscal year beginning on or after October 1, 1978, a total (as determined by the Governor of the State) of not less than 4 percent nor more than 7 1/2 percent of the sums allotted to any State with a rural population of 25 per centum or more of the total population of such State, as determined by the Bureau of the Census. The Administrator may set aside no more than 7 1/2 percent of the sums allotted to any other State for which the Governor requests such action. Such sums shall be available only for alternatives to conventional sewage treatment works for municipalities having a population of three thousand five hundred or less, or for the highly dispersed sections of larger municipalities, as defined by the Administrator.

(i) Set-aside for innovative and alternative projects

Not less than 1/2 of 1 percent of funds allotted to a State for each of the fiscal years ending September 30, 1979, through September 30, 1990, under subsection (c) of this section shall be expended only for increasing the Federal share of grants for construction of treatment works utilizing innovative processes and techniques pursuant to section 1282(a)(2) of this title. Including the expenditures authorized by the preceding sentence, a total of 2 percent of the funds allotted to a State for each of the fiscal years ending September 30, 1979, and September 30, 1980, and 3 percent of the funds allotted to a State for the fiscal year ending September 30, 1981, under subsection (c) of this section shall be expended only for increasing grants for construction of treatment works pursuant to section 1282(a)(2) of this title. Including the expenditures authorized by the first sentence of this subsection, a total (as determined by the Governor of the State) of not less than 4 percent nor more than 7 1/2 percent of the funds allotted to such State under subsection (c) of this section for each of the fiscal years ending September 30, 1982, through September 30, 1990, shall be expended only for increasing the Federal share of grants for construction of treatment works pursuant to section 1282(a)(2) of this title.

(j) Water quality management plan; reservation of funds for nonpoint source management

(1) The Administrator shall reserve each fiscal year not to exceed 1 per centum of the sums allotted and available for obligation to each State under this section for each fiscal year beginning on or after October 1, 1981, or $100,000, whichever amount is the greater.

(2) Such sums shall be used by the Administrator to make grants to the States to carry out water quality management planning, including, but not limited to—

(A) identifying most cost effective and locally acceptable facility and non-point measures to meet and maintain water quality standards;

---

[2]So in original. The period probably should be a comma.

(B) developing an implementation plan to obtain State and local financial and regulatory commitments to implement measures developed under subparagraph (A);
(C) determining the nature, extent, and causes of water quality problems in various areas of the State and interstate region, and reporting on these annually; and
(D) determining those publicly owned treatment works which should be constructed with assistance under this subchapter, in which areas and in what sequence, taking into account the relative degree of effluent reduction attained, the relative contributions to water quality of other point or nonpoint sources, and the consideration of alternatives to such construction, and implementing section 1313(e) of this title.
(3) In carrying out planning with grants made under paragraph (2) of this subsection, a State shall develop jointly with local, regional, and interstate entities, a plan for carrying out the program and give funding priority to such entities and designated or undesignated public comprehensive planning organizations to carry out the purposes of this subsection. In giving such priority, the State shall allocate at least 40 percent of the amount granted to such State for a fiscal year under paragraph (2) of this subsection to regional public comprehensive planning organizations in such State and appropriate interstate organizations for the development and implementation of the plan described in this paragraph. In any fiscal year for which the Governor, in consultation with such organizations and with the approval of the Administrator, determines that allocation of at least 40 percent of such amount to such organizations will not result in significant participation by such organizations in water quality management planning and not significantly assist in development and implementation of the plan described in this paragraph and achieving the goals of this chapter, the allocation to such organization may be less than 40 percent of such amount.
(4) All activities undertaken under this subsection shall be in coordination with other related provisions of this chapter.
(5) Nonpoint source reservation.—In addition to the sums reserved under paragraph (1), the Administrator shall reserve each fiscal year for each State 1 percent of the sums allotted and available for obligation to such State under this section for each fiscal year beginning on or after October 1, 1986, or $100,000, whichever is greater, for the purpose of carrying out section 1329 of this title. Sums so reserved in a State in any fiscal year for which such State does not request the use of such sums, to the extent such sums exceed $100,000, may be used by such State for other purposes under this subchapter.

(k) New York City Convention Center

The Administrator shall allot to the State of New York from sums authorized to be appropriated for the fiscal year ending September 30, 1982, an amount necessary to pay the entire cost of conveying sewage from the Convention Center of the city of New York to the Newtown sewage treatment plant, Brooklyn-Queens area, New York. The amount allotted under this subsection shall be in addition to and not in lieu of any other amounts authorized to be allotted to such State under this chapter.

(l) Marine estuary reservation
(1) Reservation of funds
(A) General rule
Prior to making allotments among the States under subsection (c) of this section, the Administrator shall reserve funds from sums appropriated pursuant to section 1287 of this title for each fiscal year beginning after September 30, 1986.
(B) Fiscal years 1987 and 1988
For each of fiscal years 1987 and 1988 the reservation shall be 1 percent of the sums appropriated pursuant to section 1287 of this title for such fiscal year.
(C) Fiscal years 1989 and 1990
For each of fiscal years 1989 and 1990 the reservation shall be 1 1/2 percent of the funds appropriated pursuant to section 1287 of this title for such fiscal year.
(2) Use of funds
Of the sums reserved under this subsection, two-thirds shall be available to address water quality problems of marine bays and estuaries subject to lower levels of water quality due to the impacts of discharges from combined storm water and sanitary sewer overflows from adjacent urban complexes, and one-third shall be available for the implementation of section 1330 of this title, relating to the national estuary program.

492 / Environmental Statutes

(3) Period of availability
Sums reserved under this subsection shall be subject to the period of availability for obligation established by subsection (d) of this section.

(4) Treatment of certain body of water
For purposes of this section and section 1281(n) of this title, Newark Bay, New Jersey, and the portion of the Passaic River up to Little Falls, in the vicinity of Beatties Dam, shall be treated as a marine bay and estuary.

(m) Discretionary deposits into State water pollution control revolving funds

(1) From construction grant allotments
In addition to any amounts deposited in a water pollution control revolving fund established by a State under subchapter VI of this chapter, upon request of the Governor of such State, the Administrator shall make available to the State for deposit, as capitalization grants, in such fund in any fiscal year beginning after September 30, 1986, such portion of the amounts allotted to such State under this section for such fiscal year as the Governor considers appropriate; except that (A) in fiscal year 1987, such deposit may not exceed 50 percent of the amounts allotted to such State under this section for such fiscal year, and (B) in fiscal year 1988, such deposit may not exceed 75 percent of the amounts allotted to such State under this section for this fiscal year.

(2) Notice requirement
The Governor of a State may make a request under paragraph (1) for a deposit into the water pollution control revolving fund of such State—
(A) in fiscal year 1987 only if no later than 90 days after February 4, 1987, and
(B) in each fiscal year thereafter only if 90 days before the first day of such fiscal year, the State provides notice of its intent to make such deposit.

(3) Exception
Sums reserved under section 1285(j) of this title shall not be available for obligation under this subsection.

(June 30, 1948, ch. 758, title II, Sec. 205, as added Pub. L. 92-500, Sec. 2, Oct. 18, 1972, 86 Stat. 837; amended Pub. L. 93-243, Sec. 1, Jan. 2, 1974, 87 Stat. 1069; Pub. L. 95-217, Secs. 25, 26(a), 27, 28, Dec. 27, 1977, 91 Stat. 1574, 1575; Pub. L. 96-483, Sec. 11, Oct. 21, 1980, 94 Stat. 2363; Pub. L. 97-117, Secs. 8(c), 13-16, Dec. 29, 1981, 95 Stat. 1625, 1627-1629; Pub. L. 100-4, title II, Secs. 206(a)-(c), 207-210, 212(b), title III, Sec. 316(d), Feb. 4, 1987, 101 Stat. 19-21, 27, 60; Pub. L. 105-362, title V, Sec. 501(d)(2)(C), Nov. 10, 1998, 112 Stat. 3284.)

Codification

Subsec. (f) provided that sums made available for obligation between Jan. 1, 1975, and Mar. 1, 1975, be available for obligation until Sept. 30, 1978.

Amendments

1998—Subsec. (a). Pub. L. 105-362 substituted "section 1375 of this title" for "section 1375(b) of this title" in last sentence.

1987—Subsec. (c)(2). Pub. L. 100-4, Sec. 206(a)(1), substituted "September 30, 1985, and September 30, 1986" for "and September 30, 1985".

Subsec. (c)(3). Pub. L. 100-4, Sec. 206(a)(2), added par. (3).

Subsec. (e). Pub. L. 100-4, Sec. 206(b), substituted "1985, 1986, 1987, 1988, 1989, and 1990" for "and 1985" in two places.

Subsec. (g)(1). Pub. L. 100-4, Sec. 206(c), substituted "October 1, 1994" for "October 1, 1985".

Subsec. (h). Pub. L. 100-4, Sec. 207, substituted "a total (as determined by the Governor of the State) of not less than 4 percent nor more than 7 1/2 percent" for "four per centum" and "71/2 per cent" for "four per centum".

Subsec. (i). Pub. L. 100-4, Sec. 208, amended subsec. (i) generally. Prior to amendment, subsec. (i) read as follows: "Not less than one-half of one per centum of funds allotted to a State for each of the fiscal years ending September 30, 1979, September 30, 1980, September 30, 1981, September 30, 1982, September 30, 1983, September 30, 1984, and September 30, 1985, under subsection (a) of this section shall be expended only for increasing the Federal share of grants for construction of treatment works utilizing innovative processes and techniques pursuant to section 1282(a)(2) of this title. Including the expenditures authorized by the preceding sentence, a total of two per centum of the funds allotted to a State for each of the fiscal years ending September 30, 1979, and September 30, 1980, and 3 per centum of the funds allotted to a State for the fiscal year ending September 30, 1981, under subsection (a) of this section shall be expended only for increasing grants for construction of treatment works from 75 per centum to 85 per centum pursuant to section 1282(a)(2) of this title. Including the expenditures authorized by the first sentence of this subsection, a total (as determined by the Governor of the State) of not less than 4 per centum nor more than 71/2 per centum of the funds allotted to such State for any fiscal year beginning after September 30, 1981, under subsection (c) of this section shall be expended only for increasing the Federal share of grants for construction of treatment works pursuant to section 1282(a)(2) of this title."

Subsec. (j)(3). Pub. L. 100-4, Sec. 209, inserted provision directing State to allocate at least 40 percent of amount granted under par. (2) to regional public comprehensive planning organizations and appropriate interstate organizations for development and implementation of plan, with exception for less than 40 percent allocation in certain circumstances.

Subsec. (j)(5). Pub. L. 100-4, Sec. 316(d), added par. (5).

Subsec. (l). Pub. L. 100-4, Sec. 210, added subsec. (l).

Subsec. (m). Pub. L. 100-4, Sec. 212(b), added subsec. (m).

1981—Subsec. (c). Pub. L. 97-117, Sec. 13(a), designated existing provision as par. (1) and added par. (2).

Subsec. (e). Pub. L. 97-117, Sec. 13(b), substituted "1981, 1982, 1983, 1984, and 1985" for "and 1981" in two places.

Subsec. (g)(1). Pub. L. 97-117, Sec. 14, inserted "except in the case of any fiscal year beginning on or after October 1, 1981, and ending before October 1, 1985, in which case the percentage authorized to be reserved shall not exceed 4 per centum." after "October 1, 1977," and provision that sums authorized to be reserved be in addition to and not in lieu of any other funds which may be authorized to carry out this subsection.

Subsec. (i). Pub. L. 97-117, Sec. 8(c), substituted "September 30, 1981, September 30, 1982, September 30, 1983, September 30, 1984, and September 30, 1985" for "and September 30, 1981", struck out "from 75 per centum to 85 per centum" after "innovative processes and techniques", and inserted provision that including the expenditures authorized by the first sentence of this subsection, a total, as determined by the State Governor, of not less than 4 per centum nor more than 71/2 per centum of the funds allotted to such State for any fiscal year beginning after Sept. 30, 1981, under subsec. (c) of this section be expended only for increasing the Federal share of grants for construction of treatment works pursuant to section 1282(a)(2) of this title.

Subsecs. (j), (k). Pub. L. 97-117, Secs. 15, 16, added subsecs. (j) and (k).

1980—Subsec. (g)(1). Pub. L. 96-483 inserted "of the amount authorized under section 1287 of this title for purposes" after "2 per centum".

1977—Subsec. (a). Pub. L. 95-217, Sec. 25(a), substituted "each fiscal year beginning after June 30, 1972, and before September 30, 1977" for "each fiscal year beginning after June 30, 1972".

Subsecs. (c) to (f). Pub. L. 95-217, Sec. 25(b), added subsecs. (c) to (f).

Subsecs. (g) to (i). Pub. L. 95-217, Secs. 26(a), 27, 28, added subsecs. (g) to (i).

1974—Subsec. (a). Pub. L. 93-243 inserted provisions that for the fiscal year ending June 30, 1975, the ratio shall be determined one-half on the basis of table I of House Public Works Committee Print Numbered 93-28 and one-half on the basis of table II of such print, except that no State shall receive an allotment less than that which it received for the fiscal year ending June 30, 1972, as set forth in table III of such print and substituted "June 30, 1975" for "June 30, 1974" in sentence beginning "Allotments for fiscal years".

Change of Name

Committee on Public Works and Transportation of House of Representatives treated as referring to Committee on Transportation and Infrastructure of House of Representatives by section 1(a) of Pub. L. 104-14, set out as a note preceding section 21 of Title 2, The Congress.

Termination of Trust Territory of the Pacific Islands

For termination of Trust Territory of the Pacific Islands, see note set out preceding section 1681 of Title 48, Territories and Insular Possessions.

Availability of Allotted Sums in Subsequent Years; Reallotment of Unobligated Sums

Section 7 of Pub. L. 96-483 provided that: "Notwithstanding section 205(d) of the Federal Water Pollution Control Act (33 U.S.C. 1285), sums allotted to the States for the fiscal year 1979 shall remain available for obligation for the fiscal year for which authorized and for the period of the next succeeding twenty-four months. The amount of any allotment not obligated by the end of such thirty-six month period shall be immediately reallotted by the Administrator on the basis of the same ratio as applicable to sums allotted for the then current fiscal year, except that none of the funds reallotted by the Administrator for fiscal year 1979 shall be allotted to any State which failed to obligate any of the funds being reallotted. Any sum made available to a State by reallotment under this section shall be in addition to any funds otherwise allotted to such State for grants under title II of the Federal Water Pollution Control Act [this subchapter] during any fiscal year. This section shall take effect on September 30, 1980."

Section Referred to in Other Sections

This section is referred to in sections 1254, 1259, 1266, 1281, 1282, 1283, 1329, 1377, 1382, 1383, 1384, 1414b of this title.

REIMBURSEMENT AND ADVANCED CONSTRUCTION

33 USC 1286

(a) Publicly owned treatment works construction initiated after June 30, 1966, but before July 1, 1973; reimbursement formula
Any publicly owned treatment works in a State on which construction was initiated after June 30, 1966, but before July 1, 1973, which was approved by the appropriate State water pollution control agency and which the Administrator finds meets the requirements of section 1158 of this title in effect at the time of the initiation of construction shall be reimbursed a total amount equal to the difference between the amount of Federal financial assistance, if any, received under such section 1158 of this title for such project and 50 per centum of the cost of such project, or 55 per centum of the project cost where the Administrator also determines that such treatment works was constructed in conformity with a comprehensive metropolitan treatment plan as described in section 1158(f) of this title as in effect immediately prior to October 18, 1972. Nothing in this subsection shall result in any such works receiving Federal grants from all sources in excess of 80 per centum of the cost of such project.

(b) Publicly owned treatment works construction initiated between June 30, 1956, and June 30, 1966; reimbursement formula
Any publicly owned treatment works constructed with or eligible for Federal financial assistance under this Act in a State between June 30, 1956, and June 30, 1966, which was approved by the State water pollution control agency and which the Administrator finds meets the requirements of section 1158 of this title prior to October 18, 1972 but which was constructed without assistance under such section 1158 of this title or which received such assistance in an amount less than 30 per centum of the cost of such project shall qualify for payments and reimbursement of State or local funds used for such project from sums allocated to such State under this section in an amount which shall not exceed the difference between the amount of such assistance, if any, received for such project and 30 per centum of the cost of such project.

(c) Application for reimbursement
No publicly owned treatment works shall receive any payment or reimbursement under subsection (a) or (b) of this section unless an application for such assistance is filed with the Administrator within the one year period which begins on October 18, 1972. Any application filed within such one year period may be revised from time to time, as may be necessary.

(d) Allocation of funds
The Administrator shall allocate to each qualified project under subsection (a) of this section each fiscal year for which funds are appropriated under subsection (e) of this section an amount which bears the same ratio to the unpaid balance of the reimbursement due such project as the total of such funds for such year bears to the total unpaid balance of reimbursement due all such approved projects on the date of enactment of such appropriation. The Administrator

shall allocate to each qualified project under subsection (b) of this section each fiscal year for which funds are appropriated under subsection (e) of this section an amount which bears the same ratio to the unpaid balance of the reimbursement due such project as the total of such funds for such year bears to the total unpaid balance of reimbursement due all such approved projects on the date of enactment of such appropriation.

(e) Authorization of appropriations
There is authorized to be appropriated to carry out subsection (a) of this section not to exceed $2,600,000,000 and, to carry out subsection (b) of this section, not to exceed $750,000,000. The authorizations contained in this subsection shall be the sole source of funds for reimbursements authorized by this section.

(f) Additional funds
(1) In any case where a substantial portion of the funds allotted to a State for the current fiscal year under this subchapter have been obligated under section 1281(g) of this title, or will be so obligated in a timely manner (as determined by the Administrator), and there is construction of any treatment works project without the aid of Federal funds and in accordance with all procedures and all requirements applicable to treatment works projects, except those procedures and requirements which limit construction of projects to those constructed with the aid of previously allotted Federal funds, the Administrator, upon his approval of an application made under this subsection therefor, is authorized to pay the Federal share of the cost of construction of such project when additional funds are allotted to the State under this subchapter if prior to the construction of the project the Administrator approves plans, specifications, and estimates therefor in the same manner as other treatment works projects. The Administrator may not approve an application under this subsection unless an authorization is in effect for the first fiscal year in the period for which the application requests payment and such requested payment for that fiscal year does not exceed the State's expected allotment from such authorization. The Administrator shall not be required to make such requested payment for any fiscal year—
   (A) to the extent that such payment would exceed such State's allotment of the amount appropriated for such fiscal year; and
   (B) unless such payment is for a project which, on the basis of an approved funding priority list of such State, is eligible to receive such payment based on the allotment and appropriation for such fiscal year.
To the extent that sufficient funds are not appropriated to pay the full Federal share with respect to a project for which obligations under the provisions of this subsection have been made, the Administrator shall reduce the Federal share to such amount less than 75 per centum as such appropriations do provide.
(2) In determining the allotment for any fiscal year under this subchapter, any treatment works project constructed in accordance with this section and without the aid of Federal funds shall not be considered completed until an application under the provisions of this subsection with respect to such project has been approved by the Administrator, or the availability of funds from which this project is eligible for reimbursement has expired, whichever first occurs.

(June 30, 1948, ch. 758, title II, Sec. 206, as added Pub. L. 92-500, Sec. 2, Oct. 18, 1972, 86 Stat. 838; amended Pub. L. 93-207, Sec. 1(2), Dec. 28, 1973, 87 Stat. 906; Pub. L. 95-217, Sec. 29(a), Dec. 27, 1977, 91 Stat. 1576; Pub. L. 96-483, Sec. 5, Oct. 21, 1980, 94 Stat. 2361.)

References in Text

Section 1158 of this title, referred to in subsecs. (a) and (b), refers to section 8 of act June 30, 1948, ch. 758, 62 Stat. 1158, prior to the supersedure and reenactment of act June 30, 1948, by act Oct. 18, 1972, Pub. L. 92-500, 86 Stat. 816. Provisions of section 1158 of this title are covered by this subchapter.

This Act, referred to in subsec. (b), means act June 30, 1948, ch. 758, 62 Stat. 1155, prior to the supersedure and reenactment of act June 30, 1948 by act Oct. 18, 1972, Pub. L. 92-500, 86 Stat. 816. Act June 30, 1948, ch. 758, as added by act Oct. 18, 1972, Pub. L. 92-500, 86 Stat. 816, enacted this chapter.

Amendments

1980—Subsec. (f)(1). Pub. L. 96-483 substituted "In any case where a substantial portion of the funds allotted to a State for the current fiscal year under this subchapter have been obligated under section 1281(g) of this title, or will be so obligated in a timely manner (as determined by the Administrator)" for "In any case where all funds allotted to a State under this subchapter have been obligated under section 1283 of this title", substituted "first fiscal year" for "future fiscal year", inserted "in the period" before "for which the application", substituted "and such requested payment for that fiscal year does not exceed the State's expected allotment from such authorization. The Administrator shall not be required to make such requested payment for any fiscal year—" for "which authorization will insure such payment without exceeding the State's expected allotment from such authorization.", and added subpars. (A), (B), and provisions following subpar. (B).

1977—Subsec. (a). Pub. L. 95-217 substituted "July 1, 1973" for "July 1, 1972".

1973—Subsec. (e). Pub. L. 93-207 substituted "$2,600,000,000" for "$2,000,000,000".

Application for Assistance for Publicly Owned Treatment Works Where Grants Were Made Before July 2, 1972, and on Which Construction Was Initiated Before July 1, 1973

Section 29(b) of Pub. L. 95-217 provided that applications for assistance for publicly owned treatment works for which a grant was made under this chapter before July 1, 1972, and on which construction was initiated before July 1, 1973, be filed not later than the ninetieth day after Dec. 27, 1977.

Application for Assistance

Section 2 of Pub. L. 93-207 provided that notwithstanding the requirements of subsec. (c) of this section, applications for assistance under this section could have been filed with the Administrator until Jan. 31, 1974.

Allocation of Construction Grants Appropriated for the Year Ending June 30, 1973; Interim Payments; Limitations

Section 3 of Pub. L. 93-207 provided that: "Funds available for reimbursement under Public Law 92-399 [making appropriations for Agriculture-Environmental and Consumer Protection Programs for the fiscal year ending June 30, 1973] shall be allocated in accordance with subsection (d) of section 206 of the Federal Water Pollution Control Act (86 Stat. 838) [subsec. (d) of this section], pro rata among all projects eligible under subsection (a) of such section 206 [subsec. (a) of this section] for which applications have been submitted and approved by the Administrator pursuant to such Act [this chapter]. Notwithstanding the provisions of subsection (d) of such section 206, (1) the Administrator is authorized to make interim payments to each such project for which an application has been approved on the basis of estimates of maximum pro rata entitlement of all applicants under section 206(a) and (2) for the purpose of determining allocation of sums available under Public Law 92-399, the unpaid balance of reimbursement due such projects shall be computed as of January 31, 1974. Upon completion by the Administrator of his audit and approval of all projects for which an application has been filed under subsection (a) of such section 206, the Administrator shall, within the limits of appropriated funds, allocate to each such qualified project the amount remaining, if any, of its total entitlement. Amounts allocated to projects which are later determined to be in excess of entitlement shall be available for reallocation, until expended, to other qualified projects under subsection (a) of such section 206. In no event, however, shall any payments exceed the Federal share of the cost of construction incurred to the date of the voucher covering such payment plus the Federal share of the value of the materials which have been stockpiled in the vicinity of such construction in conformity to plans and specifications for the project."

Section Referred to in Other Sections

This section is referred to in sections 1287, 1293, 1376 of this title.

AUTHORIZATION OF APPROPRIATIONS

33 USC 1287

There is authorized to be appropriated to carry out this subchapter, other than sections 1286(e), 1288 and 1289 of this title, for the fiscal year ending June 30, 1973, not to exceed $5,000,000,000, for the fiscal year ending June 30, 1974, not to exceed $6,000,000,000, and for the fiscal year ending June 30, 1975, not to exceed $7,000,000,000, and subject to such amounts as are provided in appropriation Acts, for the fiscal year ending September 30, 1977, $1,000,000,000 for the fiscal year ending September 30, 1978, $4,500,000,000 and for the fiscal years ending September 30, 1979, September 30, 1980, not to exceed $5,000,000,000; for the fiscal year ending September 30, 1981, not to exceed $2,548,837,000; and for the fiscal years ending September 30, 1982, September 30, 1983, September 30, 1984, and September 30, 1985, not to exceed $2,400,000,000 per fiscal year; and for each of the fiscal years ending September 30, 1986, September 30, 1987, and September 30, 1988, not to exceed $2,400,000,000; and for each of the fiscal years ending September 30, 1989, and September 30, 1990, not to exceed $1,200,000,000.

(June 30, 1948, ch. 758, title II, Sec. 207, as added Pub. L. 92-500, Sec. 2, Oct. 18, 1972, 86 Stat. 839; amended Pub. L. 93-207, Sec. 1(3), Dec. 28, 1973, 87 Stat. 906; Pub. L. 95-217, Sec. 30, Dec. 27, 1977, 91 Stat. 1576; Pub. L. 97-35, title XVIII, Sec. 1801(a), Aug. 13, 1981, 95 Stat. 764; Pub. L. 97-117, Sec. 17, Dec. 29, 1981, 95 Stat. 1630; Pub. L. 100-4, title II, Sec. 211, Feb. 4, 1987, 101 Stat. 21.)

Amendments

1987—Pub. L. 100-4 inserted "; and for each of the fiscal years ending September 30, 1986, September 30, 1987, and September 30, 1988, not to exceed $2,400,000,000; and for each of the fiscal years ending September 30, 1989, and September 30, 1990, not to exceed $1,200,000,000" before period at end.

1981—Pub. L. 97-117 substituted "and for the fiscal years ending September 30, 1982, September 30, 1983, September 30, 1984, and September 30, 1985, not to exceed $2,400,000,000 per fiscal year" for "and for the fiscal year ending September 30, 1982, not to exceed $0, unless there is enacted legislation establishing an allotment formula for fiscal year 1982 construction grant funds and otherwise reforming the municipal sewage treatment construction grant program under this subchapter, in which case the authorization for fiscal year 1982 shall be an amount not to exceed $2,400,000,000".

Pub. L. 97-35 substituted provisions authorizing not to exceed $2,548,837,000 for fiscal year ending Sept. 30, 1981, and not to exceed $0 for the fiscal year ending Sept. 30, 1982, unless an allotment formula is enacted, in which case the authorization is not to exceed $2,400,000,000, for provisions authorizing not to exceed $5,000,000,000 for fiscal years ending Sept. 30, 1981 and 1982.

1977—Pub. L. 95-217 inserted "and subject to such amounts as are provided in appropriation Acts, for the fiscal year ending September 30, 1977, $1,000,000,000 for the fiscal year ending September 30, 1978, $4,500,000,000 and for the fiscal years ending September 30, 1979, September 30, 1980, September 30, 1981, and September 30, 1982, not to exceed $5,000,000,000 per fiscal year".

1973—Pub. L. 93-207 inserted reference to section 1286(e) of this title.

Additional Authorization of Appropriations

Pub. L. 94-369, title III, Sec. 301, July 22, 1976, 90 Stat. 1011, provided for authorization to carry out this subchapter, other than sections 1286, 1288, and 1289, for the fiscal year ending Sept. 30, 1977, not to exceed $700,000,000, which sum (subject to amounts provided in appropriation Acts) was to be allotted to each State listed in column 1 of table IV contained in House Public Works and Transportation Committee Print numbered 94-25 in accordance with the percentages provided for such State (if any) in column 5 of such table, and such sum to be in addition to, and not in lieu of, any funds otherwise authorized and to be available until expended.

Section Referred to in Other Sections

This section is referred to in sections 1281, 1285, 1376, 1377 of this title.

AREAWIDE WASTE TREATMENT MANAGEMENT

33 USC 1288

(a) Identification and designation of areas having substantial water quality control problems
For the purpose of encouraging and facilitating the development and implementation of areawide waste treatment management plans—
  (1) The Administrator, within ninety days after October 18, 1972, and after consultation with appropriate Federal, State, and local authorities, shall by regulation publish guidelines for the identification of those areas which, as a result of urban-industrial concentrations or other factors, have substantial water quality control problems.
  (2) The Governor of each State, within sixty days after publication of the guidelines issued pursuant to paragraph (1) of this subsection, shall identify each area within the State which, as a result of urban-industrial concentrations or other factors, has substantial water quality control problems. Not later than one hundred and twenty days following such identification and after consultation with appropriate elected and other officials of local governments having jurisdiction in such areas, the Governor shall designate (A) the boundaries of each such area, and (B) a single representative organization, including elected officials from local governments or their designees, capable of developing effective areawide waste treatment management plans for such area. The Governor may in the same manner at any later time identify any additional area (or modify an existing area) for which he determines areawide waste treatment management to be appropriate, designate the boundaries of such area, and designate an organization capable of developing effective areawide waste treatment management plans for such area.
  (3) With respect to any area which, pursuant to the guidelines published under paragraph (1) of this subsection, is located in two or more States, the Governors of the respective States shall consult and cooperate in carrying out the provisions of paragraph (2), with a view toward designating the boundaries of the interstate area having common water quality control problems and for which areawide waste treatment management plans would be most effective, and toward designating, within one hundred and eighty days after publication of guidelines issued pursuant to paragraph (1) of this subsection, of a single representative organization capable of developing effective areawide waste treatment management plans for such area.
  (4) If a Governor does not act, either by designating or determining not to make a designation under paragraph (2) of this subsection, within the time required by such paragraph, or if, in the case of an interstate area, the Governors of the States involved do not designate a planning organization within the time required by paragraph (3) of this subsection, the chief elected officials of local governments within an area may by agreement designate (A) the boundaries for such an area, and (B) a single representative organization including elected officials from such local governments, or their designees, capable of developing an areawide waste treatment management plan for such area.
  (5) Existing regional agencies may be designated under paragraphs (2), (3), and (4) of this subsection.
  (6) The State shall act as a planning agency for all portions of such State which are not designated under paragraphs (2), (3), or (4) of this subsection.
  (7) Designations under this subsection shall be subject to the approval of the Administrator.
(b) Planning process
  (1) (A) Not later than one year after the date of designation of any organization under subsection (a) of this section such organization shall have in operation a continuing areawide waste treatment management planning process consistent with section 1281 of this title. Plans prepared in accordance with this process shall contain alternatives for waste treatment management, and be applicable to all wastes generated within the area involved. The initial plan prepared in accordance with such process shall be certified by the Governor and submitted to the Administrator not later than two years after the planning process is in operation.
    (B) For any agency designated after 1975 under subsection (a) of this section and for all portions of a State for which the State is required to act as the planning agency in accordance with subsection (a)(6) of this section, the initial plan prepared in accor-

dance with such process shall be certified by the Governor and submitted to the Administrator not later than three years after the receipt of the initial grant award authorized under subsection (f) of this section.
(2) Any plan prepared under such process shall include, but not be limited to—
   (A) the identification of treatment works necessary to meet the anticipated municipal and industrial waste treatment needs of the area over a twenty-year period, annually updated (including an analysis of alternative waste treatment systems), including any requirements for the acquisition of land for treatment purposes; the necessary waste water collection and urban storm water runoff systems; and a program to provide the necessary financial arrangements for the development of such treatment works, and an identification of open space and recreation opportunities that can be expected to result from improved water quality, including consideration of potential use of lands associated with treatment works and increased access to water-based recreation;
   (B) the establishment of construction priorities for such treatment works and time schedules for the initiation and completion of all treatment works;
   (C) the establishment of a regulatory program to—
       (i) implement the waste treatment management requirements of section 1281(c) of this title,
       (ii) regulate the location, modification, and construction of any facilities within such area which may result in any discharge in such area, and
       (iii) assure that any industrial or commercial wastes discharged into any treatment works in such area meet applicable pretreatment requirements;
   (D) the identification of those agencies necessary to construct, operate, and maintain all facilities required by the plan and otherwise to carry out the plan;
   (E) the identification of the measures necessary to carry out the plan (including financing), the period of time necessary to carry out the plan, the costs of carrying out the plan within such time, and the economic, social, and environmental impact of carrying out the plan within such time;
   (F) a process to (i) identify, if appropriate, agriculturally and silviculturally related nonpoint sources of pollution, including return flows from irrigated agriculture, and their cumulative effects, runoff from manure disposal areas, and from land used for livestock and crop production, and (ii) set forth procedures and methods (including land use requirements) to control to the extent feasible such sources;
   (G) a process to (i) identify, if appropriate, mine-related sources of pollution including new, current, and abandoned surface and underground mine runoff, and (ii) set forth procedures and methods (including land use requirements) to control to the extent feasible such sources;
   (H) a process to (i) identify construction activity related sources of pollution, and (ii) set forth procedures and methods (including land use requirements) to control to the extent feasible such sources;
   (I) a process to (i) identify, if appropriate, salt water intrusion into rivers, lakes, and estuaries resulting from reduction of fresh water flow from any cause, including irrigation, obstruction, ground water extraction, and diversion, and (ii) set forth procedures and methods to control such intrusion to the extent feasible where such procedures and methods are otherwise a part of the waste treatment management plan;
   (J) a process to control the disposition of all residual waste generated in such area which could affect water quality; and
   (K) a process to control the disposal of pollutants on land or in subsurface excavations within such area to protect ground and surface water quality.
(3) Areawide waste treatment management plans shall be certified annually by the Governor or his designee (or Governors or their designees, where more than one State is involved) as being consistent with applicable basin plans and such areawide waste treatment management plans shall be submitted to the Administrator for his approval.
(4) (A) Whenever the Governor of any State determines (and notifies the Administrator) that consistency with a statewide regulatory program under section 1313 of this title so requires, the requirements of clauses (F) through (K) of paragraph (2) of this subsection shall be developed and submitted by the Governor to the Administrator for approval for application to a class or category of activity throughout such State.

(B) Any program submitted under subparagraph (A) of this paragraph which, in whole or in part, is to control the discharge or other placement of dredged or fill material into the navigable waters shall include the following:
  (i) A consultation process which includes the State agency with primary jurisdiction over fish and wildlife resources.
  (ii) A process to identify and manage the discharge or other placement of dredged or fill material which adversely affects navigable waters, which shall complement and be coordinated with a State program under section 1344 of this title conducted pursuant to this chapter.
  (iii) A process to assure that any activity conducted pursuant to a best management practice will comply with the guidelines established under section 1344(b)(1) of this title, and sections 1317 and 1343 of this title.
  (iv) A process to assure that any activity conducted pursuant to a best management practice can be terminated or modified for cause including, but not limited to, the following:
     (I) violation of any condition of the best management practice;
     (II) change in any activity that requires either a temporary or permanent reduction or elimination of the discharge pursuant to the best management practice.
  (v) A process to assure continued coordination with Federal and Federal-State water-related planning and reviewing processes, including the National Wetlands Inventory.
(C) If the Governor of a State obtains approval from the Administrator of a statewide regulatory program which meets the requirements of subparagraph (B) of this paragraph and if such State is administering a permit program under section 1344 of this title, no person shall be required to obtain an individual permit pursuant to such section, or to comply with a general permit issued pursuant to such section, with respect to any appropriate activity within such State for which a best management practice has been approved by the Administrator under the program approved by the Administrator pursuant to this paragraph.
(D) (i) Whenever the Administrator determines after public hearing that a State is not administering a program approved under this section in accordance with the requirements of this section, the Administrator shall so notify the State, and if appropriate corrective action is not taken within a reasonable time, not to exceed ninety days, the Administrator shall withdraw approval of such program. The Administrator shall not withdraw approval of any such program unless he shall first have notified the State, and made public, in writing, the reasons for such withdrawal.
  (ii) In the case of a State with a program submitted and approved under this paragraph, the Administrator shall withdraw approval of such program under this subparagraph only for a substantial failure of the State to administer its program in accordance with the requirements of this paragraph.

(c) Regional operating agencies
  (1) The Governor of each State, in consultation with the planning agency designated under subsection (a) of this section, at the time a plan is submitted to the Administrator, shall designate one or more waste treatment management agencies (which may be an existing or newly created local, regional, or State agency or political subdivision) for each area designated under subsection (a) of this section and submit such designations to the Administrator.
  (2) The Administrator shall accept any such designation, unless, within 120 days of such designation, he finds that the designated management agency (or agencies) does not have adequate authority–
    (A) to carry out appropriate portions of an areawide waste treatment management plan developed under subsection (b) of this section;
    (B) to manage effectively waste treatment works and related facilities serving such area in conformance with any plan required by subsection (b) of this section;

(C) directly or by contract, to design and construct new works, and to operate and maintain new and existing works as required by any plan developed pursuant to subsection (b) of this section;
(D) to accept and utilize grants, or other funds from any source, for waste treatment management purposes;
(E) to raise revenues, including the assessment of waste treatment charges;
(F) to incur short- and long-term indebtedness;
(G) to assure in implementation of an areawide waste treatment management plan that each participating community pays its proportionate share of treatment costs;
(H) to refuse to receive any wastes from any municipality or subdivision thereof, which does not comply with any provisions of an approved plan under this section applicable to such area; and
(I) to accept for treatment industrial wastes.

(d) Conformity of works with area plan

After a waste treatment management agency having the authority required by subsection (c) of this section has been designated under such subsection for an area and a plan for such area has been approved under subsection (b) of this section, the Administrator shall not make any grant for construction of a publicly owned treatment works under section 1281(g)(1) of this title within such area except to such designated agency and for works in conformity with such plan.

(e) Permits not to conflict with approved plans

No permit under section 1342 of this title shall be issued for any point source which is in conflict with a plan approved pursuant to subsection (b) of this section.

(f) Grants

(1) The Administrator shall make grants to any agency designated under subsection (a) of this section for payment of the reasonable costs of developing and operating a continuing areawide waste treatment management planning process under subsection (b) of this section.

(2) For the two-year period beginning on the date the first grant is made under paragraph (1) of this subsection to an agency, if such first grant is made before October 1, 1977, the amount of each such grant to such agency shall be 100 per centum of the costs of developing and operating a continuing areawide waste treatment management planning process under subsection (b) of this section, and thereafter the amount granted to such agency shall not exceed 75 per centum of such costs in each succeeding one-year period. In the case of any other grant made to an agency under such paragraph (1) of this subsection, the amount of such grant shall not exceed 75 per centum of the costs of developing and operating a continuing areawide waste treatment management planning process in any year.

(3) Each applicant for a grant under this subsection shall submit to the Administrator for his approval each proposal for which a grant is applied for under this subsection. The Administrator shall act upon such proposal as soon as practicable after it has been submitted, and his approval of that proposal shall be deemed a contractual obligation of the United States for the payment of its contribution to such proposal, subject to such amounts as are provided in appropriation Acts. There is authorized to be appropriated to carry out this subsection not to exceed $50,000,000 for the fiscal year ending June 30, 1973, not to exceed $100,000,000 for the fiscal year ending June 30, 1974, not to exceed $150,000,000 per fiscal year for the fiscal years ending June 30, 1975, September 30, 1977, September 30, 1978, September 30, 1979, and September 30, 1980, not to exceed $100,000,000 per fiscal year for the fiscal years ending September 30, 1981, and September 30, 1982, and such sums as may be necessary for fiscal years 1983 through 1990.

(g) Technical assistance by Administrator

The Administrator is authorized, upon request of the Governor or the designated planning agency, and without reimbursement, to consult with, and provide technical assistance to, any agency designated under subsection (a) of this section in the development of areawide waste treatment management plans under subsection (b) of this section.

(h) Technical assistance by Secretary of the Army

(1) The Secretary of the Army, acting through the Chief of Engineers, in cooperation with the Administrator is authorized and directed, upon request of the Governor or the designated

planning organization, to consult with, and provide technical assistance to, any agency designed[1] under subsection (a) of this section in developing and operating a continuing areawide waste treatment management planning process under subsection (b) of this section.

(2) There is authorized to be appropriated to the Secretary of the Army, to carry out this subsection, not to exceed $50,000,000 per fiscal year for the fiscal years ending June 30, 1973, and June 30, 1974.

(i) State best management practices program

(1) The Secretary of the Interior, acting through the Director of the United States Fish and Wildlife Service, shall, upon request of the Governor of a State, and without reimbursement, provide technical assistance to such State in developing a statewide program for submission to the Administrator under subsection (b)(4)(B) of this section and in implementing such program after its approval.

(2) There is authorized to be appropriated to the Secretary of the Interior $6,000,000 to complete the National Wetlands Inventory of the United States, by December 31, 1981, and to provide information from such Inventory to States as it becomes available to assist such States in the development and operation of programs under this chapter.

(j) Agricultural cost sharing

(1) The Secretary of Agriculture, with the concurrence of the Administrator, and acting through the Soil Conservation Service and such other agencies of the Department of Agriculture as the Secretary may designate, is authorized and directed to establish and administer a program to enter into contracts, subject to such amounts as are provided in advance by appropriation acts, of not less than five years nor more than ten years with owners and operators having control of rural land for the purpose of installing and maintaining measures incorporating best management practices to control nonpoint source pollution for improved water quality in those States or areas for which the Administrator has approved a plan under subsection (b) of this section where the practices to which the contracts apply are certified by the management agency designated under subsection (c)(1) of this section to be consistent with such plans and will result in improved water quality. Such contracts may be entered into during the period ending not later than September 31, 1988. Under such contracts the land owner or operator shall agree—

(i) to effectuate a plan approved by a soil conservation district, where one exists, under this section for his farm, ranch, or other land substantially in accordance with the schedule outlined therein unless any requirement thereof is waived or modified by the Secretary;

(ii) to forfeit all rights to further payments or grants under the contract and refund to the United States all payments and grants received thereunder, with interest, upon his violation of the contract at any stage during the time he has control of the land if the Secretary, after considering the recommendations of the soil conservation district, where one exists, and the Administrator, determines that such violation is of such a nature as to warrant termination of the contract, or to make refunds or accept such payment adjustments as the Secretary may deem appropriate if he determines that the violation by the owner or operator does not warrant termination of the contract;

(iii) upon transfer of his right and interest in the farm, ranch, or other land during the contract period to forfeit all rights to further payments or grants under the contract and refund to the United States all payments or grants received thereunder, with interest, unless the transferee of any such land agrees with the Secretary to assume all obligations of the contract;

(iv) not to adopt any practice specified by the Secretary on the advice of the Administrator in the contract as a practice which would tend to defeat the purposes of the contract;

(v) to such additional provisions as the Secretary determines are desirable and includes in the contract to effectuate the purposes of the program or to facilitate the practical administration of the program.

---

[1] So in original. Probably should be "designated".

(2) In return for such agreement by the landowner or operator the Secretary shall agree to provide technical assistance and share the cost of carrying out those conservation practices and measures set forth in the contract for which he determines that cost sharing is appropriate and in the public interest and which are approved for cost sharing by the agency designated to implement the plan developed under subsection (b) of this section. The portion of such cost (including labor) to be shared shall be that part which the Secretary determines is necessary and appropriate to effectuate the installation of the water quality management practices and measures under the contract, but not to exceed 50 per centum of the total cost of the measures set forth in the contract; except the Secretary may increase the matching cost share where he determines that (1) the main benefits to be derived from the measures are related to improving offsite water quality, and (2) the matching share requirement would place a burden on the landowner which would probably prevent him from participating in the program.
(3) The Secretary may terminate any contract with a landowner or operator by mutual agreement with the owner or operator if the Secretary determines that such termination would be in the public interest, and may agree to such modification of contracts previously entered into as he may determine to be desirable to carry out the purposes of the program or facilitate the practical administration thereof or to accomplish equitable treatment with respect to other conservation, land use, or water quality programs.
(4) In providing assistance under this subsection the Secretary will give priority to those areas and sources that have the most significant effect upon water quality. Additional investigations or plans may be made, where necessary, to supplement approved water quality management plans, in order to determine priorities.
(5) The Secretary shall, where practicable, enter into agreements with soil conservation districts, State soil and water conservation agencies, or State water quality agencies to administer all or part of the program established in this subsection under regulations developed by the Secretary. Such agreements shall provide for the submission of such reports as the Secretary deems necessary, and for payment by the United States of such portion of the costs incurred in the administration of the program as the Secretary may deem appropriate.
(6) The contracts under this subsection shall be entered into only in areas where the management agency designated under subsection (c)(1) of this section assures an adequate level of participation by owners and operators having control of rural land in such areas. Within such areas the local soil conservation district, where one exists, together with the Secretary of Agriculture, will determine the priority of assistance among individual land owners and operators to assure that the most critical water quality problems are addressed.
(7) The Secretary, in consultation with the Administrator and subject to section 1314(k) of this title, shall, not later than September 30, 1978, promulgate regulations for carrying out this subsection and for support and cooperation with other Federal and non-Federal agencies for implementation of this subsection.
(8) This program shall not be used to authorize or finance projects that would otherwise be eligible for assistance under the terms of Public Law 83-566 [16 U.S.C. 1001 et seq.].
(9) There are hereby authorized to be appropriated to the Secretary of Agriculture $200,000,000 for fiscal year 1979, $400,000,000 for fiscal year 1980, $100,000,000 for fiscal year 1981, $100,000,000 for fiscal year 1982, and such sums as may be necessary for fiscal years 1983 through 1990, to carry out this subsection. The program authorized under this subsection shall be in addition to, and not in substitution of, other programs in such area authorized by this or any other public law.

(June 30, 1948, ch. 758, title II, Sec. 208, as added Pub. L. 92-500, Sec. 2, Oct. 18, 1972, 86 Stat. 839; amended Pub. L. 95-217, Secs. 4(e), 31, 32, 33(a), 34, 35, Dec. 27, 1977, 91 Stat. 1566, 1576-1579; Pub. L. 96-483, Sec. 1(d), (e), Oct. 21, 1980, 94 Stat. 2360; Pub. L. 100-4, title I, Sec. 101(d), (e), Feb. 4, 1987, 101 Stat. 9.)

References in Text

Public Law 83-566, referred to in subsec. (j)(8), is act Aug. 4, 1954, ch. 656, 68 Stat. 666, as amended, known as the Watershed Protection and Flood Prevention Act, which is classified generally to chapter 18 (Sec. 1001 et seq.) of Title 16, Conservation. For complete classification of this Act to the Code, see Short Title note set out under section 1001 of Title 16 and Tables.

Amendments

1987—Subsec. (f)(3). Pub. L. 100-4, Sec. 101(d), struck out "and" after "1974," and "1980," and inserted ", and such sums as may be necessary for fiscal years 1983 through 1990" after "1982".

Subsec. (j)(9). Pub. L. 100-4, Sec. 101(e), struck out "and" after "1981," and inserted "and such sums as may be necessary for fiscal years 1983 through 1990," after "1982,".

1980—Subsec. (f)(3). Pub. L. 96-483, Sec. 1(d), inserted authorization of not to exceed $100,000,000 per fiscal year for fiscal years ending Sept. 30, 1981 and 1982.

Subsec. (j)(9). Pub. L. 96-483, Sec. 1(e), inserted reference to authorization of $100,000,000 for each of fiscal years 1981 and 1982.

1977—Subsec. (b)(1). Pub. L. 95-217, Sec. 31(a), designated existing provisions as subpar. (A) and added subpar. (B).

Subsec. (b)(2)(A). Pub. L. 95-217, Sec. 32, inserted ", and an identification of open space and recreation opportunities that can be expected to result from improved water quality, including consideration of potential use of lands associated with treatment works and increased access to water-based recreation" after "development of such treatment works".

Subsec. (b)(2)(F). Pub. L. 95-217, Sec. 33(a), substituted "sources of pollution, including return flows from irrigated agriculture, and their cumulative effects," for "sources of pollution, including".

Subsec. (b)(4). Pub. L. 95-217, Sec. 34(a), designated existing provisions as subpar. (A), substituted "to the Administrator for approval for application to a class or category of activity throughout such State" for "to the Administrator for application to all regions within such State", and added subpars. (B) to (D).

Subsec. (f)(2). Pub. L. 95-217, Sec. 31(b), substituted "For the two-year period beginning on the date the first grant is made under paragraph (1) of this subsection to an agency, if such first grant is made before October 1, 1977, the amount of each such grant to such agency shall be 100 per centum of the costs of developing and operating a continuing areawide waste treatment management planning process under subsection (b) of this section, and thereafter the amount granted to such agency shall not exceed 75 per centum of such costs in each succeeding one-year period" for "The amount granted to any agency under paragraph (1) of this subsection shall be 100 per centum of the costs of developing and operating a continuing areawide waste treatment management planning process under subsection (b) of this section for each of the fiscal years ending on June 30, 1973, June 30, 1974, and June 30, 1975, and shall not exceed 75 per centum of such costs in each succeeding fiscal year" and inserted "In the case of any other grant made to an agency under such paragraph (1) of this subsection, the amount of such grant shall not exceed 75 per centum of the costs of developing and operating a continuing areawide waste treatment management planning process in any year."

Subsec. (f)(3). Pub. L. 95-217, Secs. 4(e), 31(c), substituted "and not to exceed $150,000,000 per fiscal year for the fiscal years ending June 30, 1975, September 30, 1977, September 30, 1978, September 30, 1979, and September 30, 1980" for "and not to exceed $150,000,000 for the fiscal year ending June 30, 1975" and inserted "subject to such amounts as are provided in appropriation Acts" after "contractual obligation of the United States for the payment of its contribution to such proposal".

Subsec. (i). Pub. L. 95-217, Sec. 34(b), added subsec. (i).

Subsec. (j). Pub. L. 95-217, Sec. 35, added subsec. (j).

Transfer of Functions

Enforcement functions of Secretary or other official in Department of Agriculture, insofar as they involve lands and programs under jurisdiction of that Department, relating to compliance with this chapter with respect to pre-construction, construction, and initial operation of transportation system for Canadian and Alaskan natural gas were transferred to the Federal Inspector, Office of Federal Inspector for the Alaska Natural Gas Transportation System, until the first anniversary of the date of initial operation of the Alaska Natural Gas Transportation System, see Reorg. Plan No. 1 of 1979, Secs. 102(f), 203(a), 44 F.R. 33663, 33666, 93 Stat. 1373, 1376, effective July 1, 1979, set out in the Appendix to Title 5, Government Organization and Employees. Office of Federal Inspector for the Alaska Natural Gas Transportation System abolished and functions and authority vested in Inspector transferred to Secretary of Energy by section 3012(b) of Pub. L. 102-486, set out as an Abolition of Office of Federal Inspector note under section 719e of Title 15, Commerce and Trade.

Section Referred to in Other Sections

This section is referred to in sections 1252, 1284, 1285, 1287, 1289, 1313, 1314, 1329, 1344, 1362, 1376, 1383 of this title; title 16 section 1455b; title 26 section 126; title 42 sections 300h-6, 6946, 7412.

BASIN PLANNING

33 USC 1289

(a) Preparation of Level B plans

The President, acting through the Water Resources Council, shall, as soon as practicable, prepare a Level B plan under the Water Resources Planning Act [42 U.S.C. 1962 et seq.] for all basins in the United States. All such plans shall be completed not later than January 1, 1980, except that priority in the preparation of such plans shall be given to those basins and portions thereof which are within those areas designated under paragraphs (2), (3), and (4) of subsection (a) of section 1288 of this title.

(b) Reporting requirements

The President, acting through the Water Resources Council, shall report annually to Congress on progress being made in carrying out this section. The first such report shall be submitted not later than January 31, 1973.

(c) Authorization of appropriations

There is authorized to be appropriated to carry out this section not to exceed $200,000,000.

(June 30, 1948, ch. 758, title II, Sec. 209, as added Pub. L. 92-500, Sec. 2, Oct. 18, 1972, 86 Stat. 843.)

References in Text

The Water Resources Planning Act, referred to in subsec. (a), is Pub. L. 89-80, July 22, 1965, 79 Stat. 244, as amended, which is classified generally to chapter 19B (Sec. 1962 et seq.) of Title 42, The Public Health and Welfare. For complete classification of this Act to the Code, see Short Title note set out under section 1962 of Title 42 and Tables.

Section Referred to in Other Sections

This section is referred to in sections 1287, 1313, 1376 of this title.

ANNUAL SURVEY

33 USC 1290

The Administrator shall annually make a survey to determine the efficiency of the operation and maintenance of treatment works constructed with grants made under this chapter, as compared to the efficiency planned at the time the grant was made. The results of such annual survey shall be reported to Congress not later than 90 days after the date of convening of each session of Congress.

(June 30, 1948, ch. 758, title II, Sec. 210, as added Pub. L. 92-500, Sec. 2, Oct. 18, 1972, 86 Stat. 843; amended Pub. L. 105-362, title V, Sec. 501(d)(2)(D), Nov. 10, 1998, 112 Stat. 3284.)

Amendments

1998—Pub. L. 105-362 substituted "shall be reported to Congress not later than 90 days after the date of convening of each session of Congress" for "shall be included in the report required under section 1375(a) of this title".

506 / Environmental Statutes

SEWAGE COLLECTION SYSTEMS

33 USC 1291

(a) Existing and new systems
No grant shall be made for a sewage collection system under this subchapter unless such grant (1) is for replacement or major rehabilitation of an existing collection system and is necessary to the total integrity and performance of the waste treatment works servicing such community, or (2) is for a new collection system in an existing community with sufficient existing or planned capacity adequately to treat such collected sewage and is consistent with section 1281 of this title.

(b) Use of population density as test
If the Administrator uses population density as a test for determining the eligibility of a collector sewer for assistance it shall be only for the purpose of evaluating alternatives and determining the needs for such system in relation to ground or surface water quality impact.

(c) Pollutant discharges from separate storm sewer systems
No grant shall be made under this subchapter from funds authorized for any fiscal year during the period beginning October 1, 1977, and ending September 30, 1990, for treatment works for control of pollutant discharges from separate storm sewer systems.

(June 30, 1948, ch. 758, title II, Sec. 211, as added Pub. L. 92-500, Sec. 2, Oct. 18, 1972, 86 Stat. 843; amended Pub. L. 95-217, Sec. 36, Dec. 27, 1977, 91 Stat. 1581; Pub. L. 97-117, Sec. 2(b), Dec. 29, 1981, 95 Stat. 1623; Pub. L. 100-4, title II, Sec. 206(d), Feb. 4, 1987, 101 Stat. 20.)

Amendments

1987—Subsec. (c). Pub. L. 100-4 substituted "1990" for "1985".

1981—Subsec. (c). Pub. L. 97-117 substituted "September 30, 1985" for "September 30, 1982".

1977—Pub. L. 95-217 designated existing provisions as subsec. (a) and added subsecs. (b) and (c).

Section Referred to in Other Sections

This section is referred to in section 1382 of this title.

DEFINITIONS

33 USC 1292

As used in this subchapter—
  (1) The term "construction" means any one or more of the following: preliminary planning to determine the feasibility of treatment works, engineering, architectural, legal, fiscal, or economic investigations or studies, surveys, designs, plans, working drawings, specifications, procedures, field testing of innovative or alternative waste water treatment processes and techniques meeting guidelines promulgated under section 1314(d)(3) of this title, or other necessary actions, erection, building, acquisition, alteration, remodeling, improvement, or extension of treatment works, or the inspection or supervision of any of the foregoing items.
  (2) (A) The term "treatment works" means any devices and systems used in the storage, treatment, recycling, and reclamation of municipal sewage or industrial wastes of a liquid nature to implement section 1281 of this title, or necessary to recycle or reuse water at the most economical cost over the estimated life of the works, including intercepting sewers, outfall sewers, sewage collection systems, pumping, power, and other equipment, and their appurtenances; extensions, improvements, remodeling, additions, and alterations thereof; elements essential to provide a reliable recycled supply such as standby treatment units and clear well facilities; and any works, including site acquisition of the land that will be an integral part of the treatment process (including land used for the storage of treated wastewater in land treatment systems prior to land application) or is used for ultimate disposal of residues resulting from such treatment.
  (B) In addition to the definition contained in subparagraph (A) of this paragraph, "treatment works" means any other method or system for preventing, abating, reducing, storing, treating, separating, or disposing of municipal waste, including storm water

runoff, or industrial waste, including waste in combined storm water and sanitary sewer systems. Any application for construction grants which includes wholly or in part such methods or systems shall, in accordance with guidelines published by the Administrator pursuant to subparagraph (C) of this paragraph, contain adequate data and analysis demonstrating such proposal to be, over the life of such works, the most cost efficient alternative to comply with sections 1311 or 1312 of this title, or the requirements of section 1281 of this title.

(C) For the purposes of subparagraph (B) of this paragraph, the Administrator shall, within one hundred and eighty days after October 18, 1972, publish and thereafter revise no less often than annually, guidelines for the evaluation of methods, including cost-effective analysis, described in subparagraph (B) of this paragraph.

(3) The term "replacement" as used in this subchapter means those expenditures for obtaining and installing equipment, accessories, or appurtenances during the useful life of the treatment works necessary to maintain the capacity and performance for which such works are designed and constructed.

(June 30, 1948, ch. 758, title II, Sec. 212, as added Pub. L. 92-500, Sec. 2, Oct. 18, 1972, 86 Stat. 844; amended Pub. L. 95-217, Sec. 37, Dec. 27, 1977, 91 Stat. 1581; Pub. L. 97-117, Sec. 8(d), Dec. 29, 1981, 95 Stat. 1626.)

Amendments

1981—Par. (1). Pub. L. 97-117 inserted "field testing of innovative or alternative waste water treatment processes and techniques meeting guidelines promulgated under section 1314(d)(3) of this title," after "procedures,".

1977—Par. (2)(A). Pub. L. 95-217 inserted "(including land used for the storage of treated wastewater in land treatment systems prior to land application)" after "integral part of the treatment process".

Section Referred to in Other Sections

This section is referred to in sections 1281, 1285, 1317, 1342, 1345, 1381, 1383, 1414b of this title; title 26 section 7701.

LOAN GUARANTEES

33 USC 1293

(a) State or local obligations issued exclusively to Federal Financing Bank for publicly owned treatment works; determination of eligibility of project by Administrator

Subject to the conditions of this section and to such terms and conditions as the Administrator determines to be necessary to carry out the purposes of this subchapter, the Administrator is authorized to guarantee, and to make commitments to guarantee, the principal and interest (including interest accruing between the date of default and the date of the payment in full of the guarantee) of any loan, obligation, or participation therein of any State, municipality, or intermunicipal or interstate agency issued directly and exclusively to the Federal Financing Bank to finance that part of the cost of any grant-eligible project for the construction of publicly owned treatment works not paid for with Federal financial assistance under this subchapter (other than this section), which project the Administrator has determined to be eligible for such financial assistance under this subchapter, including, but not limited to, projects eligible for reimbursement under section 1286 of this title.

(b) Conditions for issuance

No guarantee, or commitment to make a guarantee, may be made pursuant to this section—
(1) unless the Administrator certifies that the issuing body is unable to obtain on reasonable terms sufficient credit to finance its actual needs without such guarantee; and
(2) unless the Administrator determines that there is a reasonable assurance of repayment of the loan, obligation, or participation therein.

A determination of whether financing is available at reasonable rates shall be made by the Secretary of the Treasury with relationship to the current average yield on outstanding marketable obligations of municipalities of comparable maturity.

(c) Fees for application investigation and issuance of commitment guarantee
The Administrator is authorized to charge reasonable fees for the investigation of an application for a guarantee and for the issuance of a commitment to make a guarantee.

(d) Commitment for repayment
The Administrator, in determining whether there is a reasonable assurance of repayment, may require a commitment which would apply to such repayment. Such commitment may include, but not be limited to, any funds received by such grantee from the amounts appropriated under section 1286 of this title.

(June 30, 1948, ch. 758, title II, Sec. 213, as added Pub. L. 94-558, Oct. 19, 1976, 90 Stat. 2639; amended Pub. L. 96-483, Sec. 2(e), Oct. 21, 1980, 94 Stat. 2361.)

Amendments

1980—Subsec. (d). Pub. L. 96-483 struck out "(1) all or any portion of the funds retained by such grantee under section 1284(b)(3) of this title, and (2)" after "limited to".

Effective Date of 1980 Amendment

Amendment by Pub. L. 96-483 effective Dec. 27, 1977, see section 2(g) of Pub. L. 96-483, set out as a note under section 1281 of this title.

CONTAINED SPOIL DISPOSAL FACILITIES

33 USC 1293a

(a) Construction, operation, and maintenance; period; conditions; requirements
The Secretary of the Army, acting through the Chief of Engineers, is authorized to construct, operate, and maintain, subject to the provisions of subsection (c) of this section, contained spoil disposal facilities of sufficient capacity for a period not to exceed ten years, to meet the requirements of this section. Before establishing each such facility, the Secretary of the Army shall obtain the concurrence of appropriate local governments and shall consider the views and recommendations of the Administrator of the Environmental Protection Agency and shall comply with requirements of section 1171 of this title, and of the National Environmental Policy Act of 1969 [42 U.S.C. 4321 et seq.]. Section 401 of this title shall not apply to any facility authorized by this section.

(b) Time for establishment; consideration of area needs; requirements
The Secretary of the Army, acting through the Chief of Engineers, shall establish the contained spoil disposal facilities authorized in subsection (a) of this section at the earliest practicable date, taking into consideration the views and recommendations of the Administrator of the Environmental Protection Agency as to those areas which, in the Administrator's judgment, are most urgently in need of such facilities and pursuant to the requirements of the National Environmental Policy Act of 1969 [42 U.S.C. 4321 et seq.] and the Federal Water Pollution Control Act [33 U.S.C. 1251 et seq.].

(c) Written agreement requirement; terms of agreement
Prior to construction of any such facility, the appropriate State or States, interstate agency, municipality, or other appropriate political subdivision of the State shall agree in writing to (1) furnish all lands, easements, and rights-of-way necessary for the construction, operation, and maintenance of the facility; (2) contribute to the United States 25 per centum of the construction costs, such amount to be payable either in cash prior to construction, in installments during construction, or in installments, with interest at a rate to be determined by the Secretary of the Treasury, as of the beginning of the fiscal year in which construction is initiated, on the basis of the computed average interest rate payable by the Treasury upon its outstanding marketable public obligations, which are neither due or callable for redemption for fifteen years from date of issue; (3) hold and save the United States free from damages due to construction, operation, and maintenance of the facility; and (4) except as provided in subsection (f) of this section, maintain the facility after completion of its use for disposal purposes in a manner satisfactory to the Secretary of the Army.

(d) Waiver of construction costs contribution from non-Federal interests; findings of participation in waste treatment facilities for general geographical area and compliance with water quality standards; waiver of payments in event of written agreement before occurrence of findings

The requirement for appropriate non-Federal interest or interests to furnish an agreement to contribute 25 per centum of the construction costs as set forth in subsection (c) of this section shall be waived by the Secretary of the Army upon a finding by the Administrator of the Environmental Protection Agency that for the area to which such construction applies, the State or States involved, interstate agency, municipality, and other appropriate political subdivision of the State and industrial concerns are participating in and in compliance with an approved plan for the general geographical area of the dredging activity for construction, modification, expansion, or rehabilitation of waste treatment facilities and the Administrator has found that applicable water quality standards are not being violated. In the event such findings occur after the appropriate non-Federal interest or interests have entered into the agreement required by subsection (c) of this section, any payments due after the date of such findings as part of the required local contribution of 25 per centum of the construction costs shall be waived by the Secretary of the Army.

(e) Federal payment of costs for disposal of dredged spoil from project
Notwithstanding any other provision of law, all costs of disposal of dredged spoil from the project for the Great Lakes connecting channels, Michigan, shall be borne by the United States.

(f) Title to lands, easements, and rights-of-way; retention by non-Federal interests; conveyance of facilities; agreement of transferee
The participating non-Federal interest or interests shall retain title to all lands, easements, and rights-of-way furnished by it pursuant to subsection (c) of this section. A spoil disposal facility owned by a non-Federal interest or interests may be conveyed to another party only after completion of the facility's use for disposal purposes and after the transferee agrees in writing to use or maintain the facility in a manner which the Secretary of the Army determines to be satisfactory.

(g) Federal licenses or permits; charges; remission of charge
Any spoil disposal facilities constructed under the provisions of this section shall be made available to Federal licensees or permittees upon payment of an appropriate charge for such use. Twenty-five per centum of such charge shall be remitted to the participating non-Federal interest or interests except for those excused from contributing to the construction costs under subsections (d) and (e) of this section.

(h) Provisions applicable to Great Lakes and their connecting channels
This section, other than subsection (i), shall be applicable only to the Great Lakes and their connecting channels.

(i) Research, study, and experimentation program relating to dredged spoil extended to navigable waters, etc.; cooperative program; scope of program; utilization of facilities and personnel of Federal agency
The Chief of Engineers, under the direction of the Secretary of the Army, is hereby authorized to extend to all navigable waters, connecting channels, tributary streams, other waters of the United States and waters contiguous to the United States, a comprehensive program of research, study, and experimentation relating to dredged spoil. This program shall be carried out in cooperation with other Federal and State agencies, and shall include, but not be limited to, investigations on the characteristics of dredged spoil, and alternative methods of its disposal. To the extent that such study shall include the effects of such dredge spoil on water quality, the facilities and personnel of the Environmental Protection Agency shall be utilized.

(j) Period for depositing dredged materials
The Secretary of the Army, acting through the Chief of Engineers, is authorized to continue to deposit dredged materials into a contained spoil disposal facility constructed under this section until the Secretary determines that such facility is no longer needed for such purpose or that such facility is completely full.

(k) Study and monitoring program
    (1) Study
        The Secretary of the Army, acting through the Chief of Engineers, shall conduct a study of the materials disposed of in contained spoil disposal facilities constructed under this

510 / Environmental Statutes

section for the purpose of determining whether or not toxic pollutants are present in such facilities and for the purpose of determining the concentration levels of each of such pollutants in such facilities.

(2) Report

Not later than 1 year after November 17, 1988, the Secretary shall transmit to Congress a report on the results of the study conducted under paragraph (1).

(3) Inspection and monitoring program

The Secretary shall conduct a program to inspect and monitor contained spoil disposal facilities constructed under this section for the purpose of determining whether or not toxic pollutants are leaking from such facilities.

(4) Toxic pollutant defined

For purposes of this subsection, the term "toxic pollutant" means those toxic pollutants referred to in section 1311(b)(2)(C) and 1311(b)(2)(D) of this title and such other pollutants as the Secretary, in consultation with the Administrator of the Environmental Protection Agency, determines are appropriate based on their effects on human health and the environment.

(Pub. L. 91-611, title I, Sec. 123, Dec. 31, 1970, 84 Stat. 1823; Pub. L. 93-251, title I, Sec. 23, Mar. 7, 1974, 88 Stat. 20; Pub. L. 100-676, Sec. 24, Nov. 17, 1988, 102 Stat. 4027.)

References in Text

Section 1171 of this title, referred to in subsec. (a), was omitted as superseded.

The National Environmental Policy Act of 1969, referred to in subsecs. (a) and (b), is Pub. L. 91-190, Jan. 1, 1970, 83 Stat. 852, as amended, which is classified generally to chapter 55 (Sec. 4321 et seq.) of Title 42, The Public Health and Welfare. For complete classification of this Act to the Code, see Short Title note set out under section 4321 of Title 42 and Tables.

The Federal Water Pollution Control Act, referred to in subsec. (b), is act June 30, 1948, ch. 758, as amended generally by Pub. L. 92-500, Sec. 2, Oct. 18, 1972, 86 Stat. 816, which is classified generally to this chapter (Sec. 1251 et seq.). For complete classification of this Act to the Code, see Short Title note set out under section 1251 of this title and Tables.

Codification

Section was formerly classified to section 1165a of this title.

Section was not enacted as a part of the Federal Water Pollution Control Act which comprises this chapter.

Amendments

1988—Subsec. (j). Pub. L. 100-676, Sec. 24(a), added subsec. (j).

Subsec. (k). Pub. L. 100-676, Sec. 24(b), added subsec. (k).

1974—Subsec. (d). Pub. L. 93-251 inserted provision for waiver of payments in event of a written agreement before occurrence of findings.

Great Lakes Confined Disposal Facilities

Pub. L. 104-303, title V, Sec. 513, Oct. 12, 1996, 110 Stat. 3762, provided that:

"(a) Assessment.—Pursuant to the responsibilities of the Secretary under section 123 of the River and Harbor Act of 1970 (33 U.S.C. 1293a), the Secretary shall conduct an assessment of the general conditions of confined disposal facilities in the Great Lakes.

(b) Report.—Not later than 3 years after the date of the enactment of this Act [Oct. 12, 1996], the Secretary shall transmit to Congress a report on the results of the assessment conducted under subsection (a), including the following:

(1) A description of the cumulative effects of confined disposal facilities in the Great Lakes.

(2) Recommendations for specific remediation actions for each confined disposal facility in the Great Lakes.

(3) An evaluation of, and recommendations for, confined disposal facility management practices and technologies to conserve capacity at such facilities and to minimize adverse environmental effects at such facilities throughout the Great Lakes system."

PUBLIC INFORMATION AND EDUCATION ON RECYCLING AND REUSE OF WASTE-WATER, USE OF LAND TREATMENT, AND REDUCTION OF WASTEWATER VOLUME

33 USC 1294

The Administrator shall develop and operate within one year of December 27, 1977, a continuing program of public information and education on recycling and reuse of wastewater (including sludge), the use of land treatment, and methods for the reduction of wastewater volume.

(June 30, 1948, ch. 758, title II, Sec. 214, as added Pub. L. 95-217, Sec. 38, Dec. 27, 1977, 91 Stat. 1581.)

REQUIREMENTS FOR AMERICAN MATERIALS

33 USC 1295

Notwithstanding any other provision of law, no grant for which application is made after February 1, 1978, shall be made under this subchapter for any treatment works unless only such unmanufactured articles, materials, and supplies as have been mined or produced in the United States, and only such manufactured articles, materials, and supplies as have been manufactured in the United States, substantially all from articles, materials, or supplies mined, produced, or manufactured, as the case may be, in the United States will be used in such treatment works. This section shall not apply in any case where the Administrator determines, based upon those factors the Administrator deems relevant, including the available resources of the agency, it to be inconsistent with the public interest (including multilateral government procurement agreements) or the cost to be unreasonable, or if articles, materials, or supplies of the class or kind to be used or the articles, materials, or supplies from which they are manufactured are not mined, produced, or manufactured, as the case may be, in the United States in sufficient and reasonably available commercial quantities and of a satisfactory quality.

(June 30, 1948, ch. 758, title II, Sec. 215, as added Pub. L. 95-217, Sec. 39, Dec. 27, 1977, 91 Stat. 1581.)

DETERMINATION OF PRIORITY OF PROJECTS

33 USC 1296

Notwithstanding any other provision of this chapter, the determination of the priority to be given each category of projects for construction of publicly owned treatment works within each State shall be made solely by that State, except that if the Administrator, after a public hearing, determines that a specific project will not result in compliance with the enforceable requirements of this chapter, such project shall be removed from the State's priority list and such State shall submit a revised priority list. These categories shall include, but not be limited to (A) secondary treatment, (B) more stringent treatment, (C) infiltration-in-flow correction, (D) major sewer system rehabilitation, (E) new collector sewers and appurtenances, (F) new interceptors and appurtenances, and (G) correction of combined sewer overflows. Not less than 25 per centum of funds allocated to a State in any fiscal year under this subchapter for construction of publicly owned treatment works in such State shall be obligated for those types of projects referred to in clauses (D), (E), (F), and (G) of this section, if such projects are on such State's priority list for that year and are otherwise eligible for funding in that fiscal year. It is the policy of Congress that projects for wastewater treatment and management undertaken with Federal financial assistance under this chapter by any State, municipality, or intermunicipal or interstate agency shall be projects which, in the estimation of the State, are designed to achieve optimum water quality management, consistent with the public health and water quality goals and requirements of this chapter.

(June 30, 1948, ch. 758, title II, Sec. 216, as added Pub. L. 95-217, Sec. 40, Dec. 27, 1977, 91 Stat. 1582; amended Pub. L. 97-117, Sec. 18, Dec. 29, 1981, 95 Stat. 1630.)

Amendments

1981—Pub. L. 97-117 inserted provision that it is the policy of Congress that projects for wastewater treatment and management undertaken with Federal financial assistance under this chapter by any State, municipality, or intermunicipal or interstate agency be projects which, in the estimation of the State, are designed to achieve optimum water quality management, consistent with the public health and water quality goals and requirements of this chapter.

Section Referred to in Other Sections

This section is referred to in sections 1377, 1383, 1386 of this title.

GUIDELINES FOR COST-EFFECTIVENESS ANALYSIS

33 USC 1297

Any guidelines for cost-effectiveness analysis published by the Administrator under this subchapter shall provide for the identification and selection of cost effective alternatives to comply with the objectives and goals of this chapter and sections 1281(b), 1281(d), 1281(g)(2)(A), and 1311(b)(2)(B) of this title.

(June 30, 1948, ch. 758, title II, Sec. 217, as added Pub. L. 95-217, Sec. 41, Dec. 27, 1977, 91 Stat. 1582.)

COST EFFECTIVENESS

33 USC 1298

(a) Congressional statement of policy

It is the policy of Congress that a project for waste treatment and management undertaken with Federal financial assistance under this chapter by any State, municipality, or intermunicipal or interstate agency shall be considered as an overall waste treatment system for waste treatment and management, and shall be that system which constitutes the most economical and cost-effective combination of devices and systems used in the storage, treatment, recycling, and reclamation of municipal sewage or industrial wastes of a liquid nature to implement section 1281 of this title, or necessary to recycle or reuse water at the most economical cost over the estimated life of the works, including intercepting sewers, outfall sewers, sewage collection systems, pumping power, and other equipment, and their appurtenances, extension, improvements, remodeling, additions, and alterations thereof; elements essential to provide a reliable recycled supply such as standby treatment units and clear well facilities; and any works, including site acquisition of the land that will be an integral part of the treatment process (including land use for the storage of treated wastewater in land treatment systems prior to land application) or which is used for ultimate disposal of residues resulting from such treatment; water efficiency measures and devices; and any other method or system for preventing, abating, reducing, storing, treating, separating, or disposing of municipal waste, including storm water runoff, or industrial waste, including waste in combined storm water and sanitary sewer systems; to meet the requirements of this chapter.

(b) Determination by Administrator as prerequisite to approval of grant

In accordance with the policy set forth in subsection (a) of this section, before the Administrator approves any grant to any State, municipality, or intermunicipal or interstate agency for the erection, building, acquisition, alteration, remodeling, improvement, or extension of any treatment works the Administrator shall determine that the facilities plan of which such treatment works are a part constitutes the most economical and cost-effective combination of treatment works over the life of the project to meet the requirements of this chapter, including, but not limited to, consideration of construction costs, operation, maintenance, and replacement costs.

(c) Value engineering review

In furtherance of the policy set forth in subsection (a) of this section, the Administrator shall require value engineering review in connection with any treatment works, prior to approval of any grant for the erection, building, acquisition, alteration, remodeling, improvement, or extension of such treatment works, in any case in which the cost of such erection, building, acquisition, alteration, remodeling, improvement, or extension is projected to be in excess of $10,000,000. For purposes of this subsection, the term "value engineering review" means a specialized cost control technique which uses a systematic and creative approach to identify and to focus on unnecessarily high cost in a project in order to arrive at a cost saving without sacrificing the reliability or efficiency of the project.

(d) Projects affected

This section applies to projects for waste treatment and management for which no treatment works including a facilities plan for such project have received Federal financial assistance for the preparation of construction plans and specifications under this chapter before December 29, 1981.

(June 30, 1948, ch. 758, title II, Sec. 218, as added Pub. L. 97-117, Sec. 19, Dec. 29, 1981, 95 Stat. 1630.)

Section Referred to in Other Sections

This section is referred to in section 1382 of this title.

STATE CERTIFICATION OF PROJECTS

33 USC 1299

Whenever the Governor of a State which has been delegated sufficient authority to administer the construction grant program under this subchapter in that State certifies to the Administrator that a grant application meets applicable requirements of Federal and State law for assistance under this subchapter, the Administrator shall approve or disapprove such application within 45 days of the date of receipt of such application. If the Administrator does not approve or disapprove such application within 45 days of receipt, the application shall be deemed approved. If the Administrator disapproves such application the Administrator shall state in writing the reasons for such disapproval. Any grant approved or deemed approved under this section shall be subject to amounts provided in appropriation Acts.

(June 30, 1948, ch. 758, title II, Sec. 219, as added Pub. L. 97-117, Sec. 20, Dec. 29, 1981, 95 Stat. 1631.)

PILOT PROGRAM FOR ALTERNATIVE WATER SOURCE PROJECTS

33 USC 1300

(a) Policy

Nothing in this section shall be construed to affect the application of section 1251(g) of this title and all of the provisions of this section shall be carried out in accordance with the provisions of section 1251(g) of this title.

(b) In general

The Administrator may establish a pilot program to make grants to State, interstate, and intrastate water resource development agencies (including water management districts and water supply authorities), local government agencies, private utilities, and nonprofit entities for alternative water source projects to meet critical water supply needs.

(c) Eligible entity

The Administrator may make grants under this section to an entity only if the entity has authority under State law to develop or provide water for municipal, industrial, and agricultural uses in an area of the State that is experiencing critical water supply needs.

(d) Selection of projects

(1) Limitation

A project that has received funds under the reclamation and reuse program conducted under the Reclamation Projects Authorization and Adjustment Act of 1992 (43 U.S.C. 390h et seq.) shall not be eligible for grant assistance under this section.

(2) Additional consideration

In making grants under this section, the Administrator shall consider whether the project is located within the boundaries of a State or area referred to in section 391 of title 43, and within the geographic scope of the reclamation and reuse program conducted under the Reclamation Projects Authorization and Adjustment Act of 1992 (43 U.S.C. 390h et seq.).

(3) Geographical distribution
Alternative water source projects selected by the Administrator under this section shall reflect a variety of geographical and environmental conditions.
(e) Committee resolution procedure
  (1) In general
  No appropriation shall be made for any alternative water source project under this section, the total Federal cost of which exceeds $3,000,000, if such project has not been approved by a resolution adopted by the Committee on Transportation and Infrastructure of the House of Representatives or the Committee on Environment and Public Works of the Senate.
  (2) Requirements for securing consideration
  For purposes of securing consideration of approval under paragraph (1), the Administrator shall provide to a committee referred to in paragraph (1) such information as the committee requests and the non-Federal sponsor shall provide to the committee information on the costs and relative needs for the alternative water source project.
(f) Uses of grants
Amounts from grants received under this section may be used for engineering, design, construction, and final testing of alternative water source projects designed to meet critical water supply needs. Such amounts may not be used for planning, feasibility studies or for operation, maintenance, replacement, repair, or rehabilitation.
(g) Cost sharing
The Federal share of the eligible costs of an alternative water source project carried out using assistance made available under this section shall not exceed 50 percent.
(h) Reports
On or before September 30, 2004, the Administrator shall transmit to Congress a report on the results of the pilot program established under this section, including progress made toward meeting the critical water supply needs of the participants in the pilot program.
(i) Definitions
In this section, the following definitions apply:
  (1) Alternative water source project
  The term "alternative water source project" means a project designed to provide municipal, industrial, and agricultural water supplies in an environmentally sustainable manner by conserving, managing, reclaiming, or reusing water or wastewater or by treating wastewater. Such term does not include water treatment or distribution facilities.
  (2) Critical water supply needs
  The term "critical water supply needs" means existing or reasonably anticipated future water supply needs that cannot be met by existing water supplies, as identified in a comprehensive statewide or regional water supply plan or assessment projected over a planning period of at least 20 years.
(j) Authorization of appropriations
There is authorized to be appropriated to carry out this section a total of $75,000,000 for fiscal years 2002 through 2004. Such sums shall remain available until expended.

(June 30, 1948, ch. 758, title II, Sec. 220, as added Pub. L. 106-457, title VI, Sec. 602, Nov. 7, 2000, 114 Stat. 1975.)

References in Text

The Reclamation Projects Authorization and Adjustment Act of 1992, referred to in subsec. (d)(1), (2), is Pub. L. 102-575, Oct. 30, 1992, 106 Stat. 4600, as amended. Provisions relating to the reclamation and reuse program are classified generally to section 390h et seq. of Title 43, Public Lands. For complete classification of this Act to the Code, see Short Title of 1992 Amendment note set out under section 371 of Title 43 and Tables.

SEWER OVERFLOW CONTROL GRANTS

33 USC 1301

(a) In general

In any fiscal year in which the Administrator has available for obligation at least $1,350,000,000 for the purposes of section 1381 of this title—
  (1) the Administrator may make grants to States for the purpose of providing grants to a municipality or municipal entity for planning, design, and construction of treatment works to intercept, transport, control, or treat municipal combined sewer overflows and sanitary sewer overflows; and
  (2) subject to subsection (g) of this section, the Administrator may make a direct grant to a municipality or municipal entity for the purposes described in paragraph (1).

(b) Prioritization

In selecting from among municipalities applying for grants under subsection (a) of this section, a State or the Administrator shall give priority to an applicant that—
  (1) is a municipality that is a financially distressed community under subsection (c) of this section;
  (2) has implemented or is complying with an implementation schedule for the nine minimum controls specified in the CSO control policy referred to in section 1342(q)(1) of this title and has begun implementing a long-term municipal combined sewer overflow control plan or a separate sanitary sewer overflow control plan;
  (3) is requesting a grant for a project that is on a State's intended use plan pursuant to section 1386(c) of this title; or
  (4) is an Alaska Native Village.

(c) Financially distressed community
  (1) Definition
    In subsection (b) of this section, the term "financially distressed community" means a community that meets affordability criteria established by the State in which the community is located, if such criteria are developed after public review and comment.
  (2) Consideration of impact on water and sewer rates
    In determining if a community is a distressed community for the purposes of subsection (b) of this section, the State shall consider, among other factors, the extent to which the rate of growth of a community's tax base has been historically slow such that implementing a plan described in subsection (b)(2) of this section would result in a significant increase in any water or sewer rate charged by the community's publicly owned wastewater treatment facility.
  (3) Information to assist States
    The Administrator may publish information to assist States in establishing affordability criteria under paragraph (1).

(d) Cost-sharing

The Federal share of the cost of activities carried out using amounts from a grant made under subsection (a) of this section shall be not less than 55 percent of the cost. The non-Federal share of the cost may include, in any amount, public and private funds and in-kind services, and may include, notwithstanding section 1383(h) of this title, financial assistance, including loans, from a State water pollution control revolving fund.

(e) Administrative reporting requirements

If a project receives grant assistance under subsection (a) of this section and loan assistance from a State water pollution control revolving fund and the loan assistance is for 15 percent or more of the cost of the project, the project may be administered in accordance with State water pollution control revolving fund administrative reporting requirements for the purposes of streamlining such requirements.

(f) Authorization of appropriations

There is authorized to be appropriated to carry out this section $750,000,000 for each of fiscal years 2002 and 2003. Such sums shall remain available until expended.

(g) Allocation of funds
  (1) Fiscal year 2002
    Subject to subsection (h) of this section, the Administrator shall use the amounts appropriated to carry out this section for fiscal year 2002 for making grants to municipalities and municipal entities under subsection (a)(2) of this section, in accordance with the criteria set forth in subsection (b) of this section.
  (2) Fiscal year 2003
    Subject to subsection (h) of this section, the Administrator shall use the amounts appropriated to carry out this section for fiscal year 2003 as follows:
    (A) Not to exceed $250,000,000 for making grants to municipalities and municipal entities under subsection (a)(2) of this section, in accordance with the criteria set forth in subsection (b) of this section.
    (B) All remaining amounts for making grants to States under subsection (a)(1) of this section, in accordance with a formula to be established by the Administrator, after providing notice and an opportunity for public comment, that allocates to each State a proportional share of such amounts based on the total needs of the State for municipal combined sewer overflow controls and sanitary sewer overflow controls identified in the most recent survey conducted pursuant to section 1375(b)(1)[1] of this title.
(h) Administrative expenses
  Of the amounts appropriated to carry out this section for each fiscal year—
  (1) the Administrator may retain an amount not to exceed 1 percent for the reasonable and necessary costs of administering this section; and
  (2) the Administrator, or a State, may retain an amount not to exceed 4 percent of any grant made to a municipality or municipal entity under subsection (a) of this section, for the reasonable and necessary costs of administering the grant.
(i) Reports
  Not later than December 31, 2003, and periodically thereafter, the Administrator shall transmit to Congress a report containing recommended funding levels for grants under this section. The recommended funding levels shall be sufficient to ensure the continued expeditious implementation of municipal combined sewer overflow and sanitary sewer overflow controls nationwide.

(June 30, 1948, ch. 758, title II, Sec. 221, as added Pub. L. 106-554, Sec. 1(a)(4) [div. B, title I, Sec. 112(c)], Dec. 21, 2000, 114 Stat. 2763, 2763A-225.)

References in Text

Section 1375 of this title, referred to in subsec. (g)(2)(B), was amended by Pub. L. 105-362, title V, Sec. 501(d)(1), Nov. 10, 1998, 112 Stat. 3283, and, as so amended, no longer contains subsections.

Information on CSOS and SSOS

Pub. L. 106-554, Sec. 1(a)(4) [div. B, title I, Sec. 112(d)], Dec. 21, 2000, 114 Stat. 2763, 2763A-227, provided that:

"(1) Report to congress.—Not later than 3 years after the date of enactment of this Act [Dec. 21, 2000], the Administrator of the Environmental Protection Agency shall transmit to Congress a report summarizing—
  (A) the extent of the human health and environmental impacts caused by municipal combined sewer overflows and sanitary sewer overflows, including the location of discharges causing such impacts, the volume of pollutants discharged, and the constituents discharged;
  (B) the resources spent by municipalities to address these impacts; and
  (C) an evaluation of the technologies used by municipalities to address these impacts.
(2) Technology clearinghouse.—After transmitting a report under paragraph (1), the Administrator shall maintain a clearinghouse of cost-effective and efficient technologies for addressing human health and environmental impacts due to municipal combined sewer overflows and sanitary sewer overflows."

---

[1] See References in Text note below.

# SUBCHAPTER III—STANDARDS AND ENFORCEMENT

EFFLUENT LIMITATIONS

33 USC 1311

(a) Illegality of pollutant discharges except in compliance with law
Except as in compliance with this section and sections 1312, 1316, 1317, 1328, 1342, and 1344 of this title, the discharge of any pollutant by any person shall be unlawful.

(b) Timetable for achievement of objectives
In order to carry out the objective of this chapter there shall be achieved—
  (1) (A) not later than July 1, 1977, effluent limitations for point sources, other than publicly owned treatment works, (i) which shall require the application of the best practicable control technology currently available as defined by the Administrator pursuant to section 1314(b) of this title, or (ii) in the case of a discharge into a publicly owned treatment works which meets the requirements of subparagraph (B) of this paragraph, which shall require compliance with any applicable pretreatment requirements and any requirements under section 1317 of this title; and
   (B) for publicly owned treatment works in existence on July 1, 1977, or approved pursuant to section 1283 of this title prior to June 30, 1974 (for which construction must be completed within four years of approval), effluent limitations based upon secondary treatment as defined by the Administrator pursuant to section 1314(d)(1) of this title; or,
   (C) not later than July 1, 1977, any more stringent limitation, including those necessary to meet water quality standards, treatment standards, or schedules of compliance, established pursuant to any State law or regulations (under authority preserved by section 1370 of this title) or any other Federal law or regulation, or required to implement any applicable water quality standard established pursuant to this chapter.
  (2) (A) for pollutants identified in subparagraphs (C), (D), and (F) of this paragraph, effluent limitations for categories and classes of point sources, other than publicly owned treatment works, which (i) shall require application of the best available technology economically achievable for such category or class, which will result in reasonable further progress toward the national goal of eliminating the discharge of all pollutants, as determined in accordance with regulations issued by the Administrator pursuant to section 1314(b)(2) of this title, which such effluent limitations shall require the elimination of discharges of all pollutants if the Administrator finds, on the basis of information available to him (including information developed pursuant to section 1325 of this title), that such elimination is technologically and economically achievable for a category or class of point sources as determined in accordance with regulations issued by the Administrator pursuant to section 1314(b)(2) of this title, or (ii) in the case of the introduction of a pollutant into a publicly owned treatment works which meets the requirements of subparagraph (B) of this paragraph, shall require compliance with any applicable pretreatment requirements and any other requirement under section 1317 of this title;
   (B) Repealed. Pub. L. 97-117, Sec. 21(b), Dec. 29, 1981, 95 Stat. 1632.
   (C) with respect to all toxic pollutants referred to in table 1 of Committee Print Numbered 95-30 of the Committee on Public Works and Transportation of the House of Representatives compliance with effluent limitations in accordance with subparagraph (A) of this paragraph as expeditiously as practicable but in no case later than three years after the date such limitations are promulgated under section 1314(b) of this title, and in no case later than March 31, 1989;
   (D) for all toxic pollutants listed under paragraph (1) of subsection (a) of section 1317 of this title which are not referred to in subparagraph (C) of this paragraph compliance with effluent limitations in accordance with subparagraph (A) of this paragraph as expeditiously as practicable, but in no case later than three years after the date such limitations are promulgated under section 1314(b) of this title, and in no case later than March 31, 1989;

518 / Environmental Statutes

    (E) as expeditiously as practicable but in no case later than three years after the date such limitations are promulgated under section 1314(b) of this title, and in no case later than March 31, 1989, compliance with effluent limitations for categories and classes of point sources, other than publicly owned treatment works, which in the case of pollutants identified pursuant to section 1314(a)(4) of this title shall require application of the best conventional pollutant control technology as determined in accordance with regulations issued by the Administrator pursuant to section 1314(b)(4) of this title; and

    (F) for all pollutants (other than those subject to subparagraphs (C), (D), or (E) of this paragraph) compliance with effluent limitations in accordance with subparagraph (A) of this paragraph as expeditiously as practicable but in no case later than 3 years after the date such limitations are established, and in no case later than March 31, 1989.

(3) (A) for effluent limitations under paragraph (1)(A)(i) of this subsection promulgated after January 1, 1982, and requiring a level of control substantially greater or based on fundamentally different control technology than under permits for an industrial category issued before such date, compliance as expeditiously as practicable but in no case later than three years after the date such limitations are promulgated under section 1314(b) of this title, and in no case later than March 31, 1989; and

    (B) for any effluent limitation in accordance with paragraph (1)(A)(i), (2)(A)(i), or (2)(E) of this subsection established only on the basis of section 1342(a)(1) of this title in a permit issued after February 4, 1987, compliance as expeditiously as practicable but in no case later than three years after the date such limitations are established, and in no case later than March 31, 1989.

(c) Modification of timetable

The Administrator may modify the requirements of subsection (b)(2)(A) of this section with respect to any point source for which a permit application is filed after July 1, 1977, upon a showing by the owner or operator of such point source satisfactory to the Administrator that such modified requirements (1) will represent the maximum use of technology within the economic capability of the owner or operator; and (2) will result in reasonable further progress toward the elimination of the discharge of pollutants.

(d) Review and revision of effluent limitations

Any effluent limitation required by paragraph (2) of subsection (b) of this section shall be reviewed at least every five years and, if appropriate, revised pursuant to the procedure established under such paragraph.

(e) All point discharge source application of effluent limitations

Effluent limitations established pursuant to this section or section 1312 of this title shall be applied to all point sources of discharge of pollutants in accordance with the provisions of this chapter.

(f) Illegality of discharge of radiological, chemical, or biological warfare agents, high-level radioactive waste, or medical waste

Notwithstanding any other provisions of this chapter it shall be unlawful to discharge any radiological, chemical, or biological warfare agent, any high-level radioactive waste, or any medical waste, into the navigable waters.

(g) Modifications for certain nonconventional pollutants

  (1) General authority

The Administrator, with the concurrence of the State, may modify the requirements of subsection (b)(2)(A) of this section with respect to the discharge from any point source of ammonia, chlorine, color, iron, and total phenols (4AAP) (when determined by the Administrator to be a pollutant covered by subsection (b)(2)(F) of this section) and any other pollutant which the Administrator lists under paragraph (4) of this subsection.

  (2) Requirements for granting modifications

A modification under this subsection shall be granted only upon a showing by the owner or operator of a point source satisfactory to the Administrator that—

    (A) such modified requirements will result at a minimum in compliance with the requirements of subsection (b)(1)(A) or (C) of this section, whichever is applicable;

(B) such modified requirements will not result in any additional requirements on any other point or nonpoint source; and

(C) such modification will not interfere with the attainment or maintenance of that water quality which shall assure protection of public water supplies, and the protection and propagation of a balanced population of shellfish, fish, and wildlife, and allow recreational activities, in and on the water and such modification will not result in the discharge of pollutants in quantities which may reasonably be anticipated to pose an unacceptable risk to human health or the environment because of bioaccumulation, persistency in the environment, acute toxicity, chronic toxicity (including carcinogenicity, mutagenicity or teratogenicity), or synergistic propensities.

(3) Limitation on authority to apply for subsection (c) modification

If an owner or operator of a point source applies for a modification under this subsection with respect to the discharge of any pollutant, such owner or operator shall be eligible to apply for modification under subsection (c) of this section with respect to such pollutant only during the same time period as he is eligible to apply for a modification under this subsection.

(4) Procedures for listing additional pollutants

(A) General authority

Upon petition of any person, the Administrator may add any pollutant to the list of pollutants for which modification under this section is authorized (except for pollutants identified pursuant to section 1314(a)(4) of this title, toxic pollutants subject to section 1317(a) of this title, and the thermal component of discharges) in accordance with the provisions of this paragraph.

(B) Requirements for listing

(i) Sufficient information

The person petitioning for listing of an additional pollutant under this subsection shall submit to the Administrator sufficient information to make the determinations required by this subparagraph.

(ii) Toxic criteria determination

The Administrator shall determine whether or not the pollutant meets the criteria for listing as a toxic pollutant under section 1317(a) of this title.

(iii) Listing as toxic pollutant

If the Administrator determines that the pollutant meets the criteria for listing as a toxic pollutant under section 1317(a) of this title, the Administrator shall list the pollutant as a toxic pollutant under section 1317(a) of this title.

(iv) Nonconventional criteria determination

If the Administrator determines that the pollutant does not meet the criteria for listing as a toxic pollutant under such section and determines that adequate test methods and sufficient data are available to make the determinations required by paragraph (2) of this subsection with respect to the pollutant, the Administrator shall add the pollutant to the list of pollutants specified in paragraph (1) of this subsection for which modifications are authorized under this subsection.

(C) Requirements for filing of petitions

A petition for listing of a pollutant under this paragraph—

(i) must be filed not later than 270 days after the date of promulgation of an applicable effluent guideline under section 1314 of this title;

(ii) may be filed before promulgation of such guideline; and

(iii) may be filed with an application for a modification under paragraph (1) with respect to the discharge of such pollutant.

(D) Deadline for approval of petition

A decision to add a pollutant to the list of pollutants for which modifications under this subsection are authorized must be made within 270 days after the date of promulgation of an applicable effluent guideline under section 1314 of this title.

(E) Burden of proof

The burden of proof for making the determinations under subparagraph (B) shall be on the petitioner.

(5) Removal of pollutants

The Administrator may remove any pollutant from the list of pollutants for which modifications are authorized under this subsection if the Administrator determines that adequate

test methods and sufficient data are no longer available for determining whether or not modifications may be granted with respect to such pollutant under paragraph (2) of this subsection.
(h) Modification of secondary treatment requirements
The Administrator, with the concurrence of the State, may issue a permit under section 1342 of this title which modifies the requirements of subsection (b)(1)(B) of this section with respect to the discharge of any pollutant from a publicly owned treatment works into marine waters, if the applicant demonstrates to the satisfaction of the Administrator that—
(1) there is an applicable water quality standard specific to the pollutant for which the modification is requested, which has been identified under section 1314(a)(6) of this title;
(2) the discharge of pollutants in accordance with such modified requirements will not interfere, alone or in combination with pollutants from other sources, with the attainment or maintenance of that water quality which assures protection of public water supplies and the protection and propagation of a balanced, indigenous population of shellfish, fish, and wildlife, and allows recreational activities, in and on the water;
(3) the applicant has established a system for monitoring the impact of such discharge on a representative sample of aquatic biota, to the extent practicable, and the scope of such monitoring is limited to include only those scientific investigations which are necessary to study the effects of the proposed discharge;
(4) such modified requirements will not result in any additional requirements on any other point or nonpoint source;
(5) all applicable pretreatment requirements for sources introducing waste into such treatment works will be enforced;
(6) in the case of any treatment works serving a population of 50,000 or more, with respect to any toxic pollutant introduced into such works by an industrial discharger for which pollutant there is no applicable pretreatment requirement in effect, sources introducing waste into such works are in compliance with all applicable pretreatment requirements, the applicant will enforce such requirements, and the applicant has in effect a pretreatment program which, in combination with the treatment of discharges from such works, removes the same amount of such pollutant as would be removed if such works were to apply secondary treatment to discharges and if such works had no pretreatment program with respect to such pollutant;
(7) to the extent practicable, the applicant has established a schedule of activities designed to eliminate the entrance of toxic pollutants from nonindustrial sources into such treatment works;
(8) there will be no new or substantially increased discharges from the point source of the pollutant to which the modification applies above that volume of discharge specified in the permit;
(9) the applicant at the time such modification becomes effective will be discharging effluent which has received at least primary or equivalent treatment and which meets the criteria established under section 1314(a)(1) of this title after initial mixing in the waters surrounding or adjacent to the point at which such effluent is discharged.
For the purposes of this subsection the phrase "the discharge of any pollutant into marine waters" refers to a discharge into deep waters of the territorial sea or the waters of the contiguous zone, or into saline estuarine waters where there is strong tidal movement and other hydrological and geological characteristics which the Administrator determines necessary to allow compliance with paragraph (2) of this subsection, and section 1251(a)(2) of this title. For the purposes of paragraph (9), "primary or equivalent treatment" means treatment by screening, sedimentation, and skimming adequate to remove at least 30 percent of the biological oxygen demanding material and of the suspended solids in the treatment works influent, and disinfection, where appropriate. A municipality which applies secondary treatment shall be eligible to receive a permit pursuant to this subsection which modifies the requirements of subsection (b)(1)(B) of this section with respect to the discharge of any pollutant from any treatment works owned by such municipality into marine waters. No permit issued under this subsection shall authorize the discharge of sewage sludge into marine waters. In order for a permit to be issued under this subsection for the discharge of a pollutant into marine waters, such marine waters must exhibit characteristics assuring that water providing dilution does not contain significant amounts of previously discharged effluent from such treatment works.

No permit issued under this subsection shall authorize the discharge of any pollutant into saline estuarine waters which at the time of application do not support a balanced indigenous population of shellfish, fish and wildlife, or allow recreation in and on the waters or which exhibit ambient water quality below applicable water quality standards adopted for the protection of public water supplies, shellfish, fish and wildlife or recreational activities or such other standards necessary to assure support and protection of such uses. The prohibition contained in the preceding sentence shall apply without regard to the presence or absence of a causal relationship between such characteristics and the applicant's current or proposed discharge. Notwithstanding any other provisions of this subsection, no permit may be issued under this subsection for discharge of a pollutant into the New York Bight Apex consisting of the ocean waters of the Atlantic Ocean westward of 73 degrees 30 minutes west longitude and northward of 40 degrees 10 minutes north latitude.

(i) Municipal time extensions

(1) Where construction is required in order for a planned or existing publicly owned treatment works to achieve limitations under subsection (b)(1)(B) or (b)(1)(C) of this section, but (A) construction cannot be completed within the time required in such subsection, or (B) the United States has failed to make financial assistance under this chapter available in time to achieve such limitations by the time specified in such subsection, the owner or operator of such treatment works may request the Administrator (or if appropriate the State) to issue a permit pursuant to section 1342 of this title or to modify a permit issued pursuant to that section to extend such time for compliance. Any such request shall be filed with the Administrator (or if appropriate the State) within 180 days after February 4, 1987. The Administrator (or if appropriate the State) may grant such request and issue or modify such a permit, which shall contain a schedule of compliance for the publicly owned treatment works based on the earliest date by which such financial assistance will be available from the United States and construction can be completed, but in no event later than July 1, 1988, and shall contain such other terms and conditions, including those necessary to carry out subsections (b) through (g) of section 1281 of this title, section 1317 of this title, and such interim effluent limitations applicable to that treatment works as the Administrator determines are necessary to carry out the provisions of this chapter.

(2) (A) Where a point source (other than a publicly owned treatment works) will not achieve the requirements of subsections (b)(1)(A) and (b)(1)(C) of this section and—

(i) if a permit issued prior to July 1, 1977, to such point source is based upon a discharge into a publicly owned treatment works; or

(ii) if such point source (other than a publicly owned treatment works) had before July 1, 1977, a contract (enforceable against such point source) to discharge into a publicly owned treatment works; or

(iii) if either an application made before July 1, 1977, for a construction grant under this chapter for a publicly owned treatment works, or engineering or architectural plans or working drawings made before July 1, 1977, for a publicly owned treatment works, show that such point source was to discharge into such publicly owned treatment works,

and such publicly owned treatment works is presently unable to accept such discharge without construction, and in the case of a discharge to an existing publicly owned treatment works, such treatment works has an extension pursuant to paragraph (1) of this subsection, the owner or operator of such point source may request the Administrator (or if appropriate the State) to issue or modify such a permit pursuant to such section 1342 of this title to extend such time for compliance. Any such request shall be filed with the Administrator (or if appropriate the State) within 180 days after December 27, 1977, or the filing of a request by the appropriate publicly owned treatment works under paragraph (1) of this subsection, whichever is later. If the Administrator (or if appropriate the State) finds that the owner or operator of such point source has acted in good faith, he may grant such request and issue or modify such a permit, which shall contain a schedule of compliance for the point source to achieve the requirements of subsections (b)(1)(A) and (C) of this section and shall contain such other terms and conditions, including pretreatment and interim effluent limitations and water conservation requirements applicable to that point source, as the Administrator determines are necessary to carry out the provisions of this chapter.

(B) No time modification granted by the Administrator (or if appropriate the State) pursuant to paragraph (2)(A) of this subsection shall extend beyond the earliest date practicable for compliance or beyond the date of any extension granted to the appropriate publicly owned treatment works pursuant to paragraph (1) of this subsection, but in no event shall it extend beyond July 1, 1988; and no such time modification shall be granted unless (i) the publicly owned treatment works will be in operation and available to the point source before July 1, 1988, and will meet the requirements of subsections (b)(1)(B) and (C) of this section after receiving the discharge from that point source; and (ii) the point source and the publicly owned treatment works have entered into an enforceable contract requiring the point source to discharge into the publicly owned treatment works, the owner or operator of such point source to pay the costs required under section 1284 of this title, and the publicly owned treatment works to accept the discharge from the point source; and (iii) the permit for such point source requires that point source to meet all requirements under section 1317(a) and (b) of this title during the period of such time modification.

(j) Modification procedures
 (1) Any application filed under this section for a modification of the provisions of—
  (A) subsection (b)(1)(B) of this section under subsection (h) of this section shall be filed not later that[1] the 365th day which begins after December 29, 1981, except that a publicly owned treatment works which prior to December 31, 1982, had a contractual arrangement to use a portion of the capacity of an ocean outfall operated by another publicly owned treatment works which has applied for or received modification under subsection (h) of this section, may apply for a modification of subsection (h) of this section in its own right not later than 30 days after February 4, 1987, and except as provided in paragraph (5);
  (B) subsection (b)(2)(A) of this section as it applies to pollutants identified in subsection (b)(2)(F) of this section shall be filed not later than 270 days after the date of promulgation of an applicable effluent guideline under section 1314 of this title or not later than 270 days after December 27, 1977, whichever is later.
 (2) Subject to paragraph (3) of this section, any application for a modification filed under subsection (g) of this section shall not operate to stay any requirement under this chapter, unless in the judgment of the Administrator such a stay or the modification sought will not result in the discharge of pollutants in quantities which may reasonably be anticipated to pose an unacceptable risk to human health or the environment because of bioaccumulation, persistency in the environment, acute toxicity, chronic toxicity (including carcinogenicity, mutagenicity, or teratogenicity), or synergistic propensities, and that there is a substantial likelihood that the applicant will succeed on the merits of such application. In the case of an application filed under subsection (g) of this section, the Administrator may condition any stay granted under this paragraph on requiring the filing of a bond or other appropriate security to assure timely compliance with the requirements from which a modification is sought.
 (3) Compliance requirements under subsection (g).—
  (A) Effect of filing.—An application for a modification under subsection (g) of this section and a petition for listing of a pollutant as a pollutant for which modifications are authorized under such subsection shall not stay the requirement that the person seeking such modification or listing comply with effluent limitations under this chapter for all pollutants not the subject of such application or petition.
  (B) Effect of disapproval.—Disapproval of an application for a modification under subsection (g) of this section shall not stay the requirement that the person seeking such modification comply with all applicable effluent limitations under this chapter.
 (4) Deadline for subsection (g) decision.—An application for a modification with respect to a pollutant filed under subsection (g) of this section must be approved or disapproved not later than 365 days after the date of such filing; except that in any case in which a petition for listing such pollutant as a pollutant for which modifications are authorized under such subsection is approved, such application must be approved or disapproved not later than 365 days after the date of approval of such petition.

---

[1] So in original. Probably should be "than".

(5) Extension of application deadline.—
   (A) In general.—In the 180-day period beginning on October 31, 1994, the city of San Diego, California, may apply for a modification pursuant to subsection (h) of this section of the requirements of subsection (b)(1)(B) of this section with respect to biological oxygen demand and total suspended solids in the effluent discharged into marine waters.
   (B) Application.—An application under this paragraph shall include a commitment by the applicant to implement a waste water reclamation program that, at a minimum, will—
      (i) achieve a system capacity of 45,000,000 gallons of reclaimed waste water per day by January 1, 2010; and
      (ii) result in a reduction in the quantity of suspended solids discharged by the applicant into the marine environment during the period of the modification.
   (C) Additional conditions.—The Administrator may not grant a modification pursuant to an application submitted under this paragraph unless the Administrator determines that such modification will result in removal of not less than 58 percent of the biological oxygen demand (on an annual average) and not less than 80 percent of total suspended solids (on a monthly average) in the discharge to which the application applies.
   (D) Preliminary decision deadline.—The Administrator shall announce a preliminary decision on an application submitted under this paragraph not later than 1 year after the date the application is submitted.
(k) Innovative technology
   In the case of any facility subject to a permit under section 1342 of this title which proposes to comply with the requirements of subsection (b)(2)(A) or (b)(2)(E) of this section by replacing existing production capacity with an innovative production process which will result in an effluent reduction significantly greater than that required by the limitation otherwise applicable to such facility and moves toward the national goal of eliminating the discharge of all pollutants, or with the installation of an innovative control technique that has a substantial likelihood for enabling the facility to comply with the applicable effluent limitation by achieving a significantly greater effluent reduction than that required by the applicable effluent limitation and moves toward the national goal of eliminating the discharge of all pollutants, or by achieving the required reduction with an innovative system that has the potential for significantly lower costs than the systems which have been determined by the Administrator to be economically achievable, the Administrator (or the State with an approved program under section 1342 of this title, in consultation with the Administrator) may establish a date for compliance under subsection (b)(2)(A) or (b)(2)(E) of this section no later than two years after the date for compliance with such effluent limitation which would otherwise be applicable under such subsection, if it is also determined that such innovative system has the potential for industrywide application.
(l) Toxic pollutants
   Other than as provided in subsection (n) of this section, the Administrator may not modify any requirement of this section as it applies to any specific pollutant which is on the toxic pollutant list under section 1317(a)(1) of this title.
(m) Modification of effluent limitation requirements for point sources
   (1) The Administrator, with the concurrence of the State, may issue a permit under section 1342 of this title which modifies the requirements of subsections (b)(1)(A) and (b)(2)(E) of this section, and of section 1343 of this title, with respect to effluent limitations to the extent such limitations relate to biochemical oxygen demand and pH from discharges by an industrial discharger in such State into deep waters of the territorial seas, if the applicant demonstrates and the Administrator finds that—
      (A) the facility for which modification is sought is covered at the time of the enactment of this subsection by National Pollutant Discharge Elimination System permit number CA0005894 or CA0005282;
      (B) the energy and environmental costs of meeting such requirements of subsections (b)(1)(A) and (b)(2)(E) of this section and section 1343 of this title exceed by an unreasonable amount the benefits to be obtained, including the objectives of this chapter;

(C) the applicant has established a system for monitoring the impact of such discharges on a representative sample of aquatic biota;
(D) such modified requirements will not result in any additional requirements on any other point or nonpoint source;
(E) there will be no new or substantially increased discharges from the point source of the pollutant to which the modification applies above that volume of discharge specified in the permit;
(F) the discharge is into waters where there is strong tidal movement and other hydrological and geological characteristics which are necessary to allow compliance with this subsection and section 1251(a)(2) of this title;
(G) the applicant accepts as a condition to the permit a contractural[2] obligation to use funds in the amount required (but not less than $250,000 per year for ten years) for research and development of water pollution control technology, including but not limited to closed cycle technology;
(H) the facts and circumstances present a unique situation which, if relief is granted, will not establish a precedent or the relaxation of the requirements of this chapter applicable to similarly situated discharges; and
(I) no owner or operator of a facility comparable to that of the applicant situated in the United States has demonstrated that it would be put at a competitive disadvantage to the applicant (or the parent company or any subsidiary thereof) as a result of the issuance of a permit under this subsection.
(2) The effluent limitations established under a permit issued under paragraph (1) shall be sufficient to implement the applicable State water quality standards, to assure the protection of public water supplies and protection and propagation of a balanced, indigenous population of shellfish, fish, fauna, wildlife, and other aquatic organisms, and to allow recreational activities in and on the water. In setting such limitations, the Administrator shall take into account any seasonal variations and the need for an adequate margin of safety, considering the lack of essential knowledge concerning the relationship between effluent limitations and water quality and the lack of essential knowledge of the effects of discharges on beneficial uses of the receiving waters.
(3) A permit under this subsection may be issued for a period not to exceed five years, and such a permit may be renewed for one additional period not to exceed five years upon a demonstration by the applicant and a finding by the Administrator at the time of application for any such renewal that the provisions of this subsection are met.
(4) The Administrator may terminate a permit issued under this subsection if the Administrator determines that there has been a decline in ambient water quality of the receiving waters during the period of the permit even if a direct cause and effect relationship cannot be shown: Provided, That if the effluent from a source with a permit issued under this subsection is contributing to a decline in ambient water quality of the receiving waters, the Administrator shall terminate such permit.

(n) Fundamentally different factors
  (1) General rule
    The Administrator, with the concurrence of the State, may establish an alternative requirement under subsection (b)(2) of this section or section 1317(b) of this title for a facility that modifies the requirements of national effluent limitation guidelines or categorical pretreatment standards that would otherwise be applicable to such facility, if the owner or operator of such facility demonstrates to the satisfaction of the Administrator that—
    (A) the facility is fundamentally different with respect to the factors (other than cost) specified in section 1314(b) or 1314(g) of this title and considered by the Administrator in establishing such national effluent limitation guidelines or categorical pretreatment standards;
    (B) the application—
      (i) is based solely on information and supporting data submitted to the Administrator during the rulemaking for establishment of the applicable national effluent limitation guidelines or categorical pretreatment standard specifically raising the factors that are fundamentally different for such facility; or

---

[2]So in original. Probably should be "contractual".

(ii) is based on information and supporting data referred to in clause (i) and information and supporting data the applicant did not have a reasonable opportunity to submit during such rulemaking;

(C) the alternative requirement is no less stringent than justified by the fundamental difference; and

(D) the alternative requirement will not result in a non-water quality environmental impact which is markedly more adverse than the impact considered by the Administrator in establishing such national effluent limitation guideline or categorical pretreatment standard.

(2) Time limit for applications

An application for an alternative requirement which modifies the requirements of an effluent limitation or pretreatment standard under this subsection must be submitted to the Administrator within 180 days after the date on which such limitation or standard is established or revised, as the case may be.

(3) Time limit for decision

The Administrator shall approve or deny by final agency action an application submitted under this subsection within 180 days after the date such application is filed with the Administrator.

(4) Submission of information

The Administrator may allow an applicant under this subsection to submit information and supporting data until the earlier of the date the application is approved or denied or the last day that the Administrator has to approve or deny such application.

(5) Treatment of pending applications

For the purposes of this subsection, an application for an alternative requirement based on fundamentally different factors which is pending on February 4, 1987, shall be treated as having been submitted to the Administrator on the 180th day following February 4, 1987. The applicant may amend the application to take into account the provisions of this subsection.

(6) Effect of submission of application

An application for an alternative requirement under this subsection shall not stay the applicant's obligation to comply with the effluent limitation guideline or categorical pretreatment standard which is the subject of the application.

(7) Effect of denial

If an application for an alternative requirement which modifies the requirements of an effluent limitation or pretreatment standard under this subsection is denied by the Administrator, the applicant must comply with such limitation or standard as established or revised, as the case may be.

(8) Reports

By January 1, 1997, and January 1 of every odd-numbered year thereafter, the Administrator shall submit to the Committee on Environment and Public Works of the Senate and the Committee on Transportation and Infrastructure of the House of Representatives a report on the status of applications for alternative requirements which modify the requirements of effluent limitations under section 1311 or 1314 of this title or any national categorical pretreatment standard under section 1317(b) of this title filed before, on, or after February 4, 1987.

(o) Application fees

The Administrator shall prescribe and collect from each applicant fees reflecting the reasonable administrative costs incurred in reviewing and processing applications for modifications submitted to the Administrator pursuant to subsections (c), (g), (i), (k), (m), and (n) of this section, section 1314(d)(4) of this title, and section 1326(a) of this title. All amounts collected by the Administrator under this subsection shall be deposited into a special fund of the Treasury entitled "Water Permits and Related Services" which shall thereafter be available for appropriation to carry out activities of the Environmental Protection Agency for which such fees were collected.

(p) Modified permit for coal remining operations

(1) In general

Subject to paragraphs (2) through (4) of this subsection, the Administrator, or the State in any case which the State has an approved permit program under section 1342(b) of this title, may issue a permit under section 1342 of this title which modifies the requirements of subsection (b)(2)(A) of this section with respect to the pH level of any pre-existing discharge, and with respect to pre-existing discharges of iron and manganese from the remined area of any coal remining operation or with respect to the pH level or level of iron or manganese in any pre-existing discharge affected by the remining operation. Such modified requirements shall apply the best available technology economically achievable on a case-by-case basis, using best professional judgment, to set specific numerical effluent limitations in each permit.

(2) Limitations

The Administrator or the State may only issue a permit pursuant to paragraph (1) if the applicant demonstrates to the satisfaction of the Administrator or the State, as the case may be, that the coal remining operation will result in the potential for improved water quality from the remining operation but in no event shall such a permit allow the pH level of any discharge, and in no event shall such a permit allow the discharges of iron and manganese, to exceed the levels being discharged from the remined area before the coal remining operation begins. No discharge from, or affected by, the remining operation shall exceed State water quality standards established under section 1313 of this title.

(3) Definitions

For purposes of this subsection—

(A) Coal remining operation

The term "coal remining operation" means a coal mining operation which begins after February 4, 1987 at a site on which coal mining was conducted before August 3, 1977.

(B) Remined area

The term "remined area" means only that area of any coal remining operation on which coal mining was conducted before August 3, 1977.

(C) Pre-existing discharge

The term "pre-existing discharge" means any discharge at the time of permit application under this subsection.

(4) Applicability of strip mining laws

Nothing in this subsection shall affect the application of the Surface Mining Control and Reclamation Act of 1977 [30 U.S.C. 1201 et seq.] to any coal remining operation, including the application of such Act to suspended solids.

(June 30, 1948, ch. 758, title III, Sec. 301, as added Pub. L. 92-500, Sec. 2, Oct. 18, 1972, 86 Stat. 844; amended Pub. L. 95-217, Secs. 42-47, 53(c), Dec. 27, 1977, 91 Stat. 1582-1586, 1590; Pub. L. 97-117, Secs. 21, 22(a)-(d), Dec. 29, 1981, 95 Stat. 1631, 1632; Pub. L. 97-440, Jan. 8, 1983, 96 Stat. 2289; Pub. L. 100-4, title III, Secs. 301(a)-(e), 302(a)-(d), 303(a), (b)(1), (c)-(f), 304(a), 305, 306(a), (b), 307, Feb. 4, 1987, 101 Stat. 29-37; Pub. L. 100-688, title III, Sec. 3202(b), Nov. 18, 1988, 102 Stat. 4154; Pub. L. 103-431, Sec. 2, Oct. 31, 1994, 108 Stat. 4396; Pub. L. 104-66, title II, Sec. 2021(b), Dec. 21, 1995, 109 Stat. 727.)

References in Text

The Surface Mining Control and Reclamation Act of 1977, referred to in subsec. (p)(4), is Pub. L. 95-87, Aug. 3, 1977, 91 Stat. 445, as amended, which is classified generally to chapter 25 (Sec. 1201 et seq.) of Title 30, Mineral Lands and Mining. For complete classification of this Act to the Code, see Short Title note set out under section 1201 of Title 30 and Tables.

Amendments

1995—Subsec. (n)(8). Pub. L. 104-66 substituted "By January 1, 1997, and January 1 of every odd-numbered year thereafter, the Administrator shall submit to the Committee on Environment and Public Works of the Senate and the Committee on Transportation and Infrastructure" for "Every 6 months after February 4, 1987, the Administrator shall submit to the Committee on Environment and Public Works of the Senate and the Committee on Public Works and Transportation".

1994—Subsec. (j)(1)(A). Pub. L. 103-431, Sec. 2(1), inserted before semicolon at end ", and except as provided in paragraph (5)".

Subsec. (j)(5). Pub. L. 103-431, Sec. 2(2), added par. (5).

1988—Subsec. (f). Pub. L. 100-688 substituted ", any high-level radioactive waste, or any medical waste," for "or high-level radioactive waste".

1987—Subsec. (b)(2)(C). Pub. L. 100-4, Sec. 301(a), struck out "not later than July 1, 1984," before "with respect" and inserted "as expeditiously as practicable but in no case later than three years after the date such limitations are promulgated under section 1314(b) of this title, and in no case later than March 31, 1989" after "of this paragraph".

Subsec. (b)(2)(D). Pub. L. 100-4, Sec. 301(b), substituted "as expeditiously as practicable, but in no case later than three years after the date such limitations are promulgated under section 1314(b) of this title, and in no case later than March 31, 1989" for "not later than three years after the date such limitations are established".

Subsec. (b)(2)(E). Pub. L. 100-4, Sec. 301(c), substituted "as expeditiously as practicable but in no case later than three years after the date such limitations are promulgated under section 1314(b) of this title, and in no case later than March 31, 1989, compliance with" for "not later than July 1, 1984,".

Subsec. (b)(2)(F). Pub. L. 100-4, Sec. 301(d), substituted "as expeditiously as practicable but in no case" for "not" and "and in no case later than March 31, 1989" for "or not later than July 1, 1984, whichever is later, but in no case later than July 1, 1987".

Subsec. (b)(3). Pub. L. 100-4, Sec. 301(e), added par. (3).

Subsec. (g)(1). Pub. L. 100-4, Sec. 302(a), substituted par. (1) for introductory provisions of former par. (1) which read as follows: "The Administrator, with the concurrence of the State, shall modify the requirements of subsection (b)(2)(A) of this section with respect to the discharge of any pollutant (other than pollutants identified pursuant to section 1314(a)(4) of this title, toxic pollutants subject to section 1317(a) of this title, and the thermal component of discharges) from any point source upon a showing by the owner or operator of such point source satisfactory to the Administrator that—". Subpars (A) to (C) of former par. (1) were redesignated as subpars. (A) to (C) of par. (2).

Subsec. (g)(2). Pub. L. 100-4, Sec. 302(a), (d)(2), inserted introductory provisions of par. (2), and by so doing, redesignated subpars. (A) to (C) of former par. (1) as subpars. (A) to (C) of par. (2), realigned such subpars. with subpar. (A) of par. (4), and redesignated former par. (2) as (3).

Subsec. (g)(3). Pub. L. 100-4, Sec. 302(a), (d)(1), redesignated former par. (2) as (3), inserted heading, and aligned par. (3) with par. (4).

Subsec. (g)(4), (5). Pub. L. 100-4, Sec. 302(b), added pars. (4) and (5).

Subsec. (h). Pub. L. 100-4, Sec. 303(d)(2), (e), in closing provisions, inserted provision defining "primary or equivalent treatment" for purposes of par. (9) and provisions placing limitations on issuance of permits for discharge of pollutant into marine waters and saline estuarine waters and prohibiting issuance of permit for discharge of pollutant into New York Bight Apex.

Subsec. (h)(2). Pub. L. 100-4, Sec. 303(a), substituted "the discharge of pollutants in accordance with such modified requirements will not interfere, alone or in combination with pollutants from other sources," for "such modified requirements will not interfere".

Subsec. (h)(3). Pub. L. 100-4, Sec. 303(b)(1), inserted ", and the scope of such monitoring is limited to include only those scientific investigations which are necessary to study the effects of the proposed discharge" before semicolon at end.

Subsec. (h)(6) to (9). Pub. L. 100-4, Sec. 303(c), (d)(1), added par. (6), redesignated former pars. (6) and (7) as (7) and (8), respectively, substituted semicolon for period at end of par. (8), and added par. (9).

Subsec. (i)(1). Pub. L. 100-4, Sec. 304(a), substituted "February 4, 1987" for "December 27, 1977".

Subsec. (j)(1)(A). Pub. L. 100-4, Sec. 303(f), inserted before semicolon at end ", except that a publicly owned treatment works which prior to December 31, 1982, had a contractual arrangement to use a portion of the capacity of an ocean outfall operated by another publicly owned treatment works which has applied for or received modification under subsection (h) of this section, may apply for a modification of subsection (h) of this section in its own right not later than 30 days after February 4, 1987".

528 / Environmental Statutes

Subsec. (j)(2). Pub. L. 100-4, Sec. 302(c)(1), substituted "Subject to paragraph (3) of this section, any" for "Any".

Subsec. (j)(3), (4). Pub. L. 100-4, Sec. 302(c)(2), added pars. (3) and (4).

Subsec. (k). Pub. L. 100-4, Sec. 305, substituted "two years after the date for compliance with such effluent limitation which would otherwise be applicable under such subsection" for "July 1, 1987" and inserted "or (b)(2)(E)" after "(b)(2)(A)" in two places.

Subsec. (l). Pub. L. 100-4, Sec. 306(b), substituted "Other than as provided in subsection (n) of this section, the" for "The".

Subsecs. (n), (o). Pub. L. 100-4, Sec. 306(a), added subsecs. (n) and (o).

Subsec. (p). Pub. L. 100-4, Sec. 307, added subsec. (p).

1983—Subsec. (m). Pub. L. 97-440 added subsec. (m).

1981—Subsec. (b)(2)(B). Pub. L. 97-117, Sec. 21(b), struck out subpar. (B) which required that, not later than July 1, 1983, compliance by all publicly owned treatment works with the requirements in section 1281(g)(2)(A) of this title be achieved.

Subsec. (h). Pub. L. 97-117, Sec. 22(a) to (c), struck out in provision preceding par. (1) "in an existing discharge" after "discharge of any pollutant", struck out par. (8), which required the applicant to demonstrate to the satisfaction of the Administrator that any funds available to the owner of such treatment works under subchapter II of this chapter be used to achieve the degree of effluent reduction required by section 1281(b) and (g)(2)(A) of this title or to carry out the requirements of this subsection, and inserted in provision following par. (7) a further provision that a municipality which applies secondary treatment be eligible to receive a permit which modifies the requirements of subsec. (b)(1)(B) of this section with respect to the discharge of any pollutant from any treatment works owned by such municipality into marine waters and that no permit issued under this subsection authorize the discharge of sewage sludge into marine waters.

Subsec. (i)(1), (2)(B). Pub. L. 97-117, Sec. 21(a), substituted "July 1, 1988," for "July 1, 1983," wherever appearing. Par. (2)(B) contained a reference to "July 1, 1983;" which was changed to "July 1, 1988;" as the probable intent of Congress in that reference to July 1, 1983, was to the outside date for compliance for a point source other than a publicly owned treatment works and subpar. (B) allows a time extension for such a point source up to the date granted in an extension for a publicly owned treatment works, which date was extended to July 1, 1988, by Pub. L. 97-117.

Subsec. (j)(1)(A). Pub. L. 97-117, Sec. 22(d), substituted "that the 365th day which begins after December 29, 1981" for "than 270 days after December 27, 1977".

1977—Subsec. (b)(2)(A). Pub. L. 95-217, Sec. 42(b), substituted "for pollutants identified in subparagraphs (C), (D), and (F) of this paragraph" for "not later than July 1, 1983".

Subsec. (b)(2)(C) to (F). Pub. L. 95-217, Sec. 42(a), added subpars. (C) to (F).

Subsec. (g). Pub. L. 95-217, Sec. 43, added subsec. (g).

Subsec. (h). Pub. L. 95-217, Sec. 44, added subsec. (h).

Subsec. (i). Pub. L. 95-217, Sec. 45, added subsec. (i).

Subsec. (j). Pub. L. 95-217, Sec. 46, added subsec. (j).

Subsec. (k). Pub. L. 95-217, Sec. 47, added subsec. (k).

Subsec. (l). Pub. L. 95-217, Sec. 53(c), added subsec. (l).

Change of Name

Committee on Public Works and Transportation of House of Representatives treated as referring to Committee on Transportation and Infrastructure of House of Representatives by section 1(a) of Pub. L. 104-14, set out as a note preceding section 21 of Title 2, The Congress.

Effective Date of 1987 Amendment

Section 302(e) of Pub. L. 100-4 provided that:

"(1) General rule.—Except as provided in paragraph (2), the amendments made by this section [amending this section] shall apply to all requests for modifications under section 301(g) of the Federal Water Pollution Control Act [33 U.S.C. 1311(g)] pending on the date of the enactment of this Act [Feb. 4, 1987] and shall not have the effect of extending the deadline established in section 301(j)(1)(B) of such Act.

(2) Exception.—The amendments made by this section shall not affect any application for a modification with respect to the discharge of ammonia, chlorine, color, iron, or total phenols (4AAP) under section 301(g) of the Federal Water Pollution Control Act pending on the date of the enactment of this Act; except that the Administrator must approve or disapprove such application not later than 365 days after the date of such enactment."

Section 303(b)(2) of Pub. L. 100-4 provided that: "The amendment made by subsection (b) [amending this section] shall only apply to modifications and renewals of modifications which are tentatively or finally approved after the date of the enactment of this Act [Feb. 4, 1987]."

Section 303(g) of Pub. L. 100-4 provided that: "The amendments made by subsections (a), (c), (d), and (e) of this section [amending this section] shall not apply to an application for a permit under section 301(h) of the Federal Water Pollution Control Act [33 U.S.C. 1311(h)] which has been tentatively or finally approved by the Administrator before the date of the enactment of this Act [Feb. 4, 1987]; except that such amendments shall apply to all renewals of such permits after such date of enactment."

Section 304(b) of Pub. L. 100-4 provided that: "The amendment made by subsection (a) [amending this section] shall not apply to those treatment works which are subject to a compliance schedule established before the date of the enactment of this Act [Feb. 4, 1987] by a court order or a final administrative order."

Effective Date of 1981 Amendment

Section 22(e) of Pub. L. 97-117 provided that: "The amendments made by this section [amending this section] shall take effect on the date of enactment of this Act [Dec. 29, 1981], except that no applicant, other than the city of Avalon, California, who applies after the date of enactment of this Act for a permit pursuant to subsection (h) of section 301 of the Federal Water Pollution Control Act [33 U.S.C. 1311(h)] which modifies the requirements of subsection (b)(1)(B) of section 301 of such Act [33 U.S.C. 1311(b)(1)(B)] shall receive such permit during the one-year period which begins on the date of enactment of this Act."

Regulations

Section 301(f) of Pub. L. 100-4 provided that: "The Administrator shall promulgate final regulations establishing effluent limitations in accordance with sections 301(b)(2)(A) and 307(b)(1) of the Federal Water Pollution Control Act [33 U.S.C. 1311(b)(2)(A), 1317(b)(1)] for all toxic pollutants referred to in table 1 of Committee Print Numbered 95-30 of the Committee on Public Works and Transportation of the House of Representatives which are discharged from the categories of point sources in accordance with the following table:

Category	Date by which the final regulation shall be promulgated
Organic chemicals and plastics and synthetic fibers............	December 31, 1986.
Pesticides....................................	December 31, 1986."

Phosphate Fertilizer Effluent Limitation

Amendment by section 306(a), (b) of Pub. L. 100-4 not to be construed (A) to require the Administrator to permit the discharge of gypsum or gypsum waste into the navigable waters, (B) to affect the procedures and standards applicable to the Administrator in issuing permits under section 1342(a)(1)(B) of this title, and (C) to affect the authority of any State to deny or condition certification under section 1314 of this title with respect to the issuance of permits under section 1342(a)(1)(B) of this title, see section 306(c) of Pub. L. 100-4, set out as a note under section 1342 of this title.

Discharges From Point Sources in United States Virgin Islands Attributable to Manufacture of Rum; Exemption From Federal Water Pollution Control Requirements; Conditions

Pub. L. 98-67, title II, Sec. 214(g), Aug. 5, 1983, 97 Stat. 393, as amended by Pub. L. 99-514, Sec. 2, Oct. 22, 1986, 100 Stat. 2095, provided that: "Any discharge from a point source in the United States Virgin Islands in existence on the date of the enactment of this subsection [Aug. 5, 1983] which discharge is attributable to the manufacture of rum (as defined in paragraphs (3) of section 7652(c) of the Internal Revenue Code of 1986 [formerly I.R.C. 1954]) [26 U.S.C. 7652(c)(3)] shall not be subject to the requirements of section 301 (other than toxic pollutant discharges), section 306 or section 403 of the Federal Water Pollution Control Act [33 U.S.C. 1311, 1316, 1343] if—

(1) such discharge occurs at least one thousand five hundred feet into the territorial sea from the line of ordinary low water from that portion of the coast which is in direct contact with the sea, and

(2) the Governor of the United States Virgin Islands determines that such discharge will not interfere with the attainment or maintenance of that water quality which shall assure protection of public water supplies, and the protection and propagation of a balanced population of shellfish, fish, and wildlife, and allow recreational activities, in and on the water and will not result in the discharge of pollutants in quantities which may reasonably be anticipated to pose an unacceptable risk to human health or the environment because of bioaccumulation, persistency in the environment, acute toxicity, chronic toxicity (including carcinogenicity, mutagenicity, or teratogenicity), or synergistic propensities."

Certain Municipal Compliance Deadlines Unaffected; Exception

Section 21(a) of Pub. L. 97-117 provided in part that: "The amendment made by this subsection [amending this section] shall not be interpreted or applied to extend the date for compliance with section 301(b)(1)(B) or (C) of the Federal Water Pollution Control Act [33 U.S.C. 1311(b)(1)(B), (C)] beyond schedules for compliance in effect as of the date of enactment of this Act [Dec. 29, 1981], except in cases where reductions in the amount of financial assistance under this Act [Pub. L. 97-117, see Short Title of 1981 Amendment note set out under section 1251 of this title] or changed conditions affecting the rate of construction beyond the control of the owner or operator will make it impossible to complete construction by July 1, 1983."

Territorial Sea of United States

For extension of territorial sea of United States, see Proc. No. 5928, set out as a note under section 1331 of Title 43, Public Lands.

Contiguous Zone of United States

For extension of contiguous zone of United States, see Proc. No. 7219, Sept. 2, 1999, 64 F.R. 48701, set out as a note under section 1331 of Title 43, Public Lands.

Section Referred to in Other Sections

This section is referred to in sections 1255, 1292, 1293a, 1297, 1312, 1313, 1314, 1317, 1319, 1325, 1326, 1341, 1342, 1344, 1365, 1367, 1369 of this title; title 42 section 6925.

WATER QUALITY RELATED EFFLUENT LIMITATIONS

33 USC 1312

(a) Establishment
Whenever, in the judgment of the Administrator or as identified under section 1314(l) of this title, discharges of pollutants from a point source or group of point sources, with the application of effluent limitations required under section 1311(b)(2) of this title, would interfere with the attainment or maintenance of that water quality in a specific portion of the navigable waters which shall assure protection of public health, public water supplies, agricultural and industrial uses, and the protection and propagation of a balanced population of shellfish, fish and wildlife, and allow recreational activities in and on the water, effluent limitations (including alternative effluent control strategies) for such point source or sources shall be established which can reasonably be expected to contribute to the attainment or maintenance of such water quality.

(b) Modifications of effluent limitations
(1) Notice and hearing
Prior to establishment of any effluent limitation pursuant to subsection (a) of this section, the Administrator shall publish such proposed limitation and within 90 days of such publication hold a public hearing.
(2) Permits
(A) No reasonable relationship
The Administrator, with the concurrence of the State, may issue a permit which modifies the effluent limitations required by subsection (a) of this section for pollutants other than toxic pollutants if the applicant demonstrates at such hearing that (whether

or not technology or other alternative control strategies are available) there is no reasonable relationship between the economic and social costs and the benefits to be obtained (including attainment of the objective of this chapter) from achieving such limitation.
(B) Reasonable progress
The Administrator, with the concurrence of the State, may issue a permit which modifies the effluent limitations required by subsection (a) of this section for toxic pollutants for a single period not to exceed 5 years if the applicant demonstrates to the satisfaction of the Administrator that such modified requirements (i) will represent the maximum degree of control within the economic capability of the owner and operator of the source, and (ii) will result in reasonable further progress beyond the requirements of section 1311(b)(2) of this title toward the requirements of subsection (a) of this section.
(c) Delay in application of other limitations
The establishment of effluent limitations under this section shall not operate to delay the application of any effluent limitation established under section 1311 of this title.

(June 30, 1948, ch. 758, title III, Sec. 302, as added Pub. L. 92-500, Sec. 2, Oct. 18, 1972, 86 Stat. 846; amended Pub. L. 100-4, title III, Sec. 308(e), Feb. 4, 1987, 101 Stat. 39.)

Amendments

1987—Subsec. (a). Pub. L. 100-4, Sec. 308(e)(2), inserted "or as identified under section 1314(l) of this title" after "Administrator" and "public health," after "protection of".

Subsec. (b). Pub. L. 100-4, Sec. 308(e)(1), amended subsec. (b) generally. Prior to amendment, subsec. (b) read as follows:

"(1) Prior to establishment of any effluent limitation pursuant to subsection (a) of this section, the Administrator shall issue notice of intent to establish such limitation and within ninety days of such notice hold a public hearing to determine the relationship of the economic and social costs of achieving any such limitation or limitations, including any economic or social dislocation in the affected community or communities, to the social and economic benefits to be obtained (including the attainment of the objective of this chapter) and to determine whether or not such effluent limitations can be implemented with available technology or other alternative control strategies.

(2) If a person affected by such limitation demonstrates at such hearing that (whether or not such technology or other alternative control strategies are available) there is no reasonable relationship between the economic and social costs and the benefits to be obtained (including attainment of the objective of this chapter), such limitation shall not become effective and the Administrator shall adjust such limitation as it applies to such person."

Section Referred to in Other Sections

This section is referred to in sections 1292, 1311, 1313, 1314, 1319, 1341, 1342, 1365, 1367, 1369 of this title.

WATER QUALITY STANDARDS AND IMPLEMENTATION PLANS

33 USC 1313

(a) Existing water quality standards
(1) In order to carry out the purpose of this chapter, any water quality standard applicable to interstate waters which was adopted by any State and submitted to, and approved by, or is a waiting approval by, the Administrator pursuant to this Act as in effect immediately prior to October 18, 1972, shall remain in effect unless the Administrator determined that such standard is not consistent with the applicable requirements of this Act as in effect immediately prior to October 18, 1972. If the Administrator makes such a determination he shall, within three months after October 18, 1972, notify the State and specify the changes needed to meet such requirements. If such changes are not adopted by the State within ninety days after the date of such notification, the Administrator shall promulgate such changes in accordance with subsection (b) of this section.

(2) Any State which, before October 18, 1972, has adopted, pursuant to its own law, water quality standards applicable to intrastate waters shall submit such standards to the Administrator within thirty days after October 18, 1972. Each such standard shall remain in effect, in the same manner and to the same extent as any other water quality standard established under this chapter unless the Administrator determines that such standard is inconsistent with the applicable requirements of this Act as in effect immediately prior to October 18, 1972. If the Administrator makes such a determination he shall not later than the one hundred and twentieth day after the date of submission of such standards, notify the State and specify the changes needed to meet such requirements. If such changes are not adopted by the State within ninety days after such notification, the Administrator shall promulgate such changes in accordance with subsection (b) of this section.

(3) (A) Any State which prior to October 18, 1972, has not adopted pursuant to its own laws water quality standards applicable to intrastate waters shall, not later than one hundred and eighty days after October 18, 1972, adopt and submit such standards to the Administrator.

(B) If the Administrator determines that any such standards are consistent with the applicable requirements of this Act as in effect immediately prior to October 18, 1972, he shall approve such standards.

(C) If the Administrator determines that any such standards are not consistent with the applicable requirements of this Act as in effect immediately prior to October 18, 1972, he shall, not later than the ninetieth day after the date of submission of such standards, notify the State and specify the changes to meet such requirements. If such changes are not adopted by the State within ninety days after the date of notification, the Administrator shall promulgate such standards pursuant to subsection (b) of this section.

(b) Proposed regulations

(1) The Administrator shall promptly prepare and publish proposed regulations setting forth water quality standards for a State in accordance with the applicable requirements of this Act as in effect immediately prior to October 18, 1972, if—

(A) the State fails to submit water quality standards within the times prescribed in subsection (a) of this section.

(B) a water quality standard submitted by such State under subsection (a) of this section is determined by the Administrator not to be consistent with the applicable requirements of subsection (a) of this section.

(2) The Administrator shall promulgate any water quality standard published in a proposed regulation not later than one hundred and ninety days after the date he publishes any such proposed standard, unless prior to such promulgation, such State has adopted a water quality standard which the Administrator determines to be in accordance with subsection (a) of this section.

(c) Review; revised standards; publication

(1) The Governor of a State or the State water pollution control agency of such State shall from time to time (but at least once each three year period beginning with October 18, 1972) hold public hearings for the purpose of reviewing applicable water quality standards and, as appropriate, modifying and adopting standards. Results of such review shall be made available to the Administrator.

(2) (A) Whenever the State revises or adopts a new standard, such revised or new standard shall be submitted to the Administrator. Such revised or new water quality standard shall consist of the designated uses of the navigable waters involved and the water quality criteria for such waters based upon such uses. Such standards shall be such as to protect the public health or welfare, enhance the quality of water and serve the purposes of this chapter. Such standards shall be established taking into consideration their use and value for public water supplies, propagation of fish and wildlife, recreational purposes, and agricultural, industrial, and other purposes, and also taking into consideration their use and value for navigation.

(B) Whenever a State reviews water quality standards pursuant to paragraph (1) of this subsection, or revises or adopts new standards pursuant to this paragraph, such State shall adopt criteria for all toxic pollutants listed pursuant to section 1317(a)(1) of this title for which criteria have been published under section 1314(a) of this title, the discharge or presence of which in the affected waters could reasonably be expected to interfere with those designated uses adopted by the State, as necessary to support such designated uses. Such criteria shall be specific numerical criteria for such toxic pollutants. Where such numerical criteria are not available, whenever a State reviews water quality standards pursuant to paragraph (1), or revises or adopts new standards pursuant to this paragraph, such State shall adopt criteria based on biological monitoring or assessment methods consistent with information published pursuant to section 1314(a)(8) of this title. Nothing in this section shall be construed to limit or delay the use of effluent limitations or other permit conditions based on or involving biological monitoring or assessment methods or previously adopted numerical criteria.

(3) If the Administrator, within sixty days after the date of submission of the revised or new standard, determines that such standard meets the requirements of this chapter, such standard shall thereafter be the water quality standard for the applicable waters of that State. If the Administrator determines that any such revised or new standard is not consistent with the applicable requirements of this chapter, he shall not later than the ninetieth day after the date of submission of such standard notify the State and specify the changes to meet such requirements. If such changes are not adopted by the State within ninety days after the date of notification, the Administrator shall promulgate such standard pursuant to paragraph (4) of this subsection.

(4) The Administrator shall promptly prepare and publish proposed regulations setting forth a revised or new water quality standard for the navigable waters involved—
   (A) if a revised or new water quality standard submitted by such State under paragraph (3) of this subsection for such waters is determined by the Administrator not to be consistent with the applicable requirements of this chapter, or
   (B) in any case where the Administrator determines that a revised or new standard is necessary to meet the requirements of this chapter.

The Administrator shall promulgate any revised or new standard under this paragraph not later than ninety days after he publishes such proposed standards, unless prior to such promulgation, such State has adopted a revised or new water quality standard which the Administrator determines to be in accordance with this chapter.

(d) Identification of areas with insufficient controls; maximum daily load; certain effluent limitations revision

(1) (A) Each State shall identify those waters within its boundaries for which the effluent limitations required by section 1311(b)(1)(A) and section 1311(b)(1)(B) of this title are not stringent enough to implement any water quality standard applicable to such waters. The State shall establish a priority ranking for such waters, taking into account the severity of the pollution and the uses to be made of such waters.

(B) Each State shall identify those waters or parts thereof within its boundaries for which controls on thermal discharges under section 1311 of this title are not stringent enough to assure protection and propagation of a balanced indigenous population of shellfish, fish, and wildlife.

(C) Each State shall establish for the waters identified in paragraph (1)(A) of this subsection, and in accordance with the priority ranking, the total maximum daily load, for those pollutants which the Administrator identifies under section 1314(a)(2) of this title as suitable for such calculation. Such load shall be established at a level necessary to implement the applicable water quality standards with seasonal variations and a margin of safety which takes into account any lack of knowledge concerning the relationship between effluent limitations and water quality.

(D) Each State shall estimate for the waters identified in paragraph (1)(B) of this subsection the total maximum daily thermal load required to assure protection and propagation of a balanced, indigenous population of shellfish, fish, and wildlife. Such estimates shall take into account the normal water temperatures, flow rates, seasonal variations, existing sources of heat input, and the dissipative capacity of the identified waters or parts thereof. Such estimates shall include a calculation of the maximum heat input that can be made into each such part and shall include a margin of safety which takes into account any lack of knowledge concerning the development of thermal water quality criteria for such protection and propagation in the identified waters or parts thereof.

(2) Each State shall submit to the Administrator from time to time, with the first such submission not later than one hundred and eighty days after the date of publication of the first identification of pollutants under section 1314(a)(2)(D) of this title, for his approval the waters identified and the loads established under paragraphs (1)(A), (1)(B), (1)(C), and (1)(D) of this subsection. The Administrator shall either approve or disapprove such identification and load not later than thirty days after the date of submission. If the Administrator approves such identification and load, such State shall incorporate them into its current plan under subsection (e) of this section. If the Administrator disapproves such identification and load, he shall not later than thirty days after the date of such disapproval identify such waters in such State and establish such loads for such waters as he determines necessary to implement the water quality standards applicable to such waters and upon such identification and establishment the State shall incorporate them into its current plan under subsection (e) of this section.
(3) For the specific purpose of developing information, each State shall identify all waters within its boundaries which it has not identified under paragraph (1)(A) and (1)(B) of this subsection and estimate for such waters the total maximum daily load with seasonal variations and margins of safety, for those pollutants which the Administrator identifies under section 1314(a)(2) of this title as suitable for such calculation and for thermal discharges, at a level that would assure protection and propagation of a balanced indigenous population of fish, shellfish, and wildlife.
(4) Limitations on revision of certain effluent limitations.—
   (A) Standard not attained.—For waters identified under paragraph (1)(A) where the applicable water quality standard has not yet been attained, any effluent limitation based on a total maximum daily load or other waste load allocation established under this section may be revised only if (i) the cumulative effect of all such revised effluent limitations based on such total maximum daily load or waste load allocation will assure the attainment of such water quality standard, or (ii) the designated use which is not being attained is removed in accordance with regulations established under this section.
   (B) Standard attained.—For waters identified under paragraph (1)(A) where the quality of such waters equals or exceeds levels necessary to protect the designated use for such waters or otherwise required by applicable water quality standards, any effluent limitation based on a total maximum daily load or other waste load allocation established under this section, or any water quality standard established under this section, or any other permitting standard may be revised only if such revision is subject to and consistent with the antidegradation policy established under this section.

(e) Continuing planning process
   (1) Each State shall have a continuing planning process approved under paragraph (2) of this subsection which is consistent with this chapter.
   (2) Each State shall submit not later than 120 days after October 18, 1972, to the Administrator for his approval a proposed continuing planning process which is consistent with this chapter. Not later than thirty days after the date of submission of such a process the Administrator shall either approve or disapprove such process. The Administrator shall from time to time review each State's approved planning process for the purpose of insuring that such planning process is at all times consistent with this chapter. The Administrator shall not approve any State permit program under subchapter IV of this chapter for any State which does not have an approved continuing planning process under this section.
   (3) The Administrator shall approve any continuing planning process submitted to him under this section which will result in plans for all navigable waters within such State, which include, but are not limited to, the following:
      (A) effluent limitations and schedules of compliance at least as stringent as those required by section 1311(b)(1), section 1311(b)(2), section 1316, and section 1317 of this title, and at least as stringent as any requirements contained in any applicable water quality standard in effect under authority of this section;
      (B) the incorporation of all elements of any applicable area-wide waste management plans under section 1288 of this title, and applicable basin plans under section 1289 of this title;
      (C) total maximum daily load for pollutants in accordance with subsection (d) of this section;

(D) procedures for revision;
(E) adequate authority for intergovernmental cooperation;
(F) adequate implementation, including schedules of compliance, for revised or new water quality standards, under subsection (c) of this section;
(G) controls over the disposition of all residual waste from any water treatment processing;
(H) an inventory and ranking, in order of priority, of needs for construction of waste treatment works required to meet the applicable requirements of sections 1311 and 1312 of this title.

(f) Earlier compliance

Nothing in this section shall be construed to affect any effluent limitation, or schedule of compliance required by any State to be implemented prior to the dates set forth in sections 1311(b)(1) and 1311(b)(2) of this title nor to preclude any State from requiring compliance with any effluent limitation or schedule of compliance at dates earlier than such dates.

(g) Heat standards

Water quality standards relating to heat shall be consistent with the requirements of section 1326 of this title.

(h) Thermal water quality standards

For the purposes of this chapter the term "water quality standards" includes thermal water quality standards.

(i) Coastal recreation water quality criteria
   (1) Adoption by States
      (A) Initial criteria and standards

      Not later than 42 months after October 10, 2000, each State having coastal recreation waters shall adopt and submit to the Administrator water quality criteria and standards for the coastal recreation waters of the State for those pathogens and pathogen indicators for which the Administrator has published criteria under section 1314(a) of this title.

      (B) New or revised criteria and standards

      Not later than 36 months after the date of publication by the Administrator of new or revised water quality criteria under section 1314(a)(9) of this title, each State having coastal recreation waters shall adopt and submit to the Administrator new or revised water quality standards for the coastal recreation waters of the State for all pathogens and pathogen indicators to which the new or revised water quality criteria are applicable.

   (2) Failure of States to adopt
      (A) In general

      If a State fails to adopt water quality criteria and standards in accordance with paragraph (1)(A) that are as protective of human health as the criteria for pathogens and pathogen indicators for coastal recreation waters published by the Administrator, the Administrator shall promptly propose regulations for the State setting forth revised or new water quality standards for pathogens and pathogen indicators described in paragraph (1)(A) for coastal recreation waters of the State.

      (B) Exception

      If the Administrator proposes regulations for a State described in subparagraph (A) under subsection (c)(4)(B) of this section, the Administrator shall publish any revised or new standard under this subsection not later than 42 months after October 10, 2000.

   (3) Applicability

   Except as expressly provided by this subsection, the requirements and procedures of subsection (c) of this section apply to this subsection, including the requirement in subsection (c)(2)(A) of this section that the criteria protect public health and welfare.

(June 30, 1948, ch. 758, title III, Sec. 303, as added Pub. L. 92-500, Sec. 2, Oct. 18, 1972, 86 Stat. 846; amended Pub. L. 100-4, title III, Sec. 308(d), title IV, Sec. 404(b), Feb. 4, 1987, 101 Stat. 39, 68; Pub. L. 106-284, Sec. 2, Oct. 10, 2000, 114 Stat. 870.)

References in Text

This Act, referred to in subsecs. (a)(1), (2), (3)(B), (C) and (b)(1), means act June 30, 1948, ch. 758, 62 Stat. 1155, prior to the supersedure and reenactment of act June 30, 1948 by act Oct. 18, 1972, Pub. L. 92-500, 86 Stat. 816. Act June 30, 1948, ch. 758, as added by act Oct. 18, 1972, Pub. L. 92-500, 86 Stat. 816, enacted this chapter.

Amendments

2000—Subsec. (i). Pub. L. 106-284 added subsec. (i).

1987—Subsec. (c)(2). Pub. L. 100-4, Sec. 308(d), designated existing provision as subpar. (A) and added subpar. (B). Subsec. (d)(4). Pub. L. 100-4, Sec. 404(b), added par. (4).

Section Referred to in Other Sections

This section is referred to in sections 1252, 1284, 1285, 1288, 1311, 1313a, 1314, 1319, 1326, 1329, 1341, 1342, 1362, 1377, 1383, 1384 of this title; title 16 section 1455b; title 42 section 9621.

REVISED WATER QUALITY STANDARDS

33 USC 1313a

The review, revision, and adoption or promulgation of revised or new water quality standards pursuant to section 303(c) of the Federal Water Pollution Control Act [33 U.S.C. 1313(c)] shall be completed by the date three years after December 29, 1981. No grant shall be made under title II of the Federal Water Pollution Control Act [33 U.S.C. 1281 et seq.] after such date until water quality standards are reviewed and revised pursuant to section 303(c), except where the State has in good faith submitted such revised water quality standards and the Administrator has not acted to approve or disapprove such submission within one hundred and twenty days of receipt.

(Pub. L. 97-117, Sec. 24, Dec. 29, 1981, 95 Stat. 1632.)

References in Text

The Federal Water Pollution Control Act, referred to in text, is act June 30, 1948, ch. 758, as amended generally by Pub. L. 92-500, Sec. 2, Oct. 18, 1972, 86 Stat. 816. Title II of the Act is classified generally to subchapter II (Sec. 1281 et seq.) of this chapter. For complete classification of this Act to the Code, see Short Title note set out under section 1251 of this title and Tables.

Codification

Section was enacted as part of the Municipal Wastewater Treatment Construction Grant Amendments of 1981, and not as part of the Federal Water Pollution Control Act which comprises this chapter.

INFORMATION AND GUIDELINES

33 USC 1314

(a) Criteria development and publication
  (1) The Administrator, after consultation with appropriate Federal and State agencies and other interested persons, shall develop and publish, within one year after October 18, 1972 (and from time to time thereafter revise) criteria for water quality accurately reflecting the latest scientific knowledge (A) on the kind and extent of all identifiable effects on health and welfare including, but not limited to, plankton, fish, shellfish, wildlife, plant life, shorelines, beaches, esthetics, and recreation which may be expected from the presence of pollutants in any body of water, including ground water; (B) on the concentration and dispersal of pollutants, or their byproducts, through biological, physical, and chemical processes; and (C) on the effects of pollutants on biological community diversity, productivity, and stability, including information on the factors affecting rates of eutrophication and rates of organic and inorganic sedimentation for varying types of receiving waters.
  (2) The Administrator, after consultation with appropriate Federal and State agencies and other interested persons, shall develop and publish, within one year after October 18, 1972 (and from time to time thereafter revise) information (A) on the factors necessary to re-

store and maintain the chemical, physical, and biological integrity of all navigable waters, ground waters, waters of the contiguous zone, and the oceans; (B) on the factors necessary for the protection and propagation of shellfish, fish, and wildlife for classes and categories of receiving waters and to allow recreational activities in and on the water; and (C) on the measurement and classification of water quality; and (D) for the purpose of section 1313 of this title, on and the identification of pollutants suitable for maximum daily load measurement correlated with the achievement of water quality objectives.
(3) Such criteria and information and revisions thereof shall be issued to the States and shall be published in the Federal Register and otherwise made available to the public.
(4) The Administrator shall, within 90 days after December 27, 1977, and from time to time thereafter, publish and revise as appropriate information identifying conventional pollutants, including but not limited to, pollutants classified as biological oxygen demanding, suspended solids, fecal coliform, and pH. The thermal component of any discharge shall not be identified as a conventional pollutant under this paragraph.
(5) (A) The Administrator, to the extent practicable before consideration of any request under section 1311(g) of this title and within six months after December 27, 1977, shall develop and publish information on the factors necessary for the protection of public water supplies, and the protection and propagation of a balanced population of shellfish, fish and wildlife, and to allow recreational activities, in and on the water.
   (B) The Administrator, to the extent practicable before consideration of any application under section 1311(h) of this title and within six months after December 27, 1977, shall develop and publish information on the factors necessary for the protection of public water supplies, and the protection and propagation of a balanced indigenous population of shellfish, fish and wildlife, and to allow recreational activities, in and on the water.
(6) The Administrator shall, within three months after December 27, 1977, and annually thereafter, for purposes of section 1311(h) of this title publish and revise as appropriate information identifying each water quality standard in effect under this chapter or State law, the specific pollutants associated with such water quality standard, and the particular waters to which such water quality standard applies.
(7) Guidance to states.—The Administrator, after consultation with appropriate State agencies and on the basis of criteria and information published under paragraphs (1) and (2) of this subsection, shall develop and publish, within 9 months after February 4, 1987, guidance to the States on performing the identification required by subsection (l)(1) of this section.
(8) Information on water quality criteria.—The Administrator, after consultation with appropriate State agencies and within 2 years after February 4, 1987, shall develop and publish information on methods for establishing and measuring water quality criteria for toxic pollutants on other bases than pollutant-by-pollutant criteria, including biological monitoring and assessment methods.
(9) Revised criteria for coastal recreation waters.—
   (A) In general.—Not later than 5 years after October 10, 2000, after consultation and in cooperation with appropriate Federal, State, tribal, and local officials (including local health officials), the Administrator shall publish new or revised water quality criteria for pathogens and pathogen indicators (including a revised list of testing methods, as appropriate), based on the results of the studies conducted under section 1254(v) of this title, for the purpose of protecting human health in coastal recreation waters.
   (B) Reviews.—Not later than the date that is 5 years after the date of publication of water quality criteria under this paragraph, and at least once every 5 years thereafter, the Administrator shall review and, as necessary, revise the water quality criteria.
(b) Effluent limitation guidelines
For the purpose of adopting or revising effluent limitations under this chapter the Administrator shall, after consultation with appropriate Federal and State agencies and other interested persons, publish within one year of October 18, 1972, regulations, providing guidelines for effluent limitations, and, at least annually thereafter, revise, if appropriate, such regulations. Such regulations shall—
(1) (A) identify, in terms of amounts of constituents and chemical, physical, and biological characteristics of pollutants, the degree of effluent reduction attainable through the

application of the best practicable control technology currently available for classes and categories of point sources (other than publicly owned treatment works); and
   (B) specify factors to be taken into account in determining the control measures and practices to be applicable to point sources (other than publicly owned treatment works) within such categories or classes. Factors relating to the assessment of best practicable control technology currently available to comply with subsection (b)(1) of section 1311 of this title shall include consideration of the total cost of application of technology in relation to the effluent reduction benefits to be achieved from such application, and shall also take into account the age of equipment and facilities involved, the process employed, the engineering aspects of the application of various types of control techniques, process changes, non-water quality environmental impact (including energy requirements), and such other factors as the Administrator deems appropriate;
(2) (A) identify, in terms of amounts of constituents and chemical, physical, and biological characteristics of pollutants, the degree of effluent reduction attainable through the application of the best control measures and practices achievable including treatment techniques, process and procedure innovations, operating methods, and other alternatives for classes and categories of point sources (other than publicly owned treatment works); and
   (B) specify factors to be taken into account in determining the best measures and practices available to comply with subsection (b)(2) of section 1311 of this title to be applicable to any point source (other than publicly owned treatment works) within such categories or classes. Factors relating to the assessment of best available technology shall take into account the age of equipment and facilities involved, the process employed, the engineering aspects of the application of various types of control techniques, process changes, the cost of achieving such effluent reduction, non-water quality environmental impact (including energy requirements), and such other factors as the Administrator deems appropriate;
(3) identify control measures and practices available to eliminate the discharge of pollutants from categories and classes of point sources, taking into account the cost of achieving such elimination of the discharge of pollutants; and
(4) (A) identify, in terms of amounts of constituents and chemical, physical, and biological characteristics of pollutants, the degree of effluent reduction attainable through the application of the best conventional pollutant control technology (including measures and practices) for classes and categories of point sources (other than publicly owned treatment works); and
   (B) specify factors to be taken into account in determining the best conventional pollutant control technology measures and practices to comply with section 1311(b)(2)(E) of this title to be applicable to any point source (other than publicly owned treatment works) within such categories or classes. Factors relating to the assessment of best conventional pollutant control technology (including measures and practices) shall include consideration of the reasonableness of the relationship between the costs of attaining a reduction in effluents and the effluent reduction benefits derived, and the comparison of the cost and level of reduction of such pollutants from the discharge from publicly owned treatment works to the cost and level of reduction of such pollutants from a class or category of industrial sources, and shall take into account the age of equipment and facilities involved, the process employed, the engineering aspects of the application of various types of control techniques, process changes, non-water quality environmental impact (including energy requirements), and such other factors as the Administrator deems appropriate.

(c) Pollution discharge elimination procedures

The Administrator, after consultation, with appropriate Federal and State agencies and other interested persons, shall issue to the States and appropriate water pollution control agencies within 270 days after October 18, 1972 (and from time to time thereafter) information on the processes, procedures, or operating methods which result in the elimination or reduction of the discharge of pollutants to implement standards of performance under section 1316 of this title. Such information shall include technical and other data, including costs, as are available on alternative methods of elimination or reduction of the discharge of pollutants. Such infor-

mation, and revisions thereof, shall be published in the Federal Register and otherwise shall be made available to the public.
(d) Secondary treatment information; alternative waste treatment management techniques; innovative and alternative wastewater treatment processes; facilities deemed equivalent of secondary treatment
   (1) The Administrator, after consultation with appropriate Federal and State agencies and other interested persons, shall publish within sixty days after October 18, 1972 (and from time to time thereafter) information, in terms of amounts of constituents and chemical, physical, and biological characteristics of pollutants, on the degree of effluent reduction attainable through the application of secondary treatment.
   (2) The Administrator, after consultation with appropriate Federal and State agencies and other interested persons, shall publish within nine months after October 18, 1972 (and from time to time thereafter) information on alternative waste treatment management techniques and systems available to implement section 1281 of this title.
   (3) The Administrator, after consultation with appropriate Federal and State agencies and other interested persons, shall promulgate within one hundred and eighty days after December 27, 1977, guidelines for identifying and evaluating innovative and alternative wastewater treatment processes and techniques referred to in section 1281(g)(5) of this title.
   (4) For the purposes of this subsection, such biological treatment facilities as oxidation ponds, lagoons, and ditches and trickling filters shall be deemed the equivalent of secondary treatment. The Administrator shall provide guidance under paragraph (1) of this subsection on design criteria for such facilities, taking into account pollutant removal efficiencies and, consistent with the objectives of this chapter, assuring that water quality will not be adversely affected by deeming such facilities as the equivalent of secondary treatment.
(e) Best management practices for industry
   The Administrator, after consultation with appropriate Federal and State agencies and other interested persons, may publish regulations, supplemental to any effluent limitations specified under subsections (b) and (c) of this section for a class or category of point sources, for any specific pollutant which the Administrator is charged with a duty to regulate as a toxic or hazardous pollutant under section 1317(a)(1) or 1321 of this title, to control plant site runoff, spillage or leaks, sludge or waste disposal, and drainage from raw material storage which the Administrator determines are associated with or ancillary to the industrial manufacturing or treatment process within such class or category of point sources and may contribute significant amounts of such pollutants to navigable waters. Any applicable controls established under this subsection shall be included as a requirement for the purposes of section 1311, 1312, 1316, 1317, or 1343 of this title, as the case may be, in any permit issued to a point source pursuant to section 1342 of this title.
(f) Identification and evaluation of nonpoint sources of pollution; processes, procedures, and methods to control pollution
   The Administrator, after consultation with appropriate Federal and State agencies and other interested persons, shall issue to appropriate Federal agencies, the States, water pollution control agencies, and agencies designated under section 1288 of this title, within one year after October 18, 1972 (and from time to time thereafter) information including (1) guidelines for identifying and evaluating the nature and extent of nonpoint sources of pollutants, and (2) processes, procedures, and methods to control pollution resulting from—
   (A) agricultural and silvicultural activities, including runoff from fields and crop and forest lands;
   (B) mining activities, including runoff and siltation from new, currently operating, and abandoned surface and underground mines;
   (C) all construction activity, including runoff from the facilities resulting from such construction;
   (D) the disposal of pollutants in wells or in subsurface excavations;
   (E) salt water intrusion resulting from reductions of fresh water flow from any cause, including extraction of ground water, irrigation, obstruction, and diversion; and
   (F) changes in the movement, flow, or circulation of any navigable waters or ground waters, including changes caused by the construction of dams, levees, channels, causeways, or flow diversion facilities.

Such information and revisions thereof shall be published in the Federal Register and otherwise made available to the public.

(g) Guidelines for pretreatment of pollutants
  (1) For the purpose of assisting States in carrying out programs under section 1342 of this title, the Administrator shall publish, within one hundred and twenty days after October 18, 1972, and review at least annually thereafter and, if appropriate, revise guidelines for pretreatment of pollutants which he determines are not susceptible to treatment by publicly owned treatment works. Guidelines under this subsection shall be established to control and prevent the discharge into the navigable waters, the contiguous zone, or the ocean (either directly or through publicly owned treatment works) of any pollutant which interferes with, passes through, or otherwise is incompatible with such works.
  (2) When publishing guidelines under this subsection, the Administrator shall designate the category or categories of treatment works to which the guidelines shall apply.

(h) Test procedures guidelines
  The Administrator shall, within one hundred and eighty days from October 18, 1972, promulgate guidelines establishing test procedures for the analysis of pollutants that shall include the factors which must be provided in any certification pursuant to section 1341 of this title or permit application pursuant to section 1342 of this title.

(i) Guidelines for monitoring, reporting, enforcement, funding, personnel, and manpower
  The Administrator shall (1) within sixty days after October 18, 1972, promulgate guidelines for the purpose of establishing uniform application forms and other minimum requirements for the acquisition of information from owners and operators of point-sources of discharge subject to any State program under section 1342 of this title, and (2) within sixty days from October 18, 1972, promulgate guidelines establishing the minimum procedural and other elements of any State program under section 1342 of this title, which shall include:
    (A) monitoring requirements;
    (B) reporting requirements (including procedures to make information available to the public);
    (C) enforcement provisions; and
    (D) funding, personnel qualifications, and manpower requirements (including a requirement that no board or body which approves permit applications or portions thereof shall include, as a member, any person who receives, or has during the previous two years received, a significant portion of his income directly or indirectly from permit holders or applicants for a permit).

(j) Lake restoration guidance manual
  The Administrator shall, within 1 year after February 4, 1987, and biennially thereafter, publish and disseminate a lake restoration guidance manual describing methods, procedures, and processes to guide State and local efforts to improve, restore, and enhance water quality in the Nation's publicly owned lakes.

(k) Agreements with Secretaries of Agriculture, Army, and the Interior to provide maximum utilization of programs to achieve and maintain water quality; transfer of funds; authorization of appropriations
  (1) The Administrator shall enter into agreements with the Secretary of Agriculture, the Secretary of the Army, and the Secretary of the Interior, and the heads of such other departments, agencies, and instrumentalities of the United States as the Administrator determines, to provide for the maximum utilization of other Federal laws and programs for the purpose of achieving and maintaining water quality through appropriate implementation of plans approved under section 1288 of this title and nonpoint source pollution management programs approved under section 1329 of this title.
  (2) The Administrator is authorized to transfer to the Secretary of Agriculture, the Secretary of the Army, and the Secretary of the Interior and the heads of such other departments, agencies, and instrumentalities of the United States as the Administrator determines, any funds appropriated under paragraph (3) of this subsection to supplement funds otherwise appropriated to programs authorized pursuant to any agreement under paragraph (1).
  (3) There is authorized to be appropriated to carry out the provisions of this subsection, $100,000,000 per fiscal year for the fiscal years 1979 through 1983 and such sums as may be necessary for fiscal years 1984 through 1990.

(l) Individual control strategies for toxic pollutants
   (1) State list of navigable waters and development of strategies
      Not later than 2 years after February 4, 1987, each State shall submit to the Administrator for review, approval, and implementation under this subsection—
      (A) a list of those waters within the State which after the application of effluent limitations required under section 1311(b)(2) of this title cannot reasonably be anticipated to attain or maintain (i) water quality standards for such waters reviewed, revised, or adopted in accordance with section 1313(c)(2)(B) of this title, due to toxic pollutants, or (ii) that water quality which shall assure protection of public health, public water supplies, agricultural and industrial uses, and the protection and propagation of a balanced population of shellfish, fish and wildlife, and allow recreational activities in and on the water;
      (B) a list of all navigable waters in such State for which the State does not expect the applicable standard under section 1313 of this title will be achieved after the requirements of sections 1311(b), 1316, and 1317(b) of this title are met, due entirely or substantially to discharges from point sources of any toxic pollutants listed pursuant to section 1317(a) of this title;
      (C) for each segment of the navigable waters included on such lists, a determination of the specific point sources discharging any such toxic pollutant which is believed to be preventing or impairing such water quality and the amount of each such toxic pollutant discharged by each such source; and
      (D) for each such segment, an individual control strategy which the State determines will produce a reduction in the discharge of toxic pollutants from point sources identified by the State under this paragraph through the establishment of effluent limitations under section 1342 of this title and water quality standards under section 1313(c)(2)(B) of this title, which reduction is sufficient, in combination with existing controls on point and nonpoint sources of pollution, to achieve the applicable water quality standard as soon as possible, but not later than 3 years after the date of the establishment of such strategy.
   (2) Approval or disapproval
      Not later than 120 days after the last day of the 2-year period referred to in paragraph (1), the Administrator shall approve or disapprove the control strategies submitted under paragraph (1) by any State.
   (3) Administrator's action
      If a State fails to submit control strategies in accordance with paragraph (1) or the Administrator does not approve the control strategies submitted by such State in accordance with paragraph (1), then, not later than 1 year after the last day of the period referred to in paragraph (2), the Administrator, in cooperation with such State and after notice and opportunity for public comment, shall implement the requirements of paragraph (1) in such State. In the implementation of such requirements, the Administrator shall, at a minimum, consider for listing under this subsection any navigable waters for which any person submits a petition to the Administrator for listing not later than 120 days after such last day.

(m) Schedule for review of guidelines
   (1) Publication
      Within 12 months after February 4, 1987, and biennially thereafter, the Administrator shall publish in the Federal Register a plan which shall—
      (A) establish a schedule for the annual review and revision of promulgated effluent guidelines, in accordance with subsection (b) of this section;
      (B) identify categories of sources discharging toxic or nonconventional pollutants for which guidelines under subsection (b)(2) of this section and section 1316 of this title have not previously been published; and
      (C) establish a schedule for promulgation of effluent guidelines for categories identified in subparagraph (B), under which promulgation of such guidelines shall be no later than 4 years after February 4, 1987, for categories identified in the first published plan or 3 years after the publication of the plan for categories identified in later published plans.

(2) Public review
The Administrator shall provide for public review and comment on the plan prior to final publication.

(June 30, 1948, ch. 758, title III, Sec. 304, as added Pub. L. 92-500, Sec. 2, Oct. 18, 1972, 86 Stat. 850; amended Pub. L. 95-217, Secs. 48-51, 62(b), Dec. 27, 1977, 91 Stat. 1587, 1588, 1598; Pub. L. 97-117, Sec. 23, Dec. 29, 1981, 95 Stat. 1632; Pub. L. 100-4, title I, Sec. 101(f), title III, Secs. 308(a), (c), (f), 315(c), 316(e), Feb. 4, 1987, 101 Stat. 9, 38-40, 52, 61; Pub. L. 106-284, Sec. 3(b), Oct. 10, 2000, 114 Stat. 871.)

Codification

Section 50 of Pub. L. 95-217 provided in part that, upon the enactment of subsec. (e) of this section by Pub. L. 95-217 and the concurrent redesignation of former subsecs. (e) to (j) of this section as (f) to (k), respectively, all references to former subsecs. (e) to (j) be changed to (f) to (k), respectively.

Amendments

2000—Subsec. (a)(9). Pub. L. 106-284 added par. (9).

1987—Subsec. (a)(7), (8). Pub. L. 100-4, Sec. 308(c), added pars. (7) and (8). Subsec. (j). Pub. L. 100-4, Sec. 315(c), amended subsec. (j) generally. Prior to amendment, subsec. (j) read as follows: "The Administrator shall issue information biennially on methods, procedures, and processes as may be appropriate to restore and enhance the quality of the Nation's publicly owned freshwater lakes."

Subsec. (k)(1). Pub. L. 100-4, Sec. 316(e), inserted "and nonpoint source pollution management programs approved under section 1329 of this title" before period at end. Subsec. (k)(3). Pub. L. 100-4, Sec. 101(f), inserted "and such sums as may be necessary for fiscal years 1984 through 1990" after "1983". Subsec. (l). Pub. L. 100-4, Sec. 308(a), added subsec. (l). Subsec. (m). Pub. L. 100-4, Sec. 308(f), added subsec. (m).

1981—Subsec. (d)(4). Pub. L. 97-117 added par. (4).

1977—Subsec. (a)(4) to (6). Pub. L. 95-217, Sec. 48(a), added pars. (4) to (6). Subsec. (b)(4). Pub. L. 95-217, Sec. 48(b), added par. (4). Subsec. (d)(3). Pub. L. 95-217, Sec. 49, added par. (3). Subsecs. (e) to (i). Pub. L. 95-217, Sec. 50, added subsec. (e) and redesignated former subsecs. (e) to (h) as (f) to (i), respectively. Former subsec. (i) redesignated (j). Subsec. (j). Pub. L. 95-217, Secs. 50, 62(b), redesignated former subsec. (i) as (j) and substituted "shall issue information biennially on methods" for "shall, within 270 days after October 18, 1972 (and from time to time thereafter), issue such information on methods". Former subsec. (j) redesignated (k). Subsec. (k). Pub. L. 95-217, Secs. 50, 51, redesignated former subsec. (j) as (k), substituted "The Administrator shall enter into agreements with the Secretary of Agriculture, the Secretary of the Army, and the Secretary of the Interior, and the heads of such other departments, agencies, and instrumentalities of the United States as the Administrator determines, to provide the maximum utilization of other Federal laws and programs" for "The Administrator shall, within six months from October 18, 1972, enter into agreements with the Secretary of Agriculture, the Secretary of the Army, and the Secretary of the Interior to provide for the maximum utilization of the appropriate programs authorized under other Federal law to be carried out by such Secretaries" in par. (1), made conforming amendments in par. (2), and in par. (3) authorized appropriations for fiscal years 1979 through 1983.

Transfer of Functions

Enforcement functions of Secretary or other official in Department of Agriculture, insofar as they involve lands and programs under jurisdiction of that Department, relating to compliance with this chapter with respect to pre-construction, construction, and initial operation of transportation system for Canadian and Alaskan natural gas were transferred to the Federal Inspector, Office of Federal Inspector for the Alaska Natural Gas Transportation System, until the first anniversary of the date of initial operation of the Alaska Natural Gas Transportation System, see Reorg. Plan No. 1 of 1979, Secs. 102(f), 203(a), 44 F.R. 33663, 33666, 93 Stat. 1373, 1376, effective July 1, 1979, set out in the Appendix to Title 5, Government Organization and Employees. Office of Federal Inspector for the Alaska Natural Gas Transportation System abolished and functions and authority vested in Inspector transferred to Secretary of Energy by section 3012(b) of Pub. L. 102-486, set out as an Abolition of Office of Federal Inspector note under section 719e of Title 15, Commerce and Trade.

Clean Water Act / 543

Review of Effluent Guidelines Promulgated Prior to December 27, 1977

Section 73 of Pub. L. 95-217 directed Administrator, within 90 days after Dec. 27, 1977, to review every effluent guideline promulgated prior to that date which was final or interim final (other than those applicable to industrial categories listed in table 2 of Committee Print Numbered 95-30 of Committee on Public Works and Transportation of House of Representatives) and which applied to those pollutants identified pursuant to 33 U.S.C. 1314(a)(4) and, on or before July 1, 1980, to review every guideline applicable to industrial categories listed in such table 2, authorized Administrator, upon completion of each such review to make such adjustments in any such guidelines as may be necessary to carry out 33 U.S.C. 1314(b)(4), directed Administrator to publish the results of each such review, and provided for judicial review of Administrator's actions.

Contiguous Zone of United States

For extension of contiguous zone of United States, see Proc. No. 7219, set out as a note under section 1331 of Title 43, Public Lands.

Section Referred to in Other Sections

This section is referred to in sections 1254, 1255, 1281, 1284, 1288, 1292, 1311, 1312, 1313, 1315, 1317, 1322, 1323, 1329, 1342, 1344, 1369, 1376, 2408 of this title; title 42 sections 6925, 9621.

STATE REPORTS ON WATER QUALITY; TRANSMITTAL TO CONGRESS

33 USC 1315

(a) Omitted
(b) (1) Each State shall prepare and submit to the Administrator by April 1, 1975, and shall bring up to date by April 1, 1976, and biennially thereafter, a report which shall include—
    (A) a description of the water quality of all navigable waters in such State during the preceding year, with appropriate supplemental descriptions as shall be required to take into account seasonal, tidal, and other variations, correlated with the quality of water required by the objective of this chapter (as identified by the Administrator pursuant to criteria published under section 1314(a) of this title) and the water quality described in subparagraph (B) of this paragraph;
    (B) an analysis of the extent to which all navigable waters of such State provide for the protection and propagation of a balanced population of shellfish, fish, and wildlife, and allow recreational activities in and on the water;
    (C) an analysis of the extent to which the elimination of the discharge of pollutants and a level of water quality which provides for the protection and propagation of a balanced population of shellfish, fish, and wildlife and allows recreational activities in and on the water, have been or will be achieved by the requirements of this chapter, together with recommendations as to additional action necessary to achieve such objectives and for what waters such additional action is necessary;
    (D) an estimate of (i) the environmental impact, (ii) the economic and social costs necessary to achieve the objective of this chapter in such State, (iii) the economic and social benefits of such achievement, and (iv) an estimate of the date of such achievement; and
    (E) a description of the nature and extent of nonpoint sources of pollutants, and recommendations as to the programs which must be undertaken to control each category of such sources, including an estimate of the costs of implementing such programs.
(2) The Administrator shall transmit such State reports, together with an analysis thereof, to Congress on or before October 1, 1975, and October 1, 1976, and biennially thereafter.

(June 30, 1948, ch. 758, title III, Sec. 305, as added Pub. L. 92-500, Sec. 2, Oct. 18, 1972, 86 Stat. 853; amended Pub. L. 95-217, Sec. 52, Dec. 27, 1977, 91 Stat. 1589.)

Codification

Subsec. (a) authorized the Administrator, in cooperation with the States and Federal agencies, to prepare a report describing the specific quality, during 1973, of all navigable waters and waters of the contiguous zone, including an inventory of all point sources of discharge of pollutants into these waters, and identifying those navigable waters capable of supporting fish and wildlife populations and allowing recreational activities, those which could reasonably be expected to attain this level by 1977 or 1983, and those which could attain this level sooner, and submit this report to Congress on or before Jan. 1, 1974.

Amendments

1977—Subsec. (b)(1). Pub. L. 95-217, Sec. 52(1), substituted "April 1, 1975, and shall bring up to date by April 1, 1976, and biennially thereafter" for "January 1, 1975, and shall bring up to date each year thereafter" in provisions preceding subpar. (A).

Subsec. (b)(2). Pub. L. 95-217, Sec. 52(2), substituted "on or before October 1, 1975, and October 1, 1976, and biennially thereafter" for "on or before October 1, 1975, and annually thereafter".

Section Referred to in Other Sections

This section is referred to in sections 1284, 1311, 1313, 1314, 1317, 1319, 1323, 1324, 1326, 1329, 1341, 1342, 1365, 1367, 1369, 1371, 1374, 1377 of this title.

NATIONAL STANDARDS OF PERFORMANCE

33 USC 1316

(a) Definitions

For purposes of this section:
 (1) The term "standard of performance" means a standard for the control of the discharge of pollutants which reflect the greatest degree of effluent reduction which the Administrator determines to be achievable through application of the best available demonstrated control technology, processes, operating methods, or other alternatives, including, where practicable, a standard permitting no discharge of pollutants.
 (2) The term "new source" means any source, the construction of which is commenced after the publication of proposed regulations prescribing a standard of performance under this section which will be applicable to such source, if such standard is thereafter promulgated in accordance with this section.
 (3) The term "source" means any building, structure, facility, or installation from which there is or may be the discharge of pollutants.
 (4) The term "owner or operator" means any person who owns, leases, operates, controls, or supervises a source.
 (5) The term "construction" means any placement, assembly, or installation of facilities or equipment (including contractual obligations to purchase such facilities or equipment) at the premises where such equipment will be used, including preparation work at such premises.

(b) Categories of sources; Federal standards of performance for new sources
 (1) (A) The Administrator shall, within ninety days after October 18, 1972, publish (and from time to time thereafter shall revise) a list of categories of sources, which shall, at the minimum, include:
   pulp and paper mills;
   paperboard, builders paper and board mills;
   meat product and rendering processing;
   dairy product processing;
   grain mills;
   canned and preserved fruits and vegetables processing;
   canned and preserved seafood processing;
   sugar processing;
   textile mills;
   cement manufacturing;
   feedlots;
   electroplating;
   organic chemicals manufacturing;
   inorganic chemicals manufacturing;

plastic and synthetic materials manufacturing;
soap and detergent manufacturing;
fertilizer manufacturing;
petroleum refining;
iron and steel manufacturing;
nonferrous metals manufacturing;
phosphate manufacturing;
steam electric powerplants;
ferroalloy manufacturing;
leather tanning and finishing;
glass and asbestos manufacturing;
rubber processing; and
timber products processing.

(B) As soon as practicable, but in no case more than one year, after a category of sources is included in a list under subparagraph (A) of this paragraph, the Administrator shall propose and publish regulations establishing Federal standards of performance for new sources within such category. The Administrator shall afford interested persons an opportunity for written comment on such proposed regulations. After considering such comments, he shall promulgate, within one hundred and twenty days after publication of such proposed regulations, such standards with such adjustments as he deems appropriate. The Administrator shall, from time to time, as technology and alternatives change, revise such standards following the procedure required by this subsection for promulgation of such standards. Standards of performance, or revisions thereof, shall become effective upon promulgation. In establishing or revising Federal standards of performance for new sources under this section, the Administrator shall take into consideration the cost of achieving such effluent reduction, and any non-water quality, environmental impact and energy requirements.

(2) The Administrator may distinguish among classes, types, and sizes within categories of new sources for the purpose of establishing such standards and shall consider the type of process employed (including whether batch or continuous).

(3) The provisions of this section shall apply to any new source owned or operated by the United States.

(c) State enforcement of standards of performance
Each State may develop and submit to the Administrator a procedure under State law for applying and enforcing standards of performance for new sources located in such State. If the Administrator finds that the procedure and the law of any State require the application and enforcement of standards of performance to at least the same extent as required by this section, such State is authorized to apply and enforce such standards of performance (except with respect to new sources owned or operated by the United States).

(d) Protection from more stringent standards
Notwithstanding any other provision of this chapter, any point source the construction of which is commenced after October 18, 1972, and which is so constructed as to meet all applicable standards of performance shall not be subject to any more stringent standard of performance during a ten-year period beginning on the date of completion of such construction or during the period of depreciation or amortization of such facility for the purposes of section 167 or 169 (or both) of title 26 whichever period ends first.

(e) Illegality of operation of new sources in violation of applicable standards of performance
After the effective date of standards of performance promulgated under this section, it shall be unlawful for any owner or operator of any new source to operate such source in violation of any standard of performance applicable to such source.

(June 30, 1948, ch. 758, title III, Sec. 306, as added Pub. L. 92-500, Sec. 2, Oct. 18, 1972, 86 Stat. 854.)

Discharges From Point Sources in United States Virgin Islands Attributable to Manufacture of Rum; Exemption; Conditions

Discharges from point sources in the United States Virgin Islands in existence on Aug. 5, 1983, attributable to the manufacture of rum not to be subject to the requirements of this section under

546 / Environmental Statutes

certain conditions, see section 214(g) of Pub. L. 98-67, set out as a note under section 1311 of this title.

Section Referred to in Other Sections

This section is referred to in sections 1311, 1313, 1314, 1317, 1319, 1323, 1326, 1341, 1342, 1365, 1367, 1369, 1371, 1374 of this title; title 42 section 6925.

TOXIC AND PRETREATMENT EFFLUENT STANDARDS

33 USC 1317

(a) Toxic pollutant list; revision; hearing; promulgation of standards; effective date; consultation
   (1) On and after December 27, 1977, the list of toxic pollutants or combination of pollutants subject to this chapter shall consist of those toxic pollutants listed in table 1 of Committee Print Numbered 95-30 of the Committee on Public Works and Transportation of the House of Representatives, and the Administrator shall publish, not later than the thirtieth day after December 27, 1977, that list. From time to time thereafter, the Administrator may revise such list and the Administrator is authorized to add to or remove from such list any pollutant. The Administrator in publishing any revised list, including the addition or removal of any pollutant from such list, shall take into account toxicity of the pollutant, its persistence, degradability, the usual or potential presence of the affected organisms in any waters, the importance of the affected organisms, and the nature and extent of the effect of the toxic pollutant on such organisms. A determination of the Administrator under this paragraph shall be final except that if, on judicial review, such determination was based on arbitrary and capricious action of the Administrator, the Administrator shall make a redetermination.
   (2) Each toxic pollutant listed in accordance with paragraph (1) of this subsection shall be subject to effluent limitations resulting from the application of the best available technology economically achievable for the applicable category or class of point sources established in accordance with sections 1311(b)(2)(A) and 1314(b)(2) of this title. The Administrator, in his discretion, may publish in the Federal Register a proposed effluent standard (which may include a prohibition) establishing requirements for a toxic pollutant which, if an effluent limitation is applicable to a class or category of point sources, shall be applicable to such category or class only if such standard imposes more stringent requirements. Such published effluent standard (or prohibition) shall take into account the toxicity of the pollutant, its persistence, degradability, the usual or potential presence of the affected organisms in any waters, the importance of the affected organisms and the nature and extent of the effect of the toxic pollutant on such organisms, and the extent to which effective control is being or may be achieved under other regulatory authority. The Administrator shall allow a period of not less than sixty days following publication of any such proposed effluent standard (or prohibition) for written comment by interested persons on such proposed standard. In addition, if within thirty days of publication of any such proposed effluent standard (or prohibition) any interested person so requests, the Administrator shall hold a public hearing in connection therewith. Such a public hearing shall provide an opportunity for oral and written presentations, such cross-examination as the Administrator determines is appropriate on disputed issues of material fact, and the transcription of a verbatim record which shall be available to the public. After consideration of such comments and any information and material presented at any public hearing held on such proposed standard or prohibition, the Administrator shall promulgate such standard (or prohibition) with such modification as the Administrator finds are justified. Such promulgation by the Administrator shall be made within two hundred and seventy days after publication of proposed standard (or prohibition). Such standard (or prohibition) shall be final except that if, on judicial review, such standard was not based on substantial evidence, the Administrator shall promulgate a revised standard. Effluent limitations shall be established in accordance with sections 1311(b)(2)(A) and 1314(b)(2) of this title for every toxic pollutant referred to in table 1 of Committee Print Numbered 95-30 of the Committee on Public Works and Transportation of the House of Representatives as soon as practicable after December 27, 1977, but no later than July 1, 1980. Such

effluent limitations or effluent standards (or prohibitions) shall be established for every other toxic pollutant listed under paragraph (1) of this subsection as soon as practicable after it is so listed.
  (3) Each such effluent standard (or prohibition) shall be reviewed and, if appropriate, revised at least every three years.
  (4) Any effluent standard promulgated under this section shall be at that level which the Administrator determines provides an ample margin of safety.
  (5) When proposing or promulgating any effluent standard (or prohibition) under this section, the Administrator shall designate the category or categories of sources to which the effluent standard (or prohibition) shall apply. Any disposal of dredged material may be included in such a category of sources after consultation with the Secretary of the Army.
  (6) Any effluent standard (or prohibition) established pursuant to this section shall take effect on such date or dates as specified in the order promulgating such standard, but in no case, more than one year from the date of such promulgation. If the Administrator determines that compliance within one year from the date of promulgation is technologically infeasible for a category of sources, the Administrator may establish the effective date of the effluent standard (or prohibition) for such category at the earliest date upon which compliance can be feasibly attained by sources within such category, but in no event more than three years after the date of such promulgation.
  (7) Prior to publishing any regulations pursuant to this section the Administrator shall, to the maximum extent practicable within the time provided, consult with appropriate advisory committees, States, independent experts, and Federal departments and agencies.
(b) Pretreatment standards; hearing; promulgation; compliance period; revision; application to State and local laws
  (1) The Administrator shall, within one hundred and eighty days after October 18, 1972, and from time to time thereafter, publish proposed regulations establishing pretreatment standards for introduction of pollutants into treatment works (as defined in section 1292 of this title) which are publicly owned for those pollutants which are determined not to be susceptible to treatment by such treatment works or which would interfere with the operation of such treatment works. Not later than ninety days after such publication, and after opportunity for public hearing, the Administrator shall promulgate such pretreatment standards. Pretreatment standards under this subsection shall specify a time for compliance not to exceed three years from the date of promulgation and shall be established to prevent the discharge of any pollutant through treatment works (as defined in section 1292 of this title) which are publicly owned, which pollutant interferes with, passes through, or otherwise is incompatible with such works. If, in the case of any toxic pollutant under subsection (a) of this section introduced by a source into a publicly owned treatment works, the treatment by such works removes all or any part of such toxic pollutant and the discharge from such works does not violate that effluent limitation or standard which would be applicable to such toxic pollutant if it were discharged by such source other than through a publicly owned treatment works, and does not prevent sludge use or disposal by such works in accordance with section 1345 of this title, then the pretreatment requirements for the sources actually discharging such toxic pollutant into such publicly owned treatment works may be revised by the owner or operator of such works to reflect the removal of such toxic pollutant by such works.
  (2) The Administrator shall, from time to time, as control technology, processes, operating methods, or other alternatives change, revise such standards following the procedure established by this subsection for promulgation of such standards.
  (3) When proposing or promulgating any pretreatment standard under this section, the Administrator shall designate the category or categories of sources to which such standard shall apply.
  (4) Nothing in this subsection shall affect any pretreatment requirement established by any State or local law not in conflict with any pretreatment standard established under this subsection.
(c) New sources of pollutants into publicly owned treatment works
  In order to insure that any source introducing pollutants into a publicly owned treatment works, which source would be a new source subject to section 1316 of this title if it were to

discharge pollutants, will not cause a violation of the effluent limitations established for any such treatment works, the Administrator shall promulgate pretreatment standards for the category of such sources simultaneously with the promulgation of standards of performance under section 1316 of this title for the equivalent category of new sources. Such pretreatment standards shall prevent the discharge of any pollutant into such treatment works, which pollutant may interfere with, pass through, or otherwise be incompatible with such works.

(d) Operation in violation of standards unlawful

After the effective date of any effluent standard or prohibition or pretreatment standard promulgated under this section, it shall be unlawful for any owner or operator of any source to operate any source in violation of any such effluent standard or prohibition or pretreatment standard.

(e) Compliance date extension for innovative pretreatment systems

In the case of any existing facility that proposes to comply with the pretreatment standards of subsection (b) of this section by applying an innovative system that meets the requirements of section 1311(k) of this title, the owner or operator of the publicly owned treatment works receiving the treated effluent from such facility may extend the date for compliance with the applicable pretreatment standard established under this section for a period not to exceed 2 years—

(1) if the Administrator determines that the innovative system has the potential for industrywide application, and

(2) if the Administrator (or the State in consultation with the Administrator, in any case in which the State has a pretreatment program approved by the Administrator)—

(A) determines that the proposed extension will not cause the publicly owned treatment works to be in violation of its permit under section 1342 of this title or of section 1345 of this title or to contribute to such a violation, and

(B) concurs with the proposed extension.

(June 30, 1948, ch. 758, title III, Sec. 307, as added Pub. L. 92-500, Sec. 2, Oct. 18, 1972, 86 Stat. 856; amended Pub. L. 95-217, Secs. 53(a), (b), 54(a), Dec. 27, 1977, 91 Stat. 1589-1591; Pub. L. 100-4, title III, Sec. 309(a), Feb. 4, 1987, 101 Stat. 41.)

Amendments

1987—Subsec. (e). Pub. L. 100-4 added subsec. (e).

1977—Subsec. (a)(1). Pub. L. 95-217, Sec. 53(a), substituted "On and after December 27, 1977, the list of toxic pollutants or combination of pollutants subject to this chapter shall consist of those toxic pollutants listed in table 1 of Committee Print Numbered 95-30 of the Committee on Public Works and Transportation of the House of Representatives, and the Administrator shall publish, not later than the thirtieth day after December 27, 1977, that list" for "The Administrator shall, within ninety days after October 18, 1972, publish (and from time to time thereafter revise) a list which includes any toxic pollutant or combination of such pollutants for which an effluent standard (which may include a prohibition of the discharge of such pollutants or combination of such pollutants) will be established under this section" and inserted provision for the revision of the list and for the finality of the Administrator's determination except when that determination is arbitrary and capricious.

Subsec. (a)(2). Pub. L. 95-217, Sec. 53(a), expanded provisions covering effluent limitations and the establishment of effluent standards (or prohibitions), introduced provisions relating to the application of the best available technology economically achievable for the applicable category or class of point sources established in accordance with sections 1311(b)(2)(A) and 1314(b)(2) of this title, inserted provision that published effluent standards take into account the extent to which effective control is being or may be achieved under other regulatory authority, inserted provision for a sixty day minimum period following publication of proposed effluent standards for written comment, substituted two hundred and seventy days for six months as the period following publication of proposed standards during which period standards (or prohibitions) must be promulgated, and inserted provision for the finality of effluent limitations (or prohibitions) except if, on judicial review, the standard was not based on substantial evidence.

Subsec. (a)(3). Pub. L. 95-217, Sec. 53(a), struck out provision for the immediate promulgation of revised effluent standards (or prohibitions) for pollutants or combinations of pollutants if, after public hearings, the Administrator found that a modification of such proposed standards (or prohibitions) was justified. See subsec. (a)(2) of this section.

Subsec. (a)(6). Pub. L. 95-217, Sec. 53(b), inserted provision that if the Administrator determines that compliance with effluent standards (or prohibitions) within one year from the date of promulgation is technologically infeasible for a category of sources, the Administrator may establish the effective date of the effluent standard (or prohibition) for that category at the earliest date upon which compliance can be feasibly attained by sources within such category, but in no event more than three years after the date of such promulgation.

Subsec. (b)(1). Pub. L. 95-217, Sec. 54(a), inserted provision that if, in the case of any toxic pollutant under subsection (a) of this section introduced by a source into a publicly owned treatment works, the treatment by the works removes all or any part of the toxic pollutant and the discharge from the works does not violate that effluent limitation or standard which would be applicable to the toxic pollutant if it were discharged by the source other than through a publicly owned treatment works, and does not prevent sludge use or disposal by the works in accordance with section 1345 of this title, then the pretreatment requirements for the sources actually discharging the toxic pollutant into the publicly owned treatment works may be revised by the owner or operator of the works to reflect the removal of the toxic pollutant by the works.

Change of Name

Committee on Public Works and Transportation of House of Representatives treated as referring to Committee on Transportation and Infrastructure of House of Representatives by section 1(a) of Pub. L. 104-14, set out as a note preceding section 21 of Title 2, The Congress.

Increase in EPA Employees

Section 309(b) of Pub. L. 100-4 provided that: "The Administrator shall take such actions as may be necessary to increase the number of employees of the Environmental Protection Agency in order to effectively implement pretreatment requirements under section 307 of the Federal Water Pollution Control Act [33 U.S.C. 1317]."

Section Referred to in Other Sections

This section is referred to in sections 1288, 1311, 1313, 1314, 1319, 1323, 1341, 1342, 1344, 1365, 1367, 1369, 1374 of this title; title 42 sections 6924, 6925, 6939, 6939e, 9601.

RECORDS AND REPORTS; INSPECTIONS

33 USC 1318

(a) Maintenance; monitoring equipment; entry; access to information

Whenever required to carry out the objective of this chapter, including but not limited to (1) developing or assisting in the development of any effluent limitation, or other limitation, prohibition, or effluent standard, pretreatment standard, or standard of performance under this chapter; (2) determining whether any person is in violation of any such effluent limitation, or other limitation, prohibition or effluent standard, pretreatment standard, or standard of performance; (3) any requirement established under this section; or (4) carrying out sections 1315, 1321, 1342, 1344 (relating to State permit programs), 1345, and 1364 of this title—

    (A) the Administrator shall require the owner or operator of any point source to (i) establish and maintain such records, (ii) make such reports, (iii) install, use, and maintain such monitoring equipment or methods (including where appropriate, biological monitoring methods), (iv) sample such effluents (in accordance with such methods, at such locations, at such intervals, and in such manner as the Administrator shall prescribe), and (v) provide such other information as he may reasonably require; and

    (B) the Administrator or his authorized representative (including an authorized contractor acting as a representative of the Administrator), upon presentation of his credentials—

        (i) shall have a right of entry to, upon, or through any premises in which an effluent source is located or in which any records required to be maintained under clause (A) of this subsection are located, and

(ii) may at reasonable times have access to and copy any records, inspect any monitoring equipment or method required under clause (A), and sample any effluents which the owner or operator of such source is required to sample under such clause.

(b) Availability to public; trade secrets exception; penalty for disclosure of confidential information
Any records, reports, or information obtained under this section (1) shall, in the case of effluent data, be related to any applicable effluent limitations, toxic, pretreatment, or new source performance standards, and (2) shall be available to the public, except that upon a showing satisfactory to the Administrator by any person that records, reports, or information, or particular part thereof (other than effluent data), to which the Administrator has access under this section, if made public would divulge methods or processes entitled to protection as trade secrets of such person, the Administrator shall consider such record, report, or information, or particular portion thereof confidential in accordance with the purposes of section 1905 of title 18. Any authorized representative of the Administrator (including an authorized contractor acting as a representative of the Administrator) who knowingly or willfully publishes, divulges, discloses, or makes known in any manner or to any extent not authorized by law any information which is required to be considered confidential under this subsection shall be fined not more than $1,000 or imprisoned not more than 1 year, or both. Nothing in this subsection shall prohibit the Administrator or an authorized representative of the Administrator (including any authorized contractor acting as a representative of the Administrator) from disclosing records, reports, or information to other officers, employees, or authorized representatives of the United States concerned with carrying out this chapter or when relevant in any proceeding under this chapter.

(c) Application of State law
Each State may develop and submit to the Administrator procedures under State law for inspection, monitoring, and entry with respect to point sources located in such State. If the Administrator finds that the procedures and the law of any State relating to inspection, monitoring, and entry are applicable to at least the same extent as those required by this section, such State is authorized to apply and enforce its procedures for inspection, monitoring, and entry with respect to point sources located in such State (except with respect to point sources owned or operated by the United States).

(d) Access by Congress
Notwithstanding any limitation contained in this section or any other provision of law, all information reported to or otherwise obtained by the Administrator (or any representative of the Administrator) under this chapter shall be made available, upon written request of any duly authorized committee of Congress, to such committee.

(June 30, 1948, ch. 758, title III, Sec. 308, as added Pub. L. 92-500, Sec. 2, Oct. 18, 1972, 86 Stat. 858; amended Pub. L. 95-217, Sec. 67(c)(1), Dec. 27, 1977, 91 Stat. 1606; Pub. L. 100-4, title III, Sec. 310, title IV, Sec. 406(d)(1), Feb. 4, 1987, 101 Stat. 41, 73.)

Amendments

1987—Subsec. (a). Pub. L. 100-4, Sec. 406(d)(1), substituted "1345, and 1364" for "and 1364" in cl. (4).

Subsec. (a)(B). Pub. L. 100-4, Sec. 310(a)(2), inserted "(including an authorized contractor acting as a representative of the Administrator)" after "representative".

Subsec. (b). Pub. L. 100-4, Sec. 310(a)(1), substituted a period and "Any authorized representative of the Administrator (including an authorized contractor acting as a representative of the Administrator) who knowingly or willfully publishes, divulges, discloses, or makes known in any manner or to any extent not authorized by law any information which is required to be considered confidential under this subsection shall be fined not more than $1,000 or imprisoned not more than 1 year, or both. Nothing in this subsection shall prohibit the Administrator or an authorized representative of the Administrator (including any authorized contractor acting as a representative of the Administrator) from disclosing records, reports, or information to other officers, employees, or authorized representatives of the United States concerned with carrying out this chapter or when relevant in any proceeding under this chapter." for ", except that such record, report, or information may be disclosed to other officers, employees, or authorized representatives of the United States concerned with carrying out this chapter or when relevant in any proceeding under this chapter."

Subsec. (d). Pub. L. 100-4, Sec. 310(b), added subsec. (d).

1977—Subsec. (a)(4). Pub. L. 95-217 inserted "1344 (relating to State permit programs)," after "sections 1315, 1321, 1342," in provisions preceding subpar. (A).

Section Referred to in Other Sections

This section is referred to in sections 1319, 1321, 1342, 1344, 1377 of this title; title 42 sections 7412, 9606.

ENFORCEMENT

33 USC 1319

(a) State enforcement; compliance orders
   (1) Whenever, on the basis of any information available to him, the Administrator finds that any person is in violation of any condition or limitation which implements section 1311, 1312, 1316, 1317, 1318, 1328, or 1345 of this title in a permit issued by a State under an approved permit program under section 1342 or 1344 of this title he shall proceed under his authority in paragraph (3) of this subsection or he shall notify the person in alleged violation and such State of such finding. If beyond the thirtieth day after the Administrator's notification the State has not commenced appropriate enforcement action, the Administrator shall issue an order requiring such person to comply with such condition or limitation or shall bring a civil action in accordance with subsection (b) of this section.
   (2) Whenever, on the basis of information available to him, the Administrator finds that violations of permit conditions or limitations as set forth in paragraph (1) of this subsection are so widespread that such violations appear to result from a failure of the State to enforce such permit conditions or limitations effectively, he shall so notify the State. If the Administrator finds such failure extends beyond the thirtieth day after such notice, he shall give public notice of such finding. During the period beginning with such public notice and ending when such State satisfies the Administrator that it will enforce such conditions and limitations (hereafter referred to in this section as the period of "federally assumed enforcement"), except where an extension has been granted under paragraph (5)(B) of this subsection, the Administrator shall enforce any permit condition or limitation with respect to any person—
      (A) by issuing an order to comply with such condition or limitation, or
      (B) by bringing a civil action under subsection (b) of this section.
   (3) Whenever on the basis of any information available to him the Administrator finds that any person is in violation of section 1311, 1312, 1316, 1317, 1318, 1328, or 1345 of this title, or is in violation of any permit condition or limitation implementing any of such sections in a permit issued under section 1342 of this title by him or by a State or in a permit issued under section 1344 of this title by a State, he shall issue an order requiring such person to comply with such section or requirement, or he shall bring a civil action in accordance with subsection (b) of this section.
   (4) A copy of any order issued under this subsection shall be sent immediately by the Administrator to the State in which the violation occurs and other affected States. In any case in which an order under this subsection (or notice to a violator under paragraph (1) of this subsection) is issued to a corporation, a copy of such order (or notice) shall be served on any appropriate corporate officers. An order issued under this subsection relating to a violation of section 1318 of this title shall not take effect until the person to whom it is issued has had an opportunity to confer with the Administrator concerning the alleged violation.
   (5) (A) Any order issued under this subsection shall be by personal service, shall state with reasonable specificity the nature of the violation, and shall specify a time for compliance not to exceed thirty days in the case of a violation of an interim compliance schedule or operation and maintenance requirement and not to exceed a time the Administrator determines to be reasonable in the case of a violation of a final deadline, taking into account the seriousness of the violation and any good faith efforts to comply with applicable requirements.
      (B) The Administrator may, if he determines (i) that any person who is a violator of, or any person who is otherwise not in compliance with, the time requirements under this

chapter or in any permit issued under this chapter, has acted in good faith, and has made a commitment (in the form of contracts or other securities) of necessary resources to achieve compliance by the earliest possible date after July 1, 1977, but not later than April 1, 1979; (ii) that any extension under this provision will not result in the imposition of any additional controls on any other point or nonpoint source; (iii) that an application for a permit under section 1342 of this title was filed for such person prior to December 31, 1974; and (iv) that the facilities necessary for compliance with such requirements are under construction, grant an extension of the date referred to in section 1311(b)(1)(A) of this title to a date which will achieve compliance at the earliest time possible but not later than April 1, 1979.

(6) Whenever, on the basis of information available to him, the Administrator finds (A) that any person is in violation of section 1311(b)(1)(A) or (C) of this title, (B) that such person cannot meet the requirements for a time extension under section 1311(i)(2) of this title, and (C) that the most expeditious and appropriate means of compliance with this chapter by such person is to discharge into a publicly owned treatment works, then, upon request of such person, the Administrator may issue an order requiring such person to comply with this chapter at the earliest date practicable, but not later than July 1, 1983, by discharging into a publicly owned treatment works if such works concur with such order. Such order shall include a schedule of compliance.

(b) Civil actions

The Administrator is authorized to commence a civil action for appropriate relief, including a permanent or temporary injunction, for any violation for which he is authorized to issue a compliance order under subsection (a) of this section. Any action under this subsection may be brought in the district court of the United States for the district in which the defendant is located or resides or is doing business, and such court shall have jurisdiction to restrain such violation and to require compliance. Notice of the commencement of such action shall be given immediately to the appropriate State.

(c) Criminal penalties

(1) Negligent violations

Any person who—

(A) negligently violates section 1311, 1312, 1316, 1317, 1318, 1321(b)(3), 1328, or 1345 of this title, or any permit condition or limitation implementing any of such sections in a permit issued under section 1342 of this title by the Administrator or by a State, or any requirement imposed in a pretreatment program approved under section 1342(a)(3) or 1342(b)(8) of this title or in a permit issued under section 1344 of this title by the Secretary of the Army or by a State; or

(B) negligently introduces into a sewer system or into a publicly owned treatment works any pollutant or hazardous substance which such person knew or reasonably should have known could cause personal injury or property damage or, other than in compliance with all applicable Federal, State, or local requirements or permits, which causes such treatment works to violate any effluent limitation or condition in any permit issued to the treatment works under section 1342 of this title by the Administrator or a State;

shall be punished by a fine of not less than $2,500 nor more than $25,000 per day of violation, or by imprisonment for not more than 1 year, or by both. If a conviction of a person is for a violation committed after a first conviction of such person under this paragraph, punishment shall be by a fine of not more than $50,000 per day of violation, or by imprisonment of not more than 2 years, or by both.

(2) Knowing violations

Any person who—

(A) knowingly violates section 1311, 1312, 1316, 1317, 1318, 1321(b)(3), 1328, or 1345 of this title, or any permit condition or limitation implementing any of such sections in a permit issued under section 1342 of this title by the Administrator or by a State, or any requirement imposed in a pretreatment program approved under section 1342(a)(3) or 1342(b)(8) of this title or in a permit issued under section 1344 of this title by the Secretary of the Army or by a State; or

(B) knowingly introduces into a sewer system or into a publicly owned treatment works any pollutant or hazardous substance which such person knew or reasonably should have known could cause personal injury or property damage or, other than in compliance with all applicable Federal, State, or local requirements or permits, which causes such treatment works to violate any effluent limitation or condition in a permit issued to the treatment works under section 1342 of this title by the Administrator or a State; shall be punished by a fine of not less than $5,000 nor more than $50,000 per day of violation, or by imprisonment for not more than 3 years, or by both. If a conviction of a person is for a violation committed after a first conviction of such person under this paragraph, punishment shall be by a fine of not more than $100,000 per day of violation, or by imprisonment of not more than 6 years, or by both.

(3) Knowing endangerment

(A) General rule

Any person who knowingly violates section 1311, 1312, 1313, 1316, 1317, 1318, 1321(b)(3), 1328, or 1345 of this title, or any permit condition or limitation implementing any of such sections in a permit issued under section 1342 of this title by the Administrator or by a State, or in a permit issued under section 1344 of this title by the Secretary of the Army or by a State, and who knows at that time that he thereby places another person in imminent danger of death or serious bodily injury, shall, upon conviction, be subject to a fine of not more than $250,000 or imprisonment of not more than 15 years, or both. A person which is an organization shall, upon conviction of violating this subparagraph, be subject to a fine of not more than $1,000,000. If a conviction of a person is for a violation committed after a first conviction of such person under this paragraph, the maximum punishment shall be doubled with respect to both fine and imprisonment.

(B) Additional provisions

For the purpose of subparagraph (A) of this paragraph—

(i) in determining whether a defendant who is an individual knew that his conduct placed another person in imminent danger of death or serious bodily injury—

(I) the person is responsible only for actual awareness or actual belief that he possessed; and

(II) knowledge possessed by a person other than the defendant but not by the defendant himself may not be attributed to the defendant;

except that in proving the defendant's possession of actual knowledge, circumstantial evidence may be used, including evidence that the defendant took affirmative steps to shield himself from relevant information;

(ii) it is an affirmative defense to prosecution that the conduct charged was consented to by the person endangered and that the danger and conduct charged were reasonably foreseeable hazards of—

(I) an occupation, a business, or a profession; or

(II) medical treatment or medical or scientific experimentation conducted by professionally approved methods and such other person had been made aware of the risks involved prior to giving consent;

and such defense may be established under this subparagraph by a preponderance of the evidence;

(iii) the term "organization" means a legal entity, other than a government, established or organized for any purpose, and such term includes a corporation, company, association, firm, partnership, joint stock company, foundation, institution, trust, society, union, or any other association of persons; and

(iv) the term "serious bodily injury" means bodily injury which involves a substantial risk of death, unconsciousness, extreme physical pain, protracted and obvious disfigurement, or protracted loss or impairment of the function of a bodily member, organ, or mental faculty.

(4) False statements

Any person who knowingly makes any false material statement, representation, or certification in any application, record, report, plan, or other document filed or required to be maintained under this chapter or who knowingly falsifies, tampers with, or renders inaccurate any monitoring device or method required to be maintained under this chapter, shall upon conviction, be punished by a fine of not more than $10,000, or by imprisonment for not more than 2 years, or by both. If a conviction of a person is for a violation committed after a first conviction of such person under this paragraph, punishment shall be by a fine of not more than $20,000 per day of violation, or by imprisonment of not more than 4 years, or by both.

(5) Treatment of single operational upset

For purposes of this subsection, a single operational upset which leads to simultaneous violations of more than one pollutant parameter shall be treated as a single violation.

(6) Responsible corporate officer as "person"

For the purpose of this subsection, the term "person" means, in addition to the definition contained in section 1362(5) of this title, any responsible corporate officer.

(7) Hazardous substance defined

For the purpose of this subsection, the term "hazardous substance" means (A) any substance designated pursuant to section 1321(b)(2)(A) of this title, (B) any element, compound, mixture, solution, or substance designated pursuant to section 9602 of title 42, (C) any hazardous waste having the characteristics identified under or listed pursuant to section 3001 of the Solid Waste Disposal Act [42 U.S.C. 6921] (but not including any waste the regulation of which under the Solid Waste Disposal Act [42 U.S.C. 6901 et seq.] has been suspended by Act of Congress), (D) any toxic pollutant listed under section 1317(a) of this title, and (E) any imminently hazardous chemical substance or mixture with respect to which the Administrator has taken action pursuant to section 2606 of title 15.

(d) Civil penalties; factors considered in determining amount

Any person who violates section 1311, 1312, 1316, 1317, 1318, 1328, or 1345 of this title, or any permit condition or limitation implementing any of such sections in a permit issued under section 1342 of this title by the Administrator, or by a State, or in a permit issued under section 1344 of this title by a State,,[1] or any requirement imposed in a pretreatment program approved under section 1342(a)(3) or 1342(b)(8) of this title, and any person who violates any order issued by the Administrator under subsection (a) of this section, shall be subject to a civil penalty not to exceed $25,000 per day for each violation. In determining the amount of a civil penalty the court shall consider the seriousness of the violation or violations, the economic benefit (if any) resulting from the violation, any history of such violations, any good-faith efforts to comply with the applicable requirements, the economic impact of the penalty on the violator, and such other matters as justice may require. For purposes of this subsection, a single operational upset which leads to simultaneous violations of more than one pollutant parameter shall be treated as a single violation.

(e) State liability for judgments and expenses

Whenever a municipality is a party to a civil action brought by the United States under this section, the State in which such municipality is located shall be joined as a party. Such State shall be liable for payment of any judgment, or any expenses incurred as a result of complying with any judgment, entered against the municipality in such action to the extent that the laws of that State prevent the municipality from raising revenues needed to comply with such judgment.

(f) Wrongful introduction of pollutant into treatment works

Whenever, on the basis of any information available to him, the Administrator finds that an owner or operator of any source is introducing a pollutant into a treatment works in violation of subsection (d) of section 1317 of this title, the Administrator may notify the owner or operator of such treatment works and the State of such violation. If the owner or operator of the treatment works does not commence appropriate enforcement action within 30 days of the date of such notification, the Administrator may commence a civil action for appropriate relief, including but not limited to, a permanent or temporary injunction, against the owner or operator of such treatment works. In any such civil action the Administrator shall join the owner or operator of such source as a party to the action. Such action shall be brought in the district court of the United States in the district in which the treatment works is located. Such court shall have jurisdiction to restrain such violation and to require the owner or operator of the treatment works and the owner or operator of the source to take such action as may be necessary to come into compliance with this chapter. Notice of commencement of any such action shall be given to the State. Nothing in this subsection shall be construed to limit or prohibit any other authority the Administrator may have under this chapter.

---

[1] So in original.

(g) Administrative penalties
  (1) Violations
      Whenever on the basis of any information available—
      (A) the Administrator finds that any person has violated section 1311, 1312, 1316, 1317, 1318, 1328, or 1345 of this title, or has violated any permit condition or limitation implementing any of such sections in a permit issued under section 1342 of this title by the Administrator or by a State, or in a permit issued under section 1344 of this title by a State, or
      (B) the Secretary of the Army (hereinafter in this subsection referred to as the "Secretary") finds that any person has violated any permit condition or limitation in a permit issued under section 1344 of this title by the Secretary,
      the Administrator or Secretary, as the case may be, may, after consultation with the State in which the violation occurs, assess a class I civil penalty or a class II civil penalty under this subsection.
  (2) Classes of penalties
      (A) Class I
          The amount of a class I civil penalty under paragraph (1) may not exceed $10,000 per violation, except that the maximum amount of any class I civil penalty under this subparagraph shall not exceed $25,000. Before issuing an order assessing a civil penalty under this subparagraph, the Administrator or the Secretary, as the case may be, shall give to the person to be assessed such penalty written notice of the Administrator's or Secretary's proposal to issue such order and the opportunity to request, within 30 days of the date the notice is received by such person, a hearing on the proposed order. Such hearing shall not be subject to section 554 or 556 of title 5, but shall provide a reasonable opportunity to be heard and to present evidence.
      (B) Class II
          The amount of a class II civil penalty under paragraph (1) may not exceed $10,000 per day for each day during which the violation continues; except that the maximum amount of any class II civil penalty under this subparagraph shall not exceed $125,000. Except as otherwise provided in this subsection, a class II civil penalty shall be assessed and collected in the same manner, and subject to the same provisions, as in the case of civil penalties assessed and collected after notice and opportunity for a hearing on the record in accordance with section 554 of title 5. The Administrator and the Secretary may issue rules for discovery procedures for hearings under this subparagraph.
  (3) Determining amount
      In determining the amount of any penalty assessed under this subsection, the Administrator or the Secretary, as the case may be, shall take into account the nature, circumstances, extent and gravity of the violation, or violations, and, with respect to the violator, ability to pay, any prior history of such violations, the degree of culpability, economic benefit or savings (if any) resulting from the violation, and such other matters as justice may require. For purposes of this subsection, a single operational upset which leads to simultaneous violations of more than one pollutant parameter shall be treated as a single violation.
  (4) Rights of interested persons
      (A) Public notice
          Before issuing an order assessing a civil penalty under this subsection the Administrator or Secretary, as the case may be, shall provide public notice of and reasonable opportunity to comment on the proposed issuance of such order.
      (B) Presentation of evidence
          Any person who comments on a proposed assessment of a penalty under this subsection shall be given notice of any hearing held under this subsection and of the order assessing such penalty. In any hearing held under this subsection, such person shall have a reasonable opportunity to be heard and to present evidence.
      (C) Rights of interested persons to a hearing
          If no hearing is held under paragraph (2) before issuance of an order assessing a penalty under this subsection, any person who commented on the proposed assessment may petition, within 30 days after the issuance of such order, the Administrator or Secretary, as the case may be, to set aside such order and to provide a hearing on

the penalty. If the evidence presented by the petitioner in support of the petition is material and was not considered in the issuance of the order, the Administrator or Secretary shall immediately set aside such order and provide a hearing in accordance with paragraph (2)(A) in the case of a class I civil penalty and paragraph (2)(B) in the case of a class II civil penalty. If the Administrator or Secretary denies a hearing under this subparagraph, the Administrator or Secretary shall provide to the petitioner, and publish in the Federal Register, notice of and the reasons for such denial.

(5) Finality of order

An order issued under this subsection shall become final 30 days after its issuance unless a petition for judicial review is filed under paragraph (8) or a hearing is requested under paragraph (4)(C). If such a hearing is denied, such order shall become final 30 days after such denial.

(6) Effect of order

(A) Limitation on actions under other sections

Action taken by the Administrator or the Secretary, as the case may be, under this subsection shall not affect or limit the Administrator's or Secretary's authority to enforce any provision of this chapter; except that any violation—

(i) with respect to which the Administrator or the Secretary has commenced and is diligently prosecuting an action under this subsection,

(ii) with respect to which a State has commenced and is diligently prosecuting an action under a State law comparable to this subsection, or

(iii) for which the Administrator, the Secretary, or the State has issued a final order not subject to further judicial review and the violator has paid a penalty assessed under this subsection, or such comparable State law, as the case may be,

shall not be the subject of a civil penalty action under subsection (d) of this section or section 1321(b) of this title or section 1365 of this title.

(B) Applicability of limitation with respect to citizen suits

The limitations contained in subparagraph (A) on civil penalty actions under section 1365 of this title shall not apply with respect to any violation for which—

(i) a civil action under section 1365(a)(1) of this title has been filed prior to commencement of an action under this subsection, or

(ii) notice of an alleged violation of section 1365(a)(1) of this title has been given in accordance with section 1365(b)(1)(A) of this title prior to commencement of an action under this subsection and an action under section 1365(a)(1) of this title with respect to such alleged violation is filed before the 120th day after the date on which such notice is given.

(7) Effect of action on compliance

No action by the Administrator or the Secretary under this subsection shall affect any person's obligation to comply with any section of this chapter or with the terms and conditions of any permit issued pursuant to section 1342 or 1344 of this title.

(8) Judicial review

Any person against whom a civil penalty is assessed under this subsection or who commented on the proposed assessment of such penalty in accordance with paragraph (4) may obtain review of such assessment—

(A) in the case of assessment of a class I civil penalty, in the United States District Court for the District of Columbia or in the district in which the violation is alleged to have occurred, or

(B) in the case of assessment of a class II civil penalty, in United States Court of Appeals for the District of Columbia Circuit or for any other circuit in which such person resides or transacts business,

by filing a notice of appeal in such court within the 30-day period beginning on the date the civil penalty order is issued and by simultaneously sending a copy of such notice by certified mail to the Administrator or the Secretary, as the case may be, and the Attorney General. The Administrator or the Secretary shall promptly file in such court a certified copy of the record on which the order was issued. Such court shall not set aside or remand such order unless there is not substantial evidence in the record, taken as a whole, to support the finding of a violation or unless the Administrator's or Secretary's assessment of the penalty constitutes an abuse of discretion and shall not impose additional civil penalties for the same violation unless the Administrator's or Secretary's assessment of the penalty constitutes an abuse of discretion.

(9) Collection

If any person fails to pay an assessment of a civil penalty—

(A) after the order making the assessment has become final, or
(B) after a court in an action brought under paragraph (8) has entered a final judgment in favor of the Administrator or the Secretary, as the case may be,

the Administrator or the Secretary shall request the Attorney General to bring a civil action in an appropriate district court to recover the amount assessed (plus interest at currently prevailing rates from the date of the final order or the date of the final judgment, as the case may be). In such an action, the validity, amount, and appropriateness of such penalty shall not be subject to review. Any person who fails to pay on a timely basis the amount of an assessment of a civil penalty as described in the first sentence of this paragraph shall be required to pay, in addition to such amount and interest, attorneys fees and costs for collection proceedings and a quarterly nonpayment penalty for each quarter during which such failure to pay persists. Such nonpayment penalty shall be in an amount equal to 20 percent of the aggregate amount of such person's penalties and nonpayment penalties which are unpaid as of the beginning of such quarter.

(10) Subpoenas

The Administrator or Secretary, as the case may be, may issue subpoenas for the attendance and testimony of witnesses and the production of relevant papers, books, or documents in connection with hearings under this subsection. In case of contumacy or refusal to obey a subpoena issued pursuant to this paragraph and served upon any person, the district court of the United States for any district in which such person is found, resides, or transacts business, upon application by the United States and after notice to such person, shall have jurisdiction to issue an order requiring such person to appear and give testimony before the administrative law judge or to appear and produce documents before the administrative law judge, or both, and any failure to obey such order of the court may be punished by such court as a contempt thereof.

(11) Protection of existing procedures

Nothing in this subsection shall change the procedures existing on the day before February 4, 1987, under other subsections of this section for issuance and enforcement of orders by the Administrator.

(June 30, 1948, ch. 758, title III, Sec. 309, as added Pub. L. 92-500, Sec. 2, Oct. 18, 1972, 86 Stat. 859; amended Pub. L. 95-217, Secs. 54(b), 55, 56, 67(c)(2), Dec. 27, 1977, 91 Stat. 1591, 1592, 1606; Pub. L. 100-4, title III, Secs. 312, 313(a)(1), (b)(1), (c), 314(a), Feb. 4, 1987, 101 Stat. 42, 45, 46; Pub. L. 101-380, title IV, Sec. 4301(c), Aug. 18, 1990, 104 Stat. 537.)

References in Text

The Solid Waste Disposal Act, referred to in subsec. (c)(7), is title II of Pub. L. 89-272, Oct. 20, 1965, 79 Stat. 997, as amended generally by Pub. L. 94-580, Sec. 2, Oct. 21, 1976, 90 Stat. 2795, which is classified generally to chapter 82 (Sec. 6901 et seq.) of Title 42, The Public Health and Welfare. For complete classification of this Act to the Code, see Short Title note set out under section 6901 of Title 42 and Tables.

Amendments

1990—Subsec. (c)(1)(A), (2)(A), (3)(A). Pub. L. 101-380 inserted "1321(b)(3)," after "1318,".

1987—Subsec. (c). Pub. L. 100-4, Sec. 312, amended subsec. (c) generally, revising provisions of par. (1), adding pars. (2), (3), (5), and (7), redesignating former pars. (2) and (4) as (3) and (6), respectively, and revising provisions of redesignated par. (4).

Subsec. (d). Pub. L. 100-4, Sec. 313(a)(1), inserted ", or any requirement imposed in a pretreatment program approved under section 1342(a)(3) or 1342(b)(8) of this title," after second reference to "State,".

Pub. L. 100-4, Sec. 313(b)(1), substituted "$25,000 per day for each violation" for "$10,000 per day of such violation".

Pub. L. 100-4, Sec. 313(c), inserted at end "In determining the amount of a civil penalty the court shall consider the seriousness of the violation or violations, the economic benefit (if any) resulting from the violation, any history of such violations, any good-faith efforts to comply with the applicable requirements, the economic impact of the penalty on the violator, and such other matters as justice may require. For purposes of this subsection, a single operational upset which leads to simultaneous violations of more than one pollutant parameter shall be treated as a single violation."

Subsec. (g). Pub. L. 100-4, Sec. 314(a), added subsec. (g).

1977—Subsec. (a)(1). Pub. L. 95-217, Secs. 55(a), 67(c)(2)(A), substituted "1318, 1328, or 1345 of this title" for "or 1318 of this title" and "1342 or 1344 of this title" for "1342 of this title".

Subsec. (a)(2). Pub. L. 95-217, Sec. 56(a), substituted "except where an extension has been granted under paragraph (5)(B) of this subsection, the Administrator shall enforce any permit condition or limitation" for "the Administrator shall enforce any permit condition or limitation".

Subsec. (a)(3). Pub. L. 95-217, Secs. 55(b), 67(c)(2)(B), substituted "1318, 1328, or 1345 of this title" for "or 1318 of this title" and inserted "or in a permit issued under section 1344 of this title by a State" after "in a permit issued under section 1342 of this title by him or by a State".

Subsec. (a)(4). Pub. L. 95-217, Sec. 56(b), struck out provision that any order issued under this subsection had to be by personal service and had to state with reasonable specificity the nature of the violation and a time for compliance, not to exceed thirty days, which the Administrator determined to be reasonable, taking into account the seriousness of the violation and any good faith efforts to comply with applicable requirements. See section subsec. (a)(5) of this section.

Subsec. (a)(5), (6). Pub. L. 95-217, Sec. 56(c), added pars. (5) and (6).

Subsec. (c)(1). Pub. L. 95-217, Sec. 67(c)(2)(C), substituted "by a State or in a permit issued under section 1344 of this title by a State, shall be punished" for "by a State, shall be punished".

Subsec. (d). Pub. L. 95-217, Secs. 55(c), 67(c)(2)(D), substituted "1318, 1328, or 1345 of this title" for "or 1318 of this title" and inserted "or in a permit issued under section 1344 of this title by a State," after "permit issued under section 1342 of this title by the Administrator, or by a State,".

Subsec. (f). Pub. L. 95-217, Sec. 54(b), added subsec. (f).

Effective Date of 1990 Amendment

Amendment by Pub. L. 101-380 applicable to incidents occurring after Aug. 18, 1990, see section 1020 of Pub. L. 101-380, set out as an Effective Date note under section 2701 of this title.

Savings Provision

Section 313(a)(2) of Pub. L. 100-4 provided that: "No State shall be required before July 1, 1988, to modify a permit program approved or submitted under section 402 of the Federal Water Pollution Control Act [33 U.S.C. 1342] as a result of the amendment made by paragraph (1) [amending this section]."

Deposit of Certain Penalties Into Oil Spill Liability Trust Fund

Penalties paid pursuant to subsection (c) of this section and sections 1321 and 1501 et seq. of this title to be deposited in the Oil Spill Liability Trust Fund created under section 9509 of Title 26, Internal Revenue Code, see section 4304 of Pub. L. 101-380, set out as a note under section 9509 of Title 26.

Increased Penalties Not Required Under State Programs

Section 313(b)(2) of Pub. L. 100-4 provided that: "The Federal Water Pollution Control Act [33 U.S.C. 1251 et seq.] shall not be construed as requiring a State to have a civil penalty for violations described in section 309(d) of such Act [33 U.S.C. 1319(d)] which has the same monetary amount as the civil penalty established by such section, as amended by paragraph (1) [amending this section]. Nothing in this paragraph shall affect the Administrator's authority to establish or adjust by regulation a minimum acceptable State civil penalty.

Actions by Surgeon General Relating to Interstate Pollution

Act July 9, 1956, ch. 518, Sec. 5, 70 Stat. 507, provided that actions by the Surgeon General with respect to water pollutants under section 2(d) of act June 30, 1948, ch. 758, 62 Stat. 1155, as in effect prior to July 9, 1956, which had been completed prior to such date, would still be subject to the terms of section 2(d) of act June 30, 1948, in effect prior to the July 9, 1956 amendment, but that actions with respect to such pollutants would nevertheless subsequently be possible in accordance with the terms of act June 30, 1948, as amended by act July 9, 1956.

Section Referred to in Other Sections

This section is referred to in sections 1256, 1321, 1342, 1344, 1365, 1368, 1377 of this title; title 26 section 9509; title 42 sections 7412, 9606, 9607.

INTERNATIONAL POLLUTION ABATEMENT

33 USC 1320

(a) Hearing; participation by foreign nations

Whenever the Administrator, upon receipts of reports, surveys, or studies from any duly constituted international agency, has reason to believe that pollution is occurring which endangers the health or welfare of persons in a foreign country, and the Secretary of State requests him to abate such pollution, he shall give formal notification thereof to the State water pollution control agency of the State or States in which such discharge or discharges originate and to the appropriate interstate agency, if any. He shall also promptly call such a hearing, if he believes that such pollution is occurring in sufficient quantity to warrant such action, and if such foreign country has given the United States essentially the same rights with respect to the prevention and control of pollution occurring in that country as is given that country by this subsection. The Administrator, through the Secretary of State, shall invite the foreign country which may be adversely affected by the pollution to attend and participate in the hearing, and the representative of such country shall, for the purpose of the hearing and any further proceeding resulting from such hearing, have all the rights of a State water pollution control agency. Nothing in this subsection shall be construed to modify, amend, repeal, or otherwise affect the provisions of the 1909 Boundary Waters Treaty between Canada and the United States or the Water Utilization Treaty of 1944 between Mexico and the United States (59 Stat. 1219), relative to the control and abatement of pollution in waters covered by those treaties.

(b) Functions and responsibilities of Administrator not affected

The calling of a hearing under this section shall not be construed by the courts, the Administrator, or any person as limiting, modifying, or otherwise affecting the functions and responsibilities of the Administrator under this section to establish and enforce water quality requirements under this chapter.

(c) Hearing board; composition; findings of fact; recommendations; implementation of board's decision

The Administrator shall publish in the Federal Register a notice of a public hearing before a hearing board of five or more persons appointed by the Administrator. A majority of the members of the board and the chairman who shall be designated by the Administrator shall not be officers or employees of Federal, State, or local governments. On the basis of the evidence presented at such hearing, the board shall within sixty days after completion of the hearing make findings of fact as to whether or not such pollution is occurring and shall thereupon by decision, incorporating its findings therein, make such recommendations to abate the pollution as may be appropriate and shall transmit such decision and the record of the hearings to the Administrator. All such decisions shall be public. Upon receipt of such decision, the Administrator shall promptly implement the board's decision in accordance with the provisions of this chapter.

(d) Report by alleged polluter

In connection with any hearing called under this subsection, the board is authorized to require any person whose alleged activities result in discharges causing or contributing to pollution to file with it in such forms as it may prescribe, a report based on existing data, furnishing such information as may reasonably be required as to the character, kind, and quantity of such discharges and the use of facilities or other means to prevent or reduce such discharges by the person filing such a report. Such report shall be made under oath or otherwise, as the board may prescribe, and shall be filed with the board within such reasonable period as it may prescribe, unless additional time is granted by it. Upon a showing satisfactory to the board by the person filing such report that such report or portion thereof (other than effluent data), to which the Administrator has access under this section, if made public would divulge trade secrets or secret processes of such person, the board shall consider such report or portion thereof confidential for the purposes of section 1905 of title 18. If any person required to file any report under this paragraph shall fail to do so within the time fixed by the board for filing the same, and such failure shall continue for thirty days after notice of such default, such person shall forfeit to the United States the sum of $1,000 for each and every day of the continuance of such failure, which forfeiture shall be payable into the Treasury of the United States, and shall be recoverable in a civil suit in the name of the United States in the district court of the United States where such person has his principal office or in any district in which he does business. The Administrator may upon application therefor remit or mitigate any forfeiture provided for under this subsection.

(e) Compensation of board members
Board members, other than officers or employees of Federal, State, or local governments, shall be for each day (including travel-time) during which they are performing board business, entitled to receive compensation at a rate fixed by the Administrator but not in excess of the maximum rate of pay for grade GS-18, as provided in the General Schedule under section 5332 of title 5, and shall, notwithstanding the limitations of sections 5703 and 5704 of title 5, be fully reimbursed for travel, subsistence and related expenses.

(f) Enforcement proceedings
When any such recommendation adopted by the Administrator involves the institution of enforcement proceedings against any person to obtain the abatement of pollution subject to such recommendation, the Administrator shall institute such proceedings if he believes that the evidence warrants such proceedings. The district court of the United States shall consider and determine de novo all relevant issues, but shall receive in evidence the record of the proceedings before the conference or hearing board. The court shall have jurisdiction to enter such judgment and orders enforcing such judgment as it deems appropriate or to remand such proceedings to the Administrator for such further action as it may direct.

(June 30, 1948, ch. 758, title III, Sec. 310, as added Pub. L. 92-500, Sec. 2, Oct. 18, 1972, 86 Stat. 860.)

References in Other Laws to GS-16, 17, or 18 Pay Rates

References in laws to the rates of pay for GS-16, 17, or 18, or to maximum rates of pay under the General Schedule, to be considered references to rates payable under specified sections of Title 5, Government Organization and Employees, see section 529 [title I, Sec. 101(c)(1)] of Pub. L. 101-509, set out in a note under section 5376 of Title 5.

OIL AND HAZARDOUS SUBSTANCE LIABILITY

33 USC 1321

(a) Definitions
For the purpose of this section, the term—
(1) "oil" means oil of any kind or in any form, including, but not limited to, petroleum, fuel oil, sludge, oil refuse, and oil mixed with wastes other than dredged spoil;
(2) "discharge" includes, but is not limited to, any spilling, leaking, pumping, pouring, emitting, emptying or dumping, but excludes (A) discharges in compliance with a permit under section 1342 of this title, (B) discharges resulting from circumstances identified and reviewed and made a part of the public record with respect to a permit issued or modified under section 1342 of this title, and subject to a condition in such permit,,[1] (C) continuous or anticipated intermittent discharges from a point source, identified in a permit or permit application under section 1342 of this title, which are caused by events occurring within the scope of relevant operating or treatment systems, and (D) discharges incidental to mechanical removal authorized by the President under subsection (c) of this section;
(3) "vessel" means every description of watercraft or other artificial contrivance used, or capable of being used, as a means of transportation on water other than a public vessel;
(4) "public vessel" means a vessel owned or bareboat-chartered and operated by the United

---
[1]So in original.

States, or by a State or political subdivision thereof, or by a foreign nation, except when such vessel is engaged in commerce;
(5) "United States" means the States, the District of Columbia, the Commonwealth of Puerto Rico, the Commonwealth of the Northern Mariana Islands, Guam, American Samoa, the Virgin Islands, and the Trust Territory of the Pacific Islands;
(6) "owner or operator" means (A) in the case of a vessel, any person owning, operating, or chartering by demise, such vessel, and (B) in the case of an onshore facility, and an offshore facility, any person owning or operating such onshore facility or offshore facility, and (C) in the case of any abandoned offshore facility, the person who owned or operated such facility immediately prior to such abandonment;
(7) "person" includes an individual, firm, corporation, association, and a partnership.
(8) "remove" or "removal" refers to containment and removal of the oil or hazardous substances from the water and shorelines or the taking of such other actions as may be necessary to prevent, minimize, or mitigate damage to the public health or welfare, including, but not limited to, fish, shellfish, wildlife, and public and private property, shorelines, and beaches;
(9) "contiguous zone" means the entire zone established or to be established by the United States under article 24 of the Convention on the Territorial Sea and the Contiguous Zone;
(10) "onshore facility" means any facility (including, but not limited to, motor vehicles and rolling stock) of any kind located in, on, or under, any land within the United States other than submerged land;
(11) "offshore facility" means any facility of any kind located in, on, or under, any of the navigable waters of the United States, and any facility of any kind which is subject to the jurisdiction of the United States and is located in, on, or under any other waters, other than a vessel or a public vessel;
(12) "act of God" means an act occasioned by an unanticipated grave natural disaster;
(13) "barrel" means 42 United States gallons at 60 degrees Fahrenheit;
(14) "hazardous substance" means any substance designated pursuant to subsection (b)(2) of this section;
(15) "inland oil barge" means a non-self-propelled vessel carrying oil in bulk as cargo and certificated to operate only in the inland waters of the United States, while operating in such waters;
(16) "inland waters of the United States" means those waters of the United States lying inside the baseline from which the territorial sea is measured and those waters outside such baseline which are a part of the Gulf Intracoastal Waterway;
(17) "otherwise subject to the jurisdiction of the United States" means subject to the jurisdiction of the United States by virtue of United States citizenship, United States vessel documentation or numbering, or as provided for by international agreement to which the United States is a party;
(18) "Area Committee" means an Area Committee established under subsection (j) of this section;
(19) "Area Contingency Plan" means an Area Contingency Plan prepared under subsection (j) of this section;
(20) "Coast Guard District Response Group" means a Coast Guard District Response Group established under subsection (j) of this section;
(21) "Federal On-Scene Coordinator" means a Federal On-Scene Coordinator designated in the National Contingency Plan;
(22) "National Contingency Plan" means the National Contingency Plan prepared and published under subsection (d) of this section;
(23) "National Response Unit" means the National Response Unit established under subsection (j) of this section;
(24) "worst case discharge" means—
   (A) in the case of a vessel, a discharge in adverse weather conditions of its entire cargo; and
   (B) in the case of an offshore facility or onshore facility, the largest foreseeable discharge in adverse weather conditions; and

(25) "removal costs" means—
  (A) the costs of removal of oil or a hazardous substance that are incurred after it is discharged; and
  (B) in any case in which there is a substantial threat of a discharge of oil or a hazardous substance, the costs to prevent, minimize, or mitigate that threat.
(b) Congressional declaration of policy against discharges of oil or hazardous substances; designation of hazardous substances; study of higher standard of care incentives and report to Congress; liability; penalties; civil actions: penalty limitations, separate offenses, jurisdiction, mitigation of damages and costs, recovery of removal costs, alternative remedies, and withholding clearance of vessels
  (1) The Congress hereby declares that it is the policy of the United States that there should be no discharges of oil or hazardous substances into or upon the navigable waters of the United States, adjoining shorelines, or into or upon the waters of the contiguous zone, or in connection with activities under the Outer Continental Shelf Lands Act [43 U.S.C. 1331 et seq.] or the Deepwater Port Act of 1974 [33 U.S.C. 1501 et seq.], or which may affect natural resources belonging to, appertaining to, or under the exclusive management authority of the United States (including resources under the Magnuson-Stevens Fishery Conservation and Management Act [16 U.S.C. 1801 et seq.]).
  (2) (A) The Administrator shall develop, promulgate, and revise as may be appropriate, regulations designating as hazardous substances, other than oil as defined in this section, such elements and compounds which, when discharged in any quantity into or upon the navigable waters of the United States or adjoining shorelines or the waters of the contiguous zone or in connection with activities under the Outer Continental Shelf Lands Act [43 U.S.C. 1331 et seq.] or the Deepwater Port Act of 1974 [33 U.S.C. 1501 et seq.], or which may affect natural resources belonging to, appertaining to, or under the exclusive management authority of the United States (including resources under the Magnuson-Stevens Fishery Conservation and Management Act [16 U.S.C. 1801 et seq.]), present an imminent and substantial danger to the public health or welfare, including, but not limited to, fish, shellfish, wildlife, shorelines, and beaches.
  (B) The Administrator shall within 18 months after the date of enactment of this paragraph, conduct a study and report to the Congress on methods, mechanisms, and procedures to create incentives to achieve a higher standard of care in all aspects of the management and movement of hazardous substances on the part of owners, operators, or persons in charge of onshore facilities, offshore facilities, or vessels. The Administrator shall include in such study (1) limits of liability, (2) liability for third party damages, (3) penalties and fees, (4) spill prevention plans, (5) current practices in the insurance and banking industries, and (6) whether the penalty enacted in subclause (bb) of clause (iii) of subparagraph (B) of subsection (b)(2) of section 311 of Public Law 92-500 should be enacted.
  (3) The discharge of oil or hazardous substances (i) into or upon the navigable waters of the United States, adjoining shorelines, or into or upon the waters of the contiguous zone, or (ii) in connection with activities under the Outer Continental Shelf Lands Act [43 U.S.C. 1331 et seq.] or the Deepwater Port Act of 1974 [33 U.S.C. 1501 et seq.], or which may affect natural resources belonging to, appertaining to, or under the exclusive management authority of the United States (including resources under the Magnuson-Stevens Fishery Conservation and Management Act [16 U.S.C. 1801 et seq.]), in such quantities as may be harmful as determined by the President under paragraph (4) of this subsection, is prohibited, except (A) in the case of such discharges into the waters of the contiguous zone or which may affect natural resources belonging to, appertaining to, or under the exclusive management authority of the United States (including resources under the Magnuson-Stevens Fishery Conservation and Management Act), where permitted under the Protocol of 1978 Relating to the International Convention for the Prevention of Pollution from Ships, 1973, and (B) where permitted in quantities and at times and locations or under such circumstances or conditions as the President may, by regulation, determine not to be harmful. Any regulations issued under this subsection shall be consistent with maritime safety and with marine and navigation laws and regulations and applicable water quality standards.

(4) The President shall by regulation, determine for the purposes of this section those quantities of oil and any hazardous substances the discharge of which may be harmful to the public health or welfare or the environment of the United States, including but not limited to fish, shellfish, wildlife, and public and private property, shorelines, and beaches.

(5) Any person in charge of a vessel or of an onshore facility or an offshore facility shall, as soon as he has knowledge of any discharge of oil or a hazardous substance from such vessel or facility in violation of paragraph (3) of this subsection, immediately notify the appropriate agency of the United States Government of such discharge. The Federal agency shall immediately notify the appropriate State agency of any State which is, or may reasonably be expected to be, affected by the discharge of oil or a hazardous substance. Any such person (A) in charge of a vessel from which oil or a hazardous substance is discharged in violation of paragraph (3)(i) of this subsection, or (B) in charge of a vessel from which oil or a hazardous substance is discharged in violation of paragraph (3)(ii) of this subsection and who is otherwise subject to the jurisdiction of the United States at the time of the discharge, or (C) in charge of an onshore facility or an offshore facility, who fails to notify immediately such agency of such discharge shall, upon conviction, be fined in accordance with title 18, or imprisoned for not more than 5 years, or both. Notification received pursuant to this paragraph shall not be used against any such natural person in any criminal case, except a prosecution for perjury or for giving a false statement.

(6) Administrative penalties.—
   (A) Violations.—Any owner, operator, or person in charge of any vessel, onshore facility, or offshore facility—
      (i) from which oil or a hazardous substance is discharged in violation of paragraph (3), or
      (ii) who fails or refuses to comply with any regulation issued under subsection (j) of this section to which that owner, operator, or person in charge is subject,

      may be assessed a class I or class II civil penalty by the Secretary of the department in which the Coast Guard is operating or the Administrator.
   (B) Classes of penalties.—
      (i) Class i.—The amount of a class I civil penalty under subparagraph (A) may not exceed $10,000 per violation, except that the maximum amount of any class I civil penalty under this subparagraph shall not exceed $25,000. Before assessing a civil penalty under this clause, the Administrator or Secretary, as the case may be, shall give to the person to be assessed such penalty written notice of the Administrator's or Secretary's proposal to assess the penalty and the opportunity to request, within 30 days of the date the notice is received by such person, a hearing on the proposed penalty. Such hearing shall not be subject to section 554 or 556 of title 5, but shall provide a reasonable opportunity to be heard and to present evidence.
      (ii) Class ii.—The amount of a class II civil penalty under subparagraph (A) may not exceed $10,000 per day for each day during which the violation continues; except that the maximum amount of any class II civil penalty under this subparagraph shall not exceed $125,000. Except as otherwise provided in this subsection, a class II civil penalty shall be assessed and collected in the same manner, and subject to the same provisions, as in the case of civil penalties assessed and collected after notice and opportunity for a hearing on the record in accordance with section 554 of title 5. The Administrator and Secretary may issue rules for discovery procedures for hearings under this paragraph.
   (C) Rights of interested persons.—
      (i) Public notice.—Before issuing an order assessing a class II civil penalty under this paragraph the Administrator or Secretary, as the case may be, shall provide public notice of and reasonable opportunity to comment on the proposed issuance of such order.
      (ii) Presentation of evidence.—Any person who comments on a proposed assessment of a class II civil penalty under this paragraph shall be given notice of any hearing held under this paragraph and of the order assessing such penalty. In any hearing held under this paragraph, such person shall have a reasonable opportunity to be heard and to present evidence.

(iii) Rights of interested persons to a hearing.—If no hearing is held under subparagraph (B) before issuance of an order assessing a class II civil penalty under this paragraph, any person who commented on the proposed assessment may petition, within 30 days after the issuance of such order, the Administrator or Secretary, as the case may be, to set aside such order and to provide a hearing on the penalty. If the evidence presented by the petitioner in support of the petition is material and was not considered in the issuance of the order, the Administrator or Secretary shall immediately set aside such order and provide a hearing in accordance with subparagraph (B)(ii). If the Administrator or Secretary denies a hearing under this clause, the Administrator or Secretary shall provide to the petitioner, and publish in the Federal Register, notice of and the reasons for such denial.

(D) Finality of order.—An order assessing a class II civil penalty under this paragraph shall become final 30 days after its issuance unless a petition for judicial review is filed under subparagraph (G) or a hearing is requested under subparagraph (C)(iii). If such a hearing is denied, such order shall become final 30 days after such denial.

(E) Effect of order.—Action taken by the Administrator or Secretary, as the case may be, under this paragraph shall not affect or limit the Administrator's or Secretary's authority to enforce any provision of this chapter; except that any violation—
  (i) with respect to which the Administrator or Secretary has commenced and is diligently prosecuting an action to assess a class II civil penalty under this paragraph, or
  (ii) for which the Administrator or Secretary has issued a final order assessing a class II civil penalty not subject to further judicial review and the violator has paid a penalty assessed under this paragraph,
shall not be the subject of a civil penalty action under section 1319(d), 1319(g), or 1365 of this title or under paragraph (7).

(F) Effect of action on compliance.—No action by the Administrator or Secretary under this paragraph shall affect any person's obligation to comply with any section of this chapter.

(G) Judicial review.—Any person against whom a civil penalty is assessed under this paragraph or who commented on the proposed assessment of such penalty in accordance with subparagraph (C) may obtain review of such assessment—
  (i) in the case of assessment of a class I civil penalty, in the United States District Court for the District of Columbia or in the district in which the violation is alleged to have occurred, or
  (ii) in the case of assessment of a class II civil penalty, in United States Court of Appeals for the District of Columbia Circuit or for any other circuit in which such person resides or transacts business,
by filing a notice of appeal in such court within the 30-day period beginning on the date the civil penalty order is issued and by simultaneously sending a copy of such notice by certified mail to the Administrator or Secretary, as the case may be, and the Attorney General. The Administrator or Secretary shall promptly file in such court a certified copy of the record on which the order was issued. Such court shall not set aside or remand such order unless there is not substantial evidence in the record, taken as a whole, to support the finding of a violation or unless the Administrator's or Secretary's assessment of the penalty constitutes an abuse of discretion and shall not impose additional civil penalties for the same violation unless the Administrator's or Secretary's assessment of the penalty constitutes an abuse of discretion.

(H) Collection.—If any person fails to pay an assessment of a civil penalty—
  (i) after the assessment has become final, or
  (ii) after a court in an action brought under subparagraph (G) has entered a final judgment in favor of the Administrator or Secretary, as the case may be,
the Administrator or Secretary shall request the Attorney General to bring a civil action in an appropriate district court to recover the amount assessed (plus interest at currently prevailing rates from the date of the final order or the date of the final judgment, as the case may be). In such an action, the validity, amount, and appropriateness of such penalty shall not be subject to review. Any person who fails to pay on a timely basis the amount of an assessment of a civil penalty as described in the first

sentence of this subparagraph shall be required to pay, in addition to such amount and interest, attorneys fees and costs for collection proceedings and a quarterly nonpayment penalty for each quarter during which such failure to pay persists. Such nonpayment penalty shall be in an amount equal to 20 percent of the aggregate amount of such person's penalties and nonpayment penalties which are unpaid as of the beginning of such quarter.

(I) Subpoenas.–The Administrator or Secretary, as the case may be, may issue subpoenas for the attendance and testimony of witnesses and the production of relevant papers, books, or documents in connection with hearings under this paragraph. In case of contumacy or refusal to obey a subpoena issued pursuant to this subparagraph and served upon any person, the district court of the United States for any district in which such person is found, resides, or transacts business, upon application by the United States and after notice to such person, shall have jurisdiction to issue an order requiring such person to appear and give testimony before the administrative law judge or to appear and produce documents before the administrative law judge, or both, and any failure to obey such order of the court may be punished by such court as a contempt thereof.

(7) Civil penalty action.–

(A) Discharge, generally.–Any person who is the owner, operator, or person in charge of any vessel, onshore facility, or offshore facility from which oil or a hazardous substance is discharged in violation of paragraph (3), shall be subject to a civil penalty in an amount up to $25,000 per day of violation or an amount up to $1,000 per barrel of oil or unit of reportable quantity of hazardous substances discharged.

(B) Failure to remove or comply.–Any person described in subparagraph (A) who, without sufficient cause–
  (i) fails to properly carry out removal of the discharge under an order of the President pursuant to subsection (c) of this section; or
  (ii) fails to comply with an order pursuant to subsection (e)(1)(B) of this section;
shall be subject to a civil penalty in an amount up to $25,000 per day of violation or an amount up to 3 times the costs incurred by the Oil Spill Liability Trust Fund as a result of such failure.

(C) Failure to comply with regulation.–Any person who fails or refuses to comply with any regulation issued under subsection (j) of this section shall be subject to a civil penalty in an amount up to $25,000 per day of violation.

(D) Gross negligence.–In any case in which a violation of paragraph (3) was the result of gross negligence or willful misconduct of a person described in subparagraph (A), the person shall be subject to a civil penalty of not less than $100,000, and not more than $3,000 per barrel of oil or unit of reportable quantity of hazardous substance discharged.

(E) Jurisdiction.–An action to impose a civil penalty under this paragraph may be brought in the district court of the United States for the district in which the defendant is located, resides, or is doing business, and such court shall have jurisdiction to assess such penalty.

(F) Limitation.–A person is not liable for a civil penalty under this paragraph for a discharge if the person has been assessed a civil penalty under paragraph (6) for the discharge.

(8) Determination of amount.–In determining the amount of a civil penalty under paragraphs (6) and (7), the Administrator, Secretary, or the court, as the case may be, shall consider the seriousness of the violation or violations, the economic benefit to the violator, if any, resulting from the violation, the degree of culpability involved, any other penalty for the same incident, any history of prior violations, the nature, extent, and degree of success of any efforts of the violator to minimize or mitigate the effects of the discharge, the economic impact of the penalty on the violator, and any other matters as justice may require.

(9) Mitigation of damage.–In addition to establishing a penalty for the discharge of oil or a hazardous substance, the Administrator or the Secretary of the department in which the Coast Guard is operating may act to mitigate the damage to the public health or welfare caused by such discharge. The cost of such mitigation shall be deemed a cost incurred under subsection (c) of this section for the removal of such substance by the United States Government.

(10) Recovery of removal costs.—Any costs of removal incurred in connection with a discharge excluded by subsection (a)(2)(C) of this section shall be recoverable from the owner or operator of the source of the discharge in an action brought under section 1319(b) of this title.

(11) Limitation.—Civil penalties shall not be assessed under both this section and section 1319 of this title for the same discharge.

(12) Withholding clearance.—If any owner, operator, or person in charge of a vessel is liable for a civil penalty under this subsection, or if reasonable cause exists to believe that the owner, operator, or person in charge may be subject to a civil penalty under this subsection, the Secretary of the Treasury, upon the request of the Secretary of the department in which the Coast Guard is operating or the Administrator, shall with respect to such vessel refuse or revoke—

(A) the clearance required by section 91 of title 46, Appendix;

(B) a permit to proceed under section 313[2] of title 46, Appendix; and

(C) a permit to depart required under section 1443[2] of title 19;

as applicable. Clearance or a permit refused or revoked under this paragraph may be granted upon the filing of a bond or other surety satisfactory to the Secretary of the department in which the Coast Guard is operating or the Administrator.

(c) Federal removal authority

(1) General removal requirement

(A) The President shall, in accordance with the National Contingency Plan and any appropriate Area Contingency Plan, ensure effective and immediate removal of a discharge, and mitigation or prevention of a substantial threat of a discharge, of oil or a hazardous substance—

(i) into or on the navigable waters;

(ii) on the adjoining shorelines to the navigable waters;

(iii) into or on the waters of the exclusive economic zone; or

(iv) that may affect natural resources belonging to, appertaining to, or under the exclusive management authority of the United States.

(B) In carrying out this paragraph, the President may—

(i) remove or arrange for the removal of a discharge, and mitigate or prevent a substantial threat of a discharge, at any time;

(ii) direct or monitor all Federal, State, and private actions to remove a discharge; and

(iii) remove and, if necessary, destroy a vessel discharging, or threatening to discharge, by whatever means are available.

(2) Discharge posing substantial threat to public health or welfare

(A) If a discharge, or a substantial threat of a discharge, of oil or a hazardous substance from a vessel, offshore facility, or onshore facility is of such a size or character as to be a substantial threat to the public health or welfare of the United States (including but not limited to fish, shellfish, wildlife, other natural resources, and the public and private beaches and shorelines of the United States), the President shall direct all Federal, State, and private actions to remove the discharge or to mitigate or prevent the threat of the discharge.

(B) In carrying out this paragraph, the President may, without regard to any other provision of law governing contracting procedures or employment of personnel by the Federal Government—

(i) remove or arrange for the removal of the discharge, or mitigate or prevent the substantial threat of the discharge; and

(ii) remove and, if necessary, destroy a vessel discharging, or threatening to discharge, by whatever means are available.

(3) Actions in accordance with National Contingency Plan

(A) Each Federal agency, State, owner or operator, or other person participating in efforts under this subsection shall act in accordance with the National Contingency Plan or as directed by the President.

(B) An owner or operator participating in efforts under this subsection shall act in accor-

---

[2] See References in Text note below.

dance with the National Contingency Plan and the applicable response plan required under subsection (j) of this section, or as directed by the President, except that the owner or operator may deviate from the applicable response plan if the President or the Federal On-Scene Coordinator determines that deviation from the response plan would provide for a more expeditious or effective response to the spill or mitigation of its environmental effects.

(4) Exemption from liability

   (A) A person is not liable for removal costs or damages which result from actions taken or omitted to be taken in the course of rendering care, assistance, or advice consistent with the National Contingency Plan or as otherwise directed by the President relating to a discharge or a substantial threat of a discharge of oil or a hazardous substance.

   (B) Subparagraph (A) does not apply—
      (i) to a responsible party;
      (ii) to a response under the Comprehensive Environmental Response, Compensation, and Liability Act of 1980 (42 U.S.C. 9601 et seq.);
      (iii) with respect to personal injury or wrongful death; or
      (iv) if the person is grossly negligent or engages in willful misconduct.

   (C) A responsible party is liable for any removal costs and damages that another person is relieved of under subparagraph (A).

(5) Obligation and liability of owner or operator not affected

   Nothing in this subsection affects—
   (A) the obligation of an owner or operator to respond immediately to a discharge, or the threat of a discharge, of oil; or
   (B) the liability of a responsible party under the Oil Pollution Act of 1990 [33 U.S.C. 2701 et seq.].

(6) "Responsible party" defined

   For purposes of this subsection, the term "responsible party" has the meaning given that term under section 1001 of the Oil Pollution Act of 1990 [33 U.S.C. 2701].

(d) National Contingency Plan

   (1) Preparation by President

   The President shall prepare and publish a National Contingency Plan for removal of oil and hazardous substances pursuant to this section.

   (2) Contents

   The National Contingency Plan shall provide for efficient, coordinated, and effective action to minimize damage from oil and hazardous substance discharges, including containment, dispersal, and removal of oil and hazardous substances, and shall include, but not be limited to, the following:

   (A) Assignment of duties and responsibilities among Federal departments and agencies in coordination with State and local agencies and port authorities including, but not limited to, water pollution control and conservation and trusteeship of natural resources (including conservation of fish and wildlife).

   (B) Identification, procurement, maintenance, and storage of equipment and supplies.

   (C) Establishment or designation of Coast Guard strike teams, consisting of—
      (i) personnel who shall be trained, prepared, and available to provide necessary services to carry out the National Contingency Plan;
      (ii) adequate oil and hazardous substance pollution control equipment and material; and
      (iii) a detailed oil and hazardous substance pollution and prevention plan, including measures to protect fisheries and wildlife.

   (D) A system of surveillance and notice designed to safeguard against as well as ensure earliest possible notice of discharges of oil and hazardous substances and imminent threats of such discharges to the appropriate State and Federal agencies.

   (E) Establishment of a national center to provide coordination and direction for operations in carrying out the Plan.

   (F) Procedures and techniques to be employed in identifying, containing, dispersing, and removing oil and hazardous substances.

   (G) A schedule, prepared in cooperation with the States, identifying—

(i) dispersants, other chemicals, and other spill mitigating devices and substances, if any, that may be used in carrying out the Plan,
(ii) the waters in which such dispersants, other chemicals, and other spill mitigating devices and substances may be used, and
(iii) the quantities of such dispersant, other chemicals, or other spill mitigating device or substance which can be used safely in such waters,

which schedule shall provide in the case of any dispersant, chemical, spill mitigating device or substance, or waters not specifically identified in such schedule that the President, or his delegate, may, on a case-by-case basis, identify the dispersants, other chemicals, and other spill mitigating devices and substances which may be used, the waters in which they may be used, and the quantities which can be used safely in such waters.

(H) A system whereby the State or States affected by a discharge of oil or hazardous substance may act where necessary to remove such discharge and such State or States may be reimbursed in accordance with the Oil Pollution Act of 1990 [33 U.S.C. 2701 et seq.], in the case of any discharge of oil from a vessel or facility, for the reasonable costs incurred for that removal, from the Oil Spill Liability Trust Fund.

(I) Establishment of criteria and procedures to ensure immediate and effective Federal identification of, and response to, a discharge, or the threat of a discharge, that results in a substantial threat to the public health or welfare of the United States, as required under subsection (c)(2) of this section.

(J) Establishment of procedures and standards for removing a worst case discharge of oil, and for mitigating or preventing a substantial threat of such a discharge.

(K) Designation of the Federal official who shall be the Federal On-Scene Coordinator for each area for which an Area Contingency Plan is required to be prepared under subsection (j) of this section.

(L) Establishment of procedures for the coordination of activities of—
  (i) Coast Guard strike teams established under subparagraph (C);
  (ii) Federal On-Scene Coordinators designated under subparagraph (K);
  (iii) District Response Groups established under subsection (j) of this section; and
  (iv) Area Committees established under subsection (j) of this section.

(M) A fish and wildlife response plan, developed in consultation with the United States Fish and Wildlife Service, the National Oceanic and Atmospheric Administration, and other interested parties (including State fish and wildlife conservation officials), for the immediate and effective protection, rescue, and rehabilitation of, and the minimization of risk of damage to, fish and wildlife resources and their habitat that are harmed or that may be jeopardized by a discharge.

(3) Revisions and amendments

The President may, from time to time, as the President deems advisable, revise or otherwise amend the National Contingency Plan.

(4) Actions in accordance with National Contingency Plan

After publication of the National Contingency Plan, the removal of oil and hazardous substances and actions to minimize damage from oil and hazardous substance discharges shall, to the greatest extent possible, be in accordance with the National Contingency Plan.

(e) Civil enforcement

(1) Orders protecting public health

In addition to any action taken by a State or local government, when the President determines that there may be an imminent and substantial threat to the public health or welfare of the United States, including fish, shellfish, and wildlife, public and private property, shorelines, beaches, habitat, and other living and nonliving natural resources under the jurisdiction or control of the United States, because of an actual or threatened discharge of oil or a hazardous substance from a vessel or facility in violation of subsection (b) of this section, the President may—

(A) require the Attorney General to secure any relief from any person, including the owner or operator of the vessel or facility, as may be necessary to abate such endangerment; or

(B) after notice to the affected State, take any other action under this section, including issuing administrative orders, that may be necessary to protect the public health and welfare.

(2) Jurisdiction of district courts

The district courts of the United States shall have jurisdiction to grant any relief under this subsection that the public interest and the equities of the case may require.

(f) Liability for actual costs of removal

(1) Except where an owner or operator can prove that a discharge was caused solely by (A) an act of God, (B) an act of war, (C) negligence on the part of the United States Government, or (D) an act or omission of a third party without regard to whether any such act or omission was or was not negligent, or any combination of the foregoing clauses, such owner or operator of any vessel from which oil or a hazardous substance is discharged in violation of subsection (b)(3) of this section shall, notwithstanding any other provision of law, be liable to the United States Government for the actual costs incurred under subsection (c) of this section for the removal of such oil or substance by the United States Government in an amount not to exceed, in the case of an inland oil barge $125 per gross ton of such barge, or $125,000, whichever is greater, and in the case of any other vessel, $150 per gross ton of such vessel (or, for a vessel carrying oil or hazardous substances as cargo, $250,000), whichever is greater, except that where the United States can show that such discharge was the result of willful negligence or willful misconduct within the privity and knowledge of the owner, such owner or operator shall be liable to the United States Government for the full amount of such costs. Such costs shall constitute a maritime lien on such vessel which may be recovered in an action in rem in the district court of the United States for any district within which any vessel may be found. The United States may also bring an action against the owner or operator of such vessel in any court of competent jurisdiction to recover such costs.

(2) Except where an owner or operator of an onshore facility can prove that a discharge was caused solely by (A) an act of God, (B) an act of war, (C) negligence on the part of the United States Government, or (D) an act or omission of a third party without regard to whether any such act or omission was or was not negligent, or any combination of the foregoing clauses, such owner or operator of any such facility from which oil or a hazardous substance is discharged in violation of subsection (b)(3) of this section shall be liable to the United States Government for the actual costs incurred under subsection (c) of this section for the removal of such oil or substance by the United States Government in an amount not to exceed $50,000,000, except that where the United States can show that such discharge was the result of willful negligence or willful misconduct within the privity and knowledge of the owner, such owner or operator shall be liable to the United States Government for the full amount of such costs. The United States may bring an action against the owner or operator of such facility in any court of competent jurisdiction to recover such costs. The Administrator is authorized, by regulation, after consultation with the Secretary of Commerce and the Small Business Administration, to establish reasonable and equitable classifications of those onshore facilities having a total fixed storage capacity of 1,000 barrels or less which he determines because of size, type, and location do not present a substantial risk of the discharge of oil or a hazardous substance in violation of subsection (b)(3) of this section, and apply with respect to such classifications differing limits of liability which may be less than the amount contained in this paragraph.

(3) Except where an owner or operator of an offshore facility can prove that a discharge was caused solely by (A) an act of God, (B) an act of war, (C) negligence on the part of the United States Government, or (D) an act or omission of a third party without regard to whether any such act or omission was or was not negligent, or any combination of the foregoing clauses, such owner or operator of any such facility from which oil or a hazardous substance is discharged in violation of subsection (b)(3) of this section shall, notwithstanding any other provision of law, be liable to the United States Government for the actual costs incurred under subsection (c) of this section for the removal of such oil or substance by the United States Government in an amount not to exceed $50,000,000, except that where the United States can show that such discharge was the result of willful negligence or willful misconduct within the privity and knowledge of the owner, such owner or operator shall be liable to the United States Government for the full amount of

such costs. The United States may bring an action against the owner or operator of such a facility in any court of competent jurisdiction to recover such costs.

(4) The costs of removal of oil or a hazardous substance for which the owner or operator of a vessel or onshore or offshore facility is liable under subsection (f) of this section shall include any costs or expenses incurred by the Federal Government or any State government in the restoration or replacement of natural resources damaged or destroyed as a result of a discharge of oil or a hazardous substance in violation of subsection (b) of this section.

(5) The President, or the authorized representative of any State, shall act on behalf of the public as trustee of the natural resources to recover for the costs of replacing or restoring such resources. Sums recovered shall be used to restore, rehabilitate, or acquire the equivalent of such natural resources by the appropriate agencies of the Federal Government, or the State government.

(g) Third party liability

Where the owner or operator of a vessel (other than an inland oil barge) carrying oil or hazardous substances as cargo or an onshore or offshore facility which handles or stores oil or hazardous substances in bulk, from which oil or a hazardous substance is discharged in violation of subsection (b) of this section, alleges that such discharge was caused solely by an act or omission of a third party, such owner or operator shall pay to the United States Government the actual costs incurred under subsection (c) of this section for removal of such oil or substance and shall be entitled by subrogation to all rights of the United States Government to recover such costs from such third party under this subsection. In any case where an owner or operator of a vessel, of an onshore facility, or of an offshore facility, from which oil or a hazardous substance is discharged in violation of subsection (b)(3) of this section, proves that such discharge of oil or hazardous substance was caused solely by an act or omission of a third party, or was caused solely by such an act or omission in combination with an act of God, an act of war, or negligence on the part of the United States Government, such third party shall, notwithstanding any other provision of law, be liable to the United States Government for the actual costs incurred under subsection (c) of this section for removal of such oil or substance by the United States Government, except where such third party can prove that such discharge was caused solely by (A) an act of God, (B) an act of war, (C) negligence on the part of the United States Government, or (D) an act or omission of another party without regard to whether such act or omission was or was not negligent, or any combination of the foregoing clauses. If such third party was the owner or operator of a vessel which caused the discharge of oil or a hazardous substance in violation of subsection (b)(3) of this section, the liability of such third party under this subsection shall not exceed, in the case of an inland oil barge $125 per gross ton of such barge, or $125,000, whichever is greater, and in the case of any other vessel, $150 per gross ton of such vessel (or, for a vessel carrying oil or hazardous substances as cargo, $250,000), whichever is greater. In any other case the liability of such third party shall not exceed the limitation which would have been applicable to the owner or operator of the vessel or the onshore or offshore facility from which the discharge actually occurred if such owner or operator were liable. If the United States can show that the discharge of oil or a hazardous substance in violation of subsection (b)(3) of this section was the result of willful negligence or willful misconduct within the privity and knowledge of such third party, such third party shall be liable to the United States Government for the full amount of such removal costs. The United States may bring an action against the third party in any court of competent jurisdiction to recover such removal costs.

(h) Rights against third parties who caused or contributed to discharge

The liabilities established by this section shall in no way affect any rights which (1) the owner or operator of a vessel or of an onshore facility or an offshore facility may have against any third party whose acts may in any way have caused or contributed to such discharge, or (2) the United States Government may have against any third party whose actions may in any way have caused or contributed to the discharge of oil or hazardous substance.

(i) Recovery of removal costs

In any case where an owner or operator of a vessel or an onshore facility or an offshore facility from which oil or a hazardous substance is discharged in violation of subsection (b)(3) of this section acts to remove such oil or substance in accordance with regulations promulgated pursuant to this section, such owner or operator shall be entitled to recover the reasonable costs incurred in such removal upon establishing, in a suit which may be brought against the United States Government in the United States Court of Federal Claims, that such discharge was caused solely by (A) an act of God, (B) an act of war, (C) negligence on the part of the United States Government, or (D) an act or omission of a third party without regard to whether such act or omission was or was not negligent, or of any combination of the foregoing causes.

(j) National Response System

(1) In general

Consistent with the National Contingency Plan required by subsection (c)(2) of this section, as soon as practicable after October 18, 1972, and from time to time thereafter, the President shall issue regulations consistent with maritime safety and with marine and navigation laws (A) establishing methods and procedures for removal of discharged oil and hazardous substances. (B) establishing criteria for the development and implementation of local and regional oil and hazardous substance removal contingency plans, (C) establishing procedures, methods, and equipment and other requirements for equipment to prevent discharges of oil and hazardous substances from vessels and from onshore facilities and offshore facilities, and to contain such discharges, and (D) governing the inspection of vessels carrying cargoes of oil and hazardous substances and the inspection of such cargoes in order to reduce the likelihood of discharges of oil from vessels in violation of this section.

(2) National Response Unit

The Secretary of the department in which the Coast Guard is operating shall establish a National Response Unit at Elizabeth City, North Carolina. The Secretary, acting through the National Response Unit—

(A) shall compile and maintain a comprehensive computer list of spill removal resources, personnel, and equipment that is available worldwide and within the areas designated by the President pursuant to paragraph (4), and of information regarding previous spills, including data from universities, research institutions, State governments, and other nations, as appropriate, which shall be disseminated as appropriate to response groups and area committees, and which shall be available to Federal and State agencies and the public;

(B) shall provide technical assistance, equipment, and other resources requested by a Federal On-Scene Coordinator;

(C) shall coordinate use of private and public personnel and equipment to remove a worst case discharge, and to mitigate or prevent a substantial threat of such a discharge, from a vessel, offshore facility, or onshore facility operating in or near an area designated by the President pursuant to paragraph (4);

(D) may provide technical assistance in the preparation of Area Contingency Plans required under paragraph (4);

(E) shall administer Coast Guard strike teams established under the National Contingency Plan;

(F) shall maintain on file all Area Contingency Plans approved by the President under this subsection; and

(G) shall review each of those plans that affects its responsibilities under this subsection.

(3) Coast Guard District Response Groups

(A) The Secretary of the department in which the Coast Guard is operating shall establish in each Coast Guard district a Coast Guard District Response Group.

(B) Each Coast Guard District Response Group shall consist of—

(i) the Coast Guard personnel and equipment, including firefighting equipment, of each port within the district;

(ii) additional prepositioned equipment; and

(iii) a district response advisory staff.

(C) Coast Guard district response groups—

(i) shall provide technical assistance, equipment, and other resources when required by a Federal On-Scene Coordinator;

(ii) shall maintain all Coast Guard response equipment within its district;

(iii) may provide technical assistance in the preparation of Area Contingency Plans required under paragraph (4); and

(iv) shall review each of those plans that affect its area of geographic responsibility.
(4) Area Committees and Area Contingency Plans
   (A) There is established for each area designated by the President an Area Committee comprised of members appointed by the President from qualified personnel of Federal, State, and local agencies.
   (B) Each Area Committee, under the direction of the Federal On-Scene Coordinator for its area, shall—
      (i) prepare for its area the Area Contingency Plan required under subparagraph (C);
      (ii) work with State and local officials to enhance the contingency planning of those officials and to assure preplanning of joint response efforts, including appropriate procedures for mechanical recovery, dispersal, shoreline cleanup, protection of sensitive environmental areas, and protection, rescue, and rehabilitation of fisheries and wildlife; and
      (iii) work with State and local officials to expedite decisions for the use of dispersants and other mitigating substances and devices.
   (C) Each Area Committee shall prepare and submit to the President for approval an Area Contingency Plan for its area. The Area Contingency Plan shall—
      (i) when implemented in conjunction with the National Contingency Plan, be adequate to remove a worst case discharge, and to mitigate or prevent a substantial threat of such a discharge, from a vessel, offshore facility, or onshore facility operating in or near the area;
      (ii) describe the area covered by the plan, including the areas of special economic or environmental importance that might be damaged by a discharge;
      (iii) describe in detail the responsibilities of an owner or operator and of Federal, State, and local agencies in removing a discharge, and in mitigating or preventing a substantial threat of a discharge;
      (iv) list the equipment (including firefighting equipment), dispersants or other mitigating substances and devices, and personnel available to an owner or operator and Federal, State, and local agencies, to ensure an effective and immediate removal of a discharge, and to ensure mitigation or prevention of a substantial threat of a discharge;
      (v) compile a list of local scientists, both inside and outside Federal Government service, with expertise in the environmental effects of spills of the types of oil typically transported in the area, who may be contacted to provide information or, where appropriate, participate in meetings of the scientific support team convened in response to a spill, and describe the procedures to be followed for obtaining an expedited decision regarding the use of dispersants;
      (vi) describe in detail how the plan is integrated into other Area Contingency Plans and vessel, offshore facility, and onshore facility response plans approved under this subsection, and into operating procedures of the National Response Unit;
      (vii) include any other information the President requires; and
      (viii) be updated periodically by the Area Committee.
   (D) The President shall—
      (i) review and approve Area Contingency Plans under this paragraph; and
      (ii) periodically review Area Contingency Plans so approved.
(5) Tank vessel and facility response plans
   (A) The President shall issue regulations which require an owner or operator of a tank vessel or facility described in subparagraph (B) to prepare and submit to the President a plan for responding, to the maximum extent practicable, to a worst case discharge, and to a substantial threat of such a discharge, of oil or a hazardous substance.
   (B) The tank vessels and facilities referred to in subparagraph (A) are the following:
      (i) A tank vessel, as defined under section 2101 of title 46.
      (ii) An offshore facility.
      (iii) An onshore facility that, because of its location, could reasonably be expected to cause substantial harm to the environment by discharging into or on the navigable waters, adjoining shorelines, or the exclusive economic zone.

(C) A response plan required under this paragraph shall—
  (i) be consistent with the requirements of the National Contingency Plan and Area Contingency Plans;
  (ii) identify the qualified individual having full authority to implement removal actions, and require immediate communications between that individual and the appropriate Federal official and the persons providing personnel and equipment pursuant to clause (iii);
  (iii) identify, and ensure by contract or other means approved by the President the availability of, private personnel and equipment necessary to remove to the maximum extent practicable a worst case discharge (including a discharge resulting from fire or explosion), and to mitigate or prevent a substantial threat of such a discharge;
  (iv) describe the training, equipment testing, periodic unannounced drills, and response actions of persons on the vessel or at the facility, to be carried out under the plan to ensure the safety of the vessel or facility and to mitigate or prevent the discharge, or the substantial threat of a discharge;
  (v) be updated periodically; and
  (vi) be resubmitted for approval of each significant change.
(D) With respect to any response plan submitted under this paragraph for an onshore facility that, because of its location, could reasonably be expected to cause significant and substantial harm to the environment by discharging into or on the navigable waters or adjoining shorelines or the exclusive economic zone, and with respect to each response plan submitted under this paragraph for a tank vessel or offshore facility, the President shall—
  (i) promptly review such response plan;
  (ii) require amendments to any plan that does not meet the requirements of this paragraph;
  (iii) approve any plan that meets the requirements of this paragraph; and
  (iv) review each plan periodically thereafter.
(E) A tank vessel, offshore facility, or onshore facility required to prepare a response plan under this subsection may not handle, store, or transport oil unless—
  (i) in the case of a tank vessel, offshore facility, or onshore facility for which a response plan is reviewed by the President under subparagraph (D), the plan has been approved by the President; and
  (ii) the vessel or facility is operating in compliance with the plan.
(F) Notwithstanding subparagraph (E), the President may authorize a tank vessel, offshore facility, or onshore facility to operate without a response plan approved under this paragraph, until not later than 2 years after the date of the submission to the President of a plan for the tank vessel or facility, if the owner or operator certifies that the owner or operator has ensured by contract or other means approved by the President the availability of private personnel and equipment necessary to respond, to the maximum extent practicable, to a worst case discharge or a substantial threat of such a discharge.
(G) The owner or operator of a tank vessel, offshore facility, or onshore facility may not claim as a defense to liability under title I of the Oil Pollution Act of 1990 [33 U.S.C. 2701 et seq.] that the owner or operator was acting in accordance with an approved response plan.
(H) The Secretary shall maintain, in the Vessel Identification System established under chapter 125 of title 46, the dates of approval and review of a response plan under this paragraph for each tank vessel that is a vessel of the United States.
(6) Equipment requirements and inspection
Not later than 2 years after August 18, 1990, the President shall require—
(A) periodic inspection of containment booms, skimmers, vessels, and other major equipment used to remove discharges; and
(B) vessels operating on navigable waters and carrying oil or a hazardous substance in bulk as cargo to carry appropriate removal equipment that employs the best technology economically feasible and that is compatible with the safe operation of the vessel.

(7) Area drills

The President shall periodically conduct drills of removal capability, without prior notice, in areas for which Area Contingency Plans are required under this subsection and under relevant tank vessel and facility response plans. The drills may include participation by Federal, State, and local agencies, the owners and operators of vessels and facilities in the area, and private industry. The President may publish annual reports on these drills, including assessments of the effectiveness of the plans and a list of amendments made to improve plans.

(8) United States Government not liable

The United States Government is not liable for any damages arising from its actions or omissions relating to any response plan required by this section.

(k) Repealed. Pub. L. 101-380, title II, Sec. 2002(b)(2), Aug. 18, 1990, 104 Stat. 507

(l) Administration

The President is authorized to delegate the administration of this section to the heads of those Federal departments, agencies, and instrumentalities which he determines to be appropriate. Each such department, agency, and instrumentality, in order to avoid duplication of effort, shall, whenever appropriate, utilize the personnel, services, and facilities of other Federal departments, agencies, and instrumentalities.

(m) Administrative provisions

(1) For vessels

Anyone authorized by the President to enforce the provisions of this section with respect to any vessel may, except as to public vessels—

(A) board and inspect any vessel upon the navigable waters of the United States or the waters of the contiguous zone,

(B) with or without a warrant, arrest any person who in the presence or view of the authorized person violates the provisions of this section or any regulation issued thereunder, and

(C) execute any warrant or other process issued by an officer or court of competent jurisdiction.

(2) For facilities

(A) Recordkeeping

Whenever required to carry out the purposes of this section, the Administrator or the Secretary of the Department in which the Coast Guard is operating shall require the owner or operator of a facility to which this section applies to establish and maintain such records, make such reports, install, use, and maintain such monitoring equipment and methods, and provide such other information as the Administrator or Secretary, as the case may be, may require to carry out the objectives of this section.

(B) Entry and inspection

Whenever required to carry out the purposes of this section, the Administrator or the Secretary of the Department in which the Coast Guard is operating or an authorized representative of the Administrator or Secretary, upon presentation of appropriate credentials, may—

(i) enter and inspect any facility to which this section applies, including any facility at which any records are required to be maintained under subparagraph (A); and

(ii) at reasonable times, have access to and copy any records, take samples, and inspect any monitoring equipment or methods required under subparagraph (A).

(C) Arrests and execution of warrants

Anyone authorized by the Administrator or the Secretary of the department in which the Coast Guard is operating to enforce the provisions of this section with respect to any facility may—

(i) with or without a warrant, arrest any person who violates the provisions of this section or any regulation issued thereunder in the presence or view of the person so authorized; and

(ii) execute any warrant or process issued by an officer or court of competent jurisdiction.

(D) Public access
Any records, reports, or information obtained under this paragraph shall be subject to the same public access and disclosure requirements which are applicable to records, reports, and information obtained pursuant to section 1318 of this title.

(n) Jurisdiction
The several district courts of the United States are invested with jurisdiction for any actions, other than actions pursuant to subsection (i)(1) of this section, arising under this section. In the case of Guam and the Trust Territory of the Pacific Islands, such actions may be brought in the district court of Guam, and in the case of the Virgin Islands such actions may be brought in the district court of the Virgin Islands. In the case of American Samoa and the Trust Territory of the Pacific Islands, such actions may be brought in the District Court of the United States for the District of Hawaii and such court shall have jurisdiction of such actions. In the case of the Canal Zone, such actions may be brought in the United States District Court for the District of the Canal Zone.

(o) Obligation for damages unaffected; local authority not preempted; existing Federal authority not modified or affected
   (1) Nothing in this section shall affect or modify in any way the obligations of any owner or operator of any vessel, or of any owner or operator of any onshore facility or offshore facility to any person or agency under any provision of law for damages to any publicly owned or privately owned property resulting from a discharge of any oil or hazardous substance or from the removal of any such oil or hazardous substance.
   (2) Nothing in this section shall be construed as preempting any State or political subdivision thereof from imposing any requirement or liability with respect to the discharge of oil or hazardous substance into any waters within such State, or with respect to any removal activities related to such discharge.
   (3) Nothing in this section shall be construed as affecting or modifying any other existing authority of any Federal department, agency, or instrumentality, relative to onshore or offshore facilities under this chapter or any other provision of law, or to affect any State or local law not in conflict with this section.

(p) Repealed. Pub. L. 101-380, title II, Sec. 2002(b)(4), Aug. 18, 1990, 104 Stat. 507

(q) Establishment of maximum limit of liability with respect to onshore or offshore facilities
The President is authorized to establish, with respect to any class or category of onshore or offshore facilities, a maximum limit of liability under subsections (f)(2) and (3) of this section of less than $50,000,000, but not less than $8,000,000.

(r) Liability limitations not to limit liability under other legislation
Nothing in this section shall be construed to impose, or authorize the imposition of, any limitation on liability under the Outer Continental Shelf Lands Act [43 U.S.C. 1331 et seq.] or the Deepwater Port Act of 1974 [33 U.S.C. 1501 et seq.].

(s) Oil Spill Liability Trust Fund
The Oil Spill Liability Trust Fund established under section 9509 of title 26 shall be available to carry out subsections (b), (c), (d), (j), and (l) of this section as those subsections apply to discharges, and substantial threats of discharges, of oil. Any amounts received by the United States under this section shall be deposited in the Oil Spill Liability Trust Fund.

(June 30, 1948, ch. 758, title III, Sec. 311, as added Pub. L. 92-500, Sec. 2, Oct. 18, 1972, 86 Stat. 862; amended Pub. L. 93-207, Sec. 1(4), Dec. 28, 1973, 87 Stat. 906; Pub. L. 95-217, Secs. 57, 58(a)-(g), (i), (k)-(m), Dec. 27, 1977, 91 Stat. 1593-1596; Pub. L. 95-576, Sec. 1(b), Nov. 2, 1978, 92 Stat. 2467; Pub. L. 96-478, Sec. 13(b), Oct. 21, 1980, 94 Stat. 2303; Pub. L. 96-483, Sec. 8, Oct. 21, 1980, 94 Stat. 2362; Pub. L. 96-561, title II, Sec. 238(b), Dec. 22, 1980, 94 Stat. 3300; Pub. L. 97-164, title I, Sec. 161(5), Apr. 2, 1982, 96 Stat. 49; Pub. L. 100-4, title V, Sec. 502(b), Feb. 4, 1987, 101 Stat. 75; Pub. L. 101-380, title II, Sec. 2002(b), title IV, Secs. 4201(a), (b), (b)[(c)], 4202(a), (c), 4204, 4301(a), (b), 4305, 4306, Aug. 18, 1990, 104 Stat. 507, 523-527, 532, 533, 540, 541; Pub. L. 102-388, title III, Sec. 349, Oct. 6, 1992, 106 Stat. 1554; Pub. L. 102-572, title IX, Sec. 902(b)(1), Oct. 29, 1992, 106 Stat. 4516; Pub. L. 104-208, div. A, title I, Sec. 101(a) [title II, Sec. 211(b)], Sept. 30, 1996, 110 Stat. 3009, 3009-41; Pub. L. 104-324, title XI, Secs. 1143, 1144, Oct. 19, 1996, 110 Stat. 3992; Pub. L. 105-383, title IV, Sec. 411, Nov. 13, 1998, 112 Stat. 3432.)

References in Text

The Outer Continental Shelf Lands Act, referred to in subsecs. (b)(1), (2)(A), (3) and (r), is act Aug. 7, 1953, ch. 345, 67 Stat. 462, as amended, which is classified generally to subchapter III (Sec. 1331 et seq.) of chapter 29 of Title 43, Public Lands. For complete classification of this Act to the Code, see Short Title note set out under section 1331 of Title 43 and Tables.

The Deepwater Port Act of 1974, referred to in subsecs. (b)(1), (2)(A), (3) and (r), is Pub. L. 93-627, Jan. 3, 1975, 88 Stat. 2126, as amended, which is classified generally to chapter 29 (Sec. 1501 et seq.) of this title. For complete classification of this Act to the Code, see Short Title note set out under section 1501 of this title and Tables.

The Magnuson-Stevens Fishery Conservation and Management Act, referred to in subsec. (b)(1), (2)(A), (3), is Pub. L. 94-265, Apr. 13, 1976, 90 Stat. 331, as amended, which is classified principally to chapter 38 (Sec. 1801 et seq.) of Title 16, Conservation. For complete classification of this Act to the Code, see Short Title note set out under section 1801 of Title 16 and Tables.

The date of enactment of this paragraph, referred to in subsec. (b)(2)(B), probably means the date of enactment of Pub. L. 95-576, which amended subsec. (b)(2)(B) and which was approved Nov. 2, 1978.

The penalty enacted in subclause (bb) of clause (iii) of subparagraph (B) of subsection (b)(2) of section 311 of Public Law 92-500, referred to in subsec. (b)(2)(B), probably means the penalty provision of subsec. (b)(2)(B)(iii)(bb) of this section as added by Pub. L. 92-500, Sec. 2, Oct. 18, 1972, 86 Stat. 864, prior to the amendment to subsec. (b)(2)(B) by section 1(b)(3) of Pub. L. 95-576. Prior to amendment, subsec. (b)(2)(B)(iii)(bb) read as follows: "a penalty determined by the number of units discharged multiplied by the amount established for such unit under clause (iv) of this subparagraph, but such penalty shall not be more than $5,000,000 in the case of a discharge from a vessel and $500,000 in the case of a discharge from an onshore or offshore facility."

Section 313 of title 46, Appendix, referred to in subsec. (b)(12)(B), was repealed by Pub. L. 103-182, title VI, Sec. 690(a)(21), Dec. 8, 1993, 107 Stat. 2223.

Section 1443 of title 19, referred to in subsec. (b)(12)(C), was repealed by Pub. L. 103-182, title VI, Sec. 690(b)(6), Dec. 8, 1993, 107 Stat. 2223.

The Comprehensive Environmental Response, Compensation, and Liability Act of 1980, referred to in subsec. (c)(4)(B)(ii), is Pub. L. 96-510, Dec. 11, 1980, 94 Stat. 2767, as amended, which is classified principally to chapter 103 (Sec. 9601 et seq.) of Title 42, The Public Health and Welfare. For complete classification of this Act to the Code, see Short Title note set out under section 9601 of Title 42 and Tables.

The Oil Pollution Act of 1990, referred to in subsecs. (c)(5)(B), (d)(2)(H), and (j)(5)(G), is Pub. L. 101-380, Aug. 18, 1990, 104 Stat. 484, which is classified principally to chapter 40 (Sec. 2701 et seq.) of this title. Title I of the Act is classified generally to subchapter I (Sec. 2701 et seq.) of chapter 40 of this title. For complete classification of this Act to the Code, see Short Title note set out under section 2701 of this title and Tables.

Codification

August 18, 1990, referred to in subsec. (j)(6), was in the original "the date of enactment of this section", which was translated as meaning the date of enactment of Pub. L. 101-380, which enacted subsec. (j)(2) to (8), to reflect the probable intent of Congress.

Amendments

1998—Subsec. (a)(2). Pub. L. 105-383, Sec. 411(b), substituted ", (C)" for "and (C)" and inserted ", and (D) discharges incidental to mechanical removal authorized by the President under subsection (c) of this section" before semicolon at end.

Subsec. (a)(8). Pub. L. 105-383, Sec. 411(a)(1), substituted "to prevent, minimize, or mitigate damage" for "to minimize or mitigate damage".

Subsec. (a)(25). Pub. L. 105-383, Sec. 411(a)(2), added par. (25).

Subsec. (c)(4)(A). Pub. L. 105-383, Sec. 411(a)(3), inserted "relating to a discharge or a substantial threat of a discharge of oil or a hazardous substance" before period at end.

1996—Subsec. (b)(1), (2)(A), (3). Pub. L. 104-208 substituted "Magnuson-Stevens Fishery" for "Magnuson Fishery" wherever appearing.

Subsec. (c)(3)(B). Pub. L. 104-324, Sec. 1144, inserted ", except that the owner or operator may deviate from the applicable response plan if the President or the Federal On-Scene Coordinator determines that deviation from the response plan would provide for a more expeditious or effective response to the spill or mitigation of its environmental effects" before period at end.

Subsec. (j)(2)(A). Pub. L. 104-324, Sec. 1143(1), inserted "and of information regarding previous spills, including data from universities, research institutions, State governments, and other nations, as appropriate, which shall be disseminated as appropriate to response groups and area committees, and" after "paragraph (4),".

Subsec. (j)(4)(C)(v). Pub. L. 104-324, Sec. 1143(2), inserted "compile a list of local scientists, both inside and outside Federal Government service, with expertise in the environmental effects of spills of the types of oil typically transported in the area, who may be contacted to provide information or, where appropriate, participate in meetings of the scientific support team convened in response to a spill, and" before "describe".

1992—Subsec. (b)(12). Pub. L. 102-388 added par. (12).

Subsec. (i). Pub. L. 102-572 substituted "United States Court of Federal Claims" for "United States Claims Court".

1990—Subsec. (a)(8). Pub. L. 101-380, Sec. 4201(b)(1)[(c)(1)], inserted "containment and" after "refers to".

Subsec. (a)(16). Pub. L. 101-380, Sec. 4201(b)(2)[(c)(2)], substituted semicolon for period at end.

Subsec. (a)(17). Pub. L. 101-380, Sec. 4201(b)(3)[(c)(3)], substituted "otherwise" for "Otherwise" and semicolon for period at end.

Subsec. (a)(18) to (24). Pub. L. 101-380, Sec. 4201(b)(4)[(c)(4)], added pars. (18) to (24).

Subsec. (b)(4). Pub. L. 101-380, Sec. 4204, inserted "or the environment" after "the public health or welfare".

Subsec. (b)(5). Pub. L. 101-380, Sec. 4301(a), inserted after first sentence "The Federal agency shall immediately notify the appropriate State agency of any State which is, or may reasonably be expected to be, affected by the discharge of oil or a hazardous substance.", substituted "fined in accordance with title 18, United States Code, or imprisoned for not more than 5 years, or both" for "fined not more than $10,000, or imprisoned for not more than one year, or both", struck out "or information obtained by the exploitation of such notification" before "shall not be used", and inserted "natural" before "person in any".

Subsec. (b)(6) to (11). Pub. L. 101-380, Sec. 4301(b), added pars. (6) to (11) and struck out former par. (6) which related to assessment of civil penalties, limited to $5,000 for each offense, against any owner, operator, or person in charge of any onshore or offshore facility from which oil or a hazardous substance was discharged in violation of par. (3).

Subsec. (c). Pub. L. 101-380, Sec. 4201(a), amended subsec. (c) generally, substituting present provisions for provisions authorizing President to arrange for removal of discharge of oil or a hazardous substance into or upon the navigable waters of the U.S., unless he determined such removal would be properly conducted by owner or operator of the vessel causing discharge, and directed President to prepare and publish a National Contingency Plan within 60 days after October 18, 1972.

Subsec. (d). Pub. L. 101-380, Sec. 4201(b), amended subsec. (d) generally. Prior to amendment, subsec. (d) read as follows: "Whenever a marine disaster in or upon the navigable waters of the United States has created a substantial threat of a pollution hazard to the public health or welfare of the United States, including, but not limited to, fish, shellfish, and wildlife and the public and private shorelines and beaches of the United States, because of a discharge, or an imminent discharge, of large quantities of oil, or of a hazardous substance from a vessel the United States may (A) coordinate and direct all public and private efforts directed at the removal or elimination of such threat; and (B) summarily remove, and, if necessary, destroy such vessel by whatever means are available without regard to any provisions of law governing the employment of personnel or the expenditure of appropriated funds. Any expense incurred under this subsection or under the Intervention on the High Seas Act (or the convention defined in section 2(3) thereof) shall be a cost incurred by the United States Government for the purposes of subsection (f) of this section in the removal of oil or hazardous substance."

Subsec. (e). Pub. L. 101-380, Sec. 4306, amended subsec. (e) generally. Prior to amendment, subsec. (e) read as follows: "In addition to any other action taken by a State or local government, when the President determines there is an imminent and substantial threat to the public health or welfare of the United States, including, but not limited to, fish, shellfish, and wildlife and public and private property, shorelines, and beaches within the United States, because of an actual or threatened discharge of oil or hazardous substance into or upon the navigable waters of the United States from an onshore or offshore facility, the President may require the United States attorney of the district in which the threat occurs to secure such relief as may be necessary to abate such threat, and the district courts of the United States shall have jurisdiction to grant such relief as the public interest and the equities of the case may require."

Subsec. (i). Pub. L. 101-380, Sec. 2002(b)(1), struck out par. (1) designation before "In any case" and struck out pars. (2) and (3) which read as follows:

"(2) The provisions of this subsection shall not apply in any case where liability is established pursuant to the Outer Continental Shelf Lands Act, or the Deepwater Port Act of 1974.

(3) Any amount paid in accordance with a judgment of the United States Claims Court pursuant to this section shall be paid from the funds established pursuant to subsection (k) of this section."

Subsec. (j). Pub. L. 101-380, Sec. 4202(a), amended heading, inserted heading for par. (1) and realigned its margin, added pars. (2) to (8), and struck out former par. (2) which read as follows: "Any owner or operator of a vessel or an onshore facility or an offshore facility and any other person subject to any regulation issued under paragraph (1) of this subsection who fails or refuses to comply with the provisions of any such regulations, shall be liable to a civil penalty of not more than $5,000 for each such violation. This paragraph shall not apply to any owner or operator of any vessel from which oil or a hazardous substance is discharged in violation of paragraph (3)(ii) of subsection (b) of this section unless such owner, operator, or person in charge is otherwise subject to the jurisdiction of the United States. Each violation shall be a separate offense. The President may assess and compromise such penalty. No penalty shall be assessed until the owner, operator, or other person charged shall have been given notice and an opportunity for a hearing on such charge. In determining the amount of the penalty, or the amount agreed upon in compromise, the gravity of the violation, and the demonstrated good faith of the owner, operator, or other person charged in attempting to achieve rapid compliance, after notification of a violation, shall be considered by the President."

Subsec. (k). Pub. L. 101-380, Sec. 2002(b)(2), struck out subsec. (k) which authorized appropriations and supplemental appropriations to create and maintain a revolving fund to carry out subsecs. (c), (d), (i), and (l) of this section.

Subsec. (l). Pub. L. 101-380, Sec. 2002(b)(3), struck out after first sentence "Any moneys in the fund established by subsection (k) of this section shall be available to such Federal departments, agencies, and instrumentalities to carry out the provisions of subsections (c) and (i) of this section."

Subsec. (m). Pub. L. 101-380, Sec. 4305, amended subsec. (m) generally. Prior to amendment, subsec. (m) read as follows: "Anyone authorized by the President to enforce the provisions of this section may, except as to public vessels, (A) board and inspect any vessel upon the navigable waters of the United States or the waters of the contiguous zone, (B) with or without a warrant arrest any person who violates the provisions of this section or any regulation issued thereunder in his presence or view, and (C) execute any warrant or other process issued by an officer or court of competent jurisdiction."

Subsec. (o)(2). Pub. L. 101-380, Sec. 4202(c), inserted ", or with respect to any removal activities related to such discharge" after "within such State".

Subsec. (p). Pub. L. 101-380, Sec. 2002(b)(4), struck out subsec. (p) which provided for establishment and maintenance of evidence of financial responsibility by vessels over 300 gross tons carrying oil or hazardous substances.

Subsec. (s). Pub. L. 101-380, Sec. 2002(b)(5), added subsec. (s).

1987—Subsec. (a)(5). Pub. L. 100-4 substituted "the Commonwealth of the Northern Mariana Islands" for "the Canal Zone".

1982—Subsec. (i)(1), (3). Pub. L. 97-164 substituted "Claims Court" for "Court of Claims".

1980—Subsec. (b)(1), (2)(A), (3). Pub. L. 96-561 substituted "Magnuson Fishery Conservation and Management Act" for "Fishery Conservation and Management Act of 1976".

Subsec. (b)(3)(A). Pub. L. 96-478 struck out "of oil" after "in the case of such discharges" and substituted "Protocol of 1978 Relating to the International Convention for the Prevention of Pollution from Ships, 1973" for "International Convention for the Prevention of Pollution of the Sea by Oil, 1954, as amended".

Subsec. (c)(1). Pub. L. 96-561 substituted "Magnuson Fishery Conservation and Management Act" for "Fishery Conservation and Management Act of 1976".

Subsec. (k). Pub. L. 96-483 designated existing provisions as par. (1) and added par. (2).

1978—Subsec. (a)(2). Pub. L. 95-576, Sec. 1(b)(1), excluded discharges described in cls. (A) to (C) from term "discharge".

Subsec. (a)(17). Pub. L. 95-576, Sec. 1(b)(2), added par. (17).

Subsec. (b)(2)(B). Pub. L. 95-576, Sec. 1(b)(3), substituted requirement that a study be made respecting methods, mechanisms, and procedures for creating incentives to achieve higher standard of care in management and movement of hazardous substances, including consideration of enumerated items, and a report made to Congress within 18 months after Nov. 2, 1978, for provisions concerning actual removability of any designated hazardous substance, liability during two year period commencing Oct. 18, 1972 based on toxicity, degradability, and dispersal characteristics of the substance limited to $50,000 and without limitation in cases of willful negligence or willful misconduct, liability after such two year period ranging from $500 to $5,000 based on toxicity, etc., or liability for penalty determined by number of units discharged multiplied by amount established for the unit limited to $5,000,000 in the case of a discharge from a vessel and to $500,000 in the case of a discharge from onshore or offshore facility, establishment by regulation of a unit of measurement based upon the usual trade practice for each designated hazardous substance and establishment for such unit a fixed monetary amount ranging from $100 to $1,000 based on toxicity, etc.

Subsec. (b)(3). Pub. L. 95-576, Sec. 1(b)(4), substituted "such quantities as may be harmful" for "harmful quantities".

Subsec. (b)(4). Pub. L. 95-576, Sec. 1(b)(5), struck out ", to be issued as soon as possible after October 18, 1972," after "regulation" and substituted "substances" for "substance" and "discharge of which may be harmful" for "discharge of which, at such times, locations, circumstances, and conditions, will be harmful".

Subsec. (b)(5). Pub. L. 95-576, Sec. 1(b)(6), inserted "at the time of the discharge" after "otherwise subject to the jurisdiction of the United States".

Subsec. (b)(6)(A) to (E). Pub. L. 95-576, Sec. 1(b)(7), designated existing provisions as subpar. (A), inserted "at the time of the discharge" after "jurisdiction of the United States", and added subpars. (B) to (E).

1977—Subsec. (a)(11). Pub. L. 95-217, Sec. 58(k), inserted ", and any facility of any kind which is subject to the jurisdiction of the United States and is located in, on, or under any other waters," after "United States".

Subsec. (a)(15), (16). Pub. L. 95-217, Sec. 58(d)(1), added pars. (15) and (16).

Subsec. (b)(1). Pub. L. 95-217, Sec. 58(a)(1), inserted reference to activities under the Outer Continental Shelf Lands Act or the Deepwater Port Act of 1974, or which may affect natural resources belonging to, appertaining to, or under the exclusive management authority of the United States (including resources under the Fishery Conservation and Management Act of 1976).

Subsec. (b)(2)(A). Pub. L. 95-217, Sec. 58(a)(2), inserted reference to activities under the Outer Continental Shelf Lands Act or the Deepwater Port Act of 1974, or which may affect natural resources belonging to, appertaining to, or under the exclusive management authority of the United States (including resources under the Fishery Conservation and Management Act of 1976).

Subsec. (b)(2)(B)(v). Pub. L. 95-217, Sec. 57, added cl. (v).

Subsec. (b)(3). Pub. L. 95-217, Sec. 58(a)(3), (4), designated part of existing provisions preceding cl. (A) as cl. (i) and added cl. (ii), and, in cl. (A), inserted "or which may affect natural resources belonging to, appertaining to, or under the exclusive management authority of the United States (including resources under the Fishery Conservation and Management Act of 1976)" after "waters of the contiguous zone" and struck out "article IV of" before "the International Convention for the Prevention of Pollution of the Sea by Oil, 1954".

Subsec. (b)(4). Pub. L. 95-217, Sec. 58(a)(5), struck out provisions under which, in the case of the discharge of oil into or upon the waters of the contiguous zone, only those discharges which threatened the fishery resources of the contiguous zone or threatened to pollute or contribute to the pollution of the territory or the territorial sea of the United States could be determined to be harmful.

Subsec. (b)(5). Pub. L. 95-217, Sec. 58(a)(6), added cls. (A), (B), and (C) between "Any such person" and "who fails to notify".

Subsec. (b)(6). Pub. L. 95-217, Sec. 58(a)(7), (8), substituted "Any owner, operator, or person in charge of any onshore facility, or offshore facility" for "Any owner or operator of any vessel, onshore facility, or offshore facility" in provision relating to violations of par. (3) of this subsection, and inserted provisions directing the assessment of a civil penalty of not more than $5,000 for each offense by the Secretary of the department in which the Coast Guard is operating to be assessed against any owner, operator, or person in charge of any vessel from which oil or a hazardous substance is discharged in violation of paragraph (3)(i) of this subsection, and any owner, operator, or person in charge of a vessel from which oil or a hazardous substance is discharged in violation of paragraph (3)(ii) who is otherwise subject to the jurisdiction of the United States.

Subsec. (c)(1). Pub. L. 95-217, Sec. 58(b), (c)(1), inserted "or there is a substantial threat of such discharge," after "Whenever any oil or a hazardous substance is discharged," and "or in connection with activities under the Outer Continental Shelf Lands Act or the Deepwater Port Act of 1974, or which may affect natural resources belonging to, appertaining to, or under the exclusive management authority of the United States (including resources under the Fishery Conservation and Management Act of 1976)" after "waters of the contiguous zone,".

Subsec. (c)(2)(D). Pub. L. 95-217, Sec. 58(e), substituted "and imminent threats of such discharges to the appropriate State and Federal agencies;" for "to the appropriate Federal agency;".

Subsec. (d). Pub. L. 95-217, Sec. 58(c)(2), inserted "or under the Intervention on the High Seas Act (or the convention defined in section 2(3) thereof)" after "Any expense incurred under this subsection".

Subsec. (f)(1). Pub. L. 95-217, Sec. 58(d)(2), substituted ", in the case of an inland oil barge $125 per gross ton of such barge, or $125,000, whichever is greater, and in the case of any other vessel, $150 per gross ton of such vessel (or, for a vessel carrying oil or hazardous substances as cargo, $250,000), whichever is greater," for "$100 per gross ton of such vessel or $14,000,000, whichever is lesser,".

Subsec. (f)(2), (3). Pub. L. 95-217, Sec. 58(d)(5), (6), substituted "$50,000,000" for "$8,000,000".

Subsec. (f)(4), (5). Pub. L. 95-217, Sec. 58(g), added pars. (4) and (5).

Subsec. (g). Pub. L. 95-217, Sec. 58(d)(3), (f), substituted ", in the case of an inland oil barge $125 per gross ton of such barge, or $125,000, whichever is greater, and in the case of any other vessel, $150 per gross ton of such vessel (or, for a vessel carrying oil or hazardous substances as cargo, $250,000), whichever is greater" for "$100 per gross ton of such vessel or $14,000,000, whichever is the lesser" in the existing provisions and inserted provision under which, where the owner or operator of a vessel (other than an inland oil barge) carrying oil or hazardous substances as cargo or an onshore or offshore facility which handles or stores oil or hazardous substances in bulk, from which oil or a hazardous substance is discharged in violation of subsec. (b) of this section, alleges that the discharge was caused solely by an act or omission of a third party, the owner or operator must pay to the United States Government the actual costs incurred under subsec. (c) of this section for removal of the oil or substance and shall be entitled by subrogation to all rights of the United States Government to recover the costs from the third party under this subsection.

Subsec. (i)(2). Pub. L. 95-217, Sec. 58(m), inserted reference to the Deepwater Port Act of 1974.

Subsec. (j)(2). Pub. L. 95-217, Sec. 58(c)(3), inserted provision that subsec. (j)(2) shall not apply to any owner or operator of any vessel from which oil or a hazardous substance is discharged in violation of subsec. (b)(3)(ii) of this section unless the owner, operator, or person in charge is otherwise subject to the jurisdiction of the United States.

Subsec. (k). Pub. L. 95-217, Sec. 58(l), substituted "such sums as may be necessary to maintain such fund at a level of $35,000,000" for "not to exceed $35,000,000".

Subsec. (p)(1). Pub. L. 95-217, Sec. 58(d)(4), substituted ", in the case of an inland oil barge $125 per gross ton of such barge, or $125,000, whichever is greater, and in the case of any other vessel, $150 per gross ton of such vessel (or, for a vessel carrying oil or hazardous substances as cargo, $250,000), whichever is greater," for "$100 per gross ton, or $14,000,000 whichever is the lesser,".

Subsecs. (q), (r). Pub. L. 95-217, Sec. 58(i), added subsecs. (q) and (r).

1973—Subsec. (f). Pub. L. 93-207, Sec. 1(4)(A), (B), substituted "(b)(3)" for "(b)(2)" wherever appearing in pars. (1) to (3), and substituted "Administrator" for "Secretary" in last sentence of par. (2).

Subsecs. (g), (i). Pub. L. 93-207, Sec. 1(4)(C), substituted "(b)(3)" for "(b)(2)" wherever appearing.

Effective Date of 1996 Amendment

Section 101(a) [title II, Sec. 211(b)] of div. A of Pub. L. 104-208 provided that the amendment made by that section is effective 15 days after Oct. 11, 1996.

Effective Date of 1992 Amendment

Amendment by Pub. L. 102-572 effective Oct. 29, 1992, see section 911 of Pub. L. 102-572, set out as a note under section 171 of Title 28, Judiciary and Judicial Procedure.

Effective Date of 1990 Amendment

Amendment by Pub. L. 101-380 applicable to incidents occurring after Aug. 18, 1990, see section 1020 of Pub. L. 101-380, set out as an Effective Date note under section 2701 of this title.

Effective Date of 1982 Amendment

Amendment by Pub. L. 97-164 effective Oct. 1, 1982, see section 402 of Pub. L. 97-164, set out as a note under section 171 of Title 28, Judiciary and Judicial Procedure.

Effective Date of 1980 Amendments

Section 238(b) of Pub. L. 96-561 provided that the amendment made by that section is effective 15 days after Dec. 22, 1980.

Amendment by Pub. L. 96-478 effective Oct. 2, 1983, see section 14(a) of Pub. L. 96-478, set out as an Effective Date note under section 1901 of this title.

Effective Date of 1977 Amendment

Section 58(h) of Pub. L. 95-217 provided that: "The amendments made by paragraphs (5) and (6) of subsection (d) of this section [amending this section] shall take effect 180 days after the date of enactment of the Clean Water Act of 1977 [Dec. 27, 1977]."

Transfer of Functions

Enforcement functions of Administrator or other official of the Environmental Protection Agency under this section relating to spill prevention, containment and countermeasure plans with respect to pre-construction, construction, and initial operation of transportation system for Canadian and Alaskan natural gas were transferred to the Federal Inspector, Office of Federal Inspector for the Alaska Natural Gas Transportation System, until the first anniversary of the date of initial operation of the Alaska Natural Gas Transportation System, see Reorg. Plan No. 1 of 1979, Secs. 102(a), 203(a), 44 F.R. 33663, 33666, 93 Stat. 1373, 1376, effective July 1, 1979, set out in the Appendix to Title 5, Government Organization and Employees. Office of Federal Inspector for the Alaska Natural Gas Transportation System abolished and functions and authority vested in Inspector transferred to Secretary of Energy by section 3012(b) of Pub. L. 102-486, set out as an Abolition of Office of Federal Inspector note under section 719e of Title 15, Commerce and Trade.

Termination of Trust Territory of the Pacific Islands

For termination of Trust Territory of the Pacific Islands, see note set out preceding section 1681 of Title 48, Territories and Insular Possessions.

Termination of United States District Court for the District of the Canal Zone

For termination of the United States District Court for the District of the Canal Zone at end of the "transition period", being the 30-month period beginning Oct. 1, 1979, and ending midnight Mar. 31, 1982, see Paragraph 5 of Article XI of the Panama Canal Treaty of 1977 and sections 2101 and

2201 to 2203 of Pub. L. 96-70, title II, Sept. 27, 1979, 93 Stat. 493, formerly classified to sections 3831 and 3841 to 3843, respectively, of Title 22, Foreign Relations and Intercourse.

Oil Spill Liability Under Oil Pollution Act of 1990

Section 2002(a) of Pub. L. 101-380 provided that: "Subsections (f), (g), (h), and (i) of section 311 of the Federal Water Pollution Control Act (33 U.S.C. 1321) shall not apply with respect to any incident for which liability is established under section 1002 of this Act [33 U.S.C. 2702]."

Transfer of Moneys to Oil Spill Liability Trust Fund

Section 2002(b)(2) of Pub. L. 101-380 provided that: "Subsection (k) [of this section] is repealed. Any amounts remaining in the revolving fund established under that subsection shall be deposited in the [Oil Spill Liability Trust] Fund. The Fund shall assume all liability incurred by the revolving fund established under that subsection."

Revision of National Contingency Plan

Section 4201(c)[(d)] of Pub. L. 101-380 provided that: "Not later than one year after the date of the enactment of this Act [Aug. 18, 1990], the President shall revise and republish the National Contingency Plan prepared under section 311(c)(2) of the Federal Water Pollution Control Act [33 U.S.C. 1321(c)(2)] (as in effect immediately before the date of the enactment of this Act) to implement the amendments made by this section and section 4202 [amending this section]."

Implementation of National Planning and Response System

Section 4202(b) of Pub. L. 101-380 provided that:
"(1) Area committees and contingency plans.—(A) Not later than 6 months after the date of the enactment of this Act [Aug. 18, 1990], the President shall designate the areas for which Area Committees are established under section 311(j)(4) of the Federal Water Pollution Control Act [33 U.S.C. 1321(j)(4)], as amended by this Act. In designating such areas, the President shall ensure that all navigable waters, adjoining shorelines, and waters of the exclusive economic zone are subject to an Area Contingency Plan under that section.
 (B) Not later than 18 months after the date of the enactment of this Act, each Area Committee established under that section shall submit to the President the Area Contingency Plan required under that section.
 (C) Not later than 24 months after the date of the enactment of this Act, the President shall—
  (i) promptly review each plan;
  (ii) require amendments to any plan that does not meet the requirements of section 311(j)(4) of the Federal Water Pollution Control Act; and
  (iii) approve each plan that meets the requirements of that section.
(2) National response unit.—Not later than one year after the date of the enactment of this Act, the Secretary of the department in which the Coast Guard is operating shall establish a National Response Unit in accordance with section 311(j)(2) of the Federal Water Pollution Control Act, as amended by this Act.
(3) Coast guard district response groups.—Not later than 1 year after the date of the enactment of this Act, the Secretary of the department in which the Coast Guard is operating shall establish Coast Guard District Response Groups in accordance with section 311(j)(3) of the Federal Water Pollution Control Act, as amended by this Act.
(4) Tank vessel and facility response plans; transition provision; effective date of prohibition.—(A) Not later than 24 months after the date of the enactment of this Act, the President shall issue regulations for tank vessel and facility response plans under section 311(j)(5) of the Federal Water Pollution Control Act, as amended by this Act.
 (B) During the period beginning 30 months after the date of the enactment of this paragraph [Aug. 18, 1990] and ending 36 months after that date of enactment, a tank vessel or facility for which a response plan is required to be prepared under section 311(j)(5) of the Federal Water Pollution Control Act, as amended by this Act, may not handle, store, or transport oil unless the owner or operator thereof has submitted such a plan to the President.
 (C) Subparagraph (E) of section 311(j)(5) of the Federal Water Pollution Control Act, as amended by this Act, shall take effect 36 months after the date of the enactment of this Act."

Deposit of Certain Penalties Into Oil Spill Liability Trust Fund

Penalties paid pursuant to this section and sections 1319(c) and 1501 et seq. of this title to be deposited in the Oil Spill Liability Trust Fund created under section 9509 of Title 26, Internal Revenue Code, see section 4304 of Pub. L. 101-380, set out as a note under section 9509 of Title 26.

Allowable Delay in Establishing Financial Responsibility for Increase in Amounts Under 1977 Amendment

Section 58(j) of Pub. L. 95-217 provided that: "No vessel subject to the increased amounts which result from the amendments made by subsections (d)(2), (d)(3), and (d)(4) of this section [amending this section] shall be required to establish any evidence of financial responsibility under section 311(p) of the Federal Water Pollution Control Act [subsec. (p) of this section] for such increased amounts before October 1, 1978."

Territorial Sea of United States

For extension of territorial sea of United States, see Proc. No. 5928, set out as a note under section 1331 of Title 43, Public Lands.

Contiguous Zone of United States

For extension of contiguous zone of United States, see Proc. No. 7219, Sept. 2, 1999, 64 F.R. 48701, set out as a note under section 1331 of Title 43, Public Lands.

Executive Order No. 11735

Ex. Ord. No. 11735, Aug. 3, 1973, 38 F.R. 21243, as amended by Ex. Ord. No. 12418, May 5, 1983, 48 F.R. 20891, which assigned functions of the President regarding water pollution, was revoked by Ex. Ord. No. 12777, Sec. 8(i), Oct. 18, 1991, 56 F.R. 54769, set out below.

Executive Order No. 12418

Ex. Ord. No. 12418, May 5, 1983, 48 F.R. 20891, which transferred certain functions relating to the financial responsibility of vessels for water pollution and established authority of Federal agencies to respond to discharges or substantial threats of discharges of oil and hazardous substances, was revoked by Ex. Ord. No. 12777, Sec. 8(i), Oct. 18, 1991, 56 F.R. 54769, set out below.

Ex. Ord. No. 12777. Implementation of This Section and Oil Pollution Act of 1990

Ex. Ord. No. 12777, Oct. 18, 1991, 56 F.R. 54757, provided:

By the authority vested in me as President by the Constitution and the laws of the United States of America, including Section 311 of the Federal Water Pollution Control Act, ("FWPCA") (33 U.S.C. 1321), as amended by the Oil Pollution Act of 1990 (Public Law 101-380) ("OPA"), and by Section 301 of Title 3 of the United States Code, it is hereby ordered as follows:

Section 1. National Contingency Plan, Area Committees, and Area Contingency Plans. (a) Section 1 of Executive Order No. 12580 of January 23, 1987 [42 U.S.C. 9615 note], is amended to read as follows:

Section 1. National Contingency Plan.

  (a) (1) The National Contingency Plan ("the NCP"), shall provide for a National Response Team ("the NRT") composed of representatives of appropriate Federal departments and agencies for national planning and coordination of preparedness and response actions, and Regional Response Teams as the regional counterparts to the NRT for planning and coordination of regional preparedness and response actions.

  (2) The following agencies (in addition to other appropriate agencies) shall provide representatives to the National and Regional Response Teams to carry out their responsibilities under the NCP: Department of State, Department of Defense, Department of Justice, Department of the Interior, Department of Agriculture, Department of Commerce, Department of Labor, Department of Health and Human Services, Department of Transportation, Department of Energy, Environmental Protection Agency, Federal Emergency Management Agency, United States Coast Guard, and the Nuclear Regulatory Commission.

  (3) Except for periods of activation because of response action, the representative of the Environmental Protection Agency ("EPA") shall be the chairman, and the representative of the United States Coast Guard shall be the vice chairman, of the NRT and these agencies' representatives shall be co-chairs of the Regional Response Teams

("the RRTs"). When the NRT or an RRT is activated for a response action, the EPA representative shall be the chairman when the release or threatened release or discharge or threatened discharge occurs in the inland zone, and the United States Coast Guard representative shall be the chairman when the release or threatened release or discharge or threatened discharge occurs in the coastal zone, unless otherwise agreed upon by the EPA and the United States Coast Guard representatives (inland and coastal zones are defined in the NCP).

(4) The RRTs may include representatives from State governments, local governments (as agreed upon by the States), and Indian tribal governments. Subject to the functions and authorities delegated to Executive departments and agencies in other sections of this order, the NRT shall provide policy and program direction to the RRTs.

(b) (1) The responsibility for the revision of the NCP and all the other functions vested in the President by Sections 105(a), (b), (c), and (g), 125, and 301(f) of the Act, by Section 311(d)(1) of the Federal Water Pollution Control Act, and by Section 4201(c) of the Oil Pollution Act of 1990 is delegated to the Administrator of the Environmental Protection Agency ("the Administrator").

(2) The function vested in the President by Section 118(p) of the Superfund Amendments and Reauthorization Act of 1986 (Pub. L. 99-499) ("SARA") is delegated to the Administrator.

(c) In accord with Section 107(f)(2)(A) of the Act, Section 311(f)(5) of the Federal Water Pollution Control Act, as amended (33 U.S.C. 1321(f)(5)), and Section 1006(b)(1) and (2) of the Oil Pollution Act of 1990, the following shall be among those designated in the NCP as Federal trustees for natural resources:

(1) Secretary of Defense;
(2) Secretary of the Interior;
(3) Secretary of Agriculture;
(4) Secretary of Commerce;
(5) Secretary of Energy.

In the event of a spill, the above named Federal trustees for natural resources shall designate one trustee to act as Lead Administrative Trustee, the duties of which shall be defined in the regulations promulgated pursuant to Section 1006(e)(1) of OPA. If there are natural resource trustees other than those designated above which are acting in the event of a spill, those other trustees may join with the Federal trustees to name a Lead Administrative Trustee which shall exercise the duties defined in the regulations promulgated pursuant to Section 1006(e)(1) of OPA.

(d) Revisions to the NCP shall be made in consultation with members of the NRT prior to publication for notice and comment.

(e) All revisions to the NCP, whether in proposed or final form, shall be subject to review and approval by the Director of the Office of Management and Budget ("OMB")."

(b) The functions vested in the President by Section 311(j)(4) of FWPCA, and Section 4202(b)(1) of OPA [set out as a note above], respecting the designation of Areas, the appointment of Area Committee members, the requiring of information to be included in Area Contingency Plans, and the review and approval of Area Contingency Plans are delegated to the Administrator of the Environmental Protection Agency ("Administrator") for the inland zone and the Secretary of the Department in which the Coast Guard is operating for the coastal zone (inland and coastal zones are defined in the NCP).

Sec. 2. National Response System.

(a) The functions vested in the President by Section 311(j)(1)(A) of FWPCA, respecting the establishment of methods and procedures for the removal of discharged oil and hazardous substances, and by Section 311(j)(1)(B) of FWPCA respecting the establishment of criteria for the development and implementation of local and regional oil and hazardous substance removal contingency plans, are delegated to the Administrator for the inland zone and the Secretary of the Department in which the Coast Guard is operating for the coastal zone.

(b) (1) The functions vested in the President by Section 311(j)(1)(C) of FWPCA, respecting the establishment of procedures, methods, and equipment and other requirements for equipment to prevent and to contain discharges of oil and hazardous substances from non-transportation-related onshore facilities, are delegated to the Administrator.

(2) The functions vested in the President by Section 311(j)(1)(C) of FWPCA, respecting the establishment of procedures, methods, and equipment and other requirements for equipment to prevent and to contain discharges of oil and hazardous substances from vessels and transportation-related onshore facilities and deepwater ports subject to the Deepwater Ports [Port] Act of 1974 ("DPA") [33 U.S.C. 1501 et seq.], are delegated to the Secretary of Transportation.

(3) The functions vested in the President by Section 311(j)(1)(C) of FWPCA, respecting the establishment of procedures, methods, and equipment and other requirements for equipment to prevent and to contain discharges of oil and hazardous substances from offshore facilities, including associated pipelines, other than deepwater ports subject to the DPA, are delegated to the Secretary of the Interior.

(c) The functions vested in the President by Section 311(j)(1)(D) of FWPCA, respecting the inspection of vessels carrying cargoes of oil and hazardous substances and the inspection of such cargoes, are delegated to the Secretary of the Department in which the Coast Guard is operating.

(d) (1) The functions vested in the President by Section 311(j)(5) of FWPCA and Section 4202(b)(4) of OPA [set out as a note above], respecting the issuance of regulations requiring the owners or operators of non-transportation-related onshore facilities to prepare and submit response plans, the approval of means to ensure the availability of private personnel and equipment, the review and approval of such response plans, and the authorization of non-transportation-related onshore facilities to operate without approved response plans, are delegated to the Administrator.

(2) The functions vested in the President by Section 311(j)(5) of FWPCA and Section 4202(b)(4) of OPA, respecting the issuance of regulations requiring the owners or operators of tank vessels, transportation-related onshore facilities and deepwater ports subject to the DPA, to prepare and submit response plans, the approval of means to ensure the availability of private personnel and equipment, the review and approval of such response plans, and the authorization of tank vessels, transportation-related onshore facilities and deepwater ports subject to the DPA to operate without approved response plans, are delegated to the Secretary of Transportation.

(3) The functions vested in the President by Section 311(j)(5) of FWPCA and Section 4202(b)(4) of OPA, respecting the issuance of regulations requiring the owners or operators of offshore facilities, including associated pipelines, other than deepwater ports subject to the DPA, to prepare and submit response plans, the approval of means to ensure the availability of private personnel and equipment, the review and approval of such response plans, and the authorization of offshore facilities, including associated pipelines, other than deepwater ports subject to the DPA, to operate without approved response plans, are delegated to the Secretary of the Interior.

(e) (1) The functions vested in the President by Section 311(j)(6)(A) of FWPCA, respecting the requirements for periodic inspections of containment booms and equipment used to remove discharges at non-transportation-related onshore facilities, are delegated to the Administrator.

(2) The functions vested in the President by Section 311(j)(6)(A) of FWPCA, respecting the requirements for periodic inspections of containment booms and equipment used to remove discharges on vessels, and at transportation-related onshore facilities and deepwater ports subject to the DPA, are delegated to the Secretary of Transportation.

(3) The functions vested in the President by Section 311(j)(6)(A) of FWPCA, respecting the requirements for periodic inspections of containment booms and equipment used to remove discharges at offshore facilities, including associated pipelines, other than deepwater ports subject to the DPA, are delegated to the Secretary of the Interior.

(f) The functions vested in the President by Section 311(j)(6)(B) of FWPCA, respecting requirements for vessels to carry appropriate removal equipment, are delegated to the Secretary of the Department in which the Coast Guard is operating.

(g) (1) The functions vested in the President by Section 311(j)(7) of FWPCA, respecting periodic drills of removal capability under relevant response plans for onshore and offshore facilities located in the inland zone, and the publishing of annual reports on those drills, are delegated to the Administrator.

586 / Environmental Statutes

    (2) The functions vested in the President by Section 311(j)(7) of FWPCA, respecting periodic drills of removal capability under relevant response plans for tank vessels, and for onshore and offshore facilities located in the coastal zone, and the publishing of annual reports on those drills, are delegated to the Secretary of the Department in which the Coast Guard is operating.

(h) No provision of Section 2 of this order, including, but not limited to, any delegation or assignment of any function hereunder, shall in any way affect, or be construed or interpreted to affect the authority of any Department or agency, or the head of any Department or agency under any provision of law other than Section 311(j) of FWPCA or Section 4202(b)(4) of OPA.

(i) The functions vested in the President by Section 311(j) of FWPCA or Section 4202(b)(4) of OPA which have been delegated or assigned by Section 2 of this order may be redelegated to the head of any Executive department or agency with his or her consent.

Sec. 3. Removal.

The functions vested in the President by Section 311(c) of FWPCA and Section 1011 of OPA [33 U.S.C. 2711], respecting an effective and immediate removal or arrangement for removal of a discharge and mitigation or prevention of a substantial threat of a discharge of oil or a hazardous substance, the direction and monitoring of all Federal, State and private actions, the removal and destruction of a vessel, the issuance of directions, consulting with affected trustees, and removal completion determinations, are delegated to the Administrator for the inland zone and to the Secretary of the Department in which the Coast Guard is operating for the coastal zone.

Sec. 4. Liability Limit Adjustment.

(a) The functions vested in the President by Section 1004(d) of OPA [33 U.S.C. 2704(d)], respecting the establishment of limits of liability, with respect to classes or categories of non-transportation-related onshore facilities, the reporting to Congress on the desirability of adjusting limits of liability with respect to non-transportation-related onshore facilities, and the adjustment of limits of liability to reflect significant increases in the Consumer Price Index with respect to non-transportation-related onshore facilities, are delegated to the Administrator, acting in consultation with the Secretary of Transportation, the Secretary of Energy, and the Attorney General.

(b) The functions vested in the President by Section 1004(d) of OPA, respecting the establishment of limits of liability, with respect to classes or categories of transportation-related onshore facilities, the reporting to Congress on the desirability of adjusting limits of liability, with respect to vessels or transportation-related onshore facilities and deepwater ports subject to the DPA, and the adjustment of limits of liability to reflect significant increases in the Consumer Price Index with respect to vessels or transportation-related onshore facilities and deepwater ports subject to the DPA, are delegated to the Secretary of Transportation.

(c) The functions vested in the President by Section 1004(d) of OPA, respecting the reporting to Congress on the desirability of adjusting limits of liability with respect to offshore facilities, including associated pipelines, other than deepwater ports subject to the DPA, and the adjustment of limits of liability to reflect significant increases in the Consumer Price Index with respect to offshore facilities, including associated pipelines, other than deepwater ports subject to the DPA, are delegated to the Secretary of the Interior.

Sec. 5. Financial Responsibility.

(a) (1) The functions vested in the President by Section 1016(e) of OPA [33 U.S.C. 2716(e)], respecting (in the case of offshore facilities other than deepwater ports) the issuance of regulations concerning financial responsibility, the determination of acceptable methods of financial responsibility, and the specification of necessary or unacceptable terms, conditions, or defenses, are delegated to the Secretary of the Interior.

    (2) The functions vested in the President by Section 1016(e) of OPA, respecting (in the case of deepwater ports) the issuance of regulations concerning financial responsibility, the determination of acceptable methods of financial responsibility, and the specification of necessary or unacceptable terms, conditions, or defenses, are delegated to the Secretary of Transportation.

(b) (1) The functions vested in the President by Section 4303 of OPA [33 U.S.C. 2716a], respecting (in cases involving vessels) the assessment of civil penalties, the compromising, modification or remission, with or without condition, and the referral for collec-

tion of such imposed penalties, and requests to the Attorney General to secure necessary judicial relief, are delegated to the Secretary of the Department in which the Coast Guard is operating.
  (2) The functions vested in the President by Section 4303 of OPA, respecting (in cases involving offshore facilities other than deepwater ports) the assessment of civil penalties, the compromising, modification or remission, with or without condition, and the referral for collection of such imposed penalties, and requests to the Attorney General to secure necessary judicial relief, are delegated to the Secretary of the Interior.
  (3) The functions vested in the President by Section 4303 of OPA, respecting (in cases involving deepwater ports) the assessment of civil penalties, the compromising, modification or remission, with or without condition, and the referral for collection of such imposed penalties, and requests to the Attorney General to secure necessary judicial relief, are delegated to the Secretary of Transportation.

Sec. 6. Enforcement.
  (a) The functions vested in the President by Section 311(m)(1) of FWPCA, respecting the enforcement of Section 311 with respect to vessels, are delegated to the Secretary of the Department in which the Coast Guard is operating.
  (b) The functions vested in the President by Section 311(e) of FWPCA, respecting determinations of imminent and substantial threat, requesting the Attorney General to secure judicial relief, and other action including issuing administrative orders, are delegated to the Administrator for the inland zone and to the Secretary of the Department in which the Coast Guard is operating for the coastal zone.

Sec. 7. Management of the Oil Spill Liability Trust Fund and Claims.
  (a) (1) (A) The functions vested in the President by Section 1012(a)(1), (3), and (4) of OPA [33 U.S.C. 2712(a)(1), (3), (4)] respecting payment of removal costs and claims and determining consistency with the National Contingency Plan (NCP) are delegated to the Secretary of the Department in which the Coast Guard is operating.
        (B) The functions vested in the President by Section 6002(b) of the OPA [33 U.S.C. 2752(b)] respecting making amounts, not to exceed $50,000,000 and subject to normal budget controls, in any fiscal year, available from the Fund (i) to carry out Section 311(c) of FWPCA, and (ii) to initiate the assessment of natural resources damages required under Section 1006 of OPA [33 U.S.C. 2706] are delegated to the Secretary of the Department in which the Coast Guard is operating. Such Secretary shall make amounts available from the Fund to initiate the assessment of natural resources damages exclusively to the Federal trustees designated in the NCP. Such Federal trustees shall allocate such amounts among all trustees required to assess natural resources damages under Section 1006 of OPA.
    (2) The functions vested in the President by Section 1012(a)(2) of OPA [33 U.S.C. 2712(a)(2)], respecting the payment of costs and determining consistency with the NCP, are delegated to the Federal trustees designated in the NCP.
    (3) The functions vested in the President by Section 1012(a)(5) of OPA, respecting the payment of costs and expenses of departments and agencies having responsibility for the implementation, administration, and enforcement of the Oil Pollution Act of 1990 and subsections (b), (c), (d), (j) and (l) of Section 311 of FWPCA, are delegated to each head of such department and agency.
  (b) The functions vested in the President by Section 1012(c) of OPA, respecting designation of Federal officials who may obligate money, are delegated to each head of the departments and agencies to whom functions have been delegated under section 7(a) of this order for the purpose of carrying out such functions.
  (c) (1) The functions vested in the President by Section 1012(d) and (e) of OPA, respecting the obligation of the Trust Fund on the request of a Governor or pursuant to an agreement with a State, entrance into agreements with States, agreement upon terms and conditions, and the promulgation of regulations concerning such obligation and entrance into such agreement, are delegated to the Secretary of the Department in which the Coast Guard is operating, in consultation with the Administrator.
    (2) The functions vested in the President by Section 1013(e) of OPA [33 U.S.C. 2713(e)], respecting the promulgation and amendment of regulations for the presentation, filing, processing, settlement, and adjudication of claims under OPA against the Trust

Fund, are delegated to the Secretary of the Department in which the Coast Guard is operating, in consultation with the Attorney General.

(3) The functions vested in the President by Section 1012(a) of OPA, respecting the payment of costs, damages, and claims, delegated herein to the Secretary of the Department in which the Coast Guard is operating, include, inter alia, the authority to process, settle, and administratively adjudicate such costs, damages, and claims, regardless of amount.

(d) (1) The Coast Guard is designated the "appropriate agency" for the purpose of receiving the notice of discharge of oil or hazardous substances required by Section 311(b)(5) of FWPCA, and the Secretary of the Department in which the Coast Guard is operating is authorized to issue regulations implementing this designation.

(2) The functions vested in the President by Section 1014 of OPA [33 U.S.C. 2714], respecting designation of sources of discharges or threats, notification to responsible parties, promulgation of regulations respecting advertisements, the advertisement of designation, and notification of claims procedures, are delegated to the Secretary of the Department in which the Coast Guard is operating.

Sec. 8. Miscellaneous.

(a) The functions vested in the President by Section 311(b)(3) and (4) of FWPCA, as amended by the Oil Pollution Act of 1990, respecting the determination of quantities of oil and any hazardous substances the discharge of which may be harmful to the public health or welfare or the environment and the determinations of quantities, time, locations, circumstances, or conditions, which are not harmful, are delegated to the Administrator.

(b) The functions vested in the President by Section 311(d)(2)(G) of FWPCA, respecting schedules of dispersant, chemical, and other spill mitigating devices or substances, are delegated to the Administrator.

(c) The functions vested in the President by Section 1006(b)(3) and (4) of OPA [33 U.S.C. 2706(b)(3), (4)] respecting the receipt of designations of State and Indian tribe trustees for natural resources are delegated to the Administrator.

(d) The function vested in the President by Section 3004 of OPA [104 Stat. 508], with respect to encouraging the development of an international inventory of equipment and personnel, is delegated to the Secretary of the Department in which the Coast Guard is operating, in consultation with the Secretary of State.

(e) The functions vested in the President by Section 4113 of OPA [104 Stat. 516], respecting a study on the use of liners or other secondary means of containment for onshore facilities, and the implementation of the recommendations of the study, are delegated to the Administrator.

(f) The function vested in the President by Section 5002(c)(2)(D) of OPA [33 U.S.C. 2732(c)(2)(D)], respecting the designating of an employee of the Federal Government who shall represent the Federal Government on the Oil Terminal Facilities and Oil Tanker Operations Associations, is delegated to the Secretary of Transportation.

(g) The functions vested in the President by Section 5002(o) of OPA, respecting the annual certification of alternative voluntary advisory groups, are delegated to the Secretary of Transportation.

(h) The function vested in the President by Section 7001(a)(3) of OPA [33 U.S.C. 2761(a)(3)], respecting the appointment of Federal agencies to membership on the Interagency Coordinating Committee on Oil Pollution Research, is delegated to the Secretary of Transportation.

(i) Executive Order No. 11735 of August 3, 1973, Executive Order No. 12123 of February 26, 1979, Executive Order No. 12418 of May 5, 1983 and the memorandum of August 24, 1990, delegating certain authorities of the President under the Oil Pollution Act of 1990 are revoked.

Sec. 9. Consultation.

Authorities and functions delegated or assigned by this order shall be exercised subject to consultation with the Secretaries of departments and the heads of agencies with statutory responsibilities which may be significantly affected, including, but not limited to, the Department of Justice.

Sec. 10. Litigation.

(a) Notwithstanding any other provision of this order, any representation pursuant to or under this order in any judicial proceedings shall be by or through the Attorney General.

The conduct and control of all litigation arising under the Oil Pollution Act of 1990 [see Short Title note set out under section 2701 of this title] shall be the responsibility of the Attorney General.

(b) Notwithstanding any other provision of this order, the authority under the Oil Pollution Act of 1990 to require the Attorney General to commence litigation is retained by the President.

(c) Notwithstanding any other provision of this order, the Secretaries of the Departments of Transportation, Commerce, Interior, Agriculture, and/or the Administrator of the Environmental Protection Agency may request that the Attorney General commence litigation under the Oil Pollution Act of 1990.

(d) The Attorney General, in his discretion, is authorized to require that, with respect to a particular oil spill, an agency refrain from taking administrative enforcement action without first consulting with the Attorney General.

George Bush.

REPORT ON OIL SPILL RESPONDER IMMUNITY

Section 440 of Pub. L. 107-295 provided that:

"(a) Report to Congress.—Not later than January 1, 2004, the Secretary of the department in which the Coast Guard is operating, jointly with the Secretary of Commerce and the Secretary of the Interior, and after consultation with the Administrator of the Environmental Protection Agency and the Attorney General, shall submit a report to the Committee on Commerce, Science, and Transportation of the Senate and the Committee on Transportation and Infrastructure of the House of Representatives on the immunity from criminal and civil penalties provided under existing law of a private responder (other than a responsible party) in the case of the incidental take of federally listed fish or wildlife that results from, but is not the purpose of, carrying out an otherwise lawful activity conducted by that responder during an oil spill removal activity where the responder was acting in a manner consistent with the National Contingency Plan or as otherwise directed by the Federal On-Scene Coordinator for the spill, and on the circumstances under which such penalties have been or could be imposed on a private responder. The report shall take into consideration the procedures under the Inter-Agency Memorandum for addressing incidental takes.

(b) Definitions.—In this section—
  (1) the term "Federal On-Scene Coordinator" has the meaning given that term in section 311 of the Federal Water Pollution Control Act (33 U.S.C. 1321);
  (2) the term "incidental take" has the meaning given that term in the Inter-Agency Memorandum;
  (3) the term "Inter-Agency Memorandum" means the Inter-Agency Memorandum of Agreement Regarding Oil Spill Planning and Response Activities under the Federal Water Pollution Control Act's National Oil and Hazardous Substances Pollution Contingency Plan and the Endangered Species Act, effective on July 22, 2001;
  (4) the terms "National Contingency Plan", "removal", and "responsible party" have the meanings given those terms under section 1001 of the Oil Pollution Act of 1990 (33 U.S.C. 2701); and
  (5) the term "private responder" means a nongovernmental entity or individual that is carrying out an oil spill removal activity at the direction of a Federal agency or a responsible party."

Section Referred to in Other Sections

This section is referred to in sections 1266, 1314, 1318, 1319, 1322, 1376, 1402, 2701, 2702, 2703, 2704, 2712, 2735, 2752 of this title; title 8 section 1288; title 14 section 690; title 26 sections 9507, 9509; title 42 sections 6991b, 7412, 9601, 9602, 9605, 9606, 9607, 9611, 9651, 9652, 9654, 10601; title 43 sections 1653, 1656; title 46 sections 2101, 3715.

MARINE SANITATION DEVICES

33 USC 1322

(a) Definitions
   For the purpose of this section, the term—
   (1) "new vessel" includes every description of watercraft or other artificial contrivance used, or capable of being used, as a means of transportation on the navigable waters, the construction of which is initiated after promulgation of standards and regulations under this section;
   (2) "existing vessel" includes every description of watercraft or other artificial contrivance used, or capable of being used, as a means of transportation on the navigable waters, the construction of which is initiated before promulgation of standards and regulations under this section;
   (3) "public vessel" means a vessel owned or bareboat chartered and operated by the United States, by a State or political subdivision thereof, or by a foreign nation, except when such vessel is engaged in commerce;
   (4) "United States" includes the States, the District of Columbia, the Commonwealth of Puerto Rico, the Virgin Islands, Guam, American Samoa, the Canal Zone, and the Trust Territory of the Pacific Islands;
   (5) "marine sanitation device" includes any equipment for installation on board a vessel which is designed to receive, retain, treat, or discharge sewage, and any process to treat such sewage;
   (6) "sewage" means human body wastes and the wastes from toilets and other receptacles intended to receive or retain body wastes except that, with respect to commercial vessels on the Great Lakes, such term shall include graywater;
   (7) "manufacturer" means any person engaged in the manufacturing, assembling, or importation of marine sanitation devices or of vessels subject to standards and regulations promulgated under this section;
   (8) "person" means an individual, partnership, firm, corporation, association, or agency of the United States, but does not include an individual on board a public vessel;
   (9) "discharge" includes, but is not limited to, any spilling, leaking, pumping, pouring, emitting, emptying or dumping;
   (10) "commercial vessels" means those vessels used in the business of transporting property for compensation or hire, or in transporting property in the business of the owner, lessee, or operator of the vessel;
   (11) "graywater" means galley, bath, and shower water;
   (12) "discharge incidental to the normal operation of a vessel"—
      (A) means a discharge, including—
         (i) graywater, bilge water, cooling water, weather deck runoff, ballast water, oil water separator effluent, and any other pollutant discharge from the operation of a marine propulsion system, shipboard maneuvering system, crew habitability system, or installed major equipment, such as an aircraft carrier elevator or a catapult, or from a protective, preservative, or absorptive application to the hull of the vessel; and
         (ii) a discharge in connection with the testing, maintenance, and repair of a system described in clause (i) whenever the vessel is waterborne; and
      (B) does not include—
         (i) a discharge of rubbish, trash, garbage, or other such material discharged overboard;
         (ii) an air emission resulting from the operation of a vessel propulsion system, motor driven equipment, or incinerator; or
         (iii) a discharge that is not covered by part 122.3 of title 40, Code of Federal Regulations (as in effect on February 10, 1996);
   (13) "marine pollution control device" means any equipment or management practice, for installation or use on board a vessel of the Armed Forces, that is—
      (A) designed to receive, retain, treat, control, or discharge a discharge incidental to the normal operation of a vessel; and

(B) determined by the Administrator and the Secretary of Defense to be the most effective equipment or management practice to reduce the environmental impacts of the discharge consistent with the considerations set forth in subsection (n)(2)(B) of this section; and

(14) "vessel of the Armed Forces" means—
(A) any vessel owned or operated by the Department of Defense, other than a time or voyage chartered vessel; and
(B) any vessel owned or operated by the Department of Transportation that is designated by the Secretary of the department in which the Coast Guard is operating as a vessel equivalent to a vessel described in subparagraph (A).

(b) Federal standards of performance
(1) As soon as possible, after October 18, 1972, and subject to the provisions of section 1254(j) of this title, the Administrator, after consultation with the Secretary of the department in which the Coast Guard is operating, after giving appropriate consideration to the economic costs involved, and within the limits of available technology, shall promulgate Federal standards of performance for marine sanitation devices (hereafter in this section referred to as "standards") which shall be designed to prevent the discharge of untreated or inadequately treated sewage into or upon the navigable waters from new vessels and existing vessels, except vessels not equipped with installed toilet facilities. Such standards and standards established under subsection (c)(1)(B) of this section shall be consistent with maritime safety and the marine and navigation laws and regulations and shall be coordinated with the regulations issued under this subsection by the Secretary of the department in which the Coast Guard is operating. The Secretary of the department in which the Coast Guard is operating shall promulgate regulations, which are consistent with standards promulgated under this subsection and subsection (c) of this section and with maritime safety and the marine and navigation laws and regulations governing the design, construction, installation, and operation of any marine sanitation device on board such vessels.
(2) Any existing vessel equipped with a marine sanitation device on the date of promulgation of initial standards and regulations under this section, which device is in compliance with such initial standards and regulations, shall be deemed in compliance with this section until such time as the device is replaced or is found not to be in compliance with such initial standards and regulations.

(c) Initial standards; effective dates; revision; waiver
(1) (A) Initial standards and regulations under this section shall become effective for new vessels two years after promulgation; and for existing vessels five years after promulgation. Revisions of standards and regulations shall be effective upon promulgation, unless another effective date is specified, except that no revision shall take effect before the effective date of the standard or regulation being revised.
(B) The Administrator shall, with respect to commercial vessels on the Great Lakes, establish standards which require at a minimum the equivalent of secondary treatment as defined under section 1314(d) of this title. Such standards and regulations shall take effect for existing vessels after such time as the Administrator determines to be reasonable for the upgrading of marine sanitation devices to attain such standard.
(2) The Secretary of the department in which the Coast Guard is operating with regard to his regulatory authority established by this section, after consultation with the Administrator, may distinguish among classes, type, and sizes of vessels as well as between new and existing vessels, and may waive applicability of standards and regulations as necessary or appropriate for such classes, types, and sizes of vessels (including existing vessels equipped with marine sanitation devices on the date of promulgation of the initial standards required by this section), and, upon application, for individual vessels.

(d) Vessels owned and operated by the United States
The provisions of this section and the standards and regulations promulgated hereunder apply to vessels owned and operated by the United States unless the Secretary of Defense finds that compliance would not be in the interest of national security. With respect to vessels owned and operated by the Department of Defense, regulations under the last sentence of subsection (b)(1) of this section and certifications under subsection (g)(2) of this section shall be promulgated and issued by the Secretary of Defense.

(e) Pre-promulgation consultation

Before the standards and regulations under this section are promulgated, the Administrator and the Secretary of the department in which the Coast Guard is operating shall consult with the Secretary of State; the Secretary of Health and Human Services; the Secretary of Defense; the Secretary of the Treasury; the Secretary of Commerce; other interested Federal agencies; and the States and industries interested; and otherwise comply with the requirements of section 553 of title 5.

(f) Regulation by States or political subdivisions thereof; complete prohibition upon discharge of sewage

   (1) (A) Except as provided in subparagraph (B), after the effective date of the initial standards and regulations promulgated under this section, no State or political subdivision thereof shall adopt or enforce any statute or regulation of such State or political subdivision with respect to the design, manufacture, or installation or use of any marine sanitation device on any vessel subject to the provisions of this section.

   (B) A State may adopt and enforce a statute or regulation with respect to the design, manufacture, or installation or use of any marine sanitation device on a houseboat, if such statute or regulation is more stringent than the standards and regulations promulgated under this section. For purposes of this paragraph, the term "houseboat" means a vessel which, for a period of time determined by the State in which the vessel is located, is used primarily as a residence and is not used primarily as a means of transportation.

   (2) If, after promulgation of the initial standards and regulations and prior to their effective date, a vessel is equipped with a marine sanitation device in compliance with such standards and regulations and the installation and operation of such device is in accordance with such standards and regulations, such standards and regulations shall, for the purposes of paragraph (1) of this subsection, become effective with respect to such vessel on the date of such compliance.

   (3) After the effective date of the initial standards and regulations promulgated under this section, if any State determines that the protection and enhancement of the quality of some or all of the waters within such State require greater environmental protection, such State may completely prohibit the discharge from all vessels of any sewage, whether treated or not, into such waters, except that no such prohibition shall apply until the Administrator determines that adequate facilities for the safe and sanitary removal and treatment of sewage from all vessels are reasonably available for such water to which such prohibition would apply. Upon application of the State, the Administrator shall make such determination within 90 days of the date of such application.

   (4) (A) If the Administrator determines upon application by a State that the protection and enhancement of the quality of specified waters within such State requires such a prohibition, he shall by regulation completely prohibit the discharge from a vessel of any sewage (whether treated or not) into such waters.

   (B) Upon application by a State, the Administrator shall, by regulation, establish a drinking water intake zone in any waters within such State and prohibit the discharge of sewage from vessels within that zone.

(g) Sales limited to certified devices; certification of test device; recordkeeping; reports

   (1) No manufacturer of a marine sanitation device shall sell, offer for sale, or introduce or deliver for introduction in interstate commerce, or import into the United States for sale or resale any marine sanitation device manufactured after the effective date of the standards and regulations promulgated under this section unless such device is in all material respects substantially the same as a test device certified under this subsection.

   (2) Upon application of the manufacturer, the Secretary of the department in which the Coast Guard is operating shall so certify a marine sanitation device if he determines, in accordance with the provisions of this paragraph, that it meets the appropriate standards and regulations promulgated under this section. The Secretary of the department in which the Coast Guard is operating shall test or require such testing of the device in accordance with procedures set forth by the Administrator as to standards of performance and for such other purposes as may be appropriate. If the Secretary of the department in which the Coast Guard is operating determines that the device is satisfactory from the standpoint of

safety and any other requirements of maritime law or regulation, and after consideration of the design, installation, operation, material, or other appropriate factors, he shall certify the device. Any device manufactured by such manufacturer which is in all material respects substantially the same as the certified test device shall be deemed to be in conformity with the appropriate standards and regulations established under this section.

(3) Every manufacturer shall establish and maintain such records, make such reports, and provide such information as the Administrator or the Secretary of the department in which the Coast Guard is operating may reasonably require to enable him to determine whether such manufacturer has acted or is acting in compliance with this section and regulations issued thereunder and shall, upon request of an officer or employee duly designated by the Administrator or the Secretary of the department in which the Coast Guard is operating, permit such officer or employee at reasonable times to have access to and copy such records. All information reported to or otherwise obtained by the Administrator or the Secretary of the Department in which the Coast Guard is operating or their representatives pursuant to this subsection which contains or relates to a trade secret or other matter referred to in section 1905 of title 18 shall be considered confidential for the purpose of that section, except that such information may be disclosed to other officers or employees concerned with carrying out this section. This paragraph shall not apply in the case of the construction of a vessel by an individual for his own use.

(h) Sale and resale of properly equipped vessels; operability of certified marine sanitation devices

After the effective date of standards and regulations promulgated under this section, it shall be unlawful—

(1) for the manufacturer of any vessel subject to such standards and regulations to manufacture for sale, to sell or offer for sale, or to distribute for sale or resale any such vessel unless it is equipped with a marine sanitation device which is in all material respects substantially the same as the appropriate test device certified pursuant to this section;

(2) for any person, prior to the sale or delivery of a vessel subject to such standards and regulations to the ultimate purchaser, wrongfully to remove or render inoperative any certified marine sanitation device or element of design of such device installed in such vessel;

(3) for any person to fail or refuse to permit access to or copying of records or to fail to make reports or provide information required under this section; and

(4) for a vessel subject to such standards and regulations to operate on the navigable waters of the United States, if such vessel is not equipped with an operable marine sanitation device certified pursuant to this section.

(i) Jurisdiction to restrain violations; contempts

The district courts of the United States shall have jurisdictions to restrain violations of subsection (g)(1) of this section and subsections (h)(1) through (3) of this section. Actions to restrain such violations shall be brought by, and in, the name of the United States. In case of contumacy or refusal to obey a subpena served upon any person under this subsection, the district court of the United States for any district in which such person is found or resides or transacts business, upon application by the United States and after notice to such person, shall have jurisdiction to issue an order requiring such person to appear and give testimony or to appear and produce documents, and any failure to obey such order of the court may be punished by such court as a contempt thereof.

(j) Penalties

Any person who violates subsection (g)(1) of this section, clause (1) or (2) of subsection (h) of this section, or subsection (n)(8) of this section shall be liable to a civil penalty of not more than $5,000 for each violation. Any person who violates clause (4) of subsection (h) of this section or any regulation issued pursuant to this section shall be liable to a civil penalty of not more than $2,000 for each violation. Each violation shall be a separate offense. The Secretary of the department in which the Coast Guard is operating may assess and compromise any such penalty. No penalty shall be assessed until the person charged shall have been given notice and an opportunity for a hearing on such charge. In determining the amount of the penalty, or the amount agreed upon in compromise, the gravity of the violation, and the demonstrated good faith of the person charged in attempting to achieve rapid compliance, after notification of a violation, shall be considered by said Secretary.

(k) Enforcement authority
The provisions of this section shall be enforced by the Secretary of the department in which the Coast Guard is operating and he may utilize by agreement, with or without reimbursement, law enforcement officers or other personnel and facilities of the Administrator, other Federal agencies, or the States to carry out the provisions of this section. The provisions of this section may also be enforced by a State.

(l) Boarding and inspection of vessels; execution of warrants and other process
Anyone authorized by the Secretary of the department in which the Coast Guard is operating to enforce the provisions of this section may, except as to public vessels, (1) board and inspect any vessel upon the navigable waters of the United States and (2) execute any warrant or other process issued by an officer or court of competent jurisdiction.

(m) Enforcement in United States possessions
In the case of Guam and the Trust Territory of the Pacific Islands, actions arising under this section may be brought in the district court of Guam, and in the case of the Virgin Islands such actions may be brought in the district court of the Virgin Islands. In the case of American Samoa and the Trust Territory of the Pacific Islands, such actions may be brought in the District Court of the United States for the District of Hawaii and such court shall have jurisdiction of such actions. In the case of the Canal Zone, such actions may be brought in the District Court for the District of the Canal Zone.

(n) Uniform national discharge standards for vessels of Armed Forces
  (1) Applicability
  This subsection shall apply to vessels of the Armed Forces and discharges, other than sewage, incidental to the normal operation of a vessel of the Armed Forces, unless the Secretary of Defense finds that compliance with this subsection would not be in the national security interests of the United States.
  (2) Determination of discharges required to be controlled by marine pollution control devices
    (A) In general
    The Administrator and the Secretary of Defense, after consultation with the Secretary of the department in which the Coast Guard is operating, the Secretary of Commerce, and interested States, shall jointly determine the discharges incidental to the normal operation of a vessel of the Armed Forces for which it is reasonable and practicable to require use of a marine pollution control device to mitigate adverse impacts on the marine environment. Notwithstanding subsection (a)(1) of section 553 of title 5, the Administrator and the Secretary of Defense shall promulgate the determinations in accordance with such section. The Secretary of Defense shall require the use of a marine pollution control device on board a vessel of the Armed Forces in any case in which it is determined that the use of such a device is reasonable and practicable.
    (B) Considerations
    In making a determination under subparagraph (A), the Administrator and the Secretary of Defense shall take into consideration—
      (i) the nature of the discharge;
      (ii) the environmental effects of the discharge;
      (iii) the practicability of using the marine pollution control device;
      (iv) the effect that installation or use of the marine pollution control device would have on the operation or operational capability of the vessel;
      (v) applicable United States law;
      (vi) applicable international standards; and
      (vii) the economic costs of the installation and use of the marine pollution control device.
  (3) Performance standards for marine pollution control devices
    (A) In general
    For each discharge for which a marine pollution control device is determined to be required under paragraph (2), the Administrator and the Secretary of Defense, in consultation with the Secretary of the department in which the Coast Guard is operating, the Secretary of State, the Secretary of Commerce, other interested Federal agencies, and interested States, shall jointly promulgate Federal standards of performance for each marine pollution control device required with respect to the discharge. Not-

withstanding subsection (a)(1) of section 553 of title 5, the Administrator and the Secretary of Defense shall promulgate the standards in accordance with such section.
    (B) Considerations
      In promulgating standards under this paragraph, the Administrator and the Secretary of Defense shall take into consideration the matters set forth in paragraph (2)(B).
    (C) Classes, types, and sizes of vessels
      The standards promulgated under this paragraph may—
      (i) distinguish among classes, types, and sizes of vessels;
      (ii) distinguish between new and existing vessels; and
      (iii) provide for a waiver of the applicability of the standards as necessary or appropriate to a particular class, type, age, or size of vessel.
  (4) Regulations for use of marine pollution control devices
    The Secretary of Defense, after consultation with the Administrator and the Secretary of the department in which the Coast Guard is operating, shall promulgate such regulations governing the design, construction, installation, and use of marine pollution control devices on board vessels of the Armed Forces as are necessary to achieve the standards promulgated under paragraph (3).
  (5) Deadlines; effective date
    (A) Determinations
      The Administrator and the Secretary of Defense shall—
      (i) make the initial determinations under paragraph (2) not later than 2 years after February 10, 1996; and
      (ii) every 5 years—
        (I) review the determinations; and
        (II) if necessary, revise the determinations based on significant new information.
    (B) Standards
      The Administrator and the Secretary of Defense shall—
      (i) promulgate standards of performance for a marine pollution control device under paragraph (3) not later than 2 years after the date of a determination under paragraph (2) that the marine pollution control device is required; and
      (ii) every 5 years—
        (I) review the standards; and
        (II) if necessary, revise the standards, consistent with paragraph (3)(B) and based on significant new information.
    (C) Regulations
      The Secretary of Defense shall promulgate regulations with respect to a marine pollution control device under paragraph (4) as soon as practicable after the Administrator and the Secretary of Defense promulgate standards with respect to the device under paragraph (3), but not later than 1 year after the Administrator and the Secretary of Defense promulgate the standards. The regulations promulgated by the Secretary of Defense under paragraph (4) shall become effective upon promulgation unless another effective date is specified in the regulations.
    (D) Petition for review
      The Governor of any State may submit a petition requesting that the Secretary of Defense and the Administrator review a determination under paragraph (2) or a standard under paragraph (3), if there is significant new information, not considered previously, that could reasonably result in a change to the particular determination or standard after consideration of the matters set forth in paragraph (2)(B). The petition shall be accompanied by the scientific and technical information on which the petition is based. The Administrator and the Secretary of Defense shall grant or deny the petition not later than 2 years after the date of receipt of the petition.
  (6) Effect on other laws
    (A) Prohibition on regulation by States or political subdivisions of States
      Beginning on the effective date of—
      (i) a determination under paragraph (2) that it is not reasonable and practicable to require use of a marine pollution control device regarding a particular discharge incidental to the normal operation of a vessel of the Armed Forces; or
      (ii) regulations promulgated by the Secretary of Defense under paragraph (4);

except as provided in paragraph (7), neither a State nor a political subdivision of a State may adopt or enforce any statute or regulation of the State or political subdivision with respect to the discharge or the design, construction, installation, or use of any marine pollution control device required to control discharges from a vessel of the Armed Forces.
- (B) Federal laws
  This subsection shall not affect the application of section 1321 of this title to discharges incidental to the normal operation of a vessel.
- (7) Establishment of State no-discharge zones
  - (A) State prohibition
    - (i) In general
      After the effective date of—
      - (I) a determination under paragraph (2) that it is not reasonable and practicable to require use of a marine pollution control device regarding a particular discharge incidental to the normal operation of a vessel of the Armed Forces; or
      - (II) regulations promulgated by the Secretary of Defense under paragraph (4);
      if a State determines that the protection and enhancement of the quality of some or all of the waters within the State require greater environmental protection, the State may prohibit 1 or more discharges incidental to the normal operation of a vessel, whether treated or not treated, into the waters. No prohibition shall apply until the Administrator makes the determinations described in subclauses (II) and (III) of subparagraph (B)(i).
    - (ii) Documentation
      To the extent that a prohibition under this paragraph would apply to vessels of the Armed Forces and not to other types of vessels, the State shall document the technical or environmental basis for the distinction.
  - (B) Prohibition by the Administrator
    - (i) In general
      Upon application of a State, the Administrator shall by regulation prohibit the discharge from a vessel of 1 or more discharges incidental to the normal operation of a vessel, whether treated or not treated, into the waters covered by the application if the Administrator determines that—
      - (I) the protection and enhancement of the quality of the specified waters within the State require a prohibition of the discharge into the waters;
      - (II) adequate facilities for the safe and sanitary removal of the discharge incidental to the normal operation of a vessel are reasonably available for the waters to which the prohibition would apply; and
      - (III) the prohibition will not have the effect of discriminating against a vessel of the Armed Forces by reason of the ownership or operation by the Federal Government, or the military function, of the vessel.
    - (ii) Approval or disapproval
      The Administrator shall approve or disapprove an application submitted under clause (i) not later than 90 days after the date on which the application is submitted to the Administrator. Notwithstanding clause (i)(II), the Administrator shall not disapprove an application for the sole reason that there are not adequate facilities to remove any discharge incidental to the normal operation of a vessel from vessels of the Armed Forces.
  - (C) Applicability to foreign flagged vessels
    A prohibition under this paragraph—
    - (i) shall not impose any design, construction, manning, or equipment standard on a foreign flagged vessel engaged in innocent passage unless the prohibition implements a generally accepted international rule or standard; and
    - (ii) that relates to the prevention, reduction, and control of pollution shall not apply to a foreign flagged vessel engaged in transit passage unless the prohibition implements an applicable international regulation regarding the discharge of oil, oily waste, or any other noxious substance into the waters.
- (8) Prohibition relating to vessels of the Armed Forces

After the effective date of the regulations promulgated by the Secretary of Defense under paragraph (4), it shall be unlawful for any vessel of the Armed Forces subject to the regulations to—
- (A) operate in the navigable waters of the United States or the waters of the contiguous zone, if the vessel is not equipped with any required marine pollution control device meeting standards established under this subsection; or
- (B) discharge overboard any discharge incidental to the normal operation of a vessel in waters with respect to which a prohibition on the discharge has been established under paragraph (7).

(9) Enforcement

This subsection shall be enforceable, as provided in subsections (j) and (k) of this section, against any agency of the United States responsible for vessels of the Armed Forces notwithstanding any immunity asserted by the agency.

(June 30, 1948, ch. 758, title III, Sec. 312, as added Pub. L. 92-500, Sec. 2, Oct. 18, 1972, 86 Stat. 871; amended Pub. L. 95-217, Sec. 59, Dec. 27, 1977, 91 Stat. 1596; Pub. L. 96-88, title V, Sec. 509(b), Oct. 17, 1979, 93 Stat. 695; Pub. L. 100-4, title III, Sec. 311, Feb. 4, 1987, 101 Stat. 42; Pub. L. 104-106, div. A, title III, Sec. 325(b)-(c)(2), Feb. 10, 1996, 110 Stat. 254-259.)

References in Text

For definition of Canal Zone, referred to in subsecs. (a)(4) and (m), see section 3602(b) of Title 22, Foreign Relations and Intercourse.

Amendments

1996—Subsec. (a)(8). Pub. L. 104-106, Sec. 325(c)(1)(A), substituted "corporation, association, or agency of the United States," for "corporation, or association,".

Subsec. (a)(12) to (14). Pub. L. 104-106, Sec. 325(c)(1)(B), (C), added pars. (12) to (14).

Subsec. (j). Pub. L. 104-106, Sec. 325(c)(2), substituted "subsection (g)(1) of this section, clause (1) or (2) of subsection (h) of this section, or subsection (n)(8) of this section shall be liable" for "subsection (g)(1) of this section or clause (1) or (2) of subsection (h) of this section shall be liable".

Subsec. (n). Pub. L. 104-106, Sec. 325(b), added subsec. (n).

1987—Subsec. (f)(1). Pub. L. 100-4, Sec. 311(a), designated existing provision as subpar. (A), substituted "Except as provided in subparagraph (B), after" for "After", and added subpar. (B).

Subsec. (k). Pub. L. 100-4, Sec. 311(b), inserted at end "The provisions of this section may also be enforced by a State."

1977—Subsec. (a)(6). Pub. L. 95-217, Sec. 59(a), inserted "except that, with respect to commercial vessels on the Great Lakes, such term shall include graywater" after "receive or retain body wastes".

Subsec. (a)(10), (11). Pub. L. 95-217, Sec. 59(b), added pars. (10) and (11).

Subsec. (b)(1). Pub. L. 95-217, Sec. 59(c), inserted references to standards established under subsec. (c)(1)(B) of this section and to standards promulgated under subsec. (c) of this section.

Subsec. (c)(1). Pub. L. 95-217, Sec. 59(d), designated existing provisions as subpar. (A) and added subpar. (B).

Subsec. (f)(4). Pub. L. 95-217, Sec. 59(e), designated existing provisions as subpar. (A) and added subpar. (B).

Change of Name

"Secretary of Health and Human Services" substituted for "Secretary of Health, Education, and Welfare" in subsec. (e) pursuant to section 509(b) of Pub. L. 96-88 which is classified to section 3508(b) of Title 20, Education.

Termination of Trust Territory of the Pacific Islands

For termination of Trust Territory of the Pacific Islands, see note set out preceding section 1681 of Title 48, Territories and Insular Possessions.

Termination of United States District Court for the District of the Canal Zone

For termination of the United States District Court for the District of the Canal Zone at end of the "transition period", being the 30-month period beginning Oct. 1, 1979, and ending midnight Mar.

31, 1982, see Paragraph 5 of Article XI of the Panama Canal Treaty of 1977 and sections 2101 and 2201 to 2203 of Pub. L. 96-70, title II, Sept. 27, 1979, 93 Stat. 493, formerly classified to sections 3831 and 3841 to 3843, respectively, of Title 22, Foreign Relations and Intercourse.

Purpose of 1996 Amendment

Section 325(a) of Pub. L. 104-106 provided that: "The purposes of this section [amending this section and section 1362 of this title and enacting provisions set out as a note below] are to—
  (1) enhance the operational flexibility of vessels of the Armed Forces domestically and internationally;
  (2) stimulate the development of innovative vessel pollution control technology; and
  (3) advance the development by the United States Navy of environmentally sound ships."

Cooperation in National Discharge Standards Development

Section 325(d) of Pub. L. 104-106 provided that: "The Administrator of the Environmental Protection Agency and the Secretary of Defense may, by mutual agreement, with or without reimbursement, provide for the use of information, reports, personnel, or other resources of the Environmental Protection Agency or the Department of Defense to carry out section 312(n) of the Federal Water Pollution Control Act [33 U.S.C. 1322(n)] (as added by subsection (b)), including the use of the resources—
  (1) to determine—
    (A) the nature and environmental effect of discharges incidental to the normal operation of a vessel of the Armed Forces;
    (B) the practicability of using marine pollution control devices on vessels of the Armed Forces; and
    (C) the effect that installation or use of marine pollution control devices on vessels of the Armed Forces would have on the operation or operational capability of the vessels; and
  (2) to establish performance standards for marine pollution control devices on vessels of the Armed Forces."

Clean Vessels

Pub. L. 102-587, title V, subtitle F, Nov. 4, 1992, 106 Stat. 5086, provided that:

"SEC. 5601. SHORT TITLE.

This subtitle may be cited as the 'Clean Vessel Act of 1992'.

SEC. 5602. FINDINGS; PURPOSE.

(a) Findings.—The Congress finds the following:
  (1) The discharge of untreated sewage by vessels is prohibited under Federal law in all areas within the navigable waters of the United States.
  (2) The discharge of treated sewage by vessels is prohibited under either Federal or State law in many of the United States bodies of water where recreational boaters operate.
  (3) There is currently an inadequate number of pumpout stations for type III marine sanitation devices where recreational vessels normally operate.
  (4) Sewage discharged by recreational vessels because of an inadequate number of pumpout stations is a substantial contributor to localized degradation of water quality in the United States.
(b) Purpose.—The purpose of this subtitle is to provide funds to States for the construction, renovation, operation, and maintenance of pumpout stations and waste reception facilities.

SEC. 5603. DETERMINATION AND PLAN REGARDING STATE MARINE SANITATION DEVICE PUMPOUT STATION NEEDS.

(a) Survey.—Within 3 months after the notification under section 5605(b), each coastal State shall conduct a survey to determine—
  (1) the number and location of all operational pumpout stations and waste reception facilities at public and private marinas, mooring areas, docks, and other boating access facilities within the coastal zone of the State; and
  (2) the number of recreational vessels in the coastal waters of the State with type III marine sanitation devices or portable toilets, and the areas of those coastal waters where those vessels congregate.

(b) Plan.—Within 6 months after the notification under section 5605(b), and based on the survey conducted under subsection (a), each coastal State shall—
  (1) develop and submit to the Secretary of the Interior a plan for any construction or renovation of pumpout stations and waste reception facilities that are necessary to ensure that, based on the guidance issued under section 5605(a), there are pumpout stations and waste reception facilities in the State that are adequate and reasonably available to meet the needs of recreational vessels using the coastal waters of the State; and
  (2) submit to the Secretary of the Interior with that plan a list of all stations and facilities in the coastal zone of the State which are operational on the date of submittal.
(c) Plan Approval.—
  (1) In general.—Not later than 60 days after a plan is submitted by a State under subsection (b), the Secretary of the Interior shall approve or disapprove the plan, based on—
    (A) the adequacy of the survey conducted by the State under subsection (a); and
    (B) the ability of the plan, based on the guidance issued under section 5605(a), to meet the construction and renovation needs of the recreational vessels identified in the survey.
  (2) Notification of state; modification.—The Secretary of the Interior shall promptly notify the affected Governor of the approval or disapproval of a plan. If a plan is disapproved, the Secretary of the Interior shall recommend necessary modifications and return the plan to the affected Governor.
  (3) Resubmittal.—Not later than 60 days after receiving a plan returned by the Secretary of the Interior, the Governor shall make the appropriate changes and resubmit the plan.
(d) Indication of Stations and Facilities on NOAA Charts.—
  (1) In general.—The Under Secretary of Commerce for Oceans and Atmosphere shall indicate, on charts published by the National Oceanic and Atmospheric Administration for the use of operators of recreational vessels, the locations of pumpout stations and waste reception facilities.
  (2) Notification of NOAA.—
    "(A) Lists of stations and facilities.—The Secretary of the Interior shall transmit to the Under Secretary of Commerce for Oceans and Atmosphere each list of operational stations and facilities submitted by a State under subsection (b)(2), by not later than 30 days after the date of receipt of that list.
    (B) Completion of project.—The Director of the United States Fish and Wildlife Service shall notify the Under Secretary of the location of each station or facility at which a construction or renovation project is completed by a State with amounts made available under the Act of August 9, 1950 (16 U.S.C. 777a et seq. [16 U.S.C. 777 et seq.]), as amended by this subtitle, by not later than 30 days after the date of notification by a State of the completion of the project.

SEC. 5604. FUNDING.

(a) Transfer.—[Amended section 777c of Title 16, Conservation.]
(b) Access Increase.—[Amended section 777g of Title 16, Conservation.]
(c) Grant Program.—
  (1) Matching grants.—The Secretary of the Interior may obligate an amount not to exceed the amount made available under section 4(b)(2) of the Act of August 9, 1950 (16 U.S.C. 777c(b)(2), as amended by this Act), to make grants to—
    (A) coastal States to pay not more than 75 percent of the cost to a coastal State of—
      (i) conducting a survey under section 5603(a);
      (ii) developing and submitting a plan and accompanying list under section 5603(b);
      (iii) constructing and renovating pumpout stations and waste reception facilities; and
      (iv) conducting a program to educate recreational boaters about the problem of human body waste discharges from vessels and inform them of the location of pumpout stations and waste reception facilities.
    (B) inland States, which can demonstrate to the Secretary of the Interior that there are an inadequate number of pumpout stations and waste reception facilities to meet the needs of recreational vessels in the waters of that State, to pay 75 percent of the cost to that State of—
      (i) constructing and renovating pumpout stations and waste reception facilities in the inland State; and

(ii) conducting a program to educate recreational boaters about the problem of human body waste discharges from vessels and inform them of the location of pumpout stations and waste reception facilities.

(2) Priority.—In awarding grants under this subsection, the Secretary of the Interior shall give priority consideration to grant applications that—

(A) in coastal States, propose constructing and renovating pumpout stations and waste reception facilities in accordance with a coastal State's plan approved under section 5603(c);

(B) provide for public/private partnership efforts to develop and operate pumpout stations and waste receptions [sic] facilities; and

(C) propose innovative ways to increase the availability and use of pumpout stations and waste reception facilities.

(d) Disclaimer.—Nothing in this subtitle shall be interpreted to preclude a State from carrying out the provisions of this subtitle with funds other than those described in this section.

SEC. 5605. GUIDANCE AND NOTIFICATION.

(a) Issuance of Guidance.—Not later than 3 months after the date of the enactment of this subtitle [Nov. 4, 1992], the Secretary of the Interior shall, after consulting with the Administrator of the Environmental Protection Agency, the Under Secretary of Commerce for Oceans and Atmosphere, and the Commandant of the Coast Guard, issue for public comment pumpout station and waste reception facility guidance. The Secretary of the Interior shall finalize the guidance not later than 6 months after the date of enactment of this subtitle. The guidance shall include—

(1) guidance regarding the types of pumpout stations and waste reception facilities that may be appropriate for construction, renovation, operation, or maintenance with amounts available under the Act of August 9, 1950 (16 U.S.C. 777a et seq. [16 U.S.C. 777 et seq.]), as amended by this subtitle, and appropriate location of the stations and facilities within a marina or boatyard;

(2) guidance defining what constitutes adequate and reasonably available pumpout stations and waste reception facilities in boating areas;

(3) guidance on appropriate methods for disposal of vessel sewage from pumpout stations and waste reception facilities;

(4) guidance on appropriate connector fittings to facilitate the sanitary and expeditious discharge of sewage from vessels;

(5) guidance on the waters most likely to be affected by the discharge of sewage from vessels; and

(6) other information that is considered necessary to promote the establishment of pumpout facilities to reduce sewage discharges from vessels and to protect United States waters.

(b) Notification.—Not later than one month after the guidance issued under subsection (a) is finalized, the Secretary of the Interior shall provide notification in writing to the fish and wildlife, water pollution control, and coastal zone management authorities of each State, of—

(1) the availability of amounts under the Act of August 9, 1950 (16 U.S.C. 777a et seq. [16 U.S.C. 777 et seq.]) to implement the Clean Vessel Act of 1992; and

(2) the guidance developed under subsection (a).

SEC. 5606. EFFECT ON STATE FUNDING ELIGIBILITY.

This subtitle shall not be construed or applied to jeopardize any funds available to a coastal State under the Act of August 9, 1950 (16 U.S.C. 777a et seq. [16 U.S.C. 777 et seq.]), if the coastal State is, in good faith, pursuing a survey and plan designed to meet the purposes of this subtitle.

SEC. 5607. APPLICABILITY.

The requirements of section 5603 shall not apply to a coastal State if within six months after the date of enactment of this subtitle [Nov. 4, 1992] the Secretary of the Interior certifies that—

(1) the State has developed and is implementing a plan that will ensure that there will be pumpout stations and waste reception facilities adequate to meet the needs of recreational vessels in the coastal waters of the State; or

(2) existing pumpout stations and waste reception facilities in the coastal waters of the State are adequate to meet those needs.

SEC. 5608. DEFINITIONS.

For the purposes of this subtitle the term:
(1) 'coastal State'—
    (A) means a State of the United States in, or bordering on the Atlantic, Pacific, or Arctic Ocean; the Gulf of Mexico; Long Island Sound; or one or more of the Great Lakes;
    (B) includes Puerto Rico, the Virgin Islands, Guam, the Commonwealth of the Northern Mariana Islands, and American Samoa; and
    (C) does not include a State for which the ratio of the number of recreational vessels in the State numbered under chapter 123 of title 46, United States Code, to number of miles of shoreline (as that term is defined in section 926.2(d) of title 15, Code of Federal Regulations, as in effect on January 1, 1991), is less than one.
(2) 'coastal waters' means—
    (A) in the Great Lakes area, the waters within the territorial jurisdiction of the United States consisting of the Great Lakes, their connecting waters, harbors, roadsteads, and estuary-type areas such as bays, shallows, and marshes; and
    (B) in other areas, those waters, adjacent to the shorelines, which contain a measurable percentage of sea water, including sounds, bay, lagoons, bayous, ponds, and estuaries.
(3) 'coastal zone' has the same meaning that term has in section 304(1) of the Coastal Zone Management Act of 1972 (16 U.S.C. 1453(1));
(4) 'inland State' means a State which is not a coastal state;
(5) 'type III marine sanitation device' means any equipment for installation on board a vessel which is specifically designed to receive, retain, and discharge human body wastes;
(6) 'pumpout station' means a facility that pumps or receives human body wastes out of type III marine sanitation devices installed on board vessels;
(7) 'recreational vessel' means a vessel—
    "(A) manufactured for operation, or operated, primarily for pleasure; or
    "(B) leased, rented, or chartered to another for the latter's pleasure; and
(8) 'waste reception facility' means a facility specifically designed to receive wastes from portable toilets carried on vessels, and does not include lavatories."

Contiguous Zone of United States

For extension of contiguous zone of United States, see Proc. No. 7219, Sept. 2, 1999, 64 F.R. 48701, set out as a note under section 1331 of Title 43, Public Lands.

Section Referred to in Other Sections

This section is referred to in sections 1254, 1362, 1402 of this title.

FEDERAL FACILITIES POLLUTION CONTROL

33 USC 1323

(a) Each department, agency, or instrumentality of the executive, legislative, and judicial branches of the Federal Government (1) having jurisdiction over any property or facility, or (2) engaged in any activity resulting, or which may result, in the discharge or runoff of pollutants, and each officer, agent, or employee thereof in the performance of his official duties, shall be subject to, and comply with, all Federal, State, interstate, and local requirements, administrative authority, and process and sanctions respecting the control and abatement of water pollution in the same manner, and to the same extent as any nongovernmental entity including the payment of reasonable service charges. The preceding sentence shall apply (A) to any requirement whether substantive or procedural (including any recordkeeping or reporting requirement, any requirement respecting permits and any other requirement, whatsoever), (B) to the exercise of any Federal, State, or local administrative authority, and (C) to any process and sanction, whether enforced in Federal, State, or local courts or in any other manner. This subsection shall apply notwithstanding any immunity of such agencies, officers, agents, or employees under any law or rule of law. Nothing in this section shall be construed to prevent any department, agency, or instrumentality of the Federal Government, or any officer, agent, or employee thereof in the performance of his official duties, from removing to the appropriate Federal district court any proceeding to which the department, agency, or instrumentality or officer, agent, or employee thereof is subject pursuant to this section, and any such proceeding may be removed in accordance with section 1441 et seq. of title 28. No officer, agent, or employee of the United States shall be personally liable for any civil penalty arising from the performance of his official duties, for which he is not otherwise liable, and the United States shall be liable only for those civil penalties arising under Federal law or imposed by a State or local court to enforce an order or the process of such court. The President may exempt any effluent source of any department, agency, or instrumentality in the executive branch from compliance with any such a requirement if he determines it to be in the paramount interest of the United States to do so; except that no exemption may be granted from the requirements of section 1316 or 1317 of this title. No such exemptions shall be granted due to lack of appropriation unless the President shall have specifically requested such appropriation as a part of the budgetary process and the Congress shall have failed to make available such requested appropriation. Any exemption shall be for a period not in excess of one year, but additional exemptions may be granted for periods of not to exceed one year upon the President's making a new determination. The President shall report each January to the Congress all exemptions from the requirements of this section granted during the preceding calendar year, together with his reason for granting such exemption. In addition to any such exemption of a particular effluent source, the President may, if he determines it to be in the paramount interest of the United States to do so, issue regulations exempting from compliance with the requirements of this section any weaponry, equipment, aircraft, vessels, vehicles, or other classes or categories of property, and access to such property, which are owned or operated by the Armed Forces of the United States (including the Coast Guard) or by the National Guard of any State and which are uniquely military in nature. The President shall reconsider the need for such regulations at three-year intervals.

(b) (1) The Administrator shall coordinate with the head of each department, agency, or instrumentality of the Federal Government having jurisdiction over any property or facility utilizing federally owned wastewater facilities to develop a program of cooperation for utilizing wastewater control systems utilizing those innovative treatment processes and techniques for which guidelines have been promulgated under section 1314(d)(3) of this title. Such program shall include an inventory of property and facilities which could utilize such processes and techniques.

(2) Construction shall not be initiated for facilities for treatment of wastewater at any Federal property or facility after September 30, 1979, if alternative methods for wastewater treatment at such property or facility utilizing innovative treatment processes and techniques, including but not limited to methods utilizing recycle and reuse techniques and land treatment are not utilized, unless the life cycle cost of the alternative treatment works exceeds the life cycle cost of the most cost effective alternative by more than 15 per centum. The Administrator may waive the application of this paragraph in any case where the Administrator determines it to be in the public interest, or that compliance with this paragraph would interfere with the orderly compliance with conditions of a permit issued pursuant to section 1342 of this title.

(June 30, 1948, ch. 758, title III, Sec. 313, as added Pub. L. 92-500, Sec. 2, Oct. 18, 1972, 86 Stat. 875; amended Pub. L. 95-217, Secs. 60, 61(a), Dec. 27, 1977, 91 Stat. 1597, 1598.)

Amendments

1977—Subsec. (a). Pub. L. 95-217, Secs. 60, 61(a), designated existing provisions as subsec. (a) and inserted provisions making officers, agents, or employees of Federal departments, agencies, or instrumentalities subject to Federal, State, interstate, and local requirements, administrative authority, process, and sanctions respecting the control and abatement of water pollution in the same manner and to the same extent as non-governmental entities, including the payment of reasonable service charges, inserted provisions covering Federal employee liability, and inserted provisions relating to military source exemptions and the issuance of regulations covering those exemptions.

Subsec. (b). Pub. L. 95-217, Sec. 60, added subsec. (b).

Marine Guidance Systems

Pub. L. 105-383, title IV, Sec. 425(b), Nov. 13, 1998, 112 Stat. 3441, provided that: "The Secretary of Transportation shall, within 12 months after the date of the enactment of this Act [Nov. 13, 1998], evaluate and report to the Congress on the suitability of marine sector laser lighting, cold cathode lighting, and ultraviolet enhanced vision technologies for use in guiding marine vessels and traffic."

Federal Compliance With Pollution Control Standards

For provisions relating to the responsibility of the head of each Executive agency for compliance with applicable pollution control standards, see Ex. Ord. No. 12088, Oct. 13, 1978, 43 F.R. 47707, set out as a note under section 4321 of Title 42, The Public Health and Welfare.

Executive Order No. 11258

Ex. Ord. No. 11258, Nov. 17, 1965, 30 F.R. 14483, which related to prevention, control, and abatement of water pollution by federal activities, was superseded by Ex. Ord. No. 11286, July 2, 1966, 31 F.R. 9261.

Executive Order No. 11288

Ex. Ord. No. 11288, July 2, 1966, 31 F.R. 9261, which provided for prevention, control, and abatement of water pollution from federal activities, was superseded by Ex. Ord. No. 11507, Feb. 4, 1970, 35 F.R. 2573.

Section Referred to in Other Sections

This section is referred to in section 1365 of this title.

CLEAN LAKES

33 USC 1324

(a) Establishment and scope of program
  (1) State program requirements
    Each State on a biennial basis shall prepare and submit to the Administrator for his approval—
    (A) an identification and classification according to eutrophic condition of all publicly owned lakes in such State;
    (B) a description of procedures, processes, and methods (including land use requirements), to control sources of pollution of such lakes;
    (C) a description of methods and procedures, in conjunction with appropriate Federal agencies, to restore the quality of such lakes;
    (D) methods and procedures to mitigate the harmful effects of high acidity, including innovative methods of neutralizing and restoring buffering capacity of lakes and methods of removing from lakes toxic metals and other toxic substances mobilized by high acidity;
    (E) a list and description of those publicly owned lakes in such State for which uses are known to be impaired, including those lakes which are known not to meet applicable water quality standards or which require implementation of control programs to maintain compliance with applicable standards and those lakes in which water quality has deteriorated as a result of high acidity that may reasonably be due to acid deposition; and
    (F) an assessment of the status and trends of water quality in lakes in such State, including but not limited to, the nature and extent of pollution loading from point and nonpoint sources and the extent to which the use of lakes is impaired as a result of such pollution, particularly with respect to toxic pollution.
  (2) Submission as part of 1315(b)(1) report
    The information required under paragraph (1) shall be included in the report required under section 1315(b)(1) of this title, beginning with the report required under such section by April 1, 1988.
  (3) Eligibility requirement
    Beginning after April 1, 1988, a State must have submitted the information required under paragraph (1) in order to receive grant assistance under this section.

(b) Financial assistance to States
The Administrator shall provide financial assistance to States in order to carry out methods and procedures approved by him under subsection (a) of this section. The Administrator shall provide financial assistance to States to prepare the identification and classification surveys required in subsection (a)(1) of this section.

(c) Maximum amount of grant; authorization of appropriations
  (1) The amount granted to any State for any fiscal year under subsection (b) of this section shall not exceed 70 per centum of the funds expended by such State in such year for carrying out approved methods and procedures under subsection (a) of this section.
  (2) There is authorized to be appropriated $50,000,000 for each of fiscal years 2001 through 2005 for grants to States under subsection (b) of this section which such sums shall remain available until expended. The Administrator shall provide for an equitable distribution of such sums to the States with approved methods and procedures under subsection (a) of this section.

(d) Demonstration program
  (1) General requirements
    The Administrator is authorized and directed to establish and conduct at locations throughout the Nation a lake water quality demonstration program. The program shall, at a minimum—
    (A) develop cost effective technologies for the control of pollutants to preserve or enhance lake water quality while optimizing multiple lakes uses;
    (B) control nonpoint sources of pollution which are contributing to the degradation of water quality in lakes;
    (C) evaluate the feasibility of implementing regional consolidated pollution control strategies;
    (D) demonstrate environmentally preferred techniques for the removal and disposal of contaminated lake sediments;
    (E) develop improved methods for the removal of silt, stumps, aquatic growth, and other obstructions which impair the quality of lakes;
    (F) construct and evaluate silt traps and other devices or equipment to prevent or abate the deposit of sediment in lakes; and
    (G) demonstrate the costs and benefits of utilizing dredged material from lakes in the reclamation of despoiled land.
  (2) Geographical requirements
    Demonstration projects authorized by this subsection shall be undertaken to reflect a variety of geographical and environmental conditions. As a priority, the Administrator shall undertake demonstration projects at Lake Champlain, New York and Vermont; Lake Houston, Texas; Beaver Lake, Arkansas; Greenwood Lake and Belcher Creek, New Jersey; Deal Lake, New Jersey; Alcyon Lake, New Jersey; Gorton's Pond, Rhode Island; Lake Washington, Rhode Island; Lake Bomoseen, Vermont; Sauk Lake, Minnesota; Otsego Lake, New York; Oneida Lake, New York; Raystown Lake, Pennsylvania; Swan Lake, Itasca County, Minnesota; Walker Lake, Nevada; Lake Tahoe, California and Nevada; Ten Mile Lakes, Oregon; Woahink Lake, Oregon; Highland Lake, Connecticut; Lily Lake, New   Jersey; Strawbridge Lake, New Jersey; Baboosic Lake, New Hampshire; French Pond, New Hampshire; Dillon Reservoir, Ohio; Tohopekaliga Lake, Florida; Lake Apopka, Florida; Lake George, New York; Lake Wallenpaupack, Pennsylvania; Lake Allatoona, Georgia; and Lake Worth, Texas.
  (3) Reports
    Notwithstanding section 3003 of the Federal Reports Elimination and Sunset Act of 1995 (31 U.S.C. 1113 note; 109 Stat. 734-736), by January 1, 1997, and January 1 of every odd-numbered year thereafter, the Administrator shall report to the Committee on Transportation and Infrastructure of the House of Representatives and the Committee on Environment and Public Works of the Senate on work undertaken pursuant to this subsection. Upon completion of the program authorized by this subsection, the Administrator shall submit to such committees a final report on the results of such program, along with recommendations for further measures to improve the water quality of the Nation's lakes.
  (4) Authorization of appropriations

(A) In general
There is authorized to be appropriated to carry out this subsection not to exceed $40,000,000 for fiscal years beginning after September 30, 1986, to remain available until expended.
(B) Special authorizations
  (i) Amount
  There is authorized to be appropriated to carry out subsection (b) of this section with respect to subsection (a)(1)(D) of this section not to exceed $25,000,000 for fiscal years beginning after September 30, 1986, to remain available until expended.
  (ii) Distribution of funds
  The Administrator shall provide for an equitable distribution of sums appropriated pursuant to this subparagraph among States carrying out approved methods and procedures. Such distribution shall be based on the relative needs of each such State for the mitigation of the harmful effects on lakes and other surface waters of high acidity that may reasonably be due to acid deposition or acid mine drainage.
  (iii) Grants as additional assistance
  The amount of any grant to a State under this subparagraph shall be in addition to, and not in lieu of, any other Federal financial assistance.

(June 30, 1948, ch. 758, title III, Sec. 314, as added Pub. L. 92-500, Sec. 2, Oct. 18, 1972, 86 Stat. 875; amended Pub. L. 95-217, Secs. 4(f), 62(a), Dec. 27, 1977, 91 Stat. 1567, 1598; Pub. L. 96-483, Sec. 1(f), Oct. 21, 1980, 94 Stat. 2360; Pub. L. 100-4, title I, Sec. 101(g), title III, Sec. 315(a), (b), (d), Feb. 4, 1987, 101 Stat. 9, 49, 50, 52; Pub. L. 101-596, title III, Sec. 302, Nov. 16, 1990, 104 Stat. 3006; Pub. L. 104-66, title II, Sec. 2021(c), Dec. 21, 1995, 109 Stat. 727; Pub. L. 105-362, title V, Sec. 501(b), Nov. 10, 1998, 112 Stat. 3283; Pub. L. 106-457, title VII, Sec. 701, 702, Nov. 7, 2000, 114 Stat. 1976, 1977.)

Amendments

2000—Subsec. (c)(2). Pub. L. 106-457, Sec. 701 struck out "$50,000,000 for the fiscal year ending June 30, 1973; $100,000,000 for the fiscal year 1974; $150,000,000 for the fiscal year 1975, $50,000,000 for fiscal year 1977, $60,000,000 for fiscal year 1978, $60,000,000 for fiscal year 1979, $60,000,000 for fiscal year 1980, $30,000,000 for fiscal year 1981, $30,000,000 for fiscal year 1982, such sums as may be necessary for fiscal years 1983 through 1985, and $30,000,000 per fiscal year for each of the fiscal years 1986 through 1990" and inserted "$50,000,000 for each of fiscal years 2001 through 2005".

Subsec. (d)(2). Pub. L. 106-457, Sec. 702(1) inserted "Otsego Lake, New York; Oneida Lake, New York; Raystown Lake, Pennsylvania; Swan Lake, Itasca County, Minnesota; Walker Lake, Nevada; Lake Tahoe, California and Nevada; Ten Mile Lakes, Oregon; Woahink Lake, Oregon; Highland Lake, Connecticut; Lily Lake, New Jersey; Strawbridge Lake, New Jersey; Baboosic Lake, New Hampshire; French Pond, New Hampshire; Dillon Reservoir, Ohio; Tohopekaliga Lake, Florida; Lake Apopka, Florida; Lake George, New York; Lake Wallenpaupack, Pennsylvania; Lake Allatoona, Georgia;" after "Sauk Lake, Minnesota;".

Subsec. (d)(3). Pub. L. 106-457, Sec. 702(2) struck out "By" and inserted "Notwithstanding section 3003 of the Federal Reports Elimination and Sunset Act of 1995 (31 U.S.C. 1113 note; 109 Stat. 734-736), by".

Subsec. (d)(4)(B)(i). Pub. L. 106-457, Sec. 703(3) substituted "$25,000,000" for "$15,000,000".

1998—Subsec. (a)(3), (4). Pub. L. 105-362 redesignated par. (4) as (3) and struck out heading and text of par. (3). Text read as follows: "Not later than 180 days after receipt from the States of the biennial information required under paragraph (1), the Administrator shall submit to the Committee on Public Works and Transportation of the House of Representatives and the Committee on Environment and Public Works of the Senate a report on the status of water quality in lakes in the United States, including the effectiveness of the methods and procedures described in paragraph (1)(D)."

1995—Subsec. (d)(3). Pub. L. 104-66 substituted "By January 1, 1997, and January 1 of every odd-numbered year thereafter, the Administrator shall report to the Committee on Transportation and Infrastructure" for "The Administrator shall report annually to the Committee on Public Works and Transportation".

1990—Subsec. (d)(2). Pub. L. 101-596 inserted "Lake Champlain, New York and Vermont;" before "Lake Houston, Texas".

1987—Subsec. (a). Pub. L. 100-4, Sec. 315(a), amended subsec. (a) generally. Prior to amendment, subsec. (a) read as follows: "Each State shall prepare or establish, and submit to the Administrator for his approval—
  (1) an identification and classification according to eutrophic condition of all publicly owned fresh water lakes in such State;
  (2) procedures, processes, and methods (including land use requirements), to control sources of pollution of such lakes; and
  (3) methods and procedures, in conjunction with appropriate Federal agencies, to restore the quality of such lakes."

Subsec. (b). Pub. L. 100-4, Sec. 315(d)(1), substituted "subsection (a) of this section" for "this section" in first sentence.

Subsec. (c)(1). Pub. L. 100-4, Sec. 315(d)(2), substituted "subsection (b) of this section" for first reference to "this section" and "subsection (a) of this section" for second reference to "this section".

Subsec. (c)(2). Pub. L. 100-4, Secs. 101(g), 315(d)(3), struck out "and" after "1981," and inserted ", such sums as may be necessary for fiscal years 1983 through 1985, and $30,000,000 per fiscal year for each of the fiscal years 1986 through 1990" after "1982", and substituted "subsection (b) of this section" for first reference to "this section" and "subsection (a) of this section" for second reference to "this section".

Subsec. (d). Pub. L. 100-4, Sec. 315(b), added subsec. (d).

1980—Subsec. (c)(2). Pub. L. 96-483 inserted authorization of $30,000,000 for each of fiscal years 1981 and 1982.

1977—Subsec. (b). Pub. L. 95-217, Sec. 62(a), inserted provision directing the Administrator to provide financial assistance to States to prepare the identification and classification surveys required in subsec. (a)(1) of this section.

Subsec. (c)(2). Pub. L. 95-217, Sec. 4(f), substituted "$150,000,000 for the fiscal year 1975, $50,000,000 for fiscal year 1977, $60,000,000 for fiscal year 1978, $60,000,000 for fiscal year 1979, and $60,000,000 for fiscal year 1980" for "and $150,000,000 for the fiscal year 1975".

Section Referred to in Other Sections

This section is referred to in sections 1329, 1376, 1377 of this title.

NATIONAL STUDY COMMISSION

33 USC 1325

(a) Establishment
   There is established a National Study Commission, which shall make a full and complete investigation and study of all of the technological aspects of achieving, and all aspects of the total economic, social, and environmental effects of achieving or not achieving, the effluent limitations and goals set forth for 1983 in section 1311(b)(2) of this title.

(b) Membership; chairman
   Such Commission shall be composed of fifteen members, including five members of the Senate, who are members of the Environment and Public Works committee, appointed by the President of the Senate, five members of the House, who are members of the Public Works and Transportation committee, appointed by the Speaker of the House, and five members of the public appointed by the President. The Chairman of such Commission shall be elected from among its members.

(c) Contract authority
   In the conduct of such study, the Commission is authorized to contract with the National Academy of Sciences and the National Academy of Engineering (acting through the National Research Council), the National Institute of Ecology, Brookings Institution, and other nongovernmental entities, for the investigation of matters within their competence.

Clean Water Act / 607

(d) Cooperation of departments, agencies, and instrumentalities of executive branch
The heads of the departments, agencies and instrumentalities of the executive branch of the Federal Government shall cooperate with the Commission in carrying out the requirements of this section, and shall furnish to the Commission such information as the Commission deems necessary to carry out this section.

(e) Report to Congress
A report shall be submitted to the Congress of the results of such investigation and study, together with recommendations, not later than three years after October 18, 1972.

(f) Compensation and allowances
The members of the Commission who are not officers or employees of the United States, while attending conferences or meetings of the Commission or while otherwise serving at the request of the Chairman shall be entitled to receive compensation at a rate not in excess of the maximum rate of pay for Grade GS-18, as provided in the General Schedule under section 5332 of title 5, including traveltime and while away from their homes or regular places of business they may be allowed travel expenses, including per diem in lieu of subsistence as authorized by law for persons in the Government service employed intermittently.

(g) Appointment of personnel
In addition to authority to appoint personnel subject to the provisions of title 5 governing appointments in the competitive service, and to pay such personnel in accordance with the provisions of chapter 51 and subchapter III of chapter 53 of such title relating to classification and General Schedule pay rates, the Commission shall have authority to enter into contracts with private or public organizations who shall furnish the Commission with such administrative and technical personnel as may be necessary to carry out the purpose of this section. Personnel furnished by such organizations under this subsection are not, and shall not be considered to be, Federal employees for any purposes, but in the performance of their duties shall be guided by the standards which apply to employees of the legislative branches under rules 41 and 43[1] of the Senate and House of Representatives, respectively.

(h) Authorization of appropriation
There is authorized to be appropriated, for use in carrying out this section, not to exceed $17,250,000.

(June 30, 1948, ch. 758, title III, Sec. 315, as added Pub. L. 92-500, Sec. 2, Oct. 18, 1972, 86 Stat. 875; amended Pub. L. 93-207, Sec. 1(5), Dec. 28, 1973, 87 Stat. 906; Pub. L. 93-592, Sec. 5, Jan. 2, 1975, 88 Stat. 1925; Pub. L. 94-238, Mar. 23, 1976, 90 Stat. 250; H. Res. 988, Oct. 8, 1974; S. Res. 4, Feb. 4, 1977.)

References in Text

Travel expenses, including per diem in lieu of subsistence as authorized by law, referred to subsec. (f), probably refers to the allowances authorized by section 5703 of Title 5, Government Organization and Employees.

The General Schedule, referred to in subsec. (g), is set out under section 5332 of Title 5.

The Rules of the House of Representatives for the One Hundred Sixth Congress were adopted and amended generally by House Resolution No. 5, One Hundred Sixth Congress, Jan. 6, 1999. Provisions formerly appearing in rule 43, referred to in subsec. (g), are now contained in rule XXIV.

Amendments

1976—Subsec. (h). Pub. L. 94-238 substituted "$17,250,000" for "$17,000,000".

1975—Subsec. (h). Pub. L. 93-592 substituted "$17,000,000" for "$15,000,000".

1973—Subsecs. (g), (h). Pub. L. 93-207 added subsec. (g) and redesignated former subsec. (g) as (h).

Change of Name

Committee on Public Works of Senate abolished and replaced by Committee on Environment and Public Works of Senate, effective Feb. 11, 1977. See Rule XXV of Standing Rules of Senate, as amended by Senate Resolution No. 4 (popularly cited as the "Committee System Reorganization Amendments of 1977"), approved Feb. 4, 1977.

Committee on Public Works of House of Representatives changed to Committee on Public Works and Transportation of House of Representatives, effective Jan. 3, 1975, by House Resolution No.

---

[1] See References in Text note below.

608 / Environmental Statutes

988, 93d Congress. Committee on Public Works and Transportation of House of Representatives treated as referring to Committee on Transportation and Infrastructure of House of Representatives by section 1(a) of Pub. L. 104-14, set out as a note preceding section 21 of Title 2, The Congress.

References in Other Laws to GS-16, 17, or 18 Pay Rates

References in laws to the rates of pay for GS-16, 17, or 18, or to maximum rates of pay under the General Schedule, to be considered references to rates payable under specified sections of Title 5, Government Organization and Employees, see section 529 [title I, Sec. 101(c)(1)] of Pub. L. 101-509, set out in a note under section 5376 of Title 5.

Section Referred to in Other Sections

This section is referred to in sections 1311, 1376 of this title.

THERMAL DISCHARGES

33 USC 1326

(a) Effluent limitations that will assure protection and propagation of balanced, indigenous population of shellfish, fish, and wildlife
With respect to any point source otherwise subject to the provisions of section 1311 of this title or section 1316 of this title, whenever the owner or operator of any such source, after opportunity for public hearing, can demonstrate to the satisfaction of the Administrator (or, if appropriate, the State) that any effluent limitation proposed for the control of the thermal component of any discharge from such source will require effluent limitations more stringent than necessary to assure the projection and propagation of a balanced, indigenous population of shellfish, fish, and wildlife in and on the body of water into which the discharge is to be made, the Administrator (or, if appropriate, the State) may impose an effluent limitation under such sections for such plant, with respect to the thermal component of such discharge (taking into account the interaction of such thermal component with other pollutants), that will assure the protection and propagation of a balanced, indigenous population of shellfish, fish, and wildlife in and on that body of water.

(b) Cooling water intake structures
Any standard established pursuant to section 1311 of this title or section 1316 of this title and applicable to a point source shall require that the location, design, construction, and capacity of cooling water intake structures reflect the best technology available for minimizing adverse environmental impact.

(c) Period of protection from more stringent effluent limitations following discharge point source modification commenced after October 18, 1972
Notwithstanding any other provision of this chapter, any point source of a discharge having a thermal component, the modification of which point source is commenced after October 18, 1972, and which, as modified, meets effluent limitations established under section 1311 of this title or, if more stringent, effluent limitations established under section 1313 of this title and which effluent limitations will assure protection and propagation of a balanced, indigenous population of shellfish, fish, and wildlife in or on the water into which the discharge is made, shall not be subject to any more stringent effluent limitation with respect to the thermal component of its discharge during a ten year period beginning on the date of completion of such modification or during the period of depreciation or amortization of such facility for the purpose of section 167 or 169 (or both) of title 26, whichever period ends first.

(June 30, 1948, ch. 758, title III, Sec. 316, as added Pub. L. 92-500, Sec. 2, Oct. 18, 1972, 86 Stat. 876; amended Pub. L. 99-514, Sec. 2, Oct. 22, 1986, 100 Stat. 2095.)

Amendments

1986—Subsec. (c). Pub. L. 99-514 substituted "Internal Revenue Code of 1986" for "Internal Revenue Code of 1954", which for purposes of codification was translated as "title 26" thus requiring no change in text.

Section Referred to in Other Sections

This section is referred to in sections 1254, 1311, 1313, 1342 of this title.

33 USC 1327

Omitted.

Codification

Section, act June 30, 1948, ch. 758, title III, Sec. 317, as added Oct. 18, 1972, Pub. L. 92-500, Sec. 2, 86 Stat. 877, authorized Administrator to investigate and study feasibility of alternate methods of financing cost of preventing, controlling, and abating pollution as directed by Water Quality Improvement Act of 1970 and to report to Congress, not later than two years after Oct. 18, 1972, the results of investigation and study accompanied by recommendations for financing these programs for fiscal years beginning after 1976.

AQUACULTURE

33 USC 1328

(a) Authority to permit discharge of specific pollutants
   The Administrator is authorized, after public hearings, to permit the discharge of a specific pollutant or pollutants under controlled conditions associated with an approved aquaculture project under Federal or State supervision pursuant to section 1342 of this title.

(b) Procedures and guidelines
   The Administrator shall by regulation establish any procedures and guidelines which the Administrator deems necessary to carry out this section. Such regulations shall require the application to such discharge of each criterion, factor, procedure, and requirement applicable to a permit issued under section 1342 of this title, as the Administrator determines necessary to carry out the objective of this chapter.

(c) State administration
   Each State desiring to administer its own permit program within its jurisdiction for discharge of a specific pollutant or pollutants under controlled conditions associated with an approved aquaculture project may do so if upon submission of such program the Administrator determines such program is adequate to carry out the objective of this chapter.

(June 30, 1948, ch. 758, title III, Sec. 318, as added Pub. L. 92-500, Sec. 2, Oct. 18, 1972, 86 Stat. 877; amended Pub. L. 95-217, Sec. 63, Dec. 27, 1977, 91 Stat. 1599.)

Amendments

1977—Subsec. (a). Pub. L. 95-217 inserted "pursuant to section 1342 of this title" after "Federal or State supervision".

Subsec. (b). Pub. L. 95-217 struck out ", not later than January 1, 1974," after "The Administrator shall by regulation" in existing provisions and inserted provisions that the regulations require the application to the discharge of each criterion, factor, procedure, and requirement applicable to a permit issued under section 1342 of this title, as the Administrator determines necessary to carry out the objectives of this chapter.

Subsec. (c). Pub. L. 95-217 added subsec. (c).

Section Referred to in Other Sections

This section is referred to in sections 1311, 1319, 1342 of this title.

NONPOINT SOURCE MANAGEMENT PROGRAMS

33 USC 1329

(a) State assessment reports
   (1) Contents
      The Governor of each State shall, after notice and opportunity for public comment, prepare and submit to the Administrator for approval, a report which—

(A) identifies those navigable waters within the State which, without additional action to control nonpoint sources of pollution, cannot reasonably be expected to attain or maintain applicable water quality standards or the goals and requirements of this chapter;

(B) identifies those categories and subcategories of nonpoint sources or, where appropriate, particular nonpoint sources which add significant pollution to each portion of the navigable waters identified under subparagraph (A) in amounts which contribute to such portion not meeting such water quality standards or such goals and requirements;

(C) describes the process, including intergovernmental coordination and public participation, for identifying best management practices and measures to control each category and subcategory of nonpoint sources and, where appropriate, particular nonpoint sources identified under subparagraph (B) and to reduce, to the maximum extent practicable, the level of pollution resulting from such category, subcategory, or source; and

(D) identifies and describes State and local programs for controlling pollution added from nonpoint sources to, and improving the quality of, each such portion of the navigable waters, including but not limited to those programs which are receiving Federal assistance under subsections (h) and (i) of this section.

(2) Information used in preparation

In developing the report required by this section, the State (A) may rely upon information developed pursuant to sections 1288, 1313(e), 1314(f), 1315(b), and 1324 of this title, and other information as appropriate, and (B) may utilize appropriate elements of the waste treatment management plans developed pursuant to sections 1288(b) and 1313 of this title, to the extent such elements are consistent with and fulfill the requirements of this section.

(b) State management programs

(1) In general

The Governor of each State, for that State or in combination with adjacent States, shall, after notice and opportunity for public comment, prepare and submit to the Administrator for approval a management program which such State proposes to implement in the first four fiscal years beginning after the date of submission of such management program for controlling pollution added from nonpoint sources to the navigable waters within the State and improving the quality of such waters.

(2) Specific contents

Each management program proposed for implementation under this subsection shall include each of the following:

(A) An identification of the best management practices and measures which will be undertaken to reduce pollutant loadings resulting from each category, subcategory, or particular nonpoint source designated under paragraph (1)(B), taking into account the impact of the practice on ground water quality.

(B) An identification of programs (including, as appropriate, nonregulatory or regulatory programs for enforcement, technical assistance, financial assistance, education, training, technology transfer, and demonstration projects) to achieve implementation of the best management practices by the categories, subcategories, and particular nonpoint sources designated under subparagraph (A).

(C) A schedule containing annual milestones for (i) utilization of the program implementation methods identified in subparagraph (B), and (ii) implementation of the best management practices identified in subparagraph (A) by the categories, subcategories, or particular nonpoint sources designated under paragraph (1)(B). Such schedule shall provide for utilization of the best management practices at the earliest practicable date.

(D) A certification of the attorney general of the State or States (or the chief attorney of any State water pollution control agency which has independent legal counsel) that the laws of the State or States, as the case may be, provide adequate authority to implement such management program or, if there is not such adequate authority, a list of such additional authorities as will be necessary to implement such management

program. A schedule and commitment by the State or States to seek such additional authorities as expeditiously as practicable.
  (E) Sources of Federal and other assistance and funding (other than assistance provided under subsections (h) and (i) of this section) which will be available in each of such fiscal years for supporting implementation of such practices and measures and the purposes for which such assistance will be used in each of such fiscal years.
  (F) An identification of Federal financial assistance programs and Federal development projects for which the State will review individual assistance applications or development projects for their effect on water quality pursuant to the procedures set forth in Executive Order 12372 as in effect on September 17, 1983, to determine whether such assistance applications or development projects would be consistent with the program prepared under this subsection; for the purposes of this subparagraph, identification shall not be limited to the assistance programs or development projects subject to Executive Order 12372 but may include any programs listed in the most recent Catalog of Federal Domestic Assistance which may have an effect on the purposes and objectives of the State's nonpoint source pollution management program.
 (3) Utilization of local and private experts
  In developing and implementing a management program under this subsection, a State shall, to the maximum extent practicable, involve local public and private agencies and organizations which have expertise in control of nonpoint sources of pollution.
 (4) Development on watershed basis
  A State shall, to the maximum extent practicable, develop and implement a management program under this subsection on a watershed-by-watershed basis within such State.
(c) Administrative provisions
 (1) Cooperation requirement
  Any report required by subsection (a) of this section and any management program and report required by subsection (b) of this section shall be developed in cooperation with local, substate regional, and interstate entities which are actively planning for the implementation of nonpoint source pollution controls and have either been certified by the Administrator in accordance with section 1288 of this title, have worked jointly with the State on water quality management planning under section 1285(j) of this title, or have been designated by the State legislative body or Governor as water quality management planning agencies for their geographic areas.
 (2) Time period for submission of reports and management programs
  Each report and management program shall be submitted to the Administrator during the 18-month period beginning on February 4, 1987.
(d) Approval or disapproval of reports and management programs
 (1) Deadline
  Subject to paragraph (2), not later than 180 days after the date of submission to the Administrator of any report or management program under this section (other than subsections (h), (i), and (k) of this section), the Administrator shall either approve or disapprove such report or management program, as the case may be. The Administrator may approve a portion of a management program under this subsection. If the Administrator does not disapprove a report, management program, or portion of a management program in such 180-day period, such report, management program, or portion shall be deemed approved for purposes of this section.
 (2) Procedure for disapproval
  If, after notice and opportunity for public comment and consultation with appropriate Federal and State agencies and other interested persons, the Administrator determines that—
  (A) the proposed management program or any portion thereof does not meet the requirements of subsection (b)(2) of this section or is not likely to satisfy, in whole or in part, the goals and requirements of this chapter;
  (B) adequate authority does not exist, or adequate resources are not available, to implement such program or portion;
  (C) the schedule for implementing such program or portion is not sufficiently expeditious; or

(D) the practices and measures proposed in such program or portion are not adequate to reduce the level of pollution in navigable waters in the State resulting from nonpoint sources and to improve the quality of navigable waters in the State;

the Administrator shall within 6 months of the receipt of the proposed program notify the State of any revisions or modifications necessary to obtain approval. The State shall thereupon have an additional 3 months to submit its revised management program and the Administrator shall approve or disapprove such revised program within three months of receipt.

(3) Failure of State to submit report

If a Governor of a State does not submit the report required by subsection (a) of this section within the period specified by subsection (c)(2) of this section, the Administrator shall, within 30 months after February 4, 1987, prepare a report for such State which makes the identifications required by paragraphs (1)(A) and (1)(B) of subsection (a) of this section. Upon completion of the requirement of the preceding sentence and after notice and opportunity for comment, the Administrator shall report to Congress on his actions pursuant to this section.

(e) Local management programs; technical assistance

If a State fails to submit a management program under subsection (b) of this section or the Administrator does not approve such a management program, a local public agency or organization which has expertise in, and authority to, control water pollution resulting from nonpoint sources in any area of such State which the Administrator determines is of sufficient geographic size may, with approval of such State, request the Administrator to provide, and the Administrator shall provide, technical assistance to such agency or organization in developing for such area a management program which is described in subsection (b) of this section and can be approved pursuant to subsection (d) of this section. After development of such management program, such agency or organization shall submit such management program to the Administrator for approval. If the Administrator approves such management program, such agency or organization shall be eligible to receive financial assistance under subsection (h) of this section for implementation of such management program as if such agency or organization were a State for which a report submitted under subsection (a) of this section and a management program submitted under subsection (b) of this section were approved under this section. Such financial assistance shall be subject to the same terms and conditions as assistance provided to a State under subsection (h) of this section.

(f) Technical assistance for States

Upon request of a State, the Administrator may provide technical assistance to such State in developing a management program approved under subsection (b) of this section for those portions of the navigable waters requested by such State.

(g) Interstate management conference

(1) Convening of conference; notification; purpose

If any portion of the navigable waters in any State which is implementing a management program approved under this section is not meeting applicable water quality standards or the goals and requirements of this chapter as a result, in whole or in part, of pollution from nonpoint sources in another State, such State may petition the Administrator to convene, and the Administrator shall convene, a management conference of all States which contribute significant pollution resulting from nonpoint sources to such portion. If, on the basis of information available, the Administrator determines that a State is not meeting applicable water quality standards or the goals and requirements of this chapter as a result, in whole or in part, of significant pollution from nonpoint sources in another State, the Administrator shall notify such States. The Administrator may convene a management conference under this paragraph not later than 180 days after giving such notification, whether or not the State which is not meeting such standards requests such conference. The purpose of such conference shall be to develop an agreement among such States to reduce the level of pollution in such portion resulting from nonpoint sources and to improve the water quality of such portion. Nothing in such agreement shall supersede or abrogate rights to quantities of water which have been established by interstate water compacts, Supreme Court decrees, or State water laws. This subsection shall not apply to any pollution which is subject to the Colorado River Basin Salinity Control Act [43 U.S.C.

1571 et seq.]. The requirement that the Administrator convene a management conference shall not be subject to the provisions of section 1365 of this title.

    (2) State management program requirement

    To the extent that the States reach agreement through such conference, the management programs of the States which are parties to such agreements and which contribute significant pollution to the navigable waters or portions thereof not meeting applicable water quality standards or goals and requirements of this chapter will be revised to reflect such agreement. Such management programs shall be consistent with Federal and State law.

(h) Grant program

    (1) Grants for implementation of management programs

    Upon application of a State for which a report submitted under subsection (a) of this section and a management program submitted under subsection (b) of this section is approved under this section, the Administrator shall make grants, subject to such terms and conditions as the Administrator considers appropriate, under this subsection to such State for the purpose of assisting the State in implementing such management program. Funds reserved pursuant to section 1285(j)(5) of this title may be used to develop and implement such management program.

    (2) Applications

    An application for a grant under this subsection in any fiscal year shall be in such form and shall contain such other information as the Administrator may require, including an identification and description of the best management practices and measures which the State proposes to assist, encourage, or require in such year with the Federal assistance to be provided under the grant.

    (3) Federal share

    The Federal share of the cost of each management program implemented with Federal assistance under this subsection in any fiscal year shall not exceed 60 percent of the cost incurred by the State in implementing such management program and shall be made on condition that the non-Federal share is provided from non-Federal sources.

    (4) Limitation on grant amounts

    Notwithstanding any other provision of this subsection, not more than 15 percent of the amount appropriated to carry out this subsection may be used to make grants to any one State, including any grants to any local public agency or organization with authority to control pollution from nonpoint sources in any area of such State.

    (5) Priority for effective mechanisms

    For each fiscal year beginning after September 30, 1987, the Administrator may give priority in making grants under this subsection, and shall give consideration in determining the Federal share of any such grant, to States which have implemented or are proposing to implement management programs which will—

        (A) control particularly difficult or serious nonpoint source pollution problems, including, but not limited to, problems resulting from mining activities;

        (B) implement innovative methods or practices for controlling nonpoint sources of pollution, including regulatory programs where the Administrator deems appropriate;

        (C) control interstate nonpoint source pollution problems; or

        (D) carry out ground water quality protection activities which the Administrator determines are part of a comprehensive nonpoint source pollution control program, including research, planning, ground water assessments, demonstration programs, enforcement, technical assistance, education, and training to protect ground water quality from nonpoint sources of pollution.

    (6) Availability for obligation

    The funds granted to each State pursuant to this subsection in a fiscal year shall remain available for obligation by such State for the fiscal year for which appropriated. The amount of any such funds not obligated by the end of such fiscal year shall be available to the Administrator for granting to other States under this subsection in the next fiscal year.

    (7) Limitation on use of funds

    States may use funds from grants made pursuant to this section for financial assistance to persons only to the extent that such assistance is related to the costs of demonstration projects.

(8) Satisfactory progress
No grant may be made under this subsection in any fiscal year to a State which in the preceding fiscal year received a grant under this subsection unless the Administrator determines that such State made satisfactory progress in such preceding fiscal year in meeting the schedule specified by such State under subsection (b)(2) of this section.

(9) Maintenance of effort
No grant may be made to a State under this subsection in any fiscal year unless such State enters into such agreements with the Administrator as the Administrator may require to ensure that such State will maintain its aggregate expenditures from all other sources for programs for controlling pollution added to the navigable waters in such State from nonpoint sources and improving the quality of such waters at or above the average level of such expenditures in its two fiscal years preceding February 4, 1987.

(10) Request for information
The Administrator may request such information, data, and reports as he considers necessary to make the determination of continuing eligibility for grants under this section.

(11) Reporting and other requirements
Each State shall report to the Administrator on an annual basis concerning (A) its progress in meeting the schedule of milestones submitted pursuant to subsection (b)(2)(C) of this section, and (B) to the extent that appropriate information is available, reductions in nonpoint source pollutant loading and improvements in water quality for those navigable waters or watersheds within the State which were identified pursuant to subsection (a)(1)(A) of this section resulting from implementation of the management program.

(12) Limitation on administrative costs
For purposes of this subsection, administrative costs in the form of salaries, overhead, or indirect costs for services provided and charged against activities and programs carried out with a grant under this subsection shall not exceed in any fiscal year 10 percent of the amount of the grant in such year, except that costs of implementing enforcement and regulatory activities, education, training, technical assistance, demonstration projects, and technology transfer programs shall not be subject to this limitation.

(i) Grants for protecting groundwater quality
(1) Eligible applicants and activities
Upon application of a State for which a report submitted under subsection (a) of this section and a plan submitted under subsection (b) of this section is approved under this section, the Administrator shall make grants under this subsection to such State for the purpose of assisting such State in carrying out groundwater quality protection activities which the Administrator determines will advance the State toward implementation of a comprehensive nonpoint source pollution control program. Such activities shall include, but not be limited to, research, planning, groundwater assessments, demonstration programs, enforcement, technical assistance, education and training to protect the quality of groundwater and to prevent contamination of groundwater from nonpoint sources of pollution.

(2) Applications
An application for a grant under this subsection shall be in such form and shall contain such information as the Administrator may require.

(3) Federal share; maximum amount
The Federal share of the cost of assisting a State in carrying out groundwater protection activities in any fiscal year under this subsection shall be 50 percent of the costs incurred by the State in carrying out such activities, except that the maximum amount of Federal assistance which any State may receive under this subsection in any fiscal year shall not exceed $150,000.

(j) Authorization of appropriations
There is authorized to be appropriated to carry out subsections (h) and (i) of this section not to exceed $70,000,000 for fiscal year 1988, $100,000,000 per fiscal year for each of fiscal years 1989 and 1990, and $130,000,000 for fiscal year 1991; except that for each of such fiscal years not to exceed $7,500,000 may be made available to carry out subsection (i) of this section. Sums appropriated pursuant to this subsection shall remain available until expended.

Clean Water Act / 615

(k) Consistency of other programs and projects with management programs
The Administrator shall transmit to the Office of Management and Budget and the appropriate Federal departments and agencies a list of those assistance programs and development projects identified by each State under subsection (b)(2)(F) of this section for which individual assistance applications and projects will be reviewed pursuant to the procedures set forth in Executive Order 12372 as in effect on September 17, 1983. Beginning not later than sixty days after receiving notification by the Administrator, each Federal department and agency shall modify existing regulations to allow States to review individual development projects and assistance applications under the identified Federal assistance programs and shall accommodate, according to the requirements and definitions of Executive Order 12372, as in effect on September 17, 1983, the concerns of the State regarding the consistency of such applications or projects with the State nonpoint source pollution management program.

(l) Collection of information
The Administrator shall collect and make available, through publications and other appropriate means, information pertaining to management practices and implementation methods, including, but not limited to, (1) information concerning the costs and relative efficiencies of best management practices for reducing nonpoint source pollution; and (2) available data concerning the relationship between water quality and implementation of various management practices to control nonpoint sources of pollution.

(m) Set aside for administrative personnel
Not less than 5 percent of the funds appropriated pursuant to subsection (j) of this section for any fiscal year shall be available to the Administrator to maintain personnel levels at the Environmental Protection Agency at levels which are adequate to carry out this section in such year.

(June 30, 1948, ch. 758, title III, Sec. 319, as added Pub. L. 100-4, title III, Sec. 316(a), Feb. 4, 1987, 101 Stat. 52; amended Pub. L. 105-362, title V, Sec. 501(c), Nov. 10, 1998, 112 Stat. 3283.)

References in Text

Executive Order 12372, referred to in subsecs. (b)(2)(F) and (k), is Ex. Ord. No. 12372, July 14, 1982, 47 F.R. 30959, as amended, which is set out under section 6506 of Title 31, Money and Finance.

The Colorado River Basin Salinity Control Act, referred to in subsec. (g)(1), is Pub. L. 93-320, June 24, 1974, 88 Stat. 266, as amended, which is classified principally to chapter 32A (Sec. 1571 et seq.) of Title 43, Public Lands. For complete classification of this Act to the Code, see Short Title note set out under section 1571 of Title 43 and Tables.

Amendments

1998—Subsec. (i)(4). Pub. L. 105-362, Sec. 501(c)(1), struck out heading and text of par. (4). Text read as follows: "The Administrator shall include in each report transmitted under subsection (m) of this section a report on the activities and programs implemented under this subsection during the preceding fiscal year."

Subsecs. (m), (n). Pub. L. 105-362, Sec. 501(c)(2), (3), redesignated subsec. (n) as (m) and struck out heading and text of former subsec. (m) which related to reports of Administrator.

Section Referred to in Other Sections

This section is referred to in sections 1268, 1270, 1281, 1285, 1314, 1330, 1377, 1381, 1383, 1386, 1414b of this title; title 16 section 1455b; title 42 section 300j-3c.

NATIONAL ESTUARY PROGRAM

33 USC 1330

(a) Management conference
   (1) Nomination of estuaries
      The Governor of any State may nominate to the Administrator an estuary lying in whole or in part within the State as an estuary of national significance and request a management conference to develop a comprehensive management plan for the estuary. The nomi-

nation shall document the need for the conference, the likelihood of success, and information relating to the factors in paragraph (2).
  (2) Convening of conference
    (A) In general
    In any case where the Administrator determines, on his own initiative or upon nomination of a State under paragraph (1), that the attainment or maintenance of that water quality in an estuary which assures protection of public water supplies and the protection and propagation of a balanced, indigenous population of shellfish, fish, and wildlife, and allows recreational activities, in and on the water, requires the control of point and nonpoint sources of pollution to supplement existing controls of pollution in more than one State, the Administrator shall select such estuary and convene a management conference.
    (B) Priority consideration
    The Administrator shall give priority consideration under this section to Long Island Sound, New York and Connecticut; Narragansett Bay, Rhode Island; Buzzards Bay, Massachusetts; Massachusetts Bay, Massachusetts (including Cape Cod Bay and Boston Harbor); Puget Sound, Washington; New York-New Jersey Harbor, New York and New Jersey; Delaware Bay, Delaware and New Jersey; Delaware Inland Bays, Delaware; Albemarle Sound, North Carolina; Sarasota Bay, Florida; San Francisco Bay, California; Santa Monica Bay, California; Galveston Bay, Texas; Barataria-Terrebonne Bay estuary complex, Louisiana; Indian River Lagoon, Florida; Lake Pontchartrain Basin, Louisiana and Mississippi; and Peconic Bay, New York.
  (3) Boundary dispute exception
  In any case in which a boundary between two States passes through an estuary and such boundary is disputed and is the subject of an action in any court, the Administrator shall not convene a management conference with respect to such estuary before a final adjudication has been made of such dispute.
(b) Purposes of conference
  The purposes of any management conference convened with respect to an estuary under this subsection shall be to—
  (1) assess trends in water quality, natural resources, and uses of the estuary;
  (2) collect, characterize, and assess data on toxics, nutrients, and natural resources within the estuarine zone to identify the causes of environmental problems;
  (3) develop the relationship between the inplace loads and point and nonpoint loadings of pollutants to the estuarine zone and the potential uses of the zone, water quality, and natural resources;
  (4) develop a comprehensive conservation and management plan that recommends priority corrective actions and compliance schedules addressing point and nonpoint sources of pollution to restore and maintain the chemical, physical, and biological integrity of the estuary, including restoration and maintenance of water quality, a balanced indigenous population of shellfish, fish and wildlife, and recreational activities in the estuary, and assure that the designated uses of the estuary are protected;
  (5) develop plans for the coordinated implementation of the plan by the States as well as Federal and local agencies participating in the conference;
  (6) monitor the effectiveness of actions taken pursuant to the plan; and
  (7) review all Federal financial assistance programs and Federal development projects in accordance with the requirements of Executive Order 12372, as in effect on September 17, 1983, to determine whether such assistance program or project would be consistent with and further the purposes and objectives of the plan prepared under this section.
  For purposes of paragraph (7), such programs and projects shall not be limited to the assistance programs and development projects subject to Executive Order 12372, but may include any programs listed in the most recent Catalog of Federal Domestic Assistance which may have an effect on the purposes and objectives of the plan developed under this section.
(c) Members of conference
  The members of a management conference convened under this section shall include, at a minimum, the Administrator and representatives of—
  (1) each State and foreign nation located in whole or in part in the estuarine zone of the estuary for which the conference is convened;

(2) international, interstate, or regional agencies or entities having jurisdiction over all or a significant part of the estuary;
(3) each interested Federal agency, as determined appropriate by the Administrator;
(4) local governments having jurisdiction over any land or water within the estuarine zone, as determined appropriate by the Administrator; and
(5) affected industries, public and private educational institutions, and the general public, as determined appropriate by the Administrator.

(d) Utilization of existing data

In developing a conservation and management plan under this section, the management conference shall survey and utilize existing reports, data, and studies relating to the estuary that have been developed by or made available to Federal, interstate, State, and local agencies.

(e) Period of conference

A management conference convened under this section shall be convened for a period not to exceed 5 years. Such conference may be extended by the Administrator, and if terminated after the initial period, may be reconvened by the Administrator at any time thereafter, as may be necessary to meet the requirements of this section.

(f) Approval and implementation of plans

(1) Approval

Not later than 120 days after the completion of a conservation and management plan and after providing for public review and comment, the Administrator shall approve such plan if the plan meets the requirements of this section and the affected Governor or Governors concur.

(2) Implementation

Upon approval of a conservation and management plan under this section, such plan shall be implemented. Funds authorized to be appropriated under subchapters II and VI of this chapter and section 1329 of this title may be used in accordance with the applicable requirements of this chapter to assist States with the implementation of such plan.

(g) Grants

(1) Recipients

The Administrator is authorized to make grants to State, interstate, and regional water pollution control agencies and entities, State coastal zone management agencies, interstate agencies, other public or nonprofit private agencies, institutions, organizations, and individuals.

(2) Purposes

Grants under this subsection shall be made to pay for activities necessary for the development and implementation of a comprehensive conservation and management plan under this section.

(3) Federal share

The Federal share of a grant to any person (including a State, interstate, or regional agency or entity) under this subsection for a fiscal year—
(A) shall not exceed—
  (i) 75 percent of the annual aggregate costs of the development of a comprehensive conservation and management plan; and
  (ii) 50 percent of the annual aggregate costs of the implementation of the plan; and
(B) shall be made on condition that the non-Federal share of the costs are provided from non-Federal sources.

(h) Grant reporting

Any person (including a State, interstate, or regional agency or entity) that receives a grant under subsection (g) of this section shall report to the Administrator not later than 18 months after receipt of such grant and biennially thereafter on the progress being made under this section.

(i) Authorization of appropriations

There are authorized to be appropriated to the Administrator not to exceed $35,000,000 for each of fiscal years 2001 through 2005 for—
(1) expenses related to the administration of management conferences under this section, not to exceed 10 percent of the amount appropriated under this subsection;
(2) making grants under subsection (g) of this section; and

618 / Environmental Statutes

(3) monitoring the implementation of a conservation and management plan by the management conference or by the Administrator, in any case in which the conference has been terminated.

The Administrator shall provide up to $5,000,000 per fiscal year of the sums authorized to be appropriated under this subsection to the Administrator of the National Oceanic and Atmospheric Administration to carry out subsection (j) of this section.

(j) Research
 (1) Programs
  In order to determine the need to convene a management conference under this section or at the request of such a management conference, the Administrator shall coordinate and implement, through the National Marine Pollution Program Office and the National Marine Fisheries Service of the National Oceanic and Atmospheric Administration, as appropriate, for one or more estuarine zones—
  (A) a long-term program of trend assessment monitoring measuring variations in pollutant concentrations, marine ecology, and other physical or biological environmental parameters which may affect estuarine zones, to provide the Administrator the capacity to determine the potential and actual effects of alternative management strategies and measures;
  (B) a program of ecosystem assessment assisting in the development of (i) baseline studies which determine the state of estuarine zones and the effects of natural and anthropogenic changes, and (ii) predictive models capable of translating information on specific discharges or general pollutant loadings within estuarine zones into a set of probable effects on such zones;
  (C) a comprehensive water quality sampling program for the continuous monitoring of nutrients, chlorine, acid precipitation dissolved oxygen, and potentially toxic pollutants (including organic chemicals and metals) in estuarine zones, after consultation with interested State, local, interstate, or international agencies and review and analysis of all environmental sampling data presently collected from estuarine zones; and
  (D) a program of research to identify the movements of nutrients, sediments and pollutants through estuarine zones and the impact of nutrients, sediments, and pollutants on water quality, the ecosystem, and designated or potential uses of the estuarine zones.
 (2) Reports
  The Administrator, in cooperation with the Administrator of the National Oceanic and Atmospheric Administration, shall submit to the Congress no less often than biennially a comprehensive report on the activities authorized under this subsection including—
  (A) a listing of priority monitoring and research needs;
  (B) an assessment of the state and health of the Nation's estuarine zones, to the extent evaluated under this subsection;
  (C) a discussion of pollution problems and trends in pollutant concentrations with a direct or indirect effect on water quality, the ecosystem, and designated or potential uses of each estuarine zone, to the extent evaluated under this subsection; and
  (D) an evaluation of pollution abatement activities and management measures so far implemented to determine the degree of improvement toward the objectives expressed in subsection (b)(4) of this section.

(k) Definitions
 For purposes of this section, the terms "estuary" and "estuarine zone" have the meanings such terms have in section 1254(n)(3) of this title, except that the term "estuarine zone" shall also include associated aquatic ecosystems and those portions of tributaries draining into the estuary up to the historic height of migration of anadromous fish or the historic head of tidal influence, whichever is higher.

(June 30, 1948, ch. 758, title III, Sec. 320, as added Pub. L. 100-4, title III, Sec. 317(b), Feb. 4, 1987, 101 Stat. 61; amended Pub. L. 100-202, Sec. 101(f) [title II, 201], Dec. 22, 1987, 101 Stat. 1329-187, 1329-197; Pub. L. 100-653, title X, Sec. 1004, Nov. 14, 1988, 102 Stat. 3836; Pub. L. 100-688, title II, Sec. 2001, Nov. 18, 1988, 102 Stat. 4151; Pub. L. 105-362, title V, Sec. 501(a)(2), Nov. 10, 1998, 112 Stat. 3283; Pub. L. 106-457, title III, Sec. 301-303, Nov. 7, 2000, 114 Stat. 1972.)

References in Text

Executive Order 12372, referred to in subsec. (b), is Ex. Ord. No. 12372, July 14, 1982, 47 F.R. 30959, as amended, which is set out under section 6506 of Title 31, Money and Finance.

Amendments

2000–Subsec. (a)(2)(B). Pub. L. 106-457, Sec. 301, inserted "Lake Pontchartrain Basin, Louisiana and Mississippi;" before "and Peconic Bay, New York."

Subsec. (g)(2), (3). Pub. L. 106-457, Sec. 302, amended generally pars. (g)(2) and (3), which previously read: "(2) Purposes–Grants under this subsection shall be made to pay for assisting research, surveys, studies, and modeling and other technical work necessary for the development of a conservation and management plan under this section.

(3) Federal share

The amount of grants to any person (including a State, interstate, or regional agency or entity) under this subsection for a fiscal year shall not exceed 75 percent of the costs of such research, survey, studies, and work and shall be made on condition that the non-Federal share of such costs are provided from non-Federal sources."

Subsec (i). Pub. L. 106-457, Sec. 303, struck out "$12,000,000 per fiscal year for each of fiscal years 1987, 1988, 1989, 1990, and 1991" and inserted "$35,000,000 for each of fiscal years 2001 through 2005".

1998–Subsec. (k). Pub. L. 105-362 substituted "section 1254(n)(3)" for "section 1254(n)(4)".

1988–Subsec. (a)(2)(B). Pub. L. 100-653, Sec. 1004, and Pub. L. 100-688, Sec. 2001(1), made identical amendments, inserting "Massachusetts Bay, Massachusetts (including Cape Cod Bay and Boston Harbor);" after "Buzzards Bay, Massachusetts;".

Pub. L. 100-688, Sec. 2001(2), substituted "California; Galveston" for "California; and Galveston".

Pub. L. 100-688, Sec. 2001(3), which directed insertion of "; Barataria-Terrebonne Bay estuary complex, Louisiana; Indian River Lagoon, Florida; and Peconic Bay, New York" after "Galveston Bay, Texas;" was executed by making insertion after "Galveston Bay, Texas" as probable intent of Congress.

1987–Subsec. (a)(2)(B). Pub. L. 100-202 inserted "Santa Monica Bay, California;".

Massachusetts Bay Protection; Definition; Findings and Purpose; Funding Sources

Sections 1002, 1003, 1005 of title X of Pub. L. 100-653 provided that:

"SEC. 1002. DEFINITION.

For purposes of this title [amending section 1330 of this title and enacting provisions set out as notes under sections 1251 and 1330 of this title], the term 'Massachusetts Bay' includes Massachusetts Bay, Cape Cod Bay, and Boston Harbor, consisting of an area extending from Cape Ann, Massachusetts south to the northern reach of Cape Cod, Massachusetts.

SEC. 1003. FINDINGS AND PURPOSE.

(a) Findings.–The Congress finds and declares that—
  (1) Massachusetts Bay comprises a single major estuarine and oceanographic system extending from Cape Ann, Massachusetts south to the northern reaches of Cape Cod, encompassing Boston Harbor, Massachusetts Bay, and Cape Cod Bay;
  (2) several major riverine systems, including the Charles, Neponset, and Mystic Rivers, drain the watersheds of eastern Massachusetts into the Bay;
  (3) the shorelines of Massachusetts Bay, first occupied in the middle 1600's, are home to over 4 million people and support a thriving industrial and recreational economy;
  (4) Massachusetts Bay supports important commercial fisheries, including lobsters, finfish, and shellfisheries, and is home to or frequented by several endangered species and marine mammals;
  (5) Massachusetts Bay also constitutes an important recreational resource, providing fishing, swimming, and boating opportunities to the region;
  (6) rapidly expanding coastal populations and pollution pose increasing threats to the long-term health and integrity of Massachusetts Bay;

(7) while the cleanup of Boston Harbor will contribute significantly to improving the overall environmental quality of Massachusetts Bay, expanded efforts encompassing the entire ecosystem will be necessary to ensure its long-term health;

(8) the concerted efforts of all levels of Government, the private sector, and the public at large will be necessary to protect and enhance the environmental integrity of Massachusetts Bay; and

(9) the designation of Massachusetts Bay as an Estuary of National Significance and the development of a comprehensive plan for protecting and restoring the Bay may contribute significantly to its long-term health and environmental integrity.

(b) Purpose.—The purpose of this title is to protect and enhance the environmental quality of Massachusetts Bay by providing for its designation as an Estuary of National Significance and by providing for the preparation of a comprehensive restoration plan for the Bay.

SEC. 1005. FUNDING SOURCES.

Within one year of enactment [Nov. 14, 1988], the Administrator of the United States Environmental Protection Agency and the Governor of Massachusetts shall undertake to identify and make available sources of funding to support activities pertaining to Massachusetts Bay undertaken pursuant to or authorized by section 320 of the Clean Water Act [33 U.S.C. 1330], and shall make every effort to coordinate existing research, monitoring or control efforts with such activities."

Purposes and Policies of National Estuary Program

Section 317(a) of Pub. L. 100-4 provided that:
(1) Findings.—Congress finds and declares that—
   (A) the Nation's estuaries are of great importance for fish and wildlife resources and recreation and economic opportunity;
   (B) maintaining the health and ecological integrity of these estuaries is in the national interest;
   (C) increasing coastal population, development, and other direct and indirect uses of these estuaries threaten their health and ecological integrity;
   (D) long-term planning and management will contribute to the continued productivity of these areas, and will maximize their utility to the Nation; and
   (E) better coordination among Federal and State programs affecting estuaries will increase the effectiveness and efficiency of the national effort to protect, preserve, and restore these areas.
(2) Purposes.—The purposes of this section [enacting this section] are to—
   (A) identify nationally significant estuaries that are threatened by pollution, development, or overuse;
   (B) promote comprehensive planning for, and conservation and management of, nationally significant estuaries;
   (C) encourage the preparation of management plans for estuaries of national significance; and
   (D) enhance the coordination of estuarine research."

Section Referred to in Other Sections

This section is referred to in sections 1269, 1270, 1285, 1381, 1383, 1386, 1414b of this title; title 16 sections 1447c, 1455b; title 42 section 7412.

SUBCHAPTER IV—PERMITS AND LICENSES

CERTIFICATION

33 USC 1341

(a) Compliance with applicable requirements; application; procedures; license suspension
  (1) Any applicant for a Federal license or permit to conduct any activity including, but not limited to, the construction or operation of facilities, which may result in any discharge into the navigable waters, shall provide the licensing or permitting agency a certification from the State in which the discharge originates or will originate, or, if appropriate, from the interstate water pollution control agency having jurisdiction over the navigable waters at the point where the discharge originates or will originate, that any such discharge will comply with the applicable provisions of sections 1311, 1312, 1313, 1316, and 1317 of this title. In the case of any such activity for which there is not an applicable effluent limitation or other limitation under sections 1311(b) and 1312 of this title, and there is not an applicable standard under sections 1316 and 1317 of this title, the State shall so certify, except that any such certification shall not be deemed to satisfy section 1371(c) of this title. Such State or interstate agency shall establish procedures for public notice in the case of all applications for certification by it and, to the extent it deems appropriate, procedures for public hearings in connection with specific applications. In any case where a State or interstate agency has no authority to give such a certification, such certification shall be from the Administrator. If the State, interstate agency, or Administrator, as the case may be, fails or refuses to act on a request for certification, within a reasonable period of time (which shall not exceed one year) after receipt of such request, the certification requirements of this subsection shall be waived with respect to such Federal application. No license or permit shall be granted until the certification required by this section has been obtained or has been waived as provided in the preceding sentence. No license or permit shall be granted if certification has been denied by the State, interstate agency, or the Administrator, as the case may be.
  (2) Upon receipt of such application and certification the licensing or permitting agency shall immediately notify the Administrator of such application and certification. Whenever such a discharge may affect, as determined by the Administrator, the quality of the waters of any other State, the Administrator within thirty days of the date of notice of application for such Federal license or permit shall so notify such other State, the licensing or permitting agency, and the applicant. If, within sixty days after receipt of such notification, such other State determines that such discharge will affect the quality of its waters so as to violate any water quality requirements in such State, and within such sixty-day period notifies the Administrator and the licensing or permitting agency in writing of its objection to the issuance of such license or permit and requests a public hearing on such objection, the licensing or permitting agency shall hold such a hearing. The Administrator shall at such hearing submit his evaluation and recommendations with respect to any such objection to the licensing or permitting agency. Such agency, based upon the recommendations of such State, the Administrator, and upon any additional evidence, if any, presented to the agency at the hearing, shall condition such license or permit in such manner as may be necessary to insure compliance with applicable water quality requirements. If the imposition of conditions cannot insure such compliance such agency shall not issue such license or permit.
  (3) The certification obtained pursuant to paragraph (1) of this subsection with respect to the construction of any facility shall fulfill the requirements of this subsection with respect to certification in connection with any other Federal license or permit required for the operation of such facility unless, after notice to the certifying State, agency, or Administrator, as the case may be, which shall be given by the Federal agency to whom application is made for such operating license or permit, the State, or if appropriate, the interstate agency or the Administrator, notifies such agency within sixty days after receipt of such notice that there is no longer reasonable assurance that there will be compliance with the applicable provisions of sections 1311, 1312, 1313, 1316, and 1317 of this title because of changes since the construction license or permit certification was issued in (A) the construction or op-

eration of the facility, (B) the characteristics of the waters into which such discharge is made, (C) the water quality criteria applicable to such waters or (D) applicable effluent limitations or other requirements. This paragraph shall be inapplicable in any case where the applicant for such operating license or permit has failed to provide the certifying State, or, if appropriate, the interstate agency or the Administrator, with notice of any proposed changes in the construction or operation of the facility with respect to which a construction license or permit has been granted, which changes may result in violation of section 1311, 1312, 1313, 1316, or 1317 of this title.

(4) Prior to the initial operation of any federally licensed or permitted facility or activity which may result in any discharge into the navigable waters and with respect to which a certification has been obtained pursuant to paragraph (1) of this subsection, which facility or activity is not subject to a Federal operating license or permit, the licensee or permittee shall provide an opportunity for such certifying State, or, if appropriate, the interstate agency or the Administrator to review the manner in which the facility or activity shall be operated or conducted for the purposes of assuring that applicable effluent limitations or other limitations or other applicable water quality requirements will not be violated. Upon notification by the certifying State, or if appropriate, the interstate agency or the Administrator that the operation of any such federally licensed or permitted facility or activity will violate applicable effluent limitations or other limitations or other water quality requirements such Federal agency may, after public hearing, suspend such license or permit. If such license or permit is suspended, it shall remain suspended until notification is received from the certifying State, agency, or Administrator, as the case may be, that there is reasonable assurance that such facility or activity will not violate the applicable provisions of section 1311, 1312, 1313, 1316, or 1317 of this title.

(5) Any Federal license or permit with respect to which a certification has been obtained under paragraph (1) of this subsection may be suspended or revoked by the Federal agency issuing such license or permit upon the entering of a judgment under this chapter that such facility or activity has been operated in violation of the applicable provisions of section 1311, 1312, 1313, 1316, or 1317 of this title.

(6) Except with respect to a permit issued under section 1342 of this title, in any case where actual construction of a facility has been lawfully commenced prior to April 3, 1970, no certification shall be required under this subsection for a license or permit issued after April 3, 1970, to operate such facility, except that any such license or permit issued without certification shall terminate April 3, 1973, unless prior to such termination date the person having such license or permit submits to the Federal agency which issued such license or permit a certification and otherwise meets the requirements of this section.

(b) Compliance with other provisions of law setting applicable water quality requirements

Nothing in this section shall be construed to limit the authority of any department or agency pursuant to any other provision of law to require compliance with any applicable water quality requirements. The Administrator shall, upon the request of any Federal department or agency, or State or interstate agency, or applicant, provide, for the purpose of this section, any relevant information on applicable effluent limitations, or other limitations, standards, regulations, or requirements, or water quality criteria, and shall, when requested by any such department or agency or State or interstate agency, or applicant, comment on any methods to comply with such limitations, standards, regulations, requirements, or criteria.

(c) Authority of Secretary of the Army to permit use of spoil disposal areas by Federal licensees or permittees

In order to implement the provisions of this section, the Secretary of the Army, acting through the Chief of Engineers, is authorized, if he deems it to be in the public interest, to permit the use of spoil disposal areas under his jurisdiction by Federal licensees or permittees, and to make an appropriate charge for such use. Moneys received from such licensees or permittees shall be deposited in the Treasury as miscellaneous receipts.

(d) Limitations and monitoring requirements of certification

Any certification provided under this section shall set forth any effluent limitations and other limitations, and monitoring requirements necessary to assure that any applicant for a Federal license or permit will comply with any applicable effluent limitations and other limitations, under section 1311 or 1312 of this title, standard of performance under section 1316 of this title, or prohibition, effluent standard, or pretreatment standard under section 1317 of this title, and with any other appropriate requirement of State law set forth in such certification, and shall become a condition on any Federal license or permit subject to the provisions of this section.

(June 30, 1948, ch. 758, title IV, Sec. 401, as added Pub. L. 92-500, Sec. 2, Oct. 18, 1972, 86 Stat. 877; amended Pub. L. 95-217, Secs. 61(b), 64, Dec. 27, 1977, 91 Stat. 1598, 1599.)

Amendments

1977—Subsec. (a). Pub. L. 95-217 inserted reference to section 1313 of this title in pars. (1), (3), (4), and (5), struck out par. (6) which provided that no Federal agency be deemed an applicant for purposes of this subsection, and redesignated par. (7) as (6).

Section Referred to in Other Sections

This section is referred to in sections 1314, 1365, 1371, 1377, 2326a of this title.

NATIONAL POLLUTANT DISCHARGE ELIMINATION SYSTEM

33 USC 1342

(a) Permits for discharge of pollutants
  (1) Except as provided in sections 1328 and 1344 of this title, the Administrator may, after opportunity for public hearing issue a permit for the discharge of any pollutant, or combination of pollutants, notwithstanding section 1311(a) of this title, upon condition that such discharge will meet either (A) all applicable requirements under sections 1311, 1312, 1316, 1317, 1318, and 1343 of this title, or (B) prior to the taking of necessary implementing actions relating to all such requirements, such conditions as the Administrator determines are necessary to carry out the provisions of this chapter.
  (2) The Administrator shall prescribe conditions for such permits to assure compliance with the requirements of paragraph (1) of this subsection, including conditions on data and information collection, reporting, and such other requirements as he deems appropriate.
  (3) The permit program of the Administrator under paragraph (1) of this subsection, and permits issued thereunder, shall be subject to the same terms, conditions, and requirements as apply to a State permit program and permits issued thereunder under subsection (b) of this section.
  (4) All permits for discharges into the navigable waters issued pursuant to section 407 of this title shall be deemed to be permits issued under this subchapter, and permits issued under this subchapter shall be deemed to be permits issued under section 407 of this title, and shall continue in force and effect for their term unless revoked, modified, or suspended in accordance with the provisions of this chapter.
  (5) No permit for a discharge into the navigable waters shall be issued under section 407 of this title after October 18, 1972. Each application for a permit under section 407 of this title, pending on October 18, 1972, shall be deemed to be an application for a permit under this section. The Administrator shall authorize a State, which he determines has the capability of administering a permit program which will carry out the objectives of this chapter to issue permits for discharges into the navigable waters within the jurisdiction of such State. The Administrator may exercise the authority granted him by the preceding sentence only during the period which begins on October 18, 1972, and ends either on the ninetieth day after the date of the first promulgation of guidelines required by section 1314(i)(2) of this title, or the date of approval by the Administrator of a permit program for such State under subsection (b) of this section, whichever date first occurs, and no such authorization to a State shall extend beyond the last day of such period. Each such permit shall be subject to such conditions as the Administrator determines are necessary to carry out the provisions of this chapter. No such permit shall issue if the Administrator objects to such issuance.
(b) State permit programs
  At any time after the promulgation of the guidelines required by subsection (i)(2) of section 1314 of this title, the Governor of each State desiring to administer its own permit program for discharges into navigable waters within its jurisdiction may submit to the Administrator a full

and complete description of the program it proposes to establish and administer under State law or under an interstate compact. In addition, such State shall submit a statement from the attorney general (or the attorney for those State water pollution control agencies which have independent legal counsel), or from the chief legal officer in the case of an interstate agency, that the laws of such State, or the interstate compact, as the case may be, provide adequate authority to carry out the described program. The Administrator shall approve each submitted program unless he determines that adequate authority does not exist:

(1) To issue permits which—
   (A) apply, and insure compliance with, any applicable requirements of sections 1311, 1312, 1316, 1317, and 1343 of this title;
   (B) are for fixed terms not exceeding five years; and
   (C) can be terminated or modified for cause including, but not limited to, the following:
      (i) violation of any condition of the permit;
      (ii) obtaining a permit by misrepresentation, or failure to disclose fully all relevant facts;
      (iii) change in any condition that requires either a temporary or permanent reduction or elimination of the permitted discharge;
   (D) control the disposal of pollutants into wells;
(2) (A) To issue permits which apply, and insure compliance with, all applicable requirements of section 1318 of this title; or
   (B) To inspect, monitor, enter, and require reports to at least the same extent as required in section 1318 of this title;
(3) To insure that the public, and any other State the waters of which may be affected, receive notice of each application for a permit and to provide an opportunity for public hearing before a ruling on each such application;
(4) To insure that the Administrator receives notice of each application (including a copy thereof) for a permit;
(5) To insure that any State (other than the permitting State), whose waters may be affected by the issuance of a permit may submit written recommendations to the permitting State (and the Administrator) with respect to any permit application and, if any part of such written recommendations are not accepted by the permitting State, that the permitting State will notify such affected State (and the Administrator) in writing of its failure to so accept such recommendations together with its reasons for so doing;
(6) To insure that no permit will be issued if, in the judgment of the Secretary of the Army acting through the Chief of Engineers, after consultation with the Secretary of the department in which the Coast Guard is operating, anchorage and navigation of any of the navigable waters would be substantially impaired thereby;
(7) To abate violations of the permit or the permit program, including civil and criminal penalties and other ways and means of enforcement;
(8) To insure that any permit for a discharge from a publicly owned treatment works includes conditions to require the identification in terms of character and volume of pollutants of any significant source introducing pollutants subject to pretreatment standards under section 1317(b) of this title into such works and a program to assure compliance with such pretreatment standards by each such source, in addition to adequate notice to the permitting agency of (A) new introductions into such works of pollutants from any source which would be a new source as defined in section 1316 of this title if such source were discharging pollutants, (B) new introductions of pollutants into such works from a source which would be subject to section 1311 of this title if it were discharging such pollutants, or (C) a substantial change in volume or character of pollutants being introduced into such works by a source introducing pollutants into such works at the time of issuance of the permit. Such notice shall include information on the quality and quantity of effluent to be introduced into such treatment works and any anticipated impact of such change in the quantity or quality of effluent to be discharged from such publicly owned treatment works; and
(9) To insure that any industrial user of any publicly owned treatment works will comply with sections 1284(b), 1317, and 1318 of this title.

(c) Suspension of Federal program upon submission of State program; withdrawal of approval of State program; return of State program to Administrator

(1) Not later than ninety days after the date on which a State has submitted a program (or revision thereof) pursuant to subsection (b) of this section, the Administrator shall suspend the issuance of permits under subsection (a) of this section as to those discharges subject to such program unless he determines that the State permit program does not meet the requirements of subsection (b) of this section or does not conform to the guidelines issued under section 1314(i)(2) of this title. If the Administrator so determines, he shall notify the State of any revisions or modifications necessary to conform to such requirements or guidelines.

(2) Any State permit program under this section shall at all times be in accordance with this section and guidelines promulgated pursuant to section 1314(i)(2) of this title.

(3) Whenever the Administrator determines after public hearing that a State is not administering a program approved under this section in accordance with requirements of this section, he shall so notify the State and, if appropriate corrective action is not taken within a reasonable time, not to exceed ninety days, the Administrator shall withdraw approval of such program. The Administrator shall not withdraw approval of any such program unless he shall first have notified the State, and made public, in writing, the reasons for such withdrawal.

(4) Limitations on partial permit program returns and withdrawals.—
A State may return to the Administrator administration, and the Administrator may withdraw under paragraph (3) of this subsection approval, of—
  (A) a State partial permit program approved under subsection (n)(3) of this section only if the entire permit program being administered by the State department or agency at the time is returned or withdrawn; and
  (B) a State partial permit program approved under subsection (n)(4) of this section only if an entire phased component of the permit program being administered by the State at the time is returned or withdrawn.

(d) Notification of Administrator
  (1) Each State shall transmit to the Administrator a copy of each permit application received by such State and provide notice to the Administrator of every action related to the consideration of such permit application, including each permit proposed to be issued by such State.
  (2) No permit shall issue (A) if the Administrator within ninety days of the date of his notification under subsection (b)(5) of this section objects in writing to the issuance of such permit, or (B) if the Administrator within ninety days of the date of transmittal of the proposed permit by the State objects in writing to the issuance of such permit as being outside the guidelines and requirements of this chapter. Whenever the Administrator objects to the issuance of a permit under this paragraph such written objection shall contain a statement of the reasons for such objection and the effluent limitations and conditions which such permit would include if it were issued by the Administrator.
  (3) The Administrator may, as to any permit application, waive paragraph (2) of this subsection.
  (4) In any case where, after December 27, 1977, the Administrator, pursuant to paragraph (2) of this subsection, objects to the issuance of a permit, on request of the State, a public hearing shall be held by the Administrator on such objection. If the State does not resubmit such permit revised to meet such objection within 30 days after completion of the hearing, or, if no hearing is requested within 90 days after the date of such objection, the Administrator may issue the permit pursuant to subsection (a) of this section for such source in accordance with the guidelines and requirements of this chapter.

(e) Waiver of notification requirement
In accordance with guidelines promulgated pursuant to subsection (i)(2) of section 1314 of this title, the Administrator is authorized to waive the requirements of subsection (d) of this section at the time he approves a program pursuant to subsection (b) of this section for any category (including any class, type, or size within such category) of point sources within the State submitting such program.

(f) Point source categories
The Administrator shall promulgate regulations establishing categories of point sources which he determines shall not be subject to the requirements of subsection (d) of this section in any

State with a program approved pursuant to subsection (b) of this section. The Administrator may distinguish among classes, types, and sizes within any category of point sources.

(g) Other regulations for safe transportation, handling, carriage, storage, and stowage of pollutants

Any permit issued under this section for the discharge of pollutants into the navigable waters from a vessel or other floating craft shall be subject to any applicable regulations promulgated by the Secretary of the department in which the Coast Guard is operating, establishing specifications for safe transportation, handling, carriage, storage, and stowage of pollutants.

(h) Violation of permit conditions; restriction or prohibition upon introduction of pollutant by source not previously utilizing treatment works

In the event any condition of a permit for discharges from a treatment works (as defined in section 1292 of this title) which is publicly owned is violated, a State with a program approved under subsection (b) of this section or the Administrator, where no State program is approved or where the Administrator determines pursuant to section 1319(a) of this title that a State with an approved program has not commenced appropriate enforcement action with respect to such permit, may proceed in a court of competent jurisdiction to restrict or prohibit the introduction of any pollutant into such treatment works by a source not utilizing such treatment works prior to the finding that such condition was violated.

(i) Federal enforcement not limited

Nothing in this section shall be construed to limit the authority of the Administrator to take action pursuant to section 1319 of this title.

(j) Public information

A copy of each permit application and each permit issued under this section shall be available to the public. Such permit application or permit, or portion thereof, shall further be available on request for the purpose of reproduction.

(k) Compliance with permits

Compliance with a permit issued pursuant to this section shall be deemed compliance, for purposes of sections 1319 and 1365 of this title, with sections 1311, 1312, 1316, 1317, and 1343 of this title, except any standard imposed under section 1317 of this title for a toxic pollutant injurious to human health. Until December 31, 1974, in any case where a permit for discharge has been applied for pursuant to this section, but final administrative disposition of such application has not been made, such discharge shall not be a violation of (1) section 1311, 1316, or 1342 of this title, or (2) section 407 of this title, unless the Administrator or other plaintiff proves that final administrative disposition of such application has not been made because of the failure of the applicant to furnish information reasonably required or requested in order to process the application. For the 180-day period beginning on October 18, 1972, in the case of any point source discharging any pollutant or combination of pollutants immediately prior to such date which source is not subject to section 407 of this title, the discharge by such source shall not be a violation of this chapter if such a source applies for a permit for discharge pursuant to this section within such 180-day period.

(l) Limitation on permit requirement

(1) Agricultural return flows

The Administrator shall not require a permit under this section for discharges composed entirely of return flows from irrigated agriculture, nor shall the Administrator directly or indirectly, require any State to require such a permit.

(2) Stormwater runoff from oil, gas, and mining operations

The Administrator shall not require a permit under this section, nor shall the Administrator directly or indirectly require any State to require a permit, for discharges of stormwater runoff from mining operations or oil and gas exploration, production, processing, or treatment operations or transmission facilities, composed entirely of flows which are from conveyances or systems of conveyances (including but not limited to pipes, conduits, ditches, and channels) used for collecting and conveying precipitation runoff and which are not contaminated by contact with, or do not come into contact with, any overburden, raw material, intermediate products, finished product, byproduct, or waste products located on the site of such operations.

Clean Water Act / 627

(m) Additional pretreatment of conventional pollutants not required

To the extent a treatment works (as defined in section 1292 of this title) which is publicly owned is not meeting the requirements of a permit issued under this section for such treatment works as a result of inadequate design or operation of such treatment works, the Administrator, in issuing a permit under this section, shall not require pretreatment by a person introducing conventional pollutants identified pursuant to section 1314(a)(4) of this title into such treatment works other than pretreatment required to assure compliance with pretreatment standards under subsection (b)(8) of this section and section 1317(b)(1) of this title. Nothing in this subsection shall affect the Administrator's authority under sections 1317 and 1319 of this title, affect State and local authority under sections 1317(b)(4) and 1370 of this title, relieve such treatment works of its obligations to meet requirements established under this chapter, or otherwise preclude such works from pursuing whatever feasible options are available to meet its responsibility to comply with its permit under this section.

(n) Partial permit program

(1) State submission

The Governor of a State may submit under subsection (b) of this section a permit program for a portion of the discharges into the navigable waters in such State.

(2) Minimum coverage

A partial permit program under this subsection shall cover, at a minimum, administration of a major category of the discharges into the navigable waters of the State or a major component of the permit program required by subsection (b) of this section.

(3) Approval of major category partial permit programs

The Administrator may approve a partial permit program covering administration of a major category of discharges under this subsection if—

(A) such program represents a complete permit program and covers all of the discharges under the jurisdiction of a department or agency of the State; and

(B) the Administrator determines that the partial program represents a significant and identifiable part of the State program required by subsection (b) of this section.

(4) Approval of major component partial permit programs

The Administrator may approve under this subsection a partial and phased permit program covering administration of a major component (including discharge categories) of a State permit program required by subsection (b) of this section if—

(A) the Administrator determines that the partial program represents a significant and identifiable part of the State program required by subsection (b) of this section; and

(B) the State submits, and the Administrator approves, a plan for the State to assume administration by phases of the remainder of the State program required by subsection (b) of this section by a specified date not more than 5 years after submission of the partial program under this subsection and agrees to make all reasonable efforts to assume such administration by such date.

(o) Anti-backsliding

(1) General prohibition

In the case of effluent limitations established on the basis of subsection (a)(1)(B) of this section, a permit may not be renewed, reissued, or modified on the basis of effluent guidelines promulgated under section 1314(b) of this title subsequent to the original issuance of such permit, to contain effluent limitations which are less stringent than the comparable effluent limitations in the previous permit. In the case of effluent limitations established on the basis of section 1311(b)(1)(C) or section 1313(d) or (e) of this title, a permit may not be renewed, reissued, or modified to contain effluent limitations which are less stringent than the comparable effluent limitations in the previous permit except in compliance with section 1313(d)(4) of this title.

(2) Exceptions

A permit with respect to which paragraph (1) applies may be renewed, reissued, or modified to contain a less stringent effluent limitation applicable to a pollutant if—

(A) material and substantial alterations or additions to the permitted facility occurred after permit issuance which justify the application of a less stringent effluent limitation;

(B) (i) information is available which was not available at the time of permit issuance (other than revised regulations, guidance, or test methods) and which would have

justified the application of a less stringent effluent limitation at the time of permit issuance; or
    (ii) the Administrator determines that technical mistakes or mistaken interpretations of law were made in issuing the permit under subsection (a)(1)(B) of this section;
(C) a less stringent effluent limitation is necessary because of events over which the permittee has no control and for which there is no reasonably available remedy;
(D) the permittee has received a permit modification under section 1311(c), 1311(g), 1311(h), 1311(i), 1311(k), 1311(n), or 1326(a) of this title; or
(E) the permittee has installed the treatment facilities required to meet the effluent limitations in the previous permit and has properly operated and maintained the facilities but has nevertheless been unable to achieve the previous effluent limitations, in which case the limitations in the reviewed, reissued, or modified permit may reflect the level of pollutant control actually achieved (but shall not be less stringent than required by effluent guidelines in effect at the time of permit renewal, reissuance, or modification).

Subparagraph (B) shall not apply to any revised waste load allocations or any alternative grounds for translating water quality standards into effluent limitations, except where the cumulative effect of such revised allocations results in a decrease in the amount of pollutants discharged into the concerned waters, and such revised allocations are not the result of a discharger eliminating or substantially reducing its discharge of pollutants due to complying with the requirements of this chapter or for reasons otherwise unrelated to water quality.

(3) Limitations

In no event may a permit with respect to which paragraph (1) applies be renewed, reissued, or modified to contain an effluent limitation which is less stringent than required by effluent guidelines in effect at the time the permit is renewed, reissued, or modified. In no event may such a permit to discharge into waters be renewed, reissued, or modified to contain a less stringent effluent limitation if the implementation of such limitation would result in a violation of a water quality standard under section 1313 of this title applicable to such waters.

(p) Municipal and industrial stormwater discharges

(1) General rule

Prior to October 1, 1994, the Administrator or the State (in the case of a permit program approved under this section) shall not require a permit under this section for discharges composed entirely of stormwater.

(2) Exceptions

Paragraph (1) shall not apply with respect to the following stormwater discharges:
    (A) A discharge with respect to which a permit has been issued under this section before February 4, 1987.
    (B) A discharge associated with industrial activity.
    (C) A discharge from a municipal separate storm sewer system serving a population of 250,000 or more.
    (D) A discharge from a municipal separate storm sewer system serving a population of 100,000 or more but less than 250,000.
    (E) A discharge for which the Administrator or the State, as the case may be, determines that the stormwater discharge contributes to a violation of a water quality standard or is a significant contributor of pollutants to waters of the United States.

(3) Permit requirements

    (A) Industrial discharges

    Permits for discharges associated with industrial activity shall meet all applicable provisions of this section and section 1311 of this title.

    (B) Municipal discharge

    Permits for discharges from municipal storm sewers—
        (i) may be issued on a system- or jurisdiction-wide basis;
        (ii) shall include a requirement to effectively prohibit non-stormwater discharges into the storm sewers; and
        (iii) shall require controls to reduce the discharge of pollutants to the maximum extent practicable, including management practices, control techniques and system,

design and engineering methods, and such other provisions as the Administrator or the State determines appropriate for the control of such pollutants.
(4) Permit application requirements
   (A) Industrial and large municipal discharges
   Not later than 2 years after February 4, 1987, the Administrator shall establish regulations setting forth the permit application requirements for stormwater discharges described in paragraphs (2)(B) and (2)(C). Applications for permits for such discharges shall be filed no later than 3 years after February 4, 1987. Not later than 4 years after February 4, 1987, the Administrator or the State, as the case may be, shall issue or deny each such permit. Any such permit shall provide for compliance as expeditiously as practicable, but in no event later than 3 years after the date of issuance of such permit.
   (B) Other municipal discharges
   Not later than 4 years after February 4, 1987, the Administrator shall establish regulations setting forth the permit application requirements for stormwater discharges described in paragraph (2)(D). Applications for permits for such discharges shall be filed no later than 5 years after February 4, 1987. Not later than 6 years after February 4, 1987, the Administrator or the State, as the case may be, shall issue or deny each such permit. Any such permit shall provide for compliance as expeditiously as practicable, but in no event later than 3 years after the date of issuance of such permit.
(5) Studies
The Administrator, in consultation with the States, shall conduct a study for the purposes of—
   (A) identifying those stormwater discharges or classes of stormwater discharges for which permits are not required pursuant to paragraphs (1) and (2) of this subsection;
   (B) determining, to the maximum extent practicable, the nature and extent of pollutants in such discharges; and
   (C) establishing procedures and methods to control stormwater discharges to the extent necessary to mitigate impacts on water quality.
Not later than October 1, 1988, the Administrator shall submit to Congress a report on the results of the study described in subparagraphs (A) and (B). Not later than October 1, 1989, the Administrator shall submit to Congress a report on the results of the study described in subparagraph (C).
(6) Regulations
Not later than October 1, 1993, the Administrator, in consultation with State and local officials, shall issue regulations (based on the results of the studies conducted under paragraph (5)) which designate stormwater discharges, other than those discharges described in paragraph (2), to be regulated to protect water quality and shall establish a comprehensive program to regulate such designated sources. The program shall, at a minimum, (A) establish priorities, (B) establish requirements for State stormwater management programs, and (C) establish expeditious deadlines. The program may include performance standards, guidelines, guidance, and management practices and treatment requirements, as appropriate.

(q) Combined Sewer Overflows
   (1) Requirement for permits, orders, and decrees
   Each permit, order, or decree issued pursuant to this Act after the date of enactment of this subsection for a discharge from a municipal combined storm and sanitary sewer shall conform to the Combined Sewer Overflow Control Policy signed by the Administrator on April 11, 1994 (in this subsection referred to as the 'CSO control policy').
   (2) Water quality and designated use review guidance
   Not later than July 31, 2001, and after providing notice and opportunity for public comment, the Administrator shall issue guidance to facilitate the conduct of water quality and designated use reviews for municipal combined sewer overflow receiving waters.
   (3) Report
   Not later than September 1, 2001, the Administrator shall transmit to Congress a report on the progress made by the Environmental Protection Agency, States, and municipalities in implementing and enforcing the CSO control policy.

(June 30, 1948, ch. 758, title IV, Sec. 402, as added Pub. L. 92-500, Sec. 2, Oct. 18, 1972, 86 Stat. 880; amended Pub. L. 95-217, Secs. 33(c), 50, 54(c)(1), 65, 66, Dec. 27, 1977, 91 Stat. 1577, 1588, 1591, 1599, 1600; Pub. L. 100-4, title IV, Secs. 401-404(a), 404(c), formerly 404(d), 405, Feb. 4, 1987, 101 Stat. 65-67, 69, renumbered Sec. 404(c), Pub. L. 104-66, title II, Sec. 2021(e)(2), Dec. 21, 1995, 109 Stat. 727; Pub. L. 102-580, title III, Sec. 364, Oct. 31, 1992, 106 Stat. 4862; Pub. L. 106-554, Sec. 112(a), Dec. 21, 2000, 114 Stat. 2763A-224.)

Amendments

2000—Subsec. (q). Pub. L. 106-554, Sec. 112(a) added subsec. (q).

1992—Subsec. (p)(1), (6). Pub. L. 102-580 substituted "October 1, 1994" for "October 1, 1992" in par. (1) and "October 1, 1993" for "October 1, 1992" in par. (6).

1987—Subsec. (a)(1). Pub. L. 100-4, Sec. 404(c), inserted cl. (A) and (B) designations.

Subsec. (c)(1). Pub. L. 100-4, Sec. 403(b)(2), substituted "as to those discharges" for "as to those navigable waters".

Subsec. (c)(4). Pub. L. 100-4, Sec. 403(b)(1), added par. (4).

Subsec. (l). Pub. L. 100-4, Sec. 401, inserted "Limitation on permit requirement" as subsec. heading designated existing provisions as par. (1) and inserted par. heading, added par. (2), and aligned pars. (1) and (2).

Subsecs. (m) to (p). Pub. L. 100-4, Secs. 402, 403(a), 404(a), 405, added subsecs. (m) to (p).

1977—Subsec. (a)(5). Pub. L. 95-217, Sec. 50, substituted "section 1314(i)(2)" for "section 1314(h)(2)".

Subsec. (b). Pub. L. 95-217, Sec. 50, substituted in provisions preceding par. (1) "subsection (i)(2) of section 1314" for "subsection (h)(2) of section 1314".

Subsec. (b)(8). Pub. L. 95-217, Sec. 54(c)(1), inserted reference to identification in terms of character and volume of pollutants of any significant source introducing pollutants subject to pretreatment standards under section 1317(b) of this title into treatment works and programs to assure compliance with pretreatment standards by each source.

Subsec. (c)(1), (2). Pub. L. 95-217, Sec. 50, substituted "section 1314(i)(2)" for "section 1314(h)(2)".

Subsec. (d)(2). Pub. L. 95-217, Sec. 65(b), inserted provision requiring that, whenever the Administrator objects to the issuance of a permit under subsec. (d)(2) of this section, the written objection contain a statement of the reasons for the objection and the effluent limitations and conditions which the permit would include if it were issued by the Administrator.

Subsec. (d)(4). Pub. L. 95-217, Sec. 65(a), added par. (4).

Subsec. (e). Pub. L. 95-217, Sec. 50, substituted "subsection (i)(2) of section 1314" for "subsection (h)(2) of section 1314".

Subsec. (h). Pub. L. 95-217, Sec. 66, substituted "where no State program is approved or where the Administrator determines pursuant to section 1319(a) of this title that a State with an approved program has not commenced appropriate enforcement action with respect to such permit," for "where no State program is approved,".

Subsec. (l). Pub. L. 95-217, Sec. 33(c), added subsec. (l).

Transfer of Functions

Enforcement functions of Administrator or other official of the Environmental Protection Agency under this section relating to compliance with national pollutant discharge elimination system permits with respect to pre-construction, construction, and initial operation of transportation system for Canadian and Alaskan natural gas were transferred to the Federal Inspector, Office of Federal Inspector for the Alaska Natural Gas Transportation System, until the first anniversary of the date of initial operation of the Alaska Natural Gas Transportation System, see Reorg. Plan No. 1 of 1979, Secs. 102(a), 203(a), 44 F.R. 33663, 33666, 93 Stat. 1373, 1376, effective July 1, 1979, set out in the Appendix to Title 5, Government Organization and Employees. Office of Federal Inspector for the Alaska Natural Gas Transportation System abolished and functions and authority vested in Inspector transferred to Secretary of Energy by section 3012(b) of Pub. L. 102-486, set out as an Abolition of Office of Federal Inspector note under section 719e of Title 15, Commerce and Trade.

Stormwater Permit Requirements

Pub. L. 102-240, title I, Sec. 1068, Dec. 18, 1991, 105 Stat. 2007, provided that:

"(a) General Rule.—Notwithstanding the requirements of sections 402(p)(2)(B), (C), and (D) of the Federal Water Pollution Control Act [33 U.S.C. 1342(p)(2)(B), (C), (D)], permit application deadlines for stormwater discharges associated with industrial activities from facilities that are owned or operated by a municipality shall be established by the Administrator of the Environmental Protection Agency (hereinafter in this section referred to as the 'Administrator') pursuant to the requirements of this section.

(b) Permit Applications.—
   (1) Individual applications.—The Administrator shall require individual permit applications for discharges described in subsection (a) on or before October 1, 1992; except that any municipality that has participated in a timely part I group application for an industrial activity discharging stormwater that is denied such participation in a group application or for which a group application is denied shall not be required to submit an individual application until the 180th day following the date on which the denial is made.
   (2) Group applications.—With respect to group applications for permits for discharges described in subsection (a), the Administrator shall require—
      (A) part I applications on or before September 30, 1991, except that any municipality with a population of less than 250,000 shall not be required to submit a part I application before May 18, 1992; and
      (B) part II applications on or before October 1, 1992, except that any municipality with a population of less than 250,000 shall not be required to submit a part II application before May 17, 1993.

(c) Municipalities With Less Than 100,000 Population.—The Administrator shall not require any municipality with a population of less than 100,000 to apply for or obtain a permit for any stormwater discharge associated with an industrial activity other than an airport, powerplant, or uncontrolled sanitary landfill owned or operated by such municipality before October 1, 1992, unless such permit is required by section 402(p)(2)(A) or (E) of the Federal Water Pollution Control Act [33 U.S.C. 1342(p)(2)(A), (E)].

(d) Uncontrolled Sanitary Landfill Defined.—For the purposes of this section, the term 'uncontrolled sanitary landfill' means a landfill or open dump, whether in operation or closed, that does not meet the requirements for run-on and run-off controls established pursuant to subtitle D of the Solid Waste Disposal Act [42 U.S.C. 6941 et seq.].

(e) Limitation on Statutory Construction.—Nothing in this section shall be construed to affect any application or permit requirement, including any deadline, to apply for or obtain a permit for stormwater discharges subject to section 402(p)(2)(A) or (E) of the Federal Water Pollution Control Act [33 U.S.C. 1342(p)(2)(A), (E)].

(f) Regulations.—The Administrator shall issue final regulations with respect to general permits for stormwater discharges associated with industrial activity on or before February 1, 1992."

Phosphate Fertilizer Effluent Limitation

Section 306(c) of Pub. L. 100-4 provided that:
   (1) Issuance of permit.—As soon as possible after the date of the enactment of this Act [Feb. 4, 1987], but not later than 180 days after such date of enactment, the Administrator shall issue permits under section 402(a)(1)(B) of the Federal Water Pollution Control Act [33 U.S.C. 1342(a)(1)(B)] with respect to facilities—
      (A) which were under construction on or before April 8, 1974, and
      (B) for which the Administrator is proposing to revise the applicability of the effluent limitation established under section 301(b) of such Act [33 U.S.C. 1311(b)] for phosphate subcategory of the fertilizer manufacturing point source category to exclude such facilities.
   (2) Limitations on statutory construction.—Nothing in this section [amending section 1311 of this title and enacting this note] shall be construed—
      (A) to require the Administrator to permit the discharge of gypsum or gypsum waste into the navigable waters,

(B) to affect the procedures and standards applicable to the Administrator in issuing permits under section 402(a)(1)(B) of the Federal Water Pollution Control Act [33 U.S.C. 1342(a)(1)(B)], and

(C) to affect the authority of any State to deny or condition certification under section 401 of such Act [33 U.S.C. 1341] with respect to the issuance of permits under section 402(a)(1)(B) of such Act."

Log Transfer Facilities

Section 407 of Pub. L. 100-4 provided that:

"(a) Agreement.—The Administrator and Secretary of the Army shall enter into an agreement regarding coordination of permitting for log transfer facilities to designate a lead agency and to process permits required under sections 402 and 404 of the Federal Water Pollution Control Act [33 U.S.C. 1342, 1344] , where both such sections apply, for discharges associated with the construction and operation of log transfer facilities. The Administrator and Secretary are authorized to act in accordance with the terms of such agreement to assure that, to the maximum extent practicable, duplication, needless paperwork and delay in the issuance of permits, and inequitable enforcement between and among facilities in different States, shall be eliminated.

(b) Applications and Permits Before October 22, 1985.—Where both of sections 402 and 404 of the Federal Water Pollution Control Act [33 U.S.C. 1342, 1344] apply, log transfer facilities which have received a permit under section 404 of such Act before October 22, 1985, shall not be required to submit a new application for a permit under section 402 of such Act. If the Administrator determines that the terms of a permit issued on or before October 22, 1985, under section 404 of such Act satisfies the applicable requirements of sections 301, 302, 306, 307, 308, and 403 of such Act [33 U.S.C. 1311, 1312, 1316, 1317, 1318, and 1343], a separate application for a permit under section 402 of such Act shall not thereafter be required. In any case where the Administrator demonstrates, after an opportunity for a hearing, that the terms of a permit issued on or before October 22, 1985, under section 404 of such Act do not satisfy the applicable requirements of sections 301, 302, 306, 307, 308, and 403 of such Act, modifications to the existing permit under section 404 of such Act to incorporate such applicable requirements shall be issued by the Administrator as an alternative to issuance of a separate new permit under section 402 of such Act.

(c) Log Transfer Facility Defined.—For the purposes of this section, the term 'log transfer facility' means a facility which is constructed in whole or in part in waters of the United States and which is utilized for the purpose of transferring commercially harvested logs to or from a vessel or log raft, including the formation of a log raft."

Allowable Delay in Modifying Existing Approved State Permit Programs To Conform to 1977 Amendment

Section 54(c)(2) of Pub. L. 95-217 provided that any State permit program approved under this section before Dec. 27, 1977, which required modification to conform to the amendment made by section 54(c)(1) of Pub. L. 95-217, which amended subsec. (b)(8) of this section, not be required to be modified before the end of the one year period which began on Dec. 27, 1977, unless in order to make the required modification a State must amend or enact a law in which case such modification not be required for such State before the end of the two year period which began on Dec. 27, 1977.

Section Referred to in Other Sections

This section is referred to in sections 1251, 1283, 1284, 1285, 1288, 1311, 1314, 1317, 1318, 1319, 1321, 1323, 1328, 1341, 1343, 1344, 1345, 1365, 1369, 1371, 1373, 1377, 2104, 2803 of this title; title 42 sections 6903, 6924, 6925, 6939e, 9601.

OCEAN DISCHARGE CRITERIA

33 USC 1343

(a) Issuance of permits

No permit under section 1342 of this title for a discharge into the territorial sea, the waters of the contiguous zone, or the oceans shall be issued, after promulgation of guidelines established under subsection (c) of this section, except in compliance with such guidelines. Prior to the promulgation of such guidelines, a permit may be issued under such section 1342 of this title if the Administrator determines it to be in the public interest.

(b) Waiver

The requirements of subsection (d) of section 1342 of this title may not be waived in the case of permits for discharges into the territorial sea.

(c) Guidelines for determining degradation of waters

(1) The Administrator shall, within one hundred and eighty days after October 18, 1972 (and from time to time thereafter), promulgate guidelines for determining the degradation of the waters of the territorial seas, the contiguous zone, and the oceans, which shall include:

(A) the effect of disposal of pollutants on human health or welfare, including but not limited to plankton, fish, shellfish, wildlife, shorelines, and beaches;

(B) the effect of disposal of pollutants on marine life including the transfer, concentration, and dispersal of pollutants or their byproducts through biological, physical, and chemical processes; changes in marine ecosystem diversity, productivity, and stability; and species and community population changes;

(C) the effect of disposal, of pollutants on esthetic, recreation, and economic values;

(D) the persistence and permanence of the effects of disposal of pollutants;

(E) the effect of the disposal of varying rates, of particular volumes and concentrations of pollutants;

(F) other possible locations and methods of disposal or recycling of pollutants including land-based alternatives; and

(G) the effect on alternate uses of the oceans, such as mineral exploitation and scientific study.

(2) In any event where insufficient information exists on any proposed discharge to make a reasonable judgment on any of the guidelines established pursuant to this subsection no permit shall be issued under section 1342 of this title.

(June 30, 1948, ch. 758, title IV, Sec. 403, as added Pub. L. 92-500, Sec. 2, Oct. 18, 1972, 86 Stat. 883.)

Discharges From Point Sources in United States Virgin Islands Attributable to Manufacture of Rum; Exemption; Conditions

Discharges from point sources in the United States Virgin Islands in existence on Aug. 5, 1983, attributable to the manufacture of rum not to be subject to the requirements of this section under certain conditions, see section 214(g) of Pub. L. 98-67, set out as a note under section 1311 of this title.

Territorial Sea of United States

For extension of territorial sea of United States, see Proc. No. 5928, set out as a note under section 1331 of Title 43, Public Lands.

Contiguous Zone of United States

For extension of contiguous zone of United States, see Proc. No. 7219, Sept. 2, 1999, 64 F.R. 48701, set out as a note under section 1331 of Title 43, Public Lands.

Section Referred to in Other Sections

This section is referred to in sections 1254, 1288, 1311, 1314, 1342, 1344 of this title.

PERMITS FOR DREDGED OR FILL MATERIAL

33 USC 1344

(a) Discharge into navigable waters at specified disposal sites

The Secretary may issue permits, after notice and opportunity for public hearings for the discharge of dredged or fill material into the navigable waters at specified disposal sites. Not later than the fifteenth day after the date an applicant submits all the information required to complete an application for a permit under this subsection, the Secretary shall publish the notice required by this subsection.

(b) Specification for disposal sites

Subject to subsection (c) of this section, each such disposal site shall be specified for each such permit by the Secretary (1) through the application of guidelines developed by the Administrator, in conjunction with the Secretary, which guidelines shall be based upon criteria comparable to the criteria applicable to the territorial seas, the contiguous zone, and the ocean under section 1343(c) of this title, and (2) in any case where such guidelines under clause (1) alone would prohibit the specification of a site, through the application additionally of the economic impact of the site on navigation and anchorage.

(c) Denial or restriction of use of defined areas as disposal sites

The Administrator is authorized to prohibit the specification (including the withdrawal of specification) of any defined area as a disposal site, and he is authorized to deny or restrict the use of any defined area for specification (including the withdrawal of specification) as a disposal site, whenever he determines, after notice and opportunity for public hearings, that the discharge of such materials into such area will have an unacceptable adverse effect on municipal water supplies, shellfish beds and fishery areas (including spawning and breeding areas), wildlife, or recreational areas. Before making such determination, the Administrator shall consult with the Secretary. The Administrator shall set forth in writing and make public his findings and his reasons for making any determination under this subsection.

(d) "Secretary" defined

The term "Secretary" as used in this section means the Secretary of the Army, acting through the Chief of Engineers.

(e) General permits on State, regional, or nationwide basis

(1) In carrying out his functions relating to the discharge of dredged or fill material under this section, the Secretary may, after notice and opportunity for public hearing, issue general permits on a State, regional, or nationwide basis for any category of activities involving discharges of dredged or fill material if the Secretary determines that the activities in such category are similar in nature, will cause only minimal adverse environmental effects when performed separately, and will have only minimal cumulative adverse effect on the environment. Any general permit issued under this subsection shall (A) be based on the guidelines described in subsection (b)(1) of this section, and (B) set forth the requirements and standards which shall apply to any activity authorized by such general permit.

(2) No general permit issued under this subsection shall be for a period of more than five years after the date of its issuance and such general permit may be revoked or modified by the Secretary if, after opportunity for public hearing, the Secretary determines that the activities authorized by such general permit have an adverse impact on the environment or such activities are more appropriately authorized by individual permits.

(f) Non-prohibited discharge of dredged or fill material

(1) Except as provided in paragraph (2) of this subsection, the discharge of dredged or fill material—

(A) from normal farming, silviculture, and ranching activities such as plowing, seeding, cultivating, minor drainage, harvesting for the production of food, fiber, and forest products, or upland soil and water conservation practices;

(B) for the purpose of maintenance, including emergency reconstruction of recently damaged parts, of currently serviceable structures such as dikes, dams, levees, groins, riprap, breakwaters, causeways, and bridge abutments or approaches, and transportation structures;

(C) for the purpose of construction or maintenance of farm or stock ponds or irrigation ditches, or the maintenance of drainage ditches;

(D) for the purpose of construction of temporary sedimentation basins on a construction site which does not include placement of fill material into the navigable waters;

(E) for the purpose of construction or maintenance of farm roads or forest roads, or temporary roads for moving mining equipment, where such roads are constructed and maintained, in accordance with best management practices, to assure that flow and circulation patterns and chemical and biological characteristics of the navigable waters are not impaired, that the reach of the navigable waters is not reduced, and that any adverse effect on the aquatic environment will be otherwise minimized;

(F) resulting from any activity with respect to which a State has an approved program under section 1288(b)(4) of this title which meets the requirements of subparagraphs (B) and (C) of such section, is not prohibited by or otherwise subject to regulation under this section or section 1311(a) or 1342 of this title (except for effluent standards or prohibitions under section 1317 of this title).

(2) Any discharge of dredged or fill material into the navigable waters incidental to any activity having as its purpose bringing an area of the navigable waters into a use to which it was not previously subject, where the flow or circulation of navigable waters may be impaired or the reach of such waters be reduced, shall be required to have a permit under this section.

(g) State administration

(1) The Governor of any State desiring to administer its own individual and general permit program for the discharge of dredged or fill material into the navigable waters (other than those waters which are presently used, or are susceptible to use in their natural condition or by reasonable improvement as a means to transport interstate or foreign commerce shoreward to their ordinary high water mark, including all waters which are subject to the ebb and flow of the tide shoreward to their mean high water mark, or mean higher high water mark on the west coast, including wetlands adjacent thereto) within its jurisdiction may submit to the Administrator a full and complete description of the program it proposes to establish and administer under State law or under an interstate compact. In addition, such State shall submit a statement from the attorney general (or the attorney for those State agencies which have independent legal counsel), or from the chief legal officer in the case of an interstate agency, that the laws of such State, or the interstate compact, as the case may be, provide adequate authority to carry out the described program.

(2) Not later than the tenth day after the date of the receipt of the program and statement submitted by any State under paragraph (1) of this subsection, the Administrator shall provide copies of such program and statement to the Secretary and the Secretary of the Interior, acting through the Director of the United States Fish and Wildlife Service.

(3) Not later than the ninetieth day after the date of the receipt by the Administrator of the program and statement submitted by any State, under paragraph (1) of this subsection, the Secretary and the Secretary of the Interior, acting through the Director of the United States Fish and Wildlife Service, shall submit any comments with respect to such program and statement to the Administrator in writing.

(h) Determination of State's authority to issue permits under State program; approval; notification; transfers to State program

(1) Not later than the one-hundred-twentieth day after the date of the receipt by the Administrator of a program and statement submitted by any State under paragraph (1) of this subsection, the Administrator shall determine, taking into account any comments submitted by the Secretary and the Secretary of the Interior, acting through the Director of the United States Fish and Wildlife Service, pursuant to subsection (g) of this section, whether such State has the following authority with respect to the issuance of permits pursuant to such program:

(A) To issue permits which—
  (i) apply, and assure compliance with, any applicable requirements of this section, including, but not limited to, the guidelines established under subsection (b)(1) of this section, and sections 1317 and 1343 of this title;
  (ii) are for fixed terms not exceeding five years; and
  (iii) can be terminated or modified for cause including, but not limited to, the following:
    (I) violation of any condition of the permit;
    (II) obtaining a permit by misrepresentation, or failure to disclose fully all relevant facts;
    (III) change in any condition that requires either a temporary or permanent reduction or elimination of the permitted discharge.

(B) To issue permits which apply, and assure compliance with, all applicable requirements of section 1318 of this title, or to inspect, monitor, enter, and require reports to at least the same extent as required in section 1318 of this title.

(C) To assure that the public, and any other State the waters of which may be affected, receive notice of each application for a permit and to provide an opportunity for public hearing before a ruling on each such application.
(D) To assure that the Administrator receives notice of each application (including a copy thereof) for a permit.
(E) To assure that any State (other than the permitting State), whose waters may be affected by the issuance of a permit may submit written recommendations to the permitting State (and the Administrator) with respect to any permit application and, if any part of such written recommendations are not accepted by the permitting State, that the permitting State will notify such affected State (and the Administrator) in writing of its failure to so accept such recommendations together with its reasons for so doing.
(F) To assure that no permit will be issued if, in the judgment of the Secretary, after consultation with the Secretary of the department in which the Coast Guard is operating, anchorage and navigation of any of the navigable waters would be substantially impaired thereby.
(G) To abate violations of the permit or the permit program, including civil and criminal penalties and other ways and means of enforcement.
(H) To assure continued coordination with Federal and Federal-State water-related planning and review processes.
(2) If, with respect to a State program submitted under subsection (g)(1) of this section, the Administrator determines that such State—
(A) has the authority set forth in paragraph (1) of this subsection, the Administrator shall approve the program and so notify (i) such State and (ii) the Secretary, who upon subsequent notification from such State that it is administering such program, shall suspend the issuance of permits under subsections (a) and (e) of this section for activities with respect to which a permit may be issued pursuant to such State program; or
(B) does not have the authority set forth in paragraph (1) of this subsection, the Administrator shall so notify such State, which notification shall also describe the revisions or modifications necessary so that such State may resubmit such program for a determination by the Administrator under this subsection.
(3) If the Administrator fails to make a determination with respect to any program submitted by a State under subsection (g)(1) of this section within one-hundred-twenty days after the date of the receipt of such program, such program shall be deemed approved pursuant to paragraph (2)(A) of this subsection and the Administrator shall so notify such State and the Secretary who, upon subsequent notification from such State that it is administering such program, shall suspend the issuance of permits under subsection (a) and (e) of this section for activities with respect to which a permit may be issued by such State.
(4) After the Secretary receives notification from the Administrator under paragraph (2) or (3) of this subsection that a State permit program has been approved, the Secretary shall transfer any applications for permits pending before the Secretary for activities with respect to which a permit may be issued pursuant to such State program to such State for appropriate action.
(5) Upon notification from a State with a permit program approved under this subsection that such State intends to administer and enforce the terms and conditions of a general permit issued by the Secretary under subsection (e) of this section with respect to activities in such State to which such general permit applies, the Secretary shall suspend the administration and enforcement of such general permit with respect to such activities.
(i) Withdrawal of approval

Whenever the Administrator determines after public hearing that a State is not administering a program approved under subsection (h)(2)(A) of this section, in accordance with this section, including, but not limited to, the guidelines established under subsection (b)(1) of this section, the Administrator shall so notify the State, and, if appropriate corrective action is not taken within a reasonable time, not to exceed ninety days after the date of the receipt of such notification, the Administrator shall (1) withdraw approval of such program until the Administrator determines such corrective action has been taken, and (2) notify the Secretary that the Secretary shall resume the program for the issuance of permits under subsections (a) and (e) of this section for activities with respect to which the State was issuing permits and that such authority of the Secretary shall continue in effect until such time as the Administrator makes the determination described in clause (1) of this subsection and such State again has an approved program.

(j) Copies of applications for State permits and proposed general permits to be transmitted to Administrator

Each State which is administering a permit program pursuant to this section shall transmit to the Administrator (1) a copy of each permit application received by such State and provide notice to the Administrator of every action related to the consideration of such permit application, including each permit proposed to be issued by such State, and (2) a copy of each proposed general permit which such State intends to issue. Not later than the tenth day after the date of the receipt of such permit application or such proposed general permit, the Administrator shall provide copies of such permit application or such proposed general permit to the Secretary and the Secretary of the Interior, acting through the Director of the United States Fish and Wildlife Service. If the Administrator intends to provide written comments to such State with respect to such permit application or such proposed general permit, he shall so notify such State not later than the thirtieth day after the date of the receipt of such application or such proposed general permit and provide such written comments to such State, after consideration of any comments made in writing with respect to such application or such proposed general permit by the Secretary and the Secretary of the Interior, acting through the Director of the United States Fish and Wildlife Service, not later than the ninetieth day after the date of such receipt. If such State is so notified by the Administrator, it shall not issue the proposed permit until after the receipt of such comments from the Administrator, or after such ninetieth day, whichever first occurs. Such State shall not issue such proposed permit after such ninetieth day if it has received such written comments in which the Administrator objects (A) to the issuance of such proposed permit and such proposed permit is one that has been submitted to the Administrator pursuant to subsection (h)(1)(E) of this section, or (B) to the issuance of such proposed permit as being outside the requirements of this section, including, but not limited to, the guidelines developed under subsection (b)(1) of this section unless it modifies such proposed permit in accordance with such comments. Whenever the Administrator objects to the issuance of a permit under the preceding sentence such written objection shall contain a statement of the reasons for such objection and the conditions which such permit would include if it were issued by the Administrator. In any case where the Administrator objects to the issuance of a permit, on request of the State, a public hearing shall be held by the Administrator on such objection. If the State does not resubmit such permit revised to meet such objection within 30 days after completion of the hearing or, if no hearing is requested within 90 days after the date of such objection, the Secretary may issue the permit pursuant to subsection (a) or (e) of this section, as the case may be, for such source in accordance with the guidelines and requirements of this chapter.

(k) Waiver

In accordance with guidelines promulgated pursuant to subsection (i)(2) of section 1314 of this title, the Administrator is authorized to waive the requirements of subsection (j) of this section at the time of the approval of a program pursuant to subsection (h)(2)(A) of this section for any category (including any class, type, or size within such category) of discharge within the State submitting such program.

(l) Categories of discharges not subject to requirements

The Administrator shall promulgate regulations establishing categories of discharges which he determines shall not be subject to the requirements of subsection (j) of this section in any State with a program approved pursuant to subsection (h)(2)(A) of this section. The Administrator may distinguish among classes, types, and sizes within any category of discharges.

(m) Comments on permit applications or proposed general permits by Secretary of the Interior acting through Director of United States Fish and Wildlife Service

Not later than the ninetieth day after the date on which the Secretary notifies the Secretary of the Interior, acting through the Director of the United States Fish and Wildlife Service that (1) an application for a permit under subsection (a) of this section has been received by the Secretary, or (2) the Secretary proposes to issue a general permit under subsection (e) of this section, the Secretary of the Interior, acting through the Director of the United States Fish and Wildlife Service, shall submit any comments with respect to such application or such proposed general permit in writing to the Secretary.

(n) Enforcement authority not limited

Nothing in this section shall be construed to limit the authority of the Administrator to take action pursuant to section 1319 of this title.

(o) Public availability of permits and permit applications

A copy of each permit application and each permit issued under this section shall be available to the public. Such permit application or portion thereof, shall further be available on request for the purpose of reproduction.

(p) Compliance

Compliance with a permit issued pursuant to this section, including any activity carried out pursuant to a general permit issued under this section, shall be deemed compliance, for purposes of sections 1319 and 1365 of this title, with sections 1311, 1317, and 1343 of this title.

(q) Minimization of duplication, needless paperwork, and delays in issuance; agreements

Not later than the one-hundred-eightieth day after December 27, 1977, the Secretary shall enter into agreements with the Administrator, the Secretaries of the Departments of Agriculture, Commerce, Interior, and Transportation, and the heads of other appropriate Federal agencies to minimize, to the maximum extent practicable, duplication, needless paperwork, and delays in the issuance of permits under this section. Such agreements shall be developed to assure that, to the maximum extent practicable, a decision with respect to an application for a permit under subsection (a) of this section will be made not later than the ninetieth day after the date the notice for such application is published under subsection (a) of this section.

(r) Federal projects specifically authorized by Congress

The discharge of dredged or fill material as part of the construction of a Federal project specifically authorized by Congress, whether prior to or on or after December 27, 1977, is not prohibited by or otherwise subject to regulation under this section, or a State program approved under this section, or section 1311(a) or 1342 of this title (except for effluent standards or prohibitions under section 1317 of this title), if information on the effects of such discharge, including consideration of the guidelines developed under subsection (b)(1) of this section, is included in an environmental impact statement for such project pursuant to the National Environmental Policy Act of 1969 [42 U.S.C. 4321 et seq.] and such environmental impact statement has been submitted to Congress before the actual discharge of dredged or fill material in connection with the construction of such project and prior to either authorization of such project or an appropriation of funds for such construction.

(s) Violation of permits

(1) Whenever on the basis of any information available to him the Secretary finds that any person is in violation of any condition or limitation set forth in a permit issued by the Secretary under this section, the Secretary shall issue an order requiring such person to comply with such condition or limitation, or the Secretary shall bring a civil action in accordance with paragraph (3) of this subsection.

(2) A copy of any order issued under this subsection shall be sent immediately by the Secretary to the State in which the violation occurs and other affected States. Any order issued under this subsection shall be by personal service and shall state with reasonable specificity the nature of the violation, specify a time for compliance, not to exceed thirty days, which the Secretary determines is reasonable, taking into account the seriousness of the violation and any good faith efforts to comply with applicable requirements. In any case in which an order under this subsection is issued to a corporation, a copy of such order shall be served on any appropriate corporate officers.

(3) The Secretary is authorized to commence a civil action for appropriate relief, including a permanent or temporary injunction for any violation for which he is authorized to issue a compliance order under paragraph (1) of this subsection. Any action under this paragraph may be brought in the district court of the United States for the district in which the defendant is located or resides or is doing business, and such court shall have jurisdiction

to restrain such violation and to require compliance. Notice of the commencement of such acton[1] shall be given immediately to the appropriate State.

(4) Any person who violates any condition or limitation in a permit issued by the Secretary under this section, and any person who violates any order issued by the Secretary under paragraph (1) of this subsection, shall be subject to a civil penalty not to exceed $25,000 per day for each violation. In determining the amount of a civil penalty the court shall consider the seriousness of the violation or violations, the economic benefit (if any) resulting from the violation, any history of such violations, any good-faith efforts to comply with the applicable requirements, the economic impact of the penalty on the violator, and such other matters as justice may require.

(t) Navigable waters within State jurisdiction

Nothing in this section shall preclude or deny the right of any State or interstate agency to control the discharge of dredged or fill material in any portion of the navigable waters within the jurisdiction of such State, including any activity of any Federal agency, and each such agency shall comply with such State or interstate requirements both substantive and procedural to control the discharge of dredged or fill material to the same extent that any person is subject to such requirements. This section shall not be construed as affecting or impairing the authority of the Secretary to maintain navigation.

(June 30, 1948, ch. 758, title IV, Sec. 404, as added Pub. L. 92-500, Sec. 2, Oct. 18, 1972, 86 Stat. 884; amended Pub. L. 95-217, Sec. 67(a), (b), Dec. 27, 1977, 91 Stat. 1600; Pub. L. 100-4, title III, Sec. 313(d), Feb. 4, 1987, 101 Stat. 45.)

References in Text

The National Environmental Policy Act of 1969, referred to in subsec. (r), is Pub. L. 91-190, Jan. 1, 1970, 83 Stat. 852, as amended, which is classified generally to chapter 55 (Sec. 4321 et seq.) of Title 42, The Public Health and Welfare. For complete classification of this Act to the Code, see Short Title note set out under section 4321 of Title 42 and Tables.

Amendments

1987—Subsec. (s). Pub. L. 100-4 redesignated par. (5) as (4), substituted "$25,000 per day for each violation" for "$10,000 per day of such violation", inserted provision specifying factors to consider in determining the penalty amount, and struck out former par. (4) which read as follows:

"(A) Any person who willfully or negligently violates any condition or limitation in a permit issued by the Secretary under this section shall be punished by a fine of not less than $2,500 nor more than $25,000 per day of violation, or by imprisonment for not more than one year, or by both. If the conviction is for a violation committed after a first conviction of such person under this paragraph, punishment shall be by a fine of not more than $50,000 per day of violation, or by imprisonment for not more than two years, or by both.

"(B) For the purposes of this paragraph, the term 'person' shall mean, in addition to the definition contained in section 1362(5) of this title, any responsible corporate officer."

1977—Subsec. (a). Pub. L. 95-217, Sec. 67(a)(1), substituted "The Secretary" for "The Secretary of the Army, acting through the Chief of Engineers," and inserted provision that, not later than the fifteenth day after the date an applicant submits all the information required to complete an application for a permit under this subsection, the Secretary publish the notice required by this subsection. Subsecs. (b), (c). Pub. L. 95-217, Sec. 67(a)(2), substituted "the Secretary" for "the Secretary of the Army". Subsecs. (d) to (t). Pub. L. 95-217, Sec. 67(b), added subsecs. (d) to (t).

Mitigation and Mitigation Banking

Pub. L. 108-136 Section 314(b) provided: "Regulations.—(1) To ensure opportunities for Federal agency participation in mitigation banking, the Secretary of the Army, acting through the Chief of Engineers, shall issue regulations establishing performance standards and criteria for the use, consistent with section 404 of the Federal Water Pollution Control Act (33 U.S.C. 1344), of on-site, off-site, and in-lieu fee mitigation and mitigation banking as compensation for lost wetlands functions in permits issued by the Secretary of the Army under such section. To the maximum extent practicable, the regulatory standards and criteria shall maximize available credits and opportuni-

---

[1] So in original. Probably should be "action".

640 / Environmental Statutes

ties for mitigation, provide flexibility for regional variations in wetland conditions, functions and values, and apply equivalent standards and criteria to each type of compensatory mitigation."

Transfer of Functions

Enforcement functions of Administrator or other official of the Environmental Protection Agency and of Secretary or other official in Department of the Interior relating to review of the Corps of Engineers' dredged and fill material permits and such functions of Secretary of the Army, Chief of Engineers, or other official in Corps of Engineers of the United States Army relating to compliance with dredged and fill material permits issued under this section with respect to pre-construction, construction, and initial operation of transportation system for Canadian and Alaskan natural gas were transferred to the Federal Inspector, Office of Federal Inspector for the Alaska Natural Gas Transportation System, until the first anniversary of the date of initial operation of the Alaska Natural Gas Transportation System, see Reorg. Plan No. 1 of 1979, Secs. 102(a), (b), (e), 203(a), 44 F.R. 33663, 33666, 93 Stat. 1373, 1376, effective July 1, 1979, set out in the Appendix to Title 5, Government Organization and Employees. Office of Federal Inspector for the Alaska Natural Gas Transportation System abolished and functions and authority vested in Inspector transferred to Secretary of Energy by section 3012(b) of Pub. L. 102-486, set out as an Abolition of Office of Federal Inspector note under section 719e of Title 15, Commerce and Trade.

Regulatory Program

Pub. L. 106-377, Sec. 1(a)(2) [title I], Oct. 27, 2000, 114 Stat. 1441, 1441A-63, provided in part that: "For expenses necessary for administration of laws pertaining to regulation of navigable waters and wetlands, $125,000,000, to remain available until expended: Provided, That the Secretary of the Army, acting through the Chief of Engineers, is directed to use funds appropriated herein to: (1) by March 1, 2001, supplement the report, Cost Analysis For the 1999 Proposal to Issue and Modify Nationwide Permits, to reflect the Nationwide Permits actually issued on March 9, 2000, including changes in the acreage limits, preconstruction notification requirements and general conditions between the rule proposed on July 21, 1999, and the rule promulgated and published in the Federal Register; (2) after consideration of the cost analysis for the 1999 proposal to issue and modify nationwide permits and the supplement prepared pursuant to this Act [H.R. 5483, as enacted by section 1(a)(2) of Pub. L. 106-377, see Tables for classification] and by September 30, 2001, prepare, submit to Congress and publish in the Federal Register a Permit Processing Management Plan by which the Corps of Engineers will handle the additional work associated with all projected increases in the number of individual permit applications and preconstruction notifications related to the new and replacement permits and general conditions. The Permit Processing Management Plan shall include specific objective goals and criteria by which the Corps of Engineers' progress towards reducing any permit backlog can be measured; (3) beginning on December 31, 2001, and on a biannual basis thereafter, report to Congress and publish in the Federal Register, an analysis of the performance of its program as measured against the criteria set out in the Permit Processing Management Plan; (4) implement a 1-year pilot program to publish quarterly on the U.S. Army Corps of Engineer's Regulatory Program website all Regulatory Analysis and Management Systems (RAMS) data for the South Pacific Division and North Atlantic Division beginning within 30 days of the enactment of this Act [Oct. 27, 2000]; and (5) publish in Division Office websites all findings, rulings, and decisions rendered under the administrative appeals process for the Corps of Engineers Regulatory Program as established in Public Law 106-60 [113 Stat. 486]: Provided further, That, through the period ending on September 30, 2003, the Corps of Engineers shall allow any appellant to keep a verbatim record of the proceedings of the appeals conference under the aforementioned administrative appeals process: Provided further, That within 30 days of the enactment of this Act, the Secretary of the Army, acting through the Chief of Engineers, shall require all U.S. Army Corps of Engineers Divisions and Districts to record the date on which a section 404 individual permit application or nationwide permit notification is filed with the Corps of Engineers: Provided further, That the Corps of Engineers, when reporting permit processing times, shall track both the date a permit application is first received and the date the application is considered complete, as well as the reason that the application is not considered complete upon first submission."

Authority To Delegate to State of Washington Functions of the Secretary Relating to Lake Chelan, Washington

Section 76 of Pub. L. 95-217 provided that: "The Secretary of the Army, acting through the Chief of Engineers, is authorized to delegate to the State of Washington upon its request all or any part of those functions vested in such Secretary by section 404 of the Federal Water Pollution Control Act [this section] and by sections 9, 10, and 13 of the Act of March 3, 1899 [sections 401, 403, and 407 of this title], relating to Lake Chelan, Washington, if the Secretary determines (1) that such State has the authority, responsibility, and capability to carry out such functions, and (2) that such delegation is in the public interest. Such delegation shall be subject to such terms and conditions as the Secretary deems necessary, including, but not limited to, suspension and revocation for cause of such delegation."

Contiguous Zone of United States

For extension of contiguous zone of United States, see Proc. No. 7219, set out as a note under section 1331 of Title 43, Public Lands.

Section Referred to in Other Sections

This section is referred to in sections 59c-3, 59j-1, 59y, 59bb, 59bb-1, 59cc, 59dd, 59ff, 59gg, 59hh, 426p, 1251, 1285, 1288, 1311, 1318, 1319, 1342, 1377, 2104, 2317 of this title; title 16 section 3822; title 42 section 9601.

DISPOSAL OR USE OF SEWAGE SLUDGE

33 USC 1345

(a) Permit

Notwithstanding any other provision of this chapter or of any other law, in any case where the disposal of sewage sludge resulting from the operation of a treatment works as defined in section 1292 of this title (including the removal of in-place sewage sludge from one location and its deposit at another location) would result in any pollutant from such sewage sludge entering the navigable waters, such disposal is prohibited except in accordance with a permit issued by the Administrator under section 1342 of this title.

(b) Issuance of permit; regulations

The Administrator shall issue regulations governing the issuance of permits for the disposal of sewage sludge subject to subsection (a) of this section and section 1342 of this title. Such regulations shall require the application to such disposal of each criterion, factor, procedure, and requirement applicable to a permit issued under section 1342 of this title.

(c) State permit program

Each State desiring to administer its own permit program for disposal of sewage sludge subject to subsection (a) of this section within its jurisdiction may do so in accordance with section 1342 of this title.

(d) Regulations

(1) Regulations

The Administrator, after consultation with appropriate Federal and State agencies and other interested persons, shall develop and publish, within one year after December 27, 1977, and from time to time thereafter, regulations providing guidelines for the disposal of sludge and the utilization of sludge for various purposes. Such regulations shall—
(A) identify uses for sludge, including disposal;
(B) specify factors to be taken into account in determining the measures and practices applicable to each such use or disposal (including publication of information on costs);
(C) identify concentrations of pollutants which interfere with each such use or disposal.

The Administrator is authorized to revise any regulation issued under this subsection.

(2) Identification and regulation of toxic pollutants
(A) On basis of available information
(i) Proposed regulations

Not later than November 30, 1986, the Administrator shall identify those toxic pollutants which, on the basis of available information on their toxicity, persistence, concentration, mobility, or potential for exposure, may be present in sewage sludge in concentrations which may adversely affect public health or the environment, and propose regulations specifying acceptable management practices for sewage sludge containing each such toxic pollutant and establishing numerical limitations for each such pollutant for each use identified under paragraph (1)(A).

        (ii) Final regulations

Not later than August 31, 1987, and after opportunity for public hearing, the Administrator shall promulgate the regulations required by subparagraph (A)(i).

    (B) Others

        (i) Proposed regulations

Not later than July 31, 1987, the Administrator shall identify those toxic pollutants not identified under subparagraph (A)(i) which may be present in sewage sludge in concentrations which may adversely affect public health or the environment, and propose regulations specifying acceptable management practices for sewage sludge containing each such toxic pollutant and establishing numerical limitations for each pollutant for each such use identified under paragraph (1)(A).

        (ii) Final regulations

Not later than June 15, 1988, the Administrator shall promulgate the regulations required by subparagraph (B)(i).

    (C) Review

From time to time, but not less often than every 2 years, the Administrator shall review the regulations promulgated under this paragraph for the purpose of identifying additional toxic pollutants and promulgating regulations for such pollutants consistent with the requirements of this paragraph.

    (D) Minimum standards; compliance date

The management practices and numerical criteria established under subparagraphs (A), (B), and (C) shall be adequate to protect public health and the environment from any reasonably anticipated adverse effects of each pollutant. Such regulations shall require compliance as expeditiously as practicable but in no case later than 12 months after their publication, unless such regulations require the construction of new pollution control facilities, in which case the regulations shall require compliance as expeditiously as practicable but in no case later than two years from the date of their publication.

  (3) Alternative standards

For purposes of this subsection, if, in the judgment of the Administrator, it is not feasible to prescribe or enforce a numerical limitation for a pollutant identified under paragraph (2), the Administrator may instead promulgate a design, equipment, management practice, or operational standard, or combination thereof, which in the Administrator's judgment is adequate to protect public health and the environment from any reasonably anticipated adverse effects of such pollutant. In the event the Administrator promulgates a design or equipment standard under this subsection, the Administrator shall include as part of such standard such requirements as will assure the proper operation and maintenance of any such element of design or equipment.

  (4) Conditions on permits

Prior to the promulgation of the regulations required by paragraph (2), the Administrator shall impose conditions in permits issued to publicly owned treatment works under section 1342 of this title or take such other measures as the Administrator deems appropriate to protect public health and the environment from any adverse effects which may occur from toxic pollutants in sewage sludge.

  (5) Limitation on statutory construction

Nothing in this section is intended to waive more stringent requirements established by this chapter or any other law.

(e) Manner of sludge disposal

The determination of the manner of disposal or use of sludge is a local determination, except that it shall be unlawful for any person to dispose of sludge from a publicly owned treatment works or any other treatment works treating domestic sewage for any use for which regulations have been established pursuant to subsection (d) of this section, except in accordance with such regulations.

Clean Water Act / 643

(f) Implementation of regulations
  (1) Through section 1342 permits
    Any permit issued under section 1342 of this title to a publicly owned treatment works or any other treatment works treating domestic sewage shall include requirements for the use and disposal of sludge that implement the regulations established pursuant to subsection (d) of this section, unless such requirements have been included in a permit issued under the appropriate provisions of subtitle C of the Solid Waste Disposal Act [42 U.S.C. 6921 et seq.], part C of the Safe Drinking Water Act [42 U.S.C. 300h et seq.], the Marine Protection, Research, and Sanctuaries Act of 1972 [16 U.S.C. 1431 et seq., 1447 et seq.; 33 U.S.C. 1401 et seq., 2801 et seq.], or the Clean Air Act [42 U.S.C. 7401 et seq.], or under State permit programs approved by the Administrator, where the Administrator determines that such programs assure compliance with any applicable requirements of this section. Not later than December 15, 1986, the Administrator shall promulgate procedures for approval of State programs pursuant to this paragraph.
  (2) Through other permits
    In the case of a treatment works described in paragraph (1) that is not subject to section 1342 of this title and to which none of the other above listed permit programs nor approved State permit authority apply, the Administrator may issue a permit to such treatment works solely to impose requirements for the use and disposal of sludge that implement the regulations established pursuant to subsection (d) of this section. The Administrator shall include in the permit appropriate requirements to assure compliance with the regulations established pursuant to subsection (d) of this section. The Administrator shall establish procedures for issuing permits pursuant to this paragraph.
(g) Studies and projects
  (1) Grant program; information gathering
    The Administrator is authorized to conduct or initiate scientific studies, demonstration projects, and public information and education projects which are designed to promote the safe and beneficial management or use of sewage sludge for such purposes as aiding the restoration of abandoned mine sites, conditioning soil for parks and recreation areas, agricultural and horticultural uses, and other beneficial purposes. For the purposes of carrying out this subsection, the Administrator may make grants to State water pollution control agencies, other public or nonprofit agencies, institutions, organizations, and individuals. In cooperation with other Federal departments and agencies, other public and private agencies, institutions, and organizations, the Administrator is authorized to collect and disseminate information pertaining to the safe and beneficial use of sewage sludge.
  (2) Authorization of appropriations
    For the purposes of carrying out the scientific studies, demonstration projects, and public information and education projects authorized in this section, there is authorized to be appropriated for fiscal years beginning after September 30, 1986, not to exceed $5,000,000.

(June 30, 1948, ch. 758, title IV, Sec. 405, as added Pub. L. 92-500, Sec. 2, Oct. 18, 1972, 86 Stat. 884; amended Pub. L. 95-217, Secs. 54(d), 68, Dec. 27, 1977, 91 Stat. 1591, 1606; Pub. L. 100-4, title IV, Sec. 406(a)-(c), (f), Feb. 4, 1987, 101 Stat. 71, 72, 74.)

References in Text

The Solid Waste Disposal Act, referred to in subsec. (f)(1), is title II of Pub. L. 89-272, Oct. 20, 1965, 79 Stat. 997, as amended generally by Pub. L. 94-580, Sec. 2, Oct. 21, 1976, 90 Stat. 2795. Subtitle C of the Solid Waste Disposal Act is classified generally to subchapter III (Sec. 6921 et seq.) of chapter 82 of Title 42, The Public Health and Welfare. For complete classification of this Act to the Code, see Short Title note set out under section 6901 of Title 42 and Tables.

The Safe Drinking Water Act, referred to in subsec. (f)(1), is title XIV of act July 1, 1944, as added Dec. 16, 1974, Pub. L. 93-523, Sec. 2(a), 88 Stat. 1660, as amended. Part C of the Act is classified generally to part C (Sec. 300h et seq.) of subchapter XII of chapter 6A of Title 42. For complete classification of this Act to the Code, see Short Title note set out under section 201 of Title 42 and Tables.

The Marine Protection, Research, and Sanctuaries Act of 1972, referred to in subsec. (f)(1), is Pub. L. 92-532, Oct. 23, 1972, 86 Stat. 1052, as amended, which is classified generally to chapters 32 (Sec. 1431 et seq.) and 32A (Sec. 1447 et seq.) of Title 16, Conservation, and chapters 27 (Sec. 1401 et seq.) and 41 (Sec. 2801 et seq.) of this title. For complete classification of this Act to the Code, see Short Title note set out under section 1401 of this title and Tables.

The Clean Air Act, referred to in subsec. (f)(1), is act July 14, 1955, ch. 360, 69 Stat. 322, as amended, which is classified generally to chapter 85 (Sec. 7401 et seq.) of Title 42, The Public Health and Welfare. For complete classification of this Act to the Code, see Short Title note set out under section 7401 of Title 42 and Tables.

Amendments

1987—Subsec. (d). Pub. L. 100-4, Sec. 406(a), designated existing provision as par. (1), inserted heading, redesignated former pars. (1) to (3) as subpars. (A) to (C), and added pars. (2) to (5).

Pub. L. 100-4, Sec. 406(f), inserted heading "Regulations" and aligned par. (1) with par. (3) and subpars. (A) to (C) of par. (1) with subpar. (C) of par. (2).

Subsec. (e). Pub. L. 100-4, Sec. 406(b), amended subsec. (e) generally. Prior to amendment, subsec. (e) read as follows: "The determination of the manner of disposal or use of sludge is a local determination except that it shall be unlawful for the owner or operator of any publicly owned treatment works to dispose of sludge from such works for any use for which guidelines have been established pursuant to subsection (d) of this section, except in accordance with such guidelines."

Subsecs. (f), (g). Pub. L. 100-4, Sec. 406(c), added subsecs. (f) and (g).

1977—Subsec. (a). Pub. L. 95-217, Sec. 68(a), substituted "under section 1342 of this title" for "under this section".

Subsec. (b). Pub. L. 95-217, Secs. 54(d)(1), 68(b), (c), substituted "sewage sludge subject to subsection (a) of this section and section 1342 of this title" for "sewage sludge subject to this section" and struck out ", as the Administrator determines necessary to carry out the objective of this chapter" after "permit issued under section 1342 of this title".

Subsec. (c). Pub. L. 95-217, Secs. 54(d)(2), 68(d), substituted "disposal of sewage sludge subject to subsection (a) of this section within its jurisdiction may do so in accordance with section 1342 of this title" for "disposal of sewage sludge within its jurisdiction may do so if upon submission of such program the Administrator determines such program is adequate to carry out the objective of this chapter".

Subsecs. (d), (e). Pub. L. 95-217, Sec. 54(d)(3), added subsecs. (d) and (e).

Removal Credits

Section 406(e) of Pub. L. 100-4 provided that: "The part of the decision of Natural Resources Defense Council, Inc. v. U.S. Environmental Protection Agency, No. 84-3530 (3d. Cir. 1986), which addresses section 405(d) of the Federal Water Pollution Control Act [33 U.S.C. 1345(d)] is stayed until August 31, 1987, with respect to—

"(1) those publicly owned treatment works the owner or operator of which received authority to revise pretreatment requirements under section 307(b)(1) of such Act [33 U.S.C. 1317(b)(1)] before the date of the enactment of this section [Feb. 4, 1987], and

(2) those publicly owned treatment works the owner or operator of which has submitted an application for authority to revise pretreatment requirements under such section 307(b)(1) which application is pending on such date of enactment and is approved before August 31, 1987.

The Administrator shall not authorize any other removal credits under such Act [33 U.S.C. 1251 et seq.] until the Administrator issues the regulations required by paragraph (2)(A)(ii) of section 405(d) of such Act, as amended by subsection (a) of this section."

Section Referred to in Other Sections

This section is referred to in sections 1317, 1318, 1319, 1365, 1369 of this title.

COASTAL RECREATION WATER QUALITY MONITORING AND NOTIFICATION

33 USC 1346

(a) Monitoring and notification
   (1) In general

Not later than 18 months after October 10, 2000, after consultation and in cooperation with appropriate Federal, State, tribal, and local officials (including local health officials), and after providing public notice and an opportunity for comment, the Administrator shall publish performance criteria for—
  (A) monitoring and assessment (including specifying available methods for monitoring) of coastal recreation waters adjacent to beaches or similar points of access that are used by the public for attainment of applicable water quality standards for pathogens and pathogen indicators; and
  (B) the prompt notification of the public, local governments, and the Administrator of any exceeding of or likelihood of exceeding applicable water quality standards for coastal recreation waters described in subparagraph (A).
  (2) Level of protection
  The performance criteria referred to in paragraph (1) shall provide that the activities described in subparagraphs (A) and (B) of that paragraph shall be carried out as necessary for the protection of public health and safety.
(b) Program development and implementation grants
  (1) In general
  The Administrator may make grants to States and local governments to develop and implement programs for monitoring and notification for coastal recreation waters adjacent to beaches or similar points of access that are used by the public.
  (2) Limitations
    (A) In general
    The Administrator may award a grant to a State or a local government to implement a monitoring and notification program if—
      (i) the program is consistent with the performance criteria published by the Administrator under subsection (a) of this section;
      (ii) the State or local government prioritizes the use of grant funds for particular coastal recreation waters based on the use of the water and the risk to human health presented by pathogens or pathogen indicators;
      (iii) the State or local government makes available to the Administrator the factors used to prioritize the use of funds under clause (ii);
      (iv) the State or local government provides a list of discrete areas of coastal recreation waters that are subject to the program for monitoring and notification for which the grant is provided that specifies any coastal recreation waters for which fiscal constraints will prevent consistency with the performance criteria under subsection (a) of this section; and
      (v) the public is provided an opportunity to review the program through a process that provides for public notice and an opportunity for comment.
    (B) Grants to local governments
    The Administrator may make a grant to a local government under this subsection for implementation of a monitoring and notification program only if, after the 1-year period beginning on the date of publication of performance criteria under subsection (a)(1) of this section, the Administrator determines that the State is not implementing a program that meets the requirements of this subsection, regardless of whether the State has received a grant under this subsection.
  (3) Other requirements
    (A) Report
    A State recipient of a grant under this subsection shall submit to the Administrator, in such format and at such intervals as the Administrator determines to be appropriate, a report that describes—
      (i) data collected as part of the program for monitoring and notification as described in subsection (c) of this section; and
      (ii) actions taken to notify the public when water quality standards are exceeded.
    (B) Delegation
    A State recipient of a grant under this subsection shall identify each local government to which the State has delegated or intends to delegate responsibility for implementing a monitoring and notification program consistent with the performance criteria published under subsection (a) of this section (including any coastal recreation waters

for which the authority to implement a monitoring and notification program would be subject to the delegation).
    (4) Federal share
        (A) In general
            The Administrator, through grants awarded under this section, may pay up to 100 percent of the costs of developing and implementing a program for monitoring and notification under this subsection.
        (B) Non-Federal share
            The non-Federal share of the costs of developing and implementing a monitoring and notification program may be—
            (i) in an amount not to exceed 50 percent, as determined by the Administrator in consultation with State, tribal, and local government representatives; and
            (ii) provided in cash or in kind.
(c) Content of State and local government programs
    As a condition of receipt of a grant under subsection (b) of this section, a State or local government program for monitoring and notification under this section shall identify—
    (1) lists of coastal recreation waters in the State, including coastal recreation waters adjacent to beaches or similar points of access that are used by the public;
    (2) in the case of a State program for monitoring and notification, the process by which the State may delegate to local governments responsibility for implementing the monitoring and notification program;
    (3) the frequency and location of monitoring and assessment of coastal recreation waters based on—
        (A) the periods of recreational use of the waters;
        (B) the nature and extent of use during certain periods;
        (C) the proximity of the waters to known point sources and nonpoint sources of pollution; and
        (D) any effect of storm events on the waters;
    (4) (A) the methods to be used for detecting levels of pathogens and pathogen indicators that are harmful to human health; and
        (B) the assessment procedures for identifying short-term increases in pathogens and pathogen indicators that are harmful to human health in coastal recreation waters (including increases in relation to storm events);
    (5) measures for prompt communication of the occurrence, nature, location, pollutants involved, and extent of any exceeding of, or likelihood of exceeding, applicable water quality standards for pathogens and pathogen indicators to—
        (A) the Administrator, in such form as the Administrator determines to be appropriate; and
        (B) a designated official of a local government having jurisdiction over land adjoining the coastal recreation waters for which the failure to meet applicable standards is identified;
    (6) measures for the posting of signs at beaches or similar points of access, or functionally equivalent communication measures that are sufficient to give notice to the public that the coastal recreation waters are not meeting or are not expected to meet applicable water quality standards for pathogens and pathogen indicators; and
    (7) measures that inform the public of the potential risks associated with water contact activities in the coastal recreation waters that do not meet applicable water quality standards.
(d) Federal agency programs
    Not later than 3 years after October 10, 2000, each Federal agency that has jurisdiction over coastal recreation waters adjacent to beaches or similar points of access that are used by the public shall develop and implement, through a process that provides for public notice and an opportunity for comment, a monitoring and notification program for the coastal recreation waters that—
    (1) protects the public health and safety;
    (2) is consistent with the performance criteria published under subsection (a) of this section;
    (3) includes a completed report on the information specified in subsection (b)(3)(A) of this section, to be submitted to the Administrator; and
    (4) addresses the matters specified in subsection (c) of this section.

(e) Database
The Administrator shall establish, maintain, and make available to the public by electronic and other means a national coastal recreation water pollution occurrence database that provides—
   (1) the data reported to the Administrator under subsections (b)(3)(A)(i) and (d)(3) of this section; and
   (2) other information concerning pathogens and pathogen indicators in coastal recreation waters that—
      (A) is made available to the Administrator by a State or local government, from a coastal water quality monitoring program of the State or local government; and
      (B) the Administrator determines should be included.
(f) Technical assistance for monitoring floatable material
The Administrator shall provide technical assistance to States and local governments for the development of assessment and monitoring procedures for floatable material to protect public health and safety in coastal recreation waters.
(g) List of waters
   (1) In general
   Beginning not later than 18 months after the date of publication of performance criteria under subsection (a) of this section, based on information made available to the Administrator, the Administrator shall identify, and maintain a list of, discrete coastal recreation waters adjacent to beaches or similar points of access that are used by the public that—
      (A) specifies any waters described in this paragraph that are subject to a monitoring and notification program consistent with the performance criteria established under subsection (a) of this section; and
      (B) specifies any waters described in this paragraph for which there is no monitoring and notification program (including waters for which fiscal constraints will prevent the State or the Administrator from performing monitoring and notification consistent with the performance criteria established under subsection (a) of this section).
   (2) Availability
   The Administrator shall make the list described in paragraph (1) available to the public through—
      (A) publication in the Federal Register; and
      (B) electronic media.
   (3) Updates
   The Administrator shall update the list described in paragraph (1) periodically as new information becomes available.
(h) EPA implementation
In the case of a State that has no program for monitoring and notification that is consistent with the performance criteria published under subsection (a) of this section after the last day of the 3-year period beginning on the date on which the Administrator lists waters in the State under subsection (g)(1)(B) of this section, the Administrator shall conduct a monitoring and notification program for the listed waters based on a priority ranking established by the Administrator using funds appropriated for grants under subsection (i) of this section—
   (1) to conduct monitoring and notification; and
   (2) for related salaries, expenses, and travel.
(i) Authorization of appropriations
There is authorized to be appropriated for making grants under subsection (b) of this section, including implementation of monitoring and notification programs by the Administrator under subsection (h) of this section, $30,000,000 for each of fiscal years 2001 through 2005.

(June 30, 1948, ch. 758, title IV, Sec. 406, as added Pub. L. 106-284, Sec. 4, Oct. 10, 2000, 114 Stat. 872.)

Section Referred to in Other Sections

This section is referred to in section 1377 of this title.

SUBCHAPTER V—GENERAL PROVISIONS

ADMINISTRATION

33 USC 1361

(a) Authority of Administrator to prescribe regulations
   The Administrator is authorized to prescribe such regulations as are necessary to carry out his functions under this chapter.
(b) Utilization of other agency officers and employees
   The Administrator, with the consent of the head of any other agency of the United States, may utilize such officers and employees of such agency as may be found necessary to assist in carrying out the purposes of this chapter.
(c) Recordkeeping
   Each recipient of financial assistance under this chapter shall keep such records as the Administrator shall prescribe, including records which fully disclose the amount and disposition by such recipient of the proceeds of such assistance, the total cost of the project or undertaking in connection with which such assistance is given or used, and the amount of that portion of the cost of the project or undertaking supplied by other sources, and such other records as will facilitate effective audit.
(d) Audit
   The Administrator and the Comptroller General of the United States, or any of their duly authorized representatives, shall have access, for the purpose of audit and examination, to any books, documents, papers, and records of the recipients that are pertinent to the grants received under this chapter. For the purpose of carrying out audits and examinations with respect to recipients of Federal assistance under this chapter, the Administrator is authorized to enter into noncompetitive procurement contracts with independent State audit organizations, consistent with chapter 75 of title 31. Such contracts may only be entered into to the extent and in such amounts as may be provided in advance in appropriation Acts.
(e) Awards for outstanding technological achievement or innovative processes, methods, or devices in waste treatment and pollution abatement programs
   (1) It is the purpose of this subsection to authorize a program which will provide official recognition by the United States Government to those industrial organizations and political subdivisions of States which during the preceding year demonstrated an outstanding technological achievement or an innovative process, method, or device in their waste treatment and pollution abatement programs. The Administrator shall, in consultation with the appropriate State water pollution control agencies, establish regulations under which such recognition may be applied for and granted, except that no applicant shall be eligible for an award under this subsection if such applicant is not in total compliance with all applicable water quality requirements under this chapter, or otherwise does not have a satisfactory record with respect to environmental quality.
   (2) The Administrator shall award a certificate or plaque of suitable design to each industrial organization or political subdivision which qualifies for such recognition under regulations established under this subsection.
   (3) The President of the United States, the Governor of the appropriate State, the Speaker of the House of Representatives, and the President pro tempore of the Senate shall be notified of the award by the Administrator and the awarding of such recognition shall be published in the Federal Register.
(f) Detail of Environmental Protection Agency personnel to State water pollution control agencies
   Upon the request of a State water pollution control agency, personnel of the Environmental Protection Agency may be detailed to such agency for the purpose of carrying out the provisions of this chapter.

(June 30, 1948, ch. 758, title V, Sec. 501, as added Pub. L. 92-500, Sec. 2, Oct. 18, 1972, 86 Stat. 885; amended Pub. L. 100-4, title V, Sec. 501, Feb. 4, 1987, 101 Stat. 75.)

Amendments

1987—Subsec. (d). Pub. L. 100-4 inserted provision at end authorizing Administrator to enter into noncompetitive procurement contracts with independent State audit organizations, consistent with chapter 75 of title 31, but only to extent and in such amounts as provided in advance in appropriations Acts.

Environmental Court Feasibility Study

Section 9 of Pub. L. 92-500 authorized the President, acting through the Attorney General, to study the feasibility of establishing a separate court or court system with jurisdiction over environmental matters and required him to report the results of his study, together with his recommendations, to Congress not later than one year after Oct. 18, 1972.

Transfer of Public Health Service Officers

Pub. L. 89-234, Sec. 2(b)-(k), Oct. 2, 1965, 79 Stat. 904, 905, authorized the transfer of certain commissioned officers of the Public Health Service to classified positions in the Federal Water Pollution Control Administration, now the Environmental Protection Agency, where such transfer was requested within six months after the establishment of the Administration and made certain administrative provisions relating to pension and retirement rights of the transferees, sick leave benefits, group life insurance, and certain other miscellaneous provisions.

Section Referred to in Other Sections

This section is referred to in section 1283 of this title.

DEFINITIONS

33 USC 1362

Except as otherwise specifically provided, when used in this chapter:

(1) The term "State water pollution control agency" means the State agency designated by the Governor having responsibility for enforcing State laws relating to the abatement of pollution.

(2) The term "interstate agency" means an agency of two or more States established by or pursuant to an agreement or compact approved by the Congress, or any other agency of two or more States, having substantial powers or duties pertaining to the control of pollution as determined and approved by the Administrator.

(3) The term "State" means a State, the District of Columbia, the Commonwealth of Puerto Rico, the Virgin Islands, Guam, American Samoa, the Commonwealth of the Northern Mariana Islands, and the Trust Territory of the Pacific Islands.

(4) The term "municipality" means a city, town, borough, county, parish, district, association, or other public body created by or pursuant to State law and having jurisdiction over disposal of sewage, industrial wastes, or other wastes, or an Indian tribe or an authorized Indian tribal organization, or a designated and approved management agency under section 1288 of this title.

(5) The term "person" means an individual, corporation, partnership, association, State, municipality, commission, or political subdivision of a State, or any interstate body.

(6) The term "pollutant" means dredged spoil, solid waste, incinerator residue, sewage, garbage, sewage sludge, munitions, chemical wastes, biological materials, radioactive materials, heat, wrecked or discarded equipment, rock, sand, cellar dirt and industrial, municipal, and agricultural waste discharged into water. This term does not mean (A) "sewage from vessels or a discharge incidental to the normal operation of a vessel of the Armed Forces" within the meaning of section 1322 of this title; or (B) water, gas, or other material which is injected into a well to facilitate production of oil or gas, or water derived in association with oil or gas production and disposed of in a well, if the well used either to facilitate production or for disposal purposes is approved by authority of the State in which the well is located, and if such State determines that such injection or disposal will not result in the degradation of ground or surface water resources.

(7) The term "navigable waters" means the waters of the United States, including the territorial seas.

(8) The term "territorial seas" means the belt of the seas measured from the line of ordinary low water along that portion of the coast which is in direct contact with the open sea and the line marking the seaward limit of inland waters, and extending seaward a distance of three miles.

(9) The term "contiguous zone" means the entire zone established or to be established by the United States under article 24 of the Convention of the Territorial Sea and the Contiguous Zone.

(10) The term "ocean" means any portion of the high seas beyond the contiguous zone.

(11) The term "effluent limitation" means any restriction established by a State or the Administrator on quantities, rates, and concentrations of chemical, physical, biological, and other constituents which are discharged from point sources into navigable waters, the waters of the contiguous zone, or the ocean, including schedules of compliance.

(12) The term "discharge of a pollutant" and the term "discharge of pollutants" each means (A) any addition of any pollutant to navigable waters from any point source, (B) any addition of any pollutant to the waters of the contiguous zone or the ocean from any point source other than a vessel or other floating craft.

(13) The term "toxic pollutant" means those pollutants, or combinations of pollutants, including disease-causing agents, which after discharge and upon exposure, ingestion, inhalation or assimilation into any organism, either directly from the environment or indirectly by ingestion through food chains, will, on the basis of information available to the Administrator, cause death, disease, behavioral abnormalities, cancer, genetic mutations, physiological malfunctions (including malfunctions in reproduction) or physical deformations, in such organisms or their offspring.

(14) The term "point source" means any discernible, confined and discrete conveyance, including but not limited to any pipe, ditch, channel, tunnel, conduit, well, discrete fissure, container, rolling stock, concentrated animal feeding operation, or vessel or other floating craft, from which pollutants are or may be discharged. This term does not include agricultural stormwater discharges and return flows from irrigated agriculture.

(15) The term "biological monitoring" shall mean the determination of the effects on aquatic life, including accumulation of pollutants in tissue, in receiving waters due to the discharge of pollutants (A) by techniques and procedures, including sampling of organisms representative of appropriate levels of the food chain appropriate to the volume and the physical, chemical, and biological characteristics of the effluent, and (B) at appropriate frequencies and locations.

(16) The term "discharge" when used without qualification includes a discharge of a pollutant, and a discharge of pollutants.

(17) The term "schedule of compliance" means a schedule of remedial measures including an enforceable sequence of actions or operations leading to compliance with an effluent limitation, other limitation, prohibition, or standard.

(18) The term "industrial user" means those industries identified in the Standard Industrial Classification Manual, Bureau of the Budget, 1967, as amended and supplemented, under the category of "Division D–Manufacturing" and such other classes of significant waste producers as, by regulation, the Administrator deems appropriate.

(19) The term "pollution" means the man-made or man-induced alteration of the chemical, physical, biological, and radiological integrity of water.

(20) The term "medical waste" means isolation wastes; infectious agents; human blood and blood products; pathological wastes; sharps; body parts; contaminated bedding; surgical wastes and potentially contaminated laboratory wastes; dialysis wastes; and such additional medical items as the Administrator shall prescribe by regulation.

(21) Coastal recreation waters.–
  (A) In general.–The term "coastal recreation waters" means–
    (i) the Great Lakes; and
    (ii) marine coastal waters (including coastal estuaries) that are designated under section 1313(c) of this title by a State for use for swimming, bathing, surfing, or similar water contact activities.
  (B) Exclusions.–The term "coastal recreation waters" does not include–
    (i) inland waters; or

(ii) waters upstream of the mouth of a river or stream having an unimpaired natural connection with the open sea.

(22) Floatable material.–
  (A) In general.–The term "floatable material" means any foreign matter that may float or remain suspended in the water column.
  (B) Inclusions.–The term "floatable material" includes–
     (i) plastic;
     (ii) aluminum cans;
     (iii) wood products;
     (iv) bottles; and
     (v) paper products.

(23) Pathogen indicator.–The term "pathogen indicator" means a substance that indicates the potential for human infectious disease.

(June 30, 1948, ch. 758, title V, Sec. 502, as added Pub. L. 92-500, Sec. 2, Oct. 18, 1972, 86 Stat. 886; amended Pub. L. 95-217, Sec. 33(b), Dec. 27, 1977, 91 Stat. 1577; Pub. L. 100-4, title V, Secs. 502(a), 503, Feb. 4, 1987, 101 Stat. 75; Pub. L. 100-688, title III, Sec. 3202(a), Nov. 18, 1988, 102 Stat. 4154; Pub. L. 104-106, div. A, title III, Sec. 325(c)(3), Feb. 10, 1996, 110 Stat. 259; Pub. L. 106-284, Sec. 5, Oct. 10, 2000, 114 Stat. 875.)

Amendments

2000–Pars. (21) to (23). Pub. L. 106-284 added pars. (21) to (23).

1996–Par. (6)(A). Pub. L. 104-106 substituted " 'sewage from vessels or a discharge incidental to the normal operation of a vessel of the Armed Forces' " for " 'sewage from vessels' ".

1988–Par. (20). Pub. L. 100-688 added par. (20).

1987–Par. (3). Pub. L. 100-4, Sec. 502(a), inserted "the Commonwealth of the Northern Mariana Islands," after "Samoa,". Par. (14). Pub. L. 100-4, Sec. 503, inserted "agricultural stormwater discharges and" after "does not include".

1977–Par. (14). Pub. L. 95-217 inserted provision that "point source" does not include return flows from irrigated agriculture.

Termination of Trust Territory of the Pacific Islands

For termination of Trust Territory of the Pacific Islands, see note set out preceding section 1681 of Title 48, Territories and Insular Possessions.

Territorial Sea and Contiguous Zone of United States

For extension of territorial sea and contiguous zone of United States, see Proc. No. 5928 and Proc. No. 7219, respectively, set out as notes under section 1331 of Title 43, Public Lands.

Definition of "Point Source"

Section 507 of Pub. L. 100-4 provided that: "For purposes of the Federal Water Pollution Control Act [33 U.S.C. 1251 et seq.], the term 'point source' includes a landfill leachate collection system."

Section Referred to in Other Sections

This section is referred to in section 1319 of this title; title 14 section 690; title 26 section 169; title 30 section 1419; title 42 sections 9117, 9601.

WATER POLLUTION CONTROL ADVISORY BOARD

33 USC 1363

(a) Establishment; composition; terms of office
  (1) There is hereby established in the Environmental Protection Agency a Water Pollution Control Advisory Board, composed of the Administrator or his designee, who shall be Chairman, and nine members appointed by the President, none of whom shall be Federal officers or employees. The appointed members, having due regard for the purposes of this chapter, shall be selected from among representatives of various State, interstate, and local governmental agencies, of public or private interests contributing to, affected by, or

concerned with pollution, and of other public and private agencies, organizations, or groups demonstrating an active interest in the field of pollution prevention and control, as well as other individuals who are expert in this field.

(2) (A) Each member appointed by the President shall hold office for a term of three years, except that (i) any member appointed to fill a vacancy occurring prior to the expiration of the term for which his predecessor was appointed shall be appointed for the remainder of such term, and (ii) the terms of office of the members first taking office after June 30, 1956, shall expire as follows: three at the end of one year after such date, three at the end of two years after such date, and three at the end of three years after such date, as designated by the President at the time of appointment, and (iii) the term of any member under the preceding provisions shall be extended until the date on which his successor's appointment is effective. None of the members appointed by the President shall be eligible for reappointment within one year after the end of his preceding term.

(B) The members of the Board who are not officers or employees of the United States, while attending conferences or meetings of the Board or while serving at the request of the Administrator, shall be entitled to receive compensation at a rate to be fixed by the Administrator, but not exceeding $100 per diem, including travel-time, and while away from their homes or regular places of business they may be allowed travel expenses, including per diem in lieu of subsistence, as authorized by law for persons in the Government service employed intermittently.

(b) Functions
The Board shall advise, consult with, and make recommendations to the Administrator on matters of policy relating to the activities and functions of the Administrator under this chapter.

(c) Clerical and technical assistance
Such clerical and technical assistance as may be necessary to discharge the duties of the Board shall be provided from the personnel of the Environmental Protection Agency.

(June 30, 1948, ch. 758, title V, Sec. 503, as added Pub. L. 92-500, Sec. 2, Oct. 18, 1972, 86 Stat. 887.)

References in Text

Travel expenses, including per diem in lieu of subsistence as authorized by law, referred to in subsec. (a)(2)(B), probably means the allowances authorized by section 5703 of Title 5, Government Organization and Employees.

Continuation of Term of Office

Pub. L. 87-88, Sec. 6(c), July 20, 1961, 75 Stat. 207, provided that members of the Water Pollution Control Advisory Board holding office immediately preceding July 20, 1961 were to remain in office as members of the Board as established by section 6(a) of Pub. L. 87-88 until the expiration of the terms of office for which they were originally appointed.

Terms of Office of Members of Water Pollution Control Advisory Board

Act July 9, 1956, ch. 518, Sec. 3, 70 Stat. 507, provided that the terms of office of members of the Water Pollution Control Advisory Board, holding office on July 9, 1956, were to terminate at the close of business on that date.

Termination of Advisory Boards

Advisory boards in existence on Jan. 5, 1973, to terminate not later than the expiration of the 2-year period following Jan. 5, 1973, unless, in the case of a board established by the President or an officer of the Federal Government, such board is renewed by appropriate action prior to the expiration of such 2-year period, or in the case of a board established by the Congress, its duration is otherwise provided for by law. See sections 3(2) and 14 of Pub. L. 92-463, Oct. 6, 1972, 86 Stat. 770, 776, set out in the Appendix to Title 5, Government Organization and Employees.

EMERGENCY POWERS

33 USC 1364

(a) Emergency powers
Notwithstanding any other provision of this chapter, the Administrator upon receipt of evidence that a pollution source or combination of sources is presenting an imminent and substantial endangerment to the health of persons or to the welfare of persons where such endangerment is to the livelihood of such persons, such as inability to market shellfish, may bring suit on behalf of the United States in the appropriate district court to immediately restrain any person causing or contributing to the alleged pollution to stop the discharge of pollutants causing or contributing to such pollution or to take such other action as may be necessary.

(b) Repealed. Pub. L. 96-510, title III, Sec. 304(a), Dec. 11, 1980, 94 Stat. 2809

(June 30, 1948, ch. 758, title V, Sec. 504, as added Pub. L. 92-500, Sec. 2, Oct. 18, 1972, 86 Stat. 888; amended Pub. L. 95-217, Sec. 69, Dec. 27, 1977, 91 Stat. 1607; Pub. L. 96-510, title III, Sec. 304(a), Dec. 11, 1980, 94 Stat. 2809.)

Amendments

1980—Subsec. (b). Pub. L. 96-510 struck out subsec. (b) which related to emergency assistance, establishment of an emergency fund, and preparation of a contingency plan for such emergencies.

1977—Pub. L. 95-217 designated existing provisions as subsec. (a) and added subsec. (b).

Effective Date of 1980 Amendment

Amendment by Pub. L. 96-510 effective Dec. 11, 1980, see section 9652 of Title 42, The Public Health and Welfare.

Section Referred to in Other Sections

This section is referred to in sections 1256, 1318 of this title; title 42 sections 7412, 9606, 9654.

CITIZEN SUITS

33 USC 1365

(a) Authorization; jurisdiction
Except as provided in subsection (b) of this section and section 1319(g)(6) of this title, any citizen may commence a civil action on his own behalf—
  (1) against any person (including (i) the United States, and (ii) any other governmental instrumentality or agency to the extent permitted by the eleventh amendment to the Constitution) who is alleged to be in violation of (A) an effluent standard or limitation under this chapter or (B) an order issued by the Administrator or a State with respect to such a standard or limitation, or
  (2) against the Administrator where there is alleged a failure of the Administrator to perform any act or duty under this chapter which is not discretionary with the Administrator.
The district courts shall have jurisdiction, without regard to the amount in controversy or the citizenship of the parties, to enforce such an effluent standard or limitation, or such an order, or to order the Administrator to perform such act or duty, as the case may be, and to apply any appropriate civil penalties under section 1319(d) of this title.

(b) Notice
No action may be commenced—
  (1) under subsection (a)(1) of this section—
    (A) prior to sixty days after the plaintiff has given notice of the alleged violation (i) to the Administrator, (ii) to the State in which the alleged violation occurs, and (iii) to any alleged violator of the standard, limitation, or order, or
    (B) if the Administrator or State has commenced and is diligently prosecuting a civil or criminal action in a court of the United States, or a State to require compliance with the standard, limitation, or order, but in any such action in a court of the United States any citizen may intervene as a matter of right.

(2) under subsection (a)(2) of this section prior to sixty days after the plaintiff has given notice of such action to the Administrator,

except that such action may be brought immediately after such notification in the case of an action under this section respecting a violation of sections 1316 and 1317(a) of this title. Notice under this subsection shall be given in such manner as the Administrator shall prescribe by regulation.

(c) Venue; intervention by Administrator; United States interests protected
  (1) Any action respecting a violation by a discharge source of an effluent standard or limitation or an order respecting such standard or limitation may be brought under this section only in the judicial district in which such source is located.
  (2) In such action under this section, the Administrator, if not a party, may intervene as a matter of right.
  (3) Protection of interests of united states.—Whenever any action is brought under this section in a court of the United States, the plaintiff shall serve a copy of the complaint on the Attorney General and the Administrator. No consent judgment shall be entered in an action in which the United States is not a party prior to 45 days following the receipt of a copy of the proposed consent judgment by the Attorney General and the Administrator.

(d) Litigation costs
The court, in issuing any final order in any action brought pursuant to this section, may award costs of litigation (including reasonable attorney and expert witness fees) to any prevailing or substantially prevailing party, whenever the court determines such award is appropriate. The court may, if a temporary restraining order or preliminary injunction is sought, require the filing of a bond or equivalent security in accordance with the Federal Rules of Civil Procedure.

(e) Statutory or common law rights not restricted
Nothing in this section shall restrict any right which any person (or class of persons) may have under any statute or common law to seek enforcement of any effluent standard or limitation or to seek any other relief (including relief against the Administrator or a State agency).

(f) Effluent standard or limitation
For purposes of this section, the term "effluent standard or limitation under this chapter" means (1) effective July 1, 1973, an unlawful act under subsection (a) of section 1311 of this title, (2) an effluent limitation or other limitation under section 1311 or 1312 of this title; (3) standard of performance under section 1316 of this title; (4) prohibition, effluent standard or pretreatment standards under section 1317 of this title; (5) certification under section 1341 of this title; (6) a permit or condition thereof issued under section 1342 of this title, which is in effect under this chapter (including a requirement applicable by reason of section 1323 of this title); or (7) a regulation under section 1345(d) of this title,.[1]

(g) "Citizen" defined
For the purposes of this section the term "citizen" means a person or persons having an interest which is or may be adversely affected.

(h) Civil action by State Governors
A Governor of a State may commence a civil action under subsection (a) of this section, without regard to the limitations of subsection (b) of this section, against the Administrator where there is alleged a failure of the Administrator to enforce an effluent standard or limitation under this chapter the violation of which is occurring in another State and is causing an adverse effect on the public health or welfare in his State, or is causing a violation of any water quality requirement in his State.

(June 30, 1948, ch. 758, title V, Sec. 505, as added Pub. L. 92-500, Sec. 2, Oct. 18, 1972, 86 Stat. 888; amended Pub. L. 100-4, title III, Sec. 314(c), title IV, Sec. 406(d)(2), title V, Secs. 504, 505(c), Feb. 4, 1987, 101 Stat. 49, 73, 75, 76.)

References in Text

The Federal Rules of Civil Procedure, referred to in subsec. (d), are set out in the Appendix to Title 28, Judiciary and Judicial Procedure.

---

[1] So in original.

Amendments

1987—Subsec. (a). Pub. L. 100-4, Sec. 314(c), inserted "and section 1319(g)(6) of this title" after "subsection (b) of this section" in introductory text.

Subsec. (c)(3). Pub. L. 100-4, Sec. 504, added par. (3).

Subsec. (d). Pub. L. 100-4, Sec. 505(c), inserted "prevailing or substantially prevailing" before "party".

Subsec. (f). Pub. L. 100-4, Sec. 406(d)(2), added cl. (7).

Section Referred to in Other Sections

This section is referred to in sections 1319, 1321, 1329, 1342, 1344 of this title.

APPEARANCE

33 USC 1366

The Administrator shall request the Attorney General to appear and represent the United States in any civil or criminal action instituted under this chapter to which the Administrator is a party. Unless the Attorney General notifies the Administrator within a reasonable time, that he will appear in a civil action, attorneys who are officers or employees of the Environmental Protection Agency shall appear and represent the United States in such action.

(June 30, 1948, ch. 758, title V, Sec. 506, as added Pub. L. 92-500, Sec. 2, Oct. 18, 1972, 86 Stat. 889.)

EMPLOYEE PROTECTION

33 USC 1367

(a) Discrimination against persons filing, instituting, or testifying in proceedings under this chapter prohibited

No person shall fire, or in any other way discriminate against, or cause to be fired or discriminated against, any employee or any authorized representative of employees by reason of the fact that such employee or representative has filed, instituted, or caused to be filed or instituted any proceeding under this chapter, or has testified or is about to testify in any proceeding resulting from the administration or enforcement of the provisions of this chapter.

(b) Application for review; investigation; hearing; review

Any employee or a representative of employees who believes that he has been fired or otherwise discriminated against by any person in violation of subsection (a) of this section may, within thirty days after such alleged violation occurs, apply to the Secretary of Labor for a review of such firing or alleged discrimination. A copy of the application shall be sent to such person who shall be the respondent. Upon receipt of such application, the Secretary of Labor shall cause such investigation to be made as he deems appropriate. Such investigation shall provide an opportunity for a public hearing at the request of any party to such review to enable the parties to present information relating to such alleged violation. The parties shall be given written notice of the time and place of the hearing at least five days prior to the hearing. Any such hearing shall be of record and shall be subject to section 554 of title 5. Upon receiving the report of such investigation, the Secretary of Labor shall make findings of fact. If he finds that such violation did occur, he shall issue a decision, incorporating an order therein and his findings, requiring the party committing such violation to take such affirmative action to abate the violation as the Secretary of Labor deems appropriate, including, but not limited to, the rehiring or reinstatement of the employee or representative of employees to his former position with compensation. If he finds that there was no such violation, he shall issue an order denying the application. Such order issued by the Secretary of Labor under this subparagraph shall be subject to judicial review in the same manner as orders and decisions of the Administrator are subject to judicial review under this chapter.

(c) Costs and expenses

Whenever an order is issued under this section to abate such violation, at the request of the applicant, a sum equal to the aggregate amount of all costs and expenses (including the attorney's fees), as determined by the Secretary of Labor, to have been reasonably incurred by the applicant for, or in connection with, the institution and prosecution of such proceedings, shall be assessed against the person committing such violation.

(d) Deliberate violations by employee acting without direction from his employer or his agent
This section shall have no application to any employee who, acting without direction from his employer (or his agent) deliberately violates any prohibition of effluent limitation or other limitation under section 1311 or 1312 of this title, standards of performance under section 1316 of this title, effluent standard, prohibition or pretreatment standard under section 1317 of this title, or any other prohibition or limitation established under this chapter.

(e) Investigations of employment reductions
The Administrator shall conduct continuing evaluations of potential loss or shifts of employment which may result from the issuance of any effluent limitation or order under this chapter, including, where appropriate, investigating threatened plant closures or reductions in employment allegedly resulting from such limitation or order. Any employee who is discharged or laid-off, threatened with discharge or lay-off, or otherwise discriminated against by any person because of the alleged results of any effluent limitation or order issued under this chapter, or any representative of such employee, may request the Administrator to conduct a full investigation of the matter. The Administrator shall thereupon investigate the matter and, at the request of any party, shall hold public hearings on not less than five days notice, and shall at such hearings require the parties, including the employer involved, to present information relating to the actual or potential effect of such limitation or order on employment and on any alleged discharge, lay-off, or other discrimination and the detailed reasons or justification therefor. Any such hearing shall be of record and shall be subject to section 554 of title 5. Upon receiving the report of such investigation, the Administrator shall make findings of fact as to the effect of such effluent limitation or order on employment and on the alleged discharge, lay-off, or discrimination and shall make such recommendations as he deems appropriate. Such report, findings, and recommendations shall be available to the public. Nothing in this subsection shall be construed to require or authorize the Administrator to modify or withdraw any effluent limitation or order issued under this chapter.

(June 30, 1948, ch. 758, title V, Sec. 507, as added Pub. L. 92-500, Sec. 2, Oct. 18, 1972, 86 Stat. 890.)

Section Referred to in Other Sections

This section is referred to in section 1369 of this title.

FEDERAL PROCUREMENT

33 USC 1368

(a) Contracts with violators prohibited
No Federal agency may enter into any contract with any person, who has been convicted of any offense under section 1319(c) of this title, for the procurement of goods, materials, and services if such contract is to be performed at any facility at which the violation which gave rise to such conviction occurred, and if such facility is owned, leased, or supervised by such person. The prohibition in the preceding sentence shall continue until the Administrator certifies that the condition giving rise to such conviction has been corrected.

(b) Notification of agencies
The Administrator shall establish procedures to provide all Federal agencies with the notification necessary for the purposes of subsection (a) of this section.

(c) Omitted

(d) Exemptions
The President may exempt any contract, loan, or grant from all or part of the provisions of this section where he determines such exemption is necessary in the paramount interest of the United States and he shall notify the Congress of such exemption.

(e) Annual report to Congress
The President shall annually report to the Congress on measures taken in compliance with the purpose and intent of this section, including, but not limited to, the progress and problems associated with such compliance.

(f) Contractor certification or contract clause in acquisition of commercial items
  (1) No certification by a contractor, and no contract clause, may be required in the case of a contract for the acquisition of commercial items in order to implement a prohibition or requirement of this section or a prohibition or requirement issued in the implementation of this section.
  (2) In paragraph (1), the term "commercial item" has the meaning given such term in section 403(12) of title 41.

(June 30, 1948, ch. 758, title V, Sec. 508, as added Pub. L. 92-500, Sec. 2, Oct. 18, 1972, 86 Stat. 891; amended Pub. L. 103-355, title VIII, Sec. 8301(a), Oct. 13, 1994, 108 Stat. 3396.)

Codification

Subsec. (c) authorized the President to cause to be issued, not more than 180 days after October 18, 1972, an order (1) requiring each Federal agency authorized to enter into contracts or to extend Federal assistance by way of grant, loan, or contract, to effectuate the purpose and policy of this chapter, and (2) setting forth procedures, sanctions and penalties as the President determines necessary to carry out such requirement.

Amendments

1994—Subsec. (f). Pub. L. 103-355 added subsec. (f).

Effective Date of 1994 Amendment

For effective date and applicability of amendment by Pub. L. 103-355, see section 10001 of Pub. L. 103-355, set out as a note under section 251 of Title 41, Public Contracts.

Administration of Chapter With Respect to Federal Contracts, Grants, or Loans

For provisions concerning the administration of this chapter with respect to Federal contracts, grants, or loans, see Ex. Ord. No. 11738, Sept. 10, 1973, 38 F.R. 25161, set out as a note under section 7606 of Title 42, The Public Health and Welfare.

ADMINISTRATIVE PROCEDURE AND JUDICIAL REVIEW

33 USC 1369

(a) Subpenas
  (1) For purposes of obtaining information under section 1315 of this title, or carrying out section 1367(e) of this title, the Administrator may issue subpenas for the attendance and testimony of witnesses and the production of relevant papers, books, and documents, and he may administer oaths. Except for effluent data, upon a showing satisfactory to the Administrator that such papers, books, documents, or information or particular part thereof, if made public, would divulge trade secrets or secret processes, the Administrator shall consider such record, report, or information or particular portion thereof confidential in accordance with the purposes of section 1905 of title 18, except that such paper, book, document, or information may be disclosed to other officers, employees, or authorized representatives of the United States concerned with carrying out this chapter, or when relevant in any proceeding under this chapter. Witnesses summoned shall be paid the same fees and mileage that are paid witnesses in the courts of the United States. In case of contumacy or refusal to obey a subpena served upon any person under this subsection, the district court of the United States for any district in which such person is found or resides or transacts business, upon application by the United States and after notice to such person, shall have jurisdiction to issue an order requiring such person to appear and give testimony before the Administrator, to appear and produce papers, books, and documents before the Administrator, or both, and any failure to obey such order of the court may be punished by such court as a contempt thereof.
  (2) The district courts of the United States are authorized, upon application by the Administrator, to issue subpenas for attendance and testimony of witnesses and the production of relevant papers, books, and documents, for purposes of obtaining information under sections 1314(b) and (c) of this title. Any papers, books, documents, or other information or part thereof, obtained by reason of such a subpena shall be subject to the same requirements as are provided in paragraph (1) of this subsection.

658 / Environmental Statutes

(b) Review of Administrator's actions; selection of court; fees
  (1) Review of the Administrator's action (A) in promulgating any standard of performance under section 1316 of this title, (B) in making any determination pursuant to section 1316(b)(1)(C) of this title, (C) in promulgating any effluent standard, prohibition, or pretreatment standard under section 1317 of this title, (D) in making any determination as to a State permit program submitted under section 1342(b) of this title, (E) in approving or promulgating any effluent limitation or other limitation under section 1311, 1312, 1316, or 1345 of this title, (F) in issuing or denying any permit under section 1342 of this title, and (G) in promulgating any individual control strategy under section 1314(l) of this title, may be had by any interested person in the Circuit Court of Appeals of the United States for the Federal judicial district in which such person resides or transacts business which is directly affected by such action upon application by such person. Any such application shall be made within 120 days from the date of such determination, approval, promulgation, issuance or denial, or after such date only if such application is based solely on grounds which arose after such 120th day.
  (2) Action of the Administrator with respect to which review could have been obtained under paragraph (1) of this subsection shall not be subject to judicial review in any civil or criminal proceeding for enforcement.
  (3) Award of fees.—In any judicial proceeding under this subsection, the court may award costs of litigation (including reasonable attorney and expert witness fees) to any prevailing or substantially prevailing party whenever it determines that such award is appropriate.
(c) Additional evidence
  In any judicial proceeding brought under subsection (b) of this section in which review is sought of a determination under this chapter required to be made on the record after notice and opportunity for hearing, if any party applies to the court for leave to adduce additional evidence, and shows to the satisfaction of the court that such additional evidence is material and that there were reasonable grounds for the failure to adduce such evidence in the proceeding before the Administrator, the court may order such additional evidence (and evidence in rebuttal thereof) to be taken before the Administrator, in such manner and upon such terms and conditions as the court may deem proper. The Administrator may modify his findings as to the facts, or make new findings, by reason of the additional evidence so taken and he shall file such modified or new findings, and his recommendation, if any, for the modification or setting aside of his original determination, with the return of such additional evidence.

(June 30, 1948, ch. 758, title V, Sec. 509, as added Pub. L. 92-500, Sec. 2, Oct. 18, 1972, 86 Stat. 891; amended Pub. L. 93-207, Sec. 1(6), Dec. 28, 1973, 87 Stat. 906; Pub. L. 100-4, title III, Sec. 308(b), title IV, Sec. 406(d)(3), title V, Sec. 505(a), (b), Feb. 4, 1987, 101 Stat. 39, 73, 75; Pub. L. 100-236, Sec. 2, Jan. 8, 1988, 101 Stat. 1732.)

Amendments

1988—Subsec. (b)(3), (4). Pub. L. 100-236 redesignated par. (4) as (3) and struck out former par. (3) relating to venue, which provided for selection procedure in subpar. (A), administrative provisions in subpar. (B), and transfers in subpar. (C).

1987—Subsec. (b)(1). Pub. L. 100-4, Secs. 308(b), 406(d)(3), 505(a), substituted "transacts business which is directly affected by such action" for "transacts such business", "120" for "ninety", and "120th" for "ninetieth", substituted "1316, or 1345 of this title" for "or 1316 of this title" in cl. (E), and added cl. (G).

Subsec. (b)(3), (4). Pub. L. 100-4, Sec. 505(b), added pars. (3) and (4).

1973—Subsec. (b)(1)(C). Pub. L. 93-207 substituted "pretreatment" for "treatment".

Effective Date of 1988 Amendment

Amendment by Pub. L. 100-236 effective 180 days after Jan. 8, 1988, see section 3 of Pub. L. 100-236, set out as a note under section 2112 of Title 28, Judiciary and Judicial Procedure.

STATE AUTHORITY

33 USC 1370

Except as expressly provided in this chapter, nothing in this chapter shall (1) preclude or deny the right of any State or political subdivision thereof or interstate agency to adopt or enforce (A) any standard or limitation respecting discharges of pollutants, or (B) any requirement respecting control or abatement of pollution; except that if an effluent limitation, or other limitation, effluent standard, prohibition, pretreatment standard, or standard of performance is in effect under this chapter, such State or political subdivision or interstate agency may not adopt or enforce any effluent limitation, or other limitation, effluent standard, prohibition, pretreatment standard, or standard of performance which is less stringent than the effluent limitation, or other limitation, effluent standard, prohibition, pretreatment standard, or standard of performance under this chapter; or (2) be construed as impairing or in any manner affecting any right or jurisdiction of the States with respect to the waters (including boundary waters) of such States.

(June 30, 1948, ch. 758, title V, Sec. 510, as added Pub. L. 92-500, Sec. 2, Oct. 18, 1972, 86 Stat. 893.)

Section Referred to in Other Sections

This section is referred to in sections 1311, 1342 of this title.

AUTHORITY UNDER OTHER LAWS AND REGULATIONS

33 USC 1371

(a) Impairment of authority or functions of officials and agencies; treaty provisions

This chapter shall not be construed as (1) limiting the authority or functions of any officer or agency of the United States under any other law or regulation not inconsistent with this chapter; (2) affecting or impairing the authority of the Secretary of the Army (A) to maintain navigation or (B) under the Act of March 3, 1899, (30 Stat. 1112); except that any permit issued under section 1344 of this title shall be conclusive as to the effect on water quality of any discharge resulting from any activity subject to section 403 of this title, or (3) affecting or impairing the provisions of any treaty of the United States.

(b) Discharges of pollutants into navigable waters

Discharges of pollutants into the navigable waters subject to the Rivers and Harbors Act of 1910 (36 Stat. 593; 33 U.S.C. 421) and the Supervisory Harbors Act of 1888 (25 Stat. 209; 33 U.S.C. 441-451b) shall be regulated pursuant to this chapter, and not subject to such Act of 1910 and the Act of 1888 except as to effect on navigation and anchorage.

(c) Action of the Administrator deemed major Federal action; construction of the National Environmental Policy Act of 1969

(1) Except for the provision of Federal financial assistance for the purpose of assisting the construction of publicly owned treatment works as authorized by section 1281 of this title, and the issuance of a permit under section 1342 of this title for the discharge of any pollutant by a new source as defined in section 1316 of this title, no action of the Administrator taken pursuant to this chapter shall be deemed a major Federal action significantly affecting the quality of the human environment within the meaning of the National Environmental Policy Act of 1969 (83 Stat. 852) [42 U.S.C. 4321 et seq.]; and

(2) Nothing in the National Environmental Policy Act of 1969 (83 Stat. 852) shall be deemed to—

   (A) authorize any Federal agency authorized to license or permit the conduct of any activity which may result in the discharge of a pollutant into the navigable waters to review any effluent limitation or other requirement established pursuant to this chapter or the adequacy of any certification under section 1341 of this title; or

   (B) authorize any such agency to impose, as a condition precedent to the issuance of any license or permit, any effluent limitation other than any such limitation established pursuant to this chapter.

660 / Environmental Statutes

(d) Consideration of international water pollution control agreements
Notwithstanding this chapter or any other provision of law, the Administrator (1) shall not require any State to consider in the development of the ranking in order of priority of needs for the construction of treatment works (as defined in subchapter II of this chapter), any water pollution control agreement which may have been entered into between the United States and any other nation, and (2) shall not consider any such agreement in the approval of any such priority ranking.

(June 30, 1948, ch. 758, title V, Sec. 511, as added Pub. L. 92-500, Sec. 2, Oct. 18, 1972, 86 Stat. 893; amended Pub. L. 93-243, Sec. 3, Jan. 2, 1974, 87 Stat. 1069.)

References in Text

Act of March 3, 1899, referred to in subsec. (a), is act Mar. 3, 1899, ch. 425, 30 Stat. 1121, as amended, which enacted sections 401, 403, 404, 406, 407, 408, 409, 411 to 416, 418, 502, 549, and 687 of this title and amended section 686 of this title. For complete classification of this Act to the Code, see Tables.

The Rivers and Harbors Act of 1910, referred to in subsec. (b), probably means act June 23, 1910, ch. 359, 36 Stat. 593.

The Supervisory Harbors Act of 1888, referred to in subsec. (b), probably means act June 29, 1888, ch. 496, 25 Stat. 209, as amended, which is classified generally to subchapter III (Sec. 441 et seq.) of chapter 9 of this title. For complete classification of this Act to the Code, see Tables.

The National Environmental Policy Act of 1969, referred to in subsec. (c), is Pub. L. 91-190, Jan. 1, 1970, 83 Stat. 852, as amended, which is classified generally to chapter 55 (Sec. 4321 et seq.) of Title 42, The Public Health and Welfare. For complete classification of this Act to the Code, see Short Title note set out under section 4321 of Title 42 and Tables.

Amendments

1974—Subsec. (d). Pub. L. 93-243 added subsec. (d).

Section Referred to in Other Sections

This section is referred to in sections 1341, 1382 of this title.

LABOR STANDARDS

33 USC 1372

The Administrator shall take such action as may be necessary to insure that all laborers and mechanics employed by contractors or subcontractors on treatment works for which grants are made under this chapter shall be paid wages at rates not less than those prevailing for the same type of work on similar construction in the immediate locality, as determined by the Secretary of Labor, in accordance with the Davis-Bacon Act (46 Stat. 1494; 40 U.S.C., sec. 276a through 276a-5). The Secretary of Labor shall have, with respect to the labor standards specified in this subsection, the authority and functions set forth in Reorganization Plan Numbered 14 of 1950 (15 F.R. 3176) and section 276c of title 40.

(June 30, 1948, ch. 758, title V, Sec. 513, as added Pub. L. 92-500, Sec. 2, Oct. 18, 1972, 86 Stat. 894.)

References in Text

The Davis-Bacon Act, referred to in text, is act Mar. 3, 1931, ch. 411, 46 Stat. 1494, as amended, which is classified generally to sections 276a to 276a-5 of Title 40, Public Buildings, Property, and Works. For complete classification of this Act to the Code, see Short Title note set out under section 276a of Title 40 and Tables.

Reorganization Plan Numbered 14 of 1950, referred to in text, is Reorg. Plan No. 14 of 1950, eff. May 24, 1950, 15 F.R. 3176, 64 Stat. 1267, which is set out in the Appendix to Title 5, Government Organization and Employees.

Section Referred to in Other Sections

This section is referred to in section 1382 of this title.

PUBLIC HEALTH AGENCY COORDINATION

33 USC 1373

The permitting agency under section 1342 of this title shall assist the applicant for a permit under such section in coordinating the requirements of this chapter with those of the appropriate public health agencies.

(June 30, 1948, ch. 758, title V, Sec. 514, as added Pub. L. 92-500, Sec. 2, Oct. 18, 1972, 86 Stat. 894.)

EFFLUENT STANDARDS AND WATER QUALITY INFORMATION ADVISORY COMMITTEE

33 USC 1374

(a) Establishment; membership; term
   (1) There is established an Effluent Standards and Water Quality Information Advisory Committee, which shall be composed of a Chairman and eight members who shall be appointed by the Administrator within sixty days after October 18, 1972.
   (2) All members of the Committee shall be selected from the scientific community, qualified by education, training, and experience to provide, assess, and evaluate scientific and technical information on effluent standards and limitations.
   (3) Members of the Committee shall serve for a term of four years, and may be reappointed.
(b) Action on proposed regulations
   (1) No later than one hundred and eighty days prior to the date on which the Administrator is required to publish any proposed regulations required by section 1314(b) of this title, any proposed standard of performance for new sources required by section 1316 of this title, or any proposed toxic effluent standard required by section 1317 of this title, he shall transmit to the Committee a notice of intent to propose such regulations. The Chairman of the Committee within ten days after receipt of such notice may publish a notice of a public hearing by the Committee, to be held within thirty days.
   (2) No later than one hundred and twenty days after receipt of such notice, the Committee shall transmit to the Administrator such scientific and technical information as is in its possession, including that presented at any public hearing, related to the subject matter contained in such notice.
   (3) Information so transmitted to the Administrator shall constitute a part of the administrative record and comments on any proposed regulations or standards as information to be considered with other comments and information in making any final determinations.
   (4) In preparing information for transmittal, the Committee shall avail itself of the technical and scientific services of any Federal agency, including the United States Geological Survey and any national environmental laboratories which may be established.
(c) Secretary; legal counsel; compensation
   (1) The Committee shall appoint and prescribe the duties of a Secretary, and such legal counsel as it deems necessary. The Committee shall appoint such other employees as it deems necessary to exercise and fulfill its powers and responsibilities. The compensation of all employees appointed by the Committee shall be fixed in accordance with chapter 51 and subchapter III of chapter 53 of title 5.
   (2) Members of the Committee shall be entitled to receive compensation at a rate to be fixed by the President but not in excess of the maximum rate of pay for grade GS-18, as provided in the General Schedule under section 5332 of title 5.
(d) Quorum; special panel
   Five members of the Committee shall constitute a quorum, and official actions of the Committee shall be taken only on the affirmative vote of at least five members. A special panel composed of one or more members upon order of the Committee shall conduct any hearing authorized by this section and submit the transcript of such hearing to the entire Committee for its action thereon.
(e) Rules
   The Committee is authorized to make such rules as are necessary for the orderly transaction of its business.

(June 30, 1948, ch. 758, title V, Sec. 515, as added Pub. L. 92-500, Sec. 2, Oct. 18, 1972, 86 Stat. 894.)

Termination of Advisory Committees

Advisory committees in existence on Jan. 5, 1973, to terminate not later than the expiration of the 2-year period following Jan. 5, 1973, unless, in the case of a committee established by the President or an officer of the Federal Government, such committee is renewed by appropriate action prior to the expiration of such 2-year period, or in the case of a committee established by the Congress, its duration is otherwise provided by law. See section 14 of Pub. L. 92-463, Oct. 6, 1972, 86 Stat. 776, set out in the Appendix to Title 5, Government Organization and Employees.

References in Other Laws to GS-16, 17, or 18 Pay Rates

References in laws to the rates of pay for GS-16, 17, or 18, or to maximum rates of pay under the General Schedule, to be considered references to rates payable under specified sections of Title 5, Government Organization and Employees, see section 529 [title I, Sec. 101(c)(1)] of Pub. L. 101-509, set out in a note under section 5376 of Title 5.

REPORTS TO CONGRESS; DETAILED ESTIMATES AND COMPREHENSIVE STUDY ON COSTS; STATE ESTIMATES

33 USC 1375

The Administrator, in cooperation with the States, including water pollution control agencies and other water pollution control planning agencies, shall make (1) a detailed estimate of the cost of carrying out the provisions of this chapter; (2) a detailed estimate, biennially revised, of the cost of construction of all needed publicly owned treatment works in all of the States and of the cost of construction of all needed publicly owned treatment works in each of the States; (3) a comprehensive study of the economic impact on affected units of government of the cost of installation of treatment facilities; and (4) a comprehensive analysis of the national requirements for and the cost of treating municipal, industrial, and other effluent to attain the water quality objectives as established by this chapter or applicable State law. The Administrator shall submit such detailed estimate and such comprehensive study of such cost to the Congress no later than February 10 of each odd-numbered year. Whenever the Administrator, pursuant to this subsection, requests and receives an estimate of cost from a State, he shall furnish copies of such estimate together with such detailed estimate to Congress.

(June 30, 1948, ch. 758, title V, Sec. 516, as added Pub. L. 92-500, Sec. 2, Oct. 18, 1972, 86 Stat. 895; amended Pub. L. 93-243, Sec. 4, Jan. 2, 1974, 87 Stat. 1069; Pub. L. 95-217, Secs. 70-72, Dec. 27, 1977, 91 Stat. 1608, 1609; Pub. L. 100-4, title II, Sec. 212(c), Feb. 4, 1987, 101 Stat. 27; Pub. L. 104-66, title II, Sec. 2021(d), Dec. 21, 1995, 109 Stat. 727; Pub. L. 105-362, title V, Sec. 501(d)(1), Nov. 10, 1998, 112 Stat. 3283.)

Amendments

1998—Subsec. (a). Pub. L. 105-362, Sec. 501(d)(1)(A), struck out subsec. (a) which related to implementation of chapter objectives and status and progress of programs.

Subsec. (b). Pub. L. 105-362 struck out par. (1) designation, redesignated subpars. (A) to (D) as pars. (1) to (4), respectively, and struck out former par. (2) which read as follows: "Notwithstanding the second sentence of paragraph (1) of this subsection, the Administrator shall make a preliminary detailed estimate called for by subparagraph (B) of such paragraph and shall submit such preliminary detailed estimate to the Congress no later than September 3, 1974. The Administrator shall require each State to prepare an estimate of cost for such State, and shall utilize the survey form EPA-1, O.M.B. No. 158-R0017, prepared for the 1973 detailed estimate, except that such estimate shall include all costs of compliance with section 1281(g)(2)(A) of this title and water quality standards established pursuant to section 1313 of this title, and all costs of treatment works as defined in section 1292(2) of this title, including all eligible costs of constructing sewage collection systems and correcting excessive infiltration or inflow and all eligible costs of correcting combined storm and sanitary sewer problems and treating storm water flows. The survey form shall be distributed by the Administrator to each State no later than January 31, 1974."

Subsecs. (c) to (e). Pub. L. 105-362, Sec. 501(d)(1)(A), struck out subsecs. (c) to (e) which related to status of combined sewer overflows in municipal treatment works operations, legislative recommendations on program requiring coordination between water supply and wastewater control plans as condition for construction grants and public hearing, and State revolving fund report, respectively.

1995—Subsecs. (d), (e), (g). Pub. L. 104-66 redesignated subsecs. (e) and (g) as (d) and (e), respectively, and struck out former subsec. (d) which related to status reports on the use of municipal secondary effluent and sludge for agricultural and other purposes that utilize the nutrient value of treated wastewater effluent.

1987—Subsec. (g). Pub. L. 100-4 added subsec. (g).

1977—Subsecs. (c) to (e). Pub. L. 95-217 added subsecs. (c) to (e).

1974—Subsec. (b). Pub. L. 93-243 designated existing paragraph as par. (1) and cls. (1) to (4) as (A) to (D), and added par. (2).

Studies and Reports

Pub. L. 100-4, title III, Sec. 308(g), Feb. 4, 1987, 101 Stat. 40, directed Administrator to conduct a water quality improvement study and report results of such study to specified Congressional committees not later than 2 years after Feb. 4, 1987.

Pub. L. 100-4, title III, Sec. 314(b), Feb. 4, 1987, 101 Stat. 49, directed Secretary of the Army and Administrator to each prepare a report on enforcement mechanisms and to submit the reports to Congress not later than Dec. 1, 1988.

Pub. L. 100-4, title IV, Sec. 404(c), Feb. 4, 1987, 101 Stat. 69, directed Administrator to study extent to which States have adopted water quality standards in accordance with section 1313a of this title and extent to which modifications of permits issued under section 1342(a)(1)(B) of this title for the purpose of reflecting revisions of water quality standards be encouraged and to submit a report on such study to Congress not later than 2 years after Feb. 4, 1987, prior to repeal by Pub. L. 104-66, title II, Sec. 2021(e)(1), Dec. 21, 1995, 109 Stat. 727.

Pub. L. 100-4, title V, Sec. 516, Feb. 4, 1987, 101 Stat. 86, directed Administrator to conduct a study of de minimis discharges and report results of such study to specified Congressional committees not later than 1 year after Feb. 4, 1987.

Pub. L. 100-4, title V, Sec. 517, Feb. 4, 1987, 101 Stat. 86, directed Administrator to conduct a study of effectiveness of innovative and alternative wastewater processes and techniques and report results of such study to specified Congressional committees not later than 1 year after Feb. 4, 1987.

Pub. L. 100-4, title V, Sec. 518, Feb. 4, 1987, 101 Stat. 86, directed Administrator to conduct a study of testing procedures established under section 1314(h) of this title for analysis of pollutants and report results of such study to specified Congressional committees not later than 1 year after Feb. 4, 1987.

Pub. L. 100-4, title V, Sec. 519, Feb. 4, 1987, 101 Stat. 87, directed Administrator to conduct a study of pretreatment of toxic pollutants and report results of such study to specified Congressional committees not later than 4 years after Feb. 4, 1987.

Pub. L. 100-4, title V, Sec. 520, Feb. 4, 1987, 101 Stat. 87, directed Administrator, in conjunction with State and local agencies, to conduct studies of water pollution problems in aquifers and report result of such studies to Congress not later than 2 years after Feb. 4, 1987.

Pub. L. 100-4, title V, Sec. 522, Feb. 4, 1987, 101 Stat. 88, directed Administrator to conduct a study on sulfide corrosion in collection and treatment systems and report results of such study to specified Congressional committees not later than 1 year after Feb. 4, 1987.

Pub. L. 100-4, title V, Sec. 523, Feb. 4, 1987, 101 Stat. 89, directed Administrator to conduct a study of rainfall induced infiltration into sewer systems and report results of such study to Congress not later than 1 year after Feb. 4, 1987.

Pub. L. 100-4, title V, Sec. 524, Feb. 4, 1987, 101 Stat. 89, directed Administrator to conduct a study of dam water quality and report results of such study to Congress not later than Dec. 31, 1987.

Pub. L. 100-4, title V, Sec. 525, Feb. 4, 1987, 101 Stat. 89, directed Administrator to conduct a study of pollution in Lake Pend Oreille, Idaho, and the Clark Fork River and its tributaries, Idaho, Montana, and Washington, and to report to Congress findings and recommendations.

Detailed Estimates, Comprehensive Study, and Comprehensive Analysis; Report to Congress not Later Than December 31, 1982

Pub. L. 97-117, Sec. 25, Dec. 29, 1981, 95 Stat. 1633, provided that the Administrator of the Environmental Protection Agency submit to the Congress, not later than December 31, 1982, a report containing the detailed estimates, comprehensive study, and comprehensive analysis required by section 1375(b) of this title, including an estimate of the total cost and the amount of Federal funds necessary for the construction of needed publicly owned treatment facilities, such report to reflect the changes made in the Federal water pollution control program by Pub. L. 97-117 [see Short Title of 1981 Amendment note set out under section 1251 of this title]. The Administrator was to give emphasis to the effects of the amendment made by section 2(a) of Pub. L. 97-117 [amending section 1281(g)(1) of this title] in addressing water quality needs adequately and appropriately.

Study and Report to Congress by Secretary of the Interior of Financing Water Pollution Prevention, Control, and Abatement Programs

Pub. L. 91-224, title I, Sec. 109, Apr. 3, 1970, 34 Stat. 113, directed the Secretary of the Interior to conduct a full and complete investigation and study of the feasibility of all methods of financing the cost of preventing, controlling, and abating water pollution, other than methods authorized by existing law, with results of such investigation and study to be reported to Congress no later than Dec. 31, 1970, together with the recommendations of the Secretary for financing the programs for preventing, controlling, and abating water pollution for the fiscal years beginning after fiscal year 1971, including any necessary legislation.

Termination of Advisory Boards

Advisory boards in existence on Jan. 5, 1973, to terminate not later than the expiration of the 2-year period following Jan. 5, 1973, unless, in the case of a board established by the President or an officer of the Federal Government, such board is renewed by appropriate action prior to the expiration of such 2-year period, or in the case of a board established by the Congress, its duration is otherwise provided by law, see sections 3(2) and 14 of Pub. L. 92-463, Oct. 6, 1972, 86 Stat. 770, 776, set out in the Appendix to Title 5, Government Organization and Employees.

Section Referred to in Other Sections

This section is referred to in sections 1266, 1285 of this title.

REPORT ON COASTAL RECREATION WATERS

33 USC 1375a

(a) In general

Not later than 4 years after October 10, 2000, and every 4 years thereafter, the Administrator of the Environmental Protection Agency shall submit to Congress a report that includes—
   (1) recommendations concerning the need for additional water quality criteria for pathogens and pathogen indicators and other actions that should be taken to improve the quality of coastal recreation waters;
   (2) an evaluation of Federal, State, and local efforts to implement this Act, including the amendments made by this Act; and
   (3) recommendations on improvements to methodologies and techniques for monitoring of coastal recreation waters.

(b) Coordination

The Administrator of the Environmental Protection Agency may coordinate the report under this section with other reporting requirements under the Federal Water Pollution Control Act (33 U.S.C. 1251 et seq.).

(Pub. L. 106-284, Sec. 7, Oct. 10, 2000, 114 Stat. 876.)

References in Text

This Act, referred to in subsec. (a)(2), is Pub. L. 106-284, Oct. 10, 2000, 114 Stat. 870, known as the Beaches Environmental Assessment and Coastal Health Act of 2000. For complete classification of this Act to the Code, see Short Title of 2000 Amendment note set out under section 1251 of this title and Tables.

The Federal Water Pollution Control Act, referred to in subsec. (b), is act June 30, 1948, ch. 758, as amended generally by Pub. L. 92-500, Sec. 2, Oct. 18, 1972, 86 Stat. 816, which is classified generally to this chapter. For complete classification of this Act to the Code, see Short Title note set out under section 1251 of this title and Tables.

Codification

Section was enacted as part of the Beaches Environmental Assessment and Coastal Health Act of 2000, and not as part of the Federal Water Pollution Control Act which comprises this chapter.

AUTHORIZATION OF APPROPRIATIONS

33 USC 1376

There are authorized to be appropriated to carry out this chapter, other than sections 1254, 1255, 1256(a), 1257, 1258, 1262, 1263, 1264, 1265, 1286, 1287, 1288(f) and (h), 1289, 1314, 1321(c), (d), (i), (l), and (k),[1] 1324, 1325, and 1327 of this title, $250,000,000 for the fiscal year ending June 30, 1973, $300,000,000 for the fiscal year ending June 30, 1974, $350,000,000 for the fiscal year ending June 30, 1975, $100,000,000 for the fiscal year ending September 30, 1977, $150,000,000 for the fiscal year ending September 30, 1978, $150,000,000 for the fiscal year ending September 30, 1979, $150,000,000 for the fiscal year ending September 30, 1980, $150,000,000 for the fiscal year ending September 30, 1981, $161,000,000 for the fiscal year ending September 30, 1982, such sums as may be necessary for fiscal years 1983 through 1985, and $135,000,000 per fiscal year for each of the fiscal years 1986 through 1990.

(June 30, 1948, ch. 758, title V, Sec. 517, as added Pub. L. 92-500, Sec. 2, Oct. 18, 1972, 86 Stat. 896; amended Pub. L. 95-217, Sec. 4(g), Dec. 27, 1977, 91 Stat. 1567; Pub. L. 96-483, Sec. 1(g), Oct. 21, 1980, 94 Stat. 2360; Pub. L. 100-4, title I, Sec. 101(h), Feb. 4, 1987, 101 Stat. 9.)

References in Text

Section 1321(k) of this title, referred to in text, was repealed by Pub. L. 101-380, title II, Sec. 2002(b)(2), Aug. 18, 1990, 104 Stat. 507.

Amendments

1987—Pub. L. 100-4 struck out "and" after "1981," and inserted ", such sums as may be necessary for fiscal years 1983 through 1985, and $135,000,000 per fiscal year for each of the fiscal years 1986 through 1990" after "1982".

1980—Pub. L. 96-483 inserted authorization of $150,000,000 for fiscal year ending Sept. 30, 1981 and $161,000,000 for fiscal year ending Sept. 30, 1982.

1977—Pub. L. 95-217 substituted "$350,000,000 for the fiscal year ending June 30, 1975, $100,000,000 for the fiscal year ending September 30, 1977, $150,000,000 for the fiscal year ending September 30, 1978, $150,000,000 for the fiscal year ending September 30, 1979, and $150,000,000 for the fiscal year ending September 30, 1980" for "and $350,000,000 for the fiscal year ending June 30, 1975".

Authorization Approval for Funds Appropriated Before December 27, 1977, for Expenditures Through Fiscal Year Ending September 30, 1977

Section 3 of Pub. L. 95-217 provided that funds appropriated before Dec. 27, 1977 for expenditure during the fiscal year ending June 30, 1976, the transition quarter ending September 30, 1976, and the fiscal year ending September 30, 1977, under authority of this chapter were authorized for those purposes for which appropriated.

INDIAN TRIBES

33 USC 1377

(a) Policy
    Nothing in this section shall be construed to affect the application of section 1251(g) of this title, and all of the provisions of this section shall be carried out in accordance with the provi-

---

[1] See References in Text note below.

sions of such section 1251(g) of this title. Indian tribes shall be treated as States for purposes of such section 1251(g) of this title.

(b) Assessment of sewage treatment needs; report

The Administrator, in cooperation with the Director of the Indian Health Service, shall assess the need for sewage treatment works to serve Indian tribes, the degree to which such needs will be met through funds allotted to States under section 1285 of this title and priority lists under section 1296 of this title, and any obstacles which prevent such needs from being met. Not later than one year after February 4, 1987, the Administrator shall submit a report to Congress on the assessment under this subsection, along with recommendations specifying (1) how the Administrator intends to provide assistance to Indian tribes to develop waste treatment management plans and to construct treatment works under this chapter, and (2) methods by which the participation in and administration of programs under this chapter by Indian tribes can be maximized.

(c) Reservation of funds

The Administrator shall reserve each fiscal year beginning after September 30, 1986, before allotments to the States under section 1285(e) of this title, one-half of one percent of the sums appropriated under section 1287 of this title. Sums reserved under this subsection shall be available only for grants for the development of waste treatment management plans and for the construction of sewage treatment works to serve Indian tribes, as defined in subsection (h) of this section and former Indian reservations in Oklahoma (as determined by the Secretary of the Interior) and Alaska Native Villages as defined in Public Law 92-203 [43 U.S.C. 1601 et seq.].

(d) Cooperative agreements

In order to ensure the consistent implementation of the requirements of this chapter, an Indian tribe and the State or States in which the lands of such tribe are located may enter into a cooperative agreement, subject to the review and approval of the Administrator, to jointly plan and administer the requirements of this chapter.

(e) Treatment as States

The Administrator is authorized to treat an Indian tribe as a State for purposes of subchapter II of this chapter and sections 1254, 1256, 1313, 1315, 1318, 1319, 1324, 1329, 1341, 1342, 1344, and 1346 of this title to the degree necessary to carry out the objectives of this section, but only if—

(1) the Indian tribe has a governing body carrying out substantial governmental duties and powers;

(2) the functions to be exercised by the Indian tribe pertain to the management and protection of water resources which are held by an Indian tribe, held by the United States in trust for Indians, held by a member of an Indian tribe if such property interest is subject to a trust restriction on alienation, or otherwise within the borders of an Indian reservation; and

(3) the Indian tribe is reasonably expected to be capable, in the Administrator's judgment, of carrying out the functions to be exercised in a manner consistent with the terms and purposes of this chapter and of all applicable regulations.

Such treatment as a State may include the direct provision of funds reserved under subsection (c) of this section to the governing bodies of Indian tribes, and the determination of priorities by Indian tribes, where not determined by the Administrator in cooperation with the Director of the Indian Health Service. The Administrator, in cooperation with the Director of the Indian Health Service, is authorized to make grants under subchapter II of this chapter in an amount not to exceed 100 percent of the cost of a project. Not later than 18 months after February 4, 1987, the Administrator shall, in consultation with Indian tribes, promulgate final regulations which specify how Indian tribes shall be treated as States for purposes of this chapter. The Administrator shall, in promulgating such regulations, consult affected States sharing common water bodies and provide a mechanism for the resolution of any unreasonable consequences that may arise as a result of differing water quality standards that may be set by States and Indian tribes located on common bodies of water. Such mechanism shall provide for explicit consideration of relevant factors including, but not limited to, the effects of differing water quality permit requirements on upstream and downstream dischargers, economic impacts, and present and historical uses and quality of the waters subject to such standards. Such mechanism should provide for the avoidance of such unreasonable consequences in a manner consistent with the objective of this chapter.

(f) Grants for nonpoint source programs
The Administrator shall make grants to an Indian tribe under section 1329 of this title as though such tribe was a State. Not more than one-third of one percent of the amount appropriated for any fiscal year under section 1329 of this title may be used to make grants under this subsection. In addition to the requirements of section 1329 of this title, an Indian tribe shall be required to meet the requirements of paragraphs (1), (2), and (3) of subsection (d)[1] of this section in order to receive such a grant.

(g) Alaska Native organizations
No provision of this chapter shall be construed to—
  (1) grant, enlarge, or diminish, or in any way affect the scope of the governmental authority, if any, of any Alaska Native organization, including any federally-recognized tribe, traditional Alaska Native council, or Native council organized pursuant to the Act of June 18, 1934 (48 Stat. 987), over lands or persons in Alaska;
  (2) create or validate any assertion by such organization or any form of governmental authority over lands or persons in Alaska; or
  (3) in any way affect any assertion that Indian country, as defined in section 1151 of title 18, exists or does not exist in Alaska.

(h) Definitions
For purposes of this section, the term—
  (1) "Federal Indian reservation" means all land within the limits of any Indian reservation under the jurisdiction of the United States Government, notwithstanding the issuance of any patent, and including rights-of-way running through the reservation; and
  (2) "Indian tribe" means any Indian tribe, band, group, or community recognized by the Secretary of the Interior and exercising governmental authority over a Federal Indian reservation.

(June 30, 1948, ch. 758, title V, Sec. 518, as added Pub. L. 100-4, title V, Sec. 506, Feb. 4, 1987, 101 Stat. 76; amended Pub. L. 100-581, title II, Sec. 207, Nov. 1, 1988, 102 Stat. 2940; Pub. L. 106-284, Sec. 6, Oct. 10, 2000, 114 Stat. 877.)

References in Text

Public Law 92-203, referred to in subsec. (c), is Pub. L. 92-203, Dec. 18, 1971, 85 Stat. 688, as amended, known as the Alaska Native Claims Settlement Act, which is classified generally to chapter 33 (Sec. 1601 et seq.) of Title 43, Public Lands. The term "Alaska Native Villages" is defined in section 3 of Pub. L. 92-203 which is classified to section 1602 of Title 43. For complete classification of this Act to the Code, see Short Title note set out under section 1601 of Title 43 and Tables.

Act of June 18, 1934 (48 Stat. 987), referred to in subsec. (g)(1), is act June 18, 1934, ch. 576, 48 Stat. 984, as amended, popularly known as the Indian Reorganization Act, which enacted sections 461, 462, 463, 464, 465, 466 to 470, 471, 472, 473, 474, 475, 476 to 478, and 479 of Title 25, Indians. For complete classification of this Act to the Code, see Short Title note set out under section 461 of Title 25 and Tables.

Prior Provisions

A prior section 518 of act June 30, 1948, was renumbered section 519 and is set out as a note under section 1251 of this title.

Amendments

2000—Subsec. (e). Pub. L. 106-284 substituted "1344, and 1346" for "and 1344".

1988—Subsec. (c). Pub. L. 100-581 inserted ", as defined in subsection (h) of this section and former Indian reservations in Oklahoma (as determined by the Secretary of the Interior) and Alaska Native Villages as defined in Public Law 92-203" before period at end.

---

[1] So in original. Probably should be subsection "(e)".

Grants to Indian Tribes

Pub. L. 107-73, July 25, 2001, 115 Stat. 685, provided in part: "That for fiscal year 2002, and notwithstanding section 518(f) [33 U.S.C. 1377(f)] of the Federal Water Pollution Control Act, as amended, the Administrator is authorized to use the amounts appropriated for any fiscal year under section 319 of that Act [33 U.S.C. 1329] to make grants to Indian tribes pursuant to section 319(h) and 518(e) of that Act."

Pub. L. 106-377, Oct. 27, 2000, 114 Stat. 1441A-43, provided in part: "That for fiscal year 2001, and notwithstanding section 518(f) of the Federal Water Pollution Control Act [33 U.S.C. 1377(f)], as amended, the Administrator is authorized to use the amounts appropriated for any fiscal year under section 319 of that Act [33 U.S.C. 1329] to make grants to Indian tribes pursuant to section 319(h) and 518(e) of that Act."

Pub. L. 106-74, title III, Oct. 20, 1999, 113 Stat. 1083, provided in part: "That notwithstanding section 518(f) of the Federal Water Pollution Control Act [33 U.S.C. 1377(f)], the Administrator is authorized to use the amounts appropriated for any fiscal year under section 319 of that Act [33 U.S.C. 1329] to make grants to Indian tribes pursuant to section 319(h) and 518(e) of that Act".

Administrative Provisions

Pub. L. 107-73, July 25, 2001, 115 Stat. 685, provided in part: "That for fiscal year 2002, notwithstanding the limitation on amounts in section 518(c) of the Act, up to a total of 1 1/2 percent of the funds appropriated for State Revolving Funds under title VI of that Act may be reserved by the Administrator for grants under section 518(c) of such Act."

Pub. L. 106-377, Oct. 27, 2000, 114 Stat. 1441A-43, provided in part: "That for fiscal year 2001, notwithstanding the limitation on amounts in section 518(c) of the Federal Water Pollution Control Act, as amended, up to a total of 1 1/2 percent of the funds appropriated for State Revolving Funds under title VI of that Act may be reserved by the Administrator for grants under section 518(c) of such Act."

SUBCHAPTER VI—STATE WATER POLLUTION CONTROL REVOLVING FUNDS

GRANTS TO STATES FOR ESTABLISHMENT OF REVOLVING FUNDS

33 USC 1381

(a) General authority

Subject to the provisions of this subchapter, the Administrator shall make capitalization grants to each State for the purpose of establishing a water pollution control revolving fund for providing assistance (1) for construction of treatment works (as defined in section 1292 of this title) which are publicly owned, (2) for implementing a management program under section 1329 of this title, and (3) for developing and implementing a conservation and management plan under section 1330 of this title.

(b) Schedule of grant payments

The Administrator and each State shall jointly establish a schedule of payments under which the Administrator will pay to the State the amount of each grant to be made to the State under this subchapter. Such schedule shall be based on the State's intended use plan under section 1386(c) of this title, except that—
  (1) such payments shall be made in quarterly installments, and
  (2) such payments shall be made as expeditiously as possible, but in no event later than the earlier of—
    (A) 8 quarters after the date such funds were obligated by the State, or
    (B) 12 quarters after the date such funds were allotted to the State.

(June 30, 1948, ch. 758, title VI, Sec. 601, as added Pub. L. 100-4, title II, Sec. 212(a), Feb. 4, 1987, 101 Stat. 22.)

CAPITALIZATION GRANT AGREEMENTS

33 USC 1382

(a) General rule

To receive a capitalization grant with funds made available under this subchapter and section 1285(m) of this title, a State shall enter into an agreement with the Administrator which shall include but not be limited to the specifications set forth in subsection (b) of this section.

(b) Specific requirements

The Administrator shall enter into an agreement under this section with a State only after the State has established to the satisfaction of the Administrator that—
  (1) the State will accept grant payments with funds to be made available under this subchapter and section 1285(m) of this title in accordance with a payment schedule established jointly by the Administrator under section 1381(b) of this title and will deposit all such payments in the water pollution control revolving fund established by the State in accordance with this subchapter;
  (2) the State will deposit in the fund from State moneys an amount equal to at least 20 percent of the total amount of all capitalization grants which will be made to the State with funds to be made available under this subchapter and section 1285(m) of this title on or before the date on which each quarterly grant payment will be made to the State under this subchapter;
  (3) the State will enter into binding commitments to provide assistance in accordance with the requirements of this subchapter in an amount equal to 120 percent of the amount of each such grant payment within 1 year after the receipt of such grant payment;
  (4) all funds in the fund will be expended in an expeditious and timely manner;
  (5) all funds in the fund as a result of capitalization grants under this subchapter and section 1285(m) of this title will first be used to assure maintenance of progress, as determined by the Governor of the State, toward compliance with enforceable deadlines, goals, and requirements of this chapter, including the municipal compliance deadline;

(6) treatment works eligible under section 1383(c)(1) of this title which will be constructed in whole or in part before fiscal year 1995 with funds directly made available by capitalization grants under this subchapter and section 1285(m) of this title will meet the requirements of, or otherwise be treated (as determined by the Governor of the State) under sections 1281(b), 1281(g)(1), 1281(g)(2), 1281(g)(3), 1281(g)(5), 1281(g)(6), 1281(n)(1), 1281(o), 1284(a)(1), 1284(a)(2), 1284(b)(1), 1284(d)(2), 1291, 1298, 1371(c)(1), and 1372 of this title in the same manner as treatment works constructed with assistance under subchapter II of this chapter;

(7) in addition to complying with the requirements of this subchapter, the State will commit or expend each quarterly grant payment which it will receive under this subchapter in accordance with laws and procedures applicable to the commitment or expenditure of revenues of the State;

(8) in carrying out the requirements of section 1386 of this title, the State will use accounting, audit, and fiscal procedures conforming to generally accepted government accounting standards;

(9) the State will require as a condition of making a loan or providing other assistance, as described in section 1383(d) of this title, from the fund that the recipient of such assistance will maintain project accounts in accordance with generally accepted government accounting standards; and

(10) the State will make annual reports to the Administrator on the actual use of funds in accordance with section 1386(d) of this title.

(June 30, 1948, ch. 758, title VI, Sec. 602, as added Pub. L. 100-4, title II, Sec. 212(a), Feb. 4, 1987, 101 Stat. 22.)

Section Referred to in Other Sections

This section is referred to in sections 1385, 1386 of this title.

WATER POLLUTION CONTROL REVOLVING LOAN FUNDS

33 USC 1383

(a) Requirements for obligation of grant funds
Before a State may receive a capitalization grant with funds made available under this subchapter and section 1285(m) of this title, the State shall first establish a water pollution control revolving fund which complies with the requirements of this section.

(b) Administration
Each State water pollution control revolving fund shall be administered by an instrumentality of the State with such powers and limitations as may be required to operate such fund in accordance with the requirements and objectives of this chapter.

(c) Projects eligible for assistance
The amounts of funds available to each State water pollution control revolving fund shall be used only for providing financial assistance (1) to any municipality, intermunicipal, interstate, or State agency for construction of publicly owned treatment works (as defined in section 1292 of this title), (2) for the implementation of a management program established under section 1329 of this title, and (3) for development and implementation of a conservation and management plan under section 1330 of this title. The fund shall be established, maintained, and credited with repayments, and the fund balance shall be available in perpetuity for providing such financial assistance.

(d) Types of assistance
Except as otherwise limited by State law, a water pollution control revolving fund of a State under this section may be used only—
  (1) to make loans, on the condition that—
    (A) such loans are made at or below market interest rates, including interest free loans, at terms not to exceed 20 years;
    (B) annual principal and interest payments will commence not later than 1 year after completion of any project and all loans will be fully amortized not later than 20 years after project completion;

(C) the recipient of a loan will establish a dedicated source of revenue for repayment of loans; and

(D) the fund will be credited with all payments of principal and interest on all loans;

(2) to buy or refinance the debt obligation of municipalities and intermunicipal and interstate agencies within the State at or below market rates, where such debt obligations were incurred after March 7, 1985;

(3) to guarantee, or purchase insurance for, local obligations where such action would improve credit market access or reduce interest rates;

(4) as a source of revenue or security for the payment of principal and interest on revenue or general obligation bonds issued by the State if the proceeds of the sale of such bonds will be deposited in the fund;

(5) to provide loan guarantees for similar revolving funds established by municipalities or intermunicipal agencies;

(6) to earn interest on fund accounts; and

(7) for the reasonable costs of administering the fund and conducting activities under this subchapter, except that such amounts shall not exceed 4 percent of all grant awards to such fund under this subchapter.

(e) Limitation to prevent double benefits
If a State makes, from its water pollution revolving fund, a loan which will finance the cost of facility planning and the preparation of plans, specifications, and estimates for construction of publicly owned treatment works, the State shall ensure that if the recipient of such loan receives a grant under section 1281(g) of this title for construction of such treatment works and an allowance under section 1281(l)(1) of this title for non-Federal funds expended for such planning and preparation, such recipient will promptly repay such loan to the extent of such allowance.

(f) Consistency with planning requirements
A State may provide financial assistance from its water pollution control revolving fund only with respect to a project which is consistent with plans, if any, developed under sections 1285(j), 1288, 1313(e), 1329, and 1330 of this title.

(g) Priority list requirement
The State may provide financial assistance from its water pollution control revolving fund only with respect to a project for construction of a treatment works described in subsection (c)(1) of this section if such project is on the State's priority list under section 1296 of this title. Such assistance may be provided regardless of the rank of such project on such list.

(h) Eligibility of non-Federal share of construction grant projects
A State water pollution control revolving fund may provide assistance (other than under subsection (d)(1) of this section) to a municipality or intermunicipal or interstate agency with respect to the non-Federal share of the costs of a treatment works project for which such municipality or agency is receiving assistance from the Administrator under any other authority only if such assistance is necessary to allow such project to proceed.

(June 30, 1948, ch. 758, title VI, Sec. 603, as added Pub. L. 100-4, title II, Sec. 212(a), Feb. 4, 1987, 101 Stat. 23.)

Section Referred to in Other Sections

This section is referred to in section 1382 of this title.

ALLOTMENT OF FUNDS

33 USC 1384

(a) Formula
Sums authorized to be appropriated to carry out this section for each of fiscal years 1989 and 1990 shall be allotted by the Administrator in accordance with section 1285(c) of this title.

(b) Reservation of funds for planning
Each State shall reserve each fiscal year 1 percent of the sums allotted to such State under this section for such fiscal year, or $100,000, whichever amount is greater, to carry out planning under sections 1285(j) and 1313(e) of this title.

(c) Allotment period
  (1) Period of availability for grant award
      Sums allotted to a State under this section for a fiscal year shall be available for obligation by the State during the fiscal year for which sums are authorized and during the following fiscal year.
  (2) Reallotment of unobligated funds
      The amount of any allotment not obligated by the State by the last day of the 2-year period of availability established by paragraph (1) shall be immediately reallotted by the Administrator on the basis of the same ratio as is applicable to sums allotted under subchapter II of this chapter for the second fiscal year of such 2-year period. None of the funds reallotted by the Administrator shall be reallotted to any State which has not obligated all sums allotted to such State in the first fiscal year of such 2-year period.

(June 30, 1948, ch. 758, title VI, Sec. 604, as added Pub. L. 100-4, title II, Sec. 212(a), Feb. 4, 1987, 101 Stat. 25.)

Use of Capitalization Grant Funds for Construction Grants

Pub. L. 101-144, title III, Nov. 9, 1989, 103 Stat. 858, as amended by Pub. L. 101-302, title II, May 25, 1990, 104 Stat. 238, provided: "That, notwithstanding any other provision of law, sums heretofore, herein or hereafter appropriated under this heading ["Environmental Protection Agency" and "construction grants"] allotted for title VI [33 U.S.C. 1381 et seq.] capitalization grants to American Samoa, Commonwealth of the Northern Mariana Islands, Guam, the Republic of Palau (or its successor entity), Virgin Islands and the District of Columbia, may be used for title II [33 U.S.C. 1281 et seq.] construction grants at the request of the chief executive of each of the above named entities, and sums appropriated in fiscal year 1989 shall remain available for obligation until September 30, 1992."

CORRECTIVE ACTION

33 USC 1385

(a) Notification of noncompliance
    If the Administrator determines that a State has not complied with its agreement with the Administrator under section 1382 of this title or any other requirement of this subchapter, the Administrator shall notify the State of such noncompliance and the necessary corrective action.

(b) Withholding of payments
    If a State does not take corrective action within 60 days after the date a State receives notification of such action under subsection (a) of this section, the Administrator shall withhold additional payments to the State until the Administrator is satisfied that the State has taken the necessary corrective action.

(c) Reallotment of withheld payments
    If the Administrator is not satisfied that adequate corrective actions have been taken by the State within 12 months after the State is notified of such actions under subsection (a) of this section, the payments withheld from the State by the Administrator under subsection (b) of this section shall be made available for reallotment in accordance with the most recent formula for allotment of funds under this subchapter.

(June 30, 1948, ch. 758, title VI, Sec. 605, as added Pub. L. 100-4, title II, Sec. 212(a), Feb. 4, 1987, 101 Stat. 25.)

AUDITS, REPORTS, AND FISCAL CONTROLS; INTENDED USE PLAN

33 USC 1386

(a) Fiscal control and auditing procedures
    Each State electing to establish a water pollution control revolving fund under this subchapter shall establish fiscal controls and accounting procedures sufficient to assure proper accounting during appropriate accounting periods for—
    (1) payments received by the fund;

(2) disbursements made by the fund; and
(3) fund balances at the beginning and end of the accounting period.

(b) Annual Federal audits

The Administrator shall, at least on an annual basis, conduct or require each State to have independently conducted reviews and audits as may be deemed necessary or appropriate by the Administrator to carry out the objectives of this section. Audits of the use of funds deposited in the water pollution revolving fund established by such State shall be conducted in accordance with the auditing procedures of the General Accounting Office, including chapter 75 of title 31.

(c) Intended use plan

After providing for public comment and review, each State shall annually prepare a plan identifying the intended uses of the amounts available to its water pollution control revolving fund. Such intended use plan shall include, but not be limited to—

(1) a list of those projects for construction of publicly owned treatment works on the State's priority list developed pursuant to section 1296 of this title and a list of activities eligible for assistance under sections 1329 and 1330 of this title;
(2) a description of the short- and long-term goals and objectives of its water pollution control revolving fund;
(3) information on the activities to be supported, including a description of project categories, discharge requirements under subchapters III and IV of this chapter, terms of financial assistance, and communities served;
(4) assurances and specific proposals for meeting the requirements of paragraphs (3), (4), (5), and (6) of section 1382(b) of this title; and
(5) the criteria and method established for the distribution of funds.

(d) Annual report

Beginning the first fiscal year after the receipt of payments under this subchapter, the State shall provide an annual report to the Administrator describing how the State has met the goals and objectives for the previous fiscal year as identified in the plan prepared for the previous fiscal year pursuant to subsection (c) of this section, including identification of loan recipients, loan amounts, and loan terms and similar details on other forms of financial assistance provided from the water pollution control revolving fund.

(e) Annual Federal oversight review

The Administrator shall conduct an annual oversight review of each State plan prepared under subsection (c) of this section, each State report prepared under subsection (d) of this section, and other such materials as are considered necessary and appropriate in carrying out the purposes of this subchapter. After reasonable notice by the Administrator to the State or the recipient of a loan from a water pollution control revolving fund, the State or loan recipient shall make available to the Administrator such records as the Administrator reasonably requires to review and determine compliance with this subchapter.

(f) Applicability of subchapter II provisions

Except to the extent provided in this subchapter, the provisions of subchapter II of this chapter shall not apply to grants under this subchapter.

(June 30, 1948, ch. 758, title VI, Sec. 606, as added Pub. L. 100-4, title II, Sec. 212(a), Feb. 4, 1987, 101 Stat. 25.)

Section Referred to in Other Sections

This section is referred to in sections 1381, 1382 of this title.

AUTHORIZATION OF APPROPRIATIONS

33 USC 1387

There is authorized to be appropriated to carry out the purposes of this subchapter the following sums:
(1) $1,200,000,000 per fiscal year for each of fiscal years 1989 and 1990;
(2) $2,400,000,000 for fiscal year 1991;

(3) $1,800,000,000 for fiscal year 1992;
(4) $1,200,000,000 for fiscal year 1993; and
(5) $600,000,000 for fiscal year 1994.

(June 30, 1948, ch. 758, title VI, Sec. 607, as added Pub. L. 100-4, title II, Sec. 212(a), Feb. 4, 1987, 101 Stat. 26.)

ESTUARY RESTORATION
[ESTUARY RESTORATION ACT OF 2000]

PURPOSES

33 USC 2901

The purposes of this chapter are—
  (1) to promote the restoration of estuary habitat;
  (2) to develop a national estuary habitat restoration strategy for creating and maintaining effective estuary habitat restoration partnerships among public agencies at all levels of government and to establish new partnerships between the public and private sectors;
  (3) to provide Federal assistance for estuary habitat restoration projects and to promote efficient financing of such projects; and
  (4) to develop and enhance monitoring and research capabilities through the use of the environmental technology innovation program associated with the National Estuarine Research Reserve System established by section 1461 of title 16 to ensure that estuary habitat restoration efforts are based on sound scientific understanding and innovative technologies.

(Pub. L. 106-457, title I, Sec. 102, Nov. 7, 2000, 114 Stat. 1958.)

Short Title

Pub. L. 106-457, Sec. 1(a), Nov. 7, 2000, 114 Stat. 1957, provided that: "This Act [enacting this chapter, sections 1273 and 1300 of this title, and sections 277d-43 to 277d-46 of Title 22, Foreign Relations and Intercourse, amending sections 1263a, 1267, 1269, 1324, and 1330 of this title, and enacting provisions set out as notes under this section, sections 1251 and 1267 of this title, and section 277d-43 of Title 22] may be cited as the 'Estuaries and Clean Waters Act of 2000'."

Pub. L. 106-457, title I, Sec. 101, Nov. 7, 2000, 114 Stat. 1958, provided that: "This title [enacting this chapter] may be cited as the 'Estuary Restoration Act of 2000'."

Purchase of American-Made Equipment and Products

Pub. L. 106-457, title IX, Sec. 901, Nov. 7, 2000, 114 Stat. 1981, provided that:

"(a) In General.—It is the sense of Congress that, to the extent practicable, all equipment and products purchased with funds made available under this Act [see Short Title note above] should be American made.

(b) Notice to Recipients of Assistance.—The head of each Federal Agency [sic] providing financial assistance under this Act, to the extent practicable, shall provide to each recipient of the assistance a notice describing the statement made in subsection (a)."

Long-Term Estuary Assessment

Pub. L. 106-457, title IX, Sec. 902, Nov. 7, 2000, 114 Stat. 1981, provided that:

"(a) In General.—The Secretary of Commerce (acting through the Under Secretary for Oceans and Atmosphere) and the Secretary of the Interior (acting through the Director of the Geological Survey) may carry out a long-term estuary assessment project (in this section referred to as the 'project') in accordance with the requirements of this section.

(b) Purpose.—The purpose of the project shall be to establish a network of strategic environmental assessment and monitoring projects for the Mississippi River south of Vicksburg, Mississippi, and the Gulf of Mexico, in order to develop advanced long-term assessment and monitoring systems and models relating to the Mississippi River and other aquatic ecosystems, including developing equipment and techniques necessary to implement the project.

(c) Management Agreement.—To establish, operate, and implement the project, the Secretary of Commerce and the Secretary of the Interior may enter into a management agreement with a university-based consortium.

(d) Authorization of Appropriations.—There is authorized to be appropriated—

(1) $1,000,000 for fiscal year 2001 to develop the management agreement under subsection (c); and
(2) $4,000,000 for each of fiscal years 2002, 2003, 2004, and 2005 to carry out the project.

Such sums shall remain available until expended."

DEFINITIONS

33 USC 2902

In this chapter, the following definitions apply:
  (1) Council
    The term "Council" means the Estuary Habitat Restoration Council established by section 2904 of this title.
  (2) Estuary
    The term "estuary" means a part of a river or stream or other body of water that has an unimpaired connection with the open sea and where the sea water is measurably diluted with fresh water derived from land drainage. The term also includes near coastal waters and wetlands of the Great Lakes that are similar in form and function to estuaries, including the area located in the Great Lakes biogeographic region and designated as a National Estuarine Research Reserve under the Coastal Zone Management Act of 1972 (16 U.S.C. 1451 et seq.) as of November 7, 2000.
  (3) Estuary habitat
    The term "estuary habitat" means the physical, biological, and chemical elements associated with an estuary, including the complex of physical and hydrologic features and living organisms within the estuary and associated ecosystems.
  (4) Estuary habitat restoration activity
    (A) In general
      The term "estuary habitat restoration activity" means an activity that results in improving degraded estuaries or estuary habitat or creating estuary habitat (including both physical and functional restoration), with the goal of attaining a self-sustaining system integrated into the surrounding landscape.
    (B) Included activities
      The term "estuary habitat restoration activity" includes—
      (i) the reestablishment of chemical, physical, hydrologic, and biological features and components associated with an estuary;
      (ii) except as provided in subparagraph (C), the cleanup of pollution for the benefit of estuary habitat;
      (iii) the control of nonnative and invasive species in the estuary;
      (iv) the reintroduction of species native to the estuary, including through such means as planting or promoting natural succession;
      (v) the construction of reefs to promote fish and shellfish production and to provide estuary habitat for living resources; and
      (vi) other activities that improve estuary habitat.
    (C) Excluded activities
      The term "estuary habitat restoration activity" does not include an activity that—
      (i) constitutes mitigation required under any Federal or State law for the adverse effects of an activity regulated or otherwise governed by Federal or State law; or
      (ii) constitutes restoration for natural resource damages required under any Federal or State law.
  (5) Estuary habitat restoration project
    The term "estuary habitat restoration project" means a project to carry out an estuary habitat restoration activity.
  (6) Estuary habitat restoration plan
    (A) In general
      The term "estuary habitat restoration plan" means any Federal or State plan for restoration of degraded estuary habitat that was developed with the substantial participation of appropriate public and private stakeholders.

(B) Included plans and programs
The term "estuary habitat restoration plan" includes estuary habitat restoration components of—
  (i) a comprehensive conservation and management plan approved under section 1330 of this title;
  (ii) a lakewide management plan or remedial action plan developed under section 1268 of this title;
  (iii) a management plan approved under the Coastal Zone Management Act of 1972 (16 U.S.C. 1451 et seq.); and
  (iv) the interstate management plan developed pursuant to the Chesapeake Bay program under section 1267 of this title.

(7) Indian tribe
The term "Indian tribe" has the meaning given such term by section 450b of title 25.

(8) Non-Federal interest
The term "non-Federal interest" means a State, a political subdivision of a State, an Indian tribe, a regional or interstate agency, or, as provided in section 2903(f)(2) of this title, a nongovernmental organization.

(9) Secretary
The term "Secretary" means the Secretary of the Army.

(10) State
The term "State" means the States of Alabama, Alaska, California, Connecticut, Delaware, Florida, Georgia, Hawaii, Illinois, Indiana, Louisiana, Maine, Maryland, Massachusetts, Michigan, Minnesota, Mississippi, New Hampshire, New Jersey, New York, North Carolina, Ohio, Oregon, Pennsylvania, Rhode Island, South Carolina, Texas, Virginia, Washington, and Wisconsin, the District of Columbia, the Commonwealth of Puerto Rico, the Commonwealth of the Northern Mariana Islands, the United States Virgin Islands, American Samoa, and Guam.

(Pub. L. 106-457, title I, Sec. 103, Nov. 7, 2000, 114 Stat. 1958.)

References in Text

The Coastal Zone Management Act of 1972, referred to in pars. (2) and (6)(B)(iii), is title III of Pub. L. 89-454 as added by Pub. L. 92-583, Oct. 27, 1972, 86 Stat. 1280, as amended, which is classified generally to chapter 33 (Sec. 1451 et seq.) of Title 16, Conservation. For complete classification of this Act to the Code, see Short Title note set out under section 1451 of Title 16 and Tables.

ESTUARY HABITAT RESTORATION PROGRAM

33 USC 2903

(a) Establishment
There is established an estuary habitat restoration program under which the Secretary may carry out estuary habitat restoration projects and provide technical assistance in accordance with the requirements of this chapter.

(b) Origin of projects
A proposed estuary habitat restoration project shall originate from a non-Federal interest consistent with State or local laws.

(c) Selection of projects
  (1) In general
  The Secretary shall select estuary habitat restoration projects from a list of project proposals submitted by the Estuary Habitat Restoration Council under section 2904(b) of this title.
  (2) Required elements
  Each estuary habitat restoration project selected by the Secretary must—
    (A) address restoration needs identified in an estuary habitat restoration plan;
    (B) be consistent with the estuary habitat restoration strategy developed under section 2905 of this title;

(C) include a monitoring plan that is consistent with standards for monitoring developed under section 2906 of this title to ensure that short-term and long-term restoration goals are achieved; and
(D) include satisfactory assurance from the non-Federal interests proposing the project that the non-Federal interests will have adequate personnel, funding, and authority to carry out items of local cooperation and properly maintain the project.
(3) Factors for selection of projects
In selecting an estuary habitat restoration project, the Secretary shall consider the following factors:
(A) Whether the project is part of an approved Federal estuary management or habitat restoration plan.
(B) The technical feasibility of the project.
(C) The scientific merit of the project.
(D) Whether the project will encourage increased coordination and cooperation among Federal, State, and local government agencies.
(E) Whether the project fosters public-private partnerships and uses Federal resources to encourage increased private sector involvement, including consideration of the amount of private funds or in-kind contributions for an estuary habitat restoration activity.
(F) Whether the project is cost-effective.
(G) Whether the State in which the non-Federal interest is proposing the project has a dedicated source of funding to acquire or restore estuary habitat, natural areas, and open spaces for the benefit of estuary habitat restoration or protection.
(H) Other factors that the Secretary determines to be reasonable and necessary for consideration.
(4) Priority
In selecting estuary habitat restoration projects to be carried out under this chapter, the Secretary shall give priority consideration to a project if, in addition to meriting selection based on the factors under paragraph (3)—
(A) the project occurs within a watershed in which there is a program being carried out that addresses sources of pollution and other activities that otherwise would re-impair the restored habitat; or
(B) the project includes pilot testing of or a demonstration of an innovative technology having the potential for improved cost-effectiveness in estuary habitat restoration.
(d) Cost sharing
(1) Federal share
Except as provided in paragraph (2) and subsection (e)(2) of this section, the Federal share of the cost of an estuary habitat restoration project (other than the cost of operation and maintenance of the project) carried out under this chapter shall not exceed 65 percent of such cost.
(2) Innovative technology costs
The Federal share of the incremental additional cost of including in a project pilot testing of or a demonstration of an innovative technology described in subsection (c)(4)(B) of this section shall be 85 percent.
(3) Non-Federal share
The non-Federal share of the cost of an estuary habitat restoration project carried out under this chapter shall include lands, easements, rights-of-way, and relocations and may include services, or any other form of in-kind contribution determined by the Secretary to be an appropriate contribution equivalent to the monetary amount required for the non-Federal share of the activity.
(4) Operation and maintenance
The non-Federal interests shall be responsible for all costs associated with operating, maintaining, replacing, repairing, and rehabilitating all projects carried out under this section.
(e) Interim actions
(1) In general
Pending completion of the estuary habitat restoration strategy to be developed under section 2905 of this title, the Secretary may take interim actions to carry out an estuary habitat restoration activity.

Clean Water Act / 679

(2) Federal share
The Federal share of the cost of an estuary habitat restoration activity before the completion of the estuary habitat restoration strategy shall not exceed 25 percent of such cost.

(f) Cooperation of non-Federal interests
  (1) In general
  The Secretary may not carry out an estuary habitat restoration project until a non-Federal interest has entered into a written agreement with the Secretary in which the non-Federal interest agrees to—
   (A) provide all lands, easements, rights-of-way, and relocations and any other elements the Secretary determines appropriate under subsection (d)(3) of this section; and
   (B) provide for maintenance and monitoring of the project.
  (2) Nongovernmental organizations
  Notwithstanding section 1962d-5b(b) of title 42, for any project to be undertaken under this chapter, the Secretary, in consultation and coordination with appropriate State and local governmental agencies and Indian tribes, may allow a nongovernmental organization to serve as the non-Federal interest for the project.

(g) Delegation of project implementation
In carrying out this chapter, the Secretary may delegate project implementation to another Federal department or agency on a reimbursable basis if the Secretary, upon the recommendation of the Council, determines such delegation is appropriate.

(Pub. L. 106-457, title I, Sec. 104, Nov. 7, 2000, 114 Stat. 1960.)

Section Referred to in Other Sections

This section is referred to in sections 2902, 2904 of this title.

ESTABLISHMENT OF ESTUARY HABITAT RESTORATION COUNCIL

33 USC 2904

(a) Council
There is established a council to be known as the "Estuary Habitat Restoration Council".

(b) Duties
The Council shall be responsible for—
  (1) soliciting, reviewing, and evaluating project proposals and developing recommendations concerning such proposals based on the factors specified in section 2903(c)(3) of this title;
  (2) submitting to the Secretary a list of recommended projects, including a recommended priority order and any recommendation as to whether a project should be carried out by the Secretary or by another Federal department or agency under section 2903(g) of this title;
  (3) developing and transmitting to Congress a national strategy for restoration of estuary habitat;
  (4) periodically reviewing the effectiveness of the national strategy in meeting the purposes of this chapter and, as necessary, updating the national strategy; and
  (5) providing advice on the development of the database, monitoring standards, and report required under sections 2906 and 2907 of this title.

(c) Membership
The Council shall be composed of the following members:
  (1) The Secretary (or the Secretary's designee).
  (2) The Under Secretary for Oceans and Atmosphere of the Department of Commerce (or the Under Secretary's designee).
  (3) The Administrator of the Environmental Protection Agency (or the Administrator's designee).
  (4) The Secretary of the Interior, acting through the Director of the United States Fish and Wildlife Service (or such Secretary's designee).
  (5) The Secretary of Agriculture (or such Secretary's designee).
  (6) The head of any other Federal agency designated by the President to serve as an ex officio member of the Council.

(d) Prohibition of compensation
Members of the Council may not receive compensation for their service as members of the Council.
(e) Chairperson
The chairperson shall be elected by the Council from among its members for a 3-year term, except that the first elected chairperson may serve a term of fewer than 3 years.
(f) Convening of Council
   (1) First meeting
   The Secretary shall convene the first meeting of the Council not later than 60 days after November 7, 2000, for the purpose of electing a chairperson.
   (2) Additional meetings
   The chairperson shall convene additional meetings of the Council as often as appropriate to ensure that this chapter is fully carried out, but not less often than annually.
(g) Council procedures
The Council shall establish procedures for voting, the conduct of meetings, and other matters, as necessary.
(h) Public participation
Meetings of the Council shall be open to the public. The Council shall provide notice to the public of such meetings.
(i) Advice
The Council shall consult with persons with recognized scientific expertise in estuary or estuary habitat restoration, representatives of State agencies, local or regional government agencies, and nongovernmental organizations with expertise in estuary or estuary habitat restoration, and representatives of Indian tribes, agricultural interests, fishing interests, and other estuary users—
   (1) to assist the Council in the development of the estuary habitat restoration strategy to be developed under section 2905 of this title; and
   (2) to provide advice and recommendations to the Council on proposed estuary habitat restoration projects, including advice on the scientific merit, technical merit, and feasibility of a project.

(Pub. L. 106-457, title I, Sec. 105, Nov. 7, 2000, 114 Stat. 1962.)

Section Referred to in Other Sections

This section is referred to in sections 2902, 2903 of this title.

ESTUARY HABITAT RESTORATION STRATEGY

33 USC 2905

(a) In general
Not later than 1 year after November 7, 2000, the Council,[1] shall develop an estuary habitat restoration strategy designed to ensure a comprehensive approach to maximize benefits derived from estuary habitat restoration projects and to foster the coordination of Federal and non-Federal activities related to restoration of estuary habitat.
(b) Goal
The goal of the strategy shall be the restoration of 1,000,000 acres of estuary habitat by the year 2010.
(c) Integration of estuary habitat restoration plans, programs, and partnerships
In developing the estuary habitat restoration strategy, the Council shall—
   (1) conduct a review of estuary management or habitat restoration plans and Federal programs established under other laws that authorize funding for estuary habitat restoration activities; and
   (2) ensure that the estuary habitat restoration strategy is developed in a manner that is consistent with the estuary management or habitat restoration plans.

---

[1] So in original. The comma probably should not appear.

(d) Elements of the strategy
The estuary habitat restoration strategy shall include proposals, methods, and guidance on—
(1) maximizing the incentives for the creation of new public-private partnerships to carry out estuary habitat restoration projects and the use of Federal resources to encourage increased private sector involvement in estuary habitat restoration activities;
(2) ensuring that the estuary habitat restoration strategy will be implemented in a manner that is consistent with the estuary management or habitat restoration plans;
(3) promoting estuary habitat restoration projects to—
(A) provide healthy ecosystems in order to support—
(i) wildlife, including endangered and threatened species, migratory birds, and resident species of an estuary watershed; and
(ii) fish and shellfish, including commercial and recreational fisheries;
(B) improve surface and ground water quality and quantity, and flood control;
(C) provide outdoor recreation; and
(D) address other areas of concern that the Council determines to be appropriate for consideration;
(4) addressing the estimated historic losses, estimated current rate of loss, and extent of the threat of future loss or degradation of each type of estuary habitat;
(5) measuring the rate of change for each type of estuary habitat;
(6) selecting a balance of smaller and larger estuary habitat restoration projects; and
(7) ensuring equitable geographic distribution of projects funded under this chapter.
(e) Public review and comment
Before the Council adopts a final or revised estuary habitat restoration strategy, the Secretary shall publish in the Federal Register a draft of the estuary habitat restoration strategy and provide an opportunity for public review and comment.
(f) Periodic revision
Using data and information developed through project monitoring and management, and other relevant information, the Council may periodically review and update, as necessary, the estuary habitat restoration strategy.

(Pub. L. 106-457, title I, Sec. 106, Nov. 7, 2000, 114 Stat. 1963.)

Section Referred to in Other Sections

This section is referred to in sections 2903, 2904 of this title.

MONITORING OF ESTUARY HABITAT RESTORATION PROJECTS

33 USC 2906

(a) Under Secretary
In this section, the term "Under Secretary" means the Under Secretary for Oceans and Atmosphere of the Department of Commerce.
(b) Database of restoration project information
The Under Secretary, in consultation with the Council, shall develop and maintain an appropriate database of information concerning estuary habitat restoration projects carried out under this chapter, including information on project techniques, project completion, monitoring data, and other relevant information.
(c) Monitoring data standards
The Under Secretary, in consultation with the Council, shall develop standard data formats for monitoring projects, along with requirements for types of data collected and frequency of monitoring.
(d) Coordination of data
The Under Secretary shall compile information that pertains to estuary habitat restoration projects from other Federal, State, and local sources and that meets the quality control requirements and data standards established under this section.
(e) Use of existing programs
The Under Secretary shall use existing programs within the National Oceanic and Atmospheric Administration to create and maintain the database required under this section.

682 / Environmental Statutes

(f) Public availability
The Under Secretary shall make the information collected and maintained under this section available to the public.

(Pub. L. 106-457, title I, Sec. 107, Nov. 7, 2000, 114 Stat. 1964.)

Section Referred to in Other Sections

This section is referred to in sections 2903, 2904, 2907 of this title.

REPORTING

33 USC 2907

(a) In general
At the end of the third and fifth fiscal years following November 7, 2000, the Secretary, after considering the advice and recommendations of the Council, shall transmit to Congress a report on the results of activities carried out under this chapter.

(b) Contents of report
A report under subsection (a) of this section shall include—
 (1) data on the number of acres of estuary habitat restored under this chapter, including descriptions of, and partners involved with, projects selected, in progress, and completed under this chapter that comprise those acres;
 (2) information from the database established under section 2906(b) of this title related to ongoing monitoring of projects to ensure that short-term and long-term restoration goals are achieved;
 (3) an estimate of the long-term success of varying restoration techniques used in carrying out estuary habitat restoration projects;
 (4) a review of how the information described in paragraphs (1) through (3) has been incorporated in the selection and implementation of estuary habitat restoration projects;
 (5) a review of efforts made to maintain an appropriate database of restoration projects carried out under this chapter; and
 (6) a review of the measures taken to provide the information described in paragraphs (1) through (3) to persons with responsibility for assisting in the restoration of estuary habitat.

(Pub. L. 106-457, title I, Sec. 108, Nov. 7, 2000, 114 Stat. 1965.)

Section Referred to in Other Sections

This section is referred to in section 2904 of this title.

FUNDING

33 USC 2908

(a) Authorization of appropriations
 (1) Estuary habitat restoration projects
  There is authorized to be appropriated to the Secretary for carrying out and providing technical assistance for estuary habitat restoration projects—
  (A) $40,000,000 for fiscal year 2001;
  (B) $50,000,000 for each of fiscal years 2002 and 2003;
  (C) $60,000,000 for fiscal year 2004; and
  (D) $75,000,000 for fiscal year 2005.
  Such sums shall remain available until expended.
 (2) Monitoring
  There is authorized to be appropriated to the Under Secretary for Oceans and Atmosphere of the Department of Commerce for the acquisition, maintenance, and management of monitoring data on restoration projects carried out under this chapter, $1,500,000 for each of fiscal years 2001 through 2005. Such sums shall remain available until expended.

(b) Set-aside for administrative expenses of the Council
Not to exceed 3 percent of the amounts appropriated for a fiscal year under subsection (a)(1) of this section or $1,500,000, whichever is greater, may be used by the Secretary for administration and operation of the Council.

(Pub. L. 106-457, title I, Sec. 109, Nov. 7, 2000, 114 Stat. 1965.)

GENERAL PROVISIONS

33 USC 2909

(a) Agency consultation and coordination
In carrying out this chapter, the Secretary shall, as necessary, consult with, cooperate with, and coordinate its activities with the activities of other Federal departments and agencies.

(b) Cooperative agreements; memoranda of understanding
In carrying out this chapter, the Secretary may—
  (1) enter into cooperative agreements with Federal, State, and local government agencies and other entities; and
  (2) execute such memoranda of understanding as are necessary to reflect the agreements.

(c) Federal agency facilities and personnel
Federal agencies may cooperate in carrying out scientific and other programs necessary to carry out this chapter, and may provide facilities and personnel, for the purpose of assisting the Council in carrying out its duties under this chapter.

(d) Identification and mapping of dredged material disposal sites
In consultation with appropriate Federal and non-Federal public entities, the Secretary shall undertake, and update as warranted by changed conditions, surveys to identify and map sites appropriate for beneficial uses of dredged material for the protection, restoration, and creation of aquatic and ecologically related habitats, including wetlands, in order to further the purposes of this chapter.

(e) Study of bioremediation technology
  (1) In general
  Not later than 180 days after November 7, 2000, the Administrator of the Environmental Protection Agency, with the participation of the estuarine scientific community, shall begin a 2-year study on the efficacy of bioremediation products.
  (2) Requirements
  The study shall—
    (A) evaluate and assess bioremediation technology—
      (i) on low-level petroleum hydrocarbon contamination from recreational boat bilges;
      (ii) on low-level petroleum hydrocarbon contamination from stormwater discharges;
      (iii) on nonpoint petroleum hydrocarbon discharges; and
      (iv) as a first response tool for petroleum hydrocarbon spills; and
    (B) recommend management actions to optimize the return of a healthy and balanced ecosystem and make improvements in the quality and character of estuarine waters.

(Pub. L. 106-457, title I, Sec. 110, Nov. 7, 2000, 114 Stat. 1966.)

OIL POLLUTION
[OIL POLLUTION ACT OF 1990]

as amended[1]

33 U.S.C. § 2701 et seq.

SUBCHAPTER I—OIL POLLUTION LIABILITY AND COMPENSATION

DEFINITIONS

33 USC 2701

For the purposes of this Act, the term—
  (1) "act of God" means an unanticipated grave natural disaster or other natural phenomenon of an exceptional, inevitable, and irresistible character the effects of which could not have been prevented or avoided by the exercise of due care or foresight;
  (2) "barrel" means 42 United States gallons at 60 degrees fahrenheit;
  (3) "claim" means a request, made in writing for a sum certain, for compensation for damages or removal costs resulting from an incident;
  (4) "claimant" means any person or government who presents a claim for compensation under this subchapter;
  (5) "damages" means damages specified in section 2702(b) of this title, and includes the cost of assessing these damages;
  (6) "deepwater port" is a facility licensed under the Deepwater Port Act of 1974 (33 U.S.C. 1501-1524);
  (7) "discharge" means any emission (other than natural seepage), intentional or unintentional, and includes, but is not limited to, spilling, leaking, pumping, pouring, emitting, emptying, or dumping;
  (8) "exclusive economic zone" means the zone established by Presidential Proclamation Numbered 5030, dated March 10, 1983, including the ocean waters of the areas referred to as "eastern special areas" in Article 3(1) of the Agreement between the United States of America and the Union of Soviet Socialist Republics on the Maritime Boundary, signed June 1, 1990;
  (9) "facility" means any structure, group of structures, equipment, or device (other than a vessel) which is used for one or more of the following purposes: exploring for, drilling for, producing, storing, handling, transferring, processing, or transporting oil. This term includes any motor vehicle, rolling stock, or pipeline used for one or more of these purposes;
  (10) "foreign offshore unit" means a facility which is located, in whole or in part, in the territorial sea or on the continental shelf of a foreign country and which is or was used for one or more of the following purposes: exploring for, drilling for, producing, storing, handling, transferring, processing, or transporting oil produced from the seabed beneath the foreign country's territorial sea or from the foreign country's continental shelf;
  (11) "Fund" means the Oil Spill Liability Trust Fund, established by section 9509 of title 26;
  (12) "gross ton" has the meaning given that term by the Secretary under part J of title 46;
  (13) "guarantor" means any person, other than the responsible party, who provides evidence of financial responsibility for a responsible party under this Act;
  (14) "incident" means any occurrence or series of occurrences having the same origin, involving one or more vessels, facilities, or any combination thereof, resulting in the discharge or substantial threat of discharge of oil;
  (15) "Indian tribe" means any Indian tribe, band, nation, or other organized group or community, but not including any Alaska Native regional or village corporation, which is recognized as eligible for the special programs and services provided by the United States to

---

[1] Editor's note: Unless otherwise noted, text is from Title 33, Chapter 40 of U.S. Code, as amended by Pub. L. 107-295, Nov. 25, 2002, Pub. L. 106-246, July 13, 2000.

Indians because of their status as Indians and has governmental authority over lands belonging to or controlled by the tribe;

(16) "lessee" means a person holding a leasehold interest in an oil or gas lease on lands beneath navigable waters (as that term is defined in section 1301(a) of title 43) or on submerged lands of the Outer Continental Shelf, granted or maintained under applicable State law or the Outer Continental Shelf Lands Act (43 U.S.C. 1331 et seq.);

(17) "liable" or "liability" shall be construed to be the standard of liability which obtains under section 1321 of this title;

(18) "mobile offshore drilling unit" means a vessel (other than a self-elevating lift vessel) capable of use as an offshore facility;

(19) "National Contingency Plan" means the National Contingency Plan prepared and published under section 1321(d) of this title or revised under section 105 of the Comprehensive Environmental Response, Compensation, and Liability Act (42 U.S.C. 9605);

(20) "natural resources" includes land, fish, wildlife, biota, air, water, ground water, drinking water supplies, and other such resources belonging to, managed by, held in trust by, appertaining to, or otherwise controlled by the United States (including the resources of the exclusive economic zone), any State or local government or Indian tribe, or any foreign government;

(21) "navigable waters" means the waters of the United States, including the territorial sea;

(22) "offshore facility" means any facility of any kind located in, on, or under any of the navigable waters of the United States, and any facility of any kind which is subject to the jurisdiction of the United States and is located in, on, or under any other waters, other than a vessel or a public vessel;

(23) "oil" means oil of any kind or in any form, including petroleum, fuel oil, sludge, oil refuse, and oil mixed with wastes other than dredged spoil, but does not include any substance which is specifically listed or designated as a hazardous substance under subparagraphs (A) through (F) of section 101(14) of the Comprehensive Environmental Response, Compensation, and Liability Act (42 U.S.C. 9601) and which is subject to the provisions of that Act [42 U.S.C. 9601 et seq.];

(24) "onshore facility" means any facility (including, but not limited to, motor vehicles and rolling stock) of any kind located in, on, or under, any land within the United States other than submerged land;

(25) the term "Outer Continental Shelf facility" means an offshore facility which is located, in whole or in part, on the Outer Continental Shelf and is or was used for one or more of the following purposes: exploring for, drilling for, producing, storing, handling, transferring, processing, or transporting oil produced from the Outer Continental Shelf;

(26) "owner or operator" means (A) in the case of a vessel, any person owning, operating, or chartering by demise, the vessel, and (B) in the case of an onshore facility, and an offshore facility, any person owning or operating such onshore facility or offshore facility, and (C) in the case of any abandoned offshore facility, the person who owned or operated such facility immediately prior to such abandonment;

(27) "person" means an individual, corporation, partnership, association, State, municipality, commission, or political subdivision of a State, or any interstate body;

(28) "permittee" means a person holding an authorization, license, or permit for geological exploration issued under section 11 of the Outer Continental Shelf Lands Act (43 U.S.C. 1340) or applicable State law;

(29) "public vessel" means a vessel owned or bareboat chartered and operated by the United States, or by a State or political subdivision thereof, or by a foreign nation, except when the vessel is engaged in commerce;

(30) "remove" or "removal" means containment and removal of oil or a hazardous substance from water and shorelines or the taking of other actions as may be necessary to minimize or mitigate damage to the public health or welfare, including, but not limited to, fish, shellfish, wildlife, and public and private property, shorelines, and beaches;

(31) "removal costs" means the costs of removal that are incurred after a discharge of oil has occurred or, in any case in which there is a substantial threat of a discharge of oil, the costs to prevent, minimize, or mitigate oil pollution from such an incident;

(32) "responsible party" means the following:
  (A) Vessels.—In the case of a vessel, any person owning, operating, or demise chartering the vessel.
  (B) Onshore facilities.—In the case of an onshore facility (other than a pipeline), any person owning or operating the facility, except a Federal agency, State, municipality, commission, or political subdivision of a State, or any interstate body, that as the owner transfers possession and right to use the property to another person by lease, assignment, or permit.
  (C) Offshore facilities.—In the case of an offshore facility (other than a pipeline or a deepwater port licensed under the Deepwater Port Act of 1974 (33 U.S.C. 1501 et seq.)), the lessee or permittee of the area in which the facility is located or the holder of a right of use and easement granted under applicable State law or the Outer Continental Shelf Lands Act (43 U.S.C. 1301-1356) for the area in which the facility is located (if the holder is a different person than the lessee or permittee), except a Federal agency, State, municipality, commission, or political subdivision of a State, or any interstate body, that as owner transfers possession and right to use the property to another person by lease, assignment, or permit.
  (D) Deepwater ports.—In the case of a deepwater port licensed under the Deepwater Port Act of 1974 (33 U.S.C. 1501-1524), the licensee.
  (E) Pipelines.—In the case of a pipeline, any person owning or operating the pipeline.
  (F) Abandonment.—In the case of an abandoned vessel, onshore facility, deepwater port, pipeline, or offshore facility, the persons who would have been responsible parties immediately prior to the abandonment of the vessel or facility.
(33) "Secretary" means the Secretary of the department in which the Coast Guard is operating;
(34) "tank vessel" means a vessel that is constructed or adapted to carry, or that carries, oil or hazardous material in bulk as cargo or cargo residue, and that—
  (A) is a vessel of the United States;
  (B) operates on the navigable waters; or
  (C) transfers oil or hazardous material in a place subject to the jurisdiction of the United States;
(35) "territorial seas" means the belt of the seas measured from the line of ordinary low water along that portion of the coast which is in direct contact with the open sea and the line marking the seaward limit of inland waters, and extending seaward a distance of 3 miles;
(36) "United States" and "State" mean the several States of the United States, the District of Columbia, the Commonwealth of Puerto Rico, Guam, American Samoa, the United States Virgin Islands, the Commonwealth of the Northern Marianas, and any other territory or possession of the United States; and
(37) "vessel" means every description of watercraft or other artificial contrivance used, or capable of being used, as a means of transportation on water, other than a public vessel.

(Pub. L. 101-380, title I, Sec. 1001, Aug. 18, 1990, 104 Stat. 486; Pub. L. 105-383, title III, Sec. 307(a), Nov. 13, 1998, 112 Stat. 3421.)

References in Text

This Act, referred to in text, is Pub. L. 101-380, Aug. 18, 1990, 104 Stat. 484, as amended, known as the Oil Pollution Act of 1990, which is classified principally to this chapter. For complete classification of this Act to the Code, see Short Title note set out below and Tables.

The Deepwater Port Act of 1974, referred to in pars. (6) and (32)(C), (D), is Pub. L. 93-627, Jan. 3, 1975, 88 Stat. 2126, as amended, which is classified generally to chapter 29 (Sec. 1501 et seq.) of this title. For complete classification of this Act to the Code, see Short Title note set out under section 1501 of this title and Tables.

Presidential Proclamation Numbered 5030, referred to in par. (8), is Proc. No. 5030, Mar. 10, 1983, 48 F.R. 10605, which is set out as a note under section 1453 of Title 16, Conservation.

The Outer Continental Shelf Lands Act, referred to in pars. (16) and (32)(C), is act Aug. 7, 1953, ch. 345, 67 Stat. 462, as amended, which is classified generally to subchapter III (Sec. 1331 et seq.) of chapter 29 of Title 43, Public Lands. For complete classification of this Act to the Code, see Short Title note set out under section 1331 of Title 43 and Tables.

688 / Environmental Statutes

The Comprehensive Environmental Response, Compensation, and Liability Act, referred to in par. (23), probably means the Comprehensive Environmental Response, Compensation, and Liability Act of 1980, Pub. L. 96-510, Dec. 11, 1980, 94 Stat. 2767, as amended, which is classified principally to chapter 103 (Sec. 9601 et seq.) of Title 42, The Public Health and Welfare. For complete classification of this Act to the Code, see Short Title note set out under section 9601 of Title 42 and Tables.

Amendments

1998—Par. (23). Pub. L. 105-383 amended par. (23) generally. Prior to amendment, par. (23) read as follows: " 'oil' means oil of any kind or in any form, including, but not limited to, petroleum, fuel oil, sludge, oil refuse, and oil mixed with wastes other than dredged spoil, but does not include petroleum, including crude oil or any fraction thereof, which is specifically listed or designated as a hazardous substance under subparagraphs (A) through (F) of section 101(14) of the Comprehensive Environmental Response, Compensation, and Liability Act (42 U.S.C. 9601) and which is subject to the provisions of that Act;".

Effective Date

Section 1020 of title I of Pub. L. 101-380 provided that: "This Act [see Short Title of 1990 Amendments note below for classification] shall apply to an incident occurring after the date of the enactment of this Act [Aug. 18, 1990]."

Short Title of 1995 Amendment

Pub. L. 104-55, Sec. 1, Nov. 20, 1995, 109 Stat. 546, provided that: "This Act [enacting section 2720 of this title and amending sections 2704 and 2716 of this title] may be cited as the 'Edible Oil Regulatory Reform Act'."

Short Title of 1990 Amendments

Pub. L. 101-537, title II, Sec. 2001, Nov. 8, 1990, 104 Stat. 2375, and Pub. L. 101-646, title IV, Sec. 4001, Nov. 29, 1990, 104 Stat. 4788, as amended by Pub. L. 104-332, Sec. 2(h)(1), Oct. 26, 1996, 110 Stat. 4091, provided that: "This title [amending section 2761 of this title] may be cited as the 'Great Lakes Oil Pollution Research and Development Act'."

Short Title

Section 1 of Pub. L. 101-380 provided that: "This Act [enacting this chapter, sections 1642 and 1656 of Title 43, Public Lands, sections 3703a and 7505 of Title 46, Shipping, and section 1274a of the Appendix to Title 46, amending sections 1223, 1228, 1232, 1236, 1319, 1321, 1481, 1486, 1503, 1514, and 1908 of this title, section 3145 of Title 16, Conservation, sections 4612 and 9509 of Title 26, Internal Revenue Code, sections 1334, 1350, and 1653 of Title 43, sections 2101, 2302, 3318, 3715, 3718, 5116, 6101, 7101, 7106, 7107, 7109, 7302, 7502, 7503, 7701 to 7703, 8101, 8104, 8502, 8503, 8702, 9101, 9102, 9302, 9308, and 12106 of Title 46, and section 1274 of the Appendix to Title 46, repealing section 1517 of this title and sections 1811 and 1812 to 1824 of Title 43, enacting provisions set out as notes under this section, sections 1203, 1223, and 1321, of this title, section 92 of Title 14, Coast Guard, section 9509 of Title 26, sections 1334, 1651, and 1653 of Title 43, sections 3703, 3703a, and 7106 of Title 46, and section 1295 of the Appendix to Title 46, amending provisions set out as a note under section 401 of Title 23, Highways, and repealing provisions set out as a note under section 1811 of Title 43] may be cited as the 'Oil Pollution Act of 1990'."

Section Referred to in Other Sections

This section is referred to in section 1321 of this title.

ELEMENTS OF LIABILITY

33 USC 2702

(a) In general
   Notwithstanding any other provision or rule of law, and subject to the provisions of this Act, each responsible party for a vessel or a facility from which oil is discharged, or which poses the substantial threat of a discharge of oil, into or upon the navigable waters or adjoining shorelines or the exclusive economic zone is liable for the removal costs and damages specified in subsection (b) of this section that result from such incident.

(b) Covered removal costs and damages
 (1) Removal costs
  The removal costs referred to in subsection (a) of this section are—
  (A) all removal costs incurred by the United States, a State, or an Indian tribe under subsection (c), (d), (e), or (l) of section 1321 of this title, under the Intervention on the High Seas Act (33 U.S.C. 1471 et seq.), or under State law; and
  (B) any removal costs incurred by any person for acts taken by the person which are consistent with the National Contingency Plan.
 (2) Damages
  The damages referred to in subsection (a) of this section are the following:
  (A) Natural resources
   Damages for injury to, destruction of, loss of, or loss of use of, natural resources, including the reasonable costs of assessing the damage, which shall be recoverable by a United States trustee, a State trustee, an Indian tribe trustee, or a foreign trustee.
  (B) Real or personal property
   Damages for injury to, or economic losses resulting from destruction of, real or personal property, which shall be recoverable by a claimant who owns or leases that property.
  (C) Subsistence use
   Damages for loss of subsistence use of natural resources, which shall be recoverable by any claimant who so uses natural resources which have been injured, destroyed, or lost, without regard to the ownership or management of the resources.
  (D) Revenues
   Damages equal to the net loss of taxes, royalties, rents, fees, or net profit shares due to the injury, destruction, or loss of real property, personal property, or natural resources, which shall be recoverable by the Government of the United States, a State, or a political subdivision thereof.
  (E) Profits and earning capacity
   Damages equal to the loss of profits or impairment of earning capacity due to the injury, destruction, or loss of real property, personal property, or natural resources, which shall be recoverable by any claimant.
  (F) Public services
   Damages for net costs of providing increased or additional public services during or after removal activities, including protection from fire, safety, or health hazards, caused by a discharge of oil, which shall be recoverable by a State, or a political subdivision of a State.
(c) Excluded discharges
 This subchapter does not apply to any discharge—
 (1) permitted by a permit issued under Federal, State, or local law;
 (2) from a public vessel; or
 (3) from an onshore facility which is subject to the Trans-Alaska Pipeline Authorization Act (43 U.S.C. 1651 et seq.).
(d) Liability of third parties
 (1) In general
  (A) Third party treated as responsible party
   Except as provided in subparagraph (B), in any case in which a responsible party establishes that a discharge or threat of a discharge and the resulting removal costs and damages were caused solely by an act or omission of one or more third parties described in section 2703(a)(3) of this title (or solely by such an act or omission in combination with an act of God or an act of war), the third party or parties shall be treated as the responsible party or parties for purposes of determining liability under this subchapter.
  (B) Subrogation of responsible party
   If the responsible party alleges that the discharge or threat of a discharge was caused solely by an act or omission of a third party, the responsible party—
   (i) in accordance with section 2713 of this title, shall pay removal costs and damages to any claimant; and

(ii) shall be entitled by subrogation to all rights of the United States Government and the claimant to recover removal costs or damages from the third party or the Fund paid under this subsection.
(2) Limitation applied
  (A) Owner or operator of vessel or facility
    If the act or omission of a third party that causes an incident occurs in connection with a vessel or facility owned or operated by the third party, the liability of the third party shall be subject to the limits provided in section 2704 of this title as applied with respect to the vessel or facility.
  (B) Other cases
    In any other case, the liability of a third party or parties shall not exceed the limitation which would have been applicable to the responsible party of the vessel or facility from which the discharge actually occurred if the responsible party were liable.

(Pub. L. 101-380, title I, Sec. 1002, Aug. 18, 1990, 104 Stat. 489.)

References in Text

This Act, referred to in subsec. (a), is Pub. L. 101-380, Aug. 18, 1990, 104 Stat. 484, as amended, known as the Oil Pollution Act of 1990, which is classified principally to this chapter. For complete classification of this Act to the Code, see Short Title note set out under section 2701 of this title and Tables.

The Intervention on the High Seas Act, referred to in subsec. (b)(1)(A), is Pub. L. 93-248, Feb. 5, 1974, 88 Stat. 8, as amended, which is classified generally to chapter 28 (Sec. 1471 et seq.) of this title. For complete classification of this Act to the Code, see Short Title note set out under section 1471 of this title and Tables.

The Trans-Alaska Pipeline Authorization Act, referred to in subsec. (c)(3), is title II of Pub. L. 93-153, Nov. 16, 1973, 87 Stat. 584, which is classified generally to chapter 34 (Sec. 1651 et seq.) of Title 43, Public Lands. For complete classification of this Act to the Code, see Short Title note set out under section 1651 of Title 43 and Tables.

Section Referred to in Other Sections

This section is referred to in sections 2701, 2703, 2704, 2705, 2706, 2708, 2712, 2716, 2717 of this title.

DEFENSES TO LIABILITY

33 USC 2703

(a) Complete defenses
  A responsible party is not liable for removal costs or damages under section 2702 of this title if the responsible party establishes, by a preponderance of the evidence, that the discharge or substantial threat of a discharge of oil and the resulting damages or removal costs were caused solely by—
  (1) an act of God;
  (2) an act of war;
  (3) an act or omission of a third party, other than an employee or agent of the responsible party or a third party whose act or omission occurs in connection with any contractual relationship with the responsible party (except where the sole contractual arrangement arises in connection with carriage by a common carrier by rail), if the responsible party establishes, by a preponderance of the evidence, that the responsible party—
    (A) exercised due care with respect to the oil concerned, taking into consideration the characteristics of the oil and in light of all relevant facts and circumstances; and
    (B) took precautions against foreseeable acts or omissions of any such third party and the foreseeable consequences of those acts or omissions; or
  (4) any combination of paragraphs (1), (2), and (3).
(b) Defenses as to particular claimants
  A responsible party is not liable under section 2702 of this title to a claimant, to the extent that the incident is caused by the gross negligence or willful misconduct of the claimant.

(c) Limitation on complete defense
Subsection (a) of this section does not apply with respect to a responsible party who fails or refuses—
- (1) to report the incident as required by law if the responsible party knows or has reason to know of the incident;
- (2) to provide all reasonable cooperation and assistance requested by a responsible official in connection with removal activities; or
- (3) without sufficient cause, to comply with an order issued under subsection (c) or (e) of section 1321 of this title or the Intervention on the High Seas Act (33 U.S.C. 1471 et seq.).

(Pub. L. 101-380, title I, Sec. 1003, Aug. 18, 1990, 104 Stat. 491.)

References in Text

The Intervention on the High Seas Act, referred to in subsec. (c)(3), is Pub. L. 93-248, Feb. 5, 1974, 88 Stat. 8, as amended, which is classified generally to chapter 28 (Sec. 1471 et seq.) of this title. For complete classification of this Act to the Code, see Short Title note set out under section 1471 of this title and Tables.

Section Referred to in Other Sections

This section is referred to in sections 2702, 2704, 2708 of this title.

LIMITS ON LIABILITY

33 USC 2704

(a) General rule
Except as otherwise provided in this section, the total of the liability of a responsible party under section 2702 of this title and any removal costs incurred by, or on behalf of, the responsible party, with respect to each incident shall not exceed—
- (1) for a tank vessel the greater of—
  - (A) $1,200 per gross ton; or
  - (B) (i) in the case of a vessel greater than 3,000 gross tons, $10,000,000; or
    (ii) in the case of a vessel of 3,000 gross tons or less, $2,000,000;
- (2) for any other vessel, $600 per gross ton or $500,000, whichever is greater;
- (3) for an offshore facility except a deepwater port, the total of all removal costs plus $75,000,000; and
- (4) for any onshore facility and a deepwater port, $350,000,000.

(b) Division of liability for mobile offshore drilling units
- (1) Treated first as tank vessel
  For purposes of determining the responsible party and applying this Act and except as provided in paragraph (2), a mobile offshore drilling unit which is being used as an offshore facility is deemed to be a tank vessel with respect to the discharge, or the substantial threat of a discharge, of oil on or above the surface of the water.
- (2) Treated as facility for excess liability
  To the extent that removal costs and damages from any incident described in paragraph (1) exceed the amount for which a responsible party is liable (as that amount may be limited under subsection (a)(1) of this section), the mobile offshore drilling unit is deemed to be an offshore facility. For purposes of applying subsection (a)(3) of this section, the amount specified in that subsection shall be reduced by the amount for which the responsible party is liable under paragraph (1).

(c) Exceptions
- (1) Acts of responsible party
  Subsection (a) of this section does not apply if the incident was proximately caused by—
  (A) gross negligence or willful misconduct of, or
  (B) the violation of an applicable Federal safety, construction, or operating regulation by, the responsible party, an agent or employee of the responsible party, or a person acting pursuant to a contractual relationship with the responsible party (except where the sole contractual arrangement arises in connection with carriage by a common carrier by rail).

(2) Failure or refusal of responsible party
Subsection (a) of this section does not apply if the responsible party fails or refuses—
  (A) to report the incident as required by law and the responsible party knows or has reason to know of the incident;
  (B) to provide all reasonable cooperation and assistance requested by a responsible official in connection with removal activities; or
  (C) without sufficient cause, to comply with an order issued under subsection (c) or (e) of section 1321 of this title or the Intervention on the High Seas Act (33 U.S.C. 1471 et seq.).
(3) OCS facility or vessel
Notwithstanding the limitations established under subsection (a) of this section and the defenses of section 2703 of this title, all removal costs incurred by the United States Government or any State or local official or agency in connection with a discharge or substantial threat of a discharge of oil from any Outer Continental Shelf facility or a vessel carrying oil as cargo from such a facility shall be borne by the owner or operator of such facility or vessel.
(4) Certain tank vessels
Subsection (a)(1) of this section shall not apply to—
  (A) a tank vessel on which the only oil carried as cargo is an animal fat or vegetable oil, as those terms are used in section 2720 of this title; and
  (B) a tank vessel that is designated in its certificate of inspection as an oil spill response vessel (as that term is defined in section 2101 of title 46) and that is used solely for removal.

(d) Adjusting limits of liability
(1) Onshore facilities
Subject to paragraph (2), the President may establish by regulation, with respect to any class or category of onshore facility, a limit of liability under this section of less than $350,000,000, but not less than $8,000,000, taking into account size, storage capacity, oil throughput, proximity to sensitive areas, type of oil handled, history of discharges, and other factors relevant to risks posed by the class or category of facility.
(2) Deepwater ports and associated vessels
  (A) Study
  The Secretary shall conduct a study of the relative operational and environmental risks posed by the transportation of oil by vessel to deepwater ports (as defined in section 1502 of this title) versus the transportation of oil by vessel to other ports. The study shall include a review and analysis of offshore lightering practices used in connection with that transportation, an analysis of the volume of oil transported by vessel using those practices, and an analysis of the frequency and volume of oil discharges which occur in connection with the use of those practices.
  (B) Report
  Not later than 1 year after August 18, 1990, the Secretary shall submit to the Congress a report on the results of the study conducted under subparagraph (A).
  (C) Rulemaking proceeding
  If the Secretary determines, based on the results of the study conducted under this[1] subparagraph (A), that the use of deepwater ports in connection with the transportation of oil by vessel results in a lower operational or environmental risk than the use of other ports, the Secretary shall initiate, not later than the 180th day following the date of submission of the report to the Congress under subparagraph (B), a rulemaking proceeding to lower the limits of liability under this section for deepwater ports as the Secretary determines appropriate. The Secretary may establish a limit of liability of less than $350,000,000, but not less than $50,000,000, in accordance with paragraph (1).
(3) Periodic reports
The President shall, within 6 months after August 18, 1990, and from time to time thereafter, report to the Congress on the desirability of adjusting the limits of liability specified in subsection (a) of this section.

---

[1] So in original. The word "this" probably should not appear.

(4) Adjustment to reflect Consumer Price Index
The President shall, by regulations issued not less often than every 3 years, adjust the limits of liability specified in subsection (a) of this section to reflect significant increases in the Consumer Price Index.

(Pub. L. 101-380, title I, Sec. 1004, Aug. 18, 1990, 104 Stat. 491; Pub. L. 104-55, Sec. 2(d)(1), Nov. 20, 1995, 109 Stat. 546; Pub. L. 105-383, title IV, Sec. 406, Nov. 13, 1998, 112 Stat. 3429.)

References in Text

This Act, referred to in subsec. (b)(1), is Pub. L. 101-380, Aug. 18, 1990, 104 Stat. 484, as amended, known as the Oil Pollution Act of 1990, which is classified principally to this chapter. For complete classification of this Act to the Code, see Short Title note set out under section 2701 of this title and Tables.

The Intervention on the High Seas Act, referred to in subsec. (c)(2)(C), is Pub. L. 93-248, Feb. 5, 1974, 88 Stat. 8, as amended, which is classified generally to chapter 28 (Sec. 1471 et seq.) of this title. For complete classification of this Act to the Code, see Short Title note set out under section 1471 of this title and Tables.

Amendments

1998—Subsec. (a)(1). Pub. L. 105-383, Sec. 406(1), substituted comma for "(except a tank vessel on which the only oil carried as cargo is an animal fat or vegetable oil, as those terms are used in section 2720 of this title)" after "tank vessel".

Subsec. (c)(4). Pub. L. 105-383, Sec. 406(2), added par. (4).

1995—Subsec. (a)(1). Pub. L. 104-55 substituted "for a tank vessel (except a tank vessel on which the only oil carried as cargo is an animal fat or vegetable oil, as those terms are used in section 2720 of this title)" for "for a tank vessel,".

Delegation of Functions

Specific functions of President under subsec. (d) of this section delegated to Administrator of Environmental Protection Agency, Secretary of Transportation, and Secretary of the Interior by section 4 of Ex. Ord. No. 12777, Oct. 18, 1991, 56 F.R. 54763, set out as a note under section 1321 of this title.

Section Referred to in Other Sections

This section is referred to in sections 2702, 2705, 2708, 2712, 2716 of this title.

INTEREST; PARTIAL PAYMENT OF CLAIMS

33 USC 2705

(a) General rule
The responsible party or the responsible party's guarantor is liable to a claimant for interest on the amount paid in satisfaction of a claim under this Act for the period described in subsection (b) of this section. The responsible party shall establish a procedure for the payment or settlement of claims for interim, short-term damages. Payment or settlement of a claim for interim, short-term damages representing less than the full amount of damages to which the claimant ultimately may be entitled shall not preclude recovery by the claimant for damages not reflected in the paid or settled partial claim.

(b) Period
   (1) In general
   Except as provided in paragraph (2), the period for which interest shall be paid is the period beginning on the 30th day following the date on which the claim is presented to the responsible party or guarantor and ending on the date on which the claim is paid.
   (2) Exclusion of period due to offer by guarantor
   If the guarantor offers to the claimant an amount equal to or greater than that finally paid in satisfaction of the claim, the period described in paragraph (1) does not include the period beginning on the date the offer is made and ending on the date the offer is accepted. If the offer is made within 60 days after the date on which the claim is presented under section 2713(a) of this title, the period described in paragraph (1) does not include any period before the offer is accepted.

(3) Exclusion of periods in interests of justice
If in any period a claimant is not paid due to reasons beyond the control of the responsible party or because it would not serve the interests of justice, no interest shall accrue under this section during that period.
(4) Calculation of interest
The interest paid under this section shall be calculated at the average of the highest rate for commercial and finance company paper of maturities of 180 days or less obtaining on each of the days included within the period for which interest must be paid to the claimant, as published in the Federal Reserve Bulletin.
(5) Interest not subject to liability limits
  (A) In general
  Interest (including prejudgment interest) under this paragraph is in addition to damages and removal costs for which claims may be asserted under section 2702 of this title and shall be paid without regard to any limitation of liability under section 2704 of this title.
  (B) Payment by guarantor
  The payment of interest under this subsection by a guarantor is subject to section 2716(g) of this title.

(Pub. L. 101-380, title I, Sec. 1005, Aug. 18, 1990, 104 Stat. 493; Pub. L. 104-324, title XI, Sec. 1142(a), Oct. 19, 1996, 110 Stat. 3991.)

References in Text

This Act, referred to in subsec. (a), is Pub. L. 101-380, Aug. 18, 1990, 104 Stat. 484, as amended, known as the Oil Pollution Act of 1990, which is classified principally to this chapter. For complete classification of this Act to the Code, see Short Title note set out under section 2701 of this title and Tables.

Amendments

1996—Pub. L. 104-324, Sec. 1142(a)(1), inserted "; partial payment of claims" after "Interest" in section catchline.

Subsec. (a). Pub. L. 104-324, Sec. 1142(a)(2), inserted at end "The responsible party shall establish a procedure for the payment or settlement of claims for interim, short-term damages. Payment or settlement of a claim for interim, short-term damages representing less than the full amount of damages to which the claimant ultimately may be entitled shall not preclude recovery by the claimant for damages not reflected in the paid or settled partial claim."

Section Referred to in Other Sections

This section is referred to in title 16 section 1443.

NATURAL RESOURCES

33 USC 2706

(a) Liability
In the case of natural resource damages under section 2702(b)(2)(A) of this title, liability shall be—
  (1) to the United States Government for natural resources belonging to, managed by, controlled by, or appertaining to the United States;
  (2) to any State for natural resources belonging to, managed by, controlled by, or appertaining to such State or political subdivision thereof;
  (3) to any Indian tribe for natural resources belonging to, managed by, controlled by, or appertaining to such Indian tribe; and
  (4) in any case in which section 2707 of this title applies, to the government of a foreign country for natural resources belonging to, managed by, controlled by, or appertaining to such country.
(b) Designation of trustees
  (1) In general

The President, or the authorized representative of any State, Indian tribe, or foreign government, shall act on behalf of the public, Indian tribe, or foreign country as trustee of natural resources to present a claim for and to recover damages to the natural resources.
   (2) Federal trustees
      The President shall designate the Federal officials who shall act on behalf of the public as trustees for natural resources under this Act.
   (3) State trustees
      The Governor of each State shall designate State and local officials who may act on behalf of the public as trustee for natural resources under this Act and shall notify the President of the designation.
   (4) Indian tribe trustees
      The governing body of any Indian tribe shall designate tribal officials who may act on behalf of the tribe or its members as trustee for natural resources under this Act and shall notify the President of the designation.
   (5) Foreign trustees
      The head of any foreign government may designate the trustee who shall act on behalf of that government as trustee for natural resources under this Act.
(c) Functions of trustees
   (1) Federal trustees
      The Federal officials designated under subsection (b)(2) of this section—
      (A) shall assess natural resource damages under section 2702(b)(2)(A) of this title for the natural resources under their trusteeship;
      (B) may, upon request of and reimbursement from a State or Indian tribe and at the Federal officials' discretion, assess damages for the natural resources under the State's or tribe's trusteeship; and
      (C) shall develop and implement a plan for the restoration, rehabilitation, replacement, or acquisition of the equivalent, of the natural resources under their trusteeship.
   (2) State trustees
      The State and local officials designated under subsection (b)(3) of this section—
      (A) shall assess natural resource damages under section 2702(b)(2)(A) of this title for the purposes of this Act for the natural resources under their trusteeship; and
      (B) shall develop and implement a plan for the restoration, rehabilitation, replacement, or acquisition of the equivalent, of the natural resources under their trusteeship.
   (3) Indian tribe trustees
      The tribal officials designated under subsection (b)(4) of this section—
      (A) shall assess natural resource damages under section 2702(b)(2)(A) of this title for the purposes of this Act for the natural resources under their trusteeship; and
      (B) shall develop and implement a plan for the restoration, rehabilitation, replacement, or acquisition of the equivalent, of the natural resources under their trusteeship.
   (4) Foreign trustees
      The trustees designated under subsection (b)(5) of this section—
      (A) shall assess natural resource damages under section 2702(b)(2)(A) of this title for the purposes of this Act for the natural resources under their trusteeship; and
      (B) shall develop and implement a plan for the restoration, rehabilitation, replacement, or acquisition of the equivalent, of the natural resources under their trusteeship.
   (5) Notice and opportunity to be heard
      Plans shall be developed and implemented under this section only after adequate public notice, opportunity for a hearing, and consideration of all public comment.
(d) Measure of damages
   (1) In general
      The measure of natural resource damages under section 2702(b)(2)(A) of this title is—
      (A) the cost of restoring, rehabilitating, replacing, or acquiring the equivalent of, the damaged natural resources;
      (B) the diminution in value of those natural resources pending restoration; plus
      (C) the reasonable cost of assessing those damages.
   (2) Determine costs with respect to plans
      Costs shall be determined under paragraph (1) with respect to plans adopted under subsection (c) of this section.

(3) No double recovery
There shall be no double recovery under this Act for natural resource damages, including with respect to the costs of damage assessment or restoration, rehabilitation, replacement, or acquisition for the same incident and natural resource.

(e) Damage assessment regulations
(1) Regulations
The President, acting through the Under Secretary of Commerce for Oceans and Atmosphere and in consultation with the Administrator of the Environmental Protection Agency, the Director of the United States Fish and Wildlife Service, and the heads of other affected agencies, not later than 2 years after August 18, 1990, shall promulgate regulations for the assessment of natural resource damages under section 2702(b)(2)(A) of this title resulting from a discharge of oil for the purpose of this Act.
(2) Rebuttable presumption
Any determination or assessment of damages to natural resources for the purposes of this Act made under subsection (d) of this section by a Federal, State, or Indian trustee in accordance with the regulations promulgated under paragraph (1) shall have the force and effect of a rebuttable presumption on behalf of the trustee in any administrative or judicial proceeding under this Act.

(f) Use of recovered sums
Sums recovered under this Act by a Federal, State, Indian, or foreign trustee for natural resource damages under section 2702(b)(2)(A) of this title shall be retained by the trustee in a revolving trust account, without further appropriation, for use only to reimburse or pay costs incurred by the trustee under subsection (c) of this section with respect to the damaged natural resources. Any amounts in excess of those required for these reimbursements and costs shall be deposited in the Fund.

(g) Compliance
Review of actions by any Federal official where there is alleged to be a failure of that official to perform a duty under this section that is not discretionary with that official may be had by any person in the district court in which the person resides or in which the alleged damage to natural resources occurred. The court may award costs of litigation (including reasonable attorney and expert witness fees) to any prevailing or substantially prevailing party. Nothing in this subsection shall restrict any right which any person may have to seek relief under any other provision of law.

(Pub. L. 101-380, title I, Sec. 1006, Aug. 18, 1990, 104 Stat. 494.)

References in Text

This Act, referred to in subsecs. (b)(2)-(5), (c)(2)(A), (3)(A), (4)(A), (d)(3), (e), and (f), is Pub. L. 101-380, Aug. 18, 1990, 104 Stat. 484, as amended, known as the Oil Pollution Act of 1990, which is classified principally to this chapter. For complete classification of this Act to the Code, see Short Title note set out under section 2701 of this title and Tables.

Delegation of Functions

Functions of President under subsec. (b)(3) and (4) of this section delegated to Administrator of Environmental Protection Agency by section 8(c) of Ex. Ord. No. 12777, Oct. 18, 1991, 56 F.R. 54768, set out as a note under section 1321 of this title.

NOAA Oil and Hazardous Substance Spill Cost Reimbursement

Pub. L. 102-567, title II, Sec. 205, Oct. 29, 1992, 106 Stat. 4282, provided that:

"(a) Treatment of Amounts Received as Reimbursement of Expenses.–
Notwithstanding any other provision of law, amounts received by the United States as reimbursement of expenses related to oil or hazardous substance spill response activities, or natural resource damage assessment, restoration, rehabilitation, replacement, or acquisition activities, conducted (or to be conducted) by the National Oceanic and Atmospheric Administration—
(1) shall be deposited into the Fund;
(2) shall be available, without fiscal year limitation and without apportionment, for use in accordance with the law under which the activities are conducted; and
(3) shall not be considered to be an augmentation of appropriations.

(b) Application.—Subsection (a) shall apply to amounts described in subsection (a) that are received—
  (1) after the date of the enactment of this Act [Oct. 29, 1992]; or
  (2) with respect to the oil spill associated with the grounding of the EXXON VALDEZ.
(c) Definitions.—For purposes of this section—
  (1) the term 'Fund' means the Damage Assessment and Restoration Revolving Fund of the National Oceanic and Atmospheric Administration referred to in title I of Public Law 101-515 under the heading 'National Oceanic and Atmospheric Administration' (104 Stat. 2105) [set out as a note below]; and
  (2) the term 'expenses' includes incremental and base salaries, ships, aircraft, and associated indirect costs, except the term does not include base salaries and benefits of National Oceanic and Atmospheric Administration Support Coordinators."

Damage Assessment and Restoration Revolving Fund; Deposits; Availability; Transfer

Pub. L. 101-515, title I, Nov. 5, 1990, 104 Stat. 2105, provided that: "For contingency planning, response and natural resource damage assessment and restoration activities, pursuant to the Comprehensive Environmental Response, Compensation[,] and Liability Act [of 1980], as amended [42 U.S.C. 9601 et seq.], the Federal Water Pollution Control Act, as amended [33 U.S.C. 1251 et seq.], the Marine Protection, Research[,] and Sanctuaries Act [of 1972], as amended [16 U.S.C. 1431et seq., 1447 et seq.; 33 U.S.C. 1401 et seq., 2801 et seq.], and the Oil Pollution Act of 1990 [33 U.S.C. 2701 et seq.], $5,000,000 to remain available until expended: Provided, That notwithstanding any other provision of law, in fiscal year 1991 and thereafter, sums provided by any party or governmental entity for natural resource damage assessment, response or restoration activities conducted or to be conducted by the National Oceanic and Atmospheric Administration as a result of any injury to the marine environment and/or resources for which the National Oceanic and Atmospheric Administration acts as trustee of said marine environment and/or resources, shall be deposited in the Damage Assessment and Restoration Revolving Fund and said funds so deposited shall remain available until expended: Provided further, That for purposes of obligation and expenditure in fiscal year 1991 and thereafter, sums available in the Damage Assessment and Restoration Revolving Fund may be transferred, upon the approval of the Secretary of Commerce or his delegate, to the Operations, Research, and Facilities appropriation of the National Oceanic and Atmospheric Administration."

Section Referred to in Other Sections

This section is referred to in sections 2711, 2712, 2717, 2752 of this title; title 26 section 9509.

RECOVERY BY FOREIGN CLAIMANTS

33 USC 2707

(a) Required showing by foreign claimants
  (1) In general
    In addition to satisfying the other requirements of this Act, to recover removal costs or damages resulting from an incident a foreign claimant shall demonstrate that—
    (A) the claimant has not been otherwise compensated for the removal costs or damages; and
    (B) recovery is authorized by a treaty or executive agreement between the United States and the claimant's country, or the Secretary of State, in consultation with the Attorney General and other appropriate officials, has certified that the claimant's country provides a comparable remedy for United States claimants.
  (2) Exceptions
    Paragraph (1)(B) shall not apply with respect to recovery by a resident of Canada in the case of an incident described in subsection (b)(4) of this section.
(b) Discharges in foreign countries
  A foreign claimant may make a claim for removal costs and damages resulting from a discharge, or substantial threat of a discharge, of oil in or on the territorial sea, internal waters, or adjacent shoreline of a foreign country, only if the discharge is from—

(1) an Outer Continental Shelf facility or a deepwater port;
(2) a vessel in the navigable waters;
(3) a vessel carrying oil as cargo between 2 places in the United States; or
(4) a tanker that received the oil at the terminal of the pipeline constructed under the Trans-Alaska Pipeline Authorization Act (43 U.S.C. 1651 et seq.), for transportation to a place in the United States, and the discharge or threat occurs prior to delivery of the oil to that place.

(c) "Foreign claimant" defined
In this section, the term "foreign claimant" means—
(1) a person residing in a foreign country;
(2) the government of a foreign country; and
(3) an agency or political subdivision of a foreign country.

(Pub. L. 101-380, title I, Sec. 1007, Aug. 18, 1990, 104 Stat. 496.)

References in Text

This Act, referred to in subsec. (a)(1), is Pub. L. 101-380, Aug. 18, 1990, 104 Stat. 484, as amended, known as the Oil Pollution Act of 1990, which is classified principally to this chapter. For complete classification of this Act to the Code, see Short Title note set out under section 2701 of this title and Tables.

The Trans-Alaska Pipeline Authorization Act, referred to in subsec. (b)(4), is title II of Pub. L. 93-153, Nov. 16, 1973, 87 Stat. 584, which is classified generally to chapter 34 (Sec. 1651 et seq.) of Title 43, Public Lands. For complete classification of this Act to the Code, see Short Title note set out under section 1651 of Title 43 and Tables.

Section Referred to in Other Sections

This section is referred to in section 2706 of this title.

RECOVERY BY RESPONSIBLE PARTY

33 USC 2708

(a) In general
The responsible party for a vessel or facility from which oil is discharged, or which poses the substantial threat of a discharge of oil, may assert a claim for removal costs and damages under section 2713 of this title only if the responsible party demonstrates that—
(1) the responsible party is entitled to a defense to liability under section 2703 of this title; or
(2) the responsible party is entitled to a limitation of liability under section 2704 of this title.

(b) Extent of recovery
A responsible party who is entitled to a limitation of liability may assert a claim under section 2713 of this title only to the extent that the sum of the removal costs and damages incurred by the responsible party plus the amounts paid by the responsible party, or by the guarantor on behalf of the responsible party, for claims asserted under section 2713 of this title exceeds the amount to which the total of the liability under section 2702 of this title and removal costs and damages incurred by, or on behalf of, the responsible party is limited under section 2704 of this title.

(Pub. L. 101-380, title I, Sec. 1008, Aug. 18, 1990, 104 Stat. 497.)

Section Referred to in Other Sections

This section is referred to in section 2713 of this title.

CONTRIBUTION

33 USC 2709

A person may bring a civil action for contribution against any other person who is liable or potentially liable under this Act or another law. The action shall be brought in accordance with section 2717 of this title.

(Pub. L. 101-380, title I, Sec. 1009, Aug. 18, 1990, 104 Stat. 497.)

References in Text
This Act, referred to in text, is Pub. L. 101-380, Aug. 18, 1990, 104 Stat. 484, as amended, known as the Oil Pollution Act of 1990, which is classified principally to this chapter. For complete classification of this Act to the Code, see Short Title note set out under section 2701 of this title and Tables.

INDEMNIFICATION AGREEMENTS
33 USC 2710

(a) Agreements not prohibited
   Nothing in this Act prohibits any agreement to insure, hold harmless, or indemnify a party to such agreement for any liability under this Act.
(b) Liability not transferred
   No indemnification, hold harmless, or similar agreement or conveyance shall be effective to transfer liability imposed under this Act from a responsible party or from any person who may be liable for an incident under this Act to any other person.
(c) Relationship to other causes of action
   Nothing in this Act, including the provisions of subsection (b) of this section, bars a cause of action that a responsible party subject to liability under this Act, or a guarantor, has or would have, by reason of subrogation or otherwise, against any person.

(Pub. L. 101-380, title I, Sec. 1010, Aug. 18, 1990, 104 Stat. 498.)

References in Text
This Act, referred to in text, is Pub. L. 101-380, Aug. 18, 1990, 104 Stat. 484, as amended, known as the Oil Pollution Act of 1990, which is classified principally to this chapter. For complete classification of this Act to the Code, see Short Title note set out under section 2701 of this title and Tables.

CONSULTATION ON REMOVAL ACTIONS
33 USC 2711

The President shall consult with the affected trustees designated under section 2706 of this title on the appropriate removal action to be taken in connection with any discharge of oil. For the purposes of the National Contingency Plan, removal with respect to any discharge shall be considered completed when so determined by the President in consultation with the Governor or Governors of the affected States. However, this determination shall not preclude additional removal actions under applicable State law.

(Pub. L. 101-380, title I, Sec. 1011, Aug. 18, 1990, 104 Stat. 498.)

Delegation of Functions
Functions of President under this section delegated to Administrator of Environmental Protection Agency for inland zone and to Secretary of Department in which Coast Guard is operating for coastal zone by section 3 of Ex. Ord. No. 12777, Oct. 18, 1991, 56 F.R. 54757, set out as a note under section 1321 of this title.

USES OF FUND
33 USC 2712

(a) Uses generally
   The Fund shall be available to the President for—
   (1) the payment of removal costs, including the costs of monitoring removal actions, determined by the President to be consistent with the National Contingency Plan—
      (A) by Federal authorities; or
      (B) by a Governor or designated State official under subsection (d) of this section;
   (2) the payment of costs incurred by Federal, State, or Indian tribe trustees in carrying out their functions under section 2706 of this title for assessing natural resource damages and

for developing and implementing plans for the restoration, rehabilitation, replacement, or acquisition of the equivalent of damaged resources determined by the President to be consistent with the National Contingency Plan;
(3) the payment of removal costs determined by the President to be consistent with the National Contingency Plan as a result of, and damages resulting from, a discharge, or a substantial threat of a discharge, of oil from a foreign offshore unit;
(4) the payment of claims in accordance with section 2713 of this title for uncompensated removal costs determined by the President to be consistent with the National Contingency Plan or uncompensated damages;
(5) the payment of Federal administrative, operational, and personnel costs and expenses reasonably necessary for and incidental to the implementation, administration, and enforcement of this Act (including, but not limited to, sections 1004(d)(2), 1006(e), 4107, 4110, 4111, 4112, 4117, 5006, 8103, and title VII) and subsections (b), (c), (d), (j), and (l) of section 1321 of this title with respect to prevention, removal, and enforcement related to oil discharges, provided that—
   (A) not more than $25,000,000 in each fiscal year shall be available to the Secretary for operating expenses incurred by the Coast Guard;
   (B) not more than $30,000,000 each year through the end of fiscal year 1992 shall be available to establish the National Response System under section 1321(j) of this title, including the purchase and prepositioning of oil spill removal equipment; and
   (C) not more than $27,250,000 in each fiscal year shall be available to carry out subchapter IV of this chapter.
(b) Defense to liability for Fund
The Fund shall not be available to pay any claim for removal costs or damages to a particular claimant, to the extent that the incident, removal costs, or damages are caused by the gross negligence or willful misconduct of that claimant.
(c) Obligation of Fund by Federal officials
The President may promulgate regulations designating one or more Federal officials who may obligate money in accordance with subsection (a) of this section.
(d) Access to Fund by State officials
   (1) Immediate removal
   In accordance with regulations promulgated under this section, the President, upon the request of the Governor of a State or pursuant to an agreement with a State under paragraph (2), may obligate the Fund for payment in an amount not to exceed $250,000 for removal costs consistent with the National Contingency Plan required for the immediate removal of a discharge, or the mitigation or prevention of a substantial threat of a discharge, of oil.
   (2) Agreements
      (A) In general
      The President shall enter into an agreement with the Governor of any interested State to establish procedures under which the Governor or a designated State official may receive payments from the Fund for removal costs pursuant to paragraph (1).
      (B) Terms
      Agreements under this paragraph—
         (i) may include such terms and conditions as may be agreed upon by the President and the Governor of a State;
         (ii) shall provide for political subdivisions of the State to receive payments for reasonable removal costs; and
         (iii) may authorize advance payments from the Fund to facilitate removal efforts.
(e) Regulations
The President shall—
   (1) not later than 6 months after August 18, 1990, publish proposed regulations detailing the manner in which the authority to obligate the Fund and to enter into agreements under this subsection shall be exercised; and
   (2) not later than 3 months after the close of the comment period for such proposed regulations, promulgate final regulations for that purpose.

(f) Rights of subrogation
Payment of any claim or obligation by the Fund under this Act shall be subject to the United States Government acquiring by subrogation all rights of the claimant or State to recover from the responsible party.

(g) Audits
The Comptroller General shall audit all payments, obligations, reimbursements, and other uses of the Fund, to assure that the Fund is being properly administered and that claims are being appropriately and expeditiously considered. The Comptroller General shall submit to the Congress an interim report one year after August 18, 1990. The Comptroller General shall thereafter audit the Fund as is appropriate. Each Federal agency shall cooperate with the Comptroller General in carrying out this subsection.

(h) Period of limitations for claims
  (1) Removal costs
  No claim may be presented under this subchapter for recovery of removal costs for an incident unless the claim is presented within 6 years after the date of completion of all removal actions for that incident.
  (2) Damages
  No claim may be presented under this section for recovery of damages unless the claim is presented within 3 years after the date on which the injury and its connection with the discharge in question were reasonably discoverable with the exercise of due care, or in the case of natural resource damages under section 2702(b)(2)(A) of this title, if later, the date of completion of the natural resources damage assessment under section 2706(e) of this title.
  (3) Minors and incompetents
  The time limitations contained in this subsection shall not begin to run—
    (A) against a minor until the earlier of the date when such minor reaches 18 years of age or the date on which a legal representative is duly appointed for the minor, or
    (B) against an incompetent person until the earlier of the date on which such incompetent's incompetency ends or the date on which a legal representative is duly appointed for the incompetent.

(i) Limitation on payment for same costs
In any case in which the President has paid an amount from the Fund for any removal costs or damages specified under subsection (a) of this section, no other claim may be paid from the Fund for the same removal costs or damages.

(j) Obligation in accordance with plan
  (1) In general
  Except as provided in paragraph (2), amounts may be obligated from the Fund for the restoration, rehabilitation, replacement, or acquisition of natural resources only in accordance with a plan adopted under section 2706(c) of this title.
  (2) Exception
  Paragraph (1) shall not apply in a situation requiring action to avoid irreversible loss of natural resources or to prevent or reduce any continuing danger to natural resources or similar need for emergency action.

(k) Preference for private persons in area affected by discharge
  (1) In general
  In the expenditure of Federal funds for removal of oil, including for distribution of supplies, construction, and other reasonable and appropriate activities, under a contract or agreement with a private person, preference shall be given, to the extent feasible and practicable, to private persons residing or doing business primarily in the area affected by the discharge of oil.
  (2) Limitation
  This subsection shall not be considered to restrict the use of Department of Defense resources.

(Pub. L. 101-380, title I, Sec. 1012, Aug. 18, 1990, 104 Stat. 498.)

References in Text

This Act, referred to in subsecs. (a)(5) and (f), is Pub. L. 101-380, Aug. 18, 1990, 104 Stat. 484, known as the Oil Pollution Act of 1990, which is classified principally to this chapter. Sections 1004(d)(2) and 1006(e) are classified to sections 2704(d)(2) and 2706(e), respectively, of this title. Section 4107 amended section 1223 of this title and enacted provisions set out as a note under section 1223 of this title. Sections 4110 and 4111 enacted provisions set out as notes under section 3703 of Title 46, Shipping. Section 4112 is not classified to the Code. Section 4117 enacted provisions set out as a note under section 1295 of Title 46, Appendix. Section 5006 is classified to section 2736 of this title. Section 8103 enacted provisions set out as a note under section 1651 of Title 43, Public Lands. Title VII is classified to subchapter IV of this chapter. For complete classification of this Act to the Code, see Short Title note set out under section 2701 of this title and Tables.

Delegation of Functions

Functions of President under subsecs. (a)(1), (3), (4), (d), and (e) of this section delegated to Secretary of Department in which Coast Guard is operating by section 7(a)(1)(A), (c)(1), (3) of Ex. Ord. No. 12777, Oct. 18, 1991, 56 F.R. 54766, 54767, set out as a note under section 1321 of this title.

Functions of President under subsec. (a)(2) of this section delegated to Federal trustees designated in National Contingency Plan by section 7(a)(2) of Ex. Ord. No. 12777.

Functions of President under subsecs. (a)(5) and (c) of this section delegated to each head of departments and agencies having responsibility for implementation, administration, and enforcement of the Oil Pollution Act of 1990 (Pub. L. 101-380, see Tables for classification) and section 1321(b), (c), (d), (j), (l) of this title by section 7(a)(3), (b) of Ex. Ord. No. 12777.

Memorandum of the President of the United States, Aug. 24, 1990, 55 F.R. 35291, which delegated to the Secretary of the Department in which the Coast Guard is operating authority to make available from the Oil Spill Liability Trust Fund not to exceed $50,000,000 in any fiscal year to remove discharged oil or hazardous substances from navigable waters, was revoked by Ex. Ord. No. 12777, Sec. 8(i), Oct. 18, 1991, 56 F.R. 54769, set out as a note under section 1321 of this title.

Section Referred to in Other Sections

This section is referred to in sections 2713, 2736, 2752 of this title; title 26 section 9509.

CLAIMS PROCEDURE

33 USC 2713

(a) Presentation
Except as provided in subsection (b) of this section, all claims for removal costs or damages shall be presented first to the responsible party or guarantor of the source designated under section 2714(a) of this title.

(b) Presentation to Fund
  (1) In general
  Claims for removal costs or damages may be presented first to the Fund—
    (A) if the President has advertised or otherwise notified claimants in accordance with section 2714(c) of this title;
    (B) by a responsible party who may assert a claim under section 2708 of this title;
    (C) by the Governor of a State for removal costs incurred by that State; or
    (D) by a United States claimant in a case where a foreign offshore unit has discharged oil causing damage for which the Fund is liable under section 2712(a) of this title.
  (2) Limitation on presenting claim
  No claim of a person against the Fund may be approved or certified during the pendency of an action by the person in court to recover costs which are the subject of the claim.

(c) Election
If a claim is presented in accordance with subsection (a) of this section and—
  (1) each person to whom the claim is presented denies all liability for the claim, or
  (2) the claim is not settled by any person by payment within 90 days after the date upon which

(A) the claim was presented, or (B) advertising was begun pursuant to section 2714(b) of this title, whichever is later,

the claimant may elect to commence an action in court against the responsible party or guarantor or to present the claim to the Fund.

(d) Uncompensated damages

If a claim is presented in accordance with this section, including a claim for interim, short-term damages representing less than the full amount of damages to which the claimant ultimately may be entitled, and full and adequate compensation is unavailable, a claim for the uncompensated damages and removal costs may be presented to the Fund.

(e) Procedure for claims against Fund

The President shall promulgate, and may from time to time amend, regulations for the presentation, filing, processing, settlement, and adjudication of claims under this Act against the Fund.

(Pub. L. 101-380, title I, Sec. 1013, Aug. 18, 1990, 104 Stat. 501; Pub. L. 104-324, title XI, Sec. 1142(b), Oct. 19, 1996, 110 Stat. 3991.)

References in Text

This Act, referred to in subsec. (e), is Pub. L. 101-380, Aug. 18, 1990, 104 Stat. 484, as amended, known as the Oil Pollution Act of 1990, which is classified principally to this chapter. For complete classification of this Act to the Code, see Short Title note set out under section 2701 of this title and Tables.

Amendments

1996—Subsec. (d). Pub. L. 104-324 substituted "section, including a claim for interim, short-term damages representing less than the full amount of damages to which the claimant ultimately may be entitled," for "section".

Delegation of Functions

Functions of President under subsec. (e) of this section delegated to Secretary of Department in which Coast Guard is operating by section 7(c)(2) of Ex. Ord. No. 12777, Oct. 18, 1991, 56 F.R. 54767, set out as a note under section 1321 of this title.

Section Referred to in Other Sections

This section is referred to in sections 2702, 2705, 2708, 2712 of this title.

DESIGNATION OF SOURCE AND ADVERTISEMENT

33 USC 2714

(a) Designation of source and notification

When the President receives information of an incident, the President shall, where possible and appropriate, designate the source or sources of the discharge or threat. If a designated source is a vessel or a facility, the President shall immediately notify the responsible party and the guarantor, if known, of that designation.

(b) Advertisement by responsible party or guarantor

(1) If a responsible party or guarantor fails to inform the President, within 5 days after receiving notification of a designation under subsection (a) of this section, of the party's or the guarantor's denial of the designation, such party or guarantor shall advertise the designation and the procedures by which claims may be presented, in accordance with regulations promulgated by the President. Advertisement under the preceding sentence shall begin no later than 15 days after the date of the designation made under subsection (a) of this section. If advertisement is not otherwise made in accordance with this subsection, the President shall promptly and at the expense of the responsible party or the guarantor involved, advertise the designation and the procedures by which claims may be presented to the responsible party or guarantor. Advertisement under this subsection shall continue for a period of no less than 30 days.

(2) An advertisement under paragraph (1) shall state that a claimant may present a claim for interim, short-term damages representing less than the full amount of damages to which

the claimant ultimately may be entitled and that payment of such a claim shall not preclude recovery for damages not reflected in the paid or settled partial claim.
(c) Advertisement by President
If—
 (1) the responsible party and the guarantor both deny a designation within 5 days after receiving notification of a designation under subsection (a) of this section,
 (2) the source of the discharge or threat was a public vessel, or
 (3) the President is unable to designate the source or sources of the discharge or threat under subsection (a) of this section,
 the President shall advertise or otherwise notify potential claimants of the procedures by which claims may be presented to the Fund.

(Pub. L. 101-380, title I, Sec. 1014, Aug. 18, 1990, 104 Stat. 501; Pub. L. 104-324, title XI, Sec. 1142(c), Oct. 19, 1996, 110 Stat. 3991.)

Amendments

1996—Subsec. (b). Pub. L. 104-324 designated existing provisions as par. (1) and added par. (2).

Delegation of Functions

Functions of President under this section delegated to Secretary of Department in which Coast Guard is operating by section 7(d)(2) of Ex. Ord. No. 12777, Oct. 18, 1991, 56 F.R. 54768, set out as a note under section 1321 of this title.

Section Referred to in Other Sections

This section is referred to in section 2713 of this title.

SUBROGATION

33 USC 2715

(a) In general
 Any person, including the Fund, who pays compensation pursuant to this Act to any claimant for removal costs or damages shall be subrogated to all rights, claims, and causes of action that the claimant has under any other law.
(b) Interim damages
 (1) In general
  If a responsible party, a guarantor, or the Fund has made payment to a claimant for interim, short-term damages representing less than the full amount of damages to which the claimant ultimately may be entitled, subrogation under subsection (a) of this section shall apply only with respect to the portion of the claim reflected in the paid interim claim.
 (2) Final damages
  Payment of such a claim shall not foreclose a claimant's right to recovery of all damages to which the claimant otherwise is entitled under this Act or under any other law.
(c) Actions on behalf of Fund
 At the request of the Secretary, the Attorney General shall commence an action on behalf of the Fund to recover any compensation paid by the Fund to any claimant pursuant to this Act, and all costs incurred by the Fund by reason of the claim, including interest (including prejudgment interest), administrative and adjudicative costs, and attorney's fees. Such an action may be commenced against any responsible party or (subject to section 2716 of this title) guarantor, or against any other person who is liable, pursuant to any law, to the compensated claimant or to the Fund, for the cost or damages for which the compensation was paid. Such an action shall be commenced against the responsible foreign government or other responsible party to recover any removal costs or damages paid from the Fund as the result of the discharge, or substantial threat of discharge, of oil from a foreign offshore unit.

(Pub. L. 101-380, title I, Sec. 1015, Aug. 18, 1990, 104 Stat. 502; Pub. L. 104-324, title XI, Sec. 1142(d), Oct. 19, 1996, 110 Stat. 3991.)

References in Text

This Act, referred to in text, is Pub. L. 101-380, Aug. 18, 1990, 104 Stat. 484, as amended, known as the Oil Pollution Act of 1990, which is classified principally to this chapter. For complete classification of this Act to the Code, see Short Title note set out under section 2701 of this title and Tables.

Amendments

1996—Subsecs. (b), (c). Pub. L. 104-324 added subsec. (b) and redesignated former subsec. (b) as (c).

Section Referred to in Other Sections

This section is referred to in title 26 section 9509.

FINANCIAL RESPONSIBILITY

33 USC 2716

(a) Requirement

The responsible party for—
(1) any vessel over 300 gross tons (except a non-self-propelled vessel that does not carry oil as cargo or fuel) using any place subject to the jurisdiction of the United States; or
(2) any vessel using the waters of the exclusive economic zone to transship or lighter oil destined for a place subject to the jurisdiction of the United States;

shall establish and maintain, in accordance with regulations promulgated by the Secretary, evidence of financial responsibility sufficient to meet the maximum amount of liability to which the responsible party could be subjected under section 2704(a) or (d) of this title, in a case where the responsible party would be entitled to limit liability under that section. If the responsible party owns or operates more than one vessel, evidence of financial responsibility need be established only to meet the amount of the maximum liability applicable to the vessel having the greatest maximum liability.

(b) Sanctions
(1) Withholding clearance

The Secretary of the Treasury shall withhold or revoke the clearance required by section 91 of title 46, Appendix, of any vessel subject to this section that does not have the evidence of financial responsibility required for the vessel under this section.

(2) Denying entry to or detaining vessels

The Secretary may—
(A) deny entry to any vessel to any place in the United States, or to the navigable waters, or
(B) detain at the place,

any vessel that, upon request, does not produce the evidence of financial responsibility required for the vessel under this section.

(3) Seizure of vessel

Any vessel subject to the requirements of this section which is found in the navigable waters without the necessary evidence of financial responsibility for the vessel shall be subject to seizure by and forfeiture to the United States.

(c) Offshore facilities
(1) In general
(A) Evidence of financial responsibility required

Except as provided in paragraph (2), a responsible party with respect to an offshore facility that—
(i) (I) is located seaward of the line of ordinary low water along that portion of the coast that is in direct contact with the open sea and the line marking the seaward limit of inland waters; or
(II) is located in coastal inland waters, such as bays or estuaries, seaward of the line of ordinary low water along that portion of the coast that is not in direct contact with the open sea;
(ii) is used for exploring for, drilling for, producing, or transporting oil from facilities engaged in oil exploration, drilling, or production; and
(iii) has a worst-case oil spill discharge potential of more than 1,000 barrels of oil (or a lesser amount if the President determines that the risks posed by such facility justify it), shall establish and maintain evidence of financial responsibility in the amount required under subparagraph (B) or (C), as applicable.

(B) Amount required generally
Except as provided in subparagraph (C), the amount of financial responsibility for offshore facilities that meet the criteria of subparagraph (A) is—
  (i) $35,000,000 for an offshore facility located seaward of the seaward boundary of a State; or
  (ii) $10,000,000 for an offshore facility located landward of the seaward boundary of a State.
(C) Greater amount
If the President determines that an amount of financial responsibility for a responsible party greater than the amount required by subparagraph (B) is justified based on the relative operational, environmental, human health, and other risks posed by the quantity or quality of oil that is explored for, drilled for, produced, or transported by the responsible party, the evidence of financial responsibility required shall be for an amount determined by the President not exceeding $150,000,000.
(D) Multiple facilities
In a case in which a person is a responsible party for more than one facility subject to this subsection, evidence of financial responsibility need be established only to meet the amount applicable to the facility having the greatest financial responsibility requirement under this subsection.
(E) Definition
For the purpose of this paragraph, the seaward boundary of a State shall be determined in accordance with section 1301(b) of title 43.
(2) Deepwater ports
Each responsible party with respect to a deepwater port shall establish and maintain evidence of financial responsibility sufficient to meet the maximum amount of liability to which the responsible party could be subjected under section 2704(a) of this title in a case where the responsible party would be entitled to limit liability under that section. If the Secretary exercises the authority under section 2704(d)(2) of this title to lower the limit of liability for deepwater ports, the responsible party shall establish and maintain evidence of financial responsibility sufficient to meet the maximum amount of liability so established. In a case in which a person is the responsible party for more than one deepwater port, evidence of financial responsibility need be established only to meet the maximum liability applicable to the deepwater port having the greatest maximum liability.

(e)[1] Methods of financial responsibility
Financial responsibility under this section may be established by any one, or by any combination, of the following methods which the Secretary (in the case of a vessel) or the President (in the case of a facility) determines to be acceptable: evidence of insurance, surety bond, guarantee, letter of credit, qualification as a self-insurer, or other evidence of financial responsibility. Any bond filed shall be issued by a bonding company authorized to do business in the United States. In promulgating requirements under this section, the Secretary or the President, as appropriate, may specify policy or other contractual terms, conditions, or defenses which are necessary, or which are unacceptable, in establishing evidence of financial responsibility to effectuate the purposes of this Act.

(f) Claims against guarantor
(1) In general
Subject to paragraph (2), a claim for which liability may be established under section 2702 of this title may be asserted directly against any guarantor providing evidence of financial responsibility for a responsible party liable under that section for removal costs and damages to which the claim pertains. In defending against such a claim, the guarantor may invoke—
(A) all rights and defenses which would be available to the responsible party under this Act;
(B) any defense authorized under subsection (e) of this section; and
(C) the defense that the incident was caused by the willful misconduct of the responsible party.

---

[1] So in original. No subsec. (d) has been enacted.

The guarantor may not invoke any other defense that might be available in proceedings brought by the responsible party against the guarantor.

(2) Further requirement

A claim may be asserted pursuant to paragraph (1) directly against a guarantor providing evidence of financial responsibility under subsection (c)(1) of this section with respect to an offshore facility only if—

(A) the responsible party for whom evidence of financial responsibility has been provided has denied or failed to pay a claim under this Act on the basis of being insolvent, as defined under section 101(32) of title 11, and applying generally accepted accounting principles;

(B) the responsible party for whom evidence of financial responsibility has been provided has filed a petition for bankruptcy under title 11; or

(C) the claim is asserted by the United States for removal costs and damages or for compensation paid by the Fund under this Act, including costs incurred by the Fund for processing compensation claims.

(3) Rulemaking authority

Not later than 1 year after October 19, 1996, the President shall promulgate regulations to establish a process for implementing paragraph (2) in a manner that will allow for the orderly and expeditious presentation and resolution of claims and effectuate the purposes of this Act.

(g) Limitation on guarantor's liability

Nothing in this Act shall impose liability with respect to an incident on any guarantor for damages or removal costs which exceed, in the aggregate, the amount of financial responsibility which that guarantor has provided for a responsible party pursuant to this section. The total liability of the guarantor on direct action for claims brought under this Act with respect to an incident shall be limited to that amount.

(h) Continuation of regulations

Any regulation relating to financial responsibility, which has been issued pursuant to any provision of law repealed or superseded by this Act, and which is in effect on the date immediately preceding the effective date of this Act, is deemed and shall be construed to be a regulation issued pursuant to this section. Such a regulation shall remain in full force and effect unless and until superseded by a new regulation issued under this section.

(i) Unified certificate

The Secretary may issue a single unified certificate of financial responsibility for purposes of this Act and any other law.

(Pub. L. 101-380, title I, Sec. 1016, Aug. 18, 1990, 104 Stat. 502; Pub. L. 104-55, Sec. 2(d)(2), Nov. 20, 1995, 109 Stat. 547; Pub. L. 104-324, title XI, Sec. 1125(a), Oct. 19, 1996, 110 Stat. 3981.)

References in Text

This Act, referred to in subsecs. (e), (f), (g), (h), and (i), is Pub. L. 101-380, Aug. 18, 1990, 104 Stat. 484, as amended, known as the Oil Pollution Act of 1990, which is classified principally to this chapter. For complete classification of this Act to the Code, see Short Title note set out under section 2701 of this title and Tables.

The effective date of this Act, referred to in subsec. (h), is the effective date of Pub. L. 101-380 which is applicable to incidents occurring after Aug. 18, 1990, see section 1020 of Pub. L. 101-380, set out as an Effective Date note under section 2701 of this title.

Amendments

1996—Subsec. (c)(1). Pub. L. 104-324, Sec. 1125(a)(1), reenacted heading without change and amended text generally. Prior to amendment, text read as follows: "Except as provided in paragraph (2), each responsible party with respect to an offshore facility shall establish and maintain evidence of financial responsibility of $150,000,000 to meet the amount of liability to which the responsible party could be subjected under section 2704(a) of this title in a case in which the responsible party would be entitled to limit liability under that section. In a case in which a person is the responsible party for more than one facility subject to this subsection, evidence of financial responsibility need be established only to meet the maximum liability applicable to the facility having the greatest maximum liability."

708 / Environmental Statutes

Subsec. (f). Pub. L. 104-324, Sec. 1125(a)(2), reenacted heading without change and amended text generally. Prior to amendment, text read as follows: "Any claim for which liability may be established under section 2702 of this title may be asserted directly against any guarantor providing evidence of financial responsibility for a responsible party liable under that section for removal costs and damages to which the claim pertains. In defending against such a claim, the guarantor may invoke (1) all rights and defenses which would be available to the responsible party under this Act, (2) any defense authorized under subsection (e) of this section, and (3) the defense that the incident was caused by the willful misconduct of the responsible party. The guarantor may not invoke any other defense that might be available in proceedings brought by the responsible party against the guarantor."

Subsec. (g). Pub. L. 104-324, Sec. 1125(a)(3), reenacted heading without change and amended text generally. Prior to amendment, text read as follows: "Nothing in this Act shall impose liability with respect to an incident on any guarantor for damages or removal costs which exceed, in the aggregate, the amount of financial responsibility required under this Act which that guarantor has provided for a responsible party."

1995—Subsec. (a). Pub. L. 104-55 substituted "the responsible party could be subjected under section 2704(a) or (d) of this title" for ", in the case of a tank vessel, the responsible party could be subject under section 2704(a)(1) or (d) of this title, or to which, in the case of any other vessel, the responsible party could be subjected under section 2704(a)(2) or (d) of this title".

Effective Date of 1996 Amendment

Section 1125(b) of Pub. L. 104-324 provided that: "The amendment made by subsection (a)(2) [amending this section] shall not apply to any final rule issued before the date of enactment of this section [Oct. 19, 1996]."

Delegation of Functions

Specific functions of President under subsec. (e) of this section delegated to Secretary of the Interior and Secretary of Transportation by section 5(a) of Ex. Ord. No. 12777, Oct. 18, 1991, 56 F.R. 54764, set out as a note under section 1321 of this title.

Section Referred to in Other Sections

This section is referred to in sections 1503, 2705, 2715, 2716a, 2719 of this title; title 46 section 3715.

FINANCIAL RESPONSIBILITY CIVIL PENALTIES

33 USC 2716a

(a) Administrative

Any person who, after notice and an opportunity for a hearing, is found to have failed to comply with the requirements of section 2716 of this title or the regulations issued under that section, or with a denial or detention order issued under subsection (c)(2) of that section, shall be liable to the United States for a civil penalty, not to exceed $25,000 per day of violation. The amount of the civil penalty shall be assessed by the President by written notice. In determining the amount of the penalty, the President shall take into account the nature, circumstances, extent, and gravity of the violation, the degree of culpability, any history of prior violation, ability to pay, and such other matters as justice may require. The President may compromise, modify, or remit, with or without conditions, any civil penalty which is subject to imposition or which had been imposed under this paragraph. If any person fails to pay an assessed civil penalty after it has become final, the President may refer the matter to the Attorney General for collection.

(b) Judicial

In addition to, or in lieu of, assessing a penalty under subsection (a) of this section, the President may request the Attorney General to secure such relief as necessary to compel compliance with this[1] section 2716 of this title, including a judicial order terminating operations. The district courts of the United States shall have jurisdiction to grant any relief as the public interest and the equities of the case may require.

---

[1] So in original. The word "this" probably should not appear.

(Pub. L. 101-380, title IV, Sec. 4303, Aug. 18, 1990, 104 Stat. 539.)

Codification

Section was not enacted as part of title I of Pub. L. 101-380 which comprises this subchapter.

Delegation of Functions

Specific functions of President under this section delegated to Secretary of Department in which Coast Guard is operating, Secretary of the Interior, and Secretary of Transportation by section 5(b) of Ex. Ord. No. 12777, Oct. 18, 1991, 56 F.R. 54765, set out as a note under section 1321 of this title.

LITIGATION, JURISDICTION, AND VENUE

33 USC 2717

(a) Review of regulations
Review of any regulation promulgated under this Act may be had upon application by any interested person only in the Circuit Court of Appeals of the United States for the District of Columbia. Any such application shall be made within 90 days from the date of promulgation of such regulations. Any matter with respect to which review could have been obtained under this subsection shall not be subject to judicial review in any civil or criminal proceeding for enforcement or to obtain damages or recovery of response costs.

(b) Jurisdiction
Except as provided in subsections (a) and (c) of this section, the United States district courts shall have exclusive original jurisdiction over all controversies arising under this Act, without regard to the citizenship of the parties or the amount in controversy. Venue shall lie in any district in which the discharge or injury or damages occurred, or in which the defendant resides, may be found, has its principal office, or has appointed an agent for service of process. For the purposes of this section, the Fund shall reside in the District of Columbia.

(c) State court jurisdiction
A State trial court of competent jurisdiction over claims for removal costs or damages, as defined under this Act, may consider claims under this Act or State law and any final judgment of such court (when no longer subject to ordinary forms of review) shall be recognized, valid, and enforceable for all purposes of this Act.

(d) Assessment and collection of tax
The provisions of subsections (a), (b), and (c) of this section shall not apply to any controversy or other matter resulting from the assessment or collection of any tax, or to the review of any regulation promulgated under title 26.

(e) Savings provision
Nothing in this subchapter shall apply to any cause of action or right of recovery arising from any incident which occurred prior to August 18, 1990. Such claims shall be adjudicated pursuant to the law applicable on the date of the incident.

(f) Period of limitations
  (1) Damages
  Except as provided in paragraphs (3) and (4), an action for damages under this Act shall be barred unless the action is brought within 3 years after—
    (A) the date on which the loss and the connection of the loss with the discharge in question are reasonably discoverable with the exercise of due care, or
    (B) in the case of natural resource damages under section 2702(b)(2)(A) of this title, the date of completion of the natural resources damage assessment under section 2706(c) of this title.
  (2) Removal costs
  An action for recovery of removal costs referred to in section 2702(b)(1) of this title must be commenced within 3 years after completion of the removal action. In any such action described in this subsection, the court shall enter a declaratory judgment on liability for removal costs or damages that will be binding on any subsequent action or actions to recover further removal costs or damages. Except as otherwise provided in this paragraph,

an action may be commenced under this subchapter for recovery of removal costs at any time after such costs have been incurred.
(3) Contribution
No action for contribution for any removal costs or damages may be commenced more than 3 years after—
(A) the date of judgment in any action under this Act for recovery of such costs or damages, or
(B) the date of entry of a judicially approved settlement with respect to such costs or damages.
(4) Subrogation
No action based on rights subrogated pursuant to this Act by reason of payment of a claim may be commenced under this Act more than 3 years after the date of payment of such claim.
(5) Commencement
The time limitations contained herein shall not begin to run—
(A) against a minor until the earlier of the date when such minor reaches 18 years of age or the date on which a legal representative is duly appointed for such minor, or
(B) against an incompetent person until the earlier of the date on which such incompetent's incompetency ends or the date on which a legal representative is duly appointed for such incompetent.

(Pub. L. 101-380, title I, Sec. 1017, Aug. 18, 1990, 104 Stat. 504.)

References in Text

This Act, referred to in subsecs. (a), (b), (c), and (f), is Pub. L. 101-380, Aug. 18, 1990, 104 Stat. 484, as amended, known as the Oil Pollution Act of 1990, which is classified principally to this chapter. For complete classification of this Act to the Code, see Short Title note set out under section 2701 of this title and Tables.

Section Referred to in Other Sections

This section is referred to in section 2709 of this title.

RELATIONSHIP TO OTHER LAW

33 USC 2718

(a) Preservation of State authorities; Solid Waste Disposal Act
Nothing in this Act or the Act of March 3, 1851 shall—
 (1) affect, or be construed or interpreted as preempting, the authority of any State or political subdivision thereof from imposing any additional liability or requirements with respect to—
  (A) the discharge of oil or other pollution by oil within such State; or
  (B) any removal activities in connection with such a discharge; or
 (2) affect, or be construed or interpreted to affect or modify in any way the obligations or liabilities of any person under the Solid Waste Disposal Act (42 U.S.C. 6901 et seq.) or State law, including common law.
(b) Preservation of State funds
Nothing in this Act or in section 9509 of title 26 shall in any way affect, or be construed to affect, the authority of any State—
 (1) to establish, or to continue in effect, a fund any purpose of which is to pay for costs or damages arising out of, or directly resulting from, oil pollution or the substantial threat of oil pollution; or
 (2) to require any person to contribute to such a fund.
(c) Additional requirements and liabilities; penalties
Nothing in this Act, the Act of March 3, 1851 (46 U.S.C. 183 et seq.), or section 9509 of title 26, shall in any way affect, or be construed to affect, the authority of the United States or any State or political subdivision thereof—
 (1) to impose additional liability or additional requirements; or
 (2) to impose, or to determine the amount of, any fine or penalty (whether criminal or civil in nature) for any violation of law; relating to the discharge, or substantial threat of a discharge, of oil.

(d) Federal employee liability
For purposes of section 2679(b)(2)(B) of title 28, nothing in this Act shall be construed to authorize or create a cause of action against a Federal officer or employee in the officer's or employee's personal or individual capacity for any act or omission while acting within the scope of the officer's or employee's office or employment.

(Pub. L. 101-380, title I, Sec. 1018, Aug. 18, 1990, 104 Stat. 505.)

References in Text

This Act, referred to in text, is Pub. L. 101-380, Aug. 18, 1990, 104 Stat. 484, as amended, known as the Oil Pollution Act of 1990, which is classified principally to this chapter. For complete classification of this Act to the Code, see Short Title note set out under section 2701 of this title and Tables.

Act of March 3, 1851, referred to in subsecs. (a) and (c), is act Mar. 3, 1851, ch. 43, 9 Stat. 635, which was incorporated into the Revised Statutes as R.S. Secs. 4282, 4283, 4284 to 4287 and 4289, and is classified to sections 182, 183, and 184 to 188 of Title 46, Appendix, Shipping.

The Solid Waste Disposal Act, referred to in subsec. (a)(2), is title II of Pub. L. 89-272, Oct. 20, 1965, 79 Stat. 997, as amended generally by Pub. L. 94-580, Sec. 2, Oct. 21, 1976, 90 Stat. 2795, which is classified generally to chapter 82 (Sec. 6901 et seq.) of Title 42, The Public Health and Welfare. For complete classification of this Act to the Code, see Short Title note set out under section 6901 of Title 42 and Tables.

Report on Vessel Safety and Ability To Meet Legal Obligations

Pub. L. 102-241, Sec. 32, Dec. 19, 1991, 105 Stat. 2222, provided that: "Not later than one year after the date of enactment of this Act [Dec. 19, 1991], the Secretary of Transportation shall report to Congress on the effect of section 1018 of the Oil Pollution Act of 1990 (Public Law 101-380; 104 Stat. 484) [33 U.S.C. 2718] on the safety of vessels being used to transport oil and the capability of owners and operators to meet their legal obligations in the event of an oil spill."

STATE FINANCIAL RESPONSIBILITY

33 USC 2719

A State may enforce, on the navigable waters of the State, the requirements for evidence of financial responsibility under section 2716 of this title.

(Pub. L. 101-380, title I, Sec. 1019, Aug. 18, 1990, 104 Stat. 506.)

DIFFERENTIATION AMONG FATS, OILS, AND GREASES

33 USC 2720

(a) In general
Except as provided in subsection (c) of this section, in issuing or enforcing any regulation or establishing any interpretation or guideline relating to the transportation, storage, discharge, release, emission, or disposal of a fat, oil, or grease under any Federal law, the head of that Federal agency shall—
  (1) differentiate between and establish separate classes for—
    (A) animal fats and oils and greases, and fish and marine mammal oils, within the meaning of paragraph (2) of section 61(a) of title 13, and oils of vegetable origin, including oils from the seeds, nuts, and kernels referred to in paragraph (1)(A) of that section; and
    (B) other oils and greases, including petroleum; and
  (2) apply standards to different classes of fats and oils based on considerations in subsection (b) of this section.
(b) Considerations
In differentiating between the class of fats, oils, and greases described in subsection (a)(1)(A) of this section and the class of oils and greases described in subsection (a)(1)(B) of this section, the head of the Federal agency shall consider differences in the physical, chemical, biological, and other properties, and in the environmental effects, of the classes.

(c) Exception
The requirements of this Act shall not apply to the Food and Drug Administration and the Food Safety and Inspection Service.
(Pub. L. 104-55, Sec. 2, Nov. 20, 1995, 109 Stat. 546.)

References in Text

This Act, referred to in subsec. (c), is Pub. L. 104-55, Nov. 20, 1995, 109 Stat. 546, which enacted this section and amended sections 2704 and 2716 of this title. For complete classification of this Act to the Code, see Short Title of 1995 Amendment note set out under section 2701 of this title and Tables.

Codification

Section was enacted as part of the Edible Oil Regulatory Reform Act, and not as part of title I of the Oil Pollution Act of 1990 which comprises this subchapter.

Section is comprised of section 2 of Pub. L. 104-55. Subsec. (d) of section 2 of Pub. L. 104-55 amended sections 2704 and 2716 of this title.

Regulations

Pub. L. 105-277, div. A, Sec. 101(g) [title III, Sec. 343], Oct. 21, 1998, 112 Stat. 2681-439, 2681-473, provided that:

"(a) None of the funds made available by this Act or subsequent Acts may be used by the Coast Guard to issue, implement, or enforce a regulation or to establish an interpretation or guideline under the Edible Oil Regulatory Reform Act (Public Law 104-55) [see Short Title of 1995 Amendment note set out under section 2701 of this title], or the amendments made by that Act, that does not recognize and provide for, with respect to fats, oils, and greases (as described in that Act, or the amendments made by that Act) differences in—
 (1) physical, chemical, biological and other relevant properties; and
 (2) environmental effects.
(b) Not later than March 31, 1999, the Secretary of Transportation shall issue regulations amending 33 CFR 154 to comply with the requirements of Public Law 104-55."

Pub. L. 105-276, title III, Oct. 21, 1998, 112 Stat. 2499, provided that: "Not later than March 31, 1999, the Administrator of the Environmental Protection Agency shall issue regulations amending 40 C.F.R. 112 to comply with the requirements of the Edible Oil Regulatory Reform Act (Public Law 104-55) [see Short Title of 1995 Amendment note set out under section 2701 of this title]. Such regulations shall differentiate between and establish separate classes for animal fats and oils and greases, and fish and marine mammal oils (as described in that Act), and other oils and greases, and shall apply standards to such different classes of fats and oils based on differences in the physical, chemical, biological, and other properties, and in the environmental effects, of the classes. None of the funds made available by this Act or in subsequent Acts may be used by the Environmental Protection Agency to issue or to establish an interpretation or guidance relating to fats, oils, and greases (as described in Public Law 104-55) that does not comply with the requirements of the Edible Oil Regulatory Reform Act."

Sense of Congress on Implementation of Regulations Regarding Animal Fats and Vegetable Oils

Pub. L. 104-324, title XI, Sec. 1130, Oct. 19, 1996, 110 Stat. 3985, provided that:

"(a) Sense of Congress.—It is the sense of Congress that, in an effort to reduce unnecessary regulatory burdens, a regulation issued or enforced and an interpretation or guideline established pursuant to Public Law 104-55 [see Short Title of 1995 Amendment note set out under section 2701 of this title] should in any manner possible recognize and provide for the differences in the physical, chemical, biological, and other properties, and in the environmental effects, of the classes of fats, oils, and greases described under that law.

(b) Report.—Within 60 days after the date of enactment of this section [Oct. 19, 1996] and on January 1 of each year thereafter, the Secretary of Transportation shall submit a report to Congress on the extent to which the implementation by the United States Coast Guard of regulations issued or enforced, or interpretations or guidelines established, pursuant to Public Law 104-55, carry out the intent of Congress and recognize and provide for the differences in the physical, chemical, biological, and other properties, and in the environmental effects, of the classes of fats, oils, and greases described under that law."

Section Referred to in Other Sections

This section is referred to in section 2704 of this title.

Title II
Conforming Amendments[1]

OIL SPILL LIABILITY TRUST FUND

33 USC 1486

The Oil Spill Liability Trust Fund shall be available to the Secretary for actions taken under sections 1474 and 1476 of this title.

(Pub. L. 93-248, Sec. 17, Feb. 5, 1974, 88 Stat. 10; Pub. L. 101-380, title II, Sec. 2001, Aug. 18, 1990, 104 Stat. 506.)

Amendments

1990—Pub. L. 101-380 amended section generally. Prior to amendment, section read as follows: "The revolving fund established under section 1321(k) of this title shall be available to the Secretary for Federal actions and activities under section 1474 of this title."

Effective Date of 1990 Amendment

Amendment by Pub. L. 101-380 applicable to incidents occurring after Aug. 18, 1990, see section 1020 of Pub. L. 101-380, set out as an Effective Date note under section 2701 of this title.

FEDERAL WATER POLLUTION CONTROL ACT

Sec. 2002[2]

(a) Application.—Subsections (f), (g), (h), and (i) of section 311 of the Federal Water Pollution Control Act (33 U.S.C. 1321) shall not apply with respect to any incident for which liability is established under section 1002 of this Act.

(b) Conforming Amendments.—Section 311 of the Federal Water Pollution Control Act (33 U.S.C. 1321) is amended as follows:
  (1) Subsection (i) is amended by striking "(1)" after "(i)" and by striking paragraphs (2) and (3).
  (2) Subsection (k) is repealed. Any amounts remaining in the revolving fund established under that subsection shall be deposited in the Fund. The Fund shall assume all liability incurred by the revolving fund established under that subsection.
  (3) Subsection (l) is amended by striking the second sentence.
  (4) Subsection (p) is repealed.
  (5) The following is added at the end thereof: "(s) the Oil Spill Liability Trust Fund established under section 9509 of the Internal Revenue Code of 1986 (26 U.S.C. 9509F) shall be available to carry out subsections (b), (c), (d), (j), and (l) as those subsections apply to discharges, and substantial threats of discharges, of oil. Any amounts received by the United States under this section shall be deposited in the Oil Spill Liability Trust Fund."

DEEPWATER PORT ACT

Sec. 2003[2]

(a) Conforming Amendments.—The Deepwater Port Act of 1974 (33 U.S.C. 1502 et seq.) is amended—
  (1) in section 4(c)(1) by striking "section 18(l) of this Act," and inserting "section 1016 of the Oil Pollution Act of 1990"; and
  (2) by striking section 18.

---

[1]Editor's note: the following sections and excerpts, denoted as U. S. Code, were either enacted or amended by Title II (Conforming Amendments) of Pub. L. 101-380, The Oil Pollution Act of 1990, and have been ordered as in the public law for ease of reference.
[2]Editor's note: section number and text is that of Pub. L. 101-380.

Oil Pollution Act of 1990 / 715

(b) Amounts Remaining in Deepwater Port Fund.—Any amounts remaining in the Deepwater Port Liability Fund established under section 18(f) of the Deepwater Port Act of 1974 (33 U.S.C. 1517(f)) shall be deposited in the Oil Spill Liability Trust Fund established under section 302 of that title (43 U.S.C. 1812\) shall assume all liability incurred by the Deepwater Port Liability Fund.

OIL SPILL LIABILITY TRUST FUND

26 USC 9509

(a) Creation of Trust Fund
There is established in the Treasury of the United States a trust fund to be known as the "Oil Spill Liability Trust Fund", consisting of such amounts as may be appropriated or credited to such Trust Fund as provided in this section or section 9602(b).

(b) Transfers to Trust Fund
There are hereby appropriated to the Oil Spill Liability Trust Fund amounts equivalent to—
  (1) taxes received in the Treasury under section 4611 (relating to environmental tax on petroleum) to the extent attributable to the Oil Spill Liability Trust Fund financing rate under section 4611(c),
  (2) amounts recovered under the Oil Pollution Act of 1990 for damages to natural resources which are required to be deposited in the Fund under section 1006(f) of such Act,
  (3) amounts recovered by such Trust Fund under section 1015 of such Act,
  (4) amounts required to be transferred by such Act from the revolving fund established under section 311(k) of the Federal Water Pollution Control Act,
  (5) amounts required to be transferred by the Oil Pollution Act of 1990 from the Deepwater Port Liability Fund established under section 18(f) of the Deepwater Port Act of 1974,
  (6) amounts required to be transferred by the Oil Pollution Act of 1990 from the Offshore Oil Pollution Compensation Fund established under section 302 of the Outer Continental Shelf Lands Act Amendments of 1978,
  (7) amounts required to be transferred by the Oil Pollution Act of 1990 from the Trans-Alaska Pipeline Liability Fund established under section 204 of the Trans-Alaska Pipeline Authorization Act, and
  (8) any penalty paid pursuant to section 311 of the Federal Water Pollution Control Act, section 309(c) of such Act (as a result of violations of such section 311), the Deepwater Port Act of 1974, or section 207 of the Trans-Alaska Pipeline Authorization Act.

(c) Expenditures
  (1) Expenditure purposes
  Amounts in the Oil Spill Liability Trust Fund shall be available, as provided in appropriation Acts or section 6002(b) of the Oil Pollution Act of 1990, only for purposes of making expenditures—
    (A) for the payment of removal costs and other costs, expenses, claims, and damages referred to in section 1012 of such Act,
    (B) to carry out sections 5 and 7 of the Intervention on the High Seas Act relating to oil pollution or the substantial threat of oil pollution,
    (C) for the payment of liabilities incurred by the revolving fund established by section 311(k) of the Federal Water Pollution Control Act,
    (D) to carry out subsections (b), (c), (d), (j), and (l) of section 311 of the Federal Water Pollution Control Act with respect to prevention, removal, and enforcement related to oil discharges (as defined in such section),
    (E) for the payment of liabilities incurred by the Deepwater Port Liability Fund, and
    (F) for the payment of liabilities incurred by the Offshore Oil Pollution Compensation Fund.
  (2) Limitations on expenditures
    (A) $1,000,000,000 per incident, etc.
    The maximum amount which may be paid from the Oil Spill Liability Trust Fund with respect to—
      (i) any single incident shall not exceed $1,000,000,000, and

(ii) natural resource damage assessments and claims in connection with any single incident shall not exceed $500,000,000.
    (B) $30,000,000 minimum balance
    Except in the case of payments of removal costs, a payment may be made from such Trust Fund only if the amount in such Trust Fund after such payment will not be less than $30,000,000.
(d) Authority to borrow
    (1) In general
    There are authorized to be appropriated to the Oil Spill Liability Trust Fund, as repayable advances, such sums as may be necessary to carry out the purposes of such Trust Fund.
    (2) Limitation on amount outstanding
    The maximum aggregate amount of repayable advances to the Oil Spill Liability Trust Fund which is outstanding at any one time shall not exceed $1,000,000,000.
    (3) Repayment of advances
        (A) In general
        Advances made to the Oil Spill Liability Trust Fund shall be repaid, and interest on such advances shall be paid, to the general fund of the Treasury when the Secretary determines that moneys are available for such purposes in such Fund.
        (B) Final repayment
        No advance shall be made to the Oil Spill Liability Trust Fund after December 31, 1994, and all advances to such Fund shall be repaid on or before such date.
        (C) Rate of interest
        Interest on advances made pursuant to this subsection shall be—
            (i) at a rate determined by the Secretary of the Treasury (as of the close of the calendar month preceding the month in which the advance is made) to be equal to the current average market yield on outstanding marketable obligations of the United States with remaining periods to maturity comparable to the anticipated period during which the advance will be outstanding, and
            (ii) compounded annually.
(e) Liability of the United States limited to amount in Trust Fund
    (1) General rule
    Any claim filed against the Oil Spill Liability Trust Fund may be paid only out of such Trust Fund.
    (2) Coordination with other provisions
    Nothing in the Oil Pollution Act of 1990 (or in any amendment made by such Act) shall authorize the payment by the United States Government of any amount with respect to any such claim out of any source other than the Oil Spill Liability Trust Fund.
    (3) Order in which unpaid claims are to be paid
    If at any time the Oil Spill Liability Trust Fund has insufficient funds (or is unable by reason of subsection (c)(2)) to pay all of the claims out of such Trust Fund at such time, such claims shall, to the extent permitted under paragraph (1) and such subsection, be paid in full in the order in which they were finally determined.
(f) References to Oil Pollution Act of 1990
    Any reference in this section to the Oil Pollution Act of 1990 or any other Act referred to in a subparagraph of subsection (c)(1) shall be treated as a reference to such Act as in effect on the date of the enactment of this subsection.

(Added Pub. L. 99-509, title VIII, Sec. 8033(a), Oct. 21, 1986, 100 Stat. 1959, Sec. 9507; renumbered Sec. 9509, Pub. L. 99-509, title VIII, Sec. 8033(c)(2)(B), Oct. 21, 1986, 100 Stat. 1962; amended Pub. L. 100-647, title I, Sec. 1018(u)(20), Nov. 10, 1988, 102 Stat. 3591; Pub. L. 101-239, title VII, Secs. 7505(d)(2), 7811(m)(3), Dec. 19, 1989, 103 Stat. 2364, 2412; Pub. L. 101-380, title IX, Sec. 9001, Aug. 18, 1990, 104 Stat. 573.)

References in Text

The Oil Pollution Act of 1990, referred to in subsecs. (b)(2), (3), (5)-(7), (c)(1), (e)(2), and (f), is Pub. L. 101-380, Aug. 18, 1990, 104 Stat. 484, which is classified principally to chapter 40 (Sec. 2701 et seq.) of Title 33, Navigation and Navigable Waters. Sections 1006, 1012, 1015, and 6002 of the Act are classified to sections 2706, 2712, 2715, and 2752 of Title 33, respectively. For complete classification of this Act to the Code, see Short Title note set out under section 2701 of Title 33 and Tables.

Section 311 of the Federal Water Pollution Control Act, referred to in subsecs. (b)(4), (8) and (c)(1)(C), (D), is classified to section 1321 of Title 33. Subsec. (d) of section 311, which related to maritime disaster discharges, was amended generally by Pub. L. 101-380, title IV, Sec. 4201(b), Aug. 18, 1990, 104 Stat. 525. Subsec. (k) of section 311 was repealed by Pub. L. 101-380, title II, Sec. 2002(b)(2), Aug. 18, 1990, 104 Stat. 507.

The Deepwater Port Act of 1974, referred to in subsec. (b)(5), (8), is Pub. L. 93-627, Jan. 3, 1975, 88 Stat. 2126, as amended, which is classified generally to chapter 29 (Sec. 1501 et seq.) of Title 33. Section 18 of the Act was classified to section 1517 of Title 33 prior to its repeal by Pub. L. 101-380, title II, Sec. 2003(a)(2), Aug. 18, 1990, 104 Stat. 507. For complete classification of this Act to the Code, see Short Title note set out under section 1501 of Title 33 and Tables.

Section 302 of the Outer Continental Shelf Lands Act Amendments of 1978, referred to in subsec. (b)(6), was classified to section 1812 of Title 43, Public Lands, prior to its repeal by Pub. L. 101-380, title II, Sec. 2004, Aug. 18, 1990, 104 Stat. 507.

Sections 204 and 207 of the Trans-Alaska Pipeline Authorization Act, referred to in subsec. (b)(7), (8), are classified to sections 1653 and 1656, respectively, of Title 43.

Section 309(c) of the Federal Water Pollution Control Act, referred to in subsec. (b)(8), is classified to section 1319(c) of Title 33, Navigation and Navigable Waters.

Sections 5 and 7 of the Intervention on the High Seas Act, referred to in subsec. (c)(1)(B), are classified to sections 1474 and 1476, respectively, of Title 33.

The date of the enactment of this subsection, referred to in subsec. (f), probably means the date of enactment of Pub. L. 101-380, which was approved Aug. 18, 1990, and which amended subsec. (f) generally.

Amendments

1990—Subsec. (b)(2) to (8). Pub. L. 101-380, Sec. 9001(a), added pars. (2) to (8) and struck out former pars. (2) to (5) which read as follows:

"(2) amounts recovered, collected, or received under subtitle A of the Comprehensive Oil Pollution Liability and Compensation Act,

(3) amounts remaining (on January 1, 1990) in the Deepwater Port Liability Fund established by section 18(f) of the Deepwater Port Act of 1974,

(4) amounts remaining (on such date) in the Offshore Oil Pollution Compensation Fund established under section 302 of the Outer Continental Shelf Lands Act Amendments of 1978, and

(5) amounts credited to such trust fund under section 311(s) of the Federal Water Pollution Control Act."

Subsec. (c)(1). Pub. L. 101-380, Sec. 9001(b), amended par. (1) generally, substituting "Expenditure purposes" for "General expenditure purposes" in heading and substituting current text consisting of subpars. (A) to (F) for former text consisting of general provisions in subpar. (A) and special rules in subpar. (B).

Subsec. (c)(2)(A). Pub. L. 101-380, Sec. 9001(c), substituted "$1,000,000,000" for "$500,000,000" in heading and in cl. (i), and substituted "$500,000,000" for "$250,000,000" in cl. (ii).

Subsec. (c)(2)(B). Pub. L. 101-380, Sec. 9001(e)(2), substituted "payments of removal costs" for "payments described in paragraph (1)(A)(i)".

Subsec. (d)(2). Pub. L. 101-380, Sec. 9001(d)(1), substituted "$1,000,000,000" for "$500,000,000".

Subsec. (d)(3)(B). Pub. L. 101-380, Sec. 9001(d)(2), substituted "December 31, 1994" for "December 31, 1991".

Subsec. (e)(2). Pub. L. 101-380, Sec. 9001(e)(1), substituted "Oil Pollution Act of 1990" for "Comprehensive Oil Pollution Liability and Compensation Act".

Subsec. (f). Pub. L. 101-380, Sec. 9001(e)(3), substituted "References to Oil Pollution Act of 1990" for "References to Comprehensive Oil Pollution Liability and Compensation Act" in heading and amended text generally. Prior to amendment, text read as follows: "For purposes of this section, references to the Comprehensive Oil Pollution Liability and Compensation Act shall be treated as references to any law enacted before December 31, 1990, which is substantially identical to subtitle E of title VI, or subtitle D of title VIII, of H.R. 5300 of the 99th Congress as passed by the House of Representatives."

1989—Subsec. (b)(3). Pub. L. 101-239, Sec. 7811(m)(3), made technical correction to directory language of Pub. L. 100-647, see 1988 Amendment note below.

Pub. L. 101-239, Sec. 7505(d)(2)(B), substituted "(on January 1, 1990)" for "(on the 1st day the Oil Spill Liability Trust Fund financing rate under section 4611(c) applies)".

Subsec. (c)(1)(A). Pub. L. 101-239, Sec. 7505(d)(2)(C), which directed amendment of subsec. (c)(1) by striking the last sentence, was executed by striking out the last sentence of subsec. (c)(1)(A), as the probable intent of Congress. Such sentence read as follows: "For purposes of this subparagraph, references to the Comprehensive Oil Pollution Liability and Compensation Act shall be treated as references to qualified authorizing legislation (as defined in section 4611)."

Subsec. (f). Pub. L. 101-239, Sec. 7505(d)(2)(A), added subsec. (f).

1988—Subsec. (b)(3). Pub. L. 100-647, as amended by Pub. L. 101-239, Sec. 7811(m)(3), substituted "Deepwater" for "Deep Water" wherever appearing.

Effective Date of 1990 Amendment

Amendment by Pub. L. 101-380 applicable to incidents occurring after Aug. 18, 1990, see section 1020 of Pub. L. 101-380, set out as an Effective Date note under section 2701 of Title 33, Navigation and Navigable Waters.

Effective Date of 1989 Amendment

Amendment by section 7811(m)(3) of Pub. L. 101-239 effective, except as otherwise provided, as if included in the provision of the Technical and Miscellaneous Revenue Act of 1988, Pub. L. 100-647, to which such amendment relates, see section 7817 of Pub. L. 101-239, set out as a note under section 1 of this title.

Effective Date of 1988 Amendment

Amendment by Pub. L. 100-647 effective, except as otherwise provided, as if included in the provision of the Tax Reform Act of 1986, Pub. L. 99-514, to which such amendment relates, see section 1019(a) of Pub. L. 100-647, set out as a note under section 1 of this title.

Effective Date

Section 8033(c)(1) of Pub. L. 99-509 provided that: "The amendments made by this section [enacting this section] shall take effect on the commencement date (as defined in section 4611 of the Internal Revenue Code of 1954 [now 1986], as amended by this part)."

[For purposes of section 8033(c) of Pub. L. 99-509, set out as notes above and below, the commencement date is Jan. 1, 1990, see section 7505(d)(1) of Pub. L. 101-239, set out as an Effective Date of 1986 Amendment note under section 4611 of this title.]

Termination of Oil Spill Liability

Trust Fund Annual Report.—The report regarding the Oil Spill Liability Trust Fund required by the Conference Report (House Report 101-892) accompanying the Department of Transportation and Related Agencies Appropriations Act, 1991, as that requirement was amended by section 1122 of the Federal Reports Elimination and Sunset Act of 1995 (Public Law 104-66), shall no longer be submitted to the Congress.

Report on Oil Spill Liability Trust Fund

Pub. L. 104-66, title I, Sec. 1122(a), Dec. 21, 1995, 109 Stat. 724, provided that: "The quarterly report regarding the Oil Spill Liability Trust Fund required to be submitted to the House and Senate Committees on Appropriations under House Report 101-892, accompanying the appropriations for the Coast Guard in the Department of Transportation and Related Agencies Appropriations Act, 1991 [Pub. L. 101-516], shall be submitted not later than 30 days after the end of the fiscal year in which this Act is enacted and annually thereafter."

[House Report 101-892, 101st Congress, 2d Session, provided that: "The conferees direct the Coast Guard to submit quarterly reports to the House and Senate Committee on Appropriations detailing and summarizing all transfers to and expenditures from the oil spill liability trust fund. Each report shall account for each transfer to and expenditure from the fund as authorized by Section

9509 of the Internal Revenue Code of 1986, as amended, and Sections 5003 and 5004 of the Oil Pollution Act of 1990 (Public Law 101-380) [33 U.S.C. 2733, 2734]. The report shall also show amounts collectable under Section 9509(b)(2), (3), and (8) of the Internal Revenue Code of 1986. For those authorized expenditures subject to limitations, the report shall so indicate. The Coast Guard shall confer with the House and Senate Committees on Appropriations as to the format for these reports."]

Deepwater Port Liability Fund

Section 2003(b) of Pub. L. 101-380 provided that: "Any amounts remaining in the Deepwater Port Liability Fund established under section 18(f) of the Deepwater Port Act of 1974 (33 U.S.C. [former] 1517(f)) shall be deposited in the Oil Spill Liability Trust Fund established under section 9509 of the Internal Revenue Code of 1986 (26 U.S.C. 9509). The Oil Spill Liability Trust Fund shall assume all liability incurred by the Deepwater Port Liability Fund."

Offshore Oil Pollution Compensation Fund

Section 2004 of Pub. L. 101-380 provided that: "Title III of the Outer Continental Shelf Lands Act Amendments of 1978 (43 U.S.C. 1811-1824) is repealed. Any amounts remaining in the Offshore Oil Pollution Compensation Fund established under section 302 of that title (43 U.S.C. 1812) shall be deposited in the Oil Spill Liability Trust Fund established under section 9509 of the Internal Revenue Code of 1986 (26 U.S.C. 9509). The Oil Spill Liability Trust Fund shall assume all liability incurred by the Offshore Oil Pollution Compensation Fund."

Deposit of Certain Penalties Into Oil Spill Liability Trust Fund

Section 4304 of Pub. L. 101-380 provided that: "Penalties paid pursuant to section 311 of the Federal Water Pollution Control Act [33 U.S.C. 1321], section 309(c) of that Act [33 U.S.C. 1319(c)], as a result of violations of section 311 of that Act, and the Deepwater Port Act of 1974 [33 U.S.C. 1501 et seq.], shall be deposited in the Oil Spill Liability Trust Fund created under section 9509 of the Internal Revenue Code of 1986 (26 U.S.C. 9509)."

Coordination With Superfund Reauthorization

Section 8033(c)(2) of Pub. L. 99-509 provided that: "If the Superfund Amendments and Reauthorization Act of 1986 is enacted—
- (A) subsection (a) of this section shall be applied by substituting 'section 9508' for 'section 9506',
- (B) section 9507 of the Internal Revenue Code of 1954 [now 1986], as added by this section, is hereby redesignated as section 9509 of such Code, and
- (C) in lieu of the amendment made by subsection (b), the table of sections for subchapter A of chapter 98 of such Code is amended by adding after the item relating to section 9508 the following new item:
  " 'Sec. 9509. Oil Spill Liability Trust Fund.' "

Section Referred to in Other Sections

This section is referred to in title 33 sections 1321, 2701, 2718.

Title III[1]
International Oil Pollution Prevention and Removal

SENSE OF CONGRESS REGARDING PARTICIPATION IN INTERNATIONAL REGIME

Sec. 3001[2]

It is the sense of the Congress that it is in the best interests of the United States to participate in an international oil pollution liability and compensation regime that is at least as effective as Federal and State laws in preventing incidents and in guaranteeing full and prompt compensation for damages resulting from incidents.

UNITED STATES-CANADA GREAT LAKES OIL SPILL COOPERATION

Sec. 3002[2]

(a) Review.—The Secretary of State shall review relevant international agreements and treaties with the Government of Canada, including the Great Lakes Water Quality Agreement, to determine whether amendments or additional international agreements are necessary to—
   (1) prevent discharges of oil on the Great Lakes;
   (2) ensure an immediate and effective removal of oil on the Great Lakes; and
   (3) fully compensate those who are injured by a discharge of oil on the Great Lakes.
(b) Consultation.—In carrying out this section, the Secretary of State shall consult with the Department of Transportation, the Environmental Protection Agency, the National Oceanic and Atmospheric Administration, the Great Lakes States, the International Joint Commission, and other appropriate agencies.
(c) Report.—The Secretary of State shall submit a report to the Congress on the results of the review under this section within 6 months after the date of the enactment of this Act.

UNITED STATES-CANADA LAKE CHAMPLAIN OIL SPILL COOPERATION

Sec. 3003[2]

(a) Review.—The Secretary of State shall review relevant international agreements and treaties with the Government of Canada, to determine whether amendments or additional international agreements are necessary to—
   (1) prevent discharges of oil on Lake Champlain;
   (2) ensure an immediate and effective removal of oil on Lake Champlain; and
   (3) fully compensate those who are injured by a discharge of oil on Lake Champlain.
(b) Consultation.—In carrying out this section, the Secretary of State shall consult with the Department of Transportation, the Environmental Protection Agency, the National Oceanic and Atmospheric Administration, the States of Vermont and New York, the International Joint Commission, and other appropriate agencies.
(c) Report.—The Secretary of State shall submit a report to the Congress on the results of the review under this section within 6 months after the date of the enactment of this Act.

INTERNATIONAL INVENTORY OF REMOVAL EQUIPMENT AND PERSONNEL

Sec. 3004[2]

The President shall encourage appropriate international organizations to establish an international inventory of spill removal equipment and personnel.

---

[1]Editor's note: the following sections comprise Title III of Pub. L. 101-380, The Oil Pollution Act of 1990.
[2]Editor's note: section number and text is that of Pub. L. 101-380.

NEGOTIATIONS WITH CANADA CONCERNING TUG ESCORTS IN PUGET SOUND

Sec. 3005[2]

Congress urges the Secretary of State to enter into negotiations with the Government of Canada to ensure that tugboat escorts are required for all tank vessels with a capacity over 40,000 deadweight tons in the Strait of Juan de Fuca and in Haro Strait.

---

[2]Editor's note: section number and text is that of Pub. L. 101-380.

Title IV[1]
Prevention and Removal

Subtitle A— Prevention

REVIEW OF ALCOHOL AND DRUG ABUSE AND OTHER MATTERS IN ISSUING LICENSES, CERTIFICATES OF REGISTRY, AND MERCHANT MARINERS' DOCUMENTS

Sec. 4101[2]

(a) Licenses and Certificates of Registry.–Section 7101 of title 46, United States Code, is amended by adding at the end of the following:
"(g) The Secretary may not issue a license or certificate of registry under this section unless an individual applying for the license or certificate makes available to the Secretary under section 206(b)(7) of the National Driver Register Act of 1982 (23 U.S.C. 401 note), any information contained in the National Driver Register related to an offense described in section 205(a)(3) (A) or (B) of that Act committed by the individual.
(h) The Secretary may review the criminal record of an individual who applies for a license or certificate of registry under this section.
(i) The Secretary shall require the testing of an individual who applies for issuance or renewal of a license or certificate of registry under this chapter for use of a dangerous drug in violation of law or Federal regulation."

(b) Merchant Mariners' Documents.–Section 7302 of title 46, United States Code, is amended by adding at the end the following:
"(c) The Secretary may not issue a merchant mariner's document under this chapter unless the individual applying for the document makes available to the Secretary, under section 206(b)(7) of the National Driver Register Act of 1982 (23 U.S.C. 401 note), any information contained in the National Driver Register related to an offense described in section 205(a)(3) (A) or (B) of that Act committed by the individual.
(d) The Secretary may review the criminal record of an individual who applies for a merchant mariner's document under this section.
(e) The Secretary shall require the testing of an individual applying for issuance or renewal of a merchant mariner's document under this chapter for the use of a dangerous drug in violation of law or Federal regulation."

TERM OF LICENSES, CERTIFICATES OF REGISTRY, AND MERCHANT MARINERS' DOCUMENTS; CRIMINAL RECORD REVIEWS IN RENEWALS

Sec. 4102[2]

(a) Licenses.–Section 7106 of title 46, United States Code, is amended by inserting "and may be renewed for additional 5-year periods" after "is valid for 5 years."
(b) Certificates of Registry.–Section 7107 of title 46, United States Code, is amended by striking "is not limited in duration." and inserting "is valid for 5 years and may be renewed for additional 5-year periods."
(c) Merchant Mariners' Documents.–Section 7302 of title 46, United States Code, is amended by adding at the end the following:
"(f) A merchant mariner's document issued under this chapter is valid for 5 years and may be renewed for additional 5-year periods."
(d) Termination of Existing Licenses, Certificates, and Documents.–A license, certificate of registry, or merchant mariner's document issued before the date of the enactment of this section terminates on the day it would have expired if–

---

[1] Editor's note: the following sections comprise Title III of Pub. L. 101-380, The Oil Pollution Act of 1990.

[2] Editor's note: section number and text is that of Pub. L. 101-380.

(1) subsection (a), (b), and (c) were in effect on the date it was issued; and
(2) it was renewed at the end of each 5-year period under section 7106, 7107, or 7302 of title 46, United States Code.
(e) Criminal Record Review in Renewals of Licenses and Certificates Of Registry.—
  (1) In General.—Section 7109 of title 46, United States Code, is amended to read as follows:
    "§ 7109. Review of Criminal Records
    The Secretary may review the criminal record of each holder of a license or certificate of registry issued under this part who applies for renewal of that license or certificate of registry."
  (2) Clerical Amendment.—The analysis for chapter 71 of title 46, United States Code, is amended by striking the item relating to section 7109 and inserting the following:
    "§ 7109. Review of Criminal Records"

SUSPENSION AND REVOCATION OF LICENSES, CERTIFICATES OF REGISTRY, AND MERCHANT MARINERS MARINERS' DOCUMENTS FOR ALCOHOL AND DRUG ABUSE

Sec. 4103[2]

(a) Availability of Information in National Driver Register.—
  (1) In General.—Section 7702 of title 46, United States Code, is amended by adding at the end the following:
    "(c)(1) The Secretary shall request a holder of a license, certificate of registry, or merchant mariner's document to make available to the Secretary, under section 206(b)(4) of the National Driver Register Act of 1982 (23 U.S.C. 401 note), all information contained in the National Driver Register related to an offense described in section 205(a)(3) (A) or (B) of that Act committed by the individual.
    (2) The Secretary shall require the testing of the holder of a license, certificate of registry, or merchant mariner's document for use of alcohol and dangerous drugs in violation of law or Federal regulation. The testing may include preemployment (with respect to dangerous drugs only), periodic, random, reasonable cause, and post accidental testing.
    (d)(1) The Secretary may temporarily, for not more than 45 days, suspend and take possession of the license, certificate of registry, or merchant mariner's document held by an individual if, when acting under the authority of that license, certificate, or document—
      (A) that individual performs a safety sensitive function on a vessel, as determined by the Secretary; and
      (B) there is probable cause to believe that the individual—
        (i) has performed the safety sensitive function in violation of law or Federal regulation regarding use of alcohol or a dangerous drug;
        (ii) has been convicted of an offense that would prevent the issuance or renewal of the license, certificate, or document; or
        (iii) within the 3-year period preceding the initiation of a suspension proceeding, has been convicted of an offense described in section 205(a)(3) (A) or (B) of the National Driver Register Act of 1982.
    (2) If a license, certificate, or document is temporarily suspended under this section, an expedited hearing under subsection (a) of this section shall be held within 30 days after the temporary suspension."
  (2) Definition of Dangerous Drug
    (A) Section 2101 of title 46, United State Code, is amended by inserting after paragraph (8) the following new paragraph:
      "(8a) 'dangerous drug' means a narcotic drug, a controlled sub-stance, or a controlled substance analog (as defined in section 102 of the Comprehensive Drug Abuse and Control Act of 1970 (21 U.S.C. 802))."
    (B) Sections 7503(a) and 7704(a) of title 46, United States Code, are repealed.

---

[2]Editor's note: section number and text is that of Pub. L. 101-380.

724 / Environmental Statutes

(b) Bases for Suspension or Revocation.—Section 7703 of title 46, United States Code, is amended to read as follows:
"§ 7703. Bases For Suspension Or Revocation
A license, certificate of registry, or merchant mariner's document issued by the Secretary may be suspended or revoked if the holder—
  (1) when acting under the authority of that license, certificate, or document—
    (A) has violated or fails to comply with this subtitle, a regulation prescribed under this subtitle, or any other law or regulation intended to promote marine safety or to protect navigable waters; or
    (B) has committed an act of incompetence, misconduct or negligence;
  (2) is convicted of an offense that would prevent the issuance or renewal of a license, certificate of registry, or merchant mariner's document; or
  (3) with the 3-year period preceding the initiation of the suspension or revocation proceeding is convicted of an offense described in section 205(a)(3) (A) or (B) of the National Driver Register Act of 1982 (23 U.S.C. 401 note)."
(c) Termination of Revocation.—Section 7701(c) Of title 46, United States Code, is amended to read as follows:
"(c) When a license, certificate of registry, or merchant mariner's document has been revoked under this chapter, the former holder may be issued a new license, certificate of registry, or merchant mariner's document only after—
  (1) the Secretary decides, under regulations prescribed by the Secretary, that the issuance is compatible with the requirement of good discipline and safety at sea; and
  (2) the former holder provides satisfactory proof that the bases for revocation are no longer valid."

REMOVAL OF MASTER OR INDIVIDUAL IN CHARGE

Sec. 4104[2]

Section 8101 of title 46, United States Code, is amended by adding at the end the following:
"(i) When the 2 next most senior licensed officers on a vessel reasonably believe that the master or individual in charge of the vessel is under the influence of alcohol or a dangerous drug and is incapable of commanding the vessel, the next most senior master, mate, or operator licensed under section 7101(c) (1) or (3) of this title shall—
  (1) temporarily relieve the master or individual in charge;
  (2) temporarily take command of the vessel;
  (3) in the case of a vessel required to have a log under chapter 113 of this title, immediately enter the details of the incident in the log; and
  (4) report those details to the Secretary—
    (A) by the most expeditious means available; and
    (B) in written from transmitted within 12 hours after the vessel arrives at its next port."

ACCESS TO NATIONAL DRIVER REGISTER

Sec. 4105[2]

(a) Access to Register.—Section 206(b) of the National Driver Register Act of 1982 (23 U.S.C. 401 note) is amended—
  (1) by redesignating the second paragraph (5) (as added to the end of that section by section 4(b)(1) of the Rail Safety Improvement Act of 1988) as paragraph (6); and
  (2) by adding at the end the following:
    "(7)(A) Any individual who holds or who has applied for a license or certificate of registry under section 7101 of title 46, United State Code, or a merchant mariner's document under section 7302 of title 46, United States Code, may request the chief driver licensing official of a State to transmit to the Secretary of the department in which the Coast Guard is operating in accordance with subsection (a) information regarding the motor vehicle driving record of the individual.

---
[2]Editor's note: section number and text is that of Pub. L. 101-380.

(B) The Secretary—
  (i) may receive information transmitted by the chief driver licensing official of a State pursuant to a request under subparagraph (A);
  (ii) shall make the information available to the individual for review and written comment before denying, suspending, or revoking the license, certificate of registry, or merchant mariner's document of the individual based on that information and before using that information in any action taken under chapter 77 of title 46, United States Code, and
  (iii) may not otherwise divulge or use that information except for the purposes of section 7101, 7302, or 7703 of title 46, United States Code.
(C) Information regarding the motor vehicle driving record of an individual may not be transmitted to the Secretary under this paragraph if the information was entered in the Register more than 3 years before the date of the request for the information, unless the information relates to revocations or suspensions that are still in effect on the date of the request. Information submitted to the Register by States under the Act of July 14, 1960 (74 Stat. 526), or under this title shall be subject to access for the purpose of this paragraph during the transition to the Register described under section 203(c) of this title."

(b) Conforming Amendments.—
  (1) Review of Information Received from Register.—Chapter 75 of title 46, United States Code, is amended by adding at the end the following:
    "§ 7505. Review of Information in National Driver Register
    The Secretary shall make information received from the National Driver Register under section 206(b)(7) of the National Driver Register Act of 1982 (23 U.S.C. 401 note) available to an individual for review and written comment before denying, suspending, revoking, or taking any other action relating to a license, certificate of registry, or merchant mariners' document authorized to be issued for that individual under this part, based on that information."
  (2) Penalty for Negligent Operation of Vessel.—Section 2302(c) of title 46, United States Code, is amended by striking "intoxicated" and inserting "under the influence of alcohol, or a dangerous drug in violation of a law of the United States."
(c) Clerical Amendment.—The analysis for chapter 75 of title 46, United States Code, is amended by adding at the end the following:
    "7505. Review of Information in National Driver Register."

MANNING STANDARDS FOR FOREIGN TANK VESSELS

Sec. 4106[2]

(a) Standards for Tank Vessels. Section 9101(a) of title 46, United States Code, is amended to read as follows:
  "(a)(1) The Secretary shall evaluate the manning, training, qualification, and watchkeeping standards of a foreign country that issues documentation for any vessel to which chapter 37 of this title applies—
    (A) on a periodic basis; and
    (B) when the vessel is involved in a marine casualty required to be reported under section 6101(a) (4) or (5) of this title.
  (2) After each evaluation made under paragraph (1) of this subsection, the Secretary shall determine whether—
    (A) the foreign country has standards for licensing and certification of seamen that are at least equivalent to United States law or international standards accepted by the United States; and
    (B) those standards are being enforced.
  (3) If the Secretary determines under this subsection that a country has failed to maintain or enforce standards at least equivalent to United States law or international standards accepted by the United States, the Secretary shall prohibit vessels issued docu-

---

[2]Editor's note: section number and text is that of Pub. L. 101-380.

mentation by that country from entering the United States until the Secretary determines those standards have been established and are being enforced.
    (4) The Secretary may allow provisional entry of a vessel prohibited from entering the United States under paragraph (3) of this subsection if—
        (A) the owner or operator of the vessel establishes, to the satisfaction of the Secretary, that the vessel is not unsafe or a threat to the marine environment; or
        (B) the entry is necessary for the safety of the vessel or individuals on the vessel."
(b) Reporting Marine Casualties.—
    (1) Reporting Requirement.—Section 6101(a) of title 46, United States Code, is amended by adding at the end the following:
    "(5) significant harm to the environment."
    (2) Application to Foreign Vessels.—Section 6101(d) of title 46, United States Code, is amended—
        (A) by inserting "(1)" before "This part"; and
        (B) by adding at the end the following:
        "(2) This part applies, to the extent consistent with generally recognized principles of international law, to a foreign vessel constructed or adapted to carry, or that carries, oil in bulk as cargo or cargo residue involved in a marine casualty described under subsection (a)(4) or (5) in waters subject to the jurisdiction of the United States including the Exclusive Economic Zone."
(c) Technical And Conforming Amendments.—Section 9(a) of the Ports and Waterways Safety Act (33 U.S.C. 1228(a)) is amended—
    (1) in the matter preceding paragraph (1), by striking "section 4417a of the Revised Statutes, as amended," and inserting "chapter 37 of title 46, United States Code,";
    (2) in paragraph (2), by striking "section 4417a of the Revised Statutes, as amended," and inserting "chapter 37 of title 46, United States Code,"; and
    (3) in paragraph (5), by striking "section 4417(a)(11) of the Revised Statutes, as amended," and inserting "section 9101 of title 46, United States Code,".

VESSEL TRAFFIC SERVICE SYSTEMS

Sec. 4107[2]

(a) In General.—Section 4(a) of the Ports and Waterways Safety Act (33 U.S.C. 1223(a)) is amended—
    (1) by striking "Secretary may—" and inserting "Secretary—";
    (2) in paragraph (1) by striking "establish, operate, and maintain" and inserting "may construct, operate, maintain, improve, or expand";
    (3) in paragraph (2) by striking "require" and inserting "shall require appropriate";
    (4) in paragraph (3) by inserting "may" before "require";
    (5) in paragraph (4) by inserting "may" before "control"; and
    (6) in paragraph (5) by inserting "may" before "require".
(b) Direction of Vessel Movement.—
    (1) Study.—The Secretary shall conduct a study—
        (A) of whether the Secretary should be given additional authority to direct the movement of vessels on navigable waters and should exercise such authority; and
        (B) to determine and prioritize the United States ports and channels that are in need of new, expanded, or improved vessel traffic service systems, by evaluating—
            (i) the nature, volume, and frequency of vessel traffic;
            (ii) the risks of collisions, spills, and damages associated with that traffic;
            (iii) the impact of installation, expansion, or improvement of a vessel traffic service system; and
            (iv) all other relevant costs and data.
    (2) Report.—Not later than 1 year after the date of the enactment of this Act, the Secretary shall submit to the Congress a report on the results of the study conducted under paragraph (1) and recommendations for implementing the results of that study.

---

[2] Editor's note: section number and text is that of Pub. L. 101-380.

GREAT LAKES PILOTAGE

Sec. 4108[2]

(a) Individuals Who May Serve as Pilot on Undesignated Great Lake Waters.—Section 9302(b) of title 46, United States Code, is amended to read as follows:
"(b) A member of the complement of a vessel of the United States operating on register or of a vessel of Canada may serve as the pilot required on waters not designated by the President if the member is licensed under section 7101 of this title, or under equivalent provisions of Canadian law, to direct the navigation of the vessel on the waters being navigated."
(b) Penalties.—Section 9308 of title 46, United States Code, is amended in each of subsections (a), (b), and (c) by striking "$500" and inserting "no more than $10,000."

REGULATIONS

46 USC 3703[3]

(a) The Secretary shall prescribe regulations for the design, construction, alteration, repair, maintenance, operation, equipping, personnel qualification, and manning of vessels to which this chapter applies, that may be necessary for increased protection against hazards to life and property, for navigation and vessel safety, and for enhanced protection of the marine environment. The Secretary may prescribe different regulations applicable to vessels engaged in the domestic trade, and also may prescribe regulations that exceed standards set internationally. Regulations prescribed by the Secretary under this subsection are in addition to regulations prescribed under other laws that may apply to any of those vessels. Regulations prescribed under this subsection shall include requirements about—
   (1) superstructures, hulls, cargo holds or tanks, fittings, equipment, appliances, propulsion machinery, auxiliary machinery, and boilers;
   (2) the handling or stowage of cargo, the manner of handling or stowage of cargo, and the machinery and appliances used in the handling or stowage;
   (3) equipment and appliances for lifesaving, fire protection, and prevention and mitigation of damage to the marine environment;
   (4) the manning of vessels and the duties, qualifications, and training of the officers and crew;
   (5) improvements in vessel maneuvering and stopping ability and other features that reduce the possibility of marine casualties;
   (6) the reduction of cargo loss if a marine casualty occurs; and
   (7) the reduction or elimination of discharges during ballasting, deballasting, tank cleaning, cargo handling, or other such activity.
(b) In prescribing regulations under subsection (a) of this section, the Secretary shall consider the types and grades of cargo permitted to be on board a tank vessel.
(c) In prescribing regulations under subsection (a) of this section, the Secretary shall establish procedures for consulting with, and receiving and considering the views of—
   (1) interested departments, agencies, and instrumentalities of the United States Government;
   (2) officials of State and local governments;
   (3) representatives of port and harbor authorities and associations;
   (4) representatives of environmental groups; and
   (5) other interested parties knowledgeable or experienced in dealing with problems involving vessel safety, port and waterways safety, and protection of the marine environment.

(Pub. L. 98-89, Aug. 26, 1983, 97 Stat. 522.)

Historical and Revision Notes

Revised section	Source section (U.S. Code)
3703	46:391a(6)
	46:391a(12)

---

[2] Editor's note: section number and text is that of Pub. L. 101-380.

[3] Editor's note: sections 4109 and 4110 of Pub. L. 101-380 are enacted as notes to 46 USC 3703.

Section 3703 requires the Secretary to issue regulations to implement this section. Specific items are listed to be included within the regulations issued. The regulatory authority must be exercised under the Administrative Procedure Act and, in prescribing these regulations, the Secretary must consider the kinds and grades of cargo carried on board. Furthermore, in addition to any requirements of the Administrative Procedure Act, the Secretary must establish specific consultation procedures for considering the views of various specified interested officials, groups, and individuals. The procedures are intended to provide for consultation as early as possible in the regulatory process.

Studies Addressing Various Sources of Oil Spill Risk

Pub. L. 104-324, title IX, Sec. 903, Oct. 19, 1996, 110 Stat. 3947, provided that:

"(a) Study of Group-5 Fuel Oil Spills.—
  (1) Definition.—In this subsection, the term 'group-5 fuel oil' means a petroleum-based oil that has a specific gravity of greater than 1.0.
  (2) Coordination of study.—The Secretary of Transportation shall coordinate with the Marine Board of the National Research Council to conduct a study of the relative environmental and public health risks posed by discharges of group-5 fuel oil.
  (3) Matters to be included.—The study under this subsection shall include a review and analysis of—
    (A) the specific risks posed to the public health or welfare of the United States, including fish, shellfish and wildlife, public and private property, shorelines, beaches, habitat, and other natural resources under the jurisdiction or control of the United States, as a result of an actual or threatened discharge of group-5 fuel oil from a vessel or facility;
    (B) cleanup technologies currently available to address actual or threatened discharge of group-5 fuel oil; and
    (C) any technological and financial barriers that prevent the prompt remediation of discharges of group-5 fuel oil.
  (4) Report.—Not later than 18 months after the date of enactment of this Act [Oct. 19, 1996], the Secretary of Transportation shall submit to the Committee on Environment and Public Works and the Committee on Commerce, Science, and Transportation of the Senate, and the Committee on Transportation and Infrastructure of the House of Representatives a report on the results of the study under this subsection.
  (5) Rulemaking.—If the Secretary of Transportation determines, based on the results of the study under this subsection, that there are significant risks to public health or the environment resulting from the actual or threatened discharge of group-5 fuel oil from a vessel or facility that cannot be technologically or economically addressed by existing or anticipated cleanup efforts, the Secretary may initiate a rulemaking to take such action as is necessary to abate the threat.

(b) Study of Automatic Fueling Shutoff Equipment.—
  (1) Coordination of study.—The Secretary of Transportation shall coordinate with the Marine Board of the National Research Council to conduct a study of the unintentional or accidental discharge of fuel oil during lightering or fuel loading or off-loading activity.
  (2) Matters to be included.—The study under this subsection shall include a review and analysis of current monitoring and fueling practices to determine the need for automatic fuel shutoff equipment to prevent the accidental discharge of fuel oil, and whether such equipment is needed as a supplement to or replacement of existing preventive equipment or procedures.
  (3) Report.—Not later than 18 months after the date of enactment of this Act [Oct. 19, 1996], the Secretary of Transportation shall submit to the Committee on Environment and Public Works and the Committee on Commerce, Science, and Transportation of the Senate and the Committee on Transportation and Infrastructure of the House of Representatives a report on the results of the study under this subsection.
  (4) Rulemaking.—If the Secretary of Transportation determines, based on the results of the study conducted under this subsection, that the use of automatic oil shutoff equipment is necessary to prevent the actual or threatened discharge of oil during lightering or fuel loading or off[-]loading activity, the Secretary may initiate a rulemaking to take such action as is necessary to abate a threat to public health or the environment.

(c) Lightering Study.—The Secretary of Transportation shall coordinate with the Marine Board of the National Research Council on a study into the actual incidence and risk of oil spills from lightering operations off the coast of the United States. Among other things, the study shall address the manner in which existing regulations are serving to reduce oil spill risks. The study shall take into account current or proposed international rules and standards and also include recommendations on measures that would be likely to further reduce the risks of oil spills from lightering operations. Not later than 18 months after the date of enactment of this Act [Oct. 19, 1996], the Secretary shall submit a report on the study to the Committee on Commerce, Science, and Transportation of the Senate and the Committee on Transportation and Infrastructure of the House of Representatives."

Existing Tank Vessel Research

Pub. L. 104-324, title XI, Sec. 1134, Oct. 19, 1996, 110 Stat. 3985, provided that:

(a) Funding.—The Secretary of Transportation shall take steps to allocate funds appropriated for research, development, testing, and evaluation, including the combination of funds from any source available and authorized for this purpose, to ensure that any Government-sponsored project intended to evaluate double hull alternatives that provide equal or greater protection to the marine environment, or interim solutions to remediate potential environmental damage resulting from oil spills from existing tank vessels, commenced prior to the date of enactment of this section [Oct. 19, 1996], is fully funded for completion by the end of fiscal year 1997. Any vessel construction or repair necessary to carry out the purpose of this section must be performed in a shipyard located in the United States.

(b) Use of Public Vessels.—The Secretary may provide vessels owned by, or demise chartered to, and operated by the Government and not engaged in commercial service, without reimbursement, for use in and the support of projects sponsored by the Government for research, development, testing, evaluation, and demonstration of new or improved technologies that are effective in preventing or mitigating oil discharges and protecting the environment."

Oil Spill Prevention and Response Technology Test and Evaluation Program

Pub. L. 103-206, title III, Sec. 310, Dec. 20, 1993, 107 Stat. 2425, provided that:

"(a) Not later than 6 months after the date of enactment of this Act [Dec. 20, 1993], the Secretary of Transportation shall establish a program to evaluate the technological feasibility and environmental benefits of having tank vessels carry oil spill prevention and response technology. To implement the program the Secretary shall—
  (1) publish in the Federal Register an invitation for submission of proposals including plans and procedures for testing; and
  (2) review and evaluate technology using, to the maximum extent possible, existing evaluation and performance standards.

(b) The Secretary shall, to the maximum extent possible, incorporate in the program established in subsection (a), the results of existing studies and evaluations of oil spill prevention and response technology carried on tank vessels.

(c) Not later than 2 years after the date of the enactment of this Act [Dec. 20, 1993], the Secretary shall evaluate the results of the program established in subsection (a) and submit a report to Congress with recommendations on the feasibility and environmental benefits of, and appropriate equipment and utilization standards for, requiring tank vessels to carry oil spill prevention and response equipment.

(d) Not later than 6 months after the date of the enactment of this Act [Dec. 20, 1993], the Secretary shall evaluate and report to the Congress on the feasibility of using segregated ballast tanks for emergency transfer of cargo and storage of recovered oil."

Regulations Requiring Periodic Gauging of Plating Thickness for Oil Carrying Commercial Vessels

Pub. L. 101-380, title IV, Sec. 4109, Aug. 18, 1990, 104 Stat. 515, provided that: "Not later than 1 year after the date of the enactment of this Act [Aug. 18, 1990], the Secretary shall issue regulations for vessels constructed or adapted to carry, or that carry, oil in bulk as cargo or cargo residue—

(1) establishing minimum standards for plating thickness; and
(2) requiring, consistent with generally recognized principles of international law, periodic gauging of the plating thickness of all such vessels over 30 years old operating on the navigable waters or the waters of the exclusive economic zone."

Regulations Requiring Use of Overfill and Tank Level or Monitoring Devices on Oil Carrying Commercial Vessels

Pub. L. 101-380, title IV, Sec. 4110, Aug. 18, 1990, 104 Stat. 515, provided that:

"(a) Standards.—Not later than 1 year after the date of the enactment of this Act [Aug. 18, 1990], the Secretary shall establish, by regulation, minimum standards for devices for warning persons of overfills and tank levels of oil in cargo tanks and devices for monitoring the pressure of oil cargo tanks.

(b) Use.—Not later than 1 year after the date of the enactment of this Act [Aug. 18, 1990], the Secretary shall issue regulations establishing, consistent with generally recognized principles of international law, requirements concerning the use of—
(1) overfill devices, and
(2) tank level or pressure monitoring devices,
which are referred to in subsection (a) and which meet the standards established by the Secretary under subsection (a), on vessels constructed or adapted to carry, or that carry, oil in bulk as cargo or cargo residue on the navigable waters and the waters of the exclusive economic zone."

Tanker Navigation Safety Standards Study

Pub. L. 101-380, title IV, Sec. 4111, Aug. 18, 1990, 104 Stat. 515, directed Secretary, not later than 2 years after Aug. 18, 1990, to conduct a study and report to Congress on whether existing laws and regulations are adequate to ensure safe navigation of vessels transporting oil or hazardous substances in bulk on navigable waters and waters of the exclusive economic zone.

Rules Governing Operation of Vessels on Auto-Pilot or With Unattended Engine Room

Pub. L. 101-380, title IV, Sec. 4114(a), Aug. 18, 1990, 104 Stat. 517, provided that: "In order to protect life, property, and the environment, the Secretary shall initiate a rulemaking proceeding within 180 days after the date of the enactment of this Act [Aug. 18, 1990] to define the conditions under, and designate the waters upon, which tank vessels subject to section 3703 of title 46, United States Code, may operate in the navigable waters with the auto-pilot engaged or with an unattended engine room."

Regulations Requiring Escorts for Certain Tankers; "Tanker" Defined

Pub. L. 101-380, title IV, Sec. 4116(c), (d), Aug. 18, 1990, 104 Stat. 523, provided that:

"(c) Escorts for Certain Tankers.—Not later than 6 months after the date of the enactment of this Act [Aug. 18, 1990], the Secretary shall initiate issuance of regulations under section 3703(a)(3) of title 46, United States Code, to define those areas, including Prince William Sound, Alaska, and Rosario Strait and Puget Sound, Washington (including those portions of the Strait of Juan de Fuca east of Port Angeles, Haro Strait, and the Strait of Georgia subject to United States jurisdiction), on which single hulled tankers over 5,000 gross tons transporting oil in bulk shall be escorted by at least two towing vessels (as defined under section 2101 of title 46, United States Code) or other vessels considered appropriate by the Secretary.

(d) Tanker Defined.—In this section [amending section 8502 of this title] the term 'tanker' has the same meaning the term has in section 2101 of title 46, United States Code."

Section Referred to in Other Sections

This section is referred to in title 42 section 7511b.

STUDY ON TANKER NAVIGATION SAFETY STANDARDS

Sec. 4111[4]

(a) In General.—Not later than 1 year after the date of enactment of this Act, the Secretary shall initiate a study to determine whether existing laws and regulations are adequate to ensure the safe navigation of vessels transporting oil or hazardous substances in bulk on the navigable waters and the waters of the exclusive economic zone.

(b) Content.—In conducting the study required under subsection (a), the Secretary shall—
  (1) determine appropriate crew sizes on tankers;
  (2) evaluate the adequacy of qualifications and training of crewmembers on tankers;
  (3) evaluate the ability of crewmembers on tankers to take emergency actions to prevent or remove a discharge of oil or a hazardous substance from their tankers;
  (4) evaluate the adequacy of navigation equipment and systems on tankers (including sonar, electronic chart display, and satellite technology);
  (5) evaluate and test electronic means of position-reporting and identification on tankers, consider the minimum standards suitable for equipment for that purpose, and determine whether to require that equipment on tankers:
  (6) evaluate the adequacy of navigation procedures under different operating conditions, including such variable as speed, daylight, ice, tides, weather, and other conditions;
  (7) evaluate whether areas of navigable waters and the exclusive economic zone should be designated as zones where the movement of tankers should be limited or prohibited;
  (8) evaluate whether inspection standards are adequate;
  (9) review and incorporate the results of past studies, including studies conducted by the Coast Guard and the Office of Technology Assessment;
  (10) evaluate the use of computer simulator courses for training bridge officers and pilots of vessels transporting oil or hazardous substances on the navigable waters and waters of the exclusive economic zone, and determine the feasibility and practicality of mandating such training;
  (11) evaluate the size, cargo capacity, and flag nation of tankers transporting oil or hazardous substances on the navigable waters and the waters of the exclusive economic zone—
    (A) identifying changes occurring over the past 20 years in such size and cargo capacity and in vessel navigation and technology; and
    (B) evaluating the extent to which the risks or difficulties associated with tanker navigation, vessel traffic control, accidents, oil spills, and the containment an cleanup of such spills are influenced by or related to an increase in tanker size and cargo capacity; and
  (12) evaluate and test a program of remote alcohol testing for masters and pilots aboard tankers carrying significant quantities of oil.
(c) Report. Not later than 2 years after the date of enactment of this Act, the Secretary of the Army shall transmit to the Congress a report on the results of the study conducted under subsection (a), including recommendations for implementing the results of that study.

DREDGE MODIFICATION STUDY

Sec. 4112[4]

(a) Study.—The Secretary of the Army shall conduct a study and demonstration to determine the feasibility of modifying dredges to make them usable in removing discharges of oil and hazardous substances.

(b) Report.—Not later than 1 year after the date of enactment of this Act, the Secretary of the Army shall submit to the Congress a report on the results of the study conducted under subsection (a) and recommendations for implementing the results of that study.

---

[4]Editor's note: section number and text is that of Pub. L. 101-380.

USE OF LINERS

Sec. 4113[4]

(a) Study.—The President shall conduct a study to determine whether liners or other secondary means of containment should be used to prevent leaking or to aid in leak detection at onshore facilities used for the bulk storage of oil and located near navigable waters.

(b) Report.—Not later than 1 year after the date of enactment of this Act, the President shall submit to the Congress a report on the results of the study conducted under subsection (a) and recommendations to implement the results of the study.

(c) Implementation.—Not later than 6 months after the date the report required under subsection (b) is submitted to the Congress, the President shall implement the recommendations contained in the report.

TANK VESSEL MANNING

Sec. 4114[4]

(a) Rulemaking.—In order to protect life, property, and the environment, the Secretary shall initiate a rulemaking proceeding within 180 days after the date of the enactment of this Act to define the conditions under, and designate the waters upon, which tank vessels subject to section 3703 of title 46, United States Code, may operate in the navigable waters with the autopilot engaged or with an unattended engine room.

(b) Watches.—Section 8104 of title 46, United States Code, is amended by adding at the end the following new subsection:

"(n) On a tanker, a licensed individual or seaman may not be permitted to work more than 15 hours in any 24-hour period, or more than 36 hours in any 72-hour period, except in an emergency or a drill. In this subsection, 'work' includes any administrative duties associated with the vessel whether performed on board the vessel or onshore.".

(c) Manning Requirement.—Section 8101(a) of title 46, United States Code, is amended—
 (1) by striking "and" at the end of paragraph (1);
 (2) by striking the period at the end of paragraph (2) and inserting "; and"; and
 (3) by adding at the end the following new paragraph:
 "(3) a tank vessel shall consider the navigation, cargo handling, and maintenance functions of that vessel for protection of life, property, and the environment.".

(d) Standards.—Section 9102(a) of title 46, United States Code, is amended—
 (1) by striking "and" at the end of paragraph (6);
 (2) by striking the period at the end of paragraph (7) and inserting "; and"; and
 (3) by adding at the end the following new paragraph:
 "(8) instruction in vessel maintenance functions.".

(e) Records.—Section 7502 of title 46, United States Code, is amended by striking "maintain records" and inserting "maintain computerized records".

TANK VESSEL CONSTRUCTION STANDARDS

46 USC 3703a

(a) Except as otherwise provided in this section, a vessel to which this chapter applies shall be equipped with a double hull—
 (1) if it is constructed or adapted to carry, or carries, oil in bulk as cargo or cargo residue; and
 (2) when operating on the waters subject to the jurisdiction of the United States, including the Exclusive Economic Zone.

(b) This section does not apply to—
 (1) a vessel used only to respond to a discharge of oil or a hazardous substance;
 (2) a vessel of less than 5,000 gross tons as measured under section 14502 of this title, or an alternate tonnage measured under section 14302 of this title as prescribed by the Secretary under section 14104 of this title equipped with a double containment system deter-

---
[4]Editor's note: section number and text is that of Pub. L. 101-380.

mined by the Secretary to be as effective as a double hull for the prevention of a discharge of oil;
(3) before January 1, 2015—
   (A) a vessel unloading oil in bulk at a deepwater port licensed under the Deepwater Port Act of 1974 (33 U.S.C. 1501 et seq.); or
   (B) a delivering vessel that is offloading in lightering activities—
      (i) within a lightering zone established under section 3715(b)(5) of this title; and
      (ii) more than 60 miles from the baseline from which the territorial sea of the United States is measured;
(4) a vessel documented under chapter 121 of this title that was equipped with a double hull before August 12, 1992;
(5) a barge of less than 1,500 gross tons (as measured under chapter 145 of this title) carrying refined petroleum product in bulk as cargo in or adjacent to waters of the Bering Sea, Chukchi Sea, and Arctic Ocean and waters tributary thereto and in the waters of the Aleutian Islands and the Alaskan Peninsula west of 155 degrees west longitude; or
(6) a vessel in the National Defense Reserve Fleet pursuant to section 11 of the Merchant Ship Sales Act of 1946 (50 App. U.S.C. 1744).
(c) (1) In this subsection, the age of a vessel is determined from the later of the date on which the vessel—
   (A) is delivered after original construction;
   (B) is delivered after completion of a major conversion; or
   (C) had its appraised salvage value determined by the Coast Guard and is qualified for documentation under section 4136 of the Revised Statutes of the United States (46 App. U.S.C. 14).
(2) A vessel of less than 5,000 gross tons as measured under section 14502 of this title, or an alternate tonnage measured under section 14302 of this title as prescribed by the Secretary under section 14104 of this title for which a building contract or contract for major conversion was placed before June 30, 1990, and that is delivered under that contract before January 1, 1994, and a vessel of less than 5,000 gross tons as measured under section 14502 of this title, or an alternate tonnage measured under section 14302 of this title as prescribed by the Secretary under section 14104 of this title that had its appraised salvage value determined by the Coast Guard before June 30, 1990, and that qualifies for documentation under section 4136 of the Revised Statutes of the United States (46 App. U.S.C. 14) before January 1, 1994, may not operate in the navigable waters or the Exclusive Economic Zone of the United States after January 1, 2015, unless the vessel is equipped with a double hull or with a double containment system determined by the Secretary to be as effective as a double hull for the prevention of a discharge of oil.
(3) A vessel for which a building contract or contract for major conversion was placed before June 30, 1990, and that is delivered under that contract before January 1, 1994, and a vessel that had its appraised salvage value determined by the Coast Guard before June 30, 1990, and that qualifies for documentation under section 4136 of the Revised Statutes of the United States (46 App. U.S.C. 14) before January 1, 1994, may not operate in the navigable waters or Exclusive Economic Zone of the United States unless equipped with a double hull—
   (A) in the case of a vessel of at least 5,000 gross tons but less than 15,000 gross tons as measured under section 14502 of this title, or an alternate tonnage measured under section 14302 of this title as prescribed by the Secretary under section 14104 of this title—
      (i) after January 1, 1995, if the vessel is 40 years old or older and has a single hull, or is 45 years old or older and has a double bottom or double sides;
      (ii) after January 1, 1996, if the vessel is 39 years old or older and has a single hull, or is 44 years old or older and has a double bottom or double sides;
      (iii) after January 1, 1997, if the vessel is 38 years old or older and has a single hull, or is 43 years old or older and has a double bottom or double sides;
      (iv) after January 1, 1998, if the vessel is 37 years old or older and has a single hull, or is 42 years old or older and has a double bottom or double sides;
      (v) after January 1, 1999, if the vessel is 36 years old or older and has a single hull, or is 41 years old or older and has a double bottom or double sides;

734 / Environmental Statutes

        (vi) after January 1, 2000, if the vessel is 35 years old or older and has a single hull, or is 40 years old or older and has a double bottom or double sides; and
        (vii) after January 1, 2005, if the vessel is 25 years old or older and has a single hull, or is 30 years old or older and has a double bottom or double sides;
    (B) in the case of a vessel of at least 15,000 gross tons but less than 30,000 gross tons as measured under section 14502 of this title, or an alternate tonnage measured under section 14302 of this title as prescribed by the Secretary under section 14104 of this title—
        (i) after January 1, 1995, if the vessel is 40 years old or older and has a single hull, or is 45 years old or older and has a double bottom or double sides;
        (ii) after January 1, 1996, if the vessel is 38 years old or older and has a single hull, or is 43 years old or older and has a double bottom or double sides;
        (iii) after January 1, 1997, if the vessel is 36 years old or older and has a single hull, or is 41 years old or older and has a double bottom or double sides;
        (iv) after January 1, 1998, if the vessel is 34 years old or older and has a single hull, or is 39 years old or older and has a double bottom or double sides;
        (v) after January 1, 1999, if the vessel is 32 years old or older and has a single hull, or 37 years old or older and has a double bottom or double sides;
        (vi) after January 1, 2000, if the vessel is 30 years old or older and has a single hull, or is 35 years old or older and has a double bottom or double sides;
        (vii) after January 1, 2001, if the vessel is 29 years old or older and has a single hull, or is 34 years old or older and has a double bottom or double sides;
        (viii) after January 1, 2002, if the vessel is 28 years old or older and has a single hull, or is 33 years old or older and has a double bottom or double sides;
        (ix) after January 1, 2003, if the vessel is 27 years old or older and has a single hull, or is 32 years old or older and has a double bottom or double sides;
        (x) after January 1, 2004, if the vessel is 26 years old or older and has a single hull, or is 31 years old or older and has a double bottom or double sides; and
        (xi) after January 1, 2005, if the vessel is 25 years old or older and has a single hull, or is 30 years old or older and has a double bottom or double sides; and
    (C) in the case of a vessel of at least 30,000 gross tons as measured under section 14502 of this title, or an alternate tonnage measured under section 14302 of this title as prescribed by the Secretary under section 14104 of this title—
        (i) after January 1, 1995, if the vessel is 28 years old or older and has a single hull, or 33 years old or older and has a double bottom or double sides;
        (ii) after January 1, 1996, if the vessel is 27 years old or older and has a single hull, or is 32 years old or older and has a double bottom or double sides;
        (iii) after January 1, 1997, if the vessel is 26 years old or older and has a single hull, or is 31 years old or older and has a double bottom or double sides;
        (iv) after January 1, 1998, if the vessel is 25 years old or older and has a single hull, or is 30 years old or older and has a double bottom or double sides;
        (v) after January 1, 1999, if the vessel is 24 years old or older and has a single hull, or 29 years old or older and has a double bottom or double sides; and
        (vi) after January 1, 2000, if the vessel is 23 years old or older and has a single hull, or is 28 years old or older and has a double bottom or double sides.
(4) Except as provided in subsection (b) of this section—
    (A) a vessel that has a single hull may not operate after January 1, 2010; and
    (B) a vessel that has a double bottom or double sides may not operate after January 1, 2015.
(d) The operation of barges described in subsection (b)(5) outside waters described in that subsection shall be on any conditions as the Secretary may require.
(e) (1) For the purposes of this section and except as otherwise provided in paragraphs (2) and (3) of this subsection, the gross tonnage of a vessel shall be the gross tonnage that would have been recognized by the Secretary on July 1, 1997, as the tonnage measured under section 14502 of this title, or as an alternate tonnage measured under section 14302 of this title as prescribed by the Secretary under section 14104 of this title.
  (2) (A) The Secretary may waive the application of paragraph (1) to a tank vessel if—

(i) the owner of the tank vessel applies to the Secretary for the waiver before January 1, 1998;
(ii) the Secretary determines that—
  (I) the owner of the tank vessel has entered into a binding agreement to alter the tank vessel in a shipyard in the United States to reduce the gross tonnage of the tank vessel by converting a portion of the cargo tanks of the tank vessel into protectively located segregated ballast tanks; and
  (II) that conversion will result in a significant reduction in the risk of a discharge of oil;
(iii) at least 60 days before the date of the issuance of the waiver, the Secretary—
  (I) publishes notice that the Secretary has received the application and made the determinations required by clause (ii), including a description of the agreement entered into pursuant to clause (ii)(I); and
  (II) provides an opportunity for submission of comments regarding the application; and
(iv) the alterations referred to in clause (ii)(I) are completed before the later of—
  (I) the date by which the first special survey of the tank vessel is required to be completed after the date of the enactment of the National Defense Authorization Act for Fiscal Year 1998; or
  (II) July 1, 1999.
(B) A waiver under subparagraph (A) shall not be effective after the expiration of the 3-year period beginning on the first date on which the tank vessel would have been prohibited by subsection (c) from operating if the alterations referred to in subparagraph (A)(ii)(I) were not made.
(3) This subsection does not apply to a tank vessel that, before July 1, 1997, had undergone, or was the subject of a contract for, alterations that reduce the gross tonnage of the tank vessel, as shown by reliable evidence acceptable to the Secretary.

(Added Pub. L. 101-380, title IV, Sec. 4115(a), Aug. 18, 1990, 104 Stat. 517; amended Pub. L. 104-324, title VII, Sec. 715, title XI, Sec. 1103, Oct. 19, 1996, 110 Stat. 3937, 3966; Pub. L. 105-85, div. C, title XXXVI, Sec. 3606, Nov. 18, 1997, 111 Stat. 2077.)

References in Text

The Deepwater Port Act of 1974, referred to in subsec. (b)(3)(A), is Pub. L. 93-627, Jan. 3, 1975, 88 Stat. 2126, as amended, which is classified generally to chapter 29 (Sec. 1501 et seq.) of Title 33, Navigation and Navigable Waters. For complete classification of this Act to the Code, see Short Title note set out under section 1501 of Title 33 and Tables.

The date of the enactment of the National Defense Authorization Act for Fiscal Year 1998, referred to in subsec. (e)(2)(A)(iv)(I), is the date of enactment of Pub. L. 105-85, which was approved Nov. 18, 1997.

Amendments

1997—Subsec. (e). Pub. L. 105-85 added subsec. (e).

1996—Subsec. (b)(2). Pub. L. 104-324, Sec. 715(1), inserted "as measured under section 14502 of this title, or an alternate tonnage measured under section 14302 of this title as prescribed by the Secretary under section 14104 of this title" after "5,000 gross tons".

Subsec. (b)(4) to (6). Pub. L. 104-324, Sec. 1103(1), added pars. (4) to (6).

Subsec. (c)(2). Pub. L. 104-324, Sec. 715(2), inserted "as measured under section 14502 of this title, or an alternate tonnage measured under section 14302 of this title as prescribed by the Secretary under section 14104 of this title" after "5,000 gross tons" in two places.

Subsec. (c)(3)(A). Pub. L. 104-324, Sec. 715(3), inserted "as measured under section 14502 of this title, or an alternate tonnage measured under section 14302 of this title as prescribed by the Secretary under section 14104 of this title" after "15,000 gross tons".

Subsec. (c)(3)(B). Pub. L. 104-324, Sec. 715(4), inserted "as measured under section 14502 of this title, or an alternate tonnage measured under section 14302 of this title as prescribed by the Secretary under section 14104 of this title" after "30,000 gross tons".

Subsec. (c)(3)(C). Pub. L. 104-324, Sec. 715(5), inserted "as measured under section 14502 of this title, or an alternate tonnage measured under section 14302 of this title as prescribed by the Secretary under section 14104 of this title" after "30,000 gross tons".

Subsec. (d). Pub. L. 104-324, Sec. 1103(2), added subsec. (d).

Effective Date

Section applicable to incidents occurring after Aug. 18, 1990, see section 1020 of Pub. L. 101-380, set out as a note under section 2701 of Title 33, Navigation and Navigable Waters.

Tank Vessels Over 5,000 Gross Tons To Comply Until January 1, 2015, With Environmentally Protective Structural and Operational Requirements

Section 4115(b) of Pub. L. 101-380 provided that: "The Secretary shall, within 12 months after the date of the enactment of this Act [Aug. 18, 1990], complete a rulemaking proceeding and issue a final rule to require that tank vessels over 5,000 gross tons affected by section 3703a of title 46, United States Code, as added by this section, comply until January 1, 2015, with structural and operational requirements that the Secretary determines will provide as substantial protection to the environment as is economically and technologically feasible."

Study on Other Structural and Operational Tank Vessel Requirements

Pub. L. 101-380, title IV, Sec. 4115(e), Aug. 18, 1990, 104 Stat. 520, as amended by Pub. L. 105-383, title IV, Sec. 423, Nov. 13, 1998, 112 Stat. 3440, provided that:

"(1) Other requirements.—Not later than 6 months after the date of enactment of this Act [Aug. 18, 1990], the Secretary shall determine, based on recommendations from the National Academy of Sciences or other qualified organizations, whether other structural and operational tank vessel requirements will provide protection to the marine environment equal to or greater than that provided by double hulls, and shall report to the Congress that determination and recommendations for legislative action.

(2) Review and assessment.—The Secretary shall—
   (A) periodically review recommendations from the National Academy of Sciences and other qualified organizations on methods for further increasing the environmental and operational safety of tank vessels;
   (B) not later than 5 years after the date of enactment of this Act [Aug. 18, 1990], assess the impact of this section on the safety of the marine environment and the economic viability and operational makeup of the maritime oil transportation industry; and
   (C) report the results of the review and assessment to the Congress with recommendations for legislative or other action.
(3) (A) The Secretary of Transportation shall coordinate with the Marine Board of the National Research Council to conduct the necessary research and development of a rationally based equivalency assessment approach, which accounts for the overall environmental performance of alternative tank vessel designs. Notwithstanding the Coast Guard opinion of the application of sections 101 and 311 of the Clean Water Act (33 U.S.C. 1251 and 1321), the intent of this study is to establish an equivalency evaluation procedure that maintains a high standard of environmental protection, while encouraging innovative ship design. The study shall include:
   (i) development of a generalized cost spill data base, which includes all relevant costs such as clean-up costs and environmental impact costs as a function of spill size;
   (ii) refinement of the probability density functions used to establish the extent of vessel damage, based on the latest available historical damage statistics, and current research on the crash worthiness of tank vessel structures;
   (iii) development of a rationally based approach for calculating an environmental index, to assess overall outflow performance due to collisions and groundings; and
   (iv) application of the proposed index to double hull tank vessels and alternative designs currently under consideration.
(B) A Marine Board committee shall be established not later that [sic] 2 months after the date of the enactment of the Coast Guard Authorization Act of 1998 [Nov. 13, 1998]. The Secretary of Transportation shall submit to the Committee on Commerce, Science, and Transportation of the Senate and the Committee on Transportation and Infrastructure in the House of Representatives a report on the results of the study not

later than 12 months after the date of the enactment of the Coast Guard Authorization Act of 1998.
(C) Of the amounts authorized by section 1012(a)(5)(A) of this Act [33 U.S.C. 2712(a)(5)(A)], $500,000 is authorized to carry out the activities under subparagraphs (A) and (B) of this paragraph."

Territorial Sea of United States

For extension of territorial sea of United States, see Proc. No. 5928, set out as a note under section 1331 of Title 43, Public Lands.

Contiguous Zone of United States

For extension of contiguous zone of United States, see Proc. No. 7219, Sept. 2, 1999, 64 F.R. 48701, set out as a note under section 1331 of Title 43, Public Lands.

Section Referred to in Other Sections

This section is referred to in section 3715 of this title; title 50 App. section 1744.

ESTABLISHMENT OF DOUBLE HULL REQUIREMENT FOR TANK VESSELS

Sec. 4115[4]

(a) Double Hull Requirement.—Chapter 37 of title 46, United States Code, is amended by inserting after section 3703 the following new section:
"3703a. Tank vessel construction standards"
[See 46 U.S.C 3703a, Tank Vessel Construction Standards, above.]
(b) Rulemaking.—The Secretary shall, within 12 months after the date of the enactment of this Act, complete a rulemaking proceeding and issue a final rule to require that tank vessels over 5,000 gross tons affected by section 3703a of title 46, United States Code, as added by this section, comply until January 1, 2015, with structural and operational requirements that the Secretary determines will provide as substantial protection to the environment as is economically and technologically feasible.
(c) Clerical Amendment.—The analysis for chapter 37 of title 46, United States Code, is amended by inserting after the item relating to section 3703 the following:
"3703a. Tank Vessel Construction Standards.".
(d) Lightering Requirements.—Section 3715(a) of title 46, United States Code, is amended—
   (1) in paragraph (1), by striking "; and" and inserting a semicolon;
   (2) in paragraph (2), by striking the period and inserting "; and"; and
   (3) by adding at the end the following:
   "(3) the delivering and the receiving vessel had on board at the time of transfer, a certificate of financial responsibility as would have been required under section 1016 of the Oil Pollution Act of 1990, had the transfer taken place in a place subject to the jurisdiction of the United States;
   (4) the delivering and the receiving vessel had on board at the time of transfer, evidence that each vessel is operating in compliance with section 311(j) of the Federal Water Pollution Control Act (33 U.S.C. 1321(j)); and
   (5) the delivering and the receiving vessel are operating in compliance with section 3703a of this title.".
(e) Secretarial Studies.—
[See "Study on Other Structural and Operational Tank Vessel Requirements" note under 46 U.S.C 3703a above for contents of paragraph.]
(f) Vessel Financing.—Section 1104 of the Merchant Marine Act of 1936 (46 App. U.S.C. 1274) is amended—
   (1) by striking "Sec. 1104" and inserting "Sec. 1104A."; and
   (2) by inserting after section 1104A (as redesignated by paragraph (1)) the following:
   "Sec. 1104B. (a) Notwithstanding the provisions of this title, except as provided in subsection (d) of this section, the Secretary, upon the terms the Secretary may prescribe, may

---

[4]Editor's note: section number and text is that of Pub. L. 101-380.

guarantee or make a commitment to guarantee, payment of the principal of and interest on an obligation which aids in financing and refinancing, including reimbursement to an obligor for expenditures previously made, of a contract for construction or reconstruction of a vessel or vessels owned by citizens of the United States which are designed and to be employed for commercial use in the coastwise or intercoastal trade or in foreign trade as defined in section 905 of this Act if—
  (1) the construction or reconstruction by an applicant is made necessary to replace vessels the continued operation of which is denied by virtue of the imposition of a statutorily mandated change in standards for the operation of vessels, and where, as a matter of law, the applicant would otherwise be denied the right to continue operating vessels in the trades in which the applicant operated prior to the taking effect of the statutory or regulatory change;
  (2) the applicant is presently engaged in transporting cargoes in vessels of the type and class that will be constructed or reconstructed under this section, and agrees to employ vessel constructed or reconstructed under this section as replacements only for vessels made obsolete by changes in operating standards imposed by statute;
  (3) the capacity of the vessels to be constructed or reconstructed under this title will not increase the cargo carrying capacity of the vessels being replaced;
  (4) the Secretary has not made a determination that the market demand for the vessel over its useful life will diminish so as to make the granting of the guarantee fiduciarily imprudent; and
  (5) the Secretary has considered the provisions of section 1104(A)(d)(1)(A)(iii), (iv), and (v) of this title.
(b) For the purposes of this section—
  (1) the maximum term for obligations guaranteed under this program may not exceed 25 years;
  (2) obligations guaranteed may not exceed 75 percent of the actual cost or depreciated actual cost to the applicant for the construction or reconstruction of the vessel; and
  (3) reconstruction cost obligations may not be guaranteed unless the vessel after reconstruction will have a useful life of at least 15 years.
(c) (1) The Secretary shall by rule require that the applicant provide adequate security against default. The Secretary may, in addition to any fees assessed under section 1104A(e), establish a Vessel Replacement Guarantee Fund into which shall be paid by obligors under this section—
    (A) annual fees which may be an additional amount on the loan guarantee fee in section 1104A(e), not to exceed an additional 1 percent; or
    (B) fees based on the amount of the obligations versus the percentage of the obligor's fleet being replaced by vessels constructed under this section.
  (2) The Vessel Replacement Guarantee Fund shall be a subaccount in the Federal Ship Financing Fund, and shall—
    (A) be the depository for all moneys received by the Secretary under sections 1101 through 1107 of this title with respect to guarantee or commitments to guarantee made under this section;
    (B) not include investigation fees payable under section 1104A(f) which shall be paid to the Federal Ship Financing Fund; and
    (C) be the depository, whenever there shall be outstanding any notes or obligations issued by the Secretary under section 1105(d) with respect to the Vessel Replacement Guarantee Fund, for all moneys received by the Secretary under sections 1101 through 1107 from applicants under this section.
(d) The program created by this section shall, in addition to the requirements of this section, be subject to the provisions of sections 1101 through 1103; 1104A(b) (1), (4), (5), (6); 1104A(e); 1104A(f); 1104A(h); and 1105 through 1107; except that the Federal Ship Financing Fund is not liable for any guarantees or commitments to guarantee issued under this section.".

PILOTAGE

Sec. 4116[4]

(a) Pilot Required.—Section 8502(g) of title 46, United States Code, is amended to read as follows:

"(g)(1) The Secretary shall designate by regulation the areas of the approaches to and waters of Prince William Sound, Alaska, if any, on which a vessel subject to this section is not required to be under the direction and control of a pilot licensed under section 7101 of this title.

(2) In any area of Prince William Sound, Alaska, where a vessel subject to this section is required to be under the direction and control of a pilot licensed under section 7101 of this title, the pilot may not be a member of the crew of that vessel and shall be a pilot licensed by the State of Alaska who is operating under a Federal license, when the vessel is navigating waters between 60°49' North latitude and the Port of Valdez, Alaska.".

(b) Second Person Required.—Section 8502 of title 46, United States Code, is amended by adding at the end the following:

"(h) The Secretary shall designate waters on which tankers over 1,600 gross tons subject to this section shall have on the bridge a master or mate licensed to direct and control the vessel under section 7101(c)(1) of this title who is separate and distinct from the pilot required under subsection (a) of this section.".

(c) Escorts for Certain Tankers.—Not later than 6 months after the date of enactment of this Act, the Secretary shall initiate issuance of regulations under section 3703(a)(3) of title 46, United States Code, to define those areas, including Prince William Sound, Alaska, and Rosario Strait and Puget Sound, Washington (including those portions of the Strait of Juan de Fuca east of Port Angeles, Haro Strait, and the Strait of Georgia subject to United States jurisdiction), on which single hulled tankers over 5,000 gross tons transporting oil in bulk shall be escorted by at least two towing vessels (as defined under section 2101 of title 46, United State Code) or other vessels considered appropriate by the Secretary.

(d) Tanker Defined.—In this section the term "tanker" has the same meaning the term has in section 2101 of title 46, United States Code.

MARITIME POLLUTION PREVENTION TRAINING PROGRAM STUDY

Sec. 4117

The Secretary shall conduct a study to determine the feasibility of a Maritime Oil Pollution Prevention Training program to be carried out in cooperation with approved maritime training institutions. The study shall assess the costs and benefits of transferring suitable vessels to selected maritime training institutions, equipping the vessels for oil spill response, and training students in oil pollution response skills. The study shall be completed and transmitted to the Congress no later than one year after the date of the enactment of this Act.

VESSEL COMMUNICATION EQUIPMENT REGULATIONS

Sec. 4118

The Secretary shall, not later than one year after the date of the enactment of this Act, issue regulations necessary to ensure that vessels subject to the Vessel Bridge-to-Bridge Radiotelephone Act of 1971 (33 U.S.C. 1203) are also equipped as necessary to—

(1) receive radio marine navigation safety warnings; and
(2) engage in radio communications on designated frequencies with the Coast Guard, and such other vessels and stations as may be specified by the Secretary.

---

[4]Editor's note: section number and text is that of Pub. L. 101-380.

Subtitle B—Removal

FEDERAL REMOVAL AUTHORITY

Sec. 4201[1]

(a) In General.—Subsection (c) of section 311 of the Federal Water Pollution Control Act (33 U.S.C. 1321(c) is amended to read as follows: [Note: See Clean Water Act, Section 311(c) Federal Removal Authority.]

(b) National Contingency Plan.—Subsection (d) of section 311 of the Federal Water Pollution Control Act (33 U.S.C. 1321(d)) is amended to read as follows: [See Clean Water Act, Section 311(d) National Contingency Plan.]

  (b) Definitions.--Section 311(a) of the Federal Water Pollution Control Act (33 U.S.C. 1321(a))) is amended--[See paragraphs (8), and (16) to (24).]

(c) Revision of National Contingency Plan.—Not later than one year after the date of the enactment of this Act, the President shall revise and republish the national Contingency Plan prepared under section 311(c)(2) of the Federal Water Pollution Control Act (as in effect immediately before the date of the enactment of this Act) to implement the amendments made by this section and section 4202.

NATIONAL CONTINGENCY PLANNING AND RESPONSE SYSTEM

Sec. 4202[1]

(a) In General.—Subsection (j) of section 311 of the Federal Water Pollution Control Act (33 U.S.C. 1321(j) is amended– [See Clean Water Act, Section 311(j) National Response System.]

(b) Implementation.—
  (1) Area Committees and Contingency Plans.—
    (A) Not later than 6 months after the date of the enactment of this Act, the President shall designate the areas for which Area Committees are established under section 311(j)(4) of the Federal Water Pollution Control Act, as amended by this Act. In designating such areas, the President shall ensure that all navigable waters, adjoining shorelines, and waters of the exclusive economic zone are subject to an Area Contingency Plan required under that section.
    (B) Not later than 18 months after the date of the enactment of this Act, each Area Committee established under that section shall submit to the President the Area Contingency Plan required under that section.
    (C) Not later than 24 months after the date of the enactment of this Act, the President shall—
      (i) promptly review each plan;
      (ii) require amendments to any plan that does not meet the requirements of section 311(j)(4) of the Federal Water Pollution Control Act; and
      (iii) approve each plan that meets the requirements of that section.
  (2) National Response Unit.—Not later than one year after the date of the enactment of this Act, the Secretary of the department in which the Coast Guard is operating shall establish a National Response Unit in accordance with section 311(j)(4) of the Federal Water Pollution Control Act, as amended by this Act.
  (3) Coast Guard District Response Groups.—Not later than 1 year after the date of the enactment of this Act, the Secretary of the department in which the Coast Guard is operating shall establish Coast Guard District Response Groups in accordance with section 311(j)(3) of the Federal Water Pollution Control Act, as amended by this Act.
  (4) Tank Vessel and Facility Response Plans; Transition Provision; Effective Date of Prohibition.—
    (A) Not later than 24 months after the date of the enactment of this Act, the President shall issue regulations for tank vessel and facility response plans under section 311(j)(5) of the Federal Water Pollution Control Act, as amended by this Act.

---

[1]Editor's note: section number and text is that of Pub. L. 101-380.

(B) During the period beginning 30 months after the date of the enactment of this paragraph and ending 36 months after that date of enactment, a tank vessel or facility for which a response plan is required to be prepared under section 311(j)(5) of the Federal Water Pollution Control Act, as amended by this Act, may not handle, store, or transport oil unless the owner or operator thereof has submitted such a plan to the President.

(C) Subparagraph (E) of section 311(j)(5) of the Federal Water Pollution Control Act, as amended by this Act, shall take effect 36 months after the date of the enactment of this Act.

(c) State Law Not Preempted.—Section 311(o)(2) of the Federal Water Pollution Control Act (33 U.S.C. 1321(o)(2)) is amended by inserting before the period the following: ", or with respect to any removal activities related to such discharge".

COAST GUARD VESSEL DESIGN

14 USC 92 note

Pub. L. 101-380, title IV, Sec. 4203, Aug. 18, 1990, 104 Stat. 532, provided that: "The Secretary shall ensure that vessels designed and constructed to replace Coast Guard buoy tenders are equipped with oil skimming systems that are readily available and operable, and that complement the primary mission of servicing aids to navigation."

DETERMINATION OF HARMFUL QUANTITIES OF OIL AND HAZARDOUS SUBSTANCES

Sec. 4204[1]

Section 311(b)(4) of the Federal Water Pollution Control Act (33 U.S.C. 1321(b)(4) is amended by inserting "or the environment" after "the public health or welfare".

COASTWISE OIL SPILL RESPONSE COOPERATIVES

Sec. 4205[1]

Section 12106 of title 46, United States Code, is amended by adding at the end the following:
"(d)(1) A vessel may be issued a certificate of documentation with a coastwise endorsement if—
  (A) the vessel is owned by a not-for-profit oil spill response cooperative or by members of such a cooperative who dedicate the vessel to use by the cooperative;
  (B) the vessel is at least 50 percent owned by persons or entities described in section 12102(a) of this title;
  (C) the vessel otherwise qualifies under section 12106 to be employed in the coastwise trade; and
  (D) use of the vessel is restricted to—
    (i) the deployment of equipment, supplies, and personnel to recover, contain, or transport oil discharged into the navigable waters of the United States, or within the Exclusive Economic Zone, or
    (ii) for training exercises to prepare to respond to such a discharge.
(2) For purposes of the first proviso of section 27 of the Merchant Marine Act, 1920, section 2 of the Shipping Act of 1916, and section 12102(a) of this title, a vessel meeting the criteria of this subsection shall be considered to be owned exclusively by citizens of the United States."

---

[1]Editor's note: section number and text is that of Pub. L. 101-380.

Subtitle C—Penalties and Miscellaneous

FEDERAL WATER POLLUTION CONTROL ACT PENALTIES

Section 4301[1]

(a) Notice to State and Failure to Report.—Section 311(b)(5) of the Federal Water Pollution Control Act (33 U.S.C. 1321(b)(5)) is amended—
  (1) by inserting after the first sentence the following: "The Federal agency shall immediately notify the appropriate State agency of any State which is, or may reasonably be expected to be, affected by the discharge of oil or a hazardous substance.";
  (2) by striking "fined not more than $10,000, or imprisoned for not more than one year, or both" and inserting "fined in accordance with title 18, United States Code, or imprisoned for not more than 5 years, or both"; and
  (3) in the last sentence by—
    (A) striking "or information obtained by the exploitation of such notification"; and
    (B) inserting "natural" before "person".
(b) Penalties for Discharges and Violations of Regulations.—Section 311(b) of the Federal Water Pollution Control Act (33 U.S.C. 1321(b)) is amended by striking paragraph (6) and inserting the following new paragraphs: [See Clean Water Act, section 311(b)(6).]
(c) Criminal Penalties.—Section 309(c) of the Federal Water Pollution Control Act (33 U.S.C. 1319(c)) is amended by inserting after "308," each place it appears the following: "311(b)(3),".

OTHER PENALTIES

Sec. 4302[1]

(a) Negligent Operations.—Section 2302 of title 46, United States Code, is amended—
  (1) in subsection (b) by striking "shall be fined not more than $5,000, imprisoned for not more than one year, or both.", and inserting "commits a class A misdemeanor."; and
  (2) in subsection (c)—
    (A) by striking ", shall be" in the matter preceding paragraph (1);
    (B) by inserting "is" before "liable" in paragraph (1); and
    (C) by amending paragraph (2) to read as follows:
    "(2) commits a class A misdemeanor.".
(b) Inspections.—Section 3318 of title 46, United States Code, is amended—
  (1) in subsection (b) by striking "shall be fined not more than $10,000, imprisoned for not more than 5 years, or both." and inserting "commits a class D felony.";
  (2) in subsection (c) by striking "shall be fined not more than $5,000, imprisoned for not more than 5 years, or both." and inserting "commits a class D felony.";
  (3) in subsection (d) by striking "shall be fined not more than $5,000, imprisoned for not more than 5 years, or both." and inserting "commits a class D felony.";
  (4) in subsection (e) by striking "shall be fined not more than $10,000, imprisoned for not more than 2 years, or both." and inserting "commits a class A misdemeanor."; and
  (5) in the matter preceding paragraph (1) of subsection (f) by striking "shall be fined not less than $1,000, but not more than $10,000, and imprisoned for not less than 2 years but not more than 5 years," and inserting "commits a class D felony.".
(c) Carriage of Liquid Bulk Dangerous Cargoes.—Section 3718 of title 46, United States Code, is amended—
  (1) in subsection (b) by striking "shall be fined not more than $50,000, imprisoned for not more than 5 years, or both." and inserting "commits a class D felony."; and
  (2) in subsection (c) by striking "shall be fined not more than $100,000, imprisoned for not more than 10 years, or both." and inserting "commits a class C felony.".
(d) Load Lines.—Section 5116 of title 46, United States Code, is amended—
  (1) in subsection (d) by striking "shall be fined not more than $10,000, imprisoned for not more than one year, or both." and inserting "commits a class A misdemeanor."; and

---
[1] Editor's note: section number and text is that of Pub. L. 101-380.

Oil Pollution Act of 1990 / 743

 (2) in subsection (e) by striking "shall be fined not more than $10,000, imprisoned for not more than 2 years, or both." and inserting "commits a class A misdemeanor.".
(e) Complement of Inspected Vessels.—Section 8101 of title 46, United States Code, is amended—
 (1) in subsection (e) by striking "$50" and inserting "$1,000";
 (2) in subsection (f) by striking "$100, or, for a deficiency of a licensed individual, a penalty of $500." and inserting "$10,000."; and
 (3) in subsection (g) by striking "$500." and inserting "$10,000.".
(f) Watches.—Section 8104 of title 46, United States Code, is amended—
 (1) in subsection (i) by striking "$100." and inserting "$10,000."; and
 (2) in subsection (j) by striking "$500." and inserting "$10,000.".
(g) Coastwise Pilotage.—Section 8502 of title 46, United States Code, is amended—
 (1) in subsection (e) by striking "$500." and inserting "$10,000."; and
 (2) in subsection (f) by striking "$500." and inserting "$10,000.".
(h) Foreign Commerce Pilotage.—Section 8503(e) of title 46, United States Code, is amended by striking "shall be fined not more than $50,000, imprisoned for not more than five years, or both." and inserting "commits a class D felony.".
(i) Crew Requirements.—Section 8702(e) of title 46, United States Code, is amended by striking $500." and inserting "$10,000.".
(j) Ports and Waterways Safety Act.—Section 13(b) of the Port and Waterways Safety Act (33 U.S.C. 1232(b)) is amended—
 (1) in paragraph (1) by striking "shall be fined not more than $50,000 for each violation or imprisoned for not more than five years, or both." and inserting "commits a class D felony."; and
 (2) in paragraph (2) by striking "shall, in lieu of the penalties prescribed in paragraph (1), be fined not more than $100,000, or imprisoned for not more than 10 years, or both." and inserting "commits a class C felony.".
(k) Vessel Navigation.—Section 4 of the Act of April 28, 1908 (33 U.S.C. 1236), is amended—
 (1) in subsection (b) by striking "$500." and inserting "$5,000.";
 (2) in subsection (c) by striking "$500," and inserting "$5,000,"; and
 (3) in subsection (d) by striking $250." and inserting "$2,500.".
(l) Intervention on the High Seas Act.—Section 12(a) of the Intervention of the High Seas Act (33 U.S.C. 1481(a)) is amended—
 (1) in the matter preceding paragraph (1) by striking "Any person who" and inserting "A person commits a class A misdemeanor if that person"; and
 (2) in paragraph (3) by striking ", shall be fined not more than $10,000 or imprisoned not more than one year, or both".
(m) Deepwater Port Act of 1974.—Section 15(a) of the Deepwater Port Act of 1974 (33 U.S.C. 1514(a)) is amended by striking "shall on conviction be fined not more than $25,000 for each day of violation or imprisoned for not more than 1 year, or both." and inserting "commits a class A misdemeanor for each day of violation.".
(n) Act To Prevent Pollution From Ships.—Section 9(a) of the Act to Prevent Pollution from Ships (33 U.S.C. 1908(a)) is amended by striking "shall, for each violation, be fined not more than $50,000 or be imprisoned for not more than 5 years, or both." and inserting "commits a class D felony.".

FINANCIAL RESPONSIBILITY CIVIL PENALTIES

Sec. 4303[1]

(a) Administrative.—Any person who, after notice and an opportunity for a hearing, is found to have failed to comply with the requirements of section 1016 or the regulations issued under that section, or with a denial or detention order issued under subsection (c)(2) of that section, shall be liable to the United States for a civil penalty, not to exceed $25,000 per day of violation. The amount of the civil penalty shall be assessed by the President by written notice. In

---

[1]Editor's note: section number and text is that of Pub. L. 101-380.

determining the amount of the penalty, the President shall take into account the nature, circumstances, extent, and gravity of the violation, the degree of culpability, any history of prior violation, ability to pay, and such other matters as justice may require. The President may compromise, modify, or remit, with or without conditions, any civil penalty which is subject to imposition or which has been imposed under this paragraph. If any person fails to pay an assessed civil penalty after it has become final, the President may refer the matter to the Attorney General for collection.

(b) Judicial.—In addition to, or in lieu of, assessing a penalty under subsection (a), the President may request the Attorney General to secure such relief as necessary to compel compliance with this section 1016, including a judicial order terminating operations. The district courts of the United States shall have jurisdiction to grant any relief as the public interest and the inequities of the case may require.

Sec. 4304

[See "Deposit of Certain Penalties into Oil Spill Liability Trust Fund" note under 26 USC 9509 above (Oil Spill Liability Trust Fund) for contents of section 4304.]

INSPECTION AND ENTRY

Sec. 4305[1]

Section 311(m) of the Federal Water Pollution Control Act (33 U.S.C. 1321(m)) is amended to read as follows: [See Clean Water Act, Section 311(m), Administrative Provisions.]

INSPECTION AND ENTRY

Sec. 4306[1]

Section 311(e) of the Federal Water Pollution Control Act (33 U.S.C. 1321) is amended to read as follows: [See Clean Water Act, Section 311(e), Civil Enforcement.]

---

[1]Editor's note: section number and text is that of Pub. L. 101-380.

SUBCHAPTER II—PRINCE WILLIAM SOUND PROVISIONS

OIL SPILL RECOVERY INSTITUTE

33 USC 2731

(a) Establishment of Institute

The Secretary of Commerce shall provide for the establishment of a Prince William Sound Oil Spill Recovery Institute (hereinafter in this section referred to as the "Institute") through the Prince William Sound Science and Technology Institute located in Cordova, Alaska.

(b) Functions

The Institute shall conduct research and carry out educational and demonstration projects designed to—
  (1) identify and develop the best available techniques, equipment, and materials for dealing with oil spills in the arctic and subarctic marine environment; and
  (2) complement Federal and State damage assessment efforts and determine, document, assess, and understand the long-range effects of Arctic or Subarctic oil spills on the natural resources of Prince William Sound and its adjacent waters (as generally depicted on the map entitled "EXXON VALDEZ oil spill dated March 1990"), and the environment, the economy, and the lifestyle and well-being of the people who are dependent on them, except that the Institute shall not conduct studies or make recommendations on any matter which is not directly related to Arctic or Subarctic oil spills or the effects thereof.

(c) Advisory board
  (1) In general

  The policies of the Institute shall be determined by an advisory board, composed of 16 members appointed as follows:
    (A) One representative appointed by each of the Commissioners of Fish and Game, Environmental Conservation, and Natural Resources of the State of Alaska, all of whom shall be State employees.
    (B) One representative appointed by each of the Secretaries of Commerce, the Interior, and Transportation, who shall be Federal employees.
    (C) Two representatives from the fishing industry appointed by the Governor of the State of Alaska from among residents of communities in Alaska that were affected by the EXXON VALDEZ oil spill, who shall serve terms of 2 years each. Interested organizations from within the fishing industry may submit the names of qualified individuals for consideration by the Governor.
    (D) Two Alaska Natives who represent Native entities affected by the EXXON VALDEZ oil spill, at least one of whom represents an entity located in Prince William Sound, appointed by the Governor of Alaska from a list of 4 qualified individuals submitted by the Alaska Federation of Natives, who shall serve terms of 2 years each.
    (E) Two representatives from the oil and gas industry to be appointed by the Governor of the State of Alaska who shall serve terms of 2 years each. Interested organizations from within the oil and gas industry may submit the names of qualified individuals for consideration by the Governor.
    (F) Two at-large representatives from among residents of communities in Alaska that were affected by the EXXON VALDEZ oil spill who are knowledgeable about the marine environment and wildlife within Prince William Sound, and who shall serve terms of 2 years each, appointed by the remaining members of the Advisory Board. Interested parties may submit the names of qualified individuals for consideration by the Advisory Board.
    (G) One nonvoting representative of the Institute of Marine Science.
    (H) One nonvoting representative appointed by the Prince William Sound Science and Technology Institute.
  (2) Chairman

  The representative of the Secretary of Commerce shall serve as Chairman of the Advisory Board.

(3) Policies

Policies determined by the Advisory Board under this subsection shall include policies for the conduct and support, through contracts and grants awarded on a nationally competitive basis, of research, projects, and studies to be supported by the Institute in accordance with the purposes of this section.

(4) Scientific review

The Advisory Board may request a scientific review of the research program every five years by the National Academy of Sciences which shall perform the review, if requested, as part of its responsibilities under section 2761(b)(2) of this title.

(d) Scientific and technical committee

(1) In general

The Advisory Board shall establish a scientific and technical committee, composed of specialists in matters relating to oil spill containment and cleanup technology, arctic and subarctic marine ecology, and the living resources and socioeconomics of Prince William Sound and its adjacent waters, from the University of Alaska, the Institute of Marine Science, the Prince William Sound Science and Technology Institute, and elsewhere in the academic community.

(2) Functions

The Scientific and Technical Committee shall provide such advice to the Advisory Board as the Advisory Board shall request, including recommendations regarding the conduct and support of research, projects, and studies in accordance with the purposes of this section. The Advisory Board shall not request, and the Committee shall not provide, any advice which is not directly related to Arctic or Subarctic oil spills or the effects thereof.

(e) Director

The Institute shall be administered by a Director appointed by the Advisory Board. The Prince William Sound Science and Technology Institute and the Scientific and Technical Committee may each submit independent recommendations for the Advisory Board's consideration for appointment as Director. The Director may hire such staff and incur such expenses on behalf of the Institute as are authorized by the Advisory Board.

(f) Evaluation

The Secretary of Commerce may conduct an ongoing evaluation of the activities of the Institute to ensure that funds received by the Institute are used in a manner consistent with this section.

(g) Audit

The Comptroller General of the United States, and any of his or her duly authorized representatives, shall have access, for purposes of audit and examination, to any books, documents, papers, and records of the Institute and its administering agency that are pertinent to the funds received and expended by the Institute and its administering agency.

(h) Status of employees

Employees of the Institute shall not, by reason of such employment, be considered to be employees of the Federal Government for any purpose.

(i) Termination

The authorization in section 2736(b) of this title providing funding for the Institute shall terminate September 30, 2012.

(j) Use of funds

No funds made available to carry out this section may be used to initiate litigation. No funds made available to carry out this section may be used for the acquisition of real property (including buildings) or construction of any building. No more than 20 percent of funds made available to carry out this section may be used to lease necessary facilities and to administer the Institute. The Advisory Board may compensate its Federal representatives for their reasonable travel costs. None of the funds authorized by this section shall be used for any purpose other than the functions specified in subsection (b) of this section.

(k) Research

The Institute shall publish and make available to any person upon request the results of all research, educational, and demonstration projects conducted by the Institute. The Administrator shall provide a copy of all research, educational, and demonstration projects conducted by the Institute to the National Oceanic and Atmospheric Administration.

(l) "Prince William Sound and its adjacent waters" defined

In this section, the term "Prince William Sound and its adjacent waters" means such sound and waters as generally depicted on the map entitled "EXXON VALDEZ oil spill dated March 1990".

(Pub. L. 101-380, title V, Sec. 5001, Aug. 18, 1990, 104 Stat. 542; Pub. L. 104-324, title XI, Sec. 1102(a), Oct. 19, 1996, 110 Stat. 3964.)

Amendments

2002-Subsec. (i). Pub. L. 107-295, Sec. 427, struck out "10 years after October 19, 1996" and substituted "September 30, 2012."

1996—Subsec. (a). Pub. L. 104-324, Sec. 1102(a)(1), (2), struck out "to be administered by the Secretary of Commerce" after "as the 'Institute')" and substituted "located" for "and located".

Subsec. (b)(2). Pub. L. 104-324, Sec. 1102(a)(3), substituted "Arctic or Subarctic oil spills" for "the EXXON VALDEZ oil spill" in two places.

Subsec. (c)(1). Pub. L. 104-324, Sec. 1102(a)(4), substituted "16" for "18" in introductory provisions.

Subsec. (c)(1)(A). Pub. L. 104-324, Sec. 1102(a)(5), substituted ", and Natural Resources" for ", Natural Resources, and Commerce and Economic Development".

Subsec. (c)(1)(B). Pub. L. 104-324, Sec. 1102(a)(6), (8), added subpar. (B) and struck out former subpar. (B) which read as follows: "One representative appointed by each of—

   (i) the Secretaries of Commerce, the Interior, Agriculture, Transportation, and the Navy; and
   (ii) the Administrator of the Environmental Protection Agency;
   all of whom shall be Federal employees."

Subsec. (c)(1)(C). Pub. L. 104-324, Sec. 1102(a)(6), (8), added subpar. (C) and struck out former subpar. (C) which read as follows: "4 representatives appointed by the Secretary of Commerce from among residents of communities in Alaska that were affected by the EXXON VALDEZ oil spill who are knowledgeable about fisheries, other local industries, the marine environment, wildlife, public health, safety, or education. At least 2 of the representatives shall be appointed from among residents of communities located in Prince William Sound. The Secretary shall appoint residents to serve terms of 2 years each, from a list of 8 qualified individuals to be submitted by the Governor of the State of Alaska based on recommendations made by the governing body of each affected community. Each affected community may submit the names of 2 qualified individuals for the Governor's consideration. No more than 5 of the 8 qualified persons recommended by the Governor shall be members of the same political party."

Subsec. (c)(1)(D). Pub. L. 104-324, Sec. 1102(a)(6), (8), added subpar. (D) and struck out former subpar. (D) which read as follows: "3 Alaska Natives who represent Native entities affected by the EXXON VALDEZ oil spill, at least one of whom represents an entity located in Prince William Sound, to serve terms of 2 years each from a list of 6 qualified individuals submitted by the Alaska Federation of Natives."

Subsec. (c)(1)(E) to (H). Pub. L. 104-324, Sec. 1102(a)(7), (8), added subpars. (E) and (F) and redesignated former subpars. (E) and (F) as (G) and (H), respectively.

Subsec. (c)(4). Pub. L. 104-324, Sec. 1102(a)(9), added par. (4).

Subsec. (d)(2). Pub. L. 104-324, Sec. 1102(a)(10), substituted "Arctic or Subarctic oil spills" for "the EXXON VALDEZ oil spill".

Subsec. (e). Pub. L. 104-324, Sec. 1102(a)(11)-(13), substituted "appointed by the Advisory Board" for "appointed by the Secretary of Commerce", struck out ", the Advisory Board," after "Technology Institute", and substituted "Advisory Board's" for "Secretary's".

Subsec. (i). Pub. L. 104-324, Sec. 1102(a)(14), (15), inserted "authorization in section 2736(b) of this title providing funding for the" after "The" and substituted "October 19, 1996" for "August 18, 1990".

Subsec. (j). Pub. L. 104-324, Sec. 1102(a)(16), (17), struck out first sentence which read as follows: "All funds authorized for the Institute shall be provided through the National Oceanic and Atmospheric Administration.", and inserted "The Advisory Board may compensate its Federal representatives for their reasonable travel costs." after "Institute."

Termination of Advisory Boards

Advisory boards established after Jan. 5, 1973, to terminate not later than the expiration of the 2-year period beginning on the date of their establishment, unless, in the case of a board established by the President or an officer of the Federal Government, such board is renewed by appropriate action prior to the expiration of such 2-year period, or in the case of a board established by Congress, its duration is otherwise provided for by law. See sections 3(2) and 14 of Pub. L. 92-463, Oct. 6, 1972, 86 Stat. 770, 776, set out in the Appendix to Title 5, Government Organization and Employees.

Section Referred to in Other Sections

This section is referred to in sections 2736, 2761 of this title.

TERMINAL AND TANKER OVERSIGHT AND MONITORING

33 USC 2732

(a) Short title and findings
   (1) Short title
      This section may be cited as the "Oil Terminal and Oil Tanker Environmental Oversight and Monitoring Act of 1990".
   (2) Findings
      The Congress finds that—
      (A) the March 24, 1989, grounding and rupture of the fully loaded oil tanker, the EXXON VALDEZ, spilled 11 million gallons of crude oil in Prince William Sound, an environmentally sensitive area;
      (B) many people believe that complacency on the part of the industry and government personnel responsible for monitoring the operation of the Valdez terminal and vessel traffic in Prince William Sound was one of the contributing factors to the EXXON VALDEZ oil spill;
      (C) one way to combat this complacency is to involve local citizens in the process of preparing, adopting, and revising oil spill contingency plans;
      (D) a mechanism should be established which fosters the long-term partnership of industry, government, and local communities in overseeing compliance with environmental concerns in the operation of crude oil terminals;
      (E) such a mechanism presently exists at the Sullom Voe terminal in the Shetland Islands and this terminal should serve as a model for others;
      (F) because of the effective partnership that has developed at Sullom Voe, Sullom Voe is considered the safest terminal in Europe;
      (G) the present system of regulation and oversight of crude oil terminals in the United States has degenerated into a process of continual mistrust and confrontation;
      (H) only when local citizens are involved in the process will the trust develop that is necessary to change the present system from confrontation to consensus;
      (I) a pilot program patterned after Sullom Voe should be established in Alaska to further refine the concepts and relationships involved; and
      (J) similar programs should eventually be established in other major crude oil terminals in the United States because the recent oil spills in Texas, Delaware, and Rhode Island indicate that the safe transportation of crude oil is a national problem.
(b) Demonstration programs
   (1) Establishment
      There are established 2 Oil Terminal and Oil Tanker Environmental Oversight and Monitoring Demonstration Programs (hereinafter referred to as "Programs") to be carried out in the State of Alaska.
   (2) Advisory function
      The function of these Programs shall be advisory only.

(3) Purpose

The Prince William Sound Program shall be responsible for environmental monitoring of the terminal facilities in Prince William Sound and the crude oil tankers operating in Prince William Sound. The Cook Inlet Program shall be responsible for environmental monitoring of the terminal facilities and crude oil tankers operating in Cook Inlet located South of the latitude at Point Possession and North of the latitude at Amatuli Island, including offshore facilities in Cook Inlet.

(4) Suits barred

No program, association, council, committee or other organization created by this section may sue any person or entity, public or private, concerning any matter arising under this section except for the performance of contracts.

(c) Oil Terminal Facilities and Oil Tanker Operations Association

(1) Establishment

There is established an Oil Terminal Facilities and Oil Tanker Operations Association (hereinafter in this section referred to as the "Association") for each of the Programs established under subsection (b) of this section.

(2) Membership

Each Association shall be comprised of 4 individuals as follows:
- (A) One individual shall be designated by the owners and operators of the terminal facilities and shall represent those owners and operators.
- (B) One individual shall be designated by the owners and operators of the crude oil tankers calling at the terminal facilities and shall represent those owners and operators.
- (C) One individual shall be an employee of the State of Alaska, shall be designated by the Governor of the State of Alaska, and shall represent the State government.
- (D) One individual shall be an employee of the Federal Government, shall be designated by the President, and shall represent the Federal Government.

(3) Responsibilities

Each Association shall be responsible for reviewing policies relating to the operation and maintenance of the oil terminal facilities and crude oil tankers which affect or may affect the environment in the vicinity of their respective terminals. Each Association shall provide a forum among the owners and operators of the terminal facilities, the owners and operators of crude oil tankers calling at those facilities, the United States, and the State of Alaska to discuss and to make recommendations concerning all permits, plans, and site-specific regulations governing the activities and actions of the terminal facilities which affect or may affect the environment in the vicinity of the terminal facilities and of crude oil tankers calling at those facilities.

(4) Designation of existing organization

The Secretary may designate an existing nonprofit organization as an Association under this subsection if the organization is organized to meet the purposes of this section and consists of at least the individuals listed in paragraph (2).

(d) Regional Citizens' Advisory Councils

(1) Membership

There is established a Regional Citizens' Advisory Council (hereinafter in this section referred to as the "Council") for each of the programs established by subsection (b) of this section.

(2) Membership

Each Council shall be composed of voting members and nonvoting members, as follows:
- (A) Voting members

   Voting members shall be Alaska residents and, except as provided in clause (vii) of this paragraph, shall be appointed by the Governor of the State of Alaska from a list of nominees provided by each of the following interests, with one representative appointed to represent each of the following interests, taking into consideration the need for regional balance on the Council:
   - (i) Local commercial fishing industry organizations, the members of which depend on the fisheries resources of the waters in the vicinity of the terminal facilities.
   - (ii) Aquaculture associations in the vicinity of the terminal facilities.
   - (iii) Alaska Native Corporations and other Alaska Native organizations the members of which reside in the vicinity of the terminal facilities.

(iv) Environmental organizations the members of which reside in the vicinity of the terminal facilities.
(v) Recreational organizations the members of which reside in or use the vicinity of the terminal facilities.
(vi) The Alaska State Chamber of Commerce, to represent the locally based tourist industry.
(vii)(I) For the Prince William Sound Terminal Facilities Council, one representative selected by each of the following municipalities: Cordova, Whittier, Seward, Valdez, Kodiak, the Kodiak Island Borough, and the Kenai Peninsula Borough.
(II) For the Cook Inlet Terminal Facilities Council, one representative selected by each of the following municipalities: Homer, Seldovia, Anchorage, Kenai, Kodiak, the Kodiak Island Borough, and the Kenai Peninsula Borough.
(B) Nonvoting members
One ex-officio, nonvoting representative shall be designated by, and represent, each of the following:
(i) The Environmental Protection Agency.
(ii) The Coast Guard.
(iii) The National Oceanic and Atmospheric Administration.
(iv) The United States Forest Service.
(v) The Bureau of Land Management.
(vi) The Alaska Department of Environmental Conservation.
(vii) The Alaska Department of Fish and Game.
(viii) The Alaska Department of Natural Resources.
(ix) The Division of Emergency Services, Alaska Department of Military and Veterans Affairs.
(3) Terms
(A) Duration of Councils
The term of the Councils shall continue throughout the life of the operation of the Trans-Alaska Pipeline System and so long as oil is transported to or from Cook Inlet.
(B) Three years
The voting members of each Council shall be appointed for a term of 3 years except as provided for in subparagraph (C).
(C) Initial appointments
The terms of the first appointments shall be as follows:
(i) For the appointments by the Governor of the State of Alaska, one-third shall serve for 3 years, one-third shall serve for 2 years, and one-third shall serve for one year.
(ii) For the representatives of municipalities required by subsection (d)(2)(A)(vii) of this section, a drawing of lots among the appointees shall determine that one-third of that group serves for 3 years, one-third serves for 2 years, and the remainder serves for 1 year.
(4) Self-governing
Each Council shall elect its own chairperson, select its own staff, and make policies with regard to its internal operating procedures. After the initial organizational meeting called by the Secretary under subsection (i) of this section, each Council shall be self-governing.
(5) Dual membership and conflicts of interest prohibited
(A) No individual selected as a member of the Council shall serve on the Association.
(B) No individual selected as a voting member of the Council shall be engaged in any activity which might conflict with such individual carrying out his functions as a member thereof.
(6) Duties
Each Council shall—
(A) provide advice and recommendations to the Association on policies, permits, and site-specific regulations relating to the operation and maintenance of terminal facilities and crude oil tankers which affect or may affect the environment in the vicinity of the terminal facilities;
(B) monitor through the committee established under subsection (e) of this section, the environmental impacts of the operation of the terminal facilities and crude oil tankers;

(C) monitor those aspects of terminal facilities' and crude oil tankers' operations and maintenance which affect or may affect the environment in the vicinity of the terminal facilities;
(D) review through the committee established under subsection (f) of this section, the adequacy of oil spill prevention and contingency plans for the terminal facilities and the adequacy of oil spill prevention and contingency plans for crude oil tankers, operating in Prince William Sound or in Cook Inlet;
(E) provide advice and recommendations to the Association on port operations, policies and practices;
(F) recommend to the Association—
  (i) standards and stipulations for permits and site-specific regulations intended to minimize the impact of the terminal facilities' and crude oil tankers' operations in the vicinity of the terminal facilities;
  (ii) modifications of terminal facility operations and maintenance intended to minimize the risk and mitigate the impact of terminal facilities, operations in the vicinity of the terminal facilities and to minimize the risk of oil spills;
  (iii) modifications of crude oil tanker operations and maintenance in Prince William Sound and Cook Inlet intended to minimize the risk and mitigate the impact of oil spills; and
  (iv) modifications to the oil spill prevention and contingency plans for terminal facilities and for crude oil tankers in Prince William Sound and Cook Inlet intended to enhance the ability to prevent and respond to an oil spill; and
(G) create additional committees of the Council as necessary to carry out the above functions, including a scientific and technical advisory committee to the Prince William Sound Council.

(7) No estoppel
No Council shall be held liable under State or Federal law for costs or damages as a result of rendering advice under this section. Nor shall any advice given by a voting member of a Council, or program representative or agent, be grounds for estopping the interests represented by the voting Council members from seeking damages or other appropriate relief.

(8) Scientific work
In carrying out its research, development and monitoring functions, each Council is authorized to conduct its own scientific research and shall review the scientific work undertaken by or on behalf of the terminal operators or crude oil tanker operators as a result of a legal requirement to undertake that work. Each Council shall also review the relevant scientific work undertaken by or on behalf of any government entity relating to the terminal facilities or crude oil tankers. To the extent possible, to avoid unnecessary duplication, each Council shall coordinate its independent scientific work with the scientific work performed by or on behalf of the terminal operators and with the scientific work performed by or on behalf of the operators of the crude oil tankers.

(e) Committee for Terminal and Oil Tanker Operations and Environmental Monitoring
  (1) Monitoring Committee
  Each Council shall establish a standing Terminal and Oil Tanker Operations and Environmental Monitoring Committee (hereinafter in this section referred to as the "Monitoring Committee") to devise and manage a comprehensive program of monitoring the environmental impacts of the operations of terminal facilities and of crude oil tankers while operating in Prince William Sound and Cook Inlet. The membership of the Monitoring Committee shall be made up of members of the Council, citizens, and recognized scientific experts selected by the Council.

  (2) Duties
  In fulfilling its responsibilities, the Monitoring Committee shall—
    (A) advise the Council on a monitoring strategy that will permit early detection of environmental impacts of terminal facility operations and crude oil tanker operations while in Prince William Sound and Cook Inlet;
    (B) develop monitoring programs and make recommendations to the Council on the implementation of those programs;

(C) at its discretion, select and contract with universities and other scientific institutions to carry out specific monitoring projects authorized by the Council pursuant to an approved monitoring strategy;
(D) complete any other tasks assigned by the Council; and
(E) provide written reports to the Council which interpret and assess the results of all monitoring programs.

(f) Committee for Oil Spill Prevention, Safety, and Emergency Response
  (1) Technical Oil Spill Committee
  Each Council shall establish a standing technical committee (hereinafter referred to as "Oil Spill Committee") to review and assess measures designed to prevent oil spills and the planning and preparedness for responding to, containing, cleaning up, and mitigating impacts of oil spills. The membership of the Oil Spill Committee shall be made up of members of the Council, citizens, and recognized technical experts selected by the Council.
  (2) Duties
  In fulfilling its responsibilities, the Oil Spill Committee shall—
    (A) periodically review the respective oil spill prevention and contingency plans for the terminal facilities and for the crude oil tankers while in Prince William Sound or Cook Inlet, in light of new technological developments and changed circumstances;
    (B) monitor periodic drills and testing of the oil spill contingency plans for the terminal facilities and for crude oil tankers while in Prince William Sound and Cook Inlet;
    (C) study wind and water currents and other environmental factors in the vicinity of the terminal facilities which may affect the ability to prevent, respond to, contain, and clean up an oil spill;
    (D) identify highly sensitive areas which may require specific protective measures in the event of a spill in Prince William Sound or Cook Inlet;
    (E) monitor developments in oil spill prevention, containment, response, and cleanup technology;
    (F) periodically review port organization, operations, incidents, and the adequacy and maintenance of vessel traffic service systems designed to assure safe transit of crude oil tankers pertinent to terminal operations;
    (G) periodically review the standards for tankers bound for, loading at, exiting from, or otherwise using the terminal facilities;
    (H) complete any other tasks assigned by the Council; and
    (I) provide written reports to the Council outlining its findings and recommendations.

(g) Agency cooperation
  On and after the expiration of the 180-day period following August 18, 1990, each Federal department, agency, or other instrumentality shall, with respect to all permits, site-specific regulations, and other matters governing the activities and actions of the terminal facilities which affect or may affect the vicinity of the terminal facilities, consult with the appropriate Council prior to taking substantive action with respect to the permit, site-specific regulation, or other matter. This consultation shall be carried out with a view to enabling the appropriate Association and Council to review the permit, site-specific regulation, or other matters and make appropriate recommendations regarding operations, policy or agency actions. Prior consultation shall not be required if an authorized Federal agency representative reasonably believes that an emergency exists requiring action without delay.

(h) Recommendations of Council
  In the event that the Association does not adopt, or significantly modifies before adoption, any recommendation of the Council made pursuant to the authority granted to the Council in subsection (d) of this section, the Association shall provide to the Council, in writing, within 5 days of its decision, notice of its decision and a written statement of reasons for its rejection or significant modification of the recommendation.

(i) Administrative actions
  Appointments, designations, and selections of individuals to serve as members of the Associations and Councils under this section shall be submitted to the Secretary prior to the expiration of the 120-day period following August 18, 1990. On or before the expiration of the 180-

day period following August 18, 1990, the Secretary shall call an initial meeting of each Association and Council for organizational purposes.
(j) Location and compensation
  (1) Location
  Each Association and Council established by this section shall be located in the State of Alaska.
  (2) Compensation
  No member of an Association or Council shall be compensated for the member's services as a member of the Association or Council, but shall be allowed travel expenses, including per diem in lieu of subsistence, at a rate established by the Association or Council not to exceed the rates authorized for employees of agencies under sections 5702 and 5703 of title 5. However, each Council may enter into contracts to provide compensation and expenses to members of the committees created under subsections (d), (e), and (f) of this section.
(k) Funding
  (1) Requirement
  Approval of the contingency plans required of owners and operators of the Cook Inlet and Prince William Sound terminal facilities and crude oil tankers while operating in Alaskan waters in commerce with those terminal facilities shall be effective only so long as the respective Association and Council for a facility are funded pursuant to paragraph (2).
  (2) Prince William Sound Program
  The owners or operators of terminal facilities or crude oil tankers operating in Prince William Sound shall provide, on an annual basis, an aggregate amount of not more than $2,000,000, as determined by the Secretary. Such amount—
    (A) shall provide for the establishment and operation on the environmental oversight and monitoring program in Prince William Sound;
    (B) shall be adjusted annually by the Anchorage Consumer Price Index; and
    (C) may be adjusted periodically upon the mutual consent of the owners or operators of terminal facilities or crude oil tankers operating in Prince William Sound and the Prince William Sound terminal facilities Council.
  (3) Cook Inlet Program
  The owners or operators of terminal facilities, offshore facilities, or crude oil tankers operating in Cook Inlet shall provide, on an annual basis, an aggregate amount of not more than $1,000,000, as determined by the Secretary. Such amount—
    (A) shall provide for the establishment and operation of the environmental oversight and monitoring program in Cook Inlet;
    (B) shall be adjusted annually by the Anchorage Consumer Price Index; and
    (C) may be adjusted periodically upon the mutual consent of the owners or operators of terminal facilities, offshore facilities, or crude oil tankers operating in Cook Inlet and the Cook Inlet Council.
(l) Reports
  (1) Associations and Councils
  Prior to the expiration of the 36-month period following August 18, 1990, each Association and Council established by this section shall report to the President and the Congress concerning its activities under this section, together with its recommendations.
  (2) GAO
  Prior to the expiration of the 36-month period following August 18, 1990, the General Accounting Office shall report to the President and the Congress as to the handling of funds, including donated funds, by the entities carrying out the programs under this section, and the effectiveness of the demonstration programs carried out under this section, together with its recommendations.
(m) Definitions
  As used in this section, the term—
  (1) "terminal facilities" means—
    (A) in the case of the Prince William Sound Program, the entire oil terminal complex located in Valdez, Alaska, consisting of approximately 1,000 acres including all buildings, docks (except docks owned by the City of Valdez if those docks are not used for

754 / Environmental Statutes

loading of crude oil), pipes, piping, roads, ponds, tanks, crude oil tankers only while at the terminal dock, tanker escorts owned or operated by the operator of the terminal, vehicles, and other facilities associated with, and necessary for, assisting tanker movement of crude oil into and out of the oil terminal complex; and
  (B) in the case of the Cook Inlet Program, the entire oil terminal complex including all buildings, docks, pipes, piping, roads, ponds, tanks, vessels, vehicles, crude oil tankers only while at the terminal dock, tanker escorts owned or operated by the operator of the terminal, emergency spill response vessels owned or operated by the operator of the terminal, and other facilities associated with, and necessary for, assisting tanker movement of crude oil into and out of the oil terminal complex;
(2) "crude oil tanker" means a tanker (as that term is defined under section 2101 of title 46)–
  (A) in the case of the Prince William Sound Program, calling at the terminal facilities for the purpose of receiving and transporting oil to refineries, operating north of Middleston Island and bound for or exiting from Prince William Sound; and
  (B) in the case of the Cook Inlet Program, calling at the terminal facilities for the purpose of receiving and transporting oil to refineries and operating in Cook Inlet and the Gulf of Alaska north of Amatuli Island, including tankers transiting to Cook Inlet from Prince William Sound;
(3) "vicinity of the terminal facilities" means that geographical area surrounding the environment of terminal facilities which is directly affected or may be directly affected by the operation of the terminal facilities; and
(4) "Secretary" means the Secretary of Transportation.

(n) Savings clause
  (1) Regulatory authority
  Nothing in this section shall be construed as modifying, repealing, superseding, or preempting any municipal, State or Federal law or regulation, or in any way affecting litigation arising from oil spills or the rights and responsibilities of the United States or the State of Alaska, or municipalities thereof, to preserve and protect the environment through regulation of land, air, and water uses, of safety, and of related development. The monitoring provided for by this section shall be designed to help assure compliance with applicable laws and regulations and shall only extend to activities—
    (A) that would affect or have the potential to affect the vicinity of the terminal facilities and the area of crude oil tanker operations included in the Programs; and
    (B) are subject to the United States or State of Alaska, or municipality thereof, law, regulation, or other legal requirement.
  (2) Recommendations
  This subsection is not intended to prevent the Association or Council from recommending to appropriate authorities that existing legal requirements should be modified or that new legal requirements should be adopted.

(o) Alternative voluntary advisory group in lieu of Council
The requirements of subsections (c) through (l) of this section, as such subsections apply respectively to the Prince William Sound Program and the Cook Inlet Program, are deemed to have been satisfied so long as the following conditions are met:
  (1) Prince William Sound
  With respect to the Prince William Sound Program, the Alyeska Pipeline Service Company or any of its owner companies enters into a contract for the duration of the operation of the Trans-Alaska Pipeline System with the Alyeska Citizens Advisory Committee in existence on August 18, 1990, or a successor organization, to fund that Committee or organization on an annual basis in the amount provided for by subsection (k)(2)(A) of this section and the President annually certifies that the Committee or organization fosters the general goals and purposes of this section and is broadly representative of the communities and interests in the vicinity of the terminal facilities and Prince William Sound.
  (2) Cook Inlet
  With respect to the Cook Inlet Program, the terminal facilities, offshore facilities, or crude oil tanker owners and operators enter into a contract with a voluntary advisory organization to fund that organization on an annual basis and the President annually certifies that

the organization fosters the general goals and purposes of this section and is broadly representative of the communities and interests in the vicinity of the terminal facilities and Cook Inlet.

(Pub. L. 101-380, title V, Sec. 5002, Aug. 18, 1990, 104 Stat. 544.)

Delegation of Functions

Functions of President under subsecs. (c)(2)(D) and (o) of this section delegated to Secretary of Transportation by section 8(f), (g) of Ex. Ord. No. 12777, Oct. 18, 1991, 56 F.R. 54769, set out as a note under section 1321 of this title.

Prince William Sound Regional Citizens Advisory Committee

Certification of President of the United States, Mar. 21, 1991, 56 F.R. 12439, provided:

By the authority vested in me as President by the Constitution and the laws of the United States of America, including section 5002(o)(1) of the Oil Pollution Act of 1990 (Public Law 101-380, 104 Stat. 552) [33 U.S.C. 2732(o)(1)], I hereby certify for the year 1991 the following:
  (1) that the Prince William Sound Regional Citizens Advisory Committee fosters the general goals and purposes of section 5002 of the Oil Pollution Act of 1990 for the year 1991; and
  (2) that the Prince William Sound Regional Citizens Advisory Committee is broadly representative of the communities and interests in the vicinity of the terminal facilities and Prince William Sound.

This certification shall be published in the Federal Register.

George Bush.

Cook Inlet Regional Citizens Advisory Council

Certification of President of the United States, Aug. 6, 1991, 56 F.R. 37819, provided:

By the authority vested in me as President by the Constitution and the laws of the United States of America, including section 5002(o)(2) of the Oil Pollution Act of 1990 [33 U.S.C. 2732(o)(2)], I hereby certify for the year 1991 the following:
  (1) that the Cook Inlet Regional Citizens Advisory Council has met the general goals and purposes of section 5002 of the Oil Pollution Act of 1990 for the year 1991; and
  (2) that the Cook Inlet Regional Citizens Advisory Council is broadly representative of the communities and interests in the vicinity of the terminal facilities and offshore facilities in Cook Inlet.

This certification shall be published in the Federal Register.

George Bush.

BLIGH REEF LIGHT

33 USC 2733

The Secretary of Transportation shall within one year after August 18, 1990, install and ensure operation of an automated navigation light on or adjacent to Bligh Reef in Prince William Sound, Alaska, of sufficient power and height to provide long-range warning of the location of Bligh Reef.

(Pub. L. 101-380, title V, Sec. 5003, Aug. 18, 1990, 104 Stat. 553.)

Section Referred to in Other Sections

This section is referred to in section 2736 of this title.

VESSEL TRAFFIC SERVICE SYSTEM

33 USC 2734

The Secretary of Transportation shall within one year after August 18, 1990—
  (1) acquire, install, and operate such additional equipment (which may consist of radar, closed circuit television, satellite tracking systems, or other shipboard dependent surveillance), train and locate such personnel, and issue such final regulations as are necessary to increase the range of the existing VTS system in the Port of Valdez, Alaska, sufficiently to track the locations and movements of tank vessels carrying oil from the Trans-Alaska

Pipeline when such vessels are transiting Prince William Sound, Alaska, and to sound an audible alarm when such tankers depart from designated navigation routes; and
(2) submit to the Committee on Commerce, Science, and Transportation of the Senate and the Committee on Transportation and Infrastructure of the House of Representatives a report on the feasibility and desirability of instituting positive control of tank vessel movements in Prince William Sound by Coast Guard personnel using the Port of Valdez, Alaska, VTS system, as modified pursuant to paragraph (1).

(Pub. L. 101-380, title V, Sec. 5004, Aug. 18, 1990, 104 Stat. 553.)

Abolition of House Committee on Merchant Marine and Fisheries

Committee on Merchant Marine and Fisheries of House of Representatives abolished and its jurisdiction transferred by House Resolution No. 6, One Hundred Fourth Congress, Jan. 4, 1995. For treatment of references to Committee on Merchant Marine and Fisheries, see section 1(b)(3) of Pub. L. 104-14, set out as a note preceding section 21 of Title 2, The Congress.

Section Referred to in Other Sections

This section is referred to in section 2736 of this title.

EQUIPMENT AND PERSONNEL REQUIREMENTS UNDER TANK VESSEL AND FACILITY RESPONSE PLANS

33 USC 2735

(a) In general
In addition to the requirements for response plans for vessels established by section 1321(j) of this title, a response plan for a tanker loading cargo at a facility permitted under the Trans-Alaska Pipeline Authorization Act (43 U.S.C. 1651 et seq.), and a response plan for such a facility, shall provide for—
(1) prepositioned oil spill containment and removal equipment in communities and other strategic locations within the geographic boundaries of Prince William Sound, including escort vessels with skimming capability; barges to receive recovered oil; heavy duty sea boom, pumping, transferring, and lightering equipment; and other appropriate removal equipment for the protection of the environment, including fish hatcheries;
(2) the establishment of an oil spill removal organization at appropriate locations in Prince William Sound, consisting of trained personnel in sufficient numbers to immediately remove, to the maximum extent practicable, a worst case discharge or a discharge of 200,000 barrels of oil, whichever is greater;
(3) training in oil removal techniques for local residents and individuals engaged in the cultivation or production of fish or fish products in Prince William Sound;
(4) practice exercises not less than 2 times per year which test the capacity of the equipment and personnel required under this paragraph; and
(5) periodic testing and certification of equipment required under this paragraph, as required by the Secretary.
(b) Definitions
In this section—
(1) the term "Prince William Sound" means all State and Federal waters within Prince William Sound, Alaska, including the approach to Hinchenbrook Entrance out to and encompassing Seal Rocks; and
(2) the term "worst case discharge" means—
(A) in the case of a vessel, a discharge in adverse weather conditions of its entire cargo; and
(B) in the case of a facility, the largest foreseeable discharge in adverse weather conditions.

(Pub. L. 101-380, title V, Sec. 5005, Aug. 18, 1990, 104 Stat. 553; Pub. L. 102-388, title III, Sec. 354, Oct. 6, 1992, 106 Stat. 1555.)

References in Text

The Trans-Alaska Pipeline Authorization Act, referred to in subsec. (a), is title II of Pub. L. 93-153, Nov. 16, 1973, 87 Stat. 584, which is classified generally to chapter 34 (Sec. 1651 et seq.) of Title 43, Public Lands. For complete classification of this Act to the Code, see Short Title note set out under section 1651 of Title 43 and Tables.

Amendments

2002—Subsec. (2). Pub. L. 107-295 replaced "Merchant Marine and Fisheries" with "Transportation and Infrastructure."

1992—Subsec. (a). Pub. L. 102-388 substituted "tanker loading cargo at" for "tank vessel operating on Prince William Sound, or" and directed the insertion of "and a response plan for such a facility," after "(43 U.S.C. 1651 et seq.).", which was executed by making the insertion after "(43 U.S.C. 1651 et seq.)," to reflect the probable intent of Congress.

FUNDING

33 USC 2736

(a) Sections 2731, 2733, and 2734
Amounts in the Fund shall be available, without further appropriations and without fiscal year limitation, to carry out section 2731 of this title in the amount as determined in subsection (b) of this section, and to carry out sections 2733 and 2734 of this title, in an amount not to exceed $5,000,000.

(b) Use of interest only
The amount of funding to be made available annually to carry out section 2731 of this title shall be the interest produced by the Fund's investment of the $22,500,000 remaining funding authorized for the Prince William Sound Oil Spill Recovery Institute and currently deposited in the Fund and invested by the Secretary of the Treasury in income producing securities along with other funds comprising the Fund. The National Pollution Funds Center shall transfer all such accrued interest, including the interest earned from the date funds in the Trans-Alaska Liability Pipeline Fund were transferred into the Oil Spill Liability Trust Fund pursuant to section 8102(a)(2)(B)(ii), to the Prince William Sound Oil Spill Recovery Institute annually, beginning 60 days after October 19, 1996.

(c)[1] Use for section 2712
Beginning with the eleventh year following October 19, 1996, the funding authorized for the Prince William Sound Oil Spill Recovery Institute and deposited in the Fund shall thereafter be made available for purposes of section 2712 of this title in Alaska.

(c)[1] Section 2738.— Amounts in the Fund shall be available, without further appropriation and without fiscal year limitation, to carry out section 2738(b) of this title, in an amount not to exceed $5,000,000 of which up to $3,000,000 may be used for the lease payment to the Alaska SeaLife Center under section 2738(b)(2) of this title: Provided, That the entire amount is designated by the Congress as an emergency requirement pursuant to section 251(b)(2)(A) of the Balanced Budget and Emergency Deficit Control Act of 1985, as amended [2 U.S.C. 901(b)(2)(A)]: Provided further, That the entire amount shall be available only to the extent an official budget request that includes designation of the entire amount of the request as an emergency requirement as defined in the Balanced Budget and Emergency Deficit Control Act of 1985, as amended, is transmitted by the President to the Congress.

(c)[1] Section 5008.—Amounts in the Fund shall be available, without further appropriation and without fiscal year limitation, to carry out section 5008(b), in an amount not to exceed $5,000,000: Provided, That the entire amount is designated by the Congress as an emergency requirement pursuant to section 251(b)(2)(A) of the Balanced Budget and Emergency Deficit Control Act of 1985, as amended: Provided further, That the entire amount shall be available only to the extent an official budget request that includes designation of the entire amount of the request as an emergency requirement as defined in the Balanced Budget and Emergency Deficit Control Act of 1985, as amended, is transmitted by the President to the Congress.

---

[1] So in original. Three subsecs. (c) have been enacted.

(Pub. L. 101-380, title V, Sec. 5006, Aug. 18, 1990, 104 Stat. 554; Pub. L. 104-324, title XI, Sec. 1102(b), Oct. 19, 1996, 110 Stat. 3965; Pub. L. 106-246, div. B, title II, Sec. 2204(2), July 13, 2000, 114 Stat. 547; Pub. L. 106-554, Sec. 1(a)(4) [div. B, title I, Sec. 144(c)(1)(C)], Dec. 21, 2000, 114 Stat. 2763, 2763A-239.)

References in Text

Section 8102(a)(2)(B)(ii), referred to in subsec. (b), is section 8102(a)(2)(B)(ii) of Pub. L. 101-380, title VIII, Aug. 18, 1990, 104 Stat. 565, which is set out as a note under section 1653 of Title 43, Public Lands.

The Balanced Budget and Emergency Deficit Control Act of 1985, referred to in subsec. (c), is title II of Pub. L. 99-177, Dec. 12, 1985, 99 Stat. 1038, as amended, which enacted chapter 20 (Sec. 900 et seq.) and sections 654 to 656 of Title 2, The Congress, amended sections 602, 622, 631 to 642, and 651 to 653 of Title 2, sections 1104 to 1106, and 1109 of Title 31, Money and Finance, and section 911 of Title 42, The Public Health and Welfare, repealed section 661 of Title 2, enacted provisions set out as notes under section 900 of Title 2 and section 911 of Title 42, and amended provisions set out as a note under section 621 of Title 2. For complete classification of this Act to the Code, see Short Title note set out under section 900 of Title 2 and Tables.

Amendments

2000—Subsec. (c). Pub. L. 106-246 insertedthe third paragraph (c); Subsec. (c). Pub. L. 106-554 inserted "of which up to $3,000,000 may be used for the lease payment to the Alaska SeaLife Center under section 2738(b)(2) of this title" after "$5,000,000" in subsec. (c) relating to section 2738.

Pub. L. 106-246 added subsec. (c) relating to section 2738.

1996—Subsec. (a). Pub. L. 104-324, Sec. 1102(b)(1)-(3), redesignated subsec. (b) as (a), substituted "2731, 2733," for "2733" in heading, inserted "to carry out section 2731 of this title in the amount as determined in subsection (b) of this section, and" after "limitation,", and struck out heading and text of former subsec. (a). Text read as follows: "Amounts in the Fund shall be available, subject to appropriations, and shall remain available until expended, to carry out section 2731 of this title as follows:

(1) $5,000,000 shall be available for the first fiscal year beginning after August 18, 1990.
(2) $2,000,000 shall be available for each of the 9 fiscal years following the fiscal year described in paragraph (1)."

Subsecs. (b), (c). Pub. L. 104-324, Sec. 1102(b)(4), added subsecs. (b) and (c). Former subsec. (b) redesignated (a).

Section Referred to in Other Sections

This section is referred to in sections 2712, 2731, 2752, 2761 of this title.

LIMITATION

33 USC 2737

Notwithstanding any other law, tank vessels that have spilled more than 1,000,000 gallons of oil into the marine environment after March 22, 1989, are prohibited from operating on the navigable waters of Prince William Sound, Alaska.

(Pub. L. 101-380, title V, Sec. 5007, Aug. 18, 1990, 104 Stat. 554.)

NORTH PACIFIC MARINE RESEARCH INSTITUTE

33 USC 2738

(a) Institute established
The Secretary of Commerce shall establish a North Pacific Marine Research Institute (hereafter in this section referred to as the "Institute") to be administered at the Alaska SeaLife Center by the North Pacific Research Board.

(b) Functions
   The Institute shall—
   (1) conduct research and carry out education and demonstration projects on or relating to the North Pacific marine ecosystem with particular emphasis on marine mammal, sea bird, fish, and shellfish populations in the Bering Sea and Gulf of Alaska including populations located in or near Kenai Fjords National Park and the Alaska Maritime National Wildlife Refuge; and
   (2) lease, maintain, operate, and upgrade the necessary research equipment and related facilities necessary to conduct such research at the Alaska SeaLife Center.
(c) Evaluation and audit
   The Secretary of Commerce may periodically evaluate the activities of the Institute to ensure that funds received by the Institute are used in a manner consistent with this section. The Federal Advisory Committee Act [5 U.S.C. App.] shall not apply to the Institute.
(d) Status of employees
   Employees of the Institute shall not, by reason of such employment, be considered to be employees of the Federal Government for any purpose.
(e) Use of funds
   No funds made available to carry out this section may be used to initiate litigation, or for the acquisition of real property (other than facilities leased at the Alaska SeaLife Center). No more than 10 percent of the funds made available to carry out subsection (b)(1) of this section may be used to administer the Institute. The administrative funds of the Institute and the administrative funds of the North Pacific Research Board created under Public Law 105-83 may be used to jointly administer such programs at the discretion of the North Pacific Research Board.
(f) Availability of research
   The Institute shall publish and make available to any person on request the results of all research, educational, and demonstration projects conducted by the Institute. The Institute shall provide a copy of all research, educational, and demonstration projects conducted by the Institute to the National Park Service, the United States Fish and Wildlife Service, and the National Oceanic and Atmospheric Administration.
(Pub. L. 101-380, title V, Sec. 5008, as added Pub. L. 106-246, div. B, title II, Sec. 2204(1), July 13, 2000, 114 Stat. 546; amended Pub. L. 106-554, Sec. 1(a)(4) [div. B, title I, Sec. 144(c)(1)(A), (B)], Dec. 21, 2000, 114 Stat. 2763, 2763A-238, 2763A-239.)

References in Text

The Federal Advisory Committee Act, referred to in subsec. (c), is Pub. L. 92-463, Oct. 6, 1972, 86 Stat. 770, as amended, which is set out in the Appendix to Title 5, Government Organization and Employees.

Public Law 105-83, referred to in subsec. (e), is Pub. L. 105-83, Nov. 14, 1997, 111 Stat. 1543, as amended, known as the Department of the Interior and Related Agencies Appropriations Act, 1998. For complete classification of this Act to the Code, see Tables.

Amendments

2000—Pub. L. 106-246 added section "North Pacific Marine Research Institute"; Subsec. (c). Pub. L. 106-554, Sec. 1(a)(4) [div. B, title I, Sec. 144(c)(1)(A)], inserted second sentence and struck out former second sentence which read as follows: "The Comptroller General of the United States, and any of his or her duly authorized representatives, shall have access, for purposes of audit and examination, to any books, documents, papers, and records of the Institute that are pertinent to the funds received and expended by the Institute."

Subsec. (e). Pub. L. 106-554, Sec. 1(a)(4) [div. B, title I, Sec. 144(c)(1)(B)], inserted at end "The administrative funds of the Institute and the administrative funds of the North Pacific Research Board created under Public Law 105-83 may be used to jointly administer such programs at the discretion of the North Pacific Research Board."

Section Referred to in Other Sections

This section is referred to in section 2736 of this title.

SUBCHAPTER III—MISCELLANEOUS

SAVINGS PROVISION

33 USC 2751

(a) Cross-references
A reference to a law replaced by this Act, including a reference in a regulation, order, or other law, is deemed to refer to the corresponding provision of this Act.

(b) Continuation of regulations
An order, rule, or regulation in effect under a law replaced by this Act continues in effect under the corresponding provision of this Act until repealed, amended, or superseded.

(c) Rule of construction
An inference of legislative construction shall not be drawn by reason of the caption or catch line of a provision enacted by this Act.

(d) Actions and rights
Nothing in this Act shall apply to any rights and duties that matured, penalties that were incurred, and proceedings that were begun before August 18, 1990, except as provided by this section, and shall be adjudicated pursuant to the law applicable on the date prior to August 18, 1990.

(e) Admiralty and maritime law
Except as otherwise provided in this Act, this Act does not affect—
(1) admiralty and maritime law; or
(2) the jurisdiction of the district courts of the United States with respect to civil actions under admiralty and maritime jurisdiction, saving to suitors in all cases all other remedies to which they are otherwise entitled.

(Pub. L. 101-380, title VI, Sec. 6001, Aug. 18, 1990, 104 Stat. 554.)

References in Text

This Act, referred to in text, is Pub. L. 101-380, Aug. 18, 1990, 104 Stat. 484, as amended, known as the Oil Pollution Act of 1990, which is classified principally to this chapter. For complete classification of this Act to the Code, see Short Title note set out under section 2701 of this title and Tables.

ANNUAL APPROPRIATIONS

33 USC 2752

(a) Required
Except as provided in subsection (b) of this section, amounts in the Fund shall be available only as provided in annual appropriation Acts.

(b) Exceptions
Subsection (a) of this section shall not apply to sections[1] 2706(f), 2712(a)(4), or 2736 of this title, and shall not apply to an amount not to exceed $50,000,000 in any fiscal year which the President may make available from the Fund to carry out section 1321(c) of this title and to initiate the assessment of natural resources damages required under section 2706 of this title. Sums to which this subsection applies shall remain available until expended. To the extent that such amount is not adequate, the Coast Guard may obtain an advance from the Fund of such sums as may be necessary, up to a maximum of $100,000,000, and within 30 days shall notify Congress of the amount advanced and the facts and circumstances necessitating the advance. Amounts advanced shall be repaid to the Fund when, and to the extent that, removal costs are recovered by the Coast Guard from responsible parties for the discharge or substantial threat of discharge.

---

[1] So in original. Probably should be "section".

(Pub. L. 101-380, title VI, Sec. 6002, Aug. 18, 1990, 104 Stat. 555; Pub. L. 104-324, title XI, Sec. 1102(c)(1), Oct. 19, 1996, 110 Stat. 3966.)

Amendments

2002—Subsec. (b). Pub. L. 107-295 added the section "To the extent...threat of discharge."
1996—Subsec. (b). Pub. L. 104-324 substituted "2736" for "2736(b)".

Delegation of Functions

Functions of President under subsec. (b) of this section delegated to Secretary of Department in which Coast Guard is operating by section 7(a)(1)(B) of Ex. Ord. No. 12777, Oct. 18, 1991, 56 F.R. 54766, set out as a note under section 1321 of this title.

Section Referred to in Other Sections

This section is referred to in title 26 section 9509.

33 USC 2753

Repealed.

Pub. L. 104-134, title I, Sec. 101(c) [title I, Sec. 109], Apr. 26, 1996, 110 Stat. 1321-156, 1321-177; renumbered title I, Pub. L. 104-140, Sec. 1(a), May 2, 1996, 110 Stat. 1327

Section, Pub. L. 101-380, title VI, Sec. 6003, Aug. 18, 1990, 104 Stat. 555, related to protection of the Outer Banks of North Carolina.

ADMINISTRATION OF LEASING

43 USC 1334[1]

(a) Rules and regulations; amendment; cooperation with State agencies; subject matter and scope of regulations
The Secretary shall administer the provisions of this subchapter relating to the leasing of the outer Continental Shelf, and shall prescribe such rules and regulations as may be necessary to carry out such provisions. The Secretary may at any time prescribe and amend such rules and regulations as he determines to be necessary and proper in order to provide for the prevention of waste and conservation of the natural resources of the outer Continental Shelf, and the protection of correlative rights therein, and, notwithstanding any other provisions herein, such rules and regulations shall, as of their effective date, apply to all operations conducted under a lease issued or maintained under the provisions of this subchapter. In the enforcement of safety, environmental, and conservation laws and regulations, the Secretary shall cooperate with the relevant departments and agencies of the Federal Government and of the affected States. In the formulation and promulgation of regulations, the Secretary shall request and give due consideration to the views of the Attorney General with respect to matters which may affect competition. In considering any regulations and in preparing any such views, the Attorney General shall consult with the Federal Trade Commission. The regulations prescribed by the Secretary under this subsection shall include, but not be limited to, provisions—
  (1) for the suspension or temporary prohibition of any operation or activity, including production, pursuant to any lease or permit (A) at the request of a lessee, in the national interest, to facilitate proper development of a lease or to allow for the construction or negotiation for use of transportation facilities, or (B) if there is a threat of serious, irreparable, or immediate harm or damage to life (including fish and other aquatic life), to property, to any mineral deposits (in areas leased or not leased), or to the marine, coastal, or human environment, and for the extension of any permit or lease affected by suspension or prohibition under clause (A) or (B) by a period equivalent to the period of such suspension or prohibition, except that no permit or lease shall be so extended when such suspension or prohibition is the result of gross negligence or willful violation of such lease or permit, or of regulations issued with respect to such lease or permit;
  (2) with respect to cancellation of any lease or permit—

---

[1]Editor's note: the following section concerning Outer Continental Shelf Lands was amended by Sec. 6004 of Pub L. 101-380.

(A) that such cancellation may occur at any time, if the Secretary determines, after a hearing, that—
  (i) continued activity pursuant to such lease or permit would probably cause serious harm or damage to life (including fish and other aquatic life), to property, to any mineral (in areas leased or not leased), to the national security or defense, or to the marine, coastal, or human environment;
  (ii) the threat of harm or damage will not disappear or decrease to an acceptable extent within a reasonable period of time; and
  (iii) the advantages of cancellation outweigh the advantages of continuing such lease or permit force;
(B) that such cancellation shall not occur unless and until operations under such lease or permit shall have been under suspension, or temporary prohibition, by the Secretary, with due extension of any lease or permit term continuously for a period of five years, or for a lesser period upon request of the lessee;
(C) that such cancellation shall entitle the lessee to receive such compensation as he shows to the Secretary as being equal to the lesser of (i) the fair value of the canceled rights as of the date of cancellation, taking account of both anticipated revenues from the lease and anticipated costs, including costs of compliance with all applicable regulations and operating orders, liability for cleanup costs or damages, or both, in the case of an oilspill, and all other costs reasonably anticipated on the lease, or (ii) the excess, if any, over the lessee's revenues, from the lease (plus interest thereon from the date of receipt to date of reimbursement) of all consideration paid for the lease and all direct expenditures made by the lessee after the date of issuance of such lease and in connection with exploration or development, or both, pursuant to the lease (plus interest on such consideration and such expenditures from date of payment to date of reimbursement), except that (I) with respect to leases issued before September 18, 1978, such compensation shall be equal to the amount specified in clause (i) of this subparagraph; and (II) in the case of joint leases which are canceled due to the failure of one or more partners to exercise due diligence, the innocent parties shall have the right to seek damages for such loss from the responsible party or parties and the right to acquire the interests of the negligent party or parties and be issued the lease in question;
(3) for the assignment or relinquishment of a lease;
(4) for unitization, pooling, and drilling agreements;
(5) for the subsurface storage of oil and gas other than by the Federal Government;
(6) for drilling or easements necessary for exploration, development, and production;
(7) for the prompt and efficient exploration and development of a lease area; and
(8) for compliance with the national ambient air quality standards pursuant to the Clean Air Act (42 U.S.C. 7401 et seq.), to the extent that activities authorized under this subchapter significantly affect the air quality of any State.

(b) Compliance with regulations as condition for issuance, continuation, assignment, or other transfer of leases
The issuance and continuance in effect of any lease, or of any assignment or other transfer of any lease, under the provisions of this subchapter shall be conditioned upon compliance with regulations issued under this subchapter.

(c) Cancellation of nonproducing lease
Whenever the owner of a nonproducing lease fails to comply with any of the provisions of this subchapter, or of the lease, or of the regulations issued under this subchapter, such lease may be canceled by the Secretary, subject to the right of judicial review as provided in this subchapter, if such default continues for the period of thirty days after mailing of notice by registered letter to the lease owner at his record post office address.

(d) Cancellation of producing lease
Whenever the owner of any producing lease fails to comply with any of the provisions of this subchapter, of the lease, or of the regulations issued under this subchapter, such lease may be forfeited and canceled by an appropriate proceeding in any United States district court having jurisdiction under the provisions of this subchapter.

(e) Pipeline rights-of-way; forfeiture of grant

Rights-of-way through the submerged lands of the outer Continental Shelf, whether or not such lands are included in a lease maintained or issued pursuant to this subchapter, may be granted by the Secretary for pipeline purposes for the transportation of oil, natural gas, sulphur, or other minerals, or under such regulations and upon such conditions as may be prescribed by the Secretary, or where appropriate the Secretary of Transportation, including (as provided in section 1347(b) of this title) assuring maximum environmental protection by utilization of the best available and safest technologies, including the safest practices for pipeline burial and upon the express condition that oil or gas pipelines shall transport or purchase without discrimination, oil or natural gas produced from submerged lands or outer Continental Shelf lands in the vicinity of the pipelines in such proportionate amounts as the Federal Energy Regulatory Commission, in consultation with the Secretary of Energy, may, after a full hearing with due notice thereof to the interested parties, determine to be reasonable, taking into account, among other things, conservation and the prevention of waste. Failure to comply with the provisions of this section or the regulations and conditions prescribed under this section shall be grounds for forfeiture of the grant in an appropriate judicial proceeding instituted by the United States in any United States district court having jurisdiction under the provisions of this subchapter.

(f) Competitive principles governing pipeline operation
  (1) Except as provided in paragraph (2), every permit, license, easement, right-of-way, or other grant of authority for the transportation by pipeline on or across the outer Continental Shelf of oil or gas shall require that the pipeline be operated in accordance with the following competitive principles:
     (A) The pipeline must provide open and nondiscriminatory access to both owner and nonowner shippers.
     (B) Upon the specific request of one or more owner or nonowner shippers able to provide a guaranteed level of throughput, and on the condition that the shipper or shippers requesting such expansion shall be responsible for bearing their proportionate share of the costs and risks related thereto, the Federal Energy Regulatory Commission may, upon finding, after a full hearing with due notice thereof to the interested parties, that such expansion is within technological limits and economic feasibility, order a subsequent expansion of throughput capacity of any pipeline for which the permit, license, easement, right-of-way, or other grant of authority is approved or issued after September 18, 1978. This subparagraph[2] shall not apply to any such grant of authority approved or issued for the Gulf of Mexico or the Santa Barbara Channel.
  (2) The Federal Energy Regulatory Commission may, by order or regulation, exempt from any or all of the requirements of paragraph (1) of this subsection any pipeline or class of pipelines which feeds into a facility where oil and gas are first collected or a facility where oil and gas are first separated, dehydrated, or otherwise processed.
  (3) The Secretary of Energy and the Federal Energy Regulatory Commission shall consult with and give due consideration to the views of the Attorney General on specific conditions to be included in any permit, license, easement, right-of-way, or grant of authority in order to ensure that pipelines are operated in accordance with the competitive principles set forth in paragraph (1) of this subsection. In preparing any such views, the Attorney General shall consult with the Federal Trade Commission.
  (4) Nothing in this subsection shall be deemed to limit, abridge, or modify any authority of the United States under any other provision of law with respect to pipelines on or across the outer Continental Shelf.
(g) Rates of production
  (1) The leasee[3] shall produce any oil or gas, or both, obtained pursuant to an approved development and production plan, at rates consistent with any rule or order issued by the President in accordance with any provision of law.
  (2) If no rule or order referred to in paragraph (1) has been issued, the lessee shall produce such oil or gas, or both, at rates consistent with any regulation promulgated by the Secretary of Energy which is to assure the maximum rate of production which may be sustained without loss of ultimate recovery of oil or gas, or both, under sound engineering and

---

[2]So in original. Probably should be "subparagraph".
[3]So in original. Probably should be "lessee".

764 / Environmental Statutes

economic principles, and which is safe for the duration of the activity covered by the approved plan. The Secretary may permit the lessee to vary such rates if he finds that such variance is necessary.

(h) Federal action affecting outer Continental Shelf; notification; recommended changes

The head of any Federal department or agency who takes any action which has a direct and significant effect on the outer Continental Shelf or its development shall promptly notify the Secretary of such action and the Secretary shall thereafter notify the Governor of any affected State and the Secretary may thereafter recommend such changes in such action as are considered appropriate.

(i) Flaring of natural gas

After September 18, 1978, no holder of any oil and gas lease issued or maintained pursuant to this subchapter shall be permitted to flare natural gas from any well unless the Secretary finds that there is no practicable way to complete production of such gas, or that such flaring is necessary to alleviate a temporary emergency situation or to conduct testing or work-over operations.

(j) Cooperative development of common hydrocarbon-bearing areas
  (1) Findings
    (A)[4]The Congress of the United States finds that the unrestrained competitive production of hydrocarbons from a common hydrocarbon-bearing geological area underlying the Federal and State boundary may result in a number of harmful national effects, including—
      (i) the drilling of unnecessary wells, the installation of unnecessary facilities and other imprudent operating practices that result in economic waste, environmental damage, and damage to life and property;
      (ii) the physical waste of hydrocarbons and an unnecessary reduction in the amounts of hydrocarbons that can be produced from certain hydrocarbon-bearing areas; and
      (iii) the loss of correlative rights which can result in the reduced value of national hydrocarbon resources and disorders in the leasing of Federal and State resources.
  (2) Prevention of harmful effects
    The Secretary shall prevent, through the cooperative development of an area, the harmful effects of unrestrained competitive production of hydrocarbons from a common hydrocarbon-bearing area underlying the Federal and State boundary.

(Aug. 7, 1953, ch. 345, Sec. 5, 67 Stat. 464; Pub. L. 95-372, title II, Sec. 204, Sept. 18, 1978, 92 Stat. 636; Pub. L. 101-380, title VI, Sec. 6004(a), Aug. 18, 1990, 104 Stat. 558.)

References in Text

The Clean Air Act, referred to in subsec. (a)(8), is act July 14, 1955, ch. 360, 69 Stat. 322, as amended, which is classified generally to chapter 85 (Sec. 7401 et seq.) of Title 42, The Public Health and Welfare. For complete classification of this Act to the Code, see Short Title note set out under section 7401 of Title 42 and Tables.

Amendments

1990—Subsec. (j). Pub. L. 101-380 added subsec. (j).

1978—Subsec. (a). Pub. L. 95-372 expanded provisions formerly contained in subsec. (a)(1) so as to include the enforcement of safety and environmental laws and regulations, consultation with the Attorney General and the Federal Trade Commission, and regulations for the suspension or temporary prohibition of any operation or activity including production, the cancellation of leases or permits, the prompt and efficient exploration and development of a lease area, and compliance with the national ambient air quality standards to the extent that activities authorized significantly affect the air quality of any State.

Subsec. (b). Pub. L. 95-372 redesignated as subsec. (b) provisions formerly contained in subsec. (a)(2) conditioning the issuance and continuation of leases or of assignments or other transfers of leases upon compliance with regulations, and struck out provisions that had set a penalty of a fine of not more than $2,000 or imprisonment for not more than six months or both for the knowing and willful violation of rules or regulations promulgated by the Secretary. See section 1350 of this title.

---

[4]So in original. No subpar. (B) has been enacted.

Subsec. (c). Pub. L. 95-372 redesignated as subsec. (c) provisions formerly contained in subsec. (b)(1) covering the cancellation of nonproducing leases for failure of the owner to comply with any of the provisions of this subchapter, or of the lease, or of the regulations issued under this subchapter.

Subsec. (d). Pub. L. 95-372 redesignated as subsec. (d) provisions formerly contained in subsec. (b)(2) covering the cancellation and forfeiture of producing leases for failure of the owner to comply with any of the provisions of this subchapter, the lease, or regulations promulgated under this subchapter.

Subsec. (e). Pub. L. 95-372 redesignated as subsec. (e) provisions formerly contained in subsec. (c) relating to pipeline rights-of-way and inserted provisions relating to regulations prescribed by the Secretary of Transportation and assurances of maximum environmental protection through the use of the best available and safest technologies including the safest practices for pipeline burial, and substituted references to the Federal Energy Regulatory Commission and the Secretary of Energy for existing references to the Federal Power Commission and the Interstate Commerce Commission.

Subsecs. (f) to (i). Pub. L. 95-372 added subsecs. (f) to (i).

Effective Date of 1990 Amendment

Amendment by Pub. L. 101-380 applicable to incidents occurring after Aug. 18, 1990, see section 1020 of Pub. L. 101-380, set out as an Effective Date note under section 2701 of Title 33, Navigation and Navigable Waters.

Transfer of Functions

Functions vested in, or delegated to, Secretary of Energy and Department of Energy under or with respect to subsec. (g)(2) of this section, transferred to, and vested in, Secretary of the Interior, by section 100 of Pub. L. 97-257, 96 Stat. 841, set out as a note under section 7152 of Title 42, The Public Health and Welfare.

Functions of Secretary of the Interior to promulgate regulations under this subchapter which relate to fostering of competition for Federal leases, implementation of alternative bidding systems authorized for award of Federal leases, establishment of diligence requirements for operations conducted on Federal leases, setting of rates for production of Federal leases, and specifying of procedures, terms, and conditions for acquisition and disposition of Federal royalty interests taken in kind, transferred to Secretary of Energy by section 7152(b) of Title 42. Section 7152(b) of Title 42 was repealed by Pub. L. 97-100, title II, Sec. 201, Dec. 23, 1981, 95 Stat. 1407, and functions of Secretary of Energy returned to Secretary of the Interior. See House Report No. 97-315, pp. 25, 26, Nov. 5, 1981.

West Delta Field

Section 6004(b) of Pub. L. 101-380 provided that: "Section 5(j) of the Outer Continental Shelf Lands Act [43 U.S.C. 1334(j)], as added by this section, shall not be applicable with respect to Blocks 17 and 18 of the West Delta Field offshore Louisiana."

Key Largo Coral Reef Preserve

Secretary of the Interior to prescribe rules and regulations governing the protection and conservation of the coral and other mineral resources in the area designated Key Largo Coral Reef Preserve, see Proc. No. 3339, Mar. 15, 1960, 25 F.R. 2352, set out as a note under section 461 of Title 16, Conservation.

Cross References

Oil and gas leases on public lands—
    Forfeiture or cancellation of, see section 188 of Title 30, Mineral Lands and Mining.
    Rights-of-way for pipe lines, see section 185 of Title 30.
    Rules and regulations relating to, see section 189 of Title 30.
    Written relinquishment of rights under, see section 187b of Title 30.

Section Referred to in Other Sections

This section is referred to in sections 1335, 1337, 1340, 1351 of this title; title 42 section 7627.

SUBCHAPTER IV—OIL POLLUTION RESEARCH AND DEVELOPMENT PROGRAM

OIL POLLUTION RESEARCH AND DEVELOPMENT PROGRAM

33 USC 2761

(a) Interagency Coordinating Committee on Oil Pollution Research
  (1) Establishment
    There is established an Interagency Coordinating Committee on Oil Pollution Research (hereinafter in this section referred to as the "Interagency Committee").
  (2) Purposes
    The Interagency Committee shall coordinate a comprehensive program of oil pollution research, technology development, and demonstration among the Federal agencies, in cooperation and coordination with industry, universities, research institutions, State governments, and other nations, as appropriate, and shall foster cost-effective research mechanisms, including the joint funding of research.
  (3) Membership
    The Interagency Committee shall include representatives from the Department of Commerce (including the National Oceanic and Atmospheric Administration and the National Institute of Standards and Technology), the Department of Energy, the Department of the Interior (including the Minerals Management Service and the United States Fish and Wildlife Service), the Department of Transportation (including the United States Coast Guard, the Maritime Administration, and the Research and Special Projects Administration), the Department of Defense (including the Army Corps of Engineers and the Navy), the Environmental Protection Agency, the National Aeronautics and Space Administration, and the United States Fire Administration in the Federal Emergency Management Agency, as well as such other Federal agencies as the President may designate.
  A representative of the Department of Transportation shall serve as Chairman.
(b) Oil pollution research and technology plan
  (1) Implementation plan
    Within 180 days after August 18, 1990, the Interagency Committee shall submit to Congress a plan for the implementation of the oil pollution research, development, and demonstration program established pursuant to subsection (c) of this section. The research plan shall—
    (A) identify agency roles and responsibilities;
    (B) assess the current status of knowledge on oil pollution prevention, response, and mitigation technologies and effects of oil pollution on the environment;
    (C) identify significant oil pollution research gaps including an assessment of major technological deficiencies in responses to past oil discharges;
    (D) establish research priorities and goals for oil pollution technology development related to prevention, response, mitigation, and environmental effects;
    (E) estimate the resources needed to conduct the oil pollution research and development program established pursuant to subsection (c) of this section, and timetables for completing research tasks; and
    (F) identify, in consultation with the States, regional oil pollution research needs and priorities for a coordinated, multidisciplinary program of research at the regional level.
  (2) Advice and guidance
    The Chairman, through the Department of Transportation, shall contract with the National Academy of Sciences to—
    (A) provide advice and guidance in the preparation and development of the research plan; and
    (B) assess the adequacy of the plan as submitted, and submit a report to Congress on the conclusions of such assessment.

The National Institute of Standards and Technology shall provide the Interagency Committee with advice and guidance on issues relating to quality assurance and standards measurements relating to its activities under this section.

(c) Oil pollution research and development program
  (1) Establishment
    The Interagency Committee shall coordinate the establishment, by the agencies represented on the Interagency Committee, of a program for conducting oil pollution research and development, as provided in this subsection.
  (2) Innovative oil pollution technology
    The program established under this subsection shall provide for research, development, and demonstration of new or improved technologies which are effective in preventing or mitigating oil discharges and which protect the environment, including—
      (A) development of improved designs for vessels and facilities, and improved operational practices;
      (B) research, development, and demonstration of improved technologies to measure the ullage of a vessel tank, prevent discharges from tank vents, prevent discharges during lightering and bunkering operations, contain discharges on the deck of a vessel, prevent discharges through the use of vacuums in tanks, and otherwise contain discharges of oil from vessels and facilities;
      (C) research, development, and demonstration of new or improved systems of mechanical, chemical, biological, and other methods (including the use of dispersants, solvents, and bioremediation) for the recovery, removal, and disposal of oil, including evaluation of the environmental effects of the use of such systems;
      (D) research and training, in consultation with the National Response Team, to improve industry's and Government's ability to quickly and effectively remove an oil discharge, including the long-term use, as appropriate, of the National Spill Control School in Corpus Christi, Texas, and the Center for Marine Training and Safety in Galveston, Texas;
      (E) research to improve information systems for decisionmaking, including the use of data from coastal mapping, baseline data, and other data related to the environmental effects of oil discharges, and cleanup technologies;
      (F) development of technologies and methods to protect public health and safety from oil discharges, including the population directly exposed to an oil discharge;
      (G) development of technologies, methods, and standards for protecting removal personnel, including training, adequate supervision, protective equipment, maximum exposure limits, and decontamination procedures;
      (H) research and development of methods to restore and rehabilitate natural resources damaged by oil discharges;
      (I) research to evaluate the relative effectiveness and environmental impacts of bioremediation technologies; and
      (J) the demonstration of a satellite-based, dependent surveillance vessel traffic system in Narragansett Bay to evaluate the utility of such system in reducing the risk of oil discharges from vessel collisions and groundings in confined waters.
  (3) Oil pollution technology evaluation
    The program established under this subsection shall provide for oil pollution prevention and mitigation technology evaluation including—
      (A) the evaluation and testing of technologies developed independently of the research and development program established under this subsection;
      (B) the establishment, where appropriate, of standards and testing protocols traceable to national standards to measure the performance of oil pollution prevention or mitigation technologies; and
      (C) the use, where appropriate, of controlled field testing to evaluate real-world application of oil discharge prevention or mitigation technologies.
  (4) Oil pollution effects research
    (A) The Committee shall establish a research program to monitor and evaluate the environmental effects of oil discharges. Such program shall include the following elements:
      (i) The development of improved models and capabilities for predicting the environmental fate, transport, and effects of oil discharges.

(ii) The development of methods, including economic methods, to assess damages to natural resources resulting from oil discharges.
(iii) The identification of types of ecologically sensitive areas at particular risk to oil discharges and the preparation of scientific monitoring and evaluation plans, one for each of several types of ecological conditions, to be implemented in the event of major oil discharges in such areas.
(iv) The collection of environmental baseline data in ecologically sensitive areas at particular risk to oil discharges where such data are insufficient.
(B) The Department of Commerce in consultation with the Environmental Protection Agency shall monitor and scientifically evaluate the long-term environmental effects of oil discharges if—
(i) the amount of oil discharged exceeds 250,000 gallons;
(ii) the oil discharge has occurred on or after January 1, 1989; and
(iii) the Interagency Committee determines that a study of the long-term environmental effects of the discharge would be of significant scientific value, especially for preventing or responding to future oil discharges.
Areas for study may include the following sites where oil discharges have occurred: the New York/New Jersey Harbor area, where oil was discharged by an Exxon underwater pipeline, the T/B CIBRO SAVANNAH, and the M/V BT NAUTILUS; Narragansett Bay where oil was discharged by the WORLD PRODIGY; the Houston Ship Channel where oil was discharged by the RACHEL B; the Delaware River, where oil was discharged by the PRESIDENTE RIVERA, and Huntington Beach, California, where oil was discharged by the AMERICAN TRADER.
(C) Research conducted under this paragraph by, or through, the United States Fish and Wildlife Service shall be directed and coordinated by the National Wetland Research Center.
(5) Marine simulation research
The program established under this subsection shall include research on the greater use and application of geographic and vessel response simulation models, including the development of additional data bases and updating of existing data bases using, among others, the resources of the National Maritime Research Center. It shall include research and vessel simulations for—
(A) contingency plan evaluation and amendment;
(B) removal and strike team training;
(C) tank vessel personnel training; and
(D) those geographic areas where there is a significant likelihood of a major oil discharge.
(6) Demonstration projects
The United States Coast Guard, in conjunction with other such agencies in the Department of Transportation as the Secretary of Transportation may designate, shall conduct 4 port oil pollution minimization demonstration projects, one each with (A) the Port Authority of New York and New Jersey, (B) the Ports of Los Angeles and Long Beach, California, (C) the Port of New Orleans, Louisiana, and (D) ports on the Great Lakes, for the purpose of developing and demonstrating integrated port oil pollution prevention and cleanup systems which utilize the information and implement the improved practices and technologies developed from the research, development, and demonstration program established in this section. Such systems shall utilize improved technologies and management practices for reducing the risk of oil discharges, including, as appropriate, improved data access, computerized tracking of oil shipments, improved vessel tracking and navigation systems, advanced technology to monitor pipeline and tank conditions, improved oil spill response capability, improved capability to predict the flow and effects of oil discharges in both the inner and outer harbor areas for the purposes of making infrastructure decisions, and such other activities necessary to achieve the purposes of this section.
(7) Simulated environmental testing
Agencies represented on the Interagency Committee shall ensure the long-term use and operation of the Oil and Hazardous Materials Simulated Environmental Test Tank (OHMSETT) Research Center in New Jersey for oil pollution technology testing and evaluations.

(8) Regional research program
   (A) Consistent with the research plan in subsection (b) of this section, the Interagency Committee shall coordinate a program of competitive grants to universities or other research institutions, or groups of universities or research institutions, for the purposes of conducting a coordinated research program related to the regional aspects of oil pollution, such as prevention, removal, mitigation, and the effects of discharged oil on regional environments. For the purposes of this paragraph, a region means a Coast Guard district as set out in part 3 of title 33, Code of Federal Regulations (1989).
   (B) The Interagency Committee shall coordinate the publication by the agencies represented on the Interagency Committee of a solicitation for grants under this subsection. The application shall be in such form and contain such information as may be required in the published solicitation. The applications shall be reviewed by the Interagency Committee, which shall make recommendations to the appropriate granting agency represented on the Interagency Committee for awarding the grant. The granting agency shall award the grants recommended by the Interagency Committee unless the agency decides not to award the grant due to budgetary or other compelling considerations and publishes its reasons for such a determination in the Federal Register. No grants may be made by any agency from any funds authorized for this paragraph unless such grant award has first been recommended by the Interagency Committee.
   (C) Any university or other research institution, or group of universities or research institutions, may apply for a grant for the regional research program established by this paragraph. The applicant must be located in the region, or in a State a part of which is in the region, for which the project is proposed as part of the regional research program. With respect to a group application, the entity or entities which will carry out the substantial portion of the proposed research must be located in the region, or in a State a part of which is in the region, for which the project is proposed as part of the regional research program.
   (D) The Interagency Committee shall make recommendations on grants in such a manner as to ensure an appropriate balance within a region among the various aspects of oil pollution research, including prevention, removal, mitigation, and the effects of discharged oil on regional environments. In addition, the Interagency Committee shall make recommendations for grants based on the following criteria:
      (i) There is available to the applicant for carrying out this paragraph demonstrated research resources.
      (ii) The applicant demonstrates the capability of making a significant contribution to regional research needs.
      (iii) The projects which the applicant proposes to carry out under the grant are consistent with the research plan under subsection (b)(1)(F) of this section and would further the objectives of the research and development program established in this section.
   (E) Grants provided under this paragraph shall be for a period up to 3 years, subject to annual review by the granting agency, and provide not more than 80 percent of the costs of the research activities carried out in connection with the grant.
   (F) No funds made available to carry out this subsection may be used for the acquisition of real property (including buildings) or construction of any building.
   (G) Nothing in this paragraph is intended to alter or abridge the authority under existing law of any Federal agency to make grants, or enter into contracts or cooperative agreements, using funds other than those authorized in this Act for the purposes of carrying out this paragraph.
(9) Funding
   For each of the fiscal years 1991, 1992, 1993, 1994, and 1995, $6,000,000 of amounts in the Fund shall be available to carry out the regional research program in paragraph (8), such amounts to be available in equal amounts for the regional research program in each region; except that if the agencies represented on the Interagency Committee determine that regional research needs exist which cannot be addressed within such funding limits, such agencies may use their authority under paragraph (10) to make additional grants to meet such needs. For the purposes of this paragraph, the research program carried out by

the Prince William Sound Oil Spill Recovery Institute established under section 2731 of this title, shall not be eligible to receive grants under this paragraph until the authorization for funding under section 2736(b) of this title expires.

(10) Grants

In carrying out the research and development program established under this subsection, the agencies represented on the Interagency Committee may enter into contracts and cooperative agreements and make grants to universities, research institutions, and other persons. Such contracts, cooperative agreements, and grants shall address research and technology priorities set forth in the oil pollution research plan under subsection (b) of this section.

(11) Utilization of resources

In carrying out research under this section, the Department of Transportation shall continue to utilize the resources of the Research and Special Programs Administration of the Department of Transportation, to the maximum extent practicable.

(d) International cooperation

In accordance with the research plan submitted under subsection (b) of this section, the Interagency Committee shall coordinate and cooperate with other nations and foreign research entities in conducting oil pollution research, development, and demonstration activities, including controlled field tests of oil discharges.

(e) Biennial reports

The Chairman of the Interagency Committee shall submit to Congress every 2 years on October 30 a report on the activities carried out under this section in the preceding 2 fiscal years, and on activities proposed to be carried out under this section in the current 2 fiscal year period.

(f) Funding

Not to exceed $22,000,000 of amounts in the Fund shall be available annually to carry out this section except for subsection (c)(8) of this section. Of such sums—

(1) funds authorized to be appropriated to carry out the activities under subsection (c)(4) of this section shall not exceed $5,000,000 for fiscal year 1991 or $3,500,000 for any subsequent fiscal year; and

(2) not less than $3,000,000 shall be available for carrying out the activities in subsection (c)(6) of this section for fiscal years 1992, 1993, 1994, and 1995.

All activities authorized in this section, including subsection (c)(8) of this section, are subject to appropriations.

(Pub. L. 101-380, title VII, Sec. 7001, Aug. 18, 1990, 104 Stat. 559; Pub. L. 101-537, title II, Sec. 2002, Nov. 8, 1990, 104 Stat. 2375; Pub. L. 101-646, title IV, Sec. 4002, Nov. 29, 1990, 104 Stat. 4788; Pub. L. 104-324, title XI, Secs. 1102(c)(2), 1108, Oct. 19, 1996, 110 Stat. 3966, 3968; Pub. L. 104-332, Sec. 2(h)(1), (2), Oct. 26, 1996, 110 Stat. 4091.)

References in Text

This Act, referred to in subsec. (c)(8)(G), is Pub. L. 101-380, Aug. 18, 1990, 104 Stat. 484, as amended, known as the Oil Pollution Act of 1990, which is classified principally to this chapter. For complete classification of this Act to the Code, see Short Title note set out under section 2701 of this title and Tables.

Amendments

1996—Subsec. (c)(2)(D). Pub. L. 104-324, Sec. 1108, inserted ", and the Center for Marine Training and Safety in Galveston, Texas" before semicolon at end.

Subsec. (c)(6). Pub. L. 104-332, Sec. 2(h)(1), made technical amendment to Pub. L. 104-646, Sec. 4002(1). See 1990 Amendment note below.

Subsec. (c)(9). Pub. L. 104-324, Sec. 1102(c)(2), inserted "until the authorization for funding under section 2736(b) of this title expires" before period at end.

Subsec. (f). Pub. L. 104-332 made technical amendment to Pub. L. 101-646, Sec. 4002(2). See 1990 Amendment note below.

1990—Subsec. (c)(6). Pub. L. 101-537, Sec. 2002(1), and Pub. L. 101-646, Sec. 4002(1), as amended by Pub. L. 104-332, Sec. 2(h)(1), made substantially identical amendments, substituting "4" for "3" and inserting cl. (D).

Subsec. (f). Pub. L. 101-537, Sec. 2002(2), and Pub. L. 101-646, Sec. 4002(2), as amended by Pub. L. 104-332, amended subsec. (f) identically, substituting "$22,000,000" for "$21,250,000" in introductory provisions and "$3,000,000" for "$2,250,000" in par. (2).

Delegation of Functions

Functions of President under subsec. (a)(3) of this section delegated to Secretary of Transportation by section 8(h) of Ex. Ord. No. 12777, Oct. 18, 1991, 56 F.R. 54769, set out as a note under section 1321 of this title.

Section Referred to in Other Sections

This section is referred to in section 2731 of this title.

TRANS-ALASKA PIPELINE
[as amended by Title VIII of Oil Pollution Act of 1990]

CONGRESSIONAL FINDINGS AND DECLARATION

43 USC 1651

The Congress finds and declares that:

(a) The early development and delivery of oil and gas from Alaska's North Slope to domestic markets is in the national interest because of growing domestic shortages and increasing dependence upon insecure foreign sources.

(b) The Department of the Interior and other Federal agencies, have, over a long period of time, conducted extensive studies of the technical aspects and of the environmental, social, and economic impacts of the proposed trans-Alaska oil pipeline, including consideration of a trans-Canada pipeline.

(c) The earliest possible construction of a trans-Alaska oil pipeline from the North Slope of Alaska to Port Valdez in that State will make the extensive proven and potential reserves of low-sulfur oil available for domestic use and will best serve the national interest.

(d) A supplemental pipeline to connect the North Slope with a trans-Canada pipeline may be needed later and it should be studied now, but it should not be regarded as an alternative for a trans-Alaska pipeline that does not traverse a foreign country.

(Pub. L. 93-153, title II, Sec. 202, Nov. 16, 1973, 87 Stat. 584.)

Short Title of 1990 Amendment

Pub. L. 101-380, title VIII, Sec. 8001, Aug. 18, 1990, 104 Stat. 564, provided that: "This title [enacting sections 1642 and 1656 of this title, amending sections 1350 and 1653 of this title and section 3145 of Title 16, Conservation, and enacting provisions set out as notes under this section and section 1653 of this title] may be cited as the 'Trans-Alaska Pipeline System Reform Act of 1990'."

Short Title

Section 201 of title II of Pub. L. 93-153 provided that: "This title [enacting this chapter] may be cited as the 'Trans-Alaska Pipeline Authorization Act'."

Separability

Section 411 of Pub. L. 93-153 provided that: "If any provision of this Act [enacting this chapter, section 1456a of this title, and section 3512 of Title 44, Public Printing and Documents, amending section 1608 of this title, sections 45, 46, 53, and 56 of Title 15, Commerce and Trade, section 185 of Title 30, Mineral Lands and Mining, section 3502 of Title 44, and section 391a of former Title 46, Shipping, and enacting provisions set out as notes under sections 1608 and 1651 of this title, section 1904 of Title 12, Banks and Banking, section 45 of Title 15, section 791a of Title 16, Conservation, and section 1221 of Title 33, Navigation and Navigable Waters] or the applicability thereof is held invalid the remainder of this Act shall not be affected thereby."

Presidential Task Force

Pub. L. 101-380, title VIII, Sec. 8103, Aug. 18, 1990, 104 Stat. 567, established a Presidential Task Force on the Trans-Alaska Pipeline System, to conduct an audit of the Trans-Alaska Pipeline System and make recommendations to the President, Congress, and the Governor of Alaska, authorized appropriations for the Task Force, and required it to transmit its final report to the President, Congress, and the Governor no later than 2 years after the date on which funding was made available.

North Slope Crude Oil; Report on Equitable Allocation

Pub. L. 94-586, Sec. 18, Oct. 22, 1976, 90 Stat. 2916, directed that the President, within 6 months of Oct. 22, 1976, determine special expediting procedures necessary to insure the equitable allocation of North Slope crude oil to the Northern Tier States of Washington, Oregon, Idaho, Montana, Illinois, Indiana, and Idaho to carry out the provisions of section 410 of Pub. L. 93-153 [set out below], and to report his findings to Congress, such report to include a statement demonstrating the impact that the delivery system would have on reducing the dependency of New England and the Middle Atlantic States on foreign oil imports.

Trans-Canada Pipeline; Negotiations With Canada; Feasibility Study

Title III (Secs. 301-303) of Pub. L. 93-153 authorized the President to enter into negotiations with the Government of Canada to determine Canadian willingness to permit construction of pipelines or other transportation systems across its territory to bring gas and oil from Alaska's North Slope to the United States; the need for intergovernmental agreements to protect interests of any parties involved with construction, operation, and maintenance of such natural gas or oil transportation systems; terms and conditions for construction across Canadian territory; desirability of joint studies to insure environmental protection, reduce regulatory uncertainty, and insure meeting energy requirements; quantity of oil and gas for which Canada would guarantee transit; and acquisition of other energy sources so as to make unnecessary the shipment of oil from the Alaska pipeline by tanker into the Puget Sound area. The President was to report to Congress on actions taken and recommendations for further action. In addition, the Secretary of the Interior was to investigate, and to report to Congress within 2 years of Nov. 16, 1973, as to the feasibility of oil or gas pipelines from the North Slope of Alaska to connect with a pipeline through Canada that would deliver oil or gas to United States markets. Nothing in title III was to limit the authority of the Secretary or any other Federal official to grant a gas or oil pipeline right-of-way or permit, which that official was otherwise authorized by law to grant.

Exclusion of Persons From Trans-Alaska Pipeline Activities on Basis of Race, Creed, Color, National Origin, or Sex Prohibited

Section 403 of Pub. L. 93-153 provided that: "The Secretary of the Interior shall take such affirmative action as he deems necessary to assure that no person shall, on the grounds of race, creed, color, national origin, or sex, be excluded from receiving, or participating in any activity conducted under, any permit, right-of-way, public land order, or other Federal authorization granted or issued under title II [this chapter]. The Secretary of the Interior shall promulgate such rules as he deems necessary to carry out the purposes of this subsection and may enforce this subsection, and any rules promulgated under this subsection, through agency and department provisions and rules which shall be similar to those established and in effect under title VI of the Civil Rights Act of 1964 [section 2000d et seq. of Title 42, The Public Health and Welfare]."

Equitable Allocation of North Slope Crude Oil

Section 410 of Pub. L. 93-153 provided that: "The Congress declares that the crude oil on the North Slope of Alaska is an important part of the Nation's oil resources, and that the benefits of such crude oil should be equitably shared, directly or indirectly, by all regions of the country. The President shall use any authority he may have to insure an equitable allocation of available North Slope and other crude oil resources and petroleum products among all regions and all of the several States."

AUTHORIZATIONS FOR CONSTRUCTION

43 USC 1652

(a) Congressional declaration of purpose

The purpose of this chapter is to insure that, because of the extensive governmental studies already made of this project and the national interest in early delivery of North Slope oil to domestic markets, the trans-Alaska oil pipeline be constructed promptly without further administrative or judicial delay or impediment. To accomplish this purpose it is the intent of the Congress to exercise its constitutional powers to the fullest extent in the authorizations and directions herein made and in limiting judicial review of the actions taken pursuant thereto.

(b) Issuance, administration, and enforcement of rights-of-way, permits, leases, and other authorizations

The Congress hereby authorizes and directs the Secretary of the Interior and other appropriate Federal officers and agencies to issue and take all necessary action to administer and enforce rights-of-way, permits, leases, and other authorizations that are necessary for or related to the construction, operation, and maintenance of the trans-Alaska oil pipeline system, including roads and airstrips, as that system is generally described in the Final Environmental Impact Statement issued by the Department of the Interior on March 20, 1972. The route of the pipeline may be modified by the Secretary to provide during construction greater environmental protection.

(c) Applicability of statutes governing rights-of-way for pipelines through Federal lands; other statutory terms and conditions; waiver of procedural requirements; supersedure of administrative authorizations for construction

Rights-of-way, permits, leases, and other authorizations issued pursuant to this chapter by the Secretary shall be subject to the provisions of section 185 of title 30, as amended by Pub. L. 93-153 (except the provisions of subsections (h)(1), (k), (q), (w)(2), and (x)); all authorizations issued by the Secretary and other Federal officers and agencies pursuant to this chapter shall include the terms and conditions required, and may include the terms and conditions permitted, by the provisions of law that would otherwise be applicable if this chapter had not been enacted, and they may waive any procedural requirements of law or regulation which they deem desirable to waive in order to accomplish the purposes of this chapter. The direction contained in subsection (b) of this section shall supersede the provisions of any law or regulation relating to an administrative determination as to whether the authorizations for construction of the trans-Alaska oil pipeline shall be issued.

(d) National Environmental Policy Act of 1969 bypassed; issuance of authorizations for construction and operation not to be subject to judicial review; time limits on charges of invalidity or unconstitutionality; jurisdiction; hearings; review

The actions taken pursuant to this chapter which relate to the construction and completion of the pipeline system, and to the applications filed in connection therewith necessary to the pipeline's operation at full capacity, as described in the Final Environmental Impact Statement of the Department of the Interior, shall be taken without further action under the National Environmental Policy Act of 1969 [42 U.S.C. 4321 et seq.]; and the actions of the Federal officers concerning the issuance of the necessary rights-of-way, permits, leases, and other authorizations for construction and initial operation at full capacity of said pipeline system shall not be subject to judicial review under any law except that claims alleging the invalidity of this section may be brought within sixty days following November 16, 1973, and claims alleging that an action will deny rights under the Constitution of the United States, or that the action is beyond the scope of authority conferred by this chapter, may be brought within sixty days following the date of such action. A claim shall be barred unless a complaint is filed within the time specified. Any such complaint shall be filed in a United States district court, and such court shall have exclusive jurisdiction to determine such proceeding in accordance with the procedures hereinafter provided, and no other court of the United States, of any State, territory, or possession of the United States, or of the District of Columbia, shall have jurisdiction of any such claim whether in a proceeding instituted prior to or on or after November 16, 1973. Such court shall not have jurisdiction to grant any injunctive relief against the issuance of any right-of-way, permit, lease, or other authorization pursuant to this section except in conjunction with a final judgment entered in a case involving a claim filed pursuant to this section. An

774 / Environmental Statutes

interlocutory or final judgment, decree, or order of such district court may be reviewed only upon petition for a writ of certiorari to the Supreme Court of the United States.

(e) Amendment or modification of rights-of-way, permits, leases, or other authorizations

The Secretary of the Interior and the other Federal officers and agencies are authorized at any time when necessary to protect the public interest, pursuant to the authority of this section and in accordance with its provisions, to amend or modify any right-of-way, permit, lease, or other authorization issued under this chapter.

(Pub. L. 93-153, title II, Sec. 203, Nov. 16, 1973, 87 Stat. 584; Pub. L. 98-620, title IV, Sec. 402(46), Nov. 8, 1984, 98 Stat. 3360; Pub. L. 100-352, Sec. 6(c), June 27, 1988, 102 Stat. 663.)

References in Text

The National Environmental Policy Act of 1969, referred to in subsec. (d), is Pub. L. 91-190, Jan. 1, 1970, 83 Stat. 852, as amended, which is classified generally to chapter 55 (section 4321 et seq.) of Title 42, The Public Health and Welfare. For complete classification of this Act to the Code, see Short Title note set out under section 4321 of Title 42 and Tables.

Amendments

1988—Subsec. (d). Pub. L. 100-352 amended last sentence generally. Prior to amendment, last sentence read as follows: "Any review of an interlocutory or final judgment, decree, or order of such district court may be had only upon direct appeal to the Supreme Court of the United States."

1984—Subsec. (d). Pub. L. 98-620 struck out provision that any such proceeding had to be assigned for hearing at the earliest possible date, had to take precedence over all other matters pending on the docket of the district court at that time, and had to be expedited in every way by such court.

Effective Date of 1988 Amendment

Amendment by Pub. L. 100-352 effective ninety days after June 27, 1988, except that such amendment not to apply to cases pending in Supreme Court on such effective date or affect right to review or manner of reviewing judgment or decree of court which was entered before such effective date, see section 7 of Pub. L. 100-352, set out as a note under section 1254 of Title 28, Judiciary and Judicial Procedure.

Effective Date of 1984 Amendment

Amendment by Pub. L. 98-620 not applicable to cases pending on Nov. 8, 1984, see section 403 of Pub. L. 98-620, set out as a note under section 1657 of Title 28, Judiciary and Judicial Procedure.

Section Referred to in Other Sections

This section is referred to in section 1655 of this title; title 30 section 185; title 50 App. section 2406.

LIABILITY FOR DAMAGES

43 USC 1653

(a) Activities along or in vicinity of pipeline right-of-way; strict liability; limitation on liability; subrogation; emergency subsistence and other aid; exemption for State of Alaska

　(1) Except when the holder of the pipeline right-of-way granted pursuant to this chapter can prove that damages in connection with or resulting from activities along or in the vicinity of the proposed trans-Alaskan pipeline right-of-way were caused solely by an act of war or negligence of the United States, other government entity, or the damaged party, such holder shall be strictly liable to all damaged parties, public or private, without regard to fault for such damages, and without regard to ownership of any affected lands, structures, fish, wildlife, or biotic or other natural resources relied upon by Alaska Natives, Native organizations, or others for subsistence or economic purposes. Claims for such injury or damages may be determined by arbitration or judicial proceedings.

　(2) Liability under paragraph (1) of this subsection shall be limited to $350,000,000 for any one incident, and the holders of the right-of-way or permit shall be liable for any claim

Oil Pollution Act of 1990 / 775

allowed in proportion to their ownership interest in the right-of-way or permit. Liability of such holders for damages in excess of $350,000,000 shall be in accord with ordinary rules of negligence.
   (3) In any case where liability without fault is imposed pursuant to this subsection and the damages involved were caused by the negligence of a third party, the rules of subrogation shall apply in accordance with the law of the jurisdiction where the damage occurred.
   (4) Upon order of the Secretary, the holder of a right-of-way or permit shall provide emergency subsistence and other aid to an affected Alaska Native, Native organization, or other person pending expeditious filing of, and determination of, a claim under this subsection.
   (5) Where the State of Alaska is the holder of a right-of-way or permit under this chapter, the State shall not be subject to the provisions of this subsection, but the holder of the permit or right-of-way for the trans-Alaska pipeline shall be subject to this subsection with respect to facilities constructed or activities conducted under rights-of-way or permits issued to the State to the extent that such holder engages in the construction, operation, maintenance, and termination of facilities, or in other activities under rights-of-way or permits issued to the State.
(b) Control and removal of pollutants at expense of right-of-way holder
   If any area in the State of Alaska within or without the right-of-way or permit area granted under this chapter is polluted by any activities related to the Trans-Alaska Pipeline System, including operation of the terminal, conducted by or on behalf of the holder to whom such right-of-way or permit was granted, and such pollution damages or threatens to damage aquatic life, wildlife, or public or private property, the control and total removal of the pollutant shall be at the expense of such holder, including any administrative and other costs incurred by the Secretary or any other Federal or State officer or agency. Upon failure of such holder to adequately control and remove such pollutant, the Secretary, in cooperation with other Federal, State, or local agencies, or in cooperation with such holder, or both, shall have the right to accomplish the control and removal at the expense of such holder.
(c) Discharges of oil from vessels loaded at terminal facilities of pipeline; strict liability; limitation on liability; apportionment of liability; establishment and operation of Trans-Alaska Pipeline Liability Fund
   (1) Notwithstanding the provisions of any other law, if oil that has been transported through the trans-Alaska pipeline is loaded on a vessel at the terminal facilities of the pipeline, the owner and operator of the vessel (jointly and severally) and the Trans-Alaska Pipeline Liability Fund established by this subsection, shall be strictly liable without regard to fault in accordance with the provisions of this subsection for all damages, including clean-up costs, sustained by any person or entity, public or private, including residents of Canada, as the result of discharges of oil from such vessel.
   (2) Strict liability shall not be imposed under this subsection if the owner or operator of the vessel, or the Fund, can prove that the damages were caused solely by an act or war or by the negligence of the United States or other governmental agency. Strict liability shall not be imposed under this subsection with respect to the claim of a damaged party if the owner or operator of the vessel, or the Fund, can prove that the damage was caused by the negligence of such party.
   (3) Strict liability for all claims arising out of any one incident shall not exceed $100,000,000. The owner and operator of the vessel shall be jointly and severally liable for the first $14,000,000 of such claims that are allowed. Financial responsibility for $14,000,000 shall be demonstrated in accordance with the provisions of section 1321(p)[1] of title 33 before the oil is loaded. The Fund shall be liable for the balance of the claims that are allowed up to $100,000,000. If the total claims allowed exceed $100,000,000, they shall be reduced proportionately. The unpaid portion of any claim may be asserted and adjudicated under other applicable Federal or state[2] law. The Fund shall expeditiously pay claims under this subsection, including such $14,000,000, if the owner or operator of a vessel has not paid any such claim within 90 days after such claim has been submitted to such owner or operator. Upon payment of any such claim, the Fund shall be subrogated under applicable

---
[1] See References in Text note below.
[2] So in original. Probably should be capitalized.

State and Federal laws to all rights of any person entitled to recover under this subsection. In any action brought by the Fund against an owner or operator or an affiliate thereof to recover amounts under this paragraph, the Fund shall be entitled to recover prejudgment interest, costs, reasonable attorney's fees, and, in the discretion of the court, penalties.

(4) (A) The Trans-Alaska Pipeline Liability Fund is hereby established as a non-profit corporate entity that may sue and be sued in its own name. The Fund shall be administered by the holders of the trans-Alaska pipeline right-of-way under regulations prescribed by the Secretary. The Fund shall be subject to an annual audit by the Comptroller General, and a copy of the audit shall be submitted to the Congress.

(B) No present or former officer or trustee of the Fund shall be subject to any liability incurred by the Fund or by the present or former officers or trustees of the Fund, other than liability for gross negligence or willful misconduct.

(C) (i) Subject to clause (ii), each officer and each trustee of the Fund—
   (I) shall be indemnified against all claims and liabilities to which he or she has or shall become subject by reason of serving or having served as an officer or trustee, or by reason of any action taken, omitted, or neglected by him or her as an officer or trustee; and
   (II) shall be reimbursed for all attorney's fees reasonably incurred in connection with any claim or liability.
(ii) No officer or trustee shall be indemnified against, or be reimbursed for, any expenses incurred in connection with, any claim or liability arising out of his or her gross negligence or willful misconduct.

(5) The operator of the pipeline shall collect from the owner of the oil at the time it is loaded on the vessel a fee of five cents per barrel. The collection shall cease when $100,000,000 has been accumulated in the Fund, and it shall be resumed when the accumulation in the Fund falls below $100,000,000, except that after August 18, 1990, the amount to be accumulated shall be $100,000,000 or the amount determined by the trustees and certified to the Congress by the Comptroller General as necessary to pay claims arising from incidents occurring prior to August 18, 1990, and administrative costs, whichever is less.

(6) The collections under paragraph (5) shall be delivered to the Fund. Costs of administration shall be paid from the money paid to the Fund, and all sums not needed for administration and the satisfaction of claims shall be invested prudently in income-producing securities approved by the Secretary. Income from such securities shall be added to the principal of the Fund.

(7) The provisions of this subsection shall apply only to vessels engaged in transportation between the terminal facilities of the pipeline and ports under the jurisdiction of the United States. Strict liability under this subsection shall cease when the oil has first been brought ashore at a port under the jurisdiction of the United States.

(8) In any case where liability without regard to fault is imposed pursuant to this subsection and the damages involved were caused by the unseaworthiness of the vessel or by negligence, the owner and operator of the vessel, and the Fund, as the case may be shall be subrogated under applicable State and Federal laws to the rights under said laws of any person entitled to recovery hereunder. If any subrogee brings an action based on unseaworthiness of the vessel or negligence of its owner or operator, it may recover from any affiliate of the owner or operator, if the respective owner or operator fails to satisfy any claim by the subrogee allowed under this paragraph.

(9) This subsection shall not be interpreted to preempt the field of strict liability or to preclude any State from imposing additional requirements.

(10) If the Fund is unable to satisfy a claim asserted and finally determined under this subsection, the Fund may borrow the money needed to satisfy the claim from any commercial credit source, at the lowest available rate of interest, subject to approval of the Secretary.

(11) For purposes of this subsection only, the term "affiliate" includes—
   (A) Any person owned or effectively controlled by the vessel owner or operator; or
   (B) Any person that effectively controls or has the power effectively to control the vessel owner or operator by—
      (i) stock interest, or
      (ii) representation on a board of directors or similar body, or

(iii) contract or other agreement with other stockholders, or
(iv) otherwise; or
(C) Any person which is under common ownership or control with the vessel owner or operator.
(12) The term "person" means an individual, a corporation, a partnership, an association, a joint-stock company, a business trust, or an unincorporated organization.
(13) For any claims against the Fund, the term "damages" shall include, but not be limited to—
(A) the net loss of taxes, revenues, fees, royalties, rents, or other revenues incurred by a State or a political subdivision of a State due to injury, destruction, or loss of real property, personal property, or natural resources, or diminished economic activity due to a discharge of oil; and
(B) the net cost of providing increased or additional public services during or after removal activities due to a discharge of oil, including protection from fire, safety, or health hazards, incurred by a State or political subdivision of a State.
(14) Paragraphs (1) through (13) shall apply only to claims arising from incidents occurring before August 18, 1990. The Oil Pollution Act of 1990 [33 U.S.C. 2701 et seq.] shall apply to any incident, or any claims arising from an incident, occurring on or after August 18, 1990.

(Pub. L. 93-153, title II, Sec. 204, Nov. 16, 1973, 87 Stat. 586; Pub. L. 101-380, title VIII, Secs. 8101, 8102(a)(1), (4), (b)-(e), Aug. 18, 1990, 104 Stat. 565-567.)

Repeal of Subsection (c)

Pub. L. 101-380, title VIII, Sec. 8102(a)(1), (5)(A), Aug. 18, 1990, 104 Stat. 565, 566, provided that subsection (c) of this section is repealed effective 60 days after the date on which the Comptroller General certifies to Congress that: (i) all claims arising under subsection (c) of this section have been resolved, (ii) all actions for the recovery of amounts subject to subsection (c) of this section have been resolved, and (iii) all administrative expenses reasonably necessary for and incidental to the implementation of subsection (c) of this section have been paid.

References in Text

Section 1321(p) of title 33, referred to in subsec. (c)(3), was repealed by Pub. L. 101-380, title II, Sec. 2002(b)(4), Aug. 18, 1990, 104 Stat. 507.

The Oil Pollution Act of 1990, referred to in subsec. (c)(14), is Pub. L. 101-380, Aug. 18, 1990, 104 Stat. 484, which is classified principally to chapter 40 (Sec. 2701 et seq.) of Title 33, Navigation and Navigable Waters. For complete classification of this Act to the Code, see Short Title note set out under section 2701 of Title 33 and Tables.

Amendments

1990—Subsec. (a)(1). Pub. L. 101-380, Sec. 8101(a), substituted "caused solely by" for "caused by".

Subsec. (a)(2). Pub. L. 101-380, Sec. 8101(b), substituted "$350,000,000" for "$50,000,000" in two places.

Subsec. (b). Pub. L. 101-380, Sec. 8101(c), inserted "in the State of Alaska" after "any area", "related to the Trans-Alaska Pipeline System, including operation of the terminal," after "any activities", and "or State" after "any other Federal".

Subsec. (c)(2). Pub. L. 101-380, Sec. 8102(b), substituted "caused solely by" for "caused by".

Subsec. (c)(3). Pub. L. 101-380, Sec. 8102(d), inserted at end "The Fund shall expeditiously pay claims under this subsection, including such $14,000,000, if the owner or operator of a vessel has not paid any such claim within 90 days after such claim has been submitted to such owner or operator. Upon payment of any such claim, the Fund shall be subrogated under applicable State and Federal laws to all rights of any person entitled to recover under this subsection. In any action brought by the Fund against an owner or operator or an affiliate thereof to recover amounts under this paragraph, the Fund shall be entitled to recover prejudgment interest, costs, reasonable attorney's fees, and, in the discretion of the court, penalties."

Subsec. (c)(4). Pub. L. 101-380, Sec. 8102(e), designated existing provisions as par. (A) and added pars. (B) and (C).

Subsec. (c)(5). Pub. L. 101-380, Sec. 8102(a)(4), inserted before period at end of second sentence ", except that after August 18, 1990, the amount to be accumulated shall be $100,000,000 or the amount determined by the trustees and certified to the Congress by the Comptroller General as necessary to pay claims arising from incidents occurring prior to August 18, 1990, and administrative costs, whichever is less".

Subsec. (c)(13), (14). Pub. L. 101-380, Sec. 8102(c), added pars. (13) and (14).

Effective Date of 1990 Amendment

Amendment by Pub. L. 101-380 applicable to incidents occurring after Aug. 18, 1990, see section 1020 of Pub. L. 101-380, set out as an Effective Date note under section 2701 of Title 33, Navigation and Navigable Waters.

Section 8102(a)(5)(A) of Pub. L. 101-380 provided that: "The repeal by paragraph (1) [repealing subsec. (c) of this section] shall be effective 60 days after the date on which the Comptroller General of the United States certifies to the Congress that—
   (i) all claims arising under section 204(c) of the Trans-Alaska Pipeline Authorization Act (43 U.S.C. 1653(c)) have been resolved,
   (ii) all actions for the recovery of amounts subject to section 204(c) of the Trans-Alaska Pipeline Authorization Act have been resolved, and
   (iii) all administrative expenses reasonably necessary for and incidental to the implementation of section 204(c) of the Trans-Alaska Pipeline Authorization Act have been paid."

Savings Provision

Section 8102(a)(3) of Pub. L. 101-380 provided that: "The repeal made by paragraph (1) [repealing subsec. (c) of this section] shall have no effect on any right to recover or responsibility that arises from incidents subject to section 204(c) of the Trans-Alaska Pipeline Authorization Act (43 U.S.C. 1653(c)) occurring prior to the date of enactment of this Act [Aug. 18, 1990]."

Bulk Fuel Storage Tanks

Pub. L. 105-277, div. A, Sec. 101(g) [title III, Sec. 329(a), (b)], Oct. 21, 1998, 112 Stat. 2681-439, 2681-470, provided that:

"(a) Transfer of Funds.—Notwithstanding any other provision of law, the remainder of the balance in the Trans-Alaska Pipeline Liability Fund that is transferred and deposited into the Oil Spill Liability Trust Fund under section 8102(a)(2)(B)(ii) of the Oil Pollution Act of 1990 (43 U.S.C. 1653 note) after June 16, 1998 shall be used in accordance with this section.

(b) Use of Interest Only.—The interest produced from the investment of the Trans-Alaska Pipeline Liability Fund balance that is transferred and deposited into the Oil Spill Liability Trust Fund under section 8102(a)(2)(B)(ii) of the Oil Pollution Act of 1990 [Pub. L. 101-380] (43 U.S.C. 1653 note) after June 16, 1998 shall be transferred annually by the National Pollution Funds Center to the Denali Commission for a program, to be developed in consultation with the Coast Guard, to repair or replace bulk fuel storage tanks in Alaska which are not in compliance with federal law, including the Oil Pollution Act of 1990 [33 U.S.C. 2701 et seq.], or State law."

Disposition of Fund Balance

Section 8102(a)(2) of Pub. L. 101-380, as amended by Pub. L. 105-277, div. A, Sec. 101(g) [title III, Sec. 329(c)], Oct. 21, 1998, 112 Stat. 2681-439, 2681-471, provided that:

"(A) Reservation of amounts.—The trustees of the Trans-Alaska Pipeline Liability Fund (hereafter in this subsection referred to as the 'TAPS Fund') shall reserve the following amounts in the TAPS Fund—
   (i) necessary to pay claims arising under section 204(c) of the Trans-Alaska Pipeline Authorization Act (43 U.S.C. 1653(c)); and
   (ii) administrative expenses reasonably necessary for and incidental to the implementation of section 204(c) of that Act.

(B) Disposition of the balance.—After the Comptroller General of the United States certifies that the requirements of subparagraph (A) have been met, the trustees of the TAPS Fund shall dispose of the balance in the TAPS Fund after the reservation of amounts are made under subparagraph (A) by—
   (i) rebating the pro rata share of the balance to the State of Alaska for its contributions as an owner of oil, which, except as otherwise provided under article IX, section 15, of

the Alaska Constitution, shall be used for the remediation of above-ground storage tanks; and then
   (ii) transferring and depositing the remainder of the balance into the Oil Spill Liability Trust Fund established under section 9509 of the Internal Revenue Code of 1986 (26 U.S.C. 9509).
(C) Disposition of the reserved amounts.—After payment of all claims arising from an incident for which funds are reserved under subparagraph (A) and certification by the Comptroller General of the United States that the claims arising from that incident have been paid, the excess amounts, if any, for that incident shall be disposed of as set forth under subparagraphs (A) and (B).
(D) Authorization.—The amounts transferred and deposited in the Fund shall be available for the purposes of section 1012 of the Oil Pollution Act of 1990 [33 U.S.C. 2712] after funding sections 5001 [33 U.S.C. 2731] and 8103 [43 U.S.C. 1651 note] to the extent that funds have not otherwise been provided for the purposes of such sections."

Liabilities of Trustees of TAPS Fund

Section 8102(a)(5)(B) of Pub. L. 101-380 provided that: "Upon the effective date of the repeal pursuant to subparagraph (A) [see Effective Date of 1990 Amendment note above], the trustees of the TAPS Fund shall be relieved of all responsibilities under section 204(c) of the Trans-Alaska Pipeline Authorization Act [43 U.S.C. 1653(c)], but not any existing legal liability."

Preservation of Rights and Remedies of Contributors to TAPS Fund

Section 8102(a)(6) provided that: "This subsection [amending this section and enacting provisions set out as notes above] is intended expressly to preserve any and all rights and remedies of contributors to the TAPS Fund under section 1491 of title 28, United States Code (commonly referred to as the 'Tucker Act')."

Section Referred to in Other Sections

This section is referred to in title 26 section 9509.

ANTITRUST LAWS

43 USC 1654

The grant of a right-of-way, permit, lease, or other authorization pursuant to this chapter shall grant no immunity from the operation of the Federal anti-trust laws.

(Pub. L. 93-153, title II, Sec. 205, Nov. 16, 1973, 87 Stat. 588.)

References in Text

The Federal antitrust laws, referred to in text, are classified generally to chapter 1 (Sec. 1 et seq.) of Title 15, Commerce and Trade.

ROADS AND AIRPORTS

43 USC 1655

A right-of-way, permit, lease, or other authorization granted under section 1652(b) of this title for a road or airstrip as a related facility of the trans-Alaska pipeline may provide for the construction of a public road or airstrip.

(Pub. L. 93-153, title II, Sec. 206, Nov. 16, 1973, 87 Stat. 588.)

CIVIL PENALTIES

43 USC 1656

(a) Penalty
   Except as provided in subsection (c)(4) of this section, the Secretary of the Interior may assess and collect a civil penalty under this section with respect to any discharge of oil—

(1) in transit from fields or reservoirs supplying oil to the trans-Alaska pipeline; or
(2) during transportation through the trans-Alaska pipeline or handling at the terminal facilities, that causes damage to, or threatens to damage, natural resources or public or private property.

(b) Persons liable

In addition to the person causing or permitting the discharge, the owner or owners of the oil at the time the discharge occurs shall be jointly, severally, and strictly liable for the full amount of penalties assessed pursuant to this section, except that the United States and the several States, and political subdivisions thereof, shall not be liable under this section.

(c) Amount
(1) The amount of the civil penalty shall not exceed $1,000 per barrel of oil discharged.
(2) In determining the amount of civil penalty under this section, the Secretary shall consider the seriousness of the damages from the discharge, the cause of the discharge, any history of prior violations of applicable rules and laws, and the degree of success of any efforts by the violator to minimize or mitigate the effects of such discharge.
(3) The Secretary may reduce or waive the penalty imposed under this section if the discharge was solely caused by an act of war, act of God, or third party action beyond the control of the persons liable under this section.
(4) No civil penalty assessed by the Secretary pursuant to this section shall be in addition to a penalty assessed pursuant to section 1321(b) of title 33.

(d) Procedures

A civil penalty may be assessed and collected under this section only after notice and opportunity for a hearing on the record in accordance with section 554 of title 5. In any proceeding for the assessment of a civil penalty under this section, the Secretary may issue subpoenas for the attendance and testimony of witnesses and the production of relevant papers, books, and documents and may promulgate rules for discovery procedures. Any person who requested a hearing with respect to a civil penalty under this subsection and who is aggrieved by an order assessing the civil penalty may file a petition for judicial review of such order with the United States Court of Appeals for the District of Columbia circuit or for any other circuit in which such person resides or transacts business. Such a petition may only be filed within the 30-day period beginning on the date the order making such assessment was issued.

(e) State law
(1) Nothing in this section shall be construed or interpreted as preempting any State or political subdivision thereof from imposing any additional liability or requirements with respect to the discharge, or threat of discharge, of oil or other pollution by oil.
(2) Nothing in this section shall affect or modify in any way the obligations or liabilities of any person under other Federal or State law, including common law, with respect to discharges of oil.

(Pub. L. 93-153, title II, Sec. 207, as added Pub. L. 101-380, title VIII, Sec. 8202, Aug. 18, 1990, 104 Stat. 571.)

Effective Date

Section applicable to incidents occurring after Aug. 18, 1990, see section 1020 of Pub. L. 101-380, set out as a note under section 2701 of Title 33, Navigation and Navigable Waters.

Section Referred to in Other Sections

This section is referred to in title 26 section 9509.

LAND CONVEYANCES

43 USC 1642

Solely for the purpose of bringing claims that arise from the discharge of oil, the Congress confirms that all right, title, and interest of the United States in and to the lands validly selected pursuant to the Alaska Native Claims Settlement Act (43 U.S.C. 1601 et seq.) by Alaska Native corporations are deemed to have vested in the respective corporations as of March 23, 1989. This section shall take effect with respect to each Alaska Native corporation only upon its irrevocable election to accept an interim conveyance of such land and notice of such election has been formally transmitted to the Secretary of the Interior.

(Pub. L. 96-487, title XIV, Sec. 1438, as added Pub. L. 101-380, title VIII, Sec. 8301, Aug. 18, 1990, 104 Stat. 572.)

References in Text

The Alaska Native Claims Settlement Act, referred to in text, is Pub. L. 92-203, Dec. 18, 1971, 85 Stat. 688, as amended, which is classified generally to chapter 33 (Sec. 1601 et seq.) of this title. For complete classification of this Act to the Code, see Short Title note set out under section 1601 of this title and Tables.

Effective Date

Section applicable to incidents occurring after Aug. 18, 1990, see section 1020 of Pub. L. 101-380, set out as a note under section 2701 of Title 33, Navigation and Navigable Waters.

WILDLIFE RESOURCES PORTION OF STUDY AND IMPACT OF POTENTIAL OIL SPILLS IN ARCTIC OCEAN

16 USC 3145

(a) Wildlife resources

The Secretary shall work closely with the State of Alaska and Native Village and Regional Corporations in evaluating the impact of oil and gas exploration, development, production, and transportation and other human activities on the wildlife resources of these lands, including impacts on the Arctic and Porcupine caribou herds, polar bear, muskox, grizzly bear, wolf, wolverine, seabirds, shore birds, and migratory waterfowl. In addition the Secretary shall consult with the appropriate agencies of the Government of Canada in evaluating such impacts particularly with respect to the Porcupine caribou herd.

(b) Oil spills

(1) The Congress finds that—

(A) Canada has discovered commercial quantities of oil and gas in the Amalagak region of the Northwest Territory;

(B) Canada is exploring alternatives for transporting the oil from the Amalagak field to markets in Asia and the Far East;

(C) one of the options the Canadian Government is exploring involves transshipment of oil from the Amalagak field across the Beaufort Sea to tankers which would transport the oil overseas;

(D) the tankers would traverse the American Exclusive Economic Zone through the Beaufort Sea into the Chuckchi Sea and then through the Bering Straits;

(E) the Beaufort and Chuckchi Seas are vital to Alaska's Native people, providing them with subsistence in the form of walrus, seals, fish, and whales;

(F) the Secretary of the Interior has conducted Outer Continental Shelf lease sales in the Beaufort and Chuckchi Seas and oil and gas exploration is ongoing;

(G) an oil spill in the Arctic Ocean, if not properly contained and cleaned up, could have significant impacts on the indigenous people of Alaska's North Slope and on the Arctic environment; and

(H) there are no international contingency plans involving our two governments concerning containment and cleanup of an oil spill in the Arctic Ocean.

(2) (A) The Secretary of the Interior, in consultation with the Governor of Alaska, shall conduct a study of the issues of recovery of damages, contingency plans, and coordinated actions in the event of an oil spill in the Arctic Ocean.

(B) The Secretary shall, no later than January 31, 1991, transmit a report to the Congress on the findings and conclusions reached as the result of the study carried out under this subsection.

(c) Treaty negotiations

The Congress calls upon the Secretary of State, in consultation with the Secretary of the Interior, the Secretary of Transportation, and the Governor of Alaska, to begin negotiations with the Foreign Minister of Canada regarding a treaty dealing with the complex issues of recovery of damages, contingency plans, and coordinated actions in the event of an oil spill in the Arctic Ocean.

(d) Report to Congress

The Secretary of State shall report to the Congress on the Secretary's efforts pursuant to this section no later than June 1, 1991.

(Pub. L. 96-487, title X, Sec. 1005, Dec. 2, 1980, 94 Stat. 2453; Pub. L. 101-380, title VIII, Sec. 8302, Aug. 18, 1990, 104 Stat. 572.)

Amendments

1990—Pub. L. 101-380 inserted "and impact of potential oil spills in Arctic Ocean" in section catchline, designated existing text as subsec. (a), and added subsecs. (b) to (d).

Effective Date of 1990 Amendment

Amendment by Pub. L. 101-380 applicable to incidents occurring after Aug. 18, 1990, see section 1020 of Pub. L. 101-380, set out as an Effective Date note under section 2701 of Title 33, Navigation and Navigable Waters.

Study on Barren-Ground Caribou

Section 306 of Pub. L. 96-487 provided:

"(a) The Congress finds that the barren-ground caribou are a migratory species deserving of careful study and special protection, and that the Western Arctic and the Porcupine herds of such caribou are of national and international significance.

(b) The Secretary of the Interior shall conduct, and the Governor of Alaska is urged to cooperate with the Secretary in conducting, an ecological study of the barren-ground caribou herds north of the Yukon River and the herds that have been known to migrate between the United States and Canada, including, but not limited to, a determination of the seasonal migration patterns, reproduction and mortality rates, composition and age structure, behavioral characteristics, habitats (including but not limited to calving, feeding, summering and wintering areas, and key migration routes) that are critical to their natural stability and productivity and the effects on the herds of development by man, predation, and disease. In conducting this study the Secretary shall review the experience of other Arctic circumpolar countries with caribou and is authorized to enter into such contracts as he deems necessary to carry out portions or all of this study."

SAFETY OF PUBLIC WATER SYSTEMS
[Safe Drinking Water Act]

as amended[1]
42 U.S.C. § 300f et seq.

Part A—Definitions

DEFINITIONS

42 USC 300f

For purposes of this subchapter:
 (1) The term "primary drinking water regulation" means a regulation which—
    (A) applies to public water systems;
    (B) specifies contaminants which, in the judgment of the Administrator, may have any adverse effect on the health of persons;
    (C) specifies for each such contaminant either—
       (i) a maximum contaminant level, if, in the judgment of the Administrator, it is economically and technologically feasible to ascertain the level of such contaminant in water in public water systems, or
       (ii) if, in the judgment of the Administrator, it is not economically or technologically feasible to so ascertain the level of such contaminant, each treatment technique known to the Administrator which leads to a reduction in the level of such contaminant sufficient to satisfy the requirements of section 300g-1 of this title; and
    (D) contains criteria and procedures to assure a supply of drinking water which dependably complies with such maximum contaminant levels; including accepted methods for quality control and testing procedures to insure compliance with such levels and to insure proper operation and maintenance of the system, and requirements as to (i) the minimum quality of water which may be taken into the system and (ii) siting for new facilities for public water systems.
    At any time after promulgation of a regulation referred to in this paragraph, the Administrator may add equally effective quality control and testing procedures by guidance published in the Federal Register. Such procedures shall be treated as an alternative for public water systems to the quality control and testing procedures listed in the regulation.
 (2) The term "secondary drinking water regulation" which applies to public water systems and which specifies the maximum contaminant levels which, in the judgment of the Administrator, are requisite to protect the public welfare. Such regulations may apply to any contaminant in drinking water (A) which may adversely affect the odor or appearance of such water and consequently may cause a substantial number of the persons served by the public water system providing such water to discontinue its use, or (B) which may otherwise adversely affect the public welfare. Such regulations may vary accordingly to geographic and other circumstances.
 (3) The term "maximum contaminant level" means the maximum permissible level of a contaminant in water which is delivered to any user of a public water system.
 (4) Public water system.—
    (A) In general.—The term "public water system" means a system for the provision to the public of water for human consumption through pipes or other constructed conveyances, if such system has at least fifteen service connections or regularly serves at least twenty-five individuals. Such term includes (i) any collection, treatment, storage, and distribution facilities under control of the operator of such system and used primarily in connection with such system, and (ii) any collection or pretreatment storage facilities not under such control which are used primarily in connection with such system.

---

[1]Editor's note: Text from Title 42, Chapter 6A, Subchapter 12 of U.S. Code, as amended by Pub. L. 108-136, November 24, 2003; Pub. L. 107-188, June 12, 2002; Pub. L. 107-110, Jan. 8, 2002; andPub. L 106-377, October 27, 2000.

(B) Connections.—
   (i) In general.—For purposes of subparagraph (A), a connection to a system that delivers water by a constructed conveyance other than a pipe shall not be considered a connection, if—
      (I) the water is used exclusively for purposes other than residential uses (consisting of drinking, bathing, and cooking, or other similar uses);
      (II) the Administrator or the State (in the case of a State exercising primary enforcement responsibility for public water systems) determines that alternative water to achieve the equivalent level of public health protection provided by the applicable national primary drinking water regulation is provided for residential or similar uses for drinking and cooking; or
      (III) the Administrator or the State (in the case of a State exercising primary enforcement responsibility for public water systems) determines that the water provided for residential or similar uses for drinking, cooking, and bathing is centrally treated or treated at the point of entry by the provider, a pass-through entity, or the user to achieve the equivalent level of protection provided by the applicable national primary drinking water regulations.
   (ii) Irrigation districts.—An irrigation district in existence prior to May 18, 1994, that provides primarily agricultural service through a piped water system with only incidental residential or similar use shall not be considered to be a public water system if the system or the residential or similar users of the system comply with subclause (II) or (III) of clause (i).
(C) Transition period.—A water supplier that would be a public water system only as a result of modifications made to this paragraph by the Safe Drinking Water Act Amendments of 1996 shall not be considered a public water system for purposes of the Act until the date that is two years after August 6, 1996. If a water supplier does not serve 15 service connections (as defined in subparagraphs (A) and (B)) or 25 people at any time after the conclusion of the 2-year period, the water supplier shall not be considered a public water system.

(5) The term "supplier of water" means any person who owns or operates a public water system.
(6) The term "contaminant" means any physical, chemical, biological, or radiological substance or matter in water.
(7) The term "Administrator" means the Administrator of the Environmental Protection Agency.
(8) The term "Agency" means the Environmental Protection Agency.
(9) The term "Council" means the National Drinking Water Advisory Council established under section 300j-5 of this title.
(10) The term "municipality" means a city, town, or other public body created by or pursuant to State law, or an Indian Tribe.
(11) The term "Federal agency" means any department, agency, or instrumentality of the United States.
(12) The term "person" means an individual, corporation, company, association, partnership, State, municipality, or Federal agency (and includes officers, employees, and agents of any corporation, company, association, State, municipality, or Federal agency).
(13)(A) Except as provided in subparagraph (B), the term "State" includes, in addition to the several States, only the District of Columbia, Guam, the Commonwealth of Puerto Rico, the Northern Mariana Islands, the Virgin Islands, American Samoa, and the Trust Territory of the Pacific Islands.
   (B) For purposes of section 300j-12 of this title, the term "State" means each of the 50 States, the District of Columbia, and the Commonwealth of Puerto Rico.
(14) The term "Indian Tribe" means any Indian tribe having a Federally recognized governing body carrying out substantial governmental duties and powers over any area. For purposes of section 300j-12 of this title, the term includes any Native village (as defined in section 1602(c) of title 43).
(15) Community water system.—The term "community water system" means a public water system that—
   (A) serves at least 15 service connections used by year-round residents of the area served by the system; or

(B) regularly serves at least 25 year-round residents.

(16) Noncommunity water system.—The term "noncommunity water system" means a public water system that is not a community water system.

(July 1, 1944, ch. 373, title XIV, Sec. 1401, as added Pub. L. 93-523, Sec. 2(a), Dec. 16, 1974, 88 Stat. 1660; amended Pub. L. 94-317, title III, Sec. 301(b)(2), June 23, 1976, 90 Stat. 707; Pub. L. 94-484, title IX, Sec. 905(b)(1), Oct. 12, 1976, 90 Stat. 2325; Pub. L. 95-190, Sec. 8(b), Nov. 16, 1977, 91 Stat. 1397; Pub. L. 99-339, title III, Sec. 302(b), June 19, 1986, 100 Stat. 666; Pub. L. 104-182, title I, Sec. 101(a), (b)(1), Aug. 6, 1996, 110 Stat. 1615, 1616.)

References in Text

The Safe Drinking Water Act Amendments of 1996, referred to in par. (4)(C), is Pub. L. 104-182, Aug. 6, 1996, 110 Stat. 1613. For complete classification of this Act to the Code, see Short Title of 1996 Amendment note set out under section 201 of this title and Tables.

Amendments

1996—Par. (1). Pub. L. 104-182, Sec. 101(a)(1)(B), inserted at end "At any time after promulgation of a regulation referred to in this paragraph, the Administrator may add equally effective quality control and testing procedures by guidance published in the Federal Register. Such procedures shall be treated as an alternative for public water systems to the quality control and testing procedures listed in the regulation."

Par. (1)(D). Pub. L. 104-182, Sec. 101(a)(1)(A), inserted "accepted methods for" before "quality control".

Par. (4). Pub. L. 104-182, Sec. 101(b)(1), designated existing provisions as subpar. (A), inserted par. and subpar. headings, redesignated former subpars. (A) and (B) as cls. (i) and (ii), respectively, substituted "water for human consumption through pipes or other constructed conveyances" for "piped water for human consumption" in first sentence, and added subpars. (B) and (C).

Par. (13). Pub. L. 104-182, Sec. 101(a)(2), designated existing provisions as subpar. (A), substituted "Except as provided in subparagraph (B), the term" for "The term", and added subpar. (B).

Par. (14). Pub. L. 104-182, Sec. 101(a)(3), inserted at end "For purposes of section 300j-12 of this title, the term includes any Native village (as defined in section 1602(c) of title 43)."

Pars. (15), (16). Pub. L. 104-182, Sec. 101(a)(4), added pars. (15) and (16).

1986—Par. (10). Pub. L. 99-339, Sec. 302(b)(2), substituted "Indian Tribe" for "Indian tribal organization authorized by law".

Par. (14). Pub. L. 99-339, Sec. 302(b)(1), added par. (14).

1977—Par. (12). Pub. L. 95-190 expanded definition of "person" to include Federal agency, and officers, employees, and agents of any corporation, company, etc.

1976—Par. (13). Pub. L. 94-484 defined "State" to include Northern Mariana Islands.

Pub. L. 94-317 added par. (13).

Effective Date of 1996 Amendment

Section 2(b) of Pub. L. 104-182 provided that: "Except as otherwise specified in this Act [enacting sections 300g-7 to 300g-9, 300h-8, 300j-3c, and 300j-12 to 300j-18 of this title and section 1263a of Title 33, Navigation and Navigable Waters, amending this section, sections 300g-1 to 300g-6, 300h, 300h-5 to 300h-7, 300i, 300i-1, 300j to 300j-2, 300j-4 to 300j-8, 300j-11, and 300j-21 to 300j-25 of this title, sections 4701 and 4721 of Title 16, Conservation, and section 349 of Title 21, Food and Drugs, repealing section 13551 of this title, enacting provisions set out as notes under this section, sections 201, 300g-1, 300j-1, and 300j-12 of this title, section 1281 of Title 33, and section 45 of Title 40, Public Buildings, Property, and Works, and amending provisions set out as a note under section 201 of this title] or in the amendments made by this Act, this Act and the amendments made by this Act shall take effect on the date of enactment of this Act [Aug. 6, 1996]."

Short Title

This subchapter is known as the "Safe Drinking Water Act", see note set out under section 201 of this title.

Termination of Trust Territory of the Pacific Islands

For termination of Trust Territory of the Pacific Islands, see note set out preceding section 1681 of Title 48, Territories and Insular Possessions.

Effect of Public Law 104-182 on Federal Water Pollution Control Act

Section 2(c) of Pub. L. 104-182 provided that: "Except for the provisions of section 302 [42 U.S.C. 300j-12 note] (relating to transfers of funds), nothing in this Act [see Effective Date of 1996 Amendment note above] or in any amendments made by this Act to title XIV of the Public Health Service Act [this subchapter] (commonly known as the 'Safe Drinking Water Act') or any other law shall be construed by the Administrator of the Environmental Protection Agency or the courts as affecting, modifying, expanding, changing, or altering—

(1) the provisions of the Federal Water Pollution Control Act [33 U.S.C. 1251 et seq.];
(2) the duties and responsibilities of the Administrator under that Act; or
(3) the regulation or control of point or nonpoint sources of pollution discharged into waters covered by that Act.

The Administrator shall identify in the agency's annual budget all funding and full-time equivalents administering such title XIV separately from funding and staffing for the Federal Water Pollution Control Act."

Congressional Findings

Section 3 of Pub. L. 104-182 provided that: "The Congress finds that—

(1) safe drinking water is essential to the protection of public health;
(2) because the requirements of the Safe Drinking Water Act (42 U.S.C. 300f et seq.) now exceed the financial and technical capacity of some public water systems, especially many small public water systems, the Federal Government needs to provide assistance to communities to help the communities meet Federal drinking water requirements;
(3) the Federal Government commits to maintaining and improving its partnership with the States in the administration and implementation of the Safe Drinking Water Act;
(4) States play a central role in the implementation of safe drinking water programs, and States need increased financial resources and appropriate flexibility to ensure the prompt and effective development and implementation of drinking water programs;
(5) the existing process for the assessment and selection of additional drinking water contaminants needs to be revised and improved to ensure that there is a sound scientific basis for setting priorities in establishing drinking water regulations;
(6) procedures for assessing the health effects of contaminants establishing drinking water standards should be revised to provide greater opportunity for public education and participation;
(7) in considering the appropriate level of regulation for contaminants in drinking water, risk assessment, based on sound and objective science, and benefit-cost analysis are important analytical tools for improving the efficiency and effectiveness of drinking water regulations to protect human health;
(8) more effective protection of public health requires—
    (A) a Federal commitment to set priorities that will allow scarce Federal, State, and local resources to be targeted toward the drinking water problems of greatest public health concern;
    (B) maximizing the value of the different and complementary strengths and responsibilities of the Federal and State governments in those States that have primary enforcement responsibility for the Safe Drinking Water Act; and
    (C) prevention of drinking water contamination through well-trained system operators, water systems with adequate managerial, technical, and financial capacity, and enhanced protection of source waters of public water systems;
(9) compliance with the requirements of the Safe Drinking Water Act continues to be a concern at public water systems experiencing technical and financial limitations, and Federal, State, and local governments need more resources and more effective authority to attain the objectives of the Safe Drinking Water Act; and
(10) consumers served by public water systems should be provided with information on the source of the water they are drinking and its quality and safety, as well as prompt notification of any violation of drinking water regulations."

GAO Study

Section 101(b)(2) of Pub. L. 104-182 provided that: "The Comptroller General of the United States shall undertake a study to—

(A) ascertain the numbers and locations of individuals and households relying for their residential water needs, including drinking, bathing, and cooking (or other similar uses) on irrigation water systems, mining water systems, industrial water systems, or other water systems covered by section 1401(4)(B) of the Safe Drinking Water Act [par. (4)(B) of this section] that are not public water systems subject to the Safe Drinking Water Act [this subchapter];
(B) determine the sources and costs and affordability (to users and systems) of water used by such populations for their residential water needs; and
(C) review State and water system compliance with the exclusion provisions of section 1401(4)(B) of such Act.

The Comptroller General shall submit a report to the Congress within 3 years after the date of enactment of this Act [Aug. 6, 1996] containing the results of such study."

Safe Drinking Water Amendments of 1977 Restrictions on Appropriations for Research

Section 2(e) of Pub. L. 95-190 provided that: "Nothing in this Act [see Short Title of 1977 Amendment note set out under section 201 of this title] shall be construed to authorize the appropriation of any amount for research under title XIV of the Public Health Service Act [this subchapter] (relating to safe drinking water)."

Safe Drinking Water Amendments of 1977 as Not Affecting Authority of Administrator With Respect to Contaminants

Section 3(e)(2) of Pub. L. 95-190 provided that: "Nothing in this Act [see Short Title of 1977 Amendment note set out under section 201 of this title] shall be construed to alter or affect the Administrator's authority or duty under title 14 of the Public Health Service Act [this subchapter] to promulgate regulations or take other action with respect to any contaminant."

Rural Water Survey; Report to President and Congress; Authorization of Appropriations

Section 3 of Pub. L. 93-523, as amended by Pub. L. 95-190, Secs. 2(d), 3(d), Nov. 16, 1977, 91 Stat. 1393, 1394, directed Administrator of Environmental Protection Agency, after consultation with Secretary of Agriculture and the several States, to enter into arrangements with public or private entities to conduct a survey of quantity, quality, and availability of rural drinking water supplies, which survey was to include, but not be limited to, consideration of number of residents in each rural area who presently are being inadequately served by a public or private drinking water supply system, or by an individual home drinking water supply system, or who presently have limited or otherwise inadequate access to drinking water, or who, due to absence or inadequacy of a drinking water supply system, are exposed to an increased health hazard, and who have experienced incidents of chronic or acute illness, which may be attributed to inadequacy of a drinking water supply system. Survey to be completed within eighteen months of Dec. 16, 1974, and a final report thereon submitted, not later than six months after completion of survey, to President and to Congress.

Federal Compliance With Pollution Control Standards

For provisions relating to the responsibility of the head of each Executive agency for compliance with applicable pollution control standards, see Ex. Ord. No. 12088, Oct. 13, 1978, 43 F.R. 47707, set out as a note under section 4321 of this title.

Termination of Advisory Committees

Pub. L. 93-641, Sec. 6, Jan. 4, 1975, 88 Stat. 2275, set out as a note under section 217a of this title, provided that an advisory committee established pursuant to the Public Health Service Act shall terminate at such time as may be specifically prescribed by an Act of Congress enacted after Jan. 4, 1975.

Section Referred to in Other Sections

This section is referred to in sections 201, 300g-4, 300g-5, 300j-12 of this title; title 21 section 349.

Part B—Public Water Systems

COVERAGE

42 USC 300g

Subject to sections 300g-4 and 300g-5 of this title, national primary drinking water regulations under this part shall apply to each public water system in each State; except that such regulations shall not apply to a public water system—
  (1) which consists only of distribution and storage facilities (and does not have any collection and treatment facilities);
  (2) which obtains all of its water from, but is not owned or operated by, a public water system to which such regulations apply;
  (3) which does not sell water to any person; and
  (4) which is not a carrier which conveys passengers in interstate commerce.

(July 1, 1944, ch. 373, title XIV, Sec. 1411, as added Pub. L. 93-523, Sec. 2(a), Dec. 16, 1974, 88 Stat. 1662.)

NATIONAL DRINKING WATER REGULATIONS

42 USC 300g-1

(a) National primary drinking water regulations; maximum contaminant level goals; simultaneous publication of regulations and goals
  (1) Effective on June 19, 1986, each national interim or revised primary drinking water regulation promulgated under this section before June 19, 1986, shall be deemed to be a national primary drinking water regulation under subsection (b) of this section. No such regulation shall be required to comply with the standards set forth in subsection (b)(4) of this section unless such regulation is amended to establish a different maximum contaminant level after June 19, 1986.
  (2) After June 19, 1986, each recommended maximum contaminant level published before June 19, 1986, shall be treated as a maximum contaminant level goal.
  (3) Whenever a national primary drinking water regulation is proposed under subsection (b) of this section for any contaminant, the maximum contaminant level goal for such contaminant shall be proposed simultaneously. Whenever a national primary drinking water regulation is promulgated under subsection (b) of this section for any contaminant, the maximum contaminant level goal for such contaminant shall be published simultaneously.
  (4) Paragraph (3) shall not apply to any recommended maximum contaminant level published before June 19, 1986.
(b) Standards
  (1) Identification of contaminants for listing.—
    (A) General authority.—The Administrator shall, in accordance with the procedures established by this subsection, publish a maximum contaminant level goal and promulgate a national primary drinking water regulation for a contaminant (other than a contaminant referred to in paragraph (2) for which a national primary drinking water regulation has been promulgated as of August 6, 1996) if the Administrator determines that—
      (i) the contaminant may have an adverse effect on the health of persons;
      (ii) the contaminant is known to occur or there is a substantial likelihood that the contaminant will occur in public water systems with a frequency and at levels of public health concern; and
      (iii) in the sole judgment of the Administrator, regulation of such contaminant presents a meaningful opportunity for health risk reduction for persons served by public water systems.
    (B) Regulation of unregulated contaminants.—
      (i) Listing of contaminants for consideration.—
        (I) Not later than 18 months after August 6, 1996, and every 5 years thereafter, the Administrator, after consultation with the scientific community, includ-

ing the Science Advisory Board, after notice and opportunity for public comment, and after considering the occurrence data base established under section 300j-4(g) of this title, shall publish a list of contaminants which, at the time of publication, are not subject to any proposed or promulgated national primary drinking water regulation, which are known or anticipated to occur in public water systems, and which may require regulation under this subchapter.

(II) The unregulated contaminants considered under subclause (I) shall include, but not be limited to, substances referred to in section 9601(14) of this title, and substances registered as pesticides under the Federal Insecticide, Fungicide, and Rodenticide Act [7 U.S.C. 136 et seq.].

(III) The Administrator's decision whether or not to select an unregulated contaminant for a list under this clause shall not be subject to judicial review.

(ii) Determination to regulate.—

(I) Not later than 5 years after August 6, 1996, and every 5 years thereafter, the Administrator shall, after notice of the preliminary determination and opportunity for public comment, for not fewer than 5 contaminants included on the list published under clause (i), make determinations of whether or not to regulate such contaminants.

(II) A determination to regulate a contaminant shall be based on findings that the criteria of clauses (i), (ii), and (iii) of subparagraph (A) are satisfied. Such findings shall be based on the best available public health information, including the occurrence data base established under section 300j-4(g) of this title.

(III) The Administrator may make a determination to regulate a contaminant that does not appear on a list under clause (i) if the determination to regulate is made pursuant to subclause (II).

(IV) A determination under this clause not to regulate a contaminant shall be considered final agency action and subject to judicial review.

(iii) Review.—Each document setting forth the determination for a contaminant under clause (ii) shall be available for public comment at such time as the determination is published.

(C) Priorities.—In selecting unregulated contaminants for consideration under subparagraph (B), the Administrator shall select contaminants that present the greatest public health concern. The Administrator, in making such selection, shall take into consideration, among other factors of public health concern, the effect of such contaminants upon subgroups that comprise a meaningful portion of the general population (such as infants, children, pregnant women, the elderly, individuals with a history of serious illness, or other subpopulations) that are identifiable as being at greater risk of adverse health effects due to exposure to contaminants in drinking water than the general population.

(D) Urgent threats to public health.—The Administrator may promulgate an interim national primary drinking water regulation for a contaminant without making a determination for the contaminant under paragraph (4)(C), or completing the analysis under paragraph (3)(C), to address an urgent threat to public health as determined by the Administrator after consultation with and written response to any comments provided by the Secretary of Health and Human Services, acting through the director of the Centers for Disease Control and Prevention or the director of the National Institutes of Health. A determination for any contaminant in accordance with paragraph (4)(C) subject to an interim regulation under this subparagraph shall be issued, and a completed analysis meeting the requirements of paragraph (3)(C) shall be published, not later than 3 years after the date on which the regulation is promulgated and the regulation shall be repromulgated, or revised if appropriate, not later than 5 years after that date.

(E) Regulation.—For each contaminant that the Administrator determines to regulate under subparagraph (B), the Administrator shall publish maximum contaminant level goals and promulgate, by rule, national primary drinking water regulations under this subsection. The Administrator shall propose the maximum contaminant level goal and national primary drinking water regulation for a contaminant not later than 24 months after the determination to regulate under subparagraph (B), and may publish such proposed regulation concurrent with the determination to regulate. The Administrator shall publish a maximum contaminant level goal and promulgate a national primary drinking water regulation within 18 months after the proposal thereof. The Administrator, by notice in the Federal Register, may extend the deadline for such promulgation for up to 9 months.

(F) Health advisories and other actions.—The Administrator may publish health advisories (which are not regulations) or take other appropriate actions for contaminants not subject to any national primary drinking water regulation.

(2) Schedules and deadlines.—

(A) In general.—In the case of the contaminants listed in the Advance Notice of Proposed Rulemaking published in volume 47, Federal Register, page 9352, and in volume 48, Federal Register, page 45502, the Administrator shall publish maximum contaminant level goals and promulgate national primary drinking water regulations—

(i) not later than 1 year after June 19, 1986, for not fewer than 9 of the listed contaminants;

(ii) not later than 2 years after June 19, 1986, for not fewer than 40 of the listed contaminants; and

(iii) not later than 3 years after June 19, 1986, for the remainder of the listed contaminants.

(B) Substitution of contaminants.—If the Administrator identifies a drinking water contaminant the regulation of which, in the judgment of the Administrator, is more likely to be protective of public health (taking into account the schedule for regulation under subparagraph (A)) than a contaminant referred to in subparagraph (A), the Administrator may publish a maximum contaminant level goal and promulgate a national primary drinking water regulation for the identified contaminant in lieu of regulating the contaminant referred to in subparagraph (A). Substitutions may be made for not more than 7 contaminants referred to in subparagraph (A). Regulation of a contaminant identified under this subparagraph shall be in accordance with the schedule applicable to the contaminant for which the substitution is made.

(C) Disinfectants and disinfection byproducts.—The Administrator shall promulgate an Interim Enhanced Surface Water Treatment Rule, a Final Enhanced Surface Water Treatment Rule, a Stage I Disinfectants and Disinfection Byproducts Rule, and a Stage II Disinfectants and Disinfection Byproducts Rule in accordance with the schedule published in volume 59, Federal Register, page 6361 (February 10, 1994), in table III.13 of the proposed Information Collection Rule. If a delay occurs with respect to the promulgation of any rule in the schedule referred to in this subparagraph, all subsequent rules shall be completed as expeditiously as practicable but no later than a revised date that reflects the interval or intervals for the rules in the schedule.

(3) Risk assessment, management, and communication.—

(A) Use of science in decisionmaking.—In carrying out this section, and, to the degree that an Agency action is based on science, the Administrator shall use—

(i) the best available, peer-reviewed science and supporting studies conducted in accordance with sound and objective scientific practices; and

(ii) data collected by accepted methods or best available methods (if the reliability of the method and the nature of the decision justifies use of the data).

(B) Public information.—In carrying out this section, the Administrator shall ensure that the presentation of information on public health effects is comprehensive, informative, and understandable. The Administrator shall, in a document made available to the public in support of a regulation promulgated under this section, specify, to the extent practicable—

(i) each population addressed by any estimate of public health effects;

(ii) the expected risk or central estimate of risk for the specific populations;

(iii) each appropriate upper-bound or lower-bound estimate of risk;

(iv) each significant uncertainty identified in the process of the assessment of public health effects and studies that would assist in resolving the uncertainty; and

(v) peer-reviewed studies known to the Administrator that support, are directly relevant to, or fail to support any estimate of public health effects and the methodology used to reconcile inconsistencies in the scientific data.
(C) Health risk reduction and cost analysis.—
  (i) Maximum contaminant levels.—When proposing any national primary drinking water regulation that includes a maximum contaminant level, the Administrator shall, with respect to a maximum contaminant level that is being considered in accordance with paragraph (4) and each alternative maximum contaminant level that is being considered pursuant to paragraph (5) or (6)(A), publish, seek public comment on, and use for the purposes of paragraphs (4), (5), and (6) an analysis of each of the following:
    (I) Quantifiable and nonquantifiable health risk reduction benefits for which there is a factual basis in the rulemaking record to conclude that such benefits are likely to occur as the result of treatment to comply with each level.
    (II) Quantifiable and nonquantifiable health risk reduction benefits for which there is a factual basis in the rulemaking record to conclude that such benefits are likely to occur from reductions in co-occurring contaminants that may be attributed solely to compliance with the maximum contaminant level, excluding benefits resulting from compliance with other proposed or promulgated regulations.
    (III) Quantifiable and nonquantifiable costs for which there is a factual basis in the rulemaking record to conclude that such costs are likely to occur solely as a result of compliance with the maximum contaminant level, including monitoring, treatment, and other costs and excluding costs resulting from compliance with other proposed or promulgated regulations.
    (IV) The incremental costs and benefits associated with each alternative maximum contaminant level considered.
    (V) The effects of the contaminant on the general population and on groups within the general population such as infants, children, pregnant women, the elderly, individuals with a history of serious illness, or other subpopulations that are identified as likely to be greater risk of adverse health effects due to exposure to contaminants in drinking water than the general population.
    (VI) Any increased health risk that may occur as the result of compliance, including risks associated with co-occurring contaminants.
    (VII) Other relevant factors, including the quality and extent of the information, the uncertainties in the analysis supporting subclauses (I) through (VI), and factors with respect to the degree and nature of the risk.
  (ii) Treatment techniques.—When proposing a national primary drinking water regulation that includes a treatment technique in accordance with paragraph (7)(A), the Administrator shall publish and seek public comment on an analysis of the health risk reduction benefits and costs likely to be experienced as the result of compliance with the treatment technique and alternative treatment techniques that are being considered, taking into account, as appropriate, the factors described in clause (i).
  (iii) Approaches to measure and value benefits.—The Administrator may identify valid approaches for the measurement and valuation of benefits under this subparagraph, including approaches to identify consumer willingness to pay for reductions in health risks from drinking water contaminants.
  (iv) Authorization.—There are authorized to be appropriated to the Administrator, acting through the Office of Ground Water and Drinking Water, to conduct studies, assessments, and analyses in support of regulations or the development of methods, $35,000,000 for each of fiscal years 1996 through 2003.
(4) Goals and standards.—
  (A) Maximum contaminant level goals.—Each maximum contaminant level goal established under this subsection shall be set at the level at which no known or anticipated adverse effects on the health of persons occur and which allows an adequate margin of safety.

(B) Maximum contaminant levels.—Except as provided in paragraphs (5) and (6), each national primary drinking water regulation for a contaminant for which a maximum contaminant level goal is established under this subsection shall specify a maximum contaminant level for such contaminant which is as close to the maximum contaminant level goal as is feasible.
(C) Determination.—At the time the Administrator proposes a national primary drinking water regulation under this paragraph, the Administrator shall publish a determination as to whether the benefits of the maximum contaminant level justify, or do not justify, the costs based on the analysis conducted under paragraph (3)(C).
(D) Definition of feasible.—For the purposes of this subsection, the term "feasible" means feasible with the use of the best technology, treatment techniques and other means which the Administrator finds, after examination for efficacy under field conditions and not solely under laboratory conditions, are available (taking cost into consideration). For the purpose of this paragraph, granular activated carbon is feasible for the control of synthetic organic chemicals, and any technology, treatment technique, or other means found to be the best available for the control of synthetic organic chemicals must be at least as effective in controlling synthetic organic chemicals as granular activated carbon.
(E) Feasible technologies.—
 (i) In general.—Each national primary drinking water regulation which establishes a maximum contaminant level shall list the technology, treatment techniques, and other means which the Administrator finds to be feasible for purposes of meeting such maximum contaminant level, but a regulation under this subsection shall not require that any specified technology, treatment technique, or other means be used for purposes of meeting such maximum contaminant level.
 (ii) List of technologies for small systems.—The Administrator shall include in the list any technology, treatment technique, or other means that is affordable, as determined by the Administrator in consultation with the States, for small public water systems serving—
  (I) a population of 10,000 or fewer but more than 3,300;
  (II) a population of 3,300 or fewer but more than 500; and
  (III) a population of 500 or fewer but more than 25;
  and that achieves compliance with the maximum contaminant level or treatment technique, including packaged or modular systems and point-of-entry or point-of-use treatment units. Point-of-entry and point-of-use treatment units shall be owned, controlled and maintained by the public water system or by a person under contract with the public water system to ensure proper operation and maintenance and compliance with the maximum contaminant level or treatment technique and equipped with mechanical warnings to ensure that customers are automatically notified of operational problems. The Administrator shall not include in the list any point-of-use treatment technology, treatment technique, or other means to achieve compliance with a maximum contaminant level or treatment technique requirement for a microbial contaminant (or an indicator of a microbial contaminant). If the American National Standards Institute has issued product standards applicable to a specific type of point-of-entry or point-of-use treatment unit, individual units of that type shall not be accepted for compliance with a maximum contaminant level or treatment technique requirement unless they are independently certified in accordance with such standards. In listing any technology, treatment technique, or other means pursuant to this clause, the Administrator shall consider the quality of the source water to be treated.
 (iii) List of technologies that achieve compliance.—Except as provided in clause (v), not later than 2 years after August 6, 1996, and after consultation with the States, the Administrator shall issue a list of technologies that achieve compliance with the maximum contaminant level or treatment technique for each category of public water systems described in subclauses (I), (II), and (III) of clause (ii) for each national primary drinking water regulation promulgated prior to June 19, 1986.
 (iv) Additional technologies.—The Administrator may, at any time after a national primary drinking water regulation has been promulgated, supplement the list of

technologies describing additional or new or innovative treatment technologies that meet the requirements of this paragraph for categories of small public water systems described in subclauses (I), (II), and (III) of clause (ii) that are subject to the regulation.
  (v) Technologies that meet surface water treatment rule.—
  Within one year after August 6, 1996, the Administrator shall list technologies that meet the Surface Water Treatment Rule for each category of public water systems described in subclauses (I), (II), and (III) of clause (ii).
(5) Additional health risk considerations.—
  (A) In general.—Notwithstanding paragraph (4), the Administrator may establish a maximum contaminant level for a contaminant at a level other than the feasible level, if the technology, treatment techniques, and other means used to determine the feasible level would result in an increase in the health risk from drinking water by—
    (i) increasing the concentration of other contaminants in drinking water; or
    (ii) interfering with the efficacy of drinking water treatment techniques or processes that are used to comply with other national primary drinking water regulations.
  (B) Establishment of level.—If the Administrator establishes a maximum contaminant level or levels or requires the use of treatment techniques for any contaminant or contaminants pursuant to the authority of this paragraph—
    (i) the level or levels or treatment techniques shall minimize the overall risk of adverse health effects by balancing the risk from the contaminant and the risk from other contaminants the concentrations of which may be affected by the use of a treatment technique or process that would be employed to attain the maximum contaminant level or levels; and
    (ii) the combination of technology, treatment techniques, or other means required to meet the level or levels shall not be more stringent than is feasible (as defined in paragraph (4)(D)).
(6) Additional health risk reduction and cost considerations.—
  (A) In general.—Notwithstanding paragraph (4), if the Administrator determines based on an analysis conducted under paragraph (3)(C) that the benefits of a maximum contaminant level promulgated in accordance with paragraph (4) would not justify the costs of complying with the level, the Administrator may, after notice and opportunity for public comment, promulgate a maximum contaminant level for the contaminant that maximizes health risk reduction benefits at a cost that is justified by the benefits.
  (B) Exception.—The Administrator shall not use the authority of this paragraph to promulgate a maximum contaminant level for a contaminant, if the benefits of compliance with a national primary drinking water regulation for the contaminant that would be promulgated in accordance with paragraph (4) experienced by—
    (i) persons served by large public water systems; and
    (ii) persons served by such other systems as are unlikely, based on information provided by the States, to receive a variance under section 300g-4(e) of this title (relating to small system variances);
  would justify the costs to the systems of complying with the regulation. This subparagraph shall not apply if the contaminant is found almost exclusively in small systems eligible under section 300g-4(e) of this title for a small system variance.
  (C) Disinfectants and disinfection byproducts.—The Administrator may not use the authority of this paragraph to establish a maximum contaminant level in a Stage I or Stage II national primary drinking water regulation (as described in paragraph (2)(C)) for contaminants that are disinfectants or disinfection byproducts, or to establish a maximum contaminant level or treatment technique requirement for the control of cryptosporidium. The authority of this paragraph may be used to establish regulations for the use of disinfection by systems relying on ground water sources as required by paragraph (8).
  (D) Judicial review.—A determination by the Administrator that the benefits of a maximum contaminant level or treatment requirement justify or do not justify the costs of complying with the level shall be reviewed by the court pursuant to section 300j-7 of this title only as part of a review of a final national primary drinking water regulation

that has been promulgated based on the determination and shall not be set aside by the court under that section unless the court finds that the determination is arbitrary and capricious.

(7) (A) The Administrator is authorized to promulgate a national primary drinking water regulation that requires the use of a treatment technique in lieu of establishing a maximum contaminant level, if the Administrator makes a finding that it is not economically or technologically feasible to ascertain the level of the contaminant. In such case, the Administrator shall identify those treatment techniques which, in the Administrator's judgment, would prevent known or anticipated adverse effects on the health of persons to the extent feasible. Such regulations shall specify each treatment technique known to the Administrator which meets the requirements of this paragraph, but the Administrator may grant a variance from any specified treatment technique in accordance with section 300g-4(a)(3) of this title.

(B) Any schedule referred to in this subsection for the promulgation of a national primary drinking water regulation for any contaminant shall apply in the same manner if the regulation requires a treatment technique in lieu of establishing a maximum contaminant level.

(C) (i) Not later than 18 months after June 19, 1986, the Administrator shall propose and promulgate national primary drinking water regulations specifying criteria under which filtration (including coagulation and sedimentation, as appropriate) is required as a treatment technique for public water systems supplied by surface water sources. In promulgating such rules, the Administrator shall consider the quality of source waters, protection afforded by watershed management, treatment practices (such as disinfection and length of water storage) and other factors relevant to protection of health.

(ii) In lieu of the provisions of section 300g-4 of this title the Administrator shall specify procedures by which the State determines which public water systems within its jurisdiction shall adopt filtration under the criteria of clause (i). The State may require the public water system to provide studies or other information to assist in this determination. The procedures shall provide notice and opportunity for public hearing on this determination. If the State determines that filtration is required, the State shall prescribe a schedule for compliance by the public water system with the filtration requirement. A schedule shall require compliance within 18 months of a determination made under clause (iii).

(iii) Within 18 months from the time that the Administrator establishes the criteria and procedures under this subparagraph, a State with primary enforcement responsibility shall adopt any necessary regulations to implement this subparagraph. Within 12 months of adoption of such regulations the State shall make determinations regarding filtration for all the public water systems within its jurisdiction supplied by surface waters.

(iv) If a State does not have primary enforcement responsibility for public water systems, the Administrator shall have the same authority to make the determination in clause (ii) in such State as the State would have under that clause. Any filtration requirement or schedule under this subparagraph shall be treated as if it were a requirement of a national primary drinking water regulation.

(v) As an additional alternative to the regulations promulgated pursuant to clauses (i) and (iii), including the criteria for avoiding filtration contained in 40 CFR 141.71, a State exercising primary enforcement responsibility for public water systems may, on a case-by-case basis, and after notice and opportunity for public comment, establish treatment requirements as an alternative to filtration in the case of systems having uninhabited, undeveloped watersheds in consolidated ownership, and having control over access to, and activities in, those watersheds, if the State determines (and the Administrator concurs) that the quality of the source water and the alternative treatment requirements established by the State ensure greater removal or inactivation efficiencies of pathogenic organisms for which national primary drinking water regulations have been promulgated or that are of public health concern than would be achieved by the combination of filtration and chlorine disinfection (in compliance with this section).

(8) Disinfection.—At any time after the end of the 3-year period that begins on August 6, 1996, but not later than the date on which the Administrator promulgates a Stage II rulemaking for disinfectants and disinfection byproducts (as described in paragraph (2)(C)), the Administrator shall also promulgate national primary drinking water regulations requiring disinfection as a treatment technique for all public water systems, including surface water systems and, as necessary, ground water systems. After consultation with the States, the Administrator shall (as part of the regulations) promulgate criteria that the Administrator, or a State that has primary enforcement responsibility under section 300g-2 of this title, shall apply to determine whether disinfection shall be required as a treatment technique for any public water system served by ground water. The Administrator shall simultaneously promulgate a rule specifying criteria that will be used by the Administrator (or delegated State authorities) to grant variances from this requirement according to the provisions of sections 300g-4(a)(1)(B) and 300g-4(a)(3) of this title. In implementing section 300j-1(e) of this title the Administrator or the delegated State authority shall, where appropriate, give special consideration to providing technical assistance to small public water systems in complying with the regulations promulgated under this paragraph.
(9) Review and revision.—The Administrator shall, not less often than every 6 years, review and revise, as appropriate, each national primary drinking water regulation promulgated under this subchapter. Any revision of a national primary drinking water regulation shall be promulgated in accordance with this section, except that each revision shall maintain, or provide for greater, protection of the health of persons.
(10) Effective date.—A national primary drinking water regulation promulgated under this section (and any amendment thereto) shall take effect on the date that is 3 years after the date on which the regulation is promulgated unless the Administrator determines that an earlier date is practicable, except that the Administrator, or a State (in the case of an individual system), may allow up to 2 additional years to comply with a maximum contaminant level or treatment technique if the Administrator or State (in the case of an individual system) determines that additional time is necessary for capital improvements.
(11) No national primary drinking water regulation may require the addition of any substance for preventive health care purposes unrelated to contamination of drinking water.
(12) Certain contaminants.—
   (A) Arsenic.—
      (i) Schedule and standard.—Notwithstanding the deadlines set forth in paragraph (1), the Administrator shall promulgate a national primary drinking water regulation for arsenic pursuant to this subsection, in accordance with the schedule established by this paragraph.
      (ii) Study plan.—Not later than 180 days after August 6, 1996, the Administrator shall develop a comprehensive plan for study in support of drinking water rulemaking to reduce the uncertainty in assessing health risks associated with exposure to low levels of arsenic. In conducting such study, the Administrator shall consult with the National Academy of Sciences, other Federal agencies, and interested public and private entities.
      (iii) Cooperative agreements.—In carrying out the study plan, the Administrator may enter into cooperative agreements with other Federal agencies, State and local governments, and other interested public and private entities.
      (iv) Proposed regulations.—The Administrator shall propose a national primary drinking water regulation for arsenic not later than January 1, 2000.
      (v) Final regulations.—Not later than January 1, 2001, after notice and opportunity for public comment, the Administrator shall promulgate a national primary drinking water regulation for arsenic.
      (vi) Authorization.—There are authorized to be appropriated $2,500,000 for each of fiscal years 1997 through 2000 for the studies required by this paragraph.
   (B) Sulfate.—
      (i) Additional study.—Prior to promulgating a national primary drinking water regulation for sulfate, the Administrator and the Director of the Centers for Disease Control and Prevention shall jointly conduct an additional study to establish a reliable dose-response relationship for the adverse human health effects that may result from exposure to sulfate in drinking water, including the health effects that

may be experienced by groups within the general population (including infants and travelers) that are potentially at greater risk of adverse health effects as the result of such exposure. The study shall be conducted in consultation with interested States, shall be based on the best available, peer-reviewed science and supporting studies conducted in accordance with sound and objective scientific practices, and shall be completed not later than 30 months after August 6, 1996.

    (ii) Determination.—The Administrator shall include sulfate among the 5 or more contaminants for which a determination is made pursuant to paragraph (3)(B) not later than 5 years after August 6, 1996.

    (iii) Proposed and final rule.—Notwithstanding the deadlines set forth in paragraph (2), the Administrator may, pursuant to the authorities of this subsection and after notice and opportunity for public comment, promulgate a final national primary drinking water regulation for sulfate. Any such regulation shall include requirements for public notification and options for the provision of alternative water supplies to populations at risk as a means of complying with the regulation in lieu of a best available treatment technology or other means.

(13) Radon in drinking water.—

  (A) National primary drinking water regulation.—Notwithstanding paragraph (2), the Administrator shall withdraw any national primary drinking water regulation for radon proposed prior to August 6, 1996, and shall propose and promulgate a regulation for radon under this section, as amended by the Safe Drinking Water Act Amendments of 1996.

  (B) Risk assessment and studies.—

    (i) Assessment by nas.—Prior to proposing a national primary drinking water regulation for radon, the Administrator shall arrange for the National Academy of Sciences to prepare a risk assessment for radon in drinking water using the best available science in accordance with the requirements of paragraph (3). The risk assessment shall consider each of the risks associated with exposure to radon from drinking water and consider studies on the health effects of radon at levels and under conditions likely to be experienced through residential exposure. The risk assessment shall be peer-reviewed.

    (ii) Study of other measures.—The Administrator shall arrange for the National Academy of Sciences to prepare an assessment of the health risk reduction benefits associated with various mitigation measures to reduce radon levels in indoor air. The assessment may be conducted as part of the risk assessment authorized by clause (i) and shall be used by the Administrator to prepare the guidance and approve State programs under subparagraph (G).

    (iii) Other organization.—If the National Academy of Sciences declines to prepare the risk assessment or studies required by this subparagraph, the Administrator shall enter into a contract or cooperative agreement with another independent, scientific organization to prepare such assessments or studies.

  (C) Health risk reduction and cost analysis.—Not later than 30 months after August 6, 1996, the Administrator shall publish, and seek public comment on, a health risk reduction and cost analysis meeting the requirements of paragraph (3)(C) for potential maximum contaminant levels that are being considered for radon in drinking water. The Administrator shall include a response to all significant public comments received on the analysis with the preamble for the proposed rule published under subparagraph (D).

  (D) Proposed regulation.—Not later than 36 months after August 6, 1996, the Administrator shall propose a maximum contaminant level goal and a national primary drinking water regulation for radon pursuant to this section.

  (E) Final regulation.—Not later than 12 months after the date of the proposal under subparagraph (D), the Administrator shall publish a maximum contaminant level goal and promulgate a national primary drinking water regulation for radon pursuant to this section based on the risk assessment prepared pursuant to subparagraph (B) and the health risk reduction and cost analysis published pursuant to subparagraph (C). In considering the risk assessment and the health risk reduction and cost analysis in

connection with the promulgation of such a standard, the Administrator shall take into account the costs and benefits of control programs for radon from other sources.
(F) Alternative maximum contaminant level.—If the maximum contaminant level for radon in drinking water promulgated pursuant to subparagraph (E) is more stringent than necessary to reduce the contribution to radon in indoor air from drinking water to a concentration that is equivalent to the national average concentration of radon in outdoor air, the Administrator shall, simultaneously with the promulgation of such level, promulgate an alternative maximum contaminant level for radon that would result in a contribution of radon from drinking water to radon levels in indoor air equivalent to the national average concentration of radon in outdoor air. If the Administrator promulgates an alternative maximum contaminant level under this subparagraph, the Administrator shall, after notice and opportunity for public comment and in consultation with the States, publish guidelines for State programs, including criteria for multimedia measures to mitigate radon levels in indoor air, to be used by the States in preparing programs under subparagraph (G). The guidelines shall take into account data from existing radon mitigation programs and the assessment of mitigation measures prepared under subparagraph (B).
(G) Multimedia radon mitigation programs.—
  (i) In general.—A State may develop and submit a multimedia program to mitigate radon levels in indoor air for approval by the Administrator under this subparagraph. If, after notice and the opportunity for public comment, such program is approved by the Administrator, public water systems in the State may comply with the alternative maximum contaminant level promulgated under subparagraph (F) in lieu of the maximum contaminant level in the national primary drinking water regulation promulgated under subparagraph (E).
  (ii) Elements of programs.—State programs may rely on a variety of mitigation measures including public education, testing, training, technical assistance, remediation grant and loan or incentive programs, or other regulatory or nonregulatory measures. The effectiveness of elements in State programs shall be evaluated by the Administrator based on the assessment prepared by the National Academy of Sciences under subparagraph (B) and the guidelines published by the Administrator under subparagraph (F).
  (iii) Approval.—The Administrator shall approve a State program submitted under this paragraph if the health risk reduction benefits expected to be achieved by the program are equal to or greater than the health risk reduction benefits that would be achieved if each public water system in the State complied with the maximum contaminant level promulgated under subparagraph (E). The Administrator shall approve or disapprove a program submitted under this paragraph within 180 days of receipt. A program that is not disapproved during such period shall be deemed approved. A program that is disapproved may be modified to address the objections of the Administrator and be resubmitted for approval.
  (iv) Review.—The Administrator shall periodically, but not less often than every 5 years, review each multimedia mitigation program approved under this subparagraph to determine whether it continues to meet the requirements of clause (iii) and shall, after written notice to the State and an opportunity for the State to correct any deficiency in the program, withdraw approval of programs that no longer comply with such requirements.
  (v) Extension.—If, within 90 days after the promulgation of an alternative maximum contaminant level under subparagraph (F), the Governor of a State submits a letter to the Administrator committing to develop a multimedia mitigation program under this subparagraph, the effective date of the national primary drinking water regulation for radon in the State that would be applicable under paragraph (10) shall be extended for a period of 18 months.
  (vi) Local programs.—In the event that a State chooses not to submit a multimedia mitigation program for approval under this subparagraph or has submitted a program that has been disapproved, any public water system in the State may submit a program for approval by the Administrator according to the same criteria, con-

ditions, and approval process that would apply to a State program. The Administrator shall approve a multimedia mitigation program if the health risk reduction benefits expected to be achieved by the program are equal to or greater than the health risk reduction benefits that would result from compliance by the public water system with the maximum contaminant level for radon promulgated under subparagraph (E).

(14) Recycling of filter backwash.—The Administrator shall promulgate a regulation to govern the recycling of filter backwash water within the treatment process of a public water system. The Administrator shall promulgate such regulation not later than 4 years after August 6, 1996, unless such recycling has been addressed by the Administrator's Enhanced Surface Water Treatment Rule prior to such date.

(15) Variance technologies.—

(A) In general.—At the same time as the Administrator promulgates a national primary drinking water regulation for a contaminant pursuant to this section, the Administrator shall issue guidance or regulations describing the best treatment technologies, treatment techniques, or other means (referred to in this paragraph as "variance technology") for the contaminant that the Administrator finds, after examination for efficacy under field conditions and not solely under laboratory conditions, are available and affordable, as determined by the Administrator in consultation with the States, for public water systems of varying size, considering the quality of the source water to be treated. The Administrator shall identify such variance technologies for public water systems serving—

(i) a population of 10,000 or fewer but more than 3,300;
(ii) a population of 3,300 or fewer but more than 500; and
(iii) a population of 500 or fewer but more than 25,

if, considering the quality of the source water to be treated, no treatment technology is listed for public water systems of that size under paragraph (4)(E). Variance technologies identified by the Administrator pursuant to this paragraph may not achieve compliance with the maximum contaminant level or treatment technique requirement of such regulation, but shall achieve the maximum reduction or inactivation efficiency that is affordable considering the size of the system and the quality of the source water. The guidance or regulations shall not require the use of a technology from a specific manufacturer or brand.

(B) Limitation.—The Administrator shall not identify any variance technology under this paragraph, unless the Administrator has determined, considering the quality of the source water to be treated and the expected useful life of the technology, that the variance technology is protective of public health.

(C) Additional information.—The Administrator shall include in the guidance or regulations identifying variance technologies under this paragraph any assumptions supporting the public health determination referred to in subparagraph (B), where such assumptions concern the public water system to which the technology may be applied, or its source waters. The Administrator shall provide any assumptions used in determining affordability, taking into consideration the number of persons served by such systems. The Administrator shall provide as much reliable information as practicable on performance, effectiveness, limitations, costs, and other relevant factors including the applicability of variance technology to waters from surface and underground sources.

(D) Regulations and guidance.—Not later than 2 years after August 6, 1996, and after consultation with the States, the Administrator shall issue guidance or regulations under subparagraph (A) for each national primary drinking water regulation promulgated prior to August 6, 1996, for which a variance may be granted under section 300g-4(e) of this title. The Administrator may, at any time after a national primary drinking water regulation has been promulgated, issue guidance or regulations describing additional variance technologies. The Administrator shall, not less often than every 7 years, or upon receipt of a petition supported by substantial information, review variance technologies identified under this paragraph. The Administrator shall issue revised guidance or regulations if new or innovative variance technologies become available that meet the requirements of this paragraph and achieve an equal or greater reduction or inactivation efficiency than the variance technologies previously identified under this subparagraph. No public water system shall be required to replace a variance technology during the useful life of the technology for the sole reason that a more efficient variance technology has been listed under this subparagraph.

(c) Secondary regulations; publication of proposed regulations; promulgation; amendments
The Administrator shall publish proposed national secondary drinking water regulations within 270 days after December 16, 1974. Within 90 days after publication of any such regulation, he shall promulgate such regulation with such modifications as he deems appropriate. Regulations under this subsection may be amended from time to time.

(d) Regulations; public hearings; administrative consultations
Regulations under this section shall be prescribed in accordance with section 553 of title 5 (relating to rulemaking), except that the Administrator shall provide opportunity for public hearing prior to promulgation of such regulations. In proposing and promulgating regulations under this section, the Administrator shall consult with the Secretary and the National Drinking Water Advisory Council.

(e) Science Advisory Board comments
The Administrator shall request comments from the Science Advisory Board (established under the Environmental Research, Development, and Demonstration Act of 1978) prior to proposal of a maximum contaminant level goal and national primary drinking water regulation. The Board shall respond, as it deems appropriate, within the time period applicable for promulgation of the national primary drinking water standard concerned. This subsection shall, under no circumstances, be used to delay final promulgation of any national primary drinking water standard.

(July 1, 1944, ch. 373, title XIV, Sec. 1412, as added Pub. L. 93-523, Sec. 2(a), Dec. 16, 1974, 88 Stat. 1662; amended Pub. L. 95-190, Secs. 3(c), 12(a), Nov. 16, 1977, 91 Stat. 1394, 1398; Pub. L. 99-339, title I, Sec. 101(a)-(c)(1), (d), (e), June 19, 1986, 100 Stat. 642-646; Pub. L. 104-182, title I, Secs. 102(a), (c)(2), 103, 104(a), (c), 105-111(a), title V, Sec. 501(a)(1), (2), Aug. 6, 1996, 110 Stat. 1617, 1621-1623, 1625-1631, 1691.)

References in Text

The Federal Insecticide, Fungicide, and Rodenticide Act, referred to in subsec. (b)(1)(B)(i)(II), is act June 25, 1947, ch. 125, as amended generally by Pub. L. 92-516, Oct. 21, 1972, 86 Stat. 973, which is classified generally to subchapter II (Sec. 136 et seq.) of chapter 6 of Title 7, Agriculture. For complete classification of this Act to the Code, see Short Title note set out under section 136 of Title 7 and Tables.

The Safe Drinking Water Act Amendments of 1996, referred to in subsec. (b)(13)(A), is Pub. L. 104-182, Aug. 6, 1996, 110 Stat. 1613. For complete classification of this Act to the Code, see Short Title of 1996 Amendment note set out under section 201 of this title and Tables.

The Environmental Research, Development, and Demonstration Act of 1978, referred to in subsec. (e), probably means the Environmental Research, Development, and Demonstration Authorization Act of 1978 which is Pub. L. 95-155, Nov. 8, 1977, 91 Stat. 1257, as amended. Provisions of the Act establishing the Science Advisory Board are classified to section 4365 of this title. For complete classification of this Act to the Code, see Tables.

Amendments

1996—Subsec. (a)(3). Pub. L. 104-182, Sec. 102(c)(2), struck out "paragraph (1), (2), or (3) of" before "subsection (b)" in two places.

Subsec. (b). Pub. L. 104-182, Sec. 102(a), inserted heading.

Subsec. (b)(1), (2). Pub. L. 104-182, Sec. 102(a), added pars. (1) and (2) and struck out former pars. (1) and (2) which related to publication of maximum contaminant level goals and promulgation of national primary drinking water regulations for certain listed contaminants or substituted contaminants.

Subsec. (b)(3). Pub. L. 104-182, Sec. 103, added par. (3).

Pub. L. 104-182, Sec. 102(a), struck out par. (3) which related to publication of maximum contaminant level goals and promulgation of national primary drinking water regulations for contaminants, other than those referred to in pars. (1) or (2), which may have an adverse effect on human health and are known to occur in public water systems.

800 / Environmental Statutes

Subsec. (b)(4). Pub. L. 104-182, Sec. 104(a)(1), designated first sentence as subpar. (A), inserted par. and subpar. (A) headings, designated second sentence as subpar. (B), inserted subpar. (B) heading, substituted "Except as provided in paragraphs (5) and (6), each national" for "Each national" and "specify a maximum contaminant level" for "specify a maximum level", and added subpar. (C).

Subsec. (b)(4)(D). Pub. L. 104-182, Sec. 104(a)(2), (3), redesignated par. (5) as subpar. (D) of par. (4), inserted subpar. heading, and substituted "this paragraph" for "paragraph (4)".

Subsec. (b)(4)(E). Pub. L. 104-182, Secs. 104(a)(4), (5), 105, redesignated par. (6) as subpar. (E)(i) of par. (4), inserted subpar. and cl. headings, substituted "this subsection" for "this paragraph", and added cls. (ii) to (v).

Subsec. (b)(5), (6). Pub. L. 104-182, Sec. 104(a)(6), added pars. (5) and (6). Former pars. (5) and (6) redesignated subpars. (D) and (E)(i), respectively, of par. (4).

Subsec. (b)(7)(C)(v). Pub. L. 104-182, Sec. 106, added cl. (v).

Subsec. (b)(8). Pub. L. 104-182, Sec. 501(a)(2), substituted "section 300j-1(e)" for "section 300j-1(g)".

Pub. L. 104-182, Sec. 107, inserted heading, realigned margins, and substituted "At any time after the end of the 3-year period that begins on August 6, 1996, but not later than the date on which the Administrator promulgates a Stage II rulemaking for disinfectants and disinfection byproducts (as described in paragraph (2)(C)), the Administrator shall also promulgate national primary drinking water regulations requiring disinfection as a treatment technique for all public water systems, including surface water systems and, as necessary, ground water systems. After consultation with the States, the Administrator shall (as part of the regulations) promulgate criteria that the Administrator, or a State that has primary enforcement responsibility under section 300g-2 of this title, shall apply to determine whether disinfection shall be required as a treatment technique for any public water system served by ground water." for "Not later than 36 months after June 19, 1986, the Administrator shall propose and promulgate national primary drinking water regulations requiring disinfection as a treatment technique for all public water systems."

Subsec. (b)(9). Pub. L. 104-182, Sec. 104(c), amended par. (9) generally. Prior to amendment, par. (9) read as follows: "National primary drinking water regulations shall be amended whenever changes in technology, treatment techniques, and other means permit greater protection of the health of persons, but in any event such regulations shall be reviewed at least once every 3 years. Such review shall include an analysis of innovations or changes in technology, treatment techniques or other activities that have occurred over the previous 3-year period and that may provide for greater protection of the health of persons. The findings of such review shall be published in the Federal Register. If, after opportunity for public comment, the Administrator concludes that the technology, treatment techniques, or other means resulting from such innovations or changes are not feasible within the meaning of paragraph (5), an explanation of such conclusion shall be published in the Federal Register."

Subsec. (b)(10). Pub. L. 104-182, Sec. 108, amended par. (10) generally. Prior to amendment, par. (10) read as follows: "National primary drinking water regulations promulgated under this subsection (and amendments thereto) shall take effect eighteen months after the date of their promulgation. Regulations under subsection (a) of this section shall be superseded by regulations under this subsection to the extent provided by the regulations under this subsection."

Subsec. (b)(11). Pub. L. 104-182, Sec. 501(a)(1), realigned margins.

Subsec. (b)(12). Pub. L. 104-182, Sec. 109(a), added par. (12).

Subsec. (b)(13). Pub. L. 104-182, Sec. 109(b), added par. (13).

Subsec. (b)(14). Pub. L. 104-182, Sec. 110, added par. (14).

Subsec. (b)(15). Pub. L. 104-182, Sec. 111(a), added par. (15).

1986—Subsec. (a). Pub. L. 99-339, Sec. 101(a), amended subsec. (a) generally. Prior to amendment, subsec. (a) read as follows:

"(1) The Administrator shall publish proposed national interim primary drinking water regulations within 90 days after December 16, 1974. Within 180 days after December 16, 1974, he shall promulgate such regulations with such modifications as he deems appropriate. Regulations under this paragraph may be amended from time to time.

(2) National interim primary drinking water regulations promulgated under paragraph (1) shall protect health to the extent feasible, using technology, treatment techniques, and other means, which the Administrator determines are generally available (taking costs into consideration) on December 16, 1974.

(3) The interim primary regulations first promulgated under paragraph (1) shall take effect eighteen months after the date of their promulgation."

Subsec. (b)(1). Pub. L. 99-339, Sec. 101(b), substituted provisions establishing standard setting schedules and deadlines for provisions relating to establishment of maximum contaminant levels and a list of contaminants with adverse effect but of undetermined levels.

Subsec. (b)(2). Pub. L. 99-339, Sec. 101(b), substituted provisions authorizing the Administrator to substitute contaminants for those referred to in par. (1) and to supply a list of the contaminants proposed for substitution, with the decision of the Administrator to regulate such contaminant not subject to judicial review, for provisions which authorized the Administrator to publish in the Federal Register proposed revised national interim primary drinking water regulations and 180 days after the date of such proposed regulations to promulgate such revised regulations with modification as deemed appropriate.

Subsec. (b)(3). Pub. L. 99-339, Sec. 101(b), substituted provisions directing the Administrator to publish maximum contaminant level goals and promulgate national primary drinking water regulations for contaminants, other than specified in par. (1) or (2), which may have an adverse effect on health and are known or anticipated to occur in public water systems, to establish an advisory working group to aid in establishing a list of such contaminants, and to publish, within a specified time, both proposed and final goals and regulations for provisions which required that revised national primary drinking water regulations specify a maximum contaminant level or require the use of treatment techniques for each contaminant, which level or technique was to be as close to the recommended level or technique as feasible, and defined the term "feasible".

Subsec. (b)(4) to (11). Pub. L. 99-339, Sec. 101(b), (c)(1), (d), added pars. (4) to (8), redesignated former pars. (4) to (6) as pars. (9) to (11), respectively, in par. (9) substituted "National" for "Revised National" and inserted provision that review include analysis, and publication in Federal Register, of innovations in technology, treatment techniques or other activities occurring during previous three years and their feasibility, and in par. (10) substituted "National" for "Revised National".

Subsec. (e). Pub. L. 99-339, Sec. 101(e), amended subsec. (e) generally, substituting provisions which relate to the request by the Administrator of comments by the Science Advisory Board prior to proposal of a maximum contaminant level goal and national primary drinking water regulation for provisions which related to study by the National Academy of Sciences to determine the maximum contaminant levels, report to Congress, and funding therefor.

1977—Subsec. (e)(2). Pub. L. 95-190 inserted provisions relating to revisions of the required report and cl. (G).

Applicability of Prior Requirements

Section 102(b) of Pub. L. 104-182 provided that: "The requirements of subparagraphs (C) and (D) of section 1412(b)(3) of the Safe Drinking Water Act [subsec. (b)(3)(C), (D) of this section] as in effect before the date of enactment of this Act [Aug. 6, 1996], and any obligation to promulgate regulations pursuant to such subparagraphs not promulgated as of the date of enactment of this Act, are superseded by the amendments made by subsection (a) [amending this section]."

Disinfectants and Disinfection Byproducts

Section 104(b) of Pub. L. 104-182 provided that: "The Administrator of the Environmental Protection Agency may use the authority of section 1412(b)(5) of the Safe Drinking Water Act [subsec. (b)(5) of this section] (as amended by this Act) to promulgate the Stage I and Stage II Disinfectants and Disinfection Byproducts Rules as proposed in volume 59, Federal Register, page 38668 (July 29, 1994). The considerations used in the development of the July 29, 1994, proposed national primary drinking water regulation on disinfectants and disinfection byproducts shall be treated as consistent with such section 1412(b)(5) for purposes of such Stage I and Stage II rules."

Administrative Provision

Pub. L. 106-377, Sec. 1(a)(1), Oct. 27, 2000, 114 Stat. 1441A-41, provided in part: "That notwithstanding section 1412(b)(12)(A)(v) of the Safe Drinking Water Act [42 U.S.C. 300g-1], as amended, the Administrator shall promulgate a national primary drinking water regulation for arsenic not later than June 22, 2001."

Section Referred to in Other Sections

This section is referred to in sections 300f, 300g-2, 300g-3, 300g-4, 300g-5, 300j-2, 300j-3, 300j-3b, 300j-4, 300j-12, 300j-14 of this title; title 21 section 349.

STATE PRIMARY ENFORCEMENT RESPONSIBILITY

42 USC 300g-2

(a) In general

For purposes of this subchapter, a State has primary enforcement responsibility for public water systems during any period for which the Administrator determines (pursuant to regulations prescribed under subsection (b) of this section) that such State—

(1) has adopted drinking water regulations that are no less stringent than the national primary drinking water regulations promulgated by the Administrator under subsections (a) and (b) of section 300g-1 of this title not later than 2 years after the date on which the regulations are promulgated by the Administrator, except that the Administrator may provide for an extension of not more than 2 years if, after submission and review of appropriate, adequate documentation from the State, the Administrator determines that the extension is necessary and justified;

(2) has adopted and is implementing adequate procedures for the enforcement of such State regulations, including conducting such monitoring and making such inspections as the Administrator may require by regulation;

(3) will keep such records and make such reports with respect to its activities under paragraphs (1) and (2) as the Administrator may require by regulation;

(4) if it permits variances or exemptions, or both, from the requirements of its drinking water regulations which meet the requirements of paragraph (1), permits such variances and exemptions under conditions and in a manner which is not less stringent than the conditions under, and the manner in which variances and exemptions may be granted under sections 300g-4 and 300g-5 of this title;

(5) has adopted and can implement an adequate plan for the provision of safe drinking water under emergency circumstances including earthquakes, floods, hurricanes, and other natural disasters, as appropriate; and

(6) has adopted authority for administrative penalties (unless the constitution of the State prohibits the adoption of the authority) in a maximum amount—

(A) in the case of a system serving a population of more than 10,000, that is not less than $1,000 per day per violation; and

(B) in the case of any other system, that is adequate to ensure compliance (as determined by the State);

except that a State may establish a maximum limitation on the total amount of administrative penalties that may be imposed on a public water system per violation.

(b) Regulations

(1) The Administrator shall, by regulation (proposed within 180 days of December 16, 1974), prescribe the manner in which a State may apply to the Administrator for a determination that the requirements of paragraphs (1), (2), (3), and (4) of subsection (a) of this section are satisfied with respect to the State, the manner in which the determination is made, the period for which the determination will be effective, and the manner in which the Administrator may determine that such requirements are no longer met. Such regulations shall require that before a determination of the Administrator that such requirements are met or are no longer met with respect to a State may become effective, the Administrator shall notify such State of the determination and the reasons therefor and shall provide an op-

portunity for public hearing on the determination. Such regulations shall be promulgated (with such modifications as the Administrator deems appropriate) within 90 days of the publication of the proposed regulations in the Federal Register. The Administrator shall promptly notify in writing the chief executive officer of each State of the promulgation of regulations under this paragraph. Such notice shall contain a copy of the regulations and shall specify a State's authority under this subchapter when it is determined to have primary enforcement responsibility for public water systems.

   (2) When an application is submitted in accordance with the Administrator's regulations under paragraph (1), the Administrator shall within 90 days of the date on which such application is submitted (A) make the determination applied for, or (B) deny the application and notify the applicant in writing of the reasons for his denial.

(c) Interim primary enforcement authority

A State that has primary enforcement authority under this section with respect to each existing national primary drinking water regulation shall be considered to have primary enforcement authority with respect to each new or revised national primary drinking water regulation during the period beginning on the effective date of a regulation adopted and submitted by the State with respect to the new or revised national primary drinking water regulation in accordance with subsection (b)(1) of this section and ending at such time as the Administrator makes a determination under subsection (b)(2)(B) of this section with respect to the regulation.

(July 1, 1944, ch. 373, title XIV, Sec. 1413, as added Pub. L. 93-523, Sec. 2(a), Dec. 16, 1974, 88 Stat. 1665; amended Pub. L. 99-339, title I, Sec. 101(c)(2), June 19, 1986, 100 Stat. 646; Pub. L. 104-182, title I, Secs. 112, 113(b), Aug. 6, 1996, 110 Stat. 1633, 1635.)

Amendments

1996—Subsec. (a)(1). Pub. L. 104-182, Sec. 112(a)(1), amended par. (1) generally. Prior to amendment, par. (1) read as follows: "has adopted drinking water regulations which are no less stringent than the national primary drinking water regulations in effect under sections 300g-1(a) and 300g-1(b) of this title;".

Subsec. (a)(5). Pub. L. 104-182, Sec. 112(b), inserted "including earthquakes, floods, hurricanes, and other natural disasters, as appropriate" after "emergency circumstances".

Subsec. (a)(6). Pub. L. 104-182, Sec. 113(b), added par. (6).

Subsec. (c). Pub. L. 104-182, Sec. 112(a)(2), added subsec. (c).

1986—Subsec. (a)(1). Pub. L. 99-339 substituted "are no less stringent than the national primary drinking water regulations in effect under sections 300g-1(a) and 300g-1(b) of this title" for subpars. (A) and (B) which related to stringency of State drinking water regulations between period of promulgation and effective date of national interim drinking water regulations and during the period after such effective date.

Section Referred to in Other Sections

This section is referred to in sections 300g-1, 300g-3, 300g-4, 300g-7, 300j-2, 300j-12 of this title.

ENFORCEMENT OF DRINKING WATER REGULATIONS

42 USC 300g-3

(a) Notice to State and public water system; issuance of administrative order; civil action
   (1) (A) Whenever the Administrator finds during a period during which a State has primary enforcement responsibility for public water systems (within the meaning of section 300g-2(a) of this title) that any public water system—
      (i) for which a variance under section 300g-4 or an exemption under section 300g-5 of this title is not in effect, does not comply with any applicable requirement, or
      (ii) for which a variance under section 300g-4 or an exemption under section 300g-5 of this title is in effect, does not comply with any schedule or other requirement imposed pursuant thereto,
     he shall so notify the State and such public water system and provide such advice and technical assistance to such State and public water system as may be appropriate to bring the system into compliance with the requirement by the earliest feasible time.

(B) If, beyond the thirtieth day after the Administrator's notification under subparagraph (A), the State has not commenced appropriate enforcement action, the Administrator shall issue an order under subsection (g) of this section requiring the public water system to comply with such applicable requirement or the Administrator shall commence a civil action under subsection (b) of this section.
(2) Enforcement in nonprimacy states.—
(A) In general.—If, on the basis of information available to the Administrator, the Administrator finds, with respect to a period in which a State does not have primary enforcement responsibility for public water systems, that a public water system in the State—
(i) for which a variance under section 300g-4 of this title or an exemption under section 300g-5 of this title is not in effect, does not comply with any applicable requirement; or
(ii) for which a variance under section 300g-4 of this title or an exemption under section 300g-5 of this title is in effect, does not comply with any schedule or other requirement imposed pursuant to the variance or exemption;
the Administrator shall issue an order under subsection (g) of this section requiring the public water system to comply with the requirement, or commence a civil action under subsection (b) of this section.
(B) Notice.—If the Administrator takes any action pursuant to this paragraph, the Administrator shall notify an appropriate local elected official, if any, with jurisdiction over the public water system of the action prior to the time that the action is taken.
(b) Judicial determinations in appropriate Federal district courts; civil penalties, separate violations

The Administrator may bring a civil action in the appropriate United States district court to require compliance with any applicable requirement with an order issued under subsection (g) of this section, or with any schedule or other requirement imposed pursuant to a variance or exemption granted under section 300g-4 or 300g-5 of this title if—
(1) authorized under paragraph (1) or (2) of subsection (a) of this section, or
(2) if requested by (A) the chief executive officer of the State in which is located the public water system which is not in compliance with such regulation or requirement, or (B) the agency of such State which has jurisdiction over compliance by public water systems in the State with national primary drinking water regulations or State drinking water regulations.

The court may enter, in an action brought under this subsection, such judgement as protection of public health may require, taking into consideration the time necessary to comply and the availability of alternative water supplies; and, if the court determines that there has been a violation of the regulation or schedule or other requirement with respect to which the action was brought, the court may, taking into account the seriousness of the violation, the population at risk, and other appropriate factors, impose on the violator a civil penalty of not to exceed $25,000 for each day in which such violation occurs.
(c) Notice to persons served
(1) In general

Each owner or operator of a public water system shall give notice of each of the following to the persons served by the system:
(A) Notice of any failure on the part of the public water system to—
(i) comply with an applicable maximum contaminant level or treatment technique requirement of, or a testing procedure prescribed by, a national primary drinking water regulation; or
(ii) perform monitoring required by section 300j-4(a) of this title.
(B) If the public water system is subject to a variance granted under subsection (a)(1)(A), (a)(2), or (e) of section 300g-4 of this title for an inability to meet a maximum contaminant level requirement or is subject to an exemption granted under section 300g-5 of this title, notice of—
(i) the existence of the variance or exemption; and
(ii) any failure to comply with the requirements of any schedule prescribed pursuant to the variance or exemption.
(C) Notice of the concentration level of any unregulated contaminant for which the Administrator has required public notice pursuant to paragraph (2)(E).

(2) Form, manner, and frequency of notice
   (A) In general
      The Administrator shall, by regulation, and after consultation with the States, prescribe the manner, frequency, form, and content for giving notice under this subsection. The regulations shall—
      (i) provide for different frequencies of notice based on the differences between violations that are intermittent or infrequent and violations that are continuous or frequent; and
      (ii) take into account the seriousness of any potential adverse health effects that may be involved.
   (B) State requirements
      (i) In general
         A State may, by rule, establish alternative notification requirements—
         (I) with respect to the form and content of notice given under and in a manner in accordance with subparagraph (C); and
         (II) with respect to the form and content of notice given under subparagraph (D).
      (ii) Contents
         The alternative requirements shall provide the same type and amount of information as required pursuant to this subsection and regulations issued under subparagraph (A).
      (iii) Relationship to section 300g-2
         Nothing in this subparagraph shall be construed or applied to modify the requirements of section 300g-2 of this title.
   (C) Violations with potential to have serious adverse effects on human health
      Regulations issued under subparagraph (A) shall specify notification procedures for each violation by a public water system that has the potential to have serious adverse effects on human health as a result of short-term exposure. Each notice of violation provided under this subparagraph shall—
      (i) be distributed as soon as practicable after the occurrence of the violation, but not later than 24 hours after the occurrence of the violation;
      (ii) provide a clear and readily understandable explanation of—
         (I) the violation;
         (II) the potential adverse effects on human health;
         (III) the steps that the public water system is taking to correct the violation; and
         (IV) the necessity of seeking alternative water supplies until the violation is corrected;
      (iii) be provided to the Administrator or the head of the State agency that has primary enforcement responsibility under section 300g-2 of this title as soon as practicable, but not later than 24 hours after the occurrence of the violation; and
      (iv) as required by the State agency in general regulations of the State agency, or on a case-by-case basis after the consultation referred to in clause (iii), considering the health risks involved—
         (I) be provided to appropriate broadcast media;
         (II) be prominently published in a newspaper of general circulation serving the area not later than 1 day after distribution of a notice pursuant to clause (i) or the date of publication of the next issue of the newspaper; or
         (III) be provided by posting or door-to-door notification in lieu of notification by means of broadcast media or newspaper.
   (D) Written notice
      (i) In general
         Regulations issued under subparagraph (A) shall specify notification procedures for violations other than the violations covered by subparagraph (C). The procedures shall specify that a public water system shall provide written notice to each person served by the system by notice (I) in the first bill (if any) prepared after the date of occurrence of the violation, (II) in an annual report issued not later than 1 year after the date of occurrence of the violation, or (III) by mail or direct delivery as soon as practicable, but not later than 1 year after the date of occurrence of the violation.

(ii) Form and manner of notice
   The Administrator shall prescribe the form and manner of the notice to provide a clear and readily understandable explanation of the violation, any potential adverse health effects, and the steps that the system is taking to seek alternative water supplies, if any, until the violation is corrected.
(E) Unregulated contaminants
   The Administrator may require the owner or operator of a public water system to give notice to the persons served by the system of the concentration levels of an unregulated contaminant required to be monitored under section 300j-4(a) of this title.
(3) Reports
   (A) Annual report by State
      (i) In general
         Not later than January 1, 1998, and annually thereafter, each State that has primary enforcement responsibility under section 300g-2 of this title shall prepare, make readily available to the public, and submit to the Administrator an annual report on violations of national primary drinking water regulations by public water systems in the State, including violations with respect to (I) maximum contaminant levels, (II) treatment requirements, (III) variances and exemptions, and (IV) monitoring requirements determined to be significant by the Administrator after consultation with the States.
      (ii) Distribution
         The State shall publish and distribute summaries of the report and indicate where the full report is available for review.
   (B) Annual report by Administrator
      Not later than July 1, 1998, and annually thereafter, the Administrator shall prepare and make available to the public an annual report summarizing and evaluating reports submitted by States pursuant to subparagraph (A) and notices submitted by public water systems serving Indian Tribes provided to the Administrator pursuant to subparagraph (C) or (D) of paragraph (2) and making recommendations concerning the resources needed to improve compliance with this subchapter. The report shall include information about public water system compliance on Indian reservations and about enforcement activities undertaken and financial assistance provided by the Administrator on Indian reservations, and shall make specific recommendations concerning the resources needed to improve compliance with this subchapter on Indian reservations.
(4) Consumer confidence reports by community water systems
   (A) Annual reports to consumers
      The Administrator, in consultation with public water systems, environmental groups, public interest groups, risk communication experts, and the States, and other interested parties, shall issue regulations within 24 months after August 6, 1996, to require each community water system to mail to each customer of the system at least once annually a report on the level of contaminants in the drinking water purveyed by that system (referred to in this paragraph as a "consumer confidence report"). Such regulations shall provide a brief and plainly worded definition of the terms "maximum contaminant level goal", "maximum contaminant level", "variances", and "exemptions" and brief statements in plain language regarding the health concerns that resulted in regulation of each regulated contaminant. The regulations shall also include a brief and plainly worded explanation regarding contaminants that may reasonably be expected to be present in drinking water, including bottled water. The regulations shall also provide for an Environmental Protection Agency toll-free hotline that consumers can call for more information and explanation.
   (B) Contents of report
      The consumer confidence reports under this paragraph shall include, but not be limited to, each of the following:
      (i) Information on the source of the water purveyed.
      (ii) A brief and plainly worded definition of the terms "maximum contaminant level goal", "maximum contaminant level", "variances", and "exemptions" as provided in the regulations of the Administrator.

(iii) If any regulated contaminant is detected in the water purveyed by the public water system, a statement setting forth (I) the maximum contaminant level goal, (II) the maximum contaminant level, (III) the level of such contaminant in such water system, and (IV) for any regulated contaminant for which there has been a violation of the maximum contaminant level during the year concerned, the brief statement in plain language regarding the health concerns that resulted in regulation of such contaminant, as provided by the Administrator in regulations under subparagraph (A).
(iv) Information on compliance with national primary drinking water regulations, as required by the Administrator, and notice if the system is operating under a variance or exemption and the basis on which the variance or exemption was granted.
(v) Information on the levels of unregulated contaminants for which monitoring is required under section 300j-4(a)(2) of this title (including levels of cryptosporidium and radon where States determine they may be found).
(vi) A statement that the presence of contaminants in drinking water does not necessarily indicate that the drinking water poses a health risk and that more information about contaminants and potential health effects can be obtained by calling the Environmental Protection Agency hotline.

A public water system may include such additional information as it deems appropriate for public education. The Administrator may, for not more than 3 regulated contaminants other than those referred to in subclause (IV) of clause (iii), require a consumer confidence report under this paragraph to include the brief statement in plain language regarding the health concerns that resulted in regulation of the contaminant or contaminants concerned, as provided by the Administrator in regulations under subparagraph (A).

(C) Coverage

The Governor of a State may determine not to apply the mailing requirement of subparagraph (A) to a community water system serving fewer than 10,000 persons. Any such system shall—

(i) inform, in the newspaper notice required by clause (iii) or by other means, its customers that the system will not be mailing the report as required by subparagraph (A);
(ii) make the consumer confidence report available upon request to the public; and
(iii) publish the report referred to in subparagraph (A) annually in one or more local newspapers serving the area in which customers of the system are located.

(D) Alternative to publication

For any community water system which, pursuant to subparagraph (C), is not required to meet the mailing requirement of subparagraph (A) and which serves 500 persons or fewer, the community water system may elect not to comply with clause (i) or (iii) of subparagraph (C). If the community water system so elects, the system shall, at a minimum—

(i) prepare an annual consumer confidence report pursuant to subparagraph (B); and
(ii) provide notice at least once per year to each of its customers by mail, by door-to-door delivery, by posting or by other means authorized by the regulations of the Administrator that the consumer confidence report is available upon request.

(E) Alternative form and content

A State exercising primary enforcement responsibility may establish, by rule, after notice and public comment, alternative requirements with respect to the form and content of consumer confidence reports under this paragraph.

(d) Notice of noncompliance with secondary drinking water regulations

Whenever, on the basis of information available to him, the Administrator finds that within a reasonable time after national secondary drinking water regulations have been promulgated, one or more public water systems in a State do not comply with such secondary regulations, and that such noncompliance appears to result from a failure of such State to take reasonable action to assure that public water systems throughout such State meet such secondary regulations, he shall so notify the State.

(e) State authority to adopt or enforce laws or regulations respecting drinking water regulations or public water systems unaffected
Nothing in this subchapter shall diminish any authority of a State or political subdivision to adopt or enforce any law or regulation respecting drinking water regulations or public water systems, but no such law or regulation shall relieve any person of any requirement otherwise applicable under this subchapter.

(f) Notice and public hearing; availability of recommendations transmitted to State and public water system
If the Administrator makes a finding of noncompliance (described in subparagraph (A) or (B) of subsection (a)(1) of this section) with respect to a public water system in a State which has primary enforcement responsibility, the Administrator may, for the purpose of assisting that State in carrying out such responsibility and upon the petition of such State or public water system or persons served by such system, hold, after appropriate notice, public hearings for the purpose of gathering information from technical or other experts, Federal, State, or other public officials, representatives of such public water system, persons served by such system, and other interested persons on—
  (1) the ways in which such system can within the earliest feasible time be brought into compliance with the regulation or requirement with respect to which such finding was made, and
  (2) the means for the maximum feasible protection of the public health during any period in which such system is not in compliance with a national primary drinking water regulation or requirement applicable to a variance or exemption.
On the basis of such hearings the Administrator shall issue recommendations which shall be sent to such State and public water system and shall be made available to the public and communications media.

(g) Administrative order requiring compliance; notice and hearing; civil penalty; civil actions
  (1) In any case in which the Administrator is authorized to bring a civil action under this section or under section 300j-4 of this title with respect to any applicable requirement, the Administrator also may issue an order to require compliance with such applicable requirement.
  (2) An order issued under this subsection shall not take effect, in the case of a State having primary enforcement responsibility for public water systems in that State, until after the Administrator has provided the State with an opportunity to confer with the Administrator regarding the order. A copy of any order issued under this subsection shall be sent to the appropriate State agency of the State involved if the State has primary enforcement responsibility for public water systems in that State. Any order issued under this subsection shall state with reasonable specificity the nature of the violation. In any case in which an order under this subsection is issued to a corporation, a copy of such order shall be issued to appropriate corporate officers.
  (3) (A) Any person who violates, or fails or refuses to comply with, an order under this subsection shall be liable to the United States for a civil penalty of not more than $25,000 per day of violation.
    (B) In a case in which a civil penalty sought by the Administrator under this paragraph does not exceed $5,000, the penalty shall be assessed by the Administrator after notice and opportunity for a public hearing (unless the person against whom the penalty is assessed requests a hearing on the record in accordance with section 554 of title 5). In a case in which a civil penalty sought by the Administrator under this paragraph exceeds $5,000, but does not exceed $25,000, the penalty shall be assessed by the Administrator after notice and opportunity for a hearing on the record in accordance with section 554 of title 5.
    (C) Whenever any civil penalty sought by the Administrator under this subsection for a violation of an applicable requirement exceeds $25,000, the penalty shall be assessed by a civil action brought by the Administrator in the appropriate United States district court (as determined under the provisions of title 28).
    (D) If any person fails to pay an assessment of a civil penalty after it has become a final and unappealable order, or after the appropriate court of appeals has entered final judgment in favor of the Administrator, the Attorney General shall recover the amount for which such person is liable in any appropriate district court of the United States.

In any such action, the validity and appropriateness of the final order imposing the civil penalty shall not be subject to review.
(h) Consolidation incentive
  (1) In general
   An owner or operator of a public water system may submit to the State in which the system is located (if the State has primary enforcement responsibility under section 300g-2 of this title) or to the Administrator (if the State does not have primary enforcement responsibility) a plan (including specific measures and schedules) for—
   (A) the physical consolidation of the system with 1 or more other systems;
   (B) the consolidation of significant management and administrative functions of the system with 1 or more other systems; or
   (C) the transfer of ownership of the system that may reasonably be expected to improve drinking water quality.
  (2) Consequences of approval
   If the State or the Administrator approves a plan pursuant to paragraph (1), no enforcement action shall be taken pursuant to this part with respect to a specific violation identified in the approved plan prior to the date that is the earlier of the date on which consolidation is completed according to the plan or the date that is 2 years after the plan is approved.
(i) "Applicable requirement" defined
  In this section, the term "applicable requirement" means—
  (1) a requirement of section 300g-1, 300g-3, 300g-4, 300g-5, 300g-6, 300j, or 300j-4 of this title;
  (2) a regulation promulgated pursuant to a section referred to in paragraph (1);
  (3) a schedule or requirement imposed pursuant to a section referred to in paragraph (1); and
  (4) a requirement of, or permit issued under, an applicable State program for which the Administrator has made a determination that the requirements of section 300g-2 of this title have been satisfied, or an applicable State program approved pursuant to this part.

(July 1, 1944, ch. 373, title XIV, Sec. 1414, as added Pub. L. 93-523, Sec. 2(a), Dec. 16, 1974, 88 Stat. 1666; amended Pub. L. 95-190, Sec. 12(b), Nov. 16, 1977, 91 Stat. 1398; Pub. L. 99-339, title I, Secs. 102, 103, June 19, 1986, 100 Stat. 647, 648; Pub. L. 104-182, title I, Secs. 113(a), 114(a), Aug. 6, 1996, 110 Stat. 1634, 1636.)

Amendments

1996—Subsec. (a)(1)(A). Pub. L. 104-182, Sec. 113(a)(1)(A)(i)(II), substituted "with the requirement" for "with such regulation or requirement" in concluding provisions.

Subsec. (a)(1)(A)(i). Pub. L. 104-182, Sec. 113(a)(1)(A)(i)(I), substituted "any applicable requirement" for "any national primary drinking water regulation in effect under section 300g-1 of this title".

Subsec. (a)(1)(B). Pub. L. 104-182, Sec. 113(a)(1)(A)(ii), substituted "such applicable requirement" for "such regulation or requirement".

Subsec. (a)(2). Pub. L. 104-182, Sec. 113(a)(1)(B), added par. (2) and struck out former par. (2) which read as follows: "Whenever, on the basis of information available to him, the Administrator finds during a period during which a State does not have primary enforcement responsibility for public water systems that a public water system in such State—
 (A) for which a variance under section 300g-4(a)(2) or an exemption under section 300g-5(f) of this title is not in effect, does not comply with any national primary drinking water regulation in effect under section 300g-1 of this title, or
 (B) for which a variance under section 300g-4(a)(2) or an exemption under section 300g-5(f) of this title is in effect, does not comply with any schedule or other requirement imposed pursuant thereto,
the Administrator shall issue an order under subsection (g) of this section requiring the public water system to comply with such regulation or requirement or the Administrator shall commence a civil action under subsection (b) of this section."

Subsec. (b). Pub. L. 104-182, Sec. 113(a)(2), substituted "any applicable requirement" for "a national primary drinking water regulation" in introductory provisions.

Subsec. (c). Pub. L. 104-182, Sec. 114(a), amended subsec. (c) generally. Prior to amendment, subsec. (c) related to notice of owner or operator of public water system to persons served, regulations for form, manner, and frequency of notice, amendment of regulations to provide different types and frequencies of notice, and penalties.

Subsec. (g)(1). Pub. L. 104-182, Sec. 113(a)(3)(A), substituted "applicable requirement" for "regulation, schedule, or other requirement" in two places.

Subsec. (g)(2). Pub. L. 104-182, Sec. 113(a)(3)(B), substituted "effect, in the case" for "effect until after notice and opportunity for public hearing and, in the case" and "regarding the order" for "regarding the proposed order" and struck out "proposed to be" after "A copy of any order".

Subsec. (g)(3)(B). Pub. L. 104-182, Sec. 113(a)(3)(C)(i), added subpar. (B) and struck out former subpar. (B) which read as follows: "Whenever any civil penalty sought by the Administrator under this paragraph does not exceed a total of $5,000, the penalty shall be assessed by the Administrator after notice and opportunity for a hearing on the record in accordance with section 554 of title 5."

Subsec. (g)(3)(C). Pub. L. 104-182, Sec. 113(a)(3)(C)(ii), substituted "subsection for a violation of an applicable requirement exceeds $25,000" for "paragraph exceeds $5,000".

Subsecs. (h), (i). Pub. L. 104-182, Sec. 113(a)(4), added subsecs. (h) and (i).

1986—Pub. L. 99-339, Sec. 102(d)(2), substituted "Enforcement" for "Failure of State to assure enforcement" in section catchline.

Subsec. (a)(1)(A). Pub. L. 99-339, Sec. 102(a), inserted "and such public water system" after "notify the State" in provisions following cl. (ii).

Subsec. (a)(1)(B). Pub. L. 99-339, Sec. 102(b)(1), amended subpar. (B) generally, substituting provisions which relate to issuance of an order to public water system to comply with regulations, or commencement of civil action if the State has not commenced appropriate enforcement action for provisions which related to public notice of noncompliance and commencement of civil action by Administrator if State failed to take steps to obtain compliance by public water system.

Subsec. (a)(2). Pub. L. 99-339, Sec. 102(b)(2), substituted "the Administrator shall issue an order under subsection (g) of this section requiring the public water system to comply with such regulation or requirement or the Administrator shall commence a civil action under subsection (b) of this section" for "he may commence a civil action under subsection (b) of this section".

Subsec. (b). Pub. L. 99-339, Sec. 102(c), inserted ", with an order issued under subsection (g) of this section," before "or with any schedule" and substituted "there has been a violation" for "there has been a willful violation" and "$25,000" for "$5,000".

Subsec. (c). Pub. L. 99-339, Sec. 103, substituted provisions relating to amendment of regulations within fifteen months after June 19, 1986, to provide different types and frequencies of notice based on the differences between violations which are intermittent or continuous, manner and content of notices, notice required to public served by owner or operator of public water system, and civil penalty of $25,000, for provisions relating to form, manner, and frequency of notice based on three month billing period for water bills, notice required to public served by owner or operator of public water system, and civil penalty of $5,000.

Subsec. (g). Pub. L. 99-339, Sec. 102(d), added subsec. (g).

1977—Subsec. (c). Pub. L. 95-190 inserted provisions relating to frequency of required notice, and notice respecting contaminant levels, and substituted "issued under this subsection" for "thereunder".

Section Referred to in Other Sections

This section is referred to in sections 300g-4, 300g-5, 300j-7 of this title.

VARIANCES

42 USC 300g-4

(a) Characteristics of raw water sources; specific treatment technique; notice to Administrator, reasons for variance; compliance, enforcement; approval or revision of schedules and revocation of variances; review of variances and schedules; publication in Federal Register, notice and results of review; notice to State; considerations respecting abuse of discretion in granting variances or failing to prescribe schedules; State corrective action; authority of Administrator in a State without primary enforcement responsibility; alternative treatment techniques

Notwithstanding any other provision of this part, variances from national primary drinking water regulations may be granted as follows:

(1) (A) A State which has primary enforcement responsibility for public water systems may grant one or more variances from an applicable national primary drinking water regulation to one or more public water systems within its jurisdiction which, because of characteristics of the raw water sources which are reasonably available to the systems, cannot meet the requirements respecting the maximum contaminant levels of such drinking water regulation. A variance may be issued to a system on condition that the system install the best technology, treatment techniques, or other means, which the Administrator finds are available (taking costs into consideration), and based upon an evaluation satisfactory to the State that indicates that alternative sources of water are not reasonably available to the system. The Administrator shall propose and promulgate his finding of the best available technology, treatment techniques or other means available for each contaminant for purposes of this subsection at the time he proposes and promulgates a maximum contaminant level for each such contaminant. The Administrator's finding of best available technology, treatment techniques or other means for purposes of this subsection may vary depending on the number of persons served by the system or for other physical conditions related to engineering feasibility and costs of compliance with maximum contaminant levels as considered appropriate by the Administrator. Before a State may grant a variance under this subparagraph, the State must find that the variance will not result in an unreasonable risk to health. If a State grants a public water system a variance under this subparagraph, the State shall prescribe at the the[1] time the variance is granted, a schedule for—

  (i) compliance (including increments of progress) by the public water system with each containment level requirement with respect to which the variance was granted, and

  (ii) implementation by the public water system of such additional control measures as the State may require for each contaminant, subject to such contaminant level requirement, during the period ending on the date compliance with such requirement is required.

Before a schedule prescribed by a State pursuant to this subparagraph may take effect, the State shall provide notice and opportunity for a public hearing on the schedule. A notice given pursuant to the preceding sentence may cover the prescribing of more than one such schedule and a hearing held pursuant to such notice shall include each of the schedules covered by the notice. A schedule prescribed pursuant to this subparagraph for a public water system granted a variance shall require compliance by the system with each contaminant level requirement with respect to which the variance was granted as expeditiously as practicable (as the State may reasonably determine).

(B) A State which has primary enforcement responsibility for public water systems may grant to one or more public water systems within its jurisdiction one or more variances from any provision of the national primary drinking water regulation which requires the use of a specified treatment technique with respect to a contaminant if the public water system applying for the variance demonstrates to the satisfaction of the State that such treatment technique is not necessary to protect the health of persons because of the nature of the raw water source of such system. A variance granted under this subparagraph shall be conditioned on such monitoring and other requirements as the Administrator may prescribe.

(C) Before a variance proposed to be granted by a State under subparagraph (A) or (B) may take effect, such State shall provide notice and opportunity for public hearing on the proposed variance. A notice given pursuant to the preceding sentence may cover the granting of more than one variance and a hearing held pursuant to such notice shall include each of the variances covered by the notice. The State shall promptly

---

[1] So in original.

notify the Administrator of all variances granted by it. Such notification shall contain the reason for the variance (and in the case of a variance under subparagraph (A), the basis for the finding required by that subparagraph before the granting of the variance) and documentation of the need for the variance.

(D) Each public water system's variance granted by a State under subparagraph (A) shall be conditioned by the State upon compliance by the public water system with the schedule prescribed by the State pursuant to that subparagraph. The requirements of each schedule prescribed by a State pursuant to that subparagraph shall be enforceable by the State under its laws. Any requirement of a schedule on which a variance granted under that subparagraph is conditioned may be enforced under section 300g-3 of this title as if such requirement was part of a national primary drinking water regulation.

(E) Each schedule prescribed by a State pursuant to subparagraph (A) shall be deemed approved by the Administrator unless the variance for which it was prescribed is revoked by the Administrator under subparagraph (G) or the schedule is revised by the Administrator under such subparagraph.

(F) Not later than 18 months after the effective date of the interim national primary drinking water regulations the Administrator shall complete a comprehensive review of the variances granted under subparagraph (A) (and schedules prescribed pursuant thereto) and under subparagraph (B) by the States during the one-year period beginning on such effective date. The Administrator shall conduct such subsequent reviews of variances and schedules as he deems necessary to carry out the purposes of this subchapter, but each subsequent review shall be completed within each 3-year period following the completion of the first review under this subparagraph. Before conducting any review under this subparagraph, the Administrator shall publish notice of the proposed review in the Federal Register. Such notice shall (i) provide information respecting the location of data and other information respecting the variances to be reviewed (including data and other information concerning new scientific matters bearing on such variances), and (ii) advise of the opportunity to submit comments on the variances reviewed and on the need for continuing them. Upon completion of any such review, the Administrator shall publish in the Federal Register the results of his review together with findings responsive to comments submitted in connection with such review.

(G) (i) If the Administrator finds that a State has, in a substantial number of instances, abused its discretion in granting variances under subparagraph (A) or (B) or that in a substantial number of cases the State has failed to prescribe schedules in accordance with subparagraph (A), the Administrator shall notify the State of his findings. In determining if a State has abused its discretion in granting variances in a substantial number of instances, the Administrator shall consider the number of persons who are affected by the variances and if the requirements applicable to the granting of the variances were complied with. A notice under this clause shall—

(I) identify each public water system with respect to which the finding was made,
(II) specify the reasons for the finding, and
(III) as appropriate, propose revocations of specific variances or propose revised schedules or other requirements for specific public water systems granted variances, or both.

(ii) The Administrator shall provide reasonable notice and public hearing on the provisions of each notice given pursuant to clause (i) of this subparagraph. After a hearing on a notice pursuant to such clause, the Administrator shall (I) rescind the finding for which the notice was given and promptly notify the State of such rescission, or (II) promulgate (with such modifications as he deems appropriate) such variance revocations and revised schedules or other requirements proposed in such notice as he deems appropriate. Not later than 180 days after the date a notice is given pursuant to clause (i) of this subparagraph, the Administrator shall complete the hearing on the notice and take the action required by the preceding sentence.

(iii) If a State is notified under clause (i) of this subparagraph of a finding of the Administrator made with respect to a variance granted a public water system within that State or to a schedule or other requirement for a variance and if, before a revocation of such variance or a revision of such schedule or other requirement promulgated by the Administrator takes effect, the State takes corrective action with respect to such variance or schedule or other requirement which the Administrator determines makes his finding inapplicable to such variance or schedule or other requirement, the Administrator shall rescind the application of his finding to that variance on schedule or other requirement. No variance revocation or revised schedule or other requirement may take effect before the expiration of 90 days following the date of the notice in which the revocation or revised schedule or other requirement was proposed.
(2) If a State does not have primary enforcement responsibility for public water systems, the Administrator shall have the same authority to grant variances in such State as the State would have under paragraph (1) if it had primary enforcement responsibility.
(3) The Administrator may grant a variance from any treatment technique requirement of a national primary drinking water regulation upon a showing by any person that an alternative treatment technique not included in such requirement is at least as efficient in lowering the level of the contaminant with respect to which such requirement was prescribed. A variance under this paragraph shall be conditioned on the use of the alternative treatment technique which is the basis of the variance.

(b) Enforcement of schedule or other requirement

Any schedule or other requirement on which a variance granted under paragraph (1)(B) or (2) of subsection (a) of this section is conditioned may be enforced under section 300g-3 of this title as if such schedule or other requirement was part of a national primary drinking water regulation.

(c) Applications for variances; regulations: reasonable time for acting

If an application for a variance under subsection (a) of this section is made, the State receiving the application or the Administrator, as the case may be, shall act upon such application within a reasonable period (as determined under regulations prescribed by the Administrator) after the date of its submission.

(d) "Treatment technique requirement" defined

For purposes of this section, the term "treatment technique requirement" means a requirement in a national primary drinking water regulation which specifies for a contaminant (in accordance with section 300f(1)(C)(ii) of this title) each treatment technique known to the Administrator which leads to a reduction in the level of such contaminant sufficient to satisfy the requirements of section 300g-1(b) of this title.

(e) Small system variances
(1) In general

A State exercising primary enforcement responsibility for public water systems under section 300g-2 of this title (or the Administrator in nonprimacy States) may grant a variance under this subsection for compliance with a requirement specifying a maximum contaminant level or treatment technique contained in a national primary drinking water regulation to—
(A) public water systems serving 3,300 or fewer persons; and
(B) with the approval of the Administrator pursuant to paragraph (9), public water systems serving more than 3,300 persons but fewer than 10,000 persons,
if the variance meets each requirement of this subsection.
(2) Availability of variances

A public water system may receive a variance pursuant to paragraph (1), if—
(A) the Administrator has identified a variance technology under section 300g-1(b)(15) of this title that is applicable to the size and source water quality conditions of the public water system;
(B) the public water system installs, operates, and maintains, in accordance with guidance or regulations issued by the Administrator, such treatment technology, treatment technique, or other means; and

(C) the State in which the system is located determines that the conditions of paragraph (3) are met.
(3) Conditions for granting variances
A variance under this subsection shall be available only to a system—
   (A) that cannot afford to comply, in accordance with affordability criteria established by the Administrator (or the State in the case of a State that has primary enforcement responsibility under section 300g-2 of this title), with a national primary drinking water regulation, including compliance through—
      (i) treatment;
      (ii) alternative source of water supply; or
      (iii) restructuring or consolidation (unless the Administrator (or the State in the case of a State that has primary enforcement responsibility under section 300g-2 of this title) makes a written determination that restructuring or consolidation is not practicable); and
   (B) for which the Administrator (or the State in the case of a State that has primary enforcement responsibility under section 300g-2 of this title) determines that the terms of the variance ensure adequate protection of human health, considering the quality of the source water for the system and the removal efficiencies and expected useful life of the treatment technology required by the variance.
(4) Compliance schedules
A variance granted under this subsection shall require compliance with the conditions of the variance not later than 3 years after the date on which the variance is granted, except that the Administrator (or the State in the case of a State that has primary enforcement responsibility under section 300g-2 of this title) may allow up to 2 additional years to comply with a variance technology, secure an alternative source of water, restructure or consolidate if the Administrator (or the State) determines that additional time is necessary for capital improvements, or to allow for financial assistance provided pursuant to section 300j-12 of this title or any other Federal or State program.
(5) Duration of variances
The Administrator (or the State in the case of a State that has primary enforcement responsibility under section 300g-2 of this title) shall review each variance granted under this subsection not less often than every 5 years after the compliance date established in the variance to determine whether the system remains eligible for the variance and is conforming to each condition of the variance.
(6) Ineligibility for variances
A variance shall not be available under this subsection for—
   (A) any maximum contaminant level or treatment technique for a contaminant with respect to which a national primary drinking water regulation was promulgated prior to January 1, 1986; or
   (B) a national primary drinking water regulation for a microbial contaminant (including a bacterium, virus, or other organism) or an indicator or treatment technique for a microbial contaminant.
(7) Regulations and guidance
   (A) In general
   Not later than 2 years after August 6, 1996, and in consultation with the States, the Administrator shall promulgate regulations for variances to be granted under this subsection. The regulations shall, at a minimum, specify—
      (i) procedures to be used by the Administrator or a State to grant or deny variances, including requirements for notifying the Administrator and consumers of the public water system that a variance is proposed to be granted (including information regarding the contaminant and variance) and requirements for a public hearing on the variance before the variance is granted;
      (ii) requirements for the installation and proper operation of variance technology that is identified (pursuant to section 300g-1(b)(15) of this title) for small systems and the financial and technical capability to operate the treatment system, including operator training and certification;
      (iii) eligibility criteria for a variance for each national primary drinking water regulation, including requirements for the quality of the source water (pursuant to section 300g-1(b)(15)(A) of this title); and

(iv) information requirements for variance applications.
(B) Affordability criteria
Not later than 18 months after August 6, 1996, the Administrator, in consultation with the States and the Rural Utilities Service of the Department of Agriculture, shall publish information to assist the States in developing affordability criteria. The affordability criteria shall be reviewed by the States not less often than every 5 years to determine if changes are needed to the criteria.
(8) Review by the Administrator
(A) In general
The Administrator shall periodically review the program of each State that has primary enforcement responsibility for public water systems under section 300g-2 of this title with respect to variances to determine whether the variances granted by the State comply with the requirements of this subsection. With respect to affordability, the determination of the Administrator shall be limited to whether the variances granted by the State comply with the affordability criteria developed by the State.
(B) Notice and publication
If the Administrator determines that variances granted by a State are not in compliance with affordability criteria developed by the State and the requirements of this subsection, the Administrator shall notify the State in writing of the deficiencies and make public the determination.
(9) Approval of variances
A State proposing to grant a variance under this subsection to a public water system serving more than 3,300 and fewer than 10,000 persons shall submit the variance to the Administrator for review and approval prior to the issuance of the variance. The Administrator shall approve the variance if it meets each of the requirements of this subsection. The Administrator shall approve or disapprove the variance within 90 days. If the Administrator disapproves a variance under this paragraph, the Administrator shall notify the State in writing of the reasons for disapproval and the variance may be resubmitted with modifications to address the objections stated by the Administrator.
(10) Objections to variances
(A) By the Administrator
The Administrator may review and object to any variance proposed to be granted by a State, if the objection is communicated to the State not later than 90 days after the State proposes to grant the variance. If the Administrator objects to the granting of a variance, the Administrator shall notify the State in writing of each basis for the objection and propose a modification to the variance to resolve the concerns of the Administrator. The State shall make the recommended modification or respond in writing to each objection. If the State issues the variance without resolving the concerns of the Administrator, the Administrator may overturn the State decision to grant the variance if the Administrator determines that the State decision does not comply with this subsection.
(B) Petition by consumers
Not later than 30 days after a State exercising primary enforcement responsibility for public water systems under section 300g-2 of this title proposes to grant a variance for a public water system, any person served by the system may petition the Administrator to object to the granting of a variance. The Administrator shall respond to the petition and determine whether to object to the variance under subparagraph (A) not later than 60 days after the receipt of the petition.
(C) Timing
No variance shall be granted by a State until the later of the following:
(i) 90 days after the State proposes to grant a variance.
(ii) If the Administrator objects to the variance, the date on which the State makes the recommended modifications or responds in writing to each objection.

(July 1, 1944, ch. 373, title XIV, Sec. 1415, as added Pub. L. 93-523, Sec. 2(a), Dec. 16, 1974, 88 Stat. 1669; amended Pub. L. 99-339, title I, Sec. 104, June 19, 1986, 100 Stat. 649; Pub. L. 104-182, title I, Secs. 102(c)(1), 115, 116, title V, Sec. 501(a)(3), Aug. 6, 1996, 110 Stat. 1621, 1641, 1691.)

Amendments

1996—Subsec. (a)(1)(A). Pub. L. 104-182, Sec. 501(a)(3), inserted "the" before "time the variance is granted," in introductory provisions.

Pub. L. 104-182, Sec. 115, in second sentence, substituted "be issued to a system on condition that the system install" for "only be issued to a system after the system's application of" and inserted ", and based upon an evaluation satisfactory to the State that indicates that alternative sources of water are not reasonably available to the system" after "(taking costs into consideration)".

Subsec. (d). Pub. L. 104-182, Sec. 102(c)(1), substituted "section 300g-1(b)" for "section 300g-1(b)(3)".

Subsec. (e). Pub. L. 104-182, Sec. 116, added subsec. (e).

1986—Subsec. (a)(1)(A). Pub. L. 99-339, Sec. 104(1)-(3), substituted "such drinking water regulation. A variance may only be issued to a system after the system's application" for "such drinking water regulation despite application", struck out "generally" after "finds are", inserted provisions relating to proposal and promulgation by Administrator of a finding on best available technology, treatment techniques or other means available for each contaminant at time of proposal and promulgation of maximum contaminant levels, and substituted "at the time" for "within one year of the date".

Subsec. (a)(1)(A)(ii). Pub. L. 99-339, Sec. 104(4), substituted "water system of such additional control" for "water system of such control".

Section Referred to in Other Sections

This section is referred to in sections 300g, 300g-1, 300g-2, 300g-3, 300g-5, 300g-9, 300j-2, 300j-4, 300j-7, 300j-8 of this title.

EXEMPTIONS

42 USC 300g-5

(a) Requisite findings

A State which has primary enforcement responsibility may exempt any public water system within the State's jurisdiction from any requirement respecting a maximum contaminant level or any treatment technique requirement, or from both, of an applicable national primary drinking water regulation upon a finding that—

 (1) due to compelling factors (which may include economic factors, including qualification of the public water system as a system serving a disadvantaged community pursuant to section 300j-12(d) of this title), the public water system is unable to comply with such contaminant level or treatment technique requirement, or to implement measures to develop an alternative source of water supply,

 (2) the public water system was in operation on the effective date of such contaminant level or treatment technique requirement, or, for a system that was not in operation by that date, only if no reasonable alternative source of drinking water is available to such new system,

 (3) the granting of the exemption will not result in an unreasonable risk to health;[1] and

 (4) management or restructuring changes (or both) cannot reasonably be made that will result in compliance with this subchapter or, if compliance cannot be achieved, improve the quality of the drinking water.

(b) Compliance schedule and implementation of control measures; notice and hearing; dates for compliance with schedule; compliance, enforcement; approval or revision of schedules and revocation of exemptions

 (1) If a State grants a public water system an exemption under subsection (a) of this section, the State shall prescribe, at the time the exemption is granted, a schedule for—

  (A) compliance (including increments of progress or measures to develop an alternative source of water supply) by the public water system with each contaminant level requirement or treatment technique requirement with respect to which the exemption was granted, and

---

[1] So in original. The semicolon probably should be a comma.

(B) implementation by the public water system of such control measures as the State may require for each contaminant, subject to such contaminant level requirement or treatment technique requirement, during the period ending on the date compliance with such requirement is required.

Before a schedule prescribed by a State pursuant to this subsection may take effect, the State shall provide notice and opportunity for a public hearing on the schedule. A notice given pursuant to the preceding sentence may cover the prescribing of more than one such schedule and a hearing held pursuant to such notice shall include each of the schedules covered by the notice.

(2) (A) A schedule prescribed pursuant to this subsection for a public water system granted an exemption under subsection (a) of this section shall require compliance by the system with each contaminant level and treatment technique requirement with respect to which the exemption was granted as expeditiously as practicable (as the State may reasonably determine) but not later than 3 years after the otherwise applicable compliance date established in section 300g-1(b)(10) of this title.

(B) No exemption shall be granted unless the public water system establishes that—
  (i) the system cannot meet the standard without capital improvements which cannot be completed prior to the date established pursuant to section 300g-1(b)(10) of this title;
  (ii) in the case of a system which needs financial assistance for the necessary improvements, the system has entered into an agreement to obtain such financial assistance or assistance pursuant to section 300j-12 of this title, or any other Federal or State program is reasonably likely to be available within the period of the exemption; or
  (iii) the system has entered into an enforceable agreement to become a part of a regional public water system; and
  the system is taking all practicable steps to meet the standard.

(C) In the case of a system which does not serve more than a population of 3,300 and which needs financial assistance for the necessary improvements, an exemption granted under clause (i) or (ii) of subparagraph (B) may be renewed for one or more additional 2-year periods, but not to exceed a total of 6 years, if the system establishes that it is taking all practicable steps to meet the requirements of subparagraph (B).

(D) Limitation.—A public water system may not receive an exemption under this section if the system was granted a variance under section 300g-4(e) of this title.

(3) Each public water system's exemption granted by a State under subsection (a) of this section shall be conditioned by the State upon compliance by the public water system with the schedule prescribed by the State pursuant to this subsection. The requirements of each schedule prescribed by a State pursuant to this subsection shall be enforceable by the State under its laws. Any requirement of a schedule on which an exemption granted under this section is conditioned may be enforced under section 300g-3 of this title as if such requirement was part of a national primary drinking water regulation.

(4) Each schedule prescribed by a State pursuant to this subsection shall be deemed approved by the Administrator unless the exemption for which it was prescribed is revoked by the Administrator under subsection (d)(2) of this section or the schedule is revised by the Administrator under such subsection.

(c) Notice to Administrator; reasons for exemption

Each State which grants an exemption under subsection (a) of this section shall promptly notify the Administrator of the granting of such exemption. Such notification shall contain the reasons for the exemption (including the basis for the finding required by subsection (a)(3) of this section before the exemption may be granted) and document the need for the exemption.

(d) Review of exemptions and schedules; publication in Federal Register, notice and results of review; notice to State; considerations respecting abuse of discretion in granting exemptions or failing to prescribe schedules; State corrective action

(1) Not later than 18 months after the effective date of the interim national primary drinking water regulations the Administrator shall complete a comprehensive review of the exemptions granted (and schedules prescribed pursuant thereto) by the States during the one-year period beginning on such effective date. The Administrator shall conduct such sub-

sequent reviews of exemptions and schedules as he deems necessary to carry out the purposes of this subchapter, but each subsequent review shall be completed within each 3-year period following the completion of the first review under this subparagraph. Before conducting any review under this subparagraph, the Administrator shall publish notice of the proposed review in the Federal Register. Such notice shall (A) provide information respecting the location of data and other information respecting the exemptions to be reviewed (including data and other information concerning new scientific matters bearing on such exemptions), and (B) advise of the opportunity to submit comments on the exemptions reviewed and on the need for continuing them. Upon completion of any such review, the Administrator shall publish in the Federal Register the results of his review, together with findings responsive to comments submitted in connection with such review.

(2) (A) If the Administrator finds that a State has, in a substantial number of instances, abused its discretion in granting exemptions under subsection (a) of this section or failed to prescribe schedules in accordance with subsection (b) of this section, the Administrator shall notify the State of his findings. In determining if a State has abused its discretion in granting exemptions in a substantial number of instances, the Administrator shall consider the number of persons who are affected by the exemptions and if the requirements applicable to the granting of the exemptions were complied with. A notice under this subparagraph shall—
  (i) identify each exempt public water system with respect to which the finding was made,
  (ii) specify the reasons for the finding, and
  (iii) as appropriate, propose revocations of specific exemptions or propose revised schedules for specific exempt public water systems, or both.

(B) The Administrator shall provide reasonable notice and public hearing on the provisions of each notice given pursuant to subparagraph (A). After a hearing on notice pursuant to subparagraph (A), the Administrator shall (i) rescind the finding for which the notice was given and promptly notify the State of such rescission, or (ii) promulgate (with such modifications as he deems appropriate) such exemption revocations and revised schedules proposed in such notice as he deems appropriate. Not later than 180 days after the date a notice is given pursuant to subparagraph (A), the Administrator shall complete the hearing on the notice and take the action required by the preceding sentence.

(C) If a State is notified under subparagraph (A) of a finding of the Administrator made with respect to an exemption granted a public water system within that State or to a schedule prescribed pursuant to such an exemption and if before a revocation of such exemption or a revision of such schedule promulgated by the Administrator takes effect the State takes corrective action with respect to such exemption or schedule which the Administrator determines makes his finding inapplicable to such exemption or schedule, the Administrator shall rescind the application of his finding to that exemption or schedule. No exemption revocation or revised schedule may take effect before the expiration of 90 days following the date of the notice in which the revocation or revised schedule was proposed.

(e) "Treatment technique requirement" defined

For purposes of this section, the term "treatment technique requirement" means a requirement in a national primary drinking water regulation which specifies for a contaminant (in accordance with section 300f(1)(C)(ii) of this title) each treatment technique known to the Administrator which leads to a reduction in the level of such contaminant sufficient to satisfy the requirements of section 300g-1(b) of this title.

(f) Authority of Administrator in a State without primary enforcement responsibility

If a State does not have primary enforcement responsibility for public water systems, the Administrator shall have the same authority to exempt public water systems in such State from maximum contaminant level requirements and treatment technique requirements under the same conditions and in the same manner as the State would be authorized to grant exemptions under this section if it had primary enforcement responsibility.

(g) Applications for exemptions; regulations; reasonable time for acting
If an application for an exemption under this section is made, the State receiving the application or the Administrator, as the case may be, shall act upon such application within a reasonable period (as determined under regulations prescribed by the Administrator) after the date of its submission.

(July 1, 1944, ch. 373, title XIV, Sec. 1416, as added Pub. L. 93-523, Sec. 2(a), Dec. 16, 1974, 88 Stat. 1672; amended Pub. L. 95-190, Sec. 10(a), Nov. 16, 1977, 91 Stat. 1398; Pub. L. 96-502, Secs. 1, 4(b), Dec. 5, 1980, 94 Stat. 2737, 2738; Pub. L. 99-339, title I, Secs. 101(c)(4), 105, June 19, 1986, 100 Stat. 646, 649; Pub. L. 104-182, title I, Sec. 117(a), Aug. 6, 1996, 110 Stat. 1644.)

Amendments

1996—Subsec. (a)(1). Pub. L. 104-182, Sec. 117(a)(1), inserted ", including qualification of the public water system as a system serving a disadvantaged community pursuant to section 300j-12(d) of this title" after "(which may include economic factors" and "or to implement measures to develop an alternative source of water supply," after "treatment technique requirement,".

Subsec. (a)(4). Pub. L. 104-182, Sec. 117(a)(2), added par. (4).

Subsec. (b)(1)(A). Pub. L. 104-182, Sec. 117(a)(3), substituted "(including increments of progress or measures to develop an alternative source of water supply)" for "(including increments of progress)" and "requirement or treatment" for "requirement and treatment".

Subsec. (b)(2)(A). Pub. L. 104-182, Sec. 117(a)(4)(A), substituted "not later than 3 years after the otherwise applicable compliance date established in section 300g-1(b)(10) of this title." for "(except as provided in subparagraph (B))—

(i) in the case of an exemption granted with respect to a contaminant level or treatment technique requirement prescribed by the national primary drinking water regulations promulgated under section 300g-1(a) of this title, not later than 12 months after June 19, 1986; and

(ii) in the case of an exemption granted with respect to a contaminant level or treatment technique requirement prescribed by national primary drinking water regulations, other than a regulation referred to in section 300g-1(a) of this title, 12 months after the date of the issuance of the exemption."

Subsec. (b)(2)(B). Pub. L. 104-182, Sec. 117(a)(4)(A), substituted "No exemption shall be granted unless" for "The final date for compliance provided in any schedule in the case of any exemption may be extended by the State (in the case of a State which has primary enforcement responsibility) or by the Administrator (in any other case) for a period not to exceed 3 years after the date of the issuance of the exemption if" in introductory provisions.

Subsec. (b)(2)(B)(i). Pub. L. 104-182, Sec. 117(a)(4)(B), substituted "prior to the date established pursuant to section 300g-1(b)(10) of this title" for "within the period of such exemption".

Subsec. (b)(2)(B)(ii). Pub. L. 104-182, Sec. 117(a)(4)(C), inserted "or assistance pursuant to section 300j-12 of this title, or any other Federal or State program is reasonably likely to be available within the period of the exemption" after "such financial assistance".

Subsec. (b)(2)(C). Pub. L. 104-182, Sec. 117(a)(4)(D), substituted "a population of 3,300" for "500 service connections" and inserted ", but not to exceed a total of 6 years," after "for one or more additional 2-year periods".

Subsec. (b)(2)(D). Pub. L. 104-182, Sec. 117(a)(4)(E), added subpar. (D).

1986—Subsec. (b)(1). Pub. L. 99-339, Sec. 105(a)(1), substituted "at the time" for "within one year of the date".

Subsec. (b)(2)(A)(i). Pub. L. 99-339, Sec. 105(a)(2), struck out "interim" before "national primary" and substituted "not later than 12 months after June 19, 1986" for "not later than January 1, 1984".

Subsec. (b)(2)(A)(ii). Pub. L. 99-339, Sec. 105(a)(3), struck out "revised" before "national primary" and substituted "other than a regulation referred to in section 300g-1(a) of this title, 12 months after the date of the issuance of the exemption" for "not later than seven years after the date such requirement takes effect".

Subsec. (b)(2)(B). Pub. L. 99-339, Sec. 105(a)(4), amended subpar. (B) generally. Prior to amendment, subpar. (B) read as follows: "Notwithstanding clauses (i) and (ii) of subparagraph (A) of this paragraph, the final date for compliance prescribed in a schedule prescribed pursuant to this subsection for an exemption granted for a public water system which (as determined by the State granting the exemption) has entered into an enforceable agreement to become a part of a regional public water system shall—
    (i) in the case of a schedule prescribed for an exemption granted with respect to a contaminant level or treatment technique requirement prescribed by interim national primary drinking water regulations, be not later than January 1, 1986; and
    (ii) in the case of a schedule prescribed for an exemption granted with respect to a contaminant level or treatment technique requirement prescribed by revised national primary drinking water regulations, be not later than nine years after such requirement takes effect."

Subsec. (b)(2)(C). Pub. L. 99-339, Sec. 105(a)(4), added subpar. (C).

Subsec. (e). Pub. L. 99-339, Sec. 101(c)(4), substituted "300g-1(b)" for "300g-1(b)(3)".

1980—Subsec. (a)(2). Pub. L. 96-502, Sec. 4(b), substituted "treatment technique requirement, or, for a system that was not in operation by that date, only if no reasonable alternative source of drinking water is available to such new system, and" for "treatment technique requirement, and".

Subsec. (b)(2)(A)(i). Pub. L. 96-502, Sec. 1, substituted "January 1, 1984" for "January 1, 1981".

Subsec. (b)(2)(B)(i). Pub. L. 96-502, Sec. 1, substituted "January 1, 1986" for "January 1, 1983".

1977—Subsec. (b)(1). Pub. L. 95-190 substituted "contaminant" for "containment" wherever appearing.

Section Referred to in Other Sections

This section is referred to in sections 300g, 300g-2, 300g-3, 300g-9, 300j-2, 300j-7, 300j-8 of this title.

PROHIBITION ON USE OF LEAD PIPES, SOLDER, AND FLUX

42 USC 300g-6

(a) In general
  (1) Prohibitions
    (A) In general
    No person may use any pipe, any pipe or plumbing fitting or fixture, any solder, or any flux, after June 19, 1986, in the installation or repair of—
      (i) any public water system; or
      (ii) any plumbing in a residential or nonresidential facility providing water for human consumption,
    that is not lead free (within the meaning of subsection (d) of this section).
    (B) Leaded joints
    Subparagraph (A) shall not apply to leaded joints necessary for the repair of cast iron pipes.
  (2) Public notice requirements
    (A) In general
    Each owner or operator of a public water system shall identify and provide notice to persons that may be affected by lead contamination of their drinking water where such contamination results from either or both of the following:
      (i) The lead content in the construction materials of the public water distribution system.
      (ii) Corrosivity of the water supply sufficient to cause leaching of lead.
    The notice shall be provided in such manner and form as may be reasonably required by the Administrator. Notice under this paragraph shall be provided notwithstanding the absence of a violation of any national drinking water standard.

(B) Contents of notice

Notice under this paragraph shall provide a clear and readily understandable explanation of—
   (i) the potential sources of lead in the drinking water,
   (ii) potential adverse health effects,
   (iii) reasonably available methods of mitigating known or potential lead content in drinking water,
   (iv) any steps the system is taking to mitigate lead content in drinking water, and
   (v) the necessity for seeking alternative water supplies, if any.

(3) Unlawful acts

Effective 2 years after August 6, 1996, it shall be unlawful—
   (A) for any person to introduce into commerce any pipe, or any pipe or plumbing fitting or fixture, that is not lead free, except for a pipe that is used in manufacturing or industrial processing;
   (B) for any person engaged in the business of selling plumbing supplies, except manufacturers, to sell solder or flux that is not lead free; or
   (C) for any person to introduce into commerce any solder or flux that is not lead free unless the solder or flux bears a prominent label stating that it is illegal to use the solder or flux in the installation or repair of any plumbing providing water for human consumption.

(b) State enforcement

(1) Enforcement of prohibition

The requirements of subsection (a)(1) of this section shall be enforced in all States effective 24 months after June 19, 1986. States shall enforce such requirements through State or local plumbing codes, or such other means of enforcement as the State may determine to be appropriate.

(2) Enforcement of public notice requirements

The requirements of subsection (a)(2) of this section shall apply in all States effective 24 months after June 19, 1986.

(c) Penalties

If the Administrator determines that a State is not enforcing the requirements of subsection (a) of this section as required pursuant to subsection (b) of this section, the Administrator may withhold up to 5 percent of Federal funds available to that State for State program grants under section 300j-2(a) of this title.

(d) "Lead free" defined

For purposes of this section, the term "lead free"—
   (1) when used with respect to solders and flux refers to solders and flux containing not more than 0.2 percent lead;
   (2) when used with respect to pipes and pipe fittings refers to pipes and pipe fittings containing not more than 8.0 percent lead; and
   (3) when used with respect to plumbing fittings and fixtures, refers to plumbing fittings and fixtures in compliance with standards established in accordance with subsection (e) of this section.

(e) Plumbing fittings and fixtures

(1) In general

The Administrator shall provide accurate and timely technical information and assistance to qualified third-party certifiers in the development of voluntary standards and testing protocols for the leaching of lead from new plumbing fittings and fixtures that are intended by the manufacturer to dispense water for human ingestion.

(2) Standards

(A) In general

If a voluntary standard for the leaching of lead is not established by the date that is 1 year after August 6, 1996, the Administrator shall, not later than 2 years after August 6, 1996, promulgate regulations setting a health-effects-based performance standard establishing maximum leaching levels from new plumbing fittings and fixtures that are intended by the manufacturer to dispense water for human ingestion. The standard shall become effective on the date that is 5 years after the date of promulgation of the standard.

(B) Alternative requirement

If regulations are required to be promulgated under subparagraph (A) and have not been promulgated by the date that is 5 years after August 6, 1996, no person may import, manufacture, process, or distribute in commerce a new plumbing fitting or fixture, intended by the manufacturer to dispense water for human ingestion, that contains more than 4 percent lead by dry weight.

(July 1, 1944, ch. 373, title XIV, Sec. 1417, as added Pub. L. 99-339, title I, Sec. 109(a), June 19, 1986, 100 Stat. 651; amended Pub. L. 104-182, title I, Sec. 118, title V, Sec. 501(f)(1), Aug. 6, 1996, 110 Stat. 1645, 1691.)

Amendments

1996—Pub. L. 104-182, Sec. 501(f)(1), made technical amendment to section catchline and subsec. (a) designation.

Subsec. (a)(1). Pub. L. 104-182, Sec. 118(1), substituted "Prohibitions" for "Prohibition" in heading and amended text generally. Prior to amendment, text read as follows: "Any pipe, solder, or flux, which is used after June 19, 1986, in the installation or repair of—
  (A) any public water system, or
  (B) any plumbing in a residential or nonresidential facility providing water for human consumption which is connected to a public water system,
shall be lead free (within the meaning of subsection (d) of this section). This paragraph shall not apply to leaded joints necessary for the repair of cast iron pipes."

Subsec. (a)(2)(A). Pub. L. 104-182, Sec. 118(2), inserted "owner or operator of a" after "Each" in introductory provisions.

Subsec. (a)(3). Pub. L. 104-182, Sec. 118(3), added par. (3).

Subsec. (d)(3). Pub. L. 104-182, Sec. 118(4), added par. (3).

Subsec. (e). Pub. L. 104-182, Sec. 118(5), added subsec. (e).

Notification to States

Section 109(b) of Pub. L. 99-339 provided that: "The Administrator of the Environmental Protection Agency shall notify all States with respect to the requirements of section 1417 of the Public Health Service Act [this section] within 90 days after the enactment of this Act [June 19, 1986]."

Ban on Lead Water Pipes, Solder, and Flux in VA and HUD Insured or Assisted Property

Section 109(c) of Pub. L. 99-339, as amended by Pub. L. 102-54, Sec. 13(q)(2), June 13, 1991, 105 Stat. 279, provided that:

"(1) Prohibition.—The Secretary of Housing and Urban Development and the Secretary of Veterans Affairs may not insure or guarantee a mortgage or furnish assistance with respect to newly constructed residential property which contains a potable water system unless such system uses only lead free pipe, solder, and flux.

(2) Definition of lead free.—For purposes of paragraph (1) the term 'lead free'—
  (A) when used with respect to solders and flux refers to solders and flux containing not more than 0.2 percent lead, and
  (B) when used with respect to pipes and pipe fittings refers to pipes and pipe fittings containing not more than 8.0 percent lead.

(3) Effective date.—Paragraph (1) shall become effective 24 months after the enactment of this Act [June 19, 1986]."

Cross References

Housing assistance by Secretary of Veterans Affairs, see section 3701 et seq. of Title 38, Veterans' Benefits.

Housing assistance by Secretary of Housing and Urban Development, see section 1701 et seq. of Title 12, Banks and Banking.

Section Referred to in Other Sections

This section is referred to in section 300g-3 of this title.

MONITORING OF CONTAMINANTS

42 USC 300g-7

(a) Interim monitoring relief authority
 (1) In general
 A State exercising primary enforcement responsibility for public water systems may modify the monitoring requirements for any regulated or unregulated contaminants for which monitoring is required other than microbial contaminants (or indicators thereof), disinfectants and disinfection byproducts or corrosion byproducts for an interim period to provide that any public water system serving 10,000 persons or fewer shall not be required to conduct additional quarterly monitoring during an interim relief period for such contaminants if—
 (A) monitoring, conducted at the beginning of the period for the contaminant concerned and certified to the State by the public water system, fails to detect the presence of the contaminant in the ground or surface water supplying the public water system; and
 (B) the State, considering the hydrogeology of the area and other relevant factors, determines in writing that the contaminant is unlikely to be detected by further monitoring during such period.
 (2) Termination; timing of monitoring
 The interim relief period referred to in paragraph (1) shall terminate when permanent monitoring relief is adopted and approved for such State, or at the end of 36 months after August 6, 1996, whichever comes first. In order to serve as a basis for interim relief, the monitoring conducted at the beginning of the period must occur at the time determined by the State to be the time of the public water system's greatest vulnerability to the contaminant concerned in the relevant ground or surface water, taking into account in the case of pesticides the time of application of the pesticide for the source water area and the travel time for the pesticide to reach such waters and taking into account, in the case of other contaminants, seasonality of precipitation and contaminant travel time.
(b) Permanent monitoring relief authority
 (1) In general
 Each State exercising primary enforcement responsibility for public water systems under this subchapter and having an approved source water assessment program may adopt, in accordance with guidance published by the Administrator, tailored alternative monitoring requirements for public water systems in such State (as an alternative to the monitoring requirements for chemical contaminants set forth in the applicable national primary drinking water regulations) where the State concludes that (based on data available at the time of adoption concerning susceptibility, use, occurrence, or wellhead protection, or from the State's drinking water source water assessment program) such alternative monitoring would provide assurance that it complies with the Administrator's guidelines. The State program must be adequate to assure compliance with, and enforcement of, applicable national primary drinking water regulations. Alternative monitoring shall not apply to regulated microbiological contaminants (or indicators thereof), disinfectants and disinfection byproducts, or corrosion byproducts. The preceding sentence is not intended to limit other authority of the Administrator under other provisions of this subchapter to grant monitoring flexibility.
 (2) Guidelines
  (A) In general
  The Administrator shall issue, after notice and comment and at the same time as guidelines are issued for source water assessment under section 300j-13 of this title, guidelines for States to follow in proposing alternative monitoring requirements under paragraph (1) for chemical contaminants. The Administrator shall publish such guidelines in the Federal Register. The guidelines shall assure that the public health will be protected from drinking water contamination. The guidelines shall require that a State alternative monitoring program apply on a contaminant-by-contaminant basis and that, to be eligible for such alternative monitoring program, a public water system must show the State that the contaminant is not present in the drinking water supply or, if present, it is reliably and consistently below the maximum contaminant level.

(B) Definition

For purposes of subparagraph (A), the phrase "reliably and consistently below the maximum contaminant level" means that, although contaminants have been detected in a water supply, the State has sufficient knowledge of the contamination source and extent of contamination to predict that the maximum contaminant level will not be exceeded. In determining that a contaminant is reliably and consistently below the maximum contaminant level, States shall consider the quality and completeness of data, the length of time covered and the volatility or stability of monitoring results during that time, and the proximity of such results to the maximum contaminant level. Wide variations in the analytical results, or analytical results close to the maximum contaminant level, shall not be considered to be reliably and consistently below the maximum contaminant level.

(3) Effect of detection of contaminants

The guidelines issued by the Administrator under paragraph (2) shall require that if, after the monitoring program is in effect and operating, a contaminant covered by the alternative monitoring program is detected at levels at or above the maximum contaminant level or is no longer reliably or consistently below the maximum contaminant level, the public water system must either—

(A) demonstrate that the contamination source has been removed or that other action has been taken to eliminate the contamination problem; or

(B) test for the detected contaminant pursuant to the applicable national primary drinking water regulation.

(4) States not exercising primary enforcement responsibility

The Governor of any State not exercising primary enforcement responsibility under section 300g-2 of this title on August 6, 1996, may submit to the Administrator a request that the Administrator modify the monitoring requirements established by the Administrator and applicable to public water systems in that State. After consultation with the Governor, the Administrator shall modify the requirements for public water systems in that State if the request of the Governor is in accordance with each of the requirements of this subsection that apply to alternative monitoring requirements established by States that have primary enforcement responsibility. A decision by the Administrator to approve a request under this clause shall be for a period of 3 years and may subsequently be extended for periods of 5 years.

(c) Treatment as NPDWR

All monitoring relief granted by a State to a public water system for a regulated contaminant under subsection (a) or (b) of this section shall be treated as part of the national primary drinking water regulation for that contaminant.

(d) Other monitoring relief

Nothing in this section shall be construed to affect the authority of the States under applicable national primary drinking water regulations to alter monitoring requirements through waivers or other existing authorities. The Administrator shall periodically review and, as appropriate, revise such authorities.

(July 1, 1944, ch. 373, title XIV, Sec. 1418, as added Pub. L. 104-182, title I, Sec. 125(b), Aug. 6, 1996, 110 Stat. 1654.)

Section Referred to in Other Sections

This section is referred to in sections 300h-7, 300j-13 of this title.

OPERATOR CERTIFICATION

42 USC 300g-8

(a) Guidelines

Not later than 30 months after August 6, 1996, and in cooperation with the States, the Administrator shall publish guidelines in the Federal Register, after notice and opportunity for comment from interested persons, including States and public water systems, specifying minimum standards for certification (and recertification) of the operators of community and nontransient noncommunity public water systems. Such guidelines shall take into account existing State programs, the complexity of the system, and other factors aimed at providing an effective program at reasonable cost to States and public water systems, taking into account the size of the system.

(b) State programs

Beginning 2 years after the date on which the Administrator publishes guidelines under subsection (a) of this section, the Administrator shall withhold 20 percent of the funds a State is otherwise entitled to receive under section 300j-12 of this title unless the State has adopted and is implementing a program for the certification of operators of community and nontransient noncommunity public water systems that meets the requirements of the guidelines published pursuant to subsection (a) of this section or that has been submitted in compliance with subsection (c) of this section and that has not been disapproved.

(c) Existing programs

For any State exercising primary enforcement responsibility for public water systems or any other State which has an operator certification program, the guidelines under subsection (a) of this section shall allow the State to enforce such program in lieu of the guidelines under subsection (a) of this section if the State submits the program to the Administrator within 18 months after the publication of the guidelines unless the Administrator determines (within 9 months after the State submits the program to the Administrator) that such program is not substantially equivalent to such guidelines. In making this determination, an existing State program shall be presumed to be substantially equivalent to the guidelines, notwithstanding program differences, based on the size of systems or the quality of source water, providing the State program meets the overall public health objectives of the guidelines. If disapproved, the program may be resubmitted within 6 months after receipt of notice of disapproval.

(d) Expense reimbursement

  (1) In general

  The Administrator shall provide reimbursement for the costs of training, including an appropriate per diem for unsalaried operators, and certification for persons operating systems serving 3,300 persons or fewer that are required to undergo training pursuant to this section.

  (2) State grants

  The reimbursement shall be provided through grants to States with each State receiving an amount sufficient to cover the reasonable costs for training all such operators in the State, as determined by the Administrator, to the extent required by this section. Grants received by a State pursuant to this paragraph shall first be used to provide reimbursement for training and certification costs of persons operating systems serving 3,300 persons or fewer. If a State has reimbursed all such costs, the State may, after notice to the Administrator, use any remaining funds from the grant for any of the other purposes authorized for grants under section 300j-12 of this title.

  (3) Authorization

  There are authorized to be appropriated to the Administrator to provide grants for reimbursement under this section $30,000,000 for each of fiscal years 1997 through 2003.

  (4) Reservation

  If the appropriation made pursuant to paragraph (3) for any fiscal year is not sufficient to satisfy the requirements of paragraph (1), the Administrator shall, prior to any other allocation or reservation, reserve such sums as necessary from the funds appropriated pursuant to section 300j-12(m) of this title to provide reimbursement for the training and certification costs mandated by this subsection.

(July 1, 1944, ch. 373, title XIV, Sec. 1419, as added Pub. L. 104-182, title I, Sec. 123, Aug. 6, 1996, 110 Stat. 1652.)

Section Referred to in Other Sections

This section is referred to in section 300j-12 of this title.

CAPACITY DEVELOPMENT

42 USC 300g-9

(a) State authority for new systems
A State shall receive only 80 percent of the allotment that the State is otherwise entitled to receive under section 300j-12 of this title (relating to State loan funds) unless the State has obtained the legal authority or other means to ensure that all new community water systems and new nontransient, noncommunity water systems commencing operation after October 1, 1999, demonstrate technical, managerial, and financial capacity with respect to each national primary drinking water regulation in effect, or likely to be in effect, on the date of commencement of operations.

(b) Systems in significant noncompliance
  (1) List
  Beginning not later than 1 year after August 6, 1996, each State shall prepare, periodically update, and submit to the Administrator a list of community water systems and nontransient, noncommunity water systems that have a history of significant noncompliance with this subchapter (as defined in guidelines issued prior to August 6, 1996, or any revisions of the guidelines that have been made in consultation with the States) and, to the extent practicable, the reasons for noncompliance.
  (2) Report
  Not later than 5 years after August 6, 1996, and as part of the capacity development strategy of the State, each State shall report to the Administrator on the success of enforcement mechanisms and initial capacity development efforts in assisting the public water systems listed under paragraph (1) to improve technical, managerial, and financial capacity.
  (3) Withholding
  The list and report under this subsection shall be considered part of the capacity development strategy of the State required under subsection (c) of this section for purposes of the withholding requirements of section 300j-12(a)(1)(G)(i) of this title (relating to State loan funds).

(c) Capacity development strategy
  (1) In general
  Beginning 4 years after August 6, 1996, a State shall receive only—
    (A) 90 percent in fiscal year 2001;
    (B) 85 percent in fiscal year 2002; and
    (C) 80 percent in each subsequent fiscal year,
  of the allotment that the State is otherwise entitled to receive under section 300j-12 of this title (relating to State loan funds), unless the State is developing and implementing a strategy to assist public water systems in acquiring and maintaining technical, managerial, and financial capacity.
  (2) Content
  In preparing the capacity development strategy, the State shall consider, solicit public comment on, and include as appropriate—
    (A) the methods or criteria that the State will use to identify and prioritize the public water systems most in need of improving technical, managerial, and financial capacity;
    (B) a description of the institutional, regulatory, financial, tax, or legal factors at the Federal, State, or local level that encourage or impair capacity development;
    (C) a description of how the State will use the authorities and resources of this subchapter or other means to—
      (i) assist public water systems in complying with national primary drinking water regulations;
      (ii) encourage the development of partnerships between public water systems to enhance the technical, managerial, and financial capacity of the systems; and
      (iii) assist public water systems in the training and certification of operators;
    (D) a description of how the State will establish a baseline and measure improvements in capacity with respect to national primary drinking water regulations and State drinking water law; and

(E) an identification of the persons that have an interest in and are involved in the development and implementation of the capacity development strategy (including all appropriate agencies of Federal, State, and local governments, private and nonprofit public water systems, and public water system customers).

(3) Report

Not later than 2 years after the date on which a State first adopts a capacity development strategy under this subsection, and every 3 years thereafter, the head of the State agency that has primary responsibility to carry out this subchapter in the State shall submit to the Governor a report that shall also be available to the public on the efficacy of the strategy and progress made toward improving the technical, managerial, and financial capacity of public water systems in the State.

(4) Review

The decisions of the State under this section regarding any particular public water system are not subject to review by the Administrator and may not serve as the basis for withholding funds under section 300j-12 of this title.

(d) Federal assistance

(1) In general

The Administrator shall support the States in developing capacity development strategies.

(2) Informational assistance

(A) In general

Not later than 180 days after August 6, 1996, the Administrator shall—

(i) conduct a review of State capacity development efforts in existence on August 6, 1996, and publish information to assist States and public water systems in capacity development efforts; and

(ii) initiate a partnership with States, public water systems, and the public to develop information for States on recommended operator certification requirements.

(B) Publication of information

The Administrator shall publish the information developed through the partnership under subparagraph (A)(ii) not later than 18 months after August 6, 1996.

(3) Promulgation of drinking water regulations

In promulgating a national primary drinking water regulation, the Administrator shall include an analysis of the likely effect of compliance with the regulation on the technical, financial, and managerial capacity of public water systems.

(4) Guidance for new systems

Not later than 2 years after August 6, 1996, the Administrator shall publish guidance developed in consultation with the States describing legal authorities and other means to ensure that all new community water systems and new nontransient, noncommunity water systems demonstrate technical, managerial, and financial capacity with respect to national primary drinking water regulations.

(e) Variances and exemptions

Based on information obtained under subsection (c)(3) of this section, the Administrator shall, as appropriate, modify regulations concerning variances and exemptions for small public water systems to ensure flexibility in the use of the variances and exemptions. Nothing in this subsection shall be interpreted, construed, or applied to affect or alter the requirements of section 300g-4 or 300g-5 of this title.

(f) Small public water systems technology assistance centers

(1) Grant program

The Administrator is authorized to make grants to institutions of higher learning to establish and operate small public water system technology assistance centers in the United States.

(2) Responsibilities of the centers

The responsibilities of the small public water system technology assistance centers established under this subsection shall include the conduct of training and technical assistance relating to the information, performance, and technical needs of small public water systems or public water systems that serve Indian Tribes.

(3) Applications
Any institution of higher learning interested in receiving a grant under this subsection shall submit to the Administrator an application in such form and containing such information as the Administrator may require by regulation.

(4) Selection criteria
The Administrator shall select recipients of grants under this subsection on the basis of the following criteria:
  (A) The small public water system technology assistance center shall be located in a State that is representative of the needs of the region in which the State is located for addressing the drinking water needs of small and rural communities or Indian Tribes.
  (B) The grant recipient shall be located in a region that has experienced problems, or may reasonably be foreseen to experience problems, with small and rural public water systems.
  (C) The grant recipient shall have access to expertise in small public water system technology management.
  (D) The grant recipient shall have the capability to disseminate the results of small public water system technology and training programs.
  (E) The projects that the grant recipient proposes to carry out under the grant are necessary and appropriate.
  (F) The grant recipient has regional support beyond the host institution.

(5) Consortia of States
At least 2 of the grants under this subsection shall be made to consortia of States with low population densities.

(6) Authorization of appropriations
There are authorized to be appropriated to make grants under this subsection $2,000,000 for each of the fiscal years 1997 through 1999, and $5,000,000 for each of the fiscal years 2000 through 2003.

(g) Environmental finance centers
  (1) In general
  The Administrator shall provide initial funding for one or more university-based environmental finance centers for activities that provide technical assistance to State and local officials in developing the capacity of public water systems. Any such funds shall be used only for activities that are directly related to this subchapter.

  (2) National capacity development clearinghouse
  The Administrator shall establish a national public water system capacity development clearinghouse to receive and disseminate information with respect to developing, improving, and maintaining financial and managerial capacity at public water systems. The Administrator shall ensure that the clearinghouse does not duplicate other federally supported clearinghouse activities.

  (3) Capacity development techniques
  The Administrator may request an environmental finance center funded under paragraph (1) to develop and test managerial, financial, and institutional techniques for capacity development. The techniques may include capacity assessment methodologies, manual and computer based public water system rate models and capital planning models, public water system consolidation procedures, and regionalization models.

  (4) Authorization of appropriations
  There are authorized to be appropriated to carry out this subsection $1,500,000 for each of the fiscal years 1997 through 2003.

  (5) Limitation
  No portion of any funds made available under this subsection may be used for lobbying expenses.

(July 1, 1944, ch. 373, title XIV, Sec. 1420, as added Pub. L. 104-182, title I, Sec. 119, Aug. 6, 1996, 110 Stat. 1647.)

Section Referred to in Other Sections

This section is referred to in section 300j-12 of this title.

Part C—Protection of Underground Sources of Drinking Water

REGULATIONS FOR STATE PROGRAMS

42 USC 300h

(a) Publication of proposed regulations; promulgation; amendments; public hearings; administrative consultations
  (1) The Administrator shall publish proposed regulations for State underground injection control programs within 180 days after December 16, 1974. Within 180 days after publication of such proposed regulations, he shall promulgate such regulations with such modifications as he deems appropriate. Any regulation under this subsection may be amended from time to time.
  (2) Any regulation under this section shall be proposed and promulgated in accordance with section 553 of title 5 (relating to rulemaking), except that the Administrator shall provide opportunity for public hearing prior to promulgation of such regulations. In proposing and promulgating regulations under this section the Administrator shall consult with the Secretary, the National Drinking Water Advisory Council, and other appropriate Federal entities and with interested State entities.
(b) Minimum requirements; restrictions
  (1) Regulations under subsection (a) of this section for State underground injection programs shall contain minimum requirements for effective programs to prevent underground injection which endangers drinking water sources within the meaning of subsection (d)(2) of this section. Such regulations shall require that a State program, in order to be approved under section 300h-1 of this title—
    (A) shall prohibit, effective on the date on which the applicable underground injection control program takes effect, any underground injection in such State which is not authorized by a permit issued by the State (except that the regulations may permit a State to authorize underground injection by rule);
    (B) shall require (i) in the case of a program which provides for authorization of underground injection by permit, that the applicant for the permit to inject must satisfy the State that the underground injection will not endanger drinking water sources, and (ii) in the case of a program which provides for such an authorization by rule, that no rule may be promulgated which authorizes any underground injection which endangers drinking water sources;
    (C) shall include inspection, monitoring, recordkeeping, and reporting requirements; and
    (D) shall apply (i) as prescribed by section 300j-6(b)[1] of this title, to underground injections by Federal agencies, and (ii) to underground injections by any other person whether or not occurring on property owned or leased by the United States.
  (2) Regulations of the Administrator under this section for State underground injection control programs may not prescribe requirements which interfere with or impede—
    (A) the underground injection of brine or other fluids which are brought to the surface in connection with oil or natural gas production or natural gas storage operations, or
    (B) any underground injection for the secondary or tertiary recovery of oil or natural gas, unless such requirements are essential to assure that underground sources of drinking water will not be endangered by such injection.
  (3) (A) The regulations of the Administrator under this section shall permit or provide for consideration of varying geologic, hydrological, or historical conditions in different States and in different areas within a State.
    (B) (i) In prescribing regulations under this section the Administrator shall, to the extent feasible, avoid promulgation of requirements which would unnecessarily disrupt State underground injection control programs which are in effect and being enforced in a substantial number of States.
      (ii) For the purpose of this subparagraph, a regulation prescribed by the Administrator under this section shall be deemed to disrupt a State underground injection

---

[1] See References in Text note below.

control program only if it would be infeasible to comply with both such regulation and the State underground injection control program.
- (iii) For the purpose of this subparagraph, a regulation prescribed by the Administrator under this section shall be deemed unnecessary only if, without such regulation, underground sources of drinking water will not be endangered by an underground injection.
- (C) Nothing in this section shall be construed to alter or affect the duty to assure that underground sources of drinking water will not be endangered by any underground injection.

(c) Temporary permits; notice and hearing
  (1) The Administrator may, upon application of the Governor of a State which authorizes underground injection by means of permits, authorize such State to issue (without regard to subsection (b)(1)(B)(i) of this section) temporary permits for underground injection which may be effective until the, expiration of four years after December 16, 1974, if—
  - (A) the Administrator finds that the State has demonstrated that it is unable and could not reasonably have been able to process all permit applications within the time available;
  - (B) the Administrator determines the adverse effect on the environment of such temporary permits is not unwarranted;
  - (C) such temporary permits will be issued only with respect to injection wells in operation on the date on which such State's permit program approved under this part first takes effect and for which there was inadequate time to process its permit application; and
  - (D) the Administrator determines the temporary permits require the use of adequate safeguards established by rules adopted by him.
  (2) The Administrator may, upon application of the Governor of a State which authorizes underground injection by means of permits, authorize such State to issue (without regard to subsection (b)(1)(B)(i) of this section), but after reasonable notice and hearing, one or more temporary permits each of which is applicable to a particular injection well and to the underground injection of a particular fluid and which may be effective until the expiration of four years after December 16, 1974, if the State finds, on the record of such hearing—
  - (A) that technology (or other means) to permit safe injection of the fluid in accordance with the applicable underground injection control program is not generally available (taking costs into consideration);
  - (B) that injection of the fluid would be less harmful to health than the use of other available means of disposing of waste or producing the desired product; and
  - (C) that available technology or other means have been employed (and will be employed) to reduce the volume and toxicity of the fluid and to minimize the potentially adverse effect of the injection on the public health.

(d) "Underground injection" defined; underground injection endangerment of drinking water sources
  For purposes of this part:
  (1) The term "underground injection" means the subsurface emplacement of fluids by well injection. Such term does not include the underground injection of natural gas for purposes of storage.
  (2) Underground injection endangers drinking water sources if such injection may result in the presence in underground water which supplies or can reasonably be expected to supply any public water system of any contaminant, and if the presence of such contaminant may result in such system's not complying with any national primary drinking water regulation or may otherwise adversely affect the health of persons.

(July 1, 1944, ch. 373, title XIV, Sec. 1421, as added Pub. L. 93-523, Sec. 2(a), Dec. 16, 1974, 88 Stat. 1674; amended Pub. L. 95-190, Sec. 6(b), Nov. 16, 1977, 91 Stat. 1396; Pub. L. 96-502, Secs. 3, 4(c), Dec. 5, 1980, 94 Stat. 2738; Pub. L. 99-339, title II, Sec. 201(a), June 19, 1986, 100 Stat. 653; Pub. L. 104-182, title V, Sec. 501(b)(1), Aug. 6, 1996, 110 Stat. 1691.)

References in Text

Section 300j-6(b) of this title, referred to in subsec. (b)(1)(D), was repealed, and a new section 300j-6(b) relating to administrative penalty orders was added, by Pub. L. 104-182, title I, Sec. 129(a), Aug. 6, 1996, 110 Stat. 1660.

Amendments

1996—Subsec. (b)(3)(B)(i). Pub. L. 104-182 substituted "number of States" for "number or States".

1986—Subsec. (b)(2)(A). Pub. L. 99-339 inserted "or natural gas storage operations" after "production".

1980—Subsec. (b)(1)(A). Pub. L. 96-502, Sec. 4(c), substituted "effective on the date on which the applicable underground injection control program takes effect" for "effective three years after December 16, 1974".

Subsec. (d)(1). Pub. L. 96-502, Sec. 3, inserted provision that such term does not include the underground injection of natural gas for purposes of storage.

1977—Subsec. (b)(3). Pub. L. 95-190 added par. (3).

Section Referred to in Other Sections

This section is referred to in sections 300h-1, 300h-4, 300j-2, 300j-6 of this title.

STATE PRIMARY ENFORCEMENT RESPONSIBILITY

42 USC 300h-1

(a) List of States in need of a control program; amendment of list
   Within 180 days after December 16, 1974, the Administrator shall list in the Federal Register each State for which in his judgment a State underground injection control program may be necessary to assure that underground injection will not endanger drinking water sources. Such list may be amended from time to time.

(b) State applications; notice to Administrator of compliance with revised or added requirements; approval or disapproval by Administrator; duration of State primary enforcement responsibility; public hearing
   (1) (A) Each State listed under subsection (a) of this section shall within 270 days after the date of promulgation of any regulation under section 300h of this title (or, if later, within 270 days after such State is first listed under subsection (a) of this section) submit to the Administrator an application which contains a showing satisfactory to the Administrator that the State—
      (i) has adopted after reasonable notice and public hearings, and will implement, an underground injection control program which meets the requirements of regulations in effect under section 300h of this title; and
      (ii) will keep such records and make such reports with respect to its activities under its underground injection control program as the Administrator may require by regulation.

      The Administrator may, for good cause, extend the date for submission of an application by any State under this subparagraph for a period not to exceed an additional 270 days.
   (B) Within 270 days of any amendment of a regulation under section 300h of this title revising or adding any requirement respecting State underground injection control programs, each State listed under subsection (a) of this section shall submit (in such form and manner as the Administrator may require) a notice to the Administrator containing a showing satisfactory to him that the State underground injection control program meets the revised or added requirement.
   (2) Within ninety days after the State's application under paragraph (1)(A) or notice under paragraph (1)(B) and after reasonable opportunity for presentation of views, the Administrator shall by rule either approve, disapprove, or approve in part and disapprove in part, the State's underground injection control program.
   (3) If the Administrator approves the State's program under paragraph (2), the State shall have primary enforcement responsibility for underground water sources until such time as the Administrator determines, by rule, that such State no longer meets the requirements of clause (i) or (ii) of paragraph (1)(A) of this subsection.
   (4) Before promulgating any rule under paragraph (2) or (3) of this subsection, the Administrator shall provide opportunity for public hearing respecting such rule.

(c) Program by Administrator for State without primary enforcement responsibility; restrictions
   If the Administrator disapproves a State's program (or part thereof) under subsection (b)(2) of this section, if the Administrator determines under subsection (b)(3) of this section that a

State no longer meets the requirements of clause (i) or (ii) of subsection (b)(1)(A) of this section, or if a State fails to submit an application or notice before the date of expiration of the period specified in subsection (b)(1) of this section, the Administrator shall by regulation within 90 days after the date of such disapproval, determination, or expiration (as the case may be) prescribe (and may from time to time by regulation revise) a program applicable to such State meeting the requirements of section 300h(b) of this title. Such program may not include requirements which interfere with or impede—

(1) the underground injection of brine or other fluids which are brought to the surface in connection with oil or natural gas production or natural gas storage operations, or

(2) any underground injection for the secondary or tertiary recovery of oil or natural gas,

unless such requirements are essential to assure that underground sources of drinking water will not be endangered by such injection. Such program shall apply in such State to the extent that a program adopted by such State which the Administrator determines meets such requirements is not in effect. Before promulgating any regulation under this section, the Administrator shall provide opportunity for public hearing respecting such regulation.

(d) "Applicable underground injection control program" defined

For purposes of this subchapter, the term "applicable underground injection control program" with respect to a State means the program (or most recent amendment thereof) (1) which has been adopted by the State and which has been approved under subsection (b) of this section, or (2) which has been prescribed by the Administrator under subsection (c) of this section.

(e) Primary enforcement responsibility by Indian Tribe

An Indian Tribe may assume primary enforcement responsibility for underground injection control under this section consistent with such regulations as the Administrator has prescribed pursuant to this part and section 300j-11 of this title. The area over which such Indian Tribe exercises governmental jurisdiction need not have been listed under subsection (a) of this section, and such Tribe need not submit an application to assume primary enforcement responsibility within the 270-day deadline noted in subsection (b)(1)(A) of this section. Until an Indian Tribe assumes primary enforcement responsibility, the currently applicable underground injection control program shall continue to apply. If an applicable underground injection control program does not exist for an Indian Tribe, the Administrator shall prescribe such a program pursuant to subsection (c) of this section, and consistent with section 300h(b) of this title, within 270 days after June 19, 1986, unless an Indian Tribe first obtains approval to assume primary enforcement responsibility for underground injection control.

(July 1, 1944, ch. 373, title XIV, Sec. 1422, as added Pub. L. 93-523, Sec. 2(a), Dec. 16, 1974, 88 Stat. 1676; amended Pub. L. 95-190, Sec. 6(a), Nov. 16, 1977, 91 Stat. 1396; Pub. L. 99-339, title II, Sec. 201(a), title III, Sec. 302(c), June 19, 1986, 100 Stat. 653, 666.)

Amendments

1986—Subsec. (c)(1). Pub. L. 99-339, Sec. 201(a), inserted "or natural gas storage operations," after "production".

Subsec. (e). Pub. L. 99-339, Sec. 302(c), added subsec. (e).

1977—Subsec. (b)(1)(A). Pub. L. 95-190 inserted provisions relating to extension of date for submission of applications by any State.

Section Referred to in Other Sections

This section is referred to in sections 300h, 300h-2, 300h-4, 300j-2, 6924 of this title.

ENFORCEMENT OF PROGRAM

42 USC 300h-2

(a) Notice to State and violator; issuance of administrative order; civil action

(1) Whenever the Administrator finds during a period during which a State has primary enforcement responsibility for underground water sources (within the meaning of section 300h-1(b)(3) of this title or section 300h-4(c) of this title) that any person who is subject to a requirement of an applicable underground injection control program in such State is violating such requirement, he shall so notify the State and the person violating such requirement. If beyond the thirtieth day after the Administrator's notification the State

has not commenced appropriate enforcement action, the Administrator shall issue an order under subsection (c) of this section requiring the person to comply with such requirement or the Administrator shall commence a civil action under subsection (b) of this section.
    (2) Whenever the Administrator finds during a period during which a State does not have primary enforcement responsibility for underground water sources that any person subject to any requirement of any applicable underground injection control program in such State is violating such requirement, the Administrator shall issue an order under subsection (c) of this section requiring the person to comply with such requirement or the Administrator shall commence a civil action under subsection (b) of this section.
(b) Civil and criminal actions
    Civil actions referred to in paragraphs (1) and (2) of subsection (a) of this section shall be brought in the appropriate United States district court. Such court shall have jurisdiction to require compliance with any requirement of an applicable underground injection program or with an order issued under subsection (c) of this section. The court may enter such judgment as protection of public health may require. Any person who violates any requirement of an applicable underground injection control program or an order requiring compliance under subsection (c) of this section—
    (1) shall be subject to a civil penalty of not more than $25,000 for each day of such violation, and
    (2) if such violation is willful, such person may, in addition to or in lieu of the civil penalty authorized by paragraph (1), be imprisoned for not more than 3 years, or fined in accordance with title 18, or both.
(c) Administrative orders
    (1) In any case in which the Administrator is authorized to bring a civil action under this section with respect to any regulation or other requirement of this part other than those relating to—
        (A) the underground injection of brine or other fluids which are brought to the surface in connection with oil or natural gas production, or
        (B) any underground injection for the secondary or tertiary recovery of oil or natural gas, the Administrator may also issue an order under this subsection either assessing a civil penalty of not more than $10,000 for each day of violation for any past or current violation, up to a maximum administrative penalty of $125,000, or requiring compliance with such regulation or other requirement, or both.
    (2) In any case in which the Administrator is authorized to bring a civil action under this section with respect to any regulation, or other requirement of this part relating to—
        (A) the underground injection of brine or other fluids which are brought to the surface in connection with oil or natural gas production, or
        (B) any underground injection for the secondary or tertiary recovery of oil or natural gas, the Administrator may also issue an order under this subsection either assessing a civil penalty of not more than $5,000 for each day of violation for any past or current violation, up to a maximum administrative penalty of $125,000, or requiring compliance with such regulation or other requirement, or both.
    (3) (A) An order under this subsection shall be issued by the Administrator after opportunity (provided in accordance with this subparagraph) for a hearing. Before issuing the order, the Administrator shall give to the person to whom it is directed written notice of the Administrator's proposal to issue such order and the opportunity to request, within 30 days of the date the notice is received by such person, a hearing on the order. Such hearing shall not be subject to section 554 or 556 of title 5, but shall provide a reasonable opportunity to be heard and to present evidence.
        (B) The Administrator shall provide public notice of, and reasonable opportunity to comment on, any proposed order.
        (C) Any citizen who comments on any proposed order under subparagraph (B) shall be given notice of any hearing under this subsection and of any order. In any hearing held under subparagraph (A), such citizen shall have a reasonable opportunity to be heard and to present evidence.
        (D) Any order issued under this subsection shall become effective 30 days following its issuance unless an appeal is taken pursuant to paragraph (6).

(4) (A) Any order issued under this subsection shall state with reasonable specificity the nature of the violation and may specify a reasonable time for compliance.

   (B) In assessing any civil penalty under this subsection, the Administrator shall take into account appropriate factors, including (i) the seriousness of the violation; (ii) the economic benefit (if any) resulting from the violation; (iii) any history of such violations; (iv) any good-faith efforts to comply with the applicable requirements; (v) the economic impact of the penalty on the violator; and (vi) such other matters as justice may require.

(5) Any violation with respect to which the Administrator has commenced and is diligently prosecuting an action, or has issued an order under this subsection assessing a penalty, shall not be subject to an action under subsection (b) of this section or section 300h-3(c) or 300j-8 of this title, except that the foregoing limitation on civil actions under section 300j-8 of this title shall not apply with respect to any violation for which—

   (A) a civil action under section 300j-8(a)(1) of this title has been filed prior to commencement of an action under this subsection, or

   (B) a notice of violation under section 300j-8(b)(1) of this title has been given before commencement of an action under this subsection and an action under section 300j-8(a)(1) of this title is filed before 120 days after such notice is given.

(6) Any person against whom an order is issued or who commented on a proposed order pursuant to paragraph (3) may file an appeal of such order with the United States District Court for the District of Columbia or the district in which the violation is alleged to have occurred. Such an appeal may only be filed within the 30-day period beginning on the date the order is issued. Appellant shall simultaneously send a copy of the appeal by certified mail to the Administrator and to the Attorney General. The Administrator shall promptly file in such court a certified copy of the record on which such order was imposed. The district court shall not set aside or remand such order unless there is not substantial evidence on the record, taken as a whole, to support the finding of a violation or, unless the Administrator's assessment of penalty or requirement for compliance constitutes an abuse of discretion. The district court shall not impose additional civil penalties for the same violation unless the Administrator's assessment of a penalty constitutes an abuse of discretion. Notwithstanding section 300j-7(a)(2) of this title, any order issued under paragraph (3) shall be subject to judicial review exclusively under this paragraph.

(7) If any person fails to pay an assessment of a civil penalty—

   (A) after the order becomes effective under paragraph (3), or

   (B) after a court, in an action brought under paragraph (6), has entered a final judgment in favor of the Administrator, the Administrator may request the Attorney General to bring a civil action in an appropriate district court to recover the amount assessed (plus costs, attorneys' fees, and interest at currently prevailing rates from the date the order is effective or the date of such final judgment, as the case may be). In such an action, the validity, amount, and appropriateness of such penalty shall not be subject to review.

(8) The Administrator may, in connection with administrative proceedings under this subsection, issue subpoenas compelling the attendance and testimony of witnesses and subpoenas duces tecum, and may request the Attorney General to bring an action to enforce any subpoena under this section. The district courts shall have jurisdiction to enforce such subpoenas and impose sanction.

(d) State authority to adopt or enforce laws or regulations respecting underground injection unaffected

Nothing in this subchapter shall diminish any authority of a State or political subdivision to adopt or enforce any law or regulation respecting underground injection but no such law or regulation shall relieve any person of any requirement otherwise applicable under this subchapter.

(July 1, 1944, ch. 373, title XIV, Sec. 1423, as added Pub. L. 93-523, Sec. 2(a), Dec. 16, 1974, 88 Stat. 1677; amended Pub. L. 96-502, Sec. 2(b), Dec. 5, 1980, 94 Stat. 2738; Pub. L. 99-339, title II, Sec. 202, June 19, 1986, 100 Stat. 654.)

Amendments

1986—Pub. L. 99-339, Sec. 202(d), substituted "Enforcement" for "Failure of State to assure enforcement" in section catchline.

Subsec. (a)(1). Pub. L. 99-339, Sec. 202(a)(1), substituted provisions which related to issuance of an order of compliance or commencement of a civil action by the Administrator if the State has not commenced enforcement against the violator for provisions directing the Administrator to give public notice and request that the State report within 15 days thereafter as to steps taken to enforce compliance and authorizing the Administrator to commence a civil action upon failure by the State to comply timely.

Subsec. (a)(2). Pub. L. 99-339, Sec. 202(a)(2), substituted provision that the Administrator issue an order under subsec. (c) of this section or commence a civil action under subsec. (b) of this section for provision that he commence a civil action under subsec. (b)(1) of this section.

Subsec. (b). Pub. L. 99-339, Sec. 202(b), amended subsec. (b) generally, substituting provisions relating to jurisdiction of the appropriate Federal district court, entry of judgment, civil penalty of $25,000 per day, criminal liability and fine for willful violation for provisions which related to judicial determinations in appropriate Federal district courts, civil penalties of $5,000 per day, and fines of $10,000 per day for willful violations.

Subsecs. (c), (d). Pub. L. 99-339, Sec. 202(c), added subsec. (c) and redesignated former subsec. (c) as (d).

1980—Subsec. (a)(1). Pub. L. 96-502 inserted reference to section 300h-4(c) of this title.

INTERIM REGULATION OF UNDERGROUND INJECTIONS

42 USC 300h-3

(a) Necessity for well operation permit; designation of one aquifer areas
  (1) Any person may petition the Administrator to have an area of a State (or States) designated as an area in which no new underground injection well may be operated during the period beginning on the date of the designation and ending on the date on which the applicable underground injection control program covering such area takes effect unless a permit for the operation of such well has been issued by the Administrator under subsection (b) of this section. The Administrator may so designate an area within a State if he finds that the area has one aquifer which is the sole or principal drinking water source for the area and which, if contaminated, would create a significant hazard to public health.
  (2) Upon receipt of a petition under paragraph (1) of this subsection, the Administrator shall publish it in the Federal Register and shall provide an opportunity to interested persons to submit written data, views, or arguments thereon. Not later than the 30th day following the date of the publication of a petition under this paragraph in the Federal Register, the Administrator shall either make the designation for which the petition is submitted or deny the petition.
(b) Well operation permits; publication in Federal Register; notice and hearing; issuance or denial; conditions for issuance
  (1) During the period beginning on the date an area is designated under subsection (a) of this section and ending on the date the applicable underground injection control program covering such area takes effect, no new underground injection well may be operated in such area unless the Administrator has issued a permit for such operation.
  (2) Any person may petition the Administrator for the issuance of a permit for the operation of such a well in such an area. A petition submitted under this paragraph shall be submitted in such manner and contain such information as the Administrator may require by regulation. Upon receipt of such a petition, the Administrator shall publish it in the Federal Register. The Administrator shall give notice of any proceeding on a petition and shall provide opportunity for agency hearing. The Administrator shall act upon such petition on the record of any hearing held pursuant to the preceding sentence respecting such petition. Within 120 days of the publication in the Federal Register of a petition submitted under this paragraph, the Administrator shall either issue the permit for which the petition was submitted or shall deny its issuance.

(3) The Administrator may issue a permit for the operation of a new underground injection well in an area designated under subsection (a) of this section only, if he finds that the operation of such well will not cause contamination of the aquifer of such area so as to create a significant hazard to public health. The Administrator may condition the issuance of such a permit upon the use of such control measures in connection with the operation of such well, for which the permit is to be issued, as he deems necessary to assure that the operation of the well will not contaminate the aquifer of the designated area in which the well is located so as to create a significant hazard to public health.

(c) Civil penalties; separate violations; penalties for willful violations; temporary restraining order or injunction

Any person who operates a new underground injection well in violation of subsection (b) of this section, (1) shall be subject to a civil penalty of not more than $5,000 for each day in which such violation occurs, or (2) if such violation is willful, such person may, in lieu of the civil penalty authorized by clause (1), be fined not more than $10,000 for each day in which such violation occurs. If the Administrator has reason to believe that any person is violating or will violate subsection (b) of this section, he may petition the United States district court to issue a temporary restraining order or injunction (including a mandatory injunction) to enforce such subsection.

(d) "New underground injection well" defined

For purposes of this section, the term "new underground injection well" means an underground injection well whose operation was not approved by appropriate State and Federal agencies before December 16, 1974.

(e) Areas with one aquifer; publication in Federal Register; commitments for Federal financial assistance

If the Administrator determines, on his own initiative or upon petition, that an area has an aquifer which is the sole or principal drinking water source for the area and which, if contaminated, would create a significant hazard to public health, he shall publish notice of that determination in the Federal Register. After the publication of any such notice, no commitment for Federal financial assistance (through a grant, contract, loan guarantee, or otherwise) may be entered into for any project which the Administrator determines may contaminate such aquifer through a recharge zone so as to create a significant hazard to public health, but a commitment for Federal financial assistance may, if authorized under another provision of law, be entered into to plan or design the project to assure that it will not so contaminate the aquifer.

(July 1, 1944, ch. 373, title XIV, Sec. 1424, as added Pub. L. 93-523, Sec. 2(a), Dec. 16, 1974, 88 Stat. 1678.)

Section Referred to in Other Sections

This section is referred to in sections 300h-2, 300h-6 of this title.

OPTIONAL DEMONSTRATION BY STATES RELATING TO OIL OR NATURAL GAS

42 USC 300h-4

(a) Approval of State underground injection control program; alternative showing of effectiveness of program by State

For purposes of the Administrator's approval or disapproval under section 300h-1 of this title of that portion of any State underground injection control program which relates to—

(1) the underground injection of brine or other fluids which are brought to the surface in connection with oil or natural gas production or natural gas storage operations, or

(2) any underground injection for the secondary or tertiary recovery of oil or natural gas,

in lieu of the showing required under subparagraph (A) of section 300h-1(b)(1) of this title the State may demonstrate that such portion of the State program meets the requirements of subparagraphs (A) through (D) of section 300h(b)(1) of this title and represents an effective program (including adequate recordkeeping and reporting) to prevent underground injection which endangers drinking water sources.

(b) Revision or amendment of requirements of regulation; showing of effectiveness of program by State

If the Administrator revises or amends any requirement of a regulation under section 300h of this title relating to any aspect of the underground injection referred to in subsection (a) of this section, in the case of that portion of a State underground injection control program for which the demonstration referred to in subsection (a) of this section has been made, in lieu of the showing required under section 300h-1(b)(1)(B) of this title the State may demonstrate that, with respect to that aspect of such underground injection, the State program meets the requirements of subparagraphs (A) through (D) of section 300h(b)(1) of this title and represents an effective program (including adequate recordkeeping and reporting) to prevent underground injection which endangers drinking water sources.

(c) Primary enforcement responsibility of State; voiding by Administrator under duly promulgated rule
  (1) Section 300h-1(b)(3) of this title shall not apply to that portion of any State underground injection control program approved by the Administrator pursuant to a demonstration under subsection (a) of this section (and under subsection (b) of this section where applicable).
  (2) If pursuant to such a demonstration, the Administrator approves such portion of the State program, the State shall have primary enforcement responsibility with respect to that portion until such time as the Administrator determines, by rule, that such demonstration is no longer valid. Following such a determination, the Administrator may exercise the authority of subsection (c) of section 300h-1 of this title in the same manner as provided in such subsection with respect to a determination described in such subsection.
  (3) Before promulgating any rule under paragraph (2), the Administrator shall provide opportunity for public hearing respecting such rule.

(July 1, 1944, ch. 373, title XIV, Sec. 1425, as added Pub. L. 96-502, Sec. 2(a), Dec. 5, 1980, 94 Stat. 2737; amended Pub. L. 99-339, title II, Sec. 201(a), June 19, 1986, 100 Stat. 653.)

Amendments

1986—Subsec. (a)(1). Pub. L. 99-339 inserted "or natural gas storage operations," after "production".

Section Referred to in Other Sections

This section is referred to in sections 300h-2, 300j-2 of this title.

REGULATION OF STATE PROGRAMS

42 USC 300h-5

Not later than 18 months after June 19, 1986, the Administrator shall modify regulations issued under this chapter for Class I injection wells to identify monitoring methods, in addition to those in effect on November 1, 1985, including groundwater monitoring. In accordance with such regulations, the Administrator, or delegated State authority, shall determine the applicability of such monitoring methods, wherever appropriate, at locations and in such a manner as to provide the earliest possible detection of fluid migration into, or in the direction of, underground sources of drinking water from such wells, based on its assessment of the potential for fluid migration from the injection zone that may be harmful to human health or the environment. For purposes of this subsection, a class I injection well is defined in accordance with 40 CFR 146.05 as in effect on November 1, 1985.

(July 1, 1944, ch. 373, title XIV, Sec. 1426, as added Pub. L. 99-339, title II, Sec. 201(b), June 19, 1986, 100 Stat. 653; amended Pub. L. 104-66, title II, Sec. 2021(f), Dec. 21, 1995, 109 Stat. 727; Pub. L. 104-182, title V, Sec. 501(f)(2), Aug. 6, 1996, 110 Stat. 1691.)

SOLE SOURCE AQUIFER DEMONSTRATION PROGRAM

42 USC 300h-6

(a) Purpose
The purpose of this section is to establish procedures for development, implementation, and assessment of demonstration programs designed to protect critical aquifer protection areas located within areas designated as sole or principal source aquifers under section 300h-3(e) of this title.

(b) "Critical aquifer protection area" defined
For purposes of this section, the term "critical aquifer protection area" means either of the following:
  (1) All or part of an area located within an area for which an application or designation as a sole or principal source aquifer pursuant to section 300h-3(e) of this title, has been submitted and approved by the Administrator and which satisfies the criteria established by the Administrator under subsection (d) of this section.
  (2) All or part of an area which is within an aquifer designated as a sole source aquifer as of June 19, 1986, and for which an areawide ground water quality protection plan has been approved under section 208 of the Clean Water Act [33 U.S.C. 1288] prior to June 19, 1986.

(c) Application
Any State, municipal or local government or political subdivision thereof or any planning entity (including any interstate regional planning entity) that identifies a critical aquifer protection area over which it has authority or jurisdiction may apply to the Administrator for the selection of such area for a demonstration program under this section. Any applicant shall consult with other government or planning entities with authority or jurisdiction in such area prior to application. Applicants, other than the Governor, shall submit the application for a demonstration program jointly with the Governor.

(d) Criteria
Not later than 1 year after June 19, 1986, the Administrator shall, by rule, establish criteria for identifying critical aquifer protection areas under this section. In establishing such criteria, the Administrator shall consider each of the following:
  (1) The vulnerability of the aquifer to contamination due to hydrogeologic characteristics.
  (2) The number of persons or the proportion of population using the ground water as a drinking water source.
  (3) The economic, social and environmental benefits that would result to the area from maintenance of ground water of high quality.
  (4) The economic, social and environmental costs that would result from degradation of the quality of the ground water.

(e) Contents of application
An application submitted to the Administrator by any applicant for a demonstration program under this section shall meet each of the following requirements:
  (1) The application shall propose boundaries for the critical aquifer protection area within its jurisdiction.
  (2) The application shall designate or, if necessary, establish a planning entity (which shall be a public agency and which shall include representation of elected local and State governmental officials) to develop a comprehensive management plan (hereinafter in this section referred to as the "plan") for the critical protection area. Where a local government planning agency exists with adequate authority to carry out this section with respect to any proposed critical protection area, such agency shall be designated as the planning entity.
  (3) The application shall establish procedures for public participation in the development of the plan, for review, approval, and adoption of the plan, and for assistance to municipalities and other public agencies with authority under State law to implement the plan.
  (4) The application shall include a hydrogeologic assessment of surface and ground water resources within the critical protection area.
  (5) The application shall include a comprehensive management plan for the proposed protection area.

(6) The application shall include the measures and schedule proposed for implementation of such plan.
(f) Comprehensive plan
  (1) The objective of a comprehensive management plan submitted by an applicant under this section shall be to maintain the quality of the ground water in the critical protection area in a manner reasonably expected to protect human health, the environment and ground water resources. In order to achieve such objective, the plan may be designed to maintain, to the maximum extent possible, the natural vegetative and hydrogeological conditions. Each of the following elements shall be included in such a protection plan:
    (A) A map showing the detailed boundary of the critical protection area.
    (B) An identification of existing and potential point and nonpoint sources of ground water degradation.
    (C) An assessment of the relationship between activities on the land surface and ground water quality.
    (D) Specific actions and management practices to be implemented in the critical protection area to prevent adverse impacts on ground water quality.
    (E) Identification of authority adequate to implement the plan, estimates of program costs, and sources of State matching funds.
  (2) Such plan may also include the following:
    (A) A determination of the quality of the existing ground water recharged through the special protection area and the natural recharge capabilities of the special protection area watershed.
    (B) Requirements designed to maintain existing underground drinking water quality or improve underground drinking water quality if prevailing conditions fail to meet drinking water standards, pursuant to this chapter and State law.
    (C) Limits on Federal, State, and local government, financially assisted activities and projects which may contribute to degradation of such ground water or any loss of natural surface and subsurface infiltration of purification capability of the special protection watershed.
    (D) A comprehensive statement of land use management including emergency contingency planning as it pertains to the maintenance of the quality of underground sources of drinking water or to the improvement of such sources if necessary to meet drinking water standards pursuant to this chapter and State law.
    (E) Actions in the special protection area which would avoid adverse impacts on water quality, recharge capabilities, or both.
    (F) Consideration of specific techniques, which may include clustering, transfer of development rights, and other innovative measures sufficient to achieve the objectives of this section.
    (G) Consideration of the establishment of a State institution to facilitate and assist funding a development transfer credit system.
    (H) A program for State and local implementation of the plan described in this subsection in a manner that will insure the continued, uniform, consistent protection of the critical protection area in accord with the purposes of this section.
    (I) Pollution abatement measures, if appropriate.
(g) Plans under section 208 of Clean Water Act
  A plan approved before June 19, 1986, under section 208 of the Clean Water Act [33 U.S.C. 1288] to protect a sole source aquifer designated under section 300h-3(e) of this title shall be considered a comprehensive management plan for the purposes of this section.
(h) Consultation and hearings
  During the development of a comprehensive management plan under this section, the planning entity shall consult with, and consider the comments of, appropriate officials of any municipality and State or Federal agency which has jurisdiction over lands and waters within the special protection area, other concerned organizations and technical and citizen advisory committees. The planning entity shall conduct public hearings at places within the special protection area for the purpose of providing the opportunity to comment on any aspect of the plan.

(i) Approval or disapproval
Within 120 days after receipt of an application under this section, the Administrator shall approve or disapprove the application. The approval or disapproval shall be based on a determination that the critical protection area satisfies the criteria established under subsection (d) of this section and that a demonstration program for the area would provide protection for ground water quality consistent with the objectives stated in subsection (f) of this section. The Administrator shall provide to the Governor a written explanation of the reasons for the disapproval of any such application. Any petitioner may modify and resubmit any application which is not approved. Upon approval of an application, the Administrator may enter into a cooperative agreement with the applicant to establish a demonstration program under this section.

(j) Grants and reimbursement
Upon entering a cooperative agreement under subsection (i) of this section, the Administrator may provide to the applicant, on a matching basis, a grant of 50 per centum of the costs of implementing the plan established under this section. The Administrator may also reimburse the applicant of an approved plan up to 50 per centum of the costs of developing such plan, except for plans approved under section 208 of the Clean Water Act [33 U.S.C. 1288]. The total amount of grants under this section for any one aquifer, designated under section 300h-3(e) of this title, shall not exceed $4,000,000 in any one fiscal year.

(k) Activities funded under other law
No funds authorized under this section may be used to fund activities funded under other sections of this chapter or the Clean Water Act [33 U.S.C. 1251 et seq.], the Solid Waste Disposal Act [42 U.S.C. 6901 et seq.], the Comprehensive Environmental Response, Compensation, and Liability Act of 1980 [42 U.S.C. 9601 et seq.] or other environmental laws.

(l) Savings provision
Nothing under this section shall be construed to amend, supersede or abrogate rights to quantities of water which have been established by interstate water compacts, Supreme Court decrees, or State water laws; or any requirement imposed or right provided under any Federal or State environmental or public health statute.

(m) Authorization of appropriations
There are authorized to be appropriated to carry out this section not more than the following amounts:

Fiscal year:	Amount
1987	$10,000,000
1988	15,000,000
1989	17,500,000
1990	17,500,000
1991	17,500,000
1992-2003	15,000,000.

Matching grants under this section may also be used to implement or update any water quality management plan for a sole or principal source aquifer approved (before June 19, 1986) by the Administrator under section 208 of the Federal Water Pollution Control Act [33 U.S.C. 1288].

(July 1, 1944, ch. 373, title XIV, Sec. 1427, as added and amended Pub. L. 99-339, title II, Sec. 203, title III, Sec. 301(f), June 19, 1986, 100 Stat. 657, 664; Pub. L. 104-66, title II, Sec. 2021(g), Dec. 21, 1995, 109 Stat. 727; Pub. L. 104-182, title I, Sec. 120(a), title V, Sec. 501(b)(2), (f)(3), Aug. 6, 1996, 110 Stat. 1650, 1691.)

References in Text

The Clean Water Act, referred to in subsec. (k), is act June 30, 1948, ch. 758, as amended generally by Pub. L. 92-500, Sec. 2, Oct. 18, 1972, 86 Stat. 816, also known as the Federal Water Pollution Control Act, which is classified generally to chapter 26 (Sec. 1251 et seq.) of Title 33, Navigation and Navigable Waters. For complete classification of this Act to the Code, see Short Title note set out under section 1251 of Title 33 and Tables.

The Solid Waste Disposal Act, referred to in subsec. (k), is title II of Pub. L. 89-272, Oct. 20, 1965, 79 Stat. 997, as amended generally by Pub. L. 94-580, Sec. 2, Oct. 21, 1976, 90 Stat. 2795, which is classified generally to chapter 82 (Sec. 6901 et seq.) of this title. For complete classification of this Act to the Code, see Short Title note set out under section 6901 of this title and Tables.

The Comprehensive Environmental Response, Compensation, and Liability Act of 1980, referred to in subsec. (k), is Pub. L. 96-510, Dec. 11, 1980, 94 Stat. 2767, as amended, which is classified principally to chapter 103 (Sec. 9601 et seq.) of this title. For complete classification of this Act to the Code, see Short Title note set out under section 9601 of this title and Tables.

Amendments

1996—Pub. L. 104-182, Sec. 501(f)(3), made technical amendment to section catchline and subsec. (a) designation.

Subsec. (b)(1). Pub. L. 104-182, Sec. 120(a)(1), struck out "not later than 24 months after June 19, 1986," after "by the Administrator".

Subsec. (k). Pub. L. 104-182, Sec. 501(b)(2), substituted "this section" for "this subsection".

Subsec. (m). Pub. L. 104-182, Sec. 120(a)(2), inserted table item relating to fiscal years 1992 through 2003.

1995—Subsecs. (l) to (n). Pub. L. 104-66 redesignated subsecs. (m) and (n) as (l) and (m), respectively, and struck out heading and text of former subsec. (l). Text read as follows: "Not later than December 31, 1989, each State shall submit to the Administrator a report assessing the impact of the program on ground water quality and identifying those measures found to be effective in protecting ground water resources. No later than September 30, 1990, the Administrator shall submit to Congress a report summarizing the State reports, and assessing the accomplishments of the sole source aquifer demonstration program including an identification of protection methods found to be most effective and recommendations for their application to protect ground water resources from contamination whenever necessary."

1986—Subsec. (n). Pub. L. 99-339 added subsec. (n).

Section Referred to in Other Sections

This section is referred to in section 300j-14 of this title.

STATE PROGRAMS TO ESTABLISH WELLHEAD PROTECTION AREAS

42 USC 300h-7

(a) State programs

The Governor or Governor's designee of each State shall, within 3 years of June 19, 1986, adopt and submit to the Administrator a State program to protect wellhead areas within their jurisdiction from contaminants which may have any adverse effect on the health of persons. Each State program under this section shall, at a minimum—
   (1) specify the duties of State agencies, local governmental entities, and public water supply systems with respect to the development and implementation of programs required by this section;
   (2) for each wellhead, determine the wellhead protection area as defined in subsection (e) of this section based on all reasonably available hydrogeologic information on ground water flow, recharge and discharge and other information the State deems necessary to adequately determine the wellhead protection area;
   (3) identify within each wellhead protection area all potential anthropogenic sources of contaminants which may have any adverse effect on the health of persons;
   (4) describe a program that contains, as appropriate, technical assistance, financial assistance, implementation of control measures, education, training, and demonstration projects to protect the water supply within wellhead protection areas from such contaminants;
   (5) include contingency plans for the location and provision of alternate drinking water supplies for each public water system in the event of well or wellfield contamination by such contaminants; and
   (6) include a requirement that consideration be given to all potential sources of such contaminants within the expected wellhead area of a new water well which serves a public water supply system.

(b) Public participation
To the maximum extent possible, each State shall establish procedures, including but not limited to the establishment of technical and citizens' advisory committees, to encourage the public to participate in developing the protection program for wellhead areas and source water assessment programs under section 300j-13 of this title. Such procedures shall include notice and opportunity for public hearing on the State program before it is submitted to the Administrator.

(c) Disapproval
  (1) In general
  If, in the judgment of the Administrator, a State program or portion thereof under subsection (a) of this section is not adequate to protect public water systems as required by subsection (a) of this section or a State program under section 300j-13 of this title or section 300g-7(b) of this title does not meet the applicable requirements of section 300j-13 of this title or section 300g-7(b) of this title, the Administrator shall disapprove such program or portion thereof. A State program developed pursuant to subsection (a) of this section shall be deemed to be adequate unless the Administrator determines, within 9 months of the receipt of a State program, that such program (or portion thereof) is inadequate for the purpose of protecting public water systems as required by this section from contaminants that may have any adverse effect on the health of persons. A State program developed pursuant to section 300j-13 of this title or section 300g-7(b) of this title shall be deemed to meet the applicable requirements of section 300j-13 of this title or section 300g-7(b) of this title unless the Administrator determines within 9 months of the receipt of the program that such program (or portion thereof) does not meet such requirements. If the Administrator determines that a proposed State program (or any portion thereof) is disapproved, the Administrator shall submit a written statement of the reasons for such determination to the Governor of the State.
  (2) Modification and resubmission
  Within 6 months after receipt of the Administrator's written notice under paragraph (1) that any proposed State program (or portion thereof) is disapproved, the Governor or Governor's designee, shall modify the program based upon the recommendations of the Administrator and resubmit the modified program to the Administrator.

(d) Federal assistance
After the date 3 years after June 19, 1986, no State shall receive funds authorized to be appropriated under this section except for the purpose of implementing the program and requirements of paragraphs (4) and (6) of subsection (a) of this section.

(e) "Wellhead protection area" defined
As used in this section, the term "wellhead protection area" means the surface and subsurface area surrounding a water well or wellfield, supplying a public water system, through which contaminants are reasonably likely to move toward and reach such water well or wellfield. The extent of a wellhead protection area, within a State, necessary to provide protection from contaminants which may have any adverse effect on the health of persons is to be determined by the State in the program submitted under subsection (a) of this section. Not later than one year after June 19, 1986, the Administrator shall issue technical guidance which States may use in making such determinations. Such guidance may reflect such factors as the radius of influence around a well or wellfield, the depth of drawdown of the water table by such well or wellfield at any given point, the time or rate of travel of various contaminants in various hydrologic conditions, distance from the well or wellfield, or other factors affecting the likelihood of contaminants reaching the well or wellfield, taking into account available engineering pump tests or comparable data, field reconnaissance, topographic information, and the geology of the formation in which the well or wellfield is located.

(f) Prohibitions
  (1) Activities under other laws
  No funds authorized to be appropriated under this section may be used to support activities authorized by the Federal Water Pollution Control Act [33 U.S.C. 1251 et seq.], the Solid Waste Disposal Act [42 U.S.C. 6901 et seq.], the Comprehensive Environmental Response, Compensation, and Liability Act of 1980 [42 U.S.C. 9601 et seq.], or other sections of this chapter.

(2) Individual sources
No funds authorized to be appropriated under this section may be used to bring individual sources of contamination into compliance.

(g) Implementation
Each State shall make every reasonable effort to implement the State wellhead area protection program under this section within 2 years of submitting the program to the Administrator. Each State shall submit to the Administrator a biennial status report describing the State's progress in implementing the program. Such report shall include amendments to the State program for water wells sited during the biennial period.

(h) Federal agencies
Each department, agency, and instrumentality of the executive, legislative, and judicial branches of the Federal Government having jurisdiction over any potential source of contaminants identified by a State program pursuant to the provisions of subsection (a)(3) of this section shall be subject to and comply with all requirements of the State program developed according to subsection (a)(4) of this section applicable to such potential source of contaminants, both substantive and procedural, in the same manner, and to the same extent, as any other person is subject to such requirements, including payment of reasonable charges and fees. The President may exempt any potential source under the jurisdiction of any department, agency, or instrumentality in the executive branch if the President determines it to be in the paramount interest of the United States to do so. No such exemption shall be granted due to the lack of an appropriation unless the President shall have specifically requested such appropriation as part of the budgetary process and the Congress shall have failed to make available such requested appropriations.

(i) Additional requirement
(1) In general
In addition to the provisions of subsection (a) of this section, States in which there are more than 2,500 active wells at which annular injection is used as of January 1, 1986, shall include in their State program a certification that a State program exists and is being adequately enforced that provides protection from contaminants which may have any adverse effect on the health of persons and which are associated with the annular injection or surface disposal of brines associated with oil and gas production.

(2) "Annular injection" defined
For purposes of this subsection, the term "annular injection" means the reinjection of brines associated with the production of oil or gas between the production and surface casings of a conventional oil or gas producing well.

(3) Review
The Administrator shall conduct a review of each program certified under this subsection.

(4) Disapproval
If a State fails to include the certification required by this subsection or if in the judgment of the Administrator the State program certified under this subsection is not being adequately enforced, the Administrator shall disapprove the State program submitted under subsection (a) of this section.

(j) Coordination with other laws
Nothing in this section shall authorize or require any department, agency, or other instrumentality of the Federal Government or State or local government to apportion, allocate or otherwise regulate the withdrawal or beneficial use of ground or surface waters, so as to abrogate or modify any existing rights to water established pursuant to State or Federal law, including interstate compacts.

(k) Authorization of appropriations
Unless the State program is disapproved under this section, the Administrator shall make grants to the State for not less than 50 or more than 90 percent of the costs incurred by a State (as determined by the Administrator) in developing and implementing each State program under this section. For purposes of making such grants there is authorized to be appropriated not more than the following amounts:

Fiscal year:	Amount
1987	$20,000,000
1988	20,000,000
1989	35,000,000
1990	35,000,000
1991	35,000,000
1992-2003	30,000,000.

(July 1, 1944, ch. 373, title XIV, Sec. 1428, as added and amended Pub. L. 99-339, title II, Sec. 205, title III, Sec. 301(e), June 19, 1986, 100 Stat. 660, 664; Pub. L. 104-182, title I, Secs. 120(b), 132(b), title V, Sec. 501(f)(4), Aug. 6, 1996, 110 Stat. 1650, 1674, 1692.)

References in Text

The Federal Water Pollution Control Act, referred to in subsec. (f)(1), is act June 30, 1948, ch. 758, as amended generally by Pub. L. 92-500, Sec. 2, Oct. 18, 1972, 86 Stat. 816, which is classified generally to chapter 26 (Sec. 1251 et seq.) of Title 33, Navigation and Navigable Waters. For complete classification of this Act to the Code, see Short Title note set out under section 1251 of Title 33 and Tables.

The Solid Waste Disposal Act, referred to in subsec. (f)(1), is title II of Pub. L. 89-272, Oct. 20, 1965, 79 Stat. 997, as amended generally by Pub. L. 94-580, Sec. 2, Oct. 21, 1976, 90 Stat. 2795, which is classified generally to chapter 82 (Sec. 6901 et seq.) of this title. For complete classification of this Act to the Code, see Short Title note set out under section 6901 of this title and Tables.

The Comprehensive Environmental Response, Compensation, and Liability Act of 1980, referred to in subsec. (f)(1), is Pub. L. 96-510, Dec. 11, 1980, 94 Stat. 2767, as amended, which is classified principally to chapter 103 (Sec. 9601 et seq.) of this title. For complete classification of this Act to the Code, see Short Title note set out under section 9601 of this title and Tables.

Amendments

1996—Pub. L. 104-182, Sec. 501(f)(4), made technical amendment to section catchline and subsec. (a) designation.

Subsec. (b). Pub. L. 104-182, Sec. 132(b)(4), inserted before period at end of first sentence "and source water assessment programs under section 300j-13 of this title".

Subsec. (c)(1). Pub. L. 104-182, Sec. 132(b)(3), which directed substitution of "is disapproved" for "is inadequate" in third sentence, was executed by making the substitution in fourth sentence to reflect the probable intent of Congress and the amendment by Pub. L. 104-182, Sec. 132(b)(2). See below.

Pub. L. 104-182, Sec. 132(b)(2), inserted after second sentence "A State program developed pursuant to section 300j-13 of this title or section 300g-7(b) of this title shall be deemed to meet the applicable requirements of section 300j-13 of this title or section 300g-7(b) of this title unless the Administrator determines within 9 months of the receipt of the program that such program (or portion thereof) does not meet such requirements."

Pub. L. 104-182, Sec. 132(b)(1), amended first sentence generally. Prior to amendment, first sentence read as follows: "If, in the judgment of the Administrator, a State program (or portion thereof, including the definition of a wellhead protection area), is not adequate to protect public water systems as required by this section, the Administrator shall disapprove such program (or portion thereof)."

Subsec. (c)(2). Pub. L. 104-182, Sec. 132(b)(3), substituted "is disapproved" for "is inadequate".

Subsec. (k). Pub. L. 104-182, Sec. 120(b), inserted table item relating to fiscal years 1992 through 2003.

1986—Subsec. (k). Pub. L. 99-339, Sec. 301(e), added subsec. (k).

Section Referred to in Other Sections

This section is referred to in sections 300j-12, 300j-13, 300j-14 of this title.

STATE GROUND WATER PROTECTION GRANTS

42 USC 300h-8

(a) In general

The Administrator may make a grant to a State for the development and implementation of a State program to ensure the coordinated and comprehensive protection of ground water resources within the State.

(b) Guidance

Not later than 1 year after August 6, 1996, and annually thereafter, the Administrator shall publish guidance that establishes procedures for application for State ground water protection program assistance and that identifies key elements of State ground water protection programs.

(c) Conditions of grants

(1) In general

The Administrator shall award grants to States that submit an application that is approved by the Administrator. The Administrator shall determine the amount of a grant awarded pursuant to this paragraph on the basis of an assessment of the extent of ground water resources in the State and the likelihood that awarding the grant will result in sustained and reliable protection of ground water quality.

(2) Innovative program grants

The Administrator may also award a grant pursuant to this subsection for innovative programs proposed by a State for the prevention of ground water contamination.

(3) Allocation of funds

The Administrator shall, at a minimum, ensure that, for each fiscal year, not less than 1 percent of funds made available to the Administrator by appropriations to carry out this section are allocated to each State that submits an application that is approved by the Administrator pursuant to this section.

(4) Limitation on grants

No grant awarded by the Administrator may be used for a project to remediate ground water contamination.

(d) Amount of grants

The amount of a grant awarded pursuant to paragraph (1) shall not exceed 50 percent of the eligible costs of carrying out the ground water protection program that is the subject of the grant (as determined by the Administrator) for the 1-year period beginning on the date that the grant is awarded. The State shall pay a State share to cover the costs of the ground water protection program from State funds in an amount that is not less than 50 percent of the cost of conducting the program.

(e) Evaluations and reports

Not later than 3 years after August 6, 1996, and every 3 years thereafter, the Administrator shall evaluate the State ground water protection programs that are the subject of grants awarded pursuant to this section and report to the Congress on the status of ground water quality in the United States and the effectiveness of State programs for ground water protection.

(f) Authorization of appropriations

There are authorized to be appropriated to carry out this section $15,000,000 for each of fiscal years 1997 through 2003.

(July 1, 1944, ch. 373, title XIV, Sec. 1429, as added Pub. L. 104-182, title I, Sec. 131, Aug. 6, 1996, 110 Stat. 1672.)

Section Referred to in Other Sections

This section is referred to in section 300j-8 of this title.

Part D—Emergency Powers

EMERGENCY POWERS

42 USC 300i

(a) Actions authorized against imminent and substantial endangerment to health
Notwithstanding any other provision of this subchapter the Administrator, upon receipt of information that a contaminant which is present in or is likely to enter a public water system or an underground source of drinking water or that there is a threatened or potential terrorist attack (or other intentional act designed to disrupt the provision of safe drinking water or to impact adversely the safety of drinking water supplied to communities and individuals), which may present an imminent and substantial endangerment to the health of persons, and that appropriate State and local authorities have not acted to protect the health of such persons, may take such actions as he may deem necessary in order to protect the health of such persons. To the extent he determines it to be practicable in light of such imminent endangerment, he shall consult with the State and local authorities in order to confirm the correctness of the information on which action proposed to be taken under this subsection is based and to ascertain the action which such authorities are or will be taking. The action which the Administrator may take may include (but shall not be limited to) (1) issuing such orders as may be necessary to protect the health of persons who are or may be users of such system (including travelers), including orders requiring the provision of alternative water supplies by persons who caused or contributed to the endangerment, and (2) commencing a civil action for appropriate relief, including a restraining order or permanent or temporary injunction.

(b) Penalties for violations; separate offenses
Any person who violates or fails or refuses to comply with any order issued by the Administrator under subsection (a)(1) of this section may, in an action brought in the appropriate United States district court to enforce such order, be subject to a civil penalty of not to exceed $15,000 for each day in which such violation occurs or failure to comply continues.

(July 1, 1944, ch. 373, title XIV, Sec. 1431, as added Pub. L. 93-523, Sec. 2(a), Dec. 16, 1974, 88 Stat. 1680; amended Pub. L. 99-339, title II, Sec. 204, June 19, 1986, 100 Stat. 660; Pub. L. 104-182, title I, Sec. 113(d), Aug. 6, 1996, 110 Stat. 1636.)

Amendments

2002–Sub sec. (a). Pub. L. 107-188 added "or that there is a threatened or potential terrorist attack (or other intentional act designed to disrupt the provision of safe drinking water or to impact adversely the safety of drinking water supplied to communities and individuals)."

1996–Subsec. (b). Pub. L. 104-182 substituted "$15,000" for "$5,000".

1986–Subsec. (a). Pub. L. 99-339, Sec. 204(1), (2), inserted "or an underground source of drinking water" after "to enter a public water system" and "including orders requiring the provision of alternative water supplies by persons who caused or contributed to the endangerment," after "including travelers),".

Subsec. (b). Pub. L. 99-339, Sec. 204(3), struck out "willfully" after "person who" and substituted "subject to a civil penalty of not to exceed" for "fined not more than".

Section Referred to in Other Sections

This section is referred to in sections 7412, 9606 of this title.

TAMPERING WITH PUBLIC WATER SYSTEMS

42 USC 300i-1

(a) Tampering
Any person who tampers with a public water system shall be imprisoned for not more than 20 years, or fined in accordance with title 18, or both.

(b) Attempt or threat
Any person who attempts to tamper, or makes a threat to tamper, with a public drinking water system be imprisoned for not more than 10 years, or fined in accordance with title 18, or both.

(c) Civil penalty
   The Administrator may bring a civil action in the appropriate United States district court (as determined under the provisions of title 28) against any person who tampers, attempts to tamper, or makes a threat to tamper with a public water system. The court may impose on such person a civil penalty of not more than $1,000,000 for such tampering or not more than $100,000 for such attempt or threat.
(d) "Tamper" defined
   For purposes of this section, the term "tamper" means—
   (1) to introduce a contaminant into a public water system with the intention of harming persons; or
   (2) to otherwise interfere with the operation of a public water system with the intention of harming persons.

(July 1, 1944, ch. 373, title XIV, Sec. 1432, as added Pub. L. 99-339, title I, Sec. 108, June 19, 1986, 100 Stat. 651; amended Pub. L. 104-182, title V, Sec. 501(f)(5), Aug. 6, 1996, 110 Stat. 1692.)

Amendments

2002–Pub. L. 107-188 changed "5 years" to "20 years" in (a); "3 years" to "10 years" in (b); and "$50,000" to "$1,000,000" and "$20,000" to "$100,000" in (c).

1996–Pub. L. 104-182 made technical amendment to section catchline and subsec. (a) designation.

Part E—General Provisions

ASSURANCES OF AVAILABILITY OF ADEQUATE SUPPLIES OF CHEMICALS NECESSARY FOR TREATMENT OF WATER

42 USC 300j

(a) Certification of need application
   If any person who uses chlorine, activated carbon, lime, ammonia, soda ash, potassium permanganate, caustic soda, or other chemical or substance for the purpose of treating water in any public water system or in any public treatment works determines that the amount of such chemical or substance necessary to effectively treat such water is not reasonably available to him or will not be so available to him when required for the effective treatment of such water, such person may apply to the Administrator for a certification (hereinafter in this section referred to as a "certification of need") that the amount of such chemical or substance which such person requires to effectively treat such water is not reasonably available to him or will not be so available when required for the effective treatment of such water.
(b) Application requirements; publication in Federal Register; waiver, certification, issuance or denial
   (1) An application for a certification of need shall be in such form and submitted in such manner as the Administrator may require and shall (A) specify the persons the applicant determines are able to provide the chemical or substance with respect to which the application is submitted, (B) specify the persons from whom the applicant has sought such chemical or substance, and (C) contain such other information as the Administrator may require.
   (2) Upon receipt of an application under this section, the Administrator shall (A) publish in the Federal Register a notice of the receipt of the application and a brief summary of it, (B) notify in writing each person whom the President or his delegate (after consultation with the Administrator) determines could be made subject to an order required to be issued upon the issuance of the certification of need applied for in such application, and (C) provide an opportunity for the submission of written comments on such application. The requirements of the preceding sentence of this paragraph shall not apply when the Administrator for good cause finds (and incorporates the finding with a brief statement of reasons therefor in the order issued) that waiver of such requirements is necessary in order to protect the public health.

(3) Within 30 days after—
   (A) the date a notice is published under paragraph (2) in the Federal Register with respect to an application submitted under this section for the issuance of a certification of need, or
   (B) the date on which such application is received if as authorized by the second sentence of such paragraph no notice is published with respect to such application,
   the Administrator shall take action either to issue or deny the issuance of a certification of need.
(c) Certification of need; issuance; executive orders; implementation of orders; equitable apportionment of orders; factors considered
   (1) If the Administrator finds that the amount of a chemical or substance necessary for an applicant under an application submitted under this section to effectively treat water in a public water system or in a public treatment works is not reasonably available to the applicant or will not be so available to him when required for the effective treatment of such water, the Administrator shall issue a certification of need. Not later than seven days following the issuance of such certification, the President or his delegate shall issue an order requiring the provision to such person of such amounts of such chemical or substance as the Administrator deems necessary in the certification of need issued for such person. Such order shall apply to such manufactures, producers, processors, distributors, and repackagers of such chemical or substance as the President or his delegate deems necessary and appropriate, except that such order may not apply to any manufacturer, producer, or processor of such chemical or substance who manufactures, produces, or processes (as the case may be) such chemical or substance solely for its own use. Persons subject to an order issued under this section shall be given a reasonable opportunity to consult with the President or his delegate with respect to the implementation of the order.
   (2) Orders which are to be issued under paragraph (1) to manufacturers, producers, and processors of a chemical or substance shall be equitably apportioned, as far as practicable, among all manufacturers, producers, and processors of such chemical or substance; and orders which are to be issued under paragraph (1) to distributors and repackagers of a chemical or substance shall be equitably apportioned, as far as practicable, among all distributors and repackagers of such chemical or substance. In apportioning orders issued under paragraph (1) to manufacturers, producers, processors, distributors, and repackagers of chlorine, the President or his delegate shall, in carrying out the requirements of the preceding sentence, consider—
      (A) the geographical relationships and established commercial relationships between such manufacturers, producers, processors, distributors, and repackagers and the persons for whom the orders are issued;
      (B) in the case of orders to be issued to producers of chlorine, the (i) amount of chlorine historically supplied by each such producer to treat water in public water systems and public treatment works, and (ii) share of each such producer of the total annual production of chlorine in the United States; and
      (C) such other factors as the President or his delegate may determine are relevant to the apportionment of orders in accordance with the requirements of the preceding sentence.
   (3) Subject to subsection (f) of this section, any person for whom a certification of need has been issued under this subsection may upon the expiration of the order issued under paragraph (1) upon such certification apply under this section for additional certifications.
(d) Breach of contracts; defense
   There shall be available as a defense to any action brought for breach of contract in a Federal or State court arising out of delay or failure to provide, sell, or offer for sale or exchange a chemical or substance subject to an order issued pursuant to subsection (c)(1) of this section, that such delay or failure was caused solely by compliance with such order.
(e) Penalties for noncompliance with orders; temporary restraining orders and preliminary or permanent injunctions
   (1) Whoever knowingly fails to comply with any order issued pursuant to subsection (c)(1) of this section shall be fined not more than $5,000 for each such failure to comply.

(2) Whoever fails to comply with any order issued pursuant to subsection (c)(1) of this section shall be subject to a civil penalty of not more than $2,500 for each such failure to comply.

(3) Whenever the Administrator or the President or his delegate has reason to believe that any person is violating or will violate any order issued pursuant to subsection (c)(1) of this section, he may petition a United States district court to issue a temporary restraining order or preliminary or permanent injunction (including a mandatory injunction) to enforce the provision of such order.

(f) Termination date

No certification of need or order issued under this section may remain in effect for more than one year.

(July 1, 1944, ch. 373, title XIV, Sec. 1441, as added Pub. L. 93-523, Sec. 2(a), Dec. 16, 1974, 88 Stat. 1680; amended Pub. L. 95-190, Sec. 7, Nov. 16, 1977, 91 Stat. 1396; Pub. L. 96-63, Sec. 3, Sept. 6, 1979, 93 Stat. 411; Pub. L. 99-339, title III, Sec. 301(d), June 19, 1986, 100 Stat. 664; Pub. L. 104-182, title V, Sec. 501(c), Aug. 6, 1996, 110 Stat. 1691.)

Amendments

1996—Subsec. (f). Pub. L. 104-182 inserted a period after "year".

1986—Subsec. (f). Pub. L. 99-339 substituted "in effect for more than one year" for "in effect— (1) for more than one year, or (2) September 30, 1982, whichever occurs first."

1979—Subsec. (f)(2). Pub. L. 96-63 substituted "September 30, 1982" for "September 30, 1979".

1977—Subsec. (f). Pub. L. 95-190 substituted "September 30, 1979" for "June 30, 1977".

Ex. Ord. No. 11879. Delegation of Functions to Secretary of Commerce Relating to Orders for Provision of Chemicals or Substances Necessary for Treatment of Water

Ex. Ord. No. 11879, Sept. 17, 1975, 40 F.R. 43197, provided:

By virtue of the authority vested in me by Section 1441 of the Public Health Service Act, as amended by the Safe Drinking Water Act [now Safe Drinking Water Act of 1974] (88 Stat. 1680, 42 U.S.C. 300j), and as President of the United States, the Secretary of Commerce is hereby delegated, with power to redelegate to agencies, officers and employees of the Government, the functions of the President contained in said section 1441 [this section]. Those functions shall be administered under regulations or agreements which are identical or compatible with other regulations and agreements, including those provided pursuant to Executive Order No. 10480, as amended [formerly set out as a note under section 2153 of Title 50, Appendix, War and National Defense], for the allocation of similar chemicals or substances.

Gerald R. Ford.

Section Referred to in Other Sections

This section is referred to in section 300g-3 of this title.

RESEARCH, TECHNICAL ASSISTANCE, INFORMATION, TRAINING OF PERSONNEL

42 USC 300j-1

(a) Specific powers and duties of Administrator
   (1) The Administrator may conduct research, studies, and demonstrations relating to the causes, diagnosis, treatment, control, and prevention of physical and mental diseases and other impairments of man resulting directly or indirectly from contaminants in water, or to the provision of a dependably safe supply of drinking water, including—
      (A) improved methods (i) to identify and measure the existence of contaminants in drinking water (including methods which may be used by State and local health and water officials), and (ii) to identify the source of such contaminants;
      (B) improved methods to identify and measure the health effects of contaminants in drinking water;
      (C) new methods of treating raw water to prepare it for drinking, so as to improve the efficiency of water treatment and to remove contaminants from water;

(D) improved methods for providing a dependably safe supply of drinking water, including improvements in water purification and distribution, and methods of assessing the health related hazards of drinking water; and

(E) improved methods of protecting underground water sources of public water systems from contamination.

(2) Information and research facilities.—In carrying out this subchapter, the Administrator is authorized to—

(A) collect and make available information pertaining to research, investigations, and demonstrations with respect to providing a dependably safe supply of drinking water, together with appropriate recommendations in connection with the information; and

(B) make available research facilities of the Agency to appropriate public authorities, institutions, and individuals engaged in studies and research relating to this subchapter.

(3) The Administrator shall carry out a study of polychlorinated biphenyl contamination of actual or potential sources of drinking water, contamination of such sources by other substances known or suspected to be harmful to public health, the effects of such contamination, and means of removing, treating, or otherwise controlling such contamination. To assist in carrying out this paragraph, the Administrator is authorized to make grants to public agencies and private nonprofit institutions.

(4) The Administrator shall conduct a survey and study of—

(A) disposal of waste (including residential waste) which may endanger underground water which supplies, or can reasonably be expected to supply, any public water systems, and

(B) means of control of such waste disposal.

Not later than one year after December 16, 1974, he shall transmit to the Congress the results of such survey and study, together with such recommendations as he deems appropriate.

(5) The Administrator shall carry out a study of methods of underground injection which do not result in the degradation of underground drinking water sources.

(6) The Administrator shall carry out a study of methods of preventing, detecting, and dealing with surface spills of contaminants which may degrade underground water sources for public water systems.

(7) The Administrator shall carry out a study of virus contamination of drinking water sources and means of control of such contamination.

(8) The Administrator shall carry out a study of the nature and extent of the impact on underground water which supplies or can reasonably be expected to supply public water systems of (A) abandoned injection or extraction wells; (B) intensive application of pesticides and fertilizers in underground water recharge areas; and (C) ponds, pools, lagoons, pits, or other surface disposal of contaminants in underground water recharge areas.

(9) The Administrator shall conduct a comprehensive study of public water supplies and drinking water sources to determine the nature, extent, sources of and means of control of contamination by chemicals or other substances suspected of being carcinogenic. Not later than six months after December 16, 1974, he shall transmit to the Congress the initial results of such study, together with such recommendations for further review and corrective action as he deems appropriate.

(10) The Administrator shall carry out a study of the reaction of chlorine and humic acids and the effects of the contaminants which result from such reaction on public health and on the safety of drinking water, including any carcinogenic effect.

(b) Emergency situations

The Administrator is authorized to provide technical assistance and to make grants to States, or publicly owned water systems to assist in responding to and alleviating any emergency situation affecting public water systems (including sources of water for such systems) which the Administrator determines to present substantial danger to the public health. Grants provided under this subsection shall be used only to support those actions which (i) are necessary for preventing, limiting or mitigating danger to the public health in such emergency situation and (ii) would not, in the judgment of the Administrator, be taken without such emergency assistance. The Administrator may carry out the program authorized under this subsection as part of, and in accordance with the terms and conditions of, any other program of assistance for environmental emergencies which the Administrator is authorized to carry out under any

other provision of law. No limitation on appropriations for any such other program shall apply to amounts appropriated under this subparagraph.[1]
(c) Establishment of training programs and grants for training; training fees
The Administrator shall—
  (1) provide training for, and make grants for training (including postgraduate training) of (A) personnel of State agencies which have primary enforcement responsibility and of agencies or units of local government to which enforcement responsibilities have been delegated by the State, and (B) personnel who manage or operate public water systems, and
  (2) make grants for postgraduate training of individuals (including grants to educational institutions for traineeships) for purposes of qualifying such individuals to work as personnel referred to in paragraph (1).
  (3) make grants to, and enter into contracts with, any public agency, educational institution, and any other organization, in accordance with procedures prescribed by the Administrator, under which he may pay all or part of the costs (as may be determined by the Administrator) of any project or activity which is designed—
    (A) to develop, expand, or carry out a program (which may combine training education and employment) for training persons for occupations involving the public health aspects of providing safe drinking water;
    (B) to train inspectors and supervisory personnel to train or supervise persons in occupations involving the public health aspects of providing safe drinking water; or
    (C) to develop and expand the capability of programs of States and municipalities to carry out the purposes of this subchapter (other than by carrying out State programs of public water system supervision or underground water source protection (as defined in section 300j-2(c) of this title)).
  Reasonable fees may be charged for training provided under paragraph (1)(B) to persons other than personnel of State or local agencies but such training shall be provided to personnel of State or local agencies without charge.
(d) Appropriation authorization. There are authorized to be appropriated to carry out subsection (b) not more than $35,000,000 for the fiscal year 2002 and such sums as may be necessary for each fiscal year thereafter.
(e) Technical assistance. The Administrator may provide technical assistance to small public water systems to enable such systems to achieve and maintain compliance with applicable national primary drinking water regulations. Such assistance may include circuit-rider and multi-State regional technical assistance programs, training, and preliminary engineering evaluations. The Administrator shall ensure that technical assistance pursuant to this subsection is available in each State. Each nonprofit organization receiving assistance under this subsection shall consult with the State in which the assistance is to be expended or otherwise made available before using assistance to undertake activities to carry out this subsection. There are authorized to be appropriated to the Administrator to be used for such technical assistance $15,000,000 for each of the fiscal years 1997 through 2003. No portion of any State loan fund established under section 300j-12 of this title (relating to State loan funds) and no portion of any funds made available under this subsection may be used for lobbying expenses. Of the total amount appropriated under this subsection, 3 percent shall be used for technical assistance to public water systems owned or operated by Indian Tribes.

(July 1, 1944, ch. 373, title XIV, Sec. 1442, as added Pub. L. 93-523, Sec. 2(a), Dec. 16, 1974, 88 Stat. 1682; amended Pub. L. 95-190, Secs. 2(a), 3(a), (b), (e)(1), 4, 9, 10(b), 13, Nov. 16, 1977, 91 Stat. 1393-1395, 1397-1399; Pub. L. 96-63, Sec. 1, Sept. 6, 1979, 93 Stat. 411; Pub. L. 96-502, Sec. 5, Dec. 5, 1980, 94 Stat. 2738; Pub. L. 99-339, title I, Sec. 107, title III, Secs. 301(a), (g), 304(a), June 19, 1986, 100 Stat. 651, 663, 665, 667; Pub. L. 104-66, title II, Sec. 2021(h), Dec. 21, 1995, 109 Stat. 727; Pub. L. 104-182, title I, Secs. 121, 122, Aug. 6, 1996, 110 Stat. 1651.)

References in Text

Subsection (a)(2)(B) of this section, referred to in subsec. (d), was redesignated subsec. (b) of this section by Pub. L. 104-182, title I, Sec. 121(3), Aug. 6, 1996, 110 Stat. 1651.

Amendments

2002—Pub. L. 107-188 replaced "subparagraph" with "subsection" in (b) and replaced the text of (d).

1996—Subsec. (a)(2). Pub. L. 104-182, Sec. 121(4)(A), added heading and text of par. (2) and struck out former par. (2) which read as follows: "(2)(A) The Administrator shall, to the maximum extent feasible, provide technical assistance to the States and municipalities in the establishment and administration of public water system supervision programs (as defined in section 300j-2(c)(1) of this title)."

Subsec. (a)(2)(B). Pub. L. 104-182, Sec. 121(3), redesignated subpar. (B) as subsec. (b) and transferred that subsec. to appear after subsec. (a).

Subsec. (a)(3), (11). Pub. L. 104-182, Sec. 121(4)(B), (C), redesignated par. (11) as (3), transferred that par. to appear before par. (4), and struck out former par. (3) which provided that the Administrator was to conduct studies, and make periodic reports to Congress, on the costs of carrying out regulations prescribed under section 300g-1 of this title.

Subsec. (b). Pub. L. 104-182, Sec. 121(2), (3), redesignated subsec. (a)(2)(B) as subsec. (b), transferred that subsec. to appear after subsec. (a), and struck out former subsec. (b) which read as follows: "In carrying out this subchapter, the Administrator is authorized to—
(1) collect and make available information pertaining to research, investigations, and demonstrations with respect to providing a dependably safe supply of drinking water together with appropriate recommendations in connection therewith;
(2) make available research facilities of the Agency to appropriate public authorities, institutions, and individuals engaged in studies and research relating to the purposes of this subchapter;".

Subsecs. (b)(3), (c)(3). Pub. L. 104-182, Sec. 121(1), which directed redesignation of subsec. (b)(3) as par. (3) of subsec. (d) and transfer of that par. to follow par. (2) of subsec. (d), was executed by redesignating subsec. (b)(3) as par. (3) of subsec. (c) and transferring that par. to follow par. (2) of subsec. (c) to reflect the probable intent of Congress and the redesignation of subsec. (d) as (c) by Pub. L. 104-66. See 1995 Amendment note below. Moreover, subsec. (d) does not have any pars.

Subsec. (e). Pub. L. 104-182, Sec. 122, amended subsec. (e) generally. Prior to amendment, subsec. (e) read as follows: "The Administrator is authorized to provide technical assistance to small public water systems to enable such systems to achieve and maintain compliance with national drinking water regulations. Such assistance may include 'circuit-rider' programs, training, and preliminary engineering studies. There are authorized to be appropriated to carry out this subsection $10,000,000 for each of the fiscal years 1987 through 1991. Not less than the greater of—
(1) 3 percent of the amounts appropriated under this subsection, or
(2) $280,000
shall be utilized for technical assistance to public water systems owned or operated by Indian tribes."

1995—Subsecs. (c) to (g). Pub. L. 104-66 redesignated subsecs. (d), (f), and (g) as (c), (d), and (e), respectively, and struck out former subsec. (c) which read as follows: "Not later than eighteen months after November 16, 1977, the Administrator shall submit a report to Congress on the present and projected future availability of an adequate and dependable supply of safe drinking water to meet present and projected future need. Such report shall include an analysis of the future demand for drinking water and other competing uses of water, the availability and use of methods to conserve water or reduce demand, the adequacy of present measures to assure adequate and dependable supplies of safe drinking water, and the problems (financial, legal, or other) which need to be resolved in order to assure the availability of such supplies for the future. Existing information and data complied by the National Water Commission and others shall be utilized to the extent possible."

1986—Subsec. (e). Pub. L. 99-339, Sec. 304(a), struck out subsec. (e) which authorized the Administrator to make grants to public water systems which are required, under State or local law, to meet standards relating to drinking turbidity which are more stringent than the standards in effect under this subchapter.

Subsec. (f). Pub. L. 99-339, Sec. 301(a), authorized appropriations to carry out subsec. (a)(2)(B) of this section for fiscal years 1987 to 1991 and to carry out provisions of this section other than subsecs. (a)(2)(B) and (g) and provisions relating to research for fiscal years 1987 to 1991.

Subsec. (g). Pub. L. 99-339, Sec. 301(g), authorized appropriations to carry out this subsection of $10,000,000 for each of fiscal years 1987 through 1991 and specified amount to be utilized for public water systems owned or operated by Indian tribes.

Pub. L. 99-339, Sec. 107 added subsec. (g).

1980—Subsecs. (e), (f). Pub. L. 96-502 added subsec. (e) and redesignated former subsec. (e) as (f).

1979—Subsec. (e). Pub. L. 96-63 authorized appropriations of $21,405,000 for fiscal year ending Sept. 30, 1980, $30,000,000 for fiscal year ending Sept. 30, 1981, and $35,000,000 for fiscal year ending Sept. 30, 1982 for purposes other than those of subsec. (a)(2)(B) of this section and for purposes of subsec. (a)(2)(B) of this section, $8,000,000 for fiscal years 1980 through 1982.

1977—Subsec. (a)(2). Pub. L. 95-190, Secs. 9, 13, designated existing provisions as subpar. (A), added subpar. (B) and, in subpar. (B) as added, substituted provisions authorizing Administrator to make grants and provide technical assistance for any emergency situation affecting public water systems and criteria for such grants and assistance for provisions authorizing Administrator to make grants and provide technical assistance for any emergency situation respecting drinking water and criteria for determination of such situations.

Subsec. (a)(3). Pub. L. 95-190, Sec. 3(a), designated existing provisions as subpar. (A) and added subpar. (B).

Subsec. (a)(10), (11). Pub. L. 95-190, Sec. 3(e)(1), added pars. (10) and (11).

Subsec. (b)(3)(C). Pub. L. 95-190, Sec. 10(b), substituted "300j-2(c)" for "300j-2(d)".

Subsecs. (c), (d). Pub. L. 95-190, Secs. 3(b), 4, added subsecs. (c) and (d). Former subsec. (c) redesignated (e).

Subsec. (e). Pub. L. 95-190, Secs. 2(a), 3(b), redesignated former subsec. (c) as (e) and inserted provisions authorizing appropriations for fiscal years 1978 and 1979, and provisions relating to appropriations for subsec. (a)(2)(B) of this section and for research.

Scientific Research Review

Section 202 of Pub. L. 104-182 provided that:

"(a) In General.—The Administrator shall—
  (1) develop a strategic plan for drinking water research activities throughout the Environmental Protection Agency (in this section referred to as the 'Agency');
  (2) integrate that strategic plan into ongoing Agency planning activities; and
  (3) review all Agency drinking water research to ensure the research—
    (A) is of high quality; and
    (B) does not duplicate any other research being conducted by the Agency.
(b) Plan.—The Administrator shall transmit the plan to the Committees on Commerce and Science of the House of Representatives and the Committee on Environment and Public Works of the Senate and the plan shall be made available to the public."

National Center for Ground Water Research

Section 203 of Pub. L. 104-182 provided that: "The Administrator of the Environmental Protection Agency, acting through the Robert S. Kerr Environmental Research Laboratory, is authorized to reestablish a partnership between the Laboratory and the National Center for Ground Water Research, a university consortium, to conduct research, training, and technology transfer for ground water quality protection and restoration. No funds are authorized by this section."

Comparative Health Effects Assessment

Section 304(b) of Pub. L. 99-339 provided that: "The Administrator of the Environmental Protection Agency shall conduct a comparative health effects assessment, using available data, to compare the public health effects (both positive and negative) associated with water treatment chemicals and their byproducts to the public health effects associated with contaminants found in public water supplies. Not later than 18 months after the date of the enactment of this Act [June 19, 1986], the Administrator shall submit a report to the Congress setting forth the results of such assessment."

Section Referred to in Other Sections

This section is referred to in sections 300g-1, 300j-3b, 300j-12 of this title.

GRANTS FOR STATE PROGRAMS

42 USC 300j-2

(a) Public water systems supervision programs; applications for grants; allotment of sums; waiver of grant restrictions; notice of approval or disapproval of application; authorization of appropriations
  (1) From allotments made pursuant to paragraph (4), the Administrator may make grants to States to carry out public water system supervision programs.
  (2) No grant may be made under paragraph (1) unless an application therefor has been submitted to the Administrator in such form and manner as he may require. The Administrator may not approve an application of a State for its first grant under paragraph (1) unless he determines that the State—
     (A) has established or will establish within one year from the date of such grant a public water system supervision program, and
     (B) will, within that one year, assume primary enforcement responsibility for public water systems within the State.
   No grant may be made to a State under paragraph (1) for any period beginning more than one year after the date of the State's first grant unless the State has assumed and maintains primary enforcement responsibility for public water systems within the State. The prohibitions contained in the preceding two sentences shall not apply to such grants when made to Indian Tribes.
  (3) A grant under paragraph (1) shall be made to cover not more than 75 per centum of the grant recipient's costs (as determined under regulations of the Administrator) in carrying out, during the one-year period beginning on the date the grant is made, a public water system supervision program.
  (4) In each fiscal year the Administrator shall, in accordance, with regulations, allot the sums appropriated for such year under paragraph (5) among the States on the basis of population, geographical area, number of public water systems, and other relevant factors. No State shall receive less than 1 per centum of the annual appropriation for grants under paragraph (1): Provided, That the Administrator may, by regulation, reduce such percentage in accordance with the criteria specified in this paragraph: And provided further, That such percentage shall not apply to grants allotted to Guam, American Samoa, or the Virgin Islands.
  (5) The prohibition contained in the last sentence of paragraph (2) may be waived by the Administrator with respect to a grant to a State through fiscal year 1979 but such prohibition may only be waived if, in the judgment of the Administrator—
     (A) the State is making a diligent effort to assume and maintain primary enforcement responsibility for public water systems within the State;
     (B) the State has made significant progress toward assuming and maintaining such primary enforcement responsibility; and
     (C) there is reason to believe the State will assume such primary enforcement responsibility by October 1, 1979.
   The amount of any grant awarded for the fiscal years 1978 and 1979 pursuant to a waiver under this paragraph may not exceed 75 per centum of the allotment which the State would have received for such fiscal year if it had assumed and maintained such primary enforcement responsibility. The remaining 25 per centum of the amount allotted to such State for such fiscal year shall be retained by the Administrator, and the Administrator may award such amount to such State at such time as the State assumes such responsibility before the beginning of fiscal year 1980. At the beginning of each fiscal years 1979 and 1980 the amounts retained by the Administrator for any preceding fiscal year and not awarded by the beginning of fiscal year 1979 or 1980 to the States to which such amounts were originally allotted may be removed from the original allotment and reallotted for fiscal year 1979 or 1980 (as the case may be) to States which have assumed primary enforcement responsibility by the beginning of such fiscal year.
  (6) The Administrator shall notify the State of the approval or disapproval of any application for a grant under this section—
     (A) within ninety days after receipt of such application, or
     (B) not later than the first day of the fiscal year for which the grant application is made, whichever is later.

(7) Authorization.—For the purpose of making grants under paragraph (1), there are authorized to be appropriated $100,000,000 for each of fiscal years 1997 through 2003.
(8) Reservation of funds by the administrator.—If the Administrator assumes the primary enforcement responsibility of a State public water system supervision program, the Administrator may reserve from funds made available pursuant to this subsection an amount equal to the amount that would otherwise have been provided to the State pursuant to this subsection. The Administrator shall use the funds reserved pursuant to this paragraph to ensure the full and effective administration of a public water system supervision program in the State.
(9) State loan funds.—
    (A) Reservation of funds.—For any fiscal year for which the amount made available to the Administrator by appropriations to carry out this subsection is less than the amount that the Administrator determines is necessary to supplement funds made available pursuant to paragraph (8) to ensure the full and effective administration of a public water system supervision program in a State, the Administrator may reserve from the funds made available to the State under section 300j-12 of this title (relating to State loan funds) an amount that is equal to the amount of the shortfall. This paragraph shall not apply to any State not exercising primary enforcement responsibility for public water systems as of August 6, 1996.
    (B) Duty of administrator.—If the Administrator reserves funds from the allocation of a State under subparagraph (A), the Administrator shall carry out in the State each of the activities that would be required of the State if the State had primary enforcement authority under section 300g-2 of this title.
(b) Underground water source protection programs; applications for grants; allotment of sums; authorization of appropriations
    (1) From allotments made pursuant to paragraph (4), the Administrator may make grants to States to carry out underground water source protection programs.
    (2) No grant may be made under paragraph (1) unless an application therefor has been submitted to the Administrator in such form and manner as he may require. No grant may be made to any State under paragraph (1) unless the State has assumed primary enforcement responsibility within two years after the date the Administrator promulgates regulations for State underground injection control programs under section 300h of this title. The prohibition contained in the preceding sentence shall not apply to such grants when made to Indian Tribes.
    (3) A grant under paragraph (1) shall be made to cover not more than 75 per centum of the grant recipient's cost (as determined under regulations of the Administrator) in carrying out, during the one-year period beginning on the date the grant is made, and underground water source protection program.
    (4) In each fiscal year the Administrator shall, in accordance with regulations, allot the sums appropriated for such year under paragraph (5) among the States on the basis of population, geographical area, and other relevant factors.
    (5) For purposes of making grants under paragraph (1) there are authorized to be appropriated $5,000,000 for the fiscal year ending June 30, 1976, $7,500,000 for the fiscal year ending June 30, 1977, $10,000,000 for each of the fiscal years 1978 and 1979, $7,795,000 for the fiscal year ending September 30, 1980, $18,000,000 for the fiscal year ending September 30, 1981, and $21,000,000 for the fiscal year ending September 30, 1982. For the purpose of making grants under paragraph (1) there are authorized to be appropriated not more than the following amounts:

Fiscal year:	Amount
1987	$19,700,000
1988	19,700,000
1989	20,850,000
1990	20,850,000
1991	20,850,000
1992-2003	15,000,000.

(c) Definitions
For purposes of this section:

856 / Environmental Statutes

(1) The term "public water system supervision program" means a program for the adoption and enforcement of drinking water regulations (with such variances and exemptions from such regulations under conditions and in a manner which is not less stringent than the conditions under, and the manner in, which variances and exemptions may be granted under sections 300g-4 and 300g-5 of this title) which are no less stringent than the national primary drinking water regulations under section 300g-1 of this title, and for keeping records and making reports required by section 300g-2(a)(3) of this title.

(2) The term "underground water source protection program" means a program for the adoption and enforcement of a program which meets the requirements of regulations under section 300h of this title, and for keeping records and making reports required by section 300h-1(b)(1)(A)(ii) of this title. Such term includes, where applicable, a program which meets the requirements of section 300h-4 of this title.

(d) New York City watershed protection program

(1) In general

The Administrator is authorized to provide financial assistance to the State of New York for demonstration projects implemented as part of the watershed program for the protection and enhancement of the quality of source waters of the New York City water supply system, including projects that demonstrate, assess, or provide for comprehensive monitoring and surveillance and projects necessary to comply with the criteria for avoiding filtration contained in 40 CFR 141.71. Demonstration projects which shall be eligible for financial assistance shall be certified to the Administrator by the State of New York as satisfying the purposes of this subsection. In certifying projects to the Administrator, the State of New York shall give priority to monitoring projects that have undergone peer review.

(2) Report

Not later than 5 years after the date on which the Administrator first provides assistance pursuant to this paragraph, the Governor of the State of New York shall submit a report to the Administrator on the results of projects assisted.

(3) Matching requirements

Federal assistance provided under this subsection shall not exceed 50 percent of the total cost of the protection program being carried out for any particular watershed or ground water recharge area.

(4) Authorization

There are authorized to be appropriated to the Administrator to carry out this subsection for each of fiscal years 1997 through 2003, $15,000,000 for the purpose of providing assistance to the State of New York to carry out paragraph (1).

(July 1, 1944, ch. 373, title XIV, Sec. 1443, as added Pub. L. 93-523, Sec. 2(a), Dec. 16, 1974, 88 Stat. 1684; amended Pub. L. 95-190, Secs. 2(b), (c), 5(a), Nov. 16, 1977, 91 Stat. 1393, 1395; Pub. L. 96-63, Sec. 2, Sept. 6, 1979, 93 Stat. 411; Pub. L. 96-502, Secs. 2(c), 4(d), Dec. 5, 1980, 94 Stat. 2738; Pub. L. 99-339, title III, Secs. 301(b), (c), 302(d), June 19, 1986, 100 Stat. 664, 666; Pub. L. 104-182, title I, Secs. 120(c), 124, 128, Aug. 6, 1996, 110 Stat. 1651, 1653, 1659.)

Amendments

1996—Subsec. (a)(7). Pub. L. 104-182, Sec. 124(1), inserted heading and amended text generally. Prior to amendment, text read as follows: "For purposes of making grants under paragraph (1) there are authorized to be appropriated $15,000,000 for the fiscal year ending June 30, 1976, $25,000,000 for the fiscal year ending June 30, 1977, $35,000,000 for fiscal year 1978, $45,000,000 for fiscal year 1979, $29,450,000 for the fiscal year ending September 30, 1980, $32,000,000 for the fiscal year ending September 30, 1981, and $34,000,000 for the fiscal year ending September 30, 1982. For the purposes of making grants under paragraph (1) there are authorized to be appropriated not more than the following amounts:

Fiscal year:	Amount
1987	$37,200,000
1988	37,200,000
1989	40,150,000
1990	40,150,000
1991	40,150,000".

Subsec. (a)(8), (9). Pub. L. 104-182, Sec. 124(2), added pars. (8) and (9).

Subsec. (b)(5). Pub. L. 104-182, Sec. 120(c), inserted table item relating to fiscal years 1992 through 2003.

Subsec. (d). Pub. L. 104-182, Sec. 128, added subsec. (d).

1986—Subsec. (a)(2). Pub. L. 99-339, Sec. 302(d)(1), inserted provision that prohibitions contained in preceding two sentences not apply to such grants when made to Indian Tribes.

Subsec. (a)(7). Pub. L. 99-339, Sec. 301(b), authorized appropriations for grants under par. (1) of not more than $37,200,000 for fiscal years 1987 and 1988 and of not more than $40,150,000 for fiscal years 1989 to 1991.

Subsec. (b)(2). Pub. L. 99-339, Sec. 302(d)(2), inserted provision that prohibition contained in preceding sentence not apply to such grants when made to Indian Tribes.

Subsec. (b)(5). Pub. L. 99-339, Sec. 301(c), authorized appropriations for grants under par. (1) of not more than $19,700,000 for fiscal years 1987 and 1988 and of not more than $20,850,000 for fiscal years 1989 to 1991.

1980—Subsec. (b)(2). Pub. L. 96-502, Sec. 4(d), substituted provisions that no grant may be made to any State under par. (1) unless the State has assumed primary enforcement responsibility within two years after the date the Administrator promulgates regulations for State underground injection control programs under section 300h of this title for provisions that the Administrator may not approve an application of a State for its first grant under par. (1) unless he determines that the State has established or will establish within two years from the date of such grant an underground water source protection, and will, within such two years, assume primary enforcement responsibility for underground water sources within the State and that no grant may be made to a State under par. (1) for any period beginning more than two years after the date of the State's first grant unless the State has assumed and maintains primary enforcement responsibility for underground water sources within the State.

Subsec. (c)(2). Pub. L. 96-502, Sec. 2(c), inserted provision that such term includes, where applicable, a program which meets requirements of section 300h-4 of this title.

1979—Subsec. (a)(7). Pub. L. 96-63, Sec. 2(a), authorized appropriation of $29,450,000, $32,000,000, and $34,000,000 for fiscal years ending Sept. 30, 1980, through 1982, respectively.

Subsec. (b)(5). Pub. L. 96-63, Sec. 2(b), authorized appropriation of $7,795,000, $18,000,000, and $21,000,000 for fiscal years ending Sept. 30, 1980, through 1982, respectively.

1977—Subsec. (a)(5), (6). Pub. L. 95-190, Sec. 5(a), added pars. (5) and (6). Former par. (5) redesignated (7).

Subsec. (a)(7). Pub. L. 95-190, Secs. 2(b), 5(a), redesignated former par. (5) as (7) and authorized appropriations for fiscal years 1978 and 1979.

Subsec. (b)(5). Pub. L. 95-190, Sec. 2(c), inserted provisions authorizing appropriations for fiscal years 1978 and 1979.

Section Referred to in Other Sections

This section is referred to in sections 300g-6, 300j-1, 300j-12 of this title.

SPECIAL PROJECT GRANTS AND GUARANTEED LOANS

42 USC 300j-3

(a) Special study and demonstration project grants

The Administrator may make grants to any person for the purposes of—
  (1) assisting in the development and demonstration (including construction) of any project which will demonstrate a new or improved method, approach, or technology, for providing a dependably safe supply of drinking water to the public; and
  (2) assisting in the development and demonstration (including construction) of any project which will investigate and demonstrate health implications involved in the reclamation, recycling, and reuse of waste waters for drinking and the processes and methods for the preparation of safe and acceptable drinking water.

(b) Limitations
Grants made by the Administrator under this section shall be subject to the following limitations:
  (1) Grants under this section shall not exceed 66 2/3 per centum of the total cost of construction of any facility and 75 per centum of any other costs, as determined by the Administrator.
  (2) Grants under this section shall not be made for any project involving the construction or modification of any facilities for any public water system in a State unless such project has been approved by the State agency charged with the responsibility for safety of drinking water (or if there is no such agency in a State, by the State health authority).
  (3) Grants under this section shall not be made for any project unless the Administrator determines, after consulting the National Drinking Water Advisory Council, that such project will serve a useful purpose relating to the development and demonstration of new or improved techniques, methods, or technologies for the provision of safe water to the public for drinking.
  (4) Priority for grants under this section shall be given where there are known or potential public health hazards which require advanced technology for the removal of particles which are too small to be removed by ordinary treatment technology.
(c) Authorization of appropriations
For the purposes of making grants under subsections (a) and (b) of this section there are authorized to be appropriated $7,500,000 for the fiscal year ending June 30, 1975; and $7,500,000 for the fiscal year ending June 30, 1976; and $10,000,000 for the fiscal year ending June 30, 1977.
(d) Loan guarantees to public water systems; conditions; indebtedness limitation; regulations
The Administrator during the fiscal years ending June 30, 1975, and June 30, 1976, shall carry out a program of guaranteeing loans made by private lenders to small public water systems for the purpose of enabling such systems to meet national primary drinking water regulations prescribed under section 300g-1 of this title. No such guarantee may be made with respect to a system unless (1) such system cannot reasonably obtain financial assistance necessary to comply with such regulations from any other source, and (2) the Administrator determines that any facilities constructed with a loan guaranteed under this subsection is not likely to be made obsolete by subsequent changes in primary regulations. The aggregate amount of indebtedness guaranteed with respect to any system may not exceed $50,000. The aggregate amount of indebtedness guaranteed under this subsection may not exceed $50,000,000. The Administrator shall prescribe regulations to carry out this subsection.

(July 1, 1944, ch. 373, title XIV, Sec. 1444, as added Pub. L. 93-523, Sec. 2(a), Dec. 16, 1974, 88 Stat. 1685; amended Pub. L. 99-339, title I, Sec. 101(c)(3), June 19, 1986, 100 Stat. 646.)

Amendments

1986—Subsec. (d). Pub. L. 99-339 struck out "(including interim regulations)" before "prescribed" in first sentence.

Section Referred to in Other Sections

This section is referred to in section 300j-3b of this title.

GRANTS TO PUBLIC SECTOR AGENCIES

42 USC 300j-3a

(a) Assistance for development and demonstration projects
The Administrator of the Environmental Protection Agency shall offer grants to public sector agencies for the purposes of—
  (1) assisting in the development and demonstration (including construction) of any project which will demonstrate a new or improved method, approach, or technology for providing a dependably safe supply of drinking water to the public; and
  (2) assisting in the development and demonstration (including construction) of any project which will investigate and demonstrate health and conservation implications involved in

the reclamation, recycling, and reuse of wastewaters for drinking and agricultural use or the processes and methods for the preparation of safe and acceptable drinking water.

(b) Limitations

Grants made by the Administrator under this section shall be subject to the following limitations:

(1) Grants under this section shall not exceed 66 2/3 per centum of the total cost of construction of any facility and 75 per centum of any other costs, as determined by the Administrator.

(2) Grants under this section shall not be made for any project involving the construction or modification of any facilities for any public water system in a State unless such project has been approved by the State agency charged with the responsibility for safety of drinking water (or if there is no such agency in a State, by the State health authority).

(3) Grants under this section shall not be made for any project unless the Administrator determines, after consultation, that such project will serve a useful purpose relating to the development and demonstration of new or improved techniques, methods, or technologies for the provision of safe water to the public for drinking.

(c) Authorization of appropriations

There are authorized to be appropriated for the purposes of this section $25,000,000 for fiscal year 1978.

(Pub. L. 95-155, Sec. 5, Nov. 8, 1977, 91 Stat. 1258; Pub. L. 95-477, Sec. 7(a)(1), Oct. 18, 1978, 92 Stat. 1511.)

Codification

Section was enacted as part of the Environmental Research, Development, and Demonstration Authorization Act of 1978, and not as part of the Public Health Service Act which comprises this chapter.

Amendments

1978–Subsec. (a)(2). Pub. L. 95-477 inserted "agricultural use or" after "drinking and".

Effective Date of 1978 Amendment

Section 7(a)(2) of Pub. L. 95-477 provided that: "This subsection [amending this section] shall become effective October 1, 1978."

Section Referred to in Other Sections

This section is referred to in section 300j-3b of this title.

CONTAMINANT STANDARDS OR TREATMENT TECHNIQUE GUIDELINES

42 USC 300j-3b

(1) Not later than nine months after October 18, 1978, the Administrator shall promulgate guidelines establishing supplemental standards or treatment technique requirements for microbiological, viral, radiological, organic, and inorganic contaminants, which guidelines shall be conditions, as provided in paragraph (2), of any grant for a demonstration project for water reclamation, recycling, and reuse funded under section 300j-3a of this title or under section 300j-3(a)(2) of this title, where such project involves direct human consumption of treated wastewater. Such guidelines shall provide for sufficient control of each such contaminant, such that in the Administrator's judgement, no adverse effects on the health of persons may reasonably be anticipated to occur, allowing an adequate margin of safety.

(2) A grant referred to in paragraph (1) for a project which involves direct human consumption of treated wastewater may be awarded on or after the date of promulgation of guidelines under this section only if the applicant demonstrates to the satisfaction of the Administrator that the project—

(A) will comply with all national primary drinking water regulations under section 300g-1 of this title;

(B) will comply with all guidelines under this section; and

(C) will in other respects provide safe drinking water.

Any such grant awarded before the date of promulgation of such guidelines shall be conditioned on the applicant's agreement to comply to the maximum feasible extent with such guidelines as expeditiously as practicable following the date of promulgation thereof.
(3) Guidelines under this section may, in the discretion of the Administrator—
   (A) be nationally and uniformly applicable to all projects funded under section 300j-3a of this title or section 300j-1(a)(2)[1] of this title;
   (B) vary for different classes or categories of such projects (as determined by the Administrator);
   (C) be established and applicable on a project-by-project basis; or
   (D) any combination of the above.
(4) Nothing in this section shall be construed to prohibit or delay the award of any grant referred to in paragraph (1) prior to the date of promulgation of such guidelines.

(Pub. L. 95-477, Sec. 7(b), Oct. 18, 1978, 92 Stat. 1511.)

References in Text

Section 300j-1(a)(2) of this title, referred to in par. (3)(A), was amended by Pub. L. 104-182, title I, Sec. 121(3), (4)(A), Aug. 6, 1996, 110 Stat. 1651, to redesignate par. (2)(B) as subsec. (b) of section 300j-1, strike par. (2)(A), and add a new par. (2) relating to information and research facilities.

Codification

Section was enacted as part of the Environmental Research, Development, and Demonstration Authorization Act of 1979, and not as part of the Public Health Service Act which comprises this chapter.

NATIONAL ASSISTANCE PROGRAM FOR WATER INFRASTRUCTURE AND WATERSHEDS

42 USC 300j-3c

(a) Technical and financial assistance

The Administrator of the Environmental Protection Agency may provide technical and financial assistance in the form of grants to States (1) for the construction, rehabilitation, and improvement of water supply systems, and (2) consistent with nonpoint source management programs established under section 1329 of title 33, for source water quality protection programs to address pollutants in navigable waters for the purpose of making such waters usable by water supply systems.

(b) Limitation

Not more than 30 percent of the amounts appropriated to carry out this section in a fiscal year may be used for source water quality protection programs described in subsection (a)(2) of this section.

(c) Condition

As a condition to receiving assistance under this section, a State shall ensure that such assistance is carried out in the most cost-effective manner, as determined by the State.

(d) Authorization of appropriations
   (1) Unconditional authorization
      There are authorized to be appropriated to carry out this section $25,000,000 for each of fiscal years 1997 through 2003. Such sums shall remain available until expended.
   (2) Conditional authorization
      In addition to amounts authorized under paragraph (1), there are authorized to be appropriated to carry out this section $25,000,000 for each of fiscal years 1997 through 2003, provided that such authorization shall be in effect for a fiscal year only if at least 75 percent of the total amount of funds authorized to be appropriated for such fiscal year by section 300j-12(m) of this title are appropriated.

---

[1] See References in Text note below.

(e) Acquisition of lands
Assistance provided with funds made available under this section may be used for the acquisition of lands and other interests in lands; however, nothing in this section authorizes the acquisition of lands or other interests in lands from other than willing sellers.
(f) Federal share
The Federal share of the cost of activities for which grants are made under this section shall be 50 percent.
(g) Definitions
In this section, the following definitions apply:
(1) State
The term "State" means a State, the District of Columbia, the Commonwealth of Puerto Rico, the Virgin Islands, Guam, American Samoa, and the Commonwealth of the Northern Mariana Islands.
(2) Water supply system
The term "water supply system" means a system for the provision to the public of piped water for human consumption if such system has at least 15 service connections or regularly serves at least 25 individuals and a draw and fill system for the provision to the public of water for human consumption. Such term does not include a system owned by a Federal agency. Such term includes (A) any collection, treatment, storage, and distribution facilities under control of the operator of such system and used primarily in connection with such system, and (B) any collection or pretreatment facilities not under such control that are used primarily in connection with such system.

(Pub. L. 104-182, title IV, Sec. 401, Aug. 6, 1996, 110 Stat. 1690.)

Codification

Section was enacted as part of the Safe Drinking Water Act Amendments of 1996, and not as part of the Public Health Service Act which comprises this chapter.

RECORDS AND INSPECTIONS

42 USC 300j-4

(a) Provision of information to Administrator; monitoring program for unregulated contaminants
 (1) (A) Every person who is subject to any requirement of this subchapter or who is a grantee, shall establish and maintain such records, make such reports, conduct such monitoring, and provide such information as the Administrator may reasonably require by regulation to assist the Administrator in establishing regulations under this subchapter, in determining whether such person has acted or is acting in compliance with this subchapter, in administering any program of financial assistance under this subchapter, in evaluating the health risks of unregulated contaminants, or in advising the public of such risks. In requiring a public water system to monitor under this subsection, the Administrator may take into consideration the system size and the contaminants likely to be found in the system's drinking water.
  (B) Every person who is subject to a national primary drinking water regulation under section 300g-1 of this title shall provide such information as the Administrator may reasonably require, after consultation with the State in which such person is located if such State has primary enforcement responsibility for public water systems, on a case-by-case basis, to determine whether such person has acted or is acting in compliance with this subchapter.
  (C) Every person who is subject to a national primary drinking water regulation under section 300g-1 of this title shall provide such information as the Administrator may reasonably require to assist the Administrator in establishing regulations under section 300g-1 of this title, after consultation with States and suppliers of water. The Administrator may not require under this subparagraph the installation of treatment equipment or process changes, the testing of treatment technology, or the analysis or processing of monitoring samples, except where the Administrator provides the funding for such activities. Before exercising this authority, the Administrator shall first seek to obtain the information by voluntary submission.

(D) The Administrator shall not later than 2 years after August 6, 1996, after consultation with public health experts, representatives of the general public, and officials of State and local governments, review the monitoring requirements for not fewer than 12 contaminants identified by the Administrator, and promulgate any necessary modifications.
(2) Monitoring program for unregulated contaminants.–
  (A) Establishment.–The Administrator shall promulgate regulations establishing the criteria for a monitoring program for unregulated contaminants. The regulations shall require monitoring of drinking water supplied by public water systems and shall vary the frequency and schedule for monitoring requirements for systems based on the number of persons served by the system, the source of supply, and the contaminants likely to be found, ensuring that only a representative sample of systems serving 10,000 persons or fewer are required to monitor.
  (B) Monitoring program for certain unregulated contaminants.–
    (i) Initial list.–Not later than 3 years after August 6, 1996, and every 5 years thereafter, the Administrator shall issue a list pursuant to subparagraph (A) of not more than 30 unregulated contaminants to be monitored by public water systems and to be included in the national drinking water occurrence data base maintained pursuant to subsection (g) of this section.
    (ii) Governors' petition.–The Administrator shall include among the list of contaminants for which monitoring is required under this paragraph each contaminant recommended in a petition signed by the Governor of each of 7 or more States, unless the Administrator determines that the action would prevent the listing of other contaminants of a higher public health concern.
  (C) Monitoring plan for small and medium systems.–
    (i) In general.–Based on the regulations promulgated by the Administrator, each State may develop a representative monitoring plan to assess the occurrence of unregulated contaminants in public water systems that serve a population of 10,000 or fewer in that State. The plan shall require monitoring for systems representative of different sizes, types, and geographic locations in the State.
    (ii) Grants for small system costs.–From funds reserved under section 300j-12(o) of this title or appropriated under subparagraph (H), the Administrator shall pay the reasonable cost of such testing and laboratory analysis as are necessary to carry out monitoring under the plan.
  (D) Monitoring results.–Each public water system that conducts monitoring of unregulated contaminants pursuant to this paragraph shall provide the results of the monitoring to the primary enforcement authority for the system.
  (E) Notification.–Notification of the availability of the results of monitoring programs required under paragraph (2)(A) shall be given to the persons served by the system.
  (F) Waiver of monitoring requirement.–The Administrator shall waive the requirement for monitoring for a contaminant under this paragraph in a State, if the State demonstrates that the criteria for listing the contaminant do not apply in that State.
  (G) Analytical methods.–The State may use screening methods approved by the Administrator under subsection (i) of this section in lieu of monitoring for particular contaminants under this paragraph.
  (H) Authorization of appropriations.–There are authorized to be appropriated to carry out this paragraph $10,000,000 for each of the fiscal years 1997 through 2003.
(b) Entry of establishments, facilities, or other property; inspections; conduct of certain tests; audit and examination of records; entry restrictions; prohibition against informing of a proposed entry
  (1) Except as provided in paragraph (2), the Administrator, or representatives of the Administrator duly designated by him, upon presenting appropriate credentials and a written notice to any supplier of water or other person subject to (A) a national primary drinking water regulation prescribed under section 300g-1 of this title, (B) an applicable underground injection control program, or (C) any requirement to monitor an unregulated contaminant pursuant to subsection (a) of this section, or person in charge of any of the property of such supplier or other person referred to in clause (A), (B), or (C), is authorized to enter any establishment, facility, or other property of such supplier or other person in

order to determine whether such supplier or other person has acted or is acting in compliance with this subchapter, including for this purpose, inspection, at reasonable times, of records, files, papers, processes, controls, and facilities, or in order to test any feature of a public water system, including its raw water source. The Administrator or the Comptroller General (or any representative designated by either) shall have access for the purpose of audit and examination to any records, reports, or information of a grantee which are required to be maintained under subsection (a) of this section or which are pertinent to any financial assistance under this subchapter.

(2) No entry may be made under the first sentence of paragraph (1) in an establishment, facility, or other property of a supplier of water or other person subject to a national primary drinking water regulation if the establishment, facility, or other property is located in a State which has primary enforcement responsibility for public water systems unless, before written notice of such entry is made, the Administrator (or his representative) notifies the State agency charged with responsibility for safe drinking water of the reasons for such entry. The Administrator shall, upon a showing by the State agency that such an entry will be detrimental to the administration of the State's program of primary enforcement responsibility, take such showing into consideration in determining whether to make such entry. No State agency which receives notice under this paragraph of an entry proposed to be made under paragraph (1) may use the information contained in the notice to inform the person whose property is proposed to be entered of the proposed entry; and if a State agency so uses such information, notice to the agency under this paragraph is not required until such time as the Administrator determines the agency has provided him satisfactory assurances that it will no longer so use information contained in a notice under this paragraph.

(c) Penalty

Whoever fails or refuses to comply with any requirement of subsection (a) of this section or to allow the Administrator, the Comptroller General, or representatives of either, to enter and conduct any audit or inspection authorized by subsection (b) of this section shall be subject to a civil penalty of not to exceed $25,000.

(d) Confidential information; trade secrets and secret processes; information disclosure; "information required under this section" defined

(1) Subject to paragraph (2), upon a showing satisfactory to the Administrator by any person that any information required under this section from such person, if made public, would divulge trade secrets or secret processes of such person, the Administrator shall consider such information confidential in accordance with the purposes of section 1905 of title 18. If the applicant fails to make a showing satisfactory to the Administrator, the Administrator shall give such applicant thirty days' notice before releasing the information to which the application relates (unless the public health or safety requires an earlier release of such information).

(2) Any information required under this section (A) may be disclosed to other officers, employees, or authorized representatives of the United States concerned with carrying out this subchapter or to committees of the Congress, or when relevant in any proceeding under this subchapter, and (B) shall be disclosed to the extent it deals with the level of contaminants in drinking water. For purposes of this subsection the term "information required under this section" means any papers, books, documents, or information, or any particular part thereof, reported to or otherwise obtained by the Administrator under this section.

(e) "Grantee" and "person" defined

For purposes of this section, (1) the term "grantee" means any person who applies for or receives financial assistance, by grant, contract, or loan guarantee under this subchapter, and (2) the term "person" includes a Federal agency.

(f) Information regarding drinking water coolers

The Administrator may utilize the authorities of this section for purposes of part F of this subchapter. Any person who manufactures, imports, sells, or distributes drinking water coolers in interstate commerce shall be treated as a supplier of water for purposes of applying the provisions of this section in the case of persons subject to part F of this subchapter.

(g) Occurrence data base

(1) In general
Not later than 3 years after August 6, 1996, the Administrator shall assemble and maintain a national drinking water contaminant occurrence data base, using information on the occurrence of both regulated and unregulated contaminants in public water systems obtained under subsection (a)(1)(A) of this section or subsection (a)(2) of this section and reliable information from other public and private sources.

(2) Public input
In establishing the occurrence data base, the Administrator shall solicit recommendations from the Science Advisory Board, the States, and other interested parties concerning the development and maintenance of a national drinking water contaminant occurrence data base, including such issues as the structure and design of the data base, data input parameters and requirements, and the use and interpretation of data.

(3) Use
The data shall be used by the Administrator in making determinations under section 300g-1(b)(1) of this title with respect to the occurrence of a contaminant in drinking water at a level of public health concern.

(4) Public recommendations
The Administrator shall periodically solicit recommendations from the appropriate officials of the National Academy of Sciences and the States, and any person may submit recommendations to the Administrator, with respect to contaminants that should be included in the national drinking water contaminant occurrence data base, including recommendations with respect to additional unregulated contaminants that should be listed under subsection (a)(2) of this section. Any recommendation submitted under this clause shall be accompanied by reasonable documentation that—
  (A) the contaminant occurs or is likely to occur in drinking water; and
  (B) the contaminant poses a risk to public health.

(5) Public availability
The information from the data base shall be available to the public in readily accessible form.

(6) Regulated contaminants
With respect to each contaminant for which a national primary drinking water regulation has been established, the data base shall include information on the detection of the contaminant at a quantifiable level in public water systems (including detection of the contaminant at levels not constituting a violation of the maximum contaminant level for the contaminant).

(7) Unregulated contaminants
With respect to contaminants for which a national primary drinking water regulation has not been established, the data base shall include—
  (A) monitoring information collected by public water systems that serve a population of more than 10,000, as required by the Administrator under subsection (a) of this section;
  (B) monitoring information collected from a representative sampling of public water systems that serve a population of 10,000 or fewer; and
  (C) other reliable and appropriate monitoring information on the occurrence of the contaminants in public water systems that is available to the Administrator.

(h) Availability of information on small system technologies
For purposes of sections 300g-1(b)(4)(E) and 300g-4(e) of this title (relating to small system variance program), the Administrator may request information on the characteristics of commercially available treatment systems and technologies, including the effectiveness and performance of the systems and technologies under various operating conditions. The Administrator may specify the form, content, and submission date of information to be submitted by manufacturers, States, and other interested persons for the purpose of considering the systems and technologies in the development of regulations or guidance under sections 300g-1(b)(4)(E) and 300g-4(e) of this title.

(i) Screening methods
The Administrator shall review new analytical methods to screen for regulated contaminants and may approve such methods as are more accurate or cost-effective than established reference methods for use in compliance monitoring.

(July 1, 1944, ch. 373, title XIV, Sec. 1445, as added Pub. L. 93-523, Sec. 2(a), Dec. 16, 1974, 88 Stat. 1686; amended Pub. L. 95-190, Sec. 12(c), (d), Nov. 16, 1977, 91 Stat. 1398; Pub. L. 99-339, title I, Sec. 106, title III, Sec. 301(h), June 19, 1986, 100 Stat. 650, 665; Pub. L. 100-572, Sec. 5, Oct. 31, 1988, 102 Stat. 2889; Pub. L. 104-182, title I, Secs. 111(b), 125(a), (c), (d), 126, Aug. 6, 1996, 110 Stat. 1633, 1653, 1656-1658.)

Amendments

1996—Subsec. (a)(1). Pub. L. 104-182, Sec. 125(a), amended par. (1) generally. Prior to amendment, par. (1) read as follows: "Every person who is a supplier of water, who is or may be otherwise subject to a primary drinking water regulation prescribed under section 300g-1 of this title or to an applicable underground injection control program (as defined in section 300h-1(c) of this title), who is or may be subject to the permit requirement of section 300h-3 of this title, or to an order issued under section 300j of this title, or who is a grantee, shall establish and maintain such records, make such reports, conduct such monitoring, and provide such information as the Administrator may reasonably require by regulation to assist him in establishing regulations under this subchapter, in determining whether such person has acted or is acting in compliance with this subchapter in administering any program of financial assistance under this subchapter, in evaluating the health risks of unregulated contaminants, or in advising the public of such risks. In requiring a public water system to monitor under this subsection, the Administrator may take into consideration the system size and the contaminants likely to be found in the system's drinking water."

Subsec. (a)(2) to (8). Pub. L. 104-182, Sec. 125(c), added heading and text of par. (2) and struck out former pars. (2) to (8) which directed Administrator, not later than 18 months after June 19, 1986, to promulgate regulations requiring every public water system to conduct a monitoring program for unregulated contaminants, specified contents of regulations, provided for reporting and notification of availability of results of monitoring, waiver of monitoring requirements, and compliance by small systems, and authorized appropriations for fiscal year ending Sept. 30, 1987.

Subsec. (g). Pub. L. 104-182, Sec. 126, added subsec. (g).

Subsec. (h). Pub. L. 104-182, Sec. 111(b), added subsec. (h).

Subsec. (i). Pub. L. 104-182, Sec. 125(d), added subsec. (i).

1988—Subsec. (f). Pub. L. 100-572 added subsec. (f).

1986—Subsec. (a)(1). Pub. L. 99-339, Sec. 106(a), (b), designated existing provisions as par. (1) and inserted provisions permitting Administrator to consider size of system and contaminants likely to be found.

Subsec. (a)(2) to (7). Pub. L. 99-339, Sec. 106(b), added pars. (2) to (7).

Subsec. (a)(8). Pub. L. 99-339, Sec. 301(h), added par. (8).

Subsec. (c). Pub. L. 99-339, Sec. 106(c), substituted "shall be subject to a civil penalty of not to exceed $25,000" for "may be fined not more than $5,000".

1977—Subsec. (a). Pub. L. 95-190, Sec. 12(c), inserted provisions relating to evaluating and advising of health risks of unregulated contaminants.

Subsec. (b)(1). Pub. L. 95-190, Sec. 12(d), designated existing provisions as cls. (A) and (B) and added cl. (C) and reference to such cls. (A) to (C).

Section Referred to in Other Sections

This section is referred to in sections 300g-1, 300g-3, 300j-12, 7412, 9606 of this title.

NATIONAL DRINKING WATER ADVISORY COUNCIL

42 USC 300j-5

(a) Establishment; membership; representation of interests; term of office, vacancies; reappointment

There is established a National Drinking Water Advisory Council which shall consist of fifteen members appointed by the Administrator after consultation with the Secretary. Five members shall be appointed from the general public; five members shall be appointed from appropriate State and local agencies concerned with water hygiene and public water supply; and five members shall be appointed from representatives of private organizations or groups demonstrating an active interest in the field of water hygiene and public water supply, of which two such members shall be associated with small, rural public water systems. Each member of the Council shall hold office for a term of three years, except that—

(1) any member appointed to fill a vacancy occurring prior to the expiration of the term for which his predecessor was appointed shall be appointed for the remainder of such term; and

(2) the terms of the members first taking office shall expire as follows: Five shall expire three years after December 16, 1974, five shall expire two years after such date, and five shall expire one year after such date, as designated by the Administrator at the time of appointment.

The members of the Council shall be eligible for reappointment.

(b) Functions

The Council shall advise, consult with, and make recommendations to, the Administrator on matters relating to activities, functions, and policies of the Agency under this subchapter.

(c) Compensation and allowances; travel expenses

Members of the Council appointed under this section shall, while attending meetings or conferences of the Council or otherwise engaged in business of the Council, receive compensation and allowances at a rate to be fixed by the Administrator, but not exceeding the daily equivalent of the annual rate of basic pay in effect for grade GS-18 of the General Schedule for each day (including traveltime) during which they are engaged in the actual performance of duties vested in the Council. While away from their homes or regular places of business in the performance of services for the Council, members of the Council shall be allowed travel expenses, including per diem in lieu of subsistence, in the same manner as persons employed intermittently in the Government service are allowed expenses under section 5703(b)[1] of title 5.

(d) Advisory committee termination provision inapplicable

Section 14(a) of the Federal Advisory Committee Act (relating to termination) shall not apply to the Council.

(July 1, 1944, ch. 373, title XIV, Sec. 1446, as added Pub. L. 93-523, Sec. 2(a), Dec. 16, 1974, 88 Stat. 1688; amended Pub. L. 104-182, title I, Sec. 127, Aug. 6, 1996, 110 Stat. 1659.)

References in Text

Section 5703 of title 5, referred to in subsec. (c), was amended generally by Pub. L. 94-22, Sec. 4, May 19, 1975, 89 Stat. 85, and, as so amended, does not contain a subsec. (b).

Section 14(a) of the Federal Advisory Committee Act, referred to in subsec. (d), is section 14(a) of Pub. L. 92-463, which is set out in the Appendix to Title 5, Government Organization and Employees.

Amendments

1996—Subsec. (a). Pub. L. 104-182 inserted ", of which two such members shall be associated with small, rural public water systems" before period at end of second sentence.

Termination of Advisory Committees

Pub. L. 93-641, Sec. 6, Jan. 4, 1975, 88 Stat. 2275, set out as a note under section 217a of this title, provided that an advisory committee established pursuant to the Public Health Service Act shall terminate at such time as may be specifically prescribed by an Act of Congress enacted after Jan. 4, 1975.

References in Other Laws to GS-16, 17, or 18 Pay Rates

References in laws to the rates of pay for GS-16, 17, or 18, or to maximum rates of pay under the General Schedule, to be considered references to rates payable under specified sections of Title 5, Government Organization and Employees, see section 529 [title I, Sec. 101(c)(1)] of Pub. L. 101-509, set out in a note under section 5376 of Title 5.

---

[1] See References in Text note below.

Section Referred to in Other Sections

This section is referred to in section 300f of this title.

FEDERAL AGENCIES

42 USC 300j-6

(a) In general

Each department, agency, and instrumentality of the executive, legislative, and judicial branches of the Federal Government—
 (1) owning or operating any facility in a wellhead protection area;
 (2) engaged in any activity at such facility resulting, or which may result, in the contamination of water supplies in any such area;
 (3) owning or operating any public water system; or
 (4) engaged in any activity resulting, or which may result in, underground injection which endangers drinking water (within the meaning of section 300h(d)(2) of this title),

shall be subject to, and comply with, all Federal, State, interstate, and local requirements, both substantive and procedural (including any requirement for permits or reporting or any provisions for injunctive relief and such sanctions as may be imposed by a court to enforce such relief), respecting the protection of such wellhead areas, respecting such public water systems, and respecting any underground injection in the same manner and to the same extent as any person is subject to such requirements, including the payment of reasonable service charges. The Federal, State, interstate, and local substantive and procedural requirements referred to in this subsection include, but are not limited to, all administrative orders and all civil and administrative penalties and fines, regardless of whether such penalties or fines are punitive or coercive in nature or are imposed for isolated, intermittent, or continuing violations. The United States hereby expressly waives any immunity otherwise applicable to the United States with respect to any such substantive or procedural requirement (including, but not limited to, any injunctive relief, administrative order or civil or administrative penalty or fine referred to in the preceding sentence, or reasonable service charge). The reasonable service charges referred to in this subsection include, but are not limited to, fees or charges assessed in connection with the processing and issuance of permits, renewal of permits, amendments to permits, review of plans, studies, and other documents, and inspection and monitoring of facilities, as well as any other nondiscriminatory charges that are assessed in connection with a Federal, State, interstate, or local regulatory program respecting the protection of wellhead areas or public water systems or respecting any underground injection. Neither the United States, nor any agent, employee, or officer thereof, shall be immune or exempt from any process or sanction of any State or Federal Court[1] with respect to the enforcement of any such injunctive relief. No agent, employee, or officer of the United States shall be personally liable for any civil penalty under any Federal, State, interstate, or local law concerning the protection of wellhead areas or public water systems or concerning underground injection with respect to any act or omission within the scope of the official duties of the agent, employee, or officer. An agent, employee, or officer of the United States shall be subject to any criminal sanction (including, but not limited to, any fine or imprisonment) under any Federal or State requirement adopted pursuant to this subchapter, but no department, agency, or instrumentality of the executive, legislative, or judicial branch of the Federal Government shall be subject to any such sanction. The President may exempt any facility of any department, agency, or instrumentality in the executive branch from compliance with such a requirement if he determines it to be in the paramount interest of the United States to do so. No such exemption shall be granted due to lack of appropriation unless the President shall have specifically requested such appropriation as a part of the budgetary process and the Congress shall have failed to make available such requested appropriation. Any exemption shall be for a period not in excess of 1 year, but additional exemptions may be granted for periods not to exceed 1 year upon the President's making a new determination. The President shall report each January to the Congress all exemptions from the requirements of this section granted during the preceding calendar year, together with his reason for granting each such exemption.

---

[1] So in original. Probably should not be capitalized.

(b) Administrative penalty orders
   (1) In general
       If the Administrator finds that a Federal agency has violated an applicable requirement under this subchapter, the Administrator may issue a penalty order assessing a penalty against the Federal agency.
   (2) Penalties
       The Administrator may, after notice to the agency, assess a civil penalty against the agency in an amount not to exceed $25,000 per day per violation.
   (3) Procedure
       Before an administrative penalty order issued under this subsection becomes final, the Administrator shall provide the agency an opportunity to confer with the Administrator and shall provide the agency notice and an opportunity for a hearing on the record in accordance with chapters 5 and 7 of title 5.
   (4) Public review
       (A) In general
           Any interested person may obtain review of an administrative penalty order issued under this subsection. The review may be obtained in the United States District Court for the District of Columbia or in the United States District Court for the district in which the violation is alleged to have occurred by the filing of a complaint with the court within the 30-day period beginning on the date the penalty order becomes final. The person filing the complaint shall simultaneously send a copy of the complaint by certified mail to the Administrator and the Attorney General.
       (B) Record
           The Administrator shall promptly file in the court a certified copy of the record on which the order was issued.
       (C) Standard of review
           The court shall not set aside or remand the order unless the court finds that there is not substantial evidence in the record, taken as a whole, to support the finding of a violation or that the assessment of the penalty by the Administrator constitutes an abuse of discretion.
       (D) Prohibition on additional penalties
           The court may not impose an additional civil penalty for a violation that is subject to the order unless the court finds that the assessment constitutes an abuse of discretion by the Administrator.
(c) Limitation on State use of funds collected from Federal Government
    Unless a State law in effect on August 6, 1996, or a State constitution requires the funds to be used in a different manner, all funds collected by a State from the Federal Government from penalties and fines imposed for violation of any substantive or procedural requirement referred to in subsection (a) of this section shall be used by the State only for projects designed to improve or protect the environment or to defray the costs of environmental protection or enforcement.
(d) Indian rights and sovereignty as unaffected; "Federal agency" defined
    (1) Nothing in the Safe Drinking Water Amendments of 1977 shall be construed to alter or affect the status of American Indian lands or water rights nor to waive any sovereignty over Indian lands guaranteed by treaty or statute.
    (2) For the purposes of this chapter, the term "Federal agency" shall not be construed to refer to or include any American Indian tribe, nor to the Secretary of the Interior in his capacity as trustee of Indian lands.
(e) Washington Aqueduct
    The Secretary of the Army shall not pass the cost of any penalty assessed under this subchapter on to any customer, user, or other purchaser of drinking water from the Washington Aqueduct system, including finished water from the Dalecarlia or McMillan treatment plant.

(July 1, 1944, ch. 373, title XIV, Sec. 1447, as added Pub. L. 93-523, Sec. 2(a), Dec. 16, 1974, 88 Stat. 1688; amended Pub. L. 95-190, Sec. 8(a), (d), Nov. 16, 1977, 91 Stat. 1396, 1397; Pub. L. 104-182, title I, Sec. 129(a), (c), Aug. 6, 1996, 110 Stat. 1660, 1662.)

Safe Drinking Water Act / 869

References in Text

The Safe Drinking Water Amendments of 1977, referred to in subsec. (d)(1), is Pub. L. 95-190, Nov. 16, 1977, 91 Stat. 1393. For complete classification of this Act to the Code, see Short Title of 1977 Amendment note set out under section 201 of this title and Tables.

Amendments

1996—Subsecs. (a) to (d). Pub. L. 104-182, Sec. 129(a), added subsecs. (a) to (c), redesignated former subsec. (c) as (d), and struck out former subsecs. (a) and (b) which related to compliance by Federal agencies with Federal, State, and local requirements respecting provision of safe drinking water and respecting underground injection programs, liability for civil penalties, and waiver of compliance requirements when necessary in interest of national security.

Subsec. (e). Pub. L. 104-182, Sec. 129(c), added subsec. (e).

1977—Subsec. (a). Pub. L. 95-190, Sec. 8(a), substituted provisions relating to compliance by Federal agencies having jurisdiction over federally owned or maintained public water systems, or engaged in underground injection activities with Federal, State, and local requirements, etc., for provisions relating to compliance by Federal agencies having jurisdiction over federally owned or maintained public water systems with national primary drinking water regulations.

Subsec. (c). Pub. L. 95-190, Sec. 8(d), added subsec. (c).

Section Referred to in Other Sections

This section is referred to in sections 300h, 300j-8 of this title.

JUDICIAL REVIEW

42 USC 300j-7

(a) Courts of appeals; petition for review: actions respecting regulations; filing period; grounds arising after expiration of filing period; exclusiveness of remedy

A petition for review of—

(1) actions pertaining to the establishment of national primary drinking water regulations (including maximum contaminant level goals) may be filed only in the United States Court of Appeals for the District of Columbia circuit; and

(2) any other final action of the Administrator under this chapter may be filed in the circuit in which the petitioner resides or transacts business which is directly affected by the action.

Any such petition shall be filed within the 45-day period beginning on the date of the promulgation of the regulation or any other final Agency action with respect to which review is sought or on the date of the determination with respect to which review is sought, and may be filed after the expiration of such 45-day period if the petition is based solely on grounds arising after the expiration of such period. Action of the Administrator with respect to which review could have been obtained under this subsection shall not be subject to judicial review in any civil or criminal proceeding for enforcement or in any civil action to enjoin enforcement. In any petition concerning the assessment of a civil penalty pursuant to section 300g-3(g)(3)(B) of this title, the petitioner shall simultaneously send a copy of the complaint by certified mail to the Administrator and the Attorney General. The court shall set aside and remand the penalty order if the court finds that there is not substantial evidence in the record to support the finding of a violation or that the assessment of the penalty by the Administrator constitutes an abuse of discretion.

(b) District courts; petition for review: actions respecting variances or exemptions; filing period; grounds arising after expiration of filing period; exclusiveness of remedy

The United States district courts shall have jurisdiction of actions brought to review (1) the granting of, or the refusing to grant, a variance or exemption under section 300g-4 or 300g-5 of this title or (2) the requirements of any schedule prescribed for a variance or exemption under such section or the failure to prescribe such a schedule. Such an action may only be brought upon a petition for review filed with the court within the 45-day period beginning on the date the action sought to be reviewed is taken or, in the case of a petition to review the refusal to grant a variance or exemption or the failure to prescribe a schedule, within the 45-day period beginning on the date action is required to be taken on the variance, exemption, or schedule, as the case may be. A petition for such review may be filed after the expiration of such period if the petition is based solely on grounds arising after the expiration of such period. Action with respect to which review could have been obtained under this subsection shall not be subject to judicial review in any civil or criminal proceeding for enforcement or in any civil action to enjoin enforcement.

(c) Judicial order for additional evidence before Administrator; modified or new findings; recommendation for modification or setting aside of original determination
In any judicial proceeding in which review is sought of a determination under this subchapter required to be made on the record after notice and opportunity for hearing, if any party applies to the court for leave to adduce additional evidence and shows to the satisfaction of the court that such additional evidence is material and that there were reasonable grounds for the failure to adduce such evidence in the proceeding before the Administrator, the court may order such additional evidence (and evidence in rebuttal thereof) to be taken before the Administrator, in such manner and upon such term and conditions as the court may deem proper. The Administrator may modify his findings as to the facts, or make new findings, by reason of the additional evidence so taken, and he shall file such modified or new findings, and his recommendation, if any, for the modification or setting aside of his original determination, with the return of such additional evidence.

(July 1, 1944, ch. 373, title XIV, Sec. 1448, as added Pub. L. 93-523, Sec. 2(a), Dec. 16, 1974, 88 Stat. 1689; amended Pub. L. 99-339, title III, Sec. 303, June 19, 1986, 100 Stat. 667; Pub. L. 104-182, title I, Sec. 113(c), Aug. 6, 1996, 110 Stat. 1636.)

Amendments

1996—Subsec. (a). Pub. L. 104-182, Sec. 113(c)(2), (3), in concluding provisions, substituted "or any other final Agency action" for "or issuance of the order" and inserted at end "In any petition concerning the assessment of a civil penalty pursuant to section 300g-3(g)(3)(B) of this title, the petitioner shall simultaneously send a copy of the complaint by certified mail to the Administrator and the Attorney General. The court shall set aside and remand the penalty order if the court finds that there is not substantial evidence in the record to support the finding of a violation or that the assessment of the penalty by the Administrator constitutes an abuse of discretion."

Subsec. (a)(2). Pub. L. 104-182, Sec. 113(c)(1), substituted "any other final action" for "any other action".

1986—Subsec. (a)(1). Pub. L. 99-339, Sec. 303(1), amended par. (1) generally. Prior to amendment, par. (1) read as follows: "action of the Administrator in promulgating any national primary drinking water regulation under section 300g-1 of this title, any regulation under section 300g-2(b)(1) of this title, any regulation under section 300g-3(c) of this title, any regulation for State underground injection control programs under section 300h of this title, or any general regulation for the administration of this subchapter may be filed only in the United States Court of Appeals for the District of Columbia Circuit; and".

Subsec. (a)(2). Pub. L. 99-339, Sec. 303(2), amended par. (2) generally. Prior to amendment, par. (2) read as follows: "action of the Administrator in promulgating any other regulation under this subchapter, issuing any order under this subchapter, or making any determination under this subchapter may be filed only in the United States court of appeals for the appropriate circuit."

Section Referred to in Other Sections

This section is referred to in sections 300g-1, 300h-2, 300j-8 of this title.

CITIZEN'S CIVIL ACTION

42 USC 300j-8

(a) Persons subject to civil action; jurisdiction of enforcement proceedings
Except as provided in subsection (b) of this section, any person may commence a civil action on his own behalf—
  (1) against any person (including (A) the United States, and (B) any other governmental instrumentality or agency to the extent permitted by the eleventh amendment to the Consti-

tution) who is alleged to be in violation of any requirement prescribed by or under this subchapter;
(2) against the Administrator where there is alleged a failure of the Administrator to perform any act or duty under this subchapter which is not discretionary with the Administrator; or
(3) for the collection of a penalty by the United States Government (and associated costs and interest) against any Federal agency that fails, by the date that is 18 months after the effective date of a final order to pay a penalty assessed by the Administrator under section 300h-8(b)[1] of this title, to pay the penalty.

No action may be brought under paragraph (1) against a public water system for a violation of a requirement prescribed by or under this subchapter which occurred within the 27-month period beginning on the first day of the month in which this subchapter is enacted. The United States district courts shall have jurisdiction, without regard to the amount in controversy or the citizenship of the parties, to enforce in an action brought under this subsection any requirement prescribed by or under this subchapter or to order the Administrator to perform an act or duty described in paragraph (2), as the case may be.

(b) Conditions for commencement of civil action; notice
No civil action may be commenced—
(1) under subsection (a)(1) of this section respecting violation of a requirement prescribed by or under this subchapter—
   (A) prior to sixty days after the plaintiff has given notice of such violation (i) to the Administrator, (ii) to any alleged violator of such requirement and (iii) to the State in which the violation occurs, or
   (B) if the Administrator, the Attorney General, or the State has commenced and is diligently prosecuting a civil action in a court of the United States to require compliance with such requirement, but in any such action in a court of the United States any person may intervene as a matter of right; or
(2) under subsection (a)(2) of this section prior to sixty days after the plaintiff has given notice of such action to the Administrator; or
(3) under subsection (a)(3) of this section prior to 60 days after the plaintiff has given notice of such action to the Attorney General and to the Federal agency.

Notice required by this subsection shall be given in such manner as the Administrator shall prescribe by regulation. No person may commence a civil action under subsection (a) of this section to require a State to prescribe a schedule under section 300g-4 or 300g-5 of this title for a variance or exemption, unless such person shows to the satisfaction of the court that the State has in a substantial number of cases failed to prescribe such schedules.

(c) Intervention of right
In any action under this section, the Administrator or the Attorney General, if not a party, may intervene as a matter of right.

(d) Costs; attorney fees; expert witness fees; filing of bond
The court, in issuing any final order in any action brought under subsection (a) of this section, may award costs of litigation (including reasonable attorney and expert witness fees) to any party whenever the court determines such an award is appropriate. The court may, if a temporary restraining order or preliminary injunction is sought, require the filing of a bond or equivalent security in accordance with the Federal Rules of Civil Procedure.

(e) Availability of other relief
Nothing in this section shall restrict any right which any person (or class of persons) may have under any statute or common law to seek enforcement of any requirement prescribed by or under this subchapter or to seek any other relief. Nothing in this section or in any other law of the United States shall be construed to prohibit, exclude, or restrict any State or local government from—
(1) bringing any action or obtaining any remedy or sanction in any State or local court, or
(2) bringing any administrative action or obtaining any administrative remedy or sanction, against any agency of the United States under State or local law to enforce any requirement respecting the provision of safe drinking water or respecting any underground injection con-

---
[1] So in original. Probably should be section "300j-6(b)".

trol program. Nothing in this section shall be construed to authorize judicial review of regulations or orders of the Administrator under this subchapter, except as provided in section 300j-7 of this title. For provisions providing for application of certain requirements to such agencies in the same manner as to nongovernmental entities, see section 300j-6 of this title.

(July 1, 1944, ch. 373, title XIV, Sec. 1449, as added Pub. L. 93-523, Sec. 2(a), Dec. 16, 1974, 88 Stat. 1690; amended Pub. L. 95-190, Sec. 8(c), Nov. 16, 1977, 91 Stat. 1397; Pub. L. 104-182, title I, Sec. 129(b), Aug. 6, 1996, 110 Stat. 1662.)

References in Text

The Federal Rules of Civil Procedure, referred to in subsec. (d), are set out in the Appendix to Title 28, Judiciary and Judicial Procedure.

Amendments

1996—Subsec. (a)(3). Pub. L. 104-182, Sec. 129(b)(1), added par. (3).

Subsec. (b)(3). Pub. L. 104-182, Sec. 129(b)(2), added par. (3).

1977—Subsec. (e). Pub. L. 95-190 inserted provisions relating to suits by State or local governments for enforcement of safe drinking water, etc., requirements.

Section Referred to in Other Sections

This section is referred to in section 300h-2 of this title.

GENERAL PROVISIONS

42 USC 300j-9

(a) Regulations; delegation of functions
  (1) The Administrator is authorized to prescribe such regulations as are necessary or appropriate to carry out his functions under this subchapter.
  (2) The Administrator may delegate any of his functions under this subchapter (other than prescribing regulations) to any officer or employee of the Agency.
(b) Utilization of officers and employees of Federal agencies
  The Administrator, with the consent of the head of any other agency of the United States, may utilize such officers and employees of such agency as he deems necessary to assist him in carrying out the purposes of this subchapter.
(c) Assignment of Agency personnel to State or interstate agencies
  Upon the request of a State or interstate agency, the Administrator may assign personnel of the Agency to such State or interstate agency for the purposes of carrying out the provisions of this subchapter.
(d) Payments of grants; adjustments; advances; reimbursement; installments; conditions; eligibility for grants; "nonprofit agency or institution" defined
  (1) The Administrator may make payments of grants under this subchapter (after necessary adjustment on account of previously made underpayments or overpayments) in advance or by way of reimbursement, and in such installments and on such conditions as he may determine.
  (2) Financial assistance may be made available in the form of grants only to individuals and nonprofit agencies or institutions. For purposes of this paragraph, the term "nonprofit agency or institution" means an agency or institution no part of the net earnings of which inure, or may lawfully inure, to the benefit of any private shareholder or individual.
(e) Labor standards
  The Administrator shall take such action as may be necessary to assure compliance with provisions of the Act of March 3, 1931 (known as the Davis-Bacon Act; 40 U.S.C. 276a—276a-5). The Secretary of Labor shall have, with respect to the labor standards specified in this subsection, the authority and functions set forth in Reorganization Plan Numbered 14 of 1950 (15 F.R. 3176; 64 Stat. 1267) and section 276c of title 40.
(f) Appearance and representation of Administrator through Attorney General or attorney appointees

The Administrator shall request the Attorney General to appear and represent him in any civil action instituted under this subchapter to which the Administrator is a party. Unless, within a reasonable time, the Attorney General notifies the Administrator that he will appear in such action, attorneys appointed by the Administrator shall appear and represent him.

(g) Authority of Administrator under other provisions unaffected

The provisions of this subchapter shall not be construed as affecting any authority of the Administrator under part G of subchapter II of this chapter.

(h) Reports to Congressional committees; review by Office of Management and Budget: submittal of comments to Congressional committees

Not later than April 1 of each year, the Administrator shall submit to the Committee on Commerce, Science, and Transportation of the Senate and the Committee on Energy and Commerce of the House of Representatives a report respecting the activities of the Agency under this subchapter and containing such recommendations for legislation as he considers necessary. The report of the Administrator under this subsection which is due not later than April 1, 1975, and each subsequent report of the Administrator under this subsection shall include a statement on the actual and anticipated cost to public water systems in each State of compliance with the requirements of this subchapter. The Office of Management and Budget may review any report required by this subsection before its submission to such committees of Congress, but the Office may not revise any such report, require any revision in any such report, or delay its submission beyond the day prescribed for its submission, and may submit to such committees of Congress its comments respecting any such report.

(i) Discrimination prohibition; filing of complaint; investigation; orders of Secretary; notice and hearing; settlements; attorneys' fees; judicial review; filing of petition; procedural requirements; stay of orders; exclusiveness of remedy; civil actions for enforcement of orders; appropriate relief; mandamus proceedings; prohibition inapplicable to undirected but deliberate violations

   (1) No employer may discharge any employee or otherwise discriminate against any employee with respect to his compensation, terms, conditions, or privileges of employment because the employee (or any person acting pursuant to a request of the employee) has—
       (A) commenced, caused to be commenced, or is about to commence or cause to be commenced a proceeding under this subchapter or a proceeding for the administration or enforcement of drinking water regulations or underground injection control programs of a State,
       (B) testified or is about to testify in any such proceeding, or
       (C) assisted or participated or is about to assist or participate in any manner in such a proceeding or in any other action to carry out the purposes of this subchapter.
   (2) (A) Any employee who believes that he has been discharged or otherwise discriminated against by any person in violation of paragraph (1) may, within 30 days after such violation occurs, file (or have any person file on his behalf) a complaint with the Secretary of Labor (hereinafter in this subsection referred to as the "Secretary") alleging such discharge or discrimination. Upon receipt of such a complaint, the Secretary shall notify the person named in the complaint of the filing of the complaint.
       (B) (i) Upon receipt of a complaint filed under subparagraph (A), the Secretary shall conduct an investigation of the violation alleged in the complaint. Within 30 days of the receipt of such complaint, the Secretary shall complete such investigation and shall notify in writing the complainant (and any person acting in his behalf) and the person alleged to have committed such violation of the results of the investigation conducted pursuant to this subparagraph. Within 90 days of the receipt of such complaint the Secretary shall, unless the proceeding on the complaint is terminated by the Secretary on the basis of a settlement entered into by the Secretary and the person alleged to have committed such violation, issue an order either providing the relief prescribed by clause (ii) or denying the complaint. An order of the Secretary shall be made on the record after notice and opportunity for agency hearing. The Secretary may not enter into a settlement terminating a proceeding on a complaint without the participation and consent of the complainant.
           (ii) If in response to a complaint filed under subparagraph (A) the Secretary determines that a violation of paragraph (1) has occurred, the Secretary shall order (I)

the person who committed such violation to take affirmative action to abate the violation, (II) such person to reinstate the complainant to his former position together with the compensation (including back pay), terms, conditions, and privileges of his employment, (III) compensatory damages, and (IV) where appropriate, exemplary damages. If such an order is issued, the Secretary, at the request of the complainant, shall assess against the person against whom the order is issued a sum equal to the aggregate amount of all costs and expenses (including attorneys' fees) reasonably incurred, as determined by the Secretary, by the complainant for, or in connection with, the bringing of the complaint upon which the order was issued.

(3) (A) Any person adversely affected or aggrieved by an order issued under paragraph (2) may obtain review of the order in the United States Court of Appeals for the circuit in which the violation, with respect to which the order was issued, allegedly occurred. The petition for review must be filed within sixty days from the issuance of the Secretary's order. Review shall conform to chapter 7 of title 5. The commencement of proceedings under this subparagraph shall not, unless ordered by the court, operate as a stay of the Secretary's order.

(B) An order of the Secretary with respect to which review could have been obtained under subparagraph (A) shall not be subject to judicial review in any criminal or other civil proceeding.

(4) Whenever a person has failed to comply with an order issued under paragraph (2)(B), the Secretary shall file a civil action in the United States District Court for the district in which the violation was found to occur to enforce such order. In actions brought under this paragraph, the district courts shall have jurisdiction to grant all appropriate relief including, but not limited to, injunctive relief, compensatory, and exemplary damages.

(5) Any nondiscretionary duty imposed by this section is enforceable in mandamus proceeding brought under section 1361 of title 28.

(6) Paragraph (1) shall not apply with respect to any employee who, acting without direction from his employer (or the employer's agent), deliberately causes a violation of any requirement of this subchapter.

(July 1, 1944, ch. 373, title XIV, Sec. 1450, as added Pub. L. 93-523, Sec. 2(a), Dec. 16, 1974, 88 Stat. 1691; amended Pub. L. 98-620, title IV, Sec. 402(38), Nov. 8, 1984, 98 Stat. 3360; Pub. L. 103-437, Sec. 15(a)(2), Nov. 2, 1994, 108 Stat. 4591.)

References in Text

Act of March 3, 1931 (known as the Davis-Bacon Act; 40 U.S.C. 276a–276a-5), referred to in subsec. (e), is act Mar. 3, 1931, ch. 411, 46 Stat. 1494, as amended, which is classified generally to sections 276a to 276a-5 of Title 40, Public Buildings, Property, and Works. For complete classification of this Act to the Code, see Short Title note set out under section 276a of Title 40 and Tables.

Reorganization Plan Numbered 14 of 1950 (15 F.R. 3176; 64 Stat. 1267), referred to in subsec. (e), is set out in the Appendix to Title 5, Government Organization and Employees.

Part C of subchapter II of this chapter, referred to in subsec. (g), is classified to section 264 of this title.

Amendments

1994—Subsec. (h). Pub. L. 103-437 substituted "Committee on Commerce, Science, and Transportation of the Senate and the Committee on Energy and Commerce of the House" for "Committee on Commerce of the Senate and the Committee on Interstate and Foreign Commerce of the House".

1984—Subsec. (i)(4). Pub. L. 98-620 struck out provision which required civil actions filed under par. (4) to be heard and decided expeditiously.

Change of Name

Committee on Energy and Commerce of House of Representatives treated as referring to Committee on Commerce of House of Representatives by section 1(a) of Pub. L. 104-14, set out as a note preceding section 21 of Title 2, The Congress.

Effective Date of 1984 Amendment

Amendment by Pub. L. 98-620 not applicable to cases pending on Nov. 8, 1984, see section 403 of Pub. L. 98-620, set out as an Effective Date note under section 1657 of Title 28, Judiciary and Judicial Procedure.

Federal Rules of Civil Procedure

Injunctions, see rule 65, Title 28, Appendix, Judiciary and Judicial Procedure.

Writ of mandamus abolished in United States district courts, but relief available by appropriate action or motion, see rule 81.

APPOINTMENT OF SCIENTIFIC, ETC., PERSONNEL BY ADMINISTRATOR OF ENVIRONMENTAL PROTECTION AGENCY FOR IMPLEMENTATION OF RESPONSIBILITIES; COMPENSATION

42 USC 300j-10

To the extent that the Administrator of the Environmental Protection Agency deems such action necessary to the discharge of his functions under title XIV of the Public Health Service Act [42 U.S.C. 300f et seq.] (relating to safe drinking water) and under other provisions of law, he may appoint personnel to fill not more than thirty scientific, engineering, professional, legal, and administrative positions within the Environmental Protection Agency without regard to the civil service laws and may fix the compensation of such personnel not in excess of the maximum rate payable for GS-18 of the General Schedule under section 5332 of title 5.

(Pub. L. 95-190, Sec. 11(b), Nov. 16, 1977, 91 Stat. 1398.)

References in Text

The Public Health Service Act, referred to in text, is act July 1, 1944, ch. 373, 58 Stat. 682, as amended. Title XIV of the Public Health Service Act is classified generally to this subchapter (Sec. 300f et seq.). For complete classification of this Act to the Code, see Short Title note set out under section 201 of this title and Tables.

The civil service laws, referred to in text, are set out in Title 5, Government Organization and Employees. See, particularly, section 3301 et seq. of Title 5.

Codification

Section was enacted as part of the Safe Drinking Water Amendments of 1977, and not as part of the Public Health Service Act which comprises this chapter.

References in Other Laws to GS-16, 17, or 18 Pay Rates

References in laws to the rates of pay for GS-16, 17, or 18, or to maximum rates of pay under the General Schedule, to be considered references to rates payable under specified sections of Title 5, Government Organization and Employees, see section 529 [title I, Sec. 101(c)(1)] of Pub. L. 101-509, set out in a note under section 5376 of Title 5.

INDIAN TRIBES

42 USC 300j-11

(a) In general
   Subject to the provisions of subsection (b) of this section, the Administrator—
   (1) is authorized to treat Indian Tribes as States under this subchapter,
   (2) may delegate to such Tribes primary enforcement responsibility for public water systems and for underground injection control, and
   (3) may provide such Tribes grant and contract assistance to carry out functions provided by this subchapter.
(b) EPA regulations
   (1) Specific provisions

The Administrator shall, within 18 months after June 19, 1986, promulgate final regulations specifying those provisions of this subchapter for which it is appropriate to treat Indian Tribes as States. Such treatment shall be authorized only if:
  (A) the Indian Tribe is recognized by the Secretary of the Interior and has a governing body carrying out substantial governmental duties and powers;
  (B) the functions to be exercised by the Indian Tribe are within the area of the Tribal Government's jurisdiction; and
  (C) the Indian Tribe is reasonably expected to be capable, in the Administrator's judgment, of carrying out the functions to be exercised in a manner consistent with the terms and purposes of this subchapter and of all applicable regulations.
(2) Provisions where treatment as State inappropriate
For any provision of this subchapter where treatment of Indian Tribes as identical to States is inappropriate, administratively infeasible or otherwise inconsistent with the purposes of this subchapter, the Administrator may include in the regulations promulgated under this section, other means for administering such provision in a manner that will achieve the purpose of the provision. Nothing in this section shall be construed to allow Indian Tribes to assume or maintain primary enforcement responsibility for public water systems or for underground injection control in a manner less protective of the health of persons than such responsibility may be assumed or maintained by a State. An Indian tribe[1] shall not be required to exercise criminal enforcement jurisdiction for purposes of complying with the preceding sentence.

(July 1, 1944, ch. 373, title XIV, Sec. 1451, as added Pub. L. 99-339, title III, Sec. 302(a), June 19, 1986, 100 Stat. 665; amended Pub. L. 104-182, title V, Sec. 501(f)(6), Aug. 6, 1996, 110 Stat. 1692.)

Amendments

1996—Pub. L. 104-182 made technical amendment to section catchline and subsec. (a) designation.

Section Referred to in Other Sections

This section is referred to in section 300h-1 of this title.

STATE REVOLVING LOAN FUNDS

42 USC 300j-12

(a) General authority
  (1) Grants to States to establish State loan funds
    (A) In general
    The Administrator shall offer to enter into agreements with eligible States to make capitalization grants, including letters of credit, to the States under this subsection to further the health protection objectives of this subchapter, promote the efficient use of fund resources, and for other purposes as are specified in this subchapter.
    (B) Establishment of fund
    To be eligible to receive a capitalization grant under this section, a State shall establish a drinking water treatment revolving loan fund (referred to in this section as a "State loan fund") and comply with the other requirements of this section. Each grant to a State under this section shall be deposited in the State loan fund established by the State, except as otherwise provided in this section and in other provisions of this subchapter. No funds authorized by other provisions of this subchapter to be used for other purposes specified in this subchapter shall be deposited in any State loan fund.
    (C) Extended period
    The grant to a State shall be available to the State for obligation during the fiscal year for which the funds are authorized and during the following fiscal year, except that grants made available from funds provided prior to fiscal year 1997 shall be available for obligation during each of the fiscal years 1997 and 1998.
    (D) Allotment formula
    Except as otherwise provided in this section, funds made available to carry out this section shall be allotted to States that have entered into an agreement pursuant to this section (other than the District of Columbia) in accordance with—

---

[1] So in original. Probably should be capitalized.

(i) for each of fiscal years 1995 through 1997, a formula that is the same as the formula used to distribute public water system supervision grant funds under section 300j-2 of this title in fiscal year 1995, except that the minimum proportionate share established in the formula shall be 1 percent of available funds and the formula shall be adjusted to include a minimum proportionate share for the State of Wyoming and the District of Columbia; and

(ii) for fiscal year 1998 and each subsequent fiscal year, a formula that allocates to each State the proportional share of the State needs identified in the most recent survey conducted pursuant to subsection (h) of this section, except that the minimum proportionate share provided to each State shall be the same as the minimum proportionate share provided under clause (i).

(E) Reallotment

The grants not obligated by the last day of the period for which the grants are available shall be reallotted according to the appropriate criteria set forth in subparagraph (D), except that the Administrator may reserve and allocate 10 percent of the remaining amount for financial assistance to Indian Tribes in addition to the amount allotted under subsection (i) of this section and none of the funds reallotted by the Administrator shall be reallotted to any State that has not obligated all sums allotted to the State pursuant to this section during the period in which the sums were available for obligation.

(F) Nonprimacy States

The State allotment for a State not exercising primary enforcement responsibility for public water systems shall not be deposited in any such fund but shall be allotted by the Administrator under this subparagraph. Pursuant to section 300j-2(a)(9)(A) of this title such sums allotted under this subparagraph shall be reserved as needed by the Administrator to exercise primary enforcement responsibility under this subchapter in such State and the remainder shall be reallotted to States exercising primary enforcement responsibility for public water systems for deposit in such funds. Whenever the Administrator makes a final determination pursuant to section 300g-2(b) of this title that the requirements of section 300g-2(a) of this title are no longer being met by a State, additional grants for such State under this subchapter shall be immediately terminated by the Administrator. This subparagraph shall not apply to any State not exercising primary enforcement responsibility for public water systems as of August 6, 1996.

(G) Other programs

(i) New system capacity

Beginning in fiscal year 1999, the Administrator shall withhold 20 percent of each capitalization grant made pursuant to this section to a State unless the State has met the requirements of section 300g-9(a) of this title (relating to capacity development) and shall withhold 10 percent for fiscal year 2001, 15 percent for fiscal year 2002, and 20 percent for fiscal year 2003 if the State has not complied with the provisions of section 300g-9(c) of this title (relating to capacity development strategies). Not more than a total of 20 percent of the capitalization grants made to a State in any fiscal year may be withheld under the preceding provisions of this clause. All funds withheld by the Administrator pursuant to this clause shall be reallotted by the Administrator on the basis of the same ratio as is applicable to funds allotted under subparagraph (D). None of the funds reallotted by the Administrator pursuant to this paragraph shall be allotted to a State unless the State has met the requirements of section 300g-9 of this title (relating to capacity development).

(ii) Operator certification

The Administrator shall withhold 20 percent of each capitalization grant made pursuant to this section unless the State has met the requirements of 300g-8[1] of this title (relating to operator certification). All funds withheld by the Administrator pursuant to this clause shall be reallotted by the Administrator on the basis of the same ratio as applicable to funds allotted under subparagraph (D). None of

---

[1] So in original. Probably should be preceded by "section".

the funds reallotted by the Administrator pursuant to this paragraph shall be allotted to a State unless the State has met the requirements of section 300g-8 of this title (relating to operator certification).
- (2) Use of funds
  Except as otherwise authorized by this subchapter, amounts deposited in a State loan fund, including loan repayments and interest earned on such amounts, shall be used only for providing loans or loan guarantees, or as a source of reserve and security for leveraged loans, the proceeds of which are deposited in a State loan fund established under paragraph (1), or other financial assistance authorized under this section to community water systems and nonprofit noncommunity water systems, other than systems owned by Federal agencies. Financial assistance under this section may be used by a public water system only for expenditures (not including monitoring, operation, and maintenance expenditures) of a type or category which the Administrator has determined, through guidance, will facilitate compliance with national primary drinking water regulations applicable to the system under section 300g-1 of this title or otherwise significantly further the health protection objectives of this subchapter. The funds may also be used to provide loans to a system referred to in section 300f(4)(B) of this title for the purpose of providing the treatment described in section 300f(4)(B)(i)(III) of this title. The funds shall not be used for the acquisition of real property or interests therein, unless the acquisition is integral to a project authorized by this paragraph and the purchase is from a willing seller. Of the amount credited to any State loan fund established under this section in any fiscal year, 15 percent shall be available solely for providing loan assistance to public water systems which regularly serve fewer than 10,000 persons to the extent such funds can be obligated for eligible projects of public water systems.
- (3) Limitation
  - (A) In general
    Except as provided in subparagraph (B), no assistance under this section shall be provided to a public water system that—
    - (i) does not have the technical, managerial, and financial capability to ensure compliance with the requirements of this subchapter; or
    - (ii) is in significant noncompliance with any requirement of a national primary drinking water regulation or variance.
  - (B) Restructuring
    A public water system described in subparagraph (A) may receive assistance under this section if—
    - (i) the use of the assistance will ensure compliance; and
    - (ii) if subparagraph (A)(i) applies to the system, the owner or operator of the system agrees to undertake feasible and appropriate changes in operations (including ownership, management, accounting, rates, maintenance, consolidation, alternative water supply, or other procedures) if the State determines that the measures are necessary to ensure that the system has the technical, managerial, and financial capability to comply with the requirements of this subchapter over the long term.
  - (C) Review
    Prior to providing assistance under this section to a public water system that is in significant noncompliance with any requirement of a national primary drinking water regulation or variance, the State shall conduct a review to determine whether subparagraph (A)(i) applies to the system.
- (b) Intended use plans
  - (1) In general
    After providing for public review and comment, each State that has entered into a capitalization agreement pursuant to this section shall annually prepare a plan that identifies the intended uses of the amounts available to the State loan fund of the State.
  - (2) Contents
    An intended use plan shall include—
    - (A) a list of the projects to be assisted in the first fiscal year that begins after the date of the plan, including a description of the project, the expected terms of financial assistance, and the size of the community served;

(B) the criteria and methods established for the distribution of funds; and
(C) a description of the financial status of the State loan fund and the short-term and long-term goals of the State loan fund.
(3) Use of funds
   (A) In general
   An intended use plan shall provide, to the maximum extent practicable, that priority for the use of funds be given to projects that—
      (i) address the most serious risk to human health;
      (ii) are necessary to ensure compliance with the requirements of this subchapter (including requirements for filtration); and
      (iii) assist systems most in need on a per household basis according to State affordability criteria.
   (B) List of projects
   Each State shall, after notice and opportunity for public comment, publish and periodically update a list of projects in the State that are eligible for assistance under this section, including the priority assigned to each project and, to the extent known, the expected funding schedule for each project.

(c) Fund management
Each State loan fund under this section shall be established, maintained, and credited with repayments and interest. The fund corpus shall be available in perpetuity for providing financial assistance under this section. To the extent amounts in the fund are not required for current obligation or expenditure, such amounts shall be invested in interest bearing obligations.

(d) Assistance for disadvantaged communities
   (1) Loan subsidy
   Notwithstanding any other provision of this section, in any case in which the State makes a loan pursuant to subsection (a)(2) of this section to a disadvantaged community or to a community that the State expects to become a disadvantaged community as the result of a proposed project, the State may provide additional subsidization (including forgiveness of principal).
   (2) Total amount of subsidies
   For each fiscal year, the total amount of loan subsidies made by a State pursuant to paragraph (1) may not exceed 30 percent of the amount of the capitalization grant received by the State for the year.
   (3) "Disadvantaged community" defined
   In this subsection, the term "disadvantaged community" means the service area of a public water system that meets affordability criteria established after public review and comment by the State in which the public water system is located. The Administrator may publish information to assist States in establishing affordability criteria.

(e) State contribution
Each agreement under subsection (a) of this section shall require that the State deposit in the State loan fund from State moneys an amount equal to at least 20 percent of the total amount of the grant to be made to the State on or before the date on which the grant payment is made to the State, except that a State shall not be required to deposit such amount into the fund prior to the date on which each grant payment is made for fiscal years 1994, 1995, 1996, and 1997 if the State deposits the State contribution amount into the State loan fund prior to September 30, 1999.

(f) Types of assistance
Except as otherwise limited by State law, the amounts deposited into a State loan fund under this section may be used only—
   (1) to make loans, on the condition that—
      (A) the interest rate for each loan is less than or equal to the market interest rate, including an interest free loan;
      (B) principal and interest payments on each loan will commence not later than 1 year after completion of the project for which the loan was made, and each loan will be fully amortized not later than 20 years after the completion of the project, except that in the case of a disadvantaged community (as defined in subsection (d)(3) of this section), a State may provide an extended term for a loan, if the extended term—

(i) terminates not later than the date that is 30 years after the date of project completion; and
    (ii) does not exceed the expected design life of the project;
(C) the recipient of each loan will establish a dedicated source of revenue (or, in the case of a privately owned system, demonstrate that there is adequate security) for the repayment of the loan; and
(D) the State loan fund will be credited with all payments of principal and interest on each loan;
(2) to buy or refinance the debt obligation of a municipality or an intermunicipal or interstate agency within the State at an interest rate that is less than or equal to the market interest rate in any case in which a debt obligation is incurred after July 1, 1993;
(3) to guarantee, or purchase insurance for, a local obligation (all of the proceeds of which finance a project eligible for assistance under this section) if the guarantee or purchase would improve credit market access or reduce the interest rate applicable to the obligation;
(4) as a source of revenue or security for the payment of principal and interest on revenue or general obligation bonds issued by the State if the proceeds of the sale of the bonds will be deposited into the State loan fund; and
(5) to earn interest on the amounts deposited into the State loan fund.
(g) Administration of State loan funds
(1) Combined financial administration
Notwithstanding subsection (c) of this section, a State may (as a convenience and to avoid unnecessary administrative costs) combine, in accordance with State law, the financial administration of a State loan fund established under this section with the financial administration of any other revolving fund established by the State if otherwise not prohibited by the law under which the State loan fund was established and if the Administrator determines that—
(A) the grants under this section, together with loan repayments and interest, will be separately accounted for and used solely for the purposes specified in subsection (a) of this section; and
(B) the authority to establish assistance priorities and carry out oversight and related activities (other than financial administration) with respect to assistance remains with the State agency having primary responsibility for administration of the State program under section 300g-2 of this title, after consultation with other appropriate State agencies (as determined by the State): Provided, That in nonprimacy States eligible to receive assistance under this section, the Governor shall determine which State agency will have authority to establish priorities for financial assistance from the State loan fund.
(2) Cost of administering fund
Each State may annually use up to 4 percent of the funds allotted to the State under this section to cover the reasonable costs of administration of the programs under this section, including the recovery of reasonable costs expended to establish a State loan fund which are incurred after August 6, 1996, and to provide technical assistance to public water systems within the State. For fiscal year 1995 and each fiscal year thereafter, each State may use up to an additional 10 percent of the funds allotted to the State under this section—
(A) for public water system supervision programs under section 300j-2(a) of this title;
(B) to administer or provide technical assistance through source water protection programs;
(C) to develop and implement a capacity development strategy under section 300g-9(c) of this title; and
(D) for an operator certification program for purposes of meeting the requirements of section 300g-8 of this title,
if the State matches the expenditures with at least an equal amount of State funds. At least half of the match must be additional to the amount expended by the State for public water supervision in fiscal year 1993. An additional 2 percent of the funds annually allotted to each State under this section may be used by the State to provide technical assistance to public water systems serving 10,000 or fewer persons in the State. Funds utilized under subparagraph (B) shall not be used for enforcement actions.

(3) Guidance and regulations
The Administrator shall publish guidance and promulgate regulations as may be necessary to carry out the provisions of this section, including—
  (A) provisions to ensure that each State commits and expends funds allotted to the State under this section as efficiently as possible in accordance with this subchapter and applicable State laws;
  (B) guidance to prevent waste, fraud, and abuse; and
  (C) guidance to avoid the use of funds made available under this section to finance the expansion of any public water system in anticipation of future population growth.
The guidance and regulations shall also ensure that the States, and public water systems receiving assistance under this section, use accounting, audit, and fiscal procedures that conform to generally accepted accounting standards.
(4) State report
Each State administering a loan fund and assistance program under this subsection shall publish and submit to the Administrator a report every 2 years on its activities under this section, including the findings of the most recent audit of the fund and the entire State allotment. The Administrator shall periodically audit all State loan funds established by, and all other amounts allotted to, the States pursuant to this section in accordance with procedures established by the Comptroller General.

(h) Needs survey
The Administrator shall conduct an assessment of water system capital improvement needs of all eligible public water systems in the United States and submit a report to the Congress containing the results of the assessment within 180 days after August 6, 1996, and every 4 years thereafter.

(i) Indian Tribes
  (1) In general
  1 1/2 percent of the amounts appropriated annually to carry out this section may be used by the Administrator to make grants to Indian Tribes and Alaska Native villages that have not otherwise received either grants from the Administrator under this section or assistance from State loan funds established under this section. The grants may only be used for expenditures by tribes and villages for public water system expenditures referred to in subsection (a)(2) of this section.
  (2) Use of funds
  Funds reserved pursuant to paragraph (1) shall be used to address the most significant threats to public health associated with public water systems that serve Indian Tribes, as determined by the Administrator in consultation with the Director of the Indian Health Service and Indian Tribes.
  (3) Alaska Native villages
  In the case of a grant for a project under this subsection in an Alaska Native village, the Administrator is also authorized to make grants to the State of Alaska for the benefit of Native villages. An amount not to exceed 4 percent of the grant amount may be used by the State of Alaska for project management.
  (4) Needs assessment
  The Administrator, in consultation with the Director of the Indian Health Service and Indian Tribes, shall, in accordance with a schedule that is consistent with the needs surveys conducted pursuant to subsection (h) of this section, prepare surveys and assess the needs of drinking water treatment facilities to serve Indian Tribes, including an evaluation of the public water systems that pose the most significant threats to public health.

(j) Other areas
Of the funds annually available under this section for grants to States, the Administrator shall make allotments in accordance with section 300j-2(a)(4) of this title for the Virgin Islands, the Commonwealth of the Northern Mariana Islands, American Samoa, and Guam. The grants allotted as provided in this subsection may be provided by the Administrator to the governments of such areas, to public water systems in such areas, or to both, to be used for the public water system expenditures referred to in subsection (a)(2) of this section. The grants, and grants for the District of Columbia, shall not be deposited in State loan funds. The total allotment of grants under this section for all areas described in this subsection in any fiscal

year shall not exceed 0.33 percent of the aggregate amount made available to carry out this section in that fiscal year.
(k) Other authorized activities
   (1) In general
      Notwithstanding subsection (a)(2) of this section, a State may take each of the following actions:
      (A) Provide assistance, only in the form of a loan, to one or more of the following:
         (i) Any public water system described in subsection (a)(2) of this section to acquire land or a conservation easement from a willing seller or grantor, if the purpose of the acquisition is to protect the source water of the system from contamination and to ensure compliance with national primary drinking water regulations.
         (ii) Any community water system to implement local, voluntary source water protection measures to protect source water in areas delineated pursuant to section 300j-13 of this title, in order to facilitate compliance with national primary drinking water regulations applicable to the system under section 300g-1 of this title or otherwise significantly further the health protection objectives of this subchapter. Funds authorized under this clause may be used to fund only voluntary, incentive-based mechanisms.
         (iii) Any community water system to provide funding in accordance with section 300j-14(a)(1)(B)(i) of this title.
      (B) Provide assistance, including technical and financial assistance, to any public water system as part of a capacity development strategy developed and implemented in accordance with section 300g-9(c) of this title.
      (C) Make expenditures from the capitalization grant of the State for fiscal years 1996 and 1997 to delineate and assess source water protection areas in accordance with section 300j-13 of this title, except that funds set aside for such expenditure shall be obligated within 4 fiscal years.
      (D) Make expenditures from the fund for the establishment and implementation of wellhead protection programs under section 300h-7 of this title.
   (2) Limitation
      For each fiscal year, the total amount of assistance provided and expenditures made by a State under this subsection may not exceed 15 percent of the amount of the capitalization grant received by the State for that year and may not exceed 10 percent of that amount for any one of the following activities:
      (A) To acquire land or conservation easements pursuant to paragraph (1)(A)(i).
      (B) To provide funding to implement voluntary, incentive-based source water quality protection measures pursuant to clauses (ii) and (iii) of paragraph (1)(A).
      (C) To provide assistance through a capacity development strategy pursuant to paragraph (1)(B).
      (D) To make expenditures to delineate or assess source water protection areas pursuant to paragraph (1)(C).
      (E) To make expenditures to establish and implement wellhead protection programs pursuant to paragraph (1)(D).
   (3) Statutory construction
      Nothing in this section creates or conveys any new authority to a State, political subdivision of a State, or community water system for any new regulatory measure, or limits any authority of a State, political subdivision of a State or community water system.
(l) Savings
   The failure or inability of any public water system to receive funds under this section or any other loan or grant program, or any delay in obtaining the funds, shall not alter the obligation of the system to comply in a timely manner with all applicable drinking water standards and requirements of this subchapter.
(m) Authorization of appropriations
   There are authorized to be appropriated to carry out the purposes of this section $599,000,000 for the fiscal year 1994 and $1,000,000,000 for each of the fiscal years 1995 through 2003. To the extent amounts authorized to be appropriated under this subsection in any fiscal year are not appropriated in that fiscal year, such amounts are authorized to be appropriated in a

subsequent fiscal year (prior to the fiscal year 2004). Such sums shall remain available until expended.

(n) Health effects studies

From funds appropriated pursuant to this section for each fiscal year, the Administrator shall reserve $10,000,000 for health effects studies on drinking water contaminants authorized by the Safe Drinking Water Act Amendments of 1996. In allocating funds made available under this subsection, the Administrator shall give priority to studies concerning the health effects of cryptosporidium (as authorized by section 300j-18(c) of this title), disinfection byproducts (as authorized by section 300j-18(c) of this title), and arsenic (as authorized by section 300g-1(b)(12)(A) of this title), and the implementation of a plan for studies of subpopulations at greater risk of adverse effects (as authorized by section 300j-18(a) of this title).

(o) Monitoring for unregulated contaminants

From funds appropriated pursuant to this section for each fiscal year beginning with fiscal year 1998, the Administrator shall reserve $2,000,000 to pay the costs of monitoring for unregulated contaminants under section 300j-4(a)(2)(C) of this title.

(p) Demonstration project for State of Virginia

Notwithstanding the other provisions of this section limiting the use of funds deposited in a State loan fund from any State allotment, the State of Virginia may, as a single demonstration and with the approval of the Virginia General Assembly and the Administrator, conduct a program to demonstrate alternative approaches to intergovernmental coordination to assist in the financing of new drinking water facilities in the following rural communities in southwestern Virginia where none exists on August 6, 1996, and where such communities are experiencing economic hardship: Lee County, Wise County, Scott County, Dickenson County, Russell County, Buchanan County, Tazewell County, and the city of Norton, Virginia. The funds allotted to that State and deposited in the State loan fund may be loaned to a regional endowment fund for the purpose set forth in this subsection under a plan to be approved by the Administrator. The plan may include an advisory group that includes representatives of such counties.

(q) Small system technical assistance

The Administrator may reserve up to 2 percent of the total funds appropriated pursuant to subsection (m) of this section for each of the fiscal years 1997 through 2003 to carry out the provisions of section 300j-1(e) of this title (relating to technical assistance for small systems), except that the total amount of funds made available for such purpose in any fiscal year through appropriations (as authorized by section 300j-1(e) of this title) and reservations made pursuant to this subsection shall not exceed the amount authorized by section 300j-1(e) of this title.

(r) Evaluation

The Administrator shall conduct an evaluation of the effectiveness of the State loan funds through fiscal year 2001. The evaluation shall be submitted to the Congress at the same time as the President submits to the Congress, pursuant to section 1108 of title 31, an appropriations request for fiscal year 2003 relating to the budget of the Environmental Protection Agency.

(July 1, 1944, ch. 373, title XIV, Sec. 1452, as added Pub. L. 104-182, title I, Sec. 130, Aug. 6, 1996, 110 Stat. 1662.)

References in Text

The Safe Drinking Water Act Amendments of 1996, referred to in subsec. (n), is Pub. L. 104-182, Aug. 6, 1996, 110 Stat. 1613. For complete classification of this Act to the Code, see Short Title of 1996 Amendment note set out under section 201 of this title and Tables.

[Administration of Funds]

Pub. L. 107-73, July 25, 2001, 115 Stat. 685, provided in part: "That for fiscal year 2002, State authority under section 302(a) of Public Law 104-182 shall remain in effect: Provided further, That notwithstanding section 603(d)(7) of the Act, the limitation on the amounts in a State water pollution control revolving fund that may be used by a State to administer the fund shall not apply to amounts included as principal in loans made by such fund in fiscal year 2002 and prior years where such amounts represent costs of administering the fund to the extent that such amounts are or were deemed reasonable by the Administrator, accounted for separately from other assets in the fund, and used for eligible purposes of the fund, including administration."

Combining Fund Assets for Enhancement of Lending Capacity

Pub. L. 105-276, title III, Oct. 21, 1998, 112 Stat. 2498, provided in part: "That, consistent with section 1452(g) of the Safe Drinking Water Act (42 U.S.C. 300j-12(g)), section 302 of the Safe Drinking Water Act Amendments of 1996 (Public Law 104-182) [set out as a note below] and the accompanying joint explanatory statement of the committee of conference (H. Rept. No. 104-741 to accompany S. 1316, the Safe Drinking Water Act Amendments of 1996), and notwithstanding any other provision of law, beginning in fiscal year 1999 and thereafter, States may combine the assets of State Revolving Funds (SRFs) established under section 1452 of the Safe Drinking Water Act, as amended, and title VI of the Federal Water Pollution Control Act [33 U.S.C. 1381 et seq.], as amended, as security for bond issues to enhance the lending capacity of one or both SRFs, but not to acquire the state match for either program, provided that revenues from the bonds are allocated to the purposes of the Safe Drinking Water Act [this subchapter] and the Federal Water Pollution Control Act [33 U.S.C. 1251 et seq.] in the same portion as the funds are used as security for the bonds".

Transfer of Funds

Section 302 of Pub. L. 104-182 provided that:

"(a) In General.—Notwithstanding any other provision of law, at any time after the date 1 year after a State establishes a State loan fund pursuant to section 1452 of the Safe Drinking Water Act [this section] but prior to fiscal year 2002, a Governor of the State may—
  (1) reserve up to 33 percent of a capitalization grant made pursuant to such section 1452 and add the funds reserved to any funds provided to the State pursuant to section 601 of the Federal Water Pollution Control Act (33 U.S.C. 1381); and
  (2) reserve in any year a dollar amount up to the dollar amount that may be reserved under paragraph (1) for that year from capitalization grants made pursuant to section 601 of such Act (33 U.S.C. 1381) and add the reserved funds to any funds provided to the State pursuant to section 1452 of the Safe Drinking Water Act.
(b) Report.—Not later than 4 years after the date of enactment of this Act [Aug. 6, 1996], the Administrator shall submit a report to the Congress regarding the implementation of this section, together with the Administrator's recommendations, if any, for modifications or improvement.
(c) State Match.—Funds reserved pursuant to this section shall not be considered to be a State match of a capitalization grant required pursuant to section 1452 of the Safe Drinking Water Act or the Federal Water Pollution Control Act (33 U.S.C. 1251 et seq.)."

Section Referred to in Other Sections

This section is referred to in sections 300f, 300g-4, 300g-5, 300g-8, 300g-9, 300j-1, 300j-2, 300j-3c, 300j-4, 300j-13, 300j-14, 300j-15, 300j-18 of this title.

SOURCE WATER QUALITY ASSESSMENT

42 USC 300j-13

(a) Source water assessment
  (1) Guidance
     Within 12 months after August 6, 1996, after notice and comment, the Administrator shall publish guidance for States exercising primary enforcement responsibility for public water systems to carry out directly or through delegation (for the protection and benefit of public water systems and for the support of monitoring flexibility) a source water assessment program within the State's boundaries. Each State adopting modifications to monitoring requirements pursuant to section 300g-7(b) of this title shall, prior to adopting such modifications, have an approved source water assessment program under this section and shall carry out the program either directly or through delegation.
  (2) Program requirements
     A source water assessment program under this subsection shall—
     (A) delineate the boundaries of the assessment areas in such State from which one or more public water systems in the State receive supplies of drinking water, using all reasonably available hydrogeologic information on the sources of the supply of drink-

ing water in the State and the water flow, recharge, and discharge and any other reliable information as the State deems necessary to adequately determine such areas; and
  (B) identify for contaminants regulated under this subchapter for which monitoring is required under this subchapter (or any unregulated contaminants selected by the State, in its discretion, which the State, for the purposes of this subsection, has determined may present a threat to public health), to the extent practical, the origins within each delineated area of such contaminants to determine the susceptibility of the public water systems in the delineated area to such contaminants.
(3) Approval, implementation, and monitoring relief
A State source water assessment program under this subsection shall be submitted to the Administrator within 18 months after the Administrator's guidance is issued under this subsection and shall be deemed approved 9 months after the date of such submittal unless the Administrator disapproves the program as provided in section 300h-7(c) of this title. States shall begin implementation of the program immediately after its approval. The Administrator's approval of a State program under this subsection shall include a timetable, established in consultation with the State, allowing not more than 2 years for completion after approval of the program. Public water systems seeking monitoring relief in addition to the interim relief provided under section 300g-7(a) of this title shall be eligible for monitoring relief, consistent with section 300g-7(b) of this title, upon completion of the assessment in the delineated source water assessment area or areas concerned.
(4) Timetable
The timetable referred to in paragraph (3) shall take into consideration the availability to the State of funds under section 300j-12 of this title (relating to State loan funds) for assessments and other relevant factors. The Administrator may extend any timetable included in a State program approved under paragraph (3) to extend the period for completion by an additional 18 months.
(5) Demonstration project
The Administrator shall, as soon as practicable, conduct a demonstration project, in consultation with other Federal agencies, to demonstrate the most effective and protective means of assessing and protecting source waters serving large metropolitan areas and located on Federal lands.
(6) Use of other programs
To avoid duplication and to encourage efficiency, the program under this section may make use of any of the following:
  (A) Vulnerability assessments, sanitary surveys, and monitoring programs.
  (B) Delineations or assessments of ground water sources under a State wellhead protection program developed pursuant to this section.
  (C) Delineations or assessments of surface or ground water sources under a State pesticide management plan developed pursuant to the Pesticide and Ground Water State Management Plan Regulation (subparts I and J of part 152 of title 40, Code of Federal Regulations), promulgated under section 136a(d) of title 7.
  (D) Delineations or assessments of surface water sources under a State watershed initiative or to satisfy the watershed criterion for determining if filtration is required under the Surface Water Treatment Rule (section 141.70 of title 40, Code of Federal Regulations).
  (E) Delineations or assessments of surface or ground water sources under programs or plans pursuant to the Federal Water Pollution Control Act [33 U.S.C. 1251 et seq.].
(7) Public availability
The State shall make the results of the source water assessments conducted under this subsection available to the public.
(b) Approval and disapproval
For provisions relating to program approval and disapproval, see section 300h-7(c) of this title.
(July 1, 1944, ch. 373, title XIV, Sec. 1453, as added Pub. L. 104-182, title I, Sec. 132(a), Aug. 6, 1996, 110 Stat. 1673.)

References in Text
The Federal Water Pollution Control Act, referred to in subsec. (a)(6)(E), is act June 30, 1948, ch. 758, as amended generally by Pub. L. 92-500, Sec. 2, Oct. 18, 1972, 86 Stat. 816, which is classified generally to chapter 26 (Sec. 1251 et seq.) of Title 33, Navigation and Navigable Waters. For complete classification of this Act to the Code, see Short Title note set out under section 1251 of Title 33 and Tables.

Section Referred to in Other Sections
This section is referred to in sections 300g-7, 300h-7, 300j-12, 300j-14 of this title.

SOURCE WATER PETITION PROGRAM
42 USC 300j-14

(a) Petition program
  (1) In general
    (A) Establishment
       A State may establish a program under which an owner or operator of a community water system in the State, or a municipal or local government or political subdivision of a State, may submit a source water quality protection partnership petition to the State requesting that the State assist in the local development of a voluntary, incentive-based partnership, among the owner, operator, or government and other persons likely to be affected by the recommendations of the partnership, to—
       (i) reduce the presence in drinking water of contaminants that may be addressed by a petition by considering the origins of the contaminants, including to the maximum extent practicable the specific activities that affect the drinking water supply of a community;
       (ii) obtain financial or technical assistance necessary to facilitate establishment of a partnership, or to develop and implement recommendations of a partnership for the protection of source water to assist in the provision of drinking water that complies with national primary drinking water regulations with respect to contaminants addressed by a petition; and
       (iii) develop recommendations regarding voluntary and incentive-based strategies for the long-term protection of the source water of community water systems.
    (B) Funding
       Each State may—
       (i) use funds set aside pursuant to section 300j-12(k)(1)(A)(iii) of this title by the State to carry out a program described in subparagraph (A), including assistance to voluntary local partnerships for the development and implementation of partnership recommendations for the protection of source water such as source water quality assessment, contingency plans, and demonstration projects for partners within a source water area delineated under section 300j-13(a) of this title; and
       (ii) provide assistance in response to a petition submitted under this subsection using funds referred to in subsection (b)(2)(B) of this section.
  (2) Objectives
     The objectives of a petition submitted under this subsection shall be to—
     (A) facilitate the local development of voluntary, incentive-based partnerships among owners and operators of community water systems, governments, and other persons in source water areas; and
     (B) obtain assistance from the State in identifying resources which are available to implement the recommendations of the partnerships to address the origins of drinking water contaminants that may be addressed by a petition (including to the maximum extent practicable the specific activities contributing to the presence of the contaminants) that affect the drinking water supply of a community.
  (3) Contaminants addressed by a petition
     A petition submitted to a State under this subsection may address only those contaminants—

(A) that are pathogenic organisms for which a national primary drinking water regulation has been established or is required under section 300g-1 of this title; or
(B) for which a national primary drinking water regulation has been promulgated or proposed and that are detected by adequate monitoring methods in the source water at the intake structure or in any collection, treatment, storage, or distribution facilities by the community water systems at levels—
   (i) above the maximum contaminant level; or
   (ii) that are not reliably and consistently below the maximum contaminant level.

(4) Contents

A petition submitted under this subsection shall, at a minimum—
(A) include a delineation of the source water area in the State that is the subject of the petition;
(B) identify, to the maximum extent practicable, the origins of the drinking water contaminants that may be addressed by a petition (including to the maximum extent practicable the specific activities contributing to the presence of the contaminants) in the source water area delineated under section 300j-13 of this title;
(C) identify any deficiencies in information that will impair the development of recommendations by the voluntary local partnership to address drinking water contaminants that may be addressed by a petition;
(D) specify the efforts made to establish the voluntary local partnership and obtain the participation of—
   (i) the municipal or local government or other political subdivision of the State with jurisdiction over the source water area delineated under section 300j-13 of this title; and
   (ii) each person in the source water area delineated under section 300j-13 of this title—
      (I) who is likely to be affected by recommendations of the voluntary local partnership; and
      (II) whose participation is essential to the success of the partnership;
(E) outline how the voluntary local partnership has or will, during development and implementation of recommendations of the voluntary local partnership, identify, recognize and take into account any voluntary or other activities already being undertaken by persons in the source water area delineated under section 300j-13 of this title under Federal or State law to reduce the likelihood that contaminants will occur in drinking water at levels of public health concern; and
(F) specify the technical, financial, or other assistance that the voluntary local partnership requests of the State to develop the partnership or to implement recommendations of the partnership.

(b) Approval or disapproval of petitions

(1) In general

After providing notice and an opportunity for public comment on a petition submitted under subsection (a) of this section, the State shall approve or disapprove the petition, in whole or in part, not later than 120 days after the date of submission of the petition.

(2) Approval

The State may approve a petition if the petition meets the requirements established under subsection (a) of this section. The notice of approval shall, at a minimum, include for informational purposes—
(A) an identification of technical, financial, or other assistance that the State will provide to assist in addressing the drinking water contaminants that may be addressed by a petition based on—
   (i) the relative priority of the public health concern identified in the petition with respect to the other water quality needs identified by the State;
   (ii) any necessary coordination that the State will perform of the program established under this section with programs implemented or planned by other States under this section; and
   (iii) funds available (including funds available from a State revolving loan fund established under title VI of the Federal Water Pollution Control Act (33 U.S.C. 1381 et seq.)) or section 300j-12 of this title;

(B) a description of technical or financial assistance pursuant to Federal and State programs that is available to assist in implementing recommendations of the partnership in the petition, including—
  (i) any program established under the Federal Water Pollution Control Act (33 U.S.C. 1251 et seq.);
  (ii) the program established under section 1455b of title 16;
  (iii) the agricultural water quality protection program established under chapter 2 of subtitle D of title XII of the Food Security Act of 1985 (16 U.S.C. 3838 et seq.);
  (iv) the sole source aquifer protection program established under section 300h-6 of this title;
  (v) the community wellhead protection program established under section 300h-7 of this title;
  (vi) any pesticide or ground water management plan;
  (vii) any voluntary agricultural resource management plan or voluntary whole farm or whole ranch management plan developed and implemented under a process established by the Secretary of Agriculture; and
  (viii) any abandoned well closure program; and
(C) a description of activities that will be undertaken to coordinate Federal and State programs to respond to the petition.
(3) Disapproval
  If the State disapproves a petition submitted under subsection (a) of this section, the State shall notify the entity submitting the petition in writing of the reasons for disapproval. A petition may be resubmitted at any time if—
  (A) new information becomes available;
  (B) conditions affecting the source water that is the subject of the petition change; or
  (C) modifications are made in the type of assistance being requested.
(c) Grants to support State programs
  (1) In general
    The Administrator may make a grant to each State that establishes a program under this section that is approved under paragraph (2). The amount of each grant shall not exceed 50 percent of the cost of administering the program for the year in which the grant is available.
  (2) Approval
    In order to receive grant assistance under this subsection, a State shall submit to the Administrator for approval a plan for a source water quality protection partnership program that is consistent with the guidance published under subsection (d) of this section. The Administrator shall approve the plan if the plan is consistent with the guidance published under subsection (d) of this section.
(d) Guidance
  (1) In general
    Not later than 1 year after August 6, 1996, the Administrator, in consultation with the States, shall publish guidance to assist—
    (A) States in the development of a source water quality protection partnership program; and
    (B) municipal or local governments or political subdivisions of a State and community water systems in the development of source water quality protection partnerships and in the assessment of source water quality.
  (2) Contents of the guidance
    The guidance shall, at a minimum—
    (A) recommend procedures for the approval or disapproval by a State of a petition submitted under subsection (a) of this section;
    (B) recommend procedures for the submission of petitions developed under subsection (a) of this section;
    (C) recommend criteria for the assessment of source water areas within a State; and
    (D) describe technical or financial assistance pursuant to Federal and State programs that is available to address the contamination of sources of drinking water and to develop and respond to petitions submitted under subsection (a) of this section.

(e) Authorization of appropriations
There are authorized to be appropriated to carry out this section $5,000,000 for each of the fiscal years 1997 through 2003. Each State with a plan for a program approved under subsection (b) of this section shall receive an equitable portion of the funds available for any fiscal year.

(f) Statutory construction
Nothing in this section—
  (1) (A) creates or conveys new authority to a State, political subdivision of a State, or community water system for any new regulatory measure; or
      (B) limits any authority of a State, political subdivision, or community water system; or
  (2) precludes a community water system, municipal or local government, or political subdivision of a government from locally developing and carrying out a voluntary, incentive-based, source water quality protection partnership to address the origins of drinking water contaminants of public health concern.

(July 1, 1944, ch. 373, title XIV, Sec. 1454, as added Pub. L. 104-182, title I, Sec. 133(a), Aug. 6, 1996, 110 Stat. 1675.)

References in Text

The Federal Water Pollution Control Act, referred to in subsec. (b)(2)(A)(iii), (B)(i), is act June 30, 1948, ch. 758, as amended generally by Pub. L. 92-500, Sec. 2, Oct. 18, 1972, 86 Stat. 816, which is classified generally to chapter 26 (Sec. 1251 et seq.) of Title 33, Navigation and Navigable Waters. Title VI of the Act is classified generally to subchapter VI (Sec. 1381 et seq.) of chapter 26 of Title 33. For complete classification of this Act to the Code, see Short Title note set out under section 1251 of Title 33 and Tables.

The Food Security Act of 1985, referred to in subsec. (b)(2)(B)(iii), is Pub. L. 99-198, Dec. 23, 1985, 99 Stat. 1354, as amended. Chapter 2 of subtitle D of title XII of the Act was classified generally to part II (Sec. 3838 et seq.) of subchapter IV of chapter 58 of Title 16, Conservation, prior to repeal by Pub. L. 104-127, title III, Sec. 336(h), Apr. 4, 1996, 110 Stat. 1007. For complete classification of this Act to the Code, see Short Title of 1985 Amendment note set out under section 1281 of Title 7, Agriculture, and Tables.

Section Referred to in Other Sections

This section is referred to in section 300j-12 of this title.

WATER CONSERVATION PLAN

42 USC 300j-15

(a) Guidelines
Not later than 2 years after August 6, 1996, the Administrator shall publish in the Federal Register guidelines for water conservation plans for public water systems serving fewer than 3,300 persons, public water systems serving between 3,300 and 10,000 persons, and public water systems serving more than 10,000 persons, taking into consideration such factors as water availability and climate.

(b) Loans or grants
Within 1 year after publication of the guidelines under subsection (a) of this section, a State exercising primary enforcement responsibility for public water systems may require a public water system, as a condition of receiving a loan or grant from a State loan fund under section 300j-12 of this title, to submit with its application for such loan or grant a water conservation plan consistent with such guidelines.

(July 1, 1944, ch. 373, title XIV, Sec. 1455, as added Pub. L. 104-182, title I, Sec. 134, Aug. 6, 1996, 110 Stat. 1679.)

ASSISTANCE TO COLONIAS

42 USC 300j-16

(a) Definitions
As used in this section:

(1) Border State
The term "border State" means Arizona, California, New Mexico, and Texas.
(2) Eligible community
The term "eligible community" means a low-income community with economic hardship that—
  (A) is commonly referred to as a colonia;
  (B) is located along the United States-Mexico border (generally in an unincorporated area); and
  (C) lacks a safe drinking water supply or adequate facilities for the provision of safe drinking water for human consumption.
(b) Grants to alleviate health risks
The Administrator of the Environmental Protection Agency and the heads of other appropriate Federal agencies are authorized to award grants to a border State to provide assistance to eligible communities to facilitate compliance with national primary drinking water regulations or otherwise significantly further the health protection objectives of this subchapter.
(c) Use of funds
Each grant awarded pursuant to subsection (b) of this section shall be used to provide assistance to one or more eligible communities with respect to which the residents are subject to a significant health risk (as determined by the Administrator or the head of the Federal agency making the grant) attributable to the lack of access to an adequate and affordable drinking water supply system.
(d) Cost sharing
The amount of a grant awarded pursuant to this section shall not exceed 50 percent of the costs of carrying out the project that is the subject of the grant.
(e) Authorization of appropriations
There are authorized to be appropriated to carry out this section $25,000,000 for each of the fiscal years 1997 through 1999.

(July 1, 1944, ch. 373, title XIV, Sec. 1456, as added Pub. L. 104-182, title I, Sec. 135, Aug. 6, 1996, 110 Stat. 1679.)

ESTROGENIC SUBSTANCES SCREENING PROGRAM

42 USC 300j-17

In addition to the substances referred to in section 346a(p)(3)(B) of title 21 the Administrator may provide for testing under the screening program authorized by section 346a(p) of title 21, in accordance with the provisions of section 346a(p) of title 21, of any other substance that may be found in sources of drinking water if the Administrator determines that a substantial population may be exposed to such substance.

(July 1, 1944, ch. 373, title XIV, Sec. 1457, as added Pub. L. 104-182, title I, Sec. 136, Aug. 6, 1996, 110 Stat. 1680.)

DRINKING WATER STUDIES

42 USC 300j-18

(a) Subpopulations at greater risk
  (1) In general
  The Administrator shall conduct a continuing program of studies to identify groups within the general population that may be at greater risk than the general population of adverse health effects from exposure to contaminants in drinking water. The study shall examine whether and to what degree infants, children, pregnant women, the elderly, individuals with a history of serious illness, or other subpopulations that can be identified and characterized are likely to experience elevated health risks, including risks of cancer, from contaminants in drinking water.
  (2) Report

Not later than 4 years after August 6, 1996, and periodically thereafter as new and significant information becomes available, the Administrator shall report to the Congress on the results of the studies.
(b) Biological mechanisms
The Administrator shall conduct biomedical studies to—
  (1) understand the mechanisms by which chemical contaminants are absorbed, distributed, metabolized, and eliminated from the human body, so as to develop more accurate physiologically based models of the phenomena;
  (2) understand the effects of contaminants and the mechanisms by which the contaminants cause adverse effects (especially noncancer and infectious effects) and the variations in the effects among humans, especially subpopulations at greater risk of adverse effects, and between test animals and humans; and
  (3) develop new approaches to the study of complex mixtures, such as mixtures found in drinking water, especially to determine the prospects for synergistic or antagonistic interactions that may affect the shape of the dose-response relationship of the individual chemicals and microbes, and to examine noncancer endpoints and infectious diseases, and susceptible individuals and subpopulations.
(c) Studies on harmful substances in drinking water
  (1) Development of studies
    The Administrator shall, not later than 180 days after August 6, 1996, and after consultation with the Secretary of Health and Human Services, the Secretary of Agriculture, and, as appropriate, the heads of other Federal agencies, conduct the studies described in paragraph (2) to support the development and implementation of the most current version of each of the following:
    (A) Enhanced Surface Water Treatment Rule (59 Fed. Reg. 38832 (July 29, 1994)).
    (B) Disinfectant and Disinfection Byproducts Rule (59 Fed. Reg. 38668 (July 29, 1994)).
    (C) Ground Water Disinfection Rule (availability of draft summary announced at (57 Fed. Reg. 33960; July 31, 1992)).
  (2) Contents of studies
    The studies required by paragraph (1) shall include, at a minimum, each of the following:
    (A) Toxicological studies and, if warranted, epidemiological studies to determine what levels of exposure from disinfectants and disinfection byproducts, if any, may be associated with developmental and birth defects and other potential toxic end points.
    (B) Toxicological studies and, if warranted, epidemiological studies to quantify the carcinogenic potential from exposure to disinfection byproducts resulting from different disinfectants.
    (C) The development of dose-response curves for pathogens, including cryptosporidium and the Norwalk virus.
  (3) Authorization of appropriations
    There are authorized to be appropriated to carry out this subsection $12,500,000 for each of fiscal years 1997 through 2003.
(d) Waterborne disease occurrence study
  (1) System
    The Director of the Centers for Disease Control and Prevention, and the Administrator shall jointly—
    (A) within 2 years after August 6, 1996, conduct pilot waterborne disease occurrence studies for at least 5 major United States communities or public water systems; and
    (B) within 5 years after August 6, 1996, prepare a report on the findings of the pilot studies, and a national estimate of waterborne disease occurrence.
  (2) Training and education
    The Director and Administrator shall jointly establish a national health care provider training and public education campaign to inform both the professional health care provider community and the general public about waterborne disease and the symptoms that may be caused by infectious agents, including microbial contaminants. In developing such a campaign, they shall seek comment from interested groups and individuals, including scientists, physicians, State and local governments, environmental groups, public water systems, and vulnerable populations.

(3) Funding
There are authorized to be appropriated for each of the fiscal years 1997 through 2001, $3,000,000 to carry out this subsection. To the extent funds under this subsection are not fully appropriated, the Administrator may use not more than $2,000,000 of the funds from amounts reserved under section 300j-12(n) of this title for health effects studies for purposes of this subsection. The Administrator may transfer a portion of such funds to the Centers for Disease Control and Prevention for such purposes.

(July 1, 1944, ch. 373, title XIV, Sec. 1458, as added Pub. L. 104-182, title I, Sec. 137, Aug. 6, 1996, 110 Stat. 1680.)

Public Health Assessment of Exosure to Perchlorate

Pub. L. 108-136 provided that:

"(a) Epidemiological Study of Exposure to Perchlorate.—The Secretary of Defense shall provide for an independent epidemiological study of exposure to perchlorate in drinking water. The entity conducting the study shall—
- (1) assess the incidence of thyroid disease and measurable effects of thyroid function in relation to exposure to perchlorate;
- (2) ensure that the study is of sufficient scope and scale to permit the making of meaningful conclusions of the measurable public health threat associated with exposure to perchlorate,   especially the threat to sensitive subpopulalions; and
- (3) examine thyroid function, including measurements of urinary iodine and thyroid hormone levels, in a sufficient number of pregnant women, neonates, and infants exposed to perchlorate in drinking water and match measurements of perchlorate levels in the drinking water of each study participant in order to permit the development of meaningful conclusions on the public health threat to individuals exposed to perchlorate.

(b) Review of Effects of Perchlorate on Endocrine System.—The Secretary shall provide for an independent review of the effects of perchlorate on the human endocrine system. The entity conducting the review shall assess—
- (1) available data on human exposure to perchlorate, including clinical data and data on exposure of sensitive subpopulations, and the levels at which health effects were observed; and
- (2) available data on other substances that have endocrine effects similar to perchlorate to which the public is frequently exposed.

(c) Performance of Study and Review.—
- (1) The Secretary shall provide for the performance of the study under subsection (a) through the Centers for Disease Control and Prevention, the National Institutes of Health, or another Federal entity with experience in environmental toxicology selected by the Secretary.
- (2) The Secretary shall provide for the performance of the review under subsection (b) through the Centers for Disease Control and Prevention, the National Institutes of Health, or another appropriate Federal research entity with experience in human endocrinology selected by the Secretary. The Secretary shall ensure that the panel conducting the review is composed of individuals with expertise in human endocrinology.

(d) Reporting Requirements.—Not later than June 1, 2005, the Federal entities conducting the study and review under this section shall submit to the Secretary reports containing the results of the study and review."

Section Referred to in Other Sections

This section is referred to in section 300j-12 of this title.

Part F—Additional Requirements To Regulate Safety of Drinking Water

DEFINITIONS

42 USC 300j-21

As used in this part—
(1) Drinking water cooler
   The term "drinking water cooler" means any mechanical device affixed to drinking water supply plumbing which actively cools water for human consumption.
(2) Lead free
   The term "lead free" means, with respect to a drinking water cooler, that each part or component of the cooler which may come in contact with drinking water contains not more than 8 percent lead, except that no drinking water cooler which contains any solder, flux, or storage tank interior surface which may come in contact with drinking water shall be considered lead free if the solder, flux, or storage tank interior surface contains more than 0.2 percent lead. The Administrator may establish more stringent requirements for treating any part or component of a drinking water cooler as lead free for purposes of this part whenever he determines that any such part may constitute an important source of lead in drinking water.
(3) Local educational agency
   The term "local educational agency" means—
   (A) any local educational agency as defined in section 9101 of title 20,
   (B) the owner of any private, nonprofit elementary or secondary school building, and
   (C) the governing authority of any school operating under the defense dependent's education system provided for under the Defense Dependent's Education Act of 1978 (20 U.S.C. 921 and following).
(4) Repair
   The term "repair" means, with respect to a drinking water cooler, to take such corrective action as is necessary to ensure that water cooler is lead free.
(5) Replacement
   The term "replacement", when used with respect to a drinking water cooler, means the permanent removal of the water cooler and the installation of a lead free water cooler.
(6) School
   The term "school" means any elementary school or secondary school as defined in section 9101 of title 20 and any kindergarten or day care facility.
(7) Lead-lined tank
   The term "lead-lined tank" means a water reservoir container in a drinking water cooler which container is constructed of lead or which has an interior surface which is not lead free.

(July 1, 1944, ch. 373, title XIV, Sec. 1461, as added Pub. L. 100-572, Sec. 2(a), Oct. 31, 1988, 102 Stat. 2884; amended Pub. L. 103-382, title III, Sec. 391(p), Oct. 20, 1994, 108 Stat. 4024; Pub. L. 104-182, title V, Sec. 501(f)(7), Aug. 6, 1996, 110 Stat. 1692.)

References in Text

The Defense Dependent's Education Act of 1978, referred to in par. (3)(C), probably means the Defense Dependents' Education Act of 1978, title XIV of Pub. L. 95-561, Nov. 1, 1978, 92 Stat. 2365, as amended, which is classified principally to chapter 25A (Sec. 921 et seq.) of Title 20, Education. For complete classification of this Act to the Code, see Short Title note set out under section 921 of Title 20 and Tables.

Amendments

2002–Pub. L. 107-110 changed "8801" to "9101" in sections (3)(a) and (6).
1996–Pub. L. 104-182 made technical amendment to section catchline and first word of text.
1994–Par. (3)(A). Pub. L. 103-382, Sec. 391(p)(1), substituted "section 8801 of title 20" for "section 198 of the Elementary and Secondary Education Act of 1965 (20 U.S.C. 3381)".

894 / Environmental Statutes

Par. (6). Pub. L. 103-382, Sec. 391(p)(2), substituted "section 8801 of title 20" for "section 198 of the Elementary and Secondary Education Act of 1965 (20 U.S.C. 2854)".

RECALL OF DRINKING WATER COOLERS WITH LEAD-LINED TANKS

42 USC 300j-22

For purposes of the Consumer Product Safety Act [15 U.S.C. 2051 et seq.], all drinking water coolers identified by the Administrator on the list under section 300j-23 of this title as having a lead-lined tank shall be considered to be imminently hazardous consumer products within the meaning of section 12 of such Act (15 U.S.C. 2061). After notice and opportunity for comment, including a public hearing, the Consumer Product Safety Commission shall issue an order requiring the manufacturers and importers of such coolers to repair, replace, or recall and provide a refund for such coolers within 1 year after October 31, 1988. For purposes of enforcement, such order shall be treated as an order under section 15(d) of that Act (15 U.S.C. 2064(d)).

(July 1, 1944, ch. 373, title XIV, Sec. 1462, as added Pub. L. 100-572, Sec. 2(a), Oct. 31, 1988, 102 Stat. 2885; amended Pub. L. 104-182, title V, Sec. 501(f)(8), Aug. 6, 1996, 110 Stat. 1692.)

References in Text

The Consumer Product Safety Act, referred to in text, is Pub. L. 92-573, Oct. 27, 1972, 86 Stat. 1207, as amended, which is classified generally to chapter 47 (Sec. 2051 et seq.) of Title 15, Commerce and Trade. For complete classification of this Act to the Code, see Short Title note set out under section 2051 of Title 15 and Tables.

Amendments

1996—Pub. L. 104-182 made technical amendment to section catchline and first word of text.

DRINKING WATER COOLERS CONTAINING LEAD

42 USC 300j-23

(a) Publication of lists
   The Administrator shall, after notice and opportunity for public comment, identify each brand and model of drinking water cooler which is not lead free, including each brand and model of drinking water cooler which has a lead-lined tank. For purposes of identifying the brand and model of drinking water coolers under this subsection, the Administrator shall use the best information available to the Environmental Protection Agency. Within 100 days after October 31, 1988, the Administrator shall publish a list of each brand and model of drinking water cooler identified under this subsection. Such list shall separately identify each brand and model of cooler which has a lead-lined tank. The Administrator shall continue to gather information regarding lead in drinking water coolers and shall revise and republish the list from time to time as may be appropriate as new information or analysis becomes available regarding lead contamination in drinking water coolers.

(b) Prohibition
   No person may sell in interstate commerce, or manufacture for sale in interstate commerce, any drinking water cooler listed under subsection (a) of this section or any other drinking water cooler which is not lead free, including a lead-lined drinking water cooler.

(c) Criminal penalty
   Any person who knowingly violates the prohibition contained in subsection (b) of this section shall be imprisoned for not more than 5 years, or fined in accordance with title 18, or both.

(d) Civil penalty
   The Administrator may bring a civil action in the appropriate United States District Court (as determined under the provisions of title 28) to impose a civil penalty on any person who violates subsection (b) of this section. In any such action the court may impose on such person a civil penalty of not more than $5,000 ($50,000 in the case of a second or subsequent violation).

(July 1, 1944, ch. 373, title XIV, Sec. 1463, as added Pub. L. 100-572, Sec. 2(a), Oct. 31, 1988, 102 Stat. 2885; amended Pub. L. 104-182, title V, Sec. 501(f)(9), Aug. 6, 1996, 110 Stat. 1692.)

Amendments

1996—Pub. L. 104-182 made technical amendment to section catchline and subsec. (a) designation.

Section Referred to in Other Sections

This section is referred to in sections 300j-22, 300j-24 of this title.

LEAD CONTAMINATION IN SCHOOL DRINKING WATER

42 USC 300j-24

(a) Distribution of drinking water cooler list
Within 100 days after October 31, 1988, the Administrator shall distribute to the States a list of each brand and model of drinking water cooler identified and listed by the Administrator under section 300j-23(a) of this title.

(b) Guidance document and testing protocol
The Administrator shall publish a guidance document and a testing protocol to assist schools in determining the source and degree of lead contamination in school drinking water supplies and in remedying such contamination. The guidance document shall include guidelines for sample preservation. The guidance document shall also include guidance to assist States, schools, and the general public in ascertaining the levels of lead contamination in drinking water coolers and in taking appropriate action to reduce or eliminate such contamination. The guidance document shall contain a testing protocol for the identification of drinking water coolers which contribute to lead contamination in drinking water. Such document and protocol may be revised, republished and redistributed as the Administrator deems necessary. The Administrator shall distribute the guidance document and testing protocol to the States within 100 days after October 31, 1988.

(c) Dissemination to schools, etc.
Each State shall provide for the dissemination to local educational agencies, private nonprofit elementary or secondary schools and to day care centers of the guidance document and testing protocol published under subsection (b) of this section, together with the list of drinking water coolers published under section 300j-23(a) of this title.

(d) Remedial action program
  (1) Testing and remedying lead contamination
  Within 9 months after October 31, 1988, each State shall establish a program, consistent with this section, to assist local educational agencies in testing for, and remedying, lead contamination in drinking water from coolers and from other sources of lead contamination at schools under the jurisdiction of such agencies.
  (2) Public availability
  A copy of the results of any testing under paragraph (1) shall be available in the administrative offices of the local educational agency for inspection by the public, including teachers, other school personnel, and parents. The local educational agency shall notify parent, teacher, and employee organizations of the availability of such testing results.
  (3) Coolers
  In the case of drinking water coolers, such program shall include measures for the reduction or elimination of lead contamination from those water coolers which are not lead free and which are located in schools. Such measures shall be adequate to ensure that within 15 months after October 31, 1988, all such water coolers in schools under the jurisdiction of such agencies are repaired, replaced, permanently removed, or rendered inoperable unless the cooler is tested and found (within the limits of testing accuracy) not to contribute lead to drinking water.

(July 1, 1944, ch. 373, title XIV, Sec. 1464, as added Pub. L. 100-572, Sec. 2(a), Oct. 31, 1988, 102 Stat. 2886; amended Pub. L. 104-182, title V, Sec. 501(f)(10), Aug. 6, 1996, 110 Stat. 1692.)

Amendments

1996—Pub. L. 104-182 made technical amendment to section catchline and subsec. (a) designation.

Section Referred to in Other Sections
This section is referred to in section 300j-25 of this title.

FEDERAL ASSISTANCE FOR STATE PROGRAMS REGARDING LEAD CONTAMINATION IN SCHOOL DRINKING WATER

42 USC 300j-25

(a) School drinking water programs
The Administrator shall make grants to States to establish and carry out State programs under section 300j-24 of this title to assist local educational agencies in testing for, and remedying, lead contamination in drinking water from drinking water coolers and from other sources of lead contamination at schools under the jurisdiction of such agencies. Such grants may be used by States to reimburse local educational agencies for expenses incurred after October 31, 1988, for such testing and remedial action.

(b) Limits
Each grant under this section shall be used by the State for testing water coolers in accordance with section 300j-24 of this title, for testing for lead contamination in other drinking water supplies under section 300j-24 of this title, or for remedial action under State programs under section 300j-24 of this title. Not more than 5 percent of the grant may be used for program administration.

(c) Authorization of appropriations
There are authorized to be appropriated to carry out this section not more than $30,000,000 for fiscal year 1989, $30,000,000 for fiscal year 1990, and $30,000,000 for fiscal year 1991.

(July 1, 1944, ch. 373, title XIV, Sec. 1465, as added Pub. L. 100-572, Sec. 2(a), Oct. 31, 1988, 102 Stat. 2887; amended Pub. L. 104-182, title V, Sec. 501(d), (f)(11), Aug. 6, 1996, 110 Stat. 1691, 1692.)

Amendments
1996—Pub. L. 104-182, Sec. 501(f)(11), made technical amendment to section catchline and subsec. (a) designation.

Subsec. (b). Pub. L. 104-182, Sec. 501(d), substituted "by the State" for "as by the State".

CERTIFICATION OF TESTING LABORATORIES

42 USC 300j-26

The Administrator of the Environmental Protection Agency shall assure that programs for the certification of testing laboratories which test drinking water supplies for lead contamination certify only those laboratories which provide reliable accurate testing. The Administrator (or the State in the case of a State to which certification authority is delegated under this subsection) shall publish and make available to the public upon request the list of laboratories certified under this subsection.[1]

(Pub. L. 100-572, Sec. 4, Oct. 31, 1988, 102 Stat. 2889.)

Codification
Section enacted as part of the Lead Contamination Control Act of 1988, and not as part of the Public Health Service Act which comprises this chapter.

---

[1] So in original. Probably should be "section."